International Encyclopedia of the Social & Behavioral Sciences

International Encyclopedia of the Social & Behavioral Sciences

Neil J. Smelser

Center for Advanced Study in the Behavioral Sciences, Stanford, CA, USA

Paul B. Baltes

Max Planck Institute for Human Development, Berlin, Germany

Volume 3

2001

ELSEVIER

AMSTERDAM—PARIS—NEW YORK—OXFORD—SHANNON—SINGAPORE—TOKYO

Elsevier Science Ltd., The Boulevard, Langford Lane, Kidlington, Oxford, OX5 1GB, UK

First edition 2001

Library of Congress Cataloging-in-Publication Data
International encyclopedia of the social & behavioral sciences / editors in chief Neil J. Smelser, Paul B. Baltes. – 1st ed.
   p. cm.
  Includes bibliographical references.
  ISBN 0-08-043076-7 (set : alk. paper)
  1. Social sciences–Encyclopedias. I. Title: International encyclopedia of the social and behavioral sciences. II. Smelser, Neil J. III. Baltes, Paul B.
H41.I58 2001
300′.3–dc21   2001044791

British Library Cataloguing in Publication Data
A catalogue record for this book is available from the British Library.

ISBN 0-08-043076-7 (set : alk. paper)

∞™ The paper used in this publication meets the minimum requirements of the American National Standard for Information Sciences—Permanence of Paper for Printed Library Materials. ANSI Z39.48 1984.

Typeset by Cambridge University Press, UK.
Printed and bound in Great Britain by Polestar Wheatons Ltd., Exeter, UK.

Contents

Section Editors

ORLEY ASHENFELTER
Princeton University, Princeton, NJ,
USA
Economics

EUGÉNIE LADNER BIRCH
University of Pennsylvania,
Philadelphia, PA, USA
Urban Studies and Planning

RAYMOND BOUDON
Centre National de la Recherche
Scientifique, Paris, France
Sociology

CRAIG CALHOUN
Social Science Research Council,
New York, NY, USA
Area and International Studies

BERNARD COMRIE
Max Planck Institute for
Evolutionary Anthropology,
Leipzig, Germany
Linguistics

MARGARET W. CONKEY
University of California, Berkeley,
CA, USA
Archaeology

THOMAS D. COOK
Northwestern University, Evanston,
IL, USA
Logic of Inquiry and Research Design

WILLIAM DURHAM
Stanford University, Stanford, CA,
USA
Evolutionary Sciences

LAUREN B. EDELMAN
University of California, Berkeley,
CA, USA
Law

NANCY EISENBERG
Arizona State University, Tempe,
AZ, USA
*Developmental, Social, Personality,
and Motivational Psychology*

PAULA ENGLAND
University of Pennsylvania,
Philadelphia, PA, USA
Gender Studies

DAVID L. FEATHERMAN
University of Michigan, Ann Arbor,
MI, USA
Institutions and Infrastructure

MARCUS W. FELDMAN
Stanford University, Stanford, CA,
USA
Evolutionary Sciences and *Genetics,
Behavior, and Society*

STEPHEN E. FIENBERG
Carnegie Mellon University,
Pittsburgh, PA, USA
Statistics

MARC GALANTER
University of Wisconsin,
Madison, WI, USA
Law

WENDY GRISWOLD
Northwestern University, Evanston,
IL, USA
Expressive Forms

ULF HANNERZ
Stockholm University, Stockholm,
Sweden
Anthropology

SUSAN HANSON
Clark University, Worcester, MA,
USA
Geography

JAN M. HOEM
Max Planck Institute for
Demographic Research, Rostock,
Germany
Demography

FLORIAN HOLSBOER
Max Planck Institute of Psychiatry,
Munich, Germany
Psychiatry

AXEL HONNETH
Johann Wolfgang Goethe
University, Frankfurt, Germany
Philosophy

JAMES S. HOUSE
University of Michigan, Ann Arbor,
MI, USA
Health

SHEILA JASANOFF
Harvard University, Cambridge,
MA, USA
Science and Technology Studies

JOSEPH B. KADANE
Carnegie Mellon University,
Pittsburgh, PA, USA
Statistics

IRA KATZNELSON
Columbia University, New York,
NY, USA
Public Policy

WALTER KINTSCH
University of Colorado, Boulder,
CO, USA
*Cognitive Psychology and Cognitive
Science*

PATRICK KIRCH
University of California, Berkeley,
CA, USA
Archaeology

JÜRGEN KOCKA
Free University Berlin, Germany
History

RICHARD M. LERNER
Tufts University, Medford, MA,
USA
Integrative Concepts and Issues

A. A. J. MARLEY
McGill University, Montreal,
Canada
Mathematics and Computer Sciences

DAVID A. MARTIN
Woking, UK
Religious Studies

ALBERTO MARTINELLI
University of Milan, Italy
*Organizational and Management
Studies*

KARL ULRICH MAYER
Max Planck Institute for Human
Development, Berlin, Germany
Biographies

JAMES L. MCCLELLAND
Mellon Institute, Pittsburgh, PA,
USA
Behavioral and Cognitive Neuroscience

ROBERT MCCORMICK ADAMS
University of California, San Diego,
CA, USA
Ethics of Research and Applications

MARY BYRNE MCDONNELL
Social Science Research Council,
New York, NY, USA
Area and International Studies

JÜRGEN MITTELSTRASS
University of Konstanz, Germany
Ethics of Research and Applications

PHILIP PETTIT
Australian National University,
Canberra, ACT, Australia
Philosophy

NELSON W. POLSBY
University of California, Berkeley,
CA, USA
Political Science

KENNETH PREWITT
US Bureau of the Census,
Washington, DC, USA
Public Policy

CHARLES C. RAGIN
Northwestern University, Evanston,
IL, USA
Logic of Inquiry and Research Design

MELVIN SABSHIN
University of Maryland, Baltimore,
MD, USA
Psychiatry

MICHAEL SCHUDSON
University of California,
San Diego, CA, USA
*Media Studies and Commercial
Applications*

RALF SCHWARZER
Free University Berlin, Germany
Health

ROBERT A. SCOTT
Center for Advanced Study in the
Behavioral Sciences, Stanford, CA,
USA
Integrative Concepts and Issues

RICHARD ALLAN SHWEDER
University of Chicago, IL, USA
Modern Cultural Concerns

RICHARD F. THOMPSON
University of Southern California,
Los Angeles, CA, USA
Behavioral and Cognitive Neuroscience

BILLIE L. TURNER II
Clark University, Worcester, MA,
USA
Environmental/Ecological Sciences

PETER WAGNER
European University Institute,
Florence, Italy
*History of the Social and Behavioral
Sciences*

RÜDIGER WEHNER
University of Zurich, Switzerland
Genetics, Behavior, and Society

FRANZ E. WEINERT[†]
Max Planck Institute for
Psychological Research, Munich,
Germany
Education

G. TERENCE WILSON
Rutgers University, Piscataway, NJ,
USA
Clinical and Applied Psychology

JULIA DELIUS
Max Planck Institute for Human
Development, Berlin, Germany
Scientific Editorial Assistant

International Advisory Board

C

Campaigning: Political

At the microlevel, political campaigning involves an individual candidate attempting to win political office. At the macrolevel, political parties seek to gain seats in government for their partisans and ultimately to gain power or at least to share power in the relevant governmental arena. At each level decisions must be made about candidacies, organizations must be built, messages must be refined, strategies must be set, and the public must be convinced to support those waging a particular campaign. Only certain aspects of political campaigns are viewed by the public. Frequently, the actions taken away from public view are more determinative of success and failure.

1. The Choice of Candidates

Decisions about who will run for office involve decisions by potential candidates as to whether or not they will run and decisions by political parties, acting under a variety of rules, concerning who their candidates will be.

1.1 The Decision to Run

Individuals who run for political office must exhibit political ambition beyond the desire to simply serve their community. Campaigning for and serving in political office involves personal costs and public exposure that deter many from seeking office. However, even those ambitious for elective office must make decisions about what offices to seek and when to seek those offices (Jacobson and Kernell 1981). These decisions are based on a complex, often-implicit cost-benefit analysis. Potential candidates weigh the costs and benefits of both winning and losing. Their decision calculus can be summarized:

$$p_r = p_w (B_w - C_w) + p_l(B_l - C_l)$$

where p_r = probability of running; p_w = probability of winning; p_l = probability of losing; B_w = benefit of winning; C_w = cost of winning; B_l = benefit of losing; C_l = cost of losing.

The difficulty that potential candidates face in making these decisions relates to the uncertainty regarding virtually all of the relevant variables (Maisel

1986, Kazee 1994). Generally the rather obvious benefits far outweigh the costs of winning for those with the requisite political ambition; but costs must be weighed—loss of privacy, loss of time with family, frequently loss of income. Similarly, the evident costs of losing are almost always greater than the benefits; but some benefits do accrue to losers—making a name for oneself, building up good will with party officials. Beyond these broad generalizations, little is known about how specific candidates make individual decisions given the dazzling array of difficult-to-estimate variables (Maisel and Stone 1997).

1.2 Parties' Choices of Candidates

The ways in which political parties choose their candidates for office varies significantly from political system to political system and from party to party. The key variable in this aspect of the process relates to the extent to which party organization controls places on the ballot contrasted with voters acting independently. In the former, the process is often described as candidate recruitment, in the latter, candidate emergence.

At one extreme are those systems in which political parties slate their candidates for office, ranking candidates or placing them in safe constituencies. Most parties operating in electoral systems with proportional representation follow this procedure. It is also followed in systems with strong party systems, in which citizens vote more for parties than they do for individual candidates. Many European systems fit this description (Hix and Lord 1997).

At the other extreme are systems, of which the United States is prototypical, in which voters choose party candidates in primary elections. The shape of the electorate in primary elections varies considerably from polity to polity. In theory, primary elections are open only to members of one political party or another, but in actual practice how membership is defined varies according to local rules and can be quite restrictive or totally open. In either case, voters in the primary elections determine the party nominee, even if that nominee would not have been the choice of party officials (Maisel 1999).

Many systems are hybrids, with party officials and the voters sharing power. The US presidential nominating system stands as perhaps the most complex means of choosing party candidates. Delegates elected to national party conventions make the actual nominations. Some delegates are selected because of their positions within the party or as elected officials with party affiliations; others are chosen at party meetings (or caucuses) held in local communities; still others are chosen by the voters in primary elections, based on lists of delegate candidates approved by the presidential campaigns they seek to support (Polsby and Wildavsky 2000, Wayne 2000).

2. The Campaign Organization

In polities with strong party systems, campaign organizations tend to be party-centered. In these cases, the voters cast their ballots for candidates as representatives of a party. The party defines the campaign message and communicates it to the voters. The party raises the money to fund the campaign, does the polling necessary to understand what the electorate is thinking, and structures the campaign strategy and tactics. Typically full-time, year-round party workers perform all these functions or they are contracted out to professionals.

Where strong party systems do not exist, individual candidates must build their own organizations. In these cases, candidates are most concerned with their own elections, not that of those who share this party label. Candidates choose campaign managers whose sole goal is victory for that one candidate. They build personal organizations to handle the important functions of campaigning—doing research to develop issue positions and to counter opponents' proposals; polling the public to ascertain perceptions of the candidate and reactions to strategies; writing speeches; communicating with the press; developing and placing advertisements; sending out direct mail appeals, telephoning and leafleting the district; scheduling and preparing for candidate appearances; and perhaps most important, raising money. For larger and more expensive campaigns, all of these functions are performed by paid workers or volunteers in a candidate's own organization, or bought with campaign contributions.

Recent campaign organizations have been less able to handle all of these functions, and two means of coping have emerged. For campaigns in smaller constituencies, the candidate often performs all of these functions him or herself. They are done more or less well depending on the skill of the candidate, the time available, the level of competition, and the sophistication that is expected in campaigning for office (Maisel 1999).

Even those with relatively high budget campaigns often find that they cannot hire staff to perform all of the necessary campaign activities. These candidates frequently turn to paid political consultants, experts from outside the campaign who specialize in certain aspects of the campaign process and sell their services to many campaigns during any election cycle. Firms specialize in media advertising, polling, direct mail, telephone banks, fundraising, and virtually every other aspect of campaigning; other firms are structured to take over all or many aspects of a campaign. Some work in particular geographic areas. Others are ready to sell their services anywhere throughout an entire nation or even internationally.

3. Defining Messages and Setting Strategy

A political campaign requires getting a message to voters. To do that, a candidate must define what the message is and must devise a strategy to reach the voters who will be swayed by that message. Again, how this is to be done varies with whether the campaign in question is party-centered or candidate-centered.

For party-centered campaigns, the message is the party platform, and the voters to be reached at those in the party's core constituency and others to whom the message might appeal in a particular year. Neither the message nor the strategy vary much from year to year, though marginal changes are made as the context changes—and these marginal changes might well spell the difference between victory and defeat.

For candidate-centered campaigns these decisions are among the most crucial. Candidates must decide whether to stick with the party message or to devise one of their own; they must decide what particular issues will play best to their voters; and they must figure out who precisely those voters are. Campaign strategists divide the electorate in a variety of ways—by demographic characteristics, by economic interests, by geographic locations. The goal is to use research and polling data to determine what appeals will work with which audiences and to have the candidate address those audiences appropriately. For incumbents seeking re-election, the strategic consideration often involves relying upon strengths demonstrated earlier. For challengers, the strategy must be to find an opponent's weakness and to emphasize one's own strengths.

Effective campaign strategies remain more art than science. Professional political campaigners know what has worked in the past. But many strategists learn those lessons. The successful strategists are those who can see how to change the approach as the context changes, as is often said in the military, 'not to refight the last war but to plan for the next one.'

4. Communicating with the Voters

To be effective, a political campaign must be able to send the message it has devised to the audience it has targeted. Campaign messages are communicated in two ways, through free media and paid media.

4.1 Free Media Coverage

Political campaigns seek free media coverage in whatever form they can, whenever they can. Candidates want to be reported on in newspapers and newsmagazines; they want to grant interviews on radio; they want their events covered on television. Free media coverage is advantageous not only because there is no cost but also because the viewer sees news coverage of a candidate as giving that candidate a sense of legitimacy; the candidate is seen as part of the day's news, not as part of a paid advertisement. However, free media is uncontrolled exposure. Campaign strategists can try to structure what topics will be covered—and campaigns are exploring increasingly sophisticated means to do this—but too frequently the message delivered is very different from the message the candidate seeks to convey.

4.2 Paid Media Advertising

The opposites apply to paid advertising. Paid media—whether in the form of television, radio, or print advertisements, of Internet sites, or of direct mail—is costly and is often viewed by the prospective voter as the slanted message it in fact is. However, these paid media also have the distinct advantage of allowing a candidate to emphasize exactly the message desired. These messages can be narrowcast, that is designed for and directed to specific target audiences. These ads can create images, discuss positions, or—increasingly in recent years—attack an opponent, all in precisely the way strategists feel will be most effective for a specified audience.

The critical concerns about political campaigns today relate to paid media. Many fear that effective political messages cannot be conveyed in 30-second advertisements, the medium preferred by advertising executives. Others complain that the emphasis on negative, attack advertising has poisoned the atmosphere that surrounds political life, keeping some of the best candidates from running (Ansolabehere and Iyengar 1995). Virtually everyone bemoans the exorbitant costs of campaigns, costs spurred by reliance on paid media. However, political campaigns will continue to rely on paid media so long as they are effective in communicating a candidate's message to the target audience; for that is the means to electoral success—the ultimate message of a campaign's effectiveness.

See also: Advertising: Effects; Electoral Systems; Electronic Democracy; Mass Media, Political Economy of; Media and Social Movements; Media Effects; Media, Uses of; Party Identification; Political Machines; Political Money and Party Finance; Political Parties; Polling; Primary Elections; Voting, Sociology of; Women's Suffrage

Bibliography

Ansolabehere S A, Iyengar S 1995 *Going Negative: How Attack Ads Shrink and Polarize the Electorate*. Free Press, New York
Hix S, Lord C 1997 *Political Parties in the European Union*. St. Martin's Press, New York
Jacobson G C, Kernell S 1981 *Strategy and Choice in Congressional Elections*. Yale University Press, New Haven, CT
Kazee T A (ed.) 1994 *Who Runs for Congress? Ambition, Context, and Candidate Emergence*. Congressional Quarterly, Washington, DC
Maisel L S 1986 *From Obscurity to Oblivion: Running in the Congressional Primary*, rev. edn. University of Tennessee, Knoxville, TN
Maisel L S 1999 *Parties and Elections in America: The Electoral Process*, 3rd edn. Rowman & Littlefield, Lanham, MD
Maisel L S, Stone W J 1997 Determinants of candidate emergence in U. S. House elections: an exploratory study. *Legislative Studies Quarterly* **22**: 79 96: Current work from the Candidate Emergence Project can be found at http://socsci.colorado.cdu/CES/home.html
Polsby N W, Wildavsky A 2000 *Presidential Elections: Strategies and Structures of American Politics*, 10th edn. Chatham House Publishers, New York
Wayne S J 2000 *The Road to the White House 2000*. St. Martin's Press, New York

L. S. Maisel

Campbell, Donald Thomas (1916–96)

Donald Thomas Campbell, born November 20, 1916 in Grass Lake, Michigan, died May 6, 1996 in Bethlehem, Pennsylvania, thus ending a career marked by an array of superlatives. Prolific scholar and author, original thinker, ebullient teacher with a notable twinkle in his eye, and generous colleague, Campbell was widely regarded as the most important social science methodologist of the twentieth Century. Several of Campbell's articles vie with one another as among the most widely cited pieces of social science scholarship. Repeatedly he coined phrases any one of which most scholars would be proud to have conceived, for example, 'quasi-experiments,' 'unobtrusive measures,' 'internal and external validity,' and 'plausible rival hypotheses.' His concepts are incorporated as fundamental in several fields—psychology, sociology, anthropology, organization and management sciences, public policy, evaluation, education, and philosophy—and in common use by scholars unaware of their inventor. Moreover, Campbell's welcoming and self-critical personal style, modeled on his scholarship, led him to embrace and examine all 'plausible rival hypotheses' and endeared him to students and colleagues alike.

Campbell received his B.A. (1939) and Ph.D. (1947), both in Psychology, from the University of California (Berkeley), and taught at several institutions, including

Ohio State University (1947–50), the University of Chicago (1950–53), Syracuse University (as N.Y. State Board of Regents Albert Schweitzer Professor, 1979–82) and Lehigh University (as Distinguished University Professor of Sociology-Anthropology, Psychology and Education, 1983–96), but the majority of his scholarly years were spent as professor of psychology at Northwestern University (1953–79) with which Campbell's name and reputation are 'permanently and inextricably co-identified' (Campbell 1981).

Campbell's honors include a Fulbright Visiting Professorship in Social Psychology at Oxford (1968), the Distinguished Scientific Contribution Award from the American Psychological Association (1969), election to the National Academy of Sciences and the American Academy of Arts & Sciences (1973), the Kurt Lewin Memorial Award from the Society for the Psychological Study of Social Issues (1974), presidency of the American Psychological Association (1975), the Williams James Lectureship at Harvard (1977), the Myrdal Prize in Science (1977), and the Distinguished Contribution Award from the American Educational Research Association (1981). In addition, two annual awards are given in his name: The Donald Campbell Award for Significant Research in Social Psychology (1982–) and the Donald Campbell Award from the Policy Studies Organization, to an 'outstanding methodological innovator in public policy studies' (1983–). Campbell received honorary degrees from numerous universities, including Oslo, Michigan, Chicago, and Southern California.

But Campbell felt most honored by the vast array of books dedicated to him, a list that grew steadily in several disciplines before and after his death.

1. Major Contributions

When he died, Campbell's resumé listed more than 230 published books, monographs, and articles. Any brief discussion of his contributions must necessarily focus on a few. Best known as a methodologist, with considerable scholarly work in the areas of experimental design, measurement, and social experimentation, Campbell is perhaps remembered especially for his explorations of the concept of validity. He was also a well-regarded epistemologist with a keen interest in the sociology of science. To each domain, Campbell brought his unique mind to bear on the problem of knowledge production. In a remarkable array of works, Campbell explored from several perspectives the inevitable fallibilities inherent in both observers and methods in accurately portraying the world.

In his earliest publication, 'The Indirect Assessment of Social Attitudes' (1950), Campbell evidenced an aspect of the interests that would become the overall focus of his scholarly life: the imperfections introduced by human observers and methods, including the scientific method, in the search for veridical descrip-

tion of the physical world and mechanisms for compensating for these errors. (Campbell later declared profound 'ambivalence' toward the use of disguised measures; see Kidder and Campbell 1970.) Campbell explored the sources and loci of bias and developed and refined methods for illustrating and for minimizing these biases. For example in Jacobs and Campbell (1961) he demonstrated how consensus in the 'reality' of an arbitrarily invented but shared group norm could persist over generations of experimental subjects. In a series of crosscultural explorations Campbell and co-workers (e.g., Segall et al. 1966) explored sources of validity and invalidity in perceptions of 'in-groups' and 'out-groups,' and the differential susceptibility to perceptual illusions between European and non-European cultures.

Campbell and Fiske (1959) published 'Convergent and Discriminant Validation by the Multitrait, Multimethod Matrix,' a complex and frequently cited analysis of the need for multiple measures of underlying constructs (traits) and of the need for the demonstrated capacity of methods to distinguish among traits if one is to minimize irrelevant measurement artifacts. Since every measure is partially invalid, multiple and distinctive methods are called for to yield a 'heterogeneity of irrelevancies.' Campbell and Fiske explored the value of simultaneously deploying maximally different measures of an underlying trait (in pursuit of convergent validation) and of different traits measured the same way (in pursuit of discriminant validation). Only by demonstrating that an underlying trait can be measured in various distinct ways and that the chosen measurement strategies distinguish among measured traits, can one minimize the impact of misleading artifacts.

By the early 1960s Campbell had established an enviable reputation for the vigor and reach of his campaign for advancing the methods and theory associated with issues of validity. His reputation was further advanced with the publication with (Campbell and Stanley 1963) of 'Experimental and Quasi-experimental Designs for Research,' a widely circulated work (elaborated as Cook and Campbell 1979) in which they popularized the terms 'internal' and 'external' validity:

> Internal validity is the basic minimum without which any experiment is uninterpretable: did in fact the experimental treatment make a difference in this specific experimental instance? External validity asks the question of generalizability: To what populations, setting, treatment variables, and measurement variables can this effect be generalized? (Campbell and Stanley 1963).

Another widely cited treatise, *Unobtrusive Measures: Non-reactive Research in the Social Sciences* (Webb et al. 1966) evolved during affable lunchtime conversations with colleagues from different departments. Over several years these colleagues sought to identify relatively unbiased, nonreactive ways of measuring behavior. A frequently cited example describes ways a Chicago museum tried to identify the popularity of its exhibits. 'Obtrusive measures' included questioning visitors leaving the museum; an 'unobtrusive measure' was the frequency with which museum staff had to replace worn tiles in front of exhibits. By that index, the exhibit of baby chicks hatching live and wet from quivering eggs was by far the most popular.

Campbell's participation in an interdisciplinary conference spawned his brilliant foray into the sociology of science entitled 'Ethnocentrism of Disciplines: A Fishscale Model of Omniscience' (1969a). On reading a paper 'in an area of high relevance' to his own work by esteemed fellow social psychologist William McGuire, Campbell realized and then acknowledged that he had not 'read or read-at even half of McGuire's citations, and was not at all aware of the existence of another sizeable proportion' (Campbell 1969a). While many scholars might react with chagrin, Campbell instead reflected on how the 'highly arbitrary' organization of universities and academic fields skewed knowledge production:

> Thus anthropology is a hodgepodge of all novelties venturing into exotic lands—a hodgepodge of skin color, physical stature, agricultural practices, weapons, religious beliefs, kinship systems, history, archeology, and paleontology ... Thus psychology is a hodgepodge of sensitive subjective biography, or brain operations, or school achievement testing, of factor analysis, of Markov process mathematics, of schizophrenic families, of laboratory experiments on group structure in which persons are anonymous ... Thus economics is a hodgepodge of mathematics without data, of history of economic institutions without mathematics or theory, of an ideal model of psychological man ... (Campbell 1969a)

Campbell took a breathtaking leap when he conceived the 'myth of unidisciplinary competence,' demonstrating how social, administrative, structural, and political supports which accrue over time around arbitrary disciplines ultimately create incentives that reinforce these arrangements and punish others of equal epistemological worth. Campbell detailed the inevitable consequence—biased knowledge production—and offered a model of 'interdisciplinary narrowness' for mitigating this 'ethnocentrism of disciplines.'

By the late 1960s, following Vietnam War protests, campus unrest, and a national focus on urban inequities, Campbell began trying conscientiously to influence the design, implementation, and evaluation of social policies. In 'Reforms as Experiments' (1969b) Campbell introduced a range of real-world quasi-experiments (attempts to approach the standards of experimentation even where random assignment of subjects to conditions is unachievable)—each tested against standards of 'internal and external validity'—to the practical world of social reform. That article frequently is cited as the most important single work in the field now known as 'program evaluation.'

In a brilliant tongue-in-cheek section of this article Campbell advised 'trapped administrators whose political predicament will not allow the risk of failure' how to capitalize on 'threats to validity' to assure positive results (Campbell 1969b). For example, were they to accept the occasional 'grateful testimonial' as if it were a representative outcome, to reserve interventions for carefully selected subpopulations most likely to succeed, and to eliminate from their analyses all those who prematurely quit the program, 'successful' program outcomes could be virtually assured.

Campbell continued in various fora to insist that social scientists have both obligations and opportunities to test the relevance of their theories and methods in the service of public good. In this, Campbell's unswerving concern was with the biases affecting the generation of knowledge. For example, in his too-infrequently cited 'Assessing the Impact of Planned Social Change' (1975) Campbell again displayed remarkable methodological and sociological insight in generalizing the problem of data validity in the policy arena in the following way:

> The more any quantitative social indicator is used for social decision-making, the more subject it will be to corruption pressures, and the more apt it will be to distort and corrupt the social processes it is intended to monitor (Campbell 1975).

Corrupted indicators remain a persistent and only vaguely explored source of real-world invalidity (e.g., Cochran et al. 1980).

Another highly influential, widely circulated piece went unpublished for nearly 20 years: in 'Methods for the Experimenting Society' Campbell attempted specifically to design a strategy for a society willing to test innovations and their intended effects. He argues for a society that would

> vigorously try out possible solutions to recurrent problems and would make hard-headed, multidimensional evaluations of outcomes, and when the evaluation of one reform showed it to have been ineffective or harmful, would move on to try other alternatives (Campbell, in Overman 1988).

Surveying the multitude of societal reforms underway at the time, many of which he endorsed (e.g., Alexander Dubcek in Czechoslovakia, Salvador Allende, in Chile), Campbell argued:

> There is no such (experimenting society, committed to reality testing, self-criticism, to avoiding self-deception) anywhere today. While all nations are engaged in trying out innovative reforms, none of them are yet organized to adequately evaluate the outcomes of these reforms (Overman 1988).

After specifying requirements of such an 'experimenting society' Campbell attempted in various ways to determine conditions under which these results might be achievable. For example, after Allende was assassinated in Chile, Campbell invited Chilean social scientist Ricardo Zuñiga to Northwestern University specifically to reflect on the conditions that might allow vigorous, large-scale reforms to be tested.

Campbell made other major contributions in his application of evolutionary theory to the realm of ideas. Campbell, the eternal epistemologist, focused in particular on the joint operation of the 'blind-variation-and-selective-retention process fundamental to all inductive achievements, to all genuine increases in knowledge.' In his 'evolutionary epistemology,' which perhaps received its fullest flowering in his essay honoring Karl Popper (in Overman 1988), Campbell endorsed the natural selection paradigm for explaining the production of knowledge. Through the selective winnowing of ideas, Campbell argued, what survive over time are those ideas that are most meritorious, particularly as each is subjected to 'critical realism.'
In his William James lectures, Campbell (1977) summarized his perspective in this way:

> I am a fallibilist and antifoundationalist. No part of our system of knowledge is immune to correction. There are no firm building blocks, either as indubitable and therefore valid axioms, or in any set of posits that are unequivocal once made. Nor are there any unequivocal experiences or explicit operations on which to found a certainty of communication in lieu of a certainty of knowing.
> I am some kind of a realist, some kind of a critical, hypothetical, corrigible, scientific realist. But I am against direct realism, naive realism, and epistemological complacency (Campbell, in Overman 1988).

2. Legacy

Campbell's legacy is vast and pronounced. It affects a wide range of social scientists as well as public policy scholars and practitioners, and is reflected in the work of hundreds of his students and more distant heirs. He introduced fundamentally new ways of thinking that are taken for granted today about how we perceive, discover, and assess accumulated knowledge. Many of his concepts are now fundamental throughout the social and policy sciences. Campbell is the most important intellectual figure in the history of evaluation research. The strategies he employed in 'Reforms as Experiments' for unearthing and illustrating threats to interpretations of policy implementation are an often-cited model for exploring complex data (see Tufte 1983).

In remarkably vivid, fetching but precise language, Campbell repeatedly captured the central importance of fallibilities inherent in human observers and their methods as they accumulate knowledge about the world, and thus of the importance of multiple perspectives, the triangulation of methods, and an open process whereby ideas are tested against one another to promote the winnowing effects of competition.
Thus, in the James lectures, Campbell stated that

> We are cousins to the amoeba, and have received no direct revelation not shared with it. How then, indeed, could we know for certain? ... Our only hope as competent knowers is that we be the heirs of a substantial set of well-winnowed propositions (Campbell, in Overman 1988).

In the heady intellectual mix he created and sustained, Campbell was known for changing his mind when persuaded by carefully tested evidence, and for challenging others to do the same. For example, over the years Campbell was persuaded by sociologist Howard S. Becker and others to appreciate the falsifiability of carefully wrought case studies, in spite of their failure to live up to his long-cherished methodological criteria (Campbell, in Overman 1988). In return, he prompted qualitatively-oriented colleagues to persist in reconsidering the validity claims inherent in their own work (see, for example, Becker 1986). For this open-mindedness, Campbell is revered by quantitative and qualitative methodologists alike (see Patton 1999).

Campbell also influenced legions of colleagues to reflect honestly on their own work. He talked and wrote openly about his own insecurities and frustrations, including how late in his career he began to write, droughts in his own productivity, his discomfort with the production pressure and relentless expectation of genius when he was a young assistant professor at the University of Chicago, his frequent bouts of depression, and the times when he believed his students and colleagues 'carried him.'

He explained his messy desk cheerfully by saying that he 'filed archeologically,' and as long as no one moved things around he could find whatever he wanted. Amazed colleagues would watch him reach into a pile and pull out the precise papers relevant to their discussions.

Although its publishers have sold thousands of copies of *Experimental and Quasi-Experimental Designs for Research* and students return to it year after year, Campbell never received any royalties; he asked only for unlimited copies to give freely to his colleagues.

Consideration of Campbell's legacy would be incomplete without a discussion of his personal style, for it, too, promoted the production of knowledge while providing his colleagues with a vital and successful paradigm. It would understate Campbell's colossal influence if there were no mention of his towering warmth, kindness, and generosity, and his deeply honest and self-critical perspective on his own work (Campbell 1981). Campbell was remarkably able to reflect on his own fallibilities and to create conditions that would model his epistemology, and improve both his work and the work of others. Examples are diverse and legendary: he would often send a requested reprint accompanied by a colleague's critical rejoinder. He was always in pursuit of contrary evidence and counter-intuitive examples, particularly if they confronted his own work. He encouraged students to write minority sections to project reports if they disagreed with him or with an emerging majority. Campbell was resolutely encouraging of others and in fact was thought by some to 'suffer fools gladly.' He gave three grades: A, B, and incomplete. If the data collected in dissertations failed to support anticipated hypotheses, or failed to replicate published findings in the literature, Campbell urged students to write up the apparent reasons for the obtained results.

Over time, Campbell connected his early deep philosophical explorations to a program of practical work that will continue to guide generations of scholars and practitioners. Campbell lives on through his voluminous work in many fields, through his students, and through their adoption of his style.

See also: Evolutionary Epistemology; Experimental Design: Large-scale Social Experimentation; Experimental Design: Randomization and Social Experiments; Experimentation in Psychology, History of; External Validity; Foucault, Michel (1926–84); Internal Validity; Panel Surveys: Uses and Applications; Pearson, Karl (1857–1936); Quasi-Experimental Designs; Reform: Political; Unobtrusive Measures

Bibliography

Brewer M, Collins B 1981 *Scientific Inquiry and the Social Sciences*. Jossey-Bass, San Francisco
Campbell D T 1950 The indirect assessment of social attitudes. *Psychological Bulletin* 47(1): 15–38
Campbell D T 1969a Ethnocentrism of disciplines and the fish-scale model of omniscience. In: Sherif M, Sherif C (eds.) *Interdisciplinary Relationships in the Social Sciences*. Aldine, Chicago
Campbell D T 1969b Reforms as experiments. *American Psychologist* 24: 409–29
Campbell D T 1975 Assessing the impact of planned social change. In: Lyons G (ed.) *Social Research and Public Policies*. Public Affairs Center, Dartmouth College, Hanover, NH
Campbell D T 1977 *Descriptive Epistemology: Psychological, Sociological, and Evolutionary. William James Lectures.* Harvard University, Cambridge, MA
Campbell D T 1981 *Another Perspective on a Scholarly Career.* In: Brewer M B, Collins B E (eds.) *Scientific Inquiry and the Social Sciences*. Jossey-Bass, San Francisco
Campbell D T, Fiske D A 1959 Convergent and discriminant validation by the multitrait–multimethod matrix. *Psychological Bulletin* 56: 81–105
Campbell D T, Stanley J C 1963 Experimental and quasi-experimental designs for research on teaching. In: Gage N (ed.) *Handbook of Research on Teaching*. Rand McNally, Chicago
Cochran N, Gordon A C, Krause M 1980 Proactive records: Reflections on the village watchman. *Knowledge* 2(1): 5–18
Cook T D, Campbell D T 1979 *Quasi-experimentation Design and Analysis Issues for Field Settings*. Rand McNally, Chicago
Jacobs R C, Campbell D T 1961 The Perpetuation of an arbitrary tradition through several generations of a laboratory microculture. *Journal of Abnormal & Social Psychology* 62: 649–58
Kidder L, Campbell D T 1970 The indirect testing of social attitudes. In: Summers G (ed.) *Attitude Measurement*. Rand McNally, Chicago
Overman E S (ed.) 1988 *Methodology and Epistemology for Social Science: Selected Papers of Donald T. Campbell.* Chicago
Patton M Q 1997 *Utilization–Focused Evaluation*, 3rd edn. Sage, Beverly Hills, CA
Segall M H, Campbell D T, Herkovits M J 1966 *The Influence of Culture on Visual Perception*. Bobbs-Merrill, Indianapolis, IN
Tufte E R 1983 *The Visual Display of Quantitative Information*. Graphics Press, Cheshire, CT
Webb E J, Campbell D T, Schwartz R D, Sechrest L 1966 *Unobtrusive Measures: Nonreactive Research in the Social Sciences*. Rand McNally, Chicago

A. C. Gordon

Cancer-prone Personality, Type C

Type C has emerged as a behavioral pattern, coping style, or personality type that predisposes people to, or is a risk factor, in the onset and progression of cancer. Type C has been described as being over-cooperative, stoical or self-sacrificing, appeasing, unassertive, patient, avoiding conflict, compliant with external authorities, unexpressive, suppressing or denying negative emotions, self-sacrificing, and predisposed to experiencing hopelessness and depression (Bleiker 1995, Eysenck 1994, Temoshok 1990).

Since the mid-twentieth century, the contribution of psychosocial factors to cancer has been an important research topic. A search of the literature shows an exponential growth: while only nine publications appeared from 1951 to 1955, between 1995 to 1999 more than 300 hundred documents dealing with this topic have been published in scientific journals (Psychlit and Medline database). This article deals with the 'state of the art' of Type C and its role as a risk factor in the onset and progression of cancer.

1. Historical Overview

The belief that personality contributes to the etiology of disease is as old as the history of human thought. In the third millennium BC, Hippocrates stated that melancholic humor (caused by a surplus of black bile) caused cancer, and Galen (second century AD) observed that neoplasm was more likely to occur in melancholic and depressed than in sanguine women.

It is in the twentieth century that experimental evidence about relationships between cancer and personality are found. During the first half of the twentieth century, investigations were made from the perspective of psychoanalytical theory, and within the field of psychosomatic medicine. The most important characteristics in cancer patients found through empirical research mentioned: loss of important relationships, inability to express negative emotions, tension concerning parental relationships, and sexual problems.

Finally, it is from the second half of the twentieth century that the role of behavioral and psychosocial conditions in the onset and progression of cancer has been investigated systematically in research programs, groups, and laboratories, following a track parallel to research in Type A, Coronary prone behavior. A good deal of clinical observations and research data has been produced about a systematic link between some psychosocial factors and cancer. At the same time, there have been comprehensive reviews of psycho-oncology research, and strong criticism of its methodological flaws. Thus, before presenting the main traits constituting Type C, the most important difficulties involved in its research will be discussed.

2. Difficulties in the Study of Cancer-prone Personality, Type C

Temoshok and Heller (1984) described Type C research in a very illustrative fashion, as 'comparing apples, oranges and fruit salad,' expressing its complexity and methodological difficulties. In other words it involves different constructs, assessed through different instruments, in different samples of subjects with different types of cancer and other diseases, and using different designs.

The heterogeneity of factors contributing to the noncomparability of psycho-oncology literature can be considered in the following ways: (a) the nature and measurement of psychological phenomena, (b) cancer characteristics (type, site, and stage in the process), (c) sample characteristics, and (d) designs used.

2.1 The Nature and Measurement of Psychological Phenomena

Personality type, coping style, stress or emotional response, or behavioral pattern are constructs with a variety of conceptualizations in psychology. This problematic issue has been overcome by Eysenck (1994); in short, the subject's response to a given stressful situation cannot be understood without taking into consideration their stressor perception and the behavioral pattern used in coping with stress—both are stable personality conditions.

To this conceptual problem, a methodological one should be added. As constructs, all types of variables must be operationalized through psychological measures. From semistructured interviews and projective techniques to well-developed questionnaires, hundreds of measures have been used in psycho-oncology research, which have different psychometric

properties and different levels of generalizability, and their scores can, therefore, be generalized to different universes, presenting difficulties for the comparability of results. Over recent decades much more attention to Type C measurement has been paid, and these methodological problems have been partially overcome.

2.2 Cancer Characteristics

Cancer is not a homogeneous entity; both cancer types (melanoma, sarcoma, etc.) and cancer sites (lung, breast, skin, etc.) vary with regard to etiology, course, mortality, heritability, and risk factors. Also, cancer always implies a process, and psychological factors may act at different stages of this process; this fact introduces important research problems. For example Kreitler et al. (1993) stated that emotional repression may be a response to the threat posed by the cancer diagnosis. Several studies have dealt with the timing of psychological assessment and its relationship to cancer, but the relationships between psychosocial conditions and neoplastic processes require sophisticated and complex research designs, and these have yet to be fully developed.

2.3 Subjects/Sample Characteristics

Several authors have pointed out that sociodemographic variables may be associated with medical and environmental risk factors. Among sociodemographic characteristics, age seems to be the most important, since cancer incidence and prevalence increases with age, and several personality characteristics are also associated with age (e.g., introversion). When cancer groups are compared with other participants, age should be controlled (e.g., Fernández-Ballesteros et al. 1998).

In order to test the psychological risk factors of a given disease or illness through psychological covariation, comparison between healthy and ill subjects is not enough. It is essential to distinguish also between the target illness and other illnesses. Cancer patients have been compared, as well as with normal patients, with patients suffering from cardiovascular and digestive problems, chronic diseases and benign pathologies, and with accident victims, among others.

2.4 Designs

Science requires strategies or designs for testing hypotheses; that is, when and under what conditions units (subjects) will be observed and measured. Authors agree that the best design for studying a given risk factor is a prospective one. Subjects (recruited at random in the community or as a member of a given group) are assessed in the relevant target behaviors and psychological constructs, and are monitored until some of them develop cancer and others do not. Also, in longitudinal studies subjects already diagnosed with cancer are monitored during different stages of the illness process, from diagnosis to progression, treatment, and survival or death.

In quasiprospective designs psychological evaluation is carried out before cancer diagnosis, but this period is usually very short. This type of design is commonly used within cancer prevention programs in which all subjects are assessed in psychosocial characteristics and, after diagnosis, subjects with cancer are monitored. This type of design has two main flaws: psychological characteristics are measured when subjects have already developed cancer, and subjects attending a prevention campaign cannot be considered to be in a neutral context. Furthermore, this situation is quite heterogeneous, since while several subjects may already be suspicious about lumps or lesions, others are merely participating in a preventive—or 'normal'—situation.

In retrospective designs, subjects already diagnosed or being treated for cancer are compared with control groups in a set of psychological characteristics. Such retrospective designs are highly criticized because they do not tell us whether psychological characteristics are the cause or the result of cancer (e.g., Kreitler et al. 1993).

All of these designs can be considered as 'descriptive' or 'correlational' research strategies. However, there are also experimental designs; in these, the 'independent' variable (a psychological or personality condition) is manipulated in order to measure its causal or functional relationship with the 'dependent' variable (cancer).

In sum, several of these conceptual and methodological problems have been overcome, while others continue to be the object of criticism.

3. Personality Characteristics in Cancer Patients

Evidence from prospective, quasiprospective, retrospective, and experimental studies converges on a set of psychological characteristics that seem to act in the onset and progression of all types of cancer. Let us examine these characteristics.

3.1 Emotional Expression

This appears to be at the core of Type C. That is, suppression, repression, inhibition and/or denial of negative emotions seem to be the central characteristics of the cancer-prone personality (see *Emotions and Health*). Cancer patients (in comparison to controls) are described as anti-emotional and alexitimic, with a tendency to control their negative feelings (mainly anger, aggressiveness, hostility); they report

not feeling anger or irritation, and in their relationships they report avoiding arguments with others by using reason and logic, often contrary to their feelings. For example, in a quasiprospective study, within a breast cancer prevention program, Fernández-Ballesteros et al. (1997) compared the rationality (as well as other somatic characteristics) of healthy women ($N = 96$), women with benign breast disease ($N = 90$) and women with breast cancer ($N = 122$). Healthy women were matched with women with benign breast pathology or with breast cancer. All were assessed before diagnosis. Results show that women with breast cancer differed significantly from healthy women and those with benign breast pathology. Any other review on this topic yields the same results: emotional expression is one of the psychological hallmarks of cancer (Bleiker 1995, Eysenck 1994, Spiegel and Kato 1996, Temoshok 1990).

Unfortunately, however, experimental data does not describe the nature of these psychological characteristics, nor whether cancer subjects fail to perceive or feel their emotional internal physiological reactions or whether they simply fail to express them (verbally or otherwise).

3.2 Depression

Consideration of medical anamneses also suggests that depression is a frequent precursor of cancer; feelings of helplessness and hopelessness are also found in several studies. For example, the Western Electric Health longitudinal study monitored 2,020 employees with the purpose of investigating coronary disease risk factors. As a measure of personality and personal and social adjustment the Minnesota Multiphasic Personality Inventory (MMPI) was administered. At the 17-year follow-up, 4 percent had died of cancer. As reported by Shekelle et al. (1981), there was a twofold increase in the odds of death from cancer in men with psychological depression. This result was consistent across sites and types of cancer. Also, this association persisted after adjustments had been made for age, cigarette smoking, use of alcohol, family history of cancer, and occupational status (see *Depression, Hopelessness, Optimism, and Health*).

In spite of these impressive results, it is unclear whether these states are antecedents or consequences of cancer, and research data is inconsistent in this area.

3.3 Interpersonal Style

In the medical literature, cancer patients have been described by their doctors as 'extremely pleasant' in their interactions with them. There is evidence from retrospective, quasiprospective, and prospective studies, as well as from experimental studies, that cancer patients—in comparison to control subjects— yield significantly higher scores in tests assessing need for harmony, self-sacrifice, and unassertiveness. For example, in a quasiprospective study Fernández-Ballesteros et al. (1998) compared, in terms of need for harmony (as well as rationality), three groups of women with breast cancer (before diagnosis (74), during treatment (105), and during the follow-up (132)) with healthy women. Both personality variables correctly classified 86 percent of the participants (87 percent of the breast cancer patients and 82 percent of the healthy participants) and, moreover, no significant differences in rationality and need for harmony were found to be related to the stage of the cancer process.

This behavioral pattern can be understood as a coping style for stressful situations, as a personality characteristic, or as a defense mechanism against anxiety.

3.4 Stressors, Stress, Strain, and Coping Mechanisms

Cancer patients' anamneses usually show that an antecedent of cancer disease is a subject's life event. However, as already mentioned, it is important to differentiate between the external stressor, the subject's appraisal and coping style, and the stress reaction (see *Stress and Health Research*). As underlined by several authors, stress is the response of a given subject to their perception of a stressor—a stimulus or situation perceived as threatening. Also, however, subjects have different mechanisms for coping with stress. For example, Cooper and Faragher (1993) pointed out that subjects who experienced a stressful situation they perceived as threatening had a significantly higher cancer risk. In a retrospective study, Watson et al. (1984) compared breast cancer patients and healthy controls. Breast cancer patients were more likely than controls to report a tendency to control emotional reactions, particularly anger.

However, evidence about psychosocial influences on cancer incidence and progression comes not only from descriptive studies—there are also important experimental results. For example, Grossarth-Maticek carried out an experimental study within the Heidelberg prospective study. In 1971, 1,026 healthy persons from a random sample of the population were assessed in a wide set of psychosocial and medical variables. Also, 1,537 subjects were selected on the basis of their increased psychosocial and clinical risk of cancer or cardiovascular or circulatory disease. Criteria used included chronic depression and hopelessness, chronic excitement and anger, heavy smoking, hypertension, high blood cholesterol, and high blood sugar. From the 1,537 high-risk subjects, 100 were selected who were thought to have an especially high risk of cancer (and also of CV disease). Half of these subjects were selected randomly and given psychological therapy intended to decrease the respective risk. This therapy, which has been called 'creative novation behaviour therapy,' was developed by Grossarth-Maticek and Eysenck (1990) on the basis of cancer-prone characteristics (emotional expression, assertiveness, coping, etc.), and it was attempted to manipulate them through behavior therapy techniques. In 1983, mortality and causes of death for the 2,563 subjects of the study were ascertained. Of the selected subjects, 38 percent of risk subjects had died, as compared to 10 percent of the random sample.

In the cancer therapy group deaths were significantly fewer than in the control group, and there were no deaths from cancer. In marked contrast, 60 percent of the deaths in the control group were from cancer. Although Grossarth-Maticek's studies have been criticized for certain methodological shortcomings (questionnaires used were not in a standard form, and there was no report on psychometric properties), their impressive results are in accordance with the well-established effects of psychosocial treatment, which significantly increases survival in cancer patients (e.g., Spiegel and Kato 1996).

From descriptive and experimental studies it can be summarized that cancer-prone or Type C personality is a psychological configuration with two main conditions: (a) suppression of negative emotions (such as anger and anxiety), which includes not only lack of verbal expression of emotions but also corresponding interpersonal behaviors and (b) inappropriate stress coping mechanisms, leading to feelings of hopelessness, helplessness, and depression.

Finally, what mechanisms can be assumed to link psychological characteristics with cancer?

3.5 Mechanisms that Link Psychological Factors with Cancer

From a mentalistic and/or dualistic perspective, psychological characteristics observed in cancer patients have been considered as though the 'soul' (or mental entities) were affecting the body. This position has been brought up to date through empirical evidence from both psychological and biological literature that support the relationship between personality and emotions and the autonomic, endocrinological and immune systems.

O'Leary (1990), in her review of stress response and the immune system, referred to the fact that chronic stress is associated with a suppression of the immune function, and that personality and coping styles may enhance or degrade the immune response. As pointed out by Spiegel and Kato (1996), chronic and acute stress are associated with reductions in various measures of the immune function, and, moreover, psychological intervention positively influences hallmarks of the immune system.

In sum, as Spiegel and Kato (1996) conclude, 'there is a nonrandom relationship among various psychosocial factors and cancer incidence and progression that can only partially (underline added) be explained by behavioral, structural, or biological factors.'

4. Conclusions

Throughout the twentieth century, the empirical study of the relationship between personality and cancer has been an important research topic. During the 1980s and 1990s, several conceptual and methodological problems have been overcome.

Various designs, assessment devices, and samples have shown that a set of psychological characteristics appears to play a role in cancer onset and progression. These characteristics can be reduced to the suppression of negative emotions and to inappropriate stress coping mechanisms. Much more attention should be paid to the psychological nature of these characteristics.

Psychological treatments (manipulating the above psychological characteristics) appear to act on the cancer process, preventing cancer onset and increasing patient survival possibilities.

Scientific literature supports the hypothesis of a link between personality characteristics, stress reaction coping styles and biological systems. That is, there is evidence of a connection between personality, stress and cancer, as well as between personality, stress, and the autonomic, endocrinological, and immune systems.

These psychological characteristics can be considered as cancer risk factors. Nevertheless, Type C or cancer-prone personality should be understood in terms of its synergic interaction with other genetic, biological, and environmental conditions.

See also: Cancer: Psychosocial Aspects; Cancer Screening; Depression, Hopelessness, Optimism, and Health; Emotions and Health; Gender and Cancer; Personality and Health; Stress and Health Research

Bibliography

Bleiker E 1995 *Personality Factors and Breast Cancer*. ICG, Dordrecht, The Netherlands

Cooper C L, Faragher E B 1993 Psychosocial stress and breast cancer: the interrelationships between stress events, coping strategies and personality. *Psychological Medicine* 23: 653–62

Eysenck H J 1994 Personality, stress, and cancer: Prediction and prophylaxis. *Advances in Behavior Research and Therapy* 16: 167–215

Fernández-Ballesteros R, Ruiz M A, Garde S 1998 Emotional expression in healthy women and those with breast cancer. *British Journal of Health Psychology* 3: 41–50

Fernández-Ballesteros R, Zamarrón M D, Ruiz M A, Sebastián J, Spielberger C D 1997 Assessing emotional expression. *Personality and Individual Differences* 22: 719–29

Greer S, Watson M 1985 Towards a psychobiological model of cancer: Psychological considerations. *Social Science and Medicine* 20: 773–7

Grossarth-Maticek R, Eysenck H J 1990 Prophylactic effects of psychoanalysis on cancer-prone and coronary heart disease-prone probands, as compared with control groups and behaviour therapy groups. *Journal of Behavioral Therapy and Experimental Psychiatry* 21: 91–9

Kreitler S, Chaitchik S, Kreitler H 1993 Repressiveness: cause or results of cancer? *Psycho-oncology* 2: 43–54

O'Leary A 1990 Stress, emotion, and immune function. *Psychological Bulletin* 108: 363–82

Shekelle R B, Raynor W J, Ostfeld A M, Garron D C, Bieliauskas L A, Liu S C, Maliza C, Paul O 1981 Psychological depression and seventeen-year risk of death from cancer. *Psychosomatic Medicine* 43: 117–25

Spiegel M D, Kato P M 1996 Psychosocial influences on cancer incidence and progression. *Harvard Review of Psychiatry* 4: 10–26

Temoshok L 1990 On attempting to articulate the bio-psychosocial model: Psychological-psychophysiological homeostasis. In: Friedman H (ed.) *Personality and Disease*. Wiley, New York

Temoshok L, Heller B W 1984 On comparing apples, oranges and fruit salad: A methodological overview of medical outcome studies in psychosocial oncology. In: Cooper C L (ed.) *Psychosocial Stress and Cancer*. Wiley, New York

R. Fernández-Ballesteros

Cancer: Psychosocial Aspects

1. Introduction

Psychosocial research in oncology has been conducted since the 1950s. The initial interest in cancer onset has changed, perhaps due to the many methodological problems, to research in psychosocial consequences of a cancer, and the impact of psychosocial factors in cancer progression. Although there are some studies, in several fields of research, which show negative results, most well-controlled studies have shown positive correlations between specific psychosocial factors and quality of life during cancer treatment, cancer progression, and survival.

2. Quality of Life in Cancer Patients

The concept of quality of life (QOL) was first referenced in *Index Medicus* in 1977. Since that time, it has emerged as an important concept in cancer research in the description of conditions in cancer diagnosis and treatment that make the quality of life of patients worse, and in the use of quality of life measurements for the evaluation of new methods of treatment. QOL is defined as a concept which refers to the individual's own perceptions about the degree of satisfaction with treatment, and ability to perform in their daily life. Although impairment in several dimensions of quality of life are primarily caused by biological aspects of the disease, psychosocial research has focused on psychosocial factors that additionally modulate the intensity of subjectively experienced impairments in quality of life. Extensive psychosocial research has been done with cancer patients in the

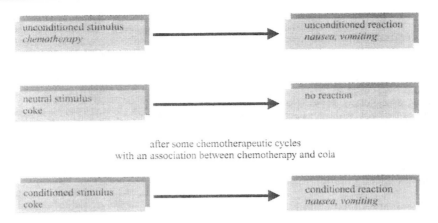

Figure 1
Learning model of classical conditioning, of anticipatory nausea and vomiting. See text for further details

initial phase of diagnosis and treatment, whereas little information is available about the problems and concerns that persist for long-term survivors. It can be assumed that, for all cancer survivors, what begins as a crisis involving diagnosis and treatment gradually becomes a chronic illness with life-long follow-up medical care, long-lasting psychological effects, and changes in social and employment relationships.

2.1 Physical Symptoms

2.1.1 Treatment-related nausea and vomiting.
It is estimated that 75 percent of the patients receiving chemotherapy will suffer from nausea or vomiting in spite of an antiemetic therapy (Morrow 1992). Nearly 25 percent of patients suffer from so-called anticipatory nausea. In these cases nausea or vomiting occur prior to the infusion of chemotherapy and is triggered by particular special odors or situations similar to stimuli experienced in previous treatment. Whereas post-chemotherapy nausea and vomiting are caused by neuropharmacological agents, anticipatory nausea and vomiting are assumed to be caused by classical processes of conditioning. Neutral stimuli (e.g., the taste of a drink like cola) that were associated with the infusion of chemotherapy (cola was mixed into the antiemetic drug that was given prior to chemotherapy), will be associated with post-chemotherapy nausea. As a consequence, its taste will release nausea even if the neuropharmacological effects of chemotherapy have passed. Taste becomes a learned stimulus for anticipatory nausea or vomiting (see Fig. 1).

Several predictors were identified as high risk factors for the development of nausea and vomiting during cancer chemotherapy: (a) antiemetic drugs; (b) physiological factors, such as age, constitutional pre-

disposition; and (c) psychological factors, such as treatment-related state anxiety or general psychological distress (Andrykowski and Gregg 1992). There are various hypothesized pathways by which a state of anxiety or distress may contribute to the experience of treatment-related nausea. First, due to the proximity of structures in the higher brain stem responsible for the release of vomiting, and noradrenergic structures that are influenced by anxiety and distress, it can be assumed that distress triggers release and intensity of nausea and vomiting through a higher noradrenergic activity. Second, it is well known from learning psychology that anxiety and distress may facilitate the process of classical conditioning. Therefore it can be assumed that distress may enhance the conditioned anticipatory nausea and vomiting.

2.1.2 Pain.
Pain is one of the most prevalent physical complaints of cancer patients. Bonica published the most comprehensive overview in 1985 (see Fig. 2). Fifty to 70 percent of cancer patients suffer from pain syndromes during the late phases of their disease; 20 to 50 percent suffer from cancer- or treatment-related pain even in early phases of their disease. In 60 to 80 percent of the cases pain syndromes are attributable to the malignancy of the tumor (tumor compression, infiltration of nerves); in 10 to 25 percent they are long-term results following operation, chemo- or radiotherapy; in 3 to 10 percent of cases the pain syndromes can be assumed to be unrelated to the cancer or treatment (e.g., migraine, arthritis). In many cases, however, it is difficult to discover the main cause of pain. It can be assumed that several psychological factors, known modulators in nonmalignant pain also influence the intensity and aversiveness of cancer-related pain. Among others, factors of depression, chronic daily stress in private life or at work, maladaptive pain-related patterns of

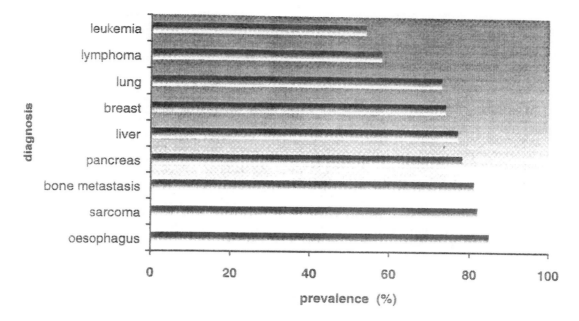

Figure 2
Prevalence of pain in different cancer diagnoses (see Bonica 1985).

thought like catastrophizing or suppressive cognitions; maladaptive pain coping strategies belong to the most important psychological factors that contribute to the chronicity of pain, e.g., chronic low pack pain (Hasenbring 1998).

2.1.3 Fatigue. Only in the last years of the twentieth century did cancer research focus on fatigue as another cancer- or treatment-related physical complaint; a national survey in the USA showed a prevalence of problems with fatigue in 76 percent of 419 chemotherapy and/or radiation-treated patients, with impairment in walking, exercising, house cleaning, or climbing stairs (Curt 2000). Cancer-related fatigue had also a significant emotional component, with 90 percent of patients reporting that fatigue contributed to a loss of control, hopelessness, isolation, lack of motivation, sadness, and frustration. A significant number of patients also reported fatigue-related social impairment, which included difficulties in shopping, expressing intimacy with a loved one, playing with children, or spending time with friends. Curt has shown that the physician recommendations tended to be nonspecific: 40 percent of physicians recommended doing nothing, 37 percent prescribed rest. Further research should focus on the biological and psychological mechanisms by which fatigue is produced and maintained, in order to develop effective interdisciplinary treatment modalities.

2.2 Body Image

Impairments of body image are mostly a direct consequence of cancer treatment. Significant impairment was seen in patients with a tumor of the head, neck, or larynx; in breast cancer patients with a resection of the mamma; and in patients with colorectal cancer and an artificial anal/sphincter praeter. Between 10 and 56 percent of the breast cancer patients develop problems in sexuality and in their partnerships. More than 50 percent of the patients with cancer of the head or neck experience a decrease in self-esteem, combined with anxiety and depression, which leads to withdrawal and social isolation (Holland and Rowland 1998).

2.3 Physical Functioning

A number of cancer patients suffer from impairment in sexual functions, in the short- and/or long-term, after cancer treatment. For instance, 75 percent of women with cancer of the cervix showed intense, continuous sexual difficulties; 33 percent gave up their sexual contacts. Patients with cancer of the prostate experience an impaired erection, which is a generally reversible consequence of injury to the autonomous nerves. Anxiety, dysfunctional patterns of thought, and feelings of shame are psychological factors eliciting avoidance behavior, which leads to persistent sexual difficulties. A study of 407 long-term survivors of bone-marrow transplantation (BMT) found sexual problems in 29 percent of the men and in 80 percent of the women (Syrjala et al. 1998). The authors recommend behavioral as well as hormonal or mechanical therapy.

2.4 Emotional Distress

Confrontation with a diagnosis of cancer is experienced as a crisis, which leads to distress in the form of, for instance, expectations of chronic suffering, acute, or long-lasting fear of death, and feelings of anxiety, depression, or anger. Patients with dysfunctional coping strategies are at risk of developing chronic anxiety and other feelings of distress; patients with intense or long-lasting emotional distress suffer more from the physical complaints described above. Extensive clinical studies have shown that 20 to 40 percent of cancer patients suffer from intense or long-lasting emotional distress (Holland and Rowland 1998). Some studies have seen intense feelings of anxiety in 80 percent of the patients immediately subsequent to cancer treatment (e.g., Hasenbring et al. 1993). Patients suffered from fear of pain caused by unfamiliar methods of treatment, by claustrophobia during computed tomography, or by anxiety because they did not know what the next steps of their therapy would entail.

2.5 Cognitive Functions

Clinical impressions suggest that a significant number of cancer patients suffer from impairment to various cognitive functions, although only a few studies have assessed cognitive functioning in cancer patients objectively. Cull et al. (1996) found 49 percent of cancer patients, with various diagnoses, suffering from impairment of concentration and memory. Cancer itself (e.g., tumor of the brain, brain metastases in breast cancer patients) and its treatment (neurotoxicity of cytostatic therapy) are known causes of cognitive impairment. Anxiety, depression, fatigue, and low psychosocial support are further possible causes of impairment of cognitive functions.

2.6 Social Relations

Fear of death, and impairment of emotional and physical functioning of cancer patients, lead to differing degrees of disturbance in their social relationships. Social roles and responsibilities in a family have to be redefined where patients suffer from significant complaints. Manne et al. (2000) reported, in a cross-sectional study with 219 cancer patients and their spouses, a significant relationship between increasing

patient functional impairment and spousal negative behaviors related to greater restrictions on the activity of the spouse and by depression.

3. Coping With Cancer-related Distress

Coping research in cancer patients has focused on cognitive and behavioral strategies that patients employ to reduce emotional distress or to change a distressing situation. A major question in cancer research has been whether specific coping responses would decrease or increase survival time. Results of different prospective cohort-studies (i.e., with two or more assessment points) indicate that several aspects of avoidance behavior, for instance, avoidance of distressing social contacts (social withdrawal), avoidance of expressing feelings of fear, anger, or regret, as well as the minimization or denial of the potential threat, are predictors of reduced survival time. For instance, Greer et al. (1979) conducted a retrospective study in women with breast cancer including a ten-year follow-up. They found that women with an active, confronting coping behavior ('fighting spirit') showed an increased survival time when compared to those who showed denial or stoic acceptance behavior. Women with signs of help-/hopelessness showed the lowest survival time. The tendency to minimization and anger were independent predictors of survival time in a further prospective study in 125 patients with metastatic melanoma, published by Butow et al. (1999).

4. Social Support

There has been extensive research into the role played by positive social relationships in the adaptation to stress. Among the variables (e.g., the number of available persons, frequency of contact with relatives, friends, etc., perceived social support, and degree of satisfaction with perceived support), perceived social support seems to be the best predictor of adaptation to cancer. Other qualitative dimensions are emotional support, instrumental, self-esteem, and appraisal support. Social support might influence patients' ability to adapt to the illness and its treatment ('stress-buffer hypothesis') or might have a direct influence on the progression of the disease ('main-effect hypothesis'). Retrospective studies in cancer patients have revealed some evidence of a positive relationship between social support and progression of the disease (Spiegel and Kato 1996). Nevertheless, there is also some evidence from recent studies for differential aspects. In a group intervention study, Helgeson et al. (2000) found that peer discussion groups in 230 women with breast cancer were helpful for women who lacked support from their partners or physicians, but harmful for women who had high levels of support. More research is needed to clarify the relationship between special aspects of social support, social networks, and the adaptation to the disease.

5. The Impact of Psychosocial Factors on Cancer Progression

Whereas psychosocial predictors of the onset of cancer have not yet been reliably identified (at the end of the twentieth century), perhaps due to methodological problems, the literature supports the idea that psychosocial variables predict cancer progression. Besides the coping styles, and the quality and amount of social support, as described above, cancer-independent distress in daily life has also been investigated in relation to cancer progression. In a study of 86 breast cancer patients, Forsén (1991) interviewed the women after surgery. Patients with more stressful life events during the year before the operation revealed an increased risk of recurrence (relative risk: 3.48) and of death (relative risk: 4.37). The role of chronic daily stress at work or in private life was seen as a high risk factor for tumor progression and for survival, after adjusting for age, diagnosis and tumor stage was explored in a further study in 51 cancer patients during their first chemotherapy (Hasenbring et al. 1993). However, some studies could not find a correlation between life events and tumor progression or survival.

6. Possible Links between Psychosocial Variables and Tumor Progression

There are a number of possible links between psychosocial factors and the progression of cancer. Chronic daily stress, the lack of social support and maladaptive strategies of coping with stress, especially when accompanied by depression (a) may change individual health behavior, which is known to be related to cancer onset or progression or (b) may directly influence endocrinological and/or immunological factors that are assumed to be precursors of cancer progression and death.

6.1 Health Behavior

Patients with increased depression as a persistent reaction to cancer, who experience intense or continuous stress (related to or independent of cancer treatment), or who lack sufficient social support may reveal more maladaptive health behaviors; for example, they tend to be less motivated to practice healthy eating habits, they are more often reliant on alcohol and smoking, and their sleep will be more frequently disturbed (Spiegel and Kato 1996). A number of epidemiological studies have shown that several of these health behaviors are significantly related to cancer progression.

6.2 Psychobiological Hypotheses

There has been extensive research that corroborates a connection between psychological distress, neuro-endocrine effects, and progression of cancer (Garssen and Goodkin 1999). Chronic stress, depression, and the lack of social support are seen to be related to hyperactivity of the hypothalamus—pituitary—adrenal axis. The possible links between stress, neuro-endocrine hyperactivity, and the progression of cancer are many. It is possible that increased cortisol can increase the onset of glucosis, which leads to a selective decrease in the growth of normal cells and enables the increase in growth of tumor cells. Another effect could be that cortisol, prolactin, or another stress-sensitive hormone, could stimulate the tumor growth directly in hormone sensitive tumors such as breast cancer. A third effect extensively researched, assumes that stress-induced hyperactivity of neuro-endocrine functions will lead to a suppression of immune functions (Andersen et al. 1994).

7. Psychosocial Intervention

Psychosocial intervention has been studied in the acute in-patient setting, primarily in order to reduce treatment-related side effects, such as nausea, vomiting, and pain, as well as in late phases of the disease in order to enhance the ability to cope with cancer-related emotional distress and to mobilize social support.

7.1 Intervention for the Reduction of Treatment-related Side Effects

There are a number of studies which have investigated the efficacy of different behavioral methods for reducing chemo- or radiotherapy-induced nausea and vomiting, and for enhancing quality of life during the acute in-patient setting, e.g., relaxation, systematic desensitization, hypnosis, and biofeedback (Carey and Burish 1988). Whilst all methods show positive effects in the reduction of nausea, vomiting, and depression, relaxation, especially in combination with guided imagery, proved to be the most effective treatment.

7.2 Interventions for Enhancing the Coping Repertoire and Quality of Life

Several single therapeutic methods were investigated which focused on emotional and social support during cancer treatment. Spiegel et al. (1989) published a first controlled, randomized intervention study of group therapy offered to women with metastatic breast cancer. For a year, sessions of seven to ten women met weekly under professional supervision. These focused on discussions about death, problems in families, on the communication with their doctors, and on methods of enhancing the quality of life during the last phases of their disease. Follow-up studies after a year revealed lower anxiety and depression, decreased pain and fatigue, and more adaptive coping strategies, when compared to a control group with nonspecific psychological support. In a ten-year follow-up significantly different survival times were observed: 36.2 months after the end of therapy in the experimental group, and 18.9 months in the control group.

Another startling group therapy study was published by Fawzy et al. (1993). They treated patients with a malignant melanoma for six weeks with a one-and-a-half-hour group session once a week. These included educational elements regarding coping with stress, seeking for social support, and relaxation/imagination. Besides a significant reduction of anxiety, depression, and fatigue, for the first time modifications in immunological variables were demonstrated. The authors found significant increases in lymphocytes, natural-killer-cell activity, and alpha-interferon induced natural-killer cytotoxicity compared to a randomized control group. In the six-year follow-up, the experimental group showed a significantly higher survival rate than did the controls, with higher survival rates in patients who showed an increase in active coping behavior.

7.3 How Can We Find Out Who Needs Professional Psychological Support?

In order to incorporate psychosocial therapy into the routine treatment of cancer patients, the question of which patients might need professional psychosocial support, and which patients would respond to the offer, has to be answered. For instance, Wellish and Wolcott (1994) tried to define criteria from their clinical experience of bone marrow transplantation that would enable the assessment of the need for psychosocial therapy based on individual coping abilities, stress in daily life, and psychiatric history. An empirical approach would be the analysis of responders and nonresponders and their determinants within randomized controlled studies (see Helgeson et al. 2000). The question 'Who needs psychological therapy?' should possibly be modified to 'Who needs which sort of psychological therapy?' because it has been shown that more than 95 percent of patients in an acute phase of their cancer treatment will accept this kind of support (Hasenbring et al. 1999).

8. Future Implications

Further research is needed to replicate the important findings of Spiegel et al. (1989) and Fawzy et al. (1993), and to answer the question of how these interventions could be implemented in the routine treatment of cancer patients. A further field of research is the investigation of the tendency towards the chronicity of physical complaints such as pain and fatigue in long-term survivors, and to identify predictors of these. It can be assumed that psychosocial factors play a significant role in association with biological predictors, which would demonstrate the necessity for adjunct psychological therapy.

See also: Cancer-prone Personality, Type C; Childhood Cancer: Psychological Aspects; Chronic Illness, Psychosocial Coping with; Chronic Illness: Quality of Life; Chronic Pain: Models and Treatment Approaches; Gender and Cancer

Bibliography

Andersen B L, Kiecolt-Glaser J K, Glaser R 1994 A biobehavioral model of cancer stress and disease course. *American Psychologist* **49**: 389–404

Andrykowksi M A, Gregg M E 1992 The role of psychological variables in post-chemotherapy nausea: Anxiety and expectation. *Psychosomatic Medicine* **54**: 48–58

Bonica J J 1985 Treatment of cancer pain: Current status and future needs. In: Fields H L, Dubner R, Cervero F (eds.) *Proceedings of the 4th World Congress on Pain: Seattle.* Raven, New York, pp. 589–616

Butow P N, Coates A S, Dunn S M 1999 Psychosocial predictors of survival in metastatic melanoma. *Journal of Clinical Oncology* **17**: 2256–63

Carey M P, Burish T G 1988 Etiology and treatment of the psychological side effects associated with cancer chemotherapy: A critical review and discussion. *Psychological Bulletin* **104**: 307–25

Cull A, Hay C, Love S B, Mackie M, Smets E, Stewart M 1996 What do cancer patients mean when they complain of concentration and memory problems? *British Journal of Cancer* **74**: 1674–9

Curt G G A 2000 The impact of fatigue on patients with cancer: Overview of fatigue 1 and 2. *The Oncologist* **5**(suppl 2): 9–12

Fawzy F I, Fawzy N W, Hyun C S, Elashoff R, Guthrie D et al. 1993 Malignant melanoma: Effects of an early structured psychiatric intervention, coping and affective state on recurrence and survival 6 years later. *Archives of General Psychiatry* **50**: 681–9

Forsén A 1991 Psychological stress as a risk factor for breast cancer. *Psychotherapy and Psychosomatics* **55**: 176–85

Garssen B, Goodkin K 1999 On the role of immunological factors as mediators between psychosocial factors and cancer progression. *Psychiatry Research* **85**: 51–61

Greer S 1991 Psychological response to cancer and survival. *Psychological Medicine* **21**: 43–9

Greer S, Morris T, Pettingale K W 1979 Psychological response to breast cancer: Effect on outcome. *Lancet* **2**111: 785–7

Hasenbring M 1998 Predictors of efficacy in treatment of chronic low back pain. *Current Opinion in Anaesthesiology* **11**: 553–8

Hasenbring M, Gassmann W, Arp K, Kollenbaum V, Schlegelberger T 1993 Belastungen, Ressourcen und Krankheitsverarbeitung im Verlauf einer Polychemotherapie: Ergebnisse einer prospektiven Längsschnittstudie. [Distress, resources and coping behavior during a polychemotherapy: results of a prospective study]. In: Muthny F A, Haag G (eds.) *Onkologie im psychosozialen Kontext.* Roland Asanger, Heidelberg, Germany

Hasenbring M, Schulz-Kindermann F, Hennings U, Florian M, Ramm G, Zander A R 1999 The efficacy of relaxation/imagery, music therapy and psychosocial support for pain relief and quality of life: First results from a randomized controlled clinical trial. *Bone Marrow Transplantation* **23**(Suppl. 1): 549

Helgeson V S, Cohen S, Schulz R, Yasko J 2000 Effects of psychosocial treatment in prolonging cancer: Who benefits from what? *Annals of the New York Academy of Science* **840**: 674–83

Holland J C, Rowland J H (eds.) 1998 *Handbook of Psychooncology* (2nd edn.). Oxford University Press, New York

Manne S L, Alfieri T, Taylor K L, Dougherty J 2000 Spousal negative responses to cancer patients: The role of social restriction, spouse mood, and relationship satisfaction. *Journal of Consulting and Clinical Psychology* **67**: 352–61

Morrow G R 1992 Behavioural factors influencing the development and expression of chemotherapy induced side effects. *British Journal of Cancer-Supplement 19: S54–60* **66**: 54–61

Spiegel D, Bloom J R, Kraemer H C, Gottheil E 1989 Effect of psychosocial treatment on survival of patients with metastatic breast cancer. *Lancet* **2**: 888–91

Spiegel D, Kato P M 1996 Psychosocial influences on cancer incidence and progression. *Harvard Review of Psychiatry* **4**: 10–26

Syrjala K L, Roth-Roemer S L, Abrams J R, Scanlan J M, Chapko M K, Visser S, Sanders J E 1998 Prevalence and predictors of sexual dysfunction in long-term survivors of marrow transplantation. *Journal of Clinical Oncology* **16**: 3148–57

Wellish D K, Wolcott D L 1994 Psychological issues in bone marrow transplantation. In: Forman S J, Blume K G, Thomas E D (eds.) *Bone Marrow Transplantation*. Blackwell-Scientific, Boston, pp. 556–570

M. I. Hasenbring

Cancer Screening

Cancer is the uncontrolled growth and spread of abnormal cells (see *Cancer: Psychosocial Aspects*; *Cancer-prone Personality, Type C*; *Childhood Cancer: Psychological Aspects*; *Gender and Cancer*; *Sun Exposure and Skin Cancer Prevention*). Typically cancer develops slowly and has a long preclinical phase. Early detection of cancer means better prognosis because of early and lighter treatment. This can lead to improved quality of life and savings for the society.

1. Difference between Screening and Testing

Screening for cancer is any kind of test performed for systematic detection or exclusion of cancer, risk factors, or susceptibility to cancer assuming that the *initiative comes from outside the individual*: from the healthcare or screening organizer. Screening sorts out apparently healthy people who probably have the screened condition from those who probably do not. A screening test need not take the form of a large-scale population intervention. It is not intended to be diagnostic. Persons with positive or suspicious findings

are checked further by diagnostic work-out. Screening is different from *testing* where the *initiative comes from the individual*, or from a health professional, *in the course of a diagnostic process* (Wilson and Jungner 1968, Health Council, Netherlands 1994). People screened are less prepared for the diagnosis and less aware about the condition they are screened for than those tested. Screening is aimed at unaware, healthy, asymptomatic people, and thus has heavier public health, social, psychological, and ethical implications than testing.

Prerequisites for successful screening (Wilson and Jungner 1968 for WHO) have been modified to be in accordance with developments in genetics (Nuffield Council of Bioethics), and specific European guidelines for mammography (x-ray of the breasts) screening have been developed (Kirkpatrick et al. 1993). In very few countries launching new screening programs is regulated by law, in some guided by recommendations. The criteria of the National Screening Committee (1998), which are based on the refined WHO criteria of 1968, are expressed as follows:

(a) The *condition* screened should be an important health problem and its natural history should be understood; it should be recognizable either at a latent or early symptomatic stage.

(b) The *test* should be simple, safe and reliable, inexpensive, and acceptable to those screened. The distribution of test values should be known, and the cut-off levels agreed upon. There should be an agreed policy for diagnostic evaluation of those with positive screening findings. The chance of physical or psychological harm to those screened should be less than the chance of benefit.

(c) The *treatment* or intervention should be effective with evidence that early treatment leads to a better outcome.

(d) The *screening program* should be clinically, socially, and ethically acceptable respecting the equity of access principle; it should also be cost-effective and managed and monitored according to quality assurance principles.

The public health rationale behind cancer screening is to reduce mortality and morbidity. The idea is to find cancer in a preclinical asymptomatic phase. Screening for risk factors or genetic susceptibility to cancer is based on the assumption that knowledge of risk affects lifestyle choices and interventions.

2. Screening Programs for Cancer

An example of cancers amenable for screening is breast cancer (the most common female cancer) screened by mammography, and also cervical cancer (by Pap smear screening). More than 1 in 10 women in industrialized countries get breast cancer in their lifetime. The natural history of breast cancer is known—there is an asymptomatic stage; treatment is more effective after early diagnosis, and based on randomized controlled studies the disease-specific mortality among women over 50 has been reduced by a third in the screened group (Kerlikowske 1995, deKoning 2000). The test is acceptable and cost-effective. When screening is carried out as a public health program, the equity of access principle is fulfilled, too. Among over 100 known types, other potential cancers for screening include prostate cancer (in many countries already more common than lung cancer among males) by serum prostate specific antigen (PSA); colorectal cancer by fecal occult blood test and sigmoidoscopy, and to a lesser extent lung, stomach, and ovarian cancer by different technologies.

Different countries implement different screening policies, some more enthusiastically than others. This shows value judgments in the interpretation of scientific evidence, as well as differences in health culture and the availability of resources. The cost of large-scale high-technology screening exceeds the resources of most societies. Low-technology options, like clinical breast examination for breast cancer and visual inspection for cervical cancer, in use in some developing countries, are often the next best, although less effective options.

3. Social and Psychological Aspects of Cancer Screening

3.1 Determinants of Screening Provision and Uptake

In society, screening can be studied both as a health service offered and an act of an individual. Different cultural and resource factors on both society and service level *determine the screening provided* (Table 1). These, plus individual factors, determine the *uptake of screening* (Marteau 1993). A tradition of centrally organized public healthcare encourages compliance, but also provides equity in access, whereas services based on self-initiation attract those people who usually take care of their health. Examples of individual level determinants are social background, health behavior in general, beliefs, perceived risk, and knowledge (Aro et al. 1999). Previous screening experience influences adherence to later screening rounds.

Theoretical models used to study determinants of cancer screening uptake have mostly been cognitive expectancy value models predicting self-initiated participation. Reasons why they are not so good at predicting behavior are probably due to the fact that, where social and service contexts are essential, the models are too individualistic, cognitive (e.g., concept of intention), and general for cancer screening. The stages of change theory can be applied to adherence to repeated screening rounds, especially if the context factors are included in the model.

3.2 Implications of Screening Provision and Uptake

Person-years saved, preferably also quality adjusted life years, are the main implications of screening uptake at the society level (Table 1). Uptake as well as provision of screening raise costs and awareness, and have an impact on values in the society. Medicalization

Table 1

Screening in a society: examples of determinants and implications of screening provision and uptake on different levels of society

	Screening provision		Screening uptake	
	Determinants	Implications	Determinants	Implications
Society level	values health policy healthcare resources	awareness costs medicalization	culture healthcare context	lives saved costs demand awareness
Service level	healthcare insurance tradition values resources	organization education access	staff invitation follow-up cost context	workload treatment
Individual level	NA[a]	awareness worry (nonattenders)	beliefs health behavior experience	inconvenience relief worry false reassurance

a not applicable

is intensified if the screened condition is seen as something bad and unwanted. Diagnostic work-out and treatment increase the amount of work needed. Since screening also detects cancers which otherwise would never become clinical, or which would appear later (overdiagnosis), the workload of the service provider is further increased.

People *invited* to, or otherwise made aware of screening, might get worried about the screened condition, and therefore refrain from participating. An invitation to screening may raise worry and a screening test may be inconvenient or bring other hazards. A *normal screening finding* brings relief, but a finding of any other sort can cause long-lasting anxiety. For those with a *false positive* finding, worry, especially cancer-specific worry, and its behavioral indicators, preoccupation with symptoms, and increased use of health services, might last long past the reassuring diagnosis (Rimer and Bluman 1997, Aro et al. 2000). Intrusive diagnostic procedures, like surgery, can be very stressful. A *true positive diagnosis* of cancer due to screening may both prolong life and improve its quality. However, this impact cannot be evaluated individually but only at a group level. Finding cancer, which would never have become clinical in a lifetime, is clearly a major adverse effect of screening. A *false negative* finding misleadingly reassures and delays diagnosis. A *true negative* finding is reassuring, assuming that screening has no adverse side effects. A good quality organized mammography screening program (for ages 50+ every two or three years) finds breast cancer in five out of 1,000 screened women, has 1:1 malignant:benign ratio of breast biopsies (Kirkpatrick et al. 1993), and a very low (even less than 1 percent) false positive rate per screening round. For a woman attending several screening rounds in a lifetime, the cumulative risk of a false positive finding rises considerably—close to 50 percent in 10 screening rounds in the US screening (Elmore et al. 1998).

While the screening uptake literature is partly based on theoretical models in predicting self-initiated attendance, literature on implications of the screening process and findings has a nearly nonexistent theoretical framework. The cognitive-behavioral models of illness anxiety rising from the tradition of psychosomatic studies have mostly been used to guide research questions and the development of methods.

4. Challenges in Studying Cancer Screening

The study of cancer screening is enriched by the examination of the determinants and implications of both provision and uptake, including the levels of society, service, and the individual. A prospective design—most easily built in organized screening programs with a planned schedule—enables the measurement of predictive determinants. Context-specific measures, in addition to standard ones, reveal valuable

factors, such as improved cancer awareness and enhanced health behavior.

Screening, however, is not the solution for cancer control. It is costly, cost-effective only among certain age or risk groups, and not globally feasible. Prevention would be better than screening for an already existing disease, but causal factors of cancer are still poorly understood. Of the predicted 20 million new cancer cases every year by 2020, up to 14 million will occur in developing countries. At present one in three to four people in industrialized countries fall ill with cancer during their lifetime. The overall five-year survival rate for cancers is over 50 percent, but for small (< 1 cm) breast cancers it exceeds 90 percent.

Screening for risk factors or susceptibility to cancer is closer to prevention than screening for disease, but has different implications. Screening for disease detects few cases, most of which would become clinical later without screening, whereas screening for risk factors finds a lot of people who will never develop the disease. Eventual screening for genetic susceptibility to cancer has to meet the criteria of good quality screening as well. Informed consent is essential and, in addition to risk notification, social and psychosocial consequences need to be understood and intervention options (lifestyle changes, choosing a partner, medication, preventive surgery, other kinds of therapy, and combinations or interactions of these) clarified. Potential screening programs need to be evaluated against accepted criteria (Hakama 1991) by healthcare technology assessment methods. Public debate and the empowerment of lay people to take part in discussions on values, ethics, screening policies, and priorities need to be encouraged. Modeling software provides one way of forecasting effects and impacts of screening where experimental studies are not acceptable or feasible. People need knowledge and skills to control the cancer problem both in the roles of decision-makers and service providers, and as individuals.

See also: Cancer-prone Personality, Type C; Cancer: Psychosocial Aspects; Childhood Cancer: Psychological Aspects; Gender and Cancer; Genetic Screening for Disease-related Characteristics; Health Behavior: Psychosocial Theories; Health Care Technology; National Health Care and Insurance Systems; Risk Screening, Testing, and Diagnosis: Ethical Aspects; Screening and Selection; Sun Exposure and Skin Cancer Prevention; Vulnerability and Perceived Susceptibility, Psychology of

Bibliography

Aro A R, Absetz P S, van Elderen T M, van der Ploeg E, van der Kamp L J T 2000 False-positive findings in mammography screening induce short-term distress—breast cancer-specific concern prevails longer. *European Journal of Cancer* **36**: 1089–97

Aro A R, de Koning H J, Absetz P, Schreck M 1999 Psychosocial predictors of first attendance for organised mammography screening. *Journal of Medical Screening* 6: 82–8

de Koning H J 2000 Assessment of nationwide cancer-screening programmes. *Lancet* 355: 80–1

Elmore J G, Barton M B, Moceri V M, Polk S, Arena P J, Flectcher S W 1998 Ten-year risk of false positive screening mammograms and clinical breast examinations. *New England Journal of Medicine* 338: 1089–96

Hakama M 1991 Screening. In: Holland W W, Detels R, Knox G, Fitzsimons B, Gardner L (eds.) *Oxford Textbook of Public Health*. Oxford University Press, Oxford, UK, Vol. 3

Health Council of the Netherlands: Committee Genetic Screening 1994 *Genetic Screening*. Health Council, publication No. 1994/22E, The Hague

Kerlikowske K, Grady D, Rubin S M, Sandrock C, Ernster V L 1995 Efficacy of screening mammography. A meta-analysis. Review. *Journal of the American Medical Association* 273: 149–54

Kirkpatrick A, Törnberg S, Thijssen M A O (eds.) 1993 *European Guidelines for Quality Assurance in Mammography Screening*. Office for the Official Publications of the European Communities. Report EUR 14821. Luxembourg

Marteau T M 1993 Health-related screening: Psychological predictors of uptake and impact. In: Maes S, Leventhal H, Johnston M (eds.) *International Review of Health Psychology*. Wiley, Chichester, UK, Vol. 2

Morrison A S 1992 *Screening in Chronic Disease*, 2nd edn. Oxford University Press, New York

National Screening Committee 1998 *First Report of the UK National Screening Committee*. Department of Health, London

Rimer B K, Bluman L G 1997 The psychosocial consequences of mammography. *Journal of the National Cancer Institute Monograph* 22: 131–8

Wilson J M C, Jungner G 1968 *The Principles and Practice of Screening for Disease*. WHO, Geneva

A. R. Aro

Cannibalism

Cannibalism is the eating of one's own kind. Of the 75 mammalian species known to eat conspecifics, three are higher primates: chimpanzees and gorillas, usually under conditions of social or environmental stress— and humans. Among these species the rarity of cannibalism, relative to the myriad opportunities and temptations to engage in it, suggests a biologically-based aversion that may have evolutionary utility. Many cultures have formulated this aversion as a taboo, or as an attitude which passively regards the behavior as unthinkable or faintly ridiculous. In most cultures where cannibalism was institutionalized (and as such is now thought to be extinct in the world), the element of taboo appeared in the guise of restrictions on the practice of cannibalism: the categories of persons eligible to eat and be eaten, the body parts consumed, and various procedural rules marking the eating of one's own kind as a special, often ritually significant, form of behavior. In societies in which cannibalism was a component of initiation into a religious cult or secret society, it was frequently the very act of violating the taboo and overcoming the fear and loathing associated with cannibalism that provided the element of ordeal common in such induction rites. In symbolic contexts, the cultural treatment of cannibalism is akin to that of incest, and in mythology the two images are often closely associated; they also raise similar explanatory problems, in that each rests upon the interaction of biological and cultural factors.

If a phylogenetic aversion toward cannibalism does exist, it is one that can be modified—though perhaps not fully abolished—by culture. Thus, from the actor's point of view the objective definition of cannibalism as applied to humans may be complicated by locally defined differences between own kind and other kind. If members of alien groups are taken to be nonhuman, eating them may not be perceived or psychologically registered as cannibalistic. Ontological distancing of this sort is not uncommon among cultures practicing cannibalism and although objectively such maneuvers may be seen as rationalizations, it is important to grant that cultural understandings are capable of creating a situation in which eating the other is palatable, even commendable, whereas eating one's own is repulsive, horrific, or insane.

As the quintessential uncivilized Other, and a projected inversion of Self, the Cannibal has been an object of fascination in many societies and for much of recorded history. Writing in the fifth century BC, Herodotus reports that man-eating is a custom among the Anthropophagi, dwelling in the wild lands north of the Black Sea, and among other groups living beyond the light of Greek civilization. In the sixteenth century, Montaigne's ironic essay *Of Cannibals* used the man-eating attributed to tribes in the New World as a foil to criticize certain European barbarities of his time. The implied 'otherness' of cannibalism appears in later literary works, such as Daniel Defoe's *Robinson Crusoe* (1719), Herman Melville's *Typee* (1846), and Joseph Conrad's *Heart of Darkness* (1902), to epitomize the exoticism of the faraway Americas, South Seas, and Africa, respectively. Today, novelists and filmmakers sometimes employ cannibal themes to convey the grotesque, nightmarish, or psychotic nature of certain situations and characters. The same fascination excites the public's appetite for accounts of present-day incidents of cannibalism under conditions of starvation or psychopathology.

As a staple figure in the world's folklore traditions, the Cannibal's otherness is usually certified by imagining the creature as not quite human: a witch, ghost, demon, giant, god, ogre, vampire, were-animal, or other monster. By negative example, the Cannibal discloses the nature of morality, sociality, and other virtues. Freudian theorists (e.g., Klein 1975) interpret such images as projections of unconscious ideas originating in early childhood. Thus, the infantile wish to devour the parent is converted into the fear of being devoured by the parent—a fear made acceptable to the ego by virtue of the parent-figure's fantastical disguise.

Types of literal cannibalism vary according to motive and circumstance; so great is the diversity, in fact, that it tends to overwhelm the common feature of ingestion and confound efforts to understand cannibalism as a unitary phenomenon. Auto-cannibalism conceivably applies to the act of eating cast-off parts of oneself—hair, nail clippings, mucous, excrement, placenta—but is perhaps better reserved for instances in which, under torture or other duress, individuals partake of their living flesh, raw or cooked. Greek mythology imagines this horror in the fate of Erisichthon, who unwisely violates a grove sacred to Ceres. As punishment, the goddess calls for Famine to visit the offender and deliver upon him a hunger so insatiable that, eventually, he devours his own body, limb by limb, unto death. Gustatory cannibalism refers to the unceremonious eating of human flesh, invariably that of an enemy, simply as food. Although reported for parts of Africa and Melanesia, some authorities doubt the existence of such culturally unadorned cannibalism; for, as Sahlins (1983, p. 88) remarks, 'cannibalism is "symbolic," even when it is "real."' Phrased slightly differently: noncannibals are fascinated by cannibalism because they don't practice it; cannibals are fascinated by cannibalism because they do. Accordingly, while human flesh is undoubtedly a potential source of high-quality protein (Harner 1977), cannibalism as a cultural practice cannot be satisfactorily explained purely as a response to particular material conditions. Epicurean cannibalism regards human flesh as a delicacy, an aesthetic normally requiring the victim to be perceived as something less than—at any rate, other than—human. Medicinal cannibalism is the ingesting of human tissue, usually that of an executed criminal, as a supposed medicine or tonic; this practice existed throughout Europe during the sixteenth, seventeenth, and eighteenth centuries (Gordon-Grube 1988). Innocent cannibalism is so named because the perpetrator is unaware that he or she is eating human flesh; thus, in Greek legend, Atreus punishes his brother Thyestes for seducing his wife, by tricking him into eating his own children. Survival cannibalism occurs under starvation conditions, such as shipwreck, military siege, and famine, in which persons normally averse to the idea are driven to the act by the will to live. That some persons under such conditions have been known to accept death instead of resorting to cannibalism attests to the psychological strength of the taboo and the corresponding revulsion many individuals feel toward the cannibal act. Survival cannibalism, especially when combined with murder, raises legal and moral issues having to do with the 'defense of necessity,' the first judicial analysis of which occurred in British courts

when, in 1884, survivors of the wrecked yacht *Mignonette* were successfully prosecuted for murder (Simpson 1984).

In works of ethnology and ethnohistory, aggressive cannibalism, usually in the context of warfare, is the most frequently reported form. For many peoples of Africa, the Americas, and the South Pacific, cannibalism is the supreme expression of hostility: killing and eating someone is the ultimate act of annihilation; reducing the hated enemy to feces is the ultimate insult. Such motives appear, also, in the large-scale cannibalism reportedly perpetrated upon 'class enemies' in China's Guangxi Province during the Cultural Revolution of 1966–1976 (Zheng 1996). In some societies the act aggressively appropriates the victim's spiritual strength, by consuming either the entire body or particular parts thereof, such as the heart, liver, genitals, or head. Early Spanish explorers reported that the Tupinamba of coastal Brazil adopted captives into their community, where they received excellent treatment and sometimes even married, before being slaughtered and eaten. Similarly, the Aztecs are said to have treated war captives with great honor and solicitude, as a prelude to sacrificing them to the gods and giving their bodies over to be eaten by the nobility. In these cases, then, cannibalism occurs in conjunction with sacrifice, but only after the victim is ennobled and made precious as an offering through incorporation into the group. Such sacrificial cannibalism is widely noted (e.g., Hogg 1966) and is shown graphically, if symbolically, in the holiest of Christian rituals—the eucharistic 'eating' of the body and blood of Christ.

As implied, most types of volitional cannibalism involve eating an enemy or, at the least, someone from outside the group ('exocannibalism'). Eating someone from within the group ('endocannibalism') usually occurs as a form of mortuary (or funerary) cannibalism, in which all or part of the body is consumed as an act of piety or affection, as a source of spiritual strength or continuity, as a kind of recycling of the spirit for the purpose of group renewal or reproduction, or as the means for assisting the spirit of the deceased to attain a desirable state in the afterlife. A premortem variant may be found in the Chinese idea (and practice) of ultimate piety, that is, a child giving a piece of his own flesh to nourish an ailing parent. The unconscious desire to incorporate the loved object—a common psychoanalytic observation—supports the notion that mortuary practices in many societies include symbolic elements that are sublimations of cannibalistic impulses or, in a more speculative vein, vestiges of actual cannibalism in the past (Sagan 1974).

As a topic of scholarly and popular interest, cannibalism was jolted by the publication of a book doubting that institutionalized cannibalism ever existed, anywhere. In *The Man-eating Myth*, author Arens (1979) argues that the centuries of reports about cannibalism in remote times or places rest on not a shred of reliable, eyewitness evidence. Instead of describing literal practices, the widespread attribution of 'cannibalism,' Arens suggests, is a derogatory racial or ethnic stereotype—a device for debasing or demonizing 'the other,' thus proving the need to govern or convert them. Scholars, he concludes, have been too quick and uncritical in accepting such attributions at face value.

The debate generated by Arens's book comes down to whether or not one is prepared to accept eyewitness accounts from missionaries, administrators, and adventurers, or the circumstantial evidences of ethnography or ethnohistory. Although few anthropologists agree with Arens's blanket dismissal of such sources, the controversy has usefully heightened both scholarly awareness of the ideological potential of 'cannibalism' and empirical rigor in studies of cannibalism as a culturally embedded, institutionalized practice (e.g., Brown and Tuzin 1983, Sanday 1986, Goldman 1999); it has also helped to inspire a body of literary and historical studies (e.g., Lestringant 1997) which examine 'cannibalism' as a metaphor in colonial discourse or in explicitly imaginary treatments of the cultural 'other.'

Of particular interest, insofar as it offers the only remaining possibility of direct evidence of willful cannibalism, is a resurgence of archaeological attention to prehistoric cannibalism and a refinement of techniques to test for it. Thus, modern taphonomic analyses of skeletal remains recovered at Anasazi sites (AD 900–1300) in the US Southwest (Turner and Turner 1999) and at Fontbrégoua Cave, a Neolithic site in southeastern France (Villa et al. 1986), strongly indicate that cannibalism occurred in those places in association with violent homicide, probably in the context of war or political terrorism. It is hoped that these new techniques may be used to test long-standing suspicions of cannibalism on the part of more ancient hominids—*Australopithecus africanus*, *Homo erectus*, *Homo neanderthalensis*, and archaic *Homo sapiens*.

See also: Ritual; Taboo

Bibliography

Arens W 1979 *The Man-eating Myth: Anthropology & Anthropophagy*. Oxford University Press, Oxford, UK
Brown P, Tuzin D (eds.) 1983 *The Ethnography of Cannibalism*. Society for Psychological Anthropology, Washington, DC
Goldman L R (ed.) 1999 *The Anthropology of Cannibalism*. Bergin and Garvey, Westport, CT
Gordon-Grube K 1988 Anthropophagy in post-renaissance Europe: The tradition of medicinal cannibalism. *American Anthropologist* **90**(2): 405–9
Harner M 1977 The ecological basis for Aztec sacrifice. *American Ethnologist* **4**(1): 117–35
Hogg G 1966 *Cannibalism and Human Sacrifice*, 1st American edn. Citadel Press, New York
Klein M 1975/1932 *The Psycho-analysis of Children* (trans. Strachey A). Dell, New York
Lestringant F 1997 *Cannibals: The Discovery and Representation of the Cannibal from Columbus to Jules Verne*. University of California Press, Berkeley, CA
Sagan E 1974 *Cannibalism: Human Aggression and Cultural Form*. Harper & Row, New York
Sahlins M 1983 Raw women, cooked men, and other 'great things' of the Fiji Islands. In: Brown P, Tuzin D (eds.) *The Ethnography of Cannibalism*. Society for Psychological Anthropology, Washington, DC, pp. 72–91
Sanday P R 1986 *Divine Hunger: Cannibalism as a Cultural System*. Cambridge University Press, Cambridge, UK
Simpson A W B 1984 *Cannibalism and the Common Law: The Story of the Tragic Last Voyage of the Mignonette and the Strange Legal Proceedings to Which it Gave Rise*. University of Chicago Press, Chicago
Turner C G II, Turner J A 1999 *Man Corn: Cannibalism and Violence in the Prehistoric American Southwest*. University of Utah Press, Salt Lake City, UT
Villa P, Bouville C, Courtin J, Helmer D, Mahieu E, Shipman P, Felluomini G, Branca M 1986 Cannibalism in the Neolithic. *Science* **233**: 431–6
Zheng Y 1996 *Scarlet Memorial: Tales of Cannibalism in Modern China* (trans. Sym T P). Westview Press, Boulder, CO

D. Tuzin

Capitalism

Capitalism is an economic system based on free market, private enterprise and ownership. The term and concept of capitalism as an exploitative socioeconomic system was initially introduced by Marxist social sciences. The spread of the term, however, was strengthened and its concept changed by the Western critiques of Marxism and socialism. Although rarely used, sociology and economics accepted the term and historiography broadly discuss its half-a-millennium development and various stages from commercial to globalized capitalism.

1. Concepts and Theories

The term, derived from *capital* (root in Latin *caput*, 'head') and related to *capitalist*, appeared in the mid-late nineteenth century in the English, German, French, and other European languages. The word *capital* had been used from the seventeenth century onward in the economic sense, meaning 'fund of money,' and later 'principal' (as opposed to *interest*). The term *capitalist* appeared in mid–late eighteenth century French, English, and American texts. The first recorded occurrence of the form *capitalism* in English is 'The sense of capitalism sobered and dignified Paul de Florac' in Thackeray's *The Newcomes* II (1854).

The spread of the term *capitalism* in common language use paralleled its use in Marxist socioeconomic theory, the appearance of *socialist/communist* economies in various countries, and the expansion of Cold War rhetoric based on the opposition of the two socioeconomic systems. The term and concept of *capitalism* as a socioeconomic system was basically introduced by the first theorists of Marxist social sciences. The spread of the concept, however, was strengthened by Western critiques of socialism and Marxism. Although rarely used, sociology and economics accepted the term and historiography broadly discussed the transition from feudalism to *capitalism*, and the various stages of capitalist development from its early commercial phase via industrial and financial *capitalism*, to its late, twentieth century characteristics. The capitalist world system is often discussed according to the pattern of advanced core and dependent, backward periphery. Development studies and economics analyze late twentieth century globalization and the increased role of transnational companies in a more inter-related, but at the same time even more polarized capitalist world economic system.

Karl Marx, who often used the terms capital, capitalist, and capitalistic, did not use the term capitalism as a noun in such basic writings as the *Communist Manifesto* and *Das Kapital*. The term appeared only later in his correspondence on the development of Russian capitalism during the late 1870s. The concept finally gained scholarly interpretation and became widely used by Marxist theory and the socialist movement in the last third of the nineteenth century. The concept was broadly used in historiography and sociology, but much less frequently in non-Marxist economics, to describe a phase of history or a set of ideas and mentality. During the twentieth century, capitalism became a popular term, especially to contrast the private-market system with socialism.

Marxist theorists interpreted the term capitalism as a socioeconomic system, a 'mode of production,' in which 'capital is not a thing but a social production relation belonging to a definite historical formation of society' (Marx 1952, Chap. 48, English trans.; first published in 1867). Capitalism is a class society basically consisting of two antagonistic classes: bourgeoisie and proletariat. The system historically came about through 'primitive accumulation,' the separation of peasantry from the means of production, and the creation of a free proletariat deprived of property, whose only saleable commodity was its labor power. The ruling class, the bourgeoisie, owns the means of production, buys the labor power, and controls all economic transactions and production processes. In the capitalistic reproduction process, capitalists who own the capital buy various types of commodities (raw material, machinery, labor power, etc.) for producing new commodities for sale. In this reproduction process money is transformed into commodities, then again into money (M–C–M). The capitalist, however, is

motivated by making profit and wants to get more money back at the end of the reproduction process (M–C–M'). The source of profit is one of the commodities—the labor power, which creates a 'surplus value.' The value of the goods produced by the workers is higher than the value of the labor power bought for a wage, which covers the expenses of the reproduction of labor power (including the reproduction of the class itself). Capitalists expropriate this 'surplus,' thus exploiting the proletariat. In capitalism, therefore, social production is in sharp contrast with individual expropriation. As a consequence, wealth is accumulated in the hands of capitalists, while the proletariat is kept in poverty. Capitalism, however, creates its own 'grave diggers'—the ever-increasing proletariat who, uniting together in the advanced West, rises up to destroy the capitalist system through a proletarian revolution. Bourgeois expropriators become expropriated and a just communist society without classes and private ownership is established.

Post-Marxian Marxism revised this theory. Eduard Bernstein, the leading theorist of the powerful German Social Democratic Party, rejected the concept of proletarian revolution in his landmark article series, *Probleme des Socialismus* (1896). He argued that capitalism has developed in a direction different from the one indicated by Marx. Poverty has not grown but diminished, and welfare reforms have been accepted peacefully. Bernstein and the Western Social Democratic movement maintained that the proletariat could realize its interests and goals by organized mass movement and parliamentary reforms. Another leading German socialist, Rudolf Hilferding, in his *Das Finanzkapital* (1909), added that modern economy created 'consciously regulated social relations.' Later he concluded in the theory of 'organized capitalism,' thus, a state-controlled welfare system.

Revolutionary socialism emerging during the first decades of twentieth century redefined contemporary capitalism as the higher or the 'last' stage of capitalism, otherwise called *imperialism*. In her *The Accumulation of Capital*, Rosa Luxemburg (1951, English trans.; first published in 1913) maintained that C would not be able to expand its markets, recruit new labor force, and mobilize new resources without a 'third person,' i.e., noncapitalist (independent farmer) sectors of the advanced countries, and, most of all, the agricultural economy of the colonies and peripheries. The Russian Vladimir I. Lenin defined imperialism as a new, expansionist stage of capitalism, which was also characterized by the domination of 'monopolies,' where the competition of small individual capitalists is replaced by the deadly competition of monopolies, not only locally but also in the international arena. According to this view, capital exports became a new instrument for exploiting backward peripheral countries. Imperialism has led to the fight for the redistribution of the colonies and spheres of interest, and this unavoidably generates wars, and leads to the proletarian revolution of the backward world. This version of Marxism was the leading ideology of the Bolshevik revolution in Russia, a revolutionary wave in Central and Eastern Europe after World War I, and the communist takeover in a series of Central and Eastern European, Asian, and African countries after World War II.

Non-Marxist scholarship did not build on the Marxist concept and interpretation of capitalism, but the term itself became commonly used in scholarship. Many twentieth century sociologists and economists used the term capitalism to mean a society and economy based on free market and entrepreneurial interest, and accepted these characteristics as the essence of capitalism, in contrast to socialism. Critiques of Marxism, therefore, contributed just as much to the spread of the term and concept of capitalism. Because of his work on the role of Protestant ethic in the development of capitalism, Max Weber played an instrumental role in making capitalism a commonly used term in scholarship. Ludwig von Mises and his disciple Friedrich von Hayek frequently used the term capitalism when launching the most radical attacks against Marxist theory and socialist economy and defending an undisturbed free market. Joseph Schumpeter's book *Capitalism, Socialism, and Democracy* (1943) emphasized the changing evolutionary character of capitalism because of its entrepreneurial interest that 'incessantly revolutionizes the economic structure from within' and with a 'creative destruction' destroys the old, outdated and creates the new.

The broadly accepted non-Marxist meaning of capitalism is rather different from the Marxist interpretation. According to the most widespread definition, capitalism is a complex socioeconomic system where the bulk of the means of production is in private hands guaranteed by modern property rights and laws. An 'invisible hand' (Adam Smith), the operation of market, regulates the entire economy, production, distribution, and labor. The market operates according to the play of supply and demand, which influence price fluctuations and automatically regulate investments and output. As the Say-law phrased it: each supply creates its demand. The market mechanism, therefore, is a self-regulating system. Capitalist entrepreneurs are acting individually and freely in a rational organization and control themselves with double-entry bookkeeping, motivated by gain and increase of profit. Capitalism, in this sense, is in sharp contrast with both its rigidly regulated feudal predecessor and contemporary rival socialism. Hereditary, almost unchangeable social status, basically noncommercialized production for local consumption, strict communal and guild regulations, and the lack of free private property, labor and market make economic relations in Feudalism rigid opposed to capitalism; and non-market economy based on state ownership and central planning contrast socialism to capitalism.

While capitalist society in its early stage has been, and in contemporary backward countries is characterized by extreme social polarization and income inequity, capitalism granted equal rights and, in principle, freedom of choice later in the advanced countries. From the 1870s on, but mostly from the 1950s, the industrial working class began shrinking, and the 'white-collar' layers, including the middle class, gradually expanded and became the most dominant layer of society. During the 1960–80s, a two-thirds to three-quarters white-collar and middle class majority dominated advanced societies.

2. Early Stages of Development

Capitalism, broadly accepted as a phase of history, is dominating the last half-a-millennium. It has also become conventional that capitalism itself had various phases and stages. Its antecedents go back to ancient history. Barter and exchange of one thing for another, as Adam Smith, the main advocate and ideologue of market capitalism argued, are a part of human nature. The pockets of private-market economy and its institutions, especially in urban settlements, flourished in medieval Europe. Moneylenders and urban merchants were its main representatives.

Its continuous development, however, began mostly from the sixteenth century. Historiography produced a vast literature on the transition from feudalism to capitalism. These writings maintain that declining productivity, a demographic crisis, and the scarcity of peasant labor generated the lowering of rents, a decrease of labor services, and an increase in peasant mobility and freedom in Western Europe. In most of these countries, consequently, serfdom was gradually loosened and disappeared by the sixteenth century. Commercialization of agriculture played a central role in the development of capitalism. The flourishing textile industry in Britain with an excess production over consumption led to the enlargement of productive capacities in an unheard scale and made England the 'workshop of the world.'

This stage between the sixteenth and eighteenth centuries is often called 'commercial capitalism' in history. The system was based on private ownership of warehouses and ships and buying and selling goods all over the world. The merchants also lent out money at interest and established connections with production. They bought and distributed raw materials for peasants who worked at home in the traditional way (putting-out system), and gradually subordinated the rural cottage industry. It led to a proto-industrialization, the development of a decentralized putting-out system coordinated by merchants, and later the establishment of (nonmechanized) factories, which introduced division of labor in the production procedure.

The emergence of capitalism, as various historians have discussed it, also gained incentive from the discovery of the 'New World.' The unlimited inflow of gold and silver from Latin America led to the accumulation of wealth. Although Spain was the main beneficiary at the beginning, most of the wealth got into the hands of Dutch and English merchants. 'It is not the importation of gold and silver—stated Adam Smith—that the discovery of America has enriched Europe ... [It] made a most essential [change] ... by opening a new inexhaustible market to all the commodities of Europe, it gave occasion to a new division of labor.' The new markets and emerging Atlantic trade enriched the commercial powers of northwest Europe and made them the core of the emerging modern world system from the sixteenth century on. This period saw the rise of modern world trade, characterized by the trade of mass consumption goods of food and textile, instead of the medieval trade of luxury goods from the near East and India. While the core countries of Western Europe sold processed industrial products, they bought unprocessed raw materials and agricultural produces from the peripheral countries of the world system: Latin America and Eastern Europe.

The rise of capitalism was strongly influenced by cultural-ideological and institutional factors. The Protestant reformation of the sixteenth century created a new work ethic and lifestyle, which was a prime mover of capitalist development. Hard work and thrift became virtues, which was in sharp contrast to parasitic noble values and lifestyle, the so-called *Hidalgo* (Spanish) and *Szlachta* (Polish) attitude. Meanwhile, the new moral code legitimized capitalist inequity: character was idealized, richness considered to be the triumph of will and work, poverty became a moral failing.

In the absolute state between the sixteenth and eighteenth centuries, centralizing policy creating uniform monetary systems, legal codes, unified and defended home markets without internal tariffs, also played an important role. The isolation of the domestic market by limiting imports was accompanied by a tremendous effort to build up a large colonial empire and a system of various privileges and stimuli for exports. The state itself became a promoter of the development of market, industry, trade, and transportation by the creation of road systems, canals, navies, and even state-owned industries. All these served to strengthen the state, but also historically paved the way for dramatic capital accumulation and modern capitalism.

2.1 Industrial Capitalism and Beyond

In the last quarter of the eighteenth century, Adam Smith published his powerful theory and ideology of the free market system, the *Wealth of Nations*, which became instrumental in the development of laissez-faire capitalism. Smith argued that from the selfish activity of the entrepreneurs, driven by profit motivation, the entire society profited, and that the individual actions, because of the self-regulating impact of the market, created an economic harmony and well being for the nation. Smith established the economic thought and popular thinking on capitalist market economy for two centuries. Political thinkers and economist of latecomer countries, however, attacked British *laissez-faire* ideology. The American Hamilton and Germans Johann-Gottlieb Fichte and Friedrich List argued against *laissez-faire* in favor of protective state interventionism.

The end of the eighteenth century is considered to be a turning point in the development of capitalism. As a consequence of the British Industrial Revolution, a new stage of more mature, as social scientists and historians called it, 'industrial capitalism' emerged and dominated the nineteenth century. Starting in Britain, the industrialization process transformed the core countries of the capitalist world system into industrialized economies with a high, sustained economic growth. Industrial capitalism, in the first period of its existence, institutionalized long working days, and exploited female and child labor ruthlessly in the factory system. Living conditions of the workers in crowded and polluted industrial cities, as described by Charles Dickens and Friedrich Engels, were extremely poor. Capitalism, however, reached its dynamic period of development. A banking revolution in Belgium and France, then, most of all, in Germany, introduced the Crédit Mobiler type, then the German type of investment banks with huge industrial portfolios. These banks played an instrumental role in industrialization. The relatively small, family-managed factories enlarged, and most of them became joint stock companies with professional management. From the mid-nineteenth century on, a European railroad system created a united European transportation network and an integrated marketplace. In this period virtually the entire globe became part of the capitalist world system. The core countries offered an unlimited market for food and raw materials. Britain and a handful of Western European countries absorbed nearly 70 percent of the world's food and raw material exports. New institutions strengthened international capitalism, such as a free trade system and the gold standard—a fiscal underpinning of the free trade system making the national currencies convertible, which was gradually introduced from the 1860s to the 1870s.

The expansion of capitalism around the turn of the nineteenth/twentieth centuries led to considerable changes in the system. Werner Sombart introduced the term of 'late capitalism,' and Rudolf Hilferding named this new period 'finance capitalism.' The concept of 'Imperialism' (Hobson) also appeared and became a leading concept of revolutionary Marxism. Some of the socialist theorists, however, such as Karl Kautsky, considered imperialism as a 'policy' of capitalism, similar to long workdays and child labor in its first phase. He maintained that capitalism could exist without colonies by introducing new policies.

Twentieth-century capitalism was characterized by the challenge of major wars, worldwide economic depression, and a significant slowing down of economic growth. More importantly, capitalism had to face the challenge of socialism, first as a movement, then as a rival socioeconomic system. A great part of the twentieth century was characterized by the struggle of the two socioeconomic systems. Capitalism reacted by a highly flexible adjustment to the new challenges. During the wars and depression, the development of state-capitalism with a strong and effective state interventionism, a return to protectionism, inflationary financing, and even state investments and planning, helped the system to respond to the new challenge. Large state-owned sectors emerged in Italy, Spain, and Poland. National planning was introduced in Germany and Hungary to cope with economic decline and unemployment. Self-regulating, *laissez-faire* market capitalism was replaced everywhere by a regulated market system. Adam Smith's theory was replaced by John Maynard Keynes' concept of state interventionism to create additional demand.

3. The Welfare State, Mixed Economy and Back to Globalized Laissez-Faire

The socialist challenge of capitalism required an effective response. The first chapter of this rivalry was opened in the late nineteenth century. Chancellor Otto von Bismarck, in his struggle with the strong German socialist movement, turned towards the introduction of welfare institutions. Pension system, health care, and other welfare institutions were introduced for workers to take the wind out of the sail of the emerging socialist movement. For these developments, the Great Depression of the early 1930s brought about a turning point. The Swedish Social Democratic government, elected in 1932, started building a welfare state. President Franklin D. Roosevelt also initiated major social legislation and the introduction of the social security system. The comprehensive system of the welfare state, however, emerged only after World War II in Western Europe. Capitalism, in contrast with its nineteenth century features, initiated widespread social legislation. Paid vacation, short workweek, nationwide pension systems, free health care, education, maternity leave, cheap housing, and many other institutions were established. Human rights were re-evaluated and the right to work, i.e., a full-employment policy, became dominant. Inequity, at least in the middle layers of the society, markedly diminished in the advanced capitalist countries.

The period after the Second World War also saw the spread of mixed economies. Almost all of the advanced Western European countries, led by France and Britain, nationalized entire sectors of their economies and established new state-owned firms in various industries.

Capitalism underwent a spectacular transformation. In his article on *The Instability of Capitalism* (1928), the leading Austrian-American economist, Joseph Schumpeter, prophesied the transformation of the system and the fading of the original meaning of capitalism. He maintained that capitalism is inherently stable and able to recover from great crises, but generates socio-intellectual effects discordant with its spirit and institutions. As a consequence, 'Capitalism is ... in so obvious process of transformation into something else ... [that] it will be merely matter of taste and terminology to call it Socialism or not.'

Towards the end of the twentieth century, capitalism adjusted to the new historical situation and markedly transformed but preserved entrepreneurial interest, market flexibility, efficiency, competitiveness, and reached its highest prosperity and fastest growth rate ever. The Western core countries of the world system successfully adjusted to a new technological-communication revolution and became the leader of new technologies and the rise of postindustrial society.

During the long period of postwar prosperity, a part of the former Asian and South European peripheries of the capitalist world system reached a higher than average growth and became an integrated and equal part of the core countries. After a long period of rivalry, capitalism emerged victorious while the parallel world system of centrally planned state socialism, which conquered one-third of the world and influenced an even greater part by its policy after World War II, collapsed in 1989–91. The former Soviet Bloc countries introduced radical market reforms, thus re-establishing capitalism. During the last third of the twentieth century, *laissez-faire* capitalism became the leading model again. Neo-liberal economics triumphed and challenged mixed economy and welfare state.

Capitalism in late twentieth century reached a new stage in its history. The main trend of this new age is globalization. National boundaries and national economies rapidly lost their importance. Multi- or transnational companies penetrated previously independent economies. Foreign direct investment became instrumental all over the world, including the advanced core countries. Towards the end of the 1990s nearly one-third of American exports and two-thirds of imports were intrafirm deliveries. About one-third of French, Dutch, and British industrial output was produced and roughly 25–40 percent of their research and development expenditure was financed by affiliates of transnational companies. In Ireland, and former state-socialist Hungary, foreign affiliates produced two-thirds of industrial output and financed roughly 70 percent of research and development expenditures.

While globalization, in some cases, contributed to a successful catching-up process with the core, it also preserved and even strengthened the core–periphery inequity. The gap between advanced core and the peripheries was growing considerably: intercountry income spread was 10:1 in 1913; 26:1 in 1950, but it increased to 40:1 at the end of the twentieth century. A newly globalized but even more polarized capitalist world system, dominated by an expanding Western core, was emerging at the turn of the millennium.

See also: Capitalism: Global; Economic History; Industrialization, Typologies and History of; Marxian Economic Thought; Marxist Social Thought, History of; Polanyi, Karl (1886–1964); Social History; Weberian Social Thought, History Of

Bibliography

Aston T H, Philpin C H E 1985 *The Brenner Debate*. Cambridge University Press, Cambridge, UK
Baldwin P 1990 *The Politics of Solidarity. Class Bases of the European Welfare State 1875–1975*. Cambridge University Press, Cambridge, UK
Hacker L M 1940 *The Triumph of American Capitalism*. Simon & Schuster, New York
Heimann E 1964 *History of Economic Doctrines*. Oxford University Press, New York
Hobson J A 1902 *Imperialism. A Study*. Nisbet & Co, London
Kautsky K 1914 *Der Imperialismus*. Neue Zeit, Berlin
List F 1904 *The National System of Political Economy*. Green and Co., London
Luxemburg R 1951 *The Accumulation of Capital*. Routledge, London
Marx K 1952 *Capital*. Encyclopedia Britannica, Chicago
Schumpeter J 1943 *Capitalism, Socialism, and Democracy*. Allen & Unwin, London
Smith A 1976 *An Inquiry into the Nature and Causes of the Wealth of Nations*. University of Chicago Press, Chicago
Sombart W 1921–8 *Der moderne Kapitalismus*. Duncker and Humbolt, Munich, Germany, Vols. I–III
Sweezy P M 1942 *The Theory of Capitalist Development. Principles of Marxian Political Economy*. Oxford University Press, New York
Wallerstein I 1974 *The Modern World System: Capitalist Agriculture and the Origins of the European World-Economy in the Sixteenth Century*. Academic Press, New York
Weber M 1992 *The Protestant Ethic and the Spirit of Capitalism*. Routledge, London

I. T. Berend

Capitalism: Global

While the idea of international capitalism has been part of political economy and related disciplines for centuries, the concept of global capitalism is of more recent origin. Despite the fact that many scholars have used the terms interchangeably, with the widespread use of the concept of globalization in the 1990s, the force of the argument for a firm distinction between these concepts has increased. International capitalism has generally been conceptualized in state-centrist terms, focused mainly on how national capitalists based on competing national economies and working through national companies operated across borders. The distinctive concept of global capitalism takes its departure from the idea of a global economy dominated by globalizing corporations and those who own and control them, and those in influential positions who serve their interests. The article traces the development of this conception of global capitalism since the 1950s, from the transitional idea of capitalist world-economy through several attempts to establish a genuinely global conception of capitalism not grounded in national economies and societies.

1. Introduction

Researchers on global capitalism have focused on three inter-related phenomena, increasingly significant since the 1960s. These are, first, the ways in which transnational corporations (TNCs) have facilitated the globalization of capital and the production of goods and services; second, the rise of new global forms of organization of the capitalist class; and third, transformations in the global scope of TNCs that own and control the mass media, notably television channels and the transnational advertising agencies and their role in promoting global brand consumer goods and the emergence of a global culture and ideology of consumerism. Theory and research on each of these three phenomena roughly coincide with attention to the economic, political and culture–ideology spheres of global capitalism.

2. Global Capitalism as an Economic System

It is no coincidence that interest in a global capitalist system in contrast to competing national capitalisms increased perceptibly from the 1950s. The context of theoretical and empirical interest in competing national capitalisms was (and for many still is) the history of colonialism and imperialism. This is overlaid with several versions of the theory that capitalist states could more or less successfully plan their own economic futures (see, for example, Keynesianism, regulation theory, and the developmental state). The concept of international capitalism, therefore, refers to a system of interacting and competing national capitalist economies, in which national elites of various types use 'their' big business (and businesses) to further national interests around the world. As direct imperialism and colonialism came to an end and as increasing numbers of very large TNCs began to emerge in the 1960s, attention began to shift decisively from national to global capitalism.

The dependency approach to development and underdevelopment of Gunder Frank and the related world-systems approach of Wallerstein, both highlighted the systemic nature of capitalism as a worldwide phenomenon over several centuries. While these theoretical innovations can be said to have prepared the ground for it, neither entirely succeeded in establishing a coherent concept of global capitalism for what came to be termed the 'age of development' from the 1950s onwards. This was due to ambivalence over their units of analysis and insufficient focus on the role of the major corporations in development in general. For example, the analysis of core, semiperiphery and periphery in the world-systems approach is based on national economies, as is the theoretically more ambitious concept of commodity chains. The simple assertion that these take place within a world-economy or global economy does not suffice for an analysis of global capitalism.

Theories of global capitalism, in the sense used here, take off from the proposition that capitalism entered a new, global phase in the second half of the twentieth century. By the end of the century, the largest TNCs had assets and annual sales far in excess of the gross national products (GNPs) of most of the countries in the world. In 2000, only about 70 countries out of a total of around 200 for which there were data, had GNPs of more than 10 billion US dollars. By contrast, the *Fortune Global 500* list of the biggest corporations by turnover reported that around 450 of them had annual sales greater than US$10 billion. This comparison, however, underestimates the economic scale of major corporations compared with sovereign states, as most TNC revenues are counted as part of the gross domestic product (GDP) of some countries. A more appropriate measure is to compare TNC revenues with government revenues. Gray (1999) has calculated that for 1997–99, the seven largest economic entities in the world were the budgets of the governments of the USA, Germany, Japan, China, Italy, UK and France, but nine of the top 20 were corporations, and of the richest 100 economic entities by revenues, 66 were TNCs. Thus, in this important sense, such well-known names as General Motors, Shell, Toyota, Unilever, Volkswagen, Nestle, Sony, Pepsico, Coca Cola, Kodak, and Xerox, the huge Japanese trading houses (and many other corporations most people have never heard of?) have more economic power at their disposal than the majority of the countries in the world. These figures indicate the gigantism of TNCs relative to the state budgets of most countries.

Not only have TNCs grown enormously in size since the 1950s, but their global reach has expanded dramatically. Many TNCs regularly earn more than half of their revenues outside the countries in which they are legally domiciled. This is not only the case for TNCs from countries with relatively small domestic markets (for example, Switzerland, Sweden, Canada, Australia), but also for those legally domiciled in the USA and Japan. While most of the biggest corporations are still headquartered in the First World, several dozen companies originating in what is conventionally called the Third World or that part of it known as the newly industrializing countries have been numbered among the 500 biggest companies by revenues in the world. This group has included the state-owned oil companies of Brazil, India, Mexico, Taiwan and Venezuela (owned by the state but increasingly run like private corporations), banks in Brazil and China, and the Korean manufacturing and trading conglomerates (chaebol), some of which have attained global brand-name status (for example, Hyundai and Samsung).

Writers who are skeptical that capitalism is a global system argue that because most major TNCs are legally domiciled in the USA, Japan and Europe, and because they trade and invest mainly between themselves, capitalism is still best analyzed in terms of national corporations. For such writers, the global economy is a myth and, consequently, there is no global capitalist system as such. Against this conclusion, proponents of the salience of a global capitalist system argue that an increasing number of corporations operating outside their countries of origin see themselves as developing global strategies of various types, as is obvious from the contents of their annual reports and other corporate publications. While all parts of all economies are clearly not equally globalizing, an increasing volume of empirical research indicates that the production and marketing processes of most major industries are being de-territorialized from their countries of origin and that these processes are being driven by the TNCs. The central issue for economic globalization is the extent to which TNCs domiciled in the USA, Japan, European and other countries can be more fruitfully conceptualized as expressing the national interest of their countries of origin (the globo-skeptic argument) or what can be conceptualized as the private interests of those who own and control them, aggregated as the interests of global capitalism. Even if historical patterns of TNC development have differed from country to country and region to region, it does not logically follow that TNCs and those who own and control them express any type of 'national' interest or national character.

The formal ownership of capital and the corporations has been transformed since the 1960s. The ownership of share capital has increased throughout the world by means of greater (though still a tiny minority in most communities) participation of the general population in stock markets and the indirect investments that hundreds of millions of people have through their pension funds and other forms of savings. This has led some to argue that economic globalization has created a popular capitalism, though others argue the more elitist thesis that the real drivers of the global capitalist system are the managers of unit trusts and pension funds. However, formal ownership does not necessarily mean effective control over capital and the resources of TNCs.

The globalization of the international financial and trading system can be fruitfully analyzed in terms of the progressive weakening of the nation-state and the growing recognition that the major institutions of global capitalism, notably TNCs and globalizing financial and trading organizations, are setting the agenda for these weakened nation-states. Theory and research on this issue has, not surprisingly, led to an increased interest in the politics of global capitalism.

3. Global Capitalism as a Political System

The politics of global capitalism is debated intensely inside and outside the social sciences. Since the disintegration of the Soviet empire from the late 1980s, the struggle between capitalism and communism has been largely replaced by the struggle between the advocates of capitalist triumphalism and the opponents of capitalist globalization. Many theorists have discussed these issues within the triadic framework of states, TNCs and international economic institutions. From this perspective, the global capitalist system is dominated by the relations between the major states and state-systems (USA, the European Union, and Japan), the major corporations, and the World Bank, the International Monetary Fund, World Trade Organisation (supplemented in some versions by other international bodies, major regional institutions, and so on).

The idea of a transnational ruling class has been suggested by several authors, notably in Cox's thesis (1987) on the emergence of a global class structure and in the work of Gill (1990) on the Trilateral Commission, where he identifies a 'developing transnational capitalist class fraction.' Sklair (2001) proposes a more explicit concept of a transnational capitalist class, and it plays a central role in his theory of the capitalist global system. Here, the transnational capitalist class is the characteristic institutional form of political transnational practices in the global capitalist system (paralleling the role of transnational corporations in the economic sphere and consumerism in the culture–ideology sphere). In this formulation the transnational capitalist class is analytically divided into four main fractions: (a) TNC executives and their local affiliates; (b) globalizing bureaucrats and politicians; (c) globalizing professionals; (d) consumerist elites (merchants and media).

A transnational capitalist class might be transnational in at least three senses. First, its members would tend to have outward-oriented global rather than inward-oriented national perspectives on a variety of issues, for example, support for free trade and neoliberal economic and social policies. Second, they would tend to be people from many countries, more and more of whom begin to consider themselves as citizens of the world as well as of their places of birth and residence (these might differ). And third, they would tend to share similar lifestyles, particularly patterns of higher education (in cosmopolitan business schools) and consumption of luxury goods and services. Theory and research to support this argument are as yet in a very embryonic phase. Nevertheless, and despite real geographical and sectoral conflicts, the whole of the transnational capitalist class shares a fundamental interest in the continued accumulation of private profit on a global scale.

Many other Marxist, anti-Marxist and Marx-inspired scholars see capitalism as a global system, but tend to conceptualize globalization in much wider terms and, thus, minimize the importance of global capitalism as an explanatory variable. The most important of these are the geographer, Harvey (1989), whose notion of time–space compression has been very influential, and the sociologist, Giddens (1990), whose conception of global capitalism is but one element in his theory of globalization as a product of late (and reflexive) modernity. Both of these contributions are significant for their attempts to build a bridge between the debates around economic, political and cultural globalization.

4. Global Capitalism as a Culture–Ideology System Dominated by Large Globalizing Media and Advertising Corporations

The third distinctive aspect of capitalism as a global system is the worldwide diffusion and increasingly concentrated ownership and control of the electronic mass media, particularly television. For example, the number of TV sets per capita has grown so rapidly in developing countries (from fewer than 10 per 1,000 population in 1970 to 145 per 1,000 in 1995, according to UNESCO) that many researchers argue that a globalizing effect due to the mass media is taking place all over the world.

Ownership and control of television, including satellite and cable systems, and associated media (like newspaper, magazine and book publishing, films, video, records/tapes/compact disks, and a wide variety of other marketing media, notably the internet), are concentrated in relatively few very large TNCs. The predominance of US-based corporations is being challenged by Japan, Europe and Australia-based groups globally, and even by Third World corporations like the Brazil-based media empire of TV Globo.

The culture–ideology of consumerism prioritizes the exceptional place of consumption and consumerism in contemporary capitalism, increasing consumption expectations and aspirations without necessarily ensuring the income to buy. The extent to which economic and environmental constraints on the private accumulation of capital challenge the global capitalist project in general and its culture–ideology of consumerism in particular, is a central issue for theory and research on the capitalist global system. Nevertheless, it should be pointed out that most scholars studying these issues of global culture do so not in terms of capitalism but in terms of the potential impact of global culture on national and local cultures and identities.

5. Crises of Global Capitalism

While Marxist and Marx-inspired theories of the inevitability of a fatal economic crisis of capitalism appear to have lost most of their adherents, at least two related but logically distinct crises of global capitalism have been identified. The first is the simultaneous creation of increasing poverty and increasing wealth within and between societies (the class polarization crisis), not to be confused with Marx's emiseration thesis which failed to predict enormous increases in wealth for rapidly expanding minorities all over the world. The second is the unsustainability of the system (the ecological crisis). These crises are often interpreted through the prism of consumerism inherent in a global capitalist system based on globalizing corporations (Sklair 2001). Globalizing corporations (in some cases rather more clearly than national governments) recognize the class crisis, but largely in marketing terms. In most communities around the world the absolute numbers of people who are becoming global consumers have been increasing rapidly over recent decades. However, it is also true that in some communities the absolute numbers of the destitute and near-destitute are also increasing, sometimes alongside the new rich consumers. The best available empirical evidence (see United Nations Development Programme Human Development Report, published annually since 1990) suggests that the gaps between rich and poor have widened since the 1980s in many parts of the world. The very poor cannot usually buy the goods and services that global capitalists sell. While there is a long way to go before consumer demand inside the rich First World is satisfied, the gap between the rich and the poor all over the world is not welcome news for TNCs. In addition to the profits lost when poor people who want to buy goods and services do not have the money or even the credit to do so, the increasing visibility of the new rich and the new poor in an age of constant global media exposure directly challenges capitalist claims that everyone eventually benefits from economic globalization.

The ecological crisis is also directly connected with consumerism, encapsulated in the political and ideological struggles over the concept of sustainable development. Since the 1980s most major TNCs have developed detailed policies in response to the challenges of environmental harm and declining stocks of resources essential for the maintenance of global capitalist consumerism. However, the persistence of problems of pollution, health risks, environmental degradation and waste management intrinsic to the system, suggests that it will be difficult to avoid ecological crisis. In this context, the attempt by TNCs and their supporters in international bureaucracies, the professions, government (globalizing bureaucrats and politicians), and the mass media to capture the idea of sustainable development and to reconcile it with capitalist globalization is worth further study.

6. Resistance to Global Capitalism

Global capitalism is often seen in terms of impersonal forces (notably market forces, free trade) wreaking havoc on the lives of ordinary and defenseless people and communities. It is not coincidental that interest in economic globalization has been accompanied by an upsurge in what has come to be known as New Social Movements (NSM) research. NSM theorists, despite their substantial differences, argue that the traditional response of the labor movement to global capitalism, based on class politics, has failed. In its place, a new analysis based on identity politics (notably of gender, sexuality, ethnicity, age, community, belief systems) has been developed, directed towards resistance to sexism, racism, environmental damage, war-mongering, capitalist exploitation and other forms of human rights abuses.

The globalization of identity politics involves the establishment of global networks of people with similar identities and interests outside the control of international, state and local authorities. There is a substantial volume of research and documentation on such developments in the women's, peace, indigenous peoples' and environmental movements, some of it in direct response to perceived TNC malpractices. This provides a series of research-rich connections for scholars influenced by postmodernist and global capitalist theories.

Serious challenges to global capitalism in the economic sphere have also come from those who 'think global and act local.' This normally involves disrupting the capacity of TNCs and global financial institutions to accumulate private profits at the expense of their workforces, their consumers and the communities that are affected by their activities. An important aspect of global capitalism is the increasing dispersal of the manufacturing process into many discrete phases carried out in many different places, popularized by Dicken (1998) as global shift. Being no longer so dependent on the production of one factory and one workforce gives capital a distinct advantage, particularly against the strike weapon that once gave tremendous negative power to the working class. Global production chains can be disrupted by strategically planned stoppages, but this is generally more of an inconvenience than a real weapon of labor against capital. The global division of labor builds flexibility into the system so that not only can capital migrate anywhere in the world to find the cheapest reliable productive sources of labor but also few groups of workers can any longer decisively 'hold capital to ransom' by withdrawing their labor. At the level of the production process, globalizing capital has a substantial advantage over labor. In this respect, the global organization of the TNCs and allied institutions like the World Bank and the WTO have generally proved to be too powerful for local labor and community organizations.

Nevertheless, global capitalists, if we are to believe their own propaganda, are continuously beset by opposition, boycott, legal challenge, and moral outrage from the consumers of their products, concerned citizens, and by disruptions from their workers. There are also many ways to be ambivalent or hostile about cultures and ideologies of consumerism, some of which the Green movement has successfully exploited.

The issue of democracy is central to the prospects for global capitalism and the struggle against it. The rule of law, freedom of association and expression, freely contested elections, as minimum conditions and however imperfectly sustained, are as necessary in the long run for mass market based global consumerist capitalism as they are for alternative social systems.

While most theory and research on capitalism continues to be state-centrist, focusing largely on how it works within specific countries, the growing influence of globalization in the social sciences appears to be encouraging more scholars to consider capitalism in the global as well as the local and/or national context.

See also: Capitalism; Economic Growth: Theory; Global History: Universal and World; Globalization and World Culture; Globalization: Geographical Aspects; Globalization: Political Aspects; Globalization, Subsuming Pluralism, Transnational Organizations, Diaspora, and Postmodernity; International Business; International Marketing; International Trade: Economic Integration; International Trade: Geographic Aspects; Marx, Karl (1818–89); Multinational Corporations; World Systems Theory

Bibliography

Cox R W 1987 *Production, Power, and World Order: Social Forces in the Making of History*. Columbia University Press, New York

Dicken P 1998 *Global Shift: Transforming the World Economy*, 3rd edn. Paul Chapman, London

Gereffi G, Korzeniewicz M (eds.) 1994 *Commodity Chains and Global Capitalism*. Praeger, Westport, CT

Giddens A 1990 *The Consequences of Modernity*. Polity Press, Cambridge, UK

Gill S 1990 *American Hegemony and the Trilateral Commission*. Cambridge University Press, Cambridge, UK

Gray C 1999 *Corporate Cash*. WEP, Eugene, OR

Harvey D 1989 *The Condition of Postmodernity*. Blackwell, Cambridge, MA

Herman E S, McChesney R 1997 *The Global Media: The New Missionaries of Corporate Capitalism*. Cassell, London

Lechner F J, Boli J (eds.) 1999 *The Globalization Reader*. Blackwell, Malden, MA

Ross R J S, Trachte K C 1990 *Global Capitalism: The New Leviathan*. State University of New York Press, Albany, NY

Sklair L 1995 *Sociology of the Global System*, 2nd edn. Johns Hopkins University Press, Baltimore, MD

Sklair L 2001 *The Transnational Capitalist Class*. Blackwell, Malden, MA

Strange S 1996 *The Retreat of the State: The Diffusion of Power in the World Economy*. Cambridge University Press, Cambridge, UK

United Nations Development Programme 1990–onwards *Human Development Report*, Oxford University Press, New York

van der Pijl K 1998 *Transnational Classes and International Relations*. Routledge, London

Wallerstein I 1979 *The Capitalist World Economy*. Cambridge University Press, Cambridge, UK

L. Sklair

Cardiovascular Conditioning: Neural Substrates

Our existence relies on our ability to alter our future behavior as a function of our past experiences, a phenomenon known as learning. This requires that a permanent record of our experiences, our memories, be stored in the brain to be recalled to guide our future actions. The last three decades of the twentieth century witnessed intense investigations of the brain areas where memories are formed and stored, and the structural changes that represent them. Many neuroscientists have adopted Pavlovian learning paradigms in animals to aid in these investigations. These relatively simple paradigms present an opportunity to identify the brain circuitry and mechanisms that contribute to learning as reflected in the acquisition of specific learned responses. Among these responses are learned cardiovascular responses, and particularly learned heart rate responses, which are the focus for this article.

1. Pavlovian Heart Rate Conditioning: A Model to Assess the Brain Circuits that Contribute to Memory

1.1 Pavlovian Conditioning

During Pavlovian conditioning the relationship among events is learned. For example, an animal learns that one event, such as the presentation of an auditory or visual stimulus, that repeatedly precedes a second event, such as the presentation of an electric shock or a pleasant morsel of food, provides information about the occurrence of the second event.

The auditory or visual stimulus is called the conditional stimulus (CS), and the electric shock or morsel of food is called the unconditional stimulus (US). This learned relationship or association is stored in memory such that subsequent presentations of the CS will elicit expectations regarding the occurrence of the US. These expectations elicit responses, called conditioned responses (CRs), which are a specific consequence of the formation and storage of the association between CS and the US. Implicit in the search for the structural changes that form the substrates for Pavlovian associative memories is the assumption that if an association between the CS and US is made, neuronal information concerning both must converge at a common brain structure(s). Thus, research directed at identifying structures involved in memory has been guided by an identification of structures where CS and US information converge.

1.2 Heart Rate Conditioning

Researchers have used heart rate CRs as model CRs to identify the areas where memories are formed and stored. These CRs are advantageous because the locations of the motor neurons that produce them are known. Thus, structures that send projections to activate these neurons leading to the expression of the CR can be identified using anatomical methodology. The subsequent identification of areas that send information to the areas that in turn activate the motor neurons, including the pathways by which CS and US information, access these areas, exposes an entire circuit that contributes to memory. Identification of the circuit permits the identification of sites of CS and US convergence and sets the stage for analyses of the structural changes that form the substrates for memory of the CS–US association.

1.3 An Early Model: Heart Rate Conditioning in the Pigeon

David Cohen (1980) was the first to use a heart rate CR to identify the components of a circuit that contributes to memory. He measured the accelerative heart rate CR in the pigeon that developed in response to a visual CS which preceded an electric current (US) applied to the foot. He believed that a systematic analysis of the flow of neuronal information, from CS and US input to CR output, should eventually lead to the identification of sites of CS and US convergence. While the pigeon model is no longer used, Cohen's strategy proved successful and was adopted by others using other models. Importantly, he identified an area where the structural changes responsible for the memory of the association potentially may occur.

That area was the avian homologue of the mammalian amygdala. Its destruction blocked the development of the CR. This finding guided future research focused on the mammalian amygdala as a component of a brain circuit that contributes to learning and memory, using a heart rate CR in the rabbit as a model response.

2. Heart Rate Conditioning in the Rabbit

2.1 Circuit Components

The heart rate decelerative, or bradycardic, CR in the rabbit has been widely used to identify the components of the circuit that contribute to memory formation and storage (see Kapp et al. 1998 and Powell 1994 for reviews). This CR develops when an acoustic CS immediately precedes either an aversive or appetitive US. The neurons comprising the final motor pathway for the expression of this CR are located in the medulla, and their axons travel via the vagus nerve to the heart. The identification of this CR pathway created the opportunity to identify the structures that may activate it. As noted in Sect. 1.3, Cohen's work pointed to the amygdala, and research in the rabbit has demonstrated an important contribution of a group of neurons in this structure to CR expression. These neurons are located in the central nucleus (ACe) and project directly and indirectly to the final motor path neurons. Electrical stimulation of the ACe produces bradycardia and lesions of the ACe markedly attenuate the development and expression of the CR (Kapp et al. 1998). Further, increases in the activity of ACe neurons developed to the CS during conditioning (Applegate et al. 1982, McEchron et al. 1995). These results suggest that these neurons excite the motor neurons leading to CR expression and are an important component of the circuit for the development and expression of the CR (Fig. 1). Recall that an assumption in the search for the neural substrates of Pavlovian associative memories is that CS and US information must converge at a common site(s). Thus, identification of the pathways conveying CS and US information to central structures such as the ACe is an important component of the analysis. The most peripheral components of the acoustic CS pathway have yet to be identified. However, research using an acoustic CS in the rat has demonstrated that destruction of neurons in the inferior colliculus, a structure that receives information from the most peripheral components of the auditory system (Fig. 1), blocks the development of several Pavlovian CRs (LeDoux 1995). The inferior colliculus in turn projects to several other auditory structures including the magnocellular component of the medical geniculate nucleus (MGm). MGm destruction blocks CR development in the rabbit (McCabe et al. 1993). The MGm projects to the lateral amygdaloid nucleus (AL), and AL neurons respond to acoustic stimuli (Quirk et al. 1995). Neurons in the AL project both directly and

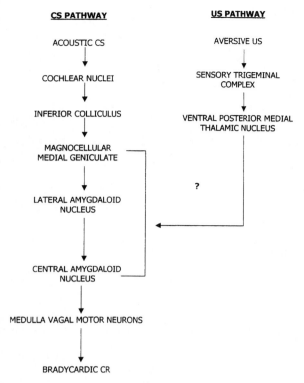

CS PATHWAY

ACOUSTIC CS

↓

COCHLEAR NUCLEI

↓

INFERIOR COLLICULUS

↓

MAGNOCELLULAR
MEDIAL GENICULATE

↓

LATERAL AMYGDALOID
NUCLEUS

↓

CENTRAL AMYGDALOID
NUCLEUS

↓

MEDULLA VAGAL MOTOR NEURONS

↓

BRADYCARDIC CR

US PATHWAY

AVERSIVE US

↓

SENSORY TRIGEMINAL
COMPLEX

↓

VENTRAL POSTERIOR MEDIAL
THALAMIC NUCLEUS

?

Figure 1
A simplified diagram of the putative structures and pathways comprising the brain circuit that contributes to the acquisition of the bradycardic CR in the rabbit

indirectly via intra-amygdaloid connections to the ACe (Fig. 1).

Less is known about the pathway by which US information gains access to central structures to converge with CS information. This pathway may be comprised of projections from spinal trigeminal complex neurons, which are activated by US presentations (McEchron et al. 1996b) and which project to the ventral posterior medial thalamic nucleus. The latter's destruction in the rabbit prevents the development of the bradycardic CR (McEchron et al. 1995). The pathway by which the US information is transmitted to converge with CS information in more central structures is at present unknown. However, recordings of neurons in the CS pathways to determine if they respond to CS and US presentations indicates sites where convergence occurs, as described in Sect. 2.2.

2.2 Potential Sites of Memory Formation: The Convergence of CS and US Information

The above research suggests that CS information accesses the amygdala, and that the ACe produces CR expression via an influence on vagal motor neurons

(Fig. 1). Does CS and US convergence occur in the amygdala, making it a potential candidate for the site where the memory is formed? Or, does convergence occur in other areas as well? With respect to the ACe, neurons within this structure are responsive to both the CS and US (McEchron et al. 1995), and the responses that develop to the CS in this nucleus during conditioning may well reflect a structural change(s) that represents the memory for the association. However, the mere development of these responses is not conclusive evidence that it is a site where this change occurs. Such responses may reflect their relay from other brain regions. For example, neurons in the rabbit and rat MGm, and in the rat AL, respond to both the CS and US (Bordi and LeDoux 1994, Romanski et al. 1993. McEchron et al. 1996a). Furthermore, responses in the MGm develop to the CS in many species during Pavlovian conditioning (Edeline et al. 1988), McEchron et al. 1995), and such changes also develop in the rat AL (Quirk et al. 1995). Thus, the responses that develop in the ACe may represent responses relayed from the MGm to the AL and from the AL to the ACe. Importantly, increases in synaptic conductivity that indicate a structural change have been demonstrated in both the MGm and AL during Pavlovian conditioning McEchron et al. 1996a, Rogan et al. 1997). The as-yet-unidentified structural substrates for these increases may well represent the neural basis for the memory of the association formed between the CS and US, and the resultant heart rate CR that develops. The extent to which increases in synaptic conductivity occur in the ACe has yet to be demonstrated. To the extent that it does occur in the ACe, then the overall picture is one in which the structural change(s) that form the substrate for the associative memory during Pavlovian conditioning may occur at several sites within the essential circuit.

As reviewed in Sect. 2.1 considerable research devoted to an identification of the essential circuit for conditioning bradycardia has focused on the amygdala and MGm. It is important to realize, however, that other brain structures also appear to contribute importantly to the development of this CR. Two in particular, the prefrontal cortex and the cerebellar vermis, make important contributions (Powell 1994, Supple and Kapp 1993). Lesions of both areas severely retard CR development, and neuronal activity develops to the CS in both areas. The functional interactions of these structures with the MGm and amygdala in the development of the bradycardic CR will be an important focus for research in the early twenty-first century. An equally important focus will be (a) a determination of the exact contribution that each of these components makes to CR development, and (b) the exact site(s) and nature of the cellular substrates for Pavlovian associative memories. Obviously, much needs to be accomplished if we are to completely understand their neural basis.

See also: Autonomic Classical and Operant Conditioning; Classical Conditioning and Clinical Psychology; Classical Conditioning, Neural Basis of; Coronary Heart Disease (CHD): Psychosocial Aspects; Eyelid Classical Conditioning; Pavlov, Ivan Petrovich (1849–1936)

Bibliography

Applegate C D, Frysinger R C, Kapp B S, Gallagher M 1982 Multiple unit activity recorded from amygdala central nucleus during Pavlovian heart rate conditioning in rabbit. *Brain Research* **238**: 457–62

Bordi F, LeDoux J E 1994 Response properties of single units in areas of rat auditory thalamus that project to the amygdala. II. Cells receiving convergent auditory and somatosensory inputs and cells antidromically activated by amygdala stimulation. *Experimental Brain Research* **98**: 275–86

Cohen D H 1980 The functional neuroanatomy of a conditioned response. In: Thompson R F, Hicks L H, Shvyrkov V B (eds.) *Neural Mechanisms of Goal Directed Behavior and Learning*. Academic Press, New York

Edeline J M, Dutrieux G, Neuenschwander-El, Massioui N 1988 Multiunit changes in hippocampus and medial geniculate body in freely behaving rats during acquisition and retention of a conditioned response to a tone. *Behavior and Neural Biology* **50**: 61–79

Kapp B S, Silvestri A J, Guarraci F A 1998 Vertebrate models of learning and memory. In: Martinez J L, Kesner R P (eds.) *Neurobiology of Learning and Memory*. Academic Press, New York

LeDoux J E 1995 Emotion: Clues from the brain. *Annual Review of Psychology* **46**: 209–35

McCabe P M, McEchron M D, Green E J, Schneiderman N 1993 Electrolytic and ibotenic acid lesions of the medial geniculate-prevent the acquisition of classically conditioned heart rate to a single acoustic stimulus in rabbits. *Brain Research* **619**: 291–8

McCabe P M, McEchron M D, Green E J, Schneiderman N 1995 Destruction of neurons in the VPM thalamus prevents rabbit heart rate conditioning. *Physiology and Behavior* **57**: 159–63

McEchron M D, Green E J, Winters R, Nolen T G, Schneiderman N, McCabe P M 1996a Changes of synaptic efficacy in the medical geniculate nucleus as a result of auditory classical conditioning. *Journal of Neuroscience* **16**: 1273–83

McEchron M D, McCabe P M, Green E J, Hitchcock J M, Schneiderman N 1996b Immunohistochemical expression of the c-Fos protein in the spinal trigeminal nucleus following presentation of a corneal airpuff stimulus. *Brain Research* **710**: 112–20

McEchron M D, McCabe P M, Green E J, Llabre M M, Schneiderman N 1995 Simultaneous single unit recording in the medial nucleus of the medial geniculate nucleus and amygdaloid central nucleus throughout habituation, acquisition, and extinction of the rabbit's classically conditioned heart rate. *Brain Research* **682**: 157–66

Powell D A 1994 Rapid associative learning: Conditioned bradycardia and its central nervous system substrates. *Intergrative Physiology and Behavioural Science*. **29**: 109–33

Quirk G J, Repa J C, LeDoux J E 1995 Fear conditioning enhances short-latency auditory responses of lateral amygdala neurons: Parallel recordings in the freely behaving rat. *Neurons* **15**: 1029–39

Rogan M J, Staubli V V, Le Douse J E 1997 Fear conditioning induces associative long-term potentiation in the amygdala. *Nature* **390**: 604–7

Romanski L M, Clugnet M C, Bordi F, LeDoux J E 1993 Somatosensory and auditory convergence in the lateral nucleus of the amygdala. *Behavioral Neuroscience* **107**: 444–50

Supple W F Jr, Kapp B S 1993 The anterior cerebellar vermis: Essential involvement in classically conditioned bradycardia in the rabbit. *Journal of Neuroscience* **13**: 3705–11

B. Kapp

Care and Gender

Care consists of the physical, emotional, and intellectual processes that enable humans to maintain their lives and activities; such activities usually are distinguished from economic production. Care is a central aspect of human life, but social scientists have only recently begun to pay careful attention to the connection of care and gender. Since most activities of care historically have belonged properly in the same sphere as the family and been the activity of women, slaves, servants, and working-class people, care has been beneath the concern of most social theorists and scientists. Changes in the roles of family and public institutions for care, as well as feminist scholars' impetus to study the concerns of women's lives, have led to the emergence of a robust field of study that explores the physical, social, political, economic, and philosophical implications of care.

1. The Growing Importance of Care for Public Concern

The long-standing devaluation of care grows out of the devaluation of its dual central aspects. On the one hand, care is about the actual physical work required to maintain and repair objects and people. On the other hand, care also denotes mental states of engagement that make central the concerns of the person, object, idea, etc. toward which the care is directed. Thus, in the English language care is associated with both burdens and woes. Even in current discussions of care some scholars emphasize the physical concerns of care, others see it as a psychological or philosophical category, while others try to combine these two elements.

The historical exclusion of care from public life and from serious scientific consideration also reflects the duality of care's nature (Tronto 1996). Aristotle began his *Politics* by distinguishing between the worlds of politics and household and relegating all the banal and daily concerns of the household as outside of the concerns of citizens. To such thinkers, care was beneath the dignity of citizens. Others have viewed care as too lofty for any serious association with public life. Realist thinkers from Augustine to Max Weber have been suspicious of attitudes of care because it was associated with ideals of Christian charity and agape, and have relegated such concerns to realms beyond public concern, either to spiritual communities or to individuals' consciences.

A major cause for this greater attention from social scientists is that care itself has changed during the industrialization since the 1850s (see *Family and Gender*; *Household Production*). Households used to be almost entirely self-contained. They produced foodstuffs, domestic products such as soap, energy, etc. for themselves. Birth, death, and illness were treated in the household with minimal assistance from others. Households consisted of people who were in various stages of their life. With the rise of industrialization, households have grown smaller, most household goods have become commodified, and professionals have begun to assist in processes of birth, death, and illness. Thus, activities that used to be conceived of as essentially private and personal became social, public, and political concerns. The development of public institutions since the eighteenth century to aid in caring for the ill and infirm (Foucault 1965) has accelerated with the development of welfare state bureaucracies (Bussemaker and van Kersbergen 1994). As care has become a more central aspect of social and political life, these questions have become more important for scholars: who cares for whom, how is care organized and paid for in different societies, and what are the practical and normative questions entailed in practices of care?

2. Conceptualizing Care

Scholars use different formulations of care depending upon the different conceptual purposes to which they employ the concept. Among these uses are: care as a sociological category; i.e., an account of how societies organize care work; care as a psychological orientation, i.e., a framework for understanding psychological differences between men and women; care as an ethical category, i.e., a basis for making ethical judgments in care settings; care as a political and philosophical perspective, i.e., a paradigm in which to understand an alternative account of human nature and values. The empirical work that ties care to gender is strongest in the psychological and sociological approaches, but within all of these accounts of care, the relationship of care to gendered activities and to the relative status of men and women in society remains central.

2.1 The Sociological Approach

Among the first issues that feminist scholars and activists noted at the beginning of the second wave of feminism was that, even in industrial societies, a deep division of labor persisted that left to women most of the tasks of caring. Marxist scholars frequently distinguished this realm of reproduction from production. Although conservatives argue that childcare and tending to the household were naturally the realm of women's work, feminists began to challenge both the gendered division of labor and the devaluation of women's work. Political platforms throughout the West provided analyses of these discrepancies and called for policy solutions such as available day care and wages for housework. Scholars soon began to explore such 'labors of love' (Finch and Groves 1983). A large sociological literature has now emerged that explores the boundaries and nature of personal care within and outside of traditional family contexts and institutionalized care in society.

2.2 The Psychological Approach

Gilligan's path breaking work, *In a Different Voice* (1982), is often taken as the starting point for the discussion of care. Gilligan's work challenged the basic assumption of Lawrence Kohlberg's influential account of cognitive moral development by arguing that not all moral development could be measured by a single path. Gilligan posited that, in addition to Kohlberg's account of the development of justice reasoning, psychologists needed to observe as well the development of an orientation to care. To Gilligan, three qualities describe this ethic and distinguish it from the justice approach: (a) it revolves around the moral concepts of responsibility and relationships rather than rights and rules; (b) it is tied to concrete circumstances rather than to abstract rules of morality; (c) it is an activity rather than a set of principles. Gilligan insisted that these three orientations need not be associated with gender, but her admonition was widely disregarded. Despite the absence of empirical evidence to support the claim that these two orientations distinguish between men and women, a broader public audience seized the idea that there was a gender difference in morality that distinguished men and women; men were more interested in impartial and principled conceptions of justice, and women were more interested in maintaining particular relationships of care. Arguments for care thus became associated with a political strategy to valorize the lives and experiences of women.

2.3 The Ethical Approach

Noddings (1984) transformed the assumption of women's more caring nature into a moral position.

Arguing that care was always a dyadic relationship, Noddings posited that there was a limit to the kinds of concerns that caring could address; they were limited to the kinds of relationships and life activities that occurred in intimate settings.

Ruddick's (1990) important work on 'maternal thinking' reinforced the notion that caring had its own set of moral norms and practices that might be distorted if applied in a broader context (see *Motherhood: Social and Cultural Aspects*). It is perhaps not surprising that proponents of this account of care were often exploring care relationships within social institutions and professions where women predominated, such as mothering (Ruddick 1990), nursing (Benner and Wrubel 1989), and in education (Noddings 1984).

2.4 The Political and Philosophical Perspective

Critics of the psychological and narrow ethical positions soon emerged, arguing that care was necessarily neither gendered nor limited to a narrow sphere of life (Sevenhuijsen 1998, Tronto 1993). These critics began to define care much more broadly and to think about it as an essential human activity, whose particular contours would be shaped by broader political and social decisions made in a society. Writing about the development of institutions for caring in the Scandinavian welfare states, Waerness (1984) argued that a distinctive 'rationality of care' could be discerned in agencies and practices that were involved in issues of care. This broader conception of care combines the previous frameworks: it understands care to be both work and a framework of values about work, to be both concrete physical activity and normative orientations and concerns about that activity. It combines the critical dimension of the sociological approaches that recognize the devalued nature of care with the psychological and ethical approaches that seek to reconstruct the values of the caring work and activities that are done. From this perspective, the persistence of the gendered nature of care is a sign of a broader problem in devaluing certain necessary human traits and activities, not only a devaluation of that which is seen as feminine or residing in women's sphere. Furthermore, scholars have begun to connect the devaluation of care with the devaluation of women's lives and activities. The relative powerlessness of care-givers is tied to the relatively low status of the work that they perform (Tronto 1993).

3. Care as a Challenge to How We Organize Social and Political Life

Scholars have begun to apply these various care frameworks to explore a number of arenas of social life. Concerns about care have informed how socio-logists have studied the organization of institutions to care for children, the elderly, the disabled, the infirm. Scholars in communication have begun to use a care perspective to explain how care can alternatively frame listening and communicating with others. Legal scholars have used an ethic of care to explain alternative ways to understand the legal process. Economists have begun to explore how economists' theories and policy proposals have been distorted by the failure to recognize the fact that women bear most of the costs of rearing children, while all share in the public benefits of well-reared workers and citizens (Folbre 1994).

More generally, political and social theorists have noted that to take the care perspective seriously challenges some of the basic assumptions that seem to permeate Western value systems about human life. The care perspective stresses human vulnerability and dependence. It argues that all individuals are dependent upon others and that an understanding of individuals as interdependent rather than as autonomous, is actually a more realistic portrayal of their existence. Since most contemporary political philosophies rest upon an assumption of the individual as a rational, autonomous individual, the care perspective thus raises a fundamental challenge to them.

Another set of challenges concerns how we organize social and political life by dividing the public sphere and the private sphere. Feminist scholars have long argued that the division of life into public and private spheres is one of the most important demarcations in reducing women, associated with the private, to second-class status (Pateman 1988). In contemporary industrialized societies, care is not divided easily into public and private: many previously private care concerns have become part of the purview of welfare state institutions, and many public activities are carried out to accomplish care.

4. Applying Care Perspectives: The Work of Care in Society

Since scholars actually are thinking about a variety of concerns when they discuss care, they might use the term in a variety of ways. No standard definition of care has yet emerged, in part because the following problems seem to be essentially contested within the meaning of the term: (a) does care apply to care-work that is directed at another, or can it also be directed toward the self? To include the self adds dimensions of spirituality to the conception of care. It also makes it more difficult to associate care with altruism. Yet advocates of incorporating the care of the self with other forms of care posit that introspections about the meaning of care are often important sources for thinking about care, and that there is another place within the framework of talking about care to distinguish between care for the self and care for others. (b) Does care primarily concern mental and emotional attitudes or does it primarily concern physical activities of care giving? Scholars who tend to emphasize the mental and emotional aspects of care often do so by ignoring the range of sites of care in society and emphasizing only the most familiar aspects of care, such as mothering. Scholars who focus on the activities of care, especially as carried out in social institutions often emphasize care as work to the exclusion of seeing other dimensions of care. (c) What are the best ways to describe different aspects of care? Fisher and Tronto (1990) provided a framework for dividing care into four phases: caring about, caring for, care giving, and care receiving. By thinking of care as an ideal of a complete process in which all of the phases are present, it is possible to provide a standard by which one can evaluate how effectively care is rendered in any particular setting. (d) How can one account for the power differentials in different forms of care? Other scholars have emphasized that it makes sense to classify care according to the relative power positions of those involved in the caring relationship. Thus, Waerness (1984) distinguishes between 'personal service' and 'necessary care.'

Personal service is work that one could have performed by oneself but calls upon others to do. Necessary care is the care needed by people who cannot provide such care to themselves. Necessary care may require particular expertise (e.g., providing medical or therapeutic care) or it might be care that is not specialized (e.g., helping the frail elderly with transportation needs). (e) How are needs for care determined? While on some basic level the needs for care are obvious, in any given society there can be a variety of ways to meet caring needs and to conceptualize and prioritize caring needs. For example, though elderly people may need assistance in moving about, different societies will determine that elderly parents should reside with their grown children, that public services should provide assistants to help the elderly in their homes, or that elderly people should live in specially designed communities or institutional settings designed for them. Indeed, any particular society may decide to allow people to choose among many different options in deciding how best to meet the needs of care. A society may decide to leave such decisions to individuals, to individual families, to the market, or to governmental agencies.

5. Applying Care: Philosophical Concerns About Care in Society

A number of philosophical issues has arisen as scholars have begun to think about care and gender.

5.1 The Care–Justice Debate

One central way to frame the philosophical dispute about the value of care has been to see it as a question of care versus justice. In this debate, the framework delineated by Gilligan's (1982) psychological theory is taken as definitive of a difference in orientations toward the moral world. Thus, the question becomes, are care and justice perspectives compatible? Throughout the 1980s, scholars emphasized the incompatibility of the approaches, often to the detriment of taking the care approach seriously. Kohlberg himself described care as a secondary kind of moral orientation that came into play to resolve local moral issues once the larger issues of justice had been settled. Some feminists tried to argue that the model of care was preferable to one of justice (Held 1993) while others insisted that the qualities of localness inevitably made care a flawed conception for understanding ethical issues (Jaggar 1995). Increasingly, feminist theorists resolve the care–justice debate by asserting that the two approaches were compatible and could complement each other, for example, by insisting upon the rights of care workers (Bubeck 1995, Kittay 1999) or by discussing caring in terms of rights (Tronto 1993).

5.2 Problems With Care Theories

Nevertheless, advocates of care theory recognize several serious problems in using care as a moral approach. One problem is the problem of parochialism. If people care most for those who are closest to them, how can they make judgments about the (perhaps more serious) needs for care of those who are more distant from them? Many care theorists acknowledge that such problems of parochialism, of being too partial to the needs of those to whom we are closest, require that care be supplemented with more abstract principles of justice. Care theorists might demand, for example, that justice requires that everyone be provided with minimal levels of care. At its most profound level, the problem of parochialism raises the question of what are the appropriate limits and boundaries of care. Does the ethical imperative to care stop at the family, local community, group, or nation, or is it global (Robinson 1999)?

A second serious problem is the problem of paternalism. How can approaches of care avoid the problem that care-givers often have a degree of power over the people for whom they care? The problems of abuse in care relationships are serious concerns. Even when abuse is not present, however, there is often conflict among the parties in a situation of care about how to best provide the care. Since the care-giver, especially in cases of necessary care, is usually in a position of providing the care receiver with something that the care receiver needs, givers have an upper hand in defining the situation and in determining the nature and extent of care. A third serious problem is in trying to determine a standard for good care. If care must be understood as relative to different circumstances, then on what basis can one ever judge what constitutes adequate or good care? Again, since care receivers are often in positions of receiving care, they are often in a weak position to argue for their own views of what caring should be provided and how. Even if care-givers are relatively devalued in society, they may still be in positions of power vis-à-vis their charges and possibilities for abuse or mistreatment are serious. A fourth serious problem concerns how we define equality in the light of the need for care for dependent individuals in democratic societies. If some individuals are highly dependent upon care, then in what sense can they count as the equals of other democratic citizens? Indeed, Kittay (1999) has noted that the care-givers of highly dependent people also are excluded from some aspects of social and political life by their need to care for their charges. For example, single mothers of disabled children provide exhausting hours of care which renders them unable to earn money for the household. Care workers are especially vulnerable to exploitation (Bubeck 1995).

5.3   Care and Citizenship

At another level, scholars have begun to question whether the very definition of what constitutes a citizen has to be conceived according to changes in caring practices. A model of citizenship that makes many benefits contingent on participation in paid employment disadvantages women (and those few men) who (must) leave the paid work force to fulfill their continuing care obligations to children, elders, or disabled relatives (Knijn and Kremer 1997).

6.   Areas for Future Research

Scholars throughout the industrialized world have begun to question how care fits into the framework of modern industrialized countries. As the model of the family as headed by a breadwinner and homemaker continues to decline, as more caring functions leave the household and become marketed commodities or services (Ungerson 1997) or provided by social institutions, care practices will continue to evolve. But the meaning and significance of care will also continue to evolve as individuals perceive that the relationships between care-givers and care receivers continue to be intensely personal and intimate.

One important part of care is the interpersonal relationship that it represents. To what extent can advanced societies continue to provide personal care? The professionalization of care in the last century (the growth of specialties such as doctoring, nursing, teaching, etc.) may in fact be matched by a process of deskilling of care in the next century as tasks are further differentiated and separated from one another.

Yet as important as the interpersonal dimensions of

care remain, we must keep in mind how easily such interpersonal relationships of care can mask the vast inequalities that exist when we ask, who cares for whom? People of relative privilege in the industrialized world are able to command vast amounts of necessary care and personal service. On the other hand, those who are the poorest members of the global society not only receive less essential care, they are often hired at subsistence wages to work and provide care for others. The globalizing economy has also commodified and globalized the traffic in care workers.

Even as theorists of care have warned against the parochialisms that often creep into care analyses, they have only begun to confront the question of whether there is a moral imperative to organize care on a global level. To what extent does one nation owe care to the citizens who live within another nation? To what extent can such concerns be extended before they are stretched too far to bear any resemblance to the kinds of concerns that we usually associate with 'caring'?

How much provision of care is enough? Tragically, there will always be more needs for care than there is care available in human societies. How then are difficult decisions about the allocation of care best made? In order for care to take place, there must first be a perception of the need for care. Yet as Fraser (1989) observed, needs are determined through a highly political process of needs interpretation. How can such a process occur fairly?

What constitutes good care will be variable in any society. Different people have different notions of what constitutes the best care for them. The challenge of care will be to offer options for care so that everyone can be well cared for in a manner that they find acceptable. Finally, the feminist impulse to revalue care grew out of a desire to end gender-based disparities in the provision of care. The greatest challenge to theorists of care is to see that, not only do gender-based forms of caring change to make the burdens and blessings of care equally distributed among men and women, but to do so in a way that does not reinscribe care as unequal burdens for the relatively disadvantaged.

See also: Caregiver Burden; Family and Gender; Fatherhood; Household Production; Masculinities and Femininities; Motherhood: Economic Aspects; Motherhood: Social and Cultural Aspects; Social Welfare Policies and Gender; Time-use and Gender

Bibliography

Benner P, Wrubel J 1989 *The Primacy of Caring: Stress and Coping in Health and Illness.* Addison-Wesley, Menlo Park, CA

Bubeck D 1995 *Care, Justice and Gender.* Oxford University Press, Oxford, UK

Bussemaker J, van Kersbergen K 1994 Gender and welfare

states: Some theoretical reflections. In: Sainsbury D (ed.) *Gendering Welfare States*. Sage, London

Finch J, Groves D 1983 *A Labour of Love: Women, Work and Caring*. Routledge and Kegan Paul, London

Fisher B, Tronto J C 1990 Towards a feminist theory of care. In: Abel E, Nelson M (eds.) *Circles of Care*. State University of New York Press, Albany, NY

Folbre N 1994 *Who Pays for the Kids? Gender and the Structures of Constraint*. Routledge, New York

Foucault M 1965 *Madness and Civilization*. Pantheon Books, New York

Fraser N 1989 *Unruly Practices: Power, Discourse, and Gender in Contemporary Social Theory*. University of Minnesota Press, Minneapolis, MN

Gilligan C 1982 *In a Different Voice*. Harvard University Press, Cambridge, MA

Held V 1993 *Feminist Morality: Transforming Culture, Society and Politics*. University of Chicago Press, Chicago

Jaggar A 1995 Caring as a feminist practice of moral reason. In: Held V (ed.) *Justice and Care: Essential Readings in Feminist Ethics*. Westview Press, Boulder, CO

Kittay E 1999 *Love's Labor*. Routledge, New York

Knijn T, Kremer M 1997 Gender and the caring dimension of welfare states toward inclusive citizenship. *Social Politics* **4**: 328–61

Noddings N 1984 *Caring: A Feminine Approach to Ethics and Moral Education*. University of California Press, Berkeley, CA

Pateman C 1988 *The Sexual Contract*. Stanford University Press, Stanford, CA

Robinson F 1999 *Globalizing Care*. Westview, Boulder, CO

Ruddick S 1990 *Maternal Thinking: Towards a Politics of Peace*. Beacon Press, Boston

Sevenhuijsen S L 1998 *Citizenship and the Ethics of Care*. Routledge, London

Tronto J C 1993 *Moral Boundaries*. Routledge, New York

Tronto J C 1996 The Political concept of care. In: Hirschmann N, Di Stefano C (eds.) *Revisioning the Political: Feminist Reconstructions of Traditional Concepts in Western Political Theory*. Westview Press, Boulder, CO

Ungerson C 1997 Social politics and the commodification of care. *Social Politics* **4**: 362–81

Waerness K 1984 The rationality of caring. *Economic and Industrial Democracy* **5**: 185–211

J. Tronto

Career Development, Psychology of

1. The Traditional Career Perspective

A career can be defined as a pattern of work experiences comprising the entire life span of a person and which is generally seen with regard to a number of phases or stages reflecting the transition from one stage of life to the next (= sequences of work roles). Therefore 'career' may be conceptualized with regard to the development of skills and expertise, the ability to learn, the developmental identity, and the self-concept as 'career anchor.'

The models of career development and the study of careers are always linked to the existing environmental conditions (cf. Whyte 1986 vs. Hall 1986), to a 'relationship concept' (= psychological contract) and to prevailing points of view (e.g. intra- or interorganizational) of the different sociological disciplines and the different fields of psychology (e.g., occupational, organizational, personnel, and managerial psychology). The orthodox perspective consists of the concentration on the big organization, associated with the 'bounded career' which develops within a single organization.

However, it needs to be pointed out that the situation in the field of career development research and in developing career theories must be assessed as extremely unsatisfactory, not least because it is a recent, interdisciplinary field within the field of social sciences. Several academic disciplines and their 'subfields' are working in it—a circumstance which has led to a 'fractionation' of the field which has therefore not been able to produce integrative theories of career development with the disciplines ignoring the results of the others (psychology, sociology, management science, anthropology, etc.).

The biggest part by far of empirical career research within the field of applied psychology (as also of the interdisciplinary studies) is dominated by the perspective of the 'intraorganizational career.' Here two issues play a central role: 'careers in organizations' and the 'matching' between the needs of the employee on the one hand and those of the organization on the other (cf. Holland 1997). This 'intrafirm perspective' has supported the so-called 'bounded career assumptions' for decades (as opposed to the 'boundary-less assumptions') having stressed for a major part the 'single organizational settings' (= research into career development within a single, stable organization) until today. Unfortunately, it can be observed in career research that this orthodox approach has been kept for a major part—in spite of significant changes in the organizations.

This traditional perspective of work and career, as it is also reflected by most of the classical 'models of career development' (cf. Brown and Brooks 1990, Osipow 1983, Super 1957), obviously comprises principles such as stability in the working environment (e.g., continued existence of the organization and the work role), movement by hierarchical promotion and interorganizational mobility, and a constant availability of positions and work roles in accordance with the interests, talents, and the lifestyle preferred by the person. It regards the organizations as a 'benevolent' unity playing an active role in designing the career of the individual employee or the executive, respectively. This traditional career perspective was accompanied by two institutions defining the background for the 'locus of career responsibility.' (a) The 'psychological contract,' the mutual relationships and expectations between the employee and the organization (=

unwritten contract of relationships): what an employee thinks he/she owes to the organization and what he/she thinks he/she can expect the organization to owe him for this. A psychological contract thus produces a long-term security (for both sides) and a high level of commitment and loyalty to the organization on the part of the employee. To the employee this had the advantage of having a valued job and a position which enabled him to climb up a hierarchical career ladder in scheduled steps. To the organization this model guaranteed a constant supply of talented employees with a high level of commitment, striving to take up new and enlarging roles—possibly even involving putting personal interests last. 'Downsizing,' 'head-count reductions,' and 'large-scale layoffs' have rendered this contract invalid. Employees can no longer count on a 'link' to their company going beyond the contractually agreed salary.

The second institution consists of the (b) assumption of big organizations which held a great fascination especially for psychological career research of the 1970s and 1980s and which was regarded as the basis for lifelong employment and as a model for a career context encompassing the entire working life (Ouchi 1981, Pascale and Athos 1981). Thus the 'locus of career responsibility' was determined as well. The organization was required to create stable social working conditions, and also to create an environment which offered ideal conditions to both the employees and the organization itself and which was also taking care of the personal development and the welfare of its employees. The focal point in career research was placed—even until the beginning of the 1990s—mainly on intraorganizational issues and limits itself to executive, management careers, or professional and hierarchical careers, respectively.

2. The No-boundary Organization

In the meantime, this traditional perspective of career development in organizations has dramatically changed, most of all with regard to the implicit work of the psychological 'relationships contract' involving a high level of commitment in the long term. A significant number of factors relating to changes in the design and the structure of organizations influence the nature of careers within organizations. Among other things, these include the changed work relationships and work contracts, the trend towards leaner and flatter organizations, and the increasing distribution of work to teams. The 'relational contract' became a 'transactional contract' designed for shorter terms, including a performance-based payment, a lower level of mutual commitment which can relatively easily be terminated by either side (MacNeill 1985). To the extent that organizations grow flatter, also the number of people required for leadership functions in the middle and upper management level will be reduced.

However, most of all this significantly limits the traditional possibility for career development by 'climbing up the ladder.' New environmental conditions or conditions of the surrounding field with their high degree of uncertainty are forcing organizations to abandon the practice of guiding their employees and executives over long-standing career paths and through prescribed development sequences. Within the 'boundary-less' organization this responsibility is shifted towards the person who is thus itself responsible for its career development—via different employment relationships in different organizations (= boundary-less career). It is the opposite of an inter-organizational career (= bounded career), with several meanings to this term: (a) this career surpasses the 'bounds' of different organizations; (b) there are no (classically) hierarchical principles in career development; (c) the marketability and network relations are predominant. Hall (1976) has coined the term 'protean career' for this new scenario. By this we understand a proactive process which is controlled by the person—and not by the organization. It consists of all the different experiences of a person in the fields of training and the work experience in different organizations, the change between different groups of training occupations or job roles, etc. to different employment relationships in different organizations.

Besides, it can also be observed that the growing trend towards teams, leads towards assigning management functions to these teams (e.g., in the medium managementb level) as their members are increasingly acquiring the ability of self-management. So-called 'high involvement work teams' coordinate, schedule, and distribute the work without depending on firmly established 'supervisor positions' (see *Teamwork and Team Training*). A stronger orientation towards teams in organizations should result in a less clear definition of individual tasks or work roles which are not inseparably linked to certain persons. The team members are expected to fulfill different tasks at different moments and, if required, to share their expertise with others. The ideal member of a team should have the highest possible number of different abilities and should be able to work without direct leadership. Therefore in such a team there is not much room for people who only want to give instructions or for those who are only able to carry out one single task or who want to specialize on certain tasks. This circumstance, too, will result in a more difficult career planning in the sense of a linear career path. Finally, the changes in work relations and in the 'psychological contract' have reduced the stability of the traditional career, as well as the attitudes, the loyalty, and the expectations of the employee or the executive. The employee can no longer count on a long-term commitment on the part of the employing organization, and neither can he or she necessarily count on the fact that his or her abilities will be assessed and valued on the job market.

Changes in career development require us to look at the changes in the organizational, professional, and industrial or economic context at the same time. The evolution of the forms of organizations has always been the impulse for the content and the way of professional careers. That is why career theories always reflect the current assumptions on organizations (Arthur et al. 1989). Organizational structures dictate the necessary core competencies and different organizational practices require a different 'mix' of competencies. Therefore changed 'boundary-less' organizations will employ employees with changed values (e.g., a limited commitment) and with a 'boundary-less' career oriented more towards the self. 'Boundary-less' organizations change existing career patterns. Here some 'critical dimensions' can be identified, such as the 'size' and the 'degree of centralization' determining the evolution of organizations and having various effects on the developing career concept and career systems.

3. The Reorganization of Organizations

Large-scale companies and organizations have rapidly lost to an increasing extent—at least since the end of the 1980s—their dominance, the importance of their expansion, and their fascination. Instead of vertical coordination of dominant companies, other models have been found which are more efficient and competitive at being able to cope with the fast, complex, global developments of the information and service society more effectively. Big organizations of the future will consist of multiple 'divisions' and 'joint ventures,' 'regional alliances,' private and public partnerships. In addition to this, entrepreneurs, franchisers, and smaller businessmen will supply supporting services, technologies and materials, and distribute goods. These 'boundary-less organizations' continuously change their dynamic forms and structures by expanding and reorganizing, acquiring new parts or selling old ones and even entering into partnerships with other organizations or companies for certain periods of time. During this process the old ideas of vertical coordination will increasingly vanish, just because horizontal coordination models as an alternative are better able to adapt to the specific and constantly changing interests of every company.

This revolution in the reorganization of organizations which was triggered by the global competition has given a new definition to both the work relationships and the forms of career development and newly challenges the classical career theory to paths not yet taken. In order to cope with a highly turbulent external environment which can be predicted only to a limited degree and in the short run, organizations have tried to adapt to the changed circumstances by 'reorganizing,' 'downsizing,' 'delayering,' 'flattening the pyramid,' 'teaming,' and 'outsourcing.'

However, the efforts of the organizations concerning the work relationships between employees and executives on the one hand and the companies on the other have also caused a high degree of destabilization. Additionally, a higher degree of diversification among both employees and executives can be observed (the percentage of women is constantly increasing and—most of all among executives—an increasing internationalization can be recognized). But also the attitudes and the behavior of the individual employee and executive towards the work situation has significantly changed, most of all in the fields of commitment, loyalty, and work and family.

4. New Career Competencies

Instead of 'bemoaning' these changes and to wish back work relationships and career developments from the past, it is necessary to point out chances for future development and to bring about clarity. This can best be done by newly arranging work roles, setting competencies required for the future, clarifying different career concepts and their conceptual meaning (e.g., whether it is firm-centered or person-centered), and by newly defining career success as well as career responsibility.

Usual work roles are often described as artifacts of the industrial age, as 'vehicles' which were used in order to split up work in 'packages.' By continuous reorganization, downsizing, teaming, etc., many of the old work roles or 'jobs' have been significantly changed—or totally deleted—by 'job enrichment' or 'job enlargement' measures. The changes in the working world also require new career competencies and strategies: a 'portfolio of skills' which can be translated from one work situation to others, with the focus on 'interorganizational employability'; lifelong learning in order to maintain the skills 'relevantly'; experience in 'team and project work' (so-called 'collaborative abilities'); building reputation over one's career; and, not least, the career should be consistent with the self-identity. In order to be successful in a turbulent working world, in the future more than mere 'job skills' will be required. New 'career competencies' will be necessary, so-called 'metaskills.' They are required in order to acquire new skills. Here are some examples: adaptability, tolerance of ambiguity, and uncertainty (Handy 1990).

Changes in the required core competencies can best be shown in the field of leadership and management, at the point of transition from the 'traditional organization' to the current 'network organization.' Careers in the traditional organization often used to comprise only a single technical expertise (e.g., production or sales)—but only in a few cases the understanding of several business functions. The more complicated the organizations became, the more competencies—in different compositions—were required (e.g., technical, commercial, and administrative competencies). In today's network organizations, in which independent companies are linked to each other, the objective is to provide critical expertise required for a specific project or product. Network organizations gain their particular influence by relying on their internal and external partners who, on their part, contribute to the value added chain. By doing this products and projects (from RandD to sale) can be tackled which could not be handled by a single organization on its own but which can only be handled with the help of network partners.

In order to do this, executives need 'collaborative' competencies. These consist of three components: (a) the ability to analyze a problem and develop solutions with the help of partners and networks; (b) 'partner abilities,' i.e., to develop concepts, to negotiate, and to carry them out to mutual benefit; (c) relationship management, i.e., to identify the needs of clients and partners and to meet them precisely. These career competencies, depending on the organizational structures, can finally be continued to the currently developing 'cellular organization' which no longer includes any kind of management hierarchy. The 'cells' of these organizational forms consist of, among other elements, 'self-managing teams' with their own management responsibilities which would be able to survive autonomously. However, they share their knowledge and their information with other 'cells' in order to be stronger and more competent. This organizational form does not work as 'employer' but it is a helpful mechanism in order to promote the knowledge-intensive abilities of their members in their application and enlargement.

5. New Career Concepts

So this leads us back to career responsibility as in the cellular organization it is completely placed with its members (= the locus of responsibility). The old theories for career management regard career development in the sense of narrow, sequenced, and methodical activities. Today's working world, on the other hand, is characterized by continuous changes (for both sides), by uncertainty, turbulence, limited obligations, and a lack of borders. Therefore the traditional 'organizational career,' in which the employees were expected to put their personal interests last, was replaced by a so-called 'self-centered career.' So the career model now changes into an individual process of self-responsibility. The individual explores his or her career opportunities, sets career goals, develops strategies, and searches for a relevant definition from time to time (Greenhaus et al. 1995).

In order to do this, Schein (1990) proposes a differentiation of the term 'career' into an 'internal' and an 'external' career—with the internal career relating to the subjective sense for where, i.e., in which direction, the working life will lead. The 'external' career relates to the formal phases and roles as they are defined by the organization's practices and the concepts of society regarding what an individual can expect within the professional organization. Closely related to the term of the 'internal' career is the concept of the 'career anchors' which can be equated with the self-concept of a person. This develops during the course of gaining increasing experience of life and work. It consists of talents and abilities which a person recognizes for himself or herself, of a structure of values, and of job-relevant motives and needs. The self-concept constructed in this way has a stabilizing influence on the actions and decisions of a person and becomes part of the personality—with these career anchors not being cemented forever but able to change (among other things by a change of values in the society). We differentiate between several categories of such career anchors which, according to the occupational group, can be part of the individual self-concept in order to express the respectively existing central motives, values, and needs (cf. also the works by Hogan et al. 2000). The essential categories of career anchors are: (a) autonomy/independence; (b) security/stability; (c) technical–functional competency; (d) general management competency; (e) entrepreneurial creativity; (f) lifestyle; (g) service in the sense of a service to a higher task; (h) challenge. Unlike the construction of 'career resilience,' the concept of the 'career anchor' implies that the definitions by different persons in organizations of their career regarding developing talents, motives, and values vary significantly.

Careers are currently changing in several ways. Today we cannot, or much less than in the past, assume that people will spend all their life in one job or in one special field. That is why we have to find answers to, among other things, the following questions: how can we find a transition from technical to management roles? In order to achieve an effective performance lifelong learning is required and the acquisition of ever new abilities. Neither can we assume that people will always stay employed by one company. These changes create an environment in which employees and executives regularly have to evaluate their potentials and career plans again and again in order to keep themselves 'marketable'—in connection with the opportunity to appear professionally 'attractive' to a company. Careers will develop laterally and diagonally. However, loyalty and commitment from the part of the organizations will decrease which will shift the center of responsibility and control of the career development (as mentioned before) towards the employee. The working individual is to develop a higher degree of 'resilience' during this transitional stage of shifting responsibility and control in order to become 'career self-resilient' in the working world. This construction of 'career resilience' measures the ability of an individual to change his or her career, to cope with uncertainty and with disappointments in organizational processes. This concept can be applied to all individuals and all careers.

6. *Challenges for the Field of Applied Psychology*

In these enormous processes of change in the field of career development the above-mentioned fields of applied psychology are given a number of essential tasks. However, here it is indispensable that the individual 'subfields' do not neglect the results of the others (neither those of other social sciences)—as has been done up to now. These tasks include, for one thing, the development of assessment methods and development tools in order to identify individual abilities, potentials, and talents, to determine the state of development and to provide creative approaches for 'skill-building.' This task gets all the more difficult if at the moment it is not yet known how the new requirements and roles will look like in 5–7 years. The same applies to development plans, job descriptions, and incentive systems. However, they are also included in the field of 'multi-rater feedback' tools such as the 360° feedback. A special importance is attached to 'cross-training' in order to create opportunities to acquire new abilities and skills or to enlarge existing ones. The activities in the field of 'human resources planning' must be significantly enlarged. One focal point here should be put on career planning in order to develop career paths and 'mentoring programs' (also over different organizational levels).

The development of training courses for 'boundary-less career management' or the problematic of 'career adaptability' must not be forgotten. The latter must be intensively studied by psychologists. For example, is 'career adaptability' a function of the personality? Also 'coping strategies' must be developed. Mentors must be enabled to help employees and executives to always steer their career safely in an ever-changing working world. Psychologists are able to help working people in their career development by replacing their (conservative) expectations of a continuous mobility 'upwards' by a rather cyclical and lateral career development. In 'boundary-less organizations' and 'boundary careers,' major role conflicts caused by complicated working conditions must be expected, and a substitute must be found for identifying with the organization.

With all of these psychological career activities the reliable determination of a specific need for development (especially the future need in growth areas), advisory activities, and the conduct of evaluation programs is of major importance. Here a 'dual focus,' i.e., individual and organization, is an essential requirement for successful work on the part of the psychologist. Career development programs offer their services to the employee for his or her career planning and give incentives for learning. The organization benefits from this program by developing in-house

talents, by supporting the planning for succession, and by countering discontent and decreasing commitment caused by uncertainty and instability of new work relations.

7. *Summary and Implications for Future Research*

Global competition has triggered a revolution in the reorganization of the organization. In contrast to the traditional form of the 'bounded' organization with its centralized decision making processes, vertical models of coordination, hierarchies, and career ladders, the present organization emphasizes a boundary-less concept, a vertically coordinated approach, and boundary-less career principles. New forms of organizations have dynamic shapes and structures. They rearrange themselves to adapt to changes in the environment. It was outlined how evolution of the forms of organizations has been the impulse for content and way of professional careers. In this scenario several trends were described such as the shift from bounded to boundary-less concepts; stability to instability of employment; long-term to short-term career goals; generic to firm-specific competencies; firm-centered to person-centered career approaches; relational to transactional employer–employee relationships; and the shift of career responsibility from the employer to the employee. In order to describe the evolving career management focus, a number of different concepts and terms created by researchers over the past several years have been presented: career anchors; psychological contract; protean career; internal vs. external career; self-centered career; destabilization of relationships between people and organizations; interorganizational concepts; networking; career self-resilience; interorganizational employability; high involvement work teams; collaborative competencies.

All of this raises some important questions for future research. For instance, to what extent will boundary-less organizations alter career theories and actual career mobility patterns? To what extent is career adaptability a function of personality (disposition toward proactive behavior) or age vs. a skill that can be developed? Can people learn to be adaptable? There is need for more research on what personal and developmental growth training best prepare people to engage in new career cycles and disengage from old ones? How can organizations help employees to regularly assess their skills, interests, and values so that they can figure out what kind of work experience to seek? As information technology makes new organizational forms possible, and as social values shift priorities, what should a given job consist of and how should one hire and train people for the ambiguous and changing roles? It is necessary to consider whether a career goal is helpful or an unnecessary restriction. Research is needed on new standards of career success, on new forms of work identity, on role overload (the work vs. family conflict), and new substitutes for organizational identification have to be found. It is also worth studying what support systems are needed for employees under the transactional contract and how the development of a 'spot market' mentality can be avoided? What is the impact of choice in the different employment contracts (relational vs. transactional)? A major implication of these ideas for future research is that the study of careers must be better connected to a turbulent, complex, rapidly changing environment, and it has to become multi-disciplinary.

Bibliography

Arthur M B, Hall D T, Lawrence B S (eds.) 1989 *Handbook of Career Theory*. Cambridge University Press, New York

Brown D, Brooks L (eds.) 1990 *Career Choice and Development*. Jossey-Bass, San Francisco

Greenhaus J H, Callanan G A, Kaplan E 1995 The role of goal setting in career management. *The International Journal of Career Management* 7(5): 3–12

Hall D T 1976 *Careers in Organizations*. Scott, Foresman, Glenview, IL

Hall D T 1996 *The Career is Dead: Long Live the Career*, 1st edn. Jossey-Bass, San Francisco

Hall D T (ed.) 1986 *Career Developments in Organizations*. Jossey-Bass, San Francisco

Handy C 1990 *The age of Unreasoning*. Harvard University Press, Boston

Hogan J, Hogan R, Weinert A B 2000 *The Values and Interests Inventory*. University of the Federal Armed Forces, Hamburg, Germany

Holland J L 1997 *Making Vocational Choices*, 3rd edn. Psychological Assessment Resources, Odessa, FL

MacNeill I R 1985 Relational contracts: what we do and do not know. *Wisconsin Law Review*. 3: 483–525

Osipow S H 1983 *Theories of Career Development*, 3rd edn. Prentice-Hall, Englewood Cliffs, NJ

Ouchi W G 1981 *Theory Z*. Addison-Wesley, Reading, MA

Pascale R T, Athos A G 1981 *The Art of Japanese Management*. Simon and Schuster, New York

Schein E H 1990 *Career Anchors*. University Associates, San Diego, CA

Super D E 1957 *The Psychology of Careers*, 1st edn. Harper and Row, New York

Whyte W F 1986 *The Organization Man*. Simon and Schuster, New York

A. B. Weinert

Caregiver Burden

1. Definition of Family Caregiving

The provision of assistance and support by one family member or friend to another is a pervasive aspect of everyday human interactions. Providing help to a family member with chronic illness or disability is not very different from the tasks and activities that characterize interactions among families and close friends without the presence of illness or disability. Thus, when a wife provides care to her husband with Alzheimer's disease (AD) by preparing his meals, it may be an activity she would normally do for an unimpaired husband. However, if a wife also assists her cognitively impaired husband with bathing and dressing, few would question whether or not caregiving is taking place. The difference is that providing assistance with bathing and dressing or assisting with complex medical routines clearly represents 'extra-ordinary' care and exceeds the bounds of what is 'normative' or 'usual.' Similarly, parents caring for a child with a chronic illness may need to assist with daily medical routines (e.g., insulin injections or chest physical therapy) that are time consuming and difficult and are in addition to normal parenting responsibilities. Caregiving involves significant expenditure of time and energy often for months or years, requiring the performance of tasks that may be physically demanding and unpleasant, and frequently disrupting other family and social roles of the caregiver (see *Gender Role Stress and Health*).

Although caregivers may perform tasks similar to those carried out by paid health professionals, they perform these services for no compensation and do so either voluntarily or because they feel there are no other alternatives. Because the physical and mental health consequences of taking on this role are sometimes severe, and because caregivers represent an invaluable resource to the well-being of our population, research on caregiving has become a high priority among scholars in many disciplines as well as among policy makers.

2. Prevalence of Caregiving

Although the definition and boundaries of what is meant by the term caregiving often vary depending on the purpose for which such definitions are used, there is strong consensus that regardless of how caregiving is defined, its prevalence is high. A broadly inclusive approach might argue that a caregiver is needed for every person with health-related mobility and self-care limitations which makes it difficult to take care of personal needs, such as dressing, bathing, and moving around the home. Current estimates indicate that 4 percent of the non-institutionalized US population under the age of 55 meet these criteria. Beyond the age of 55, the proportion of persons with mobility and/or self care limitations increases dramatically; fully half of the population falls into this category after age 85 (US Bureau of the Census 1990). If we assume that these individuals minimally require one caregiver, these estimates yield over 15 million caregivers in the US. Indeed, these estimates are somewhat lower than results reported in a recent national survey of caregivers which reported that there were 22.4 million households that met broad criteria for the presence of a caregiver in the past 12 months (National Alliance for Caregiving 1997).

Caregiving is not just a late life phenomenon involving the care of disabled older persons. It is estimated that 10–14 percent of children and adolescents (7.5 million) in the US have some type of chronic illness or disability; of these individuals, approximately 20–25 percent (1.5 million) have serious health conditions that impair daily functioning and thus require a caregiver. Additionally, 4.1 million individuals between the ages of 21 and 64 require personal assistance in ADLs/IADLs.

3. Who Provides Care and What Type of Care is Provided?

Caregivers to elderly individuals generally are differentiated by age and relationship to the care recipient. One large group consists of adult children, usually daughters or daughters-in-law, in their 50s and 60s; the second group of caregivers comprises spouses of care-recipients and is generally older and has a higher proportion of male caregivers than adult children caregivers (see *Gender Role Stress and Health*).

The roles and functions of family caregivers vary by type and stage of illness and include both direct and indirect activities. Direct activities can include provision of personal care assistance, such as helping with bathing, grooming, dressing, or toileting; healthcare assistance such as catheter care, giving injections, or monitoring medications; and checking and monitoring tasks, such as continuous or periodic supervision, and telephone monitoring. Indirect tasks include care management such as locating services, coordinating service use, monitoring services, or advocacy, and households tasks, such as cooking, cleaning, shopping, money management, and transportation of the family member to medical appointments or day care programs (Biegel and Schulz 1999). The intensity at which some or all of these caregiving activities are performed varies widely, with some caregivers having only limited types of involvement for a few hours per week while other caregivers might provide more than 40 hours a week of care and be on call 24 hours per day (see *Social Support and Stress*).

4. Conceptual Approaches to the Study of Caregiving

The dominant conceptual model for caregiving assumes that the onset and progression of chronic illness and physical disability is stressful for both patient and caregiver and, as such, can be studied within the framework of traditional stress-coping models. Indeed, some researchers have likened caregiving to being exposed to a severe, long-term, chronic stressor (Pearlin et al. 1995). Within this framework, objective

stressors include measures of patient disability, cognitive impairment, and problem behaviors, as well as the type and intensity of caregiving provided. Key outcome variables for the caregiver include psychological distress and burden, often referred to as caregiver burden, psychological and physical morbidity, and patient outcomes such as institutionalization and death.

Although the literature consistently shows a moderate relationship between level of patient disability and psychological distress of the caregiver, there is considerable variability in caregiver outcomes which is thought to be mediated and/or moderated by a variety of factors including economic and social support resources available to the caregiver (Haley et al. 1996), a host of individual difference factors, such as gender, personality attributes (optimism, self-esteem, self-mastery), coping strategies used, and the quality of the relationship between caregiver and care recipient (see Quittner et al. 1990, Schulz et al. 1990, 1995). Researchers have further extended basic stress-coping models to include examination of secondary stressors, such as role conflict engendered by caregiving demands (Pearlin et al. 1997), and have applied many additional theoretical perspectives borrowed from social and clinical psychology, sociology, and the health and biological sciences to help understand specific aspects of the caregiving situation. Finally, researchers interested in the health consequences of caregiving have focused on a variety of physiological mechanisms including the pituitary-adrenal axis, the sympathetic nervous system, and the immune system in their effort to identify biological modulators (Haidt and Rodin 1995, Kiecolt-Glaser et al. 1991, Vitaliano et al. 1997) of the stress-health relationship. Researchers have also shown that the stresses associated with caregiving are a risk factor for the caregiver's death (Schulz and Beach 1999). In sum, caregiving clearly provides a rich platform for the application of much of the theoretical and methodological expertise of researchers in many disciplines.

A wide range of caregiving effects have been described in the literature including disruption of family routines, psychological distress, and psychological and physical morbidity including mortality, financial hardship, and work-related problems (see *Stress and Health Research*). Feeling burdened or distressed by the demands of caregiving is the most frequently reported outcome associated with caregiving, although this is not a universal phenomenon, particularly among spousal caregivers (Zarit et al. 1986). Psychiatric morbidity such as depression and anxiety are also common. Physical health effects such as increased susceptibility to illness have been more difficult to demonstrate, although they are likely to occur in high demand situations among vulnerable (e.g., frail) caregivers. Possible mediators of illness effects are increased depression associated with caregiving and changes in health related behaviors such as sleeping and eating patterns and medical compliance. Positive effects of caregiving such as increased self-esteem, the satisfaction of knowing that one's relative is being properly cared for, as well as improved mental health have also been reported (Beach et al. 2000).

The demands and negative impacts of dementia caregiving are generally higher than nondementia caregiving (Schulz 2000). Indeed, a recent report by Ory et al. (1999) documents the ways in which dementia care is different from other types of family caregiving. Not only do dementia caregivers spend significantly more hours per week providing care than nondementia caregivers, they also report greater employment complications, caregiver strain, mental and physical health problems, reduced time for leisure and other family members, and family conflict. Factors that are likely to account for this greater level of strain include having to contend with behavioral problems of the care-recipient (e.g., wandering, aggressiveness), and the unpredictable nature and course of dementing illnesses. A number of health psychologists have focused this type of caregiving as a platform for studying mind-body phenomenon linking chronic stress to physical morbidity.

5. The Future of Caregiving

A number of important interrelated demographic, health, and social trends will shape the caregiving agenda in the future. First, there will be a worldwide increase in the number of older individuals, and possibly increased numbers of disabled individuals with longer life expectancies due to medical interventions. A key question will be the extent to which increases in life expectancy are associated with increasing years of disability. Some early evidence suggests that future cohorts of elderly individuals will be healthier and more functional than current cohorts, thus adding years to life may not necessarily increase the need for caregiving assistance. Alternatively, one can speculate that some types of medical interventions (e.g., drug therapies that enable AD patients to spend more years at home) will extend the family caregiving career. Second, future cohorts of elderly will have smaller families and fewer children available to provide care. The supply of caregivers may be further depleted by the increased and sustained labor-force participation of adult daughters, making them less available to provide care. Third, the trend toward shifting care from formal to informal care providers is likely to continue and accelerate. Caregivers increasingly will be asked to provide complex postacute care in addition to the chronic care they have provided traditionally. As these examples illustrate, caregiving issues are linked inextricably to broader demographic trends and the health and disability of our older population. At the macrolevel, caregiving and caregiver burden will have to be addressed through government policy and private sector programs.

See also: Aging and Health in Old Age; Gender Role Stress and Health; Social Support and Stress; Stress and Coping Theories; Stress and Health Research

Bibliography

Beach S R, Schulz R, Yee J L, Jackson S 2000 Negative and positive health effects of caring for a disabled spouse: Longitudinal findings from the Caregiver Health Effects Study. *Psychology and Aging* **15**: 259–71

Biegel D E, Schulz R 1999 Caregiving and caregiver interventions in aging and mental illness. *Family Relations* **48**: 345–54

Haidt J, Rodin J 1995 *Control and Efficacy: An Integrative Review*. A report to the John D. and Catherine T. MacArthur Foundation Program on Mental Health and Human Development

Haley W E, Roth D L, Coleton M I, Ford G R, West C A C, Collins R P, Isobe T L 1996 Appraisal, coping, and social support as mediators of wellbeing in black and white family caregivers of patients with Alzheimer's disease. *Journal of Consulting and Clinical Psychology* **64**: 121–9

Kiecolt-Glaser J K, Dura J R, Speicher C E, Trask O J, Glaser R 1991 Spousal caregivers of dementia victims: Longitudinal changes in immunity and health. *Psychosomatic Medicine* **53**: 345–62

National Alliance for Caregiving and the American Association of Retired Persons 1997 *Family Caregiving in the US Findings from a National Survey. Final Report*. National Alliance for Caregiving, Bethesda, MD

Ory M G, Hoffman III R R, Yee J L, Tennstedt S, Schulz R 1999 Prevalence and impact of caregiving: A detailed comparison between dementia and non-dementia caregivers. *Dementia and non-dementia caregiving. The Gerontologist* **39**: 177–85

Pearlin L I, Aneshensel C S, Le Blanc A J 1997 The forms and mechanisms of stress proliferation: The case of AIDS caregivers. *Journal of Health and Social Behavior* **38**: 223–36

Pearlin L I, Aneshensel C S, Mullan J T, Whitlatch C J 1995 Caregiving and its social support. In: Binstock R H, George L K (eds.) *Handbook of Aging and the Social Sciences*, 4th edn. Academic Press, New York, pp. 283–302

Quittner A L, Glueckauf R L, Jackson D N 1990 Chronic parenting stress: Moderating vs. mediating effects of social support. *Journal of Personality and Social Psychology* **59**: 1266–78

Schulz R (ed.) 2000 *Handbook of Dementia Caregiving*. Springer, New York

Schulz R, Beach S 1999 Caregiving as a risk factor for mortality. The caregiver health effects study. *Journal of the American Medical Association* **282**: 2215–9

Schulz R, O'Brien A T, Bookwala J, Fleissner K 1995 Psychiatric and physical morbidity effects of Alzheimer's Disease caregiving: Prevalence, correlates, and causes. *The Gerontologist* **35**: 771–91

Schulz R, Visintainer P, Williamson G M 1990 Psychiatric and physical morbidity effect of caregiving. *Journals of Gerontology: Psychological Sciences* **45**: P181–P191

US Bureau of the Census 1990 *The Need for Personal Assistance with Everyday Activities: Recipients and Caregivers. Current Population Reports* (Series P-70. Household Economic Studies). Department of Commerce, Washington, DC

Vitaliano P P, Schulz R, Kiecolt-Glaser J, Grant I 1997 Research on physiological and physical concomitants of caregiving:

Where do we go from here? *Annals of Behavioral Medicine* **19**: 117–23

Zarit S H, Todd P A, Zarit J M 1986 Subjective burden of husbands and wives of caregivers: A longitudinal study. *The Gerontologist* **26**: 260–6

R. Schulz

Caregiving in Old Age

1. Caregiving, the Area

Caregiving in old age is the provision of assistance to an elder when his or her health deteriorates, whether it is physical or mental health, or a combination of the two. Caregiving typically refers to unpaid care from members of the informal network, that is, from family or friends. It is an aspect of the more general concept of social support. However, there is no precise scientific definition of the term caregiving, and research reveals a diversity of views. For example, spouses who are providing assistance to their loved one with instrumental activities of daily living are less likely than others, such as children or siblings, to consider themselves as caregivers (more frequently referred to as carers in the UK). Think of the instance where a daughter takes her mother grocery shopping. Either one or both may define it as a chance to socialize, or as assistance, or as simply something they do together. The literature adds to the confusion with the use of a variety of terms, including caregiving, caring, assistance, interaction, and support, sometimes used synonymously and sometimes not. Despite these difficulties, the area of caregiving in old age has received much research attention from 1970 onwards.

2. In the Beginning

Interest in the area arose during the 1960s and 1970s as a practical concern. During this time, gerontologists documented the extensiveness of social ties, including caregiving, during later life. This was important within the context of the times when it was commonly believed that seniors in Western industrialized societies were largely isolated from their family, living alone, and often housed in long-term care institutions. Gerontological research recorded the falsity of these images by studying the strong interactional ties within the lives of most seniors. Researchers reported the preferred normality of 'intimacy at a distance,' in which neither seniors nor their children wish to live together but have a desire for contact. Usually seniors lived geographically proximate to at least one of their children. This period also examined the prevalence of informal, unpaid caregivers as the dominant source of assistance for elders. The informal network was the first resort for care when health declined. This was important because it established the strength of the family as a major source of interpersonal support and care during old age (Chappell 1990).

3. Reaching Maturity

By the late 1970s and especially in the 1980s, research on caregiving was burgeoning. It examined earlier assumptions of the research. For example, early research assumed contact meant assistance or contact included positive support. Research started to investigate whether and under what circumstances social interaction was indeed supportive, when assistance was positive. Research distinguished who provides support and studied the critical role of spouses among married couples and children when a spouse is not available frequently because of death. While caregiving frequently focuses on tasks of activities of daily living, either instrumental activities of daily living (IADL) such as shopping and banking, and basic activities of daily living (ADL) such as going to the toilet, eating, personal mobility, and other activities necessary for survival, the emotional aspects received little attention. Yet it was recognized that it is this emotional element that distinguishes informal care from formal or paid caregiving.

Caregivers were labeled the 'hidden victims,' 'sandwich generation,' 'generation-in-the-middle' (Brody 1981), raising the public recognition of caregiving. It was during this period that Cantor's (1979) hierarchical compensatory model, also known as the substitution model, received much attention. She argued for an orderly hierarchical selection of caregivers, determined by the primacy of the relationship between the giver and the recipient. According to this view, the most preferred caregiver was the spouse, followed by daughters, sons, other relatives, friends, and neighbors, in that order. Litwak's (1985) competing hypothesis of task specificity also gained popularity. In this instance, it was argued that persons differentially placed within society provide different types of assistance (spouses can provide emotional and other long-term needs on a continuous basis; neighbors provide short-term, sporadic, and instrumental assistance).

There was less of a focus on support from siblings, friendships, and grandchildren; most studies examined care from the spouse and children, who are the most prevalent care providers. Significant gender differences in caregiving were revealed: the fact that women tend to do the emotional and hands on work while men tend to provide advice and financial assistance (Horowitz 1981). Other studies reported that men are more likely to rely exclusively on their spouse for emotional support whereas women are more likely to rely on friends (Hess and Waring 1980); that caregivers experience burden as a result of their involvement in this role (Zarit et al. 1980); that there is generally one main care provider who does most of the work (Stone et al. 1987); and that working daughters do not provide fewer hours of caregiving than those who are not in paid labor (Brody et al. 1984).

Still other research indicated that some ethnic groups have different and more extensive caregiving than others, but disentangling how much of the variation is due to 'culture' is difficult because ethnic minority status and social class are correlated empirically. It was also during this time that the full extent of caregiving was exposed. In a review of scientific studies throughout industrialized worlds, Kane and Kane (1985) estimated that between 75 and 85 percent of all personal care to seniors comes from the informal network. Chappell (1985) reported that almost all community living elders receiving any type of assistance do so from the informal network. The lack of recognition of the care provided by caregivers and the lack of support for caregivers within formal health care systems was also documented (George 1988).

The sheer volume of research on caregiving established it as a major area and much was learned. Informal caregiving emerged as the indisputable dominant system of care in post-modern society—despite all that has been said about our individualism and lack of concern for one another. Caregiving, it became obvious, is significantly a woman's issue. Women predominate as the caregivers and the care-receivers. Caregivers are burdened and women who work do not shirk from caregiving.

4. Growth in the 1990s

By the late 1980s and early 1990s caregiving had become a popular area of gerontological research, producing studies on a multitude of facets of this topic. Studies on burden and stress continued, revealing either no differences in levels between male and female caregivers or, when differences were reported, that female caregivers experience more stress. Research on male caregivers showed their more instrumental approach to the role than women have. Positive aspects of caregiving such as feeling useful and bringing comfort to a loved one were being studied. Caregivers, furthermore, are reluctant users of formal services. However, the last decade of the twentieth century did not produce simply more of the same. It also saw another substantive shift in this area of inquiry. Caregiving became politicized.

Before this time, it was recognized within academic and practice circles as important, but it was not recognized at the political level. This changed for two major reasons. One was heightened awareness from a feminist perspective that aging and caregiving, as a woman's issue, had been more or less invisible as part of the private domain and not part of a public debate. Public policy had been operating by assuming that women's caregiver roles would simply continue (Hooyman 1990). A second major factor was the prolonged economic recession throughout industrial-

ized countries. This was related to a perceived crisis in health care system funding and paved the way for a new political rhetoric, recognizing, for the first time in the twentieth century, caregivers and community care. Indeed, family care emerged in the 1990s as a cornerstone of the new vision for health reform throughout the industrialized world.

This new-found political awareness of caregivers brought an urgency to research in this area, highlighting the need for an adequate understanding of caregiving if policies and programs were going to make assumptions about their capacities and their needs. It could not be assumed that the family is necessarily the most appropriate place for caregiving. The area of elder abuse provided an example. Programs that insist seniors stay with families could prolong abusive situations.

The current political interest in caregiving represents a rediscovery of caregiving. Although government had not previously acknowledged the role played by caregivers, they had never replaced private arrangements. In the past, governments intervened only when families and individuals were not coping and came to their attention. At the present time, governments' embrace of caregivers can be viewed skeptically as a means to cost-shift from the public purse to caregivers, largely women. A concern with increased burden for caregivers is prominent. New questions are being addressed. What are the assumptions about family caregivers in current policies? What is the impact of different service interventions on caregivers? How can the formal system support caregivers and how can caregivers be integrated with formal health care delivery? The answers to these questions promise exciting new knowledge to assist seniors and their families.

In addition, increasingly sophisticated analyses are being conducted and testing of earlier explanations continues. For example, Penning (1990) demonstrates a lack of empirical support for the concepts of the sandwich generation and generation-in-the-middle. Her research supports serial caregiving as a more apt descriptor of this phenomenon, since individuals are usually involved in raising their children, then caring for their parents, then caring for their husband rather than being engaged in all of these roles at one time. In addition to the characteristics of caregivers and the burdens of caring, researchers are beginning to study the meaning of caring. Wenger et al. (1996) suggest conceptualizing caregiving in terms of purposes and relationships rather than tasks, taking the everyday experiences of caregivers and care recipients into account. For example, one can examine a preparatory stage of anticipating care; being involved in having to provide preventive care, such as ensuring the person eats well and exercises; and being involved in the supervision of care.

New theoretical insights into the socioemotional context of relationships has direct relevance for caregiving. Lang et al. (1998) for example, finds increasingly discriminating choices in our social interactions as we age. Baltes (1996) studies etiologies (causes) of behavioral dependency such as learned helplessness, learned dependency and selective optimization with compensation and the prominent role the social environment plays in this regard. Her research directs attention to overdependency among care recipients, an under-researched area to date.

5. Conclusions

Interest in caregiving in old age arose and has continued from a pragmatic applied interest. It began with assumptions about supportive relationships and about the role of the family, and over time has focused on the complexity of both the definition of caregiving as well as its contextual fields. Only recently, has there been conceptual development in this area with current attempts to examine the meaning of the term 'caregiving' and how that varies from group to group. At the present time, complex conceptual issues are starting to be addressed—When is interaction caregiving? Whose definition counts? How are caregivers taken into account within the health care system? How can they be taken into account? Whose definitions of caregiving are appropriate for service delivery? How can the autonomy of caregivers be maintained? The conceptual issues relate to methodological issues. If the mother does not consider the daughter's efforts to be caregiving but the daughter does, whose definition does the researcher accept, if either? If the wife is cooking the meals anyway and always has, is this part of caregiving when her husband's health declines? When computing the economic value of caregiving, do we include those times and tasks governments would not provide?

Future directions for caregiving research in the short term seem more or less clear. Renewed interest in the area has been fueled by the recognition of caregivers at the political level in the new vision of health reform.

See also: Aging, Theories of; Care and Gender; Caregiver Burden; Ecology of Aging; Health Care Delivery Services; Health Care Markets: Theory and Practice; Health Care, Rationing of; Health Care Systems: Comparative; Lifespan Development: Evolutionary Perspectives; Lifespan Theories of Cognitive Development; Population Aging: Economic and Social Consequences; Psychoneuroimmunology

Bibliography

Baltes M M 1996 *Many Faces of Dependency in Old Age.* Cambridge University Press, Cambridge, UK
Brody E M 1981 Women in the middle and family help to older people. *Gerontologist* 21: 471–80
Brody E M, Johnsen P T, Fulcomer M C 1984 What should adult children do for elderly parents? Opinions and preferences of three generations of women. *Journal of Gerontology* 39: 736–46
Cantor M H 1979 Neighbors and friends: an overlooked resource in the informal support system. *Research on Aging* 1: 434–63
Chappell N L 1985 Social support and the receipt of home care services. *Gerontologist* 25: 47–54
Chappell N L 1990 Aging and social care. In: Binstock R H, George L K (eds.) *Handbook of Aging and the Social Sciences,* 3rd edn. Academic Press, San Diego, CA, pp. 438–54
George L K 1988 Why won't caregivers use community services? Unexpected findings from a respite care demonstration/evaluation. In: George L K, Fillenbaum G G, Burchett B M (eds.) *Respite Care: A Strategy for Easing Caregiver Burden: Final Report.* Duke University, Center for the Study of Aging Family Support Program. Durham, North Carolina
Hess B B, Waring J M 1980 Changing patterns of aging and family bonds in later life. In: Skolnick A, Skolnick J H (eds.) *Family in Transition.* Little, Brown, and Co., Boston, pp. 521–37
Hooyman N 1990 Women as caregivers of the elderly: social implications for social welfare policy and practice. In: Biegel D E, Blum A (eds.) *Aging and Caregiving: Theory, Research and Policy.* Sage, Newbury Park, CA, pp. 221–41
Horowitz A 1981 Sons and daughters as caregivers to older parents: Differences in role performance and consequences. Paper presented at the annual meeting of the Gerontological Society of America, Toronto
Kane R A, Kane R L 1985 The feasibility of universal long-term care benefits. *New England Journal of Medicine* 312: 1357–64
Lang F R, Staudinger U M, Carstensen L L 1998 Perspectives on socioemotional selectivity in late life: How personality and social context do (and do not) make a difference. *Journal of Gerontology* 53B: 21–30
Litwak E 1985 *Helping the Elderly: The Complementary Roles of Informal Networks and Formal Systems.* Guilford Press, New York
Penning M J 1990 Receipt of assistance by elderly people: hierarchical selection and task specificity. *The Gerontologist* 30: 220–7
Stone R, Cafferata G L, Sangl J 1987 Caregivers of the frail elderly: A national profile. *The Gerontologist* 27: 616–26
Wenger C, Grant G, Nolan M 1996 Older people as carers as well as recipients of care. In: Minichiello V, Chappell N, Kendig H, Walker A (eds.) *Sociology of Aging.* International Sociological Association, Research Committee on Aging, Australia, pp. 189–206
Zarit S H, Reever K E, Bach-Peterson J 1980 Relatives of impaired elderly: Correlates of feelings of burden. *Gerontologist* 20: 649–55

N. L. Chappell

Cargo Cults

1. Preliminary Definition

Cargo cults or movements are socio-magico-religious activities which have been occurring mainly in Melanesia (that part of Oceania comprising the island archipelagoes from Irian Jaya in the west, to the east and southeast through Papua New Guinea, the Bismarcks, Solomon, Vanuatu, Fiji, and New Caledonia) since the 1850s (Steinbauer 1971, p. 181) until the present day. They include genuine sociopolitical and economic aspirations, but are in essence millenarian in nature. That is, the activities, usually initiated by someone generally like a prophet, are directed towards obtaining or greeting an expected state of bliss or contentment, the latter being envisaged as a free access to cargo (the goods and foodstuffs offloaded from the ships and, more recently, the aircraft of industrialized countries).

2. Alternative Nomenclature

Despite the name 'cargo' the cults may be considered a subset in a local idiom of all those movements of socio-religious reform, revival, and renewal which, endemic to the Christian ambience, have been variously called millenarian, messianic, or enthusiastic movements. Although similar activities have occurred where Christian influences have been marginal, including one cargo cult (Berndt 1952), the vast bulk of recorded instances have taken place where Christianity has been more or less established.

Still, avoiding Christian associations and the local cargo idiom, bringing cargo movements into line with similar kinds of activities found elsewhere in Oceania and among the indigenous peoples of the Americas, sub-Saharan Africa, Australasia, and parts of Asia (areas which Europeans have colonized or settled), a number of alternative terms to cargo, according to apparent main emphases, have been coined. Thus Accommodation, Acculturation, Adaptation, and Adjustment, also as verbs, reveal the activities as attempts to reconcile tradition with the ways of a more powerful and intrusive culture; Crisis and Disaster stress the effects of prior traumatic natural or cultural events; Nativistic, Militant, and Denunciatory emphasize the movements as protests against foreign rule together with the attempt to resolve problems by reaching back into tradition; Dynamistic, Vitalization, and Revitalization accent a positive cultural renewal in the face of what is perceived as decay or decadence; Prophetic, Charismatic, Messianic stress the importance given to the leader of a movement; and Christian influences are more directly evoked by Holy Spirit and Salvation movements.

While some cargo cults have occurred elsewhere in Oceania, they are usefully regarded as a Melanesian phenomenon. More than 400 instances have been recorded since the 1850s, and one must assume that others, in secluded areas, have gone unrecorded. The decade after the end of World War II, during which allied forces had deployed vast quantities of war materiel and general supplies throughout Melanesia, saw acceleration in the number of instances.

3. Background

From early in the nineteenth century the many Melanesian coastal communities have been subject to the increasing pressures of Euro-American imperialism. Nonliterate and differentiated by many languages and dialects but using Pidgin (*Tok pisin*) as a *lingua franca*, these hunting, fishing, and horticultural communities with stone age technologies, came into contact with Euro-American industrialized civilizations. Colonial forms of order were imposed. New infectious diseases ravaged populations. Money, taxes, plantations, and forms of indentured and contract labor were introduced. From the earliest years, Christian missionaries of different denominations communicated their varying messages and doctrines. Fortune hunters, labor recruiters, traders, and prospectors tended to be 'rough' as well as 'ready.' In turn, Germans, British, Australians, Japanese, and Americans have warred and brought their own goods and modes of government. Through all this Melanesians tried to live within their own community organizations based upon simple subsistence economies (defined as without money, a common and factorial medium of exchange) plus, in many areas, plantation or other service labor for cash—which alone could buy cargo. Some Melanesians, vulnerable to unstable world markets, engaged in cash cropping.

4. Generalized Course of a Movement

One of the more engaging qualities of Melanesians is their phlegmatic acceptance of the wonders of modern technology. Still, what seems to have impressed them most about white people has been not their particular human vices and virtues or their military prowess, but their apparent free access to cargo: all those useful artifacts, sacks of flour and rice, canned foods, and frozen carcasses. A persistent theme of day to day life was, and in places still is, the 'secret' of that access. Often, one who alludes to the subject is regarded as a bore and ignored. Still, the problem itself remains: speculation and supposition are joined to traditional myths and, indeed, Bible stories—particularly Noah's curse on the sons of Ham (Genesis 9:25)—to explain why whites seemed to have free access to cargo while Melanesians did not. Such stories and speculations make up what Burridge (1963, p. 147) has called a myth-dream: a compost of hopes, desires, and possibilities which a prophet or visionary may bring into a focus and coherence through action instructions.

Given the context of the myth-dream, the prophet usually reports a peculiar experience: a dream or vision, an encounter with a traditional spirit entity, an ancestor perhaps, or a Christian representation such as the archangel Gabriel, Virgin Mary, Holy Spirit, or other entity. Such an experience may become part of the myth-dream even if, as often occurs, it is shrugged off. Sometimes, however, prophet, mystical encounter, and action instructions come together into cogent and persuasive synthesis. What it is that transforms a possibly overwrought imagination into an active cult or movement, which includes those who are otherwise sober, practical, and businesslike, is, so far, elusive.

Sometimes visionary, prophet, and leader are contained in the same person. At other times, depending on capacities for organizing others, they separate. The explicit objective of a movement, access to cargo, as well as the means thereto have led to the activities being called 'bizarre.' These have included: destruction of crops and/or traditional sacra; marching about with wooden 'rifles'; taking scribbled pieces of paper ('cheques') to a store; signaling for cargo with 'radios' of palm thatch; forms of 'baptism' (taken from Christian rites); orgiastic dances and sexual promiscuity (re-enacting traditional creation myths in which chaos and disorder give way to the moralities and rules of sexual access and marriage). Often there is a rider: those who do not participate will be doomed to destruction.

Failure of the cargo to arrive, or administrative action, usually bring activities to an end. Still, they may smolder and develop, as the Jon Frum movement on Tanna in Vanuatu (Guiart 1962) has done over the years into stable, if syncretic, sects. However, discussions continue, the myth-dream is kept alive. The question of the 'secret' remains: how do white people get cargo?

5. Interpretations

The kinds of interpretation of cargo cults are implicit in the nomenclature: reactions with differing emphases to the cultural stresses of Melanesian history that have been summarized in the previous sections. Socioeconomic analyses going ultimately to kinds of deprivation, especially problems attending the advent of cash, have dominated. Such interpretations tend to be historically particularist. They do not necessarily suffice for very similar kinds of movement in, for example, California where, instead of cargo, the idiom may be access to spacecraft or redemption by aliens from space. Although one is forced to consider the conditions of life of participants, these conditions are not exhausted by the purely socioeconomic or even political.

For example, in *Tok pisin* the word *wok* (= work) refers to magical rites and spells, cult activities and also to work in gardens, forests, or at sea, which last translates into food, giving feasts, making exchanges, gaining and maintaining relative status, and so political influence. Further, the symbolisms in the activities bespeak an ending of the old or present ways of life and a fresh start. This may be a movement from an economy based on exchanges of foodstuffs and valuables such as shell necklaces or chaplets of dogs' teeth, to one based upon cash which, in turn, would provide

access to cargo and, perhaps, an equivalence in criteria of status in relation to whites.

Cargo movements thus envisage the creation of a 'New Man,' with access to cargo and capable of competing with whites on their own terms. If a new heaven seems cloudy, it is mainly embodied in a typical Melanesian way in a new earth where access to cargo will reward the faithful, with more for the most astute.

The incidence of cargo cults, in particular the high concentration in former New Guinea where *Tok pisin* is/was most used, hints at other factors at work. The few occurrences in Polynesia and Micronesia, where *Tok pisin* is absent, and in the Papua New Guinea Highlands where, despite a more ordered colonial penetration, much the same socioeconomic conditions in relation to whites existed, presents problems. One answer is that in the context of the myth-dream the *Tok pisin* word *kago* (= cargo) accretes to itself a transcendent sense of redemption from perceived inequities which the English 'cargo' does not.

Furthermore, it is noticeable that cargo cults tend to occur most frequently in those areas, such as in former New Guinea excluding the Highlands, where (due in part to population depletion from introduced diseases) community organizations involved shifting political and social leaderships. In consequence, infirm political authority and ambiguities of obligation and identity—just that 'anomy and incertaintie' noted in the seventeenth century of English enthusiastic movements (Burridge 1960, p. 13). Elsewhere in Oceania as well as in the Highlands of Papua New Guinea not only were (and are) communities much larger and more stable, but the loci of obligation and political

6. Conclusion

Over the space of 70 years for the Highlands of Papua New Guinea, and an added near century for most of the peoples in the coastal and intermediate areas, Melanesians have moved from a stone age technology rich in symbolism (where every quality of human character and nuance of change in climate, vegetation, or animal behavior was charged with meaning) into an ambience where bureaucracy, science, and reason are paramount. The former qualities are discounted in favor of quantity, and symbolism is derided as superstition. In such a world, except where access to money and the goods it can buy are difficult, for most Melanesians cargo cults are becoming an anachronism.

As a note of caution, long ago cult leaders and influential Melanesians were taken to Australia where they were conducted around factories to see how cargo was made. Yet this only took the central question one step deeper: whence the ability to make cargo? Why were the necessary resources not available in New authority have persisted in reasonable certainty.

Guinea? Perhaps, following American example and in contemporary idiom, future cult activities may focus on the Book of Revelation from the Bible or be directed toward access to space vehicles. Still, they will pose much the same basic questions for social scientists, as have cargo movements. The question of just why a cult does or does not occur is still a mystery. Melanesian scholars will no doubt reveal many new nuances, but whether they will do any better in relation to their movements than Europeans have done for theirs, remains to be seen.

See also: Belief, Anthropology of; Cognitive Anthropology; Conflict: Anthropological Aspects; Economic Anthropology; Exchange in Anthropology; Horticultural Societies; Melanesia: Sociocultural Aspects; Millennialism; Political Anthropology; Political Economy in Anthropology; Symbolism in Anthropology

Bibliography

Belshaw C S 1954 *Changing Melanesia*. Oxford University Press, Melbourne, Australia
Berndt R M 1952 A cargo movement in the central Highlands of New Guinea. *Oceania* **XXIII**: 40–65, 137–58, 202–34
Burridge K O L 1960 *Mambu*. Methuen, London. [1970 Harper Torchbooks, New York; 1995 Princeton University Press, Princeton, NJ]
Burridge K 1969 *New Heaven, New Earth*. Basil Blackwell, Oxford, UK
Guiart J 1962 *Les Religions de l'Oceanie*. Presses Universitaires de France, Paris
Knox R A 1950 *Enthusiasm*. Clarendon Press, Oxford, UK
Lawrence P 1964/1971 *Road Belong Cargo*. Manchester University Press, London
Lindstrom L 1990 *Knowledge and Power in a South Pacific Society*. Smithsonian Institution Press, Washington, DC
Steinbauer F 1971 *Melanesian Cargo Cults* [trans. Wohlwill M]. George Prior Publishers, London
Trompf G W (ed.) 1990 *Cargo Cults and Millenarian Movements*. Mouton de Gruyter, Berlin
Wallace A F C 1956 Revitalization movements. *American Anthropologist* **LVIII**: 264–81
Worsley P 1957 *The Trumpet Shall Sound*. MacGibbon & Kee, London (Rev. Edn. 1968)

K. Burridge

Caribbean: Sociocultural Aspects

1. A String of Isles

The Caribbean archipelago, sometimes called the Antilles or the West Indies, comprises nearly a thousand identifiable islands and islets that spread over 2,500 miles around the Caribbean Sea. The archipelago spans southeasterly from southern Florida to the Gulf of Paria, then turns westward along the coast of Venezuela.

The islands are divided into four groups. The most northern group is the Bahamas, a string of several hundred islets, of which 29 are inhabited, that stands apart from the Antilles. The next two groups, the Antilles proper, are the demographic, economic, and cultural heart of the region. The Greater Antilles consist of the islands of Cuba, Hispaniola (comprised of Haiti and the Dominican Republic), Jamaica, Puerto Rico, and their respective dependencies. They encompass the bulk of the Antillean lands and house three-quarters of the region's inhabitants. The Lesser Antilles, which include the Leeward and Windward Islands, span like a crescent at the eastern end of the archipelago, and count about 40 inhabited isles. A fourth and looser grouping includes the islands off Venezuela, from Tobago and Trinidad to Aruba. Beyond the archipelago, most social scientists now include in the Caribbean the Colombian islands off the coast of Nicaragua and the mainland territories of the Guianas (Guyana, Suriname, Belize, and Cayenne, also known as French Guiana).

2. An Obvious Heterogeneity

Scholarly treatments of the Caribbean as a single object of study, and the related conceptualization of the region as a distinguishable sociocultural area, are both recent and controversial. Poets and novelists, such as Cuban writers Alejo Carpentier and Nicolas Guillen, were the first to herald Caribbean sociocultural unity early in the twentieth century. This call was renewed by recent literary figures such as Antonio Benitez-Rojo and Edouard Glissant. Most social scientists, however, took the old colonial boundaries for granted, dividing the region into linguistic spheres that duplicated the European dominions and across which they saw few similarities. By the early 1960s, international symposia on the region (e.g., Rubin 1960) and the comparative sketches that appeared in the *Nieuwe West Indische Gids*, *Caribbean Studies*, and *Social Economic Studies* implicitly acknowledged the overall unity of the Caribbean. Soon after, explicit treatments of the region as a single object of study— and parallel efforts to conceptualize its structural similarities—emerged in European geography (e.g., Lowenthal 1972) and North American anthropology (e.g., Mintz 1966, 1984).

The earlier reluctance of social scientists to view the Caribbean as a whole is understandable, and not just because their research evolved within European colonial studies and often reproduced the insularism of the local elites. With 40 million people spread over some 90 territories, most of which are tiny and surrounded by sea, the Caribbean displays a wide range of similarities and differences. No single sociological or cultural feature stands out as the defining essence of the region. Thus, complexity in regard to size and population and social heterogeneity within and across political boundaries are two defining themes of Caribbean Studies, even among the social scientists who question the singleness of the region (Trouillot 1992).

Social scientists today see the division of labor, past and present, as the root cause of Caribbean diversity both within and across territories (Cross and Heuman 1988). In the last five centuries, the Caribbean has experienced a wide range of labor regimes: slavery, indentured labor, sharecropping, peasant agriculture, simple commodity production in family-based enterprises, agricultural and industrial wage labor. Except for the barely known practices of its earliest inhabitants, the Arawaks and Island Caribs who probably specialized in swidden agriculture and small-scale fishing respectively, these labor regimes all reflect the incorporation of the Caribbean in the capitalist world economy. Today, while most Caribbean men and women still derive the bulk of their income from agriculture, some of the islands have specialized in offshore banking. Others have become favored hubs in assembly industries or electronic communications. Others rely heavily on tourism, especially from the United States, which now exercises unmatched economic and political power over most independent states within the region.

The political scene is as varied as the economic landscape (Stone 1985). The Caribbean bears the mark of a variety of political systems: colonies and neo-colonies with different degrees of limited autonomy; three monarchical experiments in nineteenth-century Haiti; Westminster-style parliamentarism in the former British colonies; civil and military dictatorships notably in Cuba, the Dominican Republic, Haiti, and Suriname; and various unusual and self-labeled versions of socialist rule. Elections are now the norm in most countries, but the formal adherence to democratic procedures barely hides a wide variety of practices from blatant fraud and unabashed clientelism to single-party rule and electoral divisions along ethnic lines.

This mosaic of economic and political formulas parallels an impressive variety of languages and religions. Caribbean languages include Spanish, French, English, Dutch, and Creole languages of all kinds, echoes of the many European nations that influenced the area (Taylor 1977, Christie 1996) Likewise, almost all the variations of Christianity can be found in the area. Jewish influence is not to be dismissed; nor is that of Islam. Hinduism and Buddhism strive in Trinidad and Guyana. Native Caribbean religions complete the denominational mosaic: Haitian Vodoun, Trinidadian Shango, Cuban Santeria, Jamaican Pocomania and Rastafarianism, belief systems and practices where the Old World meets the New. The influence of the Old World reaches its peak with the African contribution. Caribbean populations descend directly from regions of Africa that correspond to at least 18 contemporary states.

3. *Family Resemblance: The Shapes of History*

Beyond this profusion of traits and descent lines, the unity of the Caribbean is one of family resemblance. Different characteristics account for the likeness between any two territories within and across linguistic boundaries. Yet the web of parallelisms, relationships, and genealogies that spans the entire archipelago and spills over into the Guianas makes the area, as a whole, quite distinct from any other world region.

Caribbean family resemblance is governed by the shared experience of power. Caribbean societies evolved in the shadow of power yielded almost always vertically from within and almost always resting on the ultimate domination of Europe and, later, of Europe and the United States. Six overlapping features typify this exercise of power: (a) the decimation of the native population, which created an effective *terra nullius*, a land literally up for grabs; (b) a subaltern integration in the international order characterized by the duration and extent of external rule (thus the depth of intrusion in local life); (c) the extreme regimentation of populations that paralleled this intrusion; (d) plantation slavery as the epitome of the last two features; (e) the continuity of institutionalized—often state-enforced—exclusions and hierarchies; and (f) the no less continuous regimentation of cultural practices. Scholarship on the region now tends to address these themes singularly or in combination.

Modern Caribbean history starts in the early sixteenth century with the swift decimation of the original inhabitants of the Antilles from disease, warfare, mistreatment, and forced labor. From then on, Europeans moved through the islands as if they were empty lands to be fashioned exclusively for goals that originated elsewhere. Indeed, the Caribbean stands out in the world as an exceptional product of European colonialism. Caribbean territories have experienced Western European influence longer and more profoundly than any other area outside of Europe itself. Nowhere else have European states held onto dependencies for so long and shaped them so deeply without having to take into account the strength or relevance of native institutions. Almost everything that we now associate with the Caribbean—from sugar cane, coffee, mangoes, bananas, donkeys, and coconuts, to the people themselves, whether African or Asian in origin—was brought there as part of the European conquest.

External rule dictated the coercion of labor and the regimentation of local populations, both of which reached their peak during the 370 some years that African slavery lasted in the Caribbean. The slave trade itself lasted from about 1518 to 1873. During that time, the Caribbean imported at least four million African slaves, perhaps one third of all the Africans who came to the Americas. In comparison, the United States imported about half a million.

Caribbean slavery was plantation slavery, sponsored by European capitalists and geared toward the production of tropical crops for export. Sugar cane and coffee dominated the system, but tobacco, cotton, and indigo were also important. The impact of slavery on the cultural and social life of Caribbean populations may be the most evident feature behind Caribbean family resemblance. The role of particular territories varied during the centuries of slavery. Yet the entire region was deeply molded by that experience.

In 1791, the slaves of Saint-Domingue/Haiti, then France's most lucrative colony and perhaps the most profitable dependency of any European power, started an uprising that augured a new phase in Caribbean history. After 13 years of war, they defeated the formidable army sent by Napoleon to restore slavery and proclaimed the independence of Haiti in 1804. The Haitian Revolution signaled the end of Atlantic slavery. Throughout the century, European powers successively abolished either the slave trade or slavery itself in a process completed in the Antilles with the abolition of slavery in Puerto Rico (1873) and Cuba (1880).

Abolition did not bring an end to the plantation system or the coercion of the labor force. Hundreds of thousands of indentured laborers, mainly from China and South Asia, were brought to replace the blacks on sugar plantations. Caribbean people of South Asian descent now constitute important ethnic subgroups from Guadeloupe to Suriname and, most notably, in Trinidad and Guyana. In the latter two places, the Afro-Caribbean descendants of the former slaves found new niches in the agro-social system, becoming independent peasants or, later, part of a growing middle class tied to the state. The peasantry was even stronger in the mountainous islands of the Windwards, and in Haiti and Jamaica. At the other end of the spectrum the plantation system outlasted slavery, even without massive input of Asian labor, in places like Barbados, Cuba, Antigua, or Puerto Rico—though in Puerto Rico it coexisted with a peasantry whose roots anteceded freedom itself.

Whether paid laborers or independent peasants, Caribbean rural dwellers tend to be marginalized politically, socially, and culturally by local elites that replaced European colonizers. Indeed, the whole region is deeply marked by social exclusion based on markers such as skin color, ethnic affiliation, class origins, occupational status, religion, and language. That exclusion, often institutionalized, intensifies a regimentation of cultural practices which dates back to slavery. Explicit or tacit codes limiting the reach and value Creole speech, the denigration of Afro-Caribbean religions throughout the region, the

persecution of Rastafarians in Dominica or Jamaica, of Maroons in Suriname and of homosexuals in Cuba, are all evidence that cultural coercion continues in the Caribbean.

4. The Caribbean in the Social Sciences

Caribbean social science started long before the institutionalization of current disciplines, with the field observations and commentaries of colonists such as Bartolomé de las Casas, Jean-Baptiste Labat, Bryan Edwards, John Gabriel Stedman, and Moreau de Saint-Méry. Since then, local elites, colonial and postcolonial, have generated a huge literature that prefigures and continues to fuel the themes favored today by professional academics (Lewis 1983). Haiti and Cuba held the lead in the social sciences until the second half of the twentieth century. Since the 1960s, however, the anglophone Caribbean has generated a spectacular amount of social scholarship. The impact of the various local schools and the widespread acknowledgement outside of the region that its colonial history profoundly shaped its present give Caribbean social science a decisive historical bent.

History generates the greatest amount of scholarship about and from the region. The record begins with the colonists, includes the Haitian pioneers of postcolonial history, Thomas Madiou and Beaubrun Ardouin and mushrooms in the twentieth century with the works of Elsa Goveia, C. L. R. James, Eric Williams, Manuel Moreno Fraginals, Jean Fouchard, Walter Rodney, Barry Higman, and a number of historians from the University of the West Indies. Williams set the connection between capitalism and slavery as a central theme of Caribbean and Afro-American studies. James made the Haitian Revolution a legitimate object of study outside of Haiti. Fouchard pioneered twentieth-century studies of maroon slaves.

Today, the anglophone world—England and especially the United States—produces the greatest number of titles on Caribbean history, although contributions from Dutch researchers remain significant. The state of Caribbean historical research is summarized in UNESCO's six-volume *General History of the Caribbean*. Slave studies remain a highlight of current research, with increasingly detailed accounts of plantation life and coordinates. In recent years, the Haitian Revolution, slave resistance, the rise of peasantries, women's history, postslavery life in general, and US interventions in the region have attracted increased attention.

History's lead is not confined to the number of titles it generates. The disciplines next in line—anthropology in particular, but also geography, sociology, economics, and even political science—tend to frame their objects against a strong historical background. Because Caribbean social science cannot ignore the role of North Atlantic power in shaping the region, it constantly arks back to the consequences of colonialism, of external domination, and of the region's integration in the capitalist world economy. For instance, economics focuses as much on the plantation system, past and present, as on the global mechanisms that sustain the Caribbean's incorporation in the Atlantic world, often echoing dependency theory as exposed in continental Latin America (Beckford 1999).

Even economists not aligned with theories of dependency take power and history into account. Thus, while Sir Arthur Lewis's focus on 'the dual economy' and the 'traditional sector' won him a Nobel Memorial Prize, fellow Caribbeanists are acutely aware that the work of the St. Lucian economist was deeply involved in the history that produced the dualism he described (Lewis 1978). Within Caribbean Studies, the social sciences in general move in tandem with historiography, always taking into account the state of knowledge about where these societies come from even when the explicit purpose is to explain where they are now or where they might be going in the future.

Not surprisingly, a leading theme in Caribbean social studies has been the continuous assessment of the specific heritage of various Old World regions on particular territories when not on the entire area. Here again, social scientists have to navigate between obvious signs of blending and no less obvious signs of heterogeneity to account for their observations. Thus, local observers have produced a number of theoretical schemes—such as Cuban Fernando Ortiz's notion of 'transculturation,' later recycled by North Atlantic anthropology—to bypass the difficulties inherent in the enterprise. On the ground, however, Ortiz himself joined a number of researchers who focused on Africa's influence on social, political, and economic institutions (from female-dominated retail trade to matrifocal families), cultural beliefs and practices (from religion to language) to the arts (most notably music). The attention to gender roles and family structure is central to the work of a number of scholars, not all of whom accept the centrality of the African legacy (e.g., Smith 1988). On the other hand, the emphasis on African continuities is central to the work of Haitian Jean Price Mars, a founder of the Négritude movement, who renewed with the call for the re-evaluation of Africa first made by early nineteenth-century Haitian writers.

The more specific search for sub-Saharan 'survivals' became institutionalized in North Atlantic universities with the work of US anthropologist Melville Herskovits who saw the Caribbean as a subset of the Afro-Americas, much like his French counterpart, Roger Bastide. Price-Mars and Herskovits also share an emphasis on the 'cultural ambivalence' of Caribbean elites, torn in their eyes between their African and European heritage—an ongoing subtheme of Caribbean critical inquiries, most recently sustained by the cultural critique of Rex Nettleford and linguist Mervyn Alleyne in Jamaica. Since the late twentieth century, however, a number of writers, notably anthropologists Mintz and Price (1992) have critically re-assessed the Herskovits agenda. Many scholars now emphasize the principles and processes behind Caribbean sociocultural development rather than trace the Old World origins of singular traits, thus overlapping studies in creolization.

Creolization—the process by which newly arrived populations facing severe physical and institutional constraints generated a distinct mode of life and developed cultural beliefs and practices, including linguistic practices, that have become distinctively native to the region—has a long pedigree in Caribbean studies. Here again, the puzzle remains how to reconcile heterogeneity and family resemblance. A century after the beginning of the slave trade, local and foreign observers began to describe the features and development of Creole languages and wondered about the similarities across islands. Creole linguistics have now become a subfield with its own insular debates. Yet other aspects of the creolization process and the nature of Creole society itself remain central and cross-disciplinary themes in Caribbean social and cultural studies (Arnold 1998).

The emphasis on social and cultural blending, favored by various students of creolization, has long run counter to the emphasis on heterogeneity among observers who see Caribbean societies as unwieldy patchworks of groups solidly marked by skin color and artificially joined by power. Here again, the trend starts in colonial times. It runs through the nineteenth, and is revived in the early twentieth by writers such as Lorimer Denis and François Duvalier in Haiti. Yet it took Jamaican anthropologist Smith's application of the plural society model (1965) to give that line of research much of its firmness and exposure in Caribbean studies. Smith's work continues to fuel virulent controversies but the fundamental question it raises remains unavoidable. Given what is known of Caribbean heterogeneity, how does a social scientist relate current institutions and other elements of the social system to the cultural traditions of the peoples involved?

Yet the question leads to an impasse only if one looks for a unified content, a single essence that epitomizes Caribbeanness. The now common vision of the Caribbean as a sociocultural area where heterogeneity and family resemblance are inherently indissociable products of a history of uneven power provides the frame within which most scholars approach the region today (Mintz and Price 1985, Watts 1987)

5. The Exploding Islands

Just as the vision of the Caribbean as a single object of study becomes accepted in social science circles (e.g.,

Mintz and Price 1985, Cross and Heuman 1988) it faces new challenges in a world increasingly dominated by its powerful US neighbor (Serbin 1998). It must now contend with the growth in rural–urban migration, the crossing of borders within the region and the size and visibility of Caribbean diasporas in the North Atlantic.

Caribbean people have been moving within and across political borders since slavery days, and migration has been a major theme in Caribbean Studies since at least the 1960s. Today however, migratory flows within single islands, within the region, and away from it have reached unprecedented proportions. As peasants and rural proletarians rush to the cities, the expansion of urban slums now redefine the sociocultural landscape in all territories. The growing presence of intra-regional migrants—such as Haitian cane cutters in the Dominican Republic, Dominicans in Guadeloupe and Martinique—also questions boundaries once thought impermeable. Most important, outside contact has become part of daily local life. The number and visibility of Caribbean migrants in North Atlantic countries, and the fact that breakthroughs in transport and communications enhance their economic and cultural impact on their country of origins make diasporas an inherent part of Caribbean Studies (Brana-Shute 1983). Urban glut, and the frequency of outside contact have also increased the crime rate, notably infractions associated with drug use or trade. The concept of a single sociocultural area will have to accommodate this geographical and social remapping of the region and redraw its own heuristic boundaries accordingly.

See also: Colonialism, Anthropology of; Colonialism: Political Aspects; Colonization and Colonialism, History of; Creolization: Sociocultural Aspects; Historiography and Historical Thought: Indigenous Cultures in the Americas; Slavery as Social Institution; Slavery: Comparative Aspects; Slaves/Slavery, History of

Bibliography

Arnold A J (ed.) 1998 Who/what is 'creole'? *Plantation Society in the Americas* 5(1)

Beckford G 1972/1999 *Persistent Poverty: Underdevelopment in Plantation Economies of the Third World*. The University of the West Indies, Kingston, Jamaica

Brana-Shute R 1983 *A Bibliography of Caribbean Migration and Caribbean Immigrant Communities*. University of Florida, Gainesville, FL

Christie P 1996 *Caribbean Language Issues, Old & New: Papers in Honour of Professor Mervyn Alleyne*. University of the West Indies, Kingston, Jamaica

Cross M, Heuman G (eds.) 1988 *Labour in the Caribbean*. Macmillan Caribbean, London

Lewis G K 1983 *Main Currents in Caribbean Thought. The Historical Evolution of Caribbean Society in its Ideological Aspects, 1492–1900*. The Johns Hopkins University Press, Baltimore, MD

Lewis W A 1978 *The Evolution of the International Economic Order*. Princeton University Press, Princeton, NJ

Lowenthal D 1972 *West Indian Societies*. Oxford University Press, Oxford, UK

Mintz S W 1966 The Caribbean as a socio-cultural area. *Cahiers d'Histoire Mondiale* **IX**: 916–41

Mintz S W 1974/1984 *Caribbean Transformations*. The Johns Hopkins University Press, Baltimore, MD

Mintz S W, Price R 1976/1992 *The Birth of an African-American Culture: An Anthropological Perspective*. Beacon Press, Boston

Mintz S W, Price S 1985 *Caribbean Contours*. The Johns Hopkins University Press, Baltimore, MD

Rubin V D (ed.) 1960 *Caribbean Studies: A Symposium*. University of Washington, Seattle, WA

Serbin A 1998 *Sunset over The Islands. The Caribbean in an Age of Global and Regional Challenges*. St. Martin's Press, New York

Smith M G 1965 *The Plural Society in the British West Indies*. University of California Press, Berkeley, CA

Smith R T 1988 *Kinship and Class in the West Indies*. Cambridge University Press, Cambridge, UK

Stone C 1985 The Caribbean as a political region. In: Mintz S W, Price S (eds.) *Caribbean Contours*. The Johns Hopkins University Press, Baltimore, MD

Taylor D M 1977 *Languages of the West Indies*. The Johns Hopkins University Press, Baltimore, MD

Trouillot M-R 1992 The Caribbean region: An open frontier in anthropological theory. *Annual Review of Anthropology* **21**: 19–42

UNESCO 1997–2001 *General History of the Caribbean*. UNESCO and Macmillan Caribbean, London, 6 Vols.

Watts D 1987 *The West Indies: Patterns of Development, Culture and Environmental Change since 1492*. Cambridge University Press, Cambridge, UK

M. R. Trouillot

Cartographic Visualization

1. Setting

Assume one is interested in an overview of the population distribution of a particular area. An option would be to give a written description such as: 'in the northeast only a few small towns are found, while in the southeast....' Before one gets a clear picture, several pages could have been filled, especially if a description of the relations of the towns with other geographic phenomena such as the rivers or railroad network are also incorporated. A better option is to

Figure 1
Population distribution

tell this story using a map. Maps are the most efficient and effective means to transfer geospatial information. The map user can locate geographic objects, while the shape and color of signs and symbols representing the objects inform about their characteristics, such as the town's location and population size. Maps reveal geospatial relations and patterns, and offer the user insight into, and an overview of, the distribution of particular phenomena, such as an area's population distribution.

The map easily allows one to answer questions of the nature 'Where...? What...?, and When...?' These questions deal with the basic components of geospatial data: location, characteristics, and time, or their combination. The map discussed above and found in Fig. 1 will quickly result in answers to questions such as 'Where are the large towns located?' or 'What town has the highest number of inhabitants?' Questions regarding 'When...?' depend on the map contents. Often the map is just a snap shot in time, for instance the map in Fig. 1 depicts the status as of 1998. In answering questions, another quality of maps will be revealed—the ability to offer an abstraction of reality. It simplifies by selection, but at the same time it puts, when well designed, the remaining information in a clear perspective. The map of the area only needs the boundaries of municipalities, and a symbol for the number of people living in each town. In this particular case there is no need for roads, mountains, or other physical features. Maps like these are often static and come as they are, especially when they are printed on paper. On-screen maps sometimes allow for some interaction, such as getting data from the database behind the map.

For more complex questions one needs more than just a static map. For instance, to study the impact of

industrial development on the growth of towns one would need the possibility to generate maps depending on the nature of the question. This could be to switch layers with information on or off. This would also include the possibility to view the data in alternative visualizations. Questions are no longer the simple Where?, What?, and When?, especially if for instance specific demographic models are included, which can predict alternative future population trends based on census- and socio-economic data. These trends could be visualized in an animation. The mapping environment requires interaction and dynamics. This is what today's visualization is all about, as will become clear in the remainder of this chapter. However, according to the dictionary, visualization means 'to make visible.' From this perspective map making has always been visualization. Here the term visualization is used in the context that allows the map user to interact with the (digital on-screen) map. For a detailed discussion see (Hearnshaw and Unwin 1994, MacEachren and Taylor 1994).

2. *Visualization process*

Any map, static or dynamic, on screen or on paper, complex or simple, is created during what is called the cartographic visualization process. This process is considered to be the translation or conversion of geospatial data from a database into graphics. Predominantly these are map-like products as is schematically explained in Fig. 2. This process should be seen in the context of geospatial data handling. Geospatial data handling stands for the acquisition, storage, manipulation, and visualization of geospatial data in the context of particular applications.

During the visualization process, cartographic methods and techniques are applied. These can be considered as a kind of grammar that allows for the optimal design, production and use of maps, depending on the application. The process is guided by the phrase 'How do I say what to whom, and is it effective?' The phrase holds four key words: 'How' which refers to cartographic methods and techniques (in the case of Fig. 1 a proportional point symbol map has been

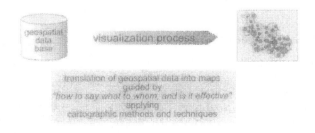

Figure 2
The cartographic visualization process

chosen); 'What' which refers to the geospatial data (Fig. 1 deals with quantitative population data); 'Whom' which refers to the map audience and the purpose of the map—(the map in Fig. 1 is rather basic and could function in a newspaper or school atlas); 'Effective' reflects the usefulness of the map (do the map readers understand the message the map intends to bring, an overview of the area's population distribution).

The producer of maps could be a professional cartographer, but could also be an expert who is mapping, for instance, vegetation stands using remote sensing images or health statistics in the slums of a city. With today's availability of web mapping tools the mapmaker could be anyone—with or without any notion of cartographic design.

The visualization process can vary greatly depending on where the visualization takes place and the purpose for which it is needed. Visualizations can be, and are, created during any phase of the geospatial data handling process. They can be simple or complex, while the production time can be short or long. Some examples are the creation of a full, traditional topographic map sheet, a newspaper map, a sketch map showing a route, a map from an electronic atlas, an animation showing the growth of a city, a three-dimensional view of a building or a mountain, or even a real-time display of traffic conditions via the World Wide Web. Other examples include 'quick and dirty' views of part of the database, the map used during the updating process, or during a geospatial analysis. The environment in which the visualization process is executed can vary considerably. It can be done on paper, on a stand-alone personal computer, or a computer linked to the World Wide Web.

Many tools are available to visualize the data. These tools consist of functions, rules, and habits. Algorithms to classify the data or smooth a coastline are samples of functions. Rules tell us, for instance, to use proportional symbols to display quantities or position an artificial light source in the northwest to create shaded relief maps. Habits, or traditions as some would call them, tell us to color the sea in blue, lowlands in green, and mountains in brown (Robinson et al. 1995, Kraak and Ormeling 1996).

3. Visualization and cartography

In the past, even dealing with incomplete and uncertain data, the visualization process nearly always resulted in an authoritative map. The maps created by a cartographer were good enough for the user. This shows that cartography, for a long time, has been very much driven by supply rather than demand. Somehow, this is still the case. However, nowadays, it is also accepted that just making a map is not the only purpose of cartography. Especially since 1980, many

people have become involved in making maps. The widespread use of Geographical Information Systems (GIS) has significantly increased the number of maps being created (Longley et al. 1999). Even the spreadsheets used by most office workers today have mapping capabilities, although most people are probably not aware of this. The opportunities offered by the World Wide Web will again lead to an incredible increase in maps produced. Some websites, such as MapQuest produce over a million maps a day! Many of these maps are not produced as final products, but rather as intermediate products to support the user in his or her work dealing with geospatial data. The map, as such, has started to play a completely new role: it is not just a communication tool but also a tool to aid the user's (visual) thinking process.

This process is being accelerated by the opportunities offered by hardware and software developments. These have changed the scientific and societal needs for geo-referenced data and, as such, for maps. New media such as CD-ROMs and the WWW not only allow for dynamic presentation but also for user interaction. Users do expect immediate and real-time access to the data and data geospatial has become abundant. This abundance of data, welcomed in some sectors, is a major problem in other sectors. One lacks the tools for user-friendly queries and retrieval when studying the massive amount of data produced by sensors, and now available via the WWW.

These developments have given the word visualization enhanced meaning, since progress in other disciplines has linked the word to more specific ways in which modern computer technology can facilitate the process of 'making visible' in real time. Specific software toolboxes have been developed, whose functionality is based on two key words: interaction and dynamics. A separate discipline called scientific visualization, has developed around it (McCormick et al. 1987), which is having a major impact on cartography as well. If applied in cartography it offers the user the possibility of instantaneously changing the appearance of the map. Interacting with the map will stimulate the user's thinking and will add a new function to the map. As well as communication, it will prompt thinking and decision-making.

Developments in scientific visualization have stimulated a model for map-based scientific visualization (DiBiase 1990). As such, it is also known as Geographical visualization (MacEachren 1995). It covers both the communication and thinking functions of the map. Communication is described as 'public visual communication' since it concerns maps aimed at a wide audience. Thinking is defined as 'private visual thinking' because it is often an individual playing with the geospatial data to determine its significance (see Fig. 3). On a lower level, different visualization stages can be recognized: each requires a different strategy from the perspective of map use, based on audience, data relations, and the need for interaction. These

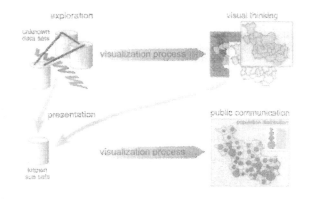

Figure 3
The visualization process: visual thinking and visual communication

stages are exploration, analysis, synthesis, and presentation.

From Fig. 3 it is obvious that presentation fits into the traditional realm of cartography, where the cartographer works on known geosptial data and creates communicative maps. These maps are often created for multiple uses. However, exploration often involves a discipline expert creating maps while dealing with unknown data. These maps are generally for a single purpose and are related to the expert's attempt to solve a problem. While dealing with the data, the expert should be able to rely on cartographic expertise provided by the software or some other means.

This process describes the 'democratization of cartography' (Morrison 1997). He explains it as 'using electronic technology, no longer does the map user depend on what the cartographer decides to put on a map. Today the user is the cartographer.' And 'users are now able to produce analyses and visualizations at will to any accuracy standard that satisfies them.'

4. *Visualization and exploration*

What is exploratory cartography? The environment has just been described: a person is trying to solve a particular geo-problem and is exploring various geo-spatial databases. Exploration also means working with unknown data. However, what is unknown for one is not necessarily unknown to others. For instance, browsing in Microsoft's Encarta World Atlas is an exploration for most of us because of its wealth of information. With products like these, such exploration takes place within boundaries set by the producers. Cartographic knowledge is incorporated in program wizards resulting in pre-designed maps. Some users feel this to be a constraint, but those same users will no longer feel constrained as soon as they follow the web links attached to this electronic atlas. This example shows that the environment, the data, and the

type of users influence one's view of what exploration entails.

Returning to the sentence driving the visualization process 'How do I say what to whom and is it effective' some similarities as well, as differences between modes of visualization: presentation and exploration. 'How' still represents the cartographic methods and techniques. However, new technology is emerging and this offers challenges and opportunities, such as animation, the application of the third dimension and virtual reality, multimedia, etc. 'I' is no longer just the cartographer, but an expert geoscientist. In the very near future, it can probably be just anyone having access to the WWW. 'What' no longer represents a relatively well-defined and known data set; at least, certainly not from the user perspective. 'To whom' seems to be simpler than before; it is not a relatively well-defined user group, but the same person represented by 'I,' the expert geoscientist in the role of cartographer. 'Effective' raises some interesting questions. When a map is used, the information to be transferred is known and, for all problems involved, can somehow be measured. But how can the visual thinking process be measured? If it is considered positively, is it because of the efficient graphics or because of the geoscientist's clever thinking? These questions become more complex if we realize that we do not even know the initial aim of the visualization in these circumstances.

The most prominent change is the shift from supply-driven cartography to a demand-driven approach. Although having many people making maps without any cartographic knowledge might seem wrong, those non-cartographers will also introduce fresh views, as for instance described by Keller and Keller (1993). They distinguish three steps in the visualization process: the first identifies the visualization goal; the second removes mental roadblocks; and the third designs the display in detail. In the second step, Keller and Keller suggest taking some distance from the discipline in order to reduce the effects of traditional constraints. Why not choose an alternative mapping method? For instance, show a video of the landscape next to a topographic map. New, fresh, creative graphics could be the result, they might also offer different insights and would probably have more impact than traditional mapping methods. During the third step, which is especially applicable in an exploratory environment, one has to decide between mapping data and visualizing phenomena.

An exploratory visualization environment offers the tools to act in the ways previously suggested. Such an environment should allow the user to look at geospatial and other geo-referenced data in any combination, at any scale, with the aim of seeing or finding geospatial patterns (which may be hidden). Geospatial patterns can be defined as variations in location, attributes or time, or a combination of any of the three geospatial components within an area of interest. One

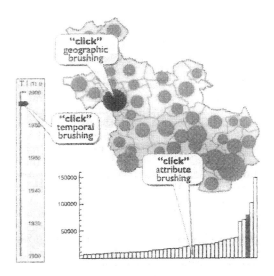

Figure 4
Brushing

of the first concepts of visual geospatial data exploration was introduced by Monmonier (1989) when he described the term brushing (see Fig. 4). This is when the selection of an object in a map automatically highlights the corresponding elements in the other graphics. Depending on the view in which one selects the objects, there is geographical brushing (clicking in the map), attribute brushing (clicking in the diagram or table), and temporal brushing (clicking on the time line). As such, the user gets an overview of the relation among geographic objects based on location, characteristics, and time.

5. Visualization Functions

What are the basic requirements of an exploratory visualization environment? The necessary functions described below all need high interactivity options.

5.1   Basic Display

Map displays need tools to allow the user to pan, zoom, scale, transform, and rotate the image contents. These geometric tools should be available and independent of the dimensionality of the displayed geospatial data. Fig. 5(a) illustrates panning and zooming facilities. Another option could be rotating the map. This last function is of particular need when displaying 3D-maps, since it also allows objects that otherwise might be hidden by other objects to be seen.

5.2   Navigation and Orientation

This involves the keys to the map. At any time, the user should be able to know where the view is located and what the symbols mean. To illustrate this function Fig. 5(b) shows a map with its marginal information as well as the coordinates at the cursor location in the map.

5.3   Query Data

During any phase of the visualization process, the user should have access to the geospatial database to query the data. The questions should not necessarily be limited to simple What? Where? or When? As Fig. 5(c) shows clicking a geographic object in the map reveals the information available in the database, as well as the hyperlinks that are attached to the object.

5.4   Multi-Scale

Combining different data sets is a common operation in an exploratory environment. The chance that these sets will have the same data density or the same level of abstraction is unlikely. Generalization operators to solve these multi-scale problems remain necessary, if not just to make sure zoom-in and zoom-out operators result in sensible maps. In Fig. 5(d) zooming-in results in a more detailed map.

5.5   Re-expression

To stimulate visual thinking, an unorthodox approach to visualization was recommended. This requires options to manipulate data behind the map or offer different mapping methods for displaying the data. An example of data manipulation is the application of several classification systems, while the use of different advanced map types to view the same data represents display differences. Fig. 5(e) illustrates how the population data shown in the figures main map can be displayed alternatively. The upper inset shows a prism map (a 3D representation of the data in which the height of the area corresponds to the attribute value; the big towns have high columns) and a cartogram (a map in which the area of a geographic unit is equal to the attribute value and not, as usually, to its geographic area; the highly populated towns take a large maps space).

5.6   Multiple Dynamically-linked Views

These tools represent a combination of multimedia and the brushing technique already mentioned. The

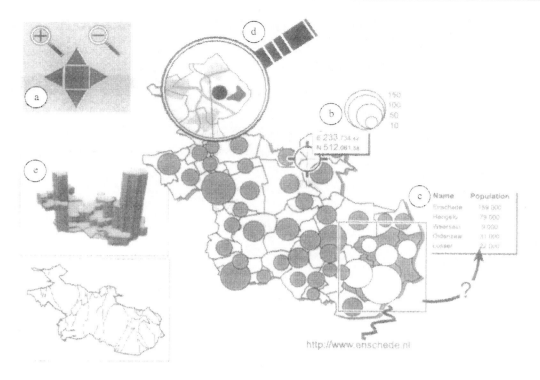

Figure 5
Exploratory cartographic functions: (a) Basic display; (b) Navigation and orientation; (c) Query; (d) Multi-scale; (e) Re-expression

user will be able to view and interact with the data in different windows, all representing related aspects of the data. These views do not necessarily contain maps; video, sound, text, etc. can all be included. Clicking an object in a particular view will show its geospatial relations to other objects or representations in all the other views (see Fig. 6).

5.7 Animation

Maps often represent complex processes that can be well expressed by animation. Animation can be used for temporal as well as non-temporal changes in geospatial data. Aspects to be solved are related to the interface (user interaction—navigation) and the legend. Since the exploratory user will also be the creator of the animation, he or she should be able to influence the flow of the animation.

6. Visualization Environments

Most cartographic components of geographical information systems can only handle one or two of the functions described in the previous section. Scientific

visualization software might have the most functions available, but it lacks the typical geo-referencing options needed to deal with geospatial data. However, operational experimental exploratory visualization environments do exist. Examples are web-based Decartes (Andrienko and Andrienko 1999) and Cartographic Data Visualizer (CDV) (Dykes 1997, Dykes 1998). As an example CDV will be discussed since it is available free as a result of academic research (http://www.geog.le.ac.uk/jad7/cdv/). Both packages primarily aim at the visualization of socio-economic census data. Fig. 6 shows a typical view on a CDV-session. The program requires a base map (administrative boundaries) and statistical data. From the menu on the left the user can select active variables and visualizations. Options are choropleth maps (or polygon maps), proportional circle maps, cartograms, and non-cartographic visualization such as dotplots and scatter diagrams. When creating these different views on the data they will all be linked together. Clicking an area in a map or a symbol in a diagram will highlight the corresponding area/symbol in the other views. The user has several options available to choose the layout of each of the views. One can also execute basic calculations to create new variables or classify the data according to different methods. CDV is by the nature

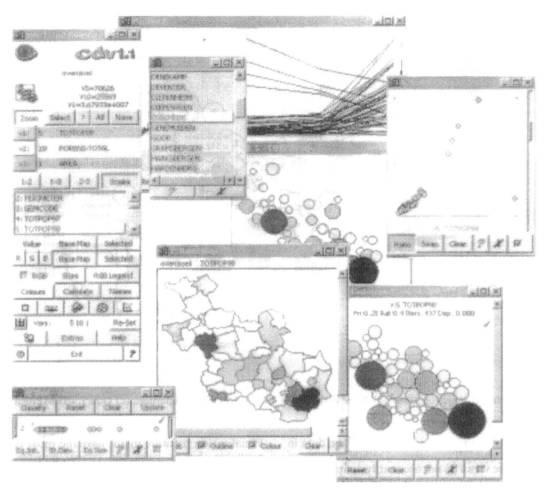

Figure 6
A typical view of a CDV session

of its functionality, capable of showing geospatial patterns that would not be apparent when single maps or diagrams would be viewed.

7. Conclusions

Packages with the functionality similar to CDV offer an advanced cartographic visualization environment. However, remembering 'How do I say what to whom, and is it effective' leaves the question open if it indeed works. From a technical point of view it certainly does, but can the user handle all those linked views. It is argued that if users can change their perspective on the data through selection and transformation, as well as alternative visualizations, meaningful relations among data variables are more likely to be revealed. For some products, this is easy to determine its

usability, for others it is quite a job. To understand how maps work is not easy (Wood 1992), especially as we change into a demand-driven mapping environment. In the supply-driven environment, it was known what the map should tell and who the customers were. Today cartographers deal partly with providing facilitating tools to visualize geospatial data. How the tools are used remains, for the moment at least, unknown. These trends will only increase as more and more maps are produced via the World Wide Web. One has to find out why someone wants to make a map, in order to be able to judge the future tools that need to be developed.

See also: Cartography; Cartography, History of; Cognitive Maps; Dynamic Mapping in Geography; Ethnic Conflict, Geography of; Geographic Information Systems; Planetary Cartography; Tactile Maps in Geography; Thematic Maps in Geography

Bibliography

Andrienko G L, Andrienko N V 1999 Interactive maps for visual data exploration. *International Journal for Geographic Information Sciences* 13: 355–74

DiBiase D 1990 Visualization in earth sciences. *Earth & Mineral Sciences, Bulletin of the College of Earth and Mineral Sciences* 59: 13–18

Dykes, J 1997 Exploring spatial data representation with dynamic graphics. *Computers and Geosciences* 23: 345–70

Dykes J A 1998 Cartographic visualization: exploratory spatial data analysis with local indicators of spatial association using Tcl/Tk and cdv. *The Statistician* 17: 485–97

Hearnshaw H M, Unwin D J (ed) 1994 *Visualization in Geographical Information System*. Wiley, Chichester, UK

Keller P R, Keller M M 1993 *Visual Cues. Practical Data Visualization*. IEEE Press, Piscataway, NJ

Kraak M-J, Ormeling F J 1996 *Cartography, the Visualization of Spatial Data*. Addison Wesley Longman, London

Longley P, Goodchild M, Maguire D M, Rhind D (eds.) 1999 *Geographical Information Systems: Principles, Techniques, Applications and Management*. Wiley, New York

MacEachren A M 1995 *How Maps Work: Representation, Visualization and Design*. Guilford Press, New York

MacEachren A M, Taylor D R F (eds.) 1994 *Visualization in Modern Cartography*. Pergamon Press, London

McCormick B H, DeFanti T A, Brown M D 1987 Visualization in Scientific Computing. *IEEE Computer Graphics* 7: 69

Monmonier, M 1989 Geographic brushing: enhancing exploratory analysis of the scatterplot matrix. *Geographical Analysis* 21: 81–4

Morrison J L 1997 Topographic mapping for the twenty first century. In: Rhind D (ed.) *Framework of the World*. Geoinformation International, Cambridge, UK, pp. 14–27

Robinson A H, Morrison J L, Muehrcke P C, Kimerling A J, Guptill S C 1995 *Elements of Cartography*. Wiley, New York

Wood D, Fels J 1992 *The Power of Maps*. Routledge, London

M. J. Kraak

Cartography

The International Cartographic Association defines cartography as 'the discipline dealing with the conception, production, dissemination and study of maps.' It goes on to say, 'A map is a symbolized image of geographic reality, representing selected features or characteristics, resulting from the creative efforts of cartographers, and is designed for use when spatial relationships are of special relevance' (International Cartographic Association 1995). Cartography, along with disciplines such as geodesy, surveying, aerial photogrammetry, and satellite remote sensing, is a component of the mapping sciences. It is closely allied with geographic information systems and geographic information science.

Cartography is most often found in geography departments in colleges and universities in the USA and Canada. It is commonly an independent department in Europe and other parts of the world. Commercial enterprises, nonprofit entities, and government agencies that produce maps generally have large cartography departments that are central to their operations.

The term 'research' within the field of cartography has at least two distinct meanings. One is the systematic gathering of information from a variety of sources for compilation into a coherent map. The other is the quest for discovery of knowledge about maps and the processes associated with them. The former definition is closely associated with commercial and nonprofit map production and the latter with academic cartography. The subject-matter of academic cartographic research ranges from historical studies of the cultural, technical, and political context of maps to the changing processes of production to the ways in which maps are used in wayfinding and in the production of knowledge. The relationship between people and maps, including symbol perception, the development of map-reading abilities, and cognitive processes in map use, have been of special interest in cartography in the late twentieth century, as have the processes by which maps are produced by computer.

Although maps are most closely associated with geography, practitioners in many disciplines and professions use the map as a device for recording and preserving information, as a tool in research, and as pedagogical illustration. As computers are used more for the process of mapping, it is no longer as strictly the domain of professional cartographers as it once was. Virtually anyone with a computer and appropriate software can produce a map. Whether this democratizing of mapping is a positive or negative development is not altogether clear. The products of nonspecialists range from misleading to highly insightful and creative. Maps are now far more widespread and are available in a more timely way to fit immediate needs than in the past, and they are becoming less constrained by convention.

Cartography and its products have a profound effect on human thinking and behavior. The map is a metaphor for the real world and is often the model that shapes it. Existing hills and valleys, rivers, and political boundaries are recorded on maps, but decisions about surface excavation, river redirection, or political redefinitions are marked on maps and become reality. The terms 'map' and 'mapping' have become common metaphors in everyday language; 'on the map' signifies importance, and 'mapping a strategy' implies attentiveness and purpose in the planning of actions.

Cartography has responded to changing social, intellectual, and technological conditions throughout history, and the permeation of computers into all aspects of life in the late twentieth century has resulted in profound changes. Cartography has transformed from a data-poor to a data-rich field, as information can now be gathered using aerial photography, global positioning systems, and satellite imaging. Inexpensive computer storage and the Internet have made it possible to share and receive massive amounts of data. Professional cartographers are now heavily involved in information management and in creating mechanisms for shared use of data. Scientific visualization in cartography, which implies the use of maps for discovery of knowledge, has gained considerable attention in recent years as a result of the ubiquity of computer usage in spatial representation.

1. Major Cartographic Concepts

Mapping Earth's surface involves the concepts of scale, projection, spatial relationships, generalization, symbolization and data modeling, and categories of maps. Some level of understanding of each of these concepts is inherent in every instance of the employment of a map.

1.1 Scale

The map is a scaled model of Earth's surface (or of the surface of some other planetary body), and the reduced size is one of its most useful features. Earth itself is too large for ready comprehension.

There are three types of scale expression commonly used on conventional maps: verbal, representative fraction (RF), and graphic (Fig. 1) (Robinson et al. 1995). Although each can refer either to distance (linear scale) or area (areal scale), linear scale is by far the more commonly used. Areal scale is generally indicated only if area is consistently scaled over the entire map. Since distance cannot be consistently scaled, no such constraint is associated with the appearance of a linear scale on a map.

Explicit scale expression is not the only indication of scale on maps (Eastman 1981, Brewer 1990). Map content and design give scale clues as well. Double-line streets, for example, immediately convey that the map shows a small area; a shaded relief background and

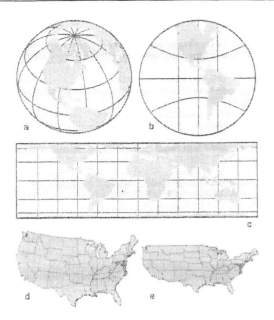

Figure 2
Five map projections showing a variety of shapes and sizes of land masses when different projection systems are applied: (a) orthographic, the projection that looks like a view of a globe, (b) gnomonic, a very distorted projection but the only one on which all great circles are straight, (c) cylindrical equal area, which preserves correct sizes of all areas but has extreme changes in linear scale, (d) Alber's, which is equal area and is commonly used for the USA, and (e) plane chart, which represents all degrees of latitude and longitude at the same length regardless of their length on Earth's surface

sparse linework indicate that the map covers a large area. Scale clues are becoming increasingly important, as the user of an animated map cannot always use an explicit expression of scale while observing the map.

1.2 Projection

The term projection refers to the system by which points on a spherical or spheroidal surface are assigned to points on a flat surface. Every point on the sphere or spheroid has a corresponding point on the flat map. Perhaps the most fundamental observation about map projections is that linear scale cannot be the same everywhere; in other words, map projections are geometrically distorted representations, in contrast to globes, which maintain a shape very close to that of the planet. There are many map projections in use and the five represented in Fig. 2 illustrate a variety of shapes and relative sizes of landmasses that can result when different systems of projection are applied.

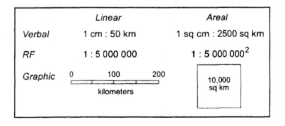

	Linear	Areal
Verbal	1 cm : 50 km	1 sq cm : 2500 sq km
RF	1 : 5 000 000	$1 : 5\,000\,000^2$
Graphic	0 100 200 kilometers	10,000 sq km

Figure 1
The three types of scale expression, illustrated in both linear and areal form

Although it is necessary to tolerate distortion when projecting Earth onto a flat surface, the distortion in map projections is systematic and in some cases highly useful. Every rectangular projection of the world, for example, has one or two straight lines on which there is no distortion and that distortion increases at right angles away from the line(s) of no distortion. Although large-area maps have major visible distortion, maps of small areas, say a city or small region have so little distortion that it has traditionally been of interest only for the most exacting measurements.

The development of geographic information systems has resulted in renewed interest in map projections because many maps have been transformed into digital files and data have to be 'unprojected' (transformed from flat map cartesian coordinates to longitude and latitude) to be compatible with other data. Even the limited amounts by which map projections affect location within small areas will affect the compatibility of multiple data sets.

Despite the impossibility of maintaining consistent linear scale on a map projection, there are two other properties that may be maintained. When, at every point on the map, maximum linear scale distortion is compensated by opposite distortion in the opposite direction, area scale is maintained. If the linear scale change is the same in every direction at each point, angles at all points will be maintained. The terms for these two categories of projection are equal-area (or equivalent), and conformal (or orthomorphic), respectively. Many projections have neither compensating nor equal changes of linear scale in opposite directions; these projections are neither equal-area nor conformal.

Some projections have special properties that make them useful for specific purposes. The Mercator projection (see *Thematic Maps in Geography*), when centered on the Equator, shows all loxodromes (or rhumb lines, i.e., lines of constant geographic direction) as straight lines. This property has been important to navigators. It was a profound development because most loxodromes on Earth (and on globes) are spirals, and the Mercator projection simplified route planning. The projection suffers from extreme deformation of area, and, like many other projections, has been used inappropriately. The Mercator maps hanging on classroom walls have led many students to think of Africa and South America as a relatively small land bodies relative to the greatly exaggerated high-latitude landmasses of Greenland and Russia.

There are over 100 named projections (see Snyder 1993), and cartographers try to choose one that is appropriate for the mapping purpose at hand. The discrete naming of projections, while providing convenient reference, obscures the fact that there are an infinite number of ways to represent Earth on flat paper. Computer construction of projections may result in revised nomenclature and increasingly tailored projections (Laskowski 1997).

1.3 Spatial Relationships

Maps show spatial relationships in a readily comprehended form. Metric relationships include distance, direction (angle), and area; topological relationships include such properties as connected to, inside, and outside. The concept of spatial relationship also includes spatial (or geometric) form; an entity may be considered to have a footprint of a point, line, or area, and if quantities are associated, the entity may be thought of as a pole, ribbon, or volume. Spatial form also includes shape (e.g., Long Island vs. Martha's Vineyard) and distribution ('more of something here than there'). The relevant spatial relationships vary with the type of map and with how they are used. Street map users want to know the street on which a feature is located and the turns and distances to reach it. Users of a world population map want to know where population is concentrated and where there are relatively empty areas.

Like the general concept of scale, spatial relationship is often taken for granted by the practiced map user. The reason for using a map is not the spatial relationship itself, but what it means. A 'hot-spot' on a map showing cancer rates suggests the need for further study and possible action; the spatial relation on the map is simply the trigger. Whether a street, population, or cancer map, it is the spatial relationships that make it a useful device. Without them, there would be no need for a map.

1.4 Generalization

As scaled representations of Earth or portions thereof, every map is generalized. Lines have fewer details in them than present in the feature on Earth's surface, and only selected features are shown. When quantities are depicted, they are usually shown by category rather than by exact value. Generalization is highly useful in focusing the map on important information instead of cluttering it with overabundant detail. It also means that some important features may not be there, not because they do not exist but because they have been generalized out of the map.

Despite the obvious necessity for generalization in making representations that are literally thousands and millions of times smaller than the original territory, it is not always understood. The small street maps of major cities that appear on road maps may be assumed by users to include every street, and a surface feature that falls between the contours of an elevation map may surprise and confuse the hiker. The failure of a map due to generalization is one of the reasons that there are very many different maps of the same area at different scales and with different selections of features. The larger the scale (i.e., the larger the representation of a given area) the less generalization is necessary and the more useful it is likely to be for finding details. The smaller the scale (the smaller the representation of a given area), the more likely it is that broad patterns will be visible because of the lack of obfuscating detail.

The relationship between scale and generalization is not an exact one. Some maps have much more detail than others of the same physical scale. The term generally applied to the degree of detail relative to size of features on Earth's surface is resolution (Tobler 1988). A map of the USA showing data by state (50 units total) has considerably coarser resolution than a map showing data by county (3,000+ units total) whether the latter map is larger, smaller, or the same size as the former.

1.5 Symbolization and Data Modeling

The very act of representing a feature with a symbol is a form of generalization. The symbol is not the original, and every map is a set of symbols. Mapmakers have been highly creative in employing symbols.

Geometrically, mapmakers can employ only points, lines, and areas as symbols on flat maps, though they may be used in such a way as to simulate the illusion of a third dimension. The use of three-dimensional media, such as molded plastic, allows the explicit use of volume as a symbol. The development of virtual reality allows the illusion not only of a third dimension but of the intersection of surfaces. Regardless of medium, the geometry of symbols generally reflects the way in which humans think of the object relative to the scale of the map. For example, a city is a large area on a street map but a point on a world map. A river on a local, large-scale engineering map is an area, but the same river appears as a line on a smaller-scale regional map. An important exception is when numerosity of symbols represents quantity. A dot map of population, for example, uses the dot to represent a quantity of persons, not an individual feature. In effect, then, dots on the map are being used to represent conceptual volume.

There are a limited number of characteristics of symbols, called 'visual variables,' which can be used to represent the characteristics of the feature represented (Bertin 1983). Darkness–lightness of the symbol and size are the most commonly used to represent quantity. Shape, color hue, and orientation most often represent differences in kind. Patterning in area symbols may also be used to distinguish characteristics of features.

The modeling of geographic space in digital files introduces a different form of representation from that on paper or similar physical medium (Peuquet 1991). Geometric concepts of point, line, area, and volume are still valid, but there is no scaled physical representation or visual symbols associated with features. Rather, numbers represent location, and codes or

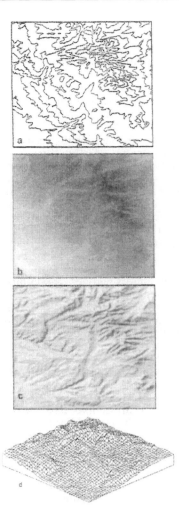

Figure 3
Four ways of representing a set of elevation data; lines are used in the contour map (a) and three-dimensional diagram (d), whereas area symbols are used in the layer shaded map (b) and in the shaded relief map (c)

descriptive terms represent what exists at a location. These digital files can be thought of as data models as opposed to a physical model. They can almost always be converted into a map, and they are usually much more flexible. A digital elevation model, for example, i.e., a file of elevation values at points, can be converted into any of the maps in Fig. 3.

1.6 Categories of Maps

Maps can be divided into two very broad categories: general reference and thematic. A general reference

Figure 4
An example of a general reference map, extracted and adapted from *The World Factbook*, CIA, 1999 ⟨http://www.cia.gov/cia/publications/factbook/⟩ (original is in color)

Figure 5
Zebra Mussels in the USA, an example of a thematic map, extracted and adapted from *National Atlas of the United States*, US Geological Survey, ⟨http://www.nationalatlas.gov/⟩ (original is in color)

map (Fig. 4) shows a variety of individual features and is generally used to find specific places, such as cities, rivers, or regions. The general reference map is selective of features in any category; only 'important' cities, rivers, or regions are identified, for example. Although lettering on the map often stands out visually, there is limited visual hierarchy among the features of the map, as all the features must be distinguishable from one another. A thematic map (Fig. 5) shows a distribution of one or more phenomena and is used to visualize spatial form. The thematic map is generally based on all the known instances of the phenomenon even though none may be shown individually. The thematic map generally has clear visual hierarchy, with the symbols representing the distribution standing out the most.

A simple twofold classification is limited, and sometimes a third is added: navigation maps. Others consider the general reference and thematic categories to be opposite ends of a scale, with individual maps fitting somewhere between. Navigation maps, such as a street guides, are near the general reference end because many different specific items are represented. They have certain thematic qualities, however, because of the focus on the features relevant to finding one's way. However, inventory maps, such as a map showing the residence of every patient with a certain disease, are close to the thematic end of the scale. They share the general reference characteristic that individual items are shown.

There is good argument that the general reference–thematic classification is more fitting of use than of maps themselves. One can look at a thematic map to see how large one political unit is relative to another, which is a function generally associated with the term 'general reference.' Likewise, one can look at a general reference map and observe overall pattern of drainage or evidence of population, a use generally associated with the term 'thematic' (Robinson and Petchenik 1976).

2. The History of Maps and Cartography

The history of cartography begins earlier than recorded time and in all likelihood had its origins in gestures and ephemeral marks in the soil (Godlewska 1997). The development of civilizations and of cartographic practice were probably highly intertwined, and at least some cartographic artifacts remain from ancient Mesopotamia and Egypt, including a clay tablet from roughly 3800 BC with mountains and a river. Extant land ownership maps date to 2000 BC. The development of grid systems, associated with less subjective and more scientific approaches to mapping, was reflected in written materials in China in the third century AD, and the earlier development of paper in China provided a flexible and highly portable physical medium for drawing maps (Thrower 1996).

The concept of the world as a sphere was basic to the development of logical representation of large areas of the world. Measurements make sense only when the curvature of the planet is taken into account. The idea seems to have had its origins with the Pythagoreans and was supported in work by Plato and Aristotle. Eratosthenes (276–196 BC), who served as the librarian at Alexandria, used the concept of the spherical Earth and the relationship between noon sun angles at different locations to measure the size of the planet. Because the exact length of a stade, the unit of measure in use at the time, is not known, it is difficult to know exactly how accurate his estimate was, but it seems to have been remarkably close and a better estimate than several that followed as scholars attempted to correct the figure. A successor in his position in the second century AD, Claudius Ptolemy, compiled the seminal tome entitled *Geographia* that contained a guide to making maps, including instructions for several map projections and the latitude-longitude location of about 8,000 places.

Mapmaking in China and South Asia is characterized by remarkable developments in roughly the same time period as the accomplishments of the ancient Greeks. There is reference to a map on silk in the third century BC, and maps were used by the military and administrators in the Han Dynasty. In later centuries, the first printed map appeared in China well before the development of printing in the West (approximately 1153 vs. 1472).

European cartography during the Middle Ages was characterized by maps that are highly schematic by modern standards but are important cultural documents of their time, having been associated with religious institutions and beliefs. One schema was a circular map with east at the top showing Asia as the upper section of the circle, separated from Europe in the lower left and Africa in the lower right by the Don River and the Nile. Europe and Africa were separated by the Mediterranean Sea. These maps are known as T-O maps, the rivers and Mediterranean forming a rough T shape and the oceans surrounding the landmasses forming the O. The second schema was a circle with north at the top and, within the circle, temperature zones that included the torrid one along the equator, bordered by the temperate zones, which in turn were bordered by frigid zones at the poles. Route maps of the time period carried far more detail than these schematic world maps, but the most remarkable detail and the most scientific approach was found in the portolan charts. These maps were used in navigation, primarily in the Mediterranean Sea, and showed intricate coastlines with hundreds of identified coastal locations. At several locations within the water are compass roses with direction lines extending from them.

Cartography in the Islamic world during the European Middle Ages, while varied, included continuation of the Greek scientific tradition. The scientific instrument called the astrolabe, a device for measuring angles to stars, was important in finding the way to Mecca. In the early 1400s, Ptolemy's *Geographia*, which had been preserved in Byzantium, reached Italy via refugees from the invading Turks. Translated into Latin, the work had an extraordinary influence on subsequent development of cartography. Systematic projection of the spherical earth to the flat map followed Ptolemaic instructions for well over a century (Thrower 1996).

Accurate mapping depends on the ability to measure both latitude and longitude accurately. Latitude, which could be measured by angles to the sun and other heavenly bodies at specific times of the day was far easier to measure than longitude, which depends on differences in time from one location to another. In a competition sponsored by the British government, John Harrison in the later half of the eighteenth century produced a chronometer that could retain accurate time at sea (Sobel 1995). It was a turning point in the accuracy of maps covering large regions of the world.

The rise of detailed scientific mapping of Earth's surface in the form of topographic mapping owes much to the Cassini family, whose influence on cartography began with the appointment of astronomer Giovanni Domenico Cassini to the Académie Royale in Paris, which along with the Royal Society of London was concerned with mapping and other scientific problems. Under his direction, maps recorded only locations that were determined by astronomical methods, and detailed measurement of a degree of latitude was undertaken at various locations to test the theory of the earth as a prolate spheroid, which affects the placement of locations on flat maps. The detailed mapping of France was continued under three more generations of the Cassinis (Jacque, César-François, and Jean) and was completed in 1793.

In the eighteenth and early nineteenth centuries, one of the most important developments in cartography was thematic mapping (Robinson 1982). With the practice of accurate base maps established, it was feasible to focus attention on the spatial arrangement of various phenomena of interest such as elevation, population, and winds. Symbol systems such as isolines, dots, and the choropleth method came into being and are commonplace in modern mapping.

Changes in cartography in the twentieth century included the use of aerial photographs in topographic mapping and changes in production technologies. The latter half of the century saw the development of satellite sensing for gathering data for maps, the deployment of global positioning systems (constellations of satellites sending signals from which latitude and longitude are determined), and the infusion of computers into mapping including the development of geographic information systems and Internet mapping. The variety of thematic mapping methods has recently undergone rapid change as attention has focused on use of the computer to overlay multiple phenomena, produce animated maps, and develop sophisticated visualizations of spatial phenomena (Thrower 1996).

The richness of cartographic history throughout the world and over many centuries is reflected in *The History of Cartography*, a monumental multi-volume series underway as this Encyclopedia is being written (Harley and Woodward 1987). The project itself is an important intellectual event in cartographic history.

See also: Cartographic Visualization; Cartography, History of; Cognitive Maps; Dynamic Mapping in Geography; Ethnic Conflict, Geography of; Geographic Information Systems; Planetary Cartography;

Tactile Maps in Geography; Thematic Maps in Geography

Bibliography

Bertin J 1983 *The Semiology of Graphics* [English translation by Berg W J]. University of Wisconsin Press, Madison, WI

Brewer C A 1990 The effect of color on the perception of map scale. In: Everett W (ed.) *Student Honors Competition Winning Papers*, Association of American Geographers, Cartography Specialty Group, Toronto, Canada

Eastman J R 1981 The perception of scale change in small-scale map series. *The American Cartographer* 8(1): 5–21

Godlewska A 1997 The idea of the map. In: Hanson S (ed.) *Ten Geographic Ideas that Changed the World.* Rutgers University Press, New Brunswick, NJ

Harley J B, Woodward D (eds.) 1987 *The History of Cartography.* University of Chicago Press, Chicago, IL

International Cartographic Association 1995 The Definition of Cartography, a statement adopted by the 10th General Assembly, Barcelona, Spain, September 3, http://www.icaci.org

Laskowski P 1997 *The Distortion Spectrum*, monograph 50. *Cartographica* 34(3): 67–95

Peuquet D 1991 Methods for structuring digital cartographic data in a personal computer environment. In: Taylor D R F (ed.) *Geographic Information Systems: The Microcomputer and Modern Cartography.* Pergamon Press, Oxford, UK

Robinson A H 1982 *Early Thematic Mapping in the History of Cartography.* University of Chicago Press, Chicago, IL

Robinson A H, Petchenik B B 1976 *The Nature of Maps: Essays toward Understanding Maps and Mapping.* University of Chicago Press, Chicago

Robinson A H, Morrison J L, Muehrcke P C, Kimerling A J, Guptill S C 1995 *Elements of Cartography*, 6th edn. Wiley, New York

Snyder J P 1993 *Flattening the Earth: Two Thousand Years of Map Projections.* University of Chicago Press, Chicago, IL

Sobel D 1995 *Longitude: The True Story of a Lone Genius Who Solved the Greatest Scientific Problem of His Time.* Walker, New York

Thrower N J W 1996 *Maps and Civilization: Cartography in Culture and Society.* University of Chicago Press, Chicago, IL

Tobler W 1988 Resolution, resampling, and all that. In: Mounsey H, Tomlinson R (eds.) *Building Databases for Global Science.* Taylor & Francis, London, pp. 129–37

J. M. Olson

Cartography, History of

Recent expansion in both the usages and definitions of the noun 'map' and the verb 'to map' have had consequences for the history of cartography as a field. Its focus is no longer biased almost exclusively towards flat, formally-constructed, professionally-produced, artifactual maps of the earth's terrestrial and marine surfaces, made in the European tradition. The increasingly adopted operational definition of 'maps' as 'graphic representations that facilitate a spatial understanding of things, concepts, conditions, processes, or events in the human world' (Harley and Woodward 1987) has increased the range of artifacts to include celestial maps and cosmographical maps of supposed worlds. It also embraces performance cartographies; spatial representation incorporated in gesture, procession, ritual, theatre, and dance. The linked constraints of paper and flatness have been abandoned to include many and mixed media and three-dimensional expressions of these, such as buildings, whole settlements, and massive earth sculptures.

1. The Field

The history of cartography as conceived in the 1940s in the first modern review of the field has been transformed (Bagrow 1951). Approximately 90 percent of that text focused on maps made in the Classical and European worlds. Although written primarily for map collectors, and not for scientists and scholars, the chronological sequencing of chapters and narrow cultural range gave the unintended impression of an evolutionary development. The field is no longer Eurocentric but encompasses maps and mapmaking in all cultures. An important consequence of this is that the historical development of mapmaking is no longer seen as unilinear. Establishing ultimate origins in prehistory may never be possible but they were certainly multiple, probably numerous, and almost certainly geographically widespread. Another consequence of the shift to a multicultural perspective is that mapmaking is no longer seen to be exclusively a specialist or even semispecialist activity. Though not as ubiquitous as speech, it has long been a widespread vernacular skill. Transformation of the field has also reduced the formerly excessive emphasis given to printed maps based either on surveys or systematic compilation and plotted on mathematically-generated graticules. Categories of what were once considered 'less accurate' derived maps are now accorded appropriate attention. These include early manuscript maps, many thematic maps, and most media maps including the cartographoons of political cartoonists.

The longer timescale, adoption of multicultural perspective, and recognition given to additional categories of maps have together increased actual and potential links between the history of cartography and other fields. Those with the histories of art, science, and technology are fairly obvious. Even so, these have not been developed as much as might have been expected. Others are beginning to be forged. Cultural anthropology is likely to be significant in relation to vernacular cartography (see, for example, Nabokov in Lewis 1998). Likewise, religious studies should contribute to the understanding of cosmographical maps and archaeoastronomy to resolving claims that some rock art incorporates celestial maps. Archaeologists of later periods are beginning to make use of maps made in or derived from the cultures being investigated (see, for example, Waselkov in Lewis 1998). The historical role of maps in relation to other modes for communicating information spatially is at last beginning to be investigated (see, for example, Fletcher 1995 and Pearce in Lewis 1998). Links with the cognitive sciences (including cognitive archaeology) will be particularly important in furthering the understanding of map use and in helping to reconstruct the early prehistory of cartography. The ultimate and most elusive question is likely to be which emerged first as the language of space among *Homo sapiens*; those currently universal features of speech referred to as spatial deixis, schematic graphics (including artifactual maps), or nongraphics (including performance cartographies)? (Twyman 1982). In trying to answer this question, links with comparative and evolutionary linguistics will be vital. Whether actual or potential, all these links will be mutually beneficial.

The substance, scope, methods, and intentions of the transformed field are being revealed by an ongoing publishing venture; the multivolume *The History of Cartography* (Harley and Woodward 1987, 1992, 1994, Woodward and Lewis 1998; with further volumes scheduled for the European Renaissance, European Enlightenment, Nineteenth Century, and Twentieth Century). Whereas, for example, Bagrow (1951) covered 'Maps of primitive peoples' in four pages, *The History of Cartography* devotes a whole volume of more than 650 pages to maps in 'traditional societies' (Woodward and Lewis 1998). Likewise, Asian, including Islamic, cartography to which Bagrow devoted 21 pages is the subject of two volumes, together containing more than 1500 pages (Harley and Woodward 1992, 1994). Whereas the index to Bagrow is approximately 95 percent personal names, and virtually devoid of topics, the volume indexes of *The History of Cartography* reveal a surprising diversity of topical content including, for example, 'accuracy,' 'alphabets,' 'ancestors,' 'animal language,' 'animism,' 'anthropology,' and 'architecture,' as well as the much less surprising 'altitude,' 'arcs,' 'astrolabes,' 'axes,' 'atlases,' and 'azimuths.'

The defining criteria of the history of cartography as announced by the editors of *The History of Cartography* in the mid-1980s (Harley and Woodward 1987) are now agreed to by a majority of those active in the field:

(a) 'acceptance of a catholic definition of "map"';

(b) 'commitment to a discussion of the manifold processes that have contributed to the form and content of individual maps';

(c) 'recognition that the primary function of cartography is ultimately related to the historically unique mental ability of map-using peoples to store, articulate, and communicate concepts and facts that have a spatial dimension';

(d) 'belief that, since cartography is nothing if not a perspective on the world, a general history of cartography ought to lay the foundations, at the very least, for a world view of its own growth.'

To these, many working in the field would now add:

(e) 'a commitment to explore the roles of maps within societies, involving reconstructing their meaning.'

These defining criteria differentiate the 'history of cartography' from 'historical cartography' the practice of compiling maps in the present from historical data. Latterly, however, 'map history' has emerged as an alternative term for 'history of cartography.' This is regrettable. The neologism 'cartographe' was introduced in 1839 for the study of early maps. The word was soon applied to the map field in general and was to appear in many European languages in the second half of the nineteenth century. It is now associated worldwide with institutions, organizations, and activities involved with the making, use, and preservation of plans, charts, and globes as well as maps in the strict sense of representations of the earth's land surface at medium to small scales.

2. Historiography

Notwithstanding the long history and near universality of maps, mapmaking, and map use, the history of cartography is a youthful field. Although there was a long but sporadic tradition of antiquaries, collectors, and some mapmakers chronicling the subject, the field only began to emerge after 1850 with the institutionalization of geography as an academic field especially in Germany. Even then it lacked identity, being treated as part of the wider history of geographical discovery and exploration. Its beginning as a modern subject began in 1935 with the founding of *Imago Mundi*, still the only international journal devoted exclusively to the field, as distinct from map collecting. Since then, the 'emergence of cartography as an independent and practical discipline' has provided 'new theoretical frameworks as well as a reinforced *raison d'être* for the study of cartographic history' (Harley and Woodward 1987).

Many of the material resources on which the emergence of the new history of cartography were based were already in place, including archives, map libraries, and private collections, but they were to become more accessible (Skelton 1972). Epistemological and methodological developments were consequences of the wider ferment of ideas and institutional changes that followed World War II. Increasing prosperity and better and more specialist librarians and bibliographers were in part responsible for the appearance of major printed catalogues of collections and regional cartobibliographies, albeit heavily biased towards Europe and North America. New printing technologies made possible the reprinting of earlier obscure but significant publications. Among these

Acta Cartographica, Vols. 1–27 (Theatrum Orbis Terrarum, Amsterdam, 1967–81) was particularly important. Most important among these publishing initiatives was the quality reproduction, often in color, of thousands of maps hitherto only accessible to a few.

The field became somewhat less dominated by geographers and historians and began to attract some of the new generation of cartographers, some of whom had trained in the military, and were interested in modern maps and in the contexts and consequences of their use. In 1972 The International Cartographic Association created a Standing Commission on the History of Cartography from an existing working group that was already preparing a handbook of cartographic terms in use before 1900 (Wallis and Robinson 1987). An international conference on the History of Cartography now meets biennially, usually preceded by a meeting of the International Society for the Curators of Early Maps. Map collectors are an important interest group, providing the field with financial and material support. The International Map Collectors' Society meets annually.

By 1994 there were more than 500 self-designated historians of cartography in the world; unequally distributed geographically with approximately 40 percent resident in continental Europe, 25 percent in North America, and 10 percent in the United Kingdom. Research interests were equally skewed with, for example, 66 respondents registering an interest in cartobibliography and 13 in projections, but only one in mining maps, two in cartouches, three in map accuracy, four in Hebrew maps, and five in tithe maps. Likewise, 19 registered an interest in Gerardus Mercator and 13 in Claudius Ptolemy but eminent cartographers from other cultures and periods were far less prominent. For example, al-Idrīsī, Timothy Pont, and Thomas Hutchins had only one registrant each. Nevertheless, the earlier collector-led, dilettante, aesthetically motivated, Eurocentric, and somewhat insular preoccupation with Renaissance and Enlightenment printed maps and mapmakers has undergone a relative decline and interest in such topics as mathematics in cartography, techniques of map production, map publishing, and surveying is increasing. Listed under the umbrella of 'Theory and Methodology' are such interests as 'cartography and cultural theory,' 'construction of knowledge space,' 'politics of projections and maps,' and 'semiotics of prehistorical maps.' (Lowenthal 1998).

In anticipating future directions of the field, the most serious limiting factors are the paucity of specialist undergraduate courses and limited opportunities for formal graduate training. For the most part, those active in the field continue to enter by chance and often in mid-career. They contribute to a rich mix of epistemologies, interests, and skills, but it could be argued that this is delaying the emergence of an overarching paradigm. Essentially, researchers do not operate within an agreed philosophy, concur on the theoretical focus of their work, or use accepted methodological procedures to solve problems identified within a theoretical framework. Conversely, most set out to investigate topics *de novo* and only rarely on the basis of what is already known. They add to knowledge but usually without extending theory. Given the paucity of graduate courses in the history of cartography, much depends on the few that do exist if the imbalance between empiricism and theory is to change. Meanwhile, it is important that the field accepts and integrates concepts, issues, and directions being developed at or beyond what many insiders now see as its periphery, often by persons who do not identify themselves with it. Important among these are the idea of maps as power, the distinction between intended and actual roles, an increased commitment to iconology, and re-examining the idea of value-free cartography.

3. The History of Mapmaking and Maps

The following outline reflects something of the enormous empirical additions made during the last quarter of the twentieth century but it is neither structured nor underpinned by a body of theory. The overriding concern has been to present a multicultural review from the earliest times to the beginning of the electronic age of geographical information systems and, in so doing, to reduce the Eurocentrism that has distorted most syntheses hitherto. Although primarily organizational, the structure does imply a working hypothesis for a developmental theory.

Cartography was originally a near-universal skill. It probably had prehistoric origins in every part of the then settled world, when map content was one or a mix of terrestrial, celestial, and cosmographical, and its roles were geographical, calendrical, and making sense of the unknown universe and linking it to the world of experience and report. The ability to read random patterns as maps was probably used in divinational practices. In so-called traditional societies, these types of cartographic activities survived until recent times. Indeed, they are still practiced in some. In Western societies some of the skills characteristic of this level of ability are still used, as when experiential sketch maps are made in communicating to others or when the scaleless topologically-structured maps provided by public transport systems are referred to.

Cartography underwent a qualitative shift in most of the world's early urban societies, where mapmaking slowly became an activity of elites but rarely a specialism. Although increasingly sophisticated and often revealing superb craftsmanship in producing artifacts of artistic quality, the basic roles of maps were still threefold, though with an increasing emphasis on terrestrial, made and used in the contexts of communicating, instructing, planning, building, administering, and record keeping. Very slowly, these societies would seem to have developed a cartographic consciousness, although the concept of 'map' as a discrete category probably remained weak.

From the later urban societies of the Middle East and the eastern Mediterranian, two further and more or less independent cartographic traditions emerged: very quickly, towards the end of the first millennium AD, Islamic terrestrial and celestial mapping; and slowly, via more complicated stages, but ultimately with greater global impact, the Classical–Christian–European tradition. Both traditions used advanced instrumentation and mathematics to achieve greater precision than in other urban societies, arguably achieved higher artistic and aesthetic standards than elsewhere, and used maps very effectively in the interests of religious, scientific, and ruling elites.

Ultimately, the European tradition achieved most, surpassing that of Islam and, without knowing it until much later, the earlier peak of cartographic achievement reached in China. The printing of maps disseminated spatially-organized information more effectively than ever before and, together with education, increasing literacy, and the mass media raised cartographic consciousness to an unprecedented level. Maps and atlases became trade items. Formal ground survey and systematically conducted censuses and inventories of many kinds replaced judicious compilation of randomly assembled intelligence as the basic sources of information. Nation-states began to map their own territories and, later on, their colonial possessions. Cosmographical mapping virtually ceased but new types of maps emerged, in particular thematic maps and large-scale national topographic map series.

After c. 1975, a fourth cartographic tradition began to emerge rapidly from the European tradition: geographical information systems. An important part of the electronic age it seems to be supplementing rather than replacing the tradition from which it emerged. If so, this will be in keeping with the historically earlier transitions between cartographic traditions.

3.1 Vernacular Terrestrial Maps

Many, perhaps most, adult members of historically traditional societies appear to have possessed the linked abilities to make certain kinds of maps and to understand those made by others in their own and similar societies. These abilities emerged in prehistory (Harley and Woodward 1987, Woodward and Lewis 1998). Artifactual, gestural, and performance maps were observed by Europeans and Euro-Americans in their early contacts with preliterate tribal societies (articles by Bassett, Davenport, Lewis, and Turnbull in Selin 1997). Less frequently, but almost as widespread, tribal peoples practicing divination were observed to interpret cartographically patterns induced on a variety of organic materials. Never constructed

according to even approximate linear scale, content was determined by the usually immediate purpose a map was made to serve. For example, physically conspicuous and culturally important ground features might be omitted, whereas minor features and unique events central to a message often dominated, usually to the exclusion of all but an essential minimum of base data. Artifactual maps were made on or with a wide range of media. Most content was terrestrial, some littoral, but very little marine. The maps were almost always short-lived and often ephemeral. In the absence of writing, many artifactual examples were made to communicate to persons not present messages about events, conditions, and proposed activities elsewhere. They were functionally undifferentiated examples of much wider systems of pictographic communication. Sometimes they were made to instruct persons present or in the course of interactive planning. Very rarely did they serve as the equivalents of the reference maps of Western societies, though some were made and from time to time remade to preserve lore. Rather, their equivalents in the latter are the experiential sketch maps of small areas used by individuals to convey local information to others. It seems likely that they manifested the cognitive and behavioral substrata from which formal cartographies later emerged but direct evidence from prehistory is, and seems likely to remain, rare and contestable. Gestural and performance maps could leave no physical evidence and most artifactual examples woulds have had short lives.

In the course of geographical discovery and exploration, Europeans routinely solicited vernacular terrestrial maps from the indigenous peoples of Africa, the Americas, the Arctic, and Australasia, often incorporating them into their own maps. They did not, however, recognise important differences between their own and the indigenes' epistemologies of terrestrial space. What appeared to be crude equivalents of their own maps were fundamentally different. Appraised retrospectively according to Western concepts of accuracy, the consequences of this led to major errors in European cartography of newly discovered areas (Lewis 1986, 1993).

3.2 Celestial and Cosmographical Maps of Shamans and Tribal Leaders

Within historical nonliterate societies, not all maps were terrestrial in content or of vernacular origin. Religious and tribal leaders often had responsibility for making, replicating, and sometimes performing celestial and cosmographical maps, as well as for preserving the lore and conducting the ceremonies with which these were associated. This was particularly so in societies preoccupied with the heavens in the contexts of calendrics and astrology and with a belief in a structured cosmos extending far beyond the world of direct experience. Celestial patterns were, for example, stitched on shamans' coats, painted on animal hides, incorporated in sand paintings, and mirrored in the organization of rooms and in the positioning of buildings within settlements and vis-à-vis each other. The rapidly developing field of archaeoastronomy is producing increasingly convincing evidence for the incorporation of celestial maps in prehistoric rock art.

The frequency, variety, and physical diversity of cosmographical maps were probably each greater than for celestial maps. In these, planar symmetry about one or more axes was a common geometrical characteristic, often incorporating an axis mundi as a third dimension. Media were very varied, including ceramics, skin drumheads, wall murals, sculpted figures, and scarification of human bodies.

There is little doubt that celestial and cosmographical maps had been made in the antecedents of these societies well before the earliest contact with Europeans. In other societies, maps had already become much more sophisticated; essentially those that had acquired scripts, evolved more advanced forms of religion, and developed large urban communities, especially Babylonia, Egypt, northern China, Persia, Islam, Mesoamerica, and the central Andes.

3.3 Cartography in Early Urban Societies

Urbanization was part cause and part consequence of increasingly complex social systems, religious institutions, civil and military administrations, and extensive trading systems. It also involved increasing specialization and the concentration of wealth. In these conditions new types and styles of maps emerged. Within each of the major urbanized regions a new cartography would appear to have emerged more or less independently. So far as is known, maps were not conceived, compiled, or made by specialist cartographers but as part only of the work of artists, scribes, engravers, sculpters, scholars, astronomers, architects, engineers, etc. The centers of map production were at first the larger urban centers, separated by hinterlands in which the vernacular, shamans', and tribal leaders' maps were almost certainly still the norm. Even in the urban centers map consciousness was probably still weak. Symptomatic of this was the absence of words for 'map' as evidenced in those languages of which there are reasonably reliable lexicons: ancient Greek and Latin, Persian, Arabic, Sanskrit, Hindi, and Chinese before 300 BC. Even so, the maps made in these societies were much more sophisticated and, by later Western standards at least, much more maplike in appearance than the vernacular shamans' and tribal leaders' maps being made elsewhere, as, perhaps, by the nonelites and reactionary groups in the towns.

Between c. 2,300 BC and 500 BC, Babylonian scribes, in addition to writing on clay tablets, used them as surfaces on which to make plans of property, land, houses, and temples, as well as small-scale maps of larger areas and the whole world as they supposed it to be (Millard in Harley and Woodward 1987).

In the fourth millennium BC, rudimentary topographic diagrams began to appear on Egyptian decorated pottery. Detailed plans were being made in ink on plaster-covered boards by the middle of the second millennium BC and cosmographical and celestial maps were being engraved in stone by the end of the first millennium BC (Shore in Harley and Woodward 1987).

In China, maps of many kinds, great complexity, and often exquisite craftsmanship were being made during and after the Warring States period (403 BC – 221 BC). Many have survived; perhaps more than for any of the other early urban societies. Among the earliest is a plan for the construction of a royal tomb, engraved on a bronze plate and inlaid with gold and silver. Others include topographic, administrative, and thematic maps on wooden boards and a map on silk showing a pattern of roads, rivers, and mountains, together with the locations of settlements, scenic sites, and places of historical interest. One of the earliest known maps to have a grid (though probably not based on it) is engraved on a stone dating from AD 1136 and may have had antecedents. There is some direct evidence for mapping according to linear scale and some textual support for this (Wanru et al. 1990 and Yee in Harley and Woodward 1994).

Surprisingly, and unexplained, there are almost no extant terrestrial maps from the Indian subcontinent for the two millennia before the advent of the Portuguese. The exceptions are a few incised potsherds from the end of the first millennium BC that have rough plans of monasteries and a few ancient sculptures depicting sacred rivers. Nevertheless, the first urban culture, the Harappan dating from the middle of the third millennium BC, had many temples and settlements that were so standard in form that they must have been based on precise plans. Furthermore, artifacts from the period have been identified as surveying instruments. Cosmographical mapping may have had its roots in temple design but the maps emerged in their complex and artistically rich forms much later in the Hindu and Jain religious traditions. Likewise, terrestrial mapping, though ultimately sophisticated, emerged late; from the middle of the seventeenth century AD onwards. In the subcontinent, therefore, early urbanization and events associated with it was not the catalyst for cartography—but two much later events were: the emergence of the great religions and contacts with Europeans (Schwartzberg in Harley and Woodward 1992).

Within months of first entering Mexico in 1519, Spaniards were presented with paintings on cloth that were itinerary maps complete with topographic details necessary for route finding. What they either did not see or recognize were three other categories of Mesoamerican cartography, terrestrial maps that incorporated accounts of history (cartographic histories); cosmographical maps showing either a horizontal cosmos divided into five quadrants or a vertical cosmos divided into layers along an *axis mundi*; and celestial maps of stars and constellations. Of these, cosmographical models were probably the oldest tradition, dating back to the Olmecs who founded urban centers as early as 1200 BC. By the first millennium AD carved stone tablets showing the cosmic layout were widespread. Celestial maps were less common but cartouches in a Mayan wall mural are believed to represent the arrangements of planets and constellations on the night of an event in AD 792. In central Mexico extant cartographic histories are numerous and elsewhere known by report. One dates from c. 1542. Made on paper, cloth, animal hides, or parchment, they were complex, iconographically sophisticated, and showed what the ruling elites wanted communities to know about their pasts. Artists, scribes, and sculpters also formed an elite but at the conquest product specialization was probably restricted to the larger urban centers. In smaller communities artists were expected to paint everything from pots to maps (Munday in Woodward and Lewis 1998).

In the years after 1532, when the Spaniards first reached the central Andean empire of the Inkas, the invaders were not given and did not report seeing maps. It is possible that flat maps did exist but that native conceptions of space and their symbolizing of it were so different from the Spaniards' experience that they were not recognized. The archaeological record certainly reveals spatial and landscape representations from the previous 2,000 years. The Nazca lines (large ground drawings) may have been made to attract and spatially direct Andean gods. Ceramics of the first millennium AD represent landscapes and buildings three dimensionally. In the years immediately before the conquest, landscapes were carved three-dimensionally on stones and even on extensive rock outcrops. Knotted string devices (khipus) may, in addition to other functions, have been used as maps. Soon after the conquest maps began to be included in native chronicles. There are long traditions of ceremonies that incorporate mapping procedures. Typically, these involve the arrangement of amulets in relation to a ground drawing of a map or plan (Gartner in Woodward and Lewis 1998).

Within 200 years of Mohammed's death in AD 632, the Islamic-Arab world extended from the Atlantic coast of North Africa in the west to the Chinese sphere in the east and was soon to extend south to the Sahara. Together with religious practices, the fostering of scholarship and science, extensive geographical exploration, and urbanization, this rapid territorial expansion stimulated cartography, in part by borrowing languishing concepts and techniques from the earlier Hellenic, Byzantine, and Persian cultures and by interacting with contemporary cultures as distant and different as medieval Europe and Hindu India. Islamic cartographic achievements were numerous and diverse: artifacts of the highest craftsmanship and artistic quality, such as astrolabes in brass incorporating pierced planisphere star maps, celestial globes, and exquisitely painted birds-eye views of cities; mathematically sophisticated circular world maps centered on Mecca, constructed in such a way that the city's distance and direction could be read directly from any locality in the Islamic world; and delicately colored cosmographical maps incorporating three divine worlds, the earth surrounded by seven heavenly spheres and a legendary encircling mountain, together with a seven-layered hell.

With the possible exception of that in China, Islamic cartography was more diverse and sophisticated than that in any of the other early urban societies. Its traditions persisted for more than a millennium. With the exception of some world maps, marine charts, and celestial globes, most maps were made for or copied from manuscript texts, to which they were generally subservient. Many of the texts were translations into Arabic from Greek, Syriac, Hebrew, Persian, Sanskrit, and Turkish. These included Ptolemy's *Almagest* and *Geography*. Islamic scientists and craftsmen were creative in adopting and adapting the techniques described in these translations. Many cartographic artifacts were used in determining religious practices but few, if any, were religious icons. Cartography was encouraged and supported by imperial patrons and many maps were linked with political power. As in all other early urban societies there were no equivalents of the modern professional cartographer. Terrestrial maps, at least, were produced by the elite for the elite for the purposes of edification, illustration, and propagation of imperial glory. With the exception of marine charts and aids to religious practice very few were practical. (Harley and Woodward 1992 and Savage-Smith, Karamustafa, and King in Selin 1997).

3.4 Cartography is European and Other Later Urban Societies

The extent to which Dark Age and medieval cartography in the western Mediterranean and Europe was influenced by that in the classical world is inadequately understood. The importance and quality of maps certainly declined in the late Roman Empire but the role of the Byzantine Empire in transmitting cartographic traditions has still to be assessed. One extant monastery map from the early ninth century AD is reminiscent of the best large-scale Roman plans. Medieval *mappae mundi* were certainly in a tradition extending from the third century AD. Some of the simple world outlines known as T-O maps made from the seventh century AD onwards were influenced by Greco-Roman philosophical tradition. Portolan charts have been claimed by a minority of authorities to have Roman, Greek, Phoenician, Egyptian, even Neolithic origins (Harvey, Woodward, and Campbell in Harley and Woodward 1987). Possible, probable, or certain though these influences from earlier cultures may have been, they were insignificant compared with that of Ptolemy (Claudius Ptolemaeus).

A second century AD Greek scholar who worked within the framework of the early Roman Empire, Ptolemy's writings were unknown in Europe until 1406, when his *Geography* was translated from Greek into Latin. Hand-copied versions, many with maps, soon began to circulate and printed editions proliferated after 1475. Written as a manual for mapmakers, the original may not have contained maps but its accounts of three projections and tables of latitudes and longitudes were sufficient for the construction of world and regional maps. The *Geography* has been called the touchstone of the Renaissance in European cartography. Before 1482 Ptolemaic maps were exclusively reconstructions but the Ulm edition of that year contained woodcut maps that incorporated recent discoveries by Europeans (Dilke 1985).

Although Ptolemaic maps continued to be published for several centuries, the influence of the ideas in the *Geography* were in the long run the more important. It insisted on carefully measured data, stressed the need for validation, promoted the idea of plotting data with reference to a graticule, and the equally important notion that the graticule could be transformed by the use of different projections, thereby preserving one property at the expense of others. Because they were in such demand, Ptolemaic maps were a factor in stimulating the map-printing technology; at first from woodblocks and, after the mid-sixteenth century, from engraved copper plates. The latter were more readily correctable and revisable than woodblocks (Woodward and Harvey in Harley and Woodward 1987).

For almost 1,000 years before the Ptolemaic impact, cartography in Europe had served the Christian church. Indeed, many, perhaps most, maps had been made by monks and clerics. The primary purpose of *mappaemundi* had been to communicate the significant events in Christian history rather than to record their precise locations, with symbolism and allegory playing major roles. The T in T-O maps separated the three known continents but also symbolized the Christian Cross, in some cases with the body of Christ superimposed on it. Many local maps and plans were of ecclesiastical buildings and church property (Woodward and Harvey in Harley and Woodward 1987). Of the main categories of maps, only the Portolan charts had a primary utilitarian function (Campbell in Harley and Woodward 1987).

The Ptolemaic impact preceded a post-Renaissance change in the role of maps from mainly religious to almost exclusively secular. It occurred during the most momentous and diverse series of developments in the history of cartography before the technical innovations of the second half of the twentieth century. From the early sixteenth century until the mid-nineteenth century Europe dominated the field. Thereafter, the USA and Canada assumed increasing importance. Voyages of discovery and overseas settlement and exploration vastly increased geographical knowledge. During and after the eighteenth-century Enlightenment, science focused attention on hitherto ignored or little known phenomena such as ocean currents and magnetic compass declination, both of which began to be mapped. New and improved instruments increased the accuracy of observations. For example, in the mid-eighteenth century the sealed spring-driven chronometer made it possible to establish longitude accurately anywhere and under virtually any condition (Sobel 1995). Navigation, travel, trade, warfare and international rivalry, settlement of newly discovered and reclaimed lands, Christian missionary activities, searching for and exploiting new and better natural resources, civil administration of increasingly complex societies with emerging senses of social responsibility, planning and civil engineering, science, tourism, popular journalism, the new academic geography that first emerged in Germany after the mid-nineteenth century, and the pedantic geography that paralleled it in the new state education systems were among the factors creating demands for and access to more, better, and different kinds of maps.

At first, those who were known to acquire maps improved their status. For example, the original commissioners of mid-sixteenth century custom-made Italian world atlases; slightly later, those who bought the standardized world atlases of the late sixteenth century Dutch cartographers Abraham Ortèlius and Gerardus Mercator; and, soon after that, the purchasers of single-country atlases such as Christopher Saxton's of England and Wales. Those who knew how to use maps, rather than just placing them in their libraries or having their names engraved on them as patrons, increased their political influence, material assets, and intellectual standing. For example, in attempting to consolidate their powers, monarchs in early modern Europe used maps to better define and expand their territories (Buisseret 1992). Known as cadastral maps, cartographic records of property ownership were important tools in the extension of land-based power (Kain and Baigent 1992). From the early eighteenth century onwards, statesmen began establishing permanent departments to map national and colonial territories, systematically, accurately, and usually at much larger scales than those, if any, already available; for example, in France (Konvitz 1987) and British India (Edney 1997). Thereafter, up-to-date topographic map series were to become hallmarks of nation-states. Governors of quasistates such as the Hudson's Bay Company attempted something similar, though less systematically (Ruggles 1991). By the eighteenth century cartographic consciousness had extended to the rural gentry and new urban middle class subscribers to monthly magazines, most of which included maps on a fairly regular basis. To conform with magazine formats and keep engraving costs down, these were small. Many illustrated current events, and were often made by eminent cartographic engravers such as Emanuel Bowen and Thomas Jefferys (Jolly 1990).

After about 1825, lithography became the popular map-printing technique in Europe. Cheaper than copper-plate engraved maps, the new maps became larger and, from the 1860s onwards, the technique was adapted to print in color. A new generation of maps and atlases began to be published, often cheaply, in large quantities, for use in schools and in the home. In the USA, however, between 1880 and 1940 wax engraving was the dominant technique in commercial cartography. One advantage was that printer's type was used for lettering on maps (Woodward 1977). Wax engraving was important in mass producing categories of widely available, cheap, and sometimes freely distributed maps that extended map consciousness among almost all sectors of the American public; railroad and domestic tourist maps after 1880 and highway maps between the two world wars. They accelerated a trend that had been stimulated by popular journalism during the Civil War. Before 1861 American newspapers rarely contained maps (Bosse 1993). Thereafter, they were to become common (Monmonier 1989).

Between 1500 and 1850 the centers of cartographic innovation and map production were in the financial cities of the densely populated, economically active regions of southern and northwestern Europe. The center of gravity of these activities were Italy (Venice, Rome, and Genoa) in the early and mid-sixteenth century, the Low Countries (Antwerp and Amsterdam) in the late sixteenth and seventeenth centuries, and France (Paris) and England (London) in the eighteenth century. Theory and techniques improved, specialisms emerged, and cartography became increasingly professionalized. By the late nineteenth century the center of gravity had crossed the North Atlantic and dispersed to cities such as New York, Washington DC, and Chicago.

One important category of maps did not conform to these general trends; maps of one or a closely related group of physical, or social, or economic phenomena. Now referred to as thematic maps, early examples were made in the late seventeenth century, rather more during the eighteenth, followed by a burgeoning in northwest Europe during the first half of the nineteenth. A consequence of growth of interest in natural history, the environment, society, and economic change, it was facilitated by scholarly periodicals and only possible once base maps existed. Much of it stemmed from the curiosity and research interests of individuals in topics as diverse as cholera, language, cereals, and volcanoes, often in attempts to demonstrate spatial correlations between two or a few phenomena (Robinson 1982). The emergence of thematic cartography heralded the great late nineteenth and twentieth century national surveys of geology, soil, landuse, etc. and the best of the national atlases published after the middle of the twentieth century.

Aerial photogrammetry, the science of obtaining accurate measurements from air photographs, was used increasingly after World War I. By the 1950s most large-scale mapping and map revision made use of it and in the 1960s and 1970s it was used to map the moon. In 1950, an even greater technical advance was heralded by the publication of the first computer-generated map. Computers are now used in every stage of mapmaking, from surveying to the compilation, design, and production of the end product. Increasingly, maps are custom made. In this respect they are similar to the vernacular maps made in traditional societies. They are not, however, grounded in individual experience or shared traditions but use software programs (geographical information systems) and digitized databases. How historians of cartography in the future will incorporate these developments into the universal history of maps and mapmaking is as yet unclear.

See also: Geography; Space and Social Theory in Geography; Spatial Analysis in Geography; Spatial Data

Bibliography

Bagrow L 1951 *Die Geschichte der Kartographie*. Safari-Verlag, Berlin. First English edition, used in preparing this article, rev. and enl. Skelton R A [trans. Paisey D L] 1964 *History of Cartography*. Harvard University Press, Cambridge, MA

Bosse D 1993 *Civil War Newspaper Maps*. Johns Hopkins University Press, Baltimore, MD

Buisseret D (ed.) 1992 *Monarchs, Ministers, and Maps: The Emergence of Cartography as a Tool of Government in Early Modern Europe*. University of Chicago Press, Chicago

Dilke O A W 1985 *Greek and Roman Maps*. Cornell University Press, Ithaca, NY

Edney M H 1997 *Mapping an Empire: The Geographic Construction of British India 1765–1843*. University of Chicago Press, Chicago

Fletcher D 1995 *The Emergence of Estate Maps: Christ Church, Oxford 1600–1840*. Oxford University Press, Oxford, UK

Harley J B, Woodward D (eds.) *The History of Cartography, Vol. 1, Cartography in Prehistoric, Ancient, and Medieval Europe and the Mediterranean, Vol. 2, book 1, 1992, Cartography in the Traditional Islamic and South Asian Societies; and Vol. 2, book 2, 1994. Cartography in the Traditional East and Southeast Asian Societies*. University of Chicago Press, Chicago

Jolly D C 1990 *Maps in British Periodicals. Part 1. Major Monthlies Before 1800*. D C Jolly, Brookline, MA

Kain R J P, Baigent E 1992 *The Cadastral Map in the Service of the State: A History of Property Mapping*. University of Chicago Press, Chicago

Konvitz J W 1987 *Cartography in France 1660–1848: Science, Engineering, and Statecraft.* University of Chicago Press, Chicago

Lewis G M 1986 Indicators of unacknowledged assimilations from Amerindian maps on Euro-American maps of North America. *Imago Mundi* **38**: 9–34

Lewis G M 1993 Metrics, geometries, signs, and language: sources of cartographic miscommunication between native and Euro-American cultures in North America. *Cartographica* **30**(1): 98–106

Lewis G M (ed.) 1998 *Cartographic Encounters: Perspectives on Native American Mapmaking and Map Use.* University of Chicago Press, Chicago

Lowenthal M A (ed.) 1998 *Who's Who in the History of Cartography: The International Guide to the Subject (D9).* Map Collector Publications Ltd. for Imago Mundi Ltd., Tring, UK

Monmonier M 1989 *Maps With The News: The Development of American Journalistic Cartography.* University of Chicago Press, Chicago

Robinson A H 1982 *Early Thematic Mapping in the History of Cartography.* University of Chicago Press, Chicago

Ruggles R I 1991 *A Country So Interesting: The Hudson's Bay Company and Two Centuries of Mapping, 1670–1870.* McGill-Queen's University Press, Montreal.

Selin H (ed.) 1997 *Encyclopaedia of the History of Science, Technology, and Medicine in Non-Western Cultures.* Kluwer Academic, Dordrecht, The Netherlands

Skelton R A 1972 *Maps: A Historical Survey of Their Study and Collecting.* University of Chicago Press, Chicago

Sobel D 1995 *Longitude.* Walker and Co., New York

Twyman M 1982 The graphic presentation of language. *Information Design Journal* **3**(1): 1–22

Wallis H M, Robinson A H (eds.) 1987 *Cartographic Innovations: An International Handbook of Mapping Terms to 1900.* Map Collector Publications, Tring, UK in association with the International Cartographic Association

Wanru C, Xihuang Z, Shengzhang H, Zhongxun N, Jincheng R, Deyuan J (eds.) 1990 *An Atlas of Ancient Maps in China— From the Warring States Period to the Yuan Dynasty (476 BC–AD 1368).* Cultural Relics Publishing House, Beijing

Woodward D 1977 *The All-American Map: Wax Engraving and its Influence on Cartography.* University of Chicago Press, Chicago

Woodward D, Lewis G M (eds.) 1998 *The History of Cartography Vol. 2, book 3, Cartography in the Traditional African, American, Arctic, Australian, and Pacific Societies.* University of Chicago Press, Chicago

G. M. Lewis

Case Study: Logic

1. The Case Study Defined

The case study is a research strategy with special implications for theoretical analysis and data collection. A single case of a particular phenomenon is examined intensively for the light that it can shed on a specific problem or question. Often several methods of data collection will be used to assemble a wide range of information about the case. One of the main benefits of a wide-range of data is that it permits a *triangulation* of research methods, thus, providing substantial verification of the particular phenomenon in question.

Researchers vary in why they choose to study a single case, but most often they do so in order to examine a proposed theory or to provide grounded and detailed information for a new theory (Glaser and Strauss 1967). Although many quantitative researchers consider the case study as a limited form of analysis, especially by comparison with methods that collect information on a large sample of instances, such a conclusion misconstrues fundamentally the main purpose of the case study. The analyst who selects and studies a single case, or even a handful of cases, is not primarily interested in statistical inference to a larger population of units, but rather in theoretical analysis and inference. Nevertheless, the findings from the study of a single case, like those from the study of a large sample of instances, always are to be regarded as tentative, awaiting further confirmation from additional studies of parallel theoretical cases.

2. Why Study the Single Case?

The intensive analysis of the case study is premised on the special advantages that it furnishes. First, the study of single cases enables the researcher to probe a particular question, or phenomenon, in great detail. Such in-depth examinations ultimately permit the researcher to acquire a degree of knowledge about the case that is typically impossible through the examination of a large number of cases. Moreover, such in-depth work also enables the researcher to pursue the examination of alternative theoretical ideas, thus ultimately arriving not merely at a thorough understanding of the empirical facts, but ideally a careful and correct appreciation of the most germane and effective theoretical argument to fit these facts (Campbell 1975).

Second, by studying a single case the researcher is able to take full account of the social, or historical, context of the phenomenon in question. Students of case studies regard context as essential to understanding the nature of the phenomenon. Take, for example, the study of children who are unruly in the classroom. The investigator may believe that such unruliness is the product of how the child relates both to his peers and teacher in the context of classroom activity. In order to appreciate and to fully understand the nature of the child's reactions, the investigator is compelled to study the child in the classroom situation (Stake 1995).

Third, the study of the single case permits the researcher to probe comprehensively into the empirical data at hand. In the study of the workings of a single community, for example, the case study researcher can explore a variety of dimensions of the community and can thereby create a multidimensional, or holistic, sense of the community rather than, let us say, a unidimensional one based upon its size or territorial breadth. In so doing the researcher can also emerge with a fuller understanding of the case in question by fashioning an integrated portrait of the case into which the various pieces, or dimensions, fit. Fourth, the case study provides boundaries to the nature of the phenomenon under investigation. The case is chosen because it represents a self-contained unit that will permit the researcher to investigate the phenomenon in isolation from other forces. Thus, educational researchers will often investigate a single classroom or school because such a case represents some unusual qualities in which they are interested (Stake 1995).

Finally, the single case is sometimes chosen because it represents a special illustration of the phenomenon under investigation. Sometimes it is portrayed as the exception to the rule, or deviant case, thereby permitting the observer to understand some more general phenomenon in greater depth.

3. How to Choose Cases

Great care must be exercised in the choice of the single case. Sometimes social scientists believe that any case may be used to explore a particular phenomenon. Indeed, there appears to have been a great deal of faulty case study research because there are few guidelines by which to select the case. In fact, the choice must always involve certain critical decisions in advance of the data collection and analysis.

First and foremost, the researcher must decide the grounds for selecting a particular unit for study. Since such selection is never based upon issues of statistical inference, the theoretical reasons for selecting the case must always be made clear—or, at least, as clear as possible—in advance of the research. For example, the sociologist R. Stephen Warner believed that broad societal changes might have a deep influence on the life of churches in America. Thus, he chose to focus on a single church, and to examine how the internal organization of the church changed over several decades during which there was marked change in American society. Second, the researcher should choose those cases that will furnish the clearest tests of the theory, or argument, in question. If a researcher is interested in the causes of revolution, then a society should be chosen where there has been a substantial and marked revolution, to examine the possible causes.

3.1 What Qualifies as a Case?

Unlike certain forms of research method, such as the sample survey, case study research can employ very different units of analysis on which to focus its theoretical attention. The earliest examples of case studies were often in-depth studies of particular *social roles*, designed to explore the nature of such roles. Other famous case studies have been done of entire *cities*, including the range of different people and organizations in such cities. More recently, social researchers have studied specific *organizations* using the case study format; specific *locales* designed to understand the nature of social groups in those locales; and even specific *individuals* whose traits exemplify special qualities for investigation (Stake 1995). In addition, the case is sometimes used very effectively to explore in rich detail the nature of *social processes* at work. One of the best illustrations of using the case study in this manner was done by the political scientist, Matthew Crenson (1971). He furnished a number of important insights into the nature and exercise of power, including the dynamics of agenda-setting, simply from the study of how political decisions were made in a single city.

4. The Case Study as a Strategy of Research

By comparison with other research methods, the case study has certain limitations. It does not permit the easy and refined manipulation of variables in the same way as an experiment does. Nor does it permit a researcher to investigate various configurations of variables that might be associated with particular outcomes, or dependent variables, like the sample survey. Most often, the case study is done using qualitative methods, thus resulting in some confusion between case studies and qualitative research (Merriam 1998). Yet there are important examples in which quantitative data also have been collected to provide key information about the single case. For example, some researchers have used time series data on a single country to examine it in depth.

4.1 The Case Study as an Inductive Tool

The case study has proven most useful for the generation of new theory. Because a single case can be examined in great depth, and because it can be studied with a variety of research tools, researchers can mine it for a great deal of information. At the same time, the careful examination of such information can furnish insights not easily acquired by other research methods. Therefore the case study is perhaps at its strongest when it is used as an inductive research instrument, allowing the researcher to construct an explanation for the phenomenon under investigation (Glaser and Strauss 1967).

4.2 The Case Study as a Deductive Tool

Yet, the study of the single case can also furnish an important tool for those observers who wish to test, or apply, deductive theories. One of the most famous illustrations of this occurs in the classic study of the International Typographers Union (Lipset et al. 1956). The authors had concluded, both on empirical and theoretical grounds, that trade unions were characterized by very rigid and tightly closed political administrations, with one clique maintaining its rule in office over a long period of time. They then chose deliberately to examine the ITU in detail, because it appeared to be the exception to the general situation. What was it about the ITU, they asked, that produced empirically disparate results from all other trade unions? This was a powerful, well-refined question. In effect, the ITU provided a comparison to all other cases: if its outcome was different, so too must have been the set of elements that brought about such an outcome. The answer, furnished through a variety of evidence, suggested that, because of their level of education, skill, and commitment to the ITU, union members of this union, as compared to others, simply were more likely to take an active role in union affairs.

The one consideration that is overlooked in using the case study as a deductive tool is that researchers may fail to specify the nature of the null hypothesis, or the likely outcome if the theory is incorrect. While most case studies have failed to consider this important feature of theory construction and testing, Yin (1994) argues that, if done carefully, such a strategy can be incorporated easily into the analysis of single, and even multiple, cases.

5. The Case Study: Seminal Illustrations

Over the years there have been a number of very significant case studies. Two, in particular, illustrate the wide variety of uses to which case study analysis can be put in the study of social phenomena.

One of the first, and surely most famous, case studies was done of the city of Muncie, Indiana (Lynd and Lynd 1929). Conducted during the course of the 1920s, the investigators and their research team wanted to uncover the full nature of a typical American city over the course of its lifetime. Part of their work involved tracing the history of the city. A large part, however, involved the collection of a wide range of information on the city's current residents, organizations, and its internal workings.

There were a variety of important discoveries, including discoveries about the nature of work life and religious life in the community, as well as about the dominance of a leading industrial family over the entire range of civic and political life of the community. It might be noted that sample surveys of city residents, or demographic data about them, would never have uncovered the full and complex portrait the Lynds were able to construct through their pioneering case study research.

A second famous case study was done of men who lived in the South End of Boston (Whyte 1943). This study, also conducted in the 1930s, was ostensibly an examination of a group of impoverished men, and how they adapted to life during the Great Depression. In fact, as Whyte so brilliantly showed, it really was a case study of a small group of men, and the way in which the nature of stratification emerged within the group, and how it influenced the behavior of individuals. It was done with great insight and care by Whyte, making it still one of the best and most influential case studies of all time.

6. Issues of Theoretical Specification: The Use of Singular Cases to Illuminate General Principles

Sometimes the study of the single case is done specifically to reveal the importance of a special configuration, or confluence, of elements that together help to explain the unique outcome of a case, and its difference from the general pattern (Campbell 1975). The logic underlying the analyst's concern is that the set of variables together constitutes the sufficient, perhaps even singular, explanation for a particular outcome, or effect. The research on the International Typographers Union by Lipset et al. (1956), for instance, pointed to the special configuration of conditions in the ITU that helped to promote internal democracy. It suggested that the special confluence of factors promoted democracy, leading to the obvious conclusion that only under certain special social and historical circumstances could such variables again come together in such a specific manner.

7. Issues of Theoretical Generalization and Refinement: The Use of Parallel and Different Cases

Because the analysis of a single case can only take the analyst so far, the best rule to follow, if possible, is to examine at least three or four pertinent cases in depth. Multiple cases permit the researcher to refine and develop theoretical arguments, and they do so precisely because case studies permit the researcher to examine cases deeply and, ultimately, to make careful comparisons among those cases.

One example will illustrate the advantages of using several cases and examining them in depth. Orum (1995) was interested in examining various theories about the origins of urban growth. Popular theories had suggested that such growth came about because of special alliances among the leading figures in different major institutional spheres, particularly local government, business, and the media. Orum suggested that such theories were limited only to contemporary circumstances and that they did not help much to explain the sources of growth in the past. Using several different cases, and studying them in great depth permitted him to come up with several important discoveries bearing upon issues of urban growth and expansion.

The first case examined was that of Milwaukee, Wisconsin. Tracing its origins back to the early nineteenth century, Orum discovered that the city seemed to go through certain stages in its growth, and that one could not simply rely on explanations of alliances among leaders of different institutional spheres. Thus, based upon intensive study, he argued that, in the earliest years, the growth of the city relied heavily on local entrepreneurs, people who promoted the city and who, among other things, sold land for it. But over time this motive force for growth changed, and the main forces turned to new economic institutions, ones that brought in growth by attracting new residents. A third stage happened when the impetus for growth shifted from the local economic enterprises, which had grown somewhat stagnant, to local government. Government sought to expand the community by adding new territory. Among other things, it also became clear in this stage that a single conception of urban growth was inappropriate; growth could take the form of new population, but also new territory. Such an insight would have been impossible had Orum relied only on the study of this single case in depth. The fourth and final phase happened as the city began to decline. In large part, the decline took place when many of its original industries left for greener pastures in other cities. Under these circumstances, a heavy burden was placed upon local government to devise ways to promote growth, either by expanding its borders or by attracting new industry through various incentives.

In effect, then, Orum's explanation for Milwaukee's growth suggested that such expansion happened by stages, and that at each stage there was a different configuration of local business and political forces responsible for such growth, and that the principal form of growth itself could vary between stages. Next, he asked whether this pattern held only for Milwaukee, or whether it could also describe the trajectory of growth and decline in other parallel industrial cities. Thus, he made comparisons in the pattern and stages of growth in Milwaukee with those in Cleveland, Ohio, a city which, on the face of it, seemed similar in many respects. In fact, the stages and forces of growth at each stage were virtually identical in Cleveland and Milwaukee. He thus argued that among American industrial cities, the nature of growth, and the forces responsible for it, showed important parallels, underscoring his argument on behalf of a stage theory of urban growth.

Finally, Orum pushed the argument one step further, wondering whether the pattern found was only characteristic of industrial growth, and cities, in America. Could the pattern of stages also apply to cities that grew up in the postindustrial era and were themselves postindustrial cities? Here he made a comparison between the patterns in Milwaukee and those in Austin, Texas, a postindustrial city he also had come to know intimately. This comparison showed that the first three stages were very similar in terms of the rapidity of growth, and in the role of entrepreneurs, local business, and local government in promoting such growth in Milwaukee and Austin alike. In the end, then, he refined his overall argument to suggest that the stage view of urban growth in America fit not only industrial-era cities, but also cities in the postindustrial era. This suggested that there appeared to be an underlying structural pattern to the growth of American cities, regardless of era. This last comparison also enabled him to draw out differences between Milwaukee and Austin, allowing for further understanding of the nature of urban growth, and difference, in the United States.

In brief, then, as the example of the various cities is intended to illustrate, the careful and systematic study of several cases can permit the researcher both to substantiate important theoretical generalizations and to refine and extend them. Again, this can be done because of the deep acquaintance the researcher gains from the study of cases, an acquaintance unlike that to be obtained with methods like surveys or experiments.

8. Conclusion

The use of a single case to develop, or to test, theoretical insights remains a very important strategy in the social sciences at the start of the twenty-first century. Indeed, it would appear to be growing in significance. But it must be executed with great care, and with a special sensitivity to theoretical issues. The major limitation in the study of the single case, or even a handful of cases, lies not in the limited number of empirical units, but in the ability of the researcher to be sensitive to issues of theory development and the gathering of relevant evidence to develop and refine that theory.

See also: Case Study: Methods and Analysis; Case-oriented Research; Human–Environment Relationship: Comparative Case Studies; Psychotherapy: Case Study; Single-subject Designs: Methodology; Time Series: General

Bibliography

Bradshaw Y, Wallace M 1991 Informing generality and explaining uniqueness: The place of case studies in comparative research. *International Journal of Comparative Sociology* **32**(1–2): 154–71

Campbell D T 1975 'Degrees of Freedom' and the case study. *Comparative Political Studies* **8**(2): 178–93

Crenson M 1971 *The Unpolitics of Air Pollution*. Johns Hopkins Press, Baltimore, MD

Feagin J R, Orum A M, Sjoberg G (eds.) 1991 *A Case for the Case Study*. University of North Carolina Press, Chapel Hill, NC

Glaser B G, Strauss A L 1967 *The Discovery of Grounded Theory: Strategies for Qualitative Research.* Aldine, Chicago

Lipset S M, Trow M, Coleman J S 1956 *Union Democracy: the Internal Politics of the International Typographical Union.* Free Press, Glencoe, IL

Lynd R, Lynd H M 1929 *Middletown: A Study in American Culture.* Harcourt Brace, New York

Merriam S B 1998 *Qualitative Research and Case Study Applications in Education.* Jossey-Bass, San Francisco

Orum A M 1995 *City-Building in America.* Westview Press, Boulder, CO

Ragin C C, Becker H S (eds.) 1992 *What Is A Case? Exploring the Foundations of Social Inquiry.* Cambridge University Press, Cambridge, UK

Ragin C, Zaret D 1983 Theory and method in comparative research: Two strategies. *Social Forces* **61**(3): 731–54

Stake R E 1995 *The Art of Case Study Research.* Sage, Thousand Oaks, CA

Warner R S 1991 Oenology: The making of *New Wine.* In: Feagin J R, Orum A M, Sjoberg G (eds.) *A Case for the Case Study.* University of North Carolina Press, Chapel Hill, NC, pp. 174–99

Whyte W F 1943 *Street Corner Society: The Social Structure of an Italian Slum.* University of Chicago Press, Chicago

Yin R K 1994 *Case Study Research: Design and Methods,* 2nd edn. Sage, Thousand Oaks, CA

A. M. Orum

Case Study: Methods and Analysis

Case study methods have been around as long as recorded history, and they presently account for a large proportion of the books and articles in anthropology, biology, economics, history, political science, psychology, sociology, and even the medical sciences. The logic of case study methods, much like that of any historian's or detective's efforts to make inferences from patterns within cases and comparisons between them, is more intuitive than the logic of statistical inference. Until relatively recently, however, the lack of formalization of the logic of case study methods inhibited them achieving their full potential for contributing to the progressive and cumulative development of theories. It is only in the last three decades that scholars have formalized case study methods and linked them to underlying arguments in the philosophy of science. Ironically, statistical methods, though less intuitive, were standardized earlier, so that attempts to formalize case study methods often misappropriated terms and concepts from statistics (McKeown 1999). More recently, case study methods have evolved from being defined 'negatively,' via contrasts to statistical methods, to being defined 'positively,' by their distinctive logic, techniques, and comparative advantages. This continuing evolution remains a contested process, but there is growing consensus on the proper procedures for carrying out case studies and the strengths and limits of such studies. It is becoming increasingly clear through this process that the comparative advantages of case study and statistical methods are largely complementary and that the two methods can thus achieve far more scientific progress together than either could alone.

1. The Definition of 'Case' and 'Case Study'

Early efforts to define 'case studies' relied on distinctions between the study of a small vs. a large number of instances of a phenomenon. Case studies thus became characterized as 'small n' studies, in contrast to 'large N' statistical studies. Related to this, one early definition stated that a 'case' is a 'phenomenon for which we report and interpret only a single measure on any pertinent variable' (Eckstein 1975). Case study researchers have increasingly rejected this definition, however, because it wrongly implies, in the language of statistics, that there is an inherent 'degrees of freedom' problem in case studies. In other words, this definition of case studies suggests that with a greater number of variables than observations on the dependent variable, case studies provided no basis for causal inference. In the view of case study researchers, however, each case includes a potentially large number of observations on intervening variables and qualitative measures of different aspects of the dependent variable, so there is not just a 'single measure' of the variables or an inherent degrees of freedom problem. This point is increasingly recognized by researchers from the statistical tradition (King et al. 1994).

In addition, the 'small *n*/large *N*' distinction implies that large *N* methods are always preferable whenever sufficient data is available. As argued below, however, case studies can serve useful theory building purposes, such as the inductive generation of new hypotheses, even when instances of a phenomenon are sufficiently numerous to allow the application of statistical methods.

For present purposes, then, a case is defined as an instance of a class of events (George 1979a, 1979b). The term 'class of events' refers here to a phenomenon of scientific interest, such as revolutions, types of governmental regime, kinds of economic system, or personality types. A case study is thus a well-defined aspect of a historical happening that the investigator selects for analysis, rather than a historical happening itself. The Cuban Missile Crisis, for example, is a historical instance of many different classes of events: cases of deterrence, coercive diplomacy, crisis management, and so on. In deciding which class of events to study and which theories to use, the researcher decides what data from the Cuban Missile Crisis is relevant to their case study of it. Of course, even if one accepts the present definition of a case, there is still room in the context of particular studies to debate such questions as: 'what is this event a case of' and 'given this phenomenon, is this event a case of it?' (Ragin and Becker 1992).

There is potential for confusion among the terms 'comparative methods,' 'case study methods,' and 'qualitative methods.' In one view the comparative method, or the use of comparisons among a small number of cases, is distinct from the case study method, which in this view involves the internal examination of single cases (see *Comparative Studies: Method and Design*). For the present purposes, however, case study methods are defined to include both within-case analysis of single cases and comparisons between or among a small number of cases. This is not an effort to claim wider meaning for the term 'case studies,' but an outgrowth of the growing consensus that the strongest means of drawing inferences from case studies is the use of a *combination* of within-case analysis and cross-case comparisons within a single study or research program, although single case studies can also play a role in theory development. As for the term 'qualitative methods,' this is sometimes used to encompass both case studies carried out with a positivist view of the philosophy of science and those implemented with a postmodern or interpretive view. This present article hews to the traditional terminology in focusing on 'case studies' as that subset of qualitative methods that has adopted a largely positivist framework.

2. The Historical Development of Case Study Methods

Case study methods have developed through several phases over the last three decades. Prior to the 1970s, 'case studies' consisted primarily of historical studies of particular events, countries, or phenomena, with little effort to cumulate results or progressively develop theories (Verba 1967). Throughout the 1970s, however, scholars who were dissatisfied with the state of case study methods, and encouraged by the example of the formalization of statistical methods, began to formalize case study methods.

First, Adam Przeworski and Henry Teune (1970) clarified the logic of 'most similar' and 'least similar' case comparisons. In the former comparison, which draws on the logic of John Stuart Mill's method of difference and mimics the experimental method, the researcher compares two cases that are similar in all but one independent variable and that differ in the outcome variable. Such a comparison may be consistent with the inference that the difference in the single independent variable that varies between the cases accounts for the difference in the dependent variable (although for a variety of reasons discussed below, this inference may be spurious). In a comparison of least similar cases, which draws on Mill's method of agreement, the researcher compares two cases that differ in all but one independent variable but that have the same value on the dependent variable. If,

Table 1
Types of case studies

Lijphart	Eckstein
atheoretical	configurative-ideographic
interpretative	disciplined-configurative
hypothesis generating	heuristic
deviant	?
theory-confirming/ infirming	crucial, most-likely, least-likely

for example, we find that teenagers are 'difficult' in both tribal societies and industrialized societies, we might be tempted to infer that it is the nature of teenagers rather than the nature of society that accounts for the difficulty of teenagers.

Arend Lijphart (1971) and Harry Eckstein (1975) contributed further to the formalization of case study methods by clarifying the differences among various types of case study research designs and theory-building goals. These authors identified similar types, although their terminology differs and Lijphart adds an important type, the 'deviant case,' for which Eckstein does not make explicit provision. Their types of case studies correspond as shown in Table 1.

The atheoretical or configurative-ideographic case study takes the form of a detailed narrative or 'story' presented in the form of a chronicle that purports to illuminate how an event came about. Such a narrative is highly specific and makes no explicit use of theory or theory-related variables. Most case studies, however, do have an explanatory purpose. These studies generally fall into the category of 'disciplined-configurative' or 'interpretive' case studies, in which general propositions are used, often implicitly, to explain specific historical cases. Another variant of such case studies is the use of cases as examples that illustrate a theory.

Heuristic case studies seek to generate new hypotheses inductively from the study of particular cases. Notably, statistical methods lack this capacity for inductively generating hypotheses, and they typically rely instead on hypotheses derived deductively or borrowed from case study research. An especially important type of case study for developing new hypotheses is the 'deviant' case study. This is the study of a case whose outcome is not predicted or explained adequately by existing theories. Unless the outcome of a deviant case turns out to be a consequence of measurement error, the case is likely to be useful for identifying variables that have been left out of existing theories. Finally, researchers can use case studies to test whether the outcomes and processes that theories predict in particular cases are in fact evident.

Eckstein's and Lijphart's contributions demonstrated that there was not just a single type of case study, but many kinds of case study research designs and many different theory-building purposes that they could serve. Their treatments differed, however, in that Lijphart relied greatly on statistical concepts and language. He was thus skeptical of the value of single case studies for building social science theories, and, consistent with the widespread preference at the time for 'large *N*' over 'small *n*' methods, he urged researchers to consider several means of either decreasing the number of variables in their models or increasing the number of cases to be studied in order to make use of statistical rather than case study methods. This advice, however, raised the risk 'conceptual stretching' (Sartori 1970), or of lumping together dissimilar cases under the same definitions. Possibly for this reason, Lijphart later placed greater emphasis instead on the controlled comparison of most similar to cases as a basis for causal inference (Lijphart 1975, Collier 1993).

Eckstein, in contrast, focused on the use of case studies for theory testing and argued that even single case studies could provide tests that might strongly support or impugn theories. In so doing, Eckstein developed the idea of a 'crucial case,' or a case that '*must closely fit* a theory if one is to have confidence in the theory's validity, or, conversely, *must not fit* equally well any rule contrary to that proposed' (Eckstein 1975, his emphasis). Eckstein argued that true crucial cases are rare, so he pointed to the alternative of 'most likely' and 'least likely' cases. A most likely case is one that is almost certain to fit a theory if the theory is true for any cases at all. The failure of a theory to explain a most likely case greatly undermines our confidence in the theory. A least likely case, conversely, is a tough test for a theory because it is a case in which the theory makes only a weak prediction. A theory's ability to explain a least likely case is strong evidence in favor of the theory. In this way, Eckstein argued, even single case studies could greatly increase or decrease our confidence in a theory or require that we alter its scope conditions.

Alexander George (1979a, 1979b) further developed case study methods by refining 'within-case' analysis and cross-case comparisons in ways that help each method compensate for the limits of the other. George argued, as Mill himself had, that the 'method of difference' and the corresponding practice of comparison of most similar cases could lead to spurious inferences. One reason for this is that no two nonexperimental cases achieve the ideal of being similar in *all* respects but one independent variable and the outcome. Thus, there is always the danger that left-out variables or residual differences in the values of the independent variables account for the difference in the outcomes of similar cases of (see *Human–Environment Relationship: Comparative Case Studies*). In addition, as Mill recognized, phenomena might be characterized by what general systems theorists have termed 'equifinality,' or the condition in which the same outcome can arise through different causal pathways or combinations of variables. Thus, there

might be no single necessary or sufficient variable for a phenomenon: it might be that either ABC or DEF causes Y, and that none of the variables A–F is itself sufficient to cause Y (see *Human–Environment Relationship: Comparative Case Studies*). In such circumstances, pair-wise comparisons of cases might wrongly reject variables that contribute to the outcome of interest in conjunction with some contexts but not with others, and might also accept as causal variables that are in fact spurious.

To compensate for these limits of controlled comparison, George developed the 'within case' methods of 'congruence testing' and 'process tracing' as means of checking on whether inferences arrived at through case comparisons were spurious (see *Pattern Matching: Methodology*). In congruence testing, the researcher checks whether the prediction a theory makes in a case, in view of the values of the case's independent variables, is congruent with the actual outcome in the case. In process tracing, the researcher examines whether the causal process a theory hypothesizes in a case is in fact evident in the sequence and values of the intervening variables in that case. Thus, process tracing might be used to test whether the residual differences between two similar cases were causal or spurious in producing a difference in these cases' outcomes. Process tracing can perform a heuristic function as well, generating new variables or hypotheses on the basis of sequences of events observed inductively in cases.

George (1979a, 1979b) also systematized case study procedures by developing what he called the method of 'structured focused comparison.' In this method, the researcher systematically: (a) specifies the research problem and the class of events to be studied; (b) defines the independent, dependent, and intervening variables of the relevant theories; (c) selects the cases to be studied and compared; (d) decides how best to characterize variance in the independent and dependent variables; and (e) formulates a detailed set of standard questions to be applied to each case. In addition, consistent with his emphasis on equifinality, George argued that case studies could be especially useful in developing what he called 'typological theories,' or contingent generalizations on '*the variety of different causal patterns* that can occur for the phenomena in question ... [and] *the conditions under which each distinctive type of causal patterns occurs*' (George 1979a, his emphasis). He thus advocated a kind of 'building block' approach to the development of theories in which each case, while rendered in terms of theoretical variables, might prove to be a distinctive causal pathway to the outcome of interest.

In the 1980s and 1990s, thousands of books and articles made use of these improvements in case study methods in a wide variety of social science research programs. Meanwhile, scholars continued to elaborate case study methods and articulate the ways in which they differed from statistical methods. David Collier, reviewing the development of case study and comparative methods, argued that these methods have advantages in defining and measuring qualitative variables in conceptually valid ways and forestalling the problem of conceptual stretching (Collier 1993). Charles Ragin argued that qualitative methods were also better than statistical methods at accounting for equifinality and complex interaction effects. Although statistical methods can model several kinds of interaction effects, Ragin noted, they can do so only at the cost of requiring a larger sample size, and models of nonlinear interactions rapidly become complex and difficult to interpret. Ragin also introduced the method of Qualitative Comparative Analysis, which uses Boolean algebra to reduce a series of comparisons of cases to the minimum number of logical statements or hypotheses that entail the results of all the cases compared (Ragin 1987). This method, he argues, makes comparisons among cases in ways that treat them inherently as configurations of variables, and that thus allow for the possibility of equifinality and complex interactions (see *Configurational Analysis*). Both Collier and Ragin also noted the limitations of case study methods, including the potential for indeterminacy when attempting to sort out rival explanations in a small number of cases, the difficulty of attaining a detailed understanding of more than a few cases, and the inability to make broad generalizations on the basis of small numbers of cases.

3. New Developments in Case Study Methods

The thousands of applications of case study methods in the last two decades have provided fertile ground for further methodological refinements. Three key recent developments include the strengthening of linkages between case study methods and the philosophy of science, the elaboration of the concept of typological theories, and the emergence of elements of consensus on the comparative advantages and limitations of case study methods.

3.1 Case Studies and the Philosophy of Science

With regard to the philosophy of science, the 'scientific realist' school of thought has emphasized that causal mechanisms, or independent stable factors that under certain conditions link causes to effects, are important to causal explanation (Little 1998). This has resonated with case study researchers' use of process tracing to uncover evidence of causal mechanisms at work. It has also provided a philosophical counterpoint to attempts by researchers from the statistical tradition to place 'causal effects,' or the expected difference in outcomes brought about by the change in a single independent variable, at the center of causal explanation (King et al. 1994). Case study researchers have argued that both causal mechanisms, which are

more easily addressed by case studies, and causal effects, which are best assessed through statistical means, are essential to the development of causal theories and causal explanations (George and Bennett 2001).

Another relevant development in the philosophy of science has been the resurgence of interest in Bayesian logic, or the logic of using new data to update prior confidence levels assigned to hypotheses. Bayesian logic differs from that of most statistics, which eschew reliance on prior probabilities. Eckstein's crucial, most likely, and least likely case study designs implicitly use a Bayesian logic, assigning prior probabilities to the likelihood of particular outcomes (McKeown 1999). One new development here is the refinement of Eckstein's approach, taking into consideration the likelihood of an outcome not just in view of one theory, but in the presence of alternative hypotheses. If a case is 'most likely' for a theory, and if the alternative hypotheses make the same prediction, then the theory will be strongly impugned if the prediction does not prove true. The failure of the theory cannot be blamed on the influence of the variables highlighted by the alternative hypotheses. Conversely, if a theory makes only a weak prediction in a 'least likely' case, the alternative hypotheses make a different prediction, but if the first theory's prediction proves true, this is the strongest possible evidence in favor of the theory (Van Evera 1997). This helps address the central problem of a Bayesian approach—that of assigning and justifying prior probabilities—even if it does not fully resolve it.

The continuing development of the logic of hypothesis testing has also been relevant to case study methods (see *Hypothesis Testing: Methodology and Limitations*). On this topic, Imre Lakatos argued that a theory can be considered progressive only if it predicts and later corroborates 'new facts,' or novel empirical content not anticipated by other theories (Lakatos 1976). This criterion helps provide a standard for judging whether process tracing, the designation of new subtypes, and the proposal of new theories from heuristic case studies are being done in a progressive or regressive way. It also provides a philosophical basis for arguing that a hypothesis can be derived from one set of observations within a case and then to some extent tested against the 'new facts' or previously unexamined or unexpected data that it predicts within that same case, although independent corroboration in other cases is usually advisable as well (Collier 1993).

3.2 Typological Theories and 'Fuzzy Logic'

A second recent development in case study methods has been the elaboration of the concept of typological theory. Typological theories occupy a middle ground between covering laws, or highly general abstract propositions, and causal mechanisms. Typological theories identify recurring conjunctions of mechanisms and provide hypotheses on the pathways through which they produce effects. Thus, like QCA, typological theories treat cases as configurations. Unlike QCA, they do not attempt to reduce the number of theoretical statements about the variables, but retain a diverse and admittedly complex set of contingent generalizations, with potentially one generalization per type. Consequently, typological theories are well suited to modeling equifinality.

To construct typological theories, researchers first specify the variables and use them to define the typological space, or the set of all mathematically possible combinations of the variables (this is sometimes termed a truth table in the philosophy of science). At first this may seem to produce an unmanageably large number of combinations: a model with five dichotomous variables, for example, would have 32 possible types. However, once the researcher begins to categorize extant cases in a preliminary way into particular types, it often becomes possible to narrow the range of cases of interest for study. Many types may remain empty, with no extant cases. Some types may be overdetermined for the outcome of interest, and hence not worthy of study unless they have an unexpected outcome. From among the cases and types that remain, the researcher can use the preliminary categorization of cases within the typological space to help identify most likely, least likely, most similar, least similar, and crucial cases for study. Cases in the typological space with unexpected outcomes, or deviant cases, can help identify new causal pathways that can be added to the existing theory in a kind of 'building block' approach (George and Bennett 2001). A related development concerns the concept of 'fuzzy logic' (Ragin 2000). Fuzzy logic treats cases as configurations but rather than using dichotomous or trichotomous variables and categorizations of cases, it allows the use of scaling to give a score on the extent to which a case fits into a certain type. In other respects, the use of fuzzy logic proceeds in ways much like those of typological theories.

3.3 The Emerging Consensus on the Strengths and Limits of Case Study Methods

A third development is that while several debates on case study methods continue, others have moved toward synthesis or even closure, and the overall picture is of an emerging consensus on the advantages limitations of case study methods. As noted above, researchers from a variety of methodological traditions have recognized that because case studies can include many observations, they do not suffer from an inherent degrees of freedom problem. At the same time, it is also widely agreed that particular case studies may suffer from indeterminacy, or an inability to exclude all but one explanation on the basis of

available process tracing evidence (Njolstad 1990). When this occurs, it may still be possible to narrow the number of plausible explanations, and it is also important to indicate as clearly as possible the extent to which the remaining hypotheses appear to be complementary, competing, and incommensurate in explaining the case.

Second, most case study researchers have readily acknowledged the limits of Mill's methods. Ragin's alternative of qualitative comparative analysis makes less restrictive assumptions, but its results are highly sensitive to changes in the measurement or coding of a single case (Goldthorpe 1997). There has thus been a movement toward typological theories and fuzzy logic, which make still less restrictive assumptions than QCA and are not so sensitive to the results of a single case. In addition, there is growing consensus that the use of within-case methods of analysis helps provide a check on the potential spuriousness of cross-case comparisons (Collier 1993, Mahoney 1999, George and Bennett 2001). Case study researchers consequently seldom if ever rely on case comparisons alone.

Third, there is growing recognition that the case selection criteria necessary for statistical studies are in some respects inappropriate for case studies. Random selection in a case study research design, for example, can result in worse biases than intentional selection (King et al. 1994). There is also increasing understanding that, consistent with the reliance of some case study designs on a Bayesian logic, case studies are sometimes intentionally selected not to be representative of some wide population but to provide the strongest possible inferences on particular theories (McKeown 1999). There is still disagreement between those who warn against any selection on the dependent variable (King et al. 1994) and those who argue that selection on the dependent variable is appropriate for some research objectives (Collier and Mahoney 1996, Ragin 2000, George and Bennett 2001). Related to this is a continuing disagreement over whether single case studies can make only limited contributions to theory building (King et al. 1994), or whether single case studies have indeed reshaped entire research programs (Rogowski 1995). There is wider agreement, however, that selection bias is potentially more severe in case studies than statistical studies because biased selection of case studies can overstate as well as understate the relationship between the independent and dependent variables (Collier and Mahoney 1996).

On the whole discussions of these issues have moved toward an emerging consensus on the comparative advantages and limitations of case study methods. These methods' advantages include the conceptualization, operationalization, and measurement of qualitative variables (conceptual validity), the avoidance of conceptual stretching, the heuristic identification of new variables and hypotheses (often through study of deviant cases), the assessment of whether statistical generalizations offer plausible or spurious explanations of individual cases, the incorporation of equifinality and complex interactions effects, and the inferences made possible by combining within-case and cross-case analyses (Collier 1993, Munck 1998, George and Bennett 2001). It is possible that new statistical methods may be able to improve upon the statistical treatment of equifinality and interaction effects, and at least narrow the gap in the treatment of this issue, but the other comparative advantages of case study methods appear to be inherent in their differences from statistical methods.

The limits of case study methods include their inappropriateness for judging the relative frequency or representativeness of cases, their weakness at performing partial correlations and establishing causal effects or causal weight, the necessarily narrow and contingent nature of their generalizations, and the danger that selection bias can be more catastrophic than in statistical studies (Collier 1993, King et al. 1994, Munck 1998, George and Bennett 2001). Fortunately, these are precisely the strengths of statistical studies.

4. Future Directions in Case Study Methods

Just as the formalization of case study methods in the 1970s inspired a generation of more sophisticated research, the recent further refinements in these methods are likely to lead to still greater sophistication in their use in the social, biological, and even physical sciences. The increasingly evident complementarity of case study and statistical methods is likely to lead toward more collaborative work by scholars using various methods. The recent interest among rational choice theorists in using case studies to test their theories, for example, is an important step in this direction (Bates et al. 1998). Because case studies, statistical methods, and formal modeling are all increasingly sophisticated, however, it is becoming less likely that a single researcher can be adept at more than one set of methods while also attaining a cutting-edge theoretical and empirical knowledge of their field. Collaboration might therefore take the form of several researchers working together using different methods, or of researchers more self-consciously building on the findings generated by those using different methods. In either form, effective collaboration requires that even as they become expert in one methodological approach, scholars must also become conversant with alternative approaches, aware of their strengths and limits, and capable of an informed reading of their substantive results.

See also: Biographical Methodology: Psychological Perspectives; Case Study: Logic; Case-oriented Research; Configurational Analysis; Human–Environment Relationship: Comparative Case Studies;

Psychotherapy: Case Study; Single-case Experimental Designs in Clinical Settings; Single-subject Designs: Methodology

Bibliography

Bates R H, Greif A, Rosenthal J, Weingast B, Levi M 1998 *Analytic Narratives*. Princeton University Press, Princeton, NJ

Collier D 1993 The comparative method. In: Finifter A W (ed.) *Political Science: the State of the Discipline II*. American Political Science Association, Washington, DC

Collier D, Mahoney J 1996 Insights and pitfalls: selection bias in qualitative research. *World Politics* **1**: 56–91

Eckstein H 1975 Case studies and theory in political science. In: Greenstein F I, Polsby N W (eds.) *Handbook of Political Science*. Addison-Wesley, Reading, MA, Vol. 7

George A L 1979a Case studies and theory development. In: Lauren P G (ed.) *Diplomacy: New Approaches in Theory, History, and Policy*. Free Press, New York

George A L 1979b The Causal nexus between cognitive beliefs and decision-making behavior: the 'Operational Code.'. In: Falkowski L S (ed.) *Psychological Models in International Politics*. Westview, Boulder, CO

George A L, Bennett A O 2001 *Case Studies and Theory Development*. MIT Press, Cambridge, MA

Goldstone J 1997 Methodological issues in comparative macro-sociology. *Comparative Social Research* **16**: 107–20

Goldthorpe J 1997 Current issues in comparative macrosociology. *Comparative Social Research* **16**: 1–26

King G, Keohane R, Verba S 1994 *Designing Social Inquiry*. Princeton University Press, Princeton, NJ

Lakatos I 1976 Falsification and the growth of scientific research programs. In: Lakatos I, Musgrave A (eds.) *Criticism and the Growth of Knowledge*. Cambridge University Press, Cambridge, UK

Lijphart A 1971 Comparative politics and the comparative method. *American Political Science Review* **65**: 682–93

Lijphart A 1975 The comparable cases strategy in comparative research. *Comparative Political Studies* **8**: 158–77

Little D 1998 *Microfoundations, Method, and Causation*. Transaction, New Brunswick, NJ

Mahoney J 1999 Nominal, ordinal, and narrative appraisal in macro-causal analysis. *American Journal of Sociology* **104**: 1154–96

McKeown T 1999 Case studies and the statistical world view. *International Organization*. **1**: 161–90

Munck G L 1998 Canons of research design in qualitative analysis. *Studies in Comparative International Development* **33**: 18–45

Njolstad O 1990 Learning from history? Case studies and the limits to theory-building. In: Gleditsch N P, Njolstad O (eds.) *Arms Races: Technological and Political Dynamics*. Sage, Newbury Park, CA

Przeworski A, Teune H 1970 *The Logic of Comparative Social Inquiry*. Wiley-Interscience, New York

Ragin C C 1987 *The Comparative Method: Moving Beyond Qualitative and Quantitative Strategies*. University of California Press, Berkeley, CA

Ragin C C 2000 *Fuzzy-Set Social Science*. University of Chicago Press, Chicago, IL

Ragin C C, Becker H S 1992 Introduction. In: Ragin C C, Becker H S (eds.) *What is a Case? Exploring the Foundations of Social Inquiry*. Cambridge University Press, Cambridge, UK

Rogowski R 1995 The role of theory and anomaly in social-scientific inference. *American Political Science Review* **89**: 467–70

Sartori G 1970 Concept misformation in comparative politics. *American Political Science Review* **64**: 1033–53

Van Evera S 1997 *Guide to Methods for Students of Political Science*. Cornell University Press Ithaca, NY

Verba S 1967 Some dilemmas in comparative research. *World Politics* **20**: 111–27

A. Bennett

Case-oriented Research

1. Introduction

Case-oriented research focuses on interconnections among parts and aspects within single cases. In this approach, the researcher attempts to make sense of each case as a singular, interpretable entity. In-depth knowledge of the cases included in a study is considered a prerequisite for the examination of patterns that might be observed across cases. Case-oriented researchers often study one case at a time, but they may also study multiple instances of a given phenomenon (e.g., comparable instances of ethnic conflict). The distinctiveness of case-oriented research is apparent when this approach is contrasted with the variable-oriented approach, where researchers focus more exclusively on cross-case patterns, without first gaining an understanding of each case.

2. Goals of Case-oriented Research

Today social scientists tend to identify case-oriented research with specific techniques of data collection linked to the observation and analysis of singular cases (e.g., direct observation of individuals at the micro level and archival research on nation-states at the macro level). While generally useful, the identity of case-oriented research with specific techniques of data collection is unfortunate, for it obscures basic differences between case-oriented research and conventional variable-oriented research. More fundamental than differences in methods of data collection is the contrast between goals (Ragin 1987). Case-oriented strategies are distinctive in that they are centrally concerned with making sense of a relatively small number of cases, selected because they are substantively or theoretically significant in some way (Eckstein 1975). Conventional variable-oriented strategies, by contrast, are centrally concerned with the problem of assessing the relationship between aspects of cases across a large number of generic 'observations,' usually with the goal of inferring general patterns that hold for a population.

For example, a researcher might use a case-oriented approach in order to study a small number of firms in an in-depth manner. Suppose these firms were all thought to be unusually successful in retaining their best employees while at the same time investing in them and thus enhancing their potential value to competing firms. To find out how they do it, a researcher would have to conduct an in-depth study of the firms in question. By contrast, a variable-oriented researcher might study the predictors of variation in rates of 'employee retention' across a large sample of firms. Is it more a matter of firm or industry characteristics? Do these two sets of factors interact? Useful answers to these questions would be based on careful analysis of relationships between variables, using data drawn from a survey of a large number of firms—the more (and the more varied), the better.

As these two examples show, what matters most is the researcher's starting point: does the researcher seek to understand specific cases or to document general patterns characterizing a population? This contrast follows a longstanding division in all of science, not just social science. Georg Henrik von Wright argues in *Explanation and Understanding* (1971) that there are two main traditions in the history of ideas regarding the conditions an explanation must satisfy in order to be considered scientifically respectable. One tradition, which he calls 'finalistic,' is anchored in the problem of making facts understandable. The other is called 'causal-mechanistic' and is anchored in the problem of prediction. The contrast between case-oriented and variable-oriented research closely parallels this fundamental division. In the two examples just described, the first researcher uses the case-oriented approach in order to make certain facts understandable, for example, the spectacular success of a handful of firms in retaining their most valuable employees; the second researcher uses the variable-oriented approach in order to derive an equation predicting levels of retention, based on a large sample of firms, and to draw inferences from this equation to an entire population.

Once the distinction between case-oriented and variable-oriented research is established and their contrasting goals acknowledged, it is clear that the importance of techniques of data collection as bearers of the 'case-oriented vs. variable-oriented' distinction begins to fade. For example, it is clear that a researcher using case-oriented methods to study a handful of firms might benefit from conducting surveys of their employees and performing a conventional variable-oriented analysis of these data. The results of the survey would contribute to this researcher's depth of knowledge about the firms in question, just as interviewing their top executives or studying their archives would contribute useful information. Likewise, it is clear that the researcher using variable-oriented methods to predict rates of retention could benefit from interviews of top executives or personnel officers to help interpret results found in the analysis of the predictors of retention. Still, the first researcher would remain focused on the problem of understanding the handful of firms in question, while the second would remain focused on the problem of explaining variation in retention rates across a large number of firms and making inferences from this sample to a population. The important point here is that data collection techniques *per se* are relatively neutral; what matters most is the researcher's goal and the contrasting research strategies that follow from different goals.

3. Logic of Case-oriented Research

The logic of case-oriented research is fundamentally configurational. Different parts of each case are understood in relation to one another and in terms of the total picture or package that they form together. The organizing idea in such research is that the parts of a case may constitute a coherent whole; that they have an integrity and coherence considered together. For example, researchers who study families often find that patterns of interpersonal accommodation are so enmeshed that a 'dysfunction' cannot be remedied without addressing many different aspects of a family all at once. Likewise, researchers who study cultures often observe that cultural traits seem to come in packages that defy easy disassembly. The 'parts' that case-oriented researchers examine can be quite varied. In macro-level research, for example, the 'parts' of a case might include institutions, path dependencies, social structures, historical patterns and trends, routine practices, cultural beliefs, singular events, event sequences, connections to other cases, the case's larger environment, and so on. What matters most is that the investigator makes sense of multiple aspects of the case in an encompassing manner, using theory as a guide.

Donald Campbell (1975) offers a rough formalization of this approach in his examination of the logic of case-oriented research. Campbell argues that at first glance the in-depth study of a single case appears to be lacking in scientific merit because there is only one case to explain and many possible explanations to choose from. He notes, however, that case-study researchers routinely 'reject' theories because they do not explain the facts of their case. Further, despite having only one case, they must often struggle to find theories that work. Why is it so difficult? The key to this puzzle is the simple fact that every theory has many implications, relevant both to features of the case in question and to causal processes and sequences operating within the case. Thus, researchers evaluate many theoretical implications relevant to their cases to see if their cases conform to expectations. Not all features of a case may be compatible with the initial theory, and the researcher must either find an alternate theory that works better, revise an existing theory, or propose an entirely new one (Walton 1992).

Campbell (1975) suggests that each separate theoretical implication can be seen as a different 'observation' for 'testing' a theory. Thus, a single case becomes many observations—some contradicting and some supporting competing theories. Collectively, competing theories and their different implications define all theoretically relevant aspects of the case in question. The researcher's task is to see which theory does the best job of explaining aspects of the case relevant not only to its own implications, but also to the implications of competing theories. Thus, after defining and selecting relevant aspects of the case, the researcher assesses the explanatory power of each theory. The theory (or combination of compatible theories) that best covers both its own implications and those of competing theories prevails and provides the basis for the investigator's representation of the case.

In the end, the researcher crafts an explanation that satisfies as many theoretical implications as possible in a coherent manner. The success of a case study hinges on (a) the number of relevant aspects of the case the researcher can encompass with his or her explanation, (b) the success of the researcher in showing that his or her portrait of the case actually makes sense of all theoretically relevant aspects, and (c) the agreement of other scholars that all relevant aspects of the case in question have in fact been addressed by the researcher in a convincing manner. Of course, the most successful case studies accomplish much more than theoretical and substantive coherence. They also may advance theory or establish important lessons for policy makers (White 1992). Still, theoretical and substantive coherence should be considered preconditions for these more ambitious goals (Yin 1994).

Campbell's (1975) argument that case-oriented researchers test multiple theoretical implications for each case underscores the configurational nature of this type of research. Because theoretical implications direct the researcher's attention to 'observations' (i.e., different aspects of a single case) that cannot be independent from one another, the researcher must make sense of them all at once, as a package. Furthermore, because different theories typically have implications about different aspects of the case, the researcher's attention is directed to a broad range of aspects, all of which may be interconnected in some way. Thus, case-oriented researchers must examine overlapping configurations of aspects as they weigh the explanatory power of competing theories.

4. Case-oriented Research on Multiple Instances

Case-oriented researchers sometimes conduct a series of case studies, selecting cases strategically so that the knowledge the cases generate accumulates. For example, a specific type of evidence that is not available in one case may prompt the investigator to select for his or her next study a case that offers this evidence. In this manner, case-oriented researchers may develop theoretical arguments in much the same way that psychoanalysts build theory from the analysis of a series of patients, admitting to their practice patients that promise to enhance their thinking and their theories in some way.

This case-by-case, grounded approach can be contrasted with a research strategy that takes *multiple instances* of a phenomenon as its starting point. For example, a researcher might be interested in the formation of green parties in Western Europe and focus on a handful of parallel cases. The key contrast between the study of multiple instances and studying a series of cases is the *timing* of the selection of cases. In serial case studies, findings from one case determine the selection of the next case; in the study of multiple instances, by contrast, the researcher identifies multiple instances of a phenomenon at the outset of an investigation. Of course, the researcher's definition of the population of cases may shift in the course of the research as the investigator learns more about the phenomenon (see Ragin 1997). The key point is that the study of multiple instances begins with a preliminary specification of relevant cases.

Designs appropriate for the case-oriented study of multiple instances are varied, with the number of cases ranging from two to as many as the researcher can study in a detailed manner. Still, there are two general approaches to the study of multiple instances: 'bottom-up' and 'top-down.' Neither strategy is practiced in pure form, and there are also many mixed and hybrid strategies in between these two hypothetical extremes, just as the there are many ways to blend and mix the study of multiple instances, chosen all at once, and the grounded selection of cases one at a time.

The bottom-up approach to multiple instances attempts to develop a more or less succinct explanation of each case, in relative isolation from other cases. Of course, it is impossible for researchers to wear blinders or to forget what they have already learned, and knowledge of one case will inevitably impinge on the examination of subsequent cases. Still, the goal of the bottom-up approach is to give each case, in effect, a separate voice and thereby allow for maximum diversity. After completing each separate case study, the researcher turns to the task of comparing cases, and each case is used as a lens for viewing other cases. The goal of this cross-fertilization of case studies is to help the researcher identify all possibly relevant factors and to revise understandings of each case using insights gained from other cases. On the basis of these comparisons, the researcher builds an analytic frame for the outcome in question, which embraces all causally relevant conditions that have some degree of cross-case relevance. In the end, the researcher builds a more complete account of each case and also develops a strong basis for identifying both cross-case

patterns and different types of cases (e.g., different paths to some outcome).

The top-down approach is more theory centered and more dependent upon prior knowledge and research. Based on existing theoretical and substantive knowledge, the researcher develops an analytic frame for the outcome under investigation, much like a survey researcher develops a questionnaire. This 'instrument' is then applied to each case in a relatively uniform and structured manner. That is, each case is 'interrogated' in much the same way. A central goal of the top-down approach, in addition to the goals of reliability and replicability, is to ensure that the cases selected for in-depth study have equal voice and the results are not skewed toward the most prominent cases, the cases with the most or best data, or the cases that the researcher simply happens to know best. While the analytic frame for the top-down approach is established at the beginning of the research, it is, of course, open to revision as researchers learn more about their cases.

The top-down approach also may be used when researchers seek to study a specific range of cases or specific categories of cases. In this approach, a preexisting analytic frame is used to guide the selection of instances for in-depth study. The goal is to select cases that maximize variation on causally relevant conditions while economizing on the number of cases. For example, a researcher might construct a two-by-two table cross-tabulating levels of two main causal conditions (e.g., high versus low levels of development and high versus low levels of democracy) and then seek to 'fill' each cell of this table with at least one case. The investigator would then conduct in-depth studies of the selected cases, knowing that important causal conditions are well represented in the set of instances chosen for examination.

5. Incongruities Between Case-oriented and Variable-oriented Research

Case-oriented research is distinct from variable-oriented research in many ways. The distinctiveness of the case-oriented approach is often overlooked, and researchers using different strategies talk past each other when discussing their methods. While some scholars emphasize philosophical differences between case-oriented and variable-oriented strategies, there are striking and profound differences between the two approaches at the 'practical level.' The practical level refers to the relatively mundane procedures researchers use when working with evidence to produce social scientific representations of what they have learned—that is, summaries of findings and patterns.

The importance of practical differences as a basis for miscommunication between case-oriented and variable-oriented researchers can be seen clearly in the contrasts between two very simple procedures: the search for commonalities across multiple instances of a phenomenon in case-oriented research and the examination of the correlation between two variables across a sample of observations in variable-oriented research. The search for commonalities is usually part of an effort to derive limited generalizations from the in-depth study of a modest number of instances. For example, a researcher might attempt to identify common antecedent conditions for an outcome these cases share. This researcher might argue further that the common antecedents are necessary conditions for the outcome—that is, if theoretical and substantive knowledge support this interpretation. For example, a researcher conducting an in-depth study of a select group of firms—those that are able to both invest in and retain their best employees—might identify causally relevant features shared by these firms. Shared features, in turn, might point to a possible formula for success and offer lessons for other firms. The search for commonalities across a select group of cases is the most basic case-oriented strategy applied to multiple instances. By contrast, the examination of a correlation between two variables across a sample of observations in variable-oriented research is usually conducted with the goal of establishing that two conditions or aspects covary. For example, high rates of retention might be correlated with high levels of employee compensation across a sample of firms. This correlation, in turn, might be interpreted causally: the researcher would argue that one reason firms differ in their employee retention rates is that they differ in how well they compensate employees.

While both procedures seem deceptively simple and straightforward, these two ways of producing results from evidence involve sharply contrasting practical orientations toward cases, outcomes, and causal conditions:

5.1 Cases

When a researcher using variable-oriented methods computes a correlation between two variables, the relevant cases become more or less invisible and variables take center stage. Furthermore, the set of cases included in the computation must be fixed before the researcher can compute the correlation. Once this set is fixed, usually at the outset of an investigation, it is rarely altered. What matters most is that the cases (which are understood as 'observations') belong to the same general 'population' and that they be drawn from this population with an eye toward randomness or representativeness or some combination of these criteria.

In a case-oriented study of commonalities, by contrast, cases have clear identities and are usually chosen specifically because of their substantive significance or theoretical relevance. Furthermore, the set of relevant cases may shift during the investigation because the researcher may decide that one or more

cases do not 'fit' with the others. For example, a researcher studying 'firms that invest in and retain their top employees' might decide that several firms originally thought to belong to this group really don't belong, and that maybe one or more that were thought to be outside this group actually belong in it. This flexibility is maintained throughout the investigation because the core concepts (e.g., 'investing in employees') may be revised as the researcher learns more about relevant instances.

5.2 Outcomes

In correlational studies researchers usually identify a 'dependent variable'—an outcome that varies across cases. Typically, such outcomes are aspects of cases that vary by level, for example, level of satisfaction, level of bureaucratization, and so on. Sometimes the outcome variable is categorical, indicating whether or not some event has occurred (e.g., filing a complaint), and sometimes it is a frequency or a rate (e.g., rate of employee retention). The important consideration, in this procedure, is that the outcome vary across 'observations.' The goal of the research typically is to explain, if possible, why cases have different values on the dependent variable. Such research is centrally concerned with the question of 'why.' For example, a researcher might seek to explain why some employees are more satisfied than average and others less so, why some firms have higher retention rates than average and others less than average, and so on.

In a case-oriented study of commonalities, by contrast, the outcome is often something that does not vary substantially across the chosen cases. In a study of firms, for example, cases might be chosen precisely because they all display the same outcome—a specific pattern of successful retention. Recall that the goal of a case-oriented study of commonalities is to identify common causal conditions linked to a specific outcome across a relatively small number of purposefully selected cases. Thus, the focus is on cases with a specific outcome, not cases that vary widely in how much they display this outcome. While the outcomes in a study of this type will not be exactly identical across cases, the researcher must demonstrate that the outcomes in the cases selected are in fact enough alike to be treated as instances of the same thing. Finally, unlike correlational studies, which are centrally concerned with the question of 'why' (as in: why some more than others?), case-oriented studies are centrally concerned with the question of 'how' (as in: how does it happen?). How do firms retain their most valuable employees?

5.3 Causal Conditions

In a correlational study, causation may be inferred from a pattern of covariation. If a variable thought to represent a cause or to be an indicator of a key causal condition is strongly correlated with the outcome variable, then the researcher may make a causal inference. Usually, the researcher will assess the relative strength of several causal variables at the same time. The typical goal is either to find out which one explains the most variation in the outcome variable or simply to assess the relative importance of the different independent variables. In effect, variables compete with each other to explain variation. In most investigations, each causal variable is considered sufficient, by itself, for the outcome or an increment in the outcome. That is, each one is considered an 'independent' variable capable of affecting the outcome variable, regardless of the values of other causal variables.

In a case-oriented study of commonalities, by contrast, causation is typically understood conjuncturally. The goal of this type of analysis is to identify the main causal conditions shared by relevant cases. Causal conditions do not compete with each other, as they do in correlational research; they combine. How they combine or 'fit together' is something that researchers try to discern using their in-depth knowledge of cases. Because all the cases have more or less the same outcome, the usual reasoning is that the causally relevant conditions shared by cases provide important clues regarding which factors must be present to produce the outcome in question. When constructing this argument, the researcher is especially sensitive to the possibility that a given causal requirement (i.e., a necessary condition) may be met in a variety of different ways.

These and other practical differences in how researchers using case-oriented versus variable-oriented methods work with evidence to produce results provide many opportunities for disjunctures in findings. For example, from the perspective of variable-oriented work, the study of commonalities across a small number of instances is fraught with analytic sins and errors: (a) The number of cases is too small and too nonrandom to warrant any kind of inference (King et al. 1994). (b) The procedure 'selects on the dependent variable' (i.e., focuses on cases all with more or less the same value on the outcome variable). This practice may deflate otherwise robust correlations (Collier 1995, Collier and Mahoney 1996, King et al. 1994). (c) Researchers may drop cases that 'don't fit' at various stages of the analysis, which seriously undermines any effort to generalize beyond the cases that remain (King et al. 1994). (d) The most important causal factors (i.e., causally relevant commonalities) do not vary and thus are impossible to assess, and so on (Lieberson 1991, 1994; Goldthorpe 1991, 1997).

Likewise, from the perspective of case-oriented work, the examination of the correlation between a causal and outcome variable across many cases is fundamentally flawed: (a) Typically, there are so many cases that there is no way for the researcher to know if they are all really comparable and thus belong together in the same analysis. (b) Fixing a population or sample boundary also fixes the assumption of homogeneity, which usually is not warranted. Investigators should be able to redefine the set of relevant cases as they learn more about them (Ragin 1997). (c) It is difficult to determine how something 'comes about' by comparing cases with different levels of the outcome. The partial instances (i.e., those with lower scores on the outcome variable) are likely to provide many false leads (Lijphart 1971, 1975, Ragin 1997). (d) It is pointless to try to isolate the 'independent' effect of any causal condition when several factors usually must combine for a particular outcome to occur (George 1979), and so on. In short, at a practical level the two approaches seem almost antithetical. It is no wonder that findings diverge and researchers often talk past each other (Rueschemeyer 1991; Ragin 1997).

6. Bridging Case-oriented and Variable-oriented Research

While the gulf between case-oriented and variable-oriented research seems great, it is possible to span it. Consider the following scenario: a researcher using case-oriented methods studies several instances of an outcome (e.g., a small number of firms that are very successful in investing in and retaining top employees) documents causally relevant commonalities, and then constructs a general, composite argument about how these firms do it. This argument leads to four specific recommendations (which might be labeled X_1 to X_4) based on the observed commonalities. A second researcher reads the report of this study and decides to evaluate it with a large sample using variable-oriented methods. This researcher collects information on a random sample of firms and finds that, as independent variables, X_1 to X_4 do *not* distinguish more successful from less successful firms, using various measures of employee retention. In short, the second researcher shows that there is no statistically significant difference in the retention rates for firms with and without these four aspects, considering these aspects one at a time or in an additive, multivariate equation.

What went wrong? Usually, the researcher using variable-oriented methods will claim that the first researcher's 'sample' was 'too small' and 'unrepresentative.' Thus, the identification of X_1 to X_4 took advantage of specific aspects of the selected cases. The first researcher might counterattack by arguing that causally relevant commonalities identified through in-depth study are very difficult to represent as 'variables,' and that the second researcher's crude attempt to operationalize them fell far short. Indeed, the first researcher might argue that it would take in-depth knowledge of each firm included in the variable-oriented study to capture these conditions appropriately and contextually.

These criticisms and countercriticisms are quite common. However, the incongruity between the two hypothetical studies can be resolved without resorting to derogation. The first researcher in this example—the one using case-oriented methods—selected on instances of the outcome and identified four causally relevant conditions shared by the firms in question. In essence, this researcher worked backwards from the outcome to causes and thus identified potential *necessary* conditions for the outcome (Ragin 2000). Are these conditions truly necessary? In part, this is an empirical question. To gain confidence, the researcher should examine as many instances of the outcome as possible, to see if they agree in displaying these four causally relevant conditions (or their causal equivalents). But it is also a question about existing knowledge. Is the argument that these four conditions are necessary consistent with theoretical and substantive knowledge? Do they make sense as necessary conditions? If the researcher's finding is consistent with existing substantive and theoretical knowledge, then the argument that these four conditions are necessary is strengthened.

How should the second researcher—the one using variable-oriented methods—respond to the argument that these four factors are necessary conditions? At a more abstract level, the specification of necessary conditions is relevant primarily to the identification of cases that are candidates for an outcome. Cases cannot be candidates for an outcome if they do not meet the necessary conditions. But many cases may meet the necessary conditions for an outcome and still not exhibit the outcome, because they lack additional conditions which, when combined with the necessary conditions, establish sufficiency for the outcome. In fact, the cases displaying the outcome may be only a small minority of those that meet the necessary conditions. Thus, while there are clear gains from specifying necessary conditions, as in the hypothetical case-oriented study, the identification of causally relevant commonalities shared by instances of an outcome does not establish the conditions that are sufficient for an outcome. Thus, the variable-oriented researcher's finding that these four conditions do not distinguish low-retention firms from high-retention firms across a large sample of firms does *not* directly challenge the argument that these conditions are necessary.

The variable-oriented analysis of these four conditions across a large sample of firms is much more directly relevant to their *sufficiency*. To show that these conditions are jointly sufficient for the outcome, it would be important to demonstrate that when these four conditions are combined the outcome follows. In other words, the variable-oriented researcher could evaluate sufficiency by examining the correspondence between the combination of the four causes, on the one hand, and the outcome, on the other, across a large sample of firms. Still, this analysis would be an evaluation of sufficiency, not necessity, and the results of this analysis would not bear in a direct manner on the claim of necessity made by the case-oriented researcher.

This sketch identifies only one of several ways to span case-oriented and variable-oriented inquiry. The general and most important point is that it *is* possible to join these two approaches if researchers are careful to distinguish between necessity and sufficiency and to separate the analysis of these two aspects. More generally, this discussion underscores the distinctiveness of case-oriented research, especially the case-oriented study of multiple instances of an outcome.

See also: Case Study: Logic; Case Study: Methods and Analysis; Classification: Conceptions in the Social Sciences; Configurational Analysis; Explanation: Conceptions in the Social Sciences; Person-centered Research; Psychotherapy: Case Study; Single-case Experimental Designs in Clinical Settings; Single-subject Designs: Methodology; Time Series: General; Triangulation: Methodology

Bibliography

Campbell D T 1975 Degrees of freedom and the case study. *Comparative Political Studies* **8**: 178–93

Collier D 1995 Translating quantitative methods for qualitative researchers: The case of selection bias. *American Political Science Review* **89**: 461–6

Collier D, Mahoney J 1996 Insights and pitfalls: Selection bias in qualitative research. *World Politics* **49**: 56–91

Eckstein H 1975 Case study and theory in political science. In: Greenstein F I, Polsby N W (eds.) *Handbook of Political Science, Volume 7, Strategies of Inquiry*. Addison-Wesley, Reading, MA

George A 1979 Case studies and theory development: The method of structured, focussed comparison. In: Lauren P G (ed.) *Diplomacy: New Approaches in History, Theory and Policy*. Free Press, New York

Goldthorpe J 1991 The uses of history in sociology: Reflections on some recent tendencies. *British Journal of Sociology* **42**: 211–30

Goldthorpe J 1997 Current issues in comparative macrosociology. *Comparative Social Research* **16**: 1–26

King G, Keohane R O, Verba S 1994 *Designing Social Inquiry: Scientific Inference in Qualitative Research*. Princeton University Press, Princeton, NJ

Lieberson S 1991 Small N's and big conclusions: An examination of the reasoning in comparative studies based on a small number of cases. *Social Forces* **70**: 307–20

Lieberson S 1994 More on the uneasy case for using Mill-type methods in small-N comparative studies. *Social Forces* **72**: 1225–37

Lijphart A 1971 Comparative politics and comparative method. *American Political Science Review* **65**: 682–93

Lijphart A 1975 The comparable cases strategy in comparative research. *Comparative Political Studies* **8**: 158–75

Ragin C C 1987 *The Comparative Method: Moving Beyond Qualitative and Quantitative Strategies*. University of California Press, Berkeley, CA

Ragin C C 1997 Turning the tables: How case-oriented research challenges variable-oriented research. *Comparative Social Research* **16**: 27–42

Ragin C C 2000 *Fuzzy-Set Social Science.* University of Chicago Press, Chicago

Rueschemeyer D 1991 Different methods—contradictory results? Research on development and democracy. In: Ragin C C (ed.) *Issues and Alternatives in Comparative Social Research.* E. J. Brill, Leiden, The Netherlands

Walton J 1992 Making the theoretical case. In: Ragin C C, Becker H S (eds.) *What Is a Case? Exploring the Foundations of Social Inquiry.* Cambridge University Press, New York

White H 1992 Cases are for identity, for explanation, or for control. In: Ragin C C, Becker H S (eds.) *What Is a Case? Exploring the Foundations of Social Inquiry.* Cambridge University Press, New York

Wright G H von 1971 *Explanation and Understanding.* Cornell University Press, Ithaca, NY

Yin R K 1994 *Case Study Research: Design and Methods,* 2nd edn. Sage, Thousand Oaks, CA

C. C. Ragin

Cassandra/Cornucopian Debate

The Cassandra/Cornucopian debate is one of many names given to an argument between two extreme positions on the prospects for human society and the environment in the face of population and economic growth. So-called Cassandras (after the Greek princess given the power of prophecy but denied the power of persuasion) contend that unchecked growth in numbers of people and material consumption rates will inevitably lead to environmental and social catastrophe. This group is alternately called doomsayers, pessimists, catastrophists, or neo-Malthusians and stereotypically is associated with ecologists and environmentalists. Cornucopians (after the Greek legend of the 'horn of plenty' that overflows with whatever its owner wishes for) believe that human ingenuity and free markets will allow the human species to adapt to any conceivable pressures caused by growth of the human enterprise. They are referred to alternately as optimists, panglossians, or exemptionists, and stereotypically are associated with free-market economists. The debate originated at least as far back as Malthus in the eighteenth century, flared up with special intensity in the late 1960s and 1970s over the issue of exhaustible natural resources, and continues in more subdued form today as reflected in the issue of global environmental change.

1. Historical Roots

The roots of the Cassandran position extend as far back as the Reverend Thomas Malthus, who in 1798 published the first and most pessimistic version of his tract *Essay on the Principle of Population* (Malthus 1798). In it, he argued that population tends to grow at a geometric rate (i.e., a constant percent increase, but ever-larger absolute increments) while necessities (particularly food supply) tend to grow at an arithmetic rate (constant absolute increments). Therefore, sustained population growth would inevitably outstrip its means of support, unless subjected to certain 'checks.' In the first edition of the essay, these 'positive checks' were war, pestilence, disease, and famine. The second edition introduced the possibility of 'preventive checks,' which included moral restraint, celibacy, late marriage, and abstinence. If the preventive checks did not slow population growth before it overran the limits of the land to support it, then the positive checks would come into play.

Malthus principally was interested in whether aid to the poor could be expected to lift them out of poverty (he concluded that it could not). Concern over the consequences of population and economic growth for human welfare and the environment has waxed and waned several times since the publication of Malthus's essay. Particularly relevant to contemporary scholarship is the growth of neo-Malthusianism since World War II. Luten (1980) traces this recent history through concern over population growth and its impact on resource use and economic growth in the 1940s and 1950s (see, e.g., Osborn 1953, Coale and Hoover 1958), to pollution and pesticides in the 1960s (notably Carson 1962), and back to population and resources in the late 1960s and 1970s (Paddock and Paddock 1967, Ehrlich 1968, Meadows et al. 1972).

The Cornucopian position has roots that extend back to the mercantilist school of economic thought in the sixteenth century, which emphasized the positive effect of population growth on economic production. It was the mercantilist economist Jean Bodin who claimed 'There is no wealth but men.' More recently, Boserup (1965, 1981) argued that increased population size and its associated demand for food itself induced new agricultural production techniques and increased density facilitated the flow and application of new knowledge. In this way a growing population aided rather than hindered development.

These points of view and others have been reflected and expanded on in Cornucopian responses to the post-war rise of neo-Malthusian concern. For example, Barnett and Morse (1963) argued that technological progress can more than offset resource scarcity, while Simon (1981, 1996) and Kahn et al. (1976) have been the most visible Cornucopian standard-bearers in recent decades.

2. Cassandras

The most recent crest of neo-Malthusian concern occurred in the 1960s and 1970s, driven by a number of writers and researchers concerned with what they saw as the inevitability of rising levels of pollution and increasingly scarce food supply and nonrenewable natural resources. Most of these arguments pointed to material consumption and especially population growth as the key drivers of these problems, and advocated immediate measures to reduce consumption and control population. For example, Hardin (1968) argued that population growth inevitably leads to the degradation of common property resources, the root of many environmental problems, and that the only solution to the 'population problem' was 'mutual coercion, mutually agreed upon,' that is, societies must agree to enforce limits upon their own reproductive behavior.

The most well-known advocate of the Cassandra position was Ehrlich, who in 1968 published *The Population Bomb*, a short popular book declaring that the struggle to feed humanity was over and had been lost; hundreds of millions were destined to starve in the coming decades. It foresaw a future so dire that it advocated consideration of a system of 'triage' in foreign aid policy first recommended by Paddock and Paddock (1967). The system would cut off aid to countries such as India deemed beyond help due to rapid population growth and dim prospects for improvements in agricultural production and would focus instead on countries such as Pakistan that might possibly avoid massive starvation with the right kind of assistance.

In 1972 the sense of impending doom was heightened further by the publication of *The Limits to Growth* (Meadows et al. 1972), a book by a group of researchers at the Massachusetts Institute of Technology that argued that the human population was approaching the limit of the planet's ability to sustain it, and without fundamental societal changes we would soon exceed that limit, triggering a dramatic increase in death rates, catastrophic environmental degradation, and social chaos. Their conclusion received an enormous amount of attention, in part because it was based on one of the first attempts to create a computer model of the world as a single system. They subjected their 'World3' model to an extensive sensitivity analysis, but in all cases it produced an 'overshoot and collapse' pattern: a surge in population followed sooner or later by a crash. The robustness of the result seemed to lend great credibility to their conclusions.

3. A Storm of Criticism

Both *The Population Bomb* and *The Limits to Growth* sold millions of copies, and this wave of academic and popular attention to a presumed approach to the planet's carrying capacity generated a storm of criticism. *The Limits to Growth* itself received special attention by academic critics (Maddox 1972, Cole et al. 1973, Nordhaus 1973, Sanderson 1994), perhaps because its basis in computer modeling gave it an aura

of academic respectability that more popular treatments lacked. Criticism covered a wide range of issues, but there were several common themes centered on the perceived lack of economic principles.

3.1 Technical Progress

Neoclassical economics views scarcity not as absolute but as relative and as a function of technology. Technical progress lowers the cost of making a resource more accessible. For example, improvements in irrigation systems make it cost effective to expand the area of irrigated land, essentially increasing the total land available for cultivation. Thus, expressing limits in fixed physical units, as was done in *World3* and in other carrying-capacity arguments, left out the crucial role of technology in expanding the pool of resources available to society.

3.2 Adjustment Mechanisms

Many critics pointed out the lack of accounting for well-known adjustment mechanisms in response to scarcity, especially price systems. In an ideal market economy, as a resource becomes relatively more scarce, its price rises. This rising price induces a host of adjustments: recycling; conservation; the development of better methods of discovery, extraction, and production; and the substitution of other goods, all of which have the effect of essentially increasing supply. An often-quoted example is that although global oil consumption rates increased between the 1970s and 1990s, oil reserves grew rather then declined over this time period—a result of price-induced improvements in exploration, extraction, and efficiency.

The *World3* model did not include a price system at all. It also aggregated the world into a single region, eliminating trade as a possibility, and aggregated over many goods so that substitution was not possible. Thus, many economists put little stock in its results, or in the conclusions of arguments that did not account for the ability of a market economy to respond to scarcity.

3.3 Methodological Weaknesses

Several critics focused on particular aspects of the methodology of *The Limits to Growth* study. Relationships between variables in the model may have been plausible, but were based on little more than the authors' intuition, ignoring theory and evidence in economics, demography, and other fields. Also, several studies showed that the 'overshoot and collapse' behavior of their model was by no means inevitable. If changes in variables were made slowly rather than suddenly, the model produced steady growth (Cole et al. 1973). If the prices were included or the possibility of substitution was allowed for, or alternative assumptions about population growth or technical change were made, model outcomes changed drastically, in some cases producing continuous growth (Nordhaus 1973).

4. Cornucopians and their Critics

In many ways the Cornucopian credo is neoclassical economic reasoning taken to an extreme. Simon was the best-known Cornucopian. In *The Ultimate Resource* (1981; a 1996 follow-up did not alter the basic message) he argued in essence that on balance people create more than they destroy, so that the more people, the better the world. While he agreed that larger populations can create short-run scarcity and environmental degradation, he believed that these problems presented challenges to which society would always adapt, improving itself in the process. In the long run, society is better off—prices are lower, the environment is cleaner, and consumption is greater—than if the problems had never arisen.

Critics of the Cornucopian position seized on several perceived weaknesses. In general, it is often argued that the theory is not testable: any scarcity or environmental degradation that is encountered can be explained away as either a market imperfection or as a short-run problem that will in fact lead to a long-run benefit. By presuming to explain everything, it explains nothing. More specific criticisms have focused on several main points.

4.1 Discontinuities

Many critics argue that Cornucopians have a blind faith that the future will repeat the past. Because resource prices have generally fallen, and by some measures and in some places the environment has improved, it is presumed that these trends will always continue. Cornucopians argue that there is no reason to expect the future to be different from the past in terms of society's ability to adapt to and benefit from scarcity-induced challenges. Cassandrans counter that there is every reason to expect the future to be different, since gradual increases in environmental degradation driven by the increasing scale of human impact are likely to eventually push ecosystems past thresholds beyond which decline will be rapid and perhaps uncontrollable.

4.2 Insufficient Accounting for Natural Science

The Cornucopian position is often accused of focusing on improvement in material consumption and human welfare at the expense of associated degradation of the environment. Many ecologists and other natural scientists considered the treatment of environmental impacts by Simon and others to be perfunctory and unconvincing at best, and deliberately misleading at worst. For example, while optimists often focused on improvements in the levels of pollution of, for example, DDT or PCBs (improvements that, Cassandras often point out, were driven in large part by the concern of environmentalists), they usually said little about larger issues such as climate change or biodiversity loss. Critics accuse them of being quick to dismiss scientific consensus when convenient to their argument, and of suggesting that such consensus was a conspiracy to obtain more research money.

4.3 Unfounded Assumptions

Simon's argument was often attacked for its reliance on the assumption of a rather mechanical link between human population numbers and the assumed stock of knowledge and other forms of social capital. Sanderson (1980) points out that Simon assumes social capital grows automatically with the size of the population, and that it has an unusually large effect on production. To some extent, population growth's positive long-run impact on economic production is built into Simon's model by assumption.

5. Winners and Losers

Although the debate is ongoing, it is possible to assess the accuracy of some of the claims made so far by the two sides. For example, Malthus has turned out to be wrong so far, because he failed to anticipate the opening up of new agricultural lands, the scope for improvements in agricultural technology, storage, and transport, and the decline in Western fertility. Similarly, the predictions of mass starvation made in the 1960s and 1970s never materialized; the Green Revolution in agriculture raised yields much more than anticipated, and developing country population growth slowed as a transition to lower fertility was begun. Nor did protracted shortages in natural resources materialize. This outcome was highlighted by a much-publicized bet made between Simon and Ehrlich in 1980. The two wagered over whether the prices of five metals (chosen by Ehrlich) would rise over the decade (indicating scarcity); Simon won on all counts as the prices of all five fell. Furthermore, as of yet there are no signs of *Limits to Growth*-type scenarios coming to pass. Supporters of the project emphasize that independent of the value of their scenarios, there was value in the attempt to model the world as a system, however crudely, as a first step toward an important new direction of research. However, Sanderson (1994) points out that *World3* was an 'evolutionary dead-end'—even the authors' own follow-up study in 1992 presented no substantial advance over the original model.

On the Cornucopian side, Simon's argument that population growth is unambiguously positive for long-term economic growth was certainly influential in countering a focus on the negative consequences of growth, but it was not adopted wholesale by economists. Mainstream economics has come to no strong conclusion on whether population growth influences economic growth. More recently, studies in Asia suggest that age structure effects of fertility reduction in some settings can stimulate growth if combined with other economic and political measures.

Some other Cornucopian articles of faith have not fared well. Nuclear energy did not solve the energy problem, as several technological optimists predicted, and while the oil price increases of the 1970s have since abated, the fossil-fuel-driven problem of global climate change has not gone away.

6. Resolution?

Attempts have been made to resolve the Cassandra/Cornucopian debate in a number of ways. Some conclude that the truth lies somewhere in between the two extremes: the outlook is neither as rosy nor as dismal as these two camps believe. Others conclude that each may have particular aspects of the story right. For example, Cornucopians may be right that we can feed an expanding population without massive famine, but Cassandras may be correct in emphasizing that this will come at great environmental cost if current trends continue.

In the absence of resolution, lessons drawn from the debate could facilitate progress on contemporary issues related to global environmental change. For example, the climate change issue has given rise to a new group of models, called integrated assessment models, which share some features with the early world-systems models: they are often global in scope, they seek to incorporate feed-backs between society and the environment, and they cover long time-scales. History offers lessons on the dangers of aggregation, the importance of grounding relationships in theory and data, and the importance of transparent assumptions and treatments of uncertainty. In addition, the debate over the Earth's capacity to sustain society has not disappeared; current manifestations include the issue of human-induced loss of 'ecosystem services' such as soil aeration, pollination, air and water purification, and element cycling. Key economic concepts left out of earlier arguments are being confronted: ecologists argue that there are no practical substitutes for ecosystem services, their supply is fixed, and their constraint on production seems to be near enough to matter. In this case, the history of the

Cassandra/Cornucopian debate may be contributing to a more productive discussion.

See also: Environmental and Resource Management; Environmental Policy; Environmental Vulnerability; Environmentalism: Philosophical Aspects; Environmentalism, Politics of; Environmentalism: Preservation and Conservation; Human–Environment Relationships; Malthus, Thomas Robert (1766–1834); Population Dynamics: Mathematic Models of Population, Development, and Natural Resources; Sustainable Development

Bibliography

Barnett H J, Morse C 1963 *Scarcity and Growth*. Johns Hopkins Press for Resources for the Future, Baltimore, MD

Boserup E 1965 *The Conditions of Agricultural Growth*. Aldine, Chicago

Boserup E 1981 *Population and Technological Change: A Study of Long-term Trends*. University of Chicago Press, Chicago

Carson R 1962 *Silent Spring*. Houghton Mifflin, Boston

Coale A J, Hoover E M 1958 *Population Growth and Economic Development in Low-income Countries*. Princeton University Press, Princeton, NJ

Cole H S D, Freeman C, Jahoda M, Pavitt K L R (eds.) 1973 *Models of Doom: A Critique of The Limits to Growth*. Universe Books, New York

Ehrlich P R 1968 *The Population Bomb*. Ballentine Books, New York

Hardin G 1968 The tragedy of the commons. *Science* **162**: 1243–8

Kahn H, Brown W, Martel L 1976 *The Next 200 Years: A Scenario for America and the World*. Morrow, New York

Luten D B 1980 Ecological optimism in the social sciences: The question of the limits to growth. *American Behavioral Scientist* **24**(1): 125–51

Maddox J R 1972 *The Doomsday Syndrome*. McGraw-Hill, New York

Malthus T R 1798/1967 *Essay on the Principle of Population*, 7th edn. Dent, London

Meadows D H, Meadows D L, Randers J 1992 *Beyond the Limits*. Chelsea Green Publishing, Post Mills, VT

Meadows D H, Meadows D L, Randers J, Behrens W W III 1972 *The Limits to Growth*. Universe Books, New York

Nordhaus W D 1973 World dynamics: Measurement without data. *The Economic Journal* **83**(332): 1156–83

Osborn F 1953 *The Limits of the Earth*. Little, Brown, Boston

Paddock W, Paddock P 1967 *Famine—1975!* Little, Brown, Boston

Sanderson W C 1980 Economic-demographic simulation models: A review of their usefulness for policy analysis. Research Report. International Institute for Applied Systems Analysis, Austria, RR-80-14

Sanderson W C 1994 Simulation models of demographic, economic, and environmental interactions. In: Lutz W (ed.) *Population–Development–Environment: Understanding their Interactions in Mauritius*. Springer-Verlag, Berlin, pp. 33–71

Simon J L 1981 *The Ultimate Resource*. Princeton University Press, Princeton, NJ
Simon J L 1996 *The Ultimate Resource 2*. Princeton University Press, Princeton, NJ

B. O'Neill

Caste

The career of caste as an anthropological concept provides a fascinating terrain on which to examine how anthropological objects come to be invented and stabilized, and the relation they bear to patterns of sociality, needs of government, and production of knowledge. Many textbooks in sociology and social anthropology represent caste as a fundamental institution of Indian society. In this view castes are ranked in a hierarchical order and are governed by rules of endogamy, commensality, and purity–pollution that put strict limits on exchange of women and food between castes. The hierarchical order, however, permits the flow of women from lower to higher castes through marriage and the flow of food from higher to lower castes. The caste system is seen to correspond to a rough division of labor, though it is recognized that certain occupations such as agriculture cut across different castes. This textbook picture of the caste system, though influential, has come under serious scrutiny in recent years as being not only ahistorical but also ignoring the power/knowledge axis in the production of social science concepts.

1. Caste as the Ideology of Indian society

Louis Dumont's (1980) *Homo Hierarchicus* has long been regarded as an outstanding contribution to the understanding of caste. Dumont argued that principles of hierarchy and holism were central for explaining the caste system. The principle of hierarchy in India, he proposed, was based upon the religious opposition between pure and impure—pollution incurred in the biological processes of life and death was removed in India not through processes of reciprocity (I bury your dead—you bury mine) but through principles of hierarchy. The task of removal of pollution was assigned to the lower castes who became permanently imbued with it. Thus the separation between castes as well as their hierarchical ordering could be derived from the opposition between pure and impure. The scheme had the simplicity and elegance to make the bewildering diversity of Indian civilization immediately knowable, especially to Western readers.

Dumont's characterization of Indian society has been challenged on the ground that what he saw as a timeless ideology was itself a result of certain practices of classification and enumeration instituted in the context of colonial administration that gave a dominant place to Brahmanical texts as representatives of Indian society. An important intervention made by McKim Marriott (1990) needs mention here. Marriott provided a significant alternative to Dumont's formulation, arguing that different transactional strategies defined the position of different castes—it was not a simple case of hierarchy versus equality but rather of a universe governed by a complex set of rules and strategies regarding matching, mixing, and marking through which different regional and local configurations of castes were generated. What was at stake for both Dumont and Marriott, despite their differences, was the representation of India as the 'other' of the modern West. They were much less interested in either the concrete historical processes through which institutions were formed or the contemporary changes in the caste system. It is instructive to compare this with the way that caste was rendered in the work of the Indian anthropologist, M. N. Srinivas. Srinivas's stake in the local and his deep concern with the way caste was shaping Indian democratic politics distinguish him from these authors.

2. The Stake in the Local

The decade of the 1950s saw the emergence of 'village studies' as an important genre of anthropological writing in India. For Srinivas the village was an indispensable site for fieldwork because of the importance he attached to what he called the 'field-view' as distinct from the overly textual view of the caste system. The two important concepts that Srinivas (1971) formulated with far reaching consequences for the study of caste were '*sanskritization*' and 'dominant caste.'

Srinivas contended that a preoccupation with textual sources had led many to assume that the caste system was a rigid hierarchical system. Attention to historical and ethnographic processes on the ground, on the other hand, showed that while individual mobility was severely restricted in the caste system, group mobility had always been possible for castes in the middle rungs through the process of *sanskritization*. This process referred to the ability of a caste group, which had achieved economic or political mobility, to stake a claim to a higher status by recasting its customs and rituals to correspond more closely to Brahmanical rituals and practices. The process of change in ritual practices and social customs was not open to everyone. However, when a caste was successful in acquiring a measure of economic or political power through physical mobility, opening up of markets, or changed political alignments, it could translate this into claims to a higher caste status. With the decline in traditional kingship brought on by the colonial rule, such functions were shifted to colonial authorities. It is one of the exquisite ironies of the colonial rule that when caste began to be recorded systematically in the census, it became a major source for claiming of higher status by various caste groups who adduced their *sanskritic* practices or their myths of origin as evidence of their higher status.

Unlike the concept of *sanskritization*, which assumed an interaction between local and regional levels, the concept of the dominant caste emerged out of an understanding of local and especially agricultural society. Srinivas (1971) argued that the ritual hierarchy of caste notwithstanding, the dominant role in village life was played by landowning peasant-proprietor castes who were rarely Brahmins. The relation between these rich peasant castes and the other castes in the village was characterized as a form of patron–client relations. Thus Srinivas argued that the horizontal solidarity of caste expressed by endogamy and commensality was counterbalanced by the vertical solidarity observable at the village level through patron–client relations. Many institutions such as fictive kinship within the village, ritual processes for creation of boundaries, and the division of labor and economic exchange, created the village as an economic, political, and ritual unit that established solidarities cutting across caste. As the general understanding of locality in the field of anthropological theory deepened, interest shifted to the mapping of specific histories through which localities were created. The search for overarching structural principles seemed less fruitful than understanding how the momentous changes that were taking place in Indian society impacted upon caste, at the local, regional, and national levels.

3. Colonial Constructions

Once the search for enduring structural principles gave way to historically grounded work, the colonial archive became an important source for understanding the nature of colonial rule and how it transformed the institution of caste. The processes of enumeration and classification played a particularly important role in this process. Although the predecessor states of the British in India did have apparatuses for counting, classifying, and controlling populations, these were tied to specific needs of the state such as revenue collection, or rising of temporary armies. The British colonial state instituted a new way of collecting information in the form of maps, settlement reports, revenue records, statistical information, censuses, folklore, narratives, to name a few.

This new form of governance, or 'rule-by-records and rule-by-reports' in the felicitous phrasing of Richard S. Smith (1986) had a decisive influence on the shaping of caste identities in the twentieth century. In the processes of classifying and enumerating the population, the British did not start with caste as if it were a natural category found on the ground. In the early phases of colonial rule the emphasis was on cadastral control. Statistics on land ownership, tenancy, crop production, and instruments of agricultural

production were geared towards standardizing methods of revenue collection and it was by no means obvious that caste rather than village would be the obvious unit for the organizing of data. According to Smith it was only around 1850 that the census in the case of Punjab was transformed from an instrument of tax to an instrument of knowledge. Earlier census reports were more pragmatic and localistic in orientation. There was considerable tension between the concerns of centrist census officials collating data in an encyclopedic manner and the local officials who were concerned with recording the nature of social groups and categories for more practical purposes such as collection for revenue or settlement of disputes (see Appadurai 1996). In order to understand the concerns of the centrist census officials who recorded information on caste for which there could have been no practical use, it is necessary to turn to the scientistic notions of race in this period.

In shifting to castes as the most natural groups around which information was to be organized on Indian society, British officials relied on their notions of race and physical types. Herbert Risley ([1908], 1969) was the most vocal proponent of using anthropometrical measures in conducting the ethnographic survey of India because, according to him, anthropometry yielded particularly good results in India by reason of the caste system, which allowed marriage only within a limited circle. Relying on such symbolism as that of dark versus light skin color and shape of nose and jaw, the category of caste was thus collapsed with that of race. Ghurye (1932) was the first Indian sociologist to criticize this view of caste and to challenge its political implications.

It is not anyone's case that the process of recording caste created this institution *ex nihilo*. What it did was to freeze the ongoing processes by which caste came to be solidified in the official imagination, and to generate the conception of community as enumerative, which had a strong influence on processes of political representation (Cohn 1984). It is important to underscore the fact that the census, gazetteers, reports, and other such forms of knowledge came to represent the power of official discourse to name and fix the status of caste groups in local imaginaries. Many caste groups began to see the census as the source for claiming higher status. Thus census commissioners were besieged with petitions challenging a particular status ascribed to a caste.

It is also interesting to see that the theories of the racial origin of castes had a serious impact on social and political mobilization, as in the anti-Brahmin movements in the South of India and in the mobilization of the untouchable castes under the leadership of Ambedkar in Western India—both of which used the idea of original settlers versus Aryan invaders. The discursive formations around caste quotas in educational institutions, government jobs, and reserved constituencies, as well as the politics of mobilization around these issues, show the interaction and circulation of categories between popular imagination and official discourse (Dirks 1992).

4. The Contemporary Context

An important paradox about caste in public life in India is that while the Constitution of India recognizes only individuals as bearers of rights and duties, and bans any discrimination based on caste or religion, the processes of democratic politics with the imperatives of grass root mobilization have created new arenas for the evolution of caste-based politics (Béteille 1996, Kothari 1970). Interestingly the legal prohibitions on caste and the political mobilization around caste reflect the contrary pulls of formal legal justice system and the imperatives of representational politics in contemporary India. This can be illustrated with the example of 'untouchability' and its contradictory careers in law, politics, and everyday life (Galanter 1972). It is not that a similar exercise cannot be done on other castes, but the example of untouchability has a particular resonance because of its unique association with the caste system.

While it could conceivably be argued that some form of caste-based discrimination is to be found in all the legal sanskritic texts, recent examination of the genealogy of the terms through which untouchability makes an appearance in discourse shows the importance of political and social processes in the negotiation of group identities in democratic societies (Charsley 1996). The term 'untouchability' is ascribed to Sir Herbert Risley ([1908], 1969) and was part of his effort to classify and rank castes in the subcontinent as a whole. While the category *shudra* occurs in the Sanskrit texts and is sometimes taken to be equivalent to 'untouchables,' its referents are varied—ranging from kings, powerful landowning castes, to castes with extreme disabilities. Prior to Risley, compilers of district gazetteers and state census reports had experimented with other terms, such as depressed classes, depressed castes, *panchamas*, *pariahs*, etc.

The use of the term 'untouchable,' in public life, owed much to the reformist politics of early twentieth century, especially to Gandhi's politics of reform and the agenda for the abolition of untouchability in the nationalist movement (Gandhi 1954). In 1931 Gandhi adopted the term *Harijan* (people of god) and increasingly substituted it for other terms in his writings. While the prototypical Harijan for Gandhi was a member of the *bhangi* caste who cleaned lavatories and was thus rendered 'unclean,' his major political opponent, Ambedkar, who himself came from the Mahar caste of Bombay Presidency, was much more interested in forging political alliances between the major agricultural dependent castes, whose low status came from their dependency rather than their polluting

occupations. Yet he preferred to retain the label 'untouchable' in his politics (Charsley 1996). In the embroilment of nationalist politics with caste mobilization, Gandhi's strategy was to retain untouchables within the fold of Hinduism while Ambedkar's attempt was to forge a new identity for them, but within the Indian civilizational context—hence the choice of neo-Buddhism as the new religion for the erstwhile untouchables (Ambedkar 1946).

The term 'untouchable,' like other such generic terms masks considerable local heterogeneity. Its importance lay in the binary division between untouchable and nonuntouchable castes created through the bureaucratic imperative of creating a single category for purposes of reservations. Under the Government of India Act of 1935, the term 'scheduled castes' replaced the earlier category of depressed classes. Though untouchability was to be the criterion for inclusion of castes into the list of scheduled castes, the names of the castes that were finally included in the state lists formed a kind of unity only through a 'common relationship their members have with government' (Dushkin 1972, p. 166). The fact that the category of untouchability was basically a twentieth century creation does not detract from either the experiences of oppression of castes grouped under this category, or the importance of the grounding of struggles for greater equality under identity politics. In fact, the creativity of the new social movements can be seen in the emergence of the term *dalit* (literally 'downtrodden') among the neo-Buddhists and scheduled castes in Maharashtra, which has become now the most commonly accepted term of self-reference by such groups. The most interesting feature of this phase of the movement of *dalits* is the emphasis not only on political action but also on representation of the experiences of untouchable castes through literature, life histories, and collection of oral literature as a critique of caste society (Murugkar 1996, Omvedt 1995).

An interesting question arises as to whether politics is the only domain within which the legacy of oppression and humiliation is articulated in contemporary India. How are caste identities performed in everyday life? Khare (1984) had suggested that instead of playing the impure foil to the Brahmin, the untouchables conduct themselves even at the community level as civilizational critics, showing a complex relationship with caste ideology. Other important ethnographies of caste show how caste identity is performed in relation to everyday activities of work and worship; how elaborate strategies for management of caste identities are evolved, and how these performances come to be experienced as forms of embodiment.

Debates on caste have shown the intricate relations between forms of esthetic, political, and social representations of caste. Simultaneously much of the scholarly agenda of research in India in recent years has been influenced by the public controversies on such issues as caste-based reservations or reintroduction of caste-based enumeration for the next decennial census. New patterns of sociality are evident in ways in which caste identity is performed in the context of family, community, economy, and polity which reconceptualize caste not as a sign of the *exotic* but of the *contemporary* repositioning of the subjects and objects of anthropology in new ways.

See also: Area and International Studies: Development in South Asia; Class: Social; Labor, Division of; Social Stratification; South Asian Studies: Culture; Subaltern History; Subaltern Studies: Cultural Concerns

Bibliography

Ambedkar B R 1946 *What Congress and Gandhi Have Done to the Untouchables.* Thacker, Bombay, India

Appadurai A 1996 Number in the colonial imagination. In: Appadurai A *Modernity at Large: Cultural Dimensions of Globalization.* University of Minnesota Press, Minneapolis, MN, pp.114–39

Béteille A 1996 Caste in contemporary India. In: Fuller C J (ed.) *Caste Today.* Oxford University Press, Delhi, India

Charsley S 1996 'Untouchable': What is in the name? *Journal of Royal Anthropological Institute* **2**: 1–23

Cohn B S 1984 The census, social structure and objectification in South Asia. *Folk* **26**: 25–49

Deliege R 1992 Replication and consensus: Untouchability, caste and ideology in India. *Man* **27**: 155–73

Dirks N B 1992 Castes of mind. *Representations* **37**: 56–78

Dumont L 1980 *Homo Hierarchicus: The Caste System and its Implications.* University of Chicago Press, Chicago

Dushkin L 1972 Scheduled caste politics. In: Mahar J M (ed.) *The Untouchables in Contemporary India.* University of Arizona Press, Tucson, AZ

Galanter M 1972 The abolition of disabilities: Untouchability and the law. In: Mahar J M (ed.) *The Untouchables in Contemporary India.* University of Arizona Press, Tucson, AZ

Gandhi M K 1954 *The Removal of Untouchability.* Navajivan Press, Ahmadabad, India

Ghurye G S 1932 *Caste and Race in India.* Kegan Paul, London

Khare R S 1984 *The Untouchable as Himself: Ideology, Identity and Pragmatism Among the Lucknow Chamars.* Cambridge University Press, Cambridge, UK

Kothari R 1970 *Caste in Indian Politics.* Orient Longmans, Delhi, India

Marriott M (ed.) 1990 *India Through Hindu Categories.* Sage, Delhi, India

Murugkar L 1991 *Dalit Panther Movement in Maharashtra: A Sociological Appraisal.* Popular Prakashan, Bombay, India

Omvedt G 1995 *Dalit Visions: The Anti-Caste Movement and the Construction of an Indian Identity.* Orient Longman, New Delhi, India

Risley H R [1908] 1969 *The People of India.* Oriental Books, New Delhi, India

Smith R S 1986 Rule-by-records and rule-by-reports: Complementary aspects of the British imperial rule of law. *Contributions to Indian Sociology* **19**(1): 153–76

Srinivas M N 1971 *Social Change in Modern India.* University of California Press, Berkeley, CA

V. Das

Categorization and Similarity Models

Imagine meeting a friend's pet, and having to decide whether it is best classified as a cat or a dog. According to prototype models of categorization, the pet is compared with mental prototypes for cat and dog, and if it is more similar to the cat prototype than to the dog prototype, then it is classified as a cat. According to exemplar models of categorization, the pet is compared with all remembered instances of cats and dogs, and if it is more similar to known cats than to known dogs, then it is classified as a cat. Notice that both types of models rely on the notion of similarity. For these models to be usefully tested and compared with each other, or with other models of categorization, similarity must be formally defined and empirically assayed, along with formal and empirical treatments of categorization. This article briefly considers empirical results and formal models of similarity and categorization, concluding that the complex but systematic behavior should eventually yield to accurate models.

1. Similarity

1.1 Empirical Assays of Similarity

The similarity of items can be assessed in many different ways. The most direct method is simply to show a person two items and ask him or her to rate their similarity or dissimilarity. Alternatively, three or more items can be presented, and the viewer is asked to put them into subgroups of apparently similar items. A different method is for the viewer to see two items and then judge whether they are the same or different. A fourth method shows the viewer a single item that must be identified; presumably the degree of confusion between items, as measured either by response time or by error rate, reflects the similarity of the items.

Although in many cases these different assays of similarity are concordant, there are a variety of situations in which they do not agree (Medin et al. 1990). For example, consider the two pairs of countries, West Germany–East Germany and Ceylon–Nepal. When asked to select the pair of countries that are most *similar* to each other, people tended to choose West Germany–East Germany. When asked to select the pair of countries that are most dissimilar from each other, people again chose West Germany–East Germany (Tversky 1977). It has also been established that even for a single method of measurement, the relative similarities of items can change depending on context. For example, in the context of hair, gray is more similar to white than it is to black, but in the context of clouds, gray is more similar to black than it is to white (Medin and Shoben 1988). Nevertheless, similarity is not an utterly unconstrained, useless theoretical construct. Rather, there are strong regularities in how similarity is affected by context and by measurement method (Goldstone 1994b; Medin et al. 1993).

1.2 Models of Similarity

Among the many models of similarity two are most prominent. Multidimensional scaling (MDS) represents items by values in a multidimensional psychological space (Shepard 1987). For example, on the dimensions of size and ferocity, the item *lion* would have values *large* and *high*. The similarity of two items, A and B, is inversely related to the distance between the items in the psychological space, denoted 'distance(A,B).' The similarity of items A and B is formally specified as

$$S(A, B) = \exp(-\text{distance}(A, B))$$
$$= \exp\left(-\left(\sum_r \alpha_r |A_r - B_r|^p\right)^{1/p}\right) \quad (1)$$

where the sum is taken over all the relevant dimensions of the space, α_r is the attention allocated to dimensions r, A_r is the value of item A on dimension r, and p is a power typically set at a value of 1 or 2 depending on whether the dimensions can be selectively attended to or not. For a review of MDS models, extensions, and some of their applications, see Ashby (1992) and Nosofsky (1992b).

A different formalization was proposed by Tversky (1977) in his 'contrast model.' In this model, items are assumed to be represented by sets of present or absent features. If A denotes the set of all relevant features in item A, then the similarity of items A and B is specified by a linear combination (i.e., a contrast) of their shared features (denoted $\mathbf{A} \cap \mathbf{B}$), the features in A that are not in B (denoted $\mathbf{A} - \mathbf{B}$), and the features in B that are not in A (denoted $\mathbf{B} - \mathbf{A}$),

$$S(A, B) = \theta f(\mathbf{A} \cap \mathbf{B}) - \alpha f(\mathbf{A} - \mathbf{B}) - \beta f(\mathbf{B} - \mathbf{A}) \quad (2)$$

where f is a function that specifies the saliences of the various features (and sets of features), and where θ, α and β are weighting factors for the influence of the shared and distinctive features.

These models have been quite successful in addressing a wide variety of phenomena in similarity data. However, all these models take for granted that there is a prespecified range of dimensions or features that considered. For example, in judging the similarity of a lion and a dog, there are an infinite number of shared features such as 'smaller than a battleship,' but these features are presumably not included in the computation of similarity. In other words, the specification of what features or dimensions are relevant to the similarity computation is critical for theories involving similarity (Goodman 1972, Murphy and Medin 1985). These formalisms can accommodate differences in relevances of the features or dimensions (by way of the salience function, f, in the contrast model, and by way of the attentional factors, α_r in the MDS model), but the processes that determine these relevances are not specified in these models.

2. Categorization

Categorization can be measured in a variety of ways. For a given item, a person can be asked to make a discrete choice among several candidate categories. Alternatively, the person can give a rating of how typical the item is of a certain category. Response times can also be measured.

In many situations, similarity is a good predictor of categorization. For example, people (in the USA) rate a robin as being highly similar to many other birds, but people do not rate a penguin as being very similar to many other birds. This similarity difference predicts that people should categorize a robin more efficiently than a penguin, which in fact occurs; people are faster to verify that 'a robin is a bird' than 'a penguin is a bird.' Similarity can also explain why people are slow to falsify the statement, 'a bat is a bird,' because a bat is similar to a bird, yet is not a bird (Smith et al. 1974).

There are also situations in which similarity apparently does not predict categorization. Consider, for example, the category of 'things to remove from a burning house.' Children and heirloom jewelry are prominent members of this category, yet they are not very similar (Barsalou 1983). As another example, consider a hypothetical three-inch diameter disk-shaped object. People will rate it as more similar to a quarter (i.e., a 25 cent coin) than to a pizza, but they categorize it as more likely to be a pizza than a quarter (Rips 1989). Some of these apparent dissociations between similarity and categorization can be reconciled if selective emphasis on particular features is taken into account. For example, children and heirloom jewelry are very similar on the dimensions of irreplaceability and portability, which are critical dimensions emphasized by a burning house. When a hypothetical three-inch diameter object also includes other features characteristic of quarters, so that there is less selective emphasis on size, then category judgments cohere with similarity judgments (Smith and Sloman 1994).

A prominent similarity-based model of categorization is the 'generalized context model' (GCM, Nosofsky 1986). In the GCM, an item to be categorized is compared with all exemplars in memory, and each exemplar 'votes' for its category with a strength proportional to the similarity of the exemplar to the item. An important quality of the GCM is that the attention paid to each stimulus dimension can be adjusted to suit the categorization at hand. An extension of the GCM includes a mechanism by which the dimensional attention strengths are learned (Kruschke 1992). Whether or not empirical evidence yet demands inclusion of prototypes, in addition to exemplars, is a matter of current debate; Nosofsky (1992a) provides a summary of tests of prototype models versus exemplar models.

Perhaps more problematic for similarity-based theories are cases in which categorization appears to be based, at least in part, on 'rules' which specify strict, necessary, and sufficient conditions. One characteristic of 'rules' is that they can be extrapolated far beyond the training exemplars. Erickson and Kruschke (1998) trained people to categorize simple geometric forms, most of which could be classified by a simple rule regarding height, and a few of which were exceptions to the rule. When tested with novel forms beyond the range of the training instances, people responded according to the rule, despite the fact that the most similar training exemplar violated the rule. Another clear case in which an abstracted rule violates exemplar similarity is presented by Shanks and Darby (1998). However, even for rules, similarity to exemplars can have an influence. Erickson and Kruschke (1998) found that rule-obeying exemplars were classified more accurately when they were similar to a high-frequency training instance than when they were similar to a lower-frequency training instance. Several other demonstrations of exemplar influence on rule use have been reported (e.g., Allen and Brooks 1991, Palmeri and Nosofsky 1995). Categorization models that combine rules with exemplars, or graded similarity, or other modifications have recently been developed (Ashby et al. 1998, Erickson and Kruschke 1998, Vandierendonck 1995).

3. Future Progress

Despite the apparent complexity of phenomena in similarity and categorization, there are systematicities that should yield to a characterization of categorization in terms of similarity. Future models of similarity and categorization will have to include (a) mechanisms than learn feature relevance that is context-sensitive; (b) mechanisms that abstract new features; and (c) mechanisms that compare representations that are more complex than feature sets or points in psychological space. An excellent discussion of these issues is provided by Goldstone (1994b). Recent progress in these directions includes models of category learning

in which the relevance of dimensions or features is learned (Kruschke 1999, Kruschke and Johansen 1999), numerous connectionist or neural-network models that create novel internal representations (for an overview see Ellis and Humphreys 1999), and models of similarity that apply to structured representations (Goldstone 1994a).

See also: Categorization and Similarity Models: Neuroscience Applications; Concept Learning and Representation: Models; Knowledge Spaces

Bibliography

Allen S W, Brooks L R 1991 Specializing the operation of an explicit rule. *Journal of Experimental Psychology: General* **120**: 3–19

Ashby F G (ed.) 1992 *Multidimensional Models of Perception and Cognition*. Erlbaum, Hillsdale, NJ

Ashby F G, Allfonso-Reese L A, Turken A U, Waldron E M 1998 A neuropsychological theory of multiple systems in category learning. *Psychological Review* **105**: 442–81

Barsalou L W 1983 Ad hoc categories. *Memory & Cognition* **11**: 211–27

Ellis R, Humphreys G W 1999 *Connectionist Psychology*. Psychology Press, Hove, East Sussex, UK

Erickson M A, Kruschke J K 1998 Rules and exemplars in category learning. *Journal of Experimental Psychology: General* **127**: 107–40

Goldstone R L 1994a Similarity, interactive activation, and mapping. *Journal of Experimental Psychology: Learning, Memory and Cognition* **20**: 3–28

Goldstone R L 1994b The role of similarity in categorization: providing a groundwork. *Cognition* **52**: 125–157

Goodman N 1972 Seven strictures on similarity. In: Goodman N (ed.) *Problems and Projects*. Bobbs-Merrill, Indianapolis, IN, pp. 437–47

Kruschke J K 1992 ALCOVE: An exemplar-based connectionist model of category learning. *Psychological Review* **99**: 22–44

Kruschke J K 1999 Toward a unified model of attention in associative learning. (Revision to appear in *The Journal of Mathematical Psychology*. Available online http://www.indiana.edu/~kruschke/tumaal.html)

Kruschke J K, Johansen M K 1999 A model of probabilistic category learning. *Journal of Experimental Psychology: Learning, Memory & Cognition*. **25**: 1083–119

Medin D L, Goldstone R L, Gentner D 1990 Similarity involving attributes and relations: Judgments of similarity and difference are not inverses. *Psychological Science* **1**: 64–9

Medin D L, Goldstone R L, Gentner D 1993 Respects for similarity. *Psychological Review* **100**: 254–78

Medin D L, Shoben E J 1988 Context and structure in conceptual combination. *Cognitive Psychology* **20**: 158–90

Murphy G L, Medin D L 1985 The role of theories in conceptual coherence. *Psychological Review* **92**: 289–316

Nosofsky R M 1986 Attention, similarity and the identification-categorization relationship. *Journal of Experimental Psychology: General* **115**: 39–57

Nosofsky R M 1992a Exemplars, prototypes, and similarity rules. In: Healy A F, Kosslyn S M, Shiffrin R M (eds.) *Essays in Honor of William K. Estes. Vol. 2: From Learning Processes to Cognitive Processes*. Erlbaum, Hillsdale, NJ, pp. 149–67

Nosofsky R M 1992b Similarity scaling and cognitive process models. *Annual Review of Psychology* **43**: 25–53

Palmeri T J, Nosofsky R M 1995 Recognition memory for exceptions to the category rule. *Journal of Experimental Psychology: Learning, Memory, & Cognition* **21**: 548–68

Rips L J 1989 Similarity, typicality, and categorization. In: Vosniadou S, Ortony A (eds.) *Similarity and Analogical Reasoning.* Cambridge University Press, Cambridge, UK, pp. 21–59

Shanks D R, Darby R J 1998 Feature- and rule-based generalization in human associative learning. *Journal of Experimental Psychology: Animal Behavior Processes B* **24**: 405–15

Shepard R N 1987 Toward a universal law of generalization for psychological science. *Science* **237**: 1317–23

Smith E E, Shoben E J, Rips L J 1974 Structure and process in semantic memory: A featural model for semantic decision. *Psychological Review* **81**: 214–41

Smith E E, Sloman S A 1994 Similarity- versus rule-based categorization. *Memory and Cognition* **22**: 377–86

Tversky A 1977 Features of similarity. *Psychological Review* **84**: 327–52

Vandierendonck A 1995 A parallel rule activation and rule synthesis model for generalization in category learning. *Psychonomic Bulletin and Review* **2**: 442–59

J. K. Kruschke

Categorization and Similarity Models: Neuroscience Applications

Categorization is the act of assigning objects or events to classes (i.e., categories). It is performed countless times every day, and is among the most important and basic of all decisions. Many different categorization models have been proposed. In several cases, models that make very different assumptions about how people learn new categories have been equally successful at accounting for a given set of categorization data. Recent advances in neuroscience have provided a new means with which to test among such competing models. The correct model of categorization will be consistent with the known neuroscience, as well as with observable categorization behavior. In addition, a knowledge of the underlying neuroscience makes it possible to develop categorization models for many groups of people that most current theories ignore (e.g., children, the elderly, people with various neurological disorders). This article reviews what is known about the neuroscience of categorization, and considers the implications of this knowledge for categorization models.

1. Structures

Categorization is not a single mental ability, but instead depends on several different abilities that use different brain structures and processes. As evidence of this, a wide variety of normal and pathological conditions have been shown to interfere with normal category learning. These include normal aging, major depression, Parkinson's disease, Alzheimer's disease, Huntington's disease, strokes, and schizophrenia (for a review, see, e.g., Ashby et al. 1998). This and other recent evidence sheds light on which neural structures do or do not participate in category learning.

1.1 Sensory Cortex

Sensory cortex refers to all cortical areas associated with sensory function. In the case of vision, this includes virtually all of the occipital cortex and much of the temporal and parietal cortex. An object must be perceived before it can be categorized, so an intact sensory cortex is necessary for normal categorization. It is not so clear, however, whether the characteristics of a category and the rules for distinguishing it from similar but different categories are learned and stored in the sensory cortex. Interest in this hypothesis has been sparked in recent years by reports of a variety of category-specific agnosias that result from damage to certain high-level visual cortical areas. Category-specific agnosia is defined as the ability to perceive or categorize most visual stimuli relatively normally, but a reduced ability to recognize exemplars from some specific category, such as inanimate objects (e.g., tools), or fruits. The most widely known of such deficits occur with human faces (i.e., prosopagnosia). Although such category-specific agnosias are consistent with the hypothesis that category structure is represented in visual cortex, they are also generally consistent with the hypothesis that visually similar objects are represented in nearby areas of the visual cortex. For example, it is well known that neighboring cells in the visual cortex tend to fire to similar stimuli. Thus, damage to some contiguous region of the visual cortex is likely to lead to perception deficits within a class of similar stimuli. In fact, specific tests have failed to rule out this similarity hypothesis.

Evidence against the hypothesis that category learning occurs in the visual cortex has been obtained in single cell recording experiments with monkeys. Several studies have found that the firing properties of cells in high-level visual areas (e.g., inferotemporal cortex) do not change when there is a switch in the category assignment of the visual stimulus to which the cell is most responsive (e.g., Rolls et al. 1977). If the categories were represented in the visual cortex, then the firing properties of visual cortical cells should change when the category memberships were switched. For example, similar studies have found changes in the responses of cells in other brain areas (e.g., amygdala) in such experiments.

1.2 Frontal Cortex

The sensory cortex projects directly to the frontal cortex, which consists roughly of the forward-most third of the cerebral cortex. With respect to category learning, two especially important structures in this region are the prefrontal cortex and the anterior cingulate, which are thought to be critical for working (i.e., short-term) memory and executive (i.e., volitional) attention—operations that are important in some types of category learning. So, it is not surprising that there is abundant evidence that these structures are critically important for learning at least some types of category structures. The most well known such evidence comes from applications of the Wisconsin Card Sorting Test (WCST). This is a widely used neuropsychological test of frontal dysfunction in which participants learn a series of categories each of which differ on only a single critical attribute (i.e., symbol color, shape, or number). Patients with frontal cortical lesions are well known to have deficits on the WCST. Activation in frontal areas, including the prefrontal cortex and the anterior cingulate, has also been found in the few extant neuroimaging studies of category learning.

The frontal cortex is the locus of human reasoning. As such, the evidence that the frontal cortex participates in category learning supports classical models of category learning (which date back to Aristotle) that assume people learn categories by reasoning about them (e.g., through an explicit process of generating and testing hypotheses about category structure).

1.3 Basal Ganglia

All of the cortical structures that have so far been discussed (sensory cortex, prefrontal cortex, anterior cingulate) project directly to the basal ganglia—a collection of subcortical structures that includes the caudate nucleus, the putamen, and the globus pallidus (other structures are also included). Patients with diseases of the basal ganglia (e.g., Parkinson's disease, Huntington's disease) are impaired in category learning (Knowlton et al. 1996a, 1996b), which suggests that these subcortical structures may contribute to the learning of new categories. Perhaps the best evidence for a basal ganglia contribution to category learning, however, comes from a long series of lesion studies in rats and monkeys. In primates, virtually all of the visual cortex projects directly to the tail of the caudate nucleus, and the cells in this area then project, via the globus pallidus and thalamus, to the prefrontal cortex and more posterior motor areas (i.e., the premotor cortex). These projections place the caudate in an ideal position to link percepts and actions, and many researchers have hypothesized that this is its primary role. Many studies have shown that lesions of the tail of the caudate nucleus impair the ability of animals to learn visual discriminations that require one response to one stimulus and a different response to some other stimulus (e.g., Packard and McGaugh 1992). Because the thalamus and visual cortex are intact in these animals, it is unlikely that their difficulty is in perceiving the stimuli. Rather, it appears that their difficulty is in learning to associate an appropriate response with each stimulus alternative.

The basal ganglia are also thought to be critical structures for procedural learning and memory, which is a phylogenetically ancient system in which simple associations between stimuli and responses are learned. For this reason, the evidence that the basal ganglia are important in category learning supports models that assume category learning depends on procedural learning and memory.

1.4 Medial Temporal Lobe

Learning about a new category requires the use of some form of memory. Oftentimes, when a person thinks of memory, he or she means the memory of facts and events (called semantic and episodic memory, respectively). It is now known that medial temporal lobe structures, including the hippocampus, the parahippocampal regions, and the entorhinal and pararhinal cortices, are critical for the consolidation of such memories. It might be expected, therefore, that such memory systems contribute significantly to category learning, especially because a number of current theories assume that people categorize a new stimulus by comparing it to memory representations of previously seen exemplars. For this reason, a number of studies have examined how amnesiacs with medial temporal lobe lesions perform in a variety of category-learning tasks. With only a few exceptions, these studies have found normal category learning, even in patients with dense amnesia that resulted from extensive lesions (e.g., Squire and Knowlton 1995). When presented with a stimulus, amnesiacs with medial temporal lobe damage are significantly impaired in judging whether they have seen that stimulus before, but their ability to assign it to the correct category is essentially normal.

These results support the hypothesis that medial temporal lobe structures are not critical for most forms of category learning, and although the issue is not yet resolved, they present a challenge to models that assume people access instance-based memories (i.e., detailed representations of previously seen category exemplars) during category learning.

2. Multiple Category Learning Systems

Another lesson learned from studying the neuroscience of categorization is that human category learning may be mediated by several different systems. This is suggested by the widely distributed neural structures that participate in category learning and by the overwhelming evidence that there are multiple memory systems. Because any category-learning system requires memory, the existence of multiple memory systems raises the possibility that each of several memory systems might have their own dedicated category-learning module. The notion that there may be multiple category-learning systems has a long history, but recently has been the subject of intense scrutiny. Among those researchers postulating multiple systems, the consensus is that one system learns explicitly and at least one learns implicitly. The explicit system is accessible to consciousness and engages in an explicit reasoning process that may involve hypothesis testing or theory construction and testing. This system is almost certainly mediated by frontal cortical structures. The implicit system is not accessible to conscious awareness. Currently, there is debate as to whether this system uses a procedural- or instance-based memory system. Much evidence supports this multiple systems hypothesis. For example, a number of studies have found qualitative differences in the way people learn categories that are best separated by an explicit rule as opposed to tasks in which no salient explicit rule will succeed.

3. COVIS (COmpetition between Verbal and Implicit Systems)

Currently, there are only a few neuropsychological theories of category learning (Ashby et al. 1998, Gluck et al. 1996, Pickering 1997). A schematic illustrating the most important neural structures and pathways of one of these is shown in Fig. 1 (Ashby et al. 1998). This

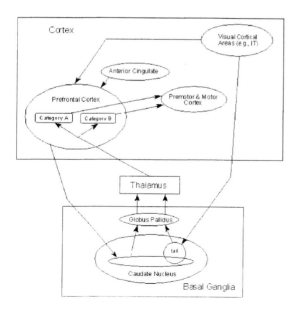

Figure 1
A schematic illustrating the COVIS model of category learning. See text for more details (IT = inferotemporal cortex)

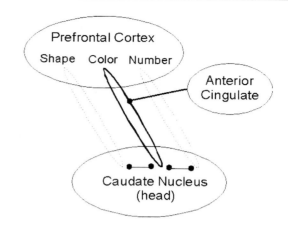

Figure 2
A schematic illustrating how the explicit system in the COVIS model of category learning operates during the Wisconsin Card Sorting Test

model, called COVIS, postulates separate, competing explicit and implicit category-learning systems that are simultaneously active at all times. Depending on the relationship between the categories to be learned, however, one system may dominate the other. There are three hierarchical levels—cortex, thalamus, and the basal ganglia. The two systems are mediated by parallel loops following the path: cortex–caudate–globus pallidus–thalamus. The posterior loop, from visual cortical areas to the tail of the caudate nucleus, mediates the implicit system. In humans, all visual areas project directly to the tail of the caudate (except Area V1), with about 10,000 visual cortical cells converging on each caudate cell. Cells in the tail of the caudate then project to the prefrontal or premotor cortex (via the globus pallidus and the thalamus). COVIS assumes that, through a procedural learning process, each caudate unit learns to associate a category label, or perhaps an abstract motor response, with a large group of visual cortical cells (Ashby and Waldron 1999).

The explicit system is mediated by an anterior loop, from the anterior cingulate and prefrontal cortex to the head of the caudate nucleus, and then back to the prefrontal cortex. Figure 2 illustrates how this system might operate for a task like the WCST. In Fig. 2, the active rule is to sort the cards by the color of the symbols pictured. This rule is maintained in working memory via the bold reverberating loop shown in the figure. If feedback indicates that this rule is incorrect, then the system must implement a different rule, perhaps one that says to sort the cards by the shape of the symbols pictured. There is evidence that implementing a new rule requires two separate operations (e.g., Owens et al. 1993). First, a new rule (e.g., sort by shape) must be selected from among the alternative salient explicit rules, and second, attention must be switched from the previously active rule to the new rule (e.g., from a rule to sort by color to a rule to sort by shape). COVIS assumes that the selection process is mediated by the anterior cingulate and prefrontal cortex, and that the switching process is mediated within the basal ganglia (Ashby et al. 1999).

See also: Categorization and Similarity Models; Concept Learning and Representation: Models; Connectionist Models of Concept Learning; Memory Models: Quantitative; Neural Networks: Biological Models and Applications; Neural Representations of Objects

Bibliography

Ashby F G, Alfonso-Reese L A, Turken A U, Waldron E M 1998 A neuropsychological theory of multiple systems in category learning. *Psychological Review* **105**: 442–81

Ashby F G, Isen A M, Turken A U 1999 A neuropsychological theory of positive affect and its influence on cognition. *Psychological Review* **106**: 529–50

Ashby F G, Waldron E M 1999 On the nature of implicit categorization. *Psychonomic Bulletin & Review* **6**: 363–78

Gluck M A, Oliver L M, Myers C E 1996 Late-training amnesic deficits in probabilistic category learning: a neurocomputational analysis. *Learning Memory* **3**: 326–40

Knowlton B J, Mangels J A, Squire L R 1996a A neostriatal habit learning system in humans. *Science* **273**: 1399–402

Knowlton B J, Squire L R, Paulsen J S, Swerdlow N R, Swenson M, Butters N 1996b Dissociations within nondeclarative memory in Huntington's disease. *Neuropsychology* **10**: 538–48

Owens A M, Roberts A C, Hodges J R, Summers B A, Polkey C E, Robbins T W 1993 Contrasting mechanisms of impaired attentional set–shifting in patients with frontal lobe damage or Parkinson's disease. *Brain* **116**: 1159–75

Packard M G, McGaugh J L 1992 Double dissociation of fornix and caudate–nucleus lesions on acquisition of two water maze tasks: further evidence for multiple memory systems. *Behavioral Neuroscience* **106**: 439–46

Pickering A D 1997 New approaches to the study of amnesic patients: what can a neurofunctional philosophy and neural network methods offer? In: Mayes A R, Downes J J (eds.) *Theories of Organic Amnesia*. Psychology Press, Hove, UK, pp. 255–300

Rolls E T, Judge S J, Sanghera M K 1977 Activity of neurones in the inferotemporal cortex of the alert monkey. *Brain Research* **130**: 229–38

Squire L R, Knowlton B J 1995 Learning about categories in the absence of memory. *Proceedings of the National Academy of Sciences, USA* **92**: 12470–4

F. G. Ashby

Catholicism

Catholicism signifies the central form that Christianity has taken in history from, at latest, the second century, but it is a form that has continued steadily to evolve. In the second millennium Catholicism has come to designate most particularly the character Christianity has assumed within the Roman Communion under the authority of the papacy.

'Catholic' is not a term to be found in the New Testament but it is already being used to characterize and designate the church in its early postapostolic period. Its primary meaning is 'universal,' signifying both Christianity's claim to be a faith unbounded by language, ethnic, or class boundaries and the insistence that local church communities must be in communion with one another: the church in Corinth or Ephesus is 'Catholic' because part of an association of communities sharing the same faith and rituals present up and down the Roman Empire and, potentially, everywhere. As such the term quickly became the church's most regularly used name, incorporated into the creeds. All Christians using the creeds, whether Roman Catholic, Orthodox, or Protestant, claim to believe in, and belong to, the Catholic Church.

The character assumed by Christianity in the second century and generally termed 'Early Catholicism' is one in which each local church is ruled by a bishop, assisted by priests (presbyters) and deacons, claiming 'succession' from the apostles. Entry is via the sacrament of baptism while regular worship is centered upon the weekly celebration of the Eucharist, renewing Jesus's last supper with his disciples. The Hebrew scriptures were retained as inspired, generally in their Greek Septuagintal form, to which was added a collection of the earliest Christian writings, the New Testament, to which apostolic authority was attributed. The shape of Catholicism had, however, been established well before the full canon of the New Testament was agreed upon, certain books remaining for long in dispute. While there was at first no formal machinery for linking local churches together in the one church, local councils of bishops from neighboring towns soon began to be called, while the churches in major cities, particularly those claiming an apostolic foundation, assumed a leading position. Among these the Church of Rome, where both Peter and Paul were martyred, came to be accorded an unquestionable preeminence from an early date.

While all the books of the New Testament are centered unequivocally upon the figure of Jesus Christ, they already suggest, particularly in the account of the first Christian martyr, Stephen, but also in concentration upon certain of the apostles, the importance for early Christianity of the personal 'witness' to Christ (the strict meaning of martyr). A cult of the martyrs, focused upon their tombs, began early and developed into a wider cult of the saints that remained a permanent characteristic of Catholicism. Furthermore virginity/celibacy was stressed from early times as an alternative road to exceptional holiness, a way later institutionalized in monasticism.

This 'Early Catholicism,' constituted by hierarchical ministry, sacraments, the canon of scripture, and the cult of the saints, was common to east and west, the Greek and Latin churches, as also to Syrian, Coptic, and Armenian churches. Despite diversities of language, liturgy, and theological tradition, Catholic Christianity was held together by the fact and theology of 'communion,' a sacramental bond of fellowship from which individuals or whole churches could be excluded on account of heretical teaching or moral deviation.

After Christianity became a privileged religion with the conversion of the emperor Constantine in the early fourth century, it grew enormously in numbers. What had hitherto been a community of a voluntary sort whose members knew that they might well have to face persecution on account of their beliefs became instead quite quickly a church of the masses, many of whose members had received very limited Christian instruction. The myths and customs of the rural population were carried on, often covered over with a thin Christian veneer. Henceforth Catholicism would be characterized by the co-existence of a clerical and monastic religious upper class with a popular religion which it would preach to generation after generation but never fully convert.

Post-Constantinian Catholicism grew too in the development of an institutional framework designed to resolve conflicts and maintain unity, although the result was often to precipitate still worse division. The most striking development of this was what came to be recognized as the 'ecumenical council' beginning with that of Nicaea (325). At the same time the authority of the major churches—Rome, Alexandria, Antioch, and then Constantinople and Jerusalem—was further accentuated. By the fifth century this had been stabilized in the theory of the 'Five Patriarchates' but, among them, Rome and Constantinople held a quite privileged position. That of Rome, with its unquestionable apostolic origins, had been there from the start, but was reinforced greatly from the late fourth century. Constantinople, the new imperial capital, claimed to be for that reason also the church's second see in dignity, though Rome denied that its own primacy was due to its civic, rather than its apostolic, status. In practice, the two co-existed for centuries, at times somewhat tensely, but also co-operatively. Rome enjoyed an increasingly effective primacy of jurisdiction throughout the Latin west but of little more than honor in the east. At the same time the advance of monasticism profoundly affected the ethos of Catholicism in both east and west.

It was only after the eleventh century that the 'Catholicism' of the western church could be distinguished clearly from the 'Orthodoxy' of the eastern. The Gregorian reform (named after Gregory VII, pope from 1073–1085) profoundly affected the western church but through the accentuation of tendencies already present. Three are crucial: the first was a large extension in the claims but, still more, the effective jurisdictional power of the papacy. Its ability to impose a defined model of ecclesiastical life was

turning 'Catholicism' into 'Roman Catholicism': a hitherto largely decentralized church was being made to conform ever more closely to rules laid down in Rome, rules which included insistence on higher moral and educational standards in the clergy and greater separation between clergy and laity. The second was a vast extension of canon law and its implementation through a hierarchy of church courts with appeal always possible to the highest courts in Rome. Canon law became the effective tool for implementing the new Gregorian ideals. The third was the law of celibacy for all the clergy. Hitherto most ordinary priests were, or had been, married, just as they had been and continued to be in the east. Henceforth in the west the married priest would be an offender, though in practice he would long continue to exist. The law of celibacy was a necessary tool for ensuring the segregation of clergy from laity, making it possible for the former to be controlled effectively by higher church authority. The 'church' became in practice more and more a clerical reality in which the laity were expected ideally to remain passive and obedient. The identification of church and clergy was accentuated further by language. The early church had allowed great linguistic flexibility but in the medieval west Latin came to have a wholly privileged position as the language of the church and its public services as well as of theology. As a range of vernaculars developed vigorously their own literatures, the ecclesiastical use of Latin became a further characteristic of Catholicism. It expressed a certain clerical universalism at odds with the national vernaculars used by the laity.

Two further developments, linked particularly with the thirteenth century, were also lastingly influential for the shaping of Catholicism and its differentiation from eastern Orthodoxy. One was the founding, beginning with the Franciscan and Dominican friars, of religious orders which were not purely monastic but, instead, active, mobile, and involved in the world around them, especially the urban world. Further societies of this sort, most notably the Jesuits in the sixteenth century, would multiply, providing a powerful, well-organized, and educated religious army at the service of the church, available not only internally but also for missionary service abroad, as the Franciscan mission to China in the fourteenth century already demonstrated. The second was scholasticism, formal systems of theology, heavily influenced by the rediscovery of Aristotle's works, which grew out of the teaching system of the new universities. Here formal logic was learned and applied in a systematization of theology very different from that of the patristic period or the continued traditions of the Greek east.

Thus, by the later Middle Ages the type of Christianity which we have come to call Catholicism was almost fully evolved—a mix of subapostolic, post-Constantinian, and medieval developments. The Reformation brought an attack on many of these developments, almost anything in fact which could not be defended with firm scriptural authority. Against this assault the papacy yielded almost nothing. It admitted moral and educational, but not doctrinal or institutional, failings. The Council of Trent (1545–63) formulated the lines of the Counter-Reformation position, emphatically reaffirming almost everything that Luther, Zwingli, and Calvin had impugned. The one major new element that it added to the character of Catholicism as a social reality was the seminary. Hitherto there had been no institutions formally established for the training of diocesan priests, who had learned what they needed to know either through the general education of a university or through a measure of apprenticeship, a son often enough learning the job from his father. The Tridentine seminary would improve greatly the effectiveness and education of the clergy but also further distance them socially from the laity, particularly on account of the 'minor seminary,' effectively a secondary school in which candidates for the priesthood would be segregated from their early teens. This could lead easily on to a further gap between the clergy and the university world, and therefore also between the clergy and modern ways of thought. While with time medieval scholasticism was ousted from the university, it would in a much degraded form continue to dominate the characteristic mindset of the clergy until the twentieth century.

Tridentine Catholicism was, nevertheless, far more creative than the term 'Counter-Reformation' might suggest. While classical Protestantism with its commitment to '*sola scriptura*' was averse to religious involvement in secular culture, the Catholicism of the sixteenth and seventeenth centuries produced its last great cultural era, the Baroque, as rich artistically as the earlier Catholic art cultures, the Romanesque and the Gothic. In art and music, as in theology and spirituality, Catholicism is by nature open to the secular and developmental, even luxuriantly. This was always true, though only in the nineteenth century did John Henry Newman justify the development of doctrine as a human and Catholic necessity, to be contrasted with Protestant insistence upon not going beyond the explicit content of scripture.

Sixteenth- and seventeenth-century Catholicism was also particularly fruitful in the literature of prayer, from the mystical writings of the Spanish Carmelites, Teresa of Avila and John of the Cross, to the Jesuit *Spiritual Exercises*, Francis de Sales' *Introduction to the Devout Life*, and countless other minor classics, many of them popular also among Protestants. Catholicism then has traditionally combined institutional rigidity with spiritual and artistic creativity. In the nineteenth century with the triumph of Ultramontanism (a name used to describe a form of Catholicism in Europe north of the Alps anxious to enhance papal authority and uniformity with Rome in contrast with the more old-fashioned Gallicanism which accepted papal supremacy but limited to a minimum papal intervention in non-Italian ecclesiastical affairs) institutional rigidity grew while creativity declined. Faced with the often anticlerical, and even antireligious, ethos of the French Revolution and later liberal movements, the Catholic Church drew in on itself as a fortress against the modern world, defining the authority of the pope at the first Vatican Council of 1870 under Pius IX (1846–78) while a little later Pius X (1903–14) condemned every form of 'modernism.' In the first decades of the twentieth century Catholicism could then appear as a consistently reactionary force, intellectually, culturally and socially. Yet it was far from being a community in decline. Modern technology made Roman centralization work in a way never previously possible. The railway brought countless pilgrims to Rome and a cult of the reigning pope among ordinary Catholics quickly developed. Pius IX, antimodern as he was, became in consequence the first 'modern' pope, almost idolized by millions. At the same time a series of apparitions of the Blessed Virgin Mary mostly to children, of which the most famous were at Lourdes in 1858 and at Fatima in 1917, much reinforced a principal focus for Catholic popular devotion, both backed by and supporting papal definitions of Mary's Immaculate Conception (1854) and Assumption into Heaven (1950). The missionary orders, mostly nineteenth-century foundations, were extending Catholicism throughout the southern hemisphere; there was a move to encourage forms of lay apostolate across Europe and North America, while for the first time there had developed a vast army of nuns at work almost everywhere. This last may have been the most significant shift. In the Middle Ages nuns were few in comparison with monks and included no active orders. Only in the seventeenth century, led by heroic women like Mary Ward and Jane Frances de Chantal, did unenclosed orders of women, committed to apostolic work as well as prayer, begin to exist despite huge clerical opposition. By the close of the nineteenth century there were more nuns in the church than priests. Silent in many ways they were forced to remain, Roman Catholicism being traditionally an intensely male-dominated and clerical form of Christianity, but a changing balance between the sexes was evident even here.

Catholicism continued to present publicly an almost unchanged face until the end of Pius XII's pontificate in 1958; highly clerical, intellectually repressed, well-organized, expansive, more tightly controlled from Rome than ever, insistent upon the use of Latin, retaining apparently untouched its medieval legacy, institutional, and liturgical. Yet processes of modernization had already gone far, intellectually especially in western Europe, institutionally elsewhere with the appointment of Asian and African bishops, and the creation of numerous cardinals to represent every continent. For the first time since the fourteenth century, the majority of cardinals were not Italian. It needed only the gentle touch of John XXIII and the calling of the Second Vatican Council (1962–5) for a truly revolutionary process to set in, only part of which was formally approved by the Council. The intellectual debate unleashed by 4 years of conciliar discussions set a movement in train which went well beyond the letter, though often not far beyond the spirit, of the Council's decrees. Within a few years Latin was replaced by the local vernacular in the liturgy and theological education; scholastic theology almost disappeared from the seminaries; hitherto frigid relationships with the Orthodox and Protestant churches gave way to a near-frenzied spate of official ecumenism.

In strictly theological terms the changes of Vatican II may seem less than revolutionary, but in the wider terms of the sociology of Catholicism, its sense of identity and shared ethos, they undoubtedly were. Symbolic ramparts, such as the denial of the cup in communion to the laity, which had been fiercely maintained against Protestantism for centuries, were dismantled quickly. It was not only that the barriers which made Catholics feel they were different—from Latin to Friday abstinence from meat—had almost disappeared, and with them the shared certainty that the pope was always right. It was also that Catholics now found themselves divided in a way that had never previously been the case in modern times. If, for Pope Paul VI (1963–1978) and the official church, Vatican II had gone just far enough this was challenged from both right and left. For the former it had gone much too far, betraying authentic Catholic values in the pursuit of ecumenism, while for the latter it had failed through evading the most awkward issues, notably that of Roman centralization. The conflict hardened particularly over two matters that refused to go away: contraception and the law of celibacy for priests. Pope Paul had prevented the Council from discussing either. Contraception was passed to a papal commission that actually recommended a change in teaching. Paul rejected the recommendation and in 1968, in the encyclical *Humanae Vitae*, reaffirmed the use of contraception to be always wrong. He was quite unprepared for the degree of open opposition this aroused and for the consequent decline in confidence in papal teaching, particularly among the more thoughtful laity, who disregarded widely the papal ban. Again, despite numerous appeals, at least to allow married men to be ordained, both he and John Paul II (1978–) repeatedly renewed insistence on the law of celibacy in face of the near-catastrophic decline in the number of priests in the western world in the 30 years following the council, due both to the withdrawal of priests from the ministry, usually to marry, and a linked fall in recruitment. A further factor was that minor seminaries were now seen as obsolete and closed almost everywhere in Europe and North America in the early postconciliar years. The credibility of the law had been internally undermined by several things:

Vatican II's praise for the married clergy of Catholic Uniate churches in the east, its permission for married men to be ordained to the diaconate, and, finally, the acceptance of married priests, especially in Britain, if they were converts who had been ministers in another church previously.

Opposition to contraception set Vatican policy against almost all international attempts to curb the rapid rise in global population. This, together with papal rejection of the ordination of women and refusal to open the door to a married priesthood, did much to restore the nineteenth-century image of official Catholicism as incurably reactionary and antimodern. At no time since the Middle Ages has the papacy appeared to matter so much within public policy as in the age of John Paul II but its image has reverted to that of Pius XII. In papal history John XXIII could seem an aberration.

Shortage of priests resulted in the closing or merging into one of many parishes, especially in France, and the transfer of duties from priests to deacons or to the laity in general. Women, who in the past had never been allowed even to serve at mass, were now enrolled in thousands as 'eucharistic ministers.' Moreover, the religious orders, both male and female, whose numbers had grown enormously between 1850 and 1960, went into rapid decline in Europe and North America. In practice a rapid declericalization of the Church's ministry was taking place. While this could be seen as advantageous, its value was partially undermined by the haphazard way in which it happened, lack of a positive pastoral strategy and continued insistence by Rome that the traditional clerical pattern remained normative.

Behind the conflicts over practice and the loss of confidence in authority there were now huge differences in theological perception. If Vatican II seemed almost unbelievably radical to Catholics content with the church of Pius XII, the policies of John Paul II seemed almost unbearably reactionary to Catholics who had found the Council a harbinger of religious liberation. Many 'progressive' Catholics, while deeply loyal to the unity of a worldwide communion and to the idea of a central 'see of unity,' not only rejected much current papal teaching, particularly that of John Paul, whose personal theology often appeared fundamentally preconciliar, but had come to share so full a sense of fellowship with Christians of other churches that intercommunion had come to be seen as obviously right and was practiced frequently with the encouragement of many priests, despite condemnation by authority. 'Conservatives' accused 'progressives' of practicing an '*à la carte*' Catholicism. 'Progressives' charged 'Conservatives' with 'integralism,' confusing the substance of Catholicism with clericalism and Ultramontanism. While 'Progressives' tended to define Catholicism in terms inclusive of the principal insights of the Reformation as constituting a necessary critique of the one-sidedness of the late medieval church,

'Conservatives' continued to define it as inherently contradictory to Protestantism. Vatican II had, in fact, led to a profound questioning of the model of Catholicism as it developed across a 1000 years from the Gregorian reform through the Counter-Reformation to the decrees of Vatican I and Ultramontanism. How far that model will in consequence alter in the long run remains unclear.

It may well be claimed that the areas where this contestation is most in evidence are also areas of church decline. As against that decline, most obvious in western Europe, is to be set a huge growth of Catholicism in Africa, Latin America, and several parts of Asia. Brazil is now the country with by far the largest number of Catholics. Here too, however, there are great differences. Latin America has suffered an acute shortage of clergy for far longer than Europe and most of the issues dividing the church in Europe are evident here too, as also in the Philippines. The advance of Pentecostal Protestantism is also altering the hitherto almost exclusively Catholic character of Latin American Christianity. Elsewhere in Asia and in most of Africa the number of priests and religious has escalated. Religious orders whose recruitment plummeted after Vatican II in their traditional areas have grown remarkably in Africa, India, and Indonesia. For the Jesuits in particular India became the most flourishing of provinces, but the growth of houses of contemplative nuns in Latin America also is noteworthy. Nevertheless throughout the southern hemisphere there are profound tensions between Roman control and local processes of inculturation and political orientation. The future of Catholicism as the principal constituent within Christianity may depend upon how far a lasting *modus vivendi* is established between pope and Curia on the one hand and the young churches of the south on the other. John Paul's understandable preoccupation with Poland and eastern Europe is unlikely to be continued by his successors. Brazil, Argentina, India, the Philippines, Nigeria, and the Congo may matter more for the shaping of Catholicism in the twenty-first century than traditional pillars such as France, Spain, Ireland, and Poland, though the mediating position of the vast church of the United States may still prove to matter most of all. While the decline in church practice or missionary enthusiasm in France or Ireland is undeniable, there is as yet little evidence to suggest that world wide the strength of Catholicism is in decline and, if the reforms of Vatican II have led to a shaking of the foundations unprecedented for many centuries, they have also contributed to a massive renewal evident above all within the third world.

See also: Catholicism and Gender; Christianity Origins: Primitive and 'Western' History; Historiography and Historical Thought: Christian Tradition; Historiography and Historical Thought: Classical Period (Especially Greece and Rome); Latin American Studies: Religion; Middle Ages, The; Orthodoxy; Reformation and Confessionalization; Religion: Evolution and Development; Religion, History of; Religion, Sociology of; Renaissance; Revolutions of 1989–90 in Eastern Central Europe; Western European Studies: Religion;

Bibliography

Alberigo G (ed.) 1995 *History of Vatican II*. Orbis, Maryknoll, NY

Aubert R 1978 *The Church in a Secularised Society*. Paulist Press, New York

Cleary E L, Stewart-Gambino H (eds.) 1992 *Conflict and Competition: The Latin-American Church in a Changing Environment*. Lynne Rienner Publishers, Boulder, CO

Duffy E 1997 *Saints and Sinners: A History of the Popes*. Yale University Press, New Haven, CT

Ellis J T 1969 *American Catholicism*. University of Chicago Press, Chicago

Flannery A 1992 *Vatican Council II: The Conciliar and Post-conciliar Documents*. Dominican Publications, Dublin, Eire

Gannon T M (ed.) 1988 *World Catholicism in Transition*. Macmillan, New York

Gifford P 1998 *African Christianity: Its Public Role*. Indiana University Press, Bloomington, IN

Greeley A M 1977 *The American Catholic: A Social Portrait*. Basic Books, New York

Hastings A 1989 *African Catholicism*. SCM Press, London

Hastings A (ed.) 1991 *Modern Catholicism*. SPCK, London

Hastings A (ed.) 1999 *A World History of Christianity*. Eerdmans, Grand Rapids, MI

Hebblethwaite P 1984 *John XXIII: Pope of the Council*. Chapman, London

Hebblethwaite P 1993 *Paul VI: The First Modern Pope*. Paulist Press, New York

Hennesey J J 1981 *American Catholics: A History of the Roman Catholic Community in the United States*. Oxford University Press, New York

Hornsby-Smith M P 1987 *Roman Catholics in England: Studies in Social Structure Since the Second World War*. Cambridge University Press, Cambridge, UK

Keough D 1990 *Church and Politics in Latin America*. St Martin's Press, New York

McBrien R P 1994 *Catholicism*. Harper, San Francisco

McBrien R P (ed.) 1995 *The Harper Collins Encyclopedia of Catholicism*. HarperCollins, New York

O'Farrell P 1977 *The Catholic Church and Community in Australia: an History*. Nelson, West Melbourne, Australia

A. Hastings

Catholicism and Gender

Christianity in its beginnings appeared to offer a gender-inclusive promise of redemption. Both women and men entered the baptismal waters to be freed from the corrupting power of the old Adam and to rise to newness of life in Christ. This vision of an inclusive community of redemption was rooted in the ministry of Jesus and the early Jesus community. Here it was suggested that women and other despised people are not just included in the existing social and cultural system, but that system itself is to be radically dismantled and turned upside down.

This vision was expressed in the baptismal formula cited in St. Paul's *Letter to the Galatians* (3:28):

> For as many of you are baptized into Christ have put on Christ. There is neither Jew nor Greek, there is neither slave nor free. There is neither male nor female, for you are all one in Christ Jesus.

Some early Christians understood this as meaning that baptism into Christ dissolved the social subordination of women to men and allowed women to preach and travel as itinerant evangelists. But this view clashed with deeply held assumptions that the female was inferior, unclean, under subjugation by nature, unable to image God.

Paul himself sought to modify this radical vision by suggesting that although this transformation of relations will happen very soon, for 'the time is later now than when we first believed,' it has not yet happened. Here and now all are to remain in their present social conditions, whether married or unmarried, slave or free.

Paul's successors sought to systematize his efforts by spiritualizing equality and splitting it from social relations, insisting that the hierarchical authority of the paterfamilias is still intact. Wives, youths, and slaves must not only continue to obey their husbands, fathers, and masters, but do so willingly.

But this conflict between egalitarian and patriarchic views of the church continued in the second century. The deutero-Pauline letter of I Timothy tries to counteract women who are claiming a public ministry by a patriarchic reading of Genesis 1–3. Women were created second and sinned first; they are under subjugation through their secondary place in God's original order of creation. Moreover, this subjugation is redoubled through their primacy in sin. They may not preach, but are to keep silence. They are saved only by accepting this subjugation in marriage, child bearing, and modest, submissive behavior.

This struggle between conflicting views of Christianity continued into the third century. By the fourth century, these more radical versions of redemptive equality had been mostly defeated. The women who flocked into celibate Christian monastic life in the fourth and fifth centuries accepted their segregation from public ministry and preaching in the church. Yet the idea continued to linger in female monasticism that the female ascetic, by virtue of renouncing marriage, was no longer under male domination.

Augustine tried to fuse these contradictions between creational patriarchy and redemptive equality. He realized that in order for woman to be redeemed in Christ she must be made in the image of God, otherwise she would have no redeemable soul. But he was also bound by Paul's dictum in I Corinthians that only the male is the image and likeness of God, and woman has only a secondary reflection of humanness under the male.

Augustine's solution was to split the image of God as a gender-neutral spiritual soul from woman's nature as female. The sex-neutral soul in woman is in the image of God and possesses a redeemable soul, but, as female, she is not in the image of God but images the body, the subjugated lower self. As female, woman was made subject to the male from the beginning, even in the original creation. This subjugation has to do with her role as wife, and sexual partner for the production of children. Furthermore, due to her primary role in leading the male into disobedience to God, woman's original subordination has now been worsened into coercive servitude. This subjugation is not changed by baptism or even by celibacy. Rather, a Christian woman should accept her subordination willingly as both her original place in creation and as punishment for her primacy in sin. This subordination will disappear only in heaven when the created order of sex, procreation, mortality, and sin is swallowed up in redemptive immortality.

This Augustinian view would be transmitted to the Middle Ages as orthodoxy to be repeated in substantially the same form by Thomas Aquinas, with the addition of the Aristotelian anthropology that defined women as biologically inferior, non-normative human beings. For Thomas Aquinas, this inferior nature of woman meant that Christ had to be a male in order to represent the fullness of human nature, only possessed by males. Only males, in turn, could represent Christ in the priesthood. Moreover, women could not exercise public authority in their own right, since they were by nature under subjugation.

Yet alternative traditions continue to lurk around the edges of the Medieval Catholic tradition, ideas of an original spiritual equality that was accessible here and now through redemptive conversion. There was also the Pentecost tradition, in which the gift of the Spirit empowers women as well as men to speak as God's prophets. In the Wisdom tradition, God coming forth to create the world is personified as female. The creating, redeeming God is imaged as both male and female.

Medieval female mystics, such as Hildegard of Bingen and Julian of Norwich, laid hold of these alternative traditions. Although accepting female subordination in marriage, they assumed that they had been freed from this subordination through celibacy and withdrawal into a female community independent of male rule, where women religiously governed their own lives. As virginal women they existed no longer as *femina*, but as *homo*, as the spiritual self made in the image and likeness of God. Through the gift of the Spirit, they had been freed from silence and called to speak as God's prophetic voice to the church and society at large, calling them to account for their sins and revealing the mysteries of God's coming transformation of the world.

Hildegard of Bingen, Julian of Norwich and other female mystics also claimed the wisdom tradition to define a feminine personification of God through which God created, sustains, and reconciles creation to God-self. The wisdom tradition enabled these female mystics to overcome the assumption that God is essentially male and so woman as woman cannot image God. As divine wisdom woman images God and God is imaged as woman. This female wisdom tradition culminates in the thought of Julian of Norwich, where femaleness is brought into the Trinity itself. As Julian puts it, 'As truly as God is our Father, so truly is God our Mother.'

The Reformation era of the sixteenth to seventeenth centuries was in many ways a setback for women. Laws that allowed women membership in guilds and control of property were narrowing. The Protestant Reformation abolished celibacy while championing the patriarchal family, where women's sole vocation was that of dutiful wife and mother. Women lost many vocations that had been available through celibate female communities.

In Catholic areas, of course, monastic life for women continued, but the narrowing of women's legal and economic opportunities also happened there. The Catholic Counter-Reformation stressed the strict cloistering of women and resisted the efforts of many creative women of the period, such as Mary Ward in England, who sought to found new non-cloistered activist orders for women. Women were either to be wives obedient to their husbands or cloistered nuns obedient to the male authorities of the church.

A few Catholic humanist thinkers, such as Erasmus, championed women's expanded education. The maverick Catholic humanist Agrippa von Nettesheim even suggested that women were originally not only spiritually equal to men, but superior in their representation of the divine Wisdom of God. Male domination was recent, and manifested not God's will or female inferiority, but simply male tyranny. But this view was deeply contrary to the trends of the times and would not be heard again until expounded by late eighteenth century feminists—for example, Mary Wollstonecraft, wh ochampioned women's rights in her treatise, *The Vindication of the Rights of Woman* (1792). Such views would not appear in Catholicism until after the Second Vatican Council in the 1960s.

There was virtually no organized Catholic participation in the first wave of American feminism that ran from the first Women's Rights Convention in Seneca Falls, New York in 1848 until the winning of women's suffrage in 1920. The reasons for this lie in several factors; first, the Catholic bishops were vehemently opposed to feminism, associating it with a secular modern apostasy to Christian and 'family' values, represented by child labor laws, the Equal Rights Amendment, birth control, divorce, liberalism, and socialism. Many bishops explicitly rejected women's suffrage itself, claiming that it would take women out of their proper sphere in the family.

The view of gender that came to prevail in nineteenth and early twentieth century Catholicism was no longer one that stressed women's inferiority, but rather their complementarity to men. Women were different and even better than men, but their specific nature lay in their passive auxiliary being. Women were 'Marylike,' rather than 'Christlike.' They are to represent the church in its submission to Christ, and to masculine leadership, not taking any such leadership themselves. In these views, Catholicism echoed and put its particular stamp on the romantic views of gender complementarity common to the period.

The conflict between official Catholicism and more egalitarian views of women has moved into the Catholic community in the post-Vatican II era. Vatican II itself largely ignored women. Women, even women religious, were absent from the delegates to the Council. Protest about women's absence by Cardinal Leon-Joseph Suenens in 1962 brought a slight change. A few women religious and laywomen were allowed as 'auditors' without vote in the later sessions of the Council. Three even served on commissions that drafted the final Council statements, specifically those on 'the Church in the Modern World' and on the 'Apostolate of the Laity.'

The final documents of the Council have a few concessions to women's new role in work and legal equality in modern society. It is said that women are claiming a new equity for themselves before the law and in fact, and the participation of women in cultural life should be acknowledged and supported by the church. These statements are echoed in Pope John XXIII's encyclical *Pacem in Terris* (1963). Here it is said that 'women are becoming ever more conscious of their human dignity, they will not tolerate being used as mere material instruments, but demand rights befitting the human person in both domestic and in public life' (Sect. 41).

These concessions to women's role in public society did not include changes in the life of the church itself, in terms of women's ordination, or in teachings on sexuality and reproduction. Both of these were being challenged in the 1960s. Mainline Protestant churches in Western Europe and North America had begun to ordain women in increasing numbers in the 1960s. In 1976 the American Episcopal Church endorsed women's ordination, a change that brought women into the priesthood in a tradition more closely allied to Catholicism.

The Roman Magisterium responded with an encyclical in that same year insisting that women could not be ordained because as women they lacked the capacity to 'image Christ.' Maleness and representation of Christ as a male were thus identified in a way that many Catholics had come to be seen as questionable. Far from ending the discussion, support groups for women's ordination among Catholics have grown since 1975 in Europe, and the United States and Canada.

Another area of contention among Catholics has been the traditional teaching that sex (allowable within marriage alone) is primarily for procreation, and cannot be separated from its procreational potential. Thus birth control (other than the rhythm method) is forbidden. As moral theologians and ordinary Catholics began increasingly to question these teachings, Pope Paul VI convened a commission to study the question in 1964. The commission met from 1964–7 and included among its members three married couples who testified to the anxiety created by lack of reliable family planning.

The commission's report voted to change the teaching to one that accepted all medically approved methods of birth control within the context of committed, child-raising families. But this official report was rejected by Pope Paul VI, who was advised by a few dissenters that such a change would threaten the church's claim to authoritative teaching. The reaffirmation of the anti-birth control teaching in the papal enclyclical *Humanae Vitae* (1968) created a storm of protest. Most lay Catholics have simply chosen to ignore the Church's teaching on this subject. Yet the Vatican, under John Paul II, has continued to insist on this teaching and even to claim that it is unchangeable, deepening the conflict between Magisterium and laity.

Recognizing the deeply conflicted state of relations of the official church to women, the American bishops voted in the early 1980s to engage in an official dialog with the US Women's Ordination Conference. At the conclusion of this dialog the bishops decided to undertake a pastoral letter on women in the church. They conducted a series of 'listening sessions' with Catholic women around the United States to hear their issues. They then began to draft an epistle that declared that men and women should be partners in home, family, and church. The epistle even condemned 'sexism' as a sin.

But the Vatican intervened in the process of drafting this letter, demanding that the condemnation of birth control and women's ordination must be strengthened, and that the model of male–female relations must be one of complementarity, not partnership. The effect of these interventions was a decision by the American bishops to table the epistle, rather than issue a document that was likely to worsen rather than improve relations with women.

This conflict between official teachings of the Vatican and a growing consciousness of their rights to equality among Catholic women (and male sup-

porters) is by no means limited to North America. Feminist theological networks grew in Western Europe in the 1980s and 1990s, and in the Catholic church in Asia, Africa, and Latin America. With an increasing crisis in the celibate male priesthood, more and more of the ministry in Catholic parishes and chaplaincies is being done by theologically trained laywomen.

Thus the conflict between the Catholic hierarchy and women, exacerbated by the reactionary policies of the pontificate of John Paul II, showed no signs of abating at the end of the twentieth century. The issues go far beyond the inclusion of a few token women in clerical office. They point to a fundamental rethinking of ancient traditions that are rooted in the male hierarchy and a view of femaleness and sexuality as expressions of inferiority and sin to be distanced from the 'purity' of sacramental office.

A thoroughgoing rethinking of these patterns any time soon in official teaching seems unlikely. But since women who claim a more egalitarian view of themselves and their right to decide about their own bodies show no signs of departing in large numbers from the Catholic church, it is likely that this conflict will continue in the foreseeable future as a deep schism of viewpoints concerning gender identity and relations among Catholics.

See also: Buddhism and Gender; Catholicism; Family and Gender; Feminist Theology; Goddess Worship (Old and New): Cultural Concerns; Islam and Gender; Judaism and Gender; Protestantism and Gender; Religion and Gender; Religion: Family and Kinship; Religion: Mobilization and Power; Religion: Morality and Social Control; Women's Religiosity

Bibliography

Boerrsen K E 1981 *Subordination and Equivalence: The Nature and Role of Women in Augustine and Thomas Aquinas.* University Press of America, Washington, DC
Kaiser R B 1986 *The Politics of Sex and Religion.* Leaven Press, Kansas City, MO
Raming I 1976 *The Exclusion of Women from the Priesthood: Divine Law or Sex Discrimination?* Trans. N Adams, Scarecrow Press, Metuchen, NJ
Ruether R R 1995 'Catholic women'. In: *In Our Own Voices: Four centuries of American women's religious writing* 1st edn., Harper, San Francisco, pp. 17–60
Ruether R R 1998 *Women and Redemption: A Theological History.* Fortress Press, Minneapolis, MN
Swidler L, Swidler A 1977 *Women Priests: A Catholic Commentary on the Vatican Declaration.* Paulist Press, New York
Weaver M J 1985 *New Catholic Women: A Contemporary Challenge to Traditional Religious Authority,* 1st edn. Harper & Row, San Francisco

R. R. Ruether

Cattell, Raymond Bernard (1905–98)

In describing the psychologist Raymond Bernard Cattell's comprehensive research program, Child, in a single sentence, gave an amazingly complete and accurate description: 'His major concern was to map out an integrated theory of human intellectual, temperamental and motivational characteristics within the context of hereditary and environmental influences using multivariate methods of analysis' (Child 1998, p. 356). In trying to convey the sweep of Cattell's theoretical and empirical work Goldberg (1968) referred to him as 'psychology's master strategist' (p. 617). Indeed, the sheer audacity of venturing into so many major research areas during one career is unlikely to be seen again for some time.

Raymond B. Cattell was born on March 20, 1905 in Staffordshire, England. He was raised in Devon, near the town of Torquay. Cattell began his academic career in chemistry at University College, London and received his Bachelor of Science degree with first class honors in 1924. Drawn to the study of psychology, Cattell began work on a doctorate at King's College, also in 1924. After completing his Ph.D. in 1929, Cattell did some teaching at University College, Exeter before becoming Director of the School Psychological Services and Clinic at Leicester in 1932.

In 1937, E. L. Thorndike invited Cattell to come for a year to Columbia University as a research associate. Subsequently, he also spent brief periods at Clark, Harvard, and Duke universities. During his time at Harvard, Cattell began seriously to develop the methodology for intensively studying the single case (P-technique factor analysis) in which he remained interested throughout his career. Cattell acknowledges that with his ' … office … having been next door to Gordon Allport's, the latter may also have played an initiating part' but goes on to lament that although Allport, too, was ' … in pursuit of uniqueness of personality … ' he had ' … some unreadiness to come to grips with statistical models' (Cattell 1984, p. 141). Exhibiting a certain disdain for those who refused to use 'proper' methods, no matter how celebrated their status, was one of Cattell's stable characteristics.

Cattell worked for a time during the latter years of World War II in the Adjutant General's Office. In 1945 he became a research professor at the University of Illinois in Urbana-Champaign and remained there until 1973 when, in part due to age restrictions then in force, he retired. He moved on to the University of Hawaii where he maintained a special appointment for a few years. When that appointment ended, Cattell stayed in Honolulu and continued to work informally with several younger colleagues and to publish an occasional paper. One of his last publications (McArdle and Cattell 1994) brought to a close his 50-year affair (Cattell 1944) with the beguiling concepts of

'parallel proportional profiles' and 'confactor rotation,' more of which will be said later.

By far the longest and most productive portion of Cattell's scientific career occurred while he was Director of the Laboratory of Personality Assessment and Group Behavior (later the Laboratory for Personality Analysis) at the University of Illinois. It was from this setting that his influence on the development of the science of psychology hit its maximum. The sheer number of big ideas and level of productivity in following them up during those years are remarkable. His success in claiming his 'fair' share of CPU time on the Illiac, the university's automatic computer, was legendary. Although by today's standards, its capacity was meager, at the time the Illiac allowed Cattell to do large factor analyses in weeks and months that would otherwise have taken years.

1. Contributions to the Methods and the Substance of Psychology

Raymond B. Cattell is an exemplar of a class of psychological researchers who were heavily invested in the application of quantitative models to the study of behavior. Also included were the likes of Cyril Burt, Hans J. Eysenck, J. P. Guilford, Charles Spearman, Godfrey Thompson, and L. L. Thurstone. Let it be said openly that this is not a list of like-minded individuals who necessarily had more in common than not. Rather, it is a list of important contributors to the development of psychology as a science who relied substantially on the models and methods of factor analysis in their empirical research pursuits. In both strategy and tactics, they differed from each other in the use of factor analytic methods.

Because of Cattell's heavy reliance on factor analysis, it is not possible to separate the substance from the methods. In fact, in an earlier review of Cattell's research program in *Theories of Personality* (Hall and Lindzey 1978), the chapter heading is 'Cattell's Factor Theory.' Therefore, a discussion of his work can be usefully begun with a methodological introduction.

At the heart of Cattell's research program lay the basic equation of the common factor model. Cattell referred to it as the factor specification equation and wrote it as:

$$a_{ji} = b_{j1} \cdot f_{1i} + b_{j2} \cdot f_{2i} + \cdots + b_{jk} \cdot f_{ki} + u_{ji}$$

where a_{ji} is a score for person i on behavior (or act) a_j, and f_{qi} ($q = 1, 2, …, k$) represent the ith person's endowments or scores on the k common factors, the b_{jq} ($q = 1, 2, …, k$) are weights (factor loadings) that specify the amount to which any individual's score on the qth factor contributes to (in Cattell's theoretical framework, *determines*) his score on variable a_j, and u_{ji} is a contribution to a_{ji} that is unique to both the behavior and the individual. The u_{ji} terms include both errors of measurement and portions of the observed score that are reliably measured, but fall outside the purview of the common factors defining the interrelations of a given set of variables.

The b_{jq} values, which Cattell referred to as situational indices (later, behavioral indices), brought the situation and the individual's traits into the same equation so that both individual and situational information could be used to predict behavior. Suppose, for example, a given individual had a very high endowment on the factor Cattell labeled Exvia, which was similar in nature to the individual differences dimension called Extraversion in many personality research and theory contexts. If, on the one hand, the b_j for Exvia with respect to performance of a given a_j was small, then that high level of Exvia had little or no bearing on that person's a_j score. On the other hand, however, if b_j for Exvia on performance of a given a_j was large, then that high level of Exvia had major influence in determining that person's a_j. By contrast, for the person with a near zero level of Exvia, little would be contributed to their performance on a_j by the Exvia factor even if the b_j for Exvia was large, because the product $b_{j,exvia} \cdot f_{exvia,i}$ would be close to zero.

This factor specification equation is thus a 'working model' of the individual differences orientation in that the differing amounts of the latent attributes possessed by different people (variation in the f_q) are 'converted' into differences in their scores on the observed variables (variation in the a_j). By knowing the amounts of a person's trait endowments and the magnitude of the contribution the traits made to manifest variables, one could predict an individual's scores on the manifest variables, that is, behavior.

Within that framework, the scientific agenda is rather clear: define the latent factors as clearly as possible, construct tests to measure them accurately, and develop empirically based estimates of the b values for the manifest variables, the a_j, of interest. Then one has made the prediction objective of science reachable and can also elaborate an explanatory system as well by detailing more and more regarding the nature of the factors (e.g., see how the factors behave across different media of observation and how stable they are across time, examine their genetic and environmental variance contributions, plot their age changes, etc.). Attacking these several objectives was a major part of Cattell's research program.

Thus, despite knowing the adaptations in the methods of the physical sciences had to be made in studying behavior, Cattell's methodological approach showed a deep reliance on fundamental principles of physical science. He believed that factors were causal influences on observable variables and that, in analytical work, when the factors had been properly rotated to their 'causal influence' identities, the factor loadings (the b_j values in the specification equation) would be proportional for a given set of behaviors (the a_j values in the specification equation) across different samples. This represented an explicit commitment to a fundamental objective of scientific research: the identification of relationships that remain *invariant* under different transformations. In his context, Cattell formalized this notion in the terms 'parallel proportional profiles' (the results) and 'confactor rotation' (the method) mentioned earlier. Along the way, he worked on the development of methods for assessing the similarity of factor loading patterns so that one could render some judgment about factorial invariance even without reaching the ideal parallel proportional profiles.

Cattell was also firmly committed to the principles of rigorous, quantitative measurement and scaling and once presented, with characteristic lack of modesty, a proposed more basic set of concepts (Cattell 1964) to replace the prevailing notions of reliability and validity. In so doing, he again challenged the status quo regarding the role of item homogeneity in evaluating the quality of measuring instruments.

Cattell placed a strict reliance on mathematical representations of phenomena of interest although, in his case, this amounted generally to using some variant of the common factor model. His insistence on the introduction of rigor into the definition of psychological concepts left its mark in a number of ways. He argued that ambiguity and confusion about concepts could be reduced by discarding as many of those in vogue as possible, discovering and defining new ones, and giving them new names to mark their unique status. In the process, he delivered such labels as 'cortertia' (cortical alertness) and 'threctia' (threat reactivity) to identify major individual differences in dimensions of personality.

A monograph on real-base, true zero scaling (Cattell 1972) illustrates the concern he held for fundamental issues of scaling, the commitment and energy with which he would attack a problem, provide a solution, and advance it for discussion and debate. Debate, however, was not always the reaction evoked by his proposals.

In addition to this strong analysis and modeling orientation, Cattell's research program was buttressed by several other key attributes. Where others might carve up the study of behavior to identify more clearly a piece for themselves in the broader scheme, Cattell did so as a way of more systematically approaching the whole. Much of his work was organized around the tripartite division of abilities, temperament, and motivation. But he enriched this classical triumvirate by distinguishing between surface and source traits, estimating heritability coefficients, and incorporating concepts of psychological states, learning theory, and situational influences. He introduced the multiple abstract variance analysis (MAVA) design to incorporate different family configurations into the estimation of heritability coefficients and in the design of correlational studies he saw not one, but six important ways to interrelate variables, persons, and occasions of measurement. He systematized the latter in a heuristic often referred to as the 'data box' or covariation chart (Cattell 1952) which is still frequently encountered in the literature.

As an example of his capacity for orderly abstraction and the willingness and ease with which he would think 'big,' Cattell was not satisfied to name and report the results of his many factor analyses. Instead, he proposed the development of a Universal Index (U. I.) of factors, the first 15 of which (U. I. 1 through U. I. 15) were to be reserved for what he considered to be the well-established human ability factors. He then proceeded to assign the next 17 numbers (U. I. 16 through U. I. 32) for factors based on objective tests on which he had published. He invited further contributions to this indexing system but, as one might expect from even a passing acquaintance with human nature, one person's proposal for a Universal Index is hardly likely to be adopted readily by others.

In addition to a frequently observed trait of successful research scientists—a desire to be first and to receive credit for it—Cattell was gifted with a high level of intelligence and capacity for abstract thought. He made up many of the items for the Culture Fair Intelligence tests (Cattell 1954) himself; took delight in the rapidity with which he could solve items from 'would be' intelligence test item writers and, in return, relished 'stumping' them with a recently written item or two of his own.

The levels of abstraction with which Cattell felt quite comfortable were in many cases a far remove from data. For example, second-order factor analyses (factor analyzing the intercorrelations of factors) were routine in his laboratory. Third-order factor analyses, while not routine, were completed on several occasions to which published papers attest. Along the way, at least one fourth-order factor analysis was conducted.

Cattell was not inclined to be tolerant of others' lack of knowledge of his system. Those who worked in his laboratory were apt to be rebuffed when they would occasionally suggest ways by which he might strengthen the bonds of communication with his readers. 'Let them go and read my 1957 book' (Cattell 1957), was the reply heard on more than one occasion to the suggestion that a little more detail might be helpful to the reader. Nor, as was already mentioned, was he kindly diposed toward those he felt were not using the multivariate tools of the trade wisely.

Cattell was an avid reader (and writer) of poetry and also enjoyed biographies from which he enriched his own writing. His enormous legacy of books, chapters, and articles, numbering well over 500 publications, exhibit many examples of his caring about the craft of writing as well as the ideas being written about. He would search for just the right word or turn of phrase—and did so amazingly quickly! When he was well into his eighties the author once asked him in what areas of his intellectual functioning he could detect losses. He responded that he didn't act on visual input as rapidly as he used to when, for instance, driving his automobile. (This was true!) But, he very quickly added, he could still retrieve adjectives, etc., quite handily when he was writing and he was very pleased about it. Some of his 'classic' remarks, many of which are buried in footnotes, will likely go unheeded by the future generations, and that will be a stylistic as well as a substantive loss. For example, his characterization of the hyperplane as 'the footprint of a causal influence' or his accusation that by developing and making widely available the by then nearly ubiquitous orthogonal analytic rotation program, Varimax, Henry Kaiser had 'put opium on the market,' are illustrative.

Cattell's deep reliance on factor analysis was symptomatic of his belief that the workings of variables should be examined with as little interference as possible from the observer. The methods of factor analysis could then be used to tease out the key patterns of relationships. As any craftsman, Cattell felt strongly about having access to proper tools and worked to evolve factor analytic methods during the length of his career. He did this both by formalizing design with the presentation of the covariation chart or 'data box' and by restlessly pushing technological developments. The ever present need for faster, more efficient methods for conducting factor analysis if his research goals were to be realized, directly resulted in software applications such as Maxplane, Procrustes, and Rotoplot to facilitate rotation of factors to a final solution. The Rotoplot program, for instance, displayed the pairwise factor (actually, reference vector) plots on an oscilloscope and filmed them by 35 mm camera mounted on the oscilloscope. As soon as the film strip could be processed, Cattell would project the plots on his office wall and write down the tangents of the angles of rotation for another run, urgently trying to achieve 'maximum simple structure' so that factors could be interpreted and the article written and submitted. At the time that Rotoplot was invented, others who were doing graphical rotation of factors were having to have each pairwise plot rendered by triangle and T-square.

2. Bridging Psychology's Past and its Future

Cattell and his research program represent an important bridge between psychology's past and its future. While he was alive, Cattell was a personal, as well as scientific link to the psychology's past. On occasion, he would tell of conversations (sometimes, encounters) with the likes of Burt, Fisher, Pearson, and Spearman. Although he was not a student of Thurstone, he seized on the tool of multiple factor analysis which Thurstone was so instrumental in bringing to psychologists and future refined it to his own ends. At the same time, his zeal in promoting, and passing along to future generations of researchers not only his substantive findings but also the methods that he thought were appropriate and necessary for psychological research, forged important links to the future. He was a prime mover in establishing the Society of Multivariate Experimental Psychology (SMEP) and the founding of the society's journal, *Multivariate Behavioral Research* (MBR). He helped to launch MBR in 1966 with a provocative lead article entitled 'Multivariate Behavioral Research and the Integrative Challenge,' in which he summarized his own version of the two general traditions of psychological research—the experimental and the individual differences traditions—and pointed out the directions for future research that would elevate the study of behavior to new levels of competence. In that same year the first edition of the *Handbook of Multivariate Experimental Psychology*, for which Cattell was both the editor and the major contributor, was published. A second edition followed 22 years later (Nesselroade and Cattell 1988).

McArdle (1984) credited Cattell with having a profound effect on the development of what is now referred to generally as 'structural modeling' the fitting of quantitative models to covariance matrices (and occasionally the associated arithmetic means, as well), which has grown to enormous proportion in current day psychological research. This connection reinforces the amazingly productive service Cattell extracted from the factor analytic model. Cattell's empirical and theoretical work, as no one else's, has helped to clarify the distinction between latent and manifest variables and the key properties of both.

The contributions that Cattell made both substantively and methodologically were many. Here, we have only touched on some of the major ones. He developed and presented one of the most systematic and encompassing theories of personality that psychology has ever seen. Along the way, he introduced a large number of methodological innovations, some of which have made their way into today's behavioral science argot with an ease that today gives no hint of Cattell's pioneering contribution. The 'scree test,' 'Procrustes' rotation, and 'P-technique' come readily to mind.

The theory of fluid and crystallized intelligence, on which Cattell collaborated closely with Horn (Horn and Cattell 1966) remains very much in currency today as far as so-called psychometrically oriented models of cognition are concerned. The apparently different age gradients of these two kinds of abilities has helped to stimulate thinking not only about the complexity of the organism and the nature of its development across the lifespan (e.g., Baltes 1987), but also about the need to consider what level of aggregation of variables is optimal for a given purpose.

Despite Cattell's strong investment in the study of human abilities (Cattell 1971), he did not neglect the temperament and motivation components of his re-

search program. For example, the fruits of his efforts to measure temperament by questionnaire, especially, are evident today in the continuing usage of the High School Personality Questionnaire (HSPQ) and the 16 Personality Factor questionnaire (16PF). Some of the work of which Cattell was most proud and for which he had the highest hopes sprang from his contributions to the study of motivation. His concept of the dynamic calculus, which was an attempt to write a systematic prediction equation for behavior that included trait, state, and dynamic aspects was refined into what he came to call structured learning theory. In the author's view, this was a key contribution in Cattell's own evaluation of his scientific legacy.

Many of the individuals who received their scientific training in Cattell's laboratory are still active and productive today. They, in turn, are passing on to their students the concepts of the data box, fluid and crystallized intelligence, covariation designs, factorial invariance, states versus traits, etc.

Despite the comprehensive perspective, the numerous insights and innovations, and the sheer bulk of his scholarly output, which spanned parts of eight different decades, Raymond B. Cattell's place in the history of psychology will not be identified without controversy for the foreseeable future. A lifetime achievement award for his contributions to psychology to be given by the American Psychological Foundation was announced in early 1997. Although Cattell had never taken kindly to the science 'establishment,' he had reached a point in his journey where such a high level of recognition for his scientific work meant something to him. But it was not to be. Some of his more philosophical, provocative writings having to do with the roles in our society of genetics, evolution, and public policy had generated bitter and sufficient resentment that, after some 'negotiating,' the award was withdrawn prior to the 1997 annual meeting of the American Psychological Association in Chicago, where it was to have been given. Cattell died the following February 2, at the age of 92.

See also: Adult Cognitive Development: Post-Piagetian Perspectives; Behavioral Assessment; Darwin, Charles Robert (1809–82); Factor Analysis and Latent Structure: Overview; Galton, Sir Francis (1822–1911); Lifespan Theories of Cognitive Development; Multivariate Analysis: Overview; Parsons, Talcott (1902–79); Personality Structure; Personality Theories; Quetelet, Adolphe (1796–1874); Thorndike, Edward Lee (1874–1949)

Bibliography

Baltes P B 1987 Theoretical propositions of life-span developmental psychology: On the dynamics between growth and decline. *Developmental Psychology* **23**(5): 611–26

Cattell R B 1944 'Parallel proportional profiles' and other principles for determining the choice of factors by rotation. *Psychometrika* **9**: 267–83

Cattell R B 1952 *Factor Analysis*. Harper, New York

Cattell R B 1954 *Culture Fair Intelligence Tests, Scales 1, 2, and 3, Forms A and B, rev. edn.* IPAT, Champaign, IL

Cattell R B 1957 *Personality and Motivation Structure and Measurement*. World Book Co., New York

Cattell R B 1964 Validity and reliability: A proposed more basic set of concepts. *Journal of Educational Psychology* **55**: 1–22

Cattell R B 1971 *Abilities: Their Structure, Growth, and Action.* Houghton Mifflin, Boston

Cattell R B 1972 Real base, true zero factor analysis. *Multivariate Behavioral Research Monographs* **72**(1): 1–162

Cattell R B 1984 The voyage of a laboratory, 1928–1984. *Multivariate Behavioral Research* **19**: 121–74

Child D 1998 Raymond Bernard Cattell (1905–1998). *British Journal of Mathematical and Statistical Psychology* **51**: 353–7

Goldberg L R 1968 Objective Personality and Motivation Tests—theoretical introduction and practical compendium—Cattel R B and Warburton F W. *Contemporary Psychology* **13**: 617–9

Hall C S, Lindzey G 1978 *Theories of Personality*, 3rd edn. Wiley, New York

Horn J L, Cattell R B 1966 Refinement and test of the theory of fluid and crystallized general intelligences. *Journal of Educational Psychology* **57**: 253–70

McArdle J J 1984 On the madness in his method: R. B. Cattell's contributions to structural equation modeling. *Multivariate Behavioral Research* **19**: 246–67

McArdle J J, Cattell R B 1994 Structural equation models of factorial invariance in parallel proportional profiles and oblique confactor problems. *Multivariate Behavioral Research* **29**(1): 63–113

Nesselroade J R, Cattell R B (eds.) 1988 *Handbook of Multivariate Experimental Psychology*, 2nd edn. Plenum, New York

J. R. Nesselroade

Causal Counterfactuals in Social Science Research

The term 'counterfactual conditional' is used in logical analyses to refer to any expression of the general form: 'If A were the case then B would be the case.' In this usage, A is usually false or untrue in the world so that A is 'contrary to fact' or counterfactual. Examples abound. 'If kangaroos had no tails, they would topple over' (Lewis 1973b). 'If an hour ago I had taken two aspirins instead of just a glass of water, my headache would now be gone' (Rubin 1978). Perhaps the most obnoxious counterfactuals in any language are those of the form: 'If I were you, I would ... .'

Lewis (1973a) observed the connection between counterfactual conditionals and references to causation. He finds these logical constructions in the language used by Hume in his famous discussion of causation. Hume defined causation twice over. He wrote 'we may define a cause to be *an object followed by another, and where all the objects, similar to the first, are followed by objects similar to the second. Or, in other words, where, if the first object had not been, the second never had existed*' (Lewis 1973a, italics are Lewis's).

Lewis draws attention to the comparison between the factual first definition where one object *is* followed by another and the counterfactual second definition where, counterfactually, it is supposed that if the first object 'had not been' the second object would not have been either.

It is the connection between counterfactuals and causation that makes them relevant to social science research. From the point of view of some authors, it is difficult, if not impossible, to make any sense of causal statements without using counterfactual language (Lewis 1973a, Holland 1986, Rubin 1978, Robins 1985, 1986). Other authors are concerned that using such language gives an emphasis to unobservable entities that is inappropriate in the analysis of empirical data (Dawid 1997, Shafer 1996). The discussion here accepts counterfactuals in discussions of causation and will explain their role in the estimation of causal effects based on the work of Neyman (1923, 1935), Rubin (1974, 1978), and others.

We begin with a simple observation. Suppose that we find that a student's test performance changes from a score of X to a score of Y after some educational intervention. We might then be tempted to attribute the pretest-posttest change, $Y - X$ to the intervening educational experience, that is, to use the gain score as a measure of the improvement due to the intervention. However, this is social science and not the tightly controlled 'before-after' measurements made in a physics laboratory. There are many other possible explanations of the gain, $Y - X$. Some of the more obvious are: simple maturation, other educational experiences occurring during the relevant time period, and differences in either the tests or the testing conditions at pre- and posttests. Cook and Campbell (1979) provide a classic list of 'threats to internal validity' that address many of the types of alternative explanations for apparent causal effects of interventions. For this reason, it is important to think about the real meaning of the attribution of cause. In this regard, Lewis's discussion of Hume serves us well. From it we see that what is important is what the value of Y *would have been* had the student *not had* the educational experiences that the intervention entailed. Call this score value, Y^*. Thus enter counterfactuals. Y^* is not directly observed for the student, that is, they *did have* the educational intervention of interest, so asking for what their posttest score *would have been* had they *not had it* is asking for information collected under conditions that are contrary to fact. Hence, it is not the difference $Y - X$ that is of interest, but the difference $Y - Y^*$, and the gain score has causal significance relative to the effect of the educational experience only if X can serve as a substitute for the counterfactual Y^*. In physical-science laboratory experiments such a substitution is often easy to make, but it is rarely believable in many social science applications of any consequence.

A formal model or language for discussing the problem of estimating causal effects (of the form $Y - Y^*$ rather than $Y - X$) was developed by Neyman (for randomized experiments) and Rubin (for a wide variety of causal studies) and will be called the Neyman/Rubin model for causal effects here.

1. Prospective Causal Studies

The Neyman/Rubin model is most easily understood in the context of a *prospective causal study* that has the general structure specified by this sequence of events.

(a) Subjects or experimental units of study are identified.

(b) Baseline or pretest information about these units is recorded.

(c) The units are either assigned to (in a controlled study) or select themselves to (in studies without the control of assignment) exposure to one of the treatment conditions or interventions of the study.

(d) These units are then subsequently exposed to their assigned or self-selected treatment condition (and each unit is affected by this exposure in a manner that is unrelated to the exposure conditions of the other units).

(e) At an appropriate later time an outcome, endpoint, or posttest measure is recorded for each unit in the study.

The type of study that this five-part schema is intended to cover includes most randomized comparative experiments as well as many types of pretest/posttest quasiexperiments or observational studies. It should be emphasized that, properly interpreted, the Neyman/Rubin model has application to other types of causal studies (see Holland 1988, Holland and Rubin 1988, Robins 1997), but, for our purposes here, prospective causal studies are already sufficiently complicated and inclusive.

The condition mentioned parenthetically in (d), that the exposure conditions of the other units do not affect the outcomes associated with a given unit, is very important, and is clearly an assumption that would not be true in general. For example, in the study of infectious diseases your vaccination will affect my likelihood of contracting polio. Rubin explicitly identifies this assumption calling it the Stable Unit-Treatment Value Assumption, or SUTVA. SUTVA will be assumed throughout this discussion.

2. The Neyman/Rubin Model

The version of the Neyman/Rubin model used here is adapted from that of Holland (1986), and differs from the original versions by Neyman (1935) and Rubin (1978) mainly in its emphasis on population quantities. One of the main benefits of this model is that it identifies certain 'counterfactual conditional expectations' as the location of key assumptions about the inferential structure of any causal study and its resulting data.

The prospective causal study begins with the 'units,' 'subjects,' or 'cases' of the study, and the ith unit is denoted by the subscript 'i.' It may help the reader to imagine that this is a discussion about a very large sample of units. Denote the population of units under study by P. For the most part P will lie quietly in the background without being noticed. The baseline information that is collected or recorded for unit i will be denoted as a *vector* of numerical information, z_i.

There is a 'causal' variable denoting a set of possible 'treatments' or 'exposure' conditions to which each unit in the study could be exposed. For simplicity we assume that these are only two treatment conditions denoted by $x = 1$ (treatment) and $x = 0$ (control). A more complicated version of this would let x be a number representing the 'strength' of the treatment level, but we will just use the dichotomous case here.

An important aspect of causal variables designating such treatments levels or intervention conditions is the assumption that the level of exposure for any unit *could have been different* from what it actually was. This condition excludes 'attributes' of units (such as race, gender, age, or pretest score) as causal variables in the sense that such attributes *cannot* have 'unit-level causal effects' in the sense that we will define below. This idea is discussed more extensively in Holland (1986, 1988), and is mentioned again in another context at the end of the present discussion. Each unit is exposed to one treatment level and the value of x to which i is exposed is denoted by x_i.

Finally we come to the outcomes or dependent variables in the study, and here is where a special notation is needed. We let $Y_i(x)$ denote the (numerical) response that would be recorded for unit i if unit i were exposed to treatment level, x. For each i, $Y_i(x)$ is a function of x. It should be emphasized that $Y_i(x)$ is not directly observed unless $x_i = x$. This is an important point because it is crucial to realize that the $\{Y_i(x)\}$ do not denote *observed data* like z_i and x_i do, but rather the $\{Y_i(x)\}$ are 'potential outcomes' that lie behind the observed values of the outcome variable. For this reason, we denote the potential observations by capital letters to distinguish them from quantities that are directly observable, which we denote by lower case letters.

The connection between the potential outcomes and the actually observed outcomes is then given by the equation

$$y_i = Y_i(x_i) \tag{1}$$

where y_i is the observed outcome or value of the dependent variable for unit i. The idea behind Equation (1) is that to get from the potential outcomes

$\{Y_i(x)\}$ to an observed outcome we must select the value of x in $Y_i(x)$ to be the value to which i is actually exposed, that is, $x = x_i$, and then we obtain y_i from the potential observations, $\{Y_i(x)\}$, via Equation (1).

The *observed data* for each unit i is the vector (z_i, x_i, y_i). The potential outcomes, $\{Y_i(x)\}$, are never observed for *all* values of x for a fixed unit, i, but only for the specific x-value to which i is actually exposed, x_i. It is sometimes said that the $\{Y_i(x)\}$ are 'counterfactual' because they are not actual observations. Here they are called *potential observations* because they could have been observed had x_i been different than it was.

It is helpful to use a notation such as, $E(y)$, to mean the average value of y_i across the (large number of) units in P. Furthermore, an expression such as

$$E(y \mid x = a) \qquad (2)$$

will mean the average value of y_i across all of the (large number of) units in P for which $x_i = a$. The use of the expectation notation is to make certain quantities clearer in their meaning, and may be justified from either a frequentist or Bayesian point of view. It should be noted that within the expectation notation, the subscript i, denoting the unit, is suppressed because, within the scope of the $E(\ )$ operator, i is averaged over.

3. Using the Neyman/Rubin Model

An important fact about the Neyman/Rubin model is the Fundamental Problem of Causal Inference (Holland 1986), which is: It is impossible in principle to *observe* $Y_i(x)$ for more than one value of x for any one unit, i. Any procedure that claims to have avoided the Fundamental Problem of Causal Inference can always be shown to be based on untestable assumptions. Sometimes such assumptions are plausible, and sometimes they are not.

A basic definition that we are now in a position to make is that of a 'unit-level causal effect.' Because we are restricting attention to the simple case of two treatment levels, $x = 0/1$ we may restrict attention to these differences

$$Y_i(1) - Y_i(0) = \text{the casual effect of } x = 1$$

$$\text{relative to } x = 0 \text{ for unit } i \qquad (3)$$

In the Neyman/Rubin notation, the unit-level causal effects are the *basic* quantities of interest in causal inference. However, the Fundamental Problem of Causal Inference is now immediately seen to *be fundamental* because it implies that unit-level causal effects are, themselves, *never directly observable*. Thus, we are always reduced to making assumptions that

allow us to make some sort of conclusion or inference about these causal effects. This is the place where the Neyman/Rubin model might appear to be impractical for applied research, that is, because its most basic parameters, the unit-level causal effects, are not directly observable. Furthermore, this is exactly the place where the potential exposability of all of the levels of x to any unit is seen to be crucial to the foundations of the theory. The definition of causal effect requires this assumption so that the difference, $Y_i(1) - Y_i(0)$, is meaningful. It is the Fundamental Problem of Causal Inference and this definition of causal effect that makes causal inference both more interesting and more difficult than the simple computation of correlational and associational measures. The unit-level causal effects mimic the comparison between a 'factual' and a 'counterfactual' identified in the quote mentioned earlier from Hume by Lewis.

It is now time to introduce the notion of an Average Causal Effect (ACE). In general, an ACE is any average of unit-level causal effects. The most general ACE has the form

$$\text{ACE} = E[Y(1) - Y(0) \mid A] \qquad (4)$$

where A denotes some collection of units defined in terms of either z_i or x_i or both. In Equation (4) we again suppress the subscript i because it is being averaged over. As an example of an A in Equation (4) we might use $A = $ 'all the units in the study,' in which case the ACE is the average causal effect over all of P. But other cases might be of interest, for example, $A = $ 'all units where i is male and for whom $x_i = 1$.' In this case the ACE is for the males in treatment group 1. Here we restrict our attention to the ACE that is called the 'effect of the treatment on the treated' in which A denotes all of the units for which $x_i = 1$, that is

$$\text{ACE} = E[Y(1) - Y(0) \mid x = 1]$$

$$= E[Y(1) \mid x = 1] - E[Y(0) \mid x = 1] \qquad (5)$$

Up to now, we have simply defined the basic structure of the data collection design as well as the causal connection between the potential outcomes and the causal variable x, that is, Equation (3). We have not yet identified the connection between any quantities that could be estimated with data and the causal parameters given by either the unit-level causal effects in Equation (3) or the average causal effects in Equation (5). This leads us to the 'prima facie Average Causal Effects,' (FACEs). The FACEs are what can be estimated from the data. To parallel the ACE in Equation (5) we examine the FACE which is simply the difference between the mean of the outcome variable observed in each treatment group, that is

$$\text{FACE} = E[y \mid x = 1] - E[y \mid x = 0] \qquad (6)$$

If we substitute the definition of y in terms of the potential observations, $\{Y_i(x)\}$, that is given in Equation (1) into Equation (6) we obtain

$$FACE = E[Y(1)|x = 1] - E[Y(0)|x = 0] \qquad (7)$$

Finally if we combine Equation (5) and Equation (7) we obtain the following basic formula that relates the ACE to the FACE

$$FACE = ACE + BIAS \qquad (8)$$

where

$$BIAS = E[Y(0)|x = 1] - E[Y(0)|x = 0] \qquad (9)$$

The BIAS term contains two parts, one *factual*, that is, $E[Y(0)|x = 0] = E[y|x = 0]$, and the other *counterfactual*, that is, $E[Y(0)|x = 1]$. The factual part is just the mean of y_i for those units with $x_i = 0$. The counterfactual part is the mean of $Y_i(0)$ for those units for whom $x_i = 1$. $E[Y(0)|x = 1]$ is a quantity for which there can never be any data because the conditioning event makes the quantity being averaged over a counterfactual. Thus, it is a counterfactual conditional expectation. The value of such counterfactual parameters is that they pinpoint exactly where assumptions must be made that allows causal inference to take place using empirical data. When BIAS = 0, we have FACE = ACE and the empirical FACE equals the causal ACE.

An important condition that insures that BIAS = 0 is the construction of x_i by random assignment which forces x_i and $Y_i(0)$ to be statistically independent of each other as functions of i over P (Holland 1986). When this independence holds, $E[Y(0)|x = 1] = E[Y(0)|x = 0]$ and BIAS = 0.

4. Empty Counterfactuals

There is an unsatisfactory and rather misleading use of counterfactuals that sometimes arises in social science research. It occurs when the counterfactual condition, that is, the 'if A were the case' part could never occur in any real sense. Such empty counterfactuals arise when a nonmanipulable factor in a causal study is described as having an 'effect' on some outcome. Examples easily come about in casual causal talk. The effect of gender on salary suggests considering 'what her salary would have been had she been a man.' The effect of test performance on future employment suggests 'the job he would have had had he scored higher on the test.' The effect of English language proficiency on a math test in English suggests 'the mathematics score a non-English speaker would have received had he or she been an English speaker.' These empty counterfactuals arise when the value of a variable for a factor in a study could not have been other than the value that it was. The interesting and useful counterfactuals arise in those cases when the variable could have had a different value that it did for the individuals in a study, at least in principle. Judgment as to when a counterfactual is empty or not is not always easy and may require careful thought in many cases. Consider the examples 'if I were you, I would, ...' Lewis's kangaroo and Rubin's aspirin in the opening paragraph. These represent very different kinds of counterfactuals from this perspective. The first is as empty as they get, the emptiness of the second depends on how the kangaroo might not have a tail (our imagination vs. an axe), while Rubin's aspirin could be taken or not.

See also: Causation (Theories and Models): Conceptions in the Social Sciences; Counterfactual Reasoning: Public Policy Aspects; Counterfactual Reasoning, Qualitative: Philosophical Aspects; Counterfactual Reasoning, Quantitative: Philosophical Aspects; Internal Validity; Quasi-Experimental Designs

Bibliography

Cook T D, Campbell D T 1979 *Quasi-experimentation: Design and Analysis Issues for Field Settings*. Houghton Mifflin, Boston

Dawid A P 1997 Causal Inference without Counterfactuals. Research Report No. 188, Department of Statistical Science, University College, London

Holland P W 1986 Statistics and causal inference. *Journal of the American Statistical Association* **81**: 945–70

Holland P W 1988 Causal inference, path analysis and recursive structural equations models. In: Clogg C (ed.) *Sociological Methodology*. American Sociological Association, Washington, DC, pp. 449–84

Holland P W, Rubin D B 1988 Causal inference in retrospective studies. *Evaluation Review* **12**: 203–31

Lewis D K 1973a Causation. *Journal of Philosophy* **70**: 556–67

Lewis D K 1973b *Counterfactuals*. Harvard University Press, Cambridge, MA

Neyman J 1923 Sur les applications de la theorie des probabilites aux experiences agricoles: Essai des principes. *Roczniki Nauk Rolniczki* **10**: 1–51 (in Polish: English trans. Dabrowska D, Speed T 1991 *Statistical Science* **5**: 463–80)

Neyman J 1935 Statistical problems in agricultural experimentation. *Supplement of the Journal of the Royal Statistical Society* **2**: 107–80

Robins J M 1985 A new theory of causality in observational survival studies—Application of the healthy worker effect. *Biometrics* **41**: 311

Robins J M 1986 A new approach to causal inference in mortality studies with a sustained exposure period—application to control of the healthy worker survivor effect. *Mathematical Modelling* **7**: 1393–1512

Robins J M 1997 Causal inference from complex longitudinal data. In: Berkane M (ed.) *Latent Variable Modeling with Applications to Causality.* Springer-Verlag, New York, pp. 69–117

Rubin D B 1974 Estimating causal effects of treatments in randomized and nonrandomized studies. *Journal of Educational Psychology* **66**: 688–701

Rubin D B 1978 Bayesian inference for casual effects: The role of randomization. *Annals of Statistics* **6**: 34–58

Shafer G 1996 *The Art of Causal Conjecture.* MIT Press, Cambridge, MA

P. W. Holland

Causal Inference and Statistical Fallacies

1. Generalities

The pairing of causality and fallacies may seem idiosyncratic. In fact it nicely captures the point that many statistical fallacies, i.e., plausible-seeming arguments that give the wrong conclusion, hinge on the overinterpretation or misinterpretation of statistical associations as implying more than they properly do. The article begins by discussing three main views of causality, briefly indicating the scope for fallacious arguments and then at the end returns to discuss some fallacies in slightly more detail. See *Graphical Models: Overview.*

The very long history in the philosophical literature of discussions of causality is largely irrelevant for these purposes. It typically regards a cause as necessary and sufficient for an effect: all smokers get lung cancer, all lung cancer patients smoke. Here the concern is with situations with multiple causes, even if one is predominant, and where explicit or implicit statistical or probabilistic considerations are needed.

2. Notions of Causality

2.1 Causality as Stable Association

Suppose that a study, or preferably several different but related studies, shows that two features, C and R, of the individuals (people, firms, communities, households, etc.) under investigation are associated. That is, if we take, to be explicit, positive monotone association, individuals with high values of C tend to have high values of R and vice versa. For example C and R might be test scores at a given age in arithmetic and language, or level of crime and unemployment rate in a community.

Under what circumstances might one reasonably conclude that C is a cause of a response R, or at least make some step in the direction of that conclusion? And what would such a statement of causality mean?

2.1.1 Symmetric and directed relations. Association is a symmetric relation between two, or possibly more, features. Causality is not symmetric. That is, if C is associated with R then R is associated with C, but if C is a cause of R then R is not a cause of C. Thus the first task, given any two features C and R, is to distinguish the cases where:

(a) C and R are to be regarded as in some sense on an equal footing and treated in a conceptually symmetric way in any interpretation.

(b) One of the variables, say C, is to be regarded as explanatory to the other variable, R, regarded as a response. That is, if there is a relation, it is regarded asymmetrically.

Often significance tests for the existence of association and of dependency are identical. The distinction being studied here is a substantive one of interpretation. Failure to observe this distinction leads to the fallacy of the overinterpreted association.

2.1.2 Graphical representation. A useful graphical representation shows two variables X_1 and X_2, regarded on an equal footing, if associated, as connected by an undirected edge, whereas two variables such that C is explanatory to R, if connected, are done so by a directed edge. See Fig. 1a and Fig. 1b.

There are two possible bases for the distinction between explanatory and response variables. One is that features referring to an earlier time point are explanatory to features referring to a later time point. The second is a subject-matter working hypothesis based for example on theory or on empirical data from other kinds of investigation. Thus the weight of a child at one year is a response to maternal smoking behavior during pregnancy. In such situations the relevant time is not the time when the observation is made but the time to which the features refer, although of course observations recorded retrospectively are especially subject to recall biases.

As an example of the second type of explanatory-response relation, suppose that data are collected on diabetic patients assessing their knowledge of the disease and of their success in managing their disease, as measured by glucose control. These data may well refer to the same time point and it is not inconceivable that, for example, patients with poor glucose control are thereby encouraged to learn more about their disease. Nevertheless, as a working hypothesis, one might interpret the data assuming that knowledge, C, is explanatory to glucose control, R, considered as a response. This is represented in simple graphical form in Fig. 1b by the directed edge from C to R.

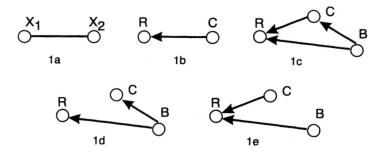

Figure 1
(a) Undirected edge between two variables X_1, X_2 on an equal footing. (b) Directed edge between explanatory variable C and response variable R. (c) General dependence of response R on B, C. (d) Special situation with $R \perp\!\!\!\perp C \,|\, B$. (e) Special situation with $B \perp\!\!\!\perp C$ corresponding in particular to randomization of C

In summary the first step towards causality is to require good reasons for regarding C as explanatory to R as a response and that any notion of causal connection between C and R, and there may be none, is that C is a cause of R, not the other way round.

We may talk about the 'fallacy of the incorrect direction' when the explanatory-response relation is identified in the wrong direction.

2.1.3 Common explanatory variables. Next, consider the possibility of one or more common explanatory variables. For this, suppose that B is potentially explanatory to C and hence also to R. There are a number of possibilities of which the most general is shown in Fig. 1c with directed edges from B to C, from C to R, and also directly from B to R. On the other hand, if the relation were that represented schematically in Fig. 1d, the only dependence between C and R is that induced by their both depending on B. Then C and R are said to be conditionally independent given B, sometimes conveniently written $R \perp\!\!\!\perp C \,|\, B$. There is no direct path from C to R that does not pass via B. Such relations are typically assessed empirically by some form of regression analysis. In such a situation, one would not regard C as a cause of R, even though in an analysis without the background variable B there is a statistical dependence between the two.

This discussion leads to one definition used in the literature of C being a cause of R, namely that there is a dependence between C and R and that the sign of that dependence is unaltered whatever variables B_1, B_2 etc., themselves explanatory to C, are considered simultaneously with C as possible sources of dependence. This definition has a long history but is best articulated by I. J. Good and P. Suppes. A corresponding notion for time series is due to N. Wiener and C. W. J. Granger. This definition underlies much

empirical statistical analysis in so far as it aims towards causal explanation.

The definition entertains all possible alternative explanatory variables. In implementation via an observational study one can at best check that the measured background variables B do not account for the dependence between C and R. The possibility that the dependence could be explained by variables explanatory to C that have not been measured, i.e., by so-called unobserved confounders, is less likely the larger the apparent effect, and can be discounted only by general plausibility arguments about the field in question. Sensitivity analysis may be helpful in this: that is, it may be worth calculating what the properties of an unobserved confounder would have to be to explain away the dependence in question. For further details see Rosenbaum (1995) and the entry *Observational Studies: Overview*.

Mistaken conclusions reached via neglect of confounders, observed or unobserved, may be called 'fallacies of the neglected confounder.'

2.1.4 Role of randomization. The situation is substantially clarified if the potential explanatory variable C is a randomized treatment allocated by the investigator. Then in the scheme sketched in Fig. 1e there can be no edge between the B's and C since such dependence would be contrary to randomization, i.e., to each individual under study being equally likely to receive each treatment possibility. In this situation an apparent dependence between C and R cannot be explained by a background variable as in Fig. 1d. It is in this sense that it is sometimes stated, especially in the statistical literature, that causality can be inferred from randomized experiments and not from observational studies. It is argued here that while other things being equal, randomized experiments are greatly to be preferred to

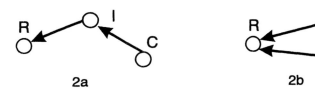

Figure 2
(a) Intermediate variable *I* accounting for overall effect of *C* after ignoring *I*; $R \amalg C | I$. (b) Correlated variables *C*, *C** on an equal footing and both explanatory to response *R*

observational studies, difficulties of interpretation, sometimes serious, remain.

2.1.5 Intermediate variables. In Sect. 2.1.4 the variables *B* have been supposed explanatory to *C* and hence to *R*. For judging a possible causal effect of *C* it would be wrong to consider in the same way variables intermediate between *C* and *R*, i.e., variables *I* that are responses to *C* and explanatory to *R*. They are valuable in clarifying the nature of any indirect path between *C* and *R*, but the use of *I* in a regression analysis of *R* and *C* would not be correct in assessing whether such a path exists. If *R* is independent of *C* given an intermediate variable *I*, but dependent on *I*, then *C* may still have caused *I* and *I* may be a cause of *R*.

For instance suppose that *C* represents assignment to a new medical regimen as compared with a control regimen and that the former, but not the latter, eventually induces lower blood pressure, *I*, which in turn induces a reduced cardiac event rate, *R*; see Fig. 2a. Does the new regime cause a reduced cardiac event rate? If *R* is conditionally independent of *C* given *I*, it would be reasonable to say that the regimen does cause a reduction in *R* and that this reduction appears to be explained via improved blood-pressure control.

2.1.6 Explanatory variables on an equal footing. In some ways an even more delicate situation arises if we consider the role of variables *C** on an equal footing with the variable *C* whose causal status is under consideration; see Fig. 2b. If the role of *C* is essentially the same whether or not *C** is conditioned, i.e., whether or not *C** is included in the regression equation, there is no problem, at least at a qualitative level. On the other hand, consider the relatively common situation where there is clear dependence on (*C*, *C**) as a pair but that either variable on its own is sufficient to explain the dependence. There are then broadly three routes to interpretation:
   (a) To regard (*C*, *C**) collectively as the possibly causal variables.
   (b) To present at least two possibilities for interpretation, one based on *C* and one on *C**.
   (c) To obtain further information clarifying the relation between *C* and *C**, establishing for instance

that *C** is explanatory to *C* and that the appropriate interpretation is to fix *C** when analysing variations of *C*.

For example, suppose that *C* and *C** are respectively measures of educational performance in arithmetic and language of a child, both measured at the same age, and that the response is some adult feature. Then the third possibility is inapplicable; the first possibility is to regard the variables as a two-dimensional measure of educational performance and to abandon, at least temporarily, any notion of separating the role of arithmetic and language.

In summary, this first broad notion of causality is that of a statistical dependency that cannot be explained away via an eligible alternative explanation.

2.2 Causality as the Effect of Intervention

2.2.1 Counterfactuals. While the notion of causality discussed in Sect. 2.1.6 is certainly important and is strongly connected with the approach adopted in many empirical statistical studies, it does not, however, directly capture a stronger interpretation of the word causal. This is connected with the idea of hypothetical intervention or modification. Suppose for simplicity of exposition that *C* takes just two possible forms, to be called presence and absence. Thus presence might be the implementation of some program of intervention, and absence a suitable control state. For monotone relations, one may say that the presence of *C* causes an increase in the response *R* if an individual with *C* present tends to have a higher *R* than that same individual would have had if *C* had been absent, other things being equal.

Slightly more explicitly, let *B* denote all variables possibly explanatory to *C* and suppose that there are no variables *C** to be considered on an equal footing to *C*. Consider for each individual two possible values of *R*, R_{pres}, R_{abs} that would arise as *C* takes on its two possible values, present and absent, and *B* is fixed. Then presence of *C* causes, say, an increase in *R* if R_{pres} is in some sense systematically greater than R_{abs}.

We now discuss this notion, which has its origins at least in part in J. Neyman's and R. A. Fisher's work on design of experiments and in the studies of H. A. Simon and has been systematically studied and fruitfully applied by D. B. Rubin.

For a given individual, only one of R_{pres} and R_{abs} can be observed, corresponding to the value of C actually holding for that individual. The other value of R is a so-called counterfactual whose introduction seems, however, essential to capture the notion hinted at above of a deeper meaning of causality.

2.2.2 Differences in counterfactuals. The simplest and least demanding relation between the two values of R is that over some populations of individuals under study the average of R_{pres} exceeds that of R_{abs}. This is a notion of an average effect and is testable empirically in favorable circumstances. A much stronger requirement is that the required inequality holds for every individual in the population of concern. Stronger still is the requirement that the difference between the two values of R is the same for all individuals, i.e., that for all individuals

$$R_{pres} - R_{abs} = \Delta$$

This is called, in the language of the theory of the design of experiments, the assumption of unit-treatment additivity.

Now these last two assumptions are clearly not directly testable and can be objected to on that account. The assumptions are indirectly testable, to a limited extent at least. If the individuals are divided into groups, for example on the basis of one or more of the background variables B, the assumptions imply for each individual observed that the difference between the two levels of R has the same sign in the first case and that it is the same, except for sampling errors, in the second. In Sect. 2.2.3 the consequences of the possibly causal variable C having a very different effect on different individuals are discussed.

2.2.3 Ignorable treatment allocation. In Sect. 2.2.2 it has been tacitly assumed throughout that the two possible values of R for each individual depend on the value of C for that individual and would be unaffected by reallocation of C to other individuals. That is, the effects of C act independently as between different individuals. These considerations have a strong bearing on the appropriate definition of a unit of study. For example, in a comparison of different methods of class teaching of children, the unit would primarily be a whole class of students, i.e., the whole group who are taught and work together.

2.2.4 Intrinsic variables. There is an important restriction implicit in this discussion. It has to be meaningful in the context in question to suppose that C for an individual might have been different from how it in fact is. This is relevant only to variables that appear solely as explanatory variables. For example they may be variables measured at base-line, i.e., at entry into a study. Any intermediate variable by its nature of being at some point a response is potentially manipulable. Purely explanatory variables can be divided into intrinsic variables, essentially defining characteristics of the individual, and potential explanatory variables, which might therefore play the role of C in the present discussion. Intrinsic variables should not be regarded as even potentially causal in the present sense. For example the gender of an individual would in most contexts be regarded as an intrinsic characteristic. The question 'what would R have been for this woman had she been a man, other things being held fixed?' is in many, although not quite all, contexts meaningless.

2.2.5 Variables to be held fixed. Finally, care is essential in defining what is to be held fixed under hypothetical changes of C. Certainly responses I to C are not fixed. Variables, B, explanatory to C are held fixed. There is an essential ambiguity for variables C^* on an equal footing with C. This is strongly connected with the issue of which explanatory variables to include in empirical regression analyses.

2.3 Causality as Explanation of a Process

There is a third notion of causality that is in some ways more in line with normal scientific usage. This is that there is some understanding, albeit provisional, of the process that leads from C to R. This understanding typically comes from theory, or often from knowledge at a hierarchical level lower than the data under immediate analysis. Sometimes, it may be possible to represent such a process by a graph without directed cycles and to visualize the causal effect by the tracing of paths from C to R via variables I intermediate between C and R. Thus the effect of diet in an epidemiological study may be related to the physiological processes underlying the disease under study, the effect of pharmaceutical products related to the pharmaco-dynamics of their action, the effect of interventions at a community level related to ideas of individual psychology, and so on.

This last notion of causality as concerned with generating processes is to be contrasted with the second view of causality as concerned with the effects of intervention and with the first view of causality as stable statistical dependence. These views are complementary, not conflicting. Goldthorpe (1998) has argued for this third view of causality as the appropriate one for sociology, with explanation via

Rational Choice Theory as an important route for interpretation.

To be satisfactory there needs to be evidence, typically arising from studies of different kinds, that such generating processes are not merely hypothesized.

3. Special Issues

3.1 Interaction Involving a Potentially Causal Variable

We now turn to the issue of interactions with a potentially causal variable. The graphical representations used in Sect. 2.3 to show the structure of various kinds of dependency and independency holding between a set of variables have the limitation, at least in the form used here, that they do not represent interaction, in particular that an effect of C may be systematically different for different groups of individuals.

This affects the role in analysis and interpretation especially of variables B that are themselves possibly explanatory to the variable C whose causal status is under consideration. So far we have been largely concerned with whether such variables could explain the effect on response of C. In more detailed discussion we should consider the possibility that the effect of C is substantially different at different levels of B. For example if B is an intrinsic feature such as gender, we consider whether the effect of C is different for men and for women. In particular, if the effects of C are in opposite directions for different levels of B we say there is a qualitative interaction, a possibility of special importance for interpretation.

Note especially, that even when C represents a randomized treatment which is automatically decoupled from preceding variables B, the possibility of serious interactions with B cannot in general be ignored; see Sect. 5.1.

Viewed slightly differently, absence of interaction is important not only in simplifying interpretation but also in enhancing generalizability and specificity. That is, an effect that has been shown to have no serious interaction with a range of potential variables is more likely to be reproduced in some new situation and more likely to have a stable subject-matter interpretation.

3.2 Unwanted Unobserved Intermediate Variable

Consider further the role of variables I referring to time points after the implementation of C. A subject-matter distinction can be drawn between on the one hand intermediate variables that are responses to C and that are explanatory to R and are part of some natural process, and on the other hand interventions into the system that may depend on C and which may be explanatory to R, but which in some sense are unwanted or inappropriate for interpretation. In the context of clinical trials, an example is the failure of patients to comply with a treatment assigned to them. Ignoring such noncompliance can lead to inappropriate intention-to-treat analysis.

Another example is in evaluations of study programs, whenever students in only one of the programs receive intensive encouragement during the evaluation period.

3.3 Aggregation

So far, little has been said about the choice of observational units for study. At a fundamental research level it may be wise to choose individuals showing the effects of interest in their simplest and most striking form. More generally, however, the choice has to be considered at two levels. There is the level at which ultimate interpretation and action is required and the level at which careful observation of largely decoupled individuals is available. For example, a criminologist comparing different sentencing or policing policies is interested in individual offenders but may be able to observe only different communities or policing areas. A nutritional epidemiologist comparing different diets is interested in individual people but may have to rely, in part at least, on consumption and mortality data from whole countries. The assumption that a dependence established on an aggregate scale, for example at a country level, has a similar interpretation at a small-scale level, for example for individual persons, involves the assumption that there are no confounders B at a person level that would account for the apparent dependency. This will typically be very hard or even impossible to check at all carefully from country-level data.

Errors rising as a result of over-aggregated units of analysis are called 'ecological fallacies' or in econometrics 'aggregation biases.' See *Ecological Inference*.

4. Bradford Hill's Conditions

The above discussion implicitly emphasizes that, while causal understanding is the aim of perhaps nearly all research work, a cautious approach is essential, especially, but by no means only, in observational studies. The most widely quoted conditions tending to make a causal interpretation more likely are those of Bradford Hill (1965), put forward in connection with the interpretation of epidemiological studies. Bradford Hill emphasized their tentative character.

For a critical discussion of these conditions, see Rothman and Greenland (1999) and for a slightly revised version of them Cox and Wermuth (1996, Sect. 8.7).

Koch gave conditions for inferring causality when the potential cause can be applied, withdrawn, and reapplied in a relatively controlled way and the pattern of response observed.

5. Some Fallacies in More Detail

The previous discussion has mentioned various points at which fallacious arguments are not only possible, but relatively common. This in no way covers the wealth of fallacious arguments possible in a statistical context, perhaps the most pervasive being the comparison of rates using inappropriate or ill-defined denominators. There is not space to discuss all these possibilities. This article is therefore concluded with three specific examples related to the main discussion of causality.

5.1 Inappropriate Reference Set for Probabilities

The first fallacy to be discussed, unlike the others, does not center around misuse of notions connected with causality, but rather with mathematically correct but inappropriate calculations of probability. Cornfield (1969) discussed a criminal case in California, People versus Collins, in which a couple had been found guilty partly on the basis of the following argument. Eye-witnesses described the crime as committed by a man with a moustache, by an Afro-American man with a beard, by an inter-racial couple in a car, by a couple in a partly yellow car, by a girl with blond hair, and by a girl with a ponytail.

Probabilities were assigned to these six features and, assuming independence, multiplied to give a probability $P = 0.8 \times 10^{-7}$, the smallness of this being argued as evidence of guilt. The California Court of Appeal rejected this argument as inappropriate, primarily because they regarded the issue as being whether there could be one or more further matching couples in the Los Angeles area. For this they argued in effect that if N is the population of the greater Los Angeles area then the number of couples with the assigned properties has a Poisson distribution of mean NP and, since one such couple is known to exist, the number has a zero-truncated Poisson distribution with parameter NP. From this the Court of Appeal calculated a probability of about 0.4 of there being one or more further couples with matching features, too high to justify a safe conviction of the original couple.

A more formal argument would use Bayes's theorem to calculate the posterior probability of guilt, assuming that the only evidence is that stated above and that the numerical assignments are reasonably accurate.

5.2 Interactive Effect Involving an Unobserved Explanatory Variable

It has been reported (Zivin and Choi 1991) that early controlled clinical trials with stroke patients were discouraging because they appeared to give differing answers to the question: do thrombolytic agents effectively improve the status of stroke patients? These are substances to dissolve blood clots, i.e., thrombi. Nowadays it is known that a stroke can be caused by a thrombus or by a burst vein. Thus, a thrombolytic agent may improve the patient's status or it may worsen it considerably, depending on the reason for the stroke. With patients of both types in any study 'treatment-unit' additivity will not hold, nor can there be 'strongly ignorable treatment allocation,' even if the study is a controlled clinical trial with random allocation of patients to one group treated with a thrombolytic agent and the other with a placebo.

Instead, observations like those in Table 1 are to be anticipated. The main response is success of treatment

Table 1

Counts, percentages and odds-ratios; the two explanatory variables are independent, $C \perp\!\!\!\perp B$, due to randomized allocation of treatments, C, to patients; depending on the patient's unobserved status, B, the thrombolitic agent has a very different chance of treatment success

R, Success of treatment	B = 1, Burst vein		B = 2, Thrombus	
	C, Thrombolytic agent		C, Thrombolytic agent	
	yes	no	yes	no
yes	6 (2 percent)	60 (20 percent)	1425 (95 percent)	300 (20 percent)
no	294	240	75	1200
sum	300	300	1500	1500
odds-ratio	0.08		16	

Table 2
Counts, percentages and the same association between R and C as measured in terms of relative chances given each level combination of A and B; strong three-factor interaction between A, B, C; response depends on each of the explanatory variables A, B, C

	$A = 1$				$A = 1$			
	$B = 1$		$B = 2$		$B = 1$		$B = 2$	
	$C = 1$	$C = 2$	$C = 1$	$C = 2$	$C = 1$	$C = 2$	$C = 1$	$C = 2$
$R = 1$	604	40	300	2000	301	2015	600	40
	(30 percent)	(20 percent)	(75 percent)	(50 percent)	(75 percent)	(50 percent)	(30 percent)	(20 percent)
$R = 2$	1396	160	100	2000	99	1985	1400	160
Sum	2000	200	400	4000	400	4000	2000	200

Relative chances for $R = 1$ comparing $C = 1$ to $C = 2$ given A, B

1.5	1.5	1.5	1.5

Table 3
Counts, percentages and relative chances obtained from Table 2 by summing over the levels of A show seemingly replicated associations for R and C given B; the actual associations between R and C, as shown in the previous table, appear reversed and $(R, C) \amalg B$

	$B = 1$		$B = 2$	
	$C = 1$	$C = 2$	$C = 1$	$C = 2$
$R = 1$	905	2055	900	2040
	(38 percent)	(49 percent)	(38 percent)	(49 percent)
$R = 2$	1495	2145	1500	2160
Sum	2400	4200	2400	4200

Relative chances for $R = 1$ comparing $C = 1$ to $C = 2$ given B

0.78	0.78

and the main explanatory variable is the type of treatment. In this example there is a ratio of 1:5 for the number of stroke patients with a burst vein to those with a thrombus. With successful randomization the patient's status will be independent of treatment, but the strong interactive effect of status and treatment on outcome cannot be avoided. Whenever it is not feasible to observe the patient's status, then the reported results of any clinical trial will strongly depend on the actual percentage of patients in the study having a thrombus as cause of the stroke. In any case, nowadays it would be unethical to include stroke patients known to have a burst vein in a clinical trial designed to study a thrombolytic agent.

5.3   Dependence Reversal

The artificial data in Table 2 illustrate that a strong three-way interaction among explanatory variables A, B, C can lead to replicated dependence reversals whenever the response R depends on each of the explanatory variables.

Here, treatment $C = 1$ is consistently better under four different conditions, since the chances for successful treatment $R = 1$ are higher for $C = 1$ if compared with $C = 2$; relative chances are even identical in the four conditions. But, this treatment appears to be consistently worse under two replications $B = 1$ and $B = 2$, i.e., when A is unobserved. In addition, in an analysis of only the three variables R, B, C, it appears as if randomization had been used successfully since $C \amalg B$.

These effects are an extreme example of what is often called the Yule-Simpson paradox. Although in a sense the word paradox is inappropriate, the possibility of this kind of dependence reversal reinforces the need for either carefully studying relations among explanatory variables or for using effective randomization procedures.

If a statistical association is to be judged as evidence for a causal hypothesis, then one should be certain that the observed associations do not mislead us about the actual associations. This is impossible without assumptions about unobserved variables even in trials with randomization (see also Stone 1993). Therefore it appears that substantial progress in establishing causes can be expected only via understanding and description of the processes which generate observed effects. See *Linear Hypothesis: Fallacies and Interpretive Problems (Simpson's Paradox)*.

6. Suggested Further Reading

The statistical aspects of causality are best approached via the discussion paper of Holland (1986), where in particular, key references to the earlier literature will be found; see also Cox and Wermuth (1996, Sect. 8.7). For general issues about observational studies, see Cochran (1965) and Rosenbaum (1995). For a philosophical perspective, see Simon (1972) and Cartwright (1989). For an interventionist view, see Rubin (1974) and for a more formal analysis still from a social science viewpoint Sobel (1995). For a development based on directed acyclic graphs, see Pearl (2000) and for the general connections with graph theory Lauritzen (2000). For an approach based on a complete specification of all independencies between a set of variables, followed by a computer-generated listing of all directed acyclic graphs consistent with those independencies, see Spirtes et al. (1993). The use of counterfactuals is criticized by Dawid (2000). The reader should be aware that many rather different interpretations of causality are involved in these discussions.

An elementary account of fallacies is given, with many interesting examples, by Huff (1954). Good (1978) gives a detailed classification of types of fallacy, again with excellent examples. See also Agresti (1983).

See also: Causation (Theories and Models): Conceptions in the Social Sciences; Causation: Physical, Mental, and Social; Explanation: Conceptions in the Social Sciences; Scientific Reasoning and Discovery, Cognitive Psychology of

Bibliography

Agresti A 1983 Fallacies, statistical. In: Kotz S, Johnson N L (eds.) *Encyclopedia of Statistical Sciences*. Wiley, New York, Vol. 3, pp. 24–8
Bradford Hill A 1965 The environment and disease: association or causation. *Proceedings of the Royal Society of Medicine* **58**: 295–300
Cartwright N 1989 *Nature's Capacities and their Measurement*. Clarendon Press, Oxford, UK
Cochran W G 1965 The planning of observational studies of human populations (with discussion). *Journal of the Royal Statistical Society* A **128**: 234–265
Cornfield J 1969 The Bayesian outlook and its application (with discussion). *Biometrics* **25**: 617–57
Cox D R, Wermuth N 1996 *Multivariate Dependencies - Models, Analysis and Interpretation*. Chapman and Hall, London
Dawid A P 2000 Causality without counterfactuals (with discussion). *Journal of the American Statistical Association* **95**: 407–48
Goldthorpe J G 1998 *Causation, Statistics and Sociology*. Economic and Social Research Institute, Dublin, Republic of Ireland
Good I J 1978 Fallacies, statistical. In: Kruskal W H, Tanur J M (eds.) *Encyclopedia of Statistics*. Free Press, New York, Vol. 1, pp. 337–49
Holland P 1986 Statistics and causal inference (with discussion). *Journal of the American Statistical Society* **81**: 945–70
Huff D 1954 *How to Lie with Statistics*. Norton, New York
Lauritzen S L 2000 Causal inference from graphical models. In: Klüppelberg C, Barndorff-Nielsen O E, Cox D R (eds.) *Complex Stochastic Systems*. Chapman and Hall/CRC, London
Pearl J 2000 *Causality: Models, Reasoning and Inference*. Cambridge University Press, Cambridge, UK
Rosenbaum P R 1995 *Observational Studies*. Springer, New York
Rothman K J, Greenland S (eds.) 1998 *Modern Epidemiology*, 2nd edn. Raven-Lippincott, Philadelphia, PA
Rubin D B 1974 Estimating causal effects of treatment in randomized and nonrandomized studies. *Journal of Educational Studies* **66**: 688–701
Simon H A 1972 Causation. In: Kruskal W H, Tanur J M (eds.) *Encyclopedia of Statistics*. Free Press, New York, Vol. 1, pp. 35–41
Sobel M E 1995 Causal inference in the social and behavioral sciences. In: Arminger G, Clogg C C, Sobel M E (eds.) *Handbook of Statistical Modeling for the Social and Behavioral Sciences*. Plenum, New York
Stone R 1993 The assumptions on which causal inferences rest. *Journal of the Royal Statistical Society* B **55**: 455–66
Spirtes P, Glymour C, Scheines R 1993 *Causation, Prediction and Search*. Springer, New York
Zivin J A, Choi D W 1991 Neue Ansätze zur Schlaganfall-Therapie. *Spektrum der Wissenschaft* **Sept**: 58–66

D. R. Cox and N. Wermuth

Causation (Theories and Models): Conceptions in the Social Sciences

Many, perhaps most problems and hypotheses in social and behavioral research concern *causal relations*. What caused the fall of communism? What caused Peter's depression? What causes aggression in general? Atkinson and Birch (1978, p. 30) consider as one of the fundamental questions in the study of motivation: 'What causes the strength of tendencies to change?' However, the idea or concept of causation is also involved in many cases in which people do not use the word 'cause.' Many concepts include the idea of causation as part of their meaning, for example, a makes b happen, a produces b, a leads to b, a has an influence on b, or b depends on a. The central importance of causation is demonstrated by the fact that social scientists continuously emphasize the difference between causal relations and mere correlations. Many research methods have been developed for drawing valid causal inferences from observations.

Causal statements are part of *explanations*. b can be explained by demonstrating that a occurred and that there is a causal law saying that whenever an event of type A takes place an event of type B necessarily follows. Although not all explanations are causal, causal explanations play a central role in science and in everyday life. Rational action is based on causal assumptions. This holds for everyday action as well as for scientific technology. If we press a switch, talk quietly to a baby, take medicine, or give up smoking, we have causal assumptions implying that what we are doing leads to a certain goal or prevents an event we don't want to happen.

1. The Concept of Cause

The concept of causation expresses a *relation* between *events*, meaning that one event is the *cause* and another the *effect*. 'a causes b' means that a makes b happen. We also speak of causation when one event prevents another from happening. a and b may be qualitative events, for example, Paul losing his job or Maria passing her exam. Causation also applies to quantitative variables, for example, the raise in price caused the drop in demand. In such a case the cause and the effect are changes of quantities. It is also possible to say that X taking a certain value is the cause for Y taking a certain value.

Causal statements can be *singular* statements or *general* ones. 'This event a caused this event b' is singular. 'A always causes B' is general. An example of a general hypothesis is 'Frustration always causes aggression' (which is not true). A general causal hypothesis which has been confirmed by empirical research is called a *causal law*. Causal statements may refer to observable as well as to unobservable events. Some causal statements connect theoretical with empirical concepts, thus functioning as *bridge principles* in testing or applying theories. For example, if an experimenter presumes that a certain treatment arouses the power motive of subjects, she accepts a causal assumption. Or if reaction time is used as an indicator of certain cognitive processes, it is presupposed that these processes have a causal influence on reaction time.

Since David Hume's famous treatise on causality, any discussion of this subject is much influenced by what he taught. Hume maintained that causal relations cannot be observed; they are inferred by the observer. We see that one billiard ball touches the other immediately before the second one begins to move. We

perceive the two events and the temporal relation between them, but we do not perceive something like a causal power or a causal link between them (Hume 1739, p. 636). Therefore, Hume defined a cause to be an event a, followed by a contiguous event b, where A is always followed by B (1748, p. 76). This is Hume's *regularity theory*, which implies that there is no causal nexus in addition to regular succession.

The view that causation is reducible to regular succession has been criticized for centuries (cf. Armstrong 1983). It has been argued, for example, that, according to the regularity theory, day causes night. Hume's view was nevertheless taken over by modern empiricists. Bertrand Russell claimed that the concept of cause was a 'relic of a bygone age' and could be replaced by the concept of functional relationship. Empiricism in turn had a considerable influence on the social sciences. Finally, however, logical empiricism (or 'logical positivism'), was severely criticized (Popper 1959, Quine 1951). Its central claims had to be given up, especially the principle that a statement is meaningful if and only if it can be verified by observation. As a consequence of this criticism, the empiricist view of causation was put into question, too, and many philosophers came to the conclusion that causation is not reducible to regular succession (Bunge 1959). The idea of regular succession does not include the idea that a *makes b happen*. 'Causation' has perhaps to be taken as a fundamental concept not capable of being defined by other concepts like succession. There is, however, still no general agreement on this problem.

In contemporary science and philosophy, *spatial contiguity* (e.g., one billiard ball touches the other) is not considered as necessary for causation. In fact, spatial contiguity as a necessary condition was already outdated in Hume's days, since Newton had developed his theory of gravitation which involves distant action. However, *temporal contiguity* is widely accepted. In the social sciences, causal statements usually presuppose that a cause precedes its effect. In principle, the idea of simultaneous causation also seems to apply. Backward causation, however, as discussed in some fields of physics, does not yet play a role in social or behavioral theories.

The idea of causation is closely connected to *counterfactual conditional statements*. Hume has given a second definition of causation which connects causes with conditionals. According to this definition, the statement that a caused b means that '*if the first object had not been, the second never had existed*' (Hume 1748, p. 76). Today this is called *counterfactual dependence*: if a had not happened, b would not have happened either; if a had happened, b would have happened, too. Lewis (1986, essays 17 and 21) defines *causation* in terms of counterfactual dependence. It is, however, controversial whether the concept of causation or the concept of counterfactual dependence is more fundamental. Some philosophers maintain that conditionals should be explained in terms of causation (Sanford 1989, Chaps. 11–14). In any case, the concepts of causation and conditionals are related to each other.

How closely are causes connected to their effects? Bunge defines causation in a way that assumes a very close connection: if A happens, then (and only then) B is always produced by it (Bunge 1959, p. 46). In this case, A is not only a sufficient condition of B, but also a necessary condition. Hume, as well as Newton, and later on, Russell, were convinced that an effect always has one and only one (type of) cause. Most contemporary social scientists instead hold that different causes can have the very same effect (a view already maintained by Machiavelli). For example, John may have been fired (b) because he stole the money (a). But he could have been fired anyway, so that stealing the money was *not necessary* for b. Being fired may have many different causes.

Interestingly, causes are often *not sufficient* either. John was only fired because his stealing was observed (c) and reported to the works management (d). a alone was not sufficient for b but a together with c and d were. This set of sufficient conditions was in turn not necessary for b since there could have been quite another set of sufficient conditions. Mackie (1974, p. 62) calls an event a of this kind an *inus condition*: a is an *insufficient* but *nonredundant* part of an *unnecessary* but *sufficient* condition of b.

In the social sciences, causal statements are often interpreted as *ceteris paribus* statements: other things being equal, A produces B. 'Ceteris paribus' does not refer to every other object and state all over the world (they never all remain unchanged, not even for a millisecond), but to those (partly unknown) states that are causally relevant for B. Consider, for example, this psychological law, known as 'the Zeigarnik effect': unfinished tasks are more easily recalled than completed ones. Obviously, this can only be true if understood as a *ceteris paribus* statement. The fact that a task has not been finished has a causal influence on recall. But there are, of course, further factors that determine whether a task will be recalled or not. Therefore, the Zeigarnik effect can only be demonstrated under certain experimental conditions: subjects work on a number of puzzles. Some of them are interrupted, some are not, and everything else is kept unchanged (as far as possible).

Since it is not always clear which additional factors have to remain unchanged, causal hypotheses are *incomplete* in a certain sense (Gadenne 1984). They can be made more complete by specifying further conditions under which the connection between A and B is supposed to hold. However, it is usually not possible to formulate a very precise hypothesis saying that A produces B provided that certain well-defined boundary conditions C hold. These 'further conditions' seem incapable of being described exactly. For example, it is usually presupposed that, during the

causal process, the system (e.g., a person, a group, an institution) exposed to A is in a 'normal state,' that is, it is not destroyed, damaged, or disturbed too much. It is assumed, for instance, that there won't be a natural catastrophe or a war, that the persons involved won't become ill or crazy, and so on. If such extraneous events do happen and prevent B from happening, this is not considered as evidence against the hypothesis. The causal statement refers to the 'normal', 'undisturbed' case.

If a is considered as a cause (maybe an *inus* condition) of b, this does not necessarily mean that a is the most immediate cause. A war may cause that some people die of hunger. This may be true, though there is a more immediate cause, namely that these people had no food just before they died, and even more immediate, physiological causes could be pointed out.

The previous remarks describe the general use of the concept of causation in the social and behavioral sciences. In addition, there are special concepts that differ from the general view. It has been claimed that in everyday language the concept of cause implies *manipulation* (Collingwood 1940, von Wright 1971). 'a is the cause of b' means that we can produce (or prevent) b by making a happen (preventing a). Now it seems to be true that many causes are actions and that people learn the concept of causation in close connection with their own behavior and its effects. However, it is implausible that this concept, once acquired, implies manipulation as part of its meaning. It is rather vice versa. The idea of manipulation by action seems to involve the idea of causation. Furthermore, people are able to use and to understand propositions about events which cannot be manipulated at all, like the explosion of a star.

In empirical social research, scientists regularly test statistical hypotheses, say, about means or correlation coefficients. In which way are these statistical hypotheses related to those causal hypotheses scientists are interested in? Usually, it seems to be presupposed that a general causal hypothesis can be tested by testing a statistical hypothesis about a parameter like a mean (cf. Erdfelder and Bredenkamp 1994). For example, if for every individual an increase in X causes an increase in Y, then for every group of individuals (and, of course, for a large population), the mean of X must be greater than the mean of Y.

But why deal with group means or correlations when the subject of research are causal relations? The reason for this is that observation and measurement are inaccurate to some degree, so that many observations have to be made in order to determine whether there is an increase or decrease in Y. In addition, to control effects of repeated measurement, it is often necessary in social research to use several research groups of individuals differing only in X (best achieved by random assignment of individuals, see below). Now, even if it is true that for every individual an increase in X causes an increase in Y, it does not follow from this that every individual of a group higher in X has a higher *measured score* in Y than every individual of a group lower in X. Therefore, one needs statistical analysis. Usually, if the statistical null hypothesis is rejected and the alternative hypothesis is accepted, this is considered as a confirmation of the causal hypothesis being tested. However, there is no total agreement about this procedure and there are some problems, concerning, for example, the logical relation between causal and statistical statements, or the connection between deciding on statistical hypotheses and the confirmation or falsification of the causal hypotheses.

It has been asked whether causal statements themselves can be interpreted as *probabilistic* statements. Suppes (1970) has presented a probabilistic theory of causality. Let the probability that B happens be higher if A occurs before: $p(B/A) > p(B)$. In this case, A seems to be something like a cause of B, it is a *prima facie* cause. A *prima facie* cause is not always a genuine cause. Suppose that there is an event A′ that precedes A, and let $p(B/A$ and $A') = p(B/A')$. Thus, A is actually quite irrelevant to B. It only appeared to be a cause, it is a *spurious* cause. If a *prima facie* cause is not spurious, it is a *genuine* cause. For a criticism of this theory see Salmon (1984, p. 193). For an advancement of the statistical approach to causation, especially with respect to the social and behavioral sciences, see Steyer (1985, Cheng 1997).

2. Causal Hypotheses and Empirical Research

Most social scientists hold (with Hume) that we cannot perceive something like a causal link between A and B. We only can perceive the events A and B themselves and their temporal relationship. The causal relation must be concluded from what we can observe. Under what conditions is it justified to conclude that certain results of observations confirm a causal statement? This is one of the major questions in the methodology of the social and behavioral sciences.

If A has always been followed by B, this can be explained by the causal hypothesis H: 'A always produces B.' It could be, however, that in every case in which A occurred, there was another event A′, unknown to the researcher, which actually caused B. Therefore, it is required that extraneous factors like A′ have to be ruled out by means of an appropriate empirical design. This is optimally done by comparing cases that differ only with respect to A (J. S. Mill's Method of Difference). For instance, individuals are randomly assigned to an experimental and a control condition. The two conditions are as similar as possible (time, rooms), except that the individuals of the experimental group are exposed to A, whereas the individuals of the control group are not. The research question is whether A causes B, or, as social scientists often say, whether there is a causal relation between

the *independent variable* X (in this simple case, X has the values A and non-A) and the *dependent variable* Y (B, non-B). If B is obtained under the experimental condition and fails to be obtained under the control condition, it is justified to consider the causal hypothesis H as confirmed (H being interpreted as a *ceteris paribus* hypothesis). This is justified because other possible causes of B were ruled out by different kinds of *control*. Some of them were *eliminated* (e.g., noise), others were *kept constant* (e.g., time, rooms, experimenter), so that they cannot be the cause of a difference between the experimental and the control condition.

In *experimental* research, X is manipulated by the researcher, whereas in *passive observational methods* (*ex post facto* design) X varies naturally. If manipulation is possible and justifiable, it has an advantage over passive variation, since it is much easier in this case to prepare two or more very similar research conditions, differing only in X. The most important method of control in social experimentation (as opposed to physical experimentation) is *randomization*. By randomly assigning individuals to experimental and control conditions, the properties of these individuals are held constant between the conditions. To be more precise, the probability distributions of these variables are held constant. In order to do this it is not necessary to know these variables, that is, one does not need to identify and measure each variable that could have an influence on Y.

In passive observational methods, one can also try to discover whether a correlation between X and Y is based on a causal relation with (the values of) X being the cause of (the values of) Y. Suppose, for instance, that people who pray regularly are healthier. It may be that praying (X) has a positive causal influence on health (Y). It could also be, however, that X and Y are both causally influenced by a third variable Z, say, a variable connected with lifestyle, or something else. In this case, the correlation between X and Y should disappear if Z is held constant. Statistically, the influence of the variable Z can be determined by calculating the *partial correlation* between X and Y adjusted for the linear regression of each on Z. If this partial correlation is close to zero, one may conclude that X is not a cause of Y. However, if one has not found a variable Z that accounts for the correlation between X and Y, this is no guarantee that such a variable does not exist.

Based on this kind of reasoning, methods have been developed for testing causal assumptions using data from passive observation (Blalock 1964). They are known under such names as *causal models*, *path analysis*, and *structural equation models*. They are especially important in sociology, economics, and political science, where it is more difficult to perform experiments than in psychology.

In addition to experimental and passive observational methods there are *quasi-experimental methods*.

These are experimental designs that allow for some control of unknown extraneous variables, though they do not use random assignment (Campbell and Stanley 1963, Cook and Campbell 1979, see also Cook and Shadish 1994).

In passive observational methods only those variables can be controlled which have been deliberately selected and measured. This is, of course, better than no control at all. Nevertheless, it cannot be ruled out that a covariation between X and Y is really due to a further variable which has not been under control. On the other hand, it should be noted that in randomized experiments, too, one can never be completely sure that every extraneous variable is under control. This follows from the trivial fact that, taken exactly, no empirical variable can be held perfectly constant, since two individuals (or groups) always exist at different space–time points. More important is that by manipulating X the experimenter may manipulate something else that, unbeknownst, has a causal influence on Y. This kind of extraneous variable cannot be controlled by randomization, but only by theoretical reflection: could the effect expected (or already found) in this experiment be caused by something else that varies with X? Is there any alternative hypothesis which also explains the difference in Y? Are there any nuisance variables connected with X? Reflections of this kind are of the utmost importance in planning experiments as well as in interpreting their results. They are not rendered superfluous by using standard designs.

In the social sciences the methodology of empirical research as presented above is usually ascribed to J. S. Mill. Mill (1843) conceived four *Inductive Methods* for discovering and proving causal relations, the most important of them being the *Method of Difference* (see above). However, he only put certain procedures already known in the Middle Ages into the form of precise rules. Robert Grosseteste (c. 1168–1253) suggested that a good way to determine whether a particular herb has a purgative effect would be to examine numerous cases in which this herb is administered under conditions where no other purgative agents are present.

Mill overrated the importance of his inductive rules. He believed that every causal law yet known in science was discovered by one of these rules. Mill's contemporary William Whewell (1794–1866), one of the intellectual fathers of Karl Popper (1959), held the opposite view: hypotheses are discovered by creative insight, a process not reducible to specific inductive rules. Today most philosophers and historians of science maintain that there are many ways of inventing hypotheses and theories and that, say, Newton and Einstein did not invent their theories with the help of Mill's rules.

However, Mill was at least partially right, since he also held that his rules play a decisive role in *proving* causal statements. The hypothetico-deductive methodology as conceived by Popper has quite similar

implications for planning and conducting empirical research as Mill's inductivism has. In order to test hypothesis H a test prediction P is derived deductively from H and some auxiliary assumptions. If non-P is observed, H is falsified—unless the auxiliary assumptions are put into question. If P is observed, this does not automatically count as a confirmation of H. The result P confirms H only if H has been *tested seriously*. A serious test requires that P cannot be explained by other hypotheses yet known in this field of research. A test is especially critical if, in addition to being serious, P contradicts other hypotheses that have been brought forward (which is known as an *experimentum crucis*). In this case, it is rather difficult for H to pass the test, and if it does, it deserves an increase in confirmation. Shortly put, this hypothetico-deductive methodology requires control of alternative explanations of B, and this in turn requires methods of control of other possible causes than A, including nuisance variables.

Since Campbell and Stanley (1963) it has become common practice to discuss the problem of causal interpretation in terms of *internal* and *external validity*. Internal validity is concerned with the singular causal statement 'a causes b.' The conclusion that a caused b is *internally valid* if the research design made it possible to control those extraneous variables that could have also produced b. However, the result that a caused b is compatible with there being further, nonredundant conditions which, in connection with a, produced b, e. g., properties of persons or the situation. Thus, the question arises whether this causal relationship also holds under different conditions. *External validity* is defined as the approximate validity with which conclusions are drawn about the generalizability of a causal relationship to and across populations of persons, settings, and times' (Cook and Campbell 1979, p. 39). External validity includes the question whether a causal relation found in laboratory research also holds under more natural conditions. Cook and Campbell (1979) expanded this view by adding *construct validity* and *statistical conclusion validity*. For a further development of these methodological criteria see Campbell (1986), Cook and Shadish (1994).

It is obvious that the problem of external validity is closely related to the *problem of induction*. Actually, the theory of internal and external validity is based on principles from Mill's *inductivistic* view as well as on elements from Popper's (1959) *hypothetico-deductive* methodology. Some supporters of a pure deductivistic view have instead proposed to dispense with any question of inductive generalizability and to formulate the problem in this way: which general hypotheses concerning the causal relation between A and B were tested in this research and which is the result? (cf. Gadenne 1984, Kruglanski and Kroy 1975). The result could be, for example, that the general hypothesis 'A and C together cause B' is confirmed, whereas the hypothesis 'A alone is sufficient for B' is falsified. The result could also be that a hypothesis which was confirmed in earlier laboratory research is now falsified in a natural setting.

Like all hypotheses and theories, causal hypotheses can be empirically confirmed though not be proven as certain. They cannot be definitely falsified either. If the result of some repeated experiments is A and non-B, the hypothesis that A *ceteris paribus* produces B is invalidated to some degree and may be given up. But even in this case it is not completely sure that the hypothesis is false. It could have happened that in all these experiments there was an uncontrolled factor F sufficient to prevent B. Furthermore, a test prediction does not usually follow from H alone; it is derived from H together with further assumptions, including singular statements describing the experimental procedure, bridge principles connecting theoretical and empirical concepts, auxiliary assumptions from other theories or even other disciplines (for example, laws concerning measuring instruments), and the assumption that extraneous variables were eliminated or held constant. Therefore, unexpected empirical results never tell us directly which assumption is false (Duhem 1954). All scientists can do is to guess which assumptions are the mistaken ones, replace them by others, and make new predictions and tests. Testing hypotheses and theories is *holistic* in this sense. Hypotheses and theories, at least nontrivial ones, are not separately testable, which renders the interpretation of results more difficult. Nevertheless, most scientists and, probably, most philosophers of science believe that although there is no verification and no conclusive falsification there is progress in empirical research. After some systematic research, it turns out that certain causal hypotheses are much better confirmed than others, and the same holds, in the long run, for whole theories. It should be noted that contemporary Popperians (often misunderstood as supporting definite falsifications) agree with this view. They do not believe that theories can be falsified easily, and do not recommend that a theory has to be given up immediately if it is contradicted by an empirical result (cf. Albert 1999).

People have a strong tendency to 'see' and to infer causal relations in their environment. Cook and Campbell (1979) speculate that this is a product of the biological evolution: causal knowledge is helpful to adapt more effectively to external circumstances, especially knowledge about manipulable causes. Though causal hypotheses in everyday life (as well as in science) are usually simplifications, they often correspond sufficiently to real processes to have survival value.

There are limits to causal thinking. First, causal statements in the social sciences, even highly confirmed ones, are *incomplete* in a certain sense (see above): whether A really produces B depends on conditions which are not yet known completely and can probably never be described in a very precise way. The causal processes in the world are so complex that even the best causal laws are presumably simplifications which do not hold without exception.

Causal thinking is compatible with the fact that there are *interactions* and *feedback processes*. Wherever people interact, that is, in the whole psychological, social, and economic area, it should be taken into account that a variable Y which is causally dependent on a variable X may have an effect on X, too. Sometimes, this effect from Y on X is so small that it can be neglected. In this case, the simplification of taking only (the values of) X as the cause and (the values of) Y as the effect is justified. But in many other cases it may lead to serious mistakes if interactions are overlooked. Even in mechanics, which is usually considered as a shining example of causal thinking, many laws are actually interaction laws, for example, Newton's third law of motion and his law of gravitation (cf. Bunge 1959).

See also: Causal Counterfactuals in Social Science Research; Causal Inference and Statistical Fallacies; Causation: Physical, Mental, and Social; Control Variable in Research; Explanation: Conceptions in the Social Sciences; External Validity; Generalization: Conceptions in the Social Sciences; Hypothesis Testing in Statistics; Hypothesis Testing: Methodology and Limitations; Internal Validity; Laboratory Experiment: Methodology; Theory: Conceptions in the Social Sciences

Bibliography

Albert H 1999 *Between Social Science, Religion, and Politics. Essays in Critical Rationalism*. Rodopi, Amsterdam

Armstrong D M 1983 *What is a Law of Nature?* Cambridge University Press, Cambridge, UK

Atkinson J W, Birch D 1978 *An Introduction to Motivation*. Van Nostrand, New York

Blalock H M Jr (ed.) 1964 *Causal Inferences in Nonexperimental Research*. The University of North Carolina Press, Chapel Hill, NC

Bunge M 1959 *Causality: The Place of the Causal Principle in Modern Science*. Harvard University Press, Cambridge, MA

Campbell D T 1986 Relabeling internal and external validity for applied social scientists. In: Tronchim W M K (eds.) 1986 *Advances in Quasi-Experimental Design Analysis: New Directions for Program Evaluation*. Jossey-Bass, San Francisco, CA, Vol. 31, pp. 67–77

Campbell D T, Stanley J C 1963 Experimental and quasi-experimental designs for research on teaching. In: Gage N L (eds.) *Handbook of Research on Teaching*. Rand McNally, Chicago

Collingwood R G 1940 *An Essay on Metaphysics*. Oxford University Press, Oxford, UK

Cook T D, Shadish W R 1994 Social experiments: Some developments over the past fifteen years. *Annual Reviews of Psychology* **45**: 545–80

Cook T D, Campbell D T 1979 *Quasi-Experimentation: Design & Analysis Issues for Field Settings*. Rand McNally, Chicago

Duhem P 1954 *The Aim and Structure of Physical Theory.* Princeton University Press, Princeton, NJ (Originally published 1908)

Erdfelder E, Bredenkamp J 1994 Hypothesenprüfung. In: Herrmann T, Tack W (eds.) *Enzyklopädie der Psychologie. Methodologische Grundlagen der Psychologie.* Hogrefe, Göttingen, pp. 604–48

Gadenne V 1984 *Theorie und Erfahrung in der psychologischen Forschung.* Tübingen, Mohr

Hume D [1739] 1978 *A Treatise of Human Nature* [Book I Selby-Bigge L A (ed.), 2nd rev. edn. Nidditch P H (ed.)]. Clarendon Press, Oxford, UK (Originally published 1739)

Hume D [1748] 1975 *An Enquiry Concerning Human Understanding.* [Selby-Bigge L A (ed.), 3rd rev. edn. Nidditch P H (ed.)]. Clarendon Press, Oxford, UK (Originally published 1748)

Kruglanski A W, Kroy M 1975 Outcome validity in experimental research: A re-conceptualization. *Journal of Representative Research in Social Psychology* 7: 168–78

Mackie J L 1974 *The Cement of the Universe.* Clarendon Press, Oxford, UK

Mill J S [1843] 1959 *A System of Logic, Ratiocinative and Inductive,* 8th edn. Longmans, London (Originally published 1843)

Popper K R 1959 *The Logic of Scientific Discovery.* Hutchinson, London

Quine W V O 1951 Two dogmas of empiricism. *The Philosophical Review* **60**: 20–43

Steyer R 1985 Causal regressive dependencies: An introduction. In: Nesselroade J R, von Eye A (eds.) *Individual Development and Social Change: Explanatory Analysis.* Academic Press, Orlando, FL, pp. 95–124

Suppes P 1970 *A Probabilistic Theory of Causality.* North-Holland, Amsterdam

von Wright G H 1971 *Explanation and Understanding.* Cornell University Press, Ithaca, NY

V. Gadenne

Causation: Physical, Mental, and Social

We invoke the notion of causation to describe many different aspects of our experience and of the world. For example, in describing the physical domain, we might say *the earthquake caused the building to collapse*; in describing the psychological or mental domain, we might say *paranoia was the cause of Oswald shooting Kennedy*; and in describing the social domain, we might say *excessive military spending caused instability in the Soviet Union*. In addition, we often use causal notions to link these various domains together. For example, we might say *her arm rose because she wanted to signal*, linking the mental domain (wanting to signal) and physical domain (her arm rising); or *social policy causes the degradation of the environment*, linking the social domain (social policy) and the physical domain (the environment). In short,

causation is a very *general* notion: it applies in and across the physical, mental, and social domains. According to many philosophers, however, there is an interesting and difficult class of problems that emerges when we focus on how causal statements in one domain—for example, the physical domain—interact with causal statements in others—for example, the social or mental domains. Problems in this class—which we will call *problems of causation in multiple domains*—is what this article is about (for causation in general, see *Causes and Laws: Philosophical Aspects*).

1. Cartesian Dualism and Gassendi's Objection

The seventeenth century philosopher and mathematician Rene Descartes famously held that, while the nature and behavior of nonhuman animals could be explained completely by the physical science of his day, various features of human beings—including in particular the fact that human thought and action are not under direct environmental control—seemed to place them beyond the reach of physical science. Descartes therefore endorsed *dualism*, the idea that every human being is a complex of a physical body located in space and subject to physical laws and an immaterial mind *not* located in space and *not* subject to physical laws. Descartes' contemporary Gassendi famously objected that dualism made a mystery of how bodily actions and movements could be caused by immaterial psychological events: 'How can there be effort directed against anything, or motion set up in it, unless there is mutual contact between what moves and is moved? And how can there be contact without a body?' (Descartes and Cottingham et al. 1984).

Gassendi's objection is an example of a problem of causation in multiple domains. It turns on the fact that there is causal contact between the mental and physical domains, something which is difficult to understand if Cartesian dualism is true. However, problems of this sort are by no means unique to the relationship between the mental and the physical, nor to Descartes' specific account of that relationship, and nor do they arise only from older ideas in science and philosophy. On the contrary, they arise from a general picture of the world which is very common in contemporary intellectual culture: *the causal hierarchy picture*.

2. The Causal Hierarchy Picture

What sort of picture of the world does contemporary science present us with? According to one common view, science presents us with a twofold picture. One part of the picture is that the world is organized into a series of levels (cf. Oppenheim and Putnam 1958). The most basic level is the physical level, which is described by the most basic science, physics. Arranged in a hierarchy on top of this level are other levels such as the chemical level, the biological level, the psychological level, and the social level, and each of these levels are described by nonbasic sciences (sometimes called *special* sciences), such as chemistry, biology, psychology, and sociology. To put things the other way around, the picture views social entities (institutions, groups, or corporations) as being composed of psychological entities (persons or individuals), which are themselves composed of biological entities (cells), which are themselves composed of chemical entities (molecules), which are themselves composed of fundamental physical entities (atoms and subatomic particles).

Another part of the picture adds causation to the hierarchy, in two distinct ways. First, it is part of the picture that, since causation is a very general notion, causal statements are true at every level. Thus, causal claims about the behavior of corporations or persons are, from the point of view of the picture, perfectly genuine and potentially true. Second, it is also part of the picture that every time a causal statement is true at some nonbasic level, there is a corresponding causal statement that is true at the basic level.

The intuitive idea behind this second point is that causal statements at higher levels require *mechanisms* at lower levels, and, ultimately, at the physical level. Thus, consider the statement, *she raised her arm because she wanted to signal*. According to the picture, this statement (if true) is made true by, and requires for its truth, a further statement drawn from a lower level, presumably a statement about neural activity and how that activity causes movement of the limbs. Or again, consider the statement, *urbanization in Australia in the twentieth century resulted in a decline of religious practice*. This statement (if true) is made true by, and requires for its truth, a further statement drawn from a lower level, presumably a statement about the thoughts and goals of particular people that made up the relevant populations. In both cases, causal statements at upper levels require mechanisms at lower levels.

Many aspects of this causal hierarchy picture have been discussed and examined in recent philosophy of (natural and social) science (see *Reduction, Varieties of*; *Social Properties (Facts and Entities): Philosophical Aspects*). But for our purposes the important point is that it raises a problem of causation in multiple domains, and in fact a whole class of such problems. Here is a simple way of seeing the issue. Consider some causal statement *S* which is putatively true at some nonbasic level *N*. Given the causal hierarchy picture, there will be another causal statement *S** which is true at the basic level *B*. However, if *S** is true, and we know it is true given our picture of science, why should we suppose *in addition* that *S* is true? Intuitively, after all, all the causal work—all the pushing and shoving—is done at the basic level. But then it is

mysterious why *S*—or any nonbasic causal claim—should be true.

While the issues are sometimes assimilated, the problem generated by the causal hierarchy picture is different from the problem that Gassendi raised for Descartes, in two respects. First, Gassendi's objection flows from the fact that, for Descartes, the physical and the mental domains are so different in nature: one is in space, the other not. But the problem raised by the causal hierarchy picture does not have its source in the fact that the mental level is so different in nature from the physical level. Its source is rather the simple fact that upper-level causal claims are *distinct from* (i.e., not identical with) lower-level claims, together with the idea that every time a causal claim is true at some nonbasic level, a corresponding causal claim will be true at the basic level. Second, the problem generated by the causal hierarchy picture is not limited to the mental and physical domains, as was Gassendi's objection. As we have seen, it arises for any nonbasic causal claim, whether in biology, psychology, or social theory. So long as one supposes that there are causal claims at these levels, a problem of causation of multiple domains can be raised.

We can now see the significance of the problem of causation in multiple domains for contemporary thought. On the one hand, we have a picture of the world, the causal hierarchy picture, which is presented to us by science and therefore has a reasonable claim to be our best and most sophisticated picture of the world. On the other hand, the problem of causation in multiple domains apparently tells us that picture cannot be right, because the picture itself makes it hard to see how any nonbasic causal statements can be true.

3. The Exclusion Argument

We have so far been concerned with presenting the problem generated by the causal hierarchy picture in an informal way. However, it is desirable to be a bit more explicit about the reasoning which leads to the problem. The crucial fact about this reasoning is that it exploits a principle about causation often called *the exclusion principle* (Kim 1993, Yablo 1992). As we shall shortly see, the precise formulation of this principle is a matter of controversy, but a reasonable initial formulation is (E1):

(E1) If e_1 causes e_2, then there is no event e_3 such that: (a) e_3 is not identical to e_1; and (b) e_3 causes e_2

Intuitively, the idea here is that the discovery of a cause for some phenomenon usually means that other causes have been ruled out or excluded. For example, if a doctor tells you that the pain in your foot is caused by uric acid crystals in the joint of your big toe, you do not regard it as an open question whether the pain has some *other* cause—calcium crystals, for example.

With the exclusion principle in place, we can now be more explicit about the problem generated by the causal hierarchy picture. It is easiest to state the argument if we focus on a particular kind of causal statement, one in which a certain nonbasic event n causes a physical event p. (Later we will consider whether this assumption is misleading.) Thus, suppose that (1) is true:

(1) n causes p.

Given the causal hierarchy picture, it would seem that there must be a physical event p* which *also* causes p; hence (2) is true:

(2) p* causes p.

Now, given that n and p* are from different domains, i.e., are drawn from different levels, we may further assume that:

(3) n is distinct from (i.e. not identical to) p*.

However, the principle of exclusion—in the form of (E1)—says that, in general, no two distinct events can cause a single event. Hence:

(4) abc

(4) If n is distinct from p*, then it is not the case that both n and p* causes p.

But (1)–(4) are jointly contradictory: while any three of them might be true, all four cannot be true together. It follows (barring some subtle ambiguity) that at least one of (1)–(4) must be false. In other words, what the reasoning tells us is that the causal hierarchy picture together with the exclusion principle presents a contradiction. To solve the problem one must give up or modify either the exclusion principle or the causal hierarchy picture or both.

4. Possible Responses

The most common response to the exclusion argument is to modify the principle of exclusion. Before turning to that response, however, it is important to briefly consider some alternative possibilities.

4.1 Rejecting the Hierarchy Part of the Picture

One obvious response is to suggest that the causal hierarchy picture is a distorted picture of the world because it takes the metaphor of levels too literally.

This objection might go as follows. While it might be true that there are apparently lots of different sciences, this is only a methodological or pragmatic fact, which represents our limited epistemological access to the world. In fact, there is only a single science—physics—which genuinely explains the world. The other sciences are simply convenient descriptions which, apart from their pragmatic usefulness, will or could be dispensed with in the future.

The main problem with this position is a feature of the causal hierarchy picture that so far has not been discussed: *multiple realizability*. Earlier we saw that according to the causal hierarchy picture, entities from upper levels are composed of entities from lower levels. But it seems an obvious empirical fact that the *same* entities from an upper level might be composed of many *different* entities at lower levels. Thus, the same corporation over time might be composed of different individuals. The same mental processes in different people might be made up of different neural processes—indeed, given science fiction possibilities, they might not even be made of neural processes at all. The lesson usually drawn from multiple realizability (as these sort of facts are called) is that entities from upper levels are genuinely distinct from lower-level entities and, as a corollary, that the sciences dealing with upper-level entities are genuinely distinct from lower-level sciences (Fodor 1974); see Kim (1993) for an opposite view. However, if this *is* the right lesson, one should take seriously the hierarchy part of the causal hierarchy picture.

It is important to note that drawing this lesson from multiple realizability does not represent a return to Cartesian dualism. One can see this if one introduces another feature of the causal hierarchy picture: *supervenience*. Philosophers often say that, in the causal hierarchy picture, the upper levels supervene on the basic level, where this means that, while the upper levels in the hierarchy are distinct from the basic level, they are nevertheless wholly determined by, or are entailed by, the basic level (cf. Kim 1993). A simple way to think of supervenience is by switching metaphors from levels to patterns. To say that the psychological or the social supervene on the physical is to say that these are patterns in the physical—hence are wholly physical—it is simply that they are not patterns that physicists are interested in. To put the point a little more formally, supervenience tells us that if you imagine a possible world which completely matches the actual world in all physical respects, then you have *ipso facto* imagined a possible world that *also* matches the actual world in all psychological and social respects. But this idea is something that Descartes would have denied. According to Descartes, the psychological (and presumably the social also) is only contingently related to the physical, and thus a possible world that completely matches the actual world in physical respects is not necessarily a world that completely matches it in these other respects.

4.2   Rejecting the Causal Part of the Picture

If one cannot reject the hierarchy part of the causal hierarchy picture, can one reject the causal part? One way to develop this objection starts with the observation that it is not at all obvious that particular sciences make explicit use of causal notions. Bertrand Russell (1917) famously claimed that physics had no use for causation. More recently, many have argued convincingly that causation has no place, or at least no central place, in the explanations offered by particular special sciences such as psychology and linguistics (Chomsky 1959, Cummins 1983) and anthropology (Sperber 1996). So perhaps the proper account of the picture of the world that science presents is that it is hierarchical but not causal.

However, while it might very well be true that particular sciences do not provide explicitly causal explanations, this does not mean that various causal claims will not be *true* at the various levels. We can see this if we examine briefly the dispute been Chomsky and Skinner, surely one of the central moments of twentieth-century science (Chomsky 1959). Skinner had proposed, among other things, that the basic aim of scientific psychology and linguistics should be to provide causal explanations of human behavior—functional analysis, Skinner called it. Part of Chomsky's response to Skinner was that it is premature to suppose that scientific psychology could provide such explanations. He suggested instead that a more reasonable aim for scientific psychology would be the decomposition of certain psychological capacities and abilities, and in particular the ability on the part of a speaker to speak a language. I think it is fair to say that, in this regard, Chomsky's suggestion has been enormously influential and that most cognitive psychologists follow him in not aiming at causal explanations of behavior. However, even if this is true, it also remains true both that there *are* truths about how behavior is caused, and that these truths are in all probability multiply realized. But then we have the problem of causation of multiple domains back again.

One can imagine a more radical development of this point, where the claim at issue is not that causation plays no role in the explanations offered by special sciences, but rather that no nonbasic causal claims are true. In fact this idea has been historically popular in philosophy of mind and psychology. In part because of the influence of Wittgenstein, it was at one time very common to hear that causal talk in the psychological domain either should not be taken seriously or should be interpreted very differently from similar talk deployed in the physical domain (Ryle 1949; for criticism see Davidson 1963). But suggestions of this sort consistently underestimate the sense in which causation is an extremely abstract and general notion. W.V. Quine famously argued that the difference between the statements *cows exist* and *numbers exist* is not a difference in existence, but rather a difference between cows and numbers. Similarly, one might say that the difference between causal claims in the physical domain and e.g. the psychological domain is not a difference in causation, it is simply a difference between physics and psychology.

4.3   Rejecting the Metaphysical Presuppositions of the Picture

Finally, a number of philosophers have attempted to avoid the exclusion argument by suggesting that it only arises from mistaken metaphysical views lying behind the causal hierarchy picture. For example, in stating the exclusion argument above, we assumed that an upper-level event might cause a lower-level event—(1) summarizes just that possibility. According to some philosophers, however, this sort of 'downward causation' is deeply mysterious, and causation takes place only within levels, not across levels (cf. Kim 1993). However, if one rejects downward causation, one might reject the exclusion argument right from the start.

However, the problem with this suggestion is two-fold. First, it is not clear that downward causation is so mysterious. As we have noted a number of times, causation is an extremely general notion. There seems no reason in principle why we should not suppose that upper-level events might cause lower-level ones. Second, it seems possible to formulate the exclusion argument even if one does not start by assuming that downward causation is possible. For consider: given the causal hierarchy picture, every nonbasic event will supervene on some basic event. But then one could causally explain the presence of any nonbasic event by causally explaining the basic event on which it supervenes. This brings the problem back again: given the causal hierarchy picture, there seems no rationale for supposing that any nonbasic causal statement is true.

5.   Problems with Exclusion

If we cannot answer the exclusion argument by rejecting the causal hierarchy picture or some metaphysical presupposition of the argument, it would seem that the only option left is to give up or modify the exclusion principle. Indeed, objections to this principle are easy enough to find. Consider the spy shot by the firing squad: the first soldier on the firing squad caused his death, but so did the second. Hence the spy's death is overdetermined. But a little reflection shows that the exclusion principle as stated so far rules out cases of overdetermination *a priori*.

This objection to the exclusion principle is suggestive but limited. It is true that there are possible cases of overdetermination. But it still seems unlikely that every case of nonbasic causation should be analogous to the case of the firing squad. To accommodate the possibility of overdetermination we can reformulate the exclusion principle to read:

(E2)   If e_1 causes e_2, then (probably, in general) there is no event e_3 such that: (a) e_3 not identical to e_1; and (b) e_3 causes e_2

(E2) allows, where (E1) does not, the possibility of firing squad cases, but it also says that we can expect such cases to be the exception rather than the rule. On the other hand, it seems clear that we could formulate a probabilistic version of the exclusion argument based on (E2) which would be almost as bad as the nonprobabilistic version based on (E1).

A second objection to the exclusion principle cuts deeper, however. Consider the possibility of composition (or multiple realizability) all the way down: whenever we arrive at a potential basic level, it turns out that this level is *itself* composed at a lower level. Combining this idea with the exclusion principle yields some absurd results. For if there is composition all the way down, it is easy to see that the exclusion argument will tell us that *any* candidate causal statement is false. But this suggests that there really is something wrong with the exclusion principle. Surely a principle of causation should not have the consequence that no candidate causal claim is true!

In response to this objection, a proponent of the exclusion principle might take one of two options. First, one might deny the possibility that there is composition all the way down. However, this is a fairly desperate maneuver. It is surely an empirical question, not a question which can be decided *a priori*, whether the levels of the world simply go on forever. Second, and much more plausibly, one might revise the exclusion principle to accommodate the objection. The obvious way to do this is to replace 'identical to' in (E2) with 'supervenient on', invoking the relation we discussed in the context of multiple realizability. That would result in the following principle:

(E3)   If e_1 causes e_2, then (probably, in general) there is no event e_3 such that: (a) e_3 is not supervenient on e_1; and (b) e_3 causes e_2

This version of the exclusion principle does not have the result that, if the world is composed all the way down, none of our paradigm causal claims are true. For it is consistent with (E3) that causal claims can be true at levels which supervene on the basic level. Thus, even if we assume that there is composition at every level, it is still consistent with (E3) that some causal claims at nonbasic levels are true.

On the other hand, if it is (E3), and not (E1) or (E2), which provides the proper articulation of the exclusion

principle, then we have a response to the exclusion argument. The exclusion argument mistakes (E1) for (E3). Combining the causal hierarchy picture and (E1) yields a contradiction, but there is no problem with combining the causal hierarchy picture and (E3), for (E3) does not exclude the possibility of nonbasic causal claims.

6.   Further Questions

Problems of causation of multiple domains threaten to undermine our picture of the world. But, as we have seen, these problems arise only from a mistaken conception of the exclusion principle, i.e. only if we formulate that principle as (E1) or (E2) and not (E3). However, it would be a mistake to conclude that this is the end of the matter. For (E3) generates some further puzzling questions of its own. I will close by briefly mentioning two of these.

The first question arises when we consider the difference between (5) and (6):

(5)   For some events e_1, e_2, and e_3, if e_1 causes e_2, and if e_3 supervenes on e_1 then e_3 causes e_2

(6)   For all events e_1, e_2, and e_3, if e_1 causes e_2, and if e_3 supervenes on e_1 then e_3 causes e_2

(E3) allows the possibility that (5) is true. But it had better not allow the possibility that (6) is. For (6) is subject to counterexamples such as the following (Jackson and Pettit 1990). Suppose living in a particular neighborhood on the north side of town (e_1) makes you happy (e_2); living in a *particular* neighborhood on the north side of town entails living on the north side of town—as we might put it, living on the north side of town (e_3) supervenes on living on a particular neighborhood on the north side (e_1). Nevertheless, it might not be true that living on the north side (e_3) makes you happy (e_2)—after all, with the exception of your own particular neighborhood, you may dislike the north side, thinking of yourself as a 'south side person.' But now we are faced with a problem: if (6) is not true and (5) is, how are we to draw the line?

In order to answer this problem, Jackson and Pettit appeal to a principle of causation they call *invariance of effect under variance of realization*. They go on to develop this principle, embedding it in a framework for thinking about the relation between causation, causal explanation, and the causal hierarchy picture (especially as that applies to the social and psychological realms) which they call *program explanation* (cf. Jackson and Pettit 1990, 1992, Pettit 1993). Unfortunately, reviewing these ideas is beyond the scope of the present discussion. But the important point is that the idea that (E3) articulates the exclusion principle incurs an obligation: to explain what distinguishes the event triples $\langle e_1, e_2, e_3 \rangle$ which satisfy (5) from the event triples which don't.

The second question returns us to Gassendi's objection to Descartes. In response to Gassendi's objection, many Cartesian dualists are tempted to endorse epiphenomenalism. Epiphenomenalists accept that there is a correlation between mental events and behavioral events, but insist that the correlation in question is not causal. Rather the correlation is the product of two other relations: a nomological (or lawful) relation between brain events and psychological events, and a causal relation between brain events and behavioral events. Since these latter relations can obtain without a causal relation obtaining between mental events and behavioral events, epiphenomenalism is a possible position, no matter how counterintuitive it seems to suppose that mental events don't cause behavioral events.

The problem that epiphenomenalism presents for (E3) and our discussion of it is the following. If we restrict attention to the relation between the psychological level and the neurological level, we too have articulated a correlation between mental and behavioral events, and for us too the correlation is a product of two further relations: first, there is a supervenience relation between the mental event and the brain event; second there is a causal relation between the brain event and the behavioral event. However, why should we suppose that this correlation is causal? As the case of epiphenomenalism makes clear, the mere fact that a correlation is a product of a causal relation and some other relation does not make the correlation causal. Perhaps then, the answer we have given to the exclusion argument is no better than the epiphenomenalist answer to Gassendi?

Part of the answer to this question is that there are correlations and there are correlations. True, the fact that a correlation is the product of a causal relation and some other relation does not make it causal. But it had better not make it noncausal either—after all, *every* causal relation is a product of a causal relation and identity. So the structural similarity between the account we have offered and epiphenomenalism does not entail that account is no better than epiphenomenalism.

But there is also a somewhat deeper issue here. The world presents us with a myriad of correlations. Our concept of causation is in part a tool to divide these correlations into the causal and the noncausal. Obviously, there are some correlations which are clearly causal and some which are not. But it needs to be admitted that there are hard cases, cases in which it is difficult to say whether we have a causal correlation here or not. The causal hierarchy picture that we have been discussing presents us with such hard cases. Adopting a concept of causation that employs (E1), these cases will turn out not to be causal; adopting a concept of causation that employs (E3), they will. As

we have seen, the latter concept *does* seem a reasonable concept of causation. But defending that choice in detail requires more investigation of the concept of causation that we can enter into here.

See also: Causal Inference and Statistical Fallacies; Causation (Theories and Models): Conceptions in the Social Sciences; Causes and Laws: Philosophical Aspects; Cognitive Science: Overview; Individualism versus Collectivism: Philosophical Aspects; Intentionality and Rationality: A Continental-European Perspective; Intentionality and Rationality: An Analytic Perspective

Bibliography

Chomsky N 1959 Verbal behavior Skinner B F. *Language* **35**(1): 26–58
Cummins R 1983 *The Nature of Psychological Explanation*. MIT Press, Cambridge, MA
Davidson D 1963/1981 Actions, reasons and causes. In: Davidson D (ed.) *Essays on Actions and Events*. Oxford University Press, Oxford, UK
Descartes R Cottingham J et al. (trans.) 1984 *The Philosophical Writings of Descartes* Cambridge University Press Cambridge, UK, Vol. 2
Fodor J A 1974/1981 Special sciences: or, the disunity of science as a working hypothesis. In: Fodor J A (ed.) *Representations* 1st edn. MIT Press, Cambridge, MA
Jackson F, Pettit P 1990 Causation and the philosophy of mind. *Philosophy and Phenomenological Research* **50**: 195–214
Jackson F, Pettit P 1992 In defense of explanatory ecumenism. *Economics and Philosophy* **8**: 1–21
Kim J 1993 *Mind and Supervenience*. Cambridge University Press, Cambridge, UK
Oppenheim P Putnam H 1958 The unity of science as a working hypothesis *Minnesota Studies in Philosophy of Science* **2**: 3–36
Pettit P 1993 *The Common Mind*. Oxford, University Press, New York
Russell B 1917/1963 On the notion of cause. In: Russell B (ed.) *Mysticism and Logic*. Penguin, New York
Ryle G 1949 *The Concept of Mind*. Hutchinson's University Library london
Sperber D 1996 *Explaining Culture*. Blackwell, Oxford, UK
Yablo S 1992 Mental causation. *Philosophical Review* **101**: 245–80

D. Stoljar

Causes and Laws: Philosophical Aspects

The questions 'what makes it the case that one event causes another?' and 'what makes it the case that something is a law of nature?' are highly controversial ones for which, amongst contemporary philosophers, there is no answer that can claim orthodoxy. This article sketches some of the most influential theories of causation and lawhood.

1. Preliminaries

'Cause' and 'law' are perhaps two of the most important and fundamental concepts that human beings deploy in their attempts to understand and intervene in their environment, both in everyday life and in their scientific endeavors. When we want to explain why an event occurred, we seek out its causes. When we act, we do so because we believe the action will have certain effects. When we want to know why our environment and our fellow human beings behave in regular, predictable ways, we look for the laws that govern that behavior.

It is part of the scientist's job to discover what causes what, and to investigate what the laws of nature are. The philosopher's job, however, is a more abstract one: the philosopher wants to know what makes it the case that something—anything, be it the decay of a subatomic particle or the assassination of Archduke Ferdinand—causes something else, or that something is a law of nature—whether it is a physical, social, psychological, or any other kind of law. We know that when one strikes a match and it lights, the first event—the striking—caused the second. But this causal fact depends for its truth on more than the mere fact that the two events occurred one after the other: there must be some extra feature of the world which binds these two events together as cause to effect. Similarly, it seems that laws of nature must be more than mere regularities: it is doubtless true that all lumps of gold are smaller than a mile in diameter, but it is not a law that this is so. So genuine laws must have some extra feature, apart from regularity, which marks them off from mere 'accidental' regularities. The philosopher's job, or at least part of it, is to say what, if anything, this 'extra feature' might be.

1.1 The Basic Locutions

There are three kinds of locution which need to be distinguished from one another. First, we have statements of law, which can be said to have the form 'it is a law that all Fs are Gs'. F and G are properties or kinds of event. For instance, if it is a law that all heated metals expand, the relevant properties are being a heated metal (a property that all and only metals that are being heated instantiate) and expanding (a property that all and only expanding things instantiate). Particular heated (and therefore expanding) bits of metal are in turn said to instantiate or are instances of the law that all heated metals expand.

Laws, then, are general facts about how objects or events of a particular kind will, as a matter of law,

behave in a given kind of situation. What about causal facts? Two different kinds of causal claim, one general and one particular, need to be distinguished. On the one hand, there are general (sometimes called 'generic,' 'population-level,' or 'type-level') causal claims, which have the form 'F causes G' or 'F is a cause of G' ('smoking causes cancer'; 'poverty is a cause of crime'). Again, F and G are properties or kinds of event or object. On the other hand there are particular causal claims of the form 'c caused e' (or 'c is a cause of e'): 'the striking of the match caused the fire,' 'the assassination of Archduke Ferdinand was a cause of the First World War,' and so on. c and e here are particular events (or facts): a particular assassination and war, for example, rather than assassinations and wars in general.

1.2 Determinism vs. Indeterminism

A question that is relevant to any discussion of the nature of causes and laws is that of whether the universe is fundamentally deterministic or indeterministic. One way of putting the thesis of determinism is this: the complete state of the universe at any given time together with the laws of nature determines precisely what the complete state of the universe will be at all future times. Indeterminism is simply the denial of determinism.

The view that the universe is fundamentally indeterministic has been widely (though by no means universally) held within science since the advent of quantum mechanics; however, philosophers have only relatively recently begun to take the possibility of indeterminism seriously. One consequence of this reluctance to take indeterminism on board is that most current theories of causes and laws (with the exception of theories of general causation) originally were formulated under the assumption of determinism, and were then modified to take into account the possibility that at least some laws and causal processes are fundamentally indeterministic. The theories of laws and particular causation discussed below are presented in their simpler, deterministic form. While the indeterministic versions of the theories present additional complications and problems—for example, because they employ the notion of probability—the fundamental philosophical issues addressed by the indeterministic and deterministic versions are mostly the same (see *Probability and Chance: Philosophical Aspects*).

2. Laws of Nature

What is the difference between laws of nature and merely 'accidental' regularities? (Suppose that it is a law that all metals expand when heated and that it is merely accidentally true that all (past, present, and future) Queens of England are less than two meters tall.) A crucial difference is that laws 'support counterfactuals,' whereas accidental regularities do not. It is true of any unheated piece of metal that if it were to be heated it would expand. But it need not be true of any non-Queen of England that if she were to be Queen she would be less than 2 meters tall. If someone is currently, say, 2.05 meters tall, becoming Queen of England would not result in her losing more than 5 cm height.

Another difference is that violations of law are said to be physically impossible, whereas violations of accidental regularities are physically possible. It is physically impossible for a heated metal to fail to expand when heated; but it is perfectly possible for a Queen of England to be taller than 2 meters.

A third difference is that we tend to suppose that laws (unlike accidental regularities) 'govern' what goes on in the universe. We tend to suppose that laws of nature are rather like pieces of divine legislation: decrees that the universe must obey certain rules rather than mere general descriptions of what in fact happens.

Can an analysis of lawhood be given that does justice to these intuitions about the nature of laws? A popular view (see Armstrong 1983) is that laws are relations of necessitation between universals. To say that it is a law that all Fs are Gs is to say that there is a necessary relation, N, that holds between the universals (properties) F and G. (Following Armstrong, we can write this '$N(F, G)$.') When an object instantiates F, the instantiation of F guarantees, via N, that G will also be instantiated. Thus, $N(F, G)$—its being a law that all Fs are Gs—guarantees that all Fs will in fact be Gs.

The basic point of this 'realist' theory of laws is that it provides an 'ontological ground' for the difference between laws and accidents: accidental regularities just happen, whereas lawful regularities are grounded in and explained by a necessary relation holding between the co-occurring properties. And, on this view, sense can be made of the idea that laws govern what happens: if $N(F, G)$ holds, then G must be instantiated whenever F is instantiated.

The main rival to this conception of laws is the 'Humean' or 'regularity' conception, according to which laws are really no more than regularities. The regularity view is motivated primarily by an 'empiricist' epistemology according to which we ought not to believe in entities that we cannot perceive. Since our evidence that there are any laws of nature comes solely from the observation of regularities—when we see a law (as opposed to an accidental regularity) being instantiated we do not see any extra ontological feature—we ought not to believe that there *is* any extra ontological feature which laws have but accidental regularities lack.

A 'naïve' regularity theory, however—according to which statements of law are merely true universal generalizations—is untenable, for it simply collapses the distinction between laws and accidental regularities. If statements of law are merely true universal generalizations, then accidental regularities are themselves laws: it turns out to be a law of nature that no Queen of England is taller than 2 meters after all.

A more sophisticated version of the regularity theory is provided by the 'Ramsey–Lewis view' (after F. P. Ramsey and David Lewis (see Lewis 1973b, pp. 73–5: J. S. Mill also held a similar view.) The basic idea of the Ramsey–Lewis view is as follows. When we seek, as scientists do, to find out how the universe behaves, we are not satisfied with isolated facts about what happened in the laboratory on Tuesday afternoon, what happened when a particular patient took a particular drug, and so on. Rather, what we seek are wide-ranging generalizations that abstract as far as possible from the particularities of the laboratory or the patient. Generalizations about the heights of Queens of England or the diameters of lumps of gold apply to an extremely restricted number and range of phenomena. On the other hand, generalizations about subatomic particles, chemical reactions, the relationship between force, mass and acceleration, and so on, apply to an enormous number of diverse phenomena, and are hence much more useful and explanatorily powerful. According to the Ramsey–Lewis view, the difference between laws of nature and merely 'accidental' regularities amounts to roughly this difference between generalizations that are wide-ranging and powerful and those that are not. It is not that there is any ontological distinction between laws and accidents—laws do not have an extra feature (N, say) that accidental regularities lack; rather, it just so happens that some generalizations (the laws) are interesting and useful ways of codifying what happens in the universe, and others (the accidents) are not.

The Ramsey–Lewis view (and the Humean view of lawhood in general) diverges from the everyday, intuitive conception of laws of nature in that it does not accord laws the governing role that we ordinarily suppose them to have. At bottom, nothing makes metals expand when heated any more than anything makes any Queen of England be shorter than 2 meters. Some philosophers claim that this aspect of Humeanism takes the sting out of the alleged conflict between determinism and free will (see Swartz 1985, chaps. 10 and 11, Berofsky 1987) (see also *Free Will and Action*).

3. General Causation

3.1 Probabilistic Theories

Frequently it is claimed on cigarette packets that smoking causes heart disease; but what makes (or would make) such a claim true? The most popular kind of theory of general causation takes such claims to be made true by probabilities: what makes it true that smoking causes heart disease is that smoking raises the probability of heart disease.

What does it mean to say that smoking (*C*) raises the probability of heart disease (*E*)? One can think of the matter in roughly the following way. Fix on a particular population: Australian citizens, say, or the residents of Greater London. Now divide that population into the smokers (those members of the population who instantiate *C*) and the nonsmokers (those who don't instantiate *C*). Find out what the relative frequency of heart disease is in each group, that is, the proportion of smokers who get heart disease (call this proportion *x*) and the proportion of nonsmokers who get heart disease (*y*). If *x* > *y*, then smoking raises the probability of heart disease in the population under investigation: $\Pr(E/C) > \Pr(E/\sim C)$ (the probability of *E* given *C* is greater than the probability of *E* given the lack of *C*).

However, while the fact that *C* raises the probability of *E* gives us *prima facie* evidence for thinking that *C* causes *E*, it does not entail that *C* causes *E*. Falling barometer readings (*C*) raise the probability of rain (*E*), that is, $\Pr(E/C) > \Pr(E/\sim C)$, even though *C* does not cause *E*. Rather, *C* and *E* are both effects of a common cause: low atmospheric pressure (*F*). The correlation between *C* and *E* is spurious. We, therefore, need to refine the basic intuition that causes raise the probabilities of their effects, in order to rule out cases of spurious correlation.

One way of doing this is to 'hold fixed' other relevant factors (in this case, *F*) when assessing *C*'s probabilistic impact on *E*: rather than looking just at the correlation between *C* and *E*, we consider the correlation between *C* and *E* in the presence of *F* and, separately, in the absence of *F*. What we find in the barometer case is that $P(E/C \& F) = (P(E/\sim C \& F)$ and $P(E/C \& \sim F) = P(E/\sim C \& \sim F)$: the probabilistic correlation between *C* and *E* disappears when we hold fixed the relevant factor, and this reflects the fact that *C* does not cause *E*: falling barometer readings do not cause rain.

According to one kind of analysis (see, for instance, Suppes 1970, Skyrms 1980, Eells 1991), general causal facts are to be analyzed in terms of this kind of conditional probability. Of course, there is usually more than one factor or property (apart from the factor *C* whose causal influence we are trying to establish) that is relevant to an effect *E*, so we need to keep all such factors fixed if the probabilistic correlations are to reflect causal correlations. Call a subset of the population whose members are all the same with respect to which relevant factors (apart from *C*) they possess a 'background context'. For example, if there are two factors apart from *C* that are relevant to *E* (call them *X* & *Y*), there will be four background contexts: *X* & *Y*, *X* & ~ *Y*, ~ *X* & *Y*, and ~ *X* & ~ *Y*. Each member of the population under investigation will be a member of one and only one background context. Now we can assess the causal status of *C* with respect to *E* in each background context. According to Eells's analysis, *C* causes (or is a positive causal factor for) *E* in a particular population if and only if *C* raises the probability of *E* in every background context of that population, that is, if and only if $\Pr(E/C \text{ and } B_i) > \Pr(E/\sim C \text{ and } B_i)$ for each background context B_i. Similarly *C* is a negative causal factor for *E* if *C* lowers the probability of *E* in every background context, and *E* is causally neutral for *E* if *C* makes no difference to the probability of *E* in each background context. According to Skyrms's slightly weaker (1980) analysis, *C* causes *E* if and only if *C* raises the probability of *E* in at least one background context and *C* does not lower the probability of *E* in any background context.

Dupré (1984, 1990) has argued that analyses like Eells's and Skyrms's are too strong: they make it too hard for general causal claims to be true. Suppose that some tiny minority of the US population has some peculiar physiological condition *P* that makes smoking (*C*) a prophylactic against heart disease (*E*)—even though for everyone else in the population, smoking increases the risk of heart disease. It follows from Eells's analysis—and also from Skyrms's—that smoking does not cause heart disease in the US population, since $\Pr(E/C \& P) < \Pr(E/\sim C \& P)$. This is a result that Dupré regards as highly counterintuitive. Dupré's rival analysis takes as its starting point a method that is actually used to test causal hypotheses in the social and medical sciences: that of the controlled experiment. If one wants to know whether *C* causes *E* in a given population, one way of trying to find out is to take a random sample of the population, induce *C* in a random subset of that sample, and compare the results. The point of having a random sample is to try to insure that other factors that are relevant to *E* occur with the same relative frequency as they do in the population as a whole, and thus that the probabilistic correlation between *C* and *E* is not spurious. Dupré calls a sample that achieves this match of frequencies a fair sample. His claim is that *C* causes *E* if and only if *C* raises the probability of *E* in a fair sample of the population. This analysis yields the desired result that smoking causes heart disease in the above example, since in any fair sample those with the physiological condition *P* will be vastly outnumbered by those who lack *P*; so *C* will still raise the probability of *E* in a fair sample.

An alleged benefit of Dupré's analysis is that it makes the metaphysics of general causation—what makes general causal claims true—match up in an obvious way with actual scientific methodology, and therefore explains why the methodology of the controlled experiment can, and often does, provide a way of uncovering causal facts.

A problem with probabilistic theories of general causation, however, is that they appear to fail given the assumption that at least some features of the world are determined by prior circumstances (see Carroll 1992). For example, suppose that C causes E, but that C itself is determined by the comination of factors XYZ. Then it is not true that $Pr(E/C \& XYZ) > Pr(E/\sim C \& XYZ)$, since $Pr(E/\sim C \& XYZ)$ is undefined; hence, according to Eells's and Skyrms's analyses—and contrary to hypothesis—it is not true that C causes E.

Dupré's analysis also falls prey to this objection. Suppose that 10 percent of the population have XYZ. Then in a fair sample of Cs, 10 percent must have XYZ; similarly for a fair sample of $\sim C$s. But there can be no such fair sample of $\sim C$s, since by hypothesis there will be nobody at all who has XYZ but lacks C. So according to Dupré's analysis it is not true that C causes E.

3.2 A Deflationary View

Given the apparent failure of standard probabilistic theories of general causation, perhaps a radical change of approach is needed. The theories discussed so far seek to analyze general causation solely in terms of conditional probabilities: no mention is made of particular causation. But this may seem rather odd, for it is natural to think that general and particular causal facts are related in some way: it is natural to think that the fact that smoking causes heart disease has something to do with the fact that lots of individual smokers are caused by their smoking to get heart disease. This line of thought leads naturally to the view that general causal claims are not claims about a distinctive kind of causation—general causation—at all, but are rather merely generalizations about particular causal claims.

The generalizations in question cannot be universal generalizations: when we say that smoking causes heart disease we do not mean to imply that all smokers get heart disease as a result of smoking. But perhaps they are rather weaker generalizations, akin to 'dogs bark' or 'American men like baseball' (see Carroll 1991). According to this proposal, general causal claims do not have precisely defined truth conditions: the question of precisely what proportion of smokers need to get heart disease because they smoke in order to make it true that smoking causes heart disease no more admits of an answer than does the question of precisely what proportion of dogs need to bark in order to make it true that dogs bark.

A central issue, then, is whether there is a special, general, kind of causation that serves to make general causal claims true—a kind of causation that is distinct and relatively autonomous from particular causation—or whether general causal claims are made true solely by particular causal claims.

4. Particular Causation

4.1 Hume's View

The agenda for much of the contemporary discussion about the nature of particular causation was set by Hume (1777, Sects. IV–VII). Hume was an empiricist, believing that there could be no 'ideas' in the mind that do not somehow come from our senses. How, then, do we come to have an idea of causation: what features of the world could furnish us with that idea? Famously, Hume maintained that we do not perceive any intrinsic connection or relation between two events we judge to be causally related: we see the match being struck, and we see it light, but we do not see any causation between those two events. Causation, then, cannot be a mysterious intrinsic relation between events—for if it were, since we cannot perceive any such relation, we could have no idea of causation. (However, see Strawson 1989 for the claim that this standard interpretation of Hume is mistaken.) Hume's positive claim was that two events are related causally in virtue of contiguity (causes and their immediate effects are right next to each other in space and time), temporal priority (causes precede their effects), and constant conjunction (events similar to the cause are always followed by events similar to the effect). So, according to Hume, what makes it true that the striking caused the lighting is that the two events are contiguous (or, if there is some spatio-temporal gap between them, the events are mediated by further events so that there is a chain of contiguous events starting with the striking and ending with the lighting); the striking occurs before the lighting; and similar strikings are always followed by similar lightings. The constant conjunction requirement insures that for Hume (and for most modern day Humeans) causation is an *extrinsic* relation: a causal relation obtains between two events not purely in virtue of how those events themselves are, but in virtue of features of other events: the striking only gets to count as a cause of the lighting because other strikings are also followed by lightings.

The other notable feature of Hume's view is that it is a reductionist view: causal claims, like 'the striking of the match caused the lighting,' are made true, at bottom, not by any primitive causal feature of the world, but by noncausal features (since the fact that two events are contiguous, the fact that one occurs before the other, and the fact that they are similar to other events are not themselves causal facts).

Nowadays Hume's own analysis is regarded as untenable, for a variety of reasons. For example, the contiguity requirement rules action at a distance (one event's causing another, spatially or temporally distant event without there being a chain of events 'hooking up' the first to the last) impossible, while many philosophers think that action at a distance is at least conceptually possible. The constant conjunction requirement is obviously flawed: there can be constant conjunction without causation—for example, joint effects of a common cause are constantly conjoined but neither causes the other—and, if determinism is false (which most philosophers believe to be evident from quantum mechanics), it seems there can be causation without constant conjunction. Bombarding an atom might cause it to decay 2 seconds later even though exactly similar bombardments will not always be followed two seconds later by decay.

Nevertheless, the general issues that Hume raised are still among the main foci of dispute in contemporary philosophy of causation. In particular, the question of whether causal facts reduce to noncausal facts is the driving force behind many of the theories of causation currently on offer.

4.2 Counterfactual Analyses

Arguably the most influential analysis of causation in recent years has been Lewis's counterfactual analysis (Lewis 1973a). According to Lewis's analysis, an event *e* causally depends on event *c* if *e* counterfactually depends on *c*—which is to say, if, had *c* not occurred, *e* would not have occurred either (see *Counterfactual Reasoning, Quantitative: Philosophical Aspects*; *Counterfactual Reasoning, Qualitative: Philosophical Aspects*). A 'chain of causal dependence' is a series of events $\langle a, b, c, ..., n \rangle$ such that *b* causally depends on *a*, *c* causally depends on *b*, and so on. Finally *c* causes *e* if there is a chain of causal dependence (perhaps involving only *c* and *e* themselves, but perhaps involving many hundreds of intermediate events) from *c* to *e*.

The need for chains of dependence arises when there is no counterfactual dependence between cause and effect because of a backup mechanism or 'preempted alternative.' Suppose that the bus stop is next to the taxi rank. Susan takes the bus to work (*c*); but if the bus had been late she would have taken a taxi. She attends a 9.30 meeting (*e*). *e* does not counterfactually depend on *c*, since if Susan had missed the bus she would have taken a taxi and attended the meeting just the same. But there is some intermediate event *d*—Susan's getting off the bus at the stop outside her office, say—which counterfactually depends on *c* (if she had not got on the bus in the first place, she would not have got off it either) and upon which *e* counterfactually depends (if she had not got off at that stop—given that she was already on the bus, and it was already nearly 9.30—she would have had to walk back to her office from the next stop, and she would have missed the meeting).

Lewis's theory has been found to be subject to a number of counter-examples; and much recent work on causation has been devoted to devising alternative analyses which, while remaining true to Lewis's basic

claim that causation is to be analysed in terms of counterfactuals, add further complexities in an attempt to circumvent the problem cases (see, e.g., Menzies 1989). Lewis's theory and its successors fall squarely within the Humean tradition, since the counterfactual analysis is a reductionist project: it seeks to show how causal facts are made true by noncausal features of the world.

Not everyone, however, is a Humean. Many philosophers deny Hume's central motivating claim that causation cannot be perceived (see Anscombe 1971, Armstrong 1997, Chap. 14, Menzies 1998); and many philosophers believe for other reasons that the reductionist project is doomed. Some argue that it is subject to fatal counter-examples (see, e.g., Carroll 1994). Some argue that the features of the world to which reductionist analyses seek to reduce causal facts are themselves really causal features; hence reductionist analyses are circular and therefore unsuccessful (see Carroll 1994). Some hold that our concept or causation is so heterogeneous that no unified analysis is possible; others that if a broadly Humean analysis of causation were true it would render the pervasive regularities which the universe exhibits utterly inexplicable: it would make the apparent orderliness of nature a sort of cosmic fluke (see Strawson 1989, Chap. 5).

5. Causes and Laws

The above discussion of particular causation makes no explicit mention of any relationship between causation and laws; yet intuitively there is some relationship between, for instance, the law that all metals expand when heated and the fact that a particular piece of metal's expansion is caused by its being heated. In fact, however, laws of nature typically do have a role to play in theories of causation. Hume's constant conjunction requirement, for example, can be seen as a requirement that causes and effects are lawfully correlated (or 'fall under' a covering law). Laws of nature enter into Lewis's counterfactual analysis of causation indirectly, via his analysis of counterfactuals (see Lewis 1973b): for Lewis, the truth of 'if *A* had been the case, *B* would have been the case' requires that *B* is true at the 'closest possible world(s)' in which *A* is true; and closeness of possible worlds depends in part on the extent to which they share the same laws of nature.

In any case, the relationship between causes and laws is certainly more complex than the simple heated metal example may suggest. For one thing, lawful correlation is not sufficient for causation, for example, arsenic poisoning may be correlated lawfully with death, but it does not follow that anyone who is poisoned with arsenic and then dies is caused to die by the poisoning (since they may get hit by a bus just after they take the arsenic). Moreover, it has been argued that lawful correlation is not necessary for causation either; Anscombe (1971), for example, holds that *c* may cause *e* even though *c* and *e* do not fall under any regularity. However, a unified account of causes and laws has recently been proposed by Heathcote and Armstrong (1991): according to their view, the causal relation is (in fact, but not as a matter of necessity) identical with *N*, the relation in virtue of which laws of nature obtain.

See also: Causal Inference and Statistical Fallacies; Causation (Theories and Models): Conceptions in the Social Sciences; Causation: Physical, Mental, and Social; Counterfactual Reasoning, Qualitative: Philosophical Aspects; Counterfactual Reasoning, Quantitative: Philosophical Aspects; Determinism: Social and Economic; Empiricism, History of; Logical Positivism and Logical Empiricism; Natural Law; Probability and Chance: Philosophical Aspects

Bibliography

Anscombe G E M 1971 *Causality and Determination*. Cambridge University Press, London
Armstrong D M 1983 *What Is A Law of Nature?* Cambridge University Press, Cambridge, UK
Armstrong D M 1997 *A World of States of Affairs*. Cambridge University Press, Cambridge, UK
Berofsky B 1987 *Freedom from Necessity*. Routledge & Kegan Paul, London
Carroll J 1991 Property-level causation? *Philosophical Studies* **63**: 245–70
Carroll J 1992 The unanimity theory and probabilistic sufficiency. *Philosophy of Science* **59**: 471–79
Carroll J W 1994 *Laws of Nature*. Cambridge University Press, Cambridge, UK
Dupré J 1984 Probabilistic causality emancipated. *Midwest Studies in Philosophy* **9**: 169–75
Dupré J 1990 Probabilistic causality: A rejoinder to Ellery Eells. *Philosophy of Science* **57**: 690–8
Eells E 1991 *Probabilistic Causality*. Cambridge University Press, Cambridge, UK
Heathcote A, Armstrong D M 1991 Causes and laws. *Nous* **25**: 63–73
Hume D 1777/1975 *Enquiries Concerning Human Understanding and Concerning the Principles of Morals*, 3rd edn. Clarendon Press, Oxford, UK
Lewis D K 1973a Causation. *Journal of Philosophy* **70**: 556–67
Lewis D K 1973b *Counterfactuals*. Blackwell, Oxford, UK
Mellor D H 1995 *The Facts of Causation*. Routledge, London
Menzies P 1989 Probabilistic causation and causal processes: A critique of Lewis. *Philosophy of Science* **56**: 642–63
Menzies P 1998 How justified are Humean doubts about intrinsic causal links? *Communication and Cognition* **31**: 339–64
Skyrms B 1980 *Causal Necessity*. Yale University Press, New Haven, CT
Strawson G 1989 *The Secret Connexion*. Clarendon Press, Oxford, UK
Suppes P 1970 *A Probabilistic Theory of Causality*. North-Holland, Amsterdam
Swartz N 1985 *The Concept of Physical Law*. Cambridge University Press, New York

H. Beebee

Celebrity

1. Celebrity and Critiques of Mass Culture

The term 'celebrity' in its modern meanings began to be used in the nineteenth century, but the study of the phenomenon began in earnest with the rise of mass-produced culture, and in particular with the elaboration of an industrialized Hollywood film 'star system' in the early decades of the twentieth century. (For an excellent history of fame and fame discourse from ancient times to the near-present, see Braudy 1986.) It first emerged as a sustained focus of inquiry through mid-twentieth century criticism of mass culture, from both the left and the right. Although these works were rarely based on empirical research, and were filled with unsupported assertions about those creating and receiving celebrity images, they called attention to the mass production and management of celebrities, and to the question of the social impact of industrialized celebrity culture.

1.1 The Celebrity and Capitalist Ideology

Early perspectives on celebrity were largely theoretical, emerging as part of Marxist-influenced Frankfurt School cultural criticism of 'mass culture', 'mass society', and the 'culture industry'. Celebrities were seen as mass-produced, standardized commodities posing as unique human individuals, and celebrity discourse as a major ideological support beam for consumer capitalism. In the 1940s, Theodor Adorno and Max Horkheimer (1977), for instance, saw celebrities as the products of 'the culture industry', the cultural apparatus of mass society; Hollywood stars serve as distractions from the dissatisfactions created by industrial capitalism, and to manipulate 'the masses' into capitalism's false promises of both choice (standardized, mass-produced celebrities appear to be different individuals) and universal success (celebrities appear to demonstrate the rewards available to all).

Leo Lowenthal (1968), also writing in the 1940s, researched changes in 'mass idols' in popular magazines, charting the move from 'idols of production' (business and politics) to 'idols of consumption' (entertainment and sports); he too suggested that these popular culture heroes perpetuated the myth of an open social system, such that the existing social system is celebrated along with the star. C. Wright Mills

(1956, p. 71) wrote in the 1950s of the professional celebrity as a summary of American capitalist society's promotion of competition and winning; as 'the crowning result of the star system in a society that makes a fetish of competition', the celebrity shows that rewards go to those who win, regardless of the content of the competition. The definition of celebrities as mass-produced distractions, and their ideological role in promoting consumption, competition, individualism, and the myth of open opportunity, has continued in much contemporary cultural criticism.

1.2 Celebrity Versus Heroism

For more conservative cultural critics from the 1950s onward, the role of the celebrity system as an ideological support for capitalism was less important than its reflection of a large-scale disconnection between notoriety and merit. Such a view crystallized in the 1960s with the publication of Daniel Boorstin's *The Image* (1961), which distinguished celebrity from heroism. In an argument that presaged more recent postmodernist theory on 'simulation and simulacra' and the implosion of artifice and reality (see Baudrillard 1988), Boorstin argued that, with the growth of mass media, public relations, and electronic communication, it was possible to produce fame without any necessary relationship to outstanding action or achievement. Thus, the hero, whose fame is the result of distinctive action or exceptional, meritorious character, has been superseded by the celebrity, whose notoriety is manufactured by mass media without regard for character or achievement; the signs of greatness are mistaken for its presence. In Boorstin's definition, the celebrity is a 'human pseudo-event'. The phenomenon of celebrity is a symptom of a media-driven culture in which artifice has displaced reality, and in which merit and attention have become uncoupled. Although as Leo Braudy (1986) has shown, the oppositions between pure, 'real' fame and inauthentic 'artificial' celebrity do not fully hold up—historically, 'fame and merit have never been firmly and exclusively coupled—the conservative critical approach to celebrities as false, vulgarized heroes has pointed towards historically new features. Modern media, through the increasingly sophisticated creation, management, and reproduction of images, have an unprecedented capacity to place a person on the cultural radar screen, quickly and with no necessary reliance on the person's publicly celebrated actions or character.

2. Celebrities as Symbolic Entities

The interest shown by cultural critics in what the workings of contemporary celebrity tell us about the culture that makes it so central has been taken up in many humanities-based approaches to stars and stardom, which tend to consider the symbolic activity that takes place in and through celebrity discourse. Who gets attention, the logic goes, tell us much about the core values, or ideological contradictions, of the society giving the attention. Two themes have been particularly pervasive: the tension between egalitarian and aristocratic cultural strands; and the pursuit of the authentic self.

2.1 Celebrities as a Democratic Aristocracy

One striking feature of contemporary Western celebrity discourse is the way celebrities are treated to a cultural status that is simultaneously 'above' the rest of the populace and 'of' that populace. Celebrities are culturally constructed as a sort of elected aristocracy, both elevated and brought down by the watching crowds; the celebrity has become one symbolic means through which the population of the unfamous declares its own power to shape the public sphere (Marshall 1997). Moreover, while celebrity culture certifies some people as more deserving of attention and rewards because of their difference from the rest of the population, it also continually demonstrates that such people are ordinary, just like everyone else (Braudy 1986). Thus, popular celebrity discourse embodies an ambivalence about hierarchy in Western democracies: celebrities are celebrated for being better than, but no better than, those who watch them.

2.2 The Search for the 'Real' Self

A second outstanding feature of contemporary celebrity discourse is the thematic emphasis on getting 'behind' celebrity images to the 'true' or 'real' self. Celebrity discourse, as Richard Dyer (1991, p. 135) has demonstrated, involves a 'rhetoric of authenticity': the question of what a celebrity is 'really like', what kind of self actually resides behind the celebrity image, is a constant, whether in the form of tabloid exposés, behind-the-scenes reporting, celebrity profiles, or fan activities such as autograph-seeking. In part, this is because celebrities have the unique characteristic of appearing to audiences only in media texts, while also living in the world as actual human beings—they are images, but are 'carried in the person of people who do go on living away from their appearances in the media' (Dyer 1991, p. 135). In part, the theme of realness is the result of the increasing visibility over time of celebrity production mechanisms, raising the question of whether the celebrity image has been manufactured to attract an audience, or whether it reflects a true, deserving self (Gamson 1994). Celebrity discourse, with its heavy rhetorical emphasis on authenticity, thus manifests a larger cultural anxiety about the relationship between media images and lived realities.

3. The Political Economy of Celebrity

While many of the attempts to grapple with the unique symbolic or ideological features of contemporary celebrity have been either entirely speculative or based exclusively on textual analysis, much of the empirical research on the topic has focused on celebrity as an economic and social system. Influenced by the strategies of political economists and organizational sociologists, this research has investigated not so much the cultural meaning of celebrity as the internal organization and economic logic of the celebrity system. In contrast to approaches which assume that film stars are popularly selected for attention, for instance, such analysts tend to see celebrity as the result of 'the exigencies of controlling the production and marketing of films' (King 1986, p. 155). Although celebrities increasingly emerge in other social domains (politics, academia, etc.), most attention has been given to the major celebrity production center, the entertainment industry.

3.1 The Hollywood Star System

The pursuit of celebrity, especially in the entertainment business, became highly routinized, rationalized, and industrialized over the course of the twentieth century, with the development of industries, such as public relations, specifically devoted to the generation and management of public visibility. Celebrities are, in this context, marketing tools. In the notoriously risky entertainment business, which requires high capital investment for most of its products, a star is an insurance policy against audience disinterest, used primarily to minimize the risk of financial loss. Thus, star images are typically managed in accordance with the needs of the financiers of the vehicle with which a celebrity is associated—with film stars, for instance, a movie studio. The key nexus is not so much the celebrity and his or her audience, but the celebrity's backers, who pursue publicity, and journalists, editors, and producers, who provide it (Gamson 1994).

The structure of the star system has changed significantly over its brief lifetime. The early studio star system involved tight control of the production, exhibition, and distribution of films and their associated film-star images by several major studios; stars were under studio contracts, and studio publicity operations were responsible for producing and disseminating celebrity stories and images. When the studio oligopoly was broken up by a US Supreme Court decision in the 1950s, many more parties with a financial interest in celebrities' careers became involved in the management of celebrity images—personal publicists, managers, agents, in addition to the celebrity himself or herself, joined studio publicists in battling for control of the process. With the growth of television since the 1950s, and the explosion of celebrity-driven media outlets since the 1970s, moreover, it has become both easier to build celebrity and more difficult to retain it—hence Andy Warhol's famous declaration that eventually everyone will be world famous for 15 minutes. While Hollywood movie studios still generate a large proportion of American and international celebrities, celebrity has become less centralized, and the logic of celebrity has taken hold within a wider range of social spheres, including the worlds of literature, art, business, music, sports, and scholarship.

4. Fandom and the Reception of Celebrity

Analyses of the social and economic organization of celebrity tend to bracket questions of its cultural meanings, and textual analyses of celebrity tend to operate with untested assumptions or assertions about the meaning and impact of celebrity for audiences. Methodologically, both have tended to exclude empirical research into the meaning of celebrities and celebrity in the everyday lives of the fans or audiences encountering them. As the study of culture in general began, in the 1980s, to take more of a methodological turn towards audience research, audience-related aspects of celebrity have also come more sharply into focus. This territory remains, however, underinvestigated, in part because the study of audiences is both methodologically cumbersome and costly.

Considerable thought, if sparse research, has been devoted to the question of the fans' or audiences' relationship to celebrities. One early theory, for instance, proposed that mass media such as television facilitate a 'para-social relationship' between performers and audience members, in which the spectator comes to relate to the celebrity as if they were in a face-to-face relationship, with the 'illusion of intimacy' (Horton and Wohl 1956). Since then, largely through psychoanalytic film theory, discussions have focused on the processes by which audience members identify with celebrities, especially film stars (Tudor 1974; Stacey 1991). Various typologies of identification have been set forth, emphasizing quite a range of activities, uses, and types of attachment developed by audiences in their encounters with celebrities (Marshall 1997). This has been especially important in challenging the assumption that 'the audience' for celebrity is a homogenous mass, and that celebrities mean the same thing for all of its members. Para-social identification and celebrity hero-worship, for instance, both appear to be common stances; but ironic, playful, and irreverent interpretations of celebrity images also appear to be prevalent, especially as the pursuit of celebrity itself has become a more common focus of public discussion (Gamson 1994). Particular attention has been paid to the ways groups marginalized on the basis of race, class, gender, sexuality, ethnicity, or age make use of celebrity images for their own purposes:

building group solidarity or expressing rebelliousness and alienation, for example, through the celebration of particular types of stars (strong women, for example, or stars from their own ethnic group) (Stacey 1991).

5. *The Future of Celebrity*

While there is considerable consensus on certain distinctive features of contemporary celebrity, a tremendous amount of room remains for empirical investigations of the contours of celebrity as a socially organized system of meaning, status, identification, and pleasure; theory on the phenomenon remains much sharper and more sophisticated than research. Three areas in particular are likely to prove fruitful for future research. First, audience research can continue not only to document the range and types of audience positions vis-à-vis celebrities, but also to examine various possible explanations for the variance—audience characteristics, for instance, or qualities of different celebrity domains and types. Second, the process by which the logic of celebrity can and does spread to spheres other than entertainment, and how it may operate differently in those realms, is not well understood. Finally, nearly all of the literature on celebrity has emerged from, and focused on, the USA and the UK. Cross-cultural comparative research is a very promising, and almost entirely untapped, source of insight into the cultural, economic, political, and social logic of celebrity.

See also: Advertising: General; Charisma: Social Aspects of; Elites: Sociological Aspects; Media Effects; Media, Uses of; Reputation; Sport, Sociology of; Status and Role: Structural Aspects

Bibliography

Adorno T, Horkheimer M 1977 The culture industry: enlightenment as mass deception. In: Curran J, Gurevitch M, Woolacott J (eds.) *Mass Communication and Society*. Sage Publications, Beverly Hills, LA, pp. 349–83
Alberoni F 1972 The powerless 'elite': theory and sociological research on the phenomenon of the stars. In: McQuail D (ed.) *Sociology of Mass Communications*. Penguin Books, Harmondsworth, UK, pp. 75–98
Baudrillard J 1988 *Selected Writings*. Stanford University Press, Stanford, CA
Boorstin D J 1961 Jean Baudrillard: *The Image: A Guide to Pseudo-events in America*. Harper & Row, New York
Braudy L 1986 *The Frenzy of Renown: Fame & Its History*. Oxford University Press, New York
Dyer R 1991 A star is born and the construction of authenticity. In: Gledhill C (ed.) *Stardom: Industry of Desire*. Routledge, London, pp. 132–40
Gamson J 1994 *Claims to Fame: Celebrity in Contemporary America*. University of California Press, Berkeley, CA
Horton D, Wohl R R 1956 Mass communication and para-social interaction: observations on intimacy at a distance. *Psychiatry* **19**: 215–29

King B 1986 Stardom as an occupation. In: Kerr P (ed.) *The Hollywood Film Industry*. Routledge and Kegan Paul, London
Lowenthal L 1968 The triumph of mass idols. In: *Literature, Popular Culture, and Society*. Pacific Books, Palo Alto, CA, pp. 109–36
Marshall P D 1997 *Celebrity and Power*. University of Minnesota Press, Minneapolis, MN
Mills C W 1956 *The Power Elite*. Oxford University Press, London
Stacey J 1991 Feminine fascinations: forms of identification in star-audience relations. In: Gledhill C (ed.) *Stardom: Industry of Desire*. Routledge, London, pp. 141–66
Tudor A 1974 *Image and Influence: Studies in the Sociology of Film*. St. Martin's Press, New York

J. Gamson

Censorship and Secrecy: Legal Perspectives

1. *Secrecy*

Secrecy involves norms about the control of information, whether limiting access to it, destroying it, or prohibiting or shaping its creation. Secrecy is a general and fundamental social process known to all societies. It can characterize interaction at any level—from information that an individual withholds, to secret rites of passage of preindustrial societies, to the secrets of contemporary fraternal or business organizations, to state-held information on national security. Secrecy norms are embedded in role relationships and involve obligations and rights to withhold information, whether reciprocal or singular. In preventing or restricting communication, the legally supported form of censorship discussed here involves secrecy. Yet most secrecy (e.g., concealing information about a surprise party or aspects of one's past) does not involve formal law and the law involves secrecy in many other ways.

In a democratic society secrecy and openness reflect conflicting values and social needs and exist in an ever-changing dynamic tension. Efforts to control information occur in a rich variety of contexts. Norms about the concealment of information and restrictions on communication ideally should be considered alongside of their opposites—norms mandating the revelation of information and protecting the freedom to know and communicate. Such norms may involve formal legal rules such as Britain's Official Secrets Act or the United States' Freedom of Information Act, nonlegally binding formal policies such as a bank's refusal to reveal client information in the absence of a warrant or the consumer information voluntarily provided on some product labels, or it may involve informal expectations (close friends are expected *not to reveal* shared secrets to outsiders but are expected *to reveal* certain personal details to each other, such as true feelings about shared interests). The correlates and consequences of such variation offer rich material for analysis of the sociology of secrecy. This article reviews some selected social forms, processes, and consequences of secrecy, and the law as applied to censorship.

There is no widely agreed upon general theoretical or conceptual framework for considering secrecy issues. Given their social importance, there is a surprising lack of empirical or explanatory research seeking to understand the contours of secrecy and openness and why, and with what consequences, some forms have the support of law. Nor has there been much research contrasting different forms of legal secrecy.

Philosophers have considered ethics, (Bok 1989) students of politics the implications for democracy, (Shils 1956, Laquer 1985, Donner 1980, Moynihan 1998) and other social scientists have studied the patterning, processes, and correlates of information control rules across institutions and societies (Simmel 1964, Goffman 1969, Tefft 1980, Wilsnak 1980, Scheppele 1988). The largest body of work is by legal scholars; it emphasizes jurisprudence in often related areas such as the First Amendment, obscenity and pornography, national security and executive privilege, freedom of information, trade secrets, privacy and confidentiality, informant identities, fraud and implied warranties, but generally fails to explain broader social processes.

2. Censorship

2.1 Definitions and Differences

Censorship of communication in the modern sense is associated with large, complex, urban societies with a degree of centralized control and technical means of effectively reaching a mass audience. It involves a determination of what can, and cannot, (or in the case of nongovernmental efforts should and should not) be expressed to a broader audience in light of given political, religious, cultural, and artistic standards. Censorship may involve withholding or editing existing information, as well as preventing information from being created. In the interest of keeping material from a broader audience, content deemed to be offensive or harmful to public welfare is suppressed or regulated.

At the most general level any rule, whether codified or customary, proscribing self-expression (e.g., nudity, hairstyles, body adornment, language use) or the surveillance and suppression of personal communication (phone, mail) can be seen as a form of censorship. But our focus is primarily on state-supported efforts to control mass communication justified by claims of protecting the public interest, a

form with profound implications for a democratic society.

Censorship assumes that certain ideas and forms of expression are threatening to individual, organizational, and societal well-being, as defined by those in power, or by those involved in a moral crusade, and hence must be prohibited. It presupposes absolute standards, which must not be violated.

Much censorship assumes that all individuals, not just children, are vulnerable and need protection from offending material—whether pornography or radical criticism of existing political and religious authority. Individuals cannot be trusted to decide what they wish to see and read or to freely form their own opinions.

Some censorship is largely symbolic, offering a way to enhance social solidarity by avoiding insults to shared values (e.g., a prohibition on flag burning). It may be a form of moral education as with prohibitions on racist and sexist speech. Or masquerading under high principles of protecting public welfare and morals, it may simply involve a desire to protect the interests of the politically, economically, and religiously powerful by restricting alternative views, and criticism or delegitimation of those in power.

Among the most common historical rationales are political (sedition, treason, national security), religious (blasphemy, heresy), moral (obscenity, impiety), and social (incivility, irreverence, disorder). These of course may be interconnected. What they share is a claim that the public interest will be negatively affected by the communication.

Censorship may be located publicly relative to other legal forms of secrecy. Censorship is justified by the *protection of public welfare*. Rationales for other legally supported forms include: the *protection of private property* for trade secrets; *economic efficiency and fairness* justifications in common law disputes over secret information; the *encouragement of honest communication and/or protection from retaliation* underlying forms such as lawyer–client and doctor–patient confidentiality, the secret ballot, and a judge's *en camera* ruling that the identity of an informant need not be revealed; the protection of *intimate relations* in the case of spousal privilege; the protection against *improperly elicited confessions* underlying the Fifth Amendment; the *strategic advantage* justification of sealed warrants and indictments; and the *respect for the dignity and privacy of the person* justification for limits on the collection and use of personal information, whether involving census, tax, library, or arrest (as against conviction) records. There has been little empirical research on whether, how well, with what consequences, and under what conditions these justifications are met.

Censorship is involuntary, unlike a nondisclosure agreement that parties to a court settlement voluntarily agree to. Censorship is unitary and non-discretionary—those subject to it don't have the option of communicating. In contrast, the dyad of a confidential professional relationship is discretionary for one party, such as the client; with the client's permission, a doctor or lawyer may reveal confidential information. Censorship seeks to withhold information from a mass audience, rather than a given individual, as with controversial laws preventing revelation of the identity of birth parents to adoptees. Where information exists but censors prevent its release, it is intended to *remain secret*. In contrast are legal secrets involving a natural *cycle of revelation* such as sealed indictments and search and arrest warrants, which become known when executed, or an industry confidentiality agreement, which may expire after a few years. Censorship as a form of secrecy stands alone. It is not reciprocally and functionally linked with its opposite—the legal mandate to reveal. For example some civil grand juries compel testimony, but then promise to keep it confidential.

Censorship is distinct from government regulation of fraudulent or deceptive commercial communication, which, unlike opinion and artistic expression, offers a clearer basis for empirically determining truth, as with the Federal Trade Commission's truth in advertising requirements. Censorship is separate from restrictions on communication based on copyright infringements, where the issue is not secrecy, but wrongful use. It is also distinct from editorial gatekeeping based on other criteria such as quality, cost, demand, and relevance, and in the case of regulating public demonstrations and entertainment, public safety and order. These can of course mask a desire to censor that would not otherwise be legally supported.

Government-legitimated censorship is distinct from censorious outcomes that may result from the actions of private groups. With the separation of church and state, only censorship by government has the support of law. Nongovernmental organizations such as a religious group or social movement may prohibit, or attempt to dissuade, members and others from producing, disseminating, or reading, listening to, or viewing material deemed objectionable. They may request editorial changes, advocate boycotts, and lobby school boards, libraries, bookstores, and theaters to exclude such material.

When we look at social processes of information control such as withholding information and selective presentation, a form of censorship may sometimes be seen in propaganda, public relations, and advertising, as public and private sector actors pursue their interest in creating favorable public impressions. Consider for example cigarette companies withholding information on the health risks of smoking or tire manufacturers not revealing the knowledge that their tires are unsafe.

2.2 Historical Development

Interest in the topic is strongly related to developments in communications technology and current events. In the modern period, continuing a trend that began with the printing press, new technologies, involving newspapers, mass-produced books and magazines, radio, telegraph, telephone, television, film, audiocassettes, video, fax, and the Internet, with their unprecedented ability to reach large numbers of people relatively easily, inexpensively, and efficiently, have created demands from conflicting groups for greater openness and freedom of communication and greater control over it. The conflict and debate continues—note conflicts over cable TV and efforts to regulate content and access to the Internet.

Following revelations in the USA about Watergate and government spying and disruption of the civil rights and antiwar movements during the 1970s, the groundbreaking Freedom of Information Act was passed and the Supreme Court strongly reaffirmed the principle of no prior restraint on the press in the Pentagon Papers case (*New York Times Co. v. United States 1971*).

As the examples of Socrates who chose to die rather than to have his ideas censored (or Plato who argued for censorship of the arts), the Romans who censored plays and banished offending poets, Pope Gelasius in the fifth century who issued the first papal list of prohibited books, and the Inquisition beginning in 1231 indicate, technology is hardly needed to spur censorship.

However, demands for censorship of religious and political ideas gained significant momentum in the fifteenth century with the appearance of that most subversive of technologies (after the invention of writing)—the printing press and the subsequent spread of literacy. This broke the historic monopoly, however limited, of religious and government institutions on communication with the masses. Authorities tried and are still trying (often in vain) to control the new techniques of mass communication. Later with the separation of church and state and the increased power of the nation state, the reach of religious censorship declined (e.g., prosecution for blasphemy) while political censorship gained in importance, as did ideas of free expression, which both countered and provoked censorship.

In the West, cultural values from the Enlightenment elaborated on by Immanuel Kant and later J. S. Mill and others stressed the importance of freedom of expression and openness as central to finding the truth, and for the stability and effectiveness of democratic government. Individuals were optimistically assumed to be responsible and rational beings who would reach the best conclusions, whether involving normative or empirical truth, with full information and discussion. Scientific ideals involving the ability to question and the freedom to communicate fit here as well. For both government and science, visibility or transparency is believed to be a central factor in accountability. Later arguments emphasized that the psychological well-being and dignity of the person were best served by the freedom to express one's self and form one's own opinions. The argument based on personality has been stronger in Europe than in the USA.

In the second half of the twentieth century, with the allies' victory over fascist governments in World War II, the fall of colonialism, and the ending of the cold war, the cultural force of democratic ideals involving freedom of inquiry and expression has grown stronger. The principle of freedom of expression is contained in the First Amendment to the United States Constitution, various United Nations documents, European Constitutions, and documents such as the European Convention on Human Rights and Fundamental Freedoms. In the USA, the Supreme Court's extension of the protection of the First Amendment to the states meant that numerous nineteenth- and early twentieth-century state and local laws sanctioning censorship were in principle unconstitutional, although in practice there was often strong local support for such laws. This can be seen in struggles over education (e.g., the Scopes 'monkey' trial involving the teaching of Darwinism in Tennessee in 1925), the routine denial of First Amendment rights to labor protestors up to the 1930s and civil rights protestors through the 1960s, and various local struggles over efforts to ban books from libraries.

For Western style pluralist democracies, formal government censorship is the exception rather than the rule, at least relative to absolutist authoritarian regimes, which believe they have the only truth (whether political, religious, or moral) and do not permit opposing views. In 2000, an annual survey of press freedom found that 80 percent of the world's population lives in nations with less than a free press; about one-third of the countries were considered to have free press and broadcast systems; and one-third had systems with strong government control (Freedom House 2000). An extreme example is from the government of Iran where Salman Rushdie's book *Satanic Verses* was not only banned for being blasphemous, but a reward was offered for Rushdie's death.

Direct organizational means of government censorship must be considered separately from the availability of resources to create and distribute information and from informal means of censorship, whether by government or private interests, including self-censorship.

While freedom of expression is a central component of the modern democratic state, among democracies, there is considerable variation in censorship by content, media of communication, place, and time period. Constitutional and legislative guarantees of the individual's right to freedom of expression are not absolute. In considering the social consequences of exercising a right, courts and legislatures balance it against other rights and community needs and standards, such as the presence of the clear and present danger that Justice Holmes wrote of in *Schenck v.*

United States (1919). In the 1968 case of *United States v. O'Brien* the Supreme Court held that local laws could regulate time, place, and manner of expression if done in a content neutral fashion, narrowly tailored to serve substantial government interests and if alternative channels of expression were left open.

There is often disagreement about the social consequences of expression and how material should be defined. Does exposure to sexually or violently explicit words and images result in incitation and mimicry as some research claims (Itzin 1993, National Academy of Sciences 2000), or is it a safety valve and thus an alternative to action as others claim (Segal and McIntosh 1993, Hein 1993)? Does the prevalence of violent and sexual content reflect or create public demand? Can a reasonable consensus be reached on the distinction between pornography and erotic art? Can heterogeneous, rapidly changing societies with multiply porous borders meaningfully talk of community standards?

There has been little research on variation in censorship. Political and religious expression has generally received greater legal support than other forms such as sexual expression. Printed matter has greater protection than other media. Film, live audience presentations, the Internet, and cable TV have greater protection than conventional television and radio where there is a scarcity of spectrum. Artistic expression likely to raise the concerns of censors is generally ignored until it seeks to reach a mass audience via the media or museums. Material appropriate for adults may not be suitable for children. Freedom of expression and access to information generally have greater protection in the USA than in Europe (e.g., greater tolerance of hate and other offensive speech, and stronger freedom of information laws and protections against libel suits).

2.3 Methods of Censorship

Three major means of direct censorship are *preventive* in nature. Their goal is to stop materials deemed unacceptable from appearing, or if that is not possible, from being seen or heard by prohibiting their circulation:

Formal prepublication review. This requires would-be communicators to submit their materials for certification before publicly offering them. Soon after the invention of the printing press, the church required review and approval before anything could be printed. However impractical and difficult to enforce in the contemporary period, to varying degrees such 'prior restraint' is found in authoritarian societies, whether based on secular political (as in Cuba) or religious doctrines (as in Iran and Afghanistan) at the turn of the century. It may be seen in democracies during emergency periods such as a war. There may be formal review boards, or censors may be assigned directly to work at newspapers and broadcasting stations.

Government or interest-group monopolization of publication. Here the censors in effect are the producers and are the only ones allowed to offer mass communication. For much of its history the church was intertwined with government and was in effect the only publisher. In the former Soviet Union the press and media were government controlled and private means were prohibited.

Licensing and registration. The means of production and transmission of information may be limited to trusted groups who agree to self-censorship in light of prior restrictions. In England in the sixteenth century, printing was restricted to one official company and all books had to be cleared by religious authorities prior to publication. Four centuries later, China required that all Internet content providers be registered with the government and abide by vague content restrictions. Permission may be required to own a printing press, and in some countries, even ownership of a typewriter has been regulated.

Government subsidized programs for the arts and journalism may come with political and cultural strings attached. In the Soviet Union, sponsorship of artists' and writers' associations stressed 'socialist realism,' a doctrine that held that art should serve the purposes of the state. Those rejecting this doctrine were neither subsidized nor offered access to the public, and they risked prosecution, as with Nobel Prize winning author Alexander Solzhenitsyn.

In the USA in 1990, under prodding from Congress, The National Endowment for the Arts required that grant recipients sign a nonobscenity oath and that artistic merit be determined by taking into account general standards of decency. A federal court held that the decency clause was too broad and that public funding of art was entitled to First Amendment protection (*Karen Finley et al. v. National Endowment for the Arts and John Frohnmayer 1992*).

A related aspect involves an informal *de-licensing* in which individuals deemed to be untrustworthy relative to the official standards are prohibited from communicating. For example, during the 1950s, Hollywood film writers suspected of communist sympathies were prohibited from working in the industry via a black list.

A more subtle form of exclusion involves denying access, as when government officials provide information only to favored journalists believed to put an acceptable slant on their reports. Even where the means of communication are freely available in a legal sense, inequality in resources often means that many potential voices go unheard. Journalist A. J. Liebling has observed, 'freedom of the press is assured to those who own one.' A related issue involves the trend toward consolidation of newspapers, magazines, television, and motion pictures under fewer and fewer owners. Such monopolies are unlikely to express as wide a spectrum of viewpoints as would be found with more decentralized ownership.

A related area of licensing can be seen in local requirements that those wishing to hold a public demonstration obtain a permit. Given constitutional protections, such permits are usually granted in the USA, although there may be restrictions justified by the need to maintain public order.

In Western democracies, broadcast media (e.g., radio and television), unlike print media, are subject to licensing. The scarcity of bandwidth requires government regulation and, depending on the criteria used, can be an invitation to censorship. The US Federal Communications Commission, for example, has ambiguous rules regarding the control of broadcast content. The use of certain four letter words deemed to be indecent is prohibited. Although rarely exercised, there is the possibility of license revocation or nonrenewal for violations.

After comedian George Carlin used the word 'fuck' in a late night broadcast in 1973, the offending radio station received a warning letter from the FCC. The station then sued, claiming that FCC regulations on indecent speech violated the First Amendment. The Supreme Court (*FCC v. Pacifica Foundation 1978*) upheld the FCC action and added an additional controversial, very broad, censorship rationale known as the 'pervasiveness doctrine.' Under this doctrine, regulation is required because, 'the broadcast media have established a uniquely pervasive presence in the lives of all Americans' and offensive and indecent material delivered over the airwaves confronts the citizen, 'not only in public, but also in the privacy of the home.' Given the ease with which indecent communications may enter the home, children must be protected from unwillingly or willingly encountering them.

The elastic quality of a standard such as 'pervasiveness' could be used to justify censorship of any form, even of books and newspapers that also pervade society. Indeed, when Congress passed the Communications Decency Act in 1996 to regulate Internet content, a medium not characterized by spectrum scarcity, it was argued that the Internet pervades the home just as the radio and television do and hence must be regulated. However the Supreme Court found this Act unconstitutional in *ACLU v. Reno* in 1997. As the Internet evolves, and to the extent that it becomes a platform for delivering voice and video communications that parallel traditional broadcasts, conflicts over the appropriateness of its regulation will likely intensify.

In contrast are means applied *after the fact*, which seek literally to block or destroy communications or to punish and deter. A classic example, likely seared on the memory of anyone who has seen it on film, is the Nazis' burning of books in 1933. Materials originating from suspect sources that do not cooperate with censors and/or are from outside a country may be *categorically blocked.* This may happen through technical means as when the former Soviet Union electronically jammed communications of Radio Free Europe or through the seizure of material at borders. China has created an electronic wall around its Internet to block access to material from nonapproved sources (e.g., among sites blocked are the New York Times and CNN). Until the United States Supreme Court (*US v. One Book Entitled Ulysses 1934*) found that James Joyce's *Ulysses* was a work of art, even though it contained 'dirty words,' US customs authorities routinely seized literature deemed inappropriate. The US Postal Service prohibits the importation and domestic transmission of certain forms of obscene communication. With the 1934 decision we see the seeds of later Supreme Court rulings such as *Miller v. California 1973*, which held that work could be prohibited only if, taken as a whole, it had no redeeming value as art or science, was patently offensive, and was not in keeping with local community standards.

The conflict between the principle of no prior restraint and any modern society's legitimate need to control some communication has resulted in a variety of after-the-fact sanctions (e.g., criminal offenses involving espionage, revealing national secrets, obscenity, pornography, and incitement, injunctions to cease publication and administrative sanctions; and civil remedies such as invasion of privacy, libel, and defamation).

In the USA in 2000 (in contrast to Britain, which has an Official Secrets Act), the disclosure of properly classified information (with certain exceptions such as information on the design of nuclear weapons and the names of intelligence agents) is not a crime. However disclosing such information can result in losses of security clearance, dismissal, and fines.

Communication has a special quality. Unlike most other legally regulated subjects, most communications cannot be legally prohibited before they are offered, but once offered, legal penalties may apply. Thus, there is a paradox and some uncertainty and risk for communicators, particularly those pushing boundaries. The goal here, beyond punishment for the infraction in question, is to warn and deter others in the hope of encouraging self-censorship.

On a statistical basis, the major form of censorship in western societies is self-censorship. Publishers, editors, and producers of mass communications are aware of boundaries not to be crossed, even though there are many gray areas. Communicators generally stay within the borders, whether to avoid prosecution or lawsuits, to avoid offending various social groups, to keep the channels of government information open, to please stockholders and advertisers, or out of their sense of patriotism and morality.

Press and broadcast organizations (e.g., The National Association of Broadcasters) and the major newspapers and television networks have codes of ethics and voluntary standards. Between the time a journalist writes a story and its appearance there are several levels of review. The large broadcasting companies have internal units that review everything from advertisements to program content before they appear. When Elvis Presley appeared on national television for the first time, only his upper body was shown, given censors' concern with what was then considered to be his prurient hip shaking.

Another prevalent nongovernmental means, often undertaken to avoid the threat of more stringent government controls, involves voluntary rating systems. Here the goal is not to ban the material but to give consumers fair warning so they can make up their own mind. In the 1920s, the Motion Picture Association of America created a seal of approval for films meeting its standards. In 1968, it created its rating system (expanded in 2000) for films based on nudity and violent content. Some comic books, TV programs, music videos, video games, music, and web sites are also rated. This may be welcomed as consumer information or seen as censorship that can chill expression and create an undesirable climate, opening the door to greater control.

Technical means of information control such as the v-chip, which permits programming a television set so it will not receive material deemed objectionable, and various software filters, which screen web sites for sexual and violent content, facilitate private control. Such means are seen as more efficient than a heavy-handed government censor and more consistent with an open, highly heterogeneous society. Those who want such material have access while those who might be offended can avoid exposure.

There are degrees of censorship. More common than outright prohibition, particularly in the case of erotic material (which has received increased legal protection in recent decades in the face of local legal prohibitions that appeared in the nineteenth century), are time, place, manner, and person restrictions—whether required by government or undertaken voluntarily. Potentially offensive material is segmented and walled off from those for whom it is deemed inappropriate. For example, pornographic material may be restricted to red-light districts, to adults, and to late night programming when minors are presumed not to be watching; children may be prohibited from certain concerts, and stores may refuse to sell them violent videos.

2.4 Limitations of Censorship

While government censorship makes a symbolic statement, it is often rather impractical beyond the short run, given the ubiquitous nature and continual improvements in mass communication technologies and the leaky nature of most social systems. Of course computer-based technologies may make it easier to track whom an individual communicates with and what material they access. But on balance, technology appears more likely to be on the side of freedom of expression than the side of the censors. The ease of modern communications, in particular remote forms (such as radio, television, fax, and the Internet) whose transmission can transcend national borders and means of reproduction (such as photocopiers, scanners, audio- and videotaping, and printing through a computer) that are inexpensive and relatively easy to use and conceal limit the ability of censors. The Internet, if available, has the potential to make everyone a publisher. Its 'many to many' communication through labyrinthine networks (chat rooms, bulletin boards, and e-mail) is far more difficult to censor than the traditional 'one to many' communication of the newspaper or television station and it is less expensive.

Given the expanding scale of published material and the diffusion of communications technology that began with the printing press, government and religious bodies are forever trying to catch up. This is the case even in modern highly authoritarian settings. For example in China during the Tiananmen Square protest, fax technology kept China and the world informed of the events, and in Iran the fall of the Shah was aided by smuggled audiotapes urging his overthrow. Strong encryption, which protects messages, also makes the censor's task more difficult.

Beyond technical factors, censorship is often accompanied by demand for the censored material. Censoring material may call attention to it and make it more attractive (the forbidden fruit/banned in Boston effect). Black market demand for such material makes it likely that some individuals will take the risk of creating and distributing it, whether out of conviction or for profit. Potential communicators often find ways to avoid or deceive censors whether using satire, parable, code language, changing the name of prohibited publications, or through simply defying the law, as with the many underground 'samizdat' presses that challenged communist rule in Eastern Europe.

It is also the case that sometimes, 'the truth will out.' In a democracy illegitimate political censorship in the name of national security or executive privilege is vulnerable to discovery—note Watergate and the Iran-Contra affair. In spite of its dependence on government sources, the mass media may play an important counterbalancing role here, watching those who seek to watch. Beyond investigative reporters often using the Freedom of Information Act, such 'dirty data' may be revealed by the legal procedure of 'discovery' in court cases, by experiments and tests, by leaks, whistleblowers, and participants with a Dostoevskian compulsion to confess and by uncontrollable contingencies such as accidents (e.g., the crash of an airplane carrying Watergate 'hush' money). The more complex and important a cover-up or illegal conspiracy, the more vulnerable it is to revelation. Even most legitimately classified government secrets have a shelf life and must be revealed after 75 years.

In the long run it is also difficult for censors to deny pragmatic outcomes and those that are empirically obvious. This raises the intriguing sociology of knowledge question of the relationship between culture with its significant, but not unlimited, elasticity and a level of reality or truth that, when in conflict with culture, may erode it over time. No matter what the power of the church to prosecute Galileo for heresy and ban his work, or the amplitude of its megaphone to assert the earth was flat, it could not suppress the truth for long.

See also: Censorship and Transgressive Art; Censorship in Research and Scholarship; Communication and Democracy; Confidentiality and Statistical Disclosure Limitation; Mass Communication: Normative Frameworks; Privacy of Individuals in Social Research: Confidentiality; Secrecy, Anthropology of

Bibliography

Aumente J 1999 The role and effects of journalism and *Samizdat* leading up to 1989. In: Aumente J, Gross P, Hiebert R, Johnson O, Mills D (eds.) *Eastern European Journalism Before, During and After Communism.* Hampton Press, Cresskill, NJ

Bok S 1989 *Secrets: On the Ethics of Concealment and Revelation.* Vintage Books, New York

Coetzee J 1996 *Giving Offense: Essays on Censorship.* University of Chicago Press, Chicago

Donner F 1980 *The Age of Surveillance: the Aims and Methods of America's Political Intelligence System.* Knopf, New York

Freedom House 2000 *Press Freedom Survey 2000.* Freedom House, Washington DC

Green J (ed.) 1990 *The Encyclopedia of Censorship.* Facts on File, New York

Goffman E 1969 *Strategic Interaction.* University of Pennsylvania, Philadelphia, PA

Hein M 1993 *Sex, Sin, and Blasphemy.* Free Press, New York

Herman E, Chomsky N 1988 *Manufacturing Consent: The Political Economy of the Mass Media.* Pantheon, New York

Itzin C 1993 *Pornography: Women, Violence and Civil Liberties.* Oxford University Press, New York

Laqueur W 1985 *A World of Secrets.* Basic Books, New York

Marx G T 1984 Notes on the collection and assessment of hidden and dirty data. In: Schneider J, Kitsuse J (eds.) *Studies in the Sociology of the Social Problem.* Ablex, New York

Moynihan D 1998 *Secrecy: The American Experience.* Yale University Press, New Haven, CT

National Academy of Sciences 2000 Promoting Health: Intervention Strategies from Social and Behavioral Science Research. National Academy Press, Washington, DC

Pool I D S 1983 *Technologies of Freedom.* Belknap Press of Harvard University Press, Cambridge, MA

Popper K 1962 *The Open Society and its Enemies.* Routledge & Kegan Paul, London

Segal L, McIntosh M (eds.) 1993 *Sex Exposed: Sexuality and the Pornography Debate.* Rutgers University Press, New Brunswick, NJ

Scheppele K 1988 *Legal Secrets: Equality and Efficiency in the Common Law.* University of Chicago Press, Chicago

Shils E 1956 *The Torment of Secrecy*. Free Press, Glencoe, IL

Simmel G 1964 *The Sociology of Georg Simmel* (ed. Wolff K). Free Press, Glencoe, IL

Strum P 1999 *When the Nazis Came to Skokie: Freedom for Speech We Hate (Landmark Law Cases and American Society)*. University of Kansas Press, St. Lawrence, KS

Sunstein C 1993 *Democracy and the Problem of Free Speech*. Free Press, New York

Tefft S 1980 *Secrecy: A Cross Cultural Perspective*. Human Sciences Press, New York

Wilsnak R 1980 Information control: A conceptual framework for sociological analysis. *Urban Life* (Jan)

G. T. Marx

Censorship and Transgressive Art

'Transgressive art' violates aesthetic or broader cultural norms. It provokes, challenges, and shocks audiences, causing anger, insult, or anxiety. Restrictions such as *censorship* may result, where parties inside or outside the production process impose modifications on work, force its suppression, or induce creators to self-impose constraints on what they make in order to avert potential problems. Artistic actions and the social reactions they call out are thus organically linked. Transgression in the world of art can also be a vital source of innovation.

1. The Term Transgressive Art: Three Meanings

Transgressive art has become a buzzword in the art world of the mid- to late 1990s. In the broadest sense, it connotes *any* artwork that offends audiences. That includes creations that could be deemed blasphemous for violating religious doctrines, be they traditional religions or dominant civic creeds; work that defies social hierarchies and would be regarded as subversive by those in power; and art that deals with 'unsavory' or 'impolite' topics. *Transgressive art* thus becomes a catch-all term, embracing a wide variety of work within its scope. In this regard, art is transgressive if it is prickly. In another age, the same material might have been condemned or dismissed as obscene, heretical, or merely 'bad art.'

But '*transgressive art*' also has two more specific, and inter-related, meanings. First, *transgressive art* corresponds to philosopher Immanuel Kant's '*sublime*,' as opposed to the 'beautiful.' Whereas the beautiful is soothing, representing order and regularity, the *sublime* is surprising, it embraces the obscure, the novel, and the terrible. The *sublime* challenges the senses and produces restlessness, as opposed to satisfaction. The *sublime* excites fear; it is

unpredictable and unanticipated. Although this distinction came to prominence in the mid-eighteenth century, it has obvious relevance to the contemporary *avant garde*, for whom unsettling the status quo is a primary principle.

Second, artists have expanded the meaning of aesthetic since the mid-1980s to beyond the object, and beyond the art world. This type of art supersedes the aesthetic formalism of Clement Greenberg by actively engaging the world, critically dissecting it, and proposing an alternative future (Kester 1998). 'Art' frequently encompasses activist interventions in the art world or the larger community, uncovering disguised social processes such as power, racism, and sexism (e.g., the feminist collective Guerrilla Girls, or Hans Haacke, whose 1971 exhibition unmasking the complex operations of a Manhattan slumlord was canceled by the Guggenheim Museum because of its 'extra-esthetic' nature). It can therefore encompass process rather than object. This means expanding the concept of 'public art' beyond heroic depictions of 'great men' and their deeds, and beyond large-scale, transcendent 'masterpieces' by confirmed artistic geniuses, to face-to-face collaborations with real communities (Jacob 1995), or enlarging the definition of art to include the voices of formerly marginalized groups, presented in untraditional venues, and employing unconventional media. This can lead to the violation of norms and taboos broader than those of the art world itself. The first page of the catalogue accompanying the Whitney Museum of American Art's exhibition 'Abject Art: Repulsion and Desire in American Art' (1993) boldly represents this position: '[O]ur goal is to talk dirty in the institution and degrade its atmosphere of purity and prudery by foregrounding issues of gender and sexuality in the art exhibited' (Ben-Levi et al. 1993, p. 7). The materials in the object list included dirt, hair, excrement, dead animals, and rotting food.

1.1 The Contemporary Coalescence

Generally speaking, since the last quarter of the nineteenth century—with the rise of Impressionism, and the breakdown of the Academy system throughout Europe—artists have veered between two major aesthetic strategies. One approach has been 'art for art's sake,' where artists produce work primarily for a small group of like-minded individuals, using what could be compared to an exclusive language of expression. The other style is producing art aimed for the wider public, incorporating social and political themes. The first strategy is aesthetically daring but hermetic; the second has often been aesthetically conservative but liberally accessible. Dada and Abstract Expressionism are examples of 'art for art's sake'; the social realism that dominated art production in the United States during the Depression of the 1930s, or the work of muralists such as Diego Rivera who were active throughout the same era in Mexico, represent socially and politically oriented art.

But contemporary artists are distinctive: they frequently have mobilized *both* approaches, combining inventive techniques with urgent social issues. What has been the impetus for this dramatic innovation? Artists have been pulled from the cloister of their studios by larger social events since the mid-1980s. The AIDS crisis hit American artists in disproportionate numbers. They responded to inadequate or biased media coverage, and the relative dearth of official political responses to the epidemic, by treating this subject with an activist stance (the now-ubiquitous 'Silence = Death' logo was originally a neon installation in the window of New York City's New Museum of Contemporary Art). Furthermore, the empowerment movements that gained strength during the 1960s—particularly the civil rights movement, feminism, and gay liberation—affected the art world by expanding opportunities for artists and art administrators from these groups, as well as making artists more self-reflexive about the structure of the art world and communities beyond. Finally, conservative religious and political leaders in the United States who reacted to the success of the disenfranchised in expressing themselves led a series of attacks to cut off public funding of the arts, targeting unconventional expression. Contemporary artists have used both traditional and *transgressive* strategies to confront these pressing issues and resist these assaults.

1.2 The Fundamental Nature of Transgression

'Transgression' signifies that rules have been violated. The most useful conceptual tool to understand the significance of this is the work of anthropologist Mary Douglas on moral pollution. In order to structure interaction, every society consolidates experience into what Douglas calls '*natural categories*,' binary oppositions that consign phenomena to one classification or another. Significant *natural categories* include *sacred* and *profane*, public and private, masculine and feminine, internal and external. Societies differ in where they assign particular behaviors, but the process is basic across human groups.

Any infraction of these *natural categories* resounds throughout society, threatening the sanctity of other distinctions as well. Controversial artists have run afoul of convention, and have been prime movers in what one observer has termed a 'category crisis' (Garber 1992), a pervasive blurring of previously precise *symbolic boundaries*. All have committed these figurative affronts in some manner or another.

Such violations are not entirely new. For example, Jean-Baptiste Carpeaux produced a sculptural group for the facade of the new Paris Opéra, *La Danse* (1865–9), featuring a cluster of frenzied female dancers surrounding a *génie de la danse*. The central figure is *sexually* ambiguous, bearing the slim body of a male youth capped by a female face. S/he troubled many viewers and became the lightning rod for a heated *public controversy*, as did *Princess X*, a sculpture by Constantin Brancusi (1916). In one respect this work resembles the classic pose of a Madonna. But it also unmistakably resembles a set of male genitalia, thus challenging the categories of male and female, *sacred* and *profane*. Furthermore, a production of *The God of Vengeance* (penned by playwright Sholem Asch, 1910) ran afoul of public opinion and the law in New York City in 1922. This is the tale of Yankel, who operates a brothel in the basement while he maintains a 'wholesome' atmosphere for his wife and chaste daughter, Rivkele, upstairs. *Sacred* and *profane*, public and private are segregated—until Rivkele falls in love with one of the prostitutes. Such cause *célèbres* were novel in their time; they are much more commonplace today.

The photographer Andres Serrano's notoriety was established by *Piss Christ* (1987), where he placed a plastic crucifix into a container of his own urine. Whereas many people were repulsed by the idea of mixing *sacred* and *profane* when this work came to wide public attention in 1989, one canny reviewer shifted the figure/ground perspective: instead of seeing the crucifix as being despoiled, perhaps more importantly the urine was being sanctified. After using a variety of vital fluids in his work (including milk, blood, and semen), subsequent projects have included *The Morgue* (photos that provided a peak into the generally forbidden realm of corpses, in 1992), *A History of Sex* (1997), which featured images of intergenerational *sexual* relations (an 87-year-old grandmother with her young lover), and a nude woman stroking the erect penis of a horse (underscoring the cultural regulation of 'proper' *sexual* expression and the *symbolic boundaries* of taboo).

At about the same time that Serrano was vilified, so was the photographer Robert Mapplethorpe. A significant portion of Mapplethorpe's work features *sexually* explicit or homoerotic images. A few nude or seminude portraits of children were also judged in *sexual* terms by some social critics. Mapplethorpe's extensive series of self portraits represents a range of *transgressions*: in 1978 he became the Devil incarnate with his leathers and a bullwhip stuck into his rectum; in 1980 he was the ethereal waif with lipstick pout, mascaraed eyes, and naked, vulnerable torso. From demon to *sexually* ambiguous figure, Mapplethorpe tweaked public sensibilities in the 1980s and 1990s.

Finally, the widespread outcry against Martin Scorsese's film *The Last Temptation of Christ* (1988) and Salman Rushdie's novel *The Satanic Verses* (1988) have similar origins in violations of *symbolic boundaries*. In both instances, major religious figures were demystified by focusing on their humanity, alongside their divinity. But to the fundamentalist mind, this was an unbearable assault on received wisdom and sanctified territory (Dubin 1992).

1.3 Bad Girls and Gender Deviation

As demonstrated, protection of *natural categories*, and intolerance of their combination or violation, are at the base of a significant portion of modern-day controversies about art. Feminist performance artists Karen Finley and Annie Sprinkle *transgress* social expectations of femininity, the self, and the 'proper' display of the body in public: they use 'earthy' language, vault from persona to persona, and reveal intimate parts of their bodies and their functions (Sprinkle invites audience members to examine her genitals with a flashlight; Finley smears the outside of her body with raw eggs, squirts breast milk, and rubs yams over her buttocks, upsetting the presumed order of nature). In one of her best-known acts, *We Keep Our Victims Ready*, Finley slathers her nearly naked body with chocolate she scoops out in handfuls from a heart-shaped box. Next she sprinkles herself with tiny red cinnamon candies, followed by a layer of alfalfa sprouts, and topped off with Xmas tinsel. Her body has become her canvas. Id trumps everything else in this type of expression (Dubin 1992).

Finley and Sprinkle continue the tradition of feminist 'bad girls' who have pioneered performance and 'body art' since the 1960s, such as Carolee Schneeman: in *Meat Joy* (1964) she enlisted others to join her in an uninhibited romp with raw fish, chickens, and other items; in *Interior Scroll* (1975), she literally gave birth to her art as she removed a rolled text from her vagina. In more recent times, French artist Orlan has embarked on a series of seven plastic surgeries which will transform her face into an amalgam of idealized female features: Mona Lisa, the goddess Diana, and Botticelli's Venus among them. Photographer Marina Vainshtein has altered her body in a different respect: her torso is covered with tattoos evoking the Holocaust, including skeletons, swastikas, barbed wire, crematoria, and the notorious inscription on the gate to Auschwitz, *Arbeit macht frei* ('Work leads to freedom'). Her 'project' *transgresses* traditional Jewish prohibitions against altering the body, at the same time that it symbolically re-enacts and then repossesses or 'controls' the violation committed by the Nazis when they dehumanized their victims by tattooing numbers on their skin.

These defiant women chafe at the way the female body has been objectified in the past, and challenge the constraints imposed upon them by men. The 1994 exhibition *Bad Girls* (The New Museum of Contemporary Art, New York) began with a linguistically loaded title: 'bad' becomes 'good,' a badge of honor from this perspective; and 'girl,' freighted with in-

dignity when uttered by a condescending male, becomes an affectionate code word for sisterhood. Works in the exhibition highlighted women who self-consciously work beyond the *symbolic boundaries* of prim femininity, skewering the cultural assumptions of how they should act.

Of course, male artists have used their bodies as an artistic medium as well: Vito Acconci's *Seedbed* (1971) featured the artist masturbating beneath a ramp in a New York City gallery, while visitors strolled above. Chris Burden's *Shooting Piece* (1971) involved having a friend shoot him in the arm; in *Trans-Fixed* (1974), he was crucified over the back of a Volkswagen. The late Bob Flanagan famously nailed his penis to a board. Ron Athey currently performs ritualized piercings and mutilations. These performances transgress convention, to be sure. But in vital ways they harmonize with male norms of *sexuality* and bravado, unlike their female artistic counterparts who more directly challenge *gendered* norms of behavior.

2. Transgressive Art and Social Response

During every epoch and in every conceivable place where modern cultures have developed, we can expect to observe this peculiar dialectic: a particular type of social control evolves to address specifically whatever the powers-that-be find threatening. The 'problem' inevitably calls out the 'solution.' This is what philosopher Michel Foucault described as 'perpetual spirals of power and pleasure' (Foucault 1978), which symbiotically bind opponents to one another in pitched battle. In other words, enforcing the rules and violating them both provide gratification. Prelate and infidel, prime minister and traitor, each characteristically complements the other in the struggle for ascendence.

2.1 Censorship: Different Forms

For all its flaws—it is an extremely vague term, all too promiscuously applied to depict any obstacles your opponents erect to limit, direct, and/or interfere with your absolute freedom of expression—*censorship* is the most recognizable and purposeful term we have to cover such situations. (Unlike Eskimos, with their purported multiplicity of descriptors of snow, speakers of English encounter a serious deficit of phrases characterizing constraints on expression.) 'Censorship' is a contested term; its meanings are reckoned along a variety of axes.

Censorship's visibility is one pivotal characteristic, be it overt or covert, *de jure* or *de facto*, regulative or constitutive (Jansen 1991). Much *censorship* is occult, brought to light only when taken-for-granted procedures fail to stem the tide of forbidden thoughts, or when they are unable to anticipate when and where new types of danger may erupt, and in what form. As the understanding of hegemony alerts us, the most efficient form of social control is through ideas, not by force. Whenever a society effectively socializes everyone into supporting the same core belief system, controls will seem natural, matter-of-fact, unremarked. This promotes the sort of stability where prescription and proscription dictate and regulate nearly all thought and behavior. An efflorescence of *censorship* therefore commonly signals some breakdown, an unraveling of established rules.

Censorship's essential nature and primary targets are additional attributes. Emile Durkheim's justly famous dictum asserts that deviance is to be expected even in a society of saints (Durkheim 1938). In a religious community, then, like the seventeenth century Italian monastery swept by a witch craze in Aldous Huxley's *The Devils of Loudun* (1952), blasphemy and heresy will be the shape given to doctrinal aberrations, and punishments will be meted out accordingly. In other societies where a puritanical moral system is to be defended, *censorship* will be directed at alleged instances of perversity. Whatever fashions the fundamental character of the community also shapes how the threats to it are perceived—those things which must be banished from view and from earshot.

The particular site or source of *censorship* is also critical. In its classic, perhaps purest form, *censorship* is a prerogative of government, be it civil or ecclesiastical. *Censorship* is something officials are entitled to impose, hence state *censorship*. Market *censorship* exists as well: certain groups are excluded from having their say because they lack the resources or access which would allow them to disseminate their ideas easily. Systematic exclusion from the marketplace of ideas typically parallels the exclusion from other opportunities and rewards a society may have to offer some of its citizens, but not to others, characteristically because of their race, religion, *gender*, class, or *sexual* orientation. Finally, we must consider self-*censorship*, where individuals hold themselves in check, consciously or unconsciously, either out of fear of bringing official action down upon their heads, or from the fatigue and frustration which results from continually trying to get past cultural gatekeepers and getting rebuffed.

These are, of course, ideal types. In any specific case, one or more of these forms of regulation might be operative, either simultaneously or sequentially. *Censorship* may occur at any point along the process of production or distribution of cultural goods, and in cases where hegemony maintains a stranglehold upon independent thinking, even at the point of reception and consumption (Dubin 1997).

The main examples of *transgressive art* cited earlier have all endured negative reactions and restrictions of one type or another. Carpeaux's sculptural *gender-*bending provoked extensive debate in periodicals of the day, suffered defacement with a bottle of ink, and even an order of banishment issued by Napoleon III. The salon president had Brancusi's *Princess X* removed from the Salon des Indépendants in 1920, pre-empting the possibility of adverse public response or even police action. All the cast members and the producer of *The God of Vengeance* were arrested and charged with obscenity, immorality, and indecency (they were found guilty, but their sentences were suspended; the play was forcibly closed). Theaters screening *The Last Temptation of Christ* endured bomb threats, picketing, and vandalism, and it was even banned in certain locales. Iran's Ayatollah Khomeini declared Salman Rushdie's *The Satanic Verses* blasphemous in 1989 and issued a *fatwa* or death decree against the Indian-born writer; 10 years later, Rushdie (who is now a British citizen) was tentatively beginning to make public appearances again.

Furthermore, a long and acrimonious national debate erupted in the United States over the work of Andres Serrano, Robert Mapplethorpe, and Karen Finley; it reached from the halls of Congress to backwater radio talk shows. In each case, a small amount of federal money had been appropriated by the National Endowment for the Arts (NEA) to underwrite exhibitions of their work. Senator Alphonse D'Amato ripped up the catalogue from an NEA-sponsored fellowship show that included the photo *Piss Christ*, on the Senate floor in 1989. Moreover, an enraged teenager damaged *Piss Christ* with a hammer while it was on display in an Australian museum in 1997; administrators subsequently closed the exhibition of Serrano's work 'for security reasons.' His *History of Sex* provoked bomb threats in the Netherlands.

The Contemporary Art Center in Cincinnati, and its director Dennis Barrie, were indicted for pandering pornography when it hosted a Robert Mapplethorpe retrospective in 1990 (they were acquitted). Karen Finley was denied an NEA fellowship in 1990 after she had gained notoriety as 'the chocolate-smeared woman' and became the poster girl for what conservative opponents of the NEA felt was an illegitimate use of public funds (she and three other performance artists—the 'NEA Four'—later successfully sued to have their fellowships restored). Significant threats and impediments to the unfettered circulation of these works materialized in every instance. Yet also in every instance, generally at great personal cost, the creators and their works prevailed.

3. Summing Up

One of the difficulties with the term *censorship* is that it commonly connotes finality. More accurately, *censorious* actions are part of an ongoing process of action and reaction that demonstrates a variable equilibrium. Cultural products typically display a resilience that enables them to persist, despite meeting substantial obstacles to their successful completion and circulation during particular times or in specific venues (Dubin 1999). Even in extreme situations where the creator is permanently silenced or the product destroyed, history often records the deed. Culture typically outlasts those who would crush it.

Transgressive art is commonly credited with destabilizing taboos (Ben-Levi et al. 1993) and providing a source of innovation in the art world (Graves 1998). Both views undoubtedly have merit. But it is equally true that at the beginning of the new millennium, *transgressive art* has become a norm in itself. In that respect it has become somewhat banal, incorporating shock for the sake of shock. What was on the extreme margins of comprehension and acceptability not so long ago has quickly become absorbed into the mainstream. Artists who seek to be transgressors at present are increasingly hard pressed to uncover virgin territories to explore.

This provides both an opportunity and a challenge to researchers. In the past, social scientists studied a wide variety of transgressions employing a Durkheimian, normative approach. Mary Douglas' work subsequently moved investigators toward a more structural form of analysis, continuing the predilection to analyze such phenomena under the rubric of 'deviance.' But in a *postmodern* world, these earlier frames of reference are not as adequate as they once were.

As a broad range of social breaches has become routine in contemporary society, the role, the import, or even the continued existence of an artistic *avant garde* is in question. Marginal art might no longer be 'where the action is.' Researchers may turn instead to other realms to examine creativity, the defiance of *symbolic boundaries*, and the eventual social responses. The frontiers of innovation are frequently found in the domains of science and technology. New forms of communication, insight, and philosophical exploration are as likely to spring from the Internet as from artistic styles such as Impressionism, a prime example of how art that once posed a dynamic, transgressive challenge to perception has become static, conventionalized.

Future researchers will discover fresh veins of material in the social worlds people create with and around computers. Computers alter discourse (who you contact, where, for what purposes, and with what frequency); identity and perception ('presentation of self' becomes more malleable, 'reality' more manifold); the distribution of ideas and images (the availability of sexually-oriented material); and the process of creation itself (an array of raw material can be 'sampled' and reconstructed in myriad forms). This fluidity of categories denotes and defines our *postmodern* world, and researchers will need to develop new theoretical

tools to understand these phenomena. The extent to which artists utilize the potential of new technologies will have a significant impact upon how viable their art remains as a generative force in the twenty-first century, and the degree to which social scientists will continue to study them.

See also: Art: Anthropological Aspects; Art, Sociology of; Cultural Studies: Cultural Concerns; Film: Genres and Genre Theory; Postmodernism in Sociology; Postmodernism: Philosophical Aspects; Television: Genres

Bibliography

Apel D 1997 The tattooed Jew. *New Art Examiner* **10**: 13–17
Ben-Levi J, Hauser C, Jones L C, Taylor S 1993 *Abject Art: Repulsion and Desire in American Art*. Whitney Museum of American Art, New York
Douglas M 1973 [1970] *Natural Symbols: Explorations in Cosmology*. Vintage, New York
Douglas M 1984 [1966] *Purity and Danger: An Analysis of the Concepts of Pollution and Taboo*. Routledge & K. Paul, London
Dubin S 1992 *Arresting Images: Impolitic Art and Uncivil Actions*. Routledge, New York
Dubin S 1999 *Displays of Power: Memory and Amnesia in the American Museum*. New York University Press, New York
Dubin S 1997 Pressed to the limit: printers and the problematics of censorship. *Journal of Visual Anthropology* **9**: 229–41
Durkheim E 1964 [1938] *The Rules of Sociological Method*. Free Press, New York
Foucault M 1978 *The History of Sexuality: Vol. 1: An Introduction*. Pantheon, New York
Garber M 1992 *Vested Interests: Cross-Dressing and Cultural Anxiety*. Routledge, New York
Graves L 1998 Transgressive traditions and art definitions. *Journal of Aesthetics and Art Criticism* **1**: 39–48
Jacob M J 1995 *Culture in Action: A Public Art Program of Sculpture Chicago*. Bay Press, Seattle, WA
Jansen S C 1991 *Censorship: The Knot That Binds Power and Knowledge*. Oxford University Press, New York
Kester G H 1998 *Art, Activism, and Oppositionality: Essays from Afterimage*. Duke University Press, Durham, NC
Rose B 1993 Is it art? Orlan and the transgressive act. *Art in America* **2**: 82–7
Tucker M, Tanner M, Goode Bryant L, Dunye C 1994 *Bad Girls*. MIT Press, Cambridge, MA

S. C. Dubin

Censorship in Research and Scholarship

Censorship is the suppression or alteration of speech or writing prior to publication in the interests of an alleged higher social good. The narrowest definition would limit the use of the term to authoritative action, usually, but not always applied by governments. However, historically, conflicts with prevailing religious doctrine have been a major reason for censorship imposed by clerical authorities. While that remains a major motive in some areas of the modern world, censorship has come to be associated primarily with the actions of governments. The rise of totalitarian governments in the twentieth century produced perhaps the most egregious and systematic programs of censorship in history, both as a consequence of the range of behavior over which such governments claimed sovereignty and of the ability of the modern state to impose and enforce its rules on its citizens. But democratic governments too engage in acts of censorship when their central values appear to be threatened or, more accurately perhaps, when the values of the dominant political or economic forces within them are threatened.

Censorship, as defined above, is frequently associated with patronage, especially in the academic world. Sponsors of research—governments, corporations, foundations, and individuals—are often in a position to close areas of research by not funding it, or to stop or alter the publication of the results of research seen to be inimical to their interests. Patronage, or more precisely, the threat of losing it, may also lead to acts of self-censorship by scholars. As research in the natural and social sciences has become more expensive, these forms of censorship have become increasingly common.

It is important to distinguish censorship, which is always accompanied by the threat of legitimately imposed sanctions, from disagreements that may be accompanied by efforts to persuade others not to read or listen to the offending writing or speech. The two are frequently confused, though the former prevents free speech, while the latter is, itself, an exercise of free speech.

1. Censorship and Research

Scholarship and research, by their very nature, have always been vulnerable to censorship. The questions asked, the methods used, the answers found and their implications, may challenge a prevailing orthodoxy, and in the extreme and most dramatic cases, may threaten to undermine the fundamentals of ruling regimes, secular and clerical alike. In democratic societies social science research is unlikely to be seen as threatening to the interests of the state. It is much more likely, however, to be seen as a threat to some group interest in the society and to elicit governmental action through the political supporters of that group. Indeed, since social science research, particularly large scale projects, has come to rely on governmental funding, and since the subjects of social science research often touch on and challenge deeply-held social and religious values, resisting efforts to stifle it

may, on occasion, require a degree of legislative self-restraint that democratically elected legislatures cannot be expected to muster. Two especially sensitive areas of research, sex and race, illustrate the point. For an excellent discussion of restraints on research in these areas in the United States, see Hunt *The New Know-Nothings.*

2. Censorship and Research On Sexual Behavior and Attitudes

In the United States, religion, politics, and the freedom to do research on the subject of sexual practices and attitudes clash more vividly than perhaps anywhere else. The result can be seen in a history of attempts, frequently successful, by the Congress to forbid studies of sexual behavior financed by public funds. In one instance, the research of Alfred Kinsey, the Congress reached into the private sector in an effort to cut off funding for the work. When Kinsey's two studies, *Sexual Behavior in the Human Male* (1948) and *Sexual Behavior in the Human Female* (1953) were published and captured wide public attention, religious, and political conservatives became alarmed at what they saw as publicizing depraved sexual practices, thereby contributing to the moral degradation of the society. Kinsey's research, however, was not publicly financed. Rather it was funded by grants channeled through the National Research Council by the Rockefeller Foundation. Congressional conservatives used the instrumentality of the Committee to Investigate Tax Exempt Foundations. The committee suggested that foundations that supported research like Kinsey's might well lose their tax exempt status. Whether there was any Constitutional basis for such a threat hardly mattered in the climate of the times. Shortly after the Committee Report was published, the Rockefeller Foundation ended its funding of the research. While the research continued, it did so with far less money, largely earned from the royalties of the books, and, as Hunt reports, '...much of its data went unpublished for many years; the findings of a survey completed in 1970, for instance, were not published until 1989.'

The Kinsey case was extraordinary in the attempt of the Congress to reach the private funding of research. In other respects, however, it was a precursor to future attempts to censor unpopular social science and art. Publicly funded research on sex has been constantly in trouble, and in the 1970s and 1980s, several large-scale surveys of sexual behavior that had been approved by the National Institutes of Health, were stopped when the Congress cut off funds for them by legislation or pressured political leaders in the Executive Branch to reverse NIH's decisions.

The most publicized case of the kind involved an exhibition at the Corcoran Gallery of Art in Washington DC of the work of the photographer Robert Mapplethorp. Included in the exhibition was a series of explicitly homoerotic pictures. Since the Corcoran Gallery is privately owned and largely privately financed, there was no direct way for outraged religious groups and their Congressional supporters to reach the Gallery directly. However, the exhibit was funded in part by money from the National Endowment for the Arts which, as a government agency was directly reachable both through legislation and appropriations. Both avenues were used. Appropriations were drastically reduced, and legislation imposing 'decency standards' on Endowment grants was passed. The latter was subsequently declared unconstitutional by the courts, but the Endowment, itself, has yet to recover from the episode and from the continuing implacable hostility of the religious and political right wings of American life.

3. Censorship and Research on Race

Conservative religious groups can claim credit for restraining research into matters of sexuality. But American liberal and civil rights groups can make a similar claim with respect to research that touches on race, a topic that is guaranteed to elicit emotional controversy. Two sets of events, both taking place at the intersection of race and genetics, illustrate the point. The two are similar in some respects, but also different in ways that show important shadings in evaluations of prior restraint of research.

The alleged correlation between race and intelligence has generated more emotional controversy than perhaps any other topic in the social sciences. Educational psychologist Arthur Jensen set off the debate in 1969 with an article in the Harvard Educational Review, 'How Much Can We Boost IQ and Scholastic Achievement?' Jensen, relying heavily on the literature of studies of identical twins, concluded that there is, in fact, a large component of heritability in intelligence, measured by IQ tests, and that African Americans on average were at a genetic disadvantage. Jensen's avowed purpose, as the title of his article suggested, was to force educators to confront that finding and to devise educational strategies that took it into account.

Jensen's conclusion from the data he reviewed, quite apart from the policy prescriptions that followed from it, was highly debatable in genetic terms, and it was hotly debated. There was no question of censoring his work, though some might have wished to do so if it had been possible. Jensen's work was wholly funded from private sources. He was, however, prevented from speaking on some college campuses by disruptions or the threat of them. If the term 'political correctness' is understood to describe a form of debate in which the object is to anathematize one's adversary in order to eliminate him from the debate on grounds of moral inferiority, then the Jensen episode can be seen as a warning to social scientists who would

venture into the area of race, intelligence and genetics that they did so at the risk not only of having their work attacked, which was fair enough, but of being personally vilified as pseudoscholars whose purported scholarship was merely a mask for a racist social agenda.

Twenty-five years later, the Jensen episode was replayed, with even greater intensity following the publication of *The Bell Curve* (Herrnstein and Murray 1994). The book was met by a storm of criticism, much of it scholarly and serious—the vast majority of psychologists and geneticists found their work to be wholly without merit—but some of it consisting of *ad hominum* vilification of the authors.

Neither the Jensen nor the Herrnstein–Murray cases meet the strict definition of censorship given at the outset. Rather, they are examples of what might be called 'virtual censorship' in which the threat of personal vilification may serve to prevent some scholars from addressing topics for which they can be certain that even their hypotheses, much their results, will call down on them painful personal confrontations. There is no way to know whether the Jensen and Herrnstein–Murray examples had that effect on others. However, the case of the aborted conference on Genetics and Crime demonstrates that the governmental equivalent of personal vilification, the threat of political retribution, can have that effect on even the best government agencies.

4. Genetics Race and Violence

On May 1, 1991, the National Institutes of Health awarded a grant for a conference on 'Genetic Factors in Crime: Findings, Uses and Implications.' The award was based on the recommendation of a peer review group, which had concluded the organizers had done a 'superb job of assessing the underlying scientific, legal, ethical, and public policy issues and organizing them in a thoughtful fashion.' Ten weeks later funds for the conference were frozen when NIH Director, Dr. Bernadine P. Healy, concluded that the review group's recommendation had not been strong enough for the meeting to go forward in the face of public criticism.

The public criticism that concerned Dr. Healy came from a coalition of psychiatrists and civil rights groups that argued that government sponsorship of the meeting was yet another step toward legalization of the racist idea that violence is genetically based. The Center for the Study of Psychiatry asserted there are no known genetic factors in crime, but merely raising the issue arouses racial prejudices and distracts us from the true causes of the high crime rate within the inner city, including poverty, unemployment, racism, dangerous and inadequate schools, drug abuse, family dysfunction, and a variety of other social and economic factors. And as one opponent put the more extreme argument, 'It is clear racism. It is an effort to use public money for a genocidal effort against African Americans.'

The cause was taken up by the Congressional Black Caucus and the problem facing the management of NIH became not the merits of the project or the protection of the peer review process which the NIH pioneered and developed, but the protection of the agency from the fallout of a political storm. The decision was not surprising. From the point of view of agency managers, political embarrassment leads to political problems, putting at risk agency interests, programs and careers that far outweigh the value of a single project, no matter how meritorious.

5. *Industry and Censorship*

Because social and behavioral research is not heavily funded by industry, it is unlikely that it will be heavily affected by the problems that have accompanied industry's support of scientific research, especially research in the biomedical sciences. The restraints imposed by industrial sponsors are typically motivated by concern for the protection of intellectual property, and most commonly they take the form of required delays in publication for a specified period of time to allow for review by the sponsor for intellectual property implications. There have been occasions, however, in which corporations have gone further and prohibited publication because the results of the research would be publicly embarrassing to the company, a situation more analogous to that sometimes faced by social scientists.

A potentially risk does face social scientists, even though they are not heavy recipients of corporate support. It is an indirect but real risk, especially for scholars in universities. Universities are often willing to protect their scholars from publication threatened by the government. However, if they are simultaneously accepting limitations on publication as a part of industrial contracts, their ability to hold a principled position against the government is seriously compromised. Indeed, during the 1980s and early 1990s, when it was the policy of the American government to use the Export Control Act to restrict the international dissemination of unclassified but allegedly sensitive research findings, it was common for government officials to argue that universities were willing to do for money what they would not do to protect the national interest. It is an argument that resonates powerfully with legislatures and with the public, and once it is accepted it applies to any research that can be invested with a claim of national interest. Since that is an open-ended category, the willingness of universities to accept prior restraints on publication as the price they must pay for industrial money could greatly compromise their ability, or even willingness, to defend social scientists whose work is challenged.

It is in the nature of governments and other important social interests to protect themselves from challenge or embarrassment. It is in the nature of social science to provide both from time to time. Tension between the two is, therefore, unavoidable. The main protection for social scientists in protecting their right to publish freely lies in their willingness to join together to assert it when threatened and the willingness of their employing institutions, individually and collectively, to join with them.

See also: Censorship and Secrecy: Legal Perspectives; Censorship and Transgressive Art; Civil Liberties and Human Rights; Civil Rights; Ethics and Values; Freedom/Liberty: Impact on the Social Sciences; Freedom of the Press; Fundamental Rights and Constitutional Guarantees

Bibliography

Herrnstein R J, Murray C 1994 *The Bell Curve: Intelligence and Class Structure in American Life*. The Free Press, New York
Hunt M *The New Know-Nothings: The Political Foes of the Scientific Study of Human Nature*. Transaction Publishers, New Brunswick, NJ
Jensen A 1969 *Harvard Educational Review* **39**: 1–121

R. M. Rosenzweig

Censuses: Comparative International Aspects

Over 200 countries have taken censuses within the last ten years. Because there is a desire to compare data from one country to another, the United Nations has issued guidelines for the taking of censuses. Each country may have its own way of dealing with special populations, but if the methods are documented, comparisons can be made. Countries differ in whether or not they use mail primarily or rely on census-takers to visit each unit and record the information. Many countries use sampling as part of the census operation, as part of the processing to get an early look at results, as part of an evaluation, or in an effort to reduce the burden on households by not asking every household to complete every question. Because of more recent concerns about privacy and confidentiality, some countries have challenged the use of a census and are looking at new methods of obtaining population data.

1. *Distinguishing Features of a Census*

National censuses, drawing on the sponsorship and authority of national governments typically provide information for national needs such as population counts used to reapportion legislatures. National censuses also serve local needs, such as providing population data for state and local agencies for planning for health, education, and many other services.

Because local populations may grow dramatically between censuses, many cities and states or provinces take local censuses to benefit from more up-to-date population figures. The emphasis in this article is on national censuses and their comparability. Before a census takes place, there must be agreement about what geographic areas are to be included. If new territory has been annexed since the last census, it must be clearly defined. Geographical subdivision as well as national boundaries must be clearly delineated and changes from the last census must be clearly stated.

While censuses typically strive for universality, in every country some groups are excluded. Such groups must be decided upon before the census. For example, the population residing in an embassy of a foreign country may be exempt from the census of the country in which the embassy is located. People who are living in the country as temporary workers may be exempt, though it is often a function of the amount of time they spend in the country. Military personnel and their families living outside of the country may or may not be counted. (In the USA, they have been counted in some censuses and not in others.) This is different in concept from early censuses when whole groups of citizens or residents were left out. (See *Censuses: History and Methods* for examples of censuses that counted only adult men.)

Though not essential, it has become a custom in most countries to tie the census of population to a census of housing, expanding analytical capability. However, it is also important to make provision for those persons who do not live in regular housing, such as the homeless or nomads. Provision must be made for squatters' colonies, refugee camps, defense areas, and the institutional population.

Modern censuses rely on enumeration of the individual, although often through households or institutions. This implies that data about each individual is collected and recorded, enabling cross-classification by individual characteristics. In some early censuses, or in some enumeration of hard-to-enumerate groups, aggregates from the group have been recorded, thereby prohibiting cross-classifications. In the USA, the first census of 1790 was of this type, collecting data on the number of males, number of females, but no individual data (Anderson 1988).

Another feature of a census is that it takes place at the same time, or with reference to a specific census day, at all places in the country. To get an accurate snapshot of the country, censuses must take into account all births, deaths, and immigrants as of a certain day, usually denoted as Census Day. (Weather sometimes dictates the physical enumeration of some remote areas of the country at a separate time.)

Periodicity of censuses ensures that trends can be followed. Also, comparisons among countries are more meaningful if they refer to the same time period. The United Nations has been instrumental in trying to set a schedule for censuses. The final step in producing a census is the compilation and publication of the data as soon as possible. Without dissemination, a census cannot be used effectively.

2. Coverage of Population

One of the biggest problems in comparing censuses across countries is the difference between a *de jure* and a *de facto* enumeration. A *de jure* census counts people at their usual place of residence, whether or not they were there on Census Day. The USA, for example, defines an individual's 'usual' residence as the place where one spends the majority of one's time. A *de facto* census counts people where they were present at the time of the census. In practice, most countries combine one method with some elements of the other. *De jure* residence may not coincide with legal residence. The United Nations (1992) recommends a combination of the two methods. For example, the 1980 census in Brazil was described as both *de jure* and *de facto* (Goyer and Domschke 1983).

Using the *de jure* concept means deciding, in advance of enumeration, where to count people who have more than one residence, persons who work at one location and return to their usual residence for the weekend, students at boarding school or college, members of the military who live on base but maintain a residence off base, and other such cases. Comparisons between countries that use *de jure* and *de facto* counting rules are difficult, as are those between countries using different *de jure* counting rules. Documentation of how and where people are counted is the best hope for making correct comparisons.

Another factor to be considered when preparing for a census is how to count certain special populations. A group that is difficult to count in many developed countries is the homeless. Though efforts are made to count them where they receive services such as food or shelter, there is always the chance that they are not counted or counted more than once. In some countries, the counting of nomads presents difficulties. Many approaches have been tried, such as a tribal approach in which a chief gives the information, or a water point approach in which all nomads are enumerated at water points. The treatment of civilian aliens who work in a country as seasonal workers, who cross a frontier daily to work in a country, or who are residing in a country for some work-related reason is now an important consideration in many European countries as well as the USA. The differential effect of how countries treat the special populations has an important effect on the estimated size of the world's population (UN Statistical Office 1992).

Influencing the coverage of the census is the time of the year when it is conducted. Most countries opt for a time of the year when travel is not impeded by bad weather and when people are at their usual place of residence. This may affect the principle of census taking that calls for simultaneous data collection. In the USA, Alaska is enumerated at a different time from the continental states. If some areas are impossible to reach, coverage will be biased downward. Another time-related factor is whether the enumeration takes place early in the month or mid-month. Canada has found that mid-month is helpful in the enumeration of those people who rely on a monthly check, move out of short-term housing until the next check appears, live on the streets at the end of one month and the beginning of the next, but are usually in housing at mid-month. Tests in the USA confirmed that a mid-month start would be useful there as well, and changing from the traditional April 1 Census Day to mid-March would also provide additional time in which to conduct the census (Cohen et. al 1999).

In conducting the census, several reference periods are used. For example, questions about income usually refer to income in the previous year. Questions about labor force usually refer to the week previous to Census Day, whereas questions about who was living in a household, usually refers to the night before Census Day. Having multiple reference periods can often be confusing to respondents and may affect the quality of data. The length of the enumeration period also affects coverage. The shorter the length, the more likely the census will avoid over- or undercounting. In large countries, the time span may be longer, but the extended period often leads to overcounting. Suharto (1995) points out that no country that used a *de jure* method in censuses between 1985–1994 was able to complete the census in a day, while nine countries that used a *de facto* method completed the census in one day. Though a one-day census avoids the complexity of people moving, coverage suffers. From a survey of countries that took censuses between 1985 and 1994, Suharto (1995) reported that 31 countries completed enumeration in a week. However, countries such as Colombia and the USA took well over two months. As the time period of the enumeration lengthens, coverage errors increase.

Privacy and confidentiality concerns also affect coverage (Suharto 1995). Within the last 20 years, in several countries, concerns about confidentiality have led to decreased census participation. Because census data are used for so many purposes, and public use files are now widely disseminated, the risk that individual census records may be inadvertently disclosed has raised public concern in many countries. A strict provision of census confidentiality is necessary to reassure people concerned about issues of privacy. This feeds into the need for an effective public relations program in which the legal protection of individual census information is stressed.

3. Basic Content

To be able to compare countries by census characteristics, countries need to collect data on a basic list of characteristics with common definitions. The United Nations has been very instrumental in developing a list of basic content items with their definitions. Though there is not total agreement on every item or definition, the ability to make comparisons on basic characteristics has been enhanced.

An item of great interest to many countries is the percentage of people who live in urban or rural areas. These data are regarded as an aspect of the developmental stage of a country. To be able to make cross-country comparisons, the definitions must be the same. However, there is no universal definition of urban. In some countries, it depends on population size, sometimes on the presence of a city, on whether an area has urban characteristics, or on whether agriculture is the predominant economic activity. All other areas not urban are defined as rural.

Another item of interest is that of households and families. In some countries, the terms household and family are used interchangeably. In others, however, household means one or more persons living in a dwelling, whether or not related by blood or marriage, while family is two or more persons related by blood or marriage. Thus, there can be more than one family in a household. Of interest in many international comparisons are numbers of households and families, types of households, number of one-person households, and family sizes (Goyer and Domschke 1983).

Other common characteristics for which cross-country comparisons are frequently made are: sex, age, race, ethnicity, marital status, educational attainment, literacy, religion, languages spoken, citizenship, employment status, occupation, income, and fertility. Some countries will not ask certain questions. For example, the USA will not ask a question about religion. Some questions cause uneasiness and may lead to coverage problems. Questions on citizenship in a country that has many undocumented workers may not be desirable (see *Censuses: History and Methods*).

4. Organizational Structure

In the more developed countries, there is a permanent census office. In other countries, a census office may be temporary for the period of the census. A permanent office offers many advantages, because what was learned in one census can be factored into the plans for the next. There are more likely to be staff in place who have census experience and who are aware of census concepts, definitions, and planning. In many countries, censuses are viewed as a statistical activity, carried out by an agency that handles statistical activities. In some countries, the census is carried out by a non-statistical agency, perhaps even the military. A country is more likely to participate in UN statistical activities and adopt UN recommendations if it has a statistical organization running the census.

5. Type of Enumeration

There are two main types of census enumeration. In the canvasser approach a census enumerator interviews the population in an enumeration area and records the responses on a census questionnaire. In the self-enumeration approach, the questionnaires are distributed (in advance) and a member of the household records the information about the household and its members on the questionnaire.

There are advantages and disadvantages to each method. In a country where the literacy rate is low, the canvasser approach is necessary. In the USA, the self-enumeration method is used, supplemented by the canvassing of nonrespondent households and special populations. Tests have shown that accuracy is improved in a self-enumeration approach because the household respondents are more likely to report what they know about themselves rather than being influenced by the responses from other households. In tests for the 1960 census, the US Census Bureau found that interviewers were influenced by what they thought the responses should be instead of what the facts showed. Suharto (1995) reported that in the 1985–1994 period, about three-quarters of the countries that took censuses used the canvassing approach.

6. Use of Sampling and Administrative Records

Sampling and administrative records are each efforts to supplement and improve upon enumeration. Sampling has been used for many years, and in a variety of contexts. One common way is to ask most of the population a minimum set of items and then ask a much larger set of questions of a sample of the population. In countries where this is done, the questionnaires are usually known as the long form and the short form. The long form has been under discussion in the USA as a possible deterrent to response. Though that view is not universally held, efforts are underway to replace the long form by more continuous survey activity, which would also have the benefit of providing more up-to-date data to local areas (Edmonston and Schultze 1995). Another use of sampling may occur during processing. It may be important to get an early indication of some census results, so a sample of questionnaires may be selected, coded for occupation, industry, and other items, and then only this sample is processed. This use of sampling

may still be of special value in countries with limited computer power. Sampling is also used in the quality control of the data processing. Similarly, in evaluation studies samples are often selected for coverage or content studies. Sampling has not yet been used for the follow-up of people who did not return the census questionnaire, though it was proposed in the USA for 2000. (See Cohen et al. 1999 for a description of the sampling approach the US Bureau of the Census originally recommended for 2000.)

Many people have suggested using administrative records as the basis for a census, and, indeed, administrative records in the form of a population register, augmented by housing registers is a replacement for a census in some European countries. However, there are other ways that administrative records can be used to improve the quality of data collected, add to the data, or evaluate the data. The US Census Bureau has long used a limited set of administrative records to evaluate its census data (Edmonston and Schultze 1995). One of the experiments carried out, as part of the 2000 census in the US was a test of whether the merging of several administrative record files would produce high-quality short-form information. The results of this test will be available in 2002.

7. Evaluation

In comparing censuses across countries, it is important to know about their quality. Many countries carry out Post-Enumeration Surveys to estimate the coverage of the census, or checks with administrative records or additional interviews to estimate the accuracy of the data for specific items. These evaluations can be helpful in changing questionnaire items for future censuses. For example, when people are asked how old they are the responses tend to 'heap' at the terminal digits of 0 and 5. Demographers refer to this phenomenon as age heaping. When the question is about date of birth, less age heaping results. The results of evaluation studies also facilitate comparisons of fertility, disability, and language spoken in the home. Estimates of coverage by major demographic groups within countries can help in the interpretation of differences in rates of different kinds such as mortality rates, prevalence rates, home ownership rates, crime victimization rates, and many others.

8. Census Processing and Dissemination

The entire census data-processing system needs to have been decided upon and tested before enumeration. Overexpenditure of census funds on data collection has sometimes affected the availability of funds to process the data. Occasionally a sample of the questionnaires is selected for coding and processing to facilitate early dissemination. The form and extent of the tabulations is also important and affects international comparability. It is important to have a plan for the release of census results to the government, to other data users, and to the general public. National results provide data for government policy and action. They also permit international comparisons and analysis of trends. Small area data are the planning tools used by local governments and businesses. Academic researchers analyze census data at each level and often find different results from government analysts, as well as puzzling results requiring deeper investigation. To facilitate broad analyses by diverse analysts, many countries have developed the tradition of releasing public-use samples of census records. This use of sampling (from the full census file) also helps address concerns regarding confidentiality once identifiers are removed. Currently, data are disseminated in many different forms. Most countries have traditionally published printed volumes of census data, but many have also prepared computer files of use to researchers, and a number of countries have begun to release tabulations and sample data on CD-ROM and in the form of files accessible via the Internet.

9. Alternatives to a Census

Though over 200 countries have taken censuses since 1990, several countries have recently abandoned census taking because of lack of public cooperation or vocal opposition, relying instead on other methods such as population registers, administrative records, or a combination of administrative records and household surveys to supply data needs. Also, the escalating cost of censuses has led to a consideration in many countries of other ways of satisfying data needs. The accuracy of such alternative forms on national data collection needs careful assessment, and is of special concern for international comparisons.

See also: Censuses: Demographic Issues; Policy Knowledge: Census; Population Cycles, Formal Theory of; Population Forecasts; Statistical Systems: Censuses of Population

Bibliography

Anderson M 1988 *The American Census*. Yale University Press, New Haven, CT

Cohen M L, White A A, Rust K F (eds.) 1999 *Measuring a Changing Nation: Modern Methods for the 2000 Census*. National Academy Press, Washington, DC

Edmonston B, Schultze C (eds.) 1995 *Modernizing the US Census*, National Academy Press, Washington, DC

Goyer D S, Domschke E 1983 *The Handbook of National Population Censuses, Latin America and the Caribbean, North America, and Oceania*. Greenwood Press, Westport, CT

Suharto S 1995 *Emerging Issues Related to World Population and Housing Census Program*, United Nations Statistics Division, Technical Notes

UN Statistical Office 1992 *Handbook of Population and Housing Censuses. Part 1. Planning, Organization and Administration of Population and Housing Censuses*. Department of Economic and Social Development. Statistical Office, New York

B. A. Bailar

Censuses: Demographic Issues

Censuses are designed to provide population counts for countries or areas within a country together with a range of demographic, social, and economic data on the population. Basic demographic data provide information on the size, distribution, structure (particularly age and sex), and change of populations; more broadly, demographic data systems also collect information on racial/ethnic characteristics, socioeconomic characteristics, and health (see *Demography: Twentieth-century History*). As a complete count of the population, a census differs from other demographic data systems, but serves to complement them. This article describes the essential features of a census in contrast with other demographic data systems and discusses the quality of demographic data collected in censuses, with a particular focus on age data.

1. Characteristics of a Census

A census of population is a complete counting of the number of persons in a country (or region) at a given point in time. Because of the amount of detail available in a census, both demographic and geographic, a well-conducted census forms the core of a modern governmental statistical or demographic data system. In particular, it provides population totals, geographic distributions, and characteristic data that can be used as benchmarks or reference points for other demographic and socioeconomic data.

The essential features of a census include reference to a well-defined territory and a specific point in time, or reference date. The census is designed to enumerate every person within the designated territory at the specific reference date and to collect information on their characteristics at that time. As ideal types, censuses may be either *de facto* or *de jure*, counting all the people present in the territory on the census date or all the people who 'usually' or legally live there

(Shryock and Siegel 1980, p. 92). Since these ideal types are difficult to implement, most censuses, in practice, are a mix of the two. At a national level, the most problematic groups to define and count tend to be: military, naval, and diplomatic personnel (both foreign personnel in the country and native personnel abroad); indigenous populations and nomadic groups; civilian nationals temporarily abroad; and civilian aliens temporarily in the country (including refugees and displaced persons). The United States census, for example, counts most people at their usual place of residence, a *de jure* concept, includes some persons temporarily in the country, such as foreign students, but excludes others such as foreign tourists (see *Censuses: Comparative International Aspects*).

For countries that either receive large numbers of temporary and permanent migrants or send large numbers, there may be a substantial difference between the *de facto* and *de jure* concepts. The alternative population concepts can be even more problematic for geographic subdivisions within a country than for the entire country. In addition to the groups previously listed, persons with multiple residences (e.g., vacation or seasonal homes, migrant workers, or persons with multiple job sites) may be difficult to assign properly to a specific subnational area. Defining the nature of a 'temporary' stay away from home can create difficulties in assigning residence for a variety of populations; for example, boarding students or residential college students may never return to their parental home but may be counted at either site (and, in fact, may often be erroneously counted at both sites). The specific set of residence rules used in a census can have a significant impact on the measured population size for areas with large numbers of these problematic groups, areas such as university towns or resort areas.

Although the principal purpose of censuses is to count the population, their main utility is generally the data collected on the characteristics of the population. The following sections of this article discuss the types of data collected in censuses and alternative data collection methods. Then the article addresses the quality of census data, the role of demographic methods in assessing data quality, and, more specifically, data on age and sex.

2. Census Content

Censuses collect a range of information on individuals and households (or families). In a census, the most basic geographic and demographic data are collected for *every individual* in the population, generally: location (or usual residence), age, sex, and relationship to head of household or family. Because of its broad population coverage, a census may be the only source for detailed demographic and socioeconomic information about subnational areas, especially small ones,

or for smaller subgroups of the population, such as ethnic or immigrant populations. Such detailed information is generally unobtainable in other general-purpose demographic data collection systems.

The major expense, both in time and money, in conducting a census is the set of activities involved in compiling a list of addresses or dwelling units and actually contacting each household. Thus, the marginal cost of collecting additional demographic, social, and economic data is generally not great (e.g., Edmonston and Schultze 1995, p. 46). Further, with modern sampling techniques, sufficient precision can often be obtained by embedding a sample within the census so that it is unnecessary to burden the entire population with a lengthy set of questions. The choice of whether to collect information from the entire population or a sample is determined by several factors, including legal requirements for the data, the desired degree of precision, and the cost of data collection.

Data collected in a census provide detailed measures of the demographic make-up of the population. Typical measures include: marital status, birthplace, citizenship, children ever born (or some measure of fertility), and measures of nationality, ethnicity, or race. Most modern censuses collect a range of other information on socioeconomic status, including: education (educational attainment, school enrollment, literacy), economic activity (occupation, industry, type of activity, income, commuting activity), and other social or political characteristics (language, religious affiliation or ethnicity, living arrangements).

3. Alternative, Complementary Demographic Data Collection Systems

A census is the backbone of a national statistical system, but it is only one part of a complete system. Surveys and registrations systems fill the data gaps left by a census; each system can provide data to check the completeness and accuracy of the others. The distinction between a census and a survey is often a matter of degree. One key difference is that censuses are usually designed to determine the size of the population of an area; surveys rarely do so. Sample surveys provide the same types of demographic, social, and economic data as collected in censuses. However, because of the generally smaller scale of a survey and because it is usually administered by trained and experienced interviewers, the survey can delve more deeply into various subjects than a census. The main tradeoffs involve the greater detail (categorical and geographic) and the greater precision provided by a census.

Registration systems, the third part of a demographic data system, are generally designed to count vital events: births, deaths, marriages, and entries and exits at international boundaries. They also include population registers of the entire population or segments of the population; examples of the latter include persons of draft age, workers covered by social insurance or government health systems, voters. Population registers, when active records are tallied, can share many features of a census: population coverage, geographic coverage, and content (Bogue et al. 1993, Sect. 3, p. 2). Registers differ in that the data are generally not collected simultaneously or with reference to a specific point in time. When a register is continuously updated (e.g., to take into account departures through death or emigration, additions through birth, immigration, or aging, and changes in status or residence), this discrepancy in timing is removed. While universal population registers are rare, partial registers are very common. In fact, comparisons of census counts with partial registers can provide critical checks on the coverage and accuracy of a census.

Vital registration systems count events, not people, yet they are essential for providing information on the demographic dynamics of a population. Birth and death rates are generally computed with vital registration data as the numerators and population data from a census as the denominators. Cumulative counts from birth, death, and immigration registration systems can be used to reconstruct the demographic history of a country and check the accuracy of census data or the consistency of censuses across time. Since the data in vital rates and census evaluations come from different collections systems (different registration systems, censuses, and surveys), such comparisons must be constructed carefully to maintain consistency with regard to definition of population groups, time references, and territorial coverage.

4. Accuracy of Censuses

Censuses are widely used to allocate political power, as a tool for allocating governmental resources, and a plethora of private uses. Although improvements in methods and technology have led to concomitant improvements in the quality of census data, the range of uses has sparked concerns over both the completeness of census counts and the accuracy of the information collected (Anderson and Fienberg 1999). Techniques for evaluation of completeness and accuracy can be broadly categorized as statistical in nature or demographic. The completeness of a census, or its coverage, is distinct from the accuracy of the data items collected in the census and involves both undercounts and overcounts. Undercounts or census omissions arise from failures to include persons or households in the census counts. Overcounts can arise from duplications or multiple counts of the same person, from fabrications, and from erroneous enumerations or counts of persons who are not properly part of the census universe. Problems with proper reporting of residence can present special problems

both for census accuracy and for census evaluations. Persons with no usual place of residence (such as homeless populations or migratory workers), persons with multiple residences, and persons away from their families or homes of record (such as college students, members of the armed forces) are particularly prone to being omitted, double counted, or counted in the wrong place, which results in a double error—an undercount at the proper location and an overcount at the wrong location. The numerical difference between the gross undercount and gross overcount is termed the *net* undercount of a census.

Statistical techniques for measuring census completeness and accuracy generally involve matching individual census records with a sample of individual records from another data system. Other systems used for evaluation include administrative records from registration systems, previous censuses, periodic sample surveys, and specially designed coverage evaluation (or postenumeration) surveys. Statistical evaluations offer the potential for measuring coverage according to a wide range of characteristics and for measuring both gross undercounts and gross overcounts.

Demographic techniques of census evaluation involve comparison of aggregate statistics or consistency checks, either internal or with external data sources. Because demographic evaluations do not check individual records, they measure *net* undercounts (or overcounts) rather than the gross components of census error. Most demographic evaluations rely on a version of the demographic balancing equation (Shryock and Siegel 1980, pp. 105–11). This simple equation relates the population at a point in time to the population at a previous time and the demographic components of change during the intervening interval: Population at the final point (P_1) equals

Population at the initial time (P_0) plus
Births during the interval (B) minus
Deaths during the interval (D) plus
Immigrants during the interval (I) minus
Emigrants during the interval (E),

Or

$$P_1 = P_0 + B - D + I - E$$

This equation can be applied to the total population of an entire country, an area within the country, age–sex groups (where it can be called cohort analysis), racial/ethnic populations, and other subgroups of the population. Since no demographic data are completely accurate, correction of errors in the measures of the components or assessment of the potential error in the resulting estimate is an essential part of demographic analysis of census errors.

The United States Census Bureau has applied demographic evaluation techniques to measuring coverage of recent censuses with a program called Demo-

Table 1
Demographic estimates of percent net census undercount, by race, for the
United States: 1940–90

Race	1990	1980	1970	1960	1950	1940
Total	1.8	1.2	2.7	3.1	4.1	5.4
Black	5.7	4.5	6.5	6.6	7.5	8.4
Not Black	1.3	0.8	2.2	2.7	3.8	5.0
Black Not Black difference	4.4	3.7	4.3	3.9	3.6	3.4

Source: Robinson et al. 1993, Table 2.

graphic Analysis (DA). The DA estimates draw on a variety of demographic data to construct estimates of the population by age, sex, and race—historical statistics on births beginning in 1925 (corrected for under-registration as measured in a series of registration tests), historical statistics on deaths and legal immigration since 1935, administrative data from Medicare (the national health insurance system for the elderly, also corrected for underregistration), and demographic estimates of emigration and unauthorized immigration. Comparing the DA estimates with census counts provides a consistent set of coverage estimates by age, sex, and race for the censuses of 1940 through 1990 (Robinson et al. 1993); the resulting estimates are shown in Table 1. The DA estimates show a steady pattern of improvement in census coverage from 1940 (5.4 percent net undercount) through 1980 (1.2 percent) but a worsening of coverage in 1990 (1.8 percent). The same pattern of change is apparent for both the minority Black population and the balance of the US population (largely the majority White population). However, the difference in under-coverage between the Black and non-Black population shows no such trend; in fact the 4.4 percentage point difference in coverage in the 1990 Census is the highest shown.

The demographic estimates of coverage for the series of US censuses have proved to be roughly consistent with measures derived from coverage evaluation surveys, for example, a 1990 survey estimated the net undercount at 1.6 percent, only 0.2 percentage points different from the demographic estimate (Hogan and Robinson 1993). The survey estimates, like the DA estimates, showed higher undercount rates for the Black population; further, the survey showed high undercount rates for other minorities populations (Hispanics, Asians, and American Indians) that could not be separately measured with demographic techniques.

The experience of the 1990 US Census illustrates both the strengths and potential weaknesses of demographic estimation techniques. Because of the reliance on historical data series, the demographic estimates permit a degree of precision in comparisons of change in coverage across censuses that is hard to achieve with coverage evaluation surveys, for example, sampling variability, other measurement errors, and changes in

survey design may limit comparisons across censuses, particularly those separated by several decades. For the demographic estimates across censuses, however, the degree of variability and potential biases tend to be consistent because the estimates are developed with consistent data, methods, and assumptions. The survey estimates are, however, more flexible in that they can provide many measures that are either not available from demographic methods or are subject to potentially large estimation errors; for example, coverage evaluation surveys can measure gross overcounts and undercounts, coverage error for racial and ethnic groups for which historical data may not be available, coverage of subnational geographic areas for which the required demographic measures of internal migration are not sufficiently precise, and other population groups for which the requisite demographic data may be completely missing or highly inadequate (such as owners and renters, family types, native and foreign-born populations).

The accuracy of demographic methods for evaluating census coverage ultimately depends on the availability of data and the degree of error and uncertainty in the vital statistics and other data from noncensus sources. A variety of techniques for assessing the variability in such demographic estimates have been proposed (Robinson et al. 1993, Anderson et al. 2000), but none is widely accepted or applied. Further, some methods for explicitly combining demographic techniques with survey results have been proposed to improve the accuracy of coverage measurements (e.g., Bell 1993).

A full evaluation of coverage with demographic techniques may not be achievable in many countries because of a lack of the requisite long historical series of demographic data plus supplementary data sources, such as those used for the DA estimates in the United States. However, demographic techniques can provide a variety of consistency checks that yield measures of the relative coverage of the census to an external standard or the relative coverage of different subpopulations within the same census rather than absolute measures of census net undercount. For example, analyzing the change in population between two censuses either in absolute terms with the balancing equation or as a rate of change provides an indication of the relative coverage of the two censuses. Likewise, sex ratio analysis (described below) provides a measure of relative coverage of men and women in different age groups. Checks of census totals or subtotals against independent aggregates such as birth statistics, partial registers (e.g., draft registrations, national health system enrollments), or universal registers requires correcting the aggregate data for underenrollment or definitional differences from the census. If full and accurate corrections can be made, such comparisons do provide measures of net undercoverage of the census.

5. Age, Sex, and Race/Ethnicity Data in Censuses

Perhaps the most crucial demographic data collected in a census are age and sex; consequently, they are almost universally collected in censuses and surveys. Much of the science of demography is devoted to analyzing, accounting for, or controlling for the effects of age structure on other social and economic phenomena, so that age is a factor, either explicit or implicit, in almost every demographic analysis. Differences in age composition between populations can account for many other observed differences, either in whole or in part, including differences in fertility, mortality, sex ratios, dependency, household structure, and even employment rates.

The primacy of age data requires special attention to quality, measurement of errors, and correction. While errors of coverage and reporting occur across the entire age spectrum, studies of age reporting from many countries (Ewbank 1981, Spiegelman 1968, p. 59) have documented several specific types of errors in censuses from many countries:

(a) underenumeration of specific age groups, especially young children and young adults;

(b) age misstatement around 'threshold' ages (age of majority, age of retirement);

(c) age overstatement at older ages;

(d) preference for ages ending in certain digits;

(e) failure to report age.

Whereas underenumeration is a general problem with census data, age-specific underenumeration affects the overall quality of these essential data used in other analyses. Problems in some age groups can be traced to specific types of enumeration issues. Undercounts of very young children seem to be widespread and appear to have a variety of causes, including oversight on the part of adult respondents, devaluation of female children in some societies, and overstatement of age. The other age group that seems to suffer generally from undercounts is young adults (roughly ages 15–30). These are the ages in most countries when individuals enter adulthood, marry, form new households, and leave their parental homes. The related geographic mobility and other changes of residence can easily lead to enumeration difficulties and age-selective omissions from the census count.

Age misstatement takes a variety of forms. Advantages accruing to individuals for attaining certain threshold ages can lead to reporting of these ages on the part of persons younger than the critical age because they perceive reporting older ages to be advantageous. While these ages may vary from country to country, the age of majority (often 18 or 21) and age of retirement (often 65) often show striking patterns of overstatement. At the extreme upper end of the age distribution, especially at ages 100 and over, there is a marked tendency for individuals to report exaggerated ages; this tendency is more prevalent in countries with poorer birth registration systems and in societies and groups with lower levels of literacy.

A particularly striking type of age reporting error is the tendency of individuals to prefer reporting ages ending in certain digits; this tendency is generally exhibited as a preference for ages ending in '0' or '5.' Other types of preferences can also be found including a tendency to report even-numbered ages and a tendency to prefer reporting years of birth ending in '0' or '5' which may result in different patterns of age reporting, depending on the date of the census. Because digit preference can be severe and can have serious ramifications for the use of census data, a variety of techniques have been developed to measure the phenomenon and to correct the data. The principal correction techniques involve distributing the population across age groups according to historical data on births or, more generally, 'smoothing' the age distribution while maintaining totals for certain age groups with graduation techniques developed mainly by actuaries (Shryock and Siegel 1980, pp. 201–29).

In contrast to age, classification of individuals according to sex presents no general problems in censuses. Analytic techniques are generally straightforward, relying principally on the sex ratio, conventionally defined as the number of males per 100 females. Nonetheless, analysis of sex ratios, especially by age group, can be a very powerful evaluative and analytic tool. Many factors can affect the sex ratio of a population, but the principal ones are age structure and migration patterns. The sex ratio of births falls in a fairly narrow range from 101 to 107 and is biologically determined. Differential mortality of the sexes causes this ratio to change as a birth cohort ages. In developed countries, male mortality generally exceeds female mortality at every age so that the sex ratio decreases smoothly as a birth cohort ages.

In the absence of migration, the sex ratio reaches 100 by young adulthood. Above age 50, the sex ratio decreases more sharply with age, reflecting again the higher mortality of males. As a result of these mortality patterns, older populations tend to have lower sex ratios than younger populations.

Departures from this general pattern can be indicative of underlying demographic, social, or economic phenomena or anomalies. In some countries, very high sex ratios among young children (i.e., high proportions of boys) are thought to indicate sex-selective abortions, infanticide, neglect, or conceal-ment of children. Higher sex ratios among young adults may indicate high levels of maternal mortality. In the United States, lower than expected sex ratios among adults aged 25–54 are indications of poorer census coverage among males than females. Low sex ratios can also result from excess male mortality in wartime; this effect will persist for the lifetime of the affected cohorts. Migration patterns can alter sex ratios if migration is sex-selective, as it often is. Areas with employment concentrations in extractive indus-tries (agriculture, mining), heavy manufacturing, or military often have high sex ratios as men, more than women, migrate into these areas in search of jobs. On the other hand, areas with a high concentration of jobs in 'white collar' occupations and 'office work' often have low sex ratios as more women than men are employed in these jobs.

The age and sex structure of a population encapsu-lates its demographic history. Cohorts are born, age, and die with predictable and discernable patterns; migrants into and out of an area alter the composition. A census—a snapshot of the population at a given time—provides invaluable information on this history. Analysis of the age–sex data, either alone or in combination with data from other demographic data systems such as surveys, registration systems, and previous censuses, can tell a great deal about the quality of the census data and the nature of the population.

Data on race or other similar identifiers such as ethnicity, nationality, or religion are collected in many, but not all censuses. While race data can be extra-ordinarily useful in demographic analyses and are often critical for applications of census data, the quality of these data can be quite variable. Groupings based on race (or similar identifiers) are often per-ceived in the popular mind as equivalent to demo-graphically distinct populations; that is, individuals enter or leave a race group only through the con-ventional demographic processes of birth, death, and migration. Indeed, DA as applied to race groups in the United States treats the Black and not Black popula-tions in just this manner; and for the 1940–90 results (described above), this treatment appears quite ap-propriate. However, in many modern societies, par-ticularly multiethnic ones, racial identification and ethnicity are increasingly becoming matters of per-sonal choice and self-identification rather than of societal ascription (Waters 1990). Consequently, in-dividual membership in or identification with a racial/ethnic group may change over time. This phenomenon introduces another 'component of change' into demo-graphic measures of the size of a population group. For example, because of the large numbers of indivi-duals in the United States with some American-Indian

ancestry and changes the salience of such ancestry to individual self-identification, more than half of the growth of the American-Indian population can be attributed to inconsistent measurement of this racial group across censuses (Passel 1996).

High incidences of intermarriage, changes in data collection methods, and changing societal norms all contribute to difficulties in consistently measuring racial/ethnic populations over time and across differ-ent data systems. The 2000 Census of the United States encompasses virtually all of the potential pitfalls in measuring race. For the first time, respondents to the US census are allowed (even encouraged) to respond with more than one racial identification. While this procedure offers a detailed picture of the population in 2000, it does not reflect the way such data were collected in previous censuses; individuals choosing more than one race are not classified in the same category as in previous censuses. As a result, valid comparisons with past (and future) censuses will require modification of the race groupings with so-called 'bridging' techniques; unfortunately for demo-graphic analyses, the data necessary to produce consistent group definitions across time may, at best, be approximate or may simply not be available at all.

6. Conclusion

Censuses provide the principal measure of population size for countries and geographic subdivisions within countries while also providing detailed information on the demographic, social, and economic characteristics of the population. An accurate census is a crucial feature of a national statistical system, providing baseline data and benchmarks for other collection systems. Demographic techniques, particularly for assessing age and sex structure and for analyzing changes over time, provide essential means for utiliz-ing the data and for assessing their quality. For further information on censuses and census data, see Ander-son (2000) and *Censuses: History and Methods*; *Censuses: Comparative International Aspects*.

Bibliography

Anderson M J (ed.) 2000 *Encyclopedia of the U.S. Census.* Congressional Quarterly Press, Washington, DC
Anderson M J, Daponte B O, Fienberg S E, Kadane J B, Spencer B D, Steffey D L 2000 Sampling-based adjustment of the 2000 Census: A balanced perspective. *Jurimetrics* **40**: 341–56
Anderson M J, Fienberg S E 1999 *Who Counts? The Politics of Census-Taking in Contemporary America.* Russell Sage Foun-dation, New York
Bell W R 1993 Using information from demographic analysis in post-enumeration survey estimation. *Journal of the American Statistical Association* **88**(423, September): 1106–18

Bogue D J, Arriaga E E, Anderton D L (eds.) 1993 *Readings in Population Research Methodology: Volume 1. Basic Tools.* United Nations Population Fund, Social Development Center, Chicago

Edmonston B, Schultze C L 1995 *Modernizing the U.S. Census.* National Academy Press, Washington, DC

Ewbank D C 1981 *Age Misreporting and Age-Selective Underenumeration: Sources, Patterns, and Consequences for Demographic Analysis.* Report No. 4, Committee on Population and Demography, National Academy Press, Washington, DC

Hogan H, Robinson J G 1993 What the Census Bureau's coverage evaluation programs tell us about the differential undercount. In: *Proceedings of the 1993 Research Conference on Undercounted Ethnic Populations.* US Department of Commerce, Washington, DC

Passel J S 1996 The growing American Indian population, 1960–1990: Beyond demography. In: Sandefur G D, Rindfuss R D, Cohen B (eds.) *Changing Numbers, Changing Needs: American Indian Demography and Public Health.* National Academy Press, Washington, DC

Robinson J G, Ahmed B, Das Gupta P, Woodrow K A 1993 Estimation of population coverage in the 1990 United States census based on demographic analysis. *Journal of the American Statistical Association* **88**(423): 1061–71

Shryock H S, Siegel J S 1980 *Methods and Materials of Demography*, 4th printing, rev. US Government Printing Office, Washington, DC

Spiegelman M 1968 *Introduction to Demography*, rev. edn. Harvard University Press, Cambridge, MA

Waters M C 1990 *Ethnic Options.* University of California Press, Berkeley, CA

J. S. Passel

Censuses: History and Methods

1. Definition/Overview

A census is a count of the population of a country as of a fixed date. National governments conduct censuses to determine how many people live in different areas of the country, whether the population is growing, stable, or declining in the country as a whole or in particular parts of the country. They also determine what the characteristics of the population are in terms of age, sex, ethnic background, marital status, or income. Generally governments collect the information by sending a questionnaire in the mail or an interviewer goes to every household or residential address in the country. The questionnaire asks the head of the household, or a responsible adult in the household (the respondent), to list all the people who live at the address as of a particular date, and answer a series of questions about each of them. The respondent or the interviewer is then responsible for sending the answers back to the government agency, which in turn adds up the results, or tabulates or aggregates the answers from the country overall and

for political subdivisions such as states or provinces, cities, counties, or other civil divisions. The agency usually reports the results to the public a few months or years after the census; the results are considered 'news' and are reported in the media. Since censuses aim to count the entire population of a country, they are very expensive and elaborate administrative operations, and thus are conducted relatively infrequently, generally at five to ten year intervals.

Between censuses, governments estimate the size and characteristics of the population, either by extrapolating the trends in the census into the future, estimating the population from other data systems such as tax or drivers license records, or by conducting periodic sample surveys to collect information about the population. Representative probability samples collect information from a small portion of the population, and thus can be conducted frequently, even monthly. In the USA, the Current Population Survey of around 50,000 households is conducted monthly. National governments also conduct other types of censuses, particularly of economic activity, such as an agriculture, manufacturing, or business census. Such censuses collect information on the number and characteristics of farms, businesses, or manufacturing firms. In the nineteenth century, such censuses were conducted at the same time as the population census. Today, the economic censuses are generally conducted on a different schedule from the population census (see *Statistical Systems: Censuses of Population*).

2. History

Censuses have been taken since ancient times by emperors and kings trying to assess the strength of their realms. These early censuses were conducted sporadically, and generally served to measure the tax or military capacity of a particular area. They tended to count adult men, men liable for military service, or people liable to tithe (pay taxes). For census taking of an entire population to become feasible, a uniform unit of analysis was required. Hence census taking in the West had to await the emergence of the concept of commensurate households, generally seen as a development of the Medieval European West (Herlihy 1985). The household or family served as the unit or analysis or the locus for counting the members within it.

Generally speaking the modern periodic census of all persons is an invention of the early modern period in the European West and, particularly from a New World perspective, was associated with efforts by the home country to determine the success of the overseas colonies. Thus the British Crown and the British Board of Trade ordered repeated counts of the colonial American population in the seventeenth and eighteenth centuries, starting in the 1620s in Virginia (Wells 1975, Cassedy 1969). In Canada, French efforts to count the population began in 1665–1666 when Jean Talon came to the New World on behalf of Louis XIV and took a census of what became Quebec. Censuses were continued at irregular intervals after Canada became a British colony in 1763 (Worton 1997). By the early nineteenth century, census taking began to be a regular feature of government in Western Europe and North America (Alterman 1969, Nissel 1987, Glass 1973, Desrosieres 1993, Patriarca 1996). The International Statistical Congress (established 1853) and the International Statistical Institute (established 1885) proposed and promoted the uniform regular censuses for all national states. In the twentieth century, census taking spread throughout the world. The United Nations Statistical Office compiles reports on population worldwide (Ventresca 1996).

3. Functions and Techniques

Censuses serve a variety of purposes in different countries. At a minimum a census provides a measure of the size of the population of a country, which can be compared with the population in the past, the population of other countries, and to make estimates of the likely population in the future. Governments use census information in almost all aspects of public policy, from determining how many children an educational system must serve, to determining where to put new roads. Censuses are also used to provide the denominators of other measures, e.g., measures of per capita income for a state or local area, or for such measures as crime rates or birth or death rates. Private businesses use census data for marketing analyses to determine where to locate new businesses, or to decide where to advertise particular products.

Other government agencies and private researchers use the census to provide the 'sampling frame' for other survey research. This is the address list that researchers use to determine where to conduct a sample or poll. In the USA, the Bureau of the Census or Census Bureau conducts the census during the tenth year of each decade. Each decade, the population count provides the data for reapportioning seats among the states in the House of Representatives and Electoral College, and for redrawing district boundaries for seats in the House, in state legislatures, and in local legislative districts. In Canada, a full census is taken during the first year of every decade and an abridged census is taken during the sixth year of the decade. The population data are also used to apportion seats among the provinces in the House of Commons and to draw electoral districts (see *Policy Knowledge: Census*).

Most nations create a permanent national statistical agency to take the census, such as the US Bureau of the Census or Statistics Canada. The agency in charge

generally undertakes a public review process to determine the questions to be asked. The questions vary from nation to nation depending on the particular political and social history and conditions of the country. Most censuses include basic demographic information such as the age, sex, educational background, occupation, and marital status of the individual. Race, ethnic or national origin, and religious affiliation are important questions in many nations. Further questions can include the person's place of birth, relationship to the household head; the individual's or the family's income; the type of house the household occupies; and whether the person is a citizen, has moved in the past five years, or speaks a particular language. Questions that are quite routine in one nation may be seen as quite controversial in another, depending on the history of the country. Americans do not ask questions on religious affiliation on the census since it is considered a violation of the First Amendment right to freedom of religion. Other nations, such as India, do collect such information. Questions on the number of children born to a woman were quite controversial in China in recent years because of the emphasis on the one-child policy of population limitation. In the USA, asking a question on income was considered controversial in 1940 when it was first asked. It is no longer as problematic. Questions change in response to public debate about the state of society. Americans wanted to know which households had radios in 1930, and introduced questions on housing quality in 1940. Canadians have recently begun to ask census questions on the unpaid work done in the home.

Taking a census can be divided into several phases. The statistical agency first divides the country into geographical subdivisions to be counted, and makes maps and address lists, and prepares instructions for the local census takers. In most countries, this phase requires hiring large numbers of temporary workers to do the counting, or calling upon other government employees at a local level, such as schoolteachers, to conduct the count. The central statistical agency prepares and prints the questionnaires, and distributes them to households either through the mail, or by delivery by enumerators. During the second phase of the count a responsible adult or household head in every household, family, or equivalent institution, is asked to fill out the form or respond to the enumerator and supply the required information about each member of the household. Questions for all people usually include a brief set, on a 'short' form, for example, name, age, sex, racial or ethnic status, marital status, and relationship to the household head. Generally a smaller sample of households receive a more complicated or 'long' form which can have many detailed questions on the individual's work status, income, housing, educational background, citizenship, and recent moves. The person who fills out the form or the enumerator is responsible for returning it to the statistical agency. The respondent then mails the form to the agency; the enumerator collects the form in person or the information by phone. During the third phase, the statistical agency enters the data onto a computer and adds up, or tabulates the responses for the nation, states, or provinces, and cities, towns, and other local jurisdictions. The agency also cross-tabulates the answers, reporting not merely on the number of people in a local area, but on the number of people, for example, in five-year age cohorts, for each sex, for local areas. The agency only publishes the tabulated results of the count, and keeps the individual responses confidential. In the USA, individual census responses are stored at the National Archives. After 72 years, the original forms are opened to the public for use. These original responses are frequently used by people researching the history of their families, or by those constructing genealogies.

Until the 1980s, statistical agencies published census results in large volumes of numeric tables—sometimes numbering in the hundreds of volumes. Since then, census results have become available electronically, on disc, magnetic tape, CD-ROM, or the Internet. The choice of census technique for a particular country is the result of its social and political traditions and technological capacities. The US census is highly automated, and is primarily conducted by mail. Canada sends enumerators to deliver the census form to each household; the household head fills it out and sends it in. Other nations use even more labor-intensive techniques of collecting and tabulating the data. Turkey, for example, currently requires people to stay home to await the census taker and counts the entire population on a specific Sunday census day (see *Censuses: Comparative International Aspects*).

4. National Traditions

4.1 The United States

The US census was mandated in the 1787 Constitution. At the time of the American Revolution the framers faced many problems of uniting the 13 separate colonies into a national government, including how to allocate political representation among the states, and how to levy taxes.

The initial government structure under the Articles of Confederation gave each state one vote in Congress, and required the states to collect taxes for the national government. This proved unsatisfactory since the states were of widely different sizes, tax capacity, and cultures. The 1787 Constitution derived the sovereignty of the state from the 'people of the US' and created a bicameral legislature with representation in the Senate based on the states; and representation in the House of Representatives based upon the population of each state. The Electoral College was com-posed of electors determined by summing the House and Senate members for each state. The decennial census was designed to provide the population figures for apportioning the seats in the House according to population. 'Direct taxes' levied on the states were also to be apportioned on the basis of population (Anderson 1988).

At the time of the Constitution, a racially based slave labor system also existed, and almost 20 percent of the American population were enslaved African-Americans. The framers debated whether slaves were 'persons' or 'property' and thus whether states should receive representation for their slave populations. The southern states where slavery dominated did not consider the slave population for purposes of apportioning their state legislatures, but they did consider slaves property for tax purposes. The framers could not find an easy solution to this dilemma, and developed what came to be called the Three-Fifths Compromise, which 'discounted' the size of slave population as equivalent to 60 percent of the free population when determining the apportionment of the House. The Three-Fifths Compromise thus required a separate count of slave and the free, mainly white, population. The Constitution also specified that 'Indians not taxed', that is, those Indians who were not considered part of the civil society were not to be counted in the census. The Three-Fifths Compromise was abolished with the abolition of slavery after the Civil War; the tradition of accounting for the various racial groups in the population continued after abolition.

The first census was taken in 1790. Assistant US marshals were instructed to travel the country and ask six questions at each household. These included: the name of the family head; and for each household, the number of free white males 16 and over; the number of free white males under 16; the number of white females; the number of other free people (the free colored); and the number of slaves. They totalled the figures for their local jurisdiction and sent them to the US marshal for the state that in turn totalled the figures for the state and sent them to the President. The first American census counted 3.9 million people.

In later years, the census became more elaborate, with more questions asked, and more data published (Cohen 1982). In 1850 Congress mandated a census schedule (form) with a line of questions for each person, including their name. A temporary Census Office, as it was then called, was set up in Washington to add up the tables of responses and publish the results in large volumes. By 1880 when the American population topped 50,000,000, the census was still being compiled by hand, using a primitive tally system. In 1890, the Census Office introduced machine tabulation of the responses, and each person's answers were converted to codes punched in Hollerith cards, a precursor to the IBM punch card. The cards were then run through counting machines. This innovation was the beginning of modern data processing, and led to further innovations in tabulating large amounts of data. By the 1940s, the Census Bureau commissioned the construction of the first non-defense computer, UNIVAC, to tabulate the 1950 census. By the late 1950s, the Census Bureau dispensed with the punch cards and developed an electronic scanning system, called FOSDIC, or Film Optical Scanning Device for Input to Computers, to read the answers on the census form and input the data to computer (Eckler 1972).

In 1940, the US began to collect some census information from a sample of the population, and slowly shifted the detailed questions on the census to the long form asked of only about 15–25 percent of households. In 1970 the American census became primarily a mail enumeration, as the Census Bureau developed automated address files for the country. As of the year 2000, over 90 percent of the roughly 100,000,000 residential addresses in the US receive the census form in the mail. If the Census Bureau does not receive a response, it sends an enumerator to determine if the address is correct and get the information from the household at the address.

4.2 Canada

Regular decennial censuses began in 1851 in Canada. The British North America Act of 1867 required that the census provide population counts for the apportionment of representation in the House of Commons among the four provinces of Ontario, Quebec, Nova Scotia, and New Brunswick, and for the periodic readjustment of the boundaries of electoral districts. The first census of the Dominion was taken in 1871, and counted 3.7 million people.

The first Canadian census after Confederation was also a very elaborate affair, collecting information on agriculture, livestock, animal products, industrial establishments, forest products, shipping and fisheries, mining, and public institutions as well as on population. Canada was primarily an agricultural nation at the time, and the Department of Agriculture conducted the census. In 1905 the census bureau was made a permanent government agency in the Agriculture Department. In 1918 an independent Dominion Bureau of Statistics was created with oversight for taking the census and collecting other statistical information, headed by a Chief Statistician. In 1971, the bureau was renamed Statistics Canada. Canada has a centralized statistical system, with all major statistical work conducted in the same agency (Worton 1997).

Canada began to conduct sample surveys along with the full census in 1941, introduced a quinquennial census (a census on the sixth year of the decade) in 1956, and self-enumeration in 1971. In the 1990s, the Canadian census introduced adjustment of census results to correct for errors on the basis of post-enumeration check survey. The population of Canada in 1997 was 30.3 million.

4.3 Great Britain

The first Parliamentary proposals for regular censuses of population in Britain date to the mid-eighteenth century, but they did not lead to the institutionalization of census taking until the end of the century. In late eighteenth century Britain, the publication of Thomas Malthus' Essay on the Principle of Population and concerns that the population was declining led Parliament to pass a bill 'for taking an Account of the Population of Great Britain and of the Increase or Diminution thereof.' The first count was taken in March 1801 by the Overseers of the Poor under the direction of former clerk of the House of Commons, John Rickman, and counted 9 million people. Census taking continued every decade afterwards except for the cancellation of the 1941 Census during the Second World War.

In 1837 the General Register Office was organized. The decennial census was made a responsibility of the GRO and used the administrative structure of the registration districts to organize the field portion of the count.

The 1841 census introduced individual level enumeration. The mid-nineteenth century census was particularly influenced by the ongoing medical and public health work of the GRO leaders such as William Farr. It therefore developed detailed data on occupation, age, and locale for the denominator data required for the publication of mortality and other statistics (Glass 1973, Nissel 1987).

Machine tabulation of the census was introduced in 1911. The 1920 Census Act established a permanent legislative mandate for the census. Sampling was introduced in 1951 by way of the analysis and publication of results from a 10 percent sample of the complete 1951 forms. In 1961, the census used a short form for the entire population and an additional long form for a 10 percent sample. In 1966, a one in ten sample count was taken. The results of the 1961 census were computer tabulated. By 1966 the Census Office had its own computer facilities. The population of the UK in 2000 is 59 million.

4.4 France

France established a population registration system in the late eighteenth century, and began a tradition of quinquennial census taking under Napoleon in 1801. The first census counted a population of 33 million. For much of the nineteenth century, the administration of the count was local with a small national office

(*Statistique Generale de la France* (SGF)) publishing the results tabulated locally. Individual forms were used in Paris starting in 1817; by 1876 the entire country used three standardized forms: one for the individual, one for the family or household, and a third for the building enumerated. Tabulation was done locally until 1896 when Lucien March introduced machine tabulation. The French pioneered in the analysis of occupational statistics derived from the census as a means of understanding the evolution of the economy from an agricultural and artisan basis to one characterized by professional qualifications and employees with credentials. In 1946, after World War II, the French National Statistical Agency was titled *Institut National de la Statistique et des Etudes Economiques* (INSEE) (Desrosieres 1991). The population of France at the 1999 census was 60 million.

5. Issues

Censuses provide important information about the population of a country, and can become embroiled in political or social controversy simply by reporting information relevant to ongoing issues in the society.

Complaints about the census generally involve concerns about the accuracy of the count, the propriety of particular questions, and the uses to which the data are put (see *Censuses: Demographic Issues*).

Censuses require public understanding, support, and cooperation to be successful. Concerns about government interference with private life can prevent people from cooperating with what is an essentially voluntary counting process. People may be suspicious of giving information to a government agency, or may object that particular census questions are invasions of privacy.

When such public trust is lacking, people may fail to participate. In recent times, individuals doubled up in illegal housing units, undocumented immigrants who do not reside in the country legally, or individuals who do not wish to reveal their economic or social situation to a government agency, can be reluctant to respond to a census. In the most serious challenges, people claim the results will not be held in confidence and that census should not be conducted at all. During World War II, census records from countries occupied by the Nazis, for example in the Netherlands, were used to identify Jews for detention, removal, and extermination. The effect of such use was to undermine the legitimacy of the census after World War II. In the Netherlands, which took its last regular census in 1971 and collects population information through other mechanisms, the legacy of the Nazi era was one of the major justifications for ending census taking (Seltzer 1998).

At the other side of the spectrum, political challenges can be made to the census if the census does not count the population well enough. All censuses contain errors of various kinds. Some people and addresses are missed. People may misunderstand a question, or fail to answer all the questions. Census officials have developed elaborate procedures to catch and correct errors as the data are collected, but some errors tend to remain. Since census results are often used to allocate seats in legislative bodies and government funds, such errors undermine the credibility of the census as an allocation mechanism.

In recent years, developments in statistical analysis have made it possible to measure the accuracy of censuses (Choldin 1994, Anderson and Fienberg 1999). Census results may be compared with population information from other sources, such as the records of births, deaths, and marriages in vital statistics. Census officials can also determine the level of accuracy of the count by conducting a second, sample count, (a post enumeration survey or PES) shortly after the complete census, and then matching the records of the sample and the census. Census officials estimate who is missed, and who is counted twice or in the wrong geographic location, and use these estimates to evaluate the overall accuracy of the count. Canada and Australia adjust the census results for omissions and other errors. Great Britain is planning to adjust the 2001 census (Chambers and Crudas 2000, Paice and Steel 2000).

In the USA, people who live in cities, the poor, and minorities tend to be undercounted relative to the rest of the country. Since 1970 officials representing such undercounted jurisdictions claimed that these jurisdictions have suffered loss of political representation and government funding since the apportionment and funding formulas are based on incorrect data. Mayors and leaders of civil rights organizations have pressed for adjustment of the census results, and have filed lawsuits to compel adjustment of the enumeration. The courts have not ordered adjustment of the US census results, and the question of adjustment has emerged as a political controversy in Congress. Since the late 1980s, Republicans have generally opposed adjusting for the undercount, while Democrats have supported it. The nation will debate these issues anew after the 2000 Census since the Census Bureau plans to publish results based upon both adjusted and unadjusted population counts and to provide their professional judgment indicating which data set they consider the more accurate.

Congress, states, and local governments could use adjusted counts for determining legislative districts, funding allocations, and for program evaluation, though such actions are likely to draw further court challenges.

See also: Population Cycles, Formal Theory of; Population Forecasts; Statistical Systems: Censuses of Population

Bibliography

Alterman H 1969 *Counting People: The Census in History*. Harcourt, Brace & World, New York

Anderson M 1988 *The American Census: A Social History*. Yale University Press, New Haven, CT

Anderson M, Fienberg S E 1999 *Who Counts? The Politics of Census Taking in Contemporary America*. Russell Sage Foundation, New York

Cassedy J 1969 *Demography in Early America: The Beginnings of the Statistical Mind*. Harvard University Press, Cambridge, MA

Chambers R, Cruddas M 2000 A one number census for the United Kingdom. *Chance Journal* 13(3): 38–41

Choldin H 1994 *Looking for the Last Percent: The Controversy over Census Undercounts*. Rutgers University Press, New Brunswick, NJ

Cohen P C 1982 *A Calculating People: The Spread of Numeracy in Early America*. University of Chicago Press, Chicago

Desrosieres A 1991 Official statistics and medicine in nineteenth-century France: The SGF as a case study. *Social History of Medicine* 4: 515–37

Desrosieres A 1993 *La Politique des Grands Nombres: Histoire de la Raison Statistique*. Edition La Découverte, Paris [1998 The Politics of Large Numbers: A History of Statistical Reasoning. Harvard University Press, Cambridge, MA]

Eckler A R 1972 *The Bureau of the Census*. Praeger, New York

Glass D V 1973 *Numbering the People*. Saxon House, Farnborough, UK

Herlihy D 1985 *Medieval Households*. Harvard University Press, Cambridge, MA

Paice J, Steel D 2000 Census adjustment in Australia. *Chance* 13(3): 41–2

Patriarca S 1996 *Numbers and Nationhood: Writing Statistics in Nineteenth-century Italy*. Cambridge University Press, New York

Nissel M 1987 *People Count: A History of the General Register Office*. Her Majesty's Stationery Office, London

Seltzer W 1998 Population statistics, the Holocaust, and the Nuremberg trials. *Population and Development Review* 24: 511–52

Ventresca M 1996 *When States Count: Institutional and Political Dynamics in Modern Census Establishment, 1800–1993*. Ph.D. dissertation, Stanford University, Stanford, CA

Wells R 1975 *The Population of the British Colonies in America before 1776: A Survey of Census Data*. Princeton University Press, Princeton, NJ

Worton D A 1997 *The Dominion Bureau of Statistics: A History of Canada's Central Statistics Office and its Antecedents: 1841–1972*. McGill-Queens University Press, Kingston, ON

M. Anderson

Center–Periphery Relationships

Concepts of center and periphery became increasingly prominent in the social sciences during the second half of the twentieth century. They were of diverse origins and entailed varied emphases, but these differences have not always been obvious in continued use. There has actually been a cluster of related conceptual pairs: center and periphery, but also core and periphery, metropolis and satellite, and metropolis and province. But they have not been mere synonyms. Moreover, in obscure and perhaps treacherous ways, ideas of center and periphery may occasionally have overlapped in social thought and discourse with other classical contrasts, such as modernity–tradition, or urban–folk.

The sociologist Edward Shils had a major part in introducing the center–periphery pair of concepts into the vocabulary of academic social science (cf. Greenfeld and Martin 1988). His paper 'Center and Periphery' originally appeared in 1961, but there was a close affinity between it and several of his other publications in the same period. The overall conception of society and culture in Shils's perspective was consensualist; but not, he asserted in a later comment, as merely a facile expression of the mood of the era. In his view, the importance of consensus to social life had been underestimated (Shils 1975, p. xi). Thus he concentrated on notions such as 'tradition,' 'ritual,' 'deference,' and 'charisma.'

Notably, in his 'Center and Periphery' paper, these two terms were used in a metaphorical sense—centrality had 'nothing to do with geometry and little with geography.' The center was identified with what was ultimate, irreducible, and sacred in the realm of symbols, values, and beliefs; it was also identified in the realm of action with those roles and institutions which embodied such cultural understandings and were most actively engaged in propagating them. Yet in 'Metropolis and Province in Intellectual Life', published in the same year, the facts of uneven spatial organization which are now usually linked to concepts of center and periphery become clear, and are set in what we would now describe as a transnational context. Drawing on his study of the situation of intellectuals in India, Shils argued that in their minds, people have varyingly extensive maps of the world significant to them, and that a major feature of such maps would be their portrayal of one's qualitative proximity to or distance from the metropolis (Shils 1972, p. 356).

In the former of these two papers, then, the center is a locus of excellence, of grace; the periphery defers to it. In the latter, the metropolis is a center of vitality, a seat of creativity. The province, on the other hand, Shils notes, is frequently taken to be in itself 'rude, unimaginative, awkward, unpolished, rough, petty, and narrow' (Shils 1972, p. 357). Cultural salvation lies in an involvement with the metropolis. The choice seems to be one between impoverished autonomy and enriching dependence.

If Shils was a theorist of consensus and cultural authority, the metropolis/satellite and core/periphery pairs, as inserted into the debates of the 1960s and 1970s, pointed in an entirely different direction, resonating with another political mood. 'Metropolis' and 'satellite' were the terms used by the economist

Andre Gunder Frank (1967), who had spent much of the 1960s in Latin America, studying what he described as the development of underdevelopment, and engaging with the growth of 'dependency theory.' Then in the 1970s, introducing 'world-system theory,' the sociologist Immanuel Wallerstein (e.g., 1974) contrasted 'core' with 'periphery.' Both Frank and Wallerstein were primarily concerned with political economy, and with the expanding control and exploitation of the material resources of the 'periphery' or 'satellite' on the part of the 'core' or 'metropolis.' In both instances, the emphasis was on conflict and domination within a global order.

The points of view represented by Shils, on the one hand, and by Frank and Wallerstein on the other, seem not often to be brought into direct confrontation, although over the years, they may have come to interact and blend with one another. By now, when center–periphery concepts are more passingly referred to, it is not always entirely clear which of the varieties is involved, if not some combination of them. Yet there is a field of tension here between studies focusing on distributions of material assets and the exercise of power on the one hand and studies of culture on the other; between views suggesting consensus and views emphasizing conflict; and between views treating the social organization of meaning and meaningful forms somewhat in isolation and other views which insist on setting it in the context of political and economic structures.

Probably all would accept, however, that centers and peripheries imply each other. We are dealing with relational phenomena: there is no center without periphery, no periphery unless there is a center. The particular way the center is a center is also reflected in the way the periphery is a periphery.

1. Levels and Varieties

Our conception of center–periphery relationships here is that they are relationships of inequality existing in geographical space. Such relationships, however, have been defined at very different levels of specificity. During the latter half of the twentieth century, especially in the Cold War era, the world was understood to be divided into three main segments—one Western and capitalist, one Socialist, one 'developing' and postcolonial. Here the First and the Second Worlds had their internal center–periphery structures. The Third World, on the other hand, may have had these, but also tended to be seen rather more as a periphery in its entirety, to one First or Second World center or other. At present the extreme macroview may be that of a center North and a peripheral South. Much of the cultural and political debate over center–periphery relationships remains mostly at such levels of identification. Notions such as Orientalism, Occidentalism, and Eurocentrism refer to understandings and representations of self and other in the context of these large-scale center–periphery structures.

Alternatively, identifications may indeed be made at the national level: the United States or France are seen rather more as centers than Sweden, Romania, or Burkina Faso. In other instances, centers are yet more specifically placed. Nations and regions may have their own centers in particular localities. In the study of historical civilizations, there is frequently an emphasis on centers as sites combining political power with complex ritual life and elaborated knowledge systems in the hands of specialists. A well-known paper by the anthropologists Bernard Cohn and McKim Marriott (first published in 1958), for example, delineates the complementary roles of centers and networks in the integration of Indian civilization (Cohn 1987, 78ff). In related mid-twentieth century work, as Redfield and Singer (1954), also anthropologists, discussed the cultural role of cities, they described the dynamic relationship between the 'great tradition' of early urban centers and the 'little traditions' of the surrounding peasant societies. The emphasis on the symbolic authority of the center here is clearly reminiscent of Shils's view.

Yet Redfield and Singer also noted that later urban centers, rather than refining particular local traditions, are often at the crossroads of the world, bringing together diverse traditions and serving as communication nodes for wider areas. In this the authors adumbrated recent interest in the role of particular cities in contemporary transnational center–periphery relationships. 'World cities,' such as New York, London, or Paris, may be seen as generalized, multipurpose centers, combining various kinds of power and drawing the attention of the periphery for many different reasons (Hannerz 1993, Knox and Taylor 1995). The contemporary global structure of center–periphery relationships, however, can be understood as more internally varied. Cities may be centers in particular ways to particular people, dispersed in a transnational periphery—Rome to the Catholic world; San Francisco to gay people not only from elsewhere in the United States, but also from other continents; Memphis, Tennessee, to friends of country music. As we see, attachments of very diverse kinds are involved. This means that the same people in the periphery may well be involved with several, noncompeting centers for different purposes. Yet centers of the same type can also compete in the periphery.

How do centers become centers, even drawing attention across national boundaries? Some are centers for mainly historical or mythical reasons, because something occurred there once in the past, or occurred there first, or because the memory of a charismatic figure is preserved there. They belong on the map of the significant past, or of eternal truths. Often they are intensified as centers at particular points in a ritual calendar. Many 'centers of pilgrimage' have such characteristics. Other centers are very much of the present. They draw attention and stimulate imagination from afar because they are 'where the action is' now, with regard to one or more lines of human preoccupation. The contemporary proliferation of center–periphery relationships of transnational reach is undoubtedly related to a greater ease of transportation and communication, making centers easy to get to, and easy to stay in touch with. As the participants, practitioners, adherents, activists, and employees of more subcultures, lifestyles, ideologies, occupations, or corporations use new means to extend their circles out of local or national habitats, new faraway centers are discovered, or even made. As more diasporas are generated by more migrants, old centers may also be reaffirmed, from further away.

2. Center–Periphery Diffusion

In part, it may be in the passage of culture from center to periphery that the two parties to the relationship manifest themselves. In the clearest case, the center would be always the donor, the periphery always the recipient—the center is active, the periphery is passive. Yet even if the imbalance is not quite so great, some measure of net cultural export would appear to be one conception of center–periphery influence. What is prominently involved here, consequently, is diffusion.

In a wider arena of debate about the effects of global interconnectedness, since mid-twentieth century, the preoccupation with cultural diffusion from center to periphery has often been expressed in one or the other of two ways. Post-World War II modernization theory offered a forecast of where the world was heading—where the West actually already was, more or less, and where the rest would follow, with some assistance from the center. When not drily 'value-free,' modernization theory tended to take a positive view of the changes in question. The other major way of describing cultural diffusion on a global scale was less favorably inclined. The term 'cultural imperialism,' as Tomlinson (1991, 3ff), has pointed out in a review, is a combination of two complicated concepts into one, with a considerable ideological charge. It has tended to refer to a growing dominance of western, and especially American, media and consumer goods in other parts of the world. Coca-Cola, McDonald's, and Barbie dolls have become the predictable pieces of evidence in a genre of cultural critique. Both the early form of modernization theory and the critique of cultural imperialism thus tend to offer global homogenization scenarios; implying, forecasting, or warning of the end of cultural diversity.

Such scenarios, however, have been increasingly often contested. There has been a growing attention to the multicentricity of culture, to crisscrossing cultural flows, and not least to instances of cultural counterflow, from periphery to center. While some net asymmetry of flow may yet be undeniable, many

commentators have also become less inclined to accept the assumption of passive reception at the periphery. They are much more likely to see an active periphery engaged in managing diffusion from the center: the periphery accepts this, rejects that, modifies one thing, and synthesizes something else with items from its own local cultural inventory. Metaphors of creolization and hybridity summarize this combination of cultural diffusion with creativity at the periphery.

3. Mixed Feelings

It is in the nature of their asymmetrical relationship that center and periphery take different views of it, and may even be differently aware of it. A periphery has to attend to its center. The center for its part may at times be preoccupied with its internal affairs, and may not have a clear grasp of the more widely dispersed consequences of its actions. The periphery tends to have a more developed idea of the center than vice versa.

Emotions may be attached to such linkages. Center–periphery relationships often do not leave people cold, passionless, neutral. In the consensualist view, centers generate warm, deferential attitudes at the peripheries. In a conflict perspective, in contrast, center and periphery are primarily defined by political and economic structures—and we may then see their cultural concomitants at the periphery in the responses to control, coercion, and constraint. Along such lines, the many forms of cultural resistance have been a major theme in the portrayal of center–periphery relationships. The periphery may defend itself symbolically against intrusions through a celebration of the self and its local and traditional roots, but there may also be a denigration of the other, an uncomplimentary representation of the center.

Yet the responses of the periphery to the center are not always clear-cut. For one thing, claims to center–periphery consensus now increasingly meet with skepticism. With Gramsci as a source of theoretical inspiration, observers may interpret deference in the more complicated terms of hegemony. It is likewise possible, however, that people at the periphery may be genuinely of two minds about a center. If ambivalence is a prevalent quality of social life, as Smelser (1998) has argued, perhaps this is even as common a response to a center as any more one-sidedly favorable or unfavorable stance. It may be a place one loves to hate and hates to love. One may feel that good things come from there, and at the same time resent its influence, or what may seem to be its narcissism. Especially those multipurpose centers understood to be 'where the action is,' moreover, may inspire sentiments which are positive, but instrumental or playful rather than deferential. They are among the liminal spaces of contemporary life.

All views of the center, however, and all messy feelings toward it, are not necessarily to be found in any single inhabitant of the periphery. They may rather be complicatedly distributed among its population, and such variations can be the foci of intense debates and conflicts structuring local life at the periphery.

4. The End of Center–Periphery Relationships?

With some frequency, one now hears voices criticizing center–periphery concepts, or proposing the decline of center–periphery structures. It is said that the world economy is increasingly decentered (see, e.g., Lash and Urry 1994, p. 4). Human life, it is also argued, is increasingly deterritorialized. People move quickly between places, being rooted in neither of them, and have relationships which belong in no place in particular. 'Critical masses' for cultural elaboration may be built up in cyberspace, and do not require local face-to-face contacts. As would-be centers and would-be peripheries are closely in touch, by way of electronic media or jumbo jets, the 'cultural lag' which divided them before is no longer there.

Even if they are often closer to futuristics than to the really existing world, there may be something to such arguments, At times, however, both the concepts criticized and the alternatives to them would need to be elaborated more precisely. Indeed we must be sensitive to the ambiguity of our terms, and to the actual range of variations out there. Asymmetries may indeed only be relative, culture flows are not entirely one-way, the world is crisscrossed by more symmetrical relationships as well, and there are many centers, and many kinds of centers, rather than only one. Centers also rise and decline. Center–periphery conceptualizations now deserve to be scrutinized and developed, rather than merely rejected. It is notable, too, that the end of centers and peripheries appears often proclaimed by commentators whose own vantage point is at the center—in this case not a privileged position.

See also: Dependency Theory; Globalization and World Culture; Globalization, Anthropology of; Globalization: Political Aspects; Hegemony: Anthropological Aspects; Hegemony: Cultural; Pilgrimage; World Systems Theory

Bibliography

Cohn B S 1987 *An Anthropologist among the Historians and Other Essays*. Oxford University Press, Delhi
Frank A G 1967 *Capitalism and Underdevelopment in Latin America*. Monthly Review Press, New York
Greenfeld L, Martin M (eds.) 1988 *Center: Ideas and Institutions*. University of Chicago Press, Chicago
Hannerz U 1993 The cultural role of world cities. In: Cohen A P, Fukui K (eds.) *Humanising the City?* Edinburgh University Press, Edinburgh, UK
Knox P L, Taylor P J (eds.) 1995 *World Cities in a World-system*. Cambridge University Press, Cambridge, UK
Lash S, Urry J 1994 *Economies of Signs and Space*. Sage, London
Redfield R, Singer M 1954 The cultural role of cities. *Economic Development and Cultural Change* **3**: 53–73
Shils E 1972 *The Intellectuals and the Powers*. University of Chicago Press, Chicago
Shils E 1975 *Center and Periphery*. University of Chicago Press, Chicago
Smelser N J 1998 The rational and the ambivalent in the social sciences. *American Sociological Review* **63**: 1–15
Tomlinson J 1991 *Cultural Imperialism*. Pinter, London
Wallerstein I 1974 *The Modern World-System*. Academic Press, New York

U. Hannerz

Centers for Advanced Study: International/Interdisciplinary

In the current period, scores of institutions of scholarly learning around the world include the words 'advanced study,' or some approximate translation thereof, in their formal titles. Others that might appropriately use such a title do not, often for simple historical reasons. Moreover, some institutions using the term have little in common, in structure or function, with the leading examples of such organizations. Therefore it is useful to review the main goals that have come to be associated with 'advanced study,' before considering the variety of institutional designs used to address them.

1. The Essence of 'Advanced Study'

The phrase 'advanced study' is hardly a technical term. Its superficial meaning is obvious, and for this reason its original coinage is not easy to trace for the English-speaking world. But its popularity and more restrictive meaning among scholars is quite surely a phenomenon of the twentieth century, springing directly from the creation and rapid success of the Institute for Advanced Study at Princeton University in the United States, officially incorporated in 1930. The original design of this Institute was in turn rather clearly the innovation of Abraham Flexner. In the 1920s, Flexner had become a noted student and critic of the American system of higher education through a series of publications including the *Flexner Report*, a sharp critique of the nation's medical schools. Flexner was later approached by the Bamberger family, who wished to endow a new medical college in New Jersey, to serve as an agent in this enterprize. Flexner soon came to recommend the endowment not of a medical college but of a new kind of university. His vision was of an institution without undergraduate students, in which advanced graduate students and top-flight professors would form a partnership of scholars who would 'be left to pursue their own ends in their own ways ... in tranquillity ...' As this vision crystallized, Flexner decided it should be called 'an Institute of Higher Learning or Advanced Studies.'

The phrase was launched into a realm of high visibility. It helped that one of the first recruits was Albert Einstein, soon surrounded by world-class mathematicians, physicists and cosmologists who could engage in fruitful dialogues with him.

Flexner's conception was deliberately designed as a counterweight to the conventional university. Universities, at least in America, are the long-acknowledged home for basic research and the pursuit of increasingly complex topics in the advancement of knowledge. Flexner felt that a center for advanced study, dedicated to roughly the same ends, should be different. Some said that Flexner's 'innovation' was a retreat to the simplicity of Plato's Academy. But he was attempting to address issues surrounding the interplay between the advancement of knowledge and the standard forms of modern university life.

While 'advanced study' might seem to involve the examination of extremely complex or intricate topics, a more essential definition is *research at the most remote frontiers of knowledge*, as they stand at any point in time. The core of well-established knowledge is for the most part constantly expanding. Institutions of education, including higher education, are mainly dedicated to the transmission of such bodies of 'received wisdom.' This transmission presumes at least a two-tier system of actors, being the masters who know and the young who are learning.

The frontier itself is a fuzzy region, which begins at the far edge of consolidated knowledge where doubt first rises as to the shape and meaning of what lies beyond. As one proceeds outward, fragments of knowledge become increasingly sparse, and general uncertainty increases rapidly. As with most poorly-explored zones, there is no dearth of conjecture as to what lies there, but controversy is high. There is also confidence that further exploration can in due time produce enlightenment, and hence true additions to consolidated knowledge. To explore effectively it is usually helpful to have mastered established knowledge in the terrain closest to that edge of the frontier. But once past that prerequisite—and the more advanced of graduate students have achieved that state—everyone can be an explorer at the same level. Hence Flexner's collegium of scholars was realistic, along with his welcome proviso that such a group be as liberated as possible from the routine demands of daily life, including most of the bureaucratic and teaching activities required of the typical university professor.

Conventional universities have long been organized into specific disciplines such as physics, biology, or economics. These disciplines have their own regional

frontiers, and are expert at sending out fingers of inquiry which in disciplinary terms illuminate previously unknown terrain. But deeper and richer probes that consolidate knowledge of larger areas, such as linking up several neighboring peninsulas to one another, are often best carried out by teams from multiple disciplines. This has, of course, become an increasing necessity, as the bodies of already-established knowledge within given disciplines have become so large that mastery of even the local 'consolidated knowledge' of a single narrow discipline consumes much of the education process. Therefore most centers of advanced study are more or less deliberately interdisciplinary, and even take steps to ensure that resident scholars do not segregate themselves by discipline, but are exposed to enriched stimulation from broader cross-disciplinary discussions. Scholars who have spent long periods of study and teaching in conventional universities before encountering this novel environment testify that they have sorely missed such broad-spectrum intellectual interaction ever since they first devoted themselves to a single discipline by entering graduate schools. Moreover, scientific knowledge about the natural world, as well as the symbolic world of mathematics, is notably cosmopolitan. Therefore diversity in national origins is also sought by most centers for advanced studies, given the possibility of relevant genius in any part of the world, and the impress of cultural perspectives on knowledge.

2. Illustrative Institutional Designs

The Institute for Advanced Study at Princeton is not only the original model for advanced study centers, but is probably larger in endowment and size, as well as structural complexity, than any others. By now, it has a permanent faculty of nearly two dozen, spread over four distinct schools. These faculties review applications from further scholars to be designated as Members, who reside at the Institute for periods ranging from a single term to several years in occasional cases. Such Members normally propose research projects that fit the specialized interests of scholars with permanent faculty appointments, although some Members are encouraged to work in areas which look profitable to the current faculty, but which are under-represented in the relevant school. Other scholarly visitors, in addition to those selected as Members, are also hosted for shorter periods where mutually fruitful. In all, some 200 scholars spend significant periods of time at the Institute in any given year.

The Princeton Institute began with a special focus on mathematics and classical studies, but has broadened considerably over time. The School of Mathematics continues to be the largest collegium of scholars. The School of Natural Sciences is substantial in size as well, although it has a heavy emphasis on astrophysics and particle physics. The School of Historical Studies continues to reflect its original dedication to ancient history and classical studies, but now enjoys significant representation in medieval and modern history. The School of Social Science was not added until the early 1970s, and remains the smallest of these units. In addition to the major social-science disciplines which have core representation, the School hosts Members and visitors in literature, philosophy, and even art history.

In 1954 the Center for Advanced Study in Behavioral Sciences, with the help of the Ford Foundation, opened its doors on land of Stanford University in Palo Alto, California, although it was administratively independent of that institution. It was inspired by the generic example of the Princeton Institute, but was also motivated as a response to the scant attention being given to the social and behavioral sciences in the Princeton Institute's program at the time. Although its broad goals are parallel to those at Princeton, its mode of operation differs in a number of particulars. Most notably, it has no permanent faculty appointments. Instead, a small secretariat invites nearly four dozen scholars as residential Fellows each year. Scholars are given office space and various forms of computer and research support, and are encouraged to pursue whatever reflections, research, and writing they wish. Various methods are employed to encourage informal intellectual communication between the disciplines present.

The disciplinary scope of these fellowships for the Center at Stanford is extremely broad. To be sure, the five primary social sciences—anthropology, economics, political science, psychology, and sociology—make up a majority of each cohort, especially as augmented by, typically, an ample representation of historians. But leaders in research in other diverse social science specialties, such as education, linguistics, statistics, geography, law, and philosophy appear with fair regularity from cohort to cohort. In addition, there has been on one hand routine representation from the boundaries in the form of literary studies or, occasionally, well-known authors of fiction, and on the other hand representatives of the natural sciences, including ornithologists, biomedical researchers, Nobel Laureates in biology, and even a chemist working on the social communication of insects. While the normal fellowship gives free rein to individual researchers, the Center at Stanford dedicates some fraction of slots within each cohort to 'special projects' prearranged for work on scientific or policy problems that require sustained multidisciplinary attention. On average there are about two such projects per year, participated in by a fifth to a tenth of the Fellows in residence.

The general model for the Center at Stanford has been adopted by newer advanced study institutions of interest to social and behavioral scientists. In 1970 the Netherlands Institute for Advanced Study in the Humanities and Social Sciences was founded through the efforts of an eminent Dutch linguist, E. M. Uhlenbeck, following his experience as a Fellow of the Stanford Center. Other institutions have been established in Europe with attention to the same model, such as the Institute for Advanced Study (*Wissenschaftskolleg*) in Berlin (1980), and the Swedish Collegium for Advanced Study in the Social Sciences (1985) at Uppsala. The National Humanities Center in North Carolina was also promoted largely by former Fellows of the Center at Stanford, and again modeled closely after it.

There are local adaptations in form across these institutions. For example, the Dutch Institute requires that half of its Fellows be from the Netherlands. The Berlin Institute hosts a few permanent Fellows as well as annual residential ones. The prominence of group projects or annual 'themes' varies from institution to institution. None of these centers, however, is designed to train graduate students or offer advanced degrees; instead, they are dedicated to promoting research of great distinction. They also enjoy a high degree of autonomy from specific universities as well as state or federal governments, although they may receive funding from, and engage in relationships with, such agencies.

In addition to the growing number of such large-scale centers, numerous smaller intrauniversity units with similar goals have emerged. While advanced study centers will always be vastly outnumbered by universities and other training institutions, the existence and popularity of these centers reflect an increasing awareness that the Flexner ideal for a collegium of research scholars is, under modern conditions, an indispensable part of the infrastructure desirable for the healthy advancement of knowledge.

See also: International Research: Programs and Databases; Specialization and Recombination of Specialties in the Social Sciences; Think Tanks

Bibliography

Flexner A 1960 *An Autobiography*. Simon and Schuster, New York

P. E. Converse

Central Africa: Sociocultural Aspects

Most authors define Central Africa as the vast area comprising speakers of the different western branches of Bantu. The great diversity of western Bantu populations and traditions have gradually extended, beginning 5,000 years ago, from southern Cameroon, into Equatorial Guinea, Gabon, People's Republic of Congo, the Democratic Republic of Congo, and Angola. Side to side to Ubangi and Nilotic speakers, they have moreover spread across the Central African Republic, southern Sudan, Western Uganda, Rwanda, and Burundi, to Eastern Congo, Tanzania, and Northwestern Zambia. Whereas the eastern Bantu have specialized in grain growing, the western Bantu adopted cassava and yams for staple foods. The region has been the scene of complex interactions between the local and outer worlds.

1. AD 1000 to 1880

Probably due to its sparse population, Central Africa did not develop the type of domestic markets and specialized local industries as found in West Africa. Until the late fifteenth century, it stayed out of the lines of long-distance communication such as those that had developed from coastal East Africa or along the caravan routes of West Africa. The history of precolonial Central Africa from AD 1000 can be divided broadly into two main regional developments.

With regard to the northern half of Central Africa, comprising the great equatorial forest with its northern woodland fringe and the Congo basin, linguistic and ethnographic data—common 'words and things' (Vansina 1990)—bear witness to the interaction between the farming and pastoral peoples in the forest and savanna areas north and south of the equator. The most important hunter-gatherer groups of Northern Central Africa were the matrilineal Pygmies, interacting with their agricultural neighbours and long-distance trading groups (like the salt-making Vili of Loango, and the neighboring copper-trading Tio). The Zaire river and its tributaries have been an important corridor for the transmission of cultural influences and systems of government, as well as for the trading economies of the Atlantic zone. The farming in the thinly scattered patrilineal societies of the northern and eastern corner of the rain forest remained for long untouched by the food plants originating from South America and already imported into other parts of Central Africa.

In the central part of the equatorial forest, the Mongo patrilineal societies were strongly influenced by the neighboring agriculturalists to the northwest along the Ubangi and higher up in the Sudan. Mongo Big Men, often combining agriculture and trade, tended to privilege their patrilocal household and patriclan rather than the village community as an economic stronghold and political unit, also by way of matrimonial transactions and cultic and initiatory specializations. By the sixteenth century, long-distance exchange economies of textiles and fire-arms for ivory and local captives may have connected the equatorial forest even with Egypt.

The savanna regions in the southern and western half of Central Africa saw the emergence of important political leadership roles, including kingship. Depending on the rainfall, the wooded savanna was moderately suitable for agriculture and/or pastoralism. Priests were the guardians of all reproductive resources. The extended family was the focus of physical and spiritual well-being of both living and deceased members of the patrilineage. Lineage chiefs gained control over the rain-making cults and the territorial custody of hunting traditions and the collection of tribute. From the fourteenth century, the chiefs gained regional control over iron and smithery, and particularly from the seventeenth century, over fire-arms and market-oriented commerce. This as well as their indirect involvement in the Atlantic slave trade made their power paramount over large areas in central Angola and western Congo.

2. Challenges from the Atlantic and Colonizing Europe

Unlike West and East Africa, Central Africa had not entered the maritime trade prior to the arrival of the Portuguese caravels seeking trading bases, from the 1480s onwards. Reports by Portuguese missionaries and merchants as well as occasional correspondence by western-educated Kongo, show how the foreign influence brought radical changes to Kongo kingdom and culture. The kingdom then comprised prosperous farming communities linked to a regional trade of fish and craft goods. From this period, the *nzimbu* shells in the hands of Europeans took on the functions of coinage for the previously unfamiliar purposes of wage-payment and marketing.

Portuguese traders carried Mediterranean manufactures to Kongo in exchange for raffia cloth, ivory, dye wood, and copper. The redistribution of these manufactures (such as North African textiles, iron knives, glass mirrors, glass schnapps bottles, glazed bowls, Venetian beads, and glazed china) was controlled carefully by the royal court. Moreover, Portuguese teachers, artisans, lawyers, and priests enhanced the authority of the king and his closest supporters. A number of Kongo were taken to Europe for further education. From the sixteenth century the history of the southern savanna became tragically bound up with the growth of Atlantic slave-trade. Manpower, rather than landed property as in early modern Europe, was the key to value in the Central African communities. Slave-trading of servile subjects and captives gained via long-distance marketing at the Malebo Pool (where Kinshasa would later develop) became the grim solution to local needs for foreign goods. Like any slave-trading society, the Kongo kingdoms and other neighboring equatorial kingdoms became oppressive and fractious, and deemed to collapse.

The Atlantic trade gradually came under the control of the semi-colonial Luso African community of the Loanda hinterland, Africa's first White colony. The long-distance savanna trade-routes probably became avenues for the dissemination of European goods and influence, as well as of the South American crops: maize, cassava, tobacco, tomatoes. Soon, frontier states such as Matamba and Kasanje as well as a new class of trading entrepreneurs took control over trade relations with the European powers. Following the industrial revolution in Europe, new goods were being shipped to Southern Cameroon, Gabon, and the Lower Congo. Towards the end of the eighteenth century, with the involvement of French, English and Dutch merchants, the Atlantic slave trade reached its peak.

Swahili-Arab penetration in Northeastern Zambia and Southeastern Congo in the early nineteenth century started as trade of guns and powder for ivory and slaves. It would soon overthrow the local chiefs and gain independent political power for itself.

Following Livingstone's and Stanley's 'explorations,' the 1885 Berlin Conference legitimized Europe's colonial scramble for Central Africa. The conquest of Equatorial Africa would last until the 1920s before military power, forced labor, harsh rubber exploitation, diseases, and hunger would have decimated half of the population and broken local resistance. Colonial rule gradually deprived local societies of the institutional ability to confront the exploitative forces and exogenous 'civilizing programs' imposed upon them. In the views of the colonizing masters, the bringing about of a philanthropic medical provision and wide-spread school education in the colonies was an essential feature in the international justification of political and economic colonialism. The colony's extractive economy directed at the 'so far unutilized resources' and relying on mandatory labor in lieu of tax payment, as well as its transport and communication technology were to open up the remote areas to the larger world scene. They were to 'uplift' and integrate the local populations in the new era of 'universal civilization and progress.'

Bantu traditional rule was deeply alien to the colony's display of order. Colonial state power was imposed through regulations, enticements, and direct interference, as both a text and texture, absorbing and domesticating people and events by the very acts of *writing* and administrative *ordering*. The textual economy disassembled and inserted local realities into panoptical recording and regulation. The management of people's civil identity and geographic confinement was achieved through the identity cards and mandatory 'passbooks.' Records of marriage, descent, settlement, and land use were meant to bind the populations geographically, and were authoritative for the succession to chiefly titles and for settling matrimonial and family disputes. On the other hand,

such regulatory documents were intended to modernize society by freeing the so-called *évolué* from customary collectivism. Population censuses, together with geographic and linguistic-ethnographic mapping and recording of data, allowed for a compartmentalization of languages and ethnic groups.

Unlike the nineteenth century bureaucratic nation-state in the West, the Bantu political traditions of Central Africa do not draw their inspiration from orders of visual representation and architectonic spatial models. They are moulded by organic, hydraulic, and/or animal-totemic metaphors informing political networks and strategies as an order of events, forces, sources, and relations. Membership of and alliances between particular social groups are not primarily tied to a geographic partitioning but to blood ties and to the mythical or primal space-time order in line with the constant cosmogenetic re-enactment of the reproductive and hierarchical weave between the founding ancestors, their foundational and migratory exploits, and their multiple descendents.

The functions of traditional political title holders were, and are, being thought of as prior to, and the source of, all life forms as well as the guarantee of their order. A chief represents and surpasses his subordinates by his twofold function. First, like his totemic animals (leopard, eagle, crocodile), he is a conqueror. Through enthronement, the ruler embodies the founding ancestors and represents the primal space-time order initiated by the immigration of his ancestral people and their conquest of the land. Through his body, in particular his clairvoyance and the nightly forces which he shares with his totemic animals, the ruler impersonates the founding ancestor. He imposes the qualities of a perennial hierarchical social organization, territorial unity, and moral order on his society. Second, the chief acts as the androgynous life-giver or mediator of the (re)generative processes between the land, society, man, and the 'the primal womb' in the earth. His rule is thus one of cosmic and physical regeneration, guaranteeing human, agricultural and social reproduction, and instituting commensality and sharing in his territory. In this diurnal ordering role, the chief protects his people from the nocturnal anti-rule of envy, theft, sexual abuse and sorcery. The elders, through councils, ceremonial exchange, and authoritative speech, extend the regenerative capacity into the daily weave of events and relations uniting kin groups under common rule.

In the Christian mission stations or in the plantation, mining, and industrial enterprises, ever larger numbers of individuals and families joined the workers camps and 'indigenous townships,' set up outside customary rule, on the fringes of White settlements. They thus created new ideological and physical spaces of identity and collective imagination. Indeed, from the last decades of the nineteenth century, Christian congregations set out to work side by side with the concessionary companies and the colonial administration. Their aim was to 'bring civilization and universal salvation to the Dark Continent,' as well as to 'save the individual's soul' through the removal of 'pagan African customs.' While the first decades of the missionary endeavor were directed at the adaptation of Christianity to local society and culture, from the 1930s on, missions became increasingly involved in the social engineering of the townships, echoing the dominant mood of the plantation or mining trusts and the colonial administration. From then on, church authorities designed paternalist programs to educate converts towards assimilating modern skills and dispositions. By the 1950s, the term modernization had become a new banner for the assimilationist option.

In the Belgian Congo, the colonial government had secured the agreement of the missions to manage the schools in exchange for land concessions. Nearly all mission stations developed boarding schools with enough fields, cattle, poultry, and workshops to be self-sufficient. The colonial school presented Western progress as the source of a more dignified identity on the world scene. Vinck (1995) convincingly shows the extent to which, from the 1920s in the Belgian Congo, the school books conveyed the primary symbols and values of the West. By encouraging the pupils to develop a new identity and self-image, these manuals influenced the entire political élite-to-be in post-independence Congo. The concept of State, a key notion in the school books, was the comprehensive and abstract, depersonalized expression of the new power and authority which came to dominate the various spheres of life. According to the manuals, all Whites shared in the power of the State and thus were to be considered as authorities. Colonial school books depicted traditional society and religion as dominated by sorcery and the machinations of the devil.

3. Endogenization

From the 1950s, among the second generation of those having assimilated the European civilizational capital, the frustration grew with the glaring contradiction between the promises which the colonial master had put before them and their second-rank position in the colonial institutions. A few Christian priests or pastors and élite got imbued with the Third World emancipation movement enhanced by the rapid decolonization in Asia, the 1955 Afro–Asian Conference in Bandung, the independence struggle in Algeria, the *Négritude* call for the rehabilitation of African cultures, and the Pan-Africanism radiating from Ghana and Guinea.

The militant élite used a triple banner in the battle for decolonization. First, in the terms of the Christian, humanist, and/or socialist discourses of the colonizers, they claimed the right to dignity, social emancipation, and equality. Second, their political aspir-

ations were largely drawing on European ideological discourse associating modern economic development with gradual political emancipation. They thereby became complicit with the modernizing and authoritarian endeavor of the White welfare—and nation state, however alien to people at grassroots level. Third, in the terms of western Bantu traditions, they favored a palaver model of negotiation, ceaselessly co-opting 'brothers' and 'doing things with words.'

In the 1970s, authenticity movements in various states prompted a radical shift away from assimilation of the White civilizational models, now urging people to take possession in a militant way of their own history and a dignified self-representation on the world scene. Throughout the 1970s and 1980s, artists and customers in the discos celebrated a liberation from paternalist and moralizing colonization. Today, the people in both the rural and urban milieux have become aware how much their lifestyles, modes of production, and environments are both in rupture with their parental models, and simultaneously excluded from the current economic and informational globalization of western consumerist lifestyles. The masses in the poverty-stricken suburbs have been haunted, through television and downtown scenes, by the imageries of ease and extravagance that the transcontinental mass media as well as the few very rich nationals exhibit in fine clothing, expensive cars, and luxury goods. Many are increasingly bitter about their exclusion. However, they do not fail to develop their own proud visions of society and the way things are. In the early 1990s, through the waves of demonstrations and Dead-Town protest manifestations or even uprisings, suburban people counteracted the govermental views on modernization and the neocolonial politics. Irony and parody allowed the populace to deconstruct imperialist twentieth century modernity.

Suburbanites straddle worlds through hybridity or the imaginary transgression of codes, in particular in the utopian fields of humor, daydream, and glottophagia. These are gradually furthering a cultural critique of the postcolonial situation: rather than fighting one another as ill-fortuned or discontented consumers of modern cash goods (increasingly brought in second-hand from the North), people in suburban neighborhoods and rural communities are re-exploring their genuine sense of communality, and their collective memory stored in body techniques and sensuous culture. Hybridity in many cultural expressions blurs the tradition/modernity, Bantu/western, precapitalist/capitalist oppositions that have been created by the Europeanizing tropes. Songs on the radio today in vernacular languages and along old rhythms, recalling both the collective frenzy and euphoria in the bars of the 1970s and 1980s and village festivities or rituals, are now unsettling the Reformist voices of the (post) colony which had connected city life with French or English speech and étiquette, with school education, and the petty bourgeois life style, and with the well-equipped biomedical services. The pidgnization or creolization of French or English colloquial language, and of narrative styles in songs and newspapers, vitiate modernist master-tales about the literate African city dweller and the retrograde and illiterate villager. Thousands of independent prophetic healing churches of the holy spirit, through exorcizing materialist greed and westernization of public mores, or even State politics identified with the work of *sataani* (the local term for the Christian-imported notion of Satan, referring to those engaged in illegal practices and sorcery), develop a forceful critique of the catastrophic collusion between economic modernization and people's sociocultural dispossession. At the same time, through collective trances and 'Christian' forms of telepathy and clairvoyance in the name of the holy spirit, the prophetic churches explore ways towards domesticating modernizing forces. During the ceremonial offering of money to the prophet and assistant assembly leaders, adepts may circle more than a full hour around the congregation, dancing and singing as if to re-enchant one of modernity's most striking secularizations, anonymous cash trade. The offering aims to transform the subaltern's poverty and needs into what is defined as divine grace or healing. The prophetical churches thereby speak back to global capitalism and celebrate their participation in a new economy. They subject the monetary economy to the utopian ideals of equality and solidarity proper to brotherhood and sisterhood.

See also: African Studies: Culture; African Studies: Politics; Colonization and Colonialism, History of; Fourth World; Historiography and Historical Thought: Sub-Saharan Africa; Near Middle East/North African Studies: Economics; Near Middle East/North African Studies: Society and History

Bibliography

Andersson E 1958 *Messianic popular movements in the Lower Congo*. Almqvist and Wiksells, Uppsala, Sweden
Birmingham D 1981 *Central Africa to 1870: Zambezia, Zaïre and the South Atlantic*. Cambridge University Press, Cambridge, UK
Birmingham D, Martin P M (eds.) 1983 *History of Central Africa*, 2 Vols. Longman, London
Boahen A (ed.) 1990 *General Hiistory of Africa: VII Africa under Colonial Domination 1880–1935*. Abridged edn. Unesco, Paris and Currey, London
Cairns H 1965 *Prelude to Imperialism: British Reactions to Central African Society 1840–1890*. Routledge, London
De Boeck F 1996 Postcolonialism, power and identity: Local and global perspectives in Zaire. In: Werbner R, Ranger T (eds.) *Postcolonial Identities in Africa*. Zed, London, pp. 75–106
Devisch R 1995 Frenzy, violence, and ethical renewal in Kinshasa. *Public Culture* 7: 593–629
Devisch R 1996 Pillaging Jesus: Healing churches and the villagisation of Kinshasa. *Africa* 66: 555–86
Harms R 1981 *River of Wealth and Sorrow: The Central Zaire Basin in the Era of Slave and Ivory Trade, 1500–1891*. Yale University Press, New Haven, CT
Hunt N R 1999 *A Colonial Lexicon of Birth Ritual, Medicalization and Mobility in the Congo*. Duke University Press, Durham, NC
Mazrui A A, Wondji C (eds.) 1993 *General History of Africa: VIII Africa since 1935*. Heinemann, London
Mbembe A 1992 Provisional notes on the postcolony. *Africa* 62: 3–37
Mudimbe V Y 1988 *The Invention of Africa: Gnosis, Philosophy, and the Order of Knowledge*. Indiana University Press, Bloomington, IN
Vansina J 1966 *Kingdoms of the Savanna: A History of the Central African States until European Occupation*. University of Wisconsin Press, Madison, WI
Vansina J 1990 *Paths in the Rainforests*. Currey, London
Vaughan M 1991 *Curing their Ills: Colonial Power and African Illness*. Polity Press, Cambridge, UK
Vinck H 1995 The influence of colonial ideology on schoolbooks in the Belgian Congo. *Paedagogica Historica* 31: 355–405

R. Devisch

Central America: Sociocultural Aspects

Most scholars know that a great deal of violence took place in Central America in the late twentieth century, but relatively few know the reasons for it, what its consequences were, or how it affected research on the region. The immediate causes of the violence were revolutionary attempts from the 1960s through the 1980s which led to brutal military reprisals, mainly against civilians—in Guatemala, Nicaragua, and El Salvador. The violence had an enormous economic impact on all five countries of the region (which also includes Honduras and Costa Rica), leaving already poor people much poorer. Civilians suffered the greatest casualties and many of the survivors left the region permanently, while those who remained live in heavily militarized states where 'low-intensity' conflict continues. Yet to everyone's surprise social mobilization and protest by a wide variety of disadvantaged groups also continues. The vast social changes engendered by these phenomena have encouraged a new kind of social science research, such that most now deal with regional patterns and transnational flows, history, large institutions such as the state and military, and the nature of ongoing as well as past social movements. After a brief summary of what happened in the five countries of the region, this article will discuss recent comparative and historical research projects and will then treat the way in which ethnography changed and developed to deal with the questions raised by this period of history.

1. The Central American Revolutions

Revolutionary movements began in Guatemala, El Salvador, and Nicaragua following the 1959 Cuban revolution, which inspired them. The Central American insurgencies resembled those that took place in much of Latin America, although unlike the others, in the 1970s they became significantly more violent and threatening to their national regimes, which were in turn much weaker. Small guerrilla fronts led by relatively well-educated men (most of them members of the middle or elite classes) attempted to organize peasants or rural workers in most countries of Latin American in order to seize state power—whether or not locally inspired grassroots movements were already in place. The early guerrillas, whose basic strategy was *focismo* (Wickham-Crowley 1992) worked largely in regions where they assumed popular support could be generated to overturn the old social order for a new one, but did little to describe their actual sociopolitical projects to the masses. The *focistas* operating in the 1960s suffered ignominious defeats, but became much more successful when they renewed their efforts under changed leadership in the 1970s. Several different guerrilla groups developed in each country, differing on strategy (insurrectionary versus prolonged popular war), revolutionary subject (workers, peasants, or middle groups), and international line (Russian, Chinese, or Third World). The actual number of guerrillas in Central America was never very large (from 2,000 to 10,000), but they were supported by most of the rural population in the areas where they worked. The military forces in Central America were of variable size and sophistication—greatest in Guatemala, least in Nicaragua—but always outnumbered the guerrillas by at least ten to one. By 1980 they had developed into formidable counter-insurgency powers (everywhere but in Costa Rica), being provided with arms, advisors, and tactical support by the USA (everywhere but in Nicaragua).

Nicaragua's Sandinistas had the greatest popular support and took state power in 1979, thus becoming the only successful revolution in Latin America besides Cuba. The Sandinistas were defeated in elections ten years later; but most observers agree that the human and material cost of the *contra* war (Vilas 1995) instigated by the USA explains the defeat. The Guatemalan and Salvadoran revolutionaries came close to taking power shortly after the Nicaraguan victory, and were in a strong enough position to negotiate peace accords with the military governments of their countries in the 1990s. During the civil wars, the violence visited upon the rural civilian population by the military was extremely high and indiscriminate everywhere, but especially so in Guatemala, where Maya Indians were most heavily affected. In fact, both scholars and the UN Commission on Human Rights depicted Guatemala's military actions as genocidal. Violence continued in much of the region, but now is mostly carried out by ex-soldiers and other uprooted people, unemployed by the previous cycle of violence. Nonetheless, very significant social movements, especially of indigenous people, are now taking place throughout the region.

Carlos Vilas (1995) provides an excellent general treatment of all of the phenomena described here in fewer than 200 pages. Vilas, an Argentinian sociologist, treats the cases in greater depth than other social scientists because he lived in the region for more than ten years, was in intellectual contact with revolutionary and state sectors in all five countries, and participated in the Nicaraguan attempt to establish a revolutionary social and political regime. Vilas' earlier (1987) study of the Sandinista revolution in Nicaragua is the best general study of revolution in Central America.

2. Comparative Research

What took place in Central America calls for comparative research, especially on the question of why three of its countries had major revolutionary movements, and two did not. Many such studies have been done, but few go beyond the obvious economic differences among the five countries. Most point to the pattern of export-led economic growth since the 1960s, which impoverished peasants everywhere but in Costa Rica. (The case of Honduras is usually explained by the fact that fewer peasants were displaced there.) The most useful and original comparisons have been done by Robert Williams, an economist who uses sociological, historical, and ethnographic methods in his research. Williams's first book (1986) observes that cotton and cattle production for export expanded hugely in all five countries (with considerable economic aid from the USA for its own economic reasons) and led to significant dispossession of peasants everywhere, *including in Costa Rica*. But the five Central American states handled peasant protest quite differently, with both Costa Rica and Honduras carrying out land reform and expanding services while the three other states responded with repression and militarization—which led to war. In his second book, Williams (1994) examines the social and economic factors that led to two different kinds of states in Central America—the three revolutionary countries being controlled by rigid oligarchies, the other two being led by more open political groups. He finds an explanation in the social and political relations created by the coffee-export economy (among the owners, workers, merchants), the first major postcolonial export in the region, which played a critical role in state formation. (Paige's 1997 study, which is less complete, reaches similar conclusions.)

Timothy Wickham-Crowley (1992) compares where, and to what effect guerrilla movements arose, and who participated as both leaders and cadre, as well as the military and regime responses provoked by guerrilla warfare. By treating all of the significant guerrilla-led movements in Latin America since (and including) the Cuban revolution, he provides a useful comparative context for the Central American guerrilla movements of both the 1960s and 1980s. Virtually no in-depth or ethnographic studies of one or more Central American guerrilla groups have been done. Such work may be forthcoming now that the wars are definitively over and the surviving guerrillas have returned to engage in peaceful politics in their countries. The Guatemalan and Salvadoran cases both cry out for research while the revolutionary protagonists are still alive, especially since Wickham-Crowley's controversial study is not actor based and relies on rather weak secondary materials.

An important six-volume comparative history has been produced (Rivas 1993), most of its contributors Central Americans. The coverage of the civil wars and their aftermath is quite limited and little new theoretical ground is broken in these volumes. What is innovative about this work is the consistent comparative emphasis, unusual for historians, which expands information on all of the countries and identifies the major gaps in knowledge. The economic and political events of the last quarter of the twentieth century clearly led to the comparative focus.

Two other comparative historical *and* ethnographic works are under way in which the Central and North American scholars are more equal in number. The more traditional project is being done only in Guatemala under the guidance of anthropologist Richard Adams, who has worked in Central America for nearly fifty years. The emphasis of the ethnographic project is on how ethnic relations were affected by the violence that took place in different communities. (In this regard it is little different from the early book edited by Robert Carmack in 1988.) The second project, taking place under the leadership of Jeffrey Gould, Charles Hale, and Dario Euraque, is more innovative. The historians and anthropologists conducting the research often worked in the same sites (some in all Central American countries except Costa Rica) and met frequently to discuss methods and ideas. The project focuses on the nature and meaning of the process of *mestizaje* (the creation of a single people through cultural and biological mixing, encouraged if not forced by nation-state building) during the past two centuries and into the present. Throughout Latin America *mestizaje* is assumed to have been a 'natural' and noncoercive process that took place mainly in the colonial period and thus had little to do with state building; North and Latin American historians have mostly repeated this myth as fact, despite strong evidence to the contrary. This Central American project takes the myth on with detailed historical and ethnographic case studies, which illuminate a great deal about the general pattern of ethnic,

gender, and race relations in the region. An early glimpse into the conclusions of this project can be found in Gould's (1998) book on *mestizaje* in Nicaragua. Because of its many novel components—participation of both anthropologists and historians, North and Central American scholars, and group work in interpretation—this project promises to be a landmark study.

3. Ethnographic Research

The social scientists most challenged by the revolutionary situation in Central America have been anthropologists. Anthropologists have mainly worked in particular communities of Mayan Indians in Guatemala. Such work continues, but is impaired by the limited insight into state and subject formation, social movements, and transnational flows that such bounded research can produce. Those who have stayed within community boundaries have dealt mainly with the impact of fear and community divisions on local culture (e.g., Zur 1998); those who initially dealt with the larger issues (e.g., Smith 1990) lost most of the strengths of an ethnographic approach. But in recent years ethnographers have stretched themselves to do quite innovative, multisited ethnographic research.

Jennifer Schirmer's (1998) research broke new ground by providing an ethnography of military political perception and strategizing in Guatemala—where counterinsurgency tactics were best developed, as well as more violent and politically significant than elsewhere. Schirmer interviewed hundreds of Guatemalan army officers multiple times between 1986 and 1996 about everything from the nature of the guerrilla threat to their views about the proper political role of the military in the state apparatus. Criticized when her research began on the assumption that she could only parrot military views, Schirmer's published work on Guatemala's military project is now widely recognized as providing invaluable information on the formation of a military ideology, one that was nativistic (even though strongly supported by the USA) and extremely successful. Especially revelatory is how deliberately the military increased their control over Guatemalan politics, culture, and civil society. The first stage of pacification used strictly military means, including murders of suspects and massacres of civilians; the second stage involved economic and cultural restructuring of the communities most affected by the violence (the indigenous ones) together with reorganization of national party politics and elections; the final stage was reached with the 1994 peace accords, in which the military helped to reconfigure both state and civil society. As one military officer enthused, 'We [planned] the State in all of its ramifications!' (Schirmer 1998, p. 235).

The most important of the postwar social movements that have taken place in Guatemala has been that of the indigenous Maya, who have always been the largest and most exploited group in Guatemala. They had not been politically active on their own specific causes or identity issues, however, until the late 1980s—although they certainly did participate in Guatemala's revolutionary movement. As it is presently constituted, the Maya movement is a cultural movement led by indigenous intellectuals, who take language, dress, and religious tradition to be the main (and probably safest) issues. But the political ramifications are much broader and a less well-known Maya movement is building on a more popular base, making economic and political issues central (Bastos and Camus 1993). Before the movement, the Maya majority rarely held important political offices, even where they outnumbered Ladinos. Today they play a major electoral role, are in charge of several major public institutions, and have to be taken into the political equation on all national issues. Among other things, the movement challenges North American ethnographers to take up issues of importance to the Maya (Warren 1998). An edited book on racism (Arenas et al. 1999), a major issue to Maya activists but a topic rarely addressed by anthropologists before the 1990s, fits this still small genre. Sieder (1998) edits a discussion of the Maya and other kinds of social movements—women's, human rights, and so forth.

Only Diane Nelson (1999) has attempted to characterize the Maya movement in relation to the state. This inventive work covers many different public signs of change in the cultural politics of ethnic relations in Guatemala (movies, signs, advertisements, jokes about Rigoberta Menchú) as well as real cultural politics over the past 15 years. Use of such a variety of materials allows Nelson to describe a complex social movement which has been extremely significant for the cultural reconstitution of Guatemala. In truth, Nelson treats state politics in only one chapter and on one issue, thus not producing a true ethnography of the state, but rather an entertaining postmodern pastiche of the multiple issues that surround ethnography in the Central American context—from new social movements, to new public cultures and discourses, to new kinds of reflexive positioning for activist analysts.

Closer to a true ethnography of the state is the as yet unpublished work of Finn Stepputat, a Danish cultural geographer. Over a long period he worked with several distinct indigenous groups, some of them returned refugees, as well as both Indian and Ladino state and military actors—all in one large municipality—on the implications of the violence, new social actors, and political movements of various kinds on indigenous political subjectivity. To summarize his thesis very briefly, he suggests that intensified interaction between indigenous groups and various representatives of the state (e.g., the military, Ladino representatives, and actors in foreign nongovernmental organizations) as well as social and religious leaders of various kinds, has evoked changes in indigenous subjectivity to the point that many now operate *in* the state rather than *apart from* the state. His ethnography promises to show how specific state-like operations and powers interact with those in civil society to produce modern citizens/states—a kind of ethnography of the state that will be of general interest to social science.

A very different kind of indigenous movement took place in Nicaragua during its revolution, one spearheaded by the Miskitu of the Atlantic coast, a large, remote, and politically neglected area. This much smaller group of Indians resisted the revolutionary Sandinistas, who wanted to assimilate them into the state. The dialog between the Miskitu and the Sandinistas over several years produced an agreement of autonomy for those living in the Miskitu region, but one whose economic and political features were ambiguous. Charles R Hale's (1994) analysis of Miskitu history and identity, together with the more contemporary negotiations between Miskitu of various positions, Sandinistas of various positions, and other ethnic groups in the region, is a rare ethnography of a multifaceted political movement, one that treats culture, social relations, and political consciousness as dynamic historical phenomena. Roger Lancaster (1992) writes a more typical ethnography of urban Mestizos in postrevolutionary Nicaragua, notable for its treatment of race, gender, and sexuality in the context of a ruined economy.

The only ethnography on El Salvador for any time period is that by Binford (1996) on El Mozote, the community that was eradicated by an elite Salvadoran brigade directly under the tutelage of US advisors. Binford tries to bring the dead to life in his ethnography, by piecing together the nature of their lived experiences before their community was destroyed. He also situates the destruction of this community in the complex environment of Salvadoran guerillas, military, and US support. There are literally no ethnographies written of Honduras and very little social science done on the country, even though Honduras represents an especially interesting Central American case in many respects. It has been divided between a modern, lowland banana enclave owned by the USA and a highland region backward in both economic and political development—in part because of the banana enclave; it was heavily militarized in the 1980s, yet its military governments engaged several times in significant land reform; and the peasants joined no revolutionary movements, even though they struggled for land (often successfully) for decades. The case asks for innovative ethnography on all of these features. Yet only one case of ethnographic research is now being written up (by Sarah England), which looks at another feature of life characteristic of all Central America, transnational migration. Though at least 10 percent of the Central American population are now transnational migrants, the phenomenon has been little treated by social scientists working in any Central American country. England's research on the Honduran Garifuna describes the multiple cultural identities taken on by a black, indigenous group, who move between Honduras (where they hold an indigenous identity) and North America (where they are considered black).

The final ethnography to be treated here is Marc Edelman's (1999) study of 'peasants against globalization' in Costa Rica. Costa Rica is the model Central American country, with a small, very homogeneous population, an early democratic government whose social services rival the best in Latin America, and no significant military presence in recent history. While little other innovative social science has been done there recently, Edelman's study of Costa Rican social movements during the 1980s is a gem, possible only for someone who has worked in a country for more than a decade. Combining a sophisticated political economic analysis of global neo-liberalism with a strong political ethnography of a multitude of peasant organizations which dissolve and regroup repeatedly, Edelman's book is bound to be controversial because of its opinionated stance on a multitude of issues, including the literature on social movements and globalization. It remains, however, an example of the innovative ethnography being produced in Central America because of the global nature of its problems, the complexity of its social movements, and the peculiarities of its state-level institutions—which operate on a scale small enough to invite national-level ethnography.

See also: Dependency Theory; Revolutions, Sociology of; Revolutions, Theories of; South America: Sociocultural Aspects

Bibliography

Arenas C, Hale C R, Palma G (eds.) 1999 *Racismo en Guatemala? Abriendo debate sobre un tema tabu*. Facultad Latinoamericano de ciencias sociales, Guatemala City, Guatemala

Bastos S, Camus M 1993 *Quebrando el silencio: Organizaciones del pueblo maya y sus demandas (1986–1992)*. Facultad Latinoamericano de ciencias sociales, Guatemala City, Guatemala

Binford L 1996 *The El Mozote Massacre: Anthropology and Human Rights*. University of Arizona Press, Tucson, AZ

Carmack R 1988 *Harvest of Violence: The Mayan Indians and the Guatemalan Crisis*. University of Oklahoma Press, Norma, OK

Edelman M 1999 *Peasants Against Globalization: Rural Social Movements in Costa Rica*. Stanford University Press, Stanford, CA

Gould J L 1998 *To Die in this Way: Nicaraguan Indians and the Myth of Mestizaje, 1880–1965*. Duke University Press, Durham, NC

Hale C R 1994 *Resistance and Contradiction: Miskitu Indians and the Nicaraguan State, 1894–1987*. Stanford University Press, Stanford, CA

Lancaster R N 1992 *Life is Hard: Machismo, Danger, and the Intimacy of Power in Nicaragua*. University of California Press, Berkeley, CA

Nelson D 1999 *A Finger in the Wound: Body Politics in Quincentennial Guatemala*. University of California Press, Berkeley, CA

Paige J M 1997 *Coffee and Power: Revolution and the Rise of Democracy in Central America*. Harvard University Press, Cambridge, MA

Rivas E Torres (ed.) 1993 *Historia General de Centroamerica, Tomos I–VI*. Ediciones Siruela, Madrid, Spain

Schirmer J 1998 *The Guatemalan Military Project: A Violence Called Democracy*. University of Pennsylvania Press, Philadelphia, PA

Sieder R (ed.) 1998 *Guatemala After the Peace Accords*. Institute of Latin American Studies, London

Smith C A 1990 (ed.) *Guatemalans and the State: 1540–1988*. University of Texas Press, Austin, TX

Vilas C 1987 *Perfiles de la revolucion Sandinista: Liberacion nacional y transformaciones sociales en Centroamerica*. Editorial Legasa, Madrid, Spain

Vilas C 1995 *Between Earthquakes and Volcanoes: Market, State, and the Revolutions in Central America*. Monthly Review Press, New York

Warren K B 1998 *Indigenous Movements and their Critics: Pan-Maya Activism in Guatemala*. Princeton University Press, Princeton, NJ

Wickham-Crowley T P 1992 *Guerrillas and Revolution in Latin America: A Comparative Study of Insurgents and Regimes Since 1956*. Princeton University Press, Princeton, NJ

Williams R G 1986 *Export Agriculture and the Crisis in Central America*. University of North Carolina Press, Chapel Hill, NC

Williams R G 1994 *States and Social Evolution: Coffee and the Rise of National Governments in Central America*. University of North Carolina Press, Chapel Hill, NC

Zur J N 1998 *Violent Memories: Mayan War Widows in Guatemala*. Westview Press, Boulder, CO

C. A. Smith

Ceramics in Archaeology

Ceramics, or pottery, are among the oldest and most significant technological innovations in the history of humankind, the first truly synthetic material. Being highly plastic and thus virtually infinite in the range of shapes and forms possible, offering ready surfaces for decoration, and being ubiquitous in many archaeological contexts, ceramic containers and artifacts have provided archaeologists with one of their main categories of empirical data. Studies of variation in ceramic production, style, and use have assisted archaeologists both in the construction of chronologies and in the interpretation of ancient societies.

Ceramics denotes objects made from clay and fired to achieve hardness, which range from low-fired terracottas and earthenwares (firing range 900–1200 °C), through stonewares (1200–1350 °C), to porcelains

(1300–1450 °C). Most archaeological analyses of ceramics are focused on earthenwares, which dominated pottery industries throughout most of prehistory. Aside from vessels and containers of all kinds, ceramic artifacts also include such important items as bricks and tiles, figurines and models, and tableware.

1. History of Ceramics

The earliest human experimentation with clay—including the discovery that moist clay is plastic, can be shaped, and when heated or fired will retain its shaped form—is not well documented archaeologically. Fired clay figurines are known from the Dolní Věstonice site in Czechoslovakia, dated to 30,000 BC. In the Old World, the first ceramic vessels appear in the early Jomon culture of Japan at about 10,000 BC, and in the Near East (Anatolia) at around 8500–8000 BC. Ceramics do not appear until considerably later in the New World, in several localities between 3000–2500 BC. In all cases, the origins of ceramic vessels appear to be closely associated with sedentary modes of life, and with storage either of agricultural products or of quantities of gathered plant foods (as in the Jomon case). There is a high degree of correlation between sedentism and pottery making, as evident in a world ethnographic sample where only two out of 46 pottery-making societies are nonsedentary (Arnold 1985).

The oldest known pottery in the world is the 'cord-marked' Jomon pottery industry of Japan, dating to 10,000 BC and associated with sedentary or semi-sedentary hunter-gatherers. Jomon pottery is highly distinctive, both with its cord or string-impressed surface decoration, and its elaborate modeled rims; vessel forms are typically high jars or beakers. Elsewhere in the Far East, pottery appears in parts of China by around 7000 BC, if not earlier. The Yang-shao-Culture, centered in the Yellow River valley of northern China and dating between 4800–4200 BC, is noted for its beautifully formed earthenware jars and dishes, decorated with red-and-black painted geometric designs. In later time periods, the Chinese perfected many technical aspects of ceramic production, such as the horizontal and vertical updraft kilns, the potter's wheel, and high-fired stonewares and glazes. Porcelain ceramics were innovated in China sometime around the beginning of the first millennium AD, and were widely traded throughout the Old World, and later to Europe and the Americas.

In the Near East, architectural uses of clay (e.g., for walls, floors, and roofs) are widespread by around 7500 BC, in association with the domestication of plants and animals, and the origins of sedentary village life. Pottery containers appear by 8500–8000 BC in Anatolia, and slightly later in other parts of the Near East. A variety of other clay implements and artifacts are also characteristic of early Near Eastern sites, such as clay spindle whorls and loom weights, clay sickles (with obsidian or flint blades), clay toys and models, and clay stamps and cylinder seals. Ceramic technology was not independently developed in Europe, but rather was borrowed or diffused from the Near East, in association with the spread of agriculture and a sedentary mode of existence. In the classical world, of course, Greek black- and red-figured pottery (600–400 BC) represents a high level of technical and artistic achievement, as does slightly later Roman Arretine ware (100 BC–AD 400).

Ceramic technology in the New World arose considerably later in time, evidently as an independent development; moreover, the potter's wheel and the use of glazes never developed in the New World. Between ca. 2500–2000 BC, pottery appears in several localities, including the coast of Columbia, the Pacific coast of Mexico, and in the southeastern United States. Among the outstanding pottery traditions of the New World, one must count the coastal Peruvian Nazca and Moche traditions (200 BC to AD 700) with their elaborated modeled anthropomorphic and zoomorphic vessels; the Late Classic Maya pottery which included exquisite polychrome funerary vessels; and the Pueblo pottery traditions of the southwestern United States.

2. Archaeological Approaches to Ceramics

Ceramics have played a central role in archaeological method and theory, for several reasons: (a) pottery has a long history, and is virtually ubiquitous in most sedentary societies; (b) pottery is nonperishable, and is often recovered in very large quantities from archaeological excavations; (c) pottery functioned both as utilitarian cooking, storage, and serving vessels for all strata of a society, as well as special purpose functions for elite ceremonial or funerary use; and, (d) as a highly plastic material, pottery displays seemingly infinite variation in composition, manufacturing method, shape, and decoration. These variations, moreover, were culturally conditioned, resulting in particular ceramic styles or traditions, which can be traced through time and space.

Early in the development of modern archaeology, scholars such as Flinders Petrie in Egypt, and somewhat later James Ford, Irving Rouse, and James Griffin in North America, recognized the value of ceramic studies in developing relative chronologies based on changes in ceramic style over time. Prior to the development of such absolute chronometric dating methods as radiocarbon or dendrochronology (see *Chronology, Stratigraphy, and Dating Methods in Archaeology*), the construction of ceramic chronologies were essential to developing local and regional time frames for prehistoric cultures.

With the rise of absolute dating methods in the second half of the twentieth century, archaeological studies of ceramics have shifted somewhat, with less emphasis on classification, seriation, and chronology construction, in favor of new approaches. These include detailed physical and chemical studies of ceramic composition and of production techniques and sequences, which inform archaeologists about the technology of ceramic production and use, and about the distribution and movement of ceramic vessels during their life spans. Such information in turn is useful to archaeologists who are attempting to understand prehistoric economic and sociopolitical organization.

2.1 Classification of Ceramics

As perhaps the most plastic of all material culture media known in antiquity, ceramics exhibit enormous variation—in fabric, methods of production, shape, decoration, and function—offering tremendous advantages as well as challenges to the archaeologist. In order to bring some order to this variability, archaeologists must classify pottery into sets of like objects (see *Classification and Typology (Archaeological Systematics)*). The aims and methods of ceramic classification, however, depend greatly upon the particular archaeological approach. For example, a classification which is aimed at the discovery of historical types, those which show meaningful variation over time, will most likely emphasize different aspects of variation from a classification designed to exhibit key differences in manufacturing process. The literature on archaeological classification of ceramics is vast, but useful overviews may be found in Shepard (1965), Rice (1987), and Sinopoli (1991).

Ceramic classifications may be based on a number of different kinds of variables, the most common being technological dimensions, vessel shape, and decoration. Classifications based on technological dimensions are especially useful when the aim is to understand production processes, although such dimensions may also be useful in the definition of historical types. Major technological dimensions include raw materials (especially clay and nonplastic inclusions such as mineral temper), methods of vessel forming (such as coiling or slab building, and the use of the potter's wheel), secondary treatments (such as the application of slips or glazes), and methods of firing (open air firing, use of kilns). Vessel shape may be classified formally according to various systems, such as that developed by Shepard (1965), which distinguishes between restricted and unrestricted vessels, and further between composite and inflected shapes. Vessel shape, naturally, is closely linked with vessel function. The third major category of variation used in ceramic classification is that of decoration and

surface treatment. Possible surface treatments include slipped, glazed, burnished, polished, paddle-impressed, and smoothed. Decorations may be applied by painting, stamping, incising, carving, or other methods, such as three-dimension appliqué or relief. Designs used in decorations typically consist of individual design elements, which are systematically organized into motifs and larger decorative panels, and generally follow culturally-determined rules. The classification and analysis of such design systems may be based on individual motif catalogs and set of design rules (e.g., Mead et al. 1965), or on analysis of underlying principles of symmetry (e.g., Washburn 1977).

Methods of ceramic classification also vary. Pottery producers have their own indigenous or folk classification systems, which have been the subject of considerable ethnoarchaeological study (see Sect. 2.4 below). Formal archaeological procedures for classifying pottery include the well-developed 'type-variety' system, first applied in North America and later extended to Mesoamerica. This system uses a 'binomial' nomenclature, in which a geographic name is combined with some specific technological descriptor (e.g., 'Barton incised'). Classification schemes range from simple paradigmatic classifications, to complex, hierarchical taxonomies. An alternative approach, much favored in the 1960s and 1970s, is quantitative or phenetic classification, in which 'types' are generated by a computer, following certain mathematical algorithms operating upon a number of qualitative and/or quantitative parameters. The prime example of such a numerical taxonomy of ceramics is that of Clarke (1970) for the Bell Beaker pottery complex of Great Britain.

2.2 Ceramics and Chronology

The emphasis accorded ceramic studies by archaeologists reflects the importance of using ceramic change as a means for constructing cultural chronologies. In the late nineteenth century, pioneering Egyptologist Flinders Petrie recognized that pottery vessels which had been placed in tomb groups as funerary objects showed subtle but continuous stylistic changes over time. Petrie arranged representative vessels in an inferred chronological sequence, resulting in the first seriation of pottery.

The methods of seriation were greatly refined by American archaeologists, such as Irving Rouse and James A. Ford (Ford 1962), working with ceramic assemblages from various New World localities, including the Mississippi Valley region, and the Viru Valley of Peru. Their work generated much debate concerning the methods of ceramic classification and the reality of ceramic 'types.' The fundamental principle of seriation was to define a set of historical types which displayed gradual temporal changes, with a particular type arising at some point in time, gradually increasing in popularity (hence reflected by increased frequency in archaeological assemblages), and later decreasing until the type disappeared from the archaeological record. When the frequencies of such historical types were plotted as percentage diagrams, they displayed a characteristic frequency distribution resembling the plan of a battleship, and hence were known as 'battleship curves.'

The great advantage of seriation was that it permitted the construction of cultural chronologies independent of any 'absolute' method of direct dating. Surface collections of potsherds from sites of unknown age could be tabulated according to the frequency of key ceramic types, and then chronologically ordered by arranging the frequency distributions to form 'battleship curves.' Moreover, local ceramic chronologies could be linked together using trade pottery which occurred in more than one region, or by tracing the diffusion of particular stylistic traits. With the invention of radiocarbon dating and other methods of 'absolute' dating in the later half of the twentieth century, the importance of seriation has declined, although it is still important as a cross-check on radiocarbon-based chronologies.

Pottery may also be directly dated, either by radiocarbon dating of organic inclusions within the ceramic fabric (i.e., dung or chaff included as temper), or by thermoluminescence (TL) dating. TL dating is based on the fact that when clay and other geological inclusions in pottery are fired at temperatures of $500\,°C$ or higher, electrons which had been 'trapped' in the crystal lattice structure are freed, emitting light or thermoluminescence. Following the firing process, new trapped electrons gradually accumulate in the crystalline imperfections of the pottery, as a natural consequence of radioactive decay. If ancient pottery is then reheated in the laboratory up to $500\,°C$, and the emitted light is measured and plotted as a 'glow curve' of intensity vs. temperature, the age of the specimen can be calculated, since the intensity of light emitted will be proportional to age. There are, of course, many possible complications deriving from the geological composition of the fabric, and from post-depositional conditions affecting the pottery. As a result, TL dating is less widely used than the radiocarbon method.

2.3 Compositional Studies

Within many ancient societies, pottery was produced by specialists who then traded, exchanged, or sold their wares to other nonpottery producing sectors of society, and/or to other villages or geographic localities. Moreover, pottery was frequently traded or exchanged over considerable distances. Tracing the production, distribution, and specialized use of pottery in ancient societies requires that the archaeologist be able to characterize the unique composition of a particular ceramic product, typically a mix of clay and other nonplastic inclusions (including purposefully added 'temper.') A key phase in archaeological pottery analysis is thus ceramic characterization (Bishop et al. 1982). Characterization may also include efforts at sourcing, in which the materials that make up a particular ceramic ware are traced to their geographic points of origin, such as local clay quarries or sources of sand used as temper.

A wide range of mineralogical and geo-chemical techniques have been applied to ceramic compositional analysis, whether for characterization or sourcing. Petrographic analysis of the nonplastic inclusions within a ceramic fabric, in which the specific mineral grains are identified by examining a thin section of the pottery under a polarizing microscope, is a widely used technique. X-ray diffraction, which identifies minerals by their crystalline structures, is another frequently applied method for the characterization of pottery on the basis on the temper or nonplastic inclusions. Other techniques which have been applied more recently include optical emission spectroscopy, X-ray fluorescence spectroscopy, atomic absorption spectroscopy, neutron activation analysis, proton-induced X-ray emission, Mössbauer spectroscopy, electronic microprobe analysis, and inductively-coupled plasma analysis (see Rice 1987 for a review of these and other methods).

2.4 Ethnoarchaeology and Ceramics

Given the importance of ceramics in archaeology, it is not surprising that archaeologists have turned to traditional pottery-making societies to learn more about potential variability in ceramic production, distribution, use, and discard. The study of contemporary peoples, using ethnographic methods of participant-observation, in order to gain knowledge of material culture variability which is potentially applicable to the interpretation of archaeological assemblages, is called ethnoarchaeology (see *Ethnoarchaeology*). Ceramic ethnoarchaeology (Kramer 1985) is perhaps one of them most important subfields within this topic.

Because archaeologists had long been concerned with the classification of ceramics, a number of ethnoarchaeological studies have focused on the ways in which traditional potters classified or categorized their own products. Indigenous potters typically pay little attention to the technological attributes often accorded emphasis by archaeologists (such as details of temper, paste, surface treatment, or decoration), but rather emphasize general function in their folk classifications. Thus, among the Kalinga of the Philippines, pottery vessels are distinguished by whether they are intended for cooking rice or for cooking vegetables and meat, and by their sizes (Longacre 1981). The Fulani of Cameroon (David and Hennig 1972) lexically discriminate among five size classes of jars, with secondary classification based on their intended contents.

Other ethnoarchaeological studies of pottery have focused on aspects of ceramic production, including the social role or status of potters in their societies, on ceramic distribution, on the use of vessels, their life spans, and on their breakage and discard rates (see Kramer 1985 for a general review). Such studies have aided archaeologists in their interpretations of ancient ceramics by revealing the complex linkages between behavior and material culture, demonstrating that strictly utilitarian explanations for archaeological phenomena are not always preferable, and by showing that multiple lines of evidence may help to discriminate between alternative explanations.

See also: Art: Anthropological Aspects; Art History; Chronology, Stratigraphy, and Dating Methods in Archaeology; Classification and Typology (Archaeological Systematics); Ethnoarchaeology; Intensification and Specialization, Archaeology of; Trade and Exchange, Archaeology of

Bibliography

Arnold D E 1985 *Ceramic Theory and Culture Process*. Cambridge University Press, Cambridge, UK
Bishop R L, Rands R L, Holley G R 1982 Ceramic compositional analysis in archaeological perspective. In: Schiffer M (ed.) *Advances in Archaeological Method and Theory*, Vol. 5. Academic Press, New York
Clarke D L 1970 *Beaker Pottery of Great Britain and Ireland*. Cambridge University Press, Cambridge, UK
David N, Hennig H 1972 *The Ethnography of Pottery: A Fulani Case Seen in Archaeological Perspective*. Addison-Wesley, Reading, MA
Deetz J 1965 *The Dynamics of Stylistic Change in Arikara Ceramics*. University of Illinois Press, Chicago
Ford J A 1962 *A Quantitative Method of Deriving Cultural Chronology*. Technical Manual No. 1. Pan American Union, Washington, DC
Kramer C 1985 Ceramic ethnoarchaeology. *Annual Review of Anthropology* 14: 77–120
Longacre W A 1981 Kalinga pottery, an ethnoarchaeological study. In: Hodder I, Issac G, Hammond N (eds.) *Pattern of the Past*. Cambridge University Press, Cambridge, UK
Mead S M, Birks L, Birks H, Shaw E 1975 *The Lapita Pottery Style of Fiji and its Associations*. Polynesian Society Memoir No. 38. Wellington (New Zealand)
Rice P M 1987 *Pottery Analysis: A Sourcebook*. University of Chicago Press, Chicago
Rye O S 1981 *Pottery Technology: Principles and Reconstruction*. Taraxacum, Inc., Washington, DC
Shepard A O 1965 *Ceramics for the Archaeologist*. Carnegie Institution of Washington Publication 609, Washington, DC
Sinopoli C M 1991 *Approaches to Archaeological Ceramics*. Plenum Press, New York
van der Leeuw S E, Pritchard A C (eds.) *The Many Dimensions of Pottery: Ceramics in Archaeology and Anthropology*. University of Amsterdam, Amsterdam
Washburn D K 1977 *A Symmetry Analysis of Upper Gila Area Ceramic Design*. Papers of the Peabody Museum of Anthropology and Archaeology, No. 68. Peabody Museum, Cambridge, UK

P. V. Kirch

Cerebellum: Associative Learning

Associative learning is behavioral change that accompanies the presentation of two or more stimuli at the same point in time or space. For many years, behavioral and neural scientists have studied associative learning in invertebrate and vertebrate species using standard classical and instrumental conditioning procedures in hopes of delineating neural circuits, brain structures, and brain systems that are involved in encoding learning and memory. In this article, the critical involvement of the cerebellum in associative learning is examined.

1. The Cerebellum and Classical Eyeblink Conditioning

Arguably the best-understood associative learning paradigm, from both behavioral and neurobiological perspectives, is classical conditioning of the eyeblink response. Briefly, a neutral stimulus such as a tone or light (the conditioned stimulus or CS) is presented just before an aversive stimulus such as a peri-orbital shock or corneal air puff (the unconditioned stimulus or US). Initially, the CS produces no overt movement while the US causes a reflexive eyeblink (the unconditioned response or UR). After 50–100 pairings of the CS and US, the CS begins to elicit a learned eyeblink (the conditioned response or CR). While most eyeblink conditioning experiments have involved rabbits as subjects, it appears that all mammals, including humans, learn this simple associative task at similar rates using similar brain circuitry.

For a variety of reasons that include (a) the relative simplicity of the response being monitored, (b) the great deal of control that the experimenter has over stimulus delivery, and (c) the precise timing of the learned response, this behavioral task has proven useful for delineating the neural circuitry involved in simple associative learning. Many experiments conducted since the early 1980s have demonstrated conclusively that the cerebellum contains a population of neurons that change their patterns of firing to encode the acquisition and performance of the classically conditioned eyeblink response—that is, the cerebellum's circuitry constitutes the essential learning and memory architecture for this basic associative learning procedure (see Woodruff-Pak and Steinmetz 2000, for review).

1.1 Lesion Experiments

The initial demonstrations of the involvement of the cerebellum in classical eyeblink conditioning were lesion experiments (e.g., McCormick and Thompson 1984). Lesions placed in the interpositus nucleus of the cerebellum prevented acquisition of eyeblink CRs and abolished previously learned CRs. Lavond et al. (1985) demonstrated the same lesion effect with infusions of kainic acid, which spared fibers of passage that course through or near the interpositus nucleus. Reversible lesions placed by cooling brain tissue (Clark and Lavond 1993) or injecting muscimol (Krupa et al. 1993) were also effective in abolishing CRs. Interestingly, when additional paired training was delivered without cooling or muscimol inactivation, the animals showed no savings in the rate of CR acquisition: they behaved as if they had received no previous paired training. These studies provide strong evidence that critical neuronal plasticity that underlies classical eyeblink conditioning occurs in the cerebellum.

Lesions of the cerebellar cortex have not produced as consistent results as interpositus nucleus lesions (e.g., Lavond and Steinmetz 1989). Cerebellar cortical lesions have reportedly caused retarded rates of CR acquisition, reduced CR amplitudes, or the appearance of mistimed CRs. These data indicate that the cerebellar cortex is involved in the conditioning process, but its precise role in conditioning or its interactions with the interpositus nucleus during conditioning are not well understood.

1.2 Recording Experiments

Electrophysiological recordings taken from cerebellar cortex and the interpositus nucleus have provided additional evidence for the involvement of the cerebellum in classical eyeblink conditioning (e.g., Berthier and Moore 1986, 1990). Recordings in regions of the cerebellum known to receive converging CS and US input have revealed neurons that discharge with patterns that seem to be encoding the conditioning process. Specifically, Purkinje cells were identified that discharged when the CS or US was presented. Other Purkinje cells either increased or decreased their rate of discharge in a pattern that seemed to be time-locked to execution of the behavioral CR. Purkinje cells that decreased their firing rates are particularly interesting because Purkinje cells are known to inhibit neurons in the deep cerebellar nuclei. Thus, a decrease in firing rate of a Purkinje cell could result in an increase in excitability of interpositus nucleus neurons, a result that is compatible with formation of a behavioral CR.

Similar to cerebellar cortex, neurons that developed discharge patterns highly correlated with CR performance were observed in the interpositus nucleus. Neurons that discharged to presentations of the CS and US were seen and, after learning, neurons that discharged in patterns that were time-locked with the behavioral CR were abundant. Interestingly, the onset of interpositus unit activity preceded the behavioral response by 30–60 milliseconds. These important observations provide strong evidence that *cellular activity in the interpositus nucleus is the neural substrate of the behavioral CR that is observed*. It is thought that CR-related activity generated in the interpositus nucleus activated neurons in the red nucleus which, in turn, activate neurons in the brainstem motor nuclei that are responsible for generating eyeblinks.

1.3 CS and US Pathways

Using stimulation, recording and lesion methods (e.g., Steinmetz et al. 1989), the putative pathways for projecting CS and US information from the periphery to the cerebellum have been delineated. It appears that a tone CS is projected from the ear to the cochlear nuclei which, in turn, relays tone information to the basilar pontine nuclei. The pontine nuclei then project information about the CS to the cerebellum along mossy fibers. On the US side, air puffs are known to activate corneal receptors that send projections to the trigeminal nucleus. The trigeminal nucleus, in turn, projects information about the US to the rostromedial portion of the dorsal accessory inferior olive. Climbing fibers that originate from the inferior olive then relay information about the occurrence of the US to the cerebellum.

1.4 The Cerebellum as an Associator

There is ample evidence from anatomy, electrophysiology, lesion, and microstimulation experiments that information concerning the occurrences of the CS and US converges on populations of neurons in the cerebellum. The leading models of the involvement of the cerebellum in classical eyeblink conditioning postulate that CS–US inputs converge in two locations— the interpositus nucleus and cerebellar cortex (e.g., Steinmetz 2000). Changes in the excitability of cortical and nuclear neurons, produced by convergent CS and US inputs, are thought to form the cellular bases for the learning and performance of the classically conditioned eyeblink response. In essence, the cerebellar circuitry serves as an 'associator' for discrete stimuli that are presented in the environment. This idea is certainly not new. Computational neurobiologists such as Marr (1969) have long considered the architecture of the cerebellum to be ideal for associating environmental information with teaching or reinforcing inputs. Further, models such as those of Marr have hypothesized that mossy fibers and climbing fibers serve as the environmental and teaching inputs, respectively. This architecture maps very nicely onto the known neural circuitry involved in eyeblink conditioning where the CS appears to be carried along mossy fibers and the US appears to be carried along climbing fibers.

The previous models do not, however, predict a role for the deep cerebellar nuclei in the associative learning process; rather they postulate that the deep nuclei are passive recipients of outflow from cerebellar cortex. The data collected using eyeblink conditioning suggest differently. The nuclei appear to receive convergent CS–US input, the nuclei show neuronal responses that are related to conditioning, and the reversible lesion experiments of Clark and Lavond (1993) and Krupa et al. (1993) suggest that critical cellular plasticity related to conditioning occurs in the nuclei. At this time, the most parsimonious explanation of the available data suggest that critical plasticity that underlies classical eyeblink conditioning occurs both in cerebellar cortex and in the deep cerebellar nuclei. It has been suggested that these two areas may encode different features of the conditioning, with excitability changes in nuclear cells important for generating activity that drives brainstem motor neurons responsible for eyeblink CRs, and excitability in cortical cells important for providing gain on the response and for regulating the timing of the response (e.g., Gould and Steinmetz 1996, Steinmetz 2000).

2. The Cerebellum and Other Associative Learning Paradigms

There are surprisingly few other demonstrations of the involvement of the cerebellum in associative learning. This is likely not due to a general lack of involvement of the structure in this type of learning (although see below for some limitations on cerebellar involvement in associative learning) but rather that few experiments have been conducted to explore the involvement of the cerebellum in associative learning tasks. Two exceptions are briefly described here; adaptation of the vestibulo–ocular reflex (VOR) and instrumental signaled bar-press conditioning.

2.1 Adaptation of the VOR

The VOR is a brain system used to stabilize a visual image on the retina during movement. In this reflex,

rotations of the head are detected by semicircular canals located in the inner ear, and the eyes are moved in their sockets in the direction opposite to the movement of the head. This reflex stabilizes the line of sight. The VOR is highly plastic as the gain of the reflex can be changed easily to accommodate changes in the strength or efficiency of the extraocular muscles to deal with changing levels of vestibular activation. In many respects, this can be considered to be an associative learning procedure as it is known that gain-setting of the VOR is dependent on two events: vestibular input from the semicircular canals and visual information (the relative slippage of the visual image on the retina during head movements) to determine if a change in VOR gain is needed. Over the years, a variety of studies have implicated the cerebellum and associated brainstem structures in adaptation of the VOR (Ito 1984, Lisberger 1988). In a similar way to classical eyeblink conditioning, it appears that neuronal plasticity that forms the basis of VOR adaptation occurs in discrete regions of the cerebellar cortex and in brainstem nuclei (the vestibular nuclei) that receive convergent input from the vestibular and visual systems.

Critical involvement of the cerebellum has also been demonstrated for an instrumental conditioning task that has some similarities to classical eyeblink conditioning (Steinmetz et al. 1993). In this task, rats are first shaped to press a bar to terminate a mild, pulsating foot-shock. After learning the bar-press response, the rats are placed in a signaled-training situation where they learn to avoid the foot-shocks by pressing the response bar during tone presentations. Rats reach 50–60 percent avoidance rates with about 10–12 days of training in this procedure. This associative task is somewhat similar to classical eyeblink conditioning in that a neutral stimulus (a tone) is used to signal an impending noxious stimulus (a mild foot-shock). Bilateral lesions of the dentate and interpositus nuclei in rats prevented learning of this avoidance response. Escape responding was initially high in lesioned rats, but this responding decreased over sessions. Interestingly, deep nuclear lesions seem to be effective in preventing avoidance learning only when the interval between tone onset and foot-shock onset is five seconds or less.

3. When is the Cerebellum Critical for Simple Associative Learning?

Another way to frame this question is to ask: when is the cerebellum *not* involved in associative learning? A number of experiments have addressed this issue.

First, the cerebellum appears to be necessary for associative learning when the interval of time between the stimuli being associated is relatively short. Classical eyeblink conditioning can only be obtained when the CS–US interval is 3–4 seconds or less. Longer

CS–US intervals do not produce eyeblink CRs, although a variety of other conditioned responses can be elicited. Adaptation of the VOR requires near-simultaneous occurrences of head rotation and retinal slip. As detailed above, signaled bar-press conditioning seems to be critically dependent on cerebellar function only when relatively short CS–US intervals are used. Avoidance conditioning is relatively easy to obtain with longer tone–foot-shock intervals, but cerebellar lesions appear to have no effect on these learned responses—suggesting that other brain areas are critical for active avoidance learning when intervals between the stimuli are relatively long. These observations are highly consistent with what is known about the role of the cerebellum in movement and posture—the cerebellum is intricately involved in making fine adjustments to ongoing movements during relatively brief periods of time (often referred to as movement error-correction).

Second, and related to the first point, the cerebellum seems to be critical for associative learning that involves relatively simple, discrete skeletal muscle responses. Conditioned eyeblinks, VOR adaptation, and conditioned bar-press responses require the rapid recruitment of relatively few muscles, especially when the time period allowed for responding is relatively brief. The idea that cerebellar involvement in learning may be limited by response requirements has been tested (Steinmetz et al. 1991). Rabbits were trained in two tasks: classical eyeblink conditioning, and a discriminative avoidance procedure. In the discriminative avoidance procedure, rabbits were presented with a tone and required to locomote in an activity wheel to avoid a foot-shock that was presented after the tone onset. Bilateral lesions of the interpositus nucleus of the cerebellum prevented acquisition of the conditioned eyeblink response and abolished already learned eyeblink CRs, but had no effect on the acquisition or performance of the discriminative avoidance response. While the discriminative wheel-turn avoidance task differs from eyeblink conditioning on several dimensions (e.g., it involves discrimination learning and uses a longer interstimulus interval), one of the major differences between paradigms lies in the response requirements (discrete eyeblink vs. a relatively complex, bipedal, locomotive response). Lavond and colleagues (1985) have also shown that the conditioned changes in heart-rate that are normally observed during classical eyeblink conditioning are not affected by cerebellar lesions. These data suggest that the encoding of autonomic responses during associative learning involves areas outside of the cerebellum, a finding that is compatible with a number of other studies. Together, these data suggest that the cerebellum may be involved in associative learning when relatively discrete skeletal muscle responses are conditioned.

Third, there is evidence that the cerebellum is not involved in encoding associative reward learning (i.e., learning that involves reinforcement). The rats described above that showed severe deficits in learning to avoid the signaled foot-shock after cerebellar lesions (Steinmetz et al. 1993) were trained in an appetitive version of the task. In the appetitive version of the task, a tone was presented for a 3–5 second period, and a bar press resulted in the delivery of food pellet reward. The cerebellar-lesioned rats easily learned the appetitive task even though they showed a complete inability to learn the aversively motivated task. In a more direct comparison of appetitive and aversive classical conditioning, Gibbs (1992) trained rabbits on two classical conditioning tasks before delivering lesions to the interpositus nucleus of the cerebellum. One task was standard classical eyeblink conditioning (an aversive task), while the second task was classical jaw-movement conditioning (an appetitive task). Jaw-movement conditioning involves pairing a tone CS with the delivery of water or juice (the US) into the mouth. The water or juice causes a movement of the jaw as the rabbit consumes the liquid. Several pairings of the CS and US produce an anticipatory jaw movement to the tone (the CR). Gibbs showed that in this within-subject experiment, lesions of the cerebellar deep nuclei abolished eyeblink conditioning but had no effect on jaw-movement conditioning. These data suggest that the cerebellum is involved in encoding aversively motivated associative learning but not appetitively motivated associative learning. This suggestion is not surprising given the large body of research that has detailed the involvement of forebrain structures and circuits in reward learning.

4. The Cerebellum and Associative Learning

For several years, theorists who have speculated about the function of the cerebellum have noted that the basic anatomy and architecture of the cerebellum seems to be designed for associative learning. The cerebellum receives inputs through two separate and unique systems of fibers: mossy fibers and climbing fibers, and a growing body of evidence suggests that plasticity in cerebellar neurons may be due to associative interactions that occur between these inputs. Further, classical eyeblink conditioning seems to be an ideal associative learning paradigm for studying the involvement of the cerebellum in associative learning. This procedure involves the conditioning of discrete responses, involves the presentation of an aversive or noxious US, and involves a relatively brief period of time between the presentation of the stimuli being associated. In essence, the classical eyeblink conditioning procedure could be considered the prototypical learning paradigm for engaging the cerebellum during associative learning. Further studies into cellular and systems-level cerebellar processes engaged during classical eyeblink conditioning should provide valuable data concerning the general role of the cerebellum in associating two or more external stimuli or internal events in time.

See also: Cerebellum: Cognitive Functions; Classical Conditioning, Neural Basis of; Electroencephalography: Basic Principles and Applications; Electroencephalography: Clinical Applications; Eyelid Classical Conditioning; Long-term Depression (Cerebellum); Topographic Maps in the Brain; Vestibuloocular Reflex, Adaptation of the

Bibliography

Berthier N E, Moore J W 1986 Cerebellar Purkinje cell activity related to the classically conditioned nictitating membrane response. *Experimental Brain Research* **63**: 341–50

Berthier N E, Moore J W 1990 Activity of deep cerebellar nuclear cells during classical conditioning of nictitating membrane extension in rabbits. *Experimental Brain Research* **83**: 44–54

Clark R E, Lavond D G 1993 Reversible lesions of the red nucleus during acquisition and retention of a classically conditioned behavior in rabbits. *Behavioral Neuroscience* **107**: 264–70

Gibbs C M 1992 Divergent effects of deep cerebellar lesions on two different conditioned somatomotor responses in rabbits. *Brain Research* **585**: 395–9

Gould T J, Steinmetz J E 1996 Changes in rabbit cerebellar cortical and interpositus nucleus activity during acquisition, extinction and backward classical conditioning. *Neurobiology of Learning and Memory* **65**: 17–34

Ito M 1984 *The Cerebellum and Neural Control*. Raven Press, New York

Krupa D J, Thompson J K, Thompson R F 1993 Localization of a memory trace in the mammalian brain. *Science* **260**: 989–91

Lavond D G, Hembree T L, Thompson R F 1985 Effect of kainic acid lesions of the cerebellar interpositus nucleus on eyelid conditioning in the rabbit. *Brain Research* **326**: 179–82

Lavond D G, Lincoln J S, McCormick D A, Thompson R F 1984 Effect of bilateral lesions of the dentate and interpositus cerebellar nuclei on conditioning of heart-rate and nictitating membrane/eyelid responses in the rabbit. *Brain Research* **305**: 323–30

Lavond D G, Steinmetz J E 1989 Acquisition of classical conditioning without cerebellar cortex. *Behavioral Brain Research* **33**: 113–64

Lisberger S G 1988 The neural basis of learning of simple motor skills. *Science* **242**: 728–35

Marr D 1969 A theory of cerebellar cortex. *Journal of Physiology* **202**: 437–70

McCormick D A, Thompson R F 1984 Cerebellum: essential involvement in the classically conditioned eyelid response. *Science* **223**: 296–9

Steinmetz J E 2000 Brain substrates of classical eyeblink conditioning: A highly localized but also distributed system. *Behavioral Brain Research* **110**: 13–24

Steinmetz J E, Lavond D G, Thompson R F 1989 Classical conditioning in rabbits using pontine nucleus stimulation as a conditioned stimulus and inferior olive stimulation as an unconditioned stimulus. *Synapse* **3**: 225–33

Steinmetz J E, Logue S F, Miller D P 1993 Using signaled bar-pressing tasks to study the neural substrates of appetitive and aversive learning in rats: Behavioral manipulations and cerebellar lesions. *Behavioral Neuroscience* **107**: 941–54

Steinmetz J E, Sears L L, Gabriel M, Kubota Y, Poremba A 1991 Cerebellar interpositus nucleus lesions disrupt classical nictitating membrane conditioning but not discriminative avoidance learning in rabbits. *Behavioral Brain Research* **45**: 71–80

Woodruff-Pak D S, Steinmetz J E (eds.) 2000 *Eyeblink Classical Conditioning: Animal Models*. Kluwer, Boston

J. E. Steinmetz

Cerebellum: Cognitive Functions

In the nineteenth century, researchers reached a consensus on the basis of animal ablation experiments that damage to the cerebellum leads to motor disorders but does not affect sensory or cognitive functions. In the early twentieth century Stewart and Holmes (1904) demonstrated that cerebellar lesions resulting from tumors or gunshots elicit comparable motor deficits in humans such as reduction of muscle tone, impairment of movement coordination, and deficits in the regulation of gait and posture. Voluntary movement control is severely affected, the main symptom being a disturbance of movement coordination (ataxia) which may affect the control of limb muscles and ocular muscles as well as speech control. In the view of clinical neurology, the cerebellum was thus thought to be exclusively engaged in the control of motor activity.

In the 1950s, however, a broader concept of cerebellar function was suggested, with a possible cerebellar involvement in the control of autonomic and limbic activity. Clinical observations made an important contribution to this broader concept (for a summary see Daum and Ackermann 1995). Congenital cerebellar malformations, for example, were found to be associated not only with ataxia, balance problems, and other motor deficits, but also with mental retardation. In addition, disorders such as schizophrenia and autism were related to neuropathological abnormalities of the cerebellum. The hypothesis of a cerebellar involvement in the control of emotions was further supported by findings of a modulation of fear and aggression by cerebellar stimulation for the control of epileptic seizures.

More recent concepts of cerebellar function were influenced by reports of two-way connections between the cerebellum and the cerebral cortex, findings of cognitive deficits in patients with cerebellar dysfunction, and neuroimaging reports of cerebellar activation during a range of cognitive tasks (Schmahmann 1997).

1. Anatomy of the Cerebellum

Like the cerebrum, the cerebellum consists of two hemispheres. Three functional regions can be distinguished: the centrally located vermis (Latin 'worm') and the lateral and intermediate zones in each hemisphere. Mossy fibers are the major afferents to the cerebellum, receiving their input from brain stem nuclei and spinal chord neurons. The climbing fibers, which are the second excitatory input to the cerebellum, originate from a single site in the medulla and the inferior olivary nucleus. Efferent projections are mediated by the Purkinje cells and the deep nuclei.

There are several reciprocal pathways between the cerebellum and the cerebral cortex. The cerebellum receives input via pontine nuclei from the parietal cortex, the prefrontal cortex, and the superior temporal sulcus. The cerebellum projects back to the same regions via the thalamus (Schmahmann 1997). These afferent and efferent projections imply a possible role of the cerebellum in the modification of information which is projected from the cortex to the cerebellum and sent back to the cortex.

2. Motor Learning and Motor Imagery

It is well known that the cerebellum plays a critical role in motor control, with the lateral regions of the cerebellum mediating movement planning and programing, while the medial regions are involved in the execution of movement (Dichgans and Diener 1984).

Imaging studies using positron emission tomography have also demonstrated a cerebellar role during motor learning of sequential finger movements as well as in trajectorial learning. In addition, the cerebellum was found to contribute to the monitoring and optimizing of movements by using sensory (proprioceptive) feedback (Jueptner and Weiler 1998).

Motor skill learning describes the qualitative improvement of performance through practice which ensures that movements can be performed fast, accurately, and with little attentional control. Electrophysiological and lesion studies in nonhuman primates with cerebellar hemispherectomies have demonstrated the critical contribution of the cerebellum at a stage of motor learning when performance becomes fast and accurate. Similar results were observed in patients with cerebellar dysfunction, who had problems in learning the skillful execution of serial movements (Doyon 1997).

The most frequently used motor learning paradigm is classical conditioning of the eyeblink response. An acoustic stimulus, the conditioned stimulus (CS), is paired with a corneal airpuff, the unconditioned stimulus (US), which evokes an eyeblink. After repeated pairing of the CS and the US, the eyeblink occurs to the CS but before onset of the airpuff and thereby forms a conditioned response (CR). The essential neuronal circuitry involves the convergence of CS and US information in the cerebellum and an efferent projection from the cerebellum to motor nuclei in the brain stem, which control eyeblink responses (see Thompson 1991). Patients with cerebellar dysfunction are severely impaired at acquiring eyeblink CRs, although the reflex blink to the US is unaffected. Conditioning of simultaneously recorded nonmotor autonomic and electrocortical responses are also intact (Daum et al. 1993a). The critical involvement of the cerebellum in the conditioning of motor responses has now been documented by a large number of clinical investigations, functional neuroimaging studies, and studies of physiological manipulations of cerebellar functions in normal subjects (for a summary see Schugens et al. 2000).

In motor imagery, a motor program that is stored elsewhere in the CNS is activated without any overt movement. There is some evidence that the cerebellum becomes active during motor imagery, in tasks such as silent counting and imagination of tennis training movements (Decety et al. 1990).

3. Timing

The notion that the cerebellum computes timing requirements for motor performance is supported by investigations in animals, as well as by clinical data (Keele and Ivry 1991). Keele and Ivry have argued that the lateral regions of the cerebellum are critically involved in the internal timing of motor and nonmotor behavior which requires temporal computation. They attributed the deficits in classical conditioning of cerebellar patients to problems in timing the initiation of the CR. This hypothesis is supported by the finding of an inappropriately timed CR reported by Daum et al. (1993a) and by Topka et al. (1993). Key symptoms of cerebellar symptoms, such as dysmetria (problems with precise movements) or dysdiadochokinesia (problems with fluent alternating movements), can also be interpreted within the context of deficient cerebellar timing functions. Further support for this idea stems from impairments in rhythmic tapping in cerebellar patients (Ivry et al. 1988) as well as from deficits in speech production, which reflects a decline in temporal coordination of neuromuscular interaction needed for articulation (Ackermann and Ziegler 1992). Impairments of speech perception are also consistent with the idea of a timing deficit in the nonmotor domain (Ackermann et al. 1999).

4. Cognitive Functions

The results of developmental dysfunction, such as cerebellar agenesis (absence of the cerebellum) or cerebellar hypoplasia (prenatal developmental deficits which result in loss or incomplete cerebellar development), varies from congenital apraxia to normal motor abilities. Similarly, cognitive development can range from profound mental retardation to normal status. Intellectual deficits after delayed motor development may be due to a close coupling of motor and intellectual functions in early life.

Performance of patients with cerebellar dysfunctions on standard intelligence tests is generally in the normal range. Short- and long-term declarative memory as well as priming effects are also largely unaffected in patients with cerebellar lesions (for a summary see Daum and Ackermann 1997).

With respect to skill learning, it has been argued that the neocortex may be primarily concerned with the generation/processing of specific operations, while the cerebellum serves to modulate and optimize the functions in question (Ito 1993). In support of this idea, cerebellar damage was associated with deficits in the automatization of visuomotor sequences and visuomotor skill learning (Doyon et al. 1998). As far as nonmotor skill learning is concerned, performance of patients with cerebellar dysfunction on standard perceptual and cognitive skill acquisition was largely unimpaired (Daum et al. 1993a, Helmuth et al. 1997). The acquisition and performance of language skills may be more difficult for such patients (Fiez et al. 1992); and cerebellar activations during such tasks may be related to verbal response search (Desmond et al. 1998).

The anatomical as well as functional relationship between the cerebellum and the prefrontal cortex (Kim et al. 1994) led to the investigation of cognitive functions that are thought to be associated with prefrontal or executive function. Performance on anticipatory planning tasks was found to be impaired in patients with cerebellar atrophy in some studies (Grafman et al. 1992, Hallett and Grafman 1997). Verbal fluency abilities are also associated with executive processing. In such tasks, subjects are asked to name as many items as possible of a certain semantic category or starting with a certain letter within a specific time limit. Patients with cerebellar damage may occasionally show problems with word generation tasks of this kind (Fiez et al. 1992). Such problems may, however, be influenced by slowing of speech ('dysarthria') which is a frequent symptom of cerebellar damage. This motor speech slowing may interfere with the execution of verbal fluency tasks, and lead to poorer performance in some cases.

While cerebellar activation is observed in functional neuroimaging during performance of the Wisconsin Card Sorting Test, a standard test of concept formation, perseverative tendencies do not usually occur in cerebellar patients (Daum and Ackermann 1997, Hallett and Grafman 1997). By contrast, cerebellar lesion patients had problems in attentional shifting between modalities (Akshoomhoff et al. 1992). This pattern might be explained by impaired cerebellar–prefrontal interaction where 'prefrontal' activation,

which would be associated with changing attentional behavior, is deficient due to cerebellar dysfunction.

Two-way cerebellar-parietal projections led to the investigation of visuospatial abilities that are mediated by the parietal cortex. The studies carried out so far yielded no clear evidence of a general impairment of visuospatial functions in patients with cerebellar dysfunction. Findings of difficulties of such patients with the mental manipulation of three-dimensional objects in space offers some evidence of a visuospatial processing deficit consistent with possible dysfunction of cerebellar–parietal circuits (Wallesch and Horn 1984).

5. Conclusion

In summary, the cerebellum makes an important contribution to the control of voluntary movement and movement coordination as well as to the control of balance, gait, and posture. Motor learning abilities are also largely dependent upon the functional integrity of the cerebellum. There is also strong evidence for a cerebellar role as an 'internal clock' which comes into play during the control of movement as well as during perceptual processing.

The exact nature of the cerebellar involvement in cognitive processes is so far less well understood. Possible contributions to prefrontal or executive functions and visuospatial processing remain to be specified by studies using patients with selective cerebellar lesions, adequately clinical and nonclinical matched control groups, and the use of a wide range of tests assessing different aspects of the abilities in question. Functional neuroimaging techniques also provide a good tool to study the cerebellar contribution to different cognitive abilities. A problem of imaging techniques is, however, that it is difficult to determine which brain area is critically involved in which aspects of cognitive processing, since essential and correlated activity cannot be easily distinguished. A combination of imaging techniques and transcranial magnetic stimulation, which elicits a transient lesion, may be a promising approach in this regard.

See also: Habituation; Motor Control Models: Learning and Performance; Motor Cortex; Prefrontal Cortex

Bibliography

Ackermann H, Graber S, Hertrich I, Daum I 1999 Cerebellar contributions to the perception of temporal cues within the speech and nonspeech. *Brain Lang.* **67**(3): 228–41

Ackermann H, Ziegler W 1992 Die cerebelläre Dysarthrie: Eine Literaturübersicht. *Fortschr. Neurol. Psychiat.* **60**: 28–40

Akshoomhoff N, Courchesne E, Press G, Iragui V 1992 Contribution of the cerebellum to neuropsychological functioning: Evidence from a case of cerebellar degenerative disorder. *Neuropsychologia* **30**: 315–28

Daum I, Ackermann H 1995 Cerebellar contributions to cognition. *Behavioural Brain Research* **67**: 201–10

Daum I, Ackermann H 1997 Neuropsychological abnormalities in cerebellar syndromes fact or fiction? In: Schmahmann J D (ed.) *The Cerebellum and Cognition.* Academic Press, San Diego, CA

Daum I, Ackermann H, Schugens M M, Reimold C, Dichgans J, Birbaumer N 1993a The cerebellum and cognitive functions in humans. *Behavioral Neuroscience* **107**: 411–9

Daum I, Schugens M M, Ackermann H, Lutzenberger W, Dichgans J, Birbaumer N 1993b Classical conditioning after cerebellar lesions in humans. *Behavioral Neuroscience* **107**: 748–56

Decety J, Sjöholm H, Ryding E, Sternberg G, Ingvar D H 1990 The cerebellum participates in mental activity: Tomographic measurements of regional cerebral blood flow. *Brain Research* **535**: 313–7

Desmond J E, Gabrieli J D E, Glover G H 1998 Dissociation of frontal and cerebellar activity in a cognitive task: Evidence for a distinction between selection and search. *Neuroimage* **7**: 368–76

Dichgans J, Diener H C 1984 Clinical evidence for functional compartmentalisation of the cerebellum. In: Bloedel J, Dichgans J, Precht W (eds.) *Cerebellar Functions.* Springer, Berlin, pp. 126–47

Doyon J 1997 Skill learning. Schmahmann J D (ed.) *The Cerebellum and Cognition. International Review of Neurobiology* **41**: 273–96

Doyon J, Laforce R Jr, Bouchard G, Gaudreau D, Roy J, Poirier M, Bedard P J, Bedard F, Bouchard J P 1998 Role of the striatum, cerebellum, and frontal lobes in the automatization of a repeated visuomotor sequence of movements. *Neuropsychologia* **36**: 625–41

Fiez J A, Petersen S E, Cheney M K, Raichle M E 1992 Impaired nonmotor learning and error detection associated with cerebellar damage. *Brain* **115**: 155–73

Grafman J, Litvan I, Massaquoi S, Stewart M, Sirigu A, Hallet M 1992 Cognitive planning deficits in patients with cerebellar atrophy. *Neurology* **42**: 1493–96

Hallet M, Grafman J 1997 The cerebellum and cognition: Executive function and motor skill learning. *International Review of Neurobiology* **41**: 297–323

Helmuth L L, Ivry R B, Shimizu N 1997 Preserved performance by cerebellar patients on tests of word generation, discrimination learning, and attention. *Learning and Memory* **3**(6): 456–74

Ito M 1993 Movement and thought: Identical control mechanisms by the cerebellum. *Trends in Neurosciences* **16**: 448–50

Ivry R B, Keele S W, Diener H C 1988 Dissociation of the lateral and medial cerebellum in movement timing and movement execution. *Experimental Brain Research* **73**: 167–80

Jueptner M, Weiler C 1998 A review of differences between basal ganglia and cerebellar control of movements as revealed by functional imaging studies. *Brain* **121**(8): 1437–49

Keele S W, Ivry R 1991 Does the cerebellum provide a common computation for diverse tasks. A timing hypothesis. *Annals of New York Academy of Sciences* **608**: 179–211

Kim S G, Ugurbil K, Strick P L 1994 Activation of a cerebellar output nucleus during cognitive processing. *Science* **265**: 949–51

Schugens M M, Topka H R, Daum I 2000 Eyeblink conditioning in neurological patients with motor impairments. In: Woodruff-Pak D S, Steinmetz J E (eds.) *Eyeblink Classical Conditioning: Vol. I Applications in Humans.* Kluwer Academic Publishers, Boston

Schmahmann J D (ed.) 1997 *The Cerebellum and Cognition. International Review of Neurobiology* Vol. 41

Stewart T G, Holmes G 1904 Symptomatology of cerebellar tumors: A study of forty cases. *Brain* **27**: 522–91

Thompson R F 1991 Are memory traces localized or distributed? *Neuropsychologia* **29**: 571–82

Topka H, Valls-Sole J, Massaquoi S G, Hallet M 1993 Deficit in classical conditioning in patients with cerebellar degeneration. *Brain* **116**: 961–9

Wallesch C W, Horn A 1984 Long-term effects of cerebellar pathology on cognitive functions. *Brain and Cognition* **14**: 19–25

B. Suchan and I. Daum

Cerebral Cortex: Organization and Function

If it is possible to distinguish a hierarchy of complexity in behavior, ranging from the simplest reflex to the so-called cognitive functions, and if behavior is related to the structural organization of the brain, there is no doubt that the cerebral cortex corresponds to the highest levels. The main reasons for this generally accepted notion are the following: (a) the cerebral cortex is not only the largest piece of cerebral gray matter in humans and in other mammals, but it is also the one with the most impressive system of internal connections, suggesting an essentially global operation; (b) there are good reasons to believe that most of the connections between cortical neurons are of the 'plastic' kind, i.e., they are modified through learning and thus incorporate knowledge about the world; and (c) lesions of the cerebral cortex often impair behavior in a realm that clearly belongs to the psychological level, such as language, orientation, and perception. This pre-eminence of the cerebral cortex in the control of complex behavior can be related to some of its anatomical and physiological peculiarities.

1. The Structural Type of the Cortex

The term cortex defines a class of brain structures characterized by an essentially two-dimensional layout. A 'vertical' organization along the 'thickness' of the cortex is repeated almost identically throughout the 'plane' of the cortex. The thickness of the cerebral cortex in humans varies between about 2 and 4mm (in the mouse 1mm) while in the plane the cortex of one hemisphere covers an area of about 1000cm² (in the mouse about 1cm²). Besides the cerebral cortex of mammals, the cerebellar cortex, the optic tectum, and many other structures of vertebrate and invertebrate brains are built according to a similar two-dimensional

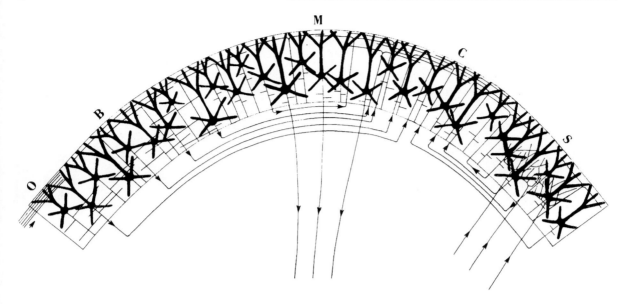

Figure 1
The basic connectivity of the cortex. Its most numerous neuronal contingent is pyramidal cells, connected into an excitatory network both locally by a rich system of axon collaterals (indicated in B) and over longer distances via the white matter beneath the cortex, terminating mainly in the upper cortical layers (indicated in C). M: primary motor cortex with axons going to the spinal cord, S: primary sensory area, receiving afferent fibers from a sensory system (via the thalamus). O: olfactory region at the edge of the cortex. From Braitenberg (1977) *On the Texture of Brains*. Springer, Berlin

scheme. What they all have in common is a diffuse projection of inputs over the whole plane, which is transformed by a unitary operation, varying from cortex to cortex, into the output. In many places the plane of the 'cortex' represents point to point some external input space such as the visual field or the surface of the body. Also, at every point of the cortical plane, output fibers leave the cortex to reach a variety of destinations, including other parts of the cortex itself. In the cerebral cortex of mammals both input and output fiber systems are on the same side of the cortical plane, forming the so-called 'hemispheric white matter' (with some minor exceptions in a marginal region, where the olfactory input enters the cortex in the uppermost layer, see olfactory input O in Fig. 1). In addition to the cortico-cortical fibers, sensory input fibers and motor output fibers shown in Fig. 1, the white matter contains a diffuse system of cortical fibers reaching the basal ganglia, as well as a system of two-way connections between cortex and thalamus.

2. Layers

As in other cortices, the input from distant places reaches the cerebral cortex predominantly at a special level of the cortical thickness. Similarly, the output to other parts of the brain takes its origin from another level. This distinction of input and output levels, together with the levels where most of the internal traffic of the cortex takes place, is at the origin of the well-known laminar structure of the cerebral cortex. The most common distinction is one of six layers, numbered (usually by Roman numerals) from the top down (from the free surface to the white matter). The most characteristic features of the various layers with respect to input and output are the following: the upper layers, layers I to III, are devoted to communication between distant parts of the cortex within or between hemispheres. Layer IV is the level at which sensory input fibers terminate (relayed from the thalamus), or fibers mostly from other parts of the cortex directly relaying such inputs. Layer V sends fibers to the basal ganglia and to distant parts of the brain or to the spinal cord. Layer VI communicates with the uppermost layers, as well as with the thalamus.

All of these statements are only statistically valid: a certain amount of thalamic fibers can also reach layers I, III, and VI, and layers IV to VI also participate to a certain degree in cortico-cortical communication. In spite of this, the distinction of the layers also gains support in the appearance of histological sections through the cortex. When the neural cell bodies are stained, the layers differ both in the number and the size of the neurons they contain. They also differ in the

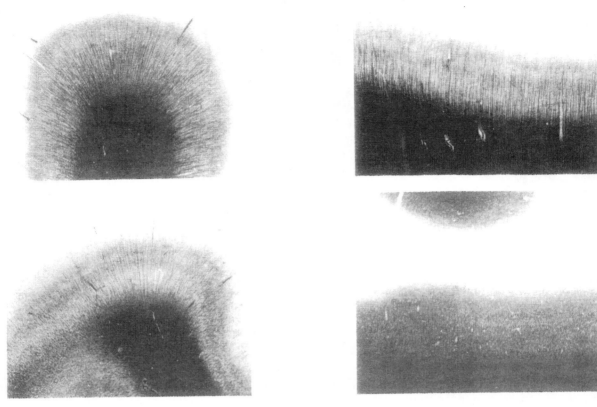

Figure 2
Examples of myeloarchitectonic differences between areas in the human cortex. Both stripes of Baillarger can be seen in the upper right (middle frontal gyrus) and lower left (Broca region), only the outer stripe can be recognized in the upper left (upper frontal gyrus) and both of them disappear in the strong myelination of the primary motor cortex (lower right). From: Braitenberg and Schüz (1989) Cortex: hohe Ordnung oder größtmögliches Durcheinander? *Spektrum der Wissenschaft* **5**: 74–86

density of fibers in myelin preparations (Fig. 2). These differences are certainly related to the different roles the layers play in cortical information handling.

The complexity of interactions both within and between layers can be appreciated by staining individual neurons in their entirety, for example with the time-honored Golgi method or with the modern techniques of intracellular injection of dyes. These methods show cortical neurons as three-dimensional devices which collect signals in the region of their dendritic trees and distribute them in the region (or regions) of their axonal terminations. The diameters of axonal and dendritic trees greatly exceed (by a factor of 10 to 100 or more) the distance between the corresponding cell bodies in the tissue. The result is an extremely dense felt of cell processes in which each neuron is interwoven with about 100,000 other neurons. Taking this into account, it follows that the

borders between the layers cannot be as sharp as they sometimes appear in textbook diagrams, since they are always crossed by dendrites and axons of many neurons in adjoining, and even more distant layers (Fig. 1).

3. Types of Neurons in the Cortex

The pattern of axonal and dendritic ramifications varies a great deal between individual neurons, depending on their localization in different layers and in different parts of the cortex. This led to the classification of a great number of neuronal types, where one overriding distinction is now accepted by most authors, that of the spiny neurons (often subsumed under the term pyramidal cells or Type I neurons), and of the spineless neurons (often subsumed under the term stellate or Type II neurons). This distinction is supported by differences in the fine structure of membrane specializations as they appear in the electron microscope both on the dendritic and axonal tree, and by electrophysiological findings. Briefly, spiny neurons receive most of their synaptic input on 'spines,' i.e., small processes emanating from the dendritic tree, and make 'excitatory' synapses onto other neurons via their axonal tree. Spineless neurons receive their synapses directly on their dendrites and 'inhibit' other neurons via their axonal tree. This distinction coincides with another anatomical feature: most spiny neurons have an axon which descends to the white matter and makes both, 'short-range connections' via local axon collaterals and 'long-range connections' somewhere else in the brain or—in most cases—somewhere else in the cortex (Fig. 1). In contrast, the axon of a spineless stellate cell does not enter the white matter and only contacts other neurons in its vicinity.

Spiny neurons are the great majority (about 85 percent) of all neurons in the cerebral cortex. This category largely coincides with that of pyramidal cells of older classifications, characterized by a bipartite dendritic tree, with several 'basal dendrites' distributed around the cell body, and one 'apical dendrite,' ascending vertically through the cortex and ramifying in upper layers (Fig. 1). There are, however, also spiny neurons without an apical dendrite, sometimes termed 'spiny stellate cells,' especially as recipients of primary sensory input in layer IV of primary sensory areas. Disregarding a subpopulation of these which does not project to the white matter, the basic connectivity of cortical neurons can be described as follows (Braitenberg and Schüz 1998).

4. The Basic Connectivity of the Cerebral Cortex

The 'skeleton cortex' (Fig. 1) consists of a large number of pyramidal cells (of the order of 10^{10} in humans), distributed throughout all layers of the cortex, and producing excitatory synapses which for the most part again contact other pyramidal cells. There is considerable divergence and convergence built into this system, since every pyramidal cell communicates with many thousands of other pyramidal cells both in its input and in its output. Thus, 'diffuse excitatory feedback' is the pre-eminent feature of the cerebral cortex. Only a small percentage of pyramidal cells project to other parts of the brain and only a few percent of the synapses in the cortex come from neurons from other parts of the brain. By far the greatest part of synaptic traffic in the cortex is internal and only involves cortical neurons.

The inhibitory stellate cells are diffusely distributed in the network of pyramidal cells. In some cases their inhibitory synapses have a strong grip on a relatively small number of cortical neurons in their vicinity (pyramidal and stellate). In other cases their inhibitory synapses are distributed more profusely, making the distinction of several classes of stellate cells possible according to the pattern of their ramification (basket cells, chandelier cells, double bouquet cells, etc.; see Peters and Jones 1984). They, too, receive their input mainly from cortical pyramidal cells. In the regions where primary sensory input (e.g., visual) enters the cortex, they may also be directly contacted by the incoming fibers.

Although the inhibitory interneurons in some cases are certainly involved in the computation which takes place in the cortical network, their role may be considered as ancillary with respect to that of the pyramidal cells. They may perhaps put a brake on neuronal activity when it threatens to explode in a runaway reaction, as may be expected in a network of elements, such as the pyramidal cells, all exciting each other. Indeed, this braking action occasionally fails, as evidenced by epileptic fits, one of the commonest forms of functional derailment in the cortex.

The comparison with other parts of the brain shows that a network of mainly excitatory connections is indeed a striking peculiarity of the cerebral cortex. In the other major parts of the brain the majority of neurons are either connected into an inhibitory network (basal ganglia) or they do not form a network among themselves but relay some input to some output in a feedforward manner (cerebellar cortex, thalamus).

5. The Basic Function

The question of what could possibly be the advantage of an immense network of interconnected excitatory neurons whose increase in size has accompanied mammalian evolution up to the crowning event of human culture, has received various tentative answers. The most convincing interpretation of cortical structure is based on the observation that the synapses between pyramidal cells, the majority of all synapses in the cortex, are of the special kind residing on dendritic spines, and on the supposition that spine-synapses are 'plastic,' i.e., modifiable by 'learning.' There is no definitive proof of this supposition, but enough indirect evidence to make it plausible (see review by Horner 1993), and, moreover, alternative explanations for the role of spines are less convincing. Be this as it may, there is little doubt that, of all parts of the brain, the cerebral cortex is the one most concerned with the acquisition of knowledge. Suffice it to say that lesions of the cerebral cortex impair complex acquired capacities, such as language.

In terms of engineering, the network of cortical pyramidal cells could be likened to a giant 'associative memory,' a device which connects together more strongly (through modifiable synapses) the neurons that are often active at the same time. Thus, events of the outside world which tend to present themselves together will be represented in the brain by neurons tied together by strong synapses. The idea that the cortex incorporates knowledge by repeating, in its synaptic connectivity, the structure of reality was spelled out in two well-known theories. In 1949, D. O. Hebb proposed 'cell assemblies' as the units of cognitive operations in the brain. These are ensembles of cortical neurons connected to each other by excitatory synapses which have been strengthened in the course of a learning process. Such cell assemblies may be thought of as representing 'objects' of the world. Due to activity reverberating among its neurons, such an assembly stays active for some time once it has been activated, a property which perhaps is at the basis of 'short-term memory.' Also, a cell assembly may become active in its entirety even if only a subset of its neurons is activated initially, in a way reminiscent of the phenomenon of 'pattern completion' well known to perceptual psychologists.

'Synfire chains' (Abeles 1991) are the other theoretical proposal based on associative memory. Quite compatible with the anatomy of the cortical network and with the physiological properties of single neurons, it is possible to imagine sets of neurons, each set when activated in synchrony, activating another such set, and this in turn another one, etc., forming long chains of activity propagating through the cortex with great selectivity and temporal precision. This scheme explains how events displayed in time (e.g., the words of a language, musical themes, complex movements, etc.) are incorporated in memory. The temporal precision postulated by this theory has been impressively verified by correlation studies on spike activity of different cortical neurons (Abeles and Prut 1996).

Between Hebbian cell assemblies representing 'objects' of the world, and Abelesian synfire chains representing 'events,' there may be transitional forms of cortical activity, all based on the idea of modifiable synapses embodying the notion of synchronous events, or of events occurring in succession, acquired through a process often called 'Hebbian learning.'

6. Cortical Areas

From the 'macroscopic layout' of the cortical network it is also possible to gain insights into its organization. It has been known for some time that restricted lesions of the cortex produce different symptoms according to their localization. This led to the definition of 'cortical areas,' distinct regions of the cortex a few centimeters across (in humans) whose reality has since been confirmed by many detailed electrophysiological studies. There are 'sensory areas' (visual, acoustic, somatosensory, olfactory), 'motor areas,' and 'association areas.' The latter in part have been recognized as secondary and tertiary stations in the elaboration of

primary sensory input, as in the case of special areas for the extraction of motion (area V5) or color (area V4) in the visual scene (Zeki 1993), or in the case of a special area (*Wernicke's area*) fed by acoustic input in the context of language, distinct from other areas concerned with acoustic perception. Evidently, besides the various sensory inputs reaching the cortex in separate regions, and the long efferent (e.g., corticospinal) axons emanating from other regions, it is the context in which the cortex operates locally that defines the areas.

Apart from the different effects of lesions, cortical areas were also delimited on the basis of subtle, and sometimes also quite evident, differences in the appearance of their layers and in the degree of myelination ('cortical architectonics'). For example, a small-celled layer IV is particularly well developed in primary sensory areas while it cannot be discerned at all in the primary motor area (Area 4). The primary motor area sticks out because of a population of very large cells in layer V, the cortico-spinal neurons. Large pyramidal cells in layer III are found in some association areas, including the speech centers. Two heavy bands of horizontal myelinated fibers (the 'stripes of Baillarger') are evident in some areas and only one such band in others (Fig. 2). Overall myelination tends to decrease towards higher association areas. Such structural differences were at the basis of 'cortical maps,' the best known of which, the map by K. Brodmann from 1909, distinguishes about 50 areas. Although this large number was met with skepticism at first, it is remarkable that many of the structural distinctions were later shown to correspond to different properties of neurons when cortical mapping was undertaken anew by microelectrode analysis. More recent maps tend to assume even higher numbers of areas.

Evidently, the neuronal network of the cortex, although built according to common principles throughout its extent, is subject to variations that adapt it locally to different kinds of input and to different kinds of computation, which the input is subjected to. The variations which appear in the Nissl (cell body) picture and in the myelin preparations (cyto- and myeloarchitectonics) are just two aspects of the underlying variations of the basic network, and indeed the two were shown by Hellwig (1993) to be related to each other by a set of simple rules.

7. Columns

Beyond the confirmation of the different nature of individual cortical areas, microelectrode neurophysiology in many cases revealed an even finer mapping within areas, the so-called 'columns.' In the primary visual area V-1 (Brodmann's area 17) certain properties to which neurons are tuned, such as responding to stimuli from the right or left eye, or to vertical, horizontal, or oblique stripes, periodically recur over the surface of the cortex at distances of about 0.5 or 1 mm (Hubel 1988). The term 'column' was chosen for these small compartments within the areas since the locally specific properties of neurons in one column tend to be similar for neurons in all, or in several layers. Columns (or slabs) of neurons with similar properties, but different in a systematic way from column to column have also been described in secondary visual areas, in the somatosensory cortex, and in the primary acoustic cortex. In many cases, these functionally defined columns can be attributed to the way the input is organized: inputs from different sources tend to enter the cortex in alternating bundles (e.g., right eye vs. left eye in the visual cortex, fibers from the same or the opposite hemisphere in the auditory and prefrontal cortex), thus imposing periodical inputs onto a largely homogeneous looking intracortical network. However, periodicity can also be found in the pattern of axonal arborizations of pyramidal cells within cortical areas where they preferably project to columns with similar functional properties (Malach et al. 1997, Yoshioka et al. 1996). Occasionally, columns may also be visible in the arrangement of cell bodies and dendritic trees (whisker representation in rodents), or as the 'cytochrome oxidase blobs' of the visual cortex. However, neither areas nor columns can be regarded as separate entities; the fiber felt is continuous across the borders between them.

8. *Connections Between Areas*

The reality of cortical areas is also evident in the pattern of connections between them. This can be studied (in animals) by injecting certain dyes locally into the cortex, which are then transported in axons either in the direction away from the cell body ('anterograde transport') or towards it ('retrograde transport') depending on the particular dye chosen. The overall picture is the following (Young et al. 1995): individual areas are connected to several other areas, but not to all. Areas can differ considerably with respect to the number of areas they are connected to. Some primary sensory areas are connected to only a few other areas; higher association areas can be connected to more than one third of all cortical areas. The majority of the connections between areas are reciprocal. In the monkey cortex, if an area A projects to another area B, there is also a projection from B to A in 82 percent of the cases. Areas that are located close to each other in the cortex, often related to the same sensory modality, are more likely to be connected, but there are also connections between areas quite far apart. Most areas are connected to their symmetrical partners in the other hemisphere. The exceptions are in parts of the visual and somatosensory areas, which do not contribute fibers to the *corpus callosum*, the main interhemispheric fiber bundle.

The strong internal connectedness of the cortex in each hemisphere is reflected also in the large volume of the hemispheric white substance (the cerebellar hemispheres by comparison have a very scanty white substance, containing only afferent and efferent fibers). In the human brain and in the brains of other large mammals, within the white matter underlying the cortex it is possible to discern about six large bundles connecting distant parts of the cortex, such as the occipito-frontal fascicle or the arcuate fascicle between the motor and the sensory speech areas. The rest of the white matter is composed of shorter fibers between neighboring areas, and to a lesser extent, of commissural fibers, connecting both hemispheres via the *corpus callosum*, and of the fibers connecting the cortex, both ways, with subcortical centers. The fact that the volume occupied by the long cortico-cortical bundles is a small fraction of the total volume of the white substance suggests that there is a hierarchical organization, with a great amount of preprocessing between neighboring areas, often within one modality, preceding the global integration.

See also: Brain Asymmetry; Brain, Evolution of; Brain: Response to Enrichment; Cingulate Cortex; Electrical Stimulation of the Brain; Functional Brain Imaging; Long-term Potentiation and Depression (Cortex); Motor Cortex; Neural Plasticity; Neural Plasticity in Auditory Cortex; Neural Plasticity in Visual Cortex; Prefrontal Cortex; Pre-motor Cortex; Split Brain; Topographic Maps in the Brain; Visual System in the Brain

Bibliography

Abeles M 1991 *Corticonics: Neural Circuits of the Cerebral Cortex*. Cambridge University Press, Cambridge, UK

Abeles M, Prut Y 1996 Spatio-temporal firing patterns in the frontal cortex of behaving monkeys. *Journal of Physiology* **90**: 249–50

Braitenberg V, Schüz A 1998 *Cortex: Statistics and Geometry of Neuronal Connectivity*, 2nd edn. *Anatomy of the Cortex: Statistics and Geometry* 1991 Springer, Berlin, Heidelberg, New York

Hebb D O 1949/1961 *Organization of Behavior. A Neuropsychological Theory*, 2nd edn. Wiley & Sons, New York

Hellwig B 1993 How the myelin picture of the human cerebral cortex can be computed from cytoarchitectural data. A bridge between von Economo and Vogt. *Journal of Brain Research* **34**(3): 387–402

Horner C H 1993 Plasticity of the dendritic spine. *Progress in Neurobiology* **41**: 281–321

Hubel D H 1988 *Eye, Brain and Vision*. The Scientific American Library, New York

Malach R, Schirman T D, Harel M, Tootell R B H, Malonek D 1997 Organization of intrinsic connections in owl monkey area MT. *Cerebral Cortex* **7**: 386–93

Peters A, Jones E G (eds.) 1984 *Cerebral Cortex, Cellular Components of the Cerebral Cortex*. Plenum Press, New York, London, Vol. 1

Yoshioka T, Blasdel G G, Levitt J B, Lund J S 1996 Relation between patterns of intrinsic lateral connectivity, ocular dominance, and cytochrome oxidase-reactive regions in macaque monkey striate cortex. *Cerebral Cortex* **6**: 297–310

Young M P, Scannell J W, Burns G 1995 *The Analysis of Cortical Connectivity.* Springer, Berlin, Heidelberg, New York

Zeki S 1993 *A Vision of the Brain.* Blackwell Scientific Publications, London, Edinburgh

A. Schüz and V. Braitenberg

Change: Methods of Studying

The themes of stability and change permeate from the Greek philosophers to the present. Following Heraklit, change seems to be a ubiquitous phenomenon: 'all is flowing (*Panta rei*)' or 'you cannot get into the same river twice.' The opposite position was held by Parmenides, who said, 'something is real only if we can say it *is*, if it was or will be, it is not real. Change is an illusion.' Stability and change are basic concepts within psychology, too. The aim of this article is to give an overview regarding methods of studying change. Therefore, in the first step, important concepts of change and stability are introduced. For each of the different concepts of stability, change is defined as absence of stability.

1. Concepts of Change and a System of Categories to Differentiate Them

1.1 Basic Concepts of Change

Traditionally, there are at least two important basic concepts of stability and change: absolute and normative stability (Baltes et al. 1977). Whereas normative stability is only defined at the group level, absolute stability can be defined at the individual *and* the group level. A definition of absolute stability for an individual is that the value of a variable for this individual does not change between occasions of measurement. Absolute stability at the group level is defined as the mean level of the group for a variable does not change between observations. Figure 1(c) shows absolute stability at the individual level for individual 3 but not for individual 1. At the same time there is stability at the group level, because the mean of the whole sample does not change. Figure 1(a) describes change in absolute stability for each individual and at the group level.

Normative stability is given if the rank order with respect to a variable does not change between two occasions of measurement. Imagine, for instance, that

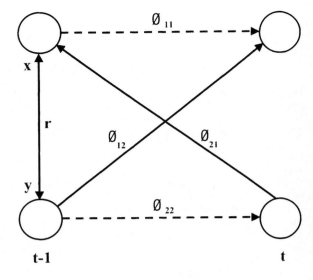

Figure 1
(a) Concepts for univariate stability/change: change of absolute value (individual and group level) but normative stability; (b) change of variability but normative stability; (c) change of rank order but absolute stability (group level)

the variable control belief is measured on two occasions. Each individual starts from a different level of control belief and then shows an increase by the same amount (cf., Fig. 1(a)). The rank correlation is 1 and, therefore, normative stability is given. Figure 1(c) illustrates change with respect to normative or rank-order stability: the rank order is reversed from time 1 to time 2. In this sample, the stability coefficient measured as rank correlation between occasions is $r = -1$.

Another concept of stability/change is stability of variability. Stability of variability requires that the variance of a variable does not change between two occasions of measurement. Figure 1(b) shows an increase in the variability across situations. The example in Fig. 1(b) demonstrates that change in the variability across occasions can occur despite absolute and normative stability. To conclude, these examples demonstrate that there exist different concepts of stability/change and that stability can be given for one concept, but not necessarily for the others.

1.2 A Classification System for Stability/Change Concepts

To gain an even fuller picture of change concepts, a classification system of change concepts will be outlined, which takes into account the following:

(a) individual change or change within groups;

(b) number of variables: univariate or multivariate change;

(c) number of and time distance between occasions: two or multiple measurements;

(d) scaling of the variables: categorial, ordinal, interval scale.

For reasons of economy, other important dimensions are not (explicitly) included within this classification:

(e) change can be located at the surface or the construct level;

(f) (measured variable or latent construct; phenotype or genotype);

(g) trend, growth, and rhythm;

(h) change of the (dimensional) structure;

(i) change in measurement error;

(j) synchronicity, asynchronicity;

(k) change and causality.

2. Examples of Important Methods for Studying Change

When outlining a system of categories for change concepts, it becomes evident that by combining the different dimensions of the system a large number of change concepts could be derived. Within this short description, however, only a subset can be explained in more detail.

2.1 Analyzing Change by Using Differences Between Two Occasions

This way of studying change is frequently used in research. The way of measuring change shown in Fig. 1(a) is based on comparing measures of one variable for a sample of individuals for two occasions. The question is whether there is a change in the mean of the variable. To analyze these questions, one computes differences between time-2 and time-1 measures. Critiques of this approach have pointed to various problems:

(a) differences are dependent on the level of the first measurement;

(b) differences are not reliable (not as much as the original variable);

(c) regression to the mean leads to systematic biases.

(a) The law of initial values states that high initial values correlate with small differences between second and first measurement and vice versa, which means that there is a negative correlation between initial status and change.

(b) From the assumptions of classical test theory, e.g., Lord (1963) derived an equation for the reliability of differences. He argued that if there are two fallible

measures, the resulting measure must be worse. This means that if there is a high correlation between the first and second measurements and the reliabilities of the single measurements are medium or high, then the reliability of the difference is low (numerical example: if $r_{11} = r_{22} = 0.84$ and $r_{12} = 0.83$, then it follows that $r_{dd} = 0.06$).

(c) Regression to the mean says that extreme values for the first occasion will probably be followed by more average values in the second measurement. The mathematical formulation for regression to the mean is $s(y_{pred}) < s(x)$ (y_{pred} are the predicted values). It can be shown easily that regression to the mean is a simple mathematical tautology depending on the assumption of equal variances for pre- and post-test.

For each of these points of critique, Rogosa (1995) gives examples that they do not hold in general and that they can be subsumed under the myths of longitudinal research. Therefore, difference scores can be used if there are only two occasion measurements.

2.2 Cross-lagged-panel Analysis

After studying change using difference scores, we turn to the study of causal relations using change measurements. Consider, for instance, the theoretical question of whether there exists a causal relationship between control belief and academic performance and vice versa. The empirical basis for computing estimates of cross-lagged-panel relationships is that a sample of individuals is measured (at least) twice with respect to (at least) two variables.

The cross-lagged-panel model contains two important cross-lagged paths (a) between control belief (time 1) and performance (time 2) and (b) between performance (time 1) and control belief (time 2). These models can be estimated and tested for significance, yielding possible causal (in the sense of time-lagged relationships; see Schmitz 1990) relationships: no causality, unidirectional causality, or bidirectional causality (feedback).

2.3 Analysis of Time Series

The data basis for analysis of time series is that at least one individual is studied for at least one variable, using many occasions of measurement. Whereas the methods in Sect. 2.1 require only a small database (two occasions measurements), for time series analysis one often needs more than 20 or even 50 data points. One might think that it would be difficult to collect such data, but in psychophysiology, behavioral observations, and diary approaches, it is feasible to collect this kind of data. One of the great advantages of the time-series approach is that one can test hypotheses also for

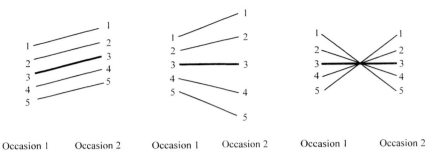

Figure 2
Cross-lagged relationships for two variables

a single individual. A typical research question may be to study the effect of an intervention (e.g., does a training have an effect on control belief?) and the identification of trends and rhythms. A variable shows a linear trend if the increase from one occasion to the next is constant. An example of a variable which shows a simple rhythm is workload measured daily: usually, the workload is high during workdays whereas at weekends people will not work. In the bi- or multivariate case one can test synchronous or asynchronous relationships (see Schmitz and Skinner 1993). Synchronous relationships occur if variables show similar patterns over time (e.g., days); they show asynchronous relationships, e.g., if one variable lags behind another variable (shows a similar pattern just one day later). One can analyze, for instance, *intra-individual* causal relationships between variables. If there are more individuals, one can perform intra-individual time-series analyzes for each individual and then combine the individual parameters at the aggregate level, as is done in hierarchical linear modeling (HLM) (Bryk and Raudenbush 1987) or in the approach proposed by Schmitz et al. (1996). Both methods can be regarded as solutions to the idiographic–nomothetic controversy. (See Fig. 2.)

3. Other Methods and Outlook

A special case of the general time-series models are chaos models, which are nonlinear.

One characteristic of chaos is the severe dependence on the initial conditions, which is often referred to as the butterfly effect. There are simple chaotic systems which can be described by only one so-called order parameter. These systems converge to homeostasis if the order parameter stays within certain limits. However, if the parameter changes slightly the system shows chaotic behavior (Alligood et al. 1997).

Sometimes the assumption of interval data is not fulfilled, and in these cases synchronicity and asynchronicity can be studied using Markov models (see Gottman and Roy 1990). If information is given on how long it takes until an event occurs, methods of

event-history analyzes can be applied (Willett and Singer 1995).

In sum, methods of studying change based on poor information—as in two-occasion measurements—can only lead to poor results (one cannot derive conclusions that are valid for individuals), whereas methods which use the information contained in rich (e.g., time-series) data can lead to rich conclusions (e.g., which are also valid for individuals). If someone is really interested in stability and change (although it requires a great deal of effort to conduct a longitudinal study), one should not always apply only simple methods (such as differences) and small data basis (such as two measurement points) for economical reasons as there are alternative methods which may provide more differentiated results. To conclude, it is time to avoid shortcomings of studying change or, as Rogosa (1995 p. 8) put it, 'Myth 1: two observations a longitudinal study make.'

See also: Chaos Theory; Event-history Analysis in Continuous Time; Event Sequence Analysis: Methods; Longitudinal Data; Longitudinal Data: Event–History Analysis in Discrete Time; Longitudinal Research: Panel Retention; Markov Models and Social Analysis; Markov Processes for Knowledge Spaces; Time Series: General

Bibliography

Alligood K T, Sauer T D, Yorke J A 1997 *Chaos. An Introduction to Dynamical Systems.* Springer, New York

Baltes P B, Reese H W, Nesselroade J R 1977 *Life-span Developmental Psychology: Introduction to Research Methods.* Brooks/Cole, Monterey, CA

Bryk A S, Raudenbush S W 1987 Application of hierarchical linear models to assessing change. *Psychological Bulletin* **101**: 147–58

Gottman J M, Roy A K 1990 *Sequential Analysis. A Guide for Behavioral Researchers.* Cambridge University Press, Cambridge, UK

Lord F M 1963 Elementary models for measuring change. In: Harris C W (ed.) *Problems in Measuring Change.* University of Wisconsin Press, Madison, WI, pp. 21–38

Rogosa D R 1995 Myths and methods: 'myths about longitudinal research' plus supplemental questions. In: Gottman J M (ed.) *The Analysis of Change*. Erlbaum, Mahwah, NJ, pp. 3–66

Schmitz B 1990 Univariate and multivariate time-series models: the analysis of intraindividual variability and intraindividual relationships. In: von Eye A (ed.) *Statistical Methods in Longitudinal Research, Volume II: Time Series and Categorical Longitudinal Data*. Academic Press, Boston, pp. 351–86

Schmitz B, Skinner E 1993 Perceived control, effort, and academic performance: interindividual, intraindividual, and multivariate time-series analyses. *Journal of Personality and Social Psychology* **64**: 1010–28

Schmitz B, Stanat P, Sang F, Tasche K G 1996 Reactive effects of a survey on the television viewing behavior of a telemetric television audience panel: a combined time-series and control group analysis. *Evaluation Review* **20**: 204–29

Willett J B, Singer J D 1995 Investigating onset, cessation, relapse, and recovery: using discrete-time survival analysis to examine the occurrence and timing of critical events. In: Gottman J M (ed.) *The Analysis of Change*. Erlbaum, Mahwah, NJ, pp. 203–59

B. Schmitz

Chaos Theory

Chaos theory is the study of deterministic difference (differential) equations that display sensitive dependence upon initial conditions (SDIC) in such a way as to generate time paths that look random.

This article (a) explains what 'chaos' is in mathematics, (b) explains why economists became interested in this concept, (c) sketches economic forces that can 'smooth' out dynamical irregularities that can lead to chaos, (d) very briefly discusses theoretical models that generate chaotic dynamical systems as equilibria, and (e) discusses empirical testing for chaos. We shall spend most of the time on (e) because even though the vast bulk of studies has not found convincing evidence for chaotic dynamics that are short term predictable (out-of-sample) using nonlinear methods with high ability to detect chaos, the quest for chaos has generated useful statistical methods.

1. Chaos

The mathematical apparatus for rigorous treatment of chaos can be quite intimidating to the nonmathematician. Therefore we shall attempt to explain the concepts verbally as much as possible. This expositional strategy will allow the reader to decide whether it is worth their while to investigate this area further. Reference to wide-ranging surveys are given.

We follow Brock (1986) for a very brief treatment of some mathematics of chaos below. A deterministic discrete time dynamical system on n-dimensional space is a system,

$$x(t+1) = F(x(t)), \quad t = 1, 2, \ldots; \ x(0) = x_0 \quad (1)$$

of n difference equations in n variables. Here F is a map from n-dimensional real space to itself, $x(t)$ and $x(t+1)$ are n-dimensional vectors at date t and $t+1$ respectively, x_0 denotes the initial condition vector, and t is time.

A useful pedagogical example is the scalar 'tent map' T from the closed interval [0, 1] to itself defined by

$$x(t+1) = T(x(t))$$

where

$$T(x) = 2x, \ x \text{ in } [0, 0.5]$$

and

$$T(x) = 2 - 2x, \ x \text{ in } [0.5, 1] \quad (2)$$

The hallmark of chaos is SDIC, i.e. for two nearby initial conditions, $x(0)$, $y(0)$, the map F magnifies the distance between them:

$$|F(x(0)) - F(y(0))| > |x(0) - y(0)|$$
$$\text{for } |x(0) - y(0)| \text{ small enough} \quad (3)$$

for most pairs of nearby initial conditions. Here $|\cdot|$ denotes a distance measure. The tent map (2) illustrates this idea nicely because $|x(0) - y(0)|$ is magnified by a factor of two for small enough $|x(0) - y(0)|$ except for the rare case where $x(0)$, $y(0)$ straddle the maximizer, $x = 0.5$.

A popular way to precisely capture the idea of SDIC and to measure it is the largest Lyapunov exponent, L, which is defined by the following limit as h tends to infinity,

$$L(x(0), v) = \text{Limit}(1/h) \ln\{|DF^h(x(0)) \cdot v|\} \quad (4)$$

Here DG denotes the n by n derivative matrix of map G, $F^h(x(0))$ denotes the application of map F to the n-vector $x(0)$ h times, v denotes a nonzero n-dimensional direction vector, '·e denotes dot product, $|\cdot|$ denotes the Euclidean norm on n-dimensional space, and ln denotes natural logarithm.

Sufficient conditions are available for $L(x(0), v)$ to exist and to be independent of $x(0)$, v for most initial conditions $x(0)$ and most vectors v. A popular definition of chaos is:

Definition (Chaos) The map F is said to be chaotic if $L > 0$.

This is not the only definition of chaotic map in the literature, but it is a popular one and we shall use it here.

The value of L for the tent map T is $L = \ln(2) > 0$ so T is chaotic by this definition of chaos. As we saw before, T displays SDIC. The quantity L measures how fast (on average per iteration) a tiny measurement error (captured by y) in the initial condition $x(0)$ is magnified by the map. If the iteration h in (2) is thought of as a forecast then $|DF^h(x(0)) \cdot v|$ represents the error in an h-horizon forecast caused by measurement error v at date zero. If $L > 0$, this error is growing exponentially as h increases by a factor $\exp(L)$. This kind of behavior is associated with deterministic maps generating random-looking time series output. Clearly the tent map example generates random-looking time series output. Another example of a type of chaotic map is a psuedo-random number generator for computers.

If the solution $\{x(t), t = 1, 2, \ldots\}$ to (1) is bounded for each initial condition, x_0, under regularity conditions the limiting behavior of chaotic dynamical systems is contained in a set A that is invariant under application of F which is called a 'strange attractor.' It is called 'strange' because it is not a rest point or a p-cycle. Here a p-cycle is a collection of p vectors, $\{x(1), x(2), \ldots, x(p)\}$, such that

$$x(2) = F(x(1)), \ x(3) = F(x(2)), \ldots,$$
$$x(p) = F(x(p-1)), \ x(1) = F(x(p)) \tag{5}$$

A rest point is a p-cycle where $p = 1$.

It is useful to briefly explain the notion of bifurcations and 'routes to chaos.' Consider a dynamical system with 'fast' and 'slow' variables, $x(t)$, and $a(t)$ where the fast variables $x(t)$ have a rate of change that is much faster than the slow variables. Write

$$x(t+1) - x(t) = f(x(t), a(t)),$$
$$a(t+1) - a(t) = eg(x(t), a(t)), \ 0 < e \ll 1, \tag{6}$$

where '$\ll 1$' means 'much less than one' to capture the idea that the second difference equation in (6) moves much more slowly than the first. Hence, it is useful sometimes to assume the fast variables have already converged to an attractor conditional on the value of the slow variables. A bifurcation value is a value of the slow variables such that passing through it leads to an abrupt change of the attractor of the fast variables. For example suppose the attractor is a rest point which abruptly changes to a p-cycle, $p > 1$; or a p-cycle which abruptly changes a more complex attractor. There is a classification theory for bifurcations (Kuznetsov (1995)).

A well-studied route to chaos in one dimensional discrete dynamical systems is the Feigenbaum cascade (and closely related Sharkovsky ordering). Here a rest point (i.e., a one-cycle) bifurcates into a two-cycle, followed by bifurcation into a four-cycle, followed by bifurcation into an eight-cycle, ..., followed by bi-furcation into a $2m$-cycle, ... to fully developed chaos as a slow 'tuning' parameter increases. This particular route to chaos is used a lot in economics (Benhabib 1992). Some economists argue that fully developed chaos is not as useful to economic science as the analysis and classification of bifurcations themselves, because the evidence from data is stronger for the existence of bifurcations.

2. Chaotic Economic Dynamics?

Even though predictability of a chaotic dynamics is futile in the long term, nonlinear prediction methods can do a good job on short term prediction when chaos is present. Consider a general stylized dynamic economic model represented by the following stochastic dynamical system

$$x(t+1) = f(R(x(t)), \ x(t)) + s \cdot n(t) \tag{7}$$

where $x(t)$ is a vector of economic quantities that represent the state vector of the economy at date t, $R(x(t))$ represents the response of economic agents to the state of the economy at date t, and the function f produces the new state vector $x(t+1)$ at date $t+1$. Here $n(t)$ denotes a stochastic process, called 'forcing noise,' (often chosen to be an independent and identically distributed sequence of mean zero, finite variance random variables) which represents outside shocks to the economic system and s denotes standard deviation of each random variable $n(t)$.

Many economic models (e.g., many of the models treated in Benhabib 1992) can be put into the mathematical form of Eqn.(7). If we define

$$F(x) = f(R(x), x) \tag{8}$$

then Eqn.(1) is a difference equation of the form (1) when $s = 0$. Since economic theory generates nonlinear dynamics it is theoretically easy to produce economic models of the form (8) that generate chaotic dynamics when external forcing noise is set equal to zero (e.g., Benhabib 1992, Boldrin's chapter in Anderson et al. 1988, Dechert 1996).

An important issue is whether, in such models, the parameter values needed to obtain chaos (especially a chaos where prediction in the near term can be improved by exploiting it) are consistent with empirical measurements in economics. For example, when real interest rates are low (as they typically are), intertemporal smoothing operations such as intertemporal arbitrage (e.g., the trading of assets across different points of time in order to profit after adjustment for interest costs and for risk bearing) tend to squash cycles and chaos in economic systems with a rich enough variety of market instruments.

Brock's chapter in Anderson et al. (1988) goes through a list of empirical plausibility checks for the magnitude of 'frictions' needed to obtain short term forecastable deterministic cycles and chaos at high to usuably (usuably from a policy-relevant predictive point of view) low frequencies in macroeconomic and financial data. Brock's general conclusion is not encouraging for the presence of persistent deterministic cycles and chaos for economic dynamics of macro variables and financial asset returns in countries with well-developed asset markets and financial markets but maybe better for countries with poorly-developed markets. It is argued that well-developed market economies just have too many instruments through which self-interested intertemporal smoothing behavior can operate to be consistent with persistent deterministic chaos or cycles at high to medium frequencies.

After all, the usual arguments behind the efficient markets hypothesis suggests that there is money lying on the table if there are potentially predictable patterns such as deterministic chaos or deterministic cycles in asset returns. That is, arbitrage opportunities are available unless interest rates are high, market instruments for arbitrage are few, risk adjustments are high, or constraints on borrowing and lending are high. Of course, none of these arguments are germane to the presence of chaos and cycles at very low frequencies. For example, Day's chapter in Pesaran and Potter (1992) is more encouraging for the presence of persistent 'complex' economic dynamics such as chaos, especially at long-term historical frequencies. However, while theory is suggestive, there is no substitute for rigorous statistical testing.

More interesting to empirical economists is whether there is evidence in economic and financial time series data for the presence of chaos. While the evidence is weak for financial data and for macroeconomic data for the presence of chaos which can be short term predicted, there does seem to be useful evidence in favor of nonlinear structure which can be predicted in the short term, conditional on appropriate information sets. The evidence for extra unconditional out-of-sample predictability (i.e., prediction of data that was not in the sample used to fit the model) using nonlinear methods appears to be weak for asset returns data. The evidence for extra conditional out-of-sample predictability of asset returns is better (LeBaron 1994). See the review of Brock et al. (1991) with especial attention to the references to Diebold, Nason, and LeBaron. However evidence for bifurcations, complex dynamics, abrupt changes, and other nonlinear phenomena seems quite strong (Dechert and Hommes 2000, see especially Chavas for animal dynamics; Carpenter et al. 1999, for ecological dynamics; LeBaron 1994, for nonlinear patterns in financial data; Dechert 1996, for an overall review of evidence).

3. New Statistical Methods

The quest for evidence of deterministic chaos, deterministic cycles, and other complex deterministic persistent patterns in economic and financial data, has inspired the development of new statistical methods. These methods have turned out to be useful in areas having nothing to do with deterministic chaos. We briefly explain two of them here. The first method is a specification test called the 'BDS test' by many writers (Bollerslev et al.'s chapter in Engle and McFadden 1994, De Grauwe et al. 1993). The method emerged out of the work that culminated in Brock et al. (1996). Here is a very brief explanation.

Suppose one formulates a model that relates a set of variables to be predicted to another set of variables called predictor variables, and fits this model to data and saves the residuals. If one has done a proper job of theorizing, model formulation, and model fitting, then the residuals should be unforecastible using histories based upon observables. The BDS test is used to formulate and carry out tests for unpredictability of residuals of fitted models. (See Brock et al. 1991 for extensive discussion and Monte Carlo work.) The BDS test has been used to test the adequancy of fitted models to data (Dechert 1996, De Grauwe et al. 1993, Pesaran and Potter 1992). The BDS test plays a similar role for nonlinear and general models as the Box and Jenkins Q-test does for auto-regressive integrated moving average (ARIMA) models (Box and Jenkins 1976). Tests like the Q-test and the BDS test are useful for testing the adequacy of fitted models and evaluating whether the evidence warrants a more costly exploration of alternatives to the null hypothesis model. See Dechert (1996) for a collection of studies where the BDS test is used in this manner.

The bootstrap-based specification test is a more sophisticated specification testing method. This method is especially relevant for detecting subtle nonlinearities in settings like finance where the economic logic dictates that any patterns are likely to be hard to detect (e.g. Maddala and Li's chapter in Maddala and Rao 1996). The idea here is to use a version of bootstrap to compute the null-model distribution of statistics gleaned from various trading strategies, and to use the data values of these statistics to suggest refinements of the null model in financially relevant directions. For example, in financial applications, the null model is sometimes taken to be a random walk. This procedure emphasizes development of statistical quantities to evaluate the null model which are motivated by the behavior that one is modeling. This method was made possible by recent technical increases in computing speed, and reduction in cost, as well as advances in computationally based inference methods such as bootstrap.

4. Conclusion and Future Directions

The study of chaos and general complex dynamics as well as general complexity theory in economics, finance, and social studies has already been fruitful in generating new methods and new evidence. This kind of work is likely to grow in prominence as computational costs fall and advances continue in computational-based methods of theory and statistical inference.

See also: Computational Psycholinguistics; Linear and Nonlinear Programming; Neural Systems and Behavior: Dynamical Systems Approaches; Self-organizing Dynamical Systems; Stochastic Dynamic Models (Choice, Response, and Time)

Bibliography

Anderson P, Arrow K, Pines D (eds.) 1988 *The Economy as an Evolving Complex System*. Addison-Wesley, Redwood City, CA

Benhabib J (ed.) 1992 *Cycles and Chaos in Economic Equilibrium*. Princeton University Press, Princeton

Box G, Jenkins G 1976 *Time Series Analysis: Forecasting and Control* (revised edn). Holden-Day, San Francisco, CA

Brock W 1986 Distinguishing random and deterministic systems (abridged version). In: Grandmont J (ed.) *Nonlinear Economic Dynamics*. Academic Press, New York

Brock W, Dechert W, Scheinkman J, LeBaron B 1996 A test for independence based upon the correlation dimension. *Econometric Reviews* **15**(3): 197–235

Brock W, Hsieh D, LeBaron B 1991 *Nonlinear Dynamics, Chaos, and Instability Statistical Theory and Economic Evidence*. MIT Press, Cambridge, MA

Carpenter S, Ludwig D, Brock W 1999 Management of eutrophication for lakes subject to potentially irreversible change. *Ecological Applications* **9**(3): 751–71

Dechert W (ed.) 1996 *Chaos Theory in Economics: Methods, Models and Evidence*. Edward Elgar, Cheltenham, UK

Dechert W, Hommes C (eds.) 2000 Complex nonlinear dynamics and computational methods. *Journal of Economic Dynamics and Control* **24**: 651–62

De Grauwe P, Dewachter H, Embrechts M 1993 *Exchange Rate Theory, Chaotic Models of Foreign Exchange Markets*. Blackwell, Oxford, UK

Engle R, McFadden D 1994 *Handbook of Econometrics*. North-Holland, Amsterdam, Vol. 4

Kuznetsov Y 1995 *Elements of Applied Bifurcation Theory*. Springer, New York

LeBaron B 1994 Chaos and nonlinear forecastibility in economics and finance. *Philosophical Transactions of the Royal Society* **348**: 397–404

Maddala G, Rao C (eds.) 1996 *Handbook of Statistics 14: Statistical Methods in Finance*. North-Holland, Amsterdam

Pesaran H, Potter S 1992 Nonlinear dynamics and econometrics. *Journal of Applied Econometrics* **7**: S1–S195

W. A. Brock

Characterization Theorems in Random Utility Theory

In random utility theory the evaluation of a stimulus by a subject is modeled by a random variable from which a sample is taken at each presentation of the stimulus. This idea, which goes back to Gustav Fechner and was further developed in psychology by Thurstone (1927), is used to explain the often observed inconsistency in choice experiments, where a subject on repeated presentations of one particular subset of alternatives does not always select the same alternative. The term 'utility' refers to a setting where the subject is requested to choose on the basis of preference (a choice context typical for economics), but it has to be stressed that the applicability of random utility models is much wider. In psychophysical experiments the criterion of choice might be, for instance, the intensity of lights, pitch of tones, perceived weight of objects, and so on. While in most instances of random utility models the distributions of the random variables are restricted to some parametric family (following Thurstone, who considered Gaussian distributed variables), the problem addressed in this entry is to characterize random utility theory in its most general form in terms of the testable restrictions it imposes on the choice data that it is supposed to model.

1. Random Utility Representation

The data of a typical choice experiment consist of the relative frequencies, or, ideally, choice probabilities $p(i, K)$ with which an alternative $i \in K$ is chosen when the subset K of alternatives is offered. The master set of n alternatives is conveniently identified with $\boldsymbol{n} = \{1, \ldots, n\}$. In principle any system of subsets may be offered, but two special cases are of both theoretical and practical interest. In a *complete system* of choice probabilities choices are obtained for every subset of $\boldsymbol{n}$ with at least two elements; if just all two-element subsets are offered, the data can be collected in a *binary choice probability* (BCP) matrix.

According to random utility theory the internal value or 'strength' of each alternative $i \in \boldsymbol{n}$ in the choice context of the experiment is modeled by a random variable $\boldsymbol{U}_i$, with all such random variables defined on the same probability space with measure Pr. The collection $\{\boldsymbol{U}_i\}_{i \in \boldsymbol{n}}$ is a *random utility* (RU) representation of the choice probabilities $p(i, K)$ whenever

$$p(i, K) = \Pr(\boldsymbol{U}_i = \max_{j \in K}\{\boldsymbol{U}_j\}), \quad i \in K \subseteq \boldsymbol{n}. \quad \text{(RU)}$$

The fact $p(i, \{i, j\}) + p(j, \{i, j\}) = 1$ for two-element subsets entails that the collection $\{\boldsymbol{U}_i\}_{i \in \boldsymbol{n}}$ is *noncoincident*, meaning that $\Pr(\boldsymbol{U}_i = \boldsymbol{U}_j) = 0$, and thus $\Pr(\boldsymbol{U}_i \geqslant \boldsymbol{U}_j) = \Pr(\boldsymbol{U}_i > \boldsymbol{U}_j)$, for $i \neq j$. This is no serious restriction; for instance, all continuous random variables have this property.

2. Representation by Rankings

The problem of interest now is to characterize RU in terms of a set of necessary and sufficient conditions on the observed choice probabilities, allowing an arbitrary joint distribution for the collection $\{U_i\}_{i \in n}$. Obviously, in RU the choice probabilities are completely determined by the $n!$ values $\Pr\{U_{i_1} > U_{i_2} > \cdots > U_{i_n}\}$ of this distribution for all rankings of the n alternatives. Any such ranking can be identified with the linear order π on n for which $i \pi j$ whenever i is ranked higher than j. Denoting the collection of linear orders on n by Π_n, choice probabilities $p(i, K)$ are said to be *induced by rankings* (IR) if there exists a probability distribution $\mathbb{P}$ on Π_n such that

$$p(i, K) = \mathbb{P}\{\pi \in \Pi_n : i \pi j \quad \text{for all} \quad j \in K \setminus \{i\}\},$$
$$i \in K \subseteq n \tag{IR}$$

As already noted by Block and Marschak (1960), RU and IR are equivalent.

In economics, where the interest is not in repeated choices by one individual, but in an aggregation of choices over many individuals, IR results immediately from the assumption that within any single person the choices derive from some fixed ranking of the alternatives (economists tend to call such choices 'rational'), with $\mathbb{P}$ collecting the relative frequencies of the rankings in the population.

The study of the representation problem for random utility models concentrates on IR rather than RU: verifying the existence of a probability distribution on a finite set of rankings turns out to be more tractable than verifying the existence of a collection of undetermined random variables.

2.1 Characterization for Complete Systems

Block and Marschak (1960) established that for a complete system of choice probabilities the linear inequalities

$$\sum_{K \subseteq J \subseteq n} (-1)^{|J \setminus K|} p(i, J) \geq 0, \quad i \in K \subseteq n \tag{BM}$$

are necessary conditions for IR, thus RU. Via an intricate combinatorial argument Falmagne (1978) then constructively showed how, given BM, a probability distribution $\mathbb{P}$ on Π_n satisfying IR can be constructed, thus proving that BM actually characterizes IR and RU in terms of testable restrictions on complete systems of observed choice probabilities.

3. The Geometry of Binary Choice Probabilities

No such definite result is available for BCP matrices, for which RU and IR specialize to

$$p_{ij} = \Pr(U_i > U_j) = \sum_{\{\pi \in \Pi_n : i \pi j\}} \mathbb{P}(\pi), \quad ij \in N$$

with p_{ij} as a shorthand for $p(i, \{i, j\})$ and with $N = \{ij : i, j \in n, i \neq j\}$ denoting the collection of ordered pairs from n.

Geometrically, any BCP matrix p is a point in $[0, 1]^N$, the unit hypercube in $n(n-1)$-dimensional real vector space indexed by N, and the collection of BCP matrices on n elements that are induced by rankings is a particular subset of this hypercube, denoted by P_n. Identifying a linear order on n with its indicator function (i.e., writing $\pi_{ij} = 1$ instead of $i \pi j$), IR can for BCP matrices be restated as

$$p \in P_n \Leftrightarrow p = \sum_{\pi \in \Pi_n} \mathbb{P}(\pi) \pi \tag{CH}$$

for some probability distribution $\mathbb{P}$, that is, for some nonnegative real numbers $\mathbb{P}(\pi)$ summing to unity. Thus, by definition, P_n constitutes the *convex hull* of the set Π_n consisting of $n!$ of the $2^{n(n-1)}$ vertices of the hypercube. By *linear duality theory* (see, e.g., Kuhn 1956) this statement is equivalent to the general criterion

$$p \in P_n \Leftrightarrow \langle c, p \rangle \leq \max_{\pi \in \Pi_n} \{\langle c, \pi \rangle\}$$

$$\text{for all integer } c \in \mathbb{R}^N, \; c \geq 0$$

where $\langle \cdot, \cdot \rangle$ is the standard inner product in $\mathbb{R}^N$. Thus, is an abstract sense, this system of linear inequalities characterizes BCP matrices p satisfying RU and IR. This solution, however, involves an infinite system of inequalities for any fixed, finite number n of alternatives, and, consequently, does not yield an effective procedure for checking whether for a given BCP matrix a random utility representation exists. (This contrasts with the solution BM for complete systems of choice probabilities.) The following standard theory makes it clear that, for any fixed n, the set P_n is in fact defined by a finite subsystem of the above infinite system. The characterization problem that remains is to find, for any n, such a finite collection of linear inequalities.

4. The Linear Description of P_n

By CH, P_n is a polytope, i.e., the convex hull of finitely many points, in $\mathbb{R}^N$. The set of vertices of P_n is Π_n, whence it is called the *linear ordering polytope*. Any polytope is alternatively described as a bounded *polyhedron*, i.e., a subset obtained as the intersection of finitely many halfspaces, or, the solution set of finitely many linear inequalities. In fact, any $p \in P_n$ satisfies the system of $\binom{n}{2}$ linear equalities (EQ)

$$p_{ij} + p_{ji} = 1, \quad ij \in N \tag{EQ}$$

each of which constrains P_n to be contained in the

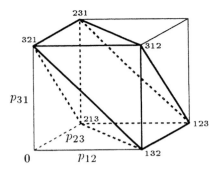

Figure 1
Unit cube with the linear ordering polytope P_3 (in bold) and vertices indicated with the corresponding rankings of $\{1, 2, 3\}$

hyperplane which is the intersection of the halfspaces defined by the two corresponding inequalities. As a consequence, P_n is not of full dimensionality in $\mathbb{R}^N$, but has (affine) dimension $n(n-1) - \binom{n}{2} = \binom{n}{2}$.

If the inequality $\langle a, p \rangle \leq a_0$ is valid for all $p \in P_n$ and the corresponding equality $\langle a, p \rangle = a_0$ is satisfied by some, but not all, $p \in P_n$, then the set $\{p \in P_n : \langle a, p \rangle = a_0\}$ is called a *face* of P_n. Geometrically, P_n is fully contained in the halfspace of $\mathbb{R}^N$ defined by this valid inequality and the face of P_n consists of the points at the boundary of P_n that lie in the hyperplane delimiting this halfspace. A face of maximum dimension, i.e., one less than the dimension P_n itself, is called a *facet* of P_n, and the corresponding valid inequality is called *facet defining*. A complete, nonredundant system of inequalities for P_n consists of facet-defining inequalities, one for each facet of P_n. Such a system is non-unique, since any two inequalities $\langle a, p \rangle \leq a_0$ and $\langle b, p \rangle \leq b_0$ that are the same modulo EQ (i.e., such that EQ entails $\langle a, p \rangle - \langle b, p \rangle = a_0 - b_0$) are equivalent and define the same face of P_n (if any). Thus, the representation problem is redefined as one of finding facet-defining inequalities for all facets of the linear ordering polytope P_n.

4.1 The Case $n = 3$ and the Triangle Inequality

The smallest nontrivial BCP-matrix $p = (p_{12}, p_{13}, p_{21}, p_{23}, p_{31}, p_{32})$ for $n = 3$ alternatives is, by (7), contained in a three-dimensional subspace of the unit hypercube of $\mathbb{R}^6$, specified, for instance, by the p_{12}, p_{23} and p_{31} coordinates. This is illustrated in Fig. 1. The polytope P_3 is the octahedron obtained as the convex hull of the six linear orders on $\{1, 2, 3\}$. These vertices and the boldface edges in Fig. 1 constitute the faces of dimension 0 and 1, respectively. The facets of P_3 are the triangular faces of the octahedron. Six of them coincide with the facets of the cube itself, correspond to the inequalities $p_{ij} \geq 0, p_{ij} \leq 1$, and thus represent no restriction on BCP matrices. The remaining two

facets, which do exclude parts of the cube from P_3, are defined by inequalities of the form

$$p_{ij} + p_{jk} + p_{ki} \leq 2, \quad i, j, k \in \mathbf{n}$$

Since this inequality can be equivalently rendered as

$$p_{ik} \leq p_{ij} + p_{jk}, \quad i, j, k \in \mathbf{n}$$

it is known as the *triangle inequality*.

Thus, for $n = 3$, the situation is simple, with the triangle inequality as necessary and sufficient condition. Since an inequality defining a facet of some P_n remains facet-defining for all higher-dimensional linear ordering polytopes, the triangle inequality is a necessary condition for all $n \geq 3$. Although the geometries of the six-dimensional P_4 and the 10-dimensional P_5 are considerably more complex than that of P_3, the triangle inequality turns out to be also sufficient for $n = 4$ and $n = 5$. It can be interpreted as 'probabilistic transitivity,' since, applied to the vertices of P_n, the inequality amounts to the transitivity property of linear orders as binary relations on $\mathbf{n}$. In this sense, EQ in one direction ($\leq$) represents a(nti)symmetry and in the reverse direction ($\geq$) completeness. (The property of (ir)reflexivity plays no role here.)

5. The General Case

In this way the picture seems nice and complete and, indeed, at some point it was conjectured that the triangle inequality would be sufficient for all n. However, for $n = 6$ soon a counterexample was found of some $p \notin P_6$, but satisfying this inequality. Thus, starting with $n = 6$, there are other facet-defining inequalities. Once this was realized, a hunt for facets started, yielding more and more inequalities, in fact whole classes of inequalities, for increasing n. (Fishburn (1992) presents history and state of the art of these developments at that point in time.) Two of the most general classes found up to now are presented next, to illustrate the complexity of the problem.

5.1 Facets Defined by Möbius Ladders

In the field of operations research, where the polytope P_n turns up in a discrete optimization context, Grötschel et al. (1985) developed techniques for proving inequalities facet-defining and defined various schemes of facet-defining inequalities in the language of graph theory. In this setup, *directed graphs* are considered with node set $\mathbf{n}$. Any arc set $A \subseteq N$ defines through its indicator function 1_A a linear functional denoted as

$$A(p) = \langle 1_A, p \rangle = \sum_{ij \in A} p_{ij}.$$

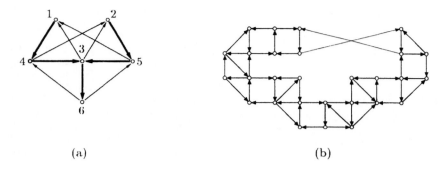

(a)   (b)

Figure 2
(a) Möbius ladder composed of one four-cycle and four three-cycles; arcs shared by two cycles in bold. (b) Möbius ladder of 21 cycles (adapted from Grötschel et al. (1985))

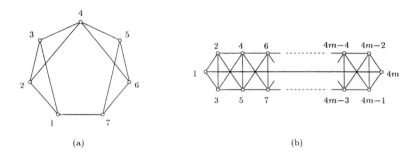

(a)   (b)

Figure 3
(a) A stability-critical graph with stability number 2. (b) An infinite family of stability-critical graphs (with stability number m)

By suitable choices for the arc set A and constant a_0 facet-defining inequalities of the form $A(p) \leqslant a_0$ may be obtained. One example follows.

Grötschel et al. (1985) call an arc set A a *Möbius ladder* basically if A is the union of an odd number k of (directed) cycles $C_1, C_2, ..., C_k$, such that each C_i is either a three-cycle or a four-cycle and the given sequence constitutes an (undirected) cycle on a higher level in the sense that any adjacent pair C_i, C_{i+1} (including C_k, C_1) has precisely one arc in common, while all nonadjacent pairs C_i, C_j are disjoint. (There are a few additional side-conditions.) For any such Möbius ladder A the inequality

$$A(p) \leqslant |A| - \frac{k+1}{2}$$

is facet defining for all linear ordering polytopes P_n for which it is defined (that is, with n equal to or exceeding the number of nodes appearing in A). Fig. 2(a) shows a small Möbius ladder, which, with $|A| = 11$ and $k = 5$, represents a facet-defining inequality for all $P_n, n \geqslant 6$. Fig. 2(b) illustrates the generality of the class of Möbius ladders by a more elaborate example, which also more explicitly shows the idea of the Möbius strip.

5.2 Facets Defined by Stability-critical Graphs

Using the techniques developed by Grötschel et al. (1985), Koppen (1995) derived another general class of facet-defining inequalities, this time in terms of *undirected graphs*. Let $G = (\boldsymbol{k}, E)$ be a connected graph with node set $\boldsymbol{k} = \{1, ..., k\}, k \geqslant 3$, and some edge set E of unordered pairs of $\boldsymbol{k}$. Let $S(\boldsymbol{k}, E)$ denote the *stability number* of G, i.e., the maximum cardinality of a *stable set* in G, where a subset of nodes of G is called stable if it does not contain an edge. G is called *stability-critical* if the removal of any one edge from G would increment the stability number (by one). Koppen (1995) proved that for any such $G = (\boldsymbol{k}, E)$ and any $2k$ distinct elements $u_1, ..., u_k, v_1, ..., v_k$ in $\boldsymbol{n}$ the inequality

$$\sum_{i \in k} p_{u_i v_i} - \sum_{\{i, j\} \in E} (p_{u_i v_j} + p_{u_j v_i}) \leqslant S(\boldsymbol{k}, E)$$

defines a facet of the linear ordering polytope $P_n, n \geqslant 2k$, if and only if G is stability-critical.

The graph in Fig. 3(a) represents such an inequality with $k = 7$ and $S(\boldsymbol{k}, E) = 2$ (any three-set contains an edge, but any edge removed introduces a stable three-set), which is facet defining for $P_n, n \geqslant 14$. In Fig. 3(b) an infinite family of stability-critical graphs is depicted, each corresponding to a new facet-defining inequality. The symmetry present here is 'accidental'; being stability-critical imposes no further structural restrictions on a graph whatsoever.

5.3 Conclusion for the Binary Case

The Möbius ladders and stability-critical graphs are just two examples of the various classes of facet-defining inequalities for BCP matrices known to date. In particular, while all cases considered here have 0–1 coefficients, facet-defining inequalities with general, unbounded integer coefficients have been found (Leung and Lee 1994, McLennan 1990, Suck 1992).

The conclusion is that, starting with the triangle inequality for $n \leqslant 5$, there is, with increasing n, a combinatorial explosion of facet-defining inequalities for P_n with no apparent structural regularities—witness the special case of stability-critical graphs alone. Thus, the problem of a complete characterization for general n seems intractable at the moment. What can be achieved on a more practical level, by computer enumeration, is obtaining a complete linear description of P_n for specific small n, $n = 6, 7, 8, \ldots$.

6. Extension to General Probabilistic Measurement

Taking an abstract, measurement-theoretic point of view, Heyer and Niederée (1992) have shown that random utility theory, as discussed above, can be generalized to other instances of probabilistic measurement (see *Measurement Theory: Probabilistic*). The basic idea is as follows (considerable extensions to more complicated relational structures and data formats are to be found in Niederée and Heyer (1997)).

Let for some finite domain of n objects, identified with n, a mapping $p: n^k \to [0, 1]$ specify 'probability data' on k-tuples of objects. Let Q be a 'quantitative' k-ary relation on $\mathbb{R}$ and $\mathscr{R}$ the set of k-ary relations on n isomorphically embeddable in $(\mathbb{R}, Q)$. Then, in this general setting, it can be shown that p has a random scale representation

$$p(i_1, \ldots, i_k) = \Pr((U_{i_1}, \ldots, U_{i_k}) \in Q)$$

for some jointly distributed collection of random variables $\{U_i\}_{i \in n}$ if and only if p is induced by a probability distribution on $\mathscr{R}$,

$$p(i_1, \ldots, i_k) = \mathbb{P}\{R \in \mathscr{R} : (i_1, \ldots, i_k) \in R\}$$

if and only if p is in the convex hull of $\mathscr{R}$, interpreted as vertices of the hypercube $[0, 1]^{n^k}$. Classical random utility theory in terms of RU, IR, and CH is simply the

special case with $k = 2$, $Q = >$ and $\mathscr{R}$ the set of linear orders on n.

The consequence is that for the general case of probability data p the characterization problem amounts to finding, for any n, a system of linear inequalities defining the facets of the polytope with vertex set $\mathscr{R}$. Some results have been obtained for other relations (Regenwetter 1996, Suck 1997). Typically, in such a case the first nontrivial facets found are the ones corresponding to the defining properties of the class of relations $\mathscr{R}$ (see the end of Sect. 4.1). The parallel with the linear order case goes further in that, quite generally, more and more facets turn up with increasing n. To date, these investigations have not resulted in characterization theorems for general n and, except for very small n, linear descriptions of the corresponding polytopes are only partly known.

See also: Decision and Choice: Random Utility Models of Choice and Response Time; Elicitation of Probabilities and Probability Distributions; Measurement Theory: Probabilistic; Preference Models with Latent Variables; Utility and Subjective Probability: Contemporary Theories; Utility and Subjective Probability: Empirical Studies

Bibliography

Block H D, Marschak J 1960 Random orderings and stochastic theories of response. In: Olkin I, Ghurye S, Hoefding W, Madow W, Mann H (eds.) *Contributions to Probability and Statistics*. Stanford University Press, Stanford, CA

Falmagne J-C 1978 A representation theorem for finite random scale systems. *Journal of Mathematical Psychology* **18**: 52–72

Fishburn P C 1992 Induced binary probabilities and the linear ordering polytope: A status report. *Mathematical Social Sciences* **23**: 67–80

Grötschel M, Jünger M, Reinelt G 1985 Facets of the linear ordering polytope. *Mathematical Programming* **33**: 43–60

Heyer D, Niederée R 1992 Generalizing the concept of binary choice systems induced by rankings: One way of probabilizing deterministic measurement structures. *Mathematical Social Sciences* **23**: 31–44

Koppen M 1995 Random utility representation of binary choice probabilities: Critical graphs yielding critical necessary conditions. *Journal of Mathematical Psychology* **39**: 21–39

Kuhn H W 1956 Solvability and consistency for linear equations and inequalities. *American Mathematical Monthly* **63**: 217–32

Leung J, Lee J 1994 More facets from fences for linear ordering and acyclic subgraph polytopes. *Discrete Applied Mathematics* **50**: 185–200

McLennan A 1990 Binary stochastic choice. In: Chipman J S, McFadden D, Richter M K (eds.) *Preferences, Uncertainty, and Optimality*. Westview, Boulder, CO

Niederée R, Heyer D 1997 Generalized random utility models and the representational theory of measurement: A conceptual link. In: Marley A A J (ed.) *Choice, Decision, and Measurement*. L. Erlbaum, Mahwah, NJ

Regenwetter M 1996 Random utility representations of finite m-ary relations. *Journal of Mathematical Psychology* **40**: 219–34

Suck R 1992 Geometric and combinatorial properties of the polytope of binary choice probabilities. *Mathematical Social Sciences* **23**: 81–102
Suck R 1997 Probabilistic biclassification and random variable representation. *Journal of Mathematical Psychology* **41**: 57–64
Thurstone L L 1927 A law of comparative judgment. *Psychological Review* **34**: 273–86

M. Koppen

Charisma and Charismatic

'Charisma' or 'gift of grace' is a theological notion that has been widely used in the social and religious sciences to describe either the hierarchical organization of religious roles or explain the growth and development of social movements based on religious inspiration or the basis of authority and leadership in society generally. In its strictly religious context, it means a divinely conferred power, being derived from the Greek *kharisma* (*kharis* favor or grace). Charismatic power is associated with the idea of the sacred as a force in human affairs. A person in possession of charisma is thought to have a talent, for example, in terms of healing or prophecy. In anthropological research, there has been considerable interest in 'shamanism' as a form of charismatic authority that depends on a capacity to have visions and to perform healing (see M. Eliade 1964). In sociology, it is conceptually part of an analytical framework that is concerned with understanding large-scale changes in religious institutions and the foundations of authority.

1. The Sociology of Charisma

In the sociology of religion, the study of charisma has been closely associated with Max Weber (1864–1920) who adopted the idea from the historical and theological research of Rudolf Sohm and Karl Holl who in turn had developed the concept in their analysis of Canon Law. Weber wrote that 'the concept of charisma' (gift of grace) is taken from the vocabulary of early Christianity. For the Christian hierocracy Rudolf Sohm, in his *Kirchenrecht*, was the first to clarify the substance of the concept, even though he did not use the same terminology. Others (for instance, Holl in *Enthusiasmus und Bussgewalt*) have clarified certain important consequences of it. It is thus nothing new (Weber 1978, pp. 1, 216). Despite Weber's modesty about the adoption of the idea, it became a fundamental dimension of his analysis of power and had far-reaching consequences for the development of the sociology of religious institutions. Weber generalized the idea and grasped its radical implications for the study of political change in human societies.

In the rise of religion certain individuals are recognized as having a capacity to experience ecstatic states that are regarded as the precondition for healing, telepathy, and divination. It is primarily through 'these extraordinary powers that have been designated by such special terms as 'mana,' 'orenda,' and the Iranian 'Maga' (the term from which our word 'magic' is derived). We shall henceforth employ the term 'charisma' for such extraordinary powers' (Weber 1963, p. 2). Such charismatic power is either inherited as a natural endowment or it is acquired by extraordinary means. The religious talent in both cases is a substance that may remain dormant in a person until it is aroused by asceticism or trance.

Weber did not dwell specifically on these features of charisma in folk religion because he wanted to employ the term to understand the secular dynamic of authority and leadership in social institutions. His main intention was to compare and contrast three types of authority: charismatic, traditional, and legal-rational. As we have seen, charismatic authority rests on the ability of a leader to inspire disciples in the belief of the authenticity of a calling. In practical terms, an authentic claim is validated by a talent such as healing, but this alone cannot be the basis of authority. In the case of genuine charisma, a follower has a duty to accept the authority of a leader. In *Economy and Society* (Weber 1978, pp. 1, 241), the term charisma is applied to a certain quality of an individual personality by virtue of which he is considered extraordinary and treated as endowed with supernatural, superhuman, or at least specifically exceptional powers or qualities. Traditional authority involves the acceptance of a rule that expresses a custom, namely an established pattern of belief or practice. Finally, legal-rational authority is typical of bureaucracies in which formal rules of conduct are underpinned by procedural norms. These forms of authority are in turn forms of compliance. Tradition depends on compliance through empathy; legal-rational authority rests on rational argument; and charismatic authority and leadership require inspiration. Weber provided many diverse illustrations of charismatic leaders including Jesus Christ, Mohammed, Napoleon, Stefan George, and the Chinese Emperor. Although the cases were heterogeneous, he argued that charismatic authority is confronted by a common problem of succession with the death of the leader. Charismatic authority is thus unstable. With the demise of the charismatic leader, the disciples typically disband, but occasionally a solution for continuity will be developed. In the case of the Christian Church, Weber argued that the charismatic authority of Christ was invested in the Church itself (as the body of Christ) and thus in the bishops who control the 'keys of grace' enjoy a vicarious authority. This 'institutionalization of charisma' becomes over time increasingly formal, bureaucratic, and impersonal. As the charismatic power of Christ becomes transformed into a set of formal procedures and bureaucratic rules, Weber spoke of the 'routinization of charisma.'

2. Forms of Religious Association

Weber's account of charisma was also an important component of his sociology of religion within which he attempted to identify different religious roles and patterns of organization. For example, he distinguished between the prophet who, as a charismatic figure, has a personal call, and the priest has authority by virtue of his service in a sacred tradition. The prophets, who often emerge from the ranks of the priesthood, are unremunerated, and depend on gifts from followers. Weber also distinguished two forms of prophecy as represented on the one hand by Buddha and on the other by Zoroaster and Muhammad. The latter are involved in 'ethical prophecy' and are conceived as instruments of God. These prophets receive a commission from God to preach a revelation and demand obedience from their disciples as an ethical duty. By contrast exemplary prophets demonstrate to their followers a salvational path through the example provided by their own lives. Exemplary prophecy was, according to Weber, characteristic of Asia; ethical prophecy, of the Abrahamic religions of the Middle East. Weber's analysis of charisma with respect to ethical prophecy in the Old Testament has been subject to considerable criticism (see Zeitlin 1984), but his conceptual framework continues to influence both sociology (see Lindholm 1990) and anthropology (see Werbner and Basu 1998).

This discussion of charisma with respect to different social roles should be seen as part of a larger sociological debate about the forms of association that characterize the social organization of religious belief and practice. Weber wanted to argue that any group that is subject to charismatic authority forms a charismatic community (*Gemeinde*) and that such a community is inherently unstable. With the death of the leader, the group either dissolves or charisma undergoes a process of routinization. The disciples have no career, no formal hierarchy, no offices, and no qualifications. The Church that provides the organizational context of the priesthood is very different. Ecclesiastical organizations require a hierarchical administration of the 'charisma of office' in which there are definite stages in clerical and administrative careers. It is clearly the case that Weber's sociology of charisma should be understood as an application of Ernest Troeltsch's 'church-sect typology' in which there is an historical oscillation between the evangelical sects and the bureaucratic churches (see Troeltsch 1931).

3. Charismatic Movements

Because Weber believed that in modern societies legal rational authority would become dominant, tradition and charisma were regarded as 'prerationalistic' and thus as characteristic of premodern societies. The notion that charismatic authority was not a resilient aspect of modern society was in turn a function of Weber's pessimistic understanding of social change in terms of secular rationalism and the erosion of religious meaning. Against Weber's assessment, the late nineteenth and twentieth centuries have been profoundly influenced by charismatic movements. Charismatic renewal has been a common theme of diverse religious movements in 'primal societies' and in the industrial societies of Europe and North America. The collapse of aboriginal or tribal societies under colonial settlement saw the spread of charismatic movements against the supremacy of White-settler societies such as the Ghost Dance among the Cheyenne and Sioux tribes of the American Plains. A Paiute prophet called Wovoka had received a vision in which through ritual dance the dead would return to restore the pristine culture of native societies. This anti-White charismatic movement subsided after the murder of Sitting Bull and the subsequent massacre of his followers at Wounded Knee in 1890. Charismatic leadership has also played a significant role in those new religious movements that have been a response to the social and economic disruptions associated with the decolonization of the Third World (see P. Worsley *The Trumpet Shall Sound* 1970).

In contexts of rapid social change, charismatic leadership is an important component of so-called 'revitalization movements' that function to create an effective transition from tribal to urban society. However, charisma is also associated with religious forms that are a response to personal alienation, isolation, and meaninglessness in the developed, industrial world. One illustration is the Family who were disciples of Charles Manson and operated in southern California in the late 1960s. Manson, who was a social dropout with a criminal record, provided a message of personal liberation based on mind-expanding drugs and found a receptive set of disciples in the cultic milieux of the American counterculture. The Manson Family offered disoriented disciples the experience of an absolute community that depended on a powerful ideology and indoctrination (see Schreck 1988). Another American illustration would be Jim Jones and the People's Temple (see Weightman 1983). These manifestations of charisma in modern society are closely associated with the dislocations of youth culture, the anomie of the modern city, and the spread of personal alienation.

4. Conclusion; Charisma in the Information Age

Weber's analysis of charisma has produced a rich legacy of sociological research, but there are serious conceptual problems associated with its application in contemporary society. The concept of charismatic movement is used to describe a variety of revivalist, nativist, messianic, and healing movements. There is considerable debate in sociology and religious studies about whether charisma in modern society is degraded and inauthentic (see Wilson 1975). The term is frequently employed to describe the fleeting popularity of political leaders whose social appeal is constructed by campaigns in the electronic media. Whereas charisma in traditional societies arises spontaneously in the collective enthusiasm for divinely inspired leaders, in modern politics it is inevitably the product of deliberate orchestration of the media. The notoriety of the Manson Family and the People's Temple was a conscious product of media attention. However, this argument indicates a persistent issue in charismatic movements, namely how to distinguish between genuine and false claims to religious authority. Biblical warnings against 'false prophets' recognized the fact that disciples could be misguided. While the term has been implausibly stretched to describe a diverse and heterogeneous range of leaders in the twentieth century from Adolf Hitler to J. F. Kennedy, it remains a basic concept in sociology and religious studies.

See also: Charisma: Social Aspects of; Folk Religion; Healing; Millennialism; New Religious Movements; Prophetism; Religion, Sociology of; Weber, Max (1864–1920)

Bibliography

Eliade M 1964 *Shamanism. Archaic Techniques of Ecstasy.* Ballingen Foundation, New York
Lindholm C 1990 *Charisma.* Blackwell, Oxford, UK
Schreck N (ed.) 1988 *The Manson File.* Amok Press, New York
Troeltsch E 1931 *The Social Teaching of the Christian Churches.* Allen and Unwin, London, 2 Vols.
Werbner P, Basu H (eds.) 1998 *Embodying Charisma Modernity Locality and the Performance of Emotion in Sufi Cults.* Routledge, London and New York
Weber M 1963 *The Sociology of Religion.* Methuen, London
Weber M 1978 *Economy and Society. An Outline of Interpretive Sociology.* University of California Press, Berkeley, CA, 2 Vols.
Weightman J M 1983 *Making Sense of the Jonestown Suicides. A Sociological History of the People's Temple.* Mellen Press, New York
Wilson B R 1975 *The Noble Savages. The Primitive Origins of Charisma and its Contemporary Survival.* University of California Press, Berkeley, CA
Zeitlin I M 1984 *Ancient Judaism Biblical Criticism from Max Weber to the Present.* Polity Press, Cambridge, UK

B. S. Turner

Charisma: Social Aspects of

The concept of charisma indicates the presence of a quality which is considered to be extraordinary and exceptional. The subject holds this quality personally, freely, and independently of his or her own will. Once this quality is socially recognized, it lends those who possess it a specific power inside the community they are part of. The explanations given for the possession of charisma—very often imputed to the arbitrary will of divinity—are crucial for the distinction between the different forms of power deriving from its possession, ranging from the authoritativeness of the prophet to the ruling of the leader, and from the magic powers of the shaman to the pure might of the fierce warrior. From the point of view of its social aspects, the concept of charisma refers to the manifestation of a specific modality of power (see *Power in Society*) inside the society, as well as to the specific form of community (see *Community Sociology*) that forms itself around the carrier of personal charisma.

1. The Origin of Charisma as a Problematic Concept

Originally, the concept of charisma appears in the New Testament literature, and almost exclusively in the epistles of the apostle Paul, where it is used with different meanings. It can in fact be: (a) a free gift from God, (b) the specific gift of a vocation, (c) a series of godly gifts following the investiture of a priest, (d) the extraordinary manifestations of the Holy Spirit that underline the evangelizing potentiality of the first Christians. Paul distinguishes between extraordinary gifts— those that do not correspond to any determined function—and exceptional spirituality, which fills the performance of ordinary functions with grace. In the spiritual life of the first communities, the charisma that resulted in the production of miraculous effects were fulfilling a function of legitimization of the acts of preaching. Moreover, they were also facilitating and increasing the efficacy of preaching. In these cases, the relation between charisma and conduct of life becomes apparent (Ducros 1937). A difference emerges, therefore, between the gift given to spread the Word, and that given to allow the subject to begin moving toward perfection. In this tradition of studies, the possession of charisma is the foundation and legitimization of the relations of the subject with the divinity that grants it, but also with the institution that guarantees the transmission of the various faith truths and of the appropriate forms of worship. Moreover, having the charisma also legitimizes its possessors in their relations with those for whom they fulfill a function of spiritual leader.

Being the leader of a community of believers for the salvation of its members is the decisive and fundamental function of the carrier of personal charisma. Having recognized the charismatic power of the leading function exercised by the 'holy people' means grasping the ideal-typical status in which every leader is a guide leading toward definitive and certain salvation, against every possible opposition. Therefore, the carrier of personal charisma ends up coinciding, in the New Testament literature, with the man of God, who intervenes in moments of crisis to show the way of perfection: the only one that truly counts for individual or collective salvation.

The considerations regarding the use of charisma in the communities of believers can be transposed also to civil communities. A long historic tradition from Plutarch to Hegel through Machiavelli, Kant, Carlyle, and the whole German Romanticism movement prepared the basic elements of the image of the charismatic leader (Cavalli 1981) that Weber would later translate into an ideal-typical figure.

2. The Concept of Charisma in Contemporary Sociology

Max Weber (1864–1920) is the author who derives the best results from this dual tradition on the social aspects of charisma. While accepting Rudolf Sohm's work on the origin of the Christian Church, Max Weber underlined different aspects of it: the idea of the supernatural gift offered for the work of a specific mission; the concepts of call, of predestination, and of election. From other works on the history of Christianity, Weber derives further developments of his theory of charisma. This is the case with Karl Holl and his studies on monasticism. For Holl, as for Rudolf Sohm, the possession of charisma is the foundation of the authority inside religious institution. Whatever its concrete manifestations—from the proof guaranteed by exceptional interventions, to the exemplary manifestation of a permanently sanctified life—the objective of charisma is to lead the community of believers after having been recognized by it.

2.1 Meanings of Charisma in Weber

In his work, Weber defines charisma many times. First of all, it is part of the sociological categories and more precisely, it is one of the ideal types of power. In the definition of 'charismatic power' the 'charisma' is

> a certain quality of an individual personality by virtue of which he is apart from ordinary men and treated as endowed with supernatural, superhuman, or at least specifically exceptional power or qualities. These, as such, are not accessible to the ordinary person, but are regarded as of divine origin or as exemplary, and on the basis of them the individual concerned is treated as a leader. In primitive circumstances this peculiar kind of deference is paid to prophets, to people with a reputation for therapeutic or legal wisdom, to leaders in the hunt, and heroes in war (Weber 1956/1968, p. 48)

The analysis of the term 'charisma' occurs also when Weber is discussing types of religious communities. Weber defines it here—not without connections to the analyses of the Durkheimian school, and

in particular, with Marcel Mauss's studies—as the collection of extraordinary powers that populate the field of magically or religiously motivated action. In this field charisma, understood as an ideal-typical form, is 'a gift that inheres in an object or person simply by virtue of natural endowment,' and it 'may be produced artificially in an object or person through some extraordinary means.' This latter definition is apparently secondary, since 'it is assumed that charismatic powers can be developed only in people or objects in which the germ already existed but would have remained dormant unless evoked by some ascetic or other regimen' (Weber 1956/1965, p. 2).

The two parts, of course, complement each other. In the analysis of charisma as a sociological category of social action, the accent is on the recognition of the exceptional quality, whatever this might be. We must also stress, however, that in the section concerning religious communities, charisma is underlined in its substantiality: It has, in other words, a specific content and expresses itself in a doctrine.

2.2 Analysis of Charisma as to Types of Religious Communities

The quality of charisma becomes more precise in its primary form as the capacity of the subject that carries it to awaken and govern the hidden powers that inhabit the natural world. This capacity can be consubstantial with the actors or activated as a consequence of an exceptional state of being, namely ecstasy. What for lay people cannot be other than an occasional experience, is for magicians a dimension characterizing the existence to which they have permanent access: 'The magician is the person who is permanently endowed with charisma.'

The success of charisma, understood in this sense, is directly connected to the capacity to force the invisible powers to yield to one's own will through the use of adequate stratagems. On the other hand, it disappears when supernatural powers assert themselves, powers that are indifferent to any kind of constraint but sensitive to veneration and worship acts. The magician is substituted by the priest or minister who is a functionary taking care of a 'regularly organized and permanent enterprise concerned with influencing the gods, in contrast with the individual and occasional efforts of magicians' (Weber 1956/1965, p. 28). The regularity of the functions and rites rendered priests as functionaries who often inherit their position and whose power seems to be separated from personal charisma.

> Yet another distinguishing quality of the priest, it is asserted, in his professional equipment of special knowledge, fixed doctrine and vocational qualifications, which brings him into contrast with sorcerers, prophets, and other types of religious functionaries who exert their influence by virtue of personal gifts (charisma) made manifest in miracle and revelation (Weber 1956/1965, p. 29).

The prophet is, in this analysis, 'a purely individual bearer of charisma, who by virtue of his mission proclaims a religious doctrine or divine commandment' (Weber 1956/1965, p. 46). It is, therefore, not so important if a new community emerges around prophets or if their followers refer more to their person than to their doctrine. What is decisive is the 'purely personal charisma' distinguishing prophets from priests or ministers, while the content of their preaching and the specificity of their actions, consisting in doctrines and ethical imperatives instead of magic, distinguish them from magicians.

2.3 Sociology of Power

Max Weber defines once more the concept of charisma when passing from the analysis of religious communities to that of political communities and, through these, to the sociology of power. It is during this third phase of his work that the social aspects of charisma are underlined. What is important to highlight is his further clarification of the emotional aspect of charisma, which is also, to a certain extent, meta-everyday, alien to the paths of rationalization that are needed for its social reproduction, but still necessary for the foundation of a new epoch. Weber arrives at the point of saying that every foundation moment is, in fact, charismatic. This connects the use of charisma not only to its social recognition but also to the processes of innovation and social transformation. He contrasts the permanent character of the traditional and the bureaucratic structures, to the foundational character of the charismatic action.

> Die Deckung allen über die Anforderungen des ökonomischen Alltags hinaus gehenden Bedarfs dagegen ist, je mehr wir historisch zurücksehen, desto mehr, prinzipiell gänzlich heterogen und zwar: charismatisch, fundiert gewesen. Das bedeutet: die 'natürlichen' Leiter in psychischer, physischer, ökonomischer, ethischer, religiöser, politischer Not waren weder angestellte Amtspersonen, noch Inhaber eines als Fachwissen erlernten und gegen Entgelt geübten 'Berufs' im heutigen Sinn dieses Wortes, sondern Träger spezifischer, als übernatürlich (im Sinne von: nicht jedermann zugänglich) gedachter Gaben des Körpers und Geistes (Weber 1956, p. 662).

Summarized in one sentence, this important quotation says that the answer to human needs, going beyond mere economic needs, is not given by experts or people holding public office but by bearers of qualities of the body and mind perceived as supernatural.

In Weber's methodology such distinctions have of course an ideal-typical character. It is therefore impossible to trace the 'pure forms' of each of them as well as to draw specific boundaries between one category and the other. This means, for example, that it is possible to find some elements of prophetic charisma in the behavior of a political leader, of a priest, or of a military leader. Likewise, magical elements can be found in religious action: This happens, for instance, when prophets use magic acts to demonstrate their own charisma.

At least three aspects of the Weberian analysis of charisma need to be recalled here: the nature of social recognition, the implicitly protesting character of charismatic power, the transformation of the exercise of charisma into everyday practice, or in other words, its 'routinization,' and, inside the everyday practice, the distinction between personal and official charisma.

2.4 Social Recognitions

The possession of charismatic qualities is connected to the social context in two ways. On the one hand it is in the social context that the recognition takes place and those possessing charisma need to be socially recognized as such by their followers. On the other hand, social recognition does not constitute the foundation of charisma. It is, on the contrary, a duty for those that are expected to recognize it. 'This recognition, psychologically born of enthusiasm or adversity and hope, involves complete personal devotion' (Weber 1956/1994, p. 33). The recognition refers, therefore, to a previous confident expectation. The nature of this expectation is that of a positive event such as a reconquest of political freedom or of supernatural salvation or, again, of a redemption capable of restoring to the entire people its place among the nations. A specific relation emerges between recognition of charisma, the diffused and extended expectation of the carrier of charismatic qualities, and the reunification around that person of a completely renewed community of followers, which aims at originating a process of renewal for the whole society. Since the entire Weberian discourse is based on ideal-typical configurations, it also has numerous variants: The social recognition of prophetic charisma has a completely different relation with 'proof' compared to magical charisma or to that of the political leader. Prophets proclaiming a 'religious doctrine or a divine imperative' need only occasionally to 'prove' the validity of their message through magical acts revealing their possession of prophetic charisma. Things look different for the magician and the leader. For them proof is the concrete result of their enterprise. Therefore, while magicians are constantly tied to the success of their own art, leaders are continually challenged to prove their charisma through (military or political) victory. As a consequence, while prophets can expect to be believed by virtue of their own testimony and are not under an obligation of certifying their own charisma through magical acts, magicians and charismatic leaders connect their credibility to the ongoing success of their extraordinary qualities.

Naturally, in cases like this, where it is not possible to find such ideal-types in their pure status in historic reality, there are many steps between one type and the other. Prophets, seen as an ideal-typical representation of charismatic power, are not just those who proclaim the 'new commandment.' They are also those who, 'as a prophetic blow and a blustering flame,' evoke 'the indefinable that pervades and reinforces big communities' (Weber 1985: p. 612, my translation). This reconnects the prophet to the charismatic leader, while the position toward the divinity (of which the prophet explicitly wants to be interpreter), as well as the social function exercised, keep the two types distinguished from each other. The prophet's function is in fact limited to the announcement of the divine message in the first case, while leaders are forced to maintain their position until victory is achieved.

2.5 Protesting Character of Charismatic Powers

The above helps us to understand the connection that Weber draws between charismatic power and situations of social crisis: The recognition of charisma, following an expectation, emerges only when a situation of social crisis looks for a solution in exceptional individuals, of whom it is possible to be devotees. From this point of view, the possession of charisma being a direct and personal gift from God, it ends up representing a kind of power implicitly in conflict with and often alternative to traditional or bureaucratic-legal power. The crisis in which the carrier of personal charisma operates is, in fact, also and mainly a crisis of leadership. In the articulation of the ideal-typical image of the 'prophet' defined as an ideal-typical case of personal charismatic power, Weber observes that the prophet almost never comes from the clergy: '... the personal call is the decisive element distinguishing the prophet from the priest. The latter lays claim to authority by virtue of his service in a sacred tradition, while the prophet's claim is based on personal revelation and charisma' (Weber 1956/1965, p. 46). This is true also in the political sector. Charismatic leaders often operate in the passage between property power and legal power and what characterizes them is not so much the content of their message as the style they use to spread it. They act driven by a duty, by virtue of which they do not present a value, but state a truth. Their message is therefore a mission they are imposing on themselves. The charisma is therefore no longer just a quality or a gift, but a 'highly asymmetric power-relationship between an inspired guide and a cohort of followers who see in him and his message the promise and anticipated achievements of a new order, to which all adhere with greater or lesser conviction' (Boudon and Bourricaud 1989, pp. 70–1). Therefore, charismatic power is based not only on the exceptional endowments of its carriers but also on the exceptional character of the social situation inside which they establish themselves, and on the promise they pro-

claim. Thus the analysis of the connection between charismatic power and utopia is introduced, where utopia is understood as the realization of a new social order. Often, though not always, Weber suggests, the mission of the carrier of charisma is of revolutionary character, since it reverses every hierarchy of values and clashes against usage, law, and tradition.

In the case of the prophet, as well as in that of the charismatic leader, charismatic power is tied to moments of crisis and transition and it is a temporary power. As such it is based on an uncertain and risky economic ground (a real 'charismatic economy'), often constituted by free offerings, gifts, or war booty. Carriers of personal charisma do not create any kind of systematic and permanent production of resources through a stable and lasting economy, nor do their followers. Charismatic power is therefore characteristic of the moments of transition *in statu nascenti* and is bound to disappear when social life goes back to normal.

2.6 Transmission of Charisma

From Weber's point of view, getting back to everyday life is, also in this case, the result of the social action of concrete social actors. In fact, the 'adherents' of the emotional community that formed itself around the carrier of charisma, as well as the 'administrative machinery' (whether constituted by followers or trustworthy people), tend to bring it about that the relation 'ends up resting, ideally and materially on a lasting fundament of unitary character.' This becomes especially evident when the problem of succession poses itself, after the demise of the carrier of charisma. The problem can be solved in different ways. Charismatic leaders can themselves, while still alive, look for a new carrier of charisma or designate a successor; the administrative machinery 'charismatically qualified' can designate a successor, or the charisma can be identified as a quality of the blood and therefore parental inheritance can affirm itself as a mechanism of succession.

Clearly, personal charisma is not always abandoned as such but it certainly tends to be subordinated to an administrative, charismatically qualified apparatus, capable of recognizing the 'signs,' or of deciding upon the norms on the basis of which the charisma can be recognized in the most rigorous possible way. Sometimes the personal charisma disappears completely, as is the case with primogeniture, which affirmed itself in the West and in Japan, where lords or monarchs are such independently of the recognition of their subjects; from this point of view, they can be completely devoid of any personal charisma.

Among these forms of transmission of charisma, of particular importance is the possibility of transmission through ritual acts, which takes a concrete form in the charisma of function. This is the case of priestly charisma and of royal charisma, both transmitted through purification, laying on of hands, and anointing. The charismatic capacities that have been acquired this way are independent of the personal qualities of those who possess them.

The transformation of charisma in everyday practice has many consequences. For example, the establishment of the principle of the charisma's inheritance extended to the administrative apparatus implies the hereditary transmission of the powers of lordship and administration of goods, therefore founding the type of the 'aristocratic state.' Moreover, the transformation of charisma in everyday practice implies the loss of the extraeconomic character, distinctive of voluntary militant adherence, in favor of a continual acquisition and redistribution of resources. The vassals are substituted by the 'taxable subjects,' the trustworthy supporters by the party's executives, the penitential charisma of the martyrs and ascetics is replaced by the official charisma of the bishops and priests.

Weber also establishes a relation to the economy: 'But the more developed the economic interdependencies of the monetary economy, the greater the pressure of the charismatic subject's everyday needs becomes' (Weber 1956/1994, p. 44). To conclude: 'Charisma typically appears early on in the development of a religious (prophetic) or political (conquering) authority. It will give way before long, however, to routine powers as soon as its authority has been assured and, above all, as soon as it has gained sway over the masses' (Weber 1956/1994, p. 44). This way the passage takes place between the charismatic and the ordinary administration.

3. Charisma as an Operational Concept in Contemporary Research

Contemporary sociology has shown interest in the Weberian concept of charisma in various ways, in the frame of a general rediscovery of this author. Important studies have been carried out in the field of political sociology where a reconstruction of the 'charismatic leader' has been accomplished. From this reconstruction a new interpretation of totalitarian dictatorships, and of the crisis of contemporary democracies, has emerged. Besides this, a second stream of research can be seen in the field of the study of the routinization processes of charisma and, in particular, of the coexistence of personal and official charisma. In fact, if we admit that among the different forms of transmission of charisma there is one that rests on ritual acts carried out by a 'charismatically qualified' authority, a substantially different situation is reached. In this new situation, the faith of the believers is not directed toward a person but toward a way of transmitting an extraordinary quality, repr-

oduced through a ritual, which is in turn guaranteed by an institution. The functional charisma does not refer to the subject anymore but to the 'belief in a state of grace, specific to the institution' (Séguy 1988). The result is a situation opposite to the initial one: 'from being a personal, unstable, and ephemeral characteristic, and by definition nontransmissible, the charisma becomes stable and enduring' (Séguy 1988, p. 18, my translation). In this way, it becomes possible to imagine a 'charismatic grace,' characteristic of the carrier of personal charisma, as opposed to an 'institutional grace.' Weber does, of course, admit the possibility that a personal charisma may hide inside a subject—for instance a priest—who carries a functional charisma. Jean Séguy does not, however, see an exceptional opposition between the two, but more a kind of kinship or elective affinity. Functional charisma is not given in an indiscriminate fashion from the charismatically qualified institution to everyone who may ask for it. It is not just the result of a charismatic education, but is founded on the pre-existence of the charisma itself inside the subject. Briefly, the institution is only a caretaker whose task is to protect the personal vocation, and therefore the gift, that the individual has received in a completely free and personal way, and to let it grow, therefore guaranteeing its realization.

4. Methodological Issues and Possible Developments

The concept of charisma has gained remarkable success in ordinary language. There, it has been assumed in its weak meaning, becoming synonymous with qualities that are functionally connected to the mere communication process. The charismatic person is first and foremost a communicator and the 'charisma' consists essentially in his or her capacity to communicate and convince. The current extension and complexity of mass media communication renders such qualities crucial for media success. The decisive character of this kind of success in the contemporary communication society renders the success of such weak understanding of the concept of charisma treacherous and misleading. In fact, even if the communicative qualities that explain media success are personal and free, they do not establish real leaderships.

When passing from the revelation of pure media success to the contents of such success, it is evident that it is not possible to put on the same level the success of a television journalist and that of the media preachers who were flourishing in the USA during the 1980s and 1990s. Nor is it possible to compare the latter with the media success of a political leader. Compared to the original Weberian conceptualization, the mere art of communicating and convincing certainly does not contain the social aspects of

1657

charisma, except in the most insignificant way. Media success does not make this carrier a 'people's leader,' nor does it make the person the carrier of a mission, which in some way transcends his or her ordinary professional task. Nothing impedes the carrier of personal charisma, spiritual as well as political, 'from the plebiscitary ruler, to the big demagog, or to the leader of a political party' (Weber, 1958, p. 50, my translation) from making constant and methodical use of the potentialities of the mass media. This does not prevent the charisma—understood here as characterized by the assumption of a leadership responsibility following an absolutely personal call and in response to a crisis situation—from expressing itself completely independently from the mediagenic qualities of the subject and, therefore, of their eventual enhancement through the mass media.

The concept of charisma, correctly interpreted in its ideal-typical meaning, is far away from being just a historically born out and conceptually concluded sociological category. Even if charisma is often connected by Weber to the infancy of societies and is supposed to come before the widespread and all-embracing process of rationalization, the 'charismatic' moment continues to cross contemporary social establishments periodically, every time they find themselves in a context of crisis. Elements of 'charismatic power' are sometimes present, not only behind official charisma but also to distinguish between the functionary of a party with a strong ideological identity and who, chosen among the holders of leadership offices, will be its actual leader. While occupying the leadership position this person will trace the boundaries of the ethic of conviction, redefining the objectives. Of course, this is not enough: In their redefinition of the objective, leaders need to lean on the main principles with which they feel themselves to be personally invested. Elements of 'personal charisma' and of 'exemplary prophecy' can therefore be found inside a party secretary as well as inside every founder of a religious movement. It was exactly among these religious movements that the term 'charisma,' among others, was reintroduced into Paul's original interpretation. The charismatic movements, which came into being in the beginning of the twentieth century within Protestant circles, have been spreading within European Catholicism since the 1970s. Based on prayer, and on biblical, theological, and spiritual growth, they consider the *charisma* as a totality of gifts given by the Holy Spirit, which is able to give life to the present Christian communities in the same way as it did to the original ones.

In many parts of his work Weber admits the possibility of a charismatic presence inside rational society, founded on instrumental rationality. This is the case with some finance managers who, thanks only to their uncommonly strong personal trustworthiness, are able to obtain conventions and agreements that others can absolutely not obtain. Such phenomena are '*in ihrer ganzen Struktur, ihrem "Geist" nach, grundverschieden von der rationalen Leitung eines regulären großkapitalistichen "Betriebs"*'... However, they are part of the 'twofold nature' of what can be called 'capitalistic spirit': '*...und ebenso das Verständnis des spezifischen Eigenart des modernen, "berufsmäßig" bürokratisierten Alltagskapitalismus ist geradezu davon abhängig, daß man diese beiden, sich überall verschlingenden, im letzen Wesen aber verschiedenen Strukturelemente begrifflich scheiden lernt*' (Weber 1956, p. 667). In a word: charismatic entrepreneurship not only is not foreign to ordinary routine bureaucratized capitalism but belongs to it, even though rationality and charisma should be conceptually distinguished.

Charisma remains therefore clearly present inside rational society, even if it is intertwined with bureaucratic-legal power and the professionally qualified bureaucracy. Rather than presenting exemplars of the pure types indicated by Weber, the concept of charisma appears to be an important conceptual tool to define and explain phenomena such as personal power and consensus in the bureaucratic-rational institutional organizations. It can work as a precious revealer of situations of latent crises as well as of conflicts—latent or open—which are growing in the society as a whole and the various institutions inside it. If it is true that we are living in an epoch 'without God or prophets' it is also true that elements of personal charisma, in its various forms, do not cease to appear, mostly, even if not exclusively, in the political and religious arenas.

See also: Authority, Social Theories of; Elites: Sociological Aspects; Ideal Type: Conceptions in the Social Sciences; Institutionalization; Judaism; Leadership in Organizations, Psychology of; Leadership, Psychology of; Legitimacy; Legitimacy, Sociology of; Organizational Climate; Organizational Culture; Organizations: Authority and Power; Organizations, Sociology of; Power in Society; Power: Political; Religion, Sociology of; Weber, Max (1864–1920)

Bibliography

Boudon R, Bourricaud F 1989 Charisma. In: Boudon R, Bourricaud F (eds.) *A Critical Dictionary of Sociology*. University of Chicago Press, Chicago, pp. 69–73

Cavalli L 1981 *Il capo carismatico*. Il Mulino, Bologna, Italy

Ducros X 1937 Charisma. In: Viller M (ed.) *Dictionnaire de Spiritualité*. G. Beauchesne, Paris, Vol. 2, pp. 503–7

Séguy J 1988 Charisme de fonction et charisme personnel: Le cas de Jean Paul II. In: Séguy J et al. (eds.) *Voyage de Jean Paul II en France*. Cerf, Paris, pp. 11–34

Shils E 1958 The concentration and dispersion of charisma: Their bearing on economic policy in underdeveloped countries. *World Politics* **11**: 1–19

Shils E 1965 Charisma, order and status. *American Sociological Review* **30**(2): 199–213

Sholem G 1974 *The Messianic Ideology in Judaism and Other Essays in Jewish Spirituality*. Schoken Books, New York

Social Compass 1982 About the theory of charisma, Special issue, **XXIX**

Weber M 1947 *The Theory of Social and Economic Organization*, 1st American edn. Oxford University Press, New York

Weber M 1956 *Wirtschaft und Gesellschaft*. J. C. B. Mohr, Tübingen, Germany

Weber M 1956/1965 *Wirtschaft und Gesellschaft*. J. C. B. Mohr, Tübingen, Germany, Vol. I, Chap. V, Sect. 1 [trans. *The Sociology of Religion*. Methuen, London]

Weber M 1956/1968 *Wirtschaft und Gesellschaft*. J. C. B. Mohr, Tübingen, Germany, Vol. I, Chap. III, Sect. 10 [trans. Eisentadt S N (ed.) *Max Weber on Charisma and Institution Building*. University of Chicago Press, Chicago

Weber M 1956/1994 *Wirtschaft und Gesellschaft* J. C. B. Mohr, Tübingen, Germany, Vol. I, Chap. III, Sect. 11–12a [trans. Heydebrand W (ed.) *Sociological Writings*. Continuum, New York]

Weber M 1958 *Politick als Beruf*. Duncker and Humbolt, Berlin

Weber M 1985 Wissenschaft als Beruf. In: Weber M (ed.) *Gesammelte Aufsätze zur Wissenschaftslehre*. J. C. B. Mohr, Tübingen, Germany, pp. 582 613

A. Zingerle (ed.) 1993 Carisma. Dinamiche dell'origine e della quotidianizzazione-Charisma. Dynamiken des ursprungs und der veralltäglichung Special issue of *Annali di Sociologia—Soziologisches Jahrbuch* **9**

S. Abbruzzese

Chemical Sciences: History and Sociology

The chemical sciences are concerned with specific kinds of matter, and their transformations. The boundaries of chemistry, notably with physics and biology, are however social constructions varying in different times and places. Chemistry is very ancient, going back into remote prehistory with cookery, the preparation of drugs and dyes, the baking of clay into ceramics, and metal-working. Its evolution into a science, where theory guides practice, and into a profession, with formal courses and qualifications, happened in the eighteenth and nineteenth centuries (Brock 1992).

1. Ancient Technologies

From very remote times, people have been using techniques and processes which we would call chemical, involving careful control, as part of a craft or art passed from father to son, mother to daughter, or master to apprentice. Indeed the word 'chemistry' is supposed to come from an ancient Egyptian word 'chem' meaning earthy: the Arabic definite article 'Al' was added to yield our 'alchemy', and dropped to give 'chymistry' and then by 1700, 'chemistry.' Early technologies, culminating in triumphs such as the making of porcelain and Japanese swords, include features we would regard as magical; but since the course of chemical reactions depends upon the purity of components, those involving natural products are hard to predict and to repeat. Recourse to prayers, incantations, and curious additives should not amaze us.

2. Metallurgy, Alchemy, and Pharmacy

Alchemy, with its objective of converting base metals into gold, which chemist-historians portrayed as absurd or dishonest, was not unreasonable. Nature was believed to be perfecting metals within her womb, and the alchemist was simply speeding up the process. If everything was composed, as Aristotle believed, of the four elements Earth, Water, Air, and Fire in different proportions, then changing these ratios would transform one substance into another, and lead might become gold. If, alternatively, Democritus and Epicurus were correct in believing that in appearance there were colors, smells, and tastes, but in reality atoms and void; then because lead, gold, and everything is made up of different arrangements of these ultimately similar atoms (or 'corpuscles'), again conversions are possible.

Alchemy began in Egypt and Babylonia, and also in China: with emphasis both upon making gold (or maybe something resembling it) using an elixir to expedite the process, and of prolonging and enhancing life by giving humans the noble and permanent qualities of gold. Pharmacy grew out of trial and error, but in the West the maverick Swiss doctor calling himself Paracelsus (1493–1541) brought alchemy into it. He introduced metallic compounds into previously herbal medicine, notably for the treatment of the new disease, syphilis, which was ravaging Europe. He publicly burnt the books of the great Greek physician, Galen, and saw chemical study as essential for medicine. His career outraged the medical establishment, but the powerful and dangerous new remedies proved irresistible to doctors and patients, and medical schools became centers for chemistry.

3. The First Chemical Theories

Until the mid-twentieth century, it was believed that alchemy was abandoned by the rational thinkers of the Scientific Revolution; especially Robert Boyle (1627–91) and Isaac Newton (1642–1727). Close examination of their manuscripts (Principe 1998) shows that both of them were in fact adepts, copying out and trying alchemical recipes, and believing that they were well on the way to a transmutation. But they were also adherents to the atomic view of matter, seeing hard and indestructible corpuscles or particles as fundamental. These formed very stable primary mixts, such as iron, gold, or sulfur, which in turn combined with each other. Unlike gravity which was universal, chemical affinity was elective: some substances reacted together, others did not. J. W. Goethe wrote a novel,

Elective Affinities (1809) exploring chemical and human bonding; chemists in eighteenth-century Germany and Sweden (the center of chemical activity) drew up tables of affinity in attempting to predict the outcome of reactions.

From Germany also came the first chemical paradigm. G. H. Stahl (1660–1734) proposed that everything which would burn contained '*phlogiston*' (Greek, flammable): this idea brought order into chemical understanding, whereas atomic ideas were vague and untestable. Moreover, in Germany Lorenz Croll in 1778 began the first chemical journal, *Chemische Annalen*, bringing into being a chemical community there (Hufbauer 1982). His example was followed in France and England by Antoine Lavoisier and William Nicholson.

4. Lavoisier's Revolution

Lavoisier (1743–94) was a wealthy man, prominent in the privatized tax system of France; his spare time he devoted to chemistry, in a splendidly equipped laboratory. Becoming a member of the Royal Academy of Sciences, the small salaried body charged with scientific research, he resolved to reform the language and theory of chemistry. As in Carl Linnaeus' botany, names should be international, clear, and free from changeable theory: while *phlogiston* should be replaced as incoherent. Stahl saw *phlogiston* emitted in burning; Lavoisier by contrast (in a classic paradigm shift) saw something absorbed from the air, leading to an increase in weight. He drew upon the work of Joseph Priestley (1733–1804), who had isolated 'vital' or 'eminently respirable' air in a British tradition of work on gases. Lavoisier christened this substance 'oxygen' (Greek, sour) because he believed that it was also responsible for acidity (generalizing from analyses of nitric and sulfuric acids). Water was a compound of oxygen with another gas, hydrogen: such elements were the basis of chemistry, rather than the hypothetical corpuscles which might concern physicists, or the Earth, Water, Air, and Fire with which Priestley's friend Thomas Jefferson (1743–1826) structured his book on Virginia. In 1794 Lavoisier was executed as a tax profiteer during Robespierre's Reign of Terror, while the left-wing views of Priestley (who continued to disagree with him over *phlogiston*) led to his exile in Pennsylvania. But their new and exciting chemistry survived and prospered (Bensaude-Vincent and Abbri 1995, Knight and Kragh 1998).

5. Electricity and Chemistry

In 1799 Alessandro Volta (1745–1827) showed that electricity was generated when two metals were dipped into water; there was no need for any animal tissue, as Luigi Galvani (1737–98) had supposed. His paper was an alarm bell, as Humphry Davy (1778–1829) put it,

and chemists everywhere repeated and extended the experiments. But results were confusing until in 1806 Davy did the careful experiments confirming his intuition that pure water is decomposed electrically into oxygen and hydrogen only. Just as Newton had found that gravity was the force behind planetary motions, so Davy inferred that electricity and chemical affinity were manifestations of one power. In 1807 he used this insight in isolating the light and reactive metals potassium and sodium, and (putting Britain back on the chemical map) went on to demonstrate, with chlorine, that Lavoisier had been wrong about acidity.

Davy had been appointed to the newly-founded Royal Institution in London's fashionable West End, where he proved himself a lecturer of enormous attractiveness, making professing a performance art (Golinski 1992, Knight 1998). The fees which men and women paid to join, and hear him, supported a research laboratory in the basement. Davy became one of the first people in Britain to make a living out of chemical research, which had previously perforce been a hobby for an aristocrat like Boyle, a minister of religion like Priestley, or a doctor like Galvani. At the Royal Institution, Davy trained (in a kind of informal apprenticeship) his successor, Michael Faraday (1791–1867), and the pursuit of Davy's insight that chemical affinity was electrical continued there.

With Lavoisier, chemistry had acquired an exact language, closer to algebra than to the evocative terms of the alchemists; and it had testable theories, for example of acidity. It is the science of the secondary qualities, of colors, smells, and tastes; it promised to be useful (chlorine for disinfecting and bleaching, for example, and oxygen for chest complaints); and it proved popular everywhere. With its connection to electricity, it became the dynamic fundamental science, concerned not just with matter but also with force; there was as yet no unified science of physics. Mechanical explanations seemed shallow; while chemistry's connections with heat, light, and electricity went deep.

6. A Mature Science

J. J. Berzelius (1779–1848) in Sweden used the unsystematic Davy's insight to create a structure for chemistry, 'dualism,' based on the idea that every compound had a positive and a negative part. He also picked up John Dalton's idea that each element was composed of atoms, identical to each other and different from those of other elements: Berzelius arranged these in an electrochemical series from oxygen, the most negative, to potassium. The number of elements known steadily grew through the century with improvements in chemical analysis.

Berzelius trained a number of chemists by having them to stay in his house, where Anna the housekeeper washed up dishes and flasks. But in the 1820s Justus Liebig (1803–73) at the University of Giessen launched the first graduate school for turning out a stream of chemists with Ph.D. degrees (Brock 1997, Morrell 1997). Liebig's success depended upon his having perfected apparatus for analyzing organic compounds; his students usually did their research on some natural product, and published it in the journal which became called *Liebigs Annalen* after its editor. They found jobs, particularly in the dye industry (Fox and Nieto-Galan 1999) and in pharmacy which were both becoming based in science rather than craft skills; many went to England, a rich country with a poor educational system. With the collapse of Napoleon's empire in 1815, the University of Berlin had emerged dedicated to research and teaching (Wissenschaft und Bildung), and the various German states began to compete in their opera houses and universities. They followed Giessen, building better laboratories and bidding for star chemists. Schools began teaching chemistry, textbooks were needed (Lundgren and Bensaude-Vincent 2000), and academic careers opened up in a field now largely separated from medicine. Universities in Britain and the USA followed the German model, usually demanding German research experience from professorial candidates.

In the 1850s chemists could agree about what things were made of, but not about formulae. Dalton had supposed that water must have the simplest possible formula, HO; Davy and others, notably Amadeo Avogadro (1776–1856), went for our H_2O formula because two volumes of hydrogen combine with one of oxygen. An atom of oxygen thus weighed either 8 or 16 times as much as one of hydrogen, and such uncertainties ran through the whole list of elements. In 1860 August Kekule (1829–96), a pioneer in working out chemical structures such as that of benzene, called for an end to this confusion through an international conference, which met in Karlsruhe. It was poorly organized, but afterwards chemists came to accept the reformulation of Avogadro's arguments by Stanislao Cannizzaro (1826–1910). With agreed atomic weights, tabular arrangement of the elements became possible; and the most successful was the Periodic Table of Dmitri Mendeleev (1834–1907).

His predictions of the properties of some hitherto undiscovered elements were startlingly accurate; and with the table (as he hoped) the student had to remember fewer brute facts. From its position an element's properties would be known. It is striking that so many bright ideas, from Dalton via Cannizzaro to Mendeleev, came from people on the periphery rather than in the great scientific centers.

7. The Fragmentation of Chemistry

In death, we rot: for we (and animals and plants) are then subject to chemical reactions which go differently while we are alive. Most people believed in a vital force which maintained life. It is claimed that Friedrich Woehler (1800–82), pupil of Berzelius and friend of Liebig, destroyed this vitalism when in 1828 he synthesized urea. In fact the chief interest in this reaction was that ammonium cyanate and urea turned out to have the same atomic constitution: their different properties were the result of different arrangements (Brooke 1995). So the story has more to do with understanding molecular structure; but the synthesis, and the work of Liebig and his students in analysis, showed that no gulf separated organic and inorganic worlds. Nevertheless, by 1848 when Berzelius died, it was clear that dualism did not fit organic compounds well, and as the chemical community grew it was convenient to separate organic chemistry, based upon carbon, from the inorganic branch. The expansion of universities led to new professorships and laboratories devoted to the specialism of organic chemistry, from which in the twentieth century emerged biochemistry.

Chemists had relied upon balances, test-tubes, condensers, blowpipes, and other apparatus difficult to manipulate. The chemist had to think with his (or occasionally her) fingers, and was proud of skills in glassblowing. Chemistry was essentially experimental, exciting and often dangerous, attractive. Then in 1860 came collaboration between Robert Bunsen, inventor of the controllable gas burner, and the physicist G. R. Kirchhoff, who found that elements heated to a high temperature have characteristic spectra. Analysis could be done by physical methods, and this optical spectroscopy was the first of what is now an armory of such techniques which has transformed the appearance of chemical laboratories (Morris and Travis, in Krige and Pestre 1997, pp. 715–40).

About the same time the new science of thermodynamics, based on energy and its transformations, brought together into classical physics sciences which had been separate, or had been part of the empire of chemistry, Davy and Faraday had been pioneers in what became a new specialism, physical chemistry, investigating energy changes in reactions, and the mechanisms, rates, and reversibility of processes. The leaders here were Wilhelm Ostwald (1853–1932) and J. H. Van't Hoff (1852–1911) who launched a journal, and promoted academic positions and laboratories. The new profession of chemical engineering was closely linked to the rise of physical chemistry. Whereas early in the nineteenth century chemists had been called in only as consultants or trouble shooters when something went wrong, by the end of it they were employed full-time (Bud and Roberts 1984). In industry, intellectual property belongs generally to the company and not the individual, and is secured by patents (Travis et al. 1998).

8. The Reduction of Chemistry

The nineteenth century was the heyday of chemistry, the golden age in which it came to maturity and seemed fundamental. The chemist and spectroscopist

William Crookes (1832 1919) followed Faraday in studying cathode rays, but J. J. Thomson in 1897 identified them as composed of subatomic corpuscles, soon named 'electrons.' The subsequent nuclear atomic model of Ernest Rutherford (1871–1937)—for whom all science was physics or stamp-collecting—and Niels Bohr (1885 1962) accounted not only for spectra, but also for the Periodic Table. Chemistry became a branch of physics (Nye 1996); the properties of gold could in principle be calculated from data about protons, neutrons, and electrons, though in practice the chemistry laboratory is essential. This meant that chemistry lost its glamor; the chemist was as ubiquitous as ever, an essential member of the teams or groups so characteristic of twentieth-century science, but playing a service role (Knight 1995).

The number of chemists has continued to grow, as has the number of new substances unknown in nature which they have synthesized. Davy wrote of the chemist being a godlike creator, and this creativity is nowadays celebrated by chemists such as Roald Hoffmann. The engineer or architect must remember the law of gravity, but to mourn that architecture has been reduced to physics would be absurd: like the poet or the painter, the chemist has to work within constraints, but that is a feature of life—indeed making creativity possible (Hoffmann and Torrance 1993).

Hoffmann, born in Poland, surviving World War II, escaping to the USA, learning chemistry there, and doing research which brought him a Nobel Prize, exemplifies another trend. Chemistry reached the West via Islam. By the eighteenth and nineteenth centuries, it was a European science, with Germany the most important center by 1900. Papers in German journals, and research experience in Germany, counted high in any pecking order; but already the USA was becoming a major power in science. There in 1916 G. N. Lewis proposed the electronic theory of chemical combination, much developed by his pupil Linus Pauling. Since 1945 the USA has been the center of things, making the English language and publication in US journals the key to prestige in research. Two world wars, and Hitler's coming to power between them, are part of the reason for this; equally important has been American prosperity, itself dependent on science. Chemistry has steadily gone West.

9. The Status of Chemistry

Davy and Liebig (Rossiter 1975) wrote famous books on agricultural chemistry, and in the nineteenth century chemical fertilizers and pesticides were unequivocally welcomed in a Europe of food shortages. Lavoisier improved French gunpowder, and later chemists produced high explosives making possible engineering achievements and also formidable weapons. All these things were seen as benefits. National

chemical societies, their academic and professional aspects sometimes in tension, were formed and enjoyed prestige (Russell et al. 1977). Although pollution from new chemical industries (as from older ones like tanning) was palpable and led to legislation, the expectation was that the chemists would be able to cure it. It did not happen: Rachel Carson's book *The Silent Spring* (1962) alerted the world to the dangers. So in the late twentieth century, despite successes such as plastics, and the array of new drugs available for medicine, chemistry is seen as boring and its applications as threatening. Chemists feel misunderstood and underappreciated.

Twentieth-century chemistry is dominated not only by universities in the Giessen tradition, but also by big-spending international companies with research laboratories, now turning towards biotechnology (Galentos and Sturchio, and Kevles, in Krige and Pestre 1997, pp. 227–52, 301–18) and by the military. Research is carried on no longer by a Woehler or a Crookes, on their own or with an assistant, but by teams of people possessing various skills. Chemistry has been taught in an impersonal way, with less hands-on experiment in a world more conscious of health and safety.

This is a strange eventful history, which was until the mid-twentieth century mainly written by participants who looked for progress. They had the advantage of being familiar with chemicals and apparatus; but professional historians of science have come to look more closely at contexts and careers. The history which emerges deserves to be known beyond the world of chemists.

See also: Archaeometry; Behavioral Neuroscience; Biomedical Sciences and Technology: History and Sociology; Ceramics in Archaeology; Cognitive Neuroscience; History of Science; Human Sciences: History and Sociology; Physical Sciences: History and Sociology; Research and Development in Organizations; Scientific Disciplines, History of; Technological Innovation

Bibliography

Bensaude-Vincent B, Abbri F 1995 *Lavoisier in European Context*. Science History, Canton, MA
Brock W H 1992 *The Fontana History of Chemistry*. Fontana, London
Brock W H 1997 *Justus von Liebig: the Chemical Gatekeeper*. Cambridge University Press, Cambridge, UK
Brooke J H 1995 *Thinking about Matter*. Ashgate Variorum, Aldershot, UK
Bud R, Roberts G K 1984 *Science versus Practice*. Manchester University Press, Manchester, UK
Fox R, Nieto-Galan A 1999 *Natural Dyestuffs*. Science History, Canton, MA

Golinski J 1992 *Science as Public Culture: Chemistry and Enlightenment in Britain, 1760–1820.* Cambridge University Press, Cambridge, UK

Hoffmann R, Torrance V 1993 *Chemistry Imagined.* Smithsonian, Washington, DC

Hufbauer K 1982 *The Formation of the German Chemical Community 1720–1795.* California University Press, Berkeley, CA

Knight D M 1995 *Ideas in Chemistry.* Athlone, London

Knight D M 1998 *Humphry Davy: Science and Power.* Cambridge University Press, Cambridge, UK

Knight D M, Kragh H 1998 *The Making of the Chemist.* Cambridge University Press, Cambridge, UK

Krige J, Pestre D 1997 *Science in the Twentieth Century.* Harwood, Amsterdam

Lundgren A, Bensaude-Vincent B 2000 *Communicating Chemistry: Textbooks and their Audiences, 1789–1939.* Science History, Canton, MA

Morrell J 1997 *Science, Culture and Politics in Britain, 1750–1870.* Ashgate Variorum, Aldershot, UK

Nye M J 1996 *Before Big Science.* Twayne, New York

Principe L 1998 *The Aspiring Adept.* Princeton University Press, Princeton, NJ

Rossiter M 1975 *The Emergence of Agricultural Science: Justus Liebig and the Americans, 1840–1880.* Yale University Press, New Haven, CT

Russell C A, Coley N G, Roberts G K 1977 *Chemists by Profession.* Open University Press, Milton Keynes, UK

Travis A S, Schröter H G, Homburg E, Morris P J T 1998 *Determinants in the Evolution of the European Chemical Industry, 1900–1939.* Kluwer, Dordrecht, The Netherlands

D. Knight

Chess Expertise, Cognitive Psychology of

Expertise may be defined as the ability of some individuals to perform at levels vastly superior to the majority. For historical and scientific reasons, research on chess expertise has played a major role in the study of expertise in general. The first reason is that chess itself has a very long history (the modern form of Western chess goes back to the sixteenth century). This has made possible an extensive study of the game, leading to the development of several 'theories' about the proper way to play by leading players such as Steinitz, Nimzowitch, and Euwe. Next, the rules of chess offer a well-specified and constrained environment that is easily formalizable. Chess is also a game flexible enough to allow multiple experimental manipulations. In addition, the presence of a rating system (the Elo system) allows one to estimate players' skill quantitatively and precisely. Compared to most other domains of expertise, this ability to measure skill is a definite advantage. Contrast this situation with, for example, the study of experts in physics or medicine, where researchers have to use very rough classifications such as novice, intermediate, and ex-

pert. Finally, there has been rich cross-fertilization between psychological research on chess expertise and research in formal fields like computer science and mathematics.

1. Chess in the Sciences

1.1 Chess in the Formal Sciences

Unsurprisingly, chess has been a favorite subject of study in the formal sciences. On several occasions, chess has been used to explore aspects of game theory; in a celebrated paper published in 1912, Zermolo formalized the concept of game tree and introduced the method of backwards induction with reference to chess. The game has also been of interest to mathematicians, for example in the field of combinatorics. However, most of the research has been made in artificial intelligence and computer science. If one ignores chess automata, most of which turned out to be fraudulent, computer chess started in earnest in 1949 with Shannon's paper describing a computer program able to play an entire game, either by full search to a specified depth or by selective search. Since that seminal work, researchers have extensively explored various techniques for improving the efficiency of search algorithms or to make search more selective (see Newell and Simon 1972, Levy and Newborn 1991). The crowning achievement of the quest for efficient search algorithms (the so-called 'brute-force' approach) was the development of Deep Blue, the first computer to beat a world champion in an official match. Deep Blue's special-purpose hardware allowed it to consider up to 200 million positions per second. By contrast, a nice example of the selective-search approach is a program written by Pitrat (1977), which uses heuristics to cut the search tree down to the same size as humans' (about 100 positions). Recently, computer chess has seen a strong interest in database theory and in the development and testing of machine-learning algorithms.

1.2 Chess in the Social and Behavioral Sciences

Expert behavior in chess has attracted the attention of various social and behavioral sciences, including psychoanalysis, psychiatry, and sociology. Questions such as 'Does extreme practice of a skill lead to madness?' 'Why are women weaker than men at chess?', 'Can oedipal compulsions lead to creativity?', and 'Why is there a high proportion of Jews among top players?' have been asked in these fields, although the answers offered are often controversial (Dextreit and Engel 1981, Holding 1985). In addition, chess has sometimes been used not as an object of study, but as a model. Two examples may suffice. In philosophy, Lasker developed a philosophical system (machology) based on the element of fight extant in a chess game. In linguistics, De Saussure made regular use of chess to illustrate the rule-like character of language. For instance, he drew an analogy between a chess game and the synchronic analysis of language: if somebody walks into a room where a chess game is being played, they can study and understand the position without knowing the moves leading to it.

2. Psychological Studies of Chess Expertise

However, in none of the social and behavioral sciences mentioned above has chess had such an impact as in psychology, where it has been used as a standard task environment for exploring expertise (Simon and Chase 1973). Several concepts, such as progressive deepening and selective search, and several experimental techniques, such as the use of verbal protocols and the use of recall tasks to study expertise, have their main source in chess research.

2.1 Brief History of Psychological Research

The first psychological investigation of chess expertise was carried out at the end of the nineteenth century by Binet, who was interested in masters' ability to play a game, or even several games, without seeing the board. This work, using questionnaires and focusing on the search for chess players' hypothetical, and probably nonexistent, concrete visual memory, no longer has much impact. Nor does the work carried out in 1927 by Djakow, Petrowski, and Rudik, who were the first psychologists to bring chess players into the laboratory. These Russians scientists, who gave a battery of psychometric tests to their subjects, were interested in the question of chess talent. Their tests measured various 'faculties of mind,' such as memory, attention, or combination power. It turned out that chess masters did not differ from lay people on most of these tests, the exception being tasks of visual memory where the stimuli bear a strong resemblance to chess-boards.

The next wave of research on chess psychology had a huge impact on expertise research and on cognitive psychology in general. It was the work of a single man, the Dutch psychologist and chess master Adriaan De Groot. In his doctoral thesis in 1946, De Groot (1978) introduced two key methods (recall of briefly presented positions, and analysis of verbal protocols collected during problem solving), which allowed him to uncover several key determinants of expertise. First, players at all levels are highly selective in their search. Even top-level players do not search much more than about one hundred positions during a 15-minute deliberation. Second, there exist almost no differences

between the search behavior of world-class grandmasters and that of weaker players, as far as measures such as depth of search, breadth of search, or branching factors are concerned. Third, players of all levels visit the same variation several times when choosing a move, a phenomenon De Groot called 'progressive deepening.' This behavior allows cognitive systems of limited capacity, such as those of humans, both to propagate information from a given branch of the search tree to other branches, and to overcome the limits of short-term memory (De Groot and Gobet 1996). Fourth, masters are able to zoom into the key features of the problem at hand very rapidly. Fifth, chess masters normally judge a position based on a single feature, which can be either static (e.g., material balance) or dynamic (e.g., potential actions). This is in sharp contrast to computer programs, which typically use a polynomial function to combine a large number of features (Levy and Newborn 1991). Sixth, chess masters have a remarkable memory for meaningful material taken from their domain, even when this material is presented for just a few seconds.

De Groot's work, and through it the ideas of the German psychologist Otto Selz, was important in shaping the revolution in cognitive psychology (Newell and Simon 1972). As the cornerstone of most current research on expert behavior, it has spawned a large number of empirical studies, the most important of which are reviewed in the next section.

2.2 Key Empirical Results

It is common to organize chess research along the following lines: perception, memory, knowledge, lookahead search, and general intelligence. Research on perception has confirmed De Groot's earlier results, and has shown that players can identify and memorize critical patterns in a position even with presentation times below one second. Automatization also affects lower levels of perception: As shown by Saariluoma (1995), the speed with which chess pieces are recognized is a function of the level of expertise. Finally, eye-tracking studies have shown that chess masters have faster eye movements, cover more of the important squares on the board, and tend to look at the intersection of squares more often than weaker players (De Groot and Gobet 1996).

Empirical studies on memory have shown that chess players' performance is mediated by variables such as depth of processing, presentation time, typicality, level of randomization, and age (for reviews, see Holding 1985, Saariluoma 1995, Gobet 1998). Interestingly, and contrary to widely held opinion, masters' superiority is maintained with briefly presented positions, even after their semantics have been destroyed by randomizing the location of pieces (Gobet and Simon 2000). While the effect is small, it is also reliable, and has been found in other domains of expertise such as programming and music.

As witnessed by the formidable time chess masters spend studying books and analyzing games, knowledge plays an important role in chess expertise. Several researchers have attempted to study knowledge directly, using techniques such as sorting experiments, questionnaires, and verbal reports. There is evidence that expertise correlates both with qualitative organization of knowledge and with quantitative amount of information stored (Freyhoff et al. 1992), reflecting findings of other domains of expertise such as physics.

While De Groot's statistics about problem solving have in most cases withstood the test of time, subsequent research has identified a few skill differences. In particular, it has been found that depth of look-ahead search varies as a function of skill (e.g., Saariluoma 1995), although the effect is rather small.

Several studies have addressed the question of whether intelligence correlates with chess skill. The general conclusion is that there is a correlation with tests measuring general intelligence, but not with tests measuring visuospatial intelligence (Doll and Mayer 1987). From these studies, it is unclear whether chess practice develops aspects of intelligence measured in IQ tests (a good candidate for explanation would be ability to think under time pressure), whether attainment of a high skill requires superior intelligence, or whether both intelligence and chess skill are causally related to a third variable, such as an ability to concentrate for long periods.

Finally, chess has been a useful domain for studying the cognitive processes that support outstanding skill in problem solving across the life span. In particular, chess has been useful in identifying compensatory mechanisms used by older adults to allow high-level performance in spite of age-related declines in perceptual, memory, and cognitive abilities (Charness 1981).

3. Theories of Problem Solving

Given the rich set of empirical data generated by chess research, it is not surprising that chess has produced several theories of expertise. It is convenient to present these theories as mainly addressing either problem solving or memory, although they often aim at a general characterization.

The first theory devoted primarily to problem-solving behavior in chess is De Groot's (1978) elaboration of Otto Selz's framework of productive thinking. Selz proposed that thinking is a continuous activity that can be described as a linear chain of operations. De Groot showed that this framework was, with a few extensions and modifications, quite

successful in accounting for chess thinking. As anticipated by Selz, players often use a hierarchy of subsidiary methods, which relates to Newell and Simon's (1972) means-end analysis. For De Groot (1978) a necessary condition for becoming a chess master is the construction through experience of two things: a highly developed and specific mode of perception, and a system of reproductory methods stored in memory.

Chess players' memory can be separated into knowledge (knowing that...) and intuitive experience (knowing how...). Selz's description of thought as a sequence of operations is also apparent in the formal models developed by the Carnegie Mellon research group centered around Herbert Simon (this research is summarized in Newell and Simon 1972). Two computer programs (written by Newell, Shaw, and Simon in 1963, and by Baylor and Simon in 1966) implemented the idea of selective search made possible by the use of heuristics. Another model, developed by Newell and Simon in 1965, used the evaluation obtained at the end of a branch to formulate six principles that dictate the generation of moves and sequences of moves. Several of these ideas have been recently combined with the chunking theory (see below) in a probabilistic model of chess thinking (Gobet 1997).

Two informal theories have also been influential in research on expertise. Holding's (1985) theory emphasizes the role of search and knowledge and suggests that human experts search in ways similar to computers. The theory discussed by Saariluoma (1995) proposes that players, while thinking about a position, access goal positions by apperception—that is, conceptual perception. They then try to close the path between the problem position and the goal position. When this is not possible, the problem space is restructured. Thus, chess thinking may be described as a sequence of apperception–restructuration cycles, which make it possible to find solutions with only limited search.

While these theories differ in their emphasis and in their specificity, going from formal computer programs to informal verbal theories, they also share a few important assumptions: They all emphasize the role of knowledge in problem solving and the high selectivity of human search.

4. Theories of Memory

One can identify four major theories of chess perception and memory in chess expertise (Gobet 1998). The most influential of them is Simon and Chase's (1973) chunking theory, which proposes that experts acquire a vast database of chunks (perceptual patterns that can be used as units) giving access to semantic memory and to procedural memory. Subsets of the chunking theory were implemented in 1973 in a computer program by Gilmartin and Simon. Based on extrapolations from the simulations, it was estimated that between 10,000 and 100,000 chunks are necessary to reach a high level of expertise. However, some weaknesses of chunking theory were uncovered by later research, mainly the fact that it underestimates storage into long-term memory (LTM), and that it underestimates the role of high-level structures such as schemata (Charness 1976, Holding 1985).

Several attempts have been made to repair these theoretical weaknesses, while still accounting for the data that chunking theory successfully explained. Holding (1985) is representative of a group of researchers emphasizing the role of high-level knowledge structures, such as schemata or prototypes. In opposition to the simple and specific structures proposed by Chase and Simon, Holding emphasizes that chess masters' memories are richly organized and general. Emphasis is also given to metaknowledge, which consists of principles for efficient search and evaluation of positions.

Ericsson and Kintsch's (1995) long-term working memory theory emphasizes that experts in various fields, including chess, can encode information into LTM more rapidly than had been postulated by traditional models of human memory. In the spirit of Selz and Newell and Simon's (1972) approaches, this theory views cognitive processes as a sequence of stable states representing end products of processing. Through acquired memory skills, these end products can be stored in LTM and can be accessed from short-term memory by means of retrieval cues. Two intertwined mechanisms allow rapid storage into LTM. The first mechanism allows encoding through a hierarchical retrieval structure; in the case of chess, the retrieval structure corresponds to the 64 squares of the board. The second mechanism allows encoding through knowledge-based associations that elaborate patterns and schemata stored in LTM. Ericsson and Kintsch (1995) suggest that these two mechanisms account for chess masters' excellent memory for chess material, as well as for their ability to plan and to evaluate alternative sequences of moves.

Gobet and Simon's (2000) template theory proposes that patterns recurring often in players' practice and study lead to the creation of more complex data structures, called templates. As with classical schemata, templates have both a core (containing the same information as chunks), and slots, where variable information can be stored. The template theory is implemented as a computer program, which acquires chunks in an unsupervised way by scanning a large database of master games. The program can simulate various data from perception, such as players' eye movements during the first five seconds of presentation of a position, and from memory, such as the role of presentation time on memory recall. A version of the program also plays (poorly) by pure pattern recognition.

One of the important challenges facing researchers in the field is to provide a coherent and integrated picture of chess thinking, combining simple perceptual structures such as Chase and Simon's chunks with more complex structures such as schemata. Long-term working memory and template theory can be seen as attempts to address this challenge.

5. Future Lines of Research

Chess expertise has been extensively studied in the past (more research has been done in psychology about chess than about all other games put together), and it is likely that this will continue in the future. In most cases, results from chess research can be generalized to other domains of expertise. While scientific understanding of expertise has grown substantially through a large number of experiments and through a wealth of theoretical developments, there is still no single theory able both to account for most of the empirical data and to simulate human behavior by playing chess at a high level of expertise. With the rapid progress in artificial intelligence and computer science, which have already produced grandmaster-level programs by brute force, it is however realistic to expect such a theory within a decade or two. In addition to this effort in computer modeling, a main research domain is likely to be neuropsychological investigation using brain imaging techniques to study the biological substrate of chess expertise.

See also: Expert Memory, Psychology of; Expertise, Acquisition of; Medical Expertise, Cognitive Psychology of; Protocol Analysis in Psychology; Short-term Memory, Cognitive Psychology of; Sports as Expertise, Psychology of; Working Memory, Psychology of

Bibliography

Charness N 1976 Memory for chess positions: Resistance to interference. *Journal of Experimental Psychology: Human Learning and Memory* **2**: 641–53

Charness N 1981 Aging and skilled problem solving. *Journal of Experimental Psychology: General* **110**: 21–38

De Groot A D 1978 *Thought and Choice in Chess*, 2nd edn. Mouton Publishers, The Hague, The Netherlands

De Groot A D, Gobet F 1996 *Perception and Memory in Chess*. Van Gorcum, Assen, The Netherlands

Dextreit J, Engel N 1981 *Jeu d'échecs et sciences humaines* [*Chess and Human Sciences*]. Payot, Paris

Doll J, Mayer U 1987 Intelligenz und Schachleistung—eine Untersuchung an Schachexperten [Intelligence and success in chess playing—an examination of chess experts]. *Psychologische Beiträge* **29**: 270–89

Ericsson K A, Kintsch W 1995 Long-term working memory. *Psychological Review* **102**: 211–45

Freyhoff H, Gruber H, Ziegler A 1992 Expertise and hierarchical knowledge representation in chess. *Psychological Research* **54**: 32–7

Gobet F 1997 A pattern-recognition theory of search in expert problem solving. *Thinking and Reasoning* **3**: 291–313

Gobet F 1998 Expert memory: A comparison of four theories. *Cognition* **66**: 115–52

Gobet F, Simon H A 2000 Five seconds or sixty? Presentation time in expert memory. *Cognitive Science*

Holding D H 1985 *The Psychology of Chess Skill.* Erlbaum, Hillsdale, NJ

Levy D, Newborn M 1991 *How Computers Play Chess.* Computer Science Press, New York

Newell A, Simon H A 1972 *Human Problem Solving.* Prentice-Hall, Englewood Cliffs, NJ

Pitrat J 1977 A chess combination program which uses plans. *Artificial Intelligence* **8**: 275–321

Saariluoma P 1995 *Chess Players' Thinking.* Routlege, London

Simon H A, Chase W G 1973 Skill in chess. *American Scientist* **61**: 393–403

F. Gobet

Chiefdoms, Archaeology of

The use of the term 'chiefdom' to refer to pre-state complex societies is a relatively recent phenomenon, beginning with Kalervo Oberg's historical classification of South and Central American societies and Marshall Sahlins's ethnographic work on Polynesian societies in the 1950s. Elman Service included 'chiefdoms' a decade later in his neoevolutionary categories of *band, tribe, chiefdom,* and *state,* and the concept became closely associated with the cultural evolutionary paradigm. Almost immediately, archaeologists began to apply the chiefdom concept to investigations of early societies such as the Mississippian towns of the southeastern USA and the Neolithic European builders of Stonehenge, which manifested some complexity but generally lacked the long-held archaeological indicators of 'civilization' (e.g., large urban centers, massive kingly tombs, written dynastic histories and legal codes, markets, and monetary systems).

1. Chiefdoms and Cultural Evolutionary Theory

Chiefdoms have been defined by some archaeologists in primarily political terms, as smaller-scale complex societies with centralized decision-making hierarchies of one or two levels above the individual village (compared to three plus levels in states). Chiefly leaders obtain their political authority through both ascription and performance (compared to largely hereditary kings), they have very generalized administrative roles (judicial, economic, ritual, military), they have few bureaucratic specialists (unlike the specialized bureaucracies of states), and they generally rely on kin-based alliances to structure political relations with subordinates (rather than the nonkin-based political institutions and formal legal codes of states). Most archaeologists would expand the definition to include social ranking that has at least some hereditary component (unlike the achieved ranking of tribal societies and the almost wholly hereditary social classes of early states) and some degree of economic centralization (control over staple production, building and managing irrigation systems, tribute mobilization, control over the production and exchange of prestige goods, and/or foreign trade monopolies). Chiefs generally maintain their political power not only through varying strategies for accumulating and disbursing material resources, but also through ideological means (manipulating cosmologies, ritual, and myth, and creating power-imbuing sacred landscapes) and military coercion. Chiefdoms rarely exist or evolve in isolation, but instead are found as clusters of interacting *peer polities* that often share aspects of elite culture, have similar structures, and compete for regional supremacy. Many chiefdoms are also part of larger *world systems* that link them to more developed states and empires.

Chiefdom-level societies have been identified by cultural anthropologists, archaeologists, and historians in many parts of the world and in many time periods (Fig. 1), often as precursors to state development but sometimes as long-term, stable structures that do not transform into more complex states (see *States and Civilizations, Archaeology of*). The Polynesian chiefdoms, the pre-Roman (Late Neolithic, Bronze Age, and Iron Age) societies of Europe, and eastern North American complex societies (particularly Mississippian Period) have received the most intense archaeological study. Archaeologists have recently expanded their use of the chiefdom model to societies in the Near East, Africa, East Asia, South Asia, Mesoamerica, South America, and western North America (Fig. 1), although the 'evolutionary status' of many as chiefdoms is controversial (e.g., the Woodland Period societies of the eastern USA, the Late Neolithic societies of Europe). Early in the development of the chiefdom concept, archaeologists identified a number of common material correlates of these types of societies (e.g., two- to three-level settlement hierarchies, monumental architecture, burials with hereditary status indicators, specialist-manufactured prestige goods, regional and interhousehold differences in wealth; see Fig. 1). However, as more of these complex societies are intensively studied by archaeologists, it has become clear that material patterns, and presumably the ideological, political,

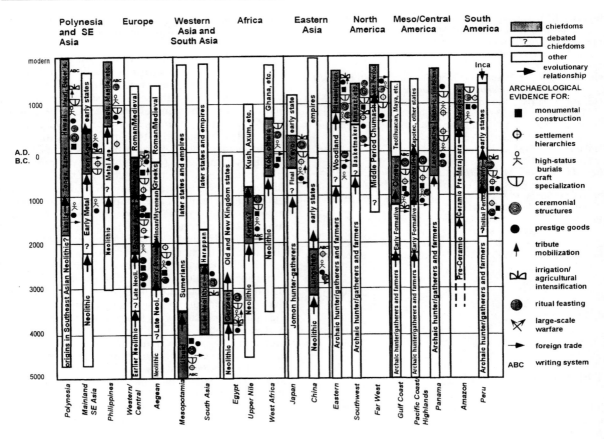

Figure 1
The chronological and geographic distribution of some chiefdoms known through archaeological and ethnographic research, with varying archaeological indicators

social, and economic structures underlying them, vary substantially (see below).

2. Critiques and Redefinition of the Chiefdom Concept

A number of recent critiques of the chiefdom concept, and cultural evolutionary models in general, have emphasized the organizational diversity and historical uniqueness that is ignored when anthropologists attempt to fit societies in broadly defined classifications and assume uniform trajectories of development. Many scholars have pointed out the great deal of variability in societies designated as 'chiefdoms.' One response to this recognized diversity has been to subdivide pre-state complex societies into developmentally distinct types, such as Robert Carneiro's 'minimal,' 'typical,' and 'maximal' chiefdoms (based on the complexity of political hierarchies), Timothy Earle's 'simple' and 'complex' chiefdoms (based on

scales of chiefly political, economic, and ritual control), and Colin Renfrew's 'group-oriented' and 'individualizing' chiefdoms (based on differing strategies of lineage versus individual aggrandizement and social display).

Other scholars have emphasized that transformations in social, political, economic, and ideological structure that have previously defined chiefdoms do not always occur together. Some archaeologists have promoted the concept of *heterarchy*—in which both hierarchical and nonhierarchical relations operate simultaneously and separately along multiple dimensions (social, economic, political, ritual)—as a better way of modeling structure and process in these societies. Other archaeologists have favored a move away from the systemic evolutionary processes implied in the chiefdom concept to 'actor-based' approaches, Marxist theories of political control, and nonmaterialist or postprocessual analyses focused on the ideological and symbolic bases for structure. Thus, while many archaeologists favor continual refinement of the chiefdom concept and its continued utility in arch-aeological research, others have advocated its abandonment.

3. Political and Social Features

Chiefdoms are characterized by partially inherited and partially achieved political leadership, reinforced through ideological manipulation, control of economic resources, and militarism. The political power of chiefs is often reflected materially in symbols of office (e.g., the jade axes of Maori chiefs and the stone maceheads of Gerzean Period Egyptian chiefs) and in monumental architecture which demonstrates a chief's ability to control and mobilize large labor forces (e.g., the henge monuments of Late Neolithic Europe, the monumental statuary of the Olmec and Easter Islanders). Chiefly centers, as the focal point of political, economic, and religious activities of chiefs, are generally archaeologically distinguishable from subordinate villages by their greater size, centrality, and presence of monumental architecture, wealth objects, and specialized production locales. Multiple levels of political authority (*paramount chiefs* and local chiefs), typical of larger-scale chiefdoms, are often archaeologically visible in regional settlement hierarchies of up to three levels.

A number of archaeologists have offered new conceptual frameworks for analyzing differing political power strategies in chiefdoms. One recent model, offered by Richard Blanton and Gary Feinman, contrasts *network* versus *corporate* strategies of political dominance, elaborating Colin Renfrew's earlier distinction between *individualizing* and *group-oriented* chiefdoms. These differing strategies are viewed as part of political dynamics in all complex societies, but political actors in a particular society may emphasize one mode of control more than the other. In a *network strategy*, political actors try to create personal networks of dominance through the strategic distribution of portable wealth and symbolic capital (e.g., ritual potency and religious knowledge). The emphasis on individual aggrandizement is archaeologically manifested in lavish individual burials, elaborate household wealth display, and competitive presentational events such as ceremonial feasting (e.g., Iron Age chiefdoms of Europe, early West African chiefdoms). The highly conflictive nature of leadership and long-term instability of political configurations are evidenced in rapidly changing settlement hierarchies. In contrast, a society emphasizing a corporate political strategy disperses power across different groups and sectors of society through bureaucratic institutions promoting consensus, solidarity, and collective action, often reinforced through archaeologically visible public architecture, collective tombs, and unifying emblems (e.g., Late Neolithic chiefdoms of Europe, Woodland Period chiefdoms of North America).

In terms of social structure, chiefdoms invariably have some form of ascribed social ranking. While social status differences are characteristic of all human societies, social ranks in chiefdoms are at least partially inherited intergenerationally. They are given structural rigidity through behavioral taboos and symbolic expression, and in most cases, there is distinct economic advantage (differential access to resources) conferred on an 'elite' stratum. Social stratification in chiefdoms is often manifested in archaeologically visible rank insignia, differential wealth in households, and varying complexity of residential architecture at settlements.

Ascribed rather than strictly achieved social ranking is most archaeologically evident in burial practices. Inherited status is generally expressed through variation in body positioning, body treatment, grave forms, and burial accompaniments which cross-cut age and sex categories, making status archaeologically distinguishable from mortuary variability, attributable to age differences, gender roles, and achieved status. Mortuary analyses based on this premise have been carried out most successfully at Mississippian, Chinese Lungshan, Egyptian Gerzean, and Bronze Age and Iron Age European cemeteries, where relatively large samples of well-preserved burials have allowed the identification of distinct social hierarchies. In cases where larger burial populations are lacking, archaeologists have frequently made an argument for the presence of elites based on finds of elaborate, often monumental 'chiefly' burials (e.g., jade-yielding Formative Period Mesoamerican tombs, the Nok mounded tombs of West Africa, the Yayoi stone-lined crypts of Japan). Status-related dietary and health differences between elites and nonelites have also been studied through zooarchaeological and paleobotanical analyses of food remains at settlements, and through osteological assessments of nutritional stress and disease in burial populations.

4. Political Economy

Just as the chiefdoms studied by archaeologists vary in political structure, they differ in the ways in which chiefs attempt to assert economic control in support of their governing institutions. Timothy Earle and Terrence D'Altroy have made a useful distinction between strategies of *staple finance* and *wealth finance* in chiefdoms. *Staple finance* involves the systematic levying of tribute payments (in the form of staple goods and/or labor) from subjugated commoners, with the revenue used to finance directly the power-enhancing activities of the chief, such as monument building, warfare, trade, and ceremonial feasting. Since control of land and its production is essential to staple finance, chiefdoms emphasizing this economic strategy generally have strongly developed institutions for land tenure (archaeologically manifested in boundary features such as walls and corporate monumental structures) and significant chiefly investment in agricultural intensification (archaeologically manifested in large-scale irrigation works, water control, and artificial terracing). Archaeological investigations suggest that the Hawaiian chiefdoms, pre-Inca South American chiefdoms, and many pre-state Mesopotamian complex societies had political economies dominated by staple finance.

Wealth finance involves the use of prestige goods or valuables as political currencies by chiefs and other elites to cement politically strategic alliances with other elites and to reward subordinates for loyalty and service (particularly associated with a *network* political strategy). Prestige goods vary according to socially defined standards of value and can be any rare or easily controlled object (e.g., jade in Lungshan China, gold in Panamanian chiefdoms, bronze in European chiefdoms, shell and copper ornaments in eastern North American chiefdoms). Politically charged wealth can be locally manufactured or obtained through foreign trade. Emerging elites control access to this political currency through support of *attached specialists* (highly skilled artisans who produce these goods wholly for elite consumption), by monopolizing valuable raw materials and technologies, by dominating trade routes, and by defining limited social contexts for their circulation (e.g., elite-controlled ceremonial feasting events). While specific chiefdoms tend to emphasize one means of economic control over another, chiefs tend to use elements of both staple finance and wealth finance in varying combinations, resulting in unique forms of political economy.

In addition to the emergence of *attached specialists*, the rise of chiefdoms is sometimes accompanied by the growth of *independent specialists*, full-time specialists producing more mundane household goods for an unrestricted set of consumers who concentrate at chiefly centers due to economies of scale. While the archaeological recovery of large-scale craft workshops containing mass production equipment (e.g., large kilns or smelting furnaces, molds, potter's wheels) is the most direct line of evidence for specialist production, such finds are rare. More often archaeologists have assessed craft production modes through analysis of the products themselves and their regional distribution. Specialized production by a limited number of concentrated, recurrently interacting, full-time craftspersons (either *attached specialists* or *independent specialists*) generally results in a more standardized product, as measured through object form, raw material, and/or decoration. In addition, specialist-produced prestige goods are largely restricted to elite centers, while household-produced domestic goods are widely dispersed throughout a region, and the socially unrestricted products of independent specialists are concentrated at, but not restricted to, regional centers.

Particularly in chiefdoms relying heavily on wealth finance, political relationships and hierarchies of authority are reinforced through the continual circulation of prestige goods, most often in the context of bride wealth exchanges (e.g., gifts of porcelain in Southeast Asia and gold in Panama), political investitures (e.g., the presentation of feather capes in Polynesia), ritualized feasting, and other politically-charged events. Of these exchange contexts, ritual feasting is particularly evident in the archaeological record. Specialized feasting paraphernalia (e.g., bronze drinking vessels in the European Iron Age, large ceramic cooking vessels in the Mississippian and Formative Mesoamerican chiefdoms), unusual food remains (e.g., large pig concentrations in Lungshan China), and their association with ritual architecture (e.g., ball courts in Mesoamerica) have been used to identify feasts which were likely aimed at political integration and competitive status display.

5. The Ideology of Rulership

Ideologies are collective representations of the social and political order in particular societies, often encoded in myths, ceremonies, and various public performances, but also frequently materialized in archaeologically visible monumental architecture, iconography, and portable objects. In both state-level societies and chiefdoms, the creation of a dominant ideology and its imposition on the populace are an important basis for power. In many chiefdoms, elites developed their own language, dialect, lexicon, and/or writing systems to control the flow of esoteric knowledge and to restrict the performance of religious rites. The archaeological contexts in which written texts are found and their decipherable content (e.g., stone stela found with monumental earthen works in Formative Period Mesoamerican centers, wooden tablet inscriptions associated with Easter Island ceremonial complexes) suggest that literacy was an elite prerogative which served to institutionalize cosmological notions and to legitimate the political and social domination of elites.

In the absence of written texts, archaeologists often infer shared cosmic orders and ruling ideologies from iconography on portable objects (e.g., the were-jaguar figurines of Formative Period Mesoamerica, 'sun' motifs and other symbols on Mississippian pottery, 'patron-deity' symbols on Egyptian Gerzean stone palettes and maces), from monumental constructions (e.g., the platform temple complexes of Polynesia, the henge monuments of Late Neolithic Europe), from material symbols in burials (e.g., painted scenes in Japanese Yayoi mounded tombs), and from the spatial organization of chiefly centers (e.g., the layout of Cahokia and other Mississippian centers). An influx of exotic symbols representing foreign cosmologies or religious beliefs (e.g., Buddhist and Hindu art and architecture in Southeast Asia, widespread Olmec styles in Formative Period Mesoamerica, Egyptian themes in the Nubian chiefly tombs of Kerma) has often been interpreted by archaeologists as a particularly effective strategy for chiefs to add to their monopolistic store of power-enhancing knowledge.

While past archaeological research has largely focused on ideologies of domination in chiefdoms, many researchers now recognize that the many individuals and social factions comprising these complex societies have distinct, and sometimes conflicting, worldviews based on personal experiences and interests. Increasingly, archaeologists are attempting to tease out diverse values and perspectives related to gender, class, ethnicity, occupation, and individuality. For example, a number of recent archaeological studies have focused on gendered views of cultural norms and social orders (e.g., Joyce Marcus's and Kent Flannery's analyses of feminine depictions in human figurines and gender-segregated work spaces in Formative Period Mesoamerica).

6. *Warfare and Militarism*

Anthropological studies have suggested that warfare in chiefdom-level societies differs from that in tribal societies by its expansionistic focus on acquisition of territory, resources, and captives, and by its concentration of military power in the hands of chiefly leaders who use it to expand their political sway. Robert Carneiro has suggested that both the rise and evolution of chiefdoms are related to warfare. Under conditions of land shortages and population stress, militarily powerful leaders systematically assault settlements along polity boundaries. Conquered enemies are incorporated into the expanding chiefdom, resulting in the elaboration of political hierarchies and the coalescence of a polity of greater complexity as well as scale. However, warfare is an almost continuous process in many chiefdoms, one of a number of forms of 'peer polity' interaction that are politically transformative. Militarism can often result in more subtle changes in power relationships among competing chiefdoms, over both the short and long term, without territorial conquest. Political loyalties may be shifted to military victors who control the ideology of warrior prestige and who increase their political currency through captured labor and valuables, resulting in larger alliance networks.

Archaeologists have focused on a variety of material evidence to document changes in the scale, intensity, and behavioral and ideological aspects of warfare in chiefdom-level societies. These include the development of fortifications or other defensive works, changes in regional settlement patterns (e.g., concentration of population in large centers, depopulation along polity boundaries, relocation of settlements to defensible positions), and systematic destruction of power-symboling architecture (e.g., dismantling of monumental architecture, toppling of statuary, burning of chiefly centers). Examples are the alternating rebuilding and burning of fortifications surrounding Iron Age European towns such as Heuneberg, the creation of 'no man's lands' between Mississippian centers, and the defacement of sacred monumental statuary on Easter Island. Osteological evidence from burials allows archaeologists to evaluate rates of violence in populations (e.g., scalping, skeletal trauma, embedded projectiles), the ritualized use of body parts in prewar and postwar ceremonialism (e.g., decapitation for trophy head taking), and debilitating physical conditions and malnutrition related to prolonged exposure to military siege. Archaeological studies of burials also allow archaeologists to identify 'warrior insignia' associated with the development of specialized warrior classes and strong ideologies of warrior prestige exemplified in the elaborate bronze horse-fittings of Bronze Age European warriors and the gold-pegged teeth of island Southeast Asian warriors. The development of new warfare technologies associated with escalating military competition can be traced archaeologically in intensified metals or stone mining, labor-saving equipment (e.g., molds) or large-scale facilities for mass production of weapons, and the adoption of horses for mounted cavalry.

7. *The Evolution of Chiefdoms*

Many archaeologists view the transition to inherited, institutionalized power and status, associated with chiefdoms but further developed in states, as the key transformation in human societies. Since the organizational dynamics of chiefdoms are viewed as similar to that of states, theories of state development are commonly applied at the chiefdom level. Early theories emphasized the managerial benefits of chieftainship as societies expanded in scale. Chiefs arose to administer irrigation works (Karl Wittfogel), coordinate localized production and exchange (Elman Service), mediate land conflicts and warfare (Robert Carneiro), ameliorate economic risk through ritual intervention (Robert Drennan), and to meet other organizational challenges.

More recently, archaeologists have criticized the functionalist nature of these theories and their simplistic emphasis on single factors, instead focusing on the varied acquisitive and power-seeking strategies of political actors as they vie for symbolic capital and control over the labor and resources of others. In this view, the origins of permanent forms of social inequality and political authority are to be found in the competitive and aggrandizing behavior of 'big men' in tribal societies. Archaeologists now examine this transformation at varying scales of analysis, ranging from the transfiguring actions and motivations of individual political actors, to multiple polities developing together through forms of *peer polity interaction*, to change-stimulating contacts with more complex states and empires (*world systems theory*). In addition, many archaeologists now recognize that not all chiefdom-level societies have unilinear evolutionary trajectories leading inevitably toward greater complexity. Many chiefdoms fail to develop state-level institutions over the long-term, instead perpetually cycling between complex and simple forms, 'devolving' into tribal societies (e.g., New Zealand's South Island Maori, possibly Amazonian societies), mysteriously collapsing (e.g., the Mississippian chiefdoms, Easter Island), or otherwise maintaining a chiefdom-level organization until eventual absorption by colonizing states and empires (e.g., many chiefdoms of the Central American Isthmus, North America, the Caribbean, island Southeast Asia, Europe and Polynesia).

See also: Big Man, Anthropology of; Conflict and War, Archaeology of; Intensification and Specialization, Archaeology of; Political Anthropology; Power in Society; States and Civilizations, Archaeology of

Bibliography

Carneiro R 1981 The chiefdom as precursor of the state. In: Jones G, Krautz R (eds.) *The Transition to Statehood in the New World*. Cambridge University Press, Cambridge, UK, pp. 37–79

Drennan R, Uribe C (eds.) 1991 *Chiefdoms in the Americas*. University Press of America, Lanham, MD

Earle T 1987 Chiefdoms in archaeological and ethnohistorical perspective. *Annual Review of Anthropology* **16**: 279–308

Earle T (ed.) 1991 *Chiefdoms: Power, Economy and Ideology*. Cambridge University Press, Cambridge, UK

Earle T 1997 *How Chiefs Come to Power*. Stanford University Press, Stanford, CA

Kirch P V 1984 *The Evolution of the Polynesian Chiefdoms*. Cambridge University Press, Cambridge, UK

Renfrew C, Shennan S (eds.) 1982 *Ranking, Resource and Exchange*. Cambridge University Press, Cambridge, UK

Yoffee N 1993 Too many chiefs. In: Yoffee N, Sherratt A (eds.) *Archaeological Theory: Who Sets the Agenda?* Cambridge University Press, Cambridge, UK, pp. 60–78

L. L. Junker

Child Abuse

Article 19 of the *Convention on the Rights of the Child*, ratified in 1989, prescribes that parties shall take all appropriate legislative, administrative, social, and educational measures to protect the child from all forms of physical or mental violence, injury or abuse, neglect or negligent treatment, maltreatment or exploitation, including sexual abuse. Until now this article has been disregarded throughout the world. In laying blame we should not only consider third-world countries (with child labor, prostitution, and soldiers) but also the rich industrial countries, where violence against children must be seen as a 'social epidemic.'

1. Forms of Child Abuse

There are four forms of child abuse:

Physical abuse. Blows or other violent actions, resulting in injuries to children, such as being beaten, hit, whipped, pushed down stairs, hurled against a wall, burned with hot water/cigarettes, jammed in doors/car windows, tortured with needles, put into cold water or pushed under water, made to eat their own faeces or drink their own urine, strangling, and poisoning.

Sexual abuse. Any action that is inflicted upon or must be tolerated by a child against their own will or any action about which the child cannot make a decision due to their physical, emotional, mental, or verbal inferiority. The offenders use their position of power and authority to satisfy their own needs at the expense of these children who thus suffer discrimination as sexual objects. Sexual abuse between children themselves is manifest when one child is much older and/or uses force.

Neglect. Considerable impact on or damage to a child's development due to a lack of care, clothing, feeding, medical care, supervision, or protection from danger.

Emotional abuse. Outright rejection, intimidation, terrorization, or isolation of a child. Actions such as verbal abuse/discrimination on a daily basis, locking a child in a dark room, tying them to a bed and many other major threats, including to their lives.

2. Prevalence of Forms of Abuse

This article draws on survey results from German-speaking countries and the United States as they are deemed to be representative of comparable statistics from modern industrial countries.

2.1 Physical Abuse

A representative survey (Pfeiffer and Wetzels 1997) of 16 to 59 year olds in Germany about their childhood experiences of physical parental violence indicates a

Table 1
Incidence of parental violence

Incidence of parental violence
Possible answers: never, rarely, occasionally, often, very often
Multiple answers were possible, N = 3241

Question	Rarely	More often than rarely
1. Throwing objects	7.0%	3.7%
2. Grabbing/pushing around	17.9%	12.1%
3. Slapping	36.0%	36.5%
4. Hitting/striking with an object	7.0%	4.6%
5. Punching, kicking	3.3%	2.6%
6. Striking, beating up	4.5%	3.5%
7. Strangling	1.4%	0.7%
8. Intentional burns	0.5%	0.4%
9. Threats with a weapon	0.6%	0.4%
10. Use of weapon	0.6%	0.3%
Total physical violence (Questions 1–10)	36.1%	38.8%
Total physical violence (Questions 5–10)	5.9%	4.7%

distinction between physical *punishment* and physical *abuse*. Physical punishment is defined as intentionally inflicting pain to control a child's behavior but without intending to cause severe injuries or damage and without violating (existing!) laws. Physical abuse definitely violates laws, as injuries to the child are either intentional or tolerated as a consequence of these violent actions. The incidences of violence observed are listed in Table 1.

Of the persons interviewed, 74.9 percent confirmed having experienced physical parental violence in their childhood, and 10.6 percent definitely suffered physical parental abuse.

2.2 Sexual Abuse

Recent retrospective studies in Germany, Austria, and Switzerland (Deegener 2000) suggest that about 15 to 25 percent of women and 5 to 10 percent of men questioned had been sexually abused in their childhood or adolescence. We believe that the approximate incidence and severity of sexual abuse in both sexes is as shown in Table 2. Almost two thirds of victims were ever only abused on one occasion. One third of cases involved repeated sexual abuse. However in the latter group, about 10 percent of cases continued over periods exceeding 12 months and extending to several years. Such long-term sexual abuse is perpetrated predominately by a victim's relatives. Between 80 and 90 percent of offenders are male.

2.3 Neglect and Emotional Abuse

If defined in conservative terms, the extent of these forms of abuse in Germany far exceeds the incidence of the other two forms. If defined in broader terms, it is not an exaggeration to say that the bullying of children is widespread and commonplace.

2.4 Statistics from the USA

The National Committee to Prevent Child Abuse (1995) indicates that over three million (suspected)

Table 2
Severity of sexual abuse

Serious sexual abuse Attempted or actual vaginal, anal, or oral violation; oral satisfaction by victim or anal penetration of offender	15%
Severe sexual abuse Victim has to masturbate in front of offender; offender masturbates in front of victim; offender fondles victim's genitals; victim has to touch offender's genitals; victim has to expose genitals to offender	35%
Less severe sexual abuse Offender attempts to touch victim's genitals; offender fondles victim's breasts; sexual kisses; French kisses	35%
Sexual abuse without physical contact Exhibitionism; victim has to watch pornographic videos; offender observes victim while bathing	15%

victims were recorded in 1994 in the USA. Almost 1300 of these children died as a result of abuse and neglect. Elders (1999) reports 3,195,000 registered cases of child abuse in 1997, with one million cases being confirmed. However, only 50 to 75 percent of all registered cases were adequately investigated. Over the years the following averages have been determined: 45 to 50 percent are cases of neglect, 25 percent of physical abuse, 10 percent of sexual abuse, 3 percent of emotional abuse, and 15 percent of other causes.

2.5 *Combination of Different Forms of Abuse*

Multiple episodes of maltreatment during childhood are more the rule than the exception. Pfeiffer and Wetzels (1997) found that even in the youngest age group (i.e., 16 to 29 year olds), approximately one sixth of adolescents and young adults in Germany had been victims of frequent or severe physical parental violence or sexual abuse (involving physical contact and abuse outside the family). Employing a rather conservative estimate, we believe that about one fifth of this young generation has been affected by physical parental violence, sexual victimization, or frequent adult partner violence.

2.6 *Assessing the Incidence of Child Abuse*

The extent of child abuse invites comparison with a global epidemic. However, in contrast to the degree of professional, political, and public attention received by other diseases, child abuse is neglected. Sadler et al. (1999) for example, estimate that the incidence of abuse is ten times higher than that of all forms of cancer. The 'costs' of child abuse are tremendously high, with the 'human costs' of the sociopsychological, cognitive, and physical consequences of abuse being inestimable. Courtney (1999) quotes a 1993 estimate for the USA, indicating that approximately 11.4 billion US$ was spent on examining abused children, providing medical care to severely injured children, treating victims and their families, and caring for children in foster families. In addition, Courtney cites Westman, who calculates that expenditure due to 'incompetent parenting' (in broad terms) in the USA amounts to about 38.6 billion US$ each year.

3. *Causes of Child Abuse*

More specific causal models are becoming accepted in research and clinical practice (Cicchetti 1989), resulting in a marked improvement in early recognition, therapy and prevention. Four groups of influences can be identified which interact within a complex reference framework:

(a) At the individual level there is the perpetrator's life history and personality, e.g., their own experiences of childhood abuse, early separation of parents, periods in (foster) homes, emotional disturbances, or alcohol and drug abuse.

(b) At the family level there are maladjusted parent–child relationships, partner conflicts and problems, etc.

(c) At the social level there are factors involving poverty, unemployment, meager and limited housing, social ghettos, and insufficient social support, etc.

(d) At the community level there are, among other things, a high tolerance of violence and aggression and a high degree of violence in their upbringing.

There are numerous interactions between these levels that may lead to (acute or protracted) familial destabilization, resulting in neglect or physical abuse. In addition to the risk factors, which may increase the probability of child abuse, one must consider the preventative factors, which reduce the risk and consequences of abuse.

4. *Consequences of Child Abuse*

Not only can child abuse influence every aspect of behavior and experience, but it can also lead to psychosomatic diseases and physical injuries (Egle et al. 2000). In addition, child abuse influences the attachment of children to their parents and their relationships with their peers. However, as the short- and long-term consequences are not specific there can be various other causes.

Whereas some research suggests that the consequences of child abuse can last throughout a person's life, other research shows that abused children suffer few (if any) adverse consequences. During the 1990s, a growing number of investigators has identified many mediating and moderating factors that can either ameliorate or exacerbate the consequences of child abuse (Masten et al. 1990, Kendall-Tackett et al. 1993, Kaplan et al. 1999):

characteristics of the child's experiences (e.g., nature, frequency, severity, type, and prior history of child abuse);

resources of the child (e.g., good social and academic competencies, endearing temperament);

vulnerability of the child (e.g., psychiatric disorder, low intelligence, insecure attachment style, early onset of the abuse);

social support of the child (e.g., good relationship with the nonabusing parent, support of significant others from outside the family, psychotherapy).

Therefore, the extent of the negative consequences of child abuse depends on complex transactional processes between vulnerability or risk factors on the one hand, and resiliency or compensatory factors on the other hand. The term 'resiliency' should not be understood to minimize the suffering of abused children or justify criticism of those children who are not resilient. However, some children from violent homes are less influenced by their abuse than others and develop effective coping skills and strategies. In this connection, the relationship between the causes and consequences of child abuse must also be considered: a low intelligence may—for example—stimulate abusive behavior by parents or caretakers, but low intelligence can also be a negative consequence of severe abusive experiences in early childhood.

Generalizing, the severity of the consequences of child abuse depends especially on the following factors: the age and developmental stage of the child, the length and severity of the abuse, and the relationship of the abuser to the victim. Therefore, long-term severe abuse of a young child perpetrated by a parent tends to produce more detrimental effects on the emotional, physical, social, and cognitive development than shorter-term abuse of an older child by a stranger. In the case of long-term physical abuse it is not uncommon to find a range of injuries inflicted at different times. The consequences of neglect remain underestimated (i.e., 'neglected neglect').

5. Prevention

The extent to which abusive educational measures (including physical punishment) are tolerated varies widely from country to country as a function of the sociocultural context. Except for legal prosecution in confirmed cases of child abuse, the rights of parents (or teachers, etc.) to employ a wide range of seemingly appropriate educational measures (including physical punishment) remain unchallenged.

In 1979 Sweden introduced a law banning physical punishment, addressing this grey zone between 'permitted' and 'illegal' educational measures. Countries such as Finland (1984), Denmark (1986), Norway (1987), and Austria (1989) followed suit. In Germany the following law was passed in 2000: 'Children have the right to a non-violent upbringing and education. Physical punishment, emotional abuse and other discriminatory measures are unacceptable.' This does not imply an increase in prosecutions. As Sweden has demonstrated successfully, the objective is rather to alter the value system and influence the 'legal hygiene,' while simultaneously strengthening the support for a nonviolent upbringing and education. An education conducted in accordance with the above-mentioned UN conventions and with the child-protection provisions found in many other constitutions would not tolerate physical punishment or other discriminatory educational measures.

Adequate prevention requires worldwide birth control, a reduction in poverty, an improvement in both socio-ecological and living conditions, the improvement of general education standards and lifelong learning (including parent training), and a reduction in the wide power and relationship gap existing between men and women, resulting from raising boys to be 'masters' and girls to be 'servants.' About one third of all cases of sexual abuse/violation are committed by male adolescents.

Furthermore, there should be independent, state-nominated representatives for minors, whose role is to replace parents at the community level and to fight for children's needs and rights in society. The young should also have more opportunities to co-determine what occurs by means of an institution such as a children's or young people's parliament. Special broad-scale support programs for families/parents at risk (such as home visits to teenage mothers or high-risk women during pregnancy) should be offered, and more assistance should be available to families in serious difficulty.

The predominant objectives of prevention need to be: (a) to interrupt the generational cycle of family violence, (b) to teach future generations humanitarian attitudes and civil behavior, and (c) to promote 'social parenting' and 'structural security' instead of 'structural violence' for all children.

There is widespread condemnation when child abuse or violent acts committed by (abused) adolescents become public, but this still tends to be little more than lip service. We tend to avoid reflecting upon our own violent relationships and actions, obscuring these by employing projections of monstrous child abusers. Appropriate responsibility for children and their futures is not being implemented for one simple reason: 'We are all against such things as child pornography, but only a few are willing to actually support programs that could save children's lives, because these cost money and comfort and require another form of living and life' (Sigusch 1996).

See also: Child Care and Child Development; Childhood Depression; Childhood Sexual Abuse and Risk for Adult Psychopathology; Children and the Law; Children, Rights of: Cultural Concerns; Family Health; Socialization in Infancy and Childhood; Violence and Effects on Children; Violence as a Problem of Health

Bibliography

Cicchetti D 1989 How research on maltreatment has informed the study of child development: perspectives from developmental psychopathology. In: Cicchetti D, Carlson V (eds.) *Child Maltreatment. Theory and Research on the Causes and Consequences of Child Abuse and Neglect*. Cambridge University Press, New York

Courtney M E 1999 The economics. *Child Abuse and Neglect* **23**: 975–86

Deegener G 2000 *Die Würde des Kindes. Plädoyer für eine Erziehung ohne Gewalt* [The dignity of the child. A plea for an upbringing without violence]. Beltz, Weinheim, Germany

Egle U T, Hoffmann S O, Joraschky P 2000 *Sexueller Mißbrauch, Mißhandlung, Vernachlässigung. Erkennung und Therapie psychischer und psychosomatischer Folgen früher Traumatisierungen* [Sexual abuse, maltreatment and neglect. Recognition and therapy of psychological and psychosomatic consequences of traumatizations at an early age]. Schattauer, Stuttgart, Germany

Elders M J 1999 The call to action. *Child Abuse and Neglect* **23**: 1003–9

Kaplan S J, Pelcovitz D, Labruna V 1999 Child and adolescent abuse and neglect research: A review of the past 10 years. Part I: Physical and emotional abuse and neglect. *Journal of the American Academy of Child and Adolescent Psychiatry* **38**: 1214–22

Kendall-Tackett K A, Meyer Williams L, Finkelhor D 1993 Impact of sexual abuse on children: A review and synthesis of recent empirical studies. *Psychological Bulletin* **113**: 164–80

Masten A S, Best K M, Garmezy N 1990 Resilience and development: Contributions from the study of children who overcome adversity. *Development and Psychopathology* **2**: 425–44

National Committee to Prevent Child Abuse (NCPCA) 1995 *Current Trends in Child Abuse Reporting and Fatalities. The Results of the 1994 Annual Fifty State Survey*. NCPCA, Chicago

Pfeiffer B, Wetzels P 1997 *Kinder als Täter und Opfer. Eine Analyse auf der Basis der PKS und einer repräsentativen Opferbefragung.* [Children as offenders and victims. An analysis of criminal statistics and victim interviews]. Forschungsbericht 68. Kriminologisches Forschungsinstitut, Hanover, Germany

Sadler, B L, Chadwick, D L, Hensler D J 1999 The summary chapter—The national call to action: Moving ahead. *Child Abuse and Neglect* **23**: 1011–18

Sigusch V 1996 Kultureller Wandel der Sexualität [Sexuality in cultural transition]. In: Sigusch V (ed.) *Sexuelle Störungen und ihre Behandlung* [Sexual disorders and their treatment]. Thieme, Stuttgart

G. Deegener

Child and Adolescent Psychiatry, Principles of

Child and adolescent psychiatry and psychotherapy comprises the diagnosis, treatment, prevention, and rehabilitation of neuropsychiatric and developmental disorders as well as behavior disturbances during childhood and adolescence. The need for a separated psychiatric discipline for children and adolescents results from age-dependent characteristics of mental disorders, strongly influenced by rapidly alternating stages of neurobiological and social development in this period of life. The discipline of child and adolescent psychiatry is now acknowledged as a medical speciality or subspecialty in many countries; however it will still need much effort to offer a specialized child mental health service worldwide.

This article provides an overview of the historical development of child psychiatry in different cultural regions, focusing on the development in Europe and the USA. A necessary distinction is made regarding the diagnostical classification system for mental disorders in childhood and adolescence in comparison to the classification system in general psychiatry. Principles of child-specific assessment and treatment are described. Further, some future perspectives in the development of a more biologically influenced child psychiatry are discussed as well as the needs for a modern child psychiatry in developing countries.

1. History

The clinical discipline of psychiatry was formed in the nineteenth century, in a situation of an increasing interest in and knowledge of psychological phenomena. In 1899, the term 'child psychiatry' was first used by the French psychiatrist M. Manheimer, who called his book *Les troubles mentaux de l' enfance*, subtitled *Précis de psychiatrie infantile*.

Four main traditions have made substantial contributions to the current body of knowledge in the field of child and adolescent psychiatry, and influenced the structure and the actual treatment concepts of child psychiatric institutions. The formerly unified disciplines of psychiatry and neurology have given rise to the tradition of neuropsychiatry, especially in some European countries. Several scientific associations still include reference to neurology. Increasing research activity in the areas of neuropsychobiology and neuropsychology confirms the need of a close linkage between these two 'brain disciplines' for a better understanding of psychiatric disorders.

A movement based on a remedial clinical tradition, promoted by Hans Asperger in Austria and Paul Moor in Switzerland, still plays a role in pediatric departments with activities in the field of child psychosomatics. In general, remedial education is an important part of the multidisciplinary children's mental healthcare service.

Developed by the pioneers of psychoanalytical work with children, like Anna Freud, Alfred Adler and Melanie Klein, the psychodynamic-psychoanalytic tradition influences etiological concepts of behavioral and personality disorders and gives implications on psychotherapeutic treatment strategies; however, behavioral therapy, often in combination with family therapy interventions, is predominant in the clinical use of psychotherapy nowadays.

The empirical, epidemiological, and statistical tradition has been established in a number of European countries, mainly the UK, Scandinavian countries, and Germany. It has been strongly influenced by the work of Michael Rutter and by research influences from the USA. This tradition created the basis of the currently used classification systems in psychiatry.

Although first considerable activities in the field of child psychiatry started in Europe in the early twentieth century, it was not until 1954 that the first European symposium of child psychiatry took place in Magglingen (Switzerland), a consequence of World War II and the ensuing political situation. At this meeting, first attempts were made to establish a unifying scientific association, which was founded in 1960 as the Union of European Pedopsychiatrists at the first European congress in Paris. Later, at a congress in Madrid in 1979, the name of the society was changed to the European Society for Child and Adolescent Psychiatry (ESCAP) (Remschmidt and van Engeland 1999).

The crystallization of child psychiatry in the USA was influenced by the growing knowledge in the field of psychiatry in Europe. A sociocultural reform, beginning in the year 1900, was the main factor contributing to the establishment of child psychiatry in the USA. The desire to protect children from social hardship resulted in the need for mental healthcare institutions. William Healy founded the first Institute of Juvenile Research in 1909 to handle child problems occurring in association with delinquency and traumatic injuries. The Orthopsychiatric Association, founded in 1924, integrated the different medical and sociopsychological professionals working in the psychiatric field. The psychiatrist Adolf Meyer installed the first department of child psychiatry at the Johns Hopkins University in the early 1930s. Leo Kanner, an immigrant from Austria, was the first chairman and published his textbook of child psychiatry in 1935. Child psychiatry was accepted as a clinical discipline in its own right in 1950. Since then, the American Academy of Child and Adolescent Psychiatry (AACAP) has made a marked contribution to the global development of a modern child and adolescent psychiatry (Schwab and Schwab-Stone 1999).

The different professionals working in the field of child psychiatry have been organized in the International Association of Child and Adolescent Psychiatry and Allied Professions (IACAPAP), founded as an umbrella organization in the 1930s. Countries from East Asia and the Pacific region present a remarkable level of medical supply and research in the field of child and adolescent psychiatry. In recent years South America, African countries, and Australia have also contributed with increasing activities to the specialization of child mental health services.

2. Epidemiology and Classification

The prevalence rates of all mental disturbances in children are estimated at about 15 percent. However, mental disorders in need of treatment occur in about half of these cases. In children with primary neuro-

logical brain dysfunctions, the prevalence of psychiatric disorders increases with the degree of the brain damage or the metabolic alteration. So, children with epilepsy suffer five times more from mental problems than unaffected children.

Psychiatric classification systems are compilations of diagnostic criteria, based on clinical experience, to define and differentiate mental disorders and establish agreement and common language among healthcare professionals and researchers. The classification of mental disorders is essential for the development of treatment concepts and a necessary precondition for epidemiological, clinical, and biological research in this field.

The 10th revision of the *International Statistical Classification of Diseases and Related Health Problems (ICD-10)*, published by the World Health Organisation (WHO) in 1992, is a comprehensive classification system of medical conditions and mental disorders, used in official medical and psychiatric nosology throughout most of the world. However, some countries (e.g., France and the USA) use compatible or modified classifications. The fourth edition of *Diagnostic and Statistical Manual of Mental Disorders (DSM-IV)*, published in 1994 by the American Psychiatric Association (APA), is the official psychiatric coding system used in the USA and is in part compatible with the ninth revision of the *International Classification of Diseases (ICD-9)*.

The mental development of children and adolescents, in contrast to that of adults, is strongly influenced by brain maturation processes and social environment. Considering this fact, the classification system in child and adolescence psychiatry is based on a multiaxial diagnostical view. The approach of the actual classification systems is atheoretical according to etiological concepts. Due to the limited knowledge about etiology and pathomechanism of the mental disorders, it is mainly the symptoms and course of a disorder that are used to define and classify the mental disorders. An approach to predict the clinical course of the disorder is associated with the description of a clinical feature. Additional contributing factors, like the intelligence level, the parent–child relationship, and the social environment are assembled by using different diagnostical axes. The impact of the disorder on psychosocial functions is assessed on Axis VI of the multiaxial diagnostic system (Remschmidt and Schmidt 1994).

ICD-10, regardless of the use of a multiaxial system, does not consider age of disease onset consistently. Apart from that, the predicted clinical course is basically used for many clinical decisions including treatment concepts (Rutter 1989). Taking into account these important facts, an appropriate version of the classification system for child and adolescent psychiatry has been developed, where age of onset and typical clinical course has been integrated. The disorders have been divided into early-onset disorders with a persistent course (e.g., autism), early-onset disorders with transient manifestation (e.g., enuresis), age-related interactional disorders (e.g., separation anxiety), young age-related disorders with sometimes recurrent episodes or chronical course (e.g., eating disorders), early-onset adult-type disorders (e.g. schizophrenia).

Even though specified diagnostic criteria are provided for each mental disorder, increasing the reliability of clinicians process of diagnosis, the professionals have to pay attention to existing mixed forms or comorbid disorders (Caron and Rutter 1991), like attention deficit/hyperactivity disorder (AD/HD) with conduct disorder or eating disorder with depressive disorder (Biederman et al. 1991).

3. Developmental Psychopathology and Pathogenesis

Mental disorders in children and adolescents are manifested in behavioral problems, affective and cognitive disturbances, and somatic concerns. The quality and severity of these problems are influenced by the developmental state. The rapid development, simultaneously on the biological and on the social level, has a strong impact on the diverse developmental tasks of a minor (Munir and Beardslee 1999).

Biological maturation, particularly in early childhood, plays a key role in the etiology of mental problems. With increasing age social adaptation and social learning becomes more prominent. The maturation of the brain and gender-specific role taking are two main factors of becoming adult. Acceleration or retardation of the biological and social maturation results in an alteration of the developmental process with behavioral problems and social disintegration in the case of existing permanent deficits.

Developmental psychopathology describes age-related aspects of mental disorders, especially the formation and alternating pattern of symptoms over time (Cicchetti and Cohen 1995). In early childhood the ability of autonomous behavior is acquired. For that, an inner representation and judgment of the child's cognitive and behavioral activities is an important precondition. Older children compare their self-image with an imagined ideal as a kind of self-control, which modifies and limits the outcome of the social learning process. Although there is an interaction between these different components, mental disorders in childhood and adolescence can be interpreted as deficits in maturation or learning processes or in their autonomous efforts. Parallel to the differentiation of cognitive, emotional, and social functions there are increasing demands on the child. Sexual development, gender-related role taking, and academic achievement all which have to be coped with adequately.

During certain periods of development, the child and adolescent have specific responsibilities. Functions according to these specific developmental demands can be easily disrupted, because they are not well established due to the rapid developmental process. Infants suffer from regulation disorders, which are often induced by the behavior of caregivers. Preschool-age children suffer from somatic, physiological dysfunction in the area of sleep, eating, speech, and elimination control, whereas in school-age children communication problems in peer groups and in the school situation appear (Esser et al. 1990). Separation anxiety, insufficient affect control, and learning disabilities are characteristic problems with increasing age. Adolescents then have to develop self-confidence, to deal with authorities and to accept their sexual identity.

Risk and protective factors, in addition to the developmental process, are effective in the pathogenesis of mental disorders. Genetically determined factors are the somatic constitution, particularly the brain function, and the pattern of personality, the temperamental factors (Rothenberger 1990).

Pervasive developmental disorders like autism have a high genetic risk (Rutter et al. 1999). Traumatic brain injuries prenatal, perinatal, or postnatal, or chronic metabolic dysfunction increase the risk of developing a mental problem. A lack of sociocultural stimulation, socioemotional deprivation, or high pressure as a result of people's inadequate expectations could be summarized as sociogenic risk factors (Rutter 1999). Language acquisition in particular strongly depends on a sociogenic balance. Intrapsychic conflicts are a result of chronic problems, like sexual or physical abuse, mental disease of a parent, delinquency in the family, distorted familiar communication. The interactive process between parents and child can amplify or otherwise reduce behavior in both directions, to a normalization or to an increased disturbance. Life events, as acute stress factors, in general play a minor role in the pathogenesis of mental disorders of children and adolescents. In the case of strong traumatic impairment, like being a victim of a rape or having a bad accident, a posttraumatic stress disorder can appear (Costello et al. 1998).

Protective factors, like social attractiveness, verbal skill, appropriate problem-solving strategies, self-consciousness, creative intelligence and interests, a pleasant life and family situation, and stable peergroup relationships can act successfully against other biological or psychosocial stress factors to reduce the risk of developing a mental disorder or in the case of manifestation to reduce symptom severity and improve clinical outcome (Laucht et al. 1997).

4. Assessment

To provide a diagnosis, child and adolescent psychiatrists examine the mental status, the psychopathological profile, and behavior of the patient;

ascertain the social and biological development, and evaluate the prior medical and psychiatric history. Further useful information can be obtained by parental interviews and school reports. Different sources of information reflect different point of views, experiences, and insights (Jensen et al. 1999). Depending on the type of disorder and the age of the child, the reliability of this information is quite different as well. The summary of information from different sources, including the child, the parents, teachers, peer group members, doctor, pediatrician, and sometimes the youth welfare department, provides the most reliable and complete picture of symptoms, functional level of the child, and influencing environmental factors.

Recognizing the level of social functioning and the performance of developmental tasks related to the child's age is a key assessment for the estimation of severity and prognosis of the disorder. Structured psychiatric interviews, rating scales, and self-report forms can be used to observe, quantify, and categorize the evaluated symptoms, for example, the Diagnostic Interview Schedule for Children-Revised (DISC-R), the Child Behavior Checklist, scales for the assessment of psychotic symptoms (Positive and Negative Symptom Rating Scale—PANS) or mood disorders (Beck Depression Inventory).

Cognitive and intellectual abilities, basic factors of a healthy mind, are age-related functions. To ascertain alterations of these functions, it is necessary to determine the social level and the state of the biological maturation. Particularly in children with mental retardation, learning disabilities, or pervasive developmental disorders a comprehensive assessment of the intellectual function (examples are Kaufman-ABC and WISC-III) is necessary to create an optimized educational and treatment program (Ollendick and Hersen 1993).

In a subgroup of patients, a defined somatic dysfunction, mainly neurological diseases, is the primary cause of mental diseases. Brain diseases (tumor, epilepsy), metabolic dysfunctions (phenylketonuria, hypothyroidism) and diseases with defined chromosomal aberrations (like Down, Angelman, and Prader-Willi syndrome) can be associated with a varied picture of mental disturbances. Therefore physical examinations and technical investigations (brain computerized scan, radiology, electroencephalography, and blood and genetic screening) are standard procedures to rule out somatic disorders and to determine the developmental state of a child. The analysis of genetic mutations, polymorphisms, and associated molecular-biological dysfunctions will provide more insight into the etiology of a psychiatric disorder which is always manifested on a neurobiological level. The early assessment of a genetically caused metabolic dysfunction (like phenylketonuria) can help to prevent the emergence of a disorder or will help, in some cases of known genetic defects (like Prader-Willi syndrome) or relevant polymorphisms associated with a disorder

(like in AD/HD), to develop better treatment strategies in the near future.

Assessment of the neuropsychological functions should be done routinely in children and adolescents with AD/HD (Barkley 1998). The core symptoms—inattention, hyperactivity, and impulsivity—need to be quantified by neuropsychological tests, in part with support of computerized methods (e.g., Continuous Performance Task, CPT). Learning disabilities, often associated with developmental or attention deficit disorders, need further examination by questionnaires and psychological tests. To rule out sensory dysfunction, visual and acoustic perception has to be assessed in cooperation with departments of ophthalmology, phonetics, and pediatric audiology.

If children are younger than four years, the psychopathological assessment is oriented on findings regarding the child's development and interactional behavior. This information can be received mainly from parental reports or, in the case of some early onset diseases, by the medical records. Semi-standardized play situations and the observation of peer group and parent–child interactions provide further information about the child's intellectual function, capacity for emotional reactions, attachment, and behavior.

5. Treatment

Psychiatric therapy in general is based on three major treatment pillars: psychotherapy, psychopharmacology, and psychosocial and family interventions. Each kind of mental disorder or disease needs a typical combination of these three therapy forms to get an optimal therapy effect. In children and adolescents the family and school environment particularly has to be taken into consideration.

For a sophisticated mental healthcare network, the cooperation of the various professional groups, including psychiatrists, psychologists, social workers, teachers, and members of administrative institutions of the government, responsible for children and adolescents, is a necessary precondition (Simeon 1990).

The treatment of mental disorders can be divided into three main groups: treatment mainly by psychotherapy, treatment mainly by a psychopharmacological intervention, and combined psychotherapeutical and pharmacological approaches. Psychosocial interventions, specially in childhood and adolescence, are in general a part of the treatment program.

A follow-up assessment over a longer time period provides information about the course of the disease. It is necessary to react early to changes in the symptomatology, to observe the social functioning of the child and adolescent, to control possible side effects of the treatment, and not to overlook the best moment to stop the treatment.

There is a group of early-onset disorders with a persistent course like mental retardation, pervasive developmental disorders, and transient developmentally dependent disorders like learning disorders, communication disorders, selective mutism, attachment and elimination disorders (encopresis, enuresis). Treatment plans are based on behavioral therapy concepts. Contingency management, self-monitoring by protocols, training of social skills and communication, and principles of classical and operant conditioning are expanded by family therapy, educational programs and cooperation with teachers, social interventions, psychomotoric and coordinative training, and in many cases additional parental guidance (Noshpitz 1981).

At the present time, there is no disorder-specific medication on the market; however, there are some substances which are successful in the reduction of single symptoms belonging to these disorders (Houts et al. 1994), like antipsychotics in autistic children (McDougle et al. 1997). An efficient medication exists only for single early-onset disorders. In the case of AD/HD, the core symptoms can be reduced about 70–80 percent by medication, mainly by the use of psychostimulants. However, children with AD/HD need an intensive behavioral and educational treatment program as well, particularly, if they suffer from an associated oppositional defiant or conduct disorder. Often their parents need additional support from parental guidance (Barkley 1998, Kazdin 1997).

The main emphasis in the treatment of mood and schizophrenic disorders, summarized as early-onset adult–type disorders, which get manifested mainly in adolescence and early adulthood, is the psychopharmacological therapy. The exception is that younger children with mood disorders often gain a clinical improvement just from psychotherapy. Antidepressive and antipsychotic medication acts quite specifically on the disturbed brain metabolism, which is, as a primary mechanism or a biological reaction on permanent psychosocial stress, the main causal factor for the disorder. Neurotransmitters like serotonin, noradrenalin, and dopamine are regulated by these substances and neuroplastical processes, which are important for the structural function of brain, are regenerated and stabilized over a longer time. Therefore the intake of most of these medications should be continued over a longer time, if there is no contraindication by serious side effects, which might occur in some cases. Although medication is necessary and the first choice of treatment, these patients need an intensive psychosocial support and training program to prevent them from social disintegration and to cover their academic achievement.

Another large group of mental diseases can be described as behavioral, emotional, age-specific interaction disorders and personality disorders. Examples are eating, anxiety and obsessive-compulsive disorders, stress reactions, and emotionally unstable personalities, called borderline personality disorder. Various behavioral therapy methods in combination with family therapy and psychosocial interventions, continued in an outpatient therapy setting, are established as the most successful kind of treatment. In a few cases, the additional use of medication can improve or accelerate the treatment success (Piccinelli et al. 1995).

Controlled clinical trials are the basis for the development of effective treatment approaches (Vitiello and Jensen 1997). Performing clinical trials in children and adolescents, either to investigate the efficacy and safety of psychotherapeutic treatment strategies or of newer psychopharmacological substances, is difficult from the legal and ethical point of view. There is the need to get a written consent from the proband or patient before starting any investigation. The proband has to be informed about targets, efficacy, and expected side effects of the planed therapy. In the case of children, especially those suffering from mental problems, an adapted, comprehensible form of information needs to be presented, and the parental authorities have to give their written consent as well. Although double-blind placebo-controlled clinical trials are the highest standard to study the efficacy and safety of newer treatment concepts, it is quite difficult from ethical point of view to carry out such a design in children.

Further aggravating circumstances hinder a fast performance of clinical trials in children and adolescents: First, the brain of a minor is not completely maturated. Brain dysfunction and resulting mental disturbances may be transient, like separation anxiety and sleep problems in early childhood. The child psychiatrist has to be aware of this fact, especially regarding the duration of medical and psychotherapeutic treatment interventions. Further, risks of pharmacological side effects and unintentional reactions to psychotherapeutic interventions are higher in children and adolescents than in adults as a consequence of the unstable somatic and mental system. Secondly, some mental disorders in children and adolescents may be triggered by an altered familiar environment with communication problems, may be with violence or sexual abuse. In these cases the treatment of the family system and not exclusively the individual therapy is the primary aim. Unintended reactions, like separation of the parents, should be mentioned as a kind of side effect.

6. Future Directions

In developing countries the scarcity of trained personnel has prevented a higher specialization of child mental health services. For professionals in developing countries the term 'child mental health' therefore covers a broad range of problems, including neurological and developmental disorders, mental retardation, educational difficulties, and psychiatric disorders. Worldwide prevalence rates, an estimation of the persons with a disorder in relation to the whole population, of about 15 percent for children with mental problems, emphasize that developing countries need support in the training and further specialization of their professionals who are responsible for child mental healthcare. Cooperative research projects, under the patronage of the WHO and of the local psychiatric associations, may be one strategy for analyzing the quantity and the quality of child mental health problems in developing countries. It is necessary to recognize characteristic patterns of mental health problems, to describe risk factors (like malnutrition, war and displacement, political oppression, poverty, child labor, urbanization, and social changes) and to develop treatment concepts in consideration of the specific sociocultural background of the community (Rahman et al. 2000).

Although the establishment of specialized mental health services in developing countries is a primary goal, improvement of the child and adolescent psychiatry in developed countries remains a permanent task. Growing insight in molecular biology increases knowledge about brain function and improves the understanding of the mind–body relation (Deutsch 1990). Genetic factors will be described, which have responsibility for the manifestation of mental diseases. Biotechnology will offer new therapeutic strategies, which have to be examined in clinical trials by child and adolescent psychiatrists.

Going one step back from the future perspectives to present problems, child and adolescent psychiatrists need to perform more controlled clinical trials assessing the efficacy and security of psychotherapeutic and psychopharmacological interventions and both in combination. It is necessary to know more about long-term courses and outcome of mental diseases in children to young adulthood and to control the efficacy of pharmacological and psychotherapeutic treatment over a longer time range. A comprehensive neuroscience research especially will increase the knowledge about disorders with an early onset and a persistent pattern of symptoms and about specific developmental-related disorders.

Some mental disorders are quite rare in children and adolescents, like manic affective disorder, so multicenter studies in many hospitals have to be designed to investigate the efficacy of therapies in a sufficient number of child and adolescent patients. Other early onset problems in children, like the different kinds of learning disabilities, need to be investigated more exactly for the development of treatment concepts with higher efficacy. Especially in developing countries with a weak school network, knowledge about learning disabilities, about efficient treatment approaches

and perhaps about their prevention, might be very helpful (Schmidt and Remschmidt 1989).

At the least the vision of child psychiatry is the prevention of diseases (Greenfield and Shore 1995). Universal prevention, comparable to vaccination strategies, is hardly reachable in psychiatry. Even selective prevention by early assessment, provisional diagnoses and early therapeutic and psychosocial interventions in identified risk groups is difficult and comprises the problem of false positive assignments with the risk of stigmatizing people. Before acute clinical symptoms occur, there is mainly the registration of unspecific problems, giving some evidence of the later manifestation of a specific mental disorder. Defined criteria of premorbid symptomatology associated with prevention concepts have not yet been established. Probably the progress in biotechnology by detecting disease-specific genetic patterns, will improve the chance of a selective prevention. A more realistic concept is that of an indicated prevention in the earliest stage of a manifested disorder with minor clinical symptoms (McGuire and Earls 1991).

See also: Adolescence, Psychiatry of; Adolescence, Sociology of; Adolescent Development, Theories of; Adolescent Health and Health Behaviors; Anxiety Disorder in Children; Behavior Therapy with Children; Childhood and Adolescence: Developmental Assets; Childhood Depression; Childhood Health; Infant and Child Development, Theories of; Mental Health Programs: Children and Adolescents; Substance Abuse in Adolescents, Prevention of

Bibliography

American Psychiatric Association 1994 *Diagnostic and Statistical Manual of Mental Disorders (DSM-IV)*, 4th edn. American Psychiatric Association, Washington, DC

Barkley R A 1998 *Attention Deficit Hyperactivity Disorder: A Handbook for Diagnosis and Treatment*, 2nd edn. Guilford Press, New York

Biederman J, Newcorn J, Sprich S 1991 Comorbidity of attention deficit hyperactivity disorder with conduct, depressive, anxiety, and other disorders. *American Journal of Psychiatry* **148**: 564–77

Brownell K D, Fairburn C G 1995 *Eating Disorders and Obesity. A Comprehensive Handbook*. Guilford Press, New York

Caron C, Rutter M 1991 Comorbidity in child psychopathology: Concepts, issues and research strategies. *Journal of Child Psychology and Psychiatry* **32**: 1063–80

Cicchetti D, Cohen D J (eds.) 1995 *Developmental Psychopathology*. Wiley, New York, Vol. 2

Costello E J, Angold A, March J, Fairbank J 1998 Life events and post traumatic stress: The development of a new measure for children and adolescents. *Psychological Medicine* **28**: 1275–88

Deutsch S I, Weizman A, Weizman R (eds.) 1990 *Application of Basic Neuroscience to Child Psychiatry*. Plenum Medical, New York

Esser G, Schmidt M H, Woerner W 1990 Epidemiology and course of psychiatric disorders in school-age children—results of a longitudinal study. *Journal of Child Psychology and Psychiatry* **31**: 243–63

Greenfield S F, Shore M F 1995 Prevention of psychiatric disorders. *Harvard Review of Psychiatry* **3**: 115–29

Houts A C, Berman J S, Abramson H 1994 Effectiveness of psychosocial and pharmacological treatments for nocturnal enuresis. *Journal of Consulting and Clinical Psychology* **62**: 737–45

Jensen P S, Rubio-Stipec M, Canino G, Bird H R, Dulcan M K, Schwab-Stone M E, Lahey B B 1999 Parent and child contributions to diagnosis of mental disorders: Are both informations always necessary? *Journal of the American Academy of Child and Adolescent Psychiatry* **38**: 1569–79

Kaplan H I, Sadock B J 1998 *Kaplan and Sadock's Synopsis of Psychiatry: Behavioral Sciences/Clinical Psychiatry.* Williams & Wilkins, Baltimore, MD

Kazdin A E 1997 Practitioner review: Psychosocial treatments for conduct disorder in children. *Journal of Child Psychology and Psychiatry* **38**: 161 78

Laucht M, Esser G, Schmidt M H 1997 Developmental outcome of infants born with biological and psychosocial risks. *Journal of Child Psychology and Psychiatry* **38**: 843–53

Lewis M 1996 *Child and Adolescent Psychiatry.* Williams & Wilkins, Baltimore, MD

McDougle C J, Holmes J P, Bronson M R, Anderson G M, Volkmar F R, Price L H, Cohen D J 1997 Risperidone treatment of children and adolescents with pervasive developmental disorders: A prospective, open label study. *Journal of the American Academy of Child and Adolescent Psychiatry* **36**: 685–93

McGuire J, Earls F 1991 Prevention of psychiatric disorders in early childhood. *Journal of Child Psychology and Psychiatry* **32**: 129–54

Munir K M, Beardslee W R 1999 Developmental psychiatry: Is there any other kind? *Harvard Review of Psychiatry* **6**: 250–62

Nathan P E, Langenbucher J W 1999 Psychopathology: Description and classification. *Annual Review of Psychology* **50**: 79–107

Nissen G, Fritze J, Trott G E 1998 *Psychopharmaka im Kindes- und Jugendalter.* Gustav Fischer Verlag, Ulm, Germany

Noshpitz J D 1981 Psychotherapy with children: Basic principles. *Current Psychiatric Therapies* **20**: 47–59

Ollendick T H, Hersen M 1993 *Handbook of Child and Adolescent Assessment.* Allyn & Bacon, Boston

Piccinelli M, Pini S, Bellantuono C, Wilkinson G 1995 Efficacy of drug treatment in obsessive-compulsive disorder. A meta-analytic review. *British Journal of Psychiatry* **166**: 424–43

Rahman A, Mubbashar M, Harrington R, Gater R 2000 Annotation: Developing child mental health services in developing countries. *Journal of Child Psychology and Psychiatry* **41**: 539–46

Remschmidt H, Schmidt M H 1985 *Kinder- und Jugendpsychiatrie in Klinik und Praxis.* Thieme, Stuttgart, Germany

Remschmidt H, Schmidt M H 1994 *Multiaxiales Klassifikationsschema für psychische Störungen des Kindes- und Jugendalters nach ICD-10 der WHO.* Huber, Bern, Switzerland

Remschmidt H, van Engeland H (eds.) 1999 *Child and Adolescent Psychiatry in Europe.* Steinkopff, Darmstadt, Germany

Reynolds W M, Johnston H F 1994 *Handbook of Depression in Children and Adolescents.* Plenum Press, New York

Rothenberger A (ed.) 1990 *Brain and Behavior in Child Psychiatry.* Springer, Berlin

Rutter M 1989 Pathways from childhood to adult life. *Journal of Child Psychology and Psychiatry* **30**: 23–51

Rutter M 1999 Psychosocial adversity and child psychopathology. *British Journal of Psychiatry* **174**: 480–93

Rutter M, Silberg J, O'Connor T, Simonoff E 1999 Genetics and child psychiatry: II Empirical research findings. *Journal of Child Psychology and Psychiatry* **40**: 19–55

Rutter M, Smith D 1995 *Psychosocial Disorders in Young People: Time Trends and Their Causes.* Wiley, Chichester, UK

Rutter M, Taylor E, Hersov L 1994 *Child and Adolescent Psychiatry.* Blackwell, Oxford, UK

Schmidt M H, Remschmidt H (eds.) 1989 *Needs and Prospects of Child and Adolescent Psychiatry.* Hogrefe & Huber, Toronto, ON

Schwab J J, Schwab-Stone M E 1999 History of child psychiatry in the USA. From social reform and psychoanalysis to psychiatry of the family. *Zeitschrift für Kinder und Jugendpsychiatrie und Psychotherapie* **27**: 277–81

Shapiro A K, Shapiro E S, Young J G, Feinberg T E 1988 *Gilles de la Tourette Syndrome.* Raven, New York

Simeon J G, Ferguson H B (eds.) 1990 *Treatment Strategies in Child and Adolescent Psychiatry.* Plenum Press, New York

Simon B 1996 The history of psychiatry: An opportunity for self-reflection and interdisciplinary dialogue. Essay review. *Psychiatry* **59**: 336–56

Steinhausen H C 1995 *Eating Disorders in Adolescence.* Walter de Gruyter, Berlin

Vitiello B, Jensen S 1997 Medication development and testing in children and adolescents—current problems, future directions. *Archives of General Psychiatry* **54**: 871–6

Wiener J M 1997 *Textbook of Child & Adolescent Psychiatry.* American Psychiatric Press, Washington, DC

World Health Organization (WHO) 1992 *The ICD-10 Classification of Mental and Behavioral Disorders-Clinical Descriptions and Diagnostic Guidelines.* WHO, Geneva

M. H. Schmidt and A. Maras

Child Care and Child Development

Childcare is regular care provided by someone other than a child's parents. Throughout human history, grandparents, siblings, and relatives have cared for young children, but since about the 1950s, nonparental childcare has become an increasingly visible and prevalent part of the lives of young children in most industrialized societies, largely because of increasing rates of maternal employment and of single-mother families. In the US, by 1997, the majority of infants and preschool children spent some time in childcare; many of them were in full-time care (35 + hours per week) (Capizzano and Adams 2000).

This rapid and dramatic change in the ecology of children's experience has raised a host of questions about the benefits and risks associated with nonparental childcare. Strong value commitments and assumptions have often influenced the questions asked. In the first wave of research in the 1970s, for example, researchers asked whether 'day care' was harmful to children; they rarely considered potential benefits. At the same time, others were investigating the benefits of 'early childhood intervention' without considering possible harmful effects. Both groups were examining systems of nonparental care for young children, but the ways they framed questions and the labels they used led to different conclusions.

1. Is Extensive Childcare Harmful?

Why might we expect nonparental childcare to be harmful for children? According to the 'maternal deprivation' view, having one primary caregiver (usually the mother) with whom to develop an early attachment relationship is critical to the socioemotional development of young children. This view implies that even very high quality nonmaternal care could impair the development of a secure attachment to the mother if it seriously reduced the amount of time that a child spends with its mother. The most commonly used measure of attachment is the Strange Situation, a laboratory procedure in which children are observed during and after brief separations from their mothers. Secure attachment is indicated when the child goes to the mother and is comforted by her. Insecure attachment may be manifested by avoiding or ignoring the mother or by clinging to her without being comforted.

A large number of early studies concluded that childcare in the preschool years did not have harmful effects on attachment security or later socioemotional development, but the evidence is more mixed with respect to extensive nonmaternal care in the first year of life. Although the majority of children who receive full-time childcare in infancy have secure attachments to their mothers, some studies find elevated rates of insecure attachment when comparing these children to those in exclusive maternal care or part-time childcare (Clarke-Stewart 1989). A major study of 1,153 infants across the US indicated that children who spent extensive time in childcare during the first 3 years of life had mothers who were slightly less sensitive in interactions with them, and that extensive care was associated with elevated rates of insecure attachment only for children whose mothers were <u>in</u>sensitive (NICHD Early Child Care Research Network 1997, 1999a, 1999b). As one reviewer concluded, 'Adverse effects on infant-mother attachment appear to occur only when infant day-care co-occurs with other risky conditions, ...' (Lamb 1997).

It does not appear that time in childcare, in and of itself, has long-term effects on most other aspects of socioemotional development, but children with extensive care from infancy on tend to be more aggressive and assertive and to be less compliant to adults in some settings than are those with less child care

experience. Many of these differences are not apparent when children have experienced high quality care (Lamb 1997).

2. Quality of Care

A second theory predicts that the effects of childcare depend on the physical and social environment provided. Harmful effects on both social and intellectual development might be expected if children receive less attention, affection, interaction, and stimulation from nonparental adults than they would from their parents. This view implies that the effects of care depend on its quality and on the quality of the home environment. Quality can be defined by the processes that occur in the setting: (a) sensitive, responsive, positive interactions of adults with children; (b) intellectually stimulating adult actions and activities, including appropriate language, reading, and play; and (c) toys, materials, and curricula that provide age-appropriate opportunities for learning. Quality can also be defined by structural characteristics, some of which can be mandated by regulatory agencies: (a) small ratios of children to adults; (b) small group sizes; (c) caregiver education and training in child development; (d) sufficient space per child; (e) a safe and clean physical environment; and (f) continuity and wages of the staff. Structural and process measures are correlated moderately with one another.

Whether process or structural indicators of quality are used, children in high-quality care have higher levels of language and intellectual skills, and perform better on academic tasks than do children in low-quality care. Although this finding is consistent across studies, there is some disagreement about whether quality produces a large enough difference to be socially significant (Lamb 1997, Scarr 1998). In one analysis, the quality of the child care environment and characteristics of the home environment during the first 3 years of life were compared as predictors of school readiness and language skill at age 3. The size of the childcare quality effect was about half that of the family environment, suggesting that childcare makes a substantial contribution to language and academic development (NICHD 1999a, 1999b). Critics have also argued that childcare effects do not last into later childhood, but evidence for long-term effects is beginning to accumulate. In a large study following children from age 4 through grade 3, children who attended higher quality childcare centers performed better on measures of cognitive skills (e.g., math and language abilities) while they were in childcare and, in many cases, through the end of second grade (Peisner-Feinberg et al. 1999).

High quality childcare also predicts social skills with peers and social competence with adults, but the relations between quality and social behavior are weaker than those between quality and cognitive/ academic performance. Some studies suggest that children's relationships with their teachers in child care forecast social skills and relations with teachers in elementary school (Howes et al. 1998, Peisner-Feinberg et al. 1999).

One problem in evaluating childcare effects is that families with more resources, better education, and more sensitive parenting styles (to name only a few attributes) place their children in higher quality childcare settings than do less advantaged families. Most recent studies have measured both family and childcare characteristics so that the independent contributions of each could be evaluated, but there is still the possibility that other unmeasured family attributes could affect childcare choices and children's cognitive and intellectual development.

Experimental studies, in which children are assigned randomly to enriched early care experiences or to control groups, demonstrate clearly that high quality early care has lasting effects on cognitive and academic skills, at least for children from economically disadvantaged families. Experiments avoid possible confounds between family and childcare attributes. The Abercedarian project enrolled children from low-income families in educational childcare from infancy until they reached school age. Children in the treatment group performed better than children in a control group (who received social and nutritional services) on tests of intelligence and school achievement throughout childhood and adolescence (Ramey et al. 2000). Less intensive early intervention programs for children ages 3–5 also produced lasting effects on children's school progress; participating children were less likely to be retained in a grade or to need special education than were children in control groups (Lazar and Darlington 1982).

The importance of childcare does not end when children enter school. Participation in formal after-school care programs that provide cognitive stimulation and positive adult interactions is associated with high academic achievement and low levels of behavior problems, particularly among low-income children (Posner and Vandell 1999). Children without adult supervision in the out-of-school hours are at risk for behavior problems and poor adjustment, particularly if they live in low-income families or unsafe neighborhoods (Pettit et al. 1999).

3. Type of Care

A great deal of childcare occurs in the child's home or someone else's home, especially for infants and toddlers. Caregivers can be grandparents, other relatives, or nonrelatives. In the US, a small percentage of infants receive center-based care, but the percentage increases as children reach ages 3–5. Many western European countries have extensive center-based care for children age 3 and over, but care settings for younger children vary considerably (Kamerman and Kahn 1991). The available data suggest both advantages and disadvantages of center-based care relative to home-based care for very young children. Infants and young children in center care show better language and cognitive development by ages 2 and 3 years than those in home-based settings of comparable quality, but they also have more communicable illnesses (e.g. colds and other respiratory illnesses) (NICHD 2000, in press).

Children attending a center or a childcare home with several other children have more experience with peers than do children in other types of home-based care. Children with extensive group experience develop better skills interacting with peers, but their caregivers also rate them higher on negative behavior (e.g. aggression, disobedience) than children in other forms of care (Lamb 1997). For young children, social skills and sociability with peers are often accompanied by a certain amount of aggression; perhaps early contact with peers leads to increases in a range of social behaviors.

4. Do Effects Differ for Children from Different Family Backgrounds?

In the US, where most childcare is funded privately, children from affluent families receive higher quality care than children from families with low and moderate incomes do. In some cases, children from very poor families receive slightly higher quality care than children from families with modest incomes, largely because of publicly funded programs for children in poverty (Phillips et al. 1994). In countries with publicly funded childcare for children from all income levels, average quality appears to be considerably better than it is in the US, and there are not wide discrepancies in quality associated with family income (Lamb 1997).

Some researchers have proposed a compensatory hypothesis: that children from disadvantaged homes might profit from childcare of reasonable or high quality because it provides more opportunities for learning and development than they receive at home. The complementary lost resources hypothesis suggests that children from highly advantaged homes may be harmed by childcare because it provides fewer opportunities than their home environments do. The evidence for these hypotheses is mixed. Almost all of the experiments exposing children to high quality care have included only economically disadvantaged children, and these children clearly profit from such care. Some investigations have found support for the lost resources notion, but most studies support the idea that high quality care provides benefits for children from a wide range of backgrounds (Lamb 1997).

5. Public Policy Issues

5.1 Public vs. Private Funding

Childcare is expensive. In some industrialized nations, public funds pay the great majority of the costs. Sweden, France, and some other countries provide large-scale publicly funded, full-day, preschool programs. In the US, at the other end of the spectrum, limited amounts of public funds are available to low-income families, and tax credits cover a small portion of childcare costs for people earning enough to owe taxes. Overall, parents pay the vast majority of the costs of care. At the same time, childcare workers and staff receive very low wages. In 1997, teachers in childcare centers, many of whom had college degrees, earned from approximately $13,000 to $19,000 per year; salaries of teaching assistants ranged from $10,500 to $12,250 per year (Whitebook et al. 1998). As a result, there is high turnover among childcare workers.

5.2 Family Leave vs. Infant Care

Care for infants is more expensive than care for preschoolers because they require more concentrated adult attention and they fare best in small groups. Many industrialized nations provide parents with paid family leave as an alternative to supplying center-based infant care (Kamerman and Kahn 1991). In the US, some workers receive paid family leave, but federal law requires only that parents receive up to 12 weeks of unpaid leave with guaranteed job security and medical benefits. Even this policy applies only to full-time, full-year workers in large organizations. As a result, many infants enter nonmaternal care between ages 2 and 3 months. There is some evidence mothers who return to work very early and whose babies have extensive nonmaternal care are less sensitive during interactions with their infants than are mothers who have more time at home (Clark et al. 1997). It may be more difficult to learn your infant's signals and respond appropriately when you spend a great deal of time at work starting very early in the child's life.

6. Conclusion

Most children in modern industrialized societies will spend a significant portion of their early lives in childcare, and many will require such care during the early school years as well. Initial fears that child care *per se* would be harmful have not been supported, but there is some evidence that extensive care, beginning in early infancy, can make it more difficult for mothers to relate sensitively to their infants. Whether childcare has positive or negative effects on children's development depends primarily on its quality. Quality is defined by sensitive, responsive, and stimulating care-givers and age-appropriate activities and curriculum. High quality care promotes cognitive, academic, and social development, and its effects last beyond the preschool years. High quality care for children from all economic levels is provided more successfully in countries that make large public investments in early care than in countries that require parents and child care staff to pay the costs of care.

7. Future Directions

Nonmaternal care is here to stay. Policy debates about what is 'good enough' care abound, and research is needed to identify thresholds of quality that make large differences, with particular attention to individual child and family characteristics. We understand how early childcare can contribute to cognitive and academic performance better than we understand how it can influence positive social behavior with both peers and adults. New designs, including experiments with random assignment, could help to answer these important questions.

See also: Divorce and Children's Social Development; Nontraditional Families and Child Development; Parenting: Attitudes and Beliefs; Parents and Teachers as Partners in Education

Bibliography

Capizzano J, Adams G 2000 *The Hours that Children under Five Spend in Child Care: Variations across States. A Report of Assessing the New Federalism.* The Urban Institute, Washington, DC

Clark R, Hyde J S, Essex M J, Klein M H 1997 Length of maternity leave and quality of mother-infant interactions. *Child Development* **68**: 364–83

Clarke-Stewart K A 1989 Infant day care: Maligned or malignant? *America Psychologist* **44**: 266–73

Howes C, Hamilton C E, Philipsen L C 1998 Stability and continuity of child-caregiver and child-peer relationships. *Child Development* **69**: 418–26

Kamerman S B, Kahn A J 1991 *Child Care, Parental Leave, and the Under-3s: Policy Innovation in Europe.* Auburn House, New York

Lamb M E 1997 Nonparental child care: Context, quality, correlates, and consequences. In: Damon W, Sigel I, Renninger K A (eds.) *Handbook of Child Psychology: Vol. 4. Child Psychology in Practice*, 5th edn. Wiley, New York, pp. 73–134

Lazar I, Darlington R 1982 Lasting effects of early education: A report from the Consortium for Longitudinal Studies. *Monographs of the Society for Research in Child Development* **47**(2-sup-3): 1–151

NICHD Early Child Care Research Network 1997 The effects of infant child care on infant-mother attachment security: Results of the NICHD study of early child care. *Child Development* **68**: 860–79

NICHD Early Child Care Research Network 1999a Child care and mother-child interaction in the first 3 years of life. *Developmental Psychology* **35**: 1399–1413

NICHD Early Child Care Network 1999b Child outcomes when child-care classrooms meet recommended standards for quality. *American Journal of Public Health* **89**: 1072–7

NICHD Early Child Care Research Network 2000 The relation of child care to cognitive and language development. *Child Development* **71**: 960–80

NICHD Early Child Care Research Network in press. Child care and common communicable illnesses: results from the NICHD Study of Early Child Care. *Archives of Pediatrics and Adolescent Medicine*

Peisner-Feinberg E S, Burchinal M R, Clifford R M, Culkin M L, Howes C, Kagan S L, Yazejian N, Byler P, Rustici J, Zelazo J 1999 *The Children of the Cost, Quality, and Outcomes Study Go to School*. University of North Carolina, Chapel Hill, NC

Pettit G S, Bates J E, Dodge K A, Meece D W 1999 The impact of after-school peer contact on early adolescent externalizing problems is moderated by parental monitoring, perceived neighborhood safety, and prior adjustment. *Child Development* **70**: 768–78

Phillips D A, Voran M, Kisker E, Howes C, Whitebook M 1994 Child care for children in poverty: Opportunity or inequity? *Child Development* **65**: 472–92

Posner J K, Vandell D L 1999 After-school activities and the development of low-income urban children: A longitudinal study. *Developmental Psychology* **35**: 868–79

Ramey C T, Campbell F A, Burchinal M R, Skinner M L, Gardner D M, Ramey S L 2000 Persistent effects of early childhood education on high-risk children and their mothers. *Applied Developmental Science* **4**: 2–14

Scarr S 1998 American child care today. *American Psychologist* **53**: 95–108

Whitebrook M, Howes C, Phillips D 1998 *Worthy Work, Unlivable Wages. The National Child Care Staffing Study, 1988–1997*. Center for Child Care Workforce, Washington, DC

A. C. Huston

Childbearing, Externalities of

In any family, lower fertility would raise income per family member at least in the short run, since the number of family members to share income would be smaller and women of reproductive age might do more market work. Would this higher per capita income justify a government policy to reduce the rate of population growth by lowering fertility? Not necessarily. By choosing to have a child, people express a preference for the child over the additional consumption that would otherwise be possible for family members. However, there may be costs and benefits to the additional child that are not directly borne by the decision-making parents, but are rather passed on to other families and to society as a whole. Such consequences, if not mediated by the market, are known as pure or technical externalities to childbearing. When they are present, then individually optimal childbearing decisions need not add up to socially optimal fertility. In this case, there is a role for government intervention to influence fertility decisions. In fact, externalities are pervasive in all societies. This article will discuss their sources, their size, and their policy implications.

1. Why Childbearing Externalities Matter

When consequences of childbearing are mediated by the market, they are called pecuniary externalities, as when an additional child reduces the wages of future workers by increasing their number. It has been shown that in this case, socially optimal fertility will not diverge from the individually optimal level (conditional on additional assumptions and a restrictive concept of social optimality; see Nerlove et al. 1987). Technical externalities do not pass through the market, as would be the case if an additional child meant higher taxes for others or a bigger hole in the ozone layer.

Economic theory asserts that in the absence of technical externalities, collective welfare will be maximized (in the sense of Pareto optimality) by individuals pursuing their own self-interest in the context of a competitive market (subject to some further conditions). In the presence of technical externalities, this is no longer so. Disregarding technical externalities, the sum of individually optimal fertility decisions should lead to the same outcome as a collective societal decision about fertility levels. With technical externalities, the outcomes would differ. Thus Garret Hardin, in a famous article, *The Tragedy of the Commons*, which first gave this issue prominence, called for 'mutual coercion, mutually agreed upon' (Hardin 1968, p. 1247). Subsequent articles by Demeny (1972), Blandy (1974), Ng (1986), Nerlove et al. (1987), and Willis (1987) developed the theory from a more rigorous economic standpoint.

Externalities to childbearing are salient in several modern policy contexts, as follows. First, in industrialized nations, fertility is on average about 1.5 children per woman, well below replacement level, leading to rapidly aging populations. Why is it so low? When old age support is provided to elders by their own adult children, this enters a couple's cost/benefit calculus and provides an incentive for higher fertility. In industrialized nations, although old age support is provided by the younger generations, this is done generally through public sector tax and transfer pension programs, rather than by the elders' own children. Thus the creation of public pension programs has created a large positive externality to childbearing: higher fertility is socially beneficial through the pension programs, but this social benefit does not impinge on individual decisions since it is the general level of fertility that matters.

Second, in developing nations, the public sector provides education and healthcare for children, so additional children impose tax costs on others, a negative externality. Governments typically spend little on the elderly in these countries, and also there are few elderly, so the public costs of children dominate. This gap between the private and social costs of children is a negative externality that is often taken to justify government intervention.

Third, in all countries additional children will place additional demands on the environment, now and in the future, and most environmental amenities (clean air, fresh water, the ozone layer, climate and CO_2 emissions, biodiversity, forest cover) are outside the market. These negative environmental externalities to childbearing are therefore potentially very important, particularly in the industrialized nations where consumption per capita is greater.

Focusing on just a few issues like these can be misleading. A proper understanding of childbearing externalities requires a more comprehensive approach.

2. Sources of Externalities

Sources of technical externalities may be grouped into (a) common resources or collective wealth, (b) public sector transfers from one age group to another, and (c) provision of public goods or social infrastructure. In addition, there is a wide range of pecuniary externalities, of which the most important is a potential adverse effect on future wages or per capita incomes. Each of these three will be briefly discussed, before we turn to a quantitative assessment.

The existence and magnitude of externalities depend on institutional context, in particular on the existence of property rights in resources and on the size of the public sector. With full property rights and no public sector, most childbearing externalities would vanish.

2.1 Common Resources or Collective Wealth

The most basic externality to childbearing occurs when an asset is commonly owned and all members of the population have free access to it. Suppose a group shares a common pasture for its cows. The larger the group, the fewer cows each will be able to graze without degrading the pasture and the cows. Each birth increases the size of the group, but if there are many families, then this diluted effect will not count in the parents' self-centered cost benefit analysis. Thus there is a negative externality. Fertility will be higher, the group larger, and all worse off than with a collective fertility decision (Hardin 1968). A similar argument could be made about environmental amenities (water, air, climate, ozone layer, etc.). Nationally-owned land, parks, and mineral or fossil fuel deposits can likewise be important sources of negative externalities.

The argument also works in the opposite direction, when collective costs are shared, as with national debt. The US national debt is roughly $20,000 per capita. Additional members of the population due to births or immigration take on a share of this obligation as taxpayers, thereby reducing what must be paid by the balance of the population. This is a positive externality to childbearing.

2.2 Public Sector Inter-age Transfers

When parents rear their children and thereby transfer income to them, and when adults transfer income to their elderly parents, no externalities to childbearing arise: the need for transfers enters into the fertility decision. When transfers take place through the public sector, however, they do lead to externalities. The most important public transfers in this context are for health, education, and pensions.

2.3 Public Goods and Social Infrastructure

The costs of providing a network of roads rises with the size of the population served within a given area, but less than proportionately to the population increase; the same applies for communications networks. These are called quasi-public goods. In addition, there are pure public goods, which by definition cost no more to provide to many people than to few. The leading example is a nation's military force, which can protect a larger population just as well as a smaller one; other examples are broadcasting, weather forecasting, and scientific research. Provision of a given level of public goods is cheaper per capita for a larger population, since the tax bill per head will be lower. Public and quasi-public goods give rise to positive externalities of childbearing.

3. Evaluation

The first attempt to evaluate childbearing externalities appears to be have been made by Lee (1991). The following discussion will draw on the more comprehensive work by Lee and Miller (1990), which included estimates for six developing nations and the USA for the early to mid-1980s. Begin with collective wealth or debt. Great variations in natural wealth, particularly for oil in Saudi Arabia and land in Brazil, lead to negative externalities that dominate other sources for these countries. For the USA, national debt is an important source of positive externalities, as it would be for many OECD nations. An effort was made to evaluate other items, but none appears to be very important. Environmental externalities were not addressed in Lee and Miller, for lack of evidence. Since then, a group of ecologists and economists have estimated the value of all the services provided by natural resources worldwide to fall within the range 16 trillion to 54 trillion dollars per year (Roush 1997). The midpoint estimate implies a negative externality of $-\$175,000$ per birth worldwide, very approximately. For most nations, this number would dominate all externalities. Despite the great uncertainty surrounding the calculation, it warns us that environmental externalities can be very large and should not be ignored.

Turn now to public sector transfers, from taxpayers to beneficiaries of various programs. When the direction of transfers is downward from older to younger ages, such as for public education, then incremental births are costly and there is a negative externality. When the direction of transfers is upward from younger to older ages, such as for public pensions and healthcare for the elderly, then incremental births reduce the old age dependency ratio, and there is a positive externality. When these three major transfer programs and other smaller ones are summed, the net direction of transfers can be found. In the USA, the net direction is strongly upward, from younger to older. These results would be even stronger for other OECD countries, since their populations are typically older and their pensions more generous than in the USA. In the developing nations evaluated other than Brazil, the net direction of transfers is downward. Like a number of other Latin American countries, but unlike most countries in Asia and Africa, Brazil has a strong pension program. It is also likely that the net direction of public transfers throughout the developing nations is strongly downward, except for those countries in Latin America that have generous unfunded public pension programs.

Now consider public goods. Expenditures on the military are the main item in this category for the USA and Saudi Arabia, but for other countries social infrastructure dominates. Public goods and social infrastructure advantages generate positive externalities to childbearing for all countries, falling in the range of two to ten times the level of gross national product (GNP) per capita.

These three broad kinds of externalities can be summed to find the net externality.

If we ignore environmental externalities, there is a substantial positive net externality to childbearing in the USA, three times as great as per capita GNP. This would probably be approximately true for other OECD countries as well. None of the developing nations evaluated has a positive externality, while Brazil and Saudi Arabia have very large negative externalities. It is striking that Kenya and Bangladesh, two countries that are generally regarded as having serious population problems, both have externalities near zero relative to GNP per capita. If global environmental externalities were taken into account at

the level discussed earlier, then all net externalities would be negative.

The estimates just discussed were based on a simple model and the analysis was done by comparative steady states. In more recent work, Lee and Miller (1997) examined fiscal impact externalities in a more detailed and nuanced manner. They projected tax payments over a very long horizon according to whether or not there was an additional birth in the base year, including the impacts of all descendants of the incremental birth as well. They found a positive net externality of US$170,000, which is six times per capita GNP for the reference year (which compares to 3.6 in Lee and Miller 1997, adjusted for non-fiscal effects). Given the increase in the cost of healthcare benefits and differences in some key assumptions, the numbers are in reasonable agreement.

4. Broader Views

The evaluations just reported are based on the narrow concept of technical externalities, following the main development of the theoretical literature. Some analysts argue for a broader view of externalities, even though the welfare implications are then no longer clear. Some stress pecuniary externalities: an additional birth will mean less land and less capital for future workers, and therefore lower productivity and wages. Nerlove et al. (1987) analyze this case, and show that under certain assumptions there is no technical externality and collective fertility decisions would not improve welfare. Nerlove et al. view parents as deriving utility from their own consumption, the number of children they have, and the future utility or consumption for their children. But it is possible that the goals of society differ from those of the individual parents. In particular, society may give the welfare of future generations greater weight than do the individual parents, or value wilderness or other aspects of the environment more highly. Society may care more about the distribution of income, or give a different weight to the welfare of women or pre-existing children than does the household decision-maker. In these cases, there is no reason to expect that the sum of individual decisions will be socially desirable, and there will be many other reasons besides technical externalities to expect a gap between the individually and socially optimal level of fertility. There may also be a different kind of externality, in which one person's fertility may influence decisions by others. For example, if one couple uses contraceptives to control fertility, that may convey information to other couples, enabling them to make a better-informed decision. Or it may alter the social norms that influence the fertility decisions of others by weakening the influence of traditional institutions opposing contraceptive use. Or some couples may imitate others. Dasgupta (1993) considers some of these possibilities.

5. Implications for Policy

The difficulty in assessing and quantifying environmental externalities, which are potentially very large for couples in industrialized nations, renders all the estimates even more uncertain. The numbers presented above are too shaky to guide policy decisions. Nevertheless it is useful to consider what they would entail if taken at face value, setting aside the question of environmental externalities.

Once the direction and magnitude of childbearing externalities have been identified, there is a clear policy implication: governments can, in principle, improve the welfare of their populations by inducing couples to have more children where externalities are positive, and fewer children where they are negative. One means to achieve this would be by internalizing the externality, such that through taxes or subsidies the couple is brought to face the full social cost or benefit of the incremental child when making its fertility decision. For example, in industrialized countries, the size of the retirement pension could be linked to each couple's fertility level; or a couple could receive a bonus of US$170,000 (say) on the birth of each child. In developing nations, each couple might be compelled to make a lump sum payment at the time of the birth of each child. In reality such policies appear to be neither practical nor desirable. They would adversely affect the well-being of children and probably fall disproportionately on the poorer segment of society in developing nations.

Nor would such policies necessarily be desirable from a theoretical perspective, because the measured externality depends sensitively on the institutional context and on public sector resource allocation. If a country has a positive externality to childbearing due to a large military establishment, the externality could be reduced by reducing the share of military expenditures in the national budget. If a country has a positive externality to childbearing due to a generous unfunded public pension program, the externality could be eliminated by switching to a funded system. If there is a large negative childbearing externality in a developing nation due to public education, note should be taken that fertility is falling rapidly in most parts of the world where it is not already low, and that transfers may soon be flowing upward across the age distribution. The existence of negative childbearing externalities reflects the ability of individual couples to pass on some of the childrearing costs to society at large. While not unimportant, this is probably not a major reason why fertility is high. More likely high fertility results in part from obstacles faced by couples in obtaining contraceptives, and in part from the absence of institutions which provide superior substi-

tutes for many of the services that children provide – from insurance against sickness, unemployment, or death of spouse, to financial institutions and reliable pension programs. It would most likely be a mistake to attempt to fine-tune policy to these measured externalities rather than to make more efficient the institutional context within which childbearing decisions are made.

See also: Family Size Preferences; Family Theory and the Realities of Childbearing Behavior; Family Theory: Economics of Childbearing; Family Theory: Feminist–Economist Critique; Family Theory: Role of Changing Values; Fertility Transition: Cultural Explanations; Fertility Transition: Economic Explanations; Gender and Reproductive Health; Motherhood: Economic Aspects; Motherhood: Social and Cultural Aspects; Personality Disorders

Bibliography

Blandy R 1974 The welfare analysis of fertility reduction. *The Economic Journal* **84**(333): 109–29

Dasgupta P 1993 *An Inquiry into Well-Being and Destitution*. Clarendon Press, Oxford, UK

Demeny P 1972 The economics of population control. In: *National Academy of Sciences, Rapid Population Growth: Consequences and Policy Implications*. Johns Hopkins University Press, Baltimore, MD

Hardin G 1968 The tragedy of the commons. *Science* **162**: 1243–8

Lee R D 1991 Evaluating externalities to childbearing in developing countries: The case of India. In: *Consequences of Rapid Population Growth in Developing Countries*. Taylor and Francis, London, pp. 297–342

Lee R D, Miller T 1990 Population growth, externalities to childbearing, and fertility policy in the Third World. Proceedings of the World Bank Annual Conference on Development Economics, 1990. Supplement to *The World Bank Economic Review* and to *The World Bank Research Observer* pp. 275–304

Lee R D, Miller T 1997 The life time fiscal impacts of immigrants and their descendants. Project on the economic demography of interage income reallocation, demography, UC Berkeley. Draft of Chapter 7 for *The New Americans, a report of the National Academy of Sciences Panel on Economic and Demographic Consequences of Immigration*. National Academy Press pp. 297–362

Nerlove M, Razin A, Sadka E 1987 *Household and Economy: Welfare Economics of Endogenous Fertility*. Academic Press, London

Ng Y 1986 The welfare economics of population control. *Population and Development Review* **12**(2): 247–66

Roush W 1997 Putting a price tag on nature's bounty. *Science* **276**: 1029

Willis R 1987 Externalities and population. In: Johnson D G, Lee R D (eds.) *Population Growth and Economic Development: Issues and Evidence*. Wisconsin University Press, Milwaukee, WI

R. D. Lee

Childhood and Adolescence: Developmental Assets

Developmental assets represent a theoretical construct first articulated in 1990 (Benson 1990). Based on a synthesis of scientific studies in pertinent fields, developmental assets identify a series of social and psychological strengths which function to enhance health outcomes for children and adolescents. The purposes of ongoing research pertaining to developmental assets are to develop new lines of scientific inquiry on the sources and consequences of strength-building approaches in child and adolescent development and to attempt to provide a conceptual roadmap to guide the design and implementation of community-wide initiatives that are aimed at promoting healthy development among children and adolescents. The conceptual, research, and application dimensions of developmental assets are described here.

1. Developmental Assets in Social and Conceptual Context

The framework of developmental assets weaves together into an *a priori* conceptual model, a set of developmental experiences, resources, and opportunities, each of which contributes to important health outcomes, conceived as both the reduction of health-compromising behaviors and the increase of positive or thriving outcomes such as school success. Though the framework is supported by scientific study, it was purposefully designed to fuel and guide community-based approaches to strengthen the natural and inherent socialization capacity of communities. Therefore, assets include the kinds of relationships, social experiences, social environments, and patterns of interaction known to promote health and over which a community has considerable control.

Developmental assets, then, represent a framework, grounded in scientific study, with the applied aim of reweaving the developmental infrastructure of a community by activating multiple sources of asset building. These include informal, nonprogrammatic relationships between adults and youth; traditional socializing systems such as families, neighborhoods, schools, congregations, and youth organizations; and the governmental, economic, and policy infrastructures which inform those socializing systems. The intent is to encourage the mobilization of asset-building efforts within many settings of a child's life and to increase those efforts for *all* children and adolescents within a community. The developmental assets framework, the theoretical underpinnings of the framework, and its partner concept of asset-building

communities are discussed in depth in a series of recent publications (e.g., Benson 1997, Benson 1998, Benson et al. 1998).

1.1 Connection to Other Areas of Scientific Inquiry

The developmental asset framework is related to several other streams of scientific study, which also seek to identify positive developmental experiences and competencies known to enhance health and well-being among adolescents. Among these is the emerging exploration of protective factors in the fields of alcohol, tobacco, and pregnancy prevention. For example, Resnick and his colleagues (1997) demonstrated the importance of family and school connections in reducing multiple forms of health risk behaviors. Similarly, the study of resiliency has identified characteristics that enable some children to navigate through and around what often are debilitating environmental risks and experiences. This has contributed considerably to our understanding of the scope and nature of social and psychological strengths (Masten et al. 1990, Rutter 1985, Werner and Smith 1992). In addition, the more applied field of youth development champions the inclusion of this emerging body of knowledge about developmental strengths into policy, programs, and practice (Pittman and Cahill 1991). The developmental asset model builds on these areas of inquiry and includes a number of elements from them in the 40 core developmental assets.

The developmental asset framework also provides a complementary approach to the paradigm of deficit reduction. A deficit reduction model is focused on reducing threats, obstacles, and risks that interfere with healthy development. Among these are abuse; neighborhood violence; access to alcohol, other drugs, and firearms; poverty; and family dysfunction. While research has shown that these factors are related to a number of negative outcomes, efforts that focus mainly on controlling or reducing them represent incomplete approaches to health promotion. As Benson and colleagues (Benson 1997, Benson et al. 1998) have discussed, approaches which depend exclusively on deficit reduction may unintentionally expand the role of professionals, programs, and policy in child and adolescent health. This may be to the detriment of more informal and natural capacities that may be rooted in the community.

The asset model provides, then, an alternative and complementary set of 'benchmarks' or targets that can be added to the necessary and influential paradigm of risk reduction. Rather than focusing solely on problems or threats to be *reduced*, it accents relationships, experiences, resources, and opportunities to be *promoted*.

1.2 Community as a Context for Human Development

The developmental asset framework is also connected, both intellectually and strategically, to the fields of community change and community building. These areas have historically focused on the economic, service, and environmental infrastructures of a city, defining both the inherent capacity of local communities for promoting civic health (Kretzman and McKnight 1993, McKnight 1995) and identifying those core processes of engaged community which can inform the health of residents. Among these emerging constructs are social trust, personal efficacy, and social capital (Sampson et al. 1997). In addition, the conceptualization and definition of the developmental assets were informed by other community research efforts focusing on the concepts of social norms, civic engagement, indigenous leadership, and community capacity building (Benson 1997, Benson et al. 1998).

2. The Developmental Asset Framework

The original configuration of 30 developmental assets (e.g., Benson 1990) was expanded to 40 developmental assets in 1996, based on analysis of data gathered on 254,000 6th–12th-grade students, additional synthesis of child and adolescent research, and consultations with researchers and practitioners (Benson 1997). The framework's conceptual foundations are based on empirical studies of child and adolescent development, as well as applied studies in prevention, health promotion, and resiliency. The development of this conceptual foundation involved a research synthesis which focused on integrating developmental experiences that are widely known to inform three types of health outcomes among adolescents: (a) the prevention of high-risk behaviors (e.g., substance use, violence, sexual intercourse, school dropout); (b) the enhancement of thriving outcomes (e.g., school success, affirmation of diversity, prosocial behavior); and (c) resiliency or the capacity to overcome adversity. The assets were framed initially around adolescent development and they are assessed through a self-report survey (Leffert et al. 1998). The assets were extended downward conceptually to include young children (birth–age 10) which then encompasses a more lifespan context (Roehlkepartain and Leffert 2000).

The conceptualization of the asset framework identified naming developmental factors that were particularly robust in predicting health outcomes and for which there was evidence that they could be generalized across gender, race/ethnicity, and family income. In addition, the assets were conceived to reflect core developmental processes which include the relationships, social experiences, social environments, patterns of interaction, norms, and competencies over

which a community of people has considerable control. That is, the assets are more about the primary processes of socialization than the equally important arenas of economy, services, and physical infrastructure of a city (Benson et al. 1998).

Because the developmental asset framework was designed not only to inform theory and research but also to have practical significance for the mobilization of communities, the 40 assets are placed in categories that have conceptual integrity and can be described easily to the residents of a community. As seen in Table 1, they are grouped into 20 external assets (i.e., environmental, contextual, and relational features of socializing systems) and 20 internal assets (i.e., skills, competencies, and commitments). The external assets include four categories: (a) support, (b) empowerment, (c) boundaries and expectations, and (d) constructive use of time. The internal assets are also placed in four categories: (a) commitment to learning, (b) positive values, (c) social competencies, and (d) positive identity. The scientific foundations for the eight categories and each of the 40 assets are described in more detail in Scales and Leffert (1999).

3. Measurement, Descriptive Data, and Prediction

Since 1996, numerous studies of 6th–12th-grade young people in public and private schools in the United States have been conducted using the *Search Institute Profiles of Student Life: Attitudes and Behaviors*, a self-report survey. This 156-item self-report survey measures the 40 developmental assets, developmental deficits (e.g., whether youth watch too much television or are victims of violence), thriving indicators (e.g., school success, physical health behaviors), and high-risk behaviors (e.g., alcohol and other substance use, antisocial behavior, school problems) (Leffert et al. 1998). The most recent aggregate sample is made up of 99,462 6th–12th-grade youth from public and alternative schools in 213 cities and towns in the United States who took the survey during the 1996–7 academic year. This sample has served as a focal point for several studies of the relation of assets to risk behaviors and thriving outcomes (Benson et al. 1998, Leffert et al. 1998, Scales et al. 2000).

3.1 Examples of Descriptive Data and the Additive Nature of Developmental Assets

The self-report survey is primarily used as a means of communicating aggregate data on a community's youth. A report, developed for each city or school district that uses the survey, often becomes a widely shared document and is used to frame a community-wide discussion and serves as a focal point to mobilize around raising healthy youth (Benson et al. 1998). A

Table 1
Forty developmental assets

External	
Support	1. *Family support*—Family life provides high levels of love and support
	2. *Positive family communication*—Young person and her or his parent(s) communicate positively, and young person is willing to seek advice and counsel from parents
	3. *Other adult relationships*—Young person receives support from three or more nonparent adults
	4. *Caring neighborhood*—Young person experiences caring neighbors
	5. *Caring school climate*—School provides a caring, encouraging environment
	6. *Parent involvement in schooling*—Parent(s) are actively involved in helping young person succeed in school
Empowerment	7. *Community values youth*—Young person perceives that community adults value youth
	8. *Youth as resources*—Young people are given useful roles in the community
	9. *Service to others*—Young person serves in the community one hour or more per week
	10. *Safety*—Young person feels safe at home, at school, and in the neighborhood
Boundaries and expectations	11. *Family boundaries*—Family has clear rules and consequences, and monitors the young person's whereabouts
	12. *School boundaries*—School provides clear rules and consequences
	13. *Neighborhood boundaries*—Neighbors take responsibility for monitoring young people's behavior
	14. *Adult role models*—Parent(s) and other adults model positive, responsible behavior
	15. *Positive peer influence*—Young person's best friends model positive, responsible behavior
	16. *High expectations*—Both parents and teachers encourage the young person to do well
Constructive use of time	17. *Creative activities*—Young person spends three or more hours per week in lessons or practice in music, theater, or other arts
	18. *Youth programs*—Young person spends three hours or more per week in sports, clubs, or organizations at school and/or in community organizations
	19. *Religious community*—Young person spends one or more hours per week in activities in a religious institution
	20. *Time at home*—Young person is out with friends 'with nothing special to do' two or fewer nights per week
Internal	
Commitment to learning	21. *Achievement motivation*—Young person is motivated to do well in school
	22. *School engagement*—Young person is actively engaged in learning
	23. *Homework*—Young person reports one or more hours of homework every school day
	24. *Bonding to school*—Young person cares about his or her school
	25. *Reading for pleasure*—Young person reads for pleasure three or more hours per week
Positive values	26. *Caring*—Young person places high value on helping other people
	27. *Equality and social justice*—Young person places high value on promoting equality and reducing hunger and poverty
	28. *Integrity*—Young person acts on convictions and stands up for her or his beliefs
	29. *Honesty*—Young person tells the truth even when it is not easy
	30. *Responsibility*—Young person accepts and takes personal responsibility
	31. *Restraint*—Young person believes it is important not to be sexually active or to use alcohol or other drugs
Social competencies	32. *Planning and decision making*—Young person knows how to plan ahead and make choices
	33. *Interpersonal competence*—Young person has empathy, sensitivity, and friendship skills
	34. *Cultural competence*—Young person has knowledge of and comfort with people of different cultural/racial/ethnic backgrounds
	35. *Resistance skills*—Young person can resist negative peer pressure and dangerous situations
	36. *Peaceful conflict resolution*—Young person seeks to resolve conflict non-violently.
Positive identity	37. *Personal power*—Young person feels he or she has control over 'things that happen to me'
	38. *Self-esteem*—Young person reports having high self-esteem
	39. *Sense of purpose*—Young person reports that 'my life has a purpose'
	40. *Positive view of personal future*—Young person is optimistic about her or his personal future

Source: 1997. Search Institute. Reproduced with permission.

Table 2
The relation of assets to patterns of high-risk behavior

High-risk behavior patterns		Percent with high-risk patterns			
Category	Definition	If 0–10 Assets	If 11–20 Assets	If 21–30 Assets	If 31–40 Assets
Alcohol	Has used alcohol three or more times in the past month or got drunk once or more in the past two weeks	53	30	11	3
Tobacco	Smokes one or more cigarettes every day or uses chewing tobacco frequently	45	21	6	1
Illicit drugs	Used illicit drugs three or more times in the past year	42	19	6	1
Sexual intercourse	Has had sexual intercourse three or more times in lifetime	33	21	10	3
Depression/ suicide	Is frequently depressed and/or has attempted suicide	40	25	13	4
Antisocial behavior	Has been involved in three or more incidents of shoplifting, trouble with police, or vandalism in the past year	52	23	7	1
Violence	Has engaged in three or more acts of fighting, hitting, injuring a person, carrying or using a weapon, or threatening physical harm in the past year	61	35	16	6
School problems	Has skipped school two or more days in the past month and/or has below a C average	43	19	7	2
Driving and alcohol	Has driven after drinking or ridden with a drinking driver three or more times in the past year	42	24	10	4
Gambling	Has gambled three or more times in the past year	34	23	13	6

Source: 1998. *Applied Developmental Science*. © Lawrence Erlbaum Associates, Inc., Hillsdale, NJ. Reproduced with permission.

dichotomous form of reporting the assets, whereby each asset is simplified into a single percentage of youth who have, or do not have, the asset, is utilized as an effective method for communicating the asset profile to diverse subgroups within a community. This also allows for a simple summation of the average number of youth assets in any given community. Based on this aggregate sample, youth report having, on average, 18 of the 40 developmental assets. As part of a standardized report, communities also receive a breakdown of the percentage of young people who report different levels of developmental assets. In the aggregate sample, 20 percent have 0–10 assets, 42 percent have 11–20, 30 percent have 21–30, and 8 percent have 31–40 (Benson et al. 1998). When these categories are combined in cross-tabulation with risk behaviors or thriving indicators, they become a significant source of information for community members. For example, Table 2 shows the percentage of 6th–12th grade youth in the aggregate sample who report that they engage in each of 10 risk behavior patterns by their level of developmental assets. The table also includes a definition of each risk behavior pattern. It is important to note that for each of the 10 risk behavior patterns, the percentage of students reporting the risk behavior declines as the level of assets rises. This same relationship between assets and risk behaviors has been observed across grade, gender, racial or ethnic group, and across all communities studied.

The opposite pattern between level of assets and positive or thriving behaviors has also been repeatedly demonstrated. For these assessments youth who report fewer assets are also less likely to report each of the thriving indicators including school success and the affirmation of diversity (Benson et al. 1998).

3.2 Grade and Gender Differences

Some variation has been observed across communities and in different subgroups of adolescents. Overall,

Table 3
Assets by grade within gender among an aggregate sample of youth surveyed in the 1996–7 school year

	All	Male		Female	
		6–8	9–12	6–8	9–12
1. Family support	64 percent	71 percent	59 percent	71 percent	60 percent
2. Positive family communication	26	30	20	35	23
3. Other adult relationships	41	37	40	44	43
4. Caring neighborhood	40	42	35	47	37
5. Caring school climate	25	26	19	34	23
6. Parent involvement in schooling	29	38	22	38	24
7. Community values youth	20	24	15	28	16
8. Youth as resources	25	29	21	31	21
9. Service to others	50	50	41	61	51
10. Safety	55	54	70	42	50
11. Family boundaries	43	43	38	48	44
12. School boundaries	46	55	35	61	41
13. Neighborhood boundaries	46	53	40	54	41
14. Adult role models	27	26	21	35	28
15. Positive peer influence	60	68	46	76	57
16. High expectations	41	50	35	50	35
17. Creative activities	19	15	13	27	21
18. Youth programs	59	59	58	59	58
19. Religious community	64	67	56	73	64
20. Time at home	50	53	45	56	48
21. Achievement motivation	63	59	54	71	71
22. School engagement	64	55	57	70	73
23. Homework	45	38	36	51	55
24. Bonding to school	51	48	45	59	54
25. Reading for pleasure	24	21	17	35	27
26. Caring	43	39	28	57	52
27. Equality and social justice	45	41	28	61	54
28. Integrity	64	53	58	65	75
29. Honesty	63	59	55	71	68
30. Responsibility	60	54	56	64	66
31. Restraint	42	53	25	67	36
32. Planning and decision making	29	24	25	32	33
33. Interpersonal competence	43	28	25	59	61
34. Cultural competence	35	31	24	46	42
35. Resistance skills	37	38	29	48	38
36. Peaceful conflict resolution	44	33	29	59	54
37. Personal power	45	40	48	41	49
38. Self-esteem	47	53	54	42	39
39. Sense of purpose	55	58	61	51	49
40. Positive view of personal future	70	70	70	70	71

$N = 99,462.$
Source: 1998. *Applied Developmental Science.* © Lawrence Erlbaum Associates, Inc., Hillsdale, NJ. Reproduced with permission.

females report experiencing more of the assets than males. With males and females across each of the asset levels, 45 percent of females report that they experience more than half of the 40 assets compared to 30 percent of males who report that they experience more than half of the assets.

When comparing the effect of grade and gender differences in each of the individual assets, at least small effects (about 0.20; Cohen 1988) are observed in about one-half of the assets, suggesting somewhat pervasive, but small, differences in the contextual experiences of boys and girls over the adolescent years (Leffert et al. 1998). In addition, a fairly consistent decline in the reports of the assets for both males and females across this age period are found. That is, young adolescents (i.e., 6th–8th graders) tend to report experiencing more of the assets than older adolescents (i.e., 9th–12th graders) (see Table 3).

3.3 Prediction of Risk Behaviors and Thriving Indicators

In reports to participating communities, analyses similar to that presented in Table 2 are included to demonstrate the relation of developmental assets to both the risk behaviors and thriving indicators. In other studies using aggregate samples, regression analyses are used to assess the extent to which the developmental assets are useful in predicting either a reduction in risk behaviors (Leffert et al. 1998) or a promotion of thriving indicators (Scales et al. 2000). Those analyses have shown that demographic variables accounted for a range of 5–14 percent of the total variance of each of the models constructed to examine risk behaviors. In each analysis, a set of the developmental assets contributed a significant amount over and above the influence of the demographic variables, accounting for a total of 21–41 percent of the variance explained in the reduction of each of the individual risk behavior patterns and for 66 percent of the variance in a composite index of risk behaviors.

Similarly, Scales and colleagues (Scales et al. 2000) examined the extent to which developmental assets predicted thriving behaviors and how it varied across different ethnic groups. The demographic variables accounted for a range of 1–8 percent of the total variance explained by each of the models and each model accounted for a total of 10–43 percent of the variance explained in the individual thriving indicators and from 47 to 54 percent of the variance explained in a thriving index.

4. Application

Developmental assets, then, have particular utility for predicting reduction in multiple forms of risk-taking and thriving behavior (e.g., Leffert et al. 1998, Scales et al. 2000). The descriptive portraits of assets from hundreds of American communities suggest that these developmental asset targets are normatively fragile. A set of comprehensive and interlocking strategies have been proposed to mobilize the inherent and natural asset-building capacity of community residents (Benson 1997, Benson et al. 1998) and community socializing systems, including families (Roehlkepartain and Leffert 2000), schools (Starkman et al. 1999), congregations (Roehlkepartain 1998), and youth-serving organizations (Nelson 1998). New conceptual and measurement efforts are underway to extend the asset framework to a series of developmental phases in the 0–20 age range.

Though the focus of this last section is on the influence of communities, it is noted here that the developmental assets construct can be applied in a wide variety of ways. For example, national youth-serving systems and their local affiliates utilize the framework for strategic planning and as a training tool for staff, boards, and volunteers. A growing number of foundations utilize the work for both frame-funding initiatives and to evaluate proposals. Professionals (e.g., social workers, counselors) utilize the framework to design interventions for individual children and adolescents.

4.1 Defining Asset-building Communities

Asset-building communities are geographies of place which maximize attentiveness to promoting developmental strengths for all children and adolescents (Benson 1997). The dynamics and processes by which communities mobilize their asset-building capacity are a relatively unexplored line of inquiry, both theoretically and empirically. An initial framework for understanding the asset-building capacity of communities provides a set of core principles (Benson 1997, Benson et al. 1998). Among these are the principles of developmental redundancy (the exposure to asset-building people and environments within multiple contexts), developmental depth (a focus on nurturing most or all assets in children and adolescents), and developmental breadth (extending, by purpose and design, the reach of asset-building energy to all children and adolescents).

In activating these core principles, five sources of asset-building potential are hypothesized to exist within all communities, each of which can be marshaled via a multiplicity of community mobilization strategies. These sources of potential asset-building influence include: (a) sustained relationships with adults, both within and beyond family; (b) peer group influence (when peers choose to activate their asset-building capacity); (c) socializing systems; (d) community-level social norms, ceremony, ritual, policy, and resource allocation; and (e) programs, including school- and community-based efforts to nurture and build skills and competencies.

In brief, asset-building communities are distinguished as relational and intergenerational places, with a critical mass of socializing institutions (e.g., families, schools, neighborhoods, youth organizations, religious communities) choosing to attend to the developmental needs of all children and adolescents. Developmental assets become a language of the common good, uniting sectors, citizens, and policy in the pursuit of shared targets for all children and adolescents. The commitment of a community and its people, institutions, and organizations is both long-term and inclusive.

Ultimately, rebuilding and strengthening the developmental infrastructure in a community are conceived less as a program implemented and managed by professionals and more as a mobilization of public will and capacity. A major target for this level of community engagement is the creation of a normative culture in which all residents are expected by virtue of their membership in the community to promote the positive development of children and adolescents.

Within the context of American society, this vision requires considerable transformation in prevailing resident and socialization systems, norms, and operating principles. As argued in numerous publications defining this conceptual model of asset-building community, American cities are typically marked by age segregation, civic disengagement, social mistrust, a loss of personal efficacy, and the lack of collaboration across systems.

4.2 Asset-building Communities: The National Movement

The marshaling of community capacity to consistently and deeply attend to the development of children and adolescents is conceived less as the implementation of a program and more the awakening of latent human and institutional potential to build developmental strengths. A series of practical tools targeted at community residents and civic leaders provides conceptual and strategic counsel for mobilizing asset-building capacity. The first asset-building initiative began in St. Louis Park, Minnesota in 1995. In the following five years, more than 500 other American communities began to craft community-wide initiatives. Organized more as a social movement than as the replication of a program, communities are encouraged to tailor their initiatives to local realities and capacities and in response to the data from local asset profiles. Because these initiatives are complex, multisector 'experiments' in changing local culture, and because they occur in a variety of rural, suburban, and urban settings, there is increasing investment in learning from these communities about innovations and effective practices in mobilizing residents and systems, with 'feedback loops' emerging to inform both the theory of community change and the development of practical resources. Several longitudinal studies will add additional insight to this evolving knowledge about the influence of community on human development.

See also: Adulthood: Developmental Tasks and Critical Life Events; Biopsychology and Health; Childhood Health; Childhood Sexual Abuse and Risk for Adult Psychopathology; Community Organization and the Life Course; Developmental Sciences, History of; Divorce and Children's Social Development; Early Childhood: Socioemotional Risks; Environments for Education; Environments for Learning; Human Development and Health; Human Development, Bioecological Theory of; Human–Environment Relationships; Infancy and Childhood: Emotional Development; Lifespan Development, Theory of; Lifespan Theories of Cognitive Development; Mental Health Programs: Children and Adolescents; Poverty and Child Development; Psychobiology of Stress and Early Child Development; Social Competence: Childhood and Adolescence

Bibliography

Benson P L 1990 *The Troubled Journey: A Portrait of 6th–12th Grade Youth.* Search Institute, Minneapolis, MN

Benson P L 1997 *All Kids Are Our Kids: What Communities Must Do To Raise Caring and Responsible Children and Adolescents.* Jossey-Bass, San Francisco, CA

Benson P L 1998 Mobilizing communities to promote developmental assets: A promising strategy for the prevention of high-risk behaviors. *Family Science Review* **11**: 220–38

Benson P L, Leffert N, Scales P C, Blyth D A 1998 Beyond the 'village' rhetoric: Creating healthy communities for children and adolescents. *Applied Developmental Science* **2**: 138–59

Cohen J 1988 *Statistical Power Analysis for the Behavioral Sciences.* Lawrence Erlbaum Associates, Inc., Hillsdale, NJ

Kretzman J P, McKnight J L 1993 *Building Communities From the Inside Out: A Path Toward Finding and Mobilizing a Community's Assets.* Center for Urban Affairs and Policy Research, Evanston, IL

Leffert N, Benson P L, Scales P C, Sharma A R, Drake D R, Blyth D A 1998 Developmental assets: Measurement and prediction of risk behaviors among adolescents. *Applied Developmental Science* **2**: 209–30

Masten A S, Best K M, Garmezy N 1990 Resilience and development: Contributions from the study of children who overcome adversity. *Development and Psychopathology* **2**: 425–44

McKnight J 1995 *The Careless Society: Community and its Counterfeits.* Basic Books, New York

Nelson L I 1998 *Helping Youth Thrive: How Youth Organizations Can—and Do—Build Developmental Assets.* Search Institute, Minneapolis, MN

Pittman K J, Cahill M 1991 *A New Vision: Promoting Youth Development.* Center for Youth Development and Policy Research, Academy for Educational Development, Washington, DC

Resnick M D, Bearman P S, Blum R W, Bauman K E, Harris K M, Jones J, Beurhring T, Sieving R E, Shew M, Ireland M, Bearinger L H, Udry J R, Tabor J 1997 Protecting adolescents from harm: Findings from the National Longitudinal Study on Adolescent Health. *Journal of the American Medical Association* **278**(10): 823–32

Roehlkepartain E 1998 *Building Assets in Congregations: A Practical Guide for Helping Youth Grow Up Healthy.* Search Institute, Minneapolis, MN

Roehlkepartain J L, Leffert N 2000 *What Young Children Need to Succeed: Working Together to Build Assets From Birth to Age 11.* Free Spirit Press, Minneapolis, MN

Rutter M 1985 Resilience in the face of adversity: Protective factors and resistance to psychiatric disorder. *British Journal of Psychiatry* **147**: 598–611

Sampson R J, Raudenbush S W, Earls F C 1997 Neighborhoods and violent crime: A multilevel study of collective efficacy. *Science* **277**: 918–24

Scales P C, Benson P L, Leffert N, Blyth D A 2000 Contribution of developmental assets to the prediction of thriving among adolescents. *Applied Developmental Science* **4**: 27–46

Scales P C, Leffert N 1999 *Developmental Assets: A Synthesis of the Scientific Research on Adolescent Development*. Search Institute, Minneapolis, MN

Starkman N, Scales P C, Roberts C 1999 *Great Places to Learn: How Asset-Building Schools Help Students Succeed*. Search Institute, Minneapolis, MN

Werner E E, Smith R S 1992 *Overcoming the Odds: High Risk Children from Birth to Adulthood*. Cornell University Press, Ithaca, NY

P. L. Benson and N. Leffert

Childhood: Anthropological Aspects

The anthropological study of childhood first documents and accounts for the variety of childhoods found around the world; second, uses the comparative ethnographic record to test hypotheses about human development; and, third, studies the mechanisms in child, family, and community life for the acquisition, internal transformations, sharing, and intergenerational transmission of culture.

A thought experiment will illustrate the anthropological point of view about childhood. Imagine a newborn, healthy infant. What is the most important thing that you could do to influence the life of that infant? Most respond by mentioning dyadic interaction with the baby: hold and touch the infant a lot; provide good nutrition and health care; provide stimulation to achieve school success; love the baby; give it wealth and social capital, and so forth. Anthropologists believe that the most important influence in human development is the *cultural setting within which the infant will grow up*. It is how, why, and by whom children are held, loved, fed, stimulated, punished, provided resources, and so forth, and how that varies so widely across human communities, that is the focus of inquiry. Shaping a whole person engaged in family and cultural community life is the 'purpose' of childhood development from an anthropological perspective. Childhood is a cultural project with goals, meanings, constant adaptation, and struggle, and anthropology provides the evidence for the startling and remarkable varieties of childhoods lived around the world. Biological, psychological, and cultural anthropologists collaborate in the study of childhood, since biology, mind, and culture are all required to understand childhood.

The study of childhood and the process of children acquiring culture 'was almost entirely neglected by anthropologists until after 1925' (Whiting 1968). Although much progress has been made, anthropology does not yet provide a single unified theory of why and how childhoods vary around the world, or of childhood acquisition of culture. Rather the field offers rich, multivariate hypotheses and data on childhood (Super and Harkness 1997).

1. The Stages of Childhood

Five stages of human growth and development are common to *Homo sapiens*: infancy, childhood, juvenility, adolescence, and adulthood (Bogin 1999). Margaret Mead described lap children (infants, aged 0–1), knee children (toddlers, 2–3), yard children (preschool, 4–5), and community children (juveniles in middle childhood, 6–12). Anthropologists analyze the cultural meaning of the very idea of 'stages,' since stages are used to account for children's behavior ('he's crying but it is OK, because he's still a toddler'), as well as to assure and define normal and appropriate development ('she is eight, and so old enough to start helping run our household'). Human cultures weave wonderful variations, meanings, and stories around pan-human maturational stages of childhood. The Beng of Ivory Coast for example, believe that young children are still partly in yet another 'stage,' a cultural world called *wrugbe*, where ancestors share life with prebirth children who are ambivalent about leaving that world. This helps explain for Beng why infants cry or are sickly: they want to return to *wrugbe*.

2. Conceptions of Childhood in Anthropology

There are a variety of perspectives on childhood in anthropology. In one view, children are socialized into a set of norms and customs that they learn and then perpetuate. In this view, children are small adults in the making, ready receptors of traditions, shaped by parents and community adults to insure continuity in cultural and moral education, competence for survival in the ecology of the community, respect for tradition, appropriate behavior and respect for elders in demeanor and gender roles.

Second, children's personalities and minds are understood as reflections of the cultural themes as well as the anxieties children grow up with (such as in the work in Bali of Bateson and Mead 1942). The focus is on the semiotics and communication of cultural meanings to children, on how these cultural patterns are absorbed and internalized, in turn reproducing the meanings as well as neurotic obsessions of their parents' cultures.

Third, the psychocultural, or personality integration model (Whiting and Whiting 1975), begins with the climate, history, and ecology of a community, which shapes child-care practices, which in turn produce psychological effects on children, effects produced by direct social learning as well as by psychodynamic processes shaping personality and defenses in children. These children become adults who then project into myths, rituals, art, and other forms (including in turn their own practices as parents) the learned patterns as well as intrapsychic conflicts produced in childhood and shared by others in their community. Children and adults alike have universal needs of the self—

hunger for recognition, reward, and material and bodily satisfaction—to which cultures respond through the cultural careers made available to children in a community (Goldschmidt 1990). Culture inevitably thwarts these hungers, leading to intrapsychic and cultural conflicts. Melford Spiro used psychodynamic and sociocultural approaches to understand the ideological, political, and ecological reasons for and consequences of the care of children by designated community caretakers, or *metapelets*, in socialist-inspired agricultural collective groups in Israel (Spiro 1975).

Fourth, anthropologists study the 'developmental niche' of childhood: everyday physical/social settings, cultural customs of care, and the psychology of the caretakers as shaped by their cultural models of parenthood that direct behavior (the goals, meanings, and rationales for parenting and being a child) (Harkness and Super 1996). Parenting of children also is shaped by the organic hardware given by our common mammalian heritage, and by socioeconomic conditions in the community. Children experience culture as it is practiced within their family's daily routine of cultural life. Cultural routines consist of activities children engage in (mealtimes, bedtimes, family visits, chores, going to church, school, play, etc.) Activities are the primary mechanisms bringing culture to and into the mind of the child. Activities consist of goals and values; tasks of an activity; the scripts for how to engage in that activity; the people present and participating in the activity; and the motives and feelings of those involved (Weisner 1996).

Finally, some anthropologists view childhood itself as a cultural construction shaped by forces within as well as outside a single cultural community. The very idea of what a child or parent is, in this view, is more the outcome of processes of power in an increasingly global political economy, in which children as well as parents, are 'constructed' or 'positioned' by these agents of power (Stephens 1995).

3. Some Cultural Influences on Children's Development

3.1 Cultural Scale and Complexity

Children in more complex societies (with occupational specialization, an extensive market economy, a nucleated settlement pattern, centralized and hierarchical political and legal system, and a centralized religious priesthood) are more likely to seek help and assistance from others, to try and dominate or control others, and to be more egoistic. Children in less complex societies are more likely to show nurturance toward other children (to offer assistance and respond to their requests), be more responsible, make more responsible suggestions to others, and do more tasks

required for family and community survival. Mothers who have heavy subsistence workloads are more likely to expect responsible work from children and use stricter discipline. Children living in extended, joint, or expanded households and family systems are more often involved in directive, aggressive interactions, while children living in smaller nuclear families are more often engaged in sociable and intimate interactions with parents and others, and fathers are more involved with children. Of course children and adults everywhere are nurturant, seek help, or are aggressive. These patterns only reflect the modal tendencies of communities, not a rigid uniformity within them (Whiting and Edwards 1988).

3.2 Gender Differences

Gender differences in children's development are recognized and shaped by all cultures (Ember 1981). Of five kinds of interpersonal behavior in children aged from three to 11—nurturance, dependency, prosocial dominance, egoistic dominance, and sociability—girls on average were more likely than boys to be nurturing toward others, while boys were more likely to be egoistically dominant and aggressive than girls. Play styles and types vary by gender (girls are more likely to do work-play and to do so nearer their homes, for instance). Women and girls do most 'mothering' of children well into the juvenile period in most cultures, so girls experience care by their own sex, while boys do not, leading to differences in early gender identification, and psychosocial and self-development. Peer groups have a tendency to segregate by gender, and children prefer same-sex children to interact with. Cultures with more mixed-age and mixed-gender groups around children are likely to have less sex-segregated roles for children. Individual differences among boys and girls, even within communities where there are strong overall gender differences, are usually substantial.

Father roles are recognized in all societies. Fathers seldom are involved in direct care of infants and young children but fathers do have complementary nurturing and affiliative roles, and are more involved in economic, protective, and didactic child training. In a study of 80 preindustrial societies, fathers were more proximate and involved with young children in monogamous, nuclear-family, and nonpatrilocal situations, and wherever mothers make relatively large contributions to family subsistence. Father involvement is related to sociocultural evolution: foraging societies report more father participation in childcare, while horticultural, agrarian/peasant, and pastoral tend to have less. There is an upswing in contemporary societies in encouraging paternal care. The cultural beliefs about gender (how women's as well as men's roles are defined by parenting), as well as the ability of fathers to provide consistently for their children, influence father involvements. Poverty and uncertain economic life, or migration and dislocation, can drastically change father as well as mother involvement in patterns of childcare.

3.3 Emotional Development

Emotional development in childhood is influenced by cultural expectations at each developmental stage about the kinds of demeanor expected. A child should show that he/she is a certain kind of cultural person with an appropriate self and identity. Cultural management of emotion relies on what Robert Levy (1973) called 'redundant cultural control.' Tahitians (Levy 1973), for example, as well as many Pacific Island, Asian and other cultures, expect children to be calm, gentle, and quiet in demeanor (except for an extended period of adolescence and youth called *taure'are'a* in Tahiti, in which adventures, autonomy, rebellion, and aggressiveness are culturally expected and common). Redundant community management of 'gentleness' includes many beliefs and practices: children are somewhat distanced from their mothers and fathers after infancy and live with peers; socialization networks are diffuse, meaning that affect towards others is diffused; severe anger is 'strongly discouraged' while mild transient episodes are tolerated; threats are common while actual aggression towards children is not; accidents are reinterpreted as punishment by spirits for aggression and this is widely believed to be true; there can be magical retaliation for serious anger; and it is generally shameful to show lack of control. A *culture complex* of many interrelated beliefs and practices of this kind is a strong sign that some emotional pattern or competence in children is of adaptive and moral importance to a society.

3.4 Basic Trust and Attachment

Basic trust and attachment are fundamental in childhood in all cultures. Anthropological studies show that a wide range of family and parenting practices can produce close affiliation and trusting attachments in children. Successful attachment does not depend on only one kind of maternal care in nuclear families, nor a specific kind of infant and toddler behavioral style. Although the individual child is named and recognized everywhere, individualism and egoistic autonomy as goals are not at all universal; rather, sociocentric and interdependent self-development are common ideals (Shweder and Bourne 1991). Chisholm (1999) proposes an evolutionary developmental hypothesis regarding trust and attachment. Environments varied during the long course of evolution. Less threatening, more favorable material and social conditions led to greater investment in fewer children, and so encouraged closer attachments to one or a few caregivers. Unfavorable conditions encouraged what are called 'insecure' or avoidant/ambivalent infant and child

attachments, since in threatening, insecure conditions that was the more adaptive, successful parental and child response likely to increase the chances of children reaching reproductive age. Most cultures provide multiple caretakers to children, not a single person, and care is 'socially distributed.' Indeed, living an entire childhood exclusively in one's natal home may well be the exception around the world. Older siblings and cousins are widely used as caretakers. Extended families in village and agrarian-based societies have high levels of multiple care of children. In India and elsewhere in Southeast Asia, for instance, there is an intense, 'relational,' childhood experience with several 'maternal' figures, a pattern found widely across cultures (Weisner and Gallimore 1977).

3.5 Developmental Goals

Anthropology does not assume that competencies valued in Western communities (verbal skills, cognitive abilities, or signs of egocentric autonomy of the self, for instance), are necessarily meaningful child developmental outcomes elsewhere, although all cultures are concerned over some version of good communication, mental ability, and self- and personhood. LeVine et al. (1994) contrast pedagogical goals (cognitive and social stimulation to prepare children for literacy and schools, as well as for an individualistic and autonomous self- and personhood away from their natal home) and pediatric goals (concern for survival, health, and physical growth of infants, and subsequent responsible engagement in family subsistence and continuity), comparing families in Boston, USA and the Gusii of western Kenya. Many parents and cultures have mixed goals, and are ambivalent about the constantly changing requirements for childhood. Anthropology has a unique point of view regarding the goals for a good childhood: the production of cultural well-being in children. Well-being is more than physical health or the attainment of skills and competence, or of successful subsequent reproduction, important as these are. Well-being is the ability of a child to engage and participate in the activities deemed desirable by a cultural community, and the psychological experiences that go along with that participation.

4. The Acquisition of Culture

The roles and settings in which children acquire culture matter for when and how children learn. Children are apprentices to more experienced community members in doing important tasks, and this apprenticeship situation is a powerful learning experience for children. Play and work blend in childhood learning. Imaginative, fantasy, toy, physical, and motoric play (including organized sports with rules) varies according to whether adults encourage it, whether it is considered 'beneficial' for children by adults because it enhances desired competencies or societies' developmental goals (such as cognitive and school-like activities in many contemporary cultures), and whether children's sheer inventiveness, creativity, and exuberance take over. The Kpelle of Liberia have children playing on 'the mother-ground,' or open public spaces where children can observe, lurk nearby, and imitate adults going about their activities in an agrarian village community. Formal schooling and the 'outside' world of employment and the nation-state contrast sharply with this mother-ground of childhood. Anthropological studies of schooling find striking differences in the culture of classrooms around the world, including different teaching practices and student expectations. Cultures vary in the 'moral and cultural curriculum' accompanying literacy and other training, classroom and peer norms, gender, and class circumstances mirrored in school practices, and daily routines of school (Tobin et al. 1989). Participation in ceremonies and rituals at times of baptism, birthdays, naming ceremonies, puberty, and marriage also are powerful influences on children's acquisition of cultural knowledge. Such ceremonies crystallize cultural beliefs and practices; they intensify emotionally, politically, and socially salient key concerns that parents and communities have about childhood, and elevate the goals the community shares for children and parents (Turner, 1967).

Multiple cultural and mental processes are involved in culture acquisition. However, the relative importance of different mental and cultural mechanisms for emotional, social, or cognitive learning is currently not well understood in anthropology. Evolved tendencies of the mind prepare children to understand the world in certain ways. For example, children in widely disparate cultural communities seem to share understandings about what living things are like and how they behave and think (Hirschfeld and Gelman 1994). Psychodynamic processes transform emotionally salient cultural information. Stories and narratives embed cultural knowledge, shape recall, and organize cultural knowledge into sequences with shared local meaning. Sociolinguistic studies of child language acquisition show wide variations in how and when parents talk to their children, and view language learning as embedded in interactional routines shaped by cultural practices, with children as active learners (Schieffelin and Ochs 1986). Cultural knowledge is available to and used by children in the form of cultural models and schemas for how to comprehend and act in the world. Neither children nor parents generally 'know that they know' most cultural knowledge, and it is not usually in conscious awareness, even as they act in accord with their culture's beliefs. Cultural beliefs and practices have powerful 'directive force' in guiding child behavior and child socialization in part because of this shared, implicit, everyday understanding put into action (D'Andrade 1995).

5. Anthropological Methods and the Study of Children

Anthropological methods for the study of children include ethnography and participant observation (Weisner 1996). These methods fit with the anthropological concept of childhoods lived in cultural pathways in naturalistic settings. Systematic observational procedures, field guides for comparative studies, and special procedures for sampling children's activities and time use enhance ethnography (Munroe and Munroe 1994). Anthropologists also use assessments standard in child development for comparing physical growth, and the cognitive and socioemotional life of children, often revising these to insure that culturally appropriate procedures and meaningful outcomes are being measured. Film and video records of childhood are invaluable for comparative studies of cultural activities, emotional expression, holding patterns, or gaze and attention.

6. Anthropology and the Study of Childhood in the Twenty-first Century

Anthropology has always been concerned with the experience and the cultural worlds of minorities, the poor and non-literate, and of those, including children, who are so often unable to give voice to and represent their own world. Life histories and autobiographical accounts have provided rich data, as in the classic *Nisa: The Life and Words of a !Kung Woman* (Shostak 1981). Scheper-Hughes (1992) describes infants and young children in deeply impoverished political-economic circumstances in urban northeastern Brazil, circumstances leading to high infant and child mortality, and anger and despair among parents (and anthropologists). Anthropological studies of African-American families and economically downwardly mobile families in the USA demonstrate how some (but not all) can rely on extended kin in their struggles with poverty. Anthropological studies of childhood disability and deviance find greater acceptance and social integration of children with physical and cognitive disabilities in many communities, as long as children are able to live as sufficiently cultural persons in their communities and are not violent or dangerous to others (Ingstad and Whyte 1995). Anthropologists are concerned with children at risk around the globe, including, for example, children under stress from academic examinations in Japan and Korea, immigrant children in Europe and elsewhere, street children, or children facing change in East Africa. Child sexual and physical abuse around the world is now a recognized concern for anthropologists. Cultural beliefs and practices regarding appropriate discipline and treatment of children clearly do vary widely, and Western notions of abuse are not universal. However, repeated and unchecked physical aggression, or intrafamilial sexual relations between close kin and children are nowhere defined as normative and acceptable (Korbin 1981). Anthropologists are concerned with children's rights, recognizing their vulnerable status and the lack of provision of basic protections for children (*Cultural Survival Quarterly*). World youth cultures are growing in importance due to the influence of the Internet and mass communications around the world. These are all topics for the anthropology of childhood in the twenty-first century. However, the comparative study of powerful local and regional cultural differences in parenting, childhood, and family life across populations around the world will continue to provide enduring scientific questions for anthropology.

See also: Adolescent Development, Theories of; Childhood Health; Children and the Law; Gender-related Development; Infancy and Childhood: Emotional Development; Life Course in History; Life Course: Sociological Aspects; Trust, Sociology of; Youth Culture, Anthropology of; Youth Culture, Sociology of

Bibliography

Bateson G, Mead M 1942 *Balinese Character*. Special Publications of the New York Academy of Sciences **2**. New York Academy of Sciences, New York

Bogin B 1999 *Patterns of Human Growth*, 2nd edn. Cambridge University Press, New York

Chisholm J 1999 *Death, Hope, and Sex. Steps to an Evolutionary Ecology of Mind and Morality*. Cambridge University Press, Cambridge, UK

Cultural Survival Quarterly. World Report on the Rights of Indigenous Peoples and Ethnic Minorities. Cambridge, MA (http://www.cs.org)

D'Andrade R 1995 *The Development of Cognitive Anthropology*. Cambridge University Press, New York

Ember C M 1981 A cross-cultural perspective on sex differences. In: Munroe R H, Munroe R L, Whiting B B (eds.) *Handbook of Cross-cultural Human Development*. Garland, New York

Goldschmidt W 1990 *The Human Career*. Blackwell, Cambridge, MA, pp. 531–80

Harkness S, Super C M (eds.) 1996 *Parents' Cultural Belief Systems: Their Origins, Expressions, and Consequences*. Guilford Press, New York

Hirschfeld L A, Gelman S A 1994 *Mapping the Mind: Domain Specificity in Cognition and Culture*. Cambridge University Press, Cambridge, UK

Ingstad B, Whyte S R 1995 *Disability and Culture*. University of California Press, Berkeley, CA

Korbin J E (ed.) 1981 *Child Abuse and Neglect: Cross-cultural Perspectives*. University of California Press, Berkeley, CA

LeVine R A 1988 Human parental care: Universal goals, cultural strategies, individual behavior. In: LeVine R A, Miller P M, West M M (eds.) *Parental Behavior in Diverse Societies. New Directions for Child Development* **40**. Jossey-Bass, San Francisco, pp. 3–12

LeVine R A, Dixon S, LeVine S, Richman A, Leiderman P H, Keefer C H, Brazelton T B 1994 *Child Care and Culture. Lessons from Africa*. Cambridge University Press, Cambridge, UK

Levy R 1973 *Tahitians. Mind and Experience in the Society Islands*. University of Chicago Press, Chicago

Munroe R L, Munroe R H 1994 Behavior across cultures: Results from observational studies. In: Lonner W J, Malpass R (eds.) *Psychology and Culture*. Allyn and Bacon, Boston, MA, pp. 107–11

Scheper-Hughes N 1992 *Death Without Weeping. The Violence of Everyday Life in Brazil*. University of California Press, Berkeley, CA

Schieffelin, B B, Ochs E (eds.) 1986 *Language Socialization Across Cultures*. Cambridge University Press, New York

Schlegel A, Barry H 1991 *Adolescence. An Anthropological Inquiry*. Free Press, New York

Shostak M 1981 *Nisa: The Life and Words of a !Kung Woman*. Harvard University Press, Cambridge, MA

Shweder R A, Bourne E J 1991 Does the concept of the person vary cross-culturally? In: *Thinking Through Cultures Expeditions in Cultural Psychology* Harvard University Press Cambridge, MA, pp. 113–55

Spiro M E 1975 *Children of the Kibbutz*, 2nd edn. Harvard University Press, Cambridge, MA

Stephens S (ed.) 1995 *Children and the Politics of Culture*. Princeton University Press, Princeton, NJ

Super C M, Harkness S 1997 The cultural structuring of child development. In: Berry J, Dasen P R, Saraswathi T S (eds.) *Handbook of Cross-cultural Psychology*, 2nd edn. Allyn and Bacon, Boston, Vol. 2, pp. 3–39

Tobin J, Wu D, Davidson D 1989 *Preschool in Three Cultures: Japan, China, and the United States*. Yale University Press, New Haven, CT

Turner V W 1967 *The Forest of Symbols*. Cornell University Press, Ithaca, NY

Weisner T S 1996 Why ethnography should be the most important method in the study of human development. In: Jessor R, Colby A, Shweder R (eds.) *Ethnography and Human Development. Context and Meaning in Social Inquiry*. University of Chicago Press, Chicago, pp. 305–24

Weisner T S, Gallimore R 1977 My brother's keeper: Child and sibling caretaking. *Current Anthropology* **18**: 169–90

Whiting J 1968 Socialization: Anthropological aspects. *International Encyclopedia of the Social Sciences* **14**: 545–51

Whiting B B, Edwards C P 1988 *Children of Different Worlds: The Formation of Social Behavior*. Harvard University Press, Cambridge, MA

Whiting J W M, Whiting B B 1975 *Children of Six Cultures: A Psychocultural Analysis*. Harvard University Press, Cambridge, MA

T. S. Weisner

Childhood Cancer: Psychological Aspects

Substantial progress in medical anticancer treatment (chemotherapy, radiotherapy, surgery, bone-marrow transplantation) has improved dramatically the long-term survival rates of children and adolescents with the diagnosis of cancer (malignant tumors, lymphomas, and leukemias). Some decades ago, the essential threat for the family was to face the death and loss of the child. Since more than two-thirds of the young patients survive, cancer in children and adolescents no longer is regarded as unevitably fatal but as a chronic disease which can result in complete cure, death' or survival with lasting neurological, orthopedical, or neuropsychological impairments.

At the end of the twentieth century, there is a consensus about the necessity of an honest explanation of the life-threatening nature of the disease to the child. The statistical survival rates, however, do not indicate the prognosis in an individual case, turning the former threat of certainty of death to the threat of uncertainty of the very personal fate. 'Damocles syndrome' is the term Koocher and O'Malley (1981) have coined to characterize the psychological situation of the family that has terminated oncological therapy but cannot be sure definitely to have defeated the disease.

1. Psychological Adaptation to Childhood Cancer as a Balance of Stress and Resources

The occurence of childhood cancer is not associated with any known predisposing social or psychological feature in the child or in the family. Its presence can be regarded a randomly occuring highly stressful life event for 'normal' families. As a consequence, psychological research and intervention is not concerned with the detection of suspected psychological causes of cancer but with an understanding of the stress impact imposed by cancer diagnosis on the child's and family's psychological functioning and well-being.

The risk of the child or the family to master or to fail the turmoils of the cancer experience may be compared to a balance with one scale pan containing all the stressors resulting from the disease and the other scale pan containing all the resources, competencies, and sources of social support to handle the stress. In some vulnerable families, the strong stressors and demands clearly outweigh only weak resources, thus increasing the probability of emotional suffering and behavioral disturbance in the child and the risk of marital discord or parental depression. Other families are characterized by resilience, i.e., the available resources are strong enough to outweigh the threatening disease impact, thus giving rise to a good adjustment and a personal sense of mastery. Actually, the large majority of patients succeed in mastering the plethora of disease and treatment-related stressors and challenges (Noll et al. 1999).

2. Enhancement of Effective Coping with Childhood Cancer by Family Counseling

Understanding adaptation to childhood cancer as a psychological balance between burden and resources may serve as a basis for effective psychological counselling strategies. Therefore, the therapeutical task on the way to enhancement of adaptation is a twofold one: the first one is to decrease stress impact and the second one is to increase resource availablity. In order to develop concrete counseling strategies for intervention, a differentiated knowledge is required of the most common and threatening sources of stress, on the one hand, and of the most powerful resources that can be mobilized, on the other. Selected typical stressors for the family of the cancer-sick child are presented in Table 1. They cover practical, emotional, social, and existential domains. As a counterpart, Table 2 shows important resources that can buffer and diminish cancer stress impact, improve adaptation, stabilize quality of life, and protect individual family members and the whole family structure from decompensation. Research has highlighted the central role of family communication behavior. For instance, the intensity of interparental exchange about disease issues is connected closely to an improved parent–child contact and a high disease related information level in

Table 1
Typical stressors, demands, and challenges frequently occurring during the course of childhood cancer

Organization of treatment (meetings with physicans, insurances, etc.)
Financial expenditures
Gathering information on cancer and its treatment
Repeated hospitalizations including the alternative to stay at home with the siblings or be in the hospital with the ill child
Treatment-related distress according to painful and frightening medical procedures (e.g., bone marrow aspirations) and treatment side-effects (e.g., nausea and vomiting due to chemotherapy)
Reduced time for recreation and holiday
Role conflict (e.g., father between ongoing job demands and family need for support)
Re-examinination of future perspectives (job perspectives of the mother; schooling of the child)
Sharing responsibility for treatment decisions (e.g., amputation in the case of bone sarkoma)
Subconscious violation, disappointment, frustration of the hope for a normal and healthy child
Religious doubts
Uncertainty of final outcome; fear of relapse, fear of loosing the child

Source: Chesler and Barbarin (1987), Noeker and Petermann (1990), Noeker et al. (1990)

Table 2
Protective family resources that enhance an effective adaptation to childhood cancer

Communication competencies
Attributing positive meanings to the situation
Commitment to the family as a unit
Engaging in active, flexible coping efforts
Balancing illness demands with other family needs
Maintaining social integration
Developing collaborative relationships with
   professionals
Ability to ask for and accept support
Clear religious or philosophical belief systems
Parenting style demonstrating consistent rules and
   expectations

Source: Koocher and O'Malley 1981, Kupst et al. 1995, Noeker and Petermann 1990, Patterson 1991

the child and the siblings. A fair and respectful sharing of the new burdens and tasks is associated with a high family coherence and stability (Noeker et al. 1990).

3. Psychological Counseling Strategies and Interventions Across Different Phases of Childhood Cancer Treatment

Based on the knowledge of typical stress and resource factors in families with childhood cancer, psychological counseling programs have been developed (Chesler and Barbarin 1987, Noeker et al. 1990). The counseling interventions are related closely to the specific stressors that characterize certain phases of treatment course. Counseling sessions may take place at the clinic or at home. Basically, all family members should join them; however, also sessions with family subsystems may be indicated, e.g., when mother and father want to find out an agreement on consistent parenting behavior. In the following, selected topics and strategies of a psychological counseling program are delineated according to the major phases of anticancer treatment process.

3.1 Supporting the Initial Coping with Cancer Diagnosis

After being told the diagnosis of childhood cancer, most parents show strong affective reactions like shock, sadness, anger, despair. The primary task of the counselor here is to show nonjudging acceptance of these emotions and to verbalize and clarify them. Ideosyncratic parental lay theories on why exactly their own child has got cancer may interfere with the medical treatment concept. When exploring these subjective disease and treatment concepts special attention has to be paid to frequent parental conceptions of feeling personally responsible and guilty for cancer manifestation (e.g., via genetics, bad food, psychological stress). Psychological clarification and

integration of the strong emotional reactions and as well as a stepwise restructuring of inappropriate disease concepts improve the parents' cognitive capacity for understanding and accepting the oncological treatment concept.

The next major counseling task is to initiate an active, mutually respectful, and supportive coping attitude and behavior within the family unit including:

(a) clarification and expression what kind of support every person in the family needs most from other family members for stabilizing outer and inner equilibrium;

(b) encouragement of open communication and expression of personal feelings, concerns, sorrows, and anxieties among the family members; and

(c) creation of a shared commitment to regard the cancer disease as a common challenge for the entire family.

3.2 Phase of Intensive Oncological Treatment

After the family has overcome the initial shock of cancer diagnosis psychological counseling should assess primary vulnerability and resource factors in the child or in the family. Factors of vulnerability that were already present before diagnosis (e.g., behavioral or developmental disorders in the child, intense sibling rivalry, marital discord, inconsistent parenting styles, socioeconomic disadvantages) may interfere with a competent adaptation to demands of disease and treatment. Their assessment improves the chances for early and preventive intervention. At least as important as the assessment of risks and deficits, however, is the exploration of strenghts and competencies. If a counselor turns the family's attention to positive experiences of crises in the past that were resolved successfully, problem-solving strategies may be reactivated that have proven specific effectivity in this individual family. In addition, psychological counseling in this phase includes:

(a) Encouraging active participation in the management of the illness;

(b) Initiating clear and practical responsibilities for the day-to-day management of additional chores and tasks; making sure that agreements are perceived as a fair sharing of the burden by every family member;

(c) Parenting issues (e.g., ways to show affection without spoiling and pity);

(d) Mobilization and acceptance of concrete social support from neighborhood or classmates; and

(e) Facilitating communication between family and healthcare team.

3.3 Positive Course: Long-term Remission of Disease and Process of Reintegration

After termination of intensive oncological therapy, anxieties stay alive in patient and family concerning a return of the disease which would require a completely new start of therapy with, however, decreased chances for cure. Families suffer from intrusive thoughts and emotions concerning cancer relapse. Cognitive-behavioral intervention strategies can support the patient and family members to observe these recurrent thoughts consciously, to accept them as a natural reaction to their unnormal situation, and at the same time, not to get too much involved every time anxieties arise. In addition, counselor and family may cautiously anticipate and go through possible responses and options for the case of an actually occuring relapse.

Termination of therapy also requires encouragment of the child to give up their sick role and corresponding privelegies and to promote the social reintegration in previous roles, groups, and obligations.

3.4 Negative Disease Course: Recurrent Relapses, End-stage of Disease, Death, and Dying

The diagnosis of cancer recurrency requires a similar accepting and verbalizing counseling behavior concerning the intense emotional reactions as in the former diagnosis shock. This process may include a clarification of ambivalent tendencies towards continuation or discontinuation of oncological treatment since the parents wish to maintain any chance for cure, on the one hand, and do not want to make the child suffer from a stressful but senseless therapy, on the other. With the worsening of treatment course, the threat of loss of the child is gradually intensified leading to the following counseling topics:

(a) Preparing parents for communication with the child on death and dying. Finding individually appropriate images integrating truth and hope;

(b) Searching for phantasies on a good way to spend the remaining time together; development of other important goals besides survival like e.g., freedom from pain; and

(c) Enhancing imagery on a suitable way of parting in dignity.

If the child actually dies, it is important to say that the therapy failed and not the child or the family. The family's engagement shown for the child should be acknowledged. Individually suitable mourning rituals may be conceived that combine keeping related to the deceased child and, at the same time, letting them go. Family members may be encouraged to take their time for mourning and grief according to their very personal needs not according to expectations of their social network (see *Bereavement*).

Summarized, many counseling interventions focus on the enhancement of open and clear family communication. The mobilization of this key resource for effective coping with the burden of childhood cancer may refer to the intrafamilial exchange of personal needs and concerns, the practical organization of day-to-day routines, or the subtle communication between parents and child about their chances of survival.

Effective extrafamilial communication may refer to establishing cooperation and agreements with the staff or to mobilizing and accepting support from the extended social network. If such competencies are not only applied but even refined during the treatment process, the 'cancer experience' may even stimulate processes of individual maturity and family coherence.

4. From a 'Protective' to an Open Approach

There follow some guidelines on how to inform children with cancer about their diagnosis. Some decades ago, a so-called 'protective' approach was preferred which consisted of not telling the child the life-theratening nature of the disease. In the meantime, not only changes in ethical considerations but also the progress in medical treatment options have led to a broad consensus that there is no responsible alternative to telling the truth even to preschool children. Today, medical progress allows the combination of the bad news of cancer diagnosis with the good news of reasonable hope for cure. Therefore, telling children the truth includes two realistic key messages: first, that death has to be expected if no treatment is performed, and second, that even treatment does not necessarily guarantee survival. Information given to the child should be appropriate to their cognitive and emotional age and maturity. In small children, showing concrete treatment procedures and instruments and offering plausible explanations for sensory experiences like vomiting during chemotherapy is more effective than abstract explanations about malignant cells. An approach that avoids telling the truth implies serious medical and psychological 'side-effects' to be considered:

(a) A child will not accept the enormously distressing treatment procedures without the awareness of the serious consequences in case of therapy refusal. Thus, true information is necessary for compliance with treatment, and compliance with treatment is necessary for medical treatment success.

(b) Children who lack plausible information on their condition tend to develop other explanations for the occurrence of their disease (Eiser 1993). A frequent one is the conception that the illness represents a punishment for own misbehavior.

(c) Trust in the parents is one of the most important psychological resources for the child to protect them from feelings of loneliness and depression. A child uncovering the parents' well-meant lies will not only have to struggle with the adversities of disease and treatment but, in addition, with social alienation.

See also: Biopsychology and Health; Cancer: Psychosocial Aspects; Cancer Screening; Childhood Health; Chronic Illness, Psychosocial Coping with; Illness: Dyadic and Collective Coping; Pain, Health Psychology of; Well-being and Health: Proactive Coping

Bibliography

Chesler M A, Barbarin O 1987 *Childhood Cancer and the Family. Meeting the Challenge of Stress and Support.* Brunner/Mazel, New York

Eiser C 1993 *Growing up with a Chronic Disease: The Impact on Children and their Families.* Kingsley, London

Koocher G P, O'Malley J E (eds.) 1981 *The Damocles Syndrome: Psychosocial Consequences of Surviving Childhood Cancer.* McGraw-Hill, New York

Kupst M J, Natta M B, Richardson C C, Schulman J L, Lavigne J V, Das L 1995 Family coping with pediatric leukemia: 10 years after treatment. *Journal of Pediatric Psychology* **20**: 601–17

Noeker M, Petermann F 1990 Treatment-related anxieties in children and adolescents with cancer. *Anxiety Research* **3**: 101–11

Noeker M, Petermann F, Bode U 1990 Family counselling in childhood cancer: Conceptualization and empirical results. In: Schmidt L R, Schwenkmezger P, Weinman J, Maes S (eds.) *Theoretical and Applied Aspects of Health Psychology.* Harwood Academic Publishers, Chur, pp. 241–53

Noll R B, Gartstein M A, Vanatta K, Correl J, Bukowski W M, Davies W H 1999 Social, emotional, and behavioral functioning of children with cancer. *Pediatrics* **103**: 71–8

Patterson J M 1991 Family resilience to the challenge of a child's disability. *Pediatric Annals* **20**: 491–99

F. Petermann and M. Noeker

Childhood Depression

Once thought to be rare or virtually nonexistent, depression in young people has been reliably documented. In this article, the meaning of depression, its clinical manifestation, and the recent history of studies in depression are discussed. Key issues in the study of depression include prevalence and course of depressive disorders in young people, gender and age differences, and comorbidity with other disorders. Topics that are the focus of current research include those familial, cognitive, and biological factors that may contribute to or maintain depression. Effective treatments for childhood or adolescent depression have begun to be identified, but many questions about optimal single or combined treatments for the disorder remain to be answered.

1. The Meaning of the Term 'Depression' in Young People

The term 'depression' in children or adolescents can refer to three different, increasingly restrictive definitions. At the least restrictive level, 'depression' refers to a negative or low mood, such as sadness. In medical terms, if the low mood persists beyond an expectable duration of time, this is a single *symptom*. It may occur in isolation or in conjunction with other symptoms. At a more restrictive level, 'depression' refers to a particular set of symptoms that frequently occur together. Such a set of symptoms is designated a *syndrome*. For instance, children with low mood often simultaneously experience boredom, low energy, and social withdrawal, among other possible symptoms. Such a syndrome can be assessed at one point in time by the use of symptom review checklists. At the most restrictive level, 'depression' refers to a psychiatric *disorder*, characterized by a significant and persistent change in the child's functioning. Depressive disorders have, in addition to a number of defining symptoms, a certain duration and course, a level of severity that causes considerable distress, and an impact on the daily functioning of the young person. Assessment of depressive disorders requires a comprehensive clinical interview, possibly accompanied by symptom checklists or rating scales.

Depression as a single symptom will not be a focus of this article. Instead the focus will be primarily on depression as a disorder, and secondarily on depression as a syndrome, since syndromal depression has been the subject of several important longitudinal studies among youths.

Depression is one of the psychiatric disorders in which disturbed mood is the core defining characteristic. Diagnoses of depression (unipolar depression) in the American Psychiatric Association (1994) nomenclature include Major Depressive Disorder and Dysthymic Disorder, both of which refer to conditions in which mood is dysphoric or low. In depression, children may report feeling sad, unhappy, bored or uninterested in usual activities, angry, or irritable, or may appear sad or tearful. By contrast, bipolar mood disorders, or manic-depressive disorders, are conditions in which mood fluctuates episodically between such dysphoric states and unusually elevated, irritable, or expansive mood states.

2. Recognition and Recent History

Recognition that depression occurs with considerable frequency in children and adolescents has been a relatively recent development. In the 1950s and 1960s, when psychoanalytic theory provided the primary conceptual model for psychiatric diagnosis and psychological assessment, clinicians rarely diagnosed depression in young people, partly because the development of superego and ego ideal functions, considered necessary to generate and maintain depression, was incomplete in youngsters. Child clinicians were also faced with the reality that their most common referral problems involved behavioral disorders or school performance problems, rather than mood problems. By the 1970s, there was recognition that depression might be 'underlying' such problems, but it was not until the emphasis on phenomenological or symptom-focused diagnosis that depression began to be assessed systematically in young people. Lewinsohn et al. (1993) have proposed that the study of affective disorders in children and adolescents really began in the 1970s when several sets of investigators, including Carlson, Cytryn, Kovacs, Poznanski, Puig-Antich, Rutter, and their colleagues demonstrated that such disorders do occur and can be reliably assessed in young people. This development corresponded to the shift in psychiatric assessment toward systematic review of presenting symptoms, and away from nondirective, inferential assessment based on play observations or patient narrative reporting.

Since the advent of symptom-driven diagnosis in US psychiatry in 1980, the same diagnostic criteria used to diagnose depressive disorders in adults have been applied to children and adolescents. At present, the diagnosis of Major Depressive Disorder (MDD) requires at least one episode in which the child has had five or more of the following symptoms, including one of the first two, for a minimum of two weeks: (a) depressed or irritable mood; (b) markedly diminished interest or pleasure in activities; (c) weight or appetite loss or gain; (d) insomnia or hypersomnia; (e) psychomotor agitation or retardation; (f) fatigue or loss of energy; (g) feelings of worthlessness or excessive guilt; (h) decreased ability to think, concentrate, or make decisions; (i) recurrent thoughts of death or suicide or a suicide attempt or plan. The diagnosis of Dysthymic Disorder (DD) is given if depressed or irritable mood is present most days for a year or more, and if mood disturbance is accompanied by two or more of six key symptoms: poor appetite or excessive eating, insomnia or hypersomnia, low energy or fatigue, low self-esteem, poor concentration or difficulty making decisions, and feelings of hopelessness. MDD and DD are not mutually exclusive, and some children or adolescents present with a long-standing DD, upon which an episode of MDD has been superimposed: a condition referred to as 'double depression.'

Parallel to the application of adult criteria to childhood depression, there have been numerous studies in the psychopathology of depression, and in its treatment, which have applied concepts and research models from the adult field and extended them to children. To give just two examples, both cognitive factors known to characterize adult depression (e.g., distortions in thinking) and cognitive therapy, which is known to be effective for adult depression, have been studied in young people. Although the use of adult diagnostic criteria for child and adolescent depression is now conventional in research and clinical practice, there continues to be controversy regarding the developmental sensitivity and adequacy of this approach. In particular, the school of thought known as developmental psychopathology (Cichetti et al. 1994) is characterized by an emphasis on understanding the multiple contributions of developmental sciences toward understanding both normal development and disorders such as depression. Merely applying the same criteria and research concepts from adults to children does not adequately account for the interactive contributions of cognitive development, family processes, school environment, and biological development to the development of mood disorders. Developmental psychopathologists seek to go beyond merely establishing that depressed children differ from nondepressed children on a set of symptoms and associated features, and to determine the conditions and processes that contribute to these differences.

3. Prevalence and Gender Differences

Prevalence of depression in children and adolescents varies across studies, in part depending on whether a syndrome (elevated scores on a continuous scale) or a diagnosed disorder (based on parent and/or child interviews) serves as the measure of depression. Fleming and Offord's (1990) review of studies showed that MDD in preadolescent children occurred in as low as 0.4 percent and as high as 2.5 percent of the samples. Upper estimates for adolescents were higher, with a range from 0.4 percent to 6.4 percent. Prevalence of DD in children ranged from 0.6 percent to 1.7 percent, and in adolescents from 1.6 percent to 8.0 percent. The subsequent Oregon Adolescent Depression Project (Lewinsohn et al. 1993) found a point prevalence of 2.57 percent for MDD and 0.53 percent for DD, and lifetime prevalence of 18.48 percent for MDD and 3.22 percent for DD in US high school students (mean age = 16.6 years).

Depression is associated with age and with gender (Birmaher et al. 1996a). Rates are higher in adolescents than in children. Phenomenology also differs to some extent by age, with adolescents with MDD more likely than children to have anhedonia, hypersomnia, weight change, or lethal suicide attempts. Among depressed children there is equal gender representation, but in adolescents the ratio is about two females to one male, similar to the pattern among adults. The reasons for gender differences in adolescent depression are the focus of considerable current research. Sociocultural pressures on girls, biological changes associated with puberty, and sex differences in cognitive coping mechanisms have been proposed as possible explanations.

4. Course of Depressive Disorders in Childhood

Kovacs and her colleagues were the first to study the course of depressive disorders in prepubertal children. Their sample consisted of children who had been referred for clinical services, and was not an epidemiological sample. The average (mean) duration of the index episode of MDD in their sample was 32 weeks and half had recovered by nine months (median duration). For DD, however, the median duration of the episode was four years. Both MDD and DD children demonstrated a high likelihood of having a second depressive episode within a nine-year follow-up period, with the risk higher among DD than among MDD children (Kovacs 1996). By contrast, children diagnosed with an Adjustment Disorder with depressed mood (one or a few depressive symptoms in reaction to a stressor) were not at risk of developing MDD during follow up.

Data from the Oregon Adolescent Depression Project (Lewinsohn et al. 1993), with an epidemiological sample, indicated that there is an extraordinarily variable duration of MDD in teenagers. Mean episode duration was 26 weeks, but median was eight weeks, with a range of 2 to 520 weeks. Seventy-five percent of the adolescents recovered by 24 weeks. Overall, about 33 percent of the adolescents who recovered from their initial episode of MDD had a second episode within four years. Adolescents with onset of MDD before age 15.5 years had longer episodes and shorter times between recovery and relapse than did adolescents with later onset.

Using syndromal measures of depression assessed on rating scales or clinician-completed symptom checklists, studies both in the USA and in the UK have demonstrated that depression during the developmental period confers an increased risk of depression during adulthood. Harrington and his colleagues (Harrington et al. 1990) have shown that depressed young people followed up an average of 18 years into adulthood have nearly a fourfold increased risk of adult depression when compared to a control group matched for nondepressive childhood symptoms.

5. Comorbidity and the Risk of Developing Bipolar Disorder

Studies from New Zealand, Puerto Rico, and the continental USA reviewed by Angold and Costello (1993) have shown that depression (either MDD or DD) in young people is very often accompanied by other disorders. The most common comorbid conditions in these studies were oppositional or conduct disorders and the various anxiety disorders. Rates of conduct or oppositional disorders in depressed children or adolescents ranged widely across studies, from 20 percent to 80 percent. Most studies showed rates of anxiety disorders between 30 percent and 50 percent, but some showed rates exceeding 70 percent. In the Oregon project, Lewinsohn and colleagues (1993) found that the most frequent comorbid diagnoses for depressed adolescents were anxiety disorder (21 percent) and substance use disorder (20 percent), with 12.4 percent of depressed teenagers having a disruptive behavior disorder.

Birmaher and colleagues (Birmaher et al. 1996a), in their review of the comorbidity literature, found that, except for substance use disorders, most of the other

comorbid conditions developed before the MDD. However, conduct disorder was sometimes found to develop after MDD and to persist after resolution of the depression. Comorbid MDD and DD, in particular, have been found to predict longer depressive episodes, more suicidality, and worse social adjustment. The presence of comorbid anxiety disorders appears to raise the risk of suicidality and of substance abuse, and to be associated with poorer response to psychotherapy. There has been particular interest in comorbid depression and disruptive behavior disorders, perhaps because these represent a combination of two distinct types of disorders, internalizing and externalizing, that would not ordinarily be expected to co-occur. Birmaher and colleagues' (1996a) review indicates that these young people are at increased risk for suicide attempts and adult criminality, and have poorer response to acute treatment, but also have more positive responses to placebo treatment and have fewer depressive recurrences.

Bipolar disorder includes distinct periods of depression and of mania. Because bipolar disorder is well recognized as distinct from unipolar depression, with a different course and different treatment requirements, it is important to assess the risk of developing bipolar disorder in depressed young people. Follow-up studies of clinically referred youths have varied in duration of follow-up period and in definition of bipolar disorder. They suggest that about 20 percent of adolescents with MDD go on to develop bipolar disorder, but the range of estimates to date varies widely. Factors that predict bipolar outcome include psychotic symptoms during the depressive episode, family history of bipolar disorder, and hypomanic reactions to antidepressant medication. There is conflicting evidence regarding the predictive utility of acute vs. prolonged onset of depression in predicting bipolar outcome. Both acute onset of severe depression in hospitalized adolescents and early onset of DD in (nonhospitalized) children have been associated with later bipolar outcome, suggesting there may be more than one path to a bipolar outcome.

6. Current Research Emphases: Psychosocial Correlates, Biology, and Treatment

Psychosocial correlates, biological correlates, and treatment efficacy and effectiveness are three areas of current research emphasis in childhood and adolescent depression. Correlates include an array of factors that are associated with and may make a causal contribution to depression or maintaining a depressive episode. Some psychosocial correlates, such as family factors and cognitive factors, can become targets of treatment in psychosocial intervention.

Compared to controls, the families of depressed young people are characterized by higher levels of parent–child and/or marital conflict, poor parent–

child communication, and more distant, less affectionate parent–child relationships (Birmaher et al. 1996a). The challenge for researchers is to determine whether these factors are specific to depression, and if so, whether they are causal.

A number of cognitive factors has been associated with depression in youths. These include cognitive distortions that emphasize negative interpretations of events, a tendency to attribute negative events to enduring and internal causes but positive events to transitory and external causes, low self-esteem, and low estimates of personal control and competence. Although such factors are present while youngsters are depressed, it is not clear whether they represent pre-existing risk factors or state-dependent correlates of the depressive episode. An important research question is to delineate the processes through which children acquire such cognitive characteristics.

Biological correlates of depression include family-genetic factors and markers of a depressed state. Children of depressed parents are more likely to develop depression than are children of nondepressed parents. Studies in adults show a significant genetic component to the transmission of mood disorders, and family interaction studies suggest that depressed parents have deficits in parenting behaviors that raise the risk of poor adaptation in their children. Both genetics and experience, therefore, are likely involved in cross-generational transmission of depression.

A number of potential biological markers of MDD have been investigated, in the desire to clarify the biological basis of the disorder. Among these are secretion of growth hormone after pharmacological challenges, abnormalities in functioning of the hypothalamic–pituitary–adrenal axis, and abnormal sleep EEG patterns. Results to date do not suggest any single marker sufficiently sensitive to or specific to childhood or adolescent MDD that can be used for diagnostic purposes.

Effective treatment is a major current focus of research. Cognitive behavior therapy (CBT) involves working with the young person to understand and to modify thoughts and behaviors that are likely contributing to depression (see *Cognitive Therapy*). Interpersonal psychotherapy (IPT) involves working with the young person to understand the impact of relationship or role conflicts on depression and to modify interpersonal patterns (see *Interpersonal Psychotherapy*). There is considerable evidence to support the efficacy of CBT both for childhood and for adolescent depression, when compared to control conditions such as a waiting list (Birmaher et al. 1996b, Reinecke et al. 1998). Most of the child study subjects have been children with a depressive syndrome, and some of the interventions have been school-based. More of the adolescent studies have involved teenagers with a depressive disorder and have been clinic-based. There have been very few studies to date comparing CBT to other active treatments. IPT has also proven more

effective than clinical monitoring for depressed adolescents, both in terms of symptom reduction and in terms of improved social functioning (Mufson et al. 1999).

Studies of older tricyclic antidepressant medications did not demonstrate efficacy in children or adolescents. A recent study by Emslie and his colleagues (Emslie et al. 1997) using fluoxetine, a selective serotonin reuptake inhibitor, did show a significantly better outcome for those on medication than for those receiving a placebo. As is true in the psychosocial treatment arena, research on medication treatment has been limited to acute or short-term treatment.

Numerous critical questions remain to be investigated. These include the relative efficacy of various psychosocial, medication, and combined treatments, the long-term efficacy of such treatments, optimal duration of treatment, and effectiveness of university- or laboratory-based interventions in the broader clinical world. It is not yet clear whether individuals who fail to respond to a first treatment will do better with an alternative. Finally, a major challenge to treatment research is to identify strategies and methods to address the comorbid conditions that so often accompany depressive disorders in young people.

See also: Anxiety Disorder in Children; Behavior Therapy with Children; Child and Adolescent Psychiatry, Principles of; Childhood Health; Depression; Depression, Clinical Psychology of; Depression, Hopelessness, Optimism, and Health; Early Childhood: Socioemotional Risks; Infancy and Childhood: Emotional Development

Bibliography

American Psychiatric Association (APA) 1994 *Diagnostic and Statistical Manual of Mental Disorders*, 4th edn. APA, Washington, DC

Angold A, Costello E 1993 Depressive comorbidity in children and adolescents. *American Journal of Psychiatry* **150**: 1779–91

Birmaher B, Ryan N, Williamson D, Brent D, Kaufman J 1996b Childhood and adolescent depression (II). *Journal of the American Academy of Child and Adolescent Psychiatry* **35**: 1575–83

Birmaher B, Ryan N, Williamson D, Brent D, Kaufman J, Dahl R, Perel J, Nelson B 1996a Childhood and adolescent depression (I). *Journal of the American Academy of Child and Adolescent Psychiatry* **35**: 1427–39

Cicchetti D, Rogosch F, Toth S 1994 A developmental psychopathology perspective on depression in children and adolescents. In: Reynolds W, Johnston H (eds.) *Handbook of Depression in Children and Adolescents*. Plenum, New York pp. 123–41

Emslie G, Rush J, Weinberg W, Kowatch R, Hughes R, Carroll W, Carmody T, Rintelmann J 1997 A double-blind, randomized, placebo-controlled trial of fluoxetine in children and adolescents with depression. *Archives of General Psychiatry* **54**: 1031–7

Fleming J E, Offord D R 1990 Epidemiology of childhood depressive disorders—a critical review. *Journal of the American Academy of Child and Adolescent Psychiatry* **29**: 571–80

Harrington R, Fudge H, Rutter M, Pickles A, Hill J 1990 Adult outcomes of childhood and adolescent depression. *Archives of General Psychiatry* **47**: 465 73

Kovacs M 1996 The course of childhood-onset depressive disorders. *Psychiatric Annals* **26**: 326–30

Lewinsohn P, Hops H, Roberts R, Seeley J, Andrews J 1993 Adolescent psychopathology. *Journal of Abnormal Psychology* **102**: 133–44

Mufson L, Weissman M, Moreau D, Garfinkel R 1999 Efficacy of interpersonal psychotherapy for depressed adolescents. *Archives of General Psychiatry* **57**: 573–9

Reinecke M A, Ryan N, DuBois D 1998 Cognitive–behavioral therapy of depression and depressive symptoms during adolescence. *Journal of the American Academy of Child and Adolescent Psychiatry* **37**: 26–34

Reynolds W, Johnston H (eds.) 1994 *Handbook of Depression in Children and Adolescents.* Plenum, New York

J. F. Curry

Childhood Health

Child health psychology is an interdisciplinary field concerned with the physical, cognitive, social, and emotional functioning and development as they relate to health and illness issues in children, adolescents, and their families. It has emerged as a separate discipline, in recognition of the unique ways in which children are affected by illness compared with adults.

There are several reasons for establishing child health psychology as a separate discipline from that of adults. First, children's understanding of health, and the causes and implications of illness, differ from those of adults. Second, children's health is important both for understanding the current health of the child and in terms of implications for adult health. Children who adopt unhealthy lifestyles tend to become adults with unhealthy lifestyles. Third, diseases that affect children may have different implications for daily life compared with conditions that affect adults. Thus, children with diabetes need insulin on a daily basis, whereas many adults may be treated by diet or medication alone. Untreated, cancer in children is rapidly fatal, but may be more chronic in adults. Fourth, the impact of childhood illness is not restricted to the individual but affects the whole family. Parents, and doctors, make decisions on behalf of children, often with little clear understanding of the child's preferences.

Child health psychology is concerned with the relationship between psychological and physical well-being. The scope of child health psychology is generally considered to include the following:

(a) psychosocial contributions to outcomes in pediatric conditions;

(b) assessment and treatment of behavioral and emotional consequences of disease;

(c) role of psychology in health care settings;

(d) promotion of health and health-related behaviors;

(e) prevention of illness and injury among children and adolescents; and

(f) training.

In reviewing the achievements of child health psychology, this initial conceptualization has been followed, though it is immediately apparent that some areas have been the focus of much greater research activity than others.

1. Psychosocial Contributions to Outcomes in Pediatric Conditions

It has been argued that chronic illness challenges the child's normal development by limiting opportunities, restricting play and activities, the attainment of autonomy, and potentially compromising family and peer relationships. These effects may differ specifically as a function of the child's age. For infants, chronic illness is most likely to affect parent–child relationships, restrict mobility, or limit opportunities to socialize with peers. Separation from parents is a key issue. For older children, the impact will have a more direct effect in terms of reduced schooling, compromised peer relationships, more time with adults, concerns about body image, and awareness of vulnerability and possible death. Cancer in adolescence may extend a period of dependency on parents and reduce opportunities to establish close interpersonal relationships with the opposite sex.

Clinically, the study of how development proceeds despite such adversity is justified in terms of increasing our understanding of normal development, offering insights where problems occur and improving clinical services. The identification of protective factors, such as parenting, is also important. In some cases, family variables may be better indicators of outcome than illness predictors. Thus, Carlson-Green et al. (1995) studied 63 children who had been treated for a brain tumor. The best predictors of children's behavior problems were family and demographic variables, while the best predictors of achievement were illness and demographic variables. The implications are that outcome following traumatic illness and treatment may be very much influenced by positive family variables. Identification of factors that moderate outcomes is of central interest in child health psychology.

2. Assessment and Treatment of Behavioral and Emotional Consequences of Disease

Measurement of psychosocial adjustment has been central to research in this area. In that a central task of childhood is to develop toward an autonomous, healthy, and well-functioning adult, adjustment has been defined in developmental-normative terms. 'Good adjustment, then, is reflected as behavior that is age-appropriate, normative and healthy, and that follows a trajectory toward positive adult functioning. Maladjustment is mainly evidenced in behavior that is inappropriate for the particular age, especially when this behavior is qualitatively pathological or clinical in nature' (Wallander and Thompson 1995 pp. 125–6).

While the basic question concerning how illness and treatment affects the child's normal development is a very real one, the issue of measurement is complex. Standardized measures that capture the kind of experiences described so graphically by parents in interview studies are not available.

Measurement of adjustment has often been based on parents' reports and most commonly is assessed using the Child Behavior Checklist (Achenbach 1991). This measure has come under considerable criticism, not least because it lacks sensitivity for work with sick children (Perrin et al. 1991). Many of the items assess somatic symptoms. As a consequence, children with cancer (or any physical illness) inevitably have higher scores than healthy children (see *Childhood Cancer: Psychological Aspects*).

Improvements in the management of a number of life threatening conditions, for example, cancer and cystic fibrosis, have led to increased survival. However, this has been achieved at the cost of often daily, frequently painful, and certainly intrusive treatment regimens, which may continue for many years. Survival alone is therefore no longer perceived to be an adequate outcome measure. A central concern must be the extent to which treatment compromises quality of life (QoL). This change in emphasis has necessitated the development of alternative means of assessing treatment outcomes. Clinicians and researchers have therefore turned to measures of QoL to provide a more comprehensive account of individual patient experience as well as information on which to base decisions about service provision. Acceptance of this broader perspective on outcomes has led to a recognition of the need to identify methods of medical management, which impose fewer restrictions on quality of life.

Quality of life is a difficult concept to define and an even more difficult one to measure. Critical to most definitions is the notion that an individual's perception of their QoL is unique, and it therefore follows that efforts must be made to elicit information directly from the individual. Proxy ratings, as provided by caregivers, are useful, but not a substitute for an individual's own information.

Only some 3 percent of trials in pediatric oncology include a measure of QoL. There are few examples of their use in intervention studies (Kazak et al. 1996). To a large extent, this can be attributed to reticence on the part of clinicians to use the measures. Objections are generally based on perceptions of poor psychometric properties. In addition, many measures lack face validity; they do not appear to tap issues of relevance to the children under study. Many measures are criticized as too long, too repetitive, or simply inappropriate.

It would be appropriate to conclude this section with some discussion of the increasing use of qualitative measures. These are preferred by some, while others acknowledge the need for qualitative measures in combination with the more conventional quantitative measures. Qualitative methods can be used in the development of quantitative measures, ensuring that the latter include issues of importance to the target population. Qualitative methods may also be the method of choice in situations involving sensitive issues or for work with very young or handicapped children (Eiser and Twamley 1999).

3. Intervention Programs

Interventions have been reported to facilitate return to school following long illness. Varni et al. (1993), for example, reported a social skills program to teach children returning to school following diagnosis with cancer how to deal with other children's questions. A number of methods were used (e.g. role-play) to prepare children for teasing and allow them to develop the skills to know what to say and save face.

Other programs are aimed at improving self-care. Holzheimer et al. (1995), for example, used a teaching video, instruction booklet, and opportunities to rehearse the desired skills, and reported improved use of an inhaler in preschool children with asthma.

Efforts to treat procedure-related pain have been reported most frequently in pediatric oncology (see *Childhood Cancer: Psychological Aspects*). Children with cancer undergo regular painful procedures (e.g., lumbar punctures and bone marrow aspirations). The earliest reports by Jay et al. (1986) described interventions based on cognitive behavior therapy, including breathing exercises and use of imagery. Filmed modeling has also been used. Although the early reports were often based on a small number of case studies, more recent work has involved randomized clinical trials. Kazak et al. (1996) reported that a combined physiological and psychological intervention was more successful than a physiological intervention alone.

Interventions for disease-related pain for children remain poorly developed, despite the very high levels of pain experienced by children with conditions such as cancer, arthritis, hemophilia, and sickle cell disease. Interventions need to target both disease-related pain and the child's perceptions of pain. Walco et al. (1999) conclude that more work is needed which documents the emergence of pain experiences and coping over time. Interventions need to be based on a variety of approaches, and target the pain experience within a social and family context.

Schools based programs for children with headaches may be particularly successful. Larsson and Carlsson (1996) randomized 26 children aged 10–15 years with chronic tension type headache to a nurse administered relaxation training intervention or no treatment control. The five-week program involved twice weekly sessions, each lasting approximately 20 minutes. Headache activity was reduced in children in the intervention group at post-treatment and six-month follow-up compared with the no treatment controls.

4. The Promotion of Health and Health-related Behaviors

Drug and alcohol use among teenagers and adolescents usually occurs in group situations, and the use of such substances has been found to be strongly motivated by self-presentational desires such as the need for social approval and peer acceptance. Family factors, including parental modeling (often parents themselves are heavy users of the substance), and the family–child relationship, are key risk factors for subsequent substance use. In addition, peer relationships appear to be strongly related to the extent of alcohol and illicit drug use. Both types of substance abuse seem to be more common among those who report academic difficulty or poor adjustment at school. Other reasons for the illicit use of alcohol and drugs include the wish to convey autonomy or rebelliousness, and the reduction of anxiety in intergroup settings. Some may use alcohol or drugs if they feel unable to cope with the pressures associated with growing up; as a sort of temporary escape from school problems, social anxieties, or home difficulties.

5. Issues Relating to Training

The nature of much of the work with children involves collaboration with other professionals: clinicians, teachers, and social services. Issues of training particularly need to address the potential obstacles to successful collaboration. There is inevitably some friction between psychologists and pediatricians in the way in which they approach research and clinical issues concerned with chronically sick children. While both share some ideals about what should be done to help children with chronic conditions and their families, their training and experience does not necessarily mean that they share the same research agenda.

6. Future Directions

Increasing recognition of the closeness between physical and psychological health has contributed to an increasing visibility of psychological factors in pediatric medicine. So too have changes in treatment. In reality, caring for the child with chronic illness is not always about achieving a cure, but should be about enhancing the QoL. As such, there is pressure to include measures of QoL as an integral part of the evaluation of clinical trials. The development of disease-specific QoL scales means that health outcomes can now be considered from a more holistic point of view. QoL measures also have a role in evaluating innovative treatments. Children undergoing bone marrow transplants necessarily experience isolation, pain, and lengthy hospitalizations, and assessments of their QoL during treatment and after are essential.

Given the increasing costs of health care, it is critical that treatments are evaluated in terms of both physical and psychological well-being. Thus, evaluations of the success or otherwise of growth hormone therapy must not be based on height alone, but consideration also needs to be given to the child's psychological well-being.

There remains scope for considerable improvements in measures available. Current work rarely draws on expertise in developmental psychology to direct the format or content of measures. There is an emerging literature documenting children's language, memory, and emotional development, much of which could be used to guide new measures. It is also important that measures are based on a theoretical framework. In the past, theory has been sparse or embedded in a model of maladjustment. It is likely that theories of normal child development will prove more useful in the future.

Despite the criticisms that can be made, there is no doubt that the establishment of a child health psychology in itself has done much to increase the profile of work with children. The difficulties involved may be considerable, but these also contribute to its attractiveness. That children have a unique perspective on life, despite the hardships of a serious illness, is without debate. From such a perspective, and for many people, work with children is therefore not only humbling, but intrinsically more satisfying, than work with other groups.

See also: Adolescent Health and Health Behaviors; Child Care and Child Development; Childhood Depression

Bibliography

Achenbach T M 1991 *Manual for the Child Behavior Checklist/4-18 and 1991 Profile*. Department of Psychiatry, University of Vermont, Burlington, VT

Bradlyn A S, Ritchey A K, Harris C V, Moore A K, O'Brien R T, Parsons S K, Pattersan K, Pollock B H 1995 Quality of life research in pediatric oncology: Research methods and barriers. *Cancer* **78**: 1333–9

Carlson-Green B, Morris R D, Krawiecki N 1995 Family and illness predictors of outcome in pediatric brain tumors. *Journal of Pediatric Psychology* **20**: 769–84

Eiser C, Cotter I, Oades P, Seamark D, Smith R 1999 Health-related quality of life measures for children. *International Journal of Cancer* **512**: 87–90

Eiser C, Twamley S 1999 Talking to children about health and illness. In: Murray M, Chamberlain K (eds.) *Qualitative Health Psychology: Theories and Methods*. Sage, London

Holzheimer L, Mohay H, Masters I B 1998 Educating young children about asthma: Comparing the effectiveness of a developmentally appropriate asthma education videotape and picture book. *Child: Care, Health and Development* **24**: 85–99

Jay S M, Elliott C, Varni J W 1986 Acute and chronic pain in adults and children with cancer. *Journal of Consulting and Clinical Psychology* **54**: 601–7

Juniper E F, Guyatt G H, Feeny D H, Ferrie P J, Griffith L E, Townsend M 1996 Measuring quality of life in children with asthma. *Quality of Life Research* **5**: 35–46

Kazak A E, Penati B, Boyer B A, Himelstein B, Brophy P, Waibel K, Blackall G F, Daller R, Johnson K 1996 A randomized controlled prospective outcome study of a psychological and intervention pharmaceutical protocol for procedural distress in pediatric leukemia. *Journal of Pediatric Psychology* **21**: 615–32

Landgraf J M, Abetz L, Ware J E 1996 *Child Health Questionnaire (CHQ): A Users Manual*. The Health Institute, New England Medical Centre

Larsson B, Carlsson J 1996 A school-based, nurse administered relaxation training for children with chronic tension-type headache. *Journal of Pediatric Psychology* **21**: 603–14

Perrin E C, Stein R E K, Drotar D 1991 Cautions in using the Child Behavior Checklist: Observations based on research about children with a chronic illness. *Journal of Pediatric Psychology* **16**: 411–21

Peterson L, Oliver K K, Brazeal T J, Bull C A 1996 A developmental exploration of expectations for and beliefs about preventing bicycle collision injuries. *Journal of Pediatric Psychology* **20**: 13–22

Varni J W, Katz E R, Colegrove R, Dolgin M 1993 The impact of social skills training on the adjustment of children with newly diagnosed cancer. *Journal of Pediatric Psychology* **18**: 751–67

Walco G A, Sterling C M, Conte P M, Engel R G 1999 Empirically supported treatments in pediatric psychology: Disease related pain. *Journal of Pediatric Psychology* **24**: 155–67

Wallander J L, Thompson R J 1995 Psychosocial adjustment of children with chronic physical conditions. In: Roberts M C (ed.) *Handbook of Pediatric Psychology*. Guilford Press, New York, Vol. 2

C. Eiser

Childhood Sexual Abuse and Risk for Adult Psychopathology

1. Overview of the Issue

Numerous studies on the prevalence, characteristics, and consequences of childhood sexual abuse (CSA) have been conducted since the 1970s, but deriving conclusions about this literature has been hampered by the wide variability in definitions and methods used across studies. Nonetheless, enough research has accumulated from both clinical and general population studies to support the claim that CSA is significantly *correlated* with increased risk for various forms of adult psychopathology. There has been disagreement, however, about whether CSA *causes* adult psychopathology. Since the 1990s, a few studies have been conducted that allow for causal interpretations about the effects of CSA on adult psychopathology.

The purpose of this article is to describe the historical and scientific development of CSA research, from early clinical studies to current studies of the general population. Definitional and methodological issues in CSA research will be discussed, and a review of recent studies that have used powerful methodologies for understanding cause-and-effect relationships will be presented. Finally, some general conclusions about the effects of CSA on adult psychopathology will be provided, and future directions for this research will be suggested.

2. The Historical Development of Research on Childhood Sexual Abuse

The evolution of CSA research, as discussed below, has followed a three-phase course that roughly parallels the progression of research found in all psychiatric epidemiological research: (a) pioneering publications and numerous clinical studies; (b) studies using non-clinical (general population) samples to estimate prevalence and correlates of CSA; and (c) studies using scientifically rigorous methods that allow for cause-and-effect conclusions about CSA and adult psychopathology.

2.1 Phase 1 Research: Pioneering Publications and Clinical Research

Modern awareness of the prevalence, characteristics, and possible consequences of CSA in the USA can be traced to the late 1970s and early 1980s. During this first phase of modern CSA research, a few pioneering publications, most notably Finkelhor's *Sexually Victimized Children* in 1979 and Russell's *Sexual Exploitation: Rape, Child Sexual Abuse, Sexual Harassment* in 1984 provided data that indicated CSA occurred frequently to children and adolescents in the USA. Following these works, public attention to CSA was further stimulated by several highly publicized media accounts of CSA, and clinical research increased dramatically. Results from early clinical studies were mostly of women, and indicated a high percentage of women reporting CSA, with many women indicating that the abuse involved family members and/or serious abuse (i.e., intercourse CSA). These studies also found that a history of CSA was associated with elevated rates of several psychological problems, including substance abuse, anxiety disorders, depression, self-injurious behaviors, and interpersonal functioning deficits. As a result of this increased attention to CSA, dramatic changes in the reporting and verification of CSA occurred in the USA: from 1976 to 1993, there was a 25-fold increase in verified cases of CSA. Although much of the original research on CSA in the 1970s and 1980s was centered on the USA, other countries, including Canada, the UK, and several European nations began or increased research on CSA.

2.2 Phase 2 Research: General Population Studies of Prevalence and Correlates of CSA

The second phase of CSA research in the early 1980s addressed a methodological limitation of earlier studies i.e., that most early studies were based on samples of children who were identified as being abused (forensic samples) or samples of adults who were in treatment (clinical samples). These studies were limited because results from forensic and clinical samples may differ significantly from results found among persons who did not report the abuse or who were not in treatment. Numerous nonclinical studies used college samples, but again, women and men in college who report a history of CSA may not generalize to the adult general population for many reasons, including that college students may over-represent socioeconomically advantaged persons and under-represent psychologically impaired persons. Some researchers have also argued that first-year college students may have very recently experienced CSA, and long-term consequences have not yet occurred.

Forensic, clinical, and college samples studies are quite important for developing a base of research to build upon, but the most scientifically rigorous sampling design is one that uses a random sample from the general population. Random sampling indicates that every person in an identified community or even an entire country has an equal chance of being selected for the study (although random samples may exclude certain age groups or persons living in institutions).

In CSA research, the basic methodology of a general population study is to ask adult participants if they experienced any sexually abusive acts during childhood (the adult retrospective recall method). Researchers also often ask participants to report the characteristics of the abuse (e.g., who was the abuser, the ages of the abuser and participant), any known effects of the abuse, and/or any current psychological problems they may be experiencing.

Over 20 adult retrospective studies with general population samples were conducted in North America in the last two decades of the twentieth century, and prevalence rates varied dramatically across studies, with about 2–62 percent in women and 3–16 percent in men. Sources of this variability include differences in (a) definitions of CSA; (b) geographical region of sample; (c) methods of data collection (telephone, mailed, or face-to-face interviews); (d) response rates; and (e) the number of questions used to ask about CSA. Definitions of CSA have varied across all studies to date, primarily in four dimensions: (a) the ages used to delimit childhood (most use 18 or 16); (b) whether or not the respondent is asked to self-define the experience as 'abusive' (e.g., asking if the experience was unwanted, the result of force or trickery, and/or was considered abusive); (c) whether or not differences in age between the respondent and the perpetrator are used to define CSA; and (d) the types of sexual activities asked about (e.g., contact only acts vs. both contact and noncontact acts).

Different definitions of CSA and the number of screening questions used most likely contribute to most of the variability across studies. Definitions that use older age cutoffs, and include both contact and noncontact acts produce higher prevalence rates. In addition, surveys that use two or more screening questions for CSA typically result in higher prevalence rates compared to surveys using only a single question. For a thorough review of how different definitions and methods influence prevalence rates of CSA, see Finkelhor (1994). In this report, Finkelhor reviews the bulk of studies to date, and concludes that about 20 percent of North American women and about 5–10 percent of North American men report a history of CSA experiences that include both contact and non-contact acts. The 20 percent estimate for women is consistent with a recent nationally representative study of women in the USA that used multiple screening items for CSA and face-to-face interviews (Vogeltanz et al. 1999). Prevalence estimates from other countries, including Australia, the UK, The Netherlands, New Zealand, Spain, Sweden, and Switzerland, appear to be fairly consistent with the North American estimates, suggesting that CSA occurs at fairly consistent rates in European and English-speaking countries.

Some of these earlier general population studies measured possible consequences of CSA, but most varied significantly in the types of psychological problems assessed and the instruments used. For example, many studies used unstandardized questions about the occurrence of numerous psychological symptoms, others used standardized questionnaires and psychological symptom checklists, and a very few used structured clinical interviews that allowed the researcher to make a clinical diagnosis for several psychological disorders. Although results from these studies varied, the majority, like earlier clinical studies, reported significant relationships between adult women's reports of experiencing CSA and their greater likelihood of experiencing current symptoms of substance abuse, depression, anxiety, sexual functioning problems, eating problems, and self-injurious behaviors. A large limitation of these studies, as with earlier clinical studies, was the relative lack of inclusion of men. Researchers preliminarily concluded that men with a history of CSA were also reporting elevated rates of various psychological problems.

In addition to reporting on the simple (bivariate) relationships between CSA and adult psychological problems in the general population, a few researchers looked at whether some characteristics of CSA might be more predictive of adult psychological problems. This preliminary data suggested that frequent and/or severe abuse, and abuse by a biological parent have been modestly, but consistently linked to a greater likelihood of problems in adulthood.

By the 1990s, several comprehensive reviews of CSA research had been published, with most authors claiming that CSA was correlated with numerous psychological problems, symptoms, or disorders. However, the majority of studies on CSA did not use methodologies that could determine if CSA *caused* adult problems, and several researchers challenged this causal assumption. The basic argument was that many persons who report a history of CSA also report that their childhood family environments were pathologic, including such problems as conflicts with parent(s), physical or emotional abuse, lack of parental warmth or caring, living with only one biological parent, and parental psychopathology. Therefore, it may be these family environment factors are the causes of adult psychopathology as well as a risk factor for the occurrence of CSA. For an example of a prominent debate on this issue, see Nash et al. (1998). As a result of these challenges, it became incumbent upon CSA researchers to address this issue in future research.

To address cause-and-effect issues in epidemiological research, researchers must use either prospective designs or rigorous multivariate studies (see a description below on these methods). This final phase of research is complex and very costly, and only a few studies to date have been rigorous enough to allow for cause-and-effect interpretations. A summary of this work is described below.

2.3 Phase 3 Research: Studies Examining the Causal Status of CSA on Adult Psychopathology

To date, only a few studies have been able to test adequately for a causal relationship between CSA and adult psychopathology. Although these studies vary in their definitions of CSA and measures of psychopathology, they are similar in three important ways. First, all the studies had large general population random samples of adults, or in one case, a nationally representative random sample of 10- to 16-year-olds. Second, all of the studies used sophisticated methodologies that allowed for some level of causal interpretation. These methods were of two types: a prospective design, in which researchers collect multiple measures from individuals over time, therefore capturing a more accurate account of what happened before and after the occurrence of CSA; or cross-

sectional multivariate designs, in which data about early family environment, the occurrence of CSA, and adult psychopathology are gathered at one point in time. Two twin studies using a cross-sectional multivariate design are also included here because the twin study provides unique information about possible genetic contributions to risk for CSA and highly shared environments. Although cross-sectional multivariate designs cannot definitively test for causal relationships, rigorous multivariate methodologies provide a high degree of confidence about causality. Finally, all of the studies used structured diagnostic interviews allowing for clinical diagnosis of psychological disorders. Although standardized questionnaires may also provide an important way of measuring levels of psychological symptoms or distress in the general population, a diagnosis provides a clear statement that the individuals being interviewed have experienced significant impairment in their lives. Diagnoses also provide information about lifetime occurrence of disorders, whereas symptom checklists typically assess only for current levels of functioning.

The studies that meet the above criteria come from the USA, Australia, and New Zealand. In the first of two general population prospective studies, Fergusson and colleagues (1996) made yearly evaluations of a New Zealand sample of over 1,000 children from birth to age 18. At age 18, CSA before age 16 and diagnosable psychological disorders were measured. Results were that CSA significantly predicted major depression, anxiety disorder, conduct disorder, substance use disorder, and suicidal behaviors after controlling for prospectively measured family environment factors. The highest risk for having a psychological disorder was found among individuals reporting CSA intercourse experiences.

Boney-McCoy and Finkelhor (1996) used a prospective design in which they interviewed a nationally representative sample of children, aged 10–16, at two times, approximately 15 months apart. Results were that sexual assaults occurring to the children after the Time 1 interview predicted Time 2 diagnoses of major depression after controlling for previous lifetime occurrence of depression, the quality of the parent–child relationship, parental education, race, and whether the child lived with both parents. However, the strength of the sexual assault–major depression association was weaker after controlling for family environment factors.

Using a large random New Zealand community sample of women, Mullen and his colleagues (1993) reported that CSA was independently related to several diagnosed psychological disorders, after controlling for inadequate parenting, parental divorce, and early physical abuse. This study also found that the severity of abuse was the strongest predictor of later problems.

Finally, two twin studies also supported the independent effects of CSA on adult psychological disorders, controlling for different aspects of family environment. Dinwiddie et al. (2000) conducted diagnostic interviews and measured CSA in 2,700 Australian twin pairs (male and female monozygotic and dizygotic pairs). A single question assessed for 'forced' CSA, and diagnoses were obtained for substance abuse, major depression, anxiety disorders, and conduct disorder. The only family environment factor measured was parental psychopathology. CSA significantly predicted all diagnoses in women and all but social phobia in men, after controlling for parental alcoholism and depression. The authors reported that when one twin reported CSA and the other twin did not (discordant for CSA), rates of disorders were not significantly different. However, further analyses revealed much higher rates of disorders among twins who were both abused (concordant), indicating that CSA may have specific effects on the development of disorders.

In the most recent and most sophisticated multivariate twin study to date, 1,411 adult female twins from the USA were given structured clinical interviews to determine lifetime diagnoses of major depression, generalized anxiety disorder, panic disorder, bulimia nervosa, alcohol dependence, drug dependence, and the presence of two or more of the disorders (comorbidity). CSA was measured using multiple screening questions to determine both contact and noncontact abuse. Several family environment factors were measured, but, uniquely, the researchers interviewed the respondents' parents, and made clinical diagnoses of disorders and obtained parent ratings of various family environment factors. Results were that self-reported CSA of any kind was significantly associated with all disorders, except bulimia nervosa, after controlling for parental (or twin) reported family environment factors and history of parental psychopathology. In all disorders (including bulimia nervosa), intercourse CSA was more strongly related to psychological disorders than any other CSA form (genital, nongenital, or any CSA). As in the previous twin study, the cotwin control analyses indicated that there are specific effects of CSA on adult psychopathology, but that shared environmental factors clearly contribute to both risk of CSA and development of future disorders.

3. Conclusions

The studies reviewed used the most scientifically rigorous methods to date for testing the causal relation between CSA and adult psychopathology. The studies also had the benefit of all using the same type of measurement for adult psychopathology, a clinical interview that used psychiatric diagnostic criteria for determining the presence of a disorder. The studies support four main conclusions. (a) The statistical relationship between CSA and adult psychopathology remains significant after controlling for certain aspects of negative family environment, although the strength of the relationship attenuates from slightly to considerably, depending on the psychological disorder being predicted. (b) The reported strength or size of the independent relationships between CSA and risk for adult psychopathology were modest, indicating that (i) family environment serves as both a risk factor for CSA and a mediator for the effects of CSA on adult psychopathology; and (ii) many individuals who report a history of CSA do not develop adult problems. (c) More severe forms of CSA i.e., intercourse CSA, lead to a greater risk of developing psychological disorders. (d) Men were under-represented in these studies, but when studied, also had similar risks to women for developing psychological disorders as a consequence of CSA history.

4. Future Directions

Research on the prevalence, characteristics, and correlates of CSA has progressed enormously in the last two decades, and findings from each phase of research have informed the next. Despite this progress, there are still some core problems that should be corrected, including the need for standard definitions of CSA, more information about what measurement strategies result in the most accurate information about CSA, and the inclusion of more men in studies. Findings from current research indicate the need for future studies of CSA that assess for a wide range of family environment factors, because it is now certain that the effects of CSA on adult psychological problems are influenced by the familial context in which children live. There is no consensus, however, on which aspects of family environment most influence responses to traumatic events such as CSA, and this research is needed. Although there is some data suggesting that more severe forms of CSA lead to greater risk for adult problems, there is still much to be learned about how characteristics of the abuse may influence later problems, and how abuse characteristics may interact with family environment factors. For example, there is no information about how family environment factors may interact with CSA differently, depending on whether or not the abuser lives in the home with the child. Finally, more information is needed about what happens after CSA, including measurement of subsequent psychological problems, coping methods, and determining what factors seem to protect individuals from developing long-term psychological problems. In order to answer these questions, CSA researchers must continue to use prospective and multivariate cross-sectional studies, but there continues to be a great need for clinical and forensic studies that can inform the direction of more costly epidemiological studies.

See also: Anxiety Disorder in Children; Behavior Therapy with Children; Child Abuse; Child and

Adolescent Psychiatry, Principles of; Child Care and Child Development; Childhood Depression; Children and the Law; Children, Rights of: Cultural Concerns; Sex Offenders, Clinical Psychology of; Violence and Effects on Children

Bibliography

Boney-McCoy S, Finkelhor D 1996 Is youth victimization related to trauma and depression after controlling for prior symptoms and family relationships? A longitudinal study. *Journal of Consulting and Clinical Psychology* **64**: 1406–16

Conte J R 1994 Child sexual abuse: Awareness and backlash. *Future of Children* **4**: 224 32

Dinwiddie S, Heath A C, Dunne M P, Bucholz K K, Madden P A F, Slutske W S, Bierut L J, Statham D B, Martin N G 2000 Early sexual abuse and lifetime psychopathology: A co-twin control study. *Psychological Medicine* **30**: 41–52

Finkelhor D 1979 *Sexually Victimized Children*. Free Press, New York

Fergusson D M, Horwood L J, Lynskey M T 1996 Childhood sexual abuse and psychiatric disorder in young adulthood, II: Psychiatric outcomes of childhood sexual abuse. *Journal of the American Academy of Child and Adolescent Psychiatry* **35**: 1365–74

Finkelhor D 1994 Current information on the scope and nature of child sexual abuse. *Future of Children* **4**: 31–53

Kendler K S, Bulik C M, Silberg J, Hettema J M, Myers J, Prescott C A 2000 Childhood sexual abuse and psychiatric and substance use disorders in women. *Archives of General Psychiatry* **57**: 953–9

Mullen P E, Martin J L, Anderson J C, Romans S E, Herbison G P 1993 Childhood sexual abuse and mental health in adult life. *British Journal of Psychiatry* **163**: 721–32

Nash M R, Neimeyer R A, Hulsey T L, Lambert W 1998 Psychopathology associated with sexual abuse: The importance of complementary designs and common ground. *Journal of Consulting and Clinical Psychology* **66**: 568–71

Rind B, Tromovitch P, Bauserman R 1998 A meta-analytic examination of assumed properties of child sexual abuse using college samples. *Psychological Bulletin* **124**: 22–53

Russell D E H 1984 *Sexual Exploitation: Rape, Child Sexual Abuse, Sexual Harassment*. Sage, Beverly Hills, CA

Vogeltanz N D, Wilsnack S C, Harris T R, Wilsnack R W, Wonderlich S A, Kristjanson A F 1999 Prevalence and risk factors for childhood sexual abuse in women: National survey findings. *Child Abuse & Neglect* **23**: 579–92

N. D. Vogeltanz-Holm

Children and the Law

The ways in which the law has positioned children have varied from society to society and over time. In part this is due to differences and changes in family life, in the material world that children inhabit, and in the way we think about children. The legal standing of children today in the West would be unrecognizable to the eighteenth century observer, who would have seen children as the property of the father. The law relating to children reflects changes in women's legal standing as well as global diversity and changing social and cultural attitudes and practices. With the rapid development of international law in the second half of the twentieth century global variations have become more visible and contested. These variations express some of the key social and political tensions raised by the changing significance of childhood at the beginning of the twenty-first century. So despite the emergence of international laws on children, the ways in which children's welfare and rights are secured differ.

1. A Brief History of Children and the Law

Under the Roman civil law doctrine of *patria potestas* the father had unlimited control over his children. This doctrine shaped Western legal systems' vesting of parental rights in the father to the exclusion of the mother until the eighteenth and nineteenth centuries. Within Anglo-American jurisprudence, the common law treated the father as the legitimate child's natural guardian. Legislative reform throughout the nineteenth century encroached upon the rights of the father, giving mothers limited rights to custody of their children in specific circumstances. By the early twentieth century the welfare of the child had become the guiding principle in disputes over children on divorce. However it was only much later in the twentieth century that the rights of mothers and fathers within marriage in relation to their children were equalized.

With the rise in divorce and parental separation in the last decades of the twentieth century and the questioning of earlier norms by the growing feminist movements (Bridgeman and Monk 2000) legislatures and policy makers considered how the welfare of those children affected could be properly safeguarded and promoted. Developments have included the emergence of alternative dispute resolution, the delegalization of family disputes and the adoption of 'no-fault' divorce (Eekelaar and Katz 1984). (See *Family Law*.)

1.1 Legitimacy

While legitimate children were seen as the property of the father, illegitimate children were seen as the property of no one. Such a child was *nullius filius* and had no legal relationship with his or her parents. The early bastardy laws were aimed at preventing illegitimate children from becoming a charge on the community—and attempted to do so by punishing the unmarried mother and the reputed father, and charging either the mother or both for the relief of the child. In the twentieth century, the status of the illegitimate child has changed substantially as has the language concerning legitimacy. Article 25(2) of the Universal Declaration of Human Rights 1948 provides that 'all children, whether born in or out of wedlock, shall enjoy the same social protection' and Article 2(2) of the United Nations Convention on the Rights of the Child 1989 (UNCRC) requires states to take all 'appropriate measures to ensure that the child is protected against all forms of discrimination or punishment on the basis of the status ... of the child's parents.' Some countries have abolished the concept of illegitimacy altogether, others have permitted legitimation by subsequent marriage and have legislated to mitigate the adverse legal consequences by extending to illegitimate children the same rights accorded to legitimate children. The parental status of the father has been increasingly recognized in some countries; others, such as those in South Asia continue to recognize only the nonmarital child's legal relationship with the mother (Goonesekere 1998).

1.2 Child Welfare and Protection

Much of the history of children and the law has been dominated by campaigns to protect children and to advance their welfare. The traditional account of the history of childhood is a story of rescue. The nineteenth century witnessed the development of agencies that were dedicated to rescuing children from abuse and neglect within the family. Societies for the prevention of cruelty to children were established in many Western cities, and by the early twentieth century there were over 34 such societies in the USA and fifteen elsewhere. By the late twentieth century, child rescue had become an international as well as national cause (Kent 1995, Van Bueren 1998).

Then, as today, there was debate surrounding the proper role of the state regarding intervention into family life. The ideology of family privacy and the idea that children were the property of their parents combined to render legislatures reluctant to encroach too far into family life. However children of poor and working class families were more visible and more intensively policed than those from wealthier and more powerful sections of the community. The 'discovery' of 'the battered child' in the middle of the twentieth century, and of child sexual abuse in the final decades, gave rise to significant changes in legal practice, such as revisions in the rules regarding the admissibility of children's testimony.

In contrast to the legislative reluctance to intervene in any substantial way with the parent–child relationship, there was considerable legislative activity in the nineteenth and twentieth centuries to protect children from exploitation and abuse outside the home and to better advance their welfare. In the public sphere in industrializing countries, laws were introduced to restrict and finally to prohibit the employment of children in various occupations (e.g., in factories and coal mines). Initially such legislation restricted the hours worked; with the advent of compulsory education laws children were further withdrawn from the labor force. Concerns about child health resulted in measures to reduce infant mortality rates and to improve diet through welfare provision such as school meals. Such measures benefited all children by improving public hygiene, but many focused on the urban poor.

1.3 Institutional Developments

The development of mass education for children in the nineteenth and twentieth centuries has resulted in the school becoming central to the experience of childhood. The law relating to children and education was controversial given that disputes over education raised issues around parental rights, religious freedom, and social justice.

Another institutional expression of the legal and social changes surrounding childhood was the growth of the juvenile court movement in the late nineteenth and early twentieth centuries (see *Juvenile Justice: International Law Perspectives*). Between 1899 and 1908, juvenile courts had been set up in states in the USA, Australia, and England (Mack 1909). Separate penal institutions for juvenile offenders had already been established with reformatories for juvenile offenders being built in the USA and England by the mid-nineteenth century. The rationale for these developments was that children were harmed by exposure to adult depravity, especially within the penal system, that children were more victims than villains, and that with timely and appropriate intervention the child could be rescued from a life of crime and immorality. In a number of jurisdictions there was no distinction made between the child who offended and the neglected child—both were seen as the victim of the socioeconomic environment. The dominance of welfare considerations in the juvenile courts, however, resulted in the neglect of procedural rights for children. Procedural justice for children in the criminal and civil justice systems became an issue in the 1960s and 1970s in a number of jurisdictions. For example in the USA the Supreme Court decision in Re Gault (1965) established that children were entitled to the protection of the Constitution.

Later the idea of a family court emerged in response to the demand that decisions taken in relation to children needed to be informed by specialist knowledge about their needs and welfare. This in turn has led to the emergence of specialist judges in some jurisdictions.

Despite significant historical variations in the position of children under the law, by the end of the twentieth century in civil proceedings the child's welfare was treated as the primary if not paramount consideration. The language used in many legal systems is no longer that of parental rights alone but rather of parental responsibility; rights that parents do enjoy must be exercised for the benefit of the child. The child is no longer seen as the property of parents.

2. The Welfare of Children

Today most legal systems consider the child's welfare to be a primary consideration in the resolution of disputes involving children—a position reinforced by the near universal signing and ratification of the UNCRC.

The law relating to children is increasingly expressed in terms of advancing their welfare though there are exceptions (see Sect. 2.2). The centrality of the welfare of the child is expressed in domestic and international law. Principle 1 of the UN Declaration of the Rights of the Child 1959 provides that in the enactment of laws for the special protection of children 'the best interests of the child shall be the paramount consideration.' This set the international benchmark for assessing legislation affecting the welfare of children until the UNCRC of 1989. The UNCRC is based on the '3 Ps': rights to protection, provision, and participation. Article 3 of the UNCRC provides that: 'In all actions concerning children, whether undertaken by public or private social welfare institutions, courts of law, administrative authorities or legislative bodies, the best interests of the child shall be a primary consideration.' Article 3 is wider than Principle 1 of the UN Declaration insofar as it states that the child's welfare shall be the primary consideration of 'public or private social welfare institutions.'

While the welfare principle is the primary concern in judicial proceedings affecting children the ability of legislation directly to safeguard and promote the welfare of children is limited by the material and ideological circumstances of their upbringing. The condition of children in the world today varies enormously; this can be seen in different mortality rates, child labor, access to education, malnutrition, the prevalence of child prostitution, and the presence of child soldiers. These issues give rise to intense debate nationally and internationally. For example, while Article 32 of the UNCRC requires states parties to the UNCRC to recognize the right of the child to be protected from economic exploitation and from performing any work that is likely to be hazardous or to interfere with the child's education' child labor, including bonded labor, is still widespread throughout South Asia and South America. The International Labour Organization Convention No.138 links the child labor issue with education and provides that the minimum age for admission to employment must not be lower than the compulsory school age and in any event should not be lower than 15.

The debates surrounding the welfare rights of children are intense because they raise questions regarding state power, whose definition of welfare prevails, and respect for the child's identity and community. These issues are contested at both the national and global level (Alston 1994).

2.1 Children and Families

The conventional account of the different ways in which children are treated by the law has two divergent strands—one that emphasizes the child's place within a particular family (belonging to a specific religious, ethnic, and cultural community) and one that offers a more individualized approach, recognizing the distinctiveness of interests even within the family. Domestic and international law sees the child's family as being the natural and proper environment for the child's upbringing; even though the concept of the family is undergoing change, ranging from increased cohabitation to gay marriage and adoption (Cornell 1998). There is considerable social value in ensuring that, within limits, parents should be free to bring up their children in a way that is consistent with their own values and beliefs. However, there is variation in how legal systems regulate family life, and in particular how they allocate powers and duties to parents and determine the circumstances in which family privacy can be overridden.

2.1.1 Child abuse. While child abuse is not confined to the family, much of the debate about the legal framework focuses on this setting. The abuse of children in 'public care' (while regularly plagued by scandal) tends to generate discussion about the accountability of welfare bureaucracies and the quality of care provided by the corporate parent. Abuse within the home gives rise to special problems for legal systems. Not only do childrearing practices vary, but some groups (e.g., the urban poor) are subject to more coercive forms of intervention than others. In some jurisdictions, for example, the grounds for intervening into family life in order to protect children are drawn in broad terms (e.g., statutes identify 'immorality' as constituting neglect and thus permit the removal of the child), while in others there is a minimum harm threshold that has to be satisfied if any intervention is to be justified. Jurisdictions vary in the degree to which they adjudicate between the competing values of parents' right to raise their children according to their own values, on the one hand, and the child's right to be protected, on the other (Schwartz-Kenney et al. 2001).

2.1.2 Relationship breakdown. The rise in relationship breakdown in the West has led to a number of significant developments.

There has been an increase in disputes over the custody of children when relationships end. Many jurisdictions have moved towards no-fault divorce, and where private ordering is unsuccessful disputes over children are increasingly resolved via mediation. Where such disputes are not resolved through mediation, court adjudication tends to focus on the welfare of the child. The enforcement of orders made in relation to custody and access, or contact, is problematic; the courts in some jurisdictions (such as the USA) at times threaten to imprison the custodial parent if they continue to refuse to allow the noncustodial parent access.

Custody disputes occasionally involve child abductions. Most states have provisions dealing with child abduction nationally and have entered into bilateral and regional treaties to deter the practice (e.g., the Inter-American Convention on the International Return of Children 1989). At the international level, the Hague Convention on the Civil Aspects of International Child Abduction (1980), which has been signed by over 50 countries including most in North and South America and Europe, focuses on the enforcement of rights of custody between contracting states. The Convention applies where a child has been wrongfully removed or retained in breach of rights of custody. The principle behind the Convention is that children who have been abducted should be returned immediately to the country from which they have been abducted and that any dispute as to custody should be resolved within that jurisdiction. Article 13 of the Hague Convention provides defenses to an order for the immediate return of the child including where the child objects and has attained an age and maturity where it is appropriate to take account of his or her views. This recognition of the autonomy rights of the child reflects how far the law has moved away from the idea that children are the property of their parents.

2.2 Juvenile Crime

While legal doctrine, procedure, and philosophy regarding the treatment of juvenile offenders vary across nations, international law at the end of the twentieth century has begun to lay down minimum rules for the administration of juvenile justice. In 1985 the UN General Assembly adopted the UN Standard Minimum Rules for the Administration of Juvenile Justice (the 'Beijing Rules'). The Beijing Rules constitute a benchmark against which national juvenile justice systems can be measured covering the investigation, prosecution, and punishment of juvenile crime.

Today the trend is towards a balancing of welfare and punishment considerations. The discrediting of aspects of the rehabilitative ideal in some countries in the 1960s and 1970s has led to a pragmatism and managerialism in juvenile justice. Increasingly juvenile offenders are segregated from adult offenders and diversion and reparation schemes have developed to reduce the risk of contamination from the formal justice system and to underscore the offender's responsibility to the victim and the wider community. However in some countries (e.g., some states in the USA) there are moves to treat juvenile offenders as if they were adults, including exposing them to the possibility of capital punishment for offences committed whilst a minor (Strater 1995).

3. The Modern Children's Rights Movement

It is now accepted that children have rights (Freeman 1997). The meaning and realization of such rights is contested locally and globally. Ideas about children's rights are linked with the child's own community and culture.

The UNCRC signals that children have civil, political, and social rights. These 'human rights' are not just concerned with the welfare of children, though many of the UNCRC's provisions are concerned with their protection (e.g., from abuse) and the adequate provisioning of childhood. The distinctive feature of the modern children's rights movement is that alongside the traditional concern with the welfare and protection rights of children it aims to promote their 'liberty rights.' The rights contained in Articles 12 to 16 of the UNCRC, are indispensable to developing respect for the children in society and to fostering their participation in the community (De Winter 1997). The UNCRC has also acted as a catalyst for the further development of children's ombudsmen (Flekkoy 1991)

However the meaning of the right to participate is contested (see Ncube 1998), and legal systems are cautious about seeing the child as a legal subject. While in a number of jurisdictions children are able to instruct lawyers to represent them in private as well as public law proceedings, invariably the court's view of that child's welfare will prevail over the child's wishes.

In short, changing views of children are effecting legal change. Children are now acknowledged as having a voice in law in an increasing number of jurisdictions. Familial relations are undergoing change pursuant to a trend towards the democratization of family life (Beck 1997). Changing views about children and human rights are bringing about a movement to end the corporal punishment of children. The UNCRC is giving rise to increased tension between the local and global positioning of the child. Debates on protecting children from traditional childrearing practices and the labeling of these as 'abusive' has given rise to critiques of universalist conceptions of rights. Yet states themselves are subject to scrutiny as to how they are meeting their obligations under the UNCRC. While the way in which the law treats children continues to be contested, the emergent language of rights concerning social and intergenerational relations threatens to subvert many established ways of treating children and to open up spaces in which children can acquire their own voice.

See also: Adoption and Foster Care: United States; Child Abuse; Children, Rights of: Cultural Concerns; Dissolution of Family in Western Nations: Cultural Concerns; Divorce and Children's Social Development; Divorce, Sociology of; Family as Institution; Family Law; Family Processes; Family Theory: Role of Changing Values; Nontraditional Families and Child Development; Poverty and Child Development; Regulation: Family and Gender; Street Children: Cultural Concerns

Bibliography

Alston P (ed.) 1994 *The Best Interests of the Child: Reconciling Culture and Human Rights*. Clarendon Press, Oxford, UK
Beck U 1997 Democratization of the family. *Childhood: A Global Journal of Child Research* **4**(2): pp. 151–68
Bridgeman J, Monk D (eds.) 2000 *Feminist Perspectives on Child Law*. Cavendish, London
Cornell D 1998 *At the Heart of Freedom: Feminism, Sex and Equality*. Princeton University Press, Princeton, NJ
De Winter M 1997 *Children as Fellow Citizens*. Radcliffe Medical Press, Oxford, UK
Eekelaar J, Katz S N (eds.) 1984 *The Resolution of Family Conflict: Comparative Legal Perspectives*. Butterworths, Toronto, Canada
Flekkoy M 1991 *A Voice for Children*. Jessica Kingsley, London
Freeman M D A 1997 *The Moral Status of the Child*. Martinus Nijhoff, The Hague, The Netherlands
Goonesekere S 1998 *Children, Law and Justice*. Sage, New Delhi, India
Kent G 1995 *Children in the International Political Economy*. St Martin's Press, New York
Mack J 1909–10 The juvenile court. *Harvard Law Review* **23**: 104–22
Ncube W (ed.) 1998 *Law, Culture, Tradition and Children's Rights in Eastern and Southern Africa*. Dartmouth, Aldershot, UK
Schwartz-Kenney B, McCauley M, Epstein M (eds.) 2001 *Child Abuse: A Global View*. Greenwood Press, Westport, CT
Strater S 1995 The juvenile death penalty: In the best interests of the child? *Loyola University Chicago Law Journal* **26**: 147–82
Van Bueren G (ed.) 1998 *Childhood Abused: Protecting Children against Torture, Cruel, Inhuman and Degrading Treatment and Punishment* (Programme on International Rights of the Child) Ashgate, Aldershot, UK

J. Roche

Children, Rights of: Cultural Concerns

The last 100 years have witnessed enormous progress in the recognition of individual human rights throughout the world. In addition, various identity groups, including women, racial, ethnic and religious minorities, the disabled, and gay males and lesbians all have claimed, and received to varying degrees, rights to equal treatment under law, nondiscrimination in employment in both the public and private sectors, and fuller integration into the economic and political life of their countries.

It is perhaps not surprising, therefore, that a worldwide movement to recognize children as a distinct subgroup with claims of rights also occurred. In 1924, the League of Nations adopted the first Declaration of the Rights of Children. In 1989, the United Nations General Assembly adopted the UN Convention on the Rights of the Child (UN Convention 1989), which has been called the 'most comprehensive and detailed of all … international human rights instruments' (Alston 1994, p.1). The Convention has been ratified by 192 of the 194 UN members. In the United States conservative political groups, concerned that the CRC undermines parental authority and gives government too much power over families, have contributed to blocking ratification. Somalia lacks an internationally recognized government, precluding ratification.

Despite the seemingly widespread acceptance of the concept of children's rights, the idea that children, individually or as a class, should have *rights* (claims enforceable against others) is actually revolutionary and problematic both in philosophical and practical terms. Determining what rights to provide children requires that societies confront fundamental value issues quite different from those entailed in recognizing other groups' claims.

First, children generally are not autonomous; they are dependent. Ideally, they are part of families; their life chances are greatly affected by the care they receive from their families. Parents need authority to fulfill these responsibilities; some highly respected child development specialists argue that giving children rights may be incompatible with sound child development (Goldstein et al. 1973). In addition, giving children rights may conflict with parental rights and privacy. However, parents do not always act in their children's best interests and the community as a whole has an interest in the development of future generations. Children have their own views and desires. Therefore, it must be decided how responsibility for the well-being and upbringing of children should be allocated between parents, families, the child, and the community as a whole.

Second, intellectual and emotional capacities develop gradually, for both biological and social reasons. These limits in capacity may conflict with claims that children should have the same liberties and privileges as adults (Purdy 1992). A theory of children's rights must address the question, what entitles persons to be full participants in a country's civil and political life?

This article reviews the historical development of children's rights. It then describes the different categories of claims made under the rubric of children's rights and discusses value issues that need to be resolved as governments, courts, and citizens seek to define the children's status in each society. It concludes by examining the challenges countries face implementing any such rights.

1. The Historical Context

For much of history children were viewed largely as nonpersons, the property and responsibility of their parents, who had a right to control their upbringing, even their very existence (Eekelaar 1986). Children (usually defined as persons under 21 or 18 years of age) also could not participate in the political or civic life of their countries.

In the mid-1800s, some countries began assuming state responsibility for promoting and protecting children's well-being. Initially, this entailed providing free public education and passage of laws protecting children from severe physical abuse by their parents. Over the next 100 years, Western industrialized countries adopted more laws affecting the status of children, including laws limiting child labor in settings outside the family, passage of compulsory school attendance laws, and greater state efforts to protect children from parental maltreatment. The idea that childhood was a period for gradual maturation and lesser responsibility also was reflected in the creation of the juvenile court, which was directed to treat, not punish, children who violated the law (Hawes 1991).

While these policies were advocated in the name of children's rights, and certainly contributed to their well-being, these were not the types of civil rights that other groups were demanding and receiving. The focus was on their protection, not their autonomy or fuller integration into the economic and political life of their countries. Moreover, except where parental behavior was seen as inimical to the social order, parents continued to have virtually total authority over their children's upbringing. In the United States, where the movement towards child protection was most evident, the US Supreme Court ruled early on that parents had a constitutional right to control their children's upbringing (Meyer v. Nebraska 1923).

In fact, these laws often were supported primarily as a means of protecting adult interests. For example, child labor laws and compulsory schooling were championed by newly emerging labor unions, which viewed the availability of child labor as a barrier to higher wages for adults (Woodhouse 1992). Proponents of the juvenile court promoted it as a needed intervention to protect society from children who were not being adequately supervised by their parents, often poor, immigrant parents (Schlossman 1977).

Since the 1960s, countries have continued expanding the protection of children's well-being. The establishment of a right to education for virtually all children throughout the world, increased state efforts to guarantee children a minimal level of material well-being, and greatly expanding state intervention into family privacy through child abuse laws have all benefited children. Moreover, during this period, in many countries children were recognized as rights-holders with respect to freedom of speech and other civil liberties and were given a greater degree of legal autonomy over the decisions affecting their lives.

Yet the scope of applicable rights remains highly contested. At the extreme, some commentators have argued for 'children's liberation,' with the complete elimination of distinctions between children and adults with respect to all political, social, and familial rights (children, as reflecting of their status, usually have not been the demanders of rights, in contrast to other groups). For example, they argued that children should have the right to vote, to decide whether to go to school, and to a share of the family income to spend as they choose (Farson 1974).

Few proponents of children's rights go this far. Most advocates propose limiting, but not eliminating, parental autonomy in controlling their children's lives and giving children increasing autonomy as they mature, in recognition that capacities develop over time. Yet even the more limited types of claims of rights raise profoundly difficult issues.

2. What is Meant by Children's Rights

The term children's rights is used to encompasses a variety of different claims (Campbell 1992). Distinguishing these categories reveals the tensions in the general concept and helps identify the issues related to the implementation of various types of claims.

2.1 Basic Human Rights

The first claim is that children are entitled to basic human rights, including the right to life itself, the right not to be 'owned' by another, the right to freedom from tobrture or other cruel punishment, and the right to be free from discrimination based on race, color, sex, religion, or national, ethnic, or social origin.

Such rights are widely accepted for adults, despite continuing problems with implementation, especially with respect to nondiscrimination based on gender, race, and ethnicity. Since these rights are not tied to competence or capacity, there is no reason for denying them to children on this basis. The critical step is accepting that children are *persons*, not chattels or incomplete human beings. The adoption of this premise by virtually all countries reflects a fundamental shift in the conception of children.

Still, application of these rights to children is not entirely unproblematic, at least with respect to the relationship of parents and children. Few countries still consider children to be the property of their parents. However, many people agree with Professor Charles Fried that 'the right to form one's child's values, one's child's life plan ... are extensions of the basic right not to be interfered with in doing these things for oneself' (Fried 1978). Yet, such a right constitutes a form of 'ownership' and may conflict with the child's right to an 'open future' and with society's interest in how future adults are socialized (Feinberg 1980).

There is no easy resolution to this conflict. Unless the state were to intervene in family life in ways that would be deemed unacceptable in most countries, parents will continue to make critical decisions for children, regardless of the child's wishes. As noted, respected child development experts assert that parents need autonomy to successfully raise their children.

Moreover, deference to parental or family authority may be demanded by a society's political, cultural, or religious traditions. In some countries, supporting parental autonomy is seen as critical to supporting political and cultural diversity. In others, the proper role of parents may be seen as teaching children to accept national cultural values and traditions, not as helping children develop into 'autonomous' adults (see generally Alston 1994). Many countries have reserved the right to apply the CRC in light of their own cultural or religious laws, although there is evidence that the CRC is influencing these values (*International Journal of Children's Rights* 1995). Whether children's rights are universal or culture specific likely will remain one of the major debates in implementing the CRC.

In fact, given that children's values and perspectives are malleable and constructed, someone will shape their values and personhood. Parents, families, neighborhoods, peers, government institutions such as schools and general cultural norms all play a part. Thus, the issue is what are the appropriate roles of the family and the state in making critical decisions, such as those regarding schooling, religion, where the child shall live, not whether children should have the right to control their own upbringing (Coons et al. 1991). This question goes to the heart of how a society defines the relationship between the state and the individual, adults and children alike.

Children also are denied some basic civil rights available to adults because societies have an interest in how they are socialized. At a minimum, children are compelled to go to school, thus restricting their liberty rights. Finally, there is still substantial debate over the status of the fetus with respect to abortion and maternal behavior during pregnancy. Because no consensus could be reached on this issue, the CRC leaves the question to each country.

Despite these problems, the recognition that children are persons, with rights, along with the acceptance of the basic premise of the CRC that in all decisions affecting children their 'best interests' shall be a primary consideration, constitutes a great advance that clearly benefits the vast majority of children.

2.2 Welfare Rights

A second category of claimed rights is that government should guarantee children a basic level of well-being; these are often called welfare rights. The CRC provides that children should have a right to 'a standard of living adequate for the child's physical, mental, spiritual, moral and social development' (ART 27), 'the enjoyment of the highest attainable standard of health ...' (ART 24), and to education (ART 28). The CRC goes beyond these basic goods, and seeks to afford children a broader set of welfare rights, including the right 'to rest and leisure, to engage in play and recreational activities appropriate to the age of the child and to participate freely in cultural life and the arts' (ART 31).

Since the 1950s, governments have assumed increasing responsibility for guaranteeing that children have adequate food, nutrition, shelter, and health care. In many countries, children benefit from general social welfare policies, which provide all citizens with universal health insurance and various forms of income support. Most industrialized countries also have partially socialized the cost of caring for children through children's allowances, paid parental leave after the birth of a child, and public provision of day care. Many less economically developed countries are moving in the same direction, despite limited financial resources.

The laggard in this regard, given its capacity, is the United States. In the late 1900s child poverty actually grew in the United States. Resistance in the US reflects, in part, the belief of many political figures that childhood poverty is caused by 'irresponsible' adult behavior, such as having children out of wedlock, and that it is impossible to provide goods to children without also giving them to adults, thereby 'rewarding' the adults' action. In addition, many politicians support the premise of libertarian theorists like Robert Nozick that there is no moral justification for the redistribution of wealth (Nozick 1974).

Even in countries that accept a welfare state, the level of support that a child should receive remains largely a political issue, not a legal right enforceable by courts. No matter how wealthy a country, tradeoffs between levels of socially provided health care, housing, education, and other welfare goods are now seen as inevitable. Courts, appropriately, are reluctant to get too deeply into these decisions. Since the scope of the claimed right is so vague, courts lack the legitimacy and authority to order elected governments to provide people with specific levels of well-being. In addition, some theorists contend that, in the political process, framing political debates in terms of moral obligations that the citizens of a country pledge to provide to each other may prove more productive thn trying to establish rights (O'Neill 1988, cf. Freeman 1992).

Another critical question is whether welfare rights should encompass the right to 'equal opportunity.' Opportunity focuses on each child's options in adulthood. Social scientists have struggled to identify the goods that must be provided to children during childhood in order to equalize their opportunities as adults. Much of the focus is on education. But opportunity is also highly influenced by the quality of parenting a child receives and the social and cultural environment in which the child is raised. A right to equal opportunity is far more difficult to guarantee than a right to basic necessities and may require restricting parental rights (Fishkin 1983).

2.3 Protection Rights

A third category of claimed rights for children is protection from inadequate care from their caretakers, especially their parents. Since giving children more protection changes their relationship with their parents and the state's relationship with parents and families, this right raises fundamental issues quite different from welfare rights.

The degree of justifiable state intrusion against a parent's will remains highly debated. Should the state treat parents as 'stewards' or 'trustees' of their children, and seek to ensure that parents provide children a high level of care, or should the state be the protector 'of last resort,' intervening only if parental care is clearly harmful?

Most countries have decided that coercive intervention should be limited to situations where the actual or threatened harm to the child's physical or emotional well-being is substantial. This approach reflects the judgement that unwanted intervention is a drastic step from the child's, as well as the parent's, perspective. It also is based on evidence that the care provided to children removed from their families sometimes is as bad or worse than the parental care (Wald 1982).

However, a few countries have adopted laws that seek to provide greater protection for children. Five countries have banned any corporal punishment of children; while these laws do not carry any significant sanctions for violation, they reflect a different conception of the rights of children and the role of the state. In recent years, evidence that early child-rearing can substantially affect a child's school readiness and performance has led to increased calls for more extensive monitoring of how each child is being reared.

In the future, governments will continue to struggle with the appropriate grounds for protective intervention. The critical task, however, will be to develop and connect children to social programs that enhance all children's well-being and future opportunities without resorting to coercive interventions. By the time protection rights must be invoked, the child has suffered substantial harm and the capacity of the state to rectify the situation is often limited (US Advisory Board 1991).

2.4 Liberty and Participation Rights

The fourth category of rights does focus on autonomy. In virtually all countries, persons under 18 lack the right to vote and to marry, they are restricted in making decisions about whether to work, and in their freedoms of expression and other civil rights. In addition, in many countries children accused of criminal behavior generally are denied some due process rights available to adults in that country, for example the right to a jury trial; these limitations have been justified as necessary to promote the rehabilitative ideals of the juvenile justice system.

In 1967, the US Supreme Court determined that children are entitled to at least some of the rights guaranteed by the free speech provision of the US Constitution (Tinker v. Des Moines Independent Community School District 1969). Since then the liberty rights of minors have been gradually increased in the US and many other countries. The CRC provides that: '(the) child shall have the right to freedom of expression; this right shall include the freedom to seek, receive and impart information and ideas of all kinds, regardless of frontiers, either orally, in writing or in print, in the form of art, or through any other media of the child's choice' (ART 13); '(s)tates parties shall respect the right of the child to freedom of thought, conscience, and religion' (ART 14); '(s)tates parties recognize the rights of the child to freedom of association and to freedom of peaceful assembly' (ART 15). Notably, the CRC does not provide adult status in other areas, such as the right to vote, marry, work, or to be from constraints imposed only on children, such as the obligation to attend school, or to be at home by a certain hour (curfew laws).

Courts, legislatures, and the drafters of the CRC have not arrived at any consistent theory justifying granting children some rights and not others. Nor have they resolved the tension between claims for special protection and for full participation. If adolescents are seen as having the maturity and capacity to make decisions about their health care, to choose what they read or see, or to vote, does it follow that they should be held fully responsible for their antisocial behavior?

The critical issues relate both to capacities and to questions about developmental needs. For some rights, such as voting or marrying, it is generally accepted that some minimum level of competence is necessary to the proper exercise of the right. Children often are denied other rights, such as unlimited access to books or movies, on the assumption that early exposure to certain materials or ideas may be harmful to them.

An overriding question is whether it makes sense to assume that the same age line should govern access to all political and civil rights. Franklin Zimring has proposed treating children as possessing a 'learner's permit,' whereby they are given increasing autonomy and responsibility over time (Zimring 1982). Different rights might be available at different ages, based on best guesses about average capacity. Age lines are inherently arbitrary; not all people attain capacities at the same age. But individualized decisions about whether someone is old enough to vote, marry, or leave school are likely, in practice, to be even more arbitrary, as is having a single age trigger all rights.

2.5 Autonomy Within the Family

The issues regarding autonomy rights are even more difficult with respect to the right of children to act independently of their parents' wishes. The extreme view, that children of any age should be free to make their own decisions, has not received acceptance. In many countries giving children any autonomy within the family would be incomprehensible. In other countries, there are debates about whether children should have a right to make certain major decisions, such as whether to have an abortion or receive treatment for substance abuse, without their parents' permission or knowledge. Advocates of giving children these rights contend that many children will be reluctant to seek out needed services if their parents are informed. Children have also been given some rights to determine important aspects of their life, such as which parent to live with in the case of divorce. The case for giving children rights is strongest with respect to decisions where parents may not be counted upon to generally act in their children's best interests.

There is no easy resolution to the tension between parental rights and children's rights. It is unrealistic to assume that children can have total liberty rights, enforceable against their parent's opposition. Asking courts to enforce most such rights would be a waste of court resources and the orders would be unenforceable as a practical matter. But giving children some rights is feasible, for example, access to drug treatment or abortion without parental permission. The question is whether the benefits of giving children autonomy with respect to the decision outweigh the harms of limiting parental oversight of their children. These rights will have to reflect the legal and social structure of each country and should not be thought of as universal children's rights.

3. The Future

The situation of children throughout much of the world has been improved substantially during the twentieth century. Concepts of rights likely contributed to these advances. The recognition that children are independent human beings with claims to special attention and resources is a major advance with respect to universal recognition of human rights (Freeman 1992).

However, further development of children's rights will require resolving the value issues often masked by rights talk. Despite the unprecedented rapidity of the ratification of the CRC, the fact that the contours of many of the proposed rights are not very clearly defined will make enforcement and monitoring by the international bodies problematic. In fact, the very vagueness of the obligations may account for the rapid ratification and almost total support of the CRC, despite the fact that many of the proposed rights seemingly conflict with deeply held cultural and religious values in many countries. Countries expect to interpret the provisions in light of their customs and values.

With respect to welfare rights, those concerned with helping children must recognize that realization of most of the proposed rights requires policies that help families, not just children. Children's well-being generally is inseparable from that of the parents. Greater provision of welfare rights should lessen the occasions that protection rights will need to be invoked. However, in establishing welfare rights countries need to ensure that when adults seek to act on behalf of children, their own needs do not take precedence.

With respect all general social policies, countries must think through the implications of the fact that children, who may constitute a third to half of the population, cannot vote. The poorest children are further disenfranchised by the general powerlessness of their parents. Some countries are making significant efforts to include the voices of children in discussions of issues related to them and to more general public policy issues. The recognition of children's right to speak for themselves could significantly alter the place of children in the state (Melton and Limber 1992).

In the poorest countries, it will be very difficult to promote any form of children's rights unless general poverty is alleviated. Many countries continue to deal with problems of street children, child prostitution, child labor, and infanticide. The advancement of children's rights in these countries will be intimately linked to women's rights, since it is unlikely that children will have economic security and greater liberty if their mothers lack these rights. It will also require wealthier countries to demonstrate concern for children beyond national borders.

Children's rights advocates sought to make the 1900s the century of the child. They were successful in many respects. Future advances will require finding adequate balances for the tensions that have been identified, as well as eliminating the negative impacts on children of discrimination based on race, class, and gender. For most children, these later factors may be greater barriers to their rights and well-being than age.

Bibliography

Alston P 1994 The best interests principle: towards a reconciliation of culture and human rights. In: Alston P (ed.) *The Best Interests of the Child*. Clarendon Press, Oxford, UK

Armstrong M, Chuulu M S, Himonga C, Letuka P, Mokobi K, Ncube W, Nhlapo T, Rwezania B, Vilakazi P 1995 Towards a cultural understanding of the interplay between children's and women's rights: an Eastern and Southern African perspective. *International Journal of Children's Rights* 3: 333–68

Campbell T 1992 The rights of the minor: as person, as child, as juvenile, as future adult. In: Alston P, Parker S, Seymour J (eds.) *Children, Rights and the Law*. Clarendon Press, Oxford, UK

Convention of the Rights of the Child 1989 G.A. Res 44/25 U.N., GAOR, 44th sess., Annex, Supp. No 49 at 167 U.N. Doc A/44/49

Coons J, Mnookin R, Sugarman S 1991 Puzzling over children's rights. *Brigham Young University Law Review* 307–50

Eekelaar J 1986 The emergence of children's rights. *Oxford Journal of Legal Studies* 6: 161–82

Farson R 1974 *Birthrights*. Macmillan, New York

Feinberg J 1980 The children's right to an open future. In: Aiken W, LaFolette H (eds.) *Whose Child? Children's Rights, Parental Authority, and State Power*. Rowman and Littlefield, Tottowa, NJ

Fishkin J S 1983 *Justice, Equal Opportunity, and The Family*. Yale University Press, New Haven, CT

Freeman M 1992 Taking children's rights more seriously. In: Alston P, Parker S, Seymour J (eds.) *Children, Rights and the Law*. Clarendon Press, Oxford, UK

Fried C 1978 *Right and Wrong*. Harvard University Press, Cambridge, MA

Goldstein J, Freud A, Solnit A J 1973 *Beyond the Best Interests of the Child*. Free Press, New York

Hawes J 1991 *The Children's Rights Movement: A History of Advocacy and Protection*. Twayne Publishers, Boston

International Journal of Children's Rights 1995 Special Issue: Multiculturalism and The Rights of the Child 3: 1–144

Melton G, Limber S 1992 What children's rights mean to children: children's own views. In: Freeman M, Vreeman R (eds.) *The Ideologies of Children's Rights*. Kluwer Academic Publishers, Dordrecht, The Netherlands

Meyer v. Nebraska 1923 *United States Supreme Court Reports* 262: 390–403

Nozick R 1974 *Anarchy, State and Utopia*. Basil Blackwell, Oxford, UK

O'Neill O 1988 Children's rights and children's lives. *Ethics* 98: 445–63

Purdy L 1992 *In Their Best Interest?* Cornell University Press, Ithaca, NY

Schlossman S L 1977 *Love and the American Delinquent*. University of Chicago Press, Chicago

Tinker v. Des Moines Independent Community School District 1969 *United States Supreme Court Reports* 393: 503–26

United States Advisory Board on Child Abuse and Neglect 1991 *Creating Caring Communities*. US Department of Health and Human Services, Washington, DC

Wald M 1982 State intervention on behalf of endangered children. *International Journal of Child Abuse and Neglect* 6: 3–45

Woodhouse B 1992 'Who Owns the Child?': *Meyer* and *Pierce* and the child as property. *William and Mary Law Review* 33: 995–1122

Zimring F 1982 *The Changing Legal World of Adolescence*. Free Press, New York/London

M. S. Wald

Children, Value of

In demography, the term 'value of children' most often refers to the benefits parents receive from having and rearing children. Benefits may accrue from the children themselves, from the experience of rearing them, or from the responses of kin, community, and society at large. Children also entail costs for parents and the 'value of children' sometimes refers to their net value (benefits less costs). Benefits and costs of children are shaped by the economic conditions of life, by forms of social organization, and by cultural beliefs and practices. The net value of children underlies parents' desires for children; childbearing desires, in combination with the ability to achieve them determine whether or not individuals or couples have children and how many children they have.

1. *Theoretical Development*

The economic value of children is a key component of fertility variation and change. In agricultural economies and during early periods of industrialization, parents and kin make the heavy investment of time and money in young children in order to reap the rewards of children's labor from adolescence onward (Schultz 1973). The old-age security value of children is particularly important in contexts where no public provisions exist for elder care (Cain 1985). For large numbers of people throughout the world, the economic value of children continues to be a primary benefit of parenthood.

For most parents in industrial societies, however, children provide very little or no economic value. Children's labor does not produce subsistence for the family nor do children often support their parents in old age. Children are extremely costly to raise and often require economic support well into the young adult years as they complete their formal education. The location and organization of paid employment produces high opportunity costs of childrearing for parental employment. Fertility declines in the twentieth century have been attributed in large part to declines in the economic value and increases in the economic costs of children to their parents (Fawcett 1983).

Of course, scholars have long recognized that the value of children extended beyond their economic benefits. Hoffman and Hoffman (1973) identified the following psychological needs fulfilled by parenthood and the experience of childrearing: (a) adult status and social identity; (b) expansion of the self (tie to a larger entity, 'immortality'); (c) morality (including religion, altruism, good of the group); (d) primary group ties, affiliation; (e) stimulation, novelty, fun; (f) creativity, accomplishment, competence; (g) power, influence, effectance; and (h) social comparison, competition. The influence of such benefits on fertility would depend on the availability of alternative mechanisms for fulfilling the identified needs. They also recognized that childrearing carried with it potential psychological costs such as stress and worry.

Recent theoretical arguments reject lists of psychological benefits as sufficient to explain why people continue to have children when they become economic liabilities. One alternative theory claims that the reduction of uncertainty is the primary goal of parenthood (Friedman et al. 1994). Those with limited access to other means for uncertainty reduction, such as stable careers and marriages, will want to become parents. Few of the hypotheses derived from this theory stand up to empirical scrutiny and those that do can be explained by the economic and social opportunity costs of children (Lehrer et al. 1996).

Building on the work of cultural anthropologists and sociologists, Schoen et al. (1997) proposed the theory that children produce social capital for parents. Social capital consists of social relationships and the social resources they provide. At birth, children strengthen parents' ties to kin. Through schooling and other activities, they link parents with community resources. As adolescents and young adults, children bring new information, ideas, and social relationships to parental households. And most parents eventually obtain in-laws and grandchildren as a consequence of parenthood. Parents may also, of course, incur loss of social capital because they have less time to maintain friendships, relationships with co-workers, or connections to social and political organizations.

While the distinctions among economic, psychological, and social benefits and costs of children make some sense (and also fit disciplinary boundaries), it is important to recognize their interrelationships. Economic subsistence comes first in a list of parental needs, so the economic value of children may be sufficient to stimulate parenthood, whether or not children have any social or psychological value. Social and psychological benefits may be viewed as extras that make the task of childrearing less burdensome, or at least

outweigh the social and psychological costs of parenthood. On the other hand, the kin and community ties produced by children may be indirect sources of economic benefits. Several of the benefits identified as psychological also have social components: primary group ties include the parents' relationship, itself a form of social capital; expansion of self includes ties to larger social groups, including kin, community, and society.

2. Measuring the Value of Children

The economic value and costs of children could be measured indirectly by estimating the value of children's labor and transfers to parents over the life course, expenditures related to childrearing, and the value of parental time that might otherwise be spent on income-producing activities (e.g., Rosenzweig 1978). Similar estimates of social or psychological values have not been attempted, and it could be argued that a shared metric for economic, social, and psychological values does not exist. Even if it were possible to measure the true net value of children, parents' perceptions of those values are what enter into fertility decisions.

The term 'value of children' is most closely associated with a set of surveys conducted in the mid-1970s in the United States, the Philippines, South Korea, Taiwan, Indonesia, and Thailand (Fawcett 1983). Although based on the psychological values of children discussed above, the surveys also contained information on the perceived economic and social benefits and costs of children. Respondents were asked open-ended questions about reasons for having or not having children and were asked to rate the importance of several lists of child benefits and costs as reasons to have or not have children or their next child. Analyses of these data remain the primary source of current knowledge about variation in the value of children.

Measures of the benefits and costs of children are also the basis for subjective-expected-utility or expectancy-value models of fertility decisions (e.g., Davidson and Jaccard 1979). Respondents are asked to rate the value of possible outcomes of having or not having a child and also the subjective probability that having or not having a child will produce the outcome. The product of those two responses comprises the importance of a given outcome as a reason to have or not have a child. Almost all of the research based on these models has focused on the total expected utility of having a child, rather than on the relative importance of specific child benefits and costs.

More recently, several European Fertility and Family Surveys and the US National Survey of Families and Households used structured importance ratings to measure the value of children to parents. In these surveys, the rating scales are more extensive than the three-point scale used for the earlier VOC surveys, but the questions do not cover all of the theoretical benefits and costs discussed above. Analyses of these data to date have combined ratings of social and psychological benefits of children into a single scale (e.g., Schoen et al. 1997).

3. Variations in the Value of Children

3.1 The Value of First and Later-born Children

First, second and higher-order births are associated with distinct benefits and costs (Bulatao 1981, Fawcett 1983). The first child confers the status of parenthood, so that benefits associated with parenthood *per se* can be acquired by having only one child. Adult status, relationship stability, parent-child interaction, and kin connections are all cited as primary reasons for becoming a parent. The first child is also associated with the greatest increase in opportunity costs, that is, constraints on parental time and energy.

The most important value of a second child is to provide a sibling for the first (Bulatao 1981). Second, children may further strengthen partnership and kin ties and provide additional opportunities for rewarding parent-child interactions. The value of higher-order births is predominantly economic—each child contributes additional labor or economic security for parents. Restrictions on parents' time are also associated with higher birth orders, but at a diminishing rate. Financial costs of children become more salient to parents at the birth of fourth and higher-order siblings.

3.2 Gender and the Value of Children

Overall, men and women perceive the values and costs associated with children in much the same way. The few differences that are observed are consistent with traditional gender roles (Fawcett 1983). Men are on average more concerned than women about the financial costs of childrearing and about having sons to continue the family name. The latter difference is particularly pronounced in patrilineal societies. Women place greater importance than do men on the work and strain of raising children, the opportunity costs of children for other activities, and the benefits of children for the marital relationship; the last difference is also larger in patrilineal than in bilineal kinship systems.

Differences in the perceived benefits of daughters and sons are also related to differences in the roles and behaviors of men and women (Fawcett 1983). Sons are valued more than daughters for kinship ties, that is, to continue the family name, and for financial assistance. These values are especially pronounced in patrilineal

family systems and where men have greater access than women to economic opportunities. Daughters are valued more than sons for household and childcare help and companionship. In patrilineal societies, the values associated with sons are produced for the most part in adulthood, those associated with daughters during childhood, consistent with the practice of daughters' leaving the parental home upon marriage. Many of the benefits of children, particularly social and psychological benefits, do not appear to differ for sons and daughters.

3.3 Socioeconomic Variation in the Value of Children

As noted above, the economic value of children is associated with agricultural and household economic production and the absence of social insurance for elderly parents. Although children also entail high economic costs in such contexts, they are necessary for survival. Industrialization and urbanization reduce the economic value of child labor and increase the costs of rearing children to be economically independent. Economic development eventually leads to the development of social insurance that reduces further the economic value of children for support in old age. As a result, children's net economic value is perceived to be lower in industrialized wealthy countries than in poorer countries with a greater dependence on agricultural and household production (Fawcett 1983).

Psychological benefits and costs of children are reported to be more important in industrial and postindustrial settings than in agricultural settings (Fawcett 1983). This difference may arise because of the priority of economic survival over psychological wellbeing, that is, children may provide psychological benefits (and costs) for parents in all settings, but these components of child value become salient only when children become irrelevant to economic survival. On the other hand, the increasing complexity and impersonal character of daily life in industrialized urban societies may produce a greater need for the love and companionship and stimulation of children. At the same time, psychological costs of childrearing may increase because kin and community take less responsibility for the supervision and care of children.

Because the social capital value of children has only recently been introduced into theoretical discussions of the value of children, it is difficult to know how such values might vary under different economic conditions. In agricultural settings there may be a stronger association between economic and social ties so that the latter are not distinguishable from the former. Only in industrial and urban societies may social capital be sufficiently separable from financial capital to identify it as a separate source of child value.

Socioeconomic variation in the value of children is also evidenced across families within societies (Fawcett 1983). A consistent finding from VOC surveys was that urban respondents place a lower economic value and a higher emotional value on children than do respondents living in rural areas. Similarly, education is inversely associated with children's economic value and directly associated with their emotional value as well as with perceived restrictions or opportunity costs of parenthood. Direct financial costs and childcare stresses do not vary substantially across countries or across individuals in different economic circumstances. Increasing economic status is associated with desire for increased child 'quality' which means greater financial and time/energy investments in each child. Thus, the perceived cost of childrearing, other than opportunity costs, remains essentially the same across socioeconomic levels.

3.4 Culture and the Value of Children

Broad cultural values may also serve as sources of specific or general values of children. Religious institutions and beliefs may support the value of children for social and psychological benefits. For example, Catholicism is viewed as a support for large-family values in the Philippines, Confucianism for the high value of sons to carry on the family name in some Asian countries. The relative values of daughters and sons are associated with broad cultural values on gender equality (Fawcett 1983).

Lesthaeghe (1983) argued that ideational change is an independent force underlying current low fertility in Western countries. He identifies the two most salient features of this change as secularization and individuation. Secularization allows more latitude to individual morality, individuation stresses the importance of personal self-actualization. Using national surveys of social and family values, Lesthaeghe and coworkers (e.g., Lesthaeghe and Meekers 1986) distinguished two dimensions of family values—a nonconformity dimension linked to partner relationships and nonmarital childbearing; and the 'meaning of parenthood,' including beliefs that children are necessary for 'fulfillment' and for marital success. Measures of secularism and individuation were strongly associated with nonconforming family values, but only weakly associated with the meaning of parenthood.

4. The Value of Children and Fertility

Studies using ratings such as those in the Value of Children Surveys have generally found that high perceived economic benefits of children are associated with a large family size. The importance of psycho-

logical benefits and restrictions on parental activities are associated with a small family size (Fawcett 1983). The relationship between perceived child values and fertility is not, however, as strong as some scholars had hoped, and the financial and time/effort costs of children are not associated with family size.

Relatively moderate associations between values of children and completed fertility should not be surprising. Specific values are associated with particular numbers of children, not consistently with large or small numbers. Child values can influence only desired fertility, so that the relationship between values and outcomes depends on the degree of fertility control. In addition, measures of the perceived value of children have often been relatively crude (e.g., 3-point response scale). When a particular parity progression is specified, when contraception is pervasive, and when precise measures of the expected value (net of cost) of children are generated, very high correlations are observed with birth intentions and eventual births (e.g., Davidson and Jaccard 1979).

See also: Demographic Transition, Second; Family Size Preferences; Family Theory: Complementarity of Economic and Social Explanations; Family Theory: Economics of Intergenerational Relations; Family Theory: Role of Changing Values; Fertility Transition: Cultural Explanations; Fertility Transition: Economic Explanations; Reproductive Rights in Affluent Nations

Bibliography

Bulatao R A 1981 Values and disvalues of children in successive childbearing decisions. *Demography* **18**: 1–25
Cain M 1985 Fertility as an adjustment to risk. In: Rossi A S (ed.) *Gender and the Life Course*. Aldine, New York
Davidson A R, Jaccard J J 1975 Population psychology: A new look at an old problem. *Journal of Personality and Social Psychology* **31**: 1073–82
Fawcett J T 1983 Perceptions of the value of children: Satisfactions and costs. In: Bulatao R A, Lee R D (eds.) *Determinants of Fertility in Developing Countries, Vol. 2: Supply and Demand for Children*. Academic Press, New York
Friedman D, Hechter M, Kanazawa S 1994 A theory of the value of children. *Demography* **31**: 375–401
Hoffman L W, Hoffman M L 1973 The value of children to parents. In: Fawcett J T (ed.) *Psychological Perspectives on Population*. Basic Books, New York
Lehrer E L, Grossbard-Shechtman S, Leasure J W 1996 'A theory of the value of children'—Comment. *Demography* **33**: 133–9
Lesthaeghe R 1983 A century of demographic and cultural change in Western Europe: An exploration of underlying dimensions. *Population and Development Review* **9**: 411–35
Lesthaeghe R, Meekers D 1986 Value changes and the dimensions of familism in the European Community. *European Journal of Population* **2**: 225–68

Rosenzweig M R 1978 The value of children's time, family size and non-household child activities in a developing country: Evidence from household data. In: Simon J L (ed.) *Research in Population Economics: An Annual Compilation of Research,* Vol. 1.

Schoen R, Kim Y J, Nathanson C A, Fields J, Astone N M 1997 Why do Americans want children? *Population and Development Review* **23**: 333–58

Schultz T 1973 The value of children: An economic perspective. *Journal of Political Economy* **81**: S2–S13

E. Thomson

Children's Play: Educational Function

Until recently, many writers have considered children's play to be a trivial and inconsequential activity; they have also disagreed on its definition. Today, however, social scientists and educators appear voracious in their study of children's play. To many researchers, play is viewed as a generative force in children's social, emotional, and cognitive development (see Rubin et al. 1983). The developmental and educational significance of play in childhood is discussed herein.

1. Classical Theories of Play

Contemporary research on the topic of children's play draws heavily from early theoretical accounts about the functional significance of the phenomenon. The 'surplus energy' theory characterized play as 'blowing off steam'. Schiller, an eighteenth-century philosopher defined play as the aimless expenditure of exuberant energy. He wrote that work satisfied the primary needs of the human species. Once these needs were met, the superfluous energy that remained resulted in play. Because children were not responsible for their own survival, they were thought to have a total energy 'surplus,' which was depleted through play. Schiller raised a number of contemporary issues in his writings. First, he considered play a symbolic activity through which the participant could transform and transcend reality and thereby gain new symbolic representations of the world. Second, he distinguished between forms of play—material superfluidity resulted in physical play, esthetic superfluidity culminated in dramatic–symbolic play. Collectively, these notions reappear in the later writings of Piaget, Vygotsky, and Bühler.

According to the relaxation theorists such as Lazarus, the purpose of play was to restore energy expended in work. Thus, labor was viewed as energy consuming, resulting in an energy deficit. This deficit could be replenished through rest or sleep, or by engaging in play.

Subsequently recapitulation theorists posited that cultural epochs were repeated sequentially in children's play; the animal stage (children's climbing and swinging); the savage stage (hunting, tag, hide-and-go-seek); the nomad stage (keeping pets); the agricultural–patriarchal stage (playing with dolls, digging in sand); and the tribal stage (team games). They also believed that play served as an outlet for the catharsis or release of unnecessary, primitive racial instincts, thereby preparing individuals for the intellectually advanced activities of the modern era. For example, Patrick suggested that contemporary occupations required abstract reasoning, concentrated attention, and coordinated eye-hand activities, all of which were presumed to be relatively recent evolutionary acquisitions. Because this worked tapped recently acquired skills, it was more taxing than physical labor. As such, relief from fatigue could be gained through play, or the practice of 'racially old' activities (e.g., hunting, fishing).

According to pre-exercise or practice theorists such as Groos, the period of childhood existed so that the organism could play. Humankind's relatively long period of immaturity was considered necessary to allow for children to practice the instinctively-based complex skills that would be essential for survival in adulthood. Thus, the adaptive function of play was to prepare children to perfect skills that they would require in adulthood.

Of further interest, Groos noted that children's play comprised 'don't have to' activities—while playing, children are more interested in the processes rather than the products of the behavior. In this regard, recent speculations concerned with effectance motivation can be traced back to Groos' writings.

Importantly, Groos noted that children's play changed with development. First, there was experimental play, which included sensory and motor practice activities. Such play evolved into constructive play and the practice of higher mental powers. The purpose of such activity was to aid in the development of self-control. Second, there was socionomic play, which included fighting and chasing, as well as imitative, social and family games (dramatic play). This form of play was thought to aid in the development of personal relationships.

Despite obvious limitations, not the least of which are limited supportive, empirical bases, these early theories continue to have an impact on how many people think about play today. For example, parents and teachers are often heard to express reservations about poor weather conditions that might keep children indoors all day. The traditionally held belief is that such restriction constrains the expenditure of surplus energy.

2. Modern Theories of Play

Several common themes run across modern twentieth-century interpretations of children's play. These include the belief that: (a) children need to play in order to express themselves or to relieve themselves of anxieties and fears; and (b) play both causes and reflects developments in social, cognitive, and linguistic prowess.

2.1 Psychoanalytic Theory

Freud (1961) believed that play provided children with important avenues for the expression of wish fulfillment and the mastery of traumatic events. He argued that play allowed the child to transcend the rigid sanctions of reality thereby serving as a safe context within which the child could vent socially unacceptable impulses. Freud addressed the mastery aspect of play through the repetition compulsion, a psychic mechanism that allows individuals to cope with traumatic events through a compulsive repetition of components of the disturbing events. Children were thought to use play to become active masters of situations in which they were once passive victims. For example, if her mother, for not tidying up her room, scolded a young child, the child may re-enact the scene numerous times with a doll, casting herself in the role of angry mother.

More recently, psychoanalytic theorists have expanded on Freud's conceptualizations of play. For example, with regard to wish fulfillment, Peller noted that children's choices of roles are often based on feelings of love, admiration, fear, or anger for a particular person. Such roles allow children to fulfill the wish to be like certain others. With regard to mastery, Erikson believed play served to allow the child to integrate biological and social spheres of functioning. Through play, children create model situations in which aspects of the past are re-lived, the present represented and renewed, and the future anticipated.

2.2 Piaget

Piaget (1962) suggested that play represented the purest form of assimilation. In assimilation, children incorporate events, objects, or situations into existing ways of thinking. Thus, as 'pure assimilation,' play was not considered an avenue to cognitive growth, but rather as a reflection of the child's present level of cognitive development.

Borrowing largely from Karl Bühler and Spencer, Piaget described three stages in the development of play. Practice play first appeared in infancy, consisting of sensorimotor actions (e.g., clapping hands). Through this 'functional exercise,' Piaget believed that children acquired and honed the basic motor skills inherent in their everyday activities. Symbolic play, appearing around the second year, required an implied representation of absent objects (e.g., pretending to bake a cake while in the sand box). In contrast with practice play, where actions were exercised and elaborated for their functional value, symbolic play al-

lowed the exercise of actions for their representational value. Games-with-rules was the last structural category to develop; this type of play activity necessarily incorporated social coordination and a basic understanding of social relationships.

2.3 Vygotsky

Like Piaget, Vygotsky (1967) framed play within a larger psychological theory of children's cognition. Vygotsky argued that children used symbolic play as an essential link in the association of abstract meanings and their associated concrete objects. Symbolic play was useful in allowing children to conceive of meanings independently of the objects that they may represent. Thus, unlike Piaget, Vygotsky argued that play was not a reflection of egocentrism, but rather a symbolic process that brings into being the mediating role of signs. For example, when children first begin to use words, the word is perceived as a property of the object rather than as a sign denoting the object. The child grasps the external structure of the word–object relation earlier than the internal structure of the sign–referent relationship. The fusion of word with object follows the more general fusion of action and object. In infancy, the child relates to things as 'objects of action.' For higher mental processes to develop, things must become 'objects of thought' and practical actions must become mental representations (e.g., volitional choice). Play precipitates this emancipation of meaning from object to action. The central event responsible for the emancipation is the use of one object (e.g., a stick) to substitute for another (a real space ship), or the use of one action (a jump) to denote another (a space launch). To Vygotsky, movement in the field of meaning is the predominant feature of play.

2.4 Other Modern Theories

Drive modulation theorists proposed that excessively high and excessively low levels of stimulation are aversive; play is used as a means of modulating the arousal associated with this aversion. For example, when confronted with a novel object, specific exploration allowed the child to explore its features and relieve arousal through increasing familiarity with the object. Following specific exploration, an optimal level of arousal is sought through diverse exploration, or stimulus-seeking activity. This latter form of exploration, or play, increases stimulation when we are 'bored' and continues until arousal reaches an optimal level. Thus, play is viewed as a stimulus-producing activity that is generated by low levels of arousal.

Recent theoretical accounts have emphasized the role of play, particularly pretense, in the development of children's theory of mind (e.g., Lillard 1998), including the provision of opportunities to build and expand mental representations. Further, educational thinkers have posited that creativity and flexibility is promoted by children's play (e.g., Bruner 1972). Accordingly, play allows the exploration of new combinations of behaviors and ideas within a psychologically safe milieu. Through play, children develop behavioral 'prototypes' that may be used subsequently in more 'serious' contexts. For example, a young child may button and unbutton her doll's dress many times, and thereafter incorporate her accomplishments from this play session when dressing herself. As such, the means become more important than the ends, and since accomplishing goals is not important in play, children are free to experiment with new and unusual combinations of behavior.

Finally, linguists have proposed ways in which play may help children perfect newly acquired language skills and increase conscious awareness of linguistic rules. Play provides a superior context within which children may gain valuable language practice as they experiment with the meaning, the structure, and the function of language (Davidson 1996). Play conversations also work to improve communication skills. These skills, in turn, are important components of many developmental acquisitions attained during childhood, particularly narrative representation, social cognition, intersubjectivity, and fantasy play. Goncu (1993), for example, has suggested that the improvisational processes typical of social pretend play are critical to the development of intersubjectivity (i.e., the development of a mutual understanding between play participants). These processes prepare children for an ever increasingly complex social life within which a variety of interactional contexts exist that range from the more ritualized and structured to the more improvisational. Within each of these interactional contexts, however, are elements of both improvisation and social structure (Sawyer 1997). Thus, among the unique properties of children's peer play are its framed and improvisational nature, each which the child must master.

3. Issues in Defining Play

It is one thing to think about *why* play exists in the human repertoire; it is something else altogether to define it. Following from Rubin et al. (1983), the following characteristics, when taken together, define play.

(a) Play is not governed by appetitive drives, compliance with social demands, or by inducements external to the behavior itself; instead play is intrinsically motivated.

(b) Play is spontaneous, free from external sanctions, and its goals are self-imposed.

(c) Play asks 'What can I do with this object or person?' This question differentiates play from exploration, which asks 'What is this object (or person) and what I do with it (him or her)?'

(d) Play is not a serious rendition of an activity or a behavior it resembles; instead it consists of activities that can be labeled as pretense

(e) Play is free from externally imposed rules—this characteristic distinguishes play from games-with-rules.

(f) Play involves active engagement—this distinguishes play from daydreaming, lounging, and aimless loafing.

4. Developmental Progressions in Children's Play

Between the periods of infancy and middle childhood, children's play undergoes an evolution in both form and content. These progressions are reviewed briefly below.

4.1 Infant and Toddler Play

By the end of the first year, infants begin to demonstrate rapid growth in representational thinking. Decontextualized behavior, which is first demonstrated in the first year, involves the 'out of context' production of familiar behavior. For example, the infant may close her eyes, put her head on a pillow, and lie in a curled position at a time of day (e.g., mid-morning), and in a context (e.g., playground) that is detached from the situational context when and where sleeping or napping occurs. By the middle of the second year, the toddler coordinates the use of several objects in his or her demonstrations of decontextualized behavior (e.g., a 'Teddy Bear' is fed from an empty cup).

This latter use of objects in pretense captures the essence of the second developmental component of play, self-other relationships. When pretense appears at about 12 months, it is centered around the child's own body (e.g., the child feeds herself). Roughly between 15 and 21 months, play becomes other-referenced; however, the 'other' is typically an inanimate object, as in the 'Teddy Bear' example noted above. Moreover, during this period, when others are involved in pretense activities, they are passive recipients of the child's behavior. Beyond 20 months, and increasingly so up to about 30 months, the child gains the ability to 'step out' of the play situation and to manipulate the 'other' as if it were an active agent (e.g., the Teddy Bear 'feeds' a doll with a plastic spoon). The developmental significance of these accomplishments should not be easily underestimated. Advances in maturity of play reflect the young child's increasing ability to symbolically represent things, actions, roles, and relationships.

A third component of play is the use of substitute objects. The ability to identify one object with another (e.g., a stick is used as a laser gun) is paradigmatic of symbolic representation. The fourth component of play is the coordination and sequencing of pretense. Between the ages of 12 and 20 months, toddlers' pretend acts become increasingly coordinated into meaningful sequences. At first, the child produces a single pretend gesture (drinking from a plastic cup); later, the child relates, in succession, the same act to the self and then to others (drinks from the cup, feeds the Teddy Bear from the cup). Subsequently, in a multi-scheme combination, the young child is able to coordinate different sequential acts (pours tea, feeds the Teddy Bear, puts bear to sleep). By the end of the second year, children indicate verbally that these coordinated sequences are planned prior to execution (child self-verbalizes sequence of pretend behavior prior to acting).

4.2 The Play of Preschoolers and Elementary School-age Children

The above noted constituents of play are mastered prior to or near the child's second birthday. These elements of play become increasingly shared with others as children mature. But why is shared or social pretense important? As noted above, there are several functions of sociodramatic play. Such play creates a context for mastering the communication of meaning. It provides opportunities for children to learn to control and compromise; these opportunities arise during discussions and negotiations concerning pretend roles and scripts and the rules guiding the pretend episodes. Also, social pretense allows for a 'safe' context within which children can explore and discuss issues of intimacy and trust.

By 36 months, children are generally able to communicate pretend scripts to adults and peers; by five years, they can discuss, assign, and enact play themes while continuing to add novel components. By the middle years of childhood, social pretend becomes a venue for self-disclosure and the sharing of confidences especially among close friends.

5. Correlates and Outcomes of Play

5.1 Play and Cognitive Development

Children (three- to five-year-olds) who engage frequently in sociodramatic and constructive play tend to perform better on tests of intelligence than their age-mates who are more inclined to play in a sensorimotor fashion. Interestingly, children who frequently play in a constructive fashion (e.g., building things; constructing puzzles) are likely to be proficient at solving convergent problems (problems with a single solution). Those who frequently play in a dramatic fashion are likely to be proficient at solving divergent problems (problems with multiple solutions).

5.2 Play and Social Development

Because successful participation in social pretense requires many of the skills theorized to be associated with the achievement of competent peer relationships, this type of play is viewed as a marker of social competence from toddlerhood to the middle and late childhood years. Preschoolers who frequently engage in sociodramatic play are more socially skilled than their age-mates who infrequently engage in such activity. Moreover, results from various training studies indicate that instruction in sociodramatic play is associated with increases in cooperation, social participation, and role-taking skills (see Rubin et al. 1983 for a review).

5.3 Play and Language Development

The mechanisms by which play may aid in the development of linguistic competencies are straightforward. Children frequently play with the different forms and rules of language. This play may take the form of repeating strings of nonsense syllables (phonology), substituting words of the same grammatical category (syntax), or intentionally distorting meaning through nonsense and jokes (semantics). As a result, language play may help children perfect newly acquired language skills and increase conscious awareness of linguistic rules, as well as provide a superior context in which the child may gain valuable language practice.

Generally speaking, particular phases in the development of symbolic play and language tend to co-occur. For example, sociodramatic play appears to be an important factor in the development of oral language development and vocabulary, story production, story comprehension, communication of meaning, and the early development of literacy (Davidson 1996, Shore 1995). Indeed, it has been reported that training children to engage in pretense with others improves their language skills, literacy development, and mathematical thinking (see Fromberg and Bergen 1998 for relevant reviews).

6. Summary and Conclusions

It is clear that play is a developmental phenomenon of significant proportion. Not only does it seem to provide a window into the child's cognitive and socio-emotional being, but it also appears to be a propelling force for the development of cognitive, language, and socio-emotional skills. Thus, play should be considered an informal, enjoyable, and relatively stress-free means of providing children with intellectual and social stimulation.

See also: Cognitive Development in Childhood and Adolescence; Infant and Child Development, Theories of; Personality Development in Childhood; Play and Development in Children; Play, Anthropology of; Social Cognition in Childhood; Socialization and Education: Theoretical Perspectives

Bibliography

Bruner J S 1972 The nature and uses of immaturity. *American Psychologist* **27**: 687–708

Davidson J I F 1996 *Emergent Literacy and Dramatic Play in Early Education*. Delmar, Albany, NY

Freud S 1961 *Beyond the Pleasure Principle*. Norton, New York

Fromberg D P, Bergen D 1998 *Play from Birth to Twelve and Beyond: Contexts, Perspectives and Meanings*. Garland, New York

Goncu A 1993 Development of intersubjectivity in social pretend play. *Human Development* **36**: 185–98

Howes C 1992 *The Collaborative Construction of Pretend*. State University of New York Press, New York

Lillard A S 1998 Playing with a theory of mind. In: Saracho O N, Spodek B (eds.) *Multiple Perspectives on Play in Early Childhood Education*. State University of New York Press, Albany, NY, pp. 11–33

Piaget J 1962 *Play, Dreams, and Imitation in Childhood*. Norton, New York

Rubin K H, Fein G G, Vandenberg B 1983 Play. In: Mussen P H (ed.) *Handbook of Child Psychology: Socialization, Personality and Social Development*. Wiley, New York, Vol. 4, pp. 693–774

Sawyer R K 1997 *Pretend Play as Improvisation. Conversations in the Preschool Classroom*. Lawrence Erlbaum Associates, Mahwah, NJ

Shore C 1995 *Individual Differences in Language Development*. Sage, Thousand Oaks, CA

Vygotsky L S 1967 Play and its role in the mental development of the child. *Soviet Psychology* **12**: 62–76

K. H. Rubin

China: Sociocultural Aspects

China as a political entity must be distinguished from China conceived in cultural terms. Within the political boundaries of China are many groups that are not generally considered to be ethnically or culturally Chinese (Han), although they are Chinese citizens. By the same token there are significant populations generally considered to be ethnically Chinese living outside China's political boundaries—'overseas Chinese' (*huaqiao*). This article discusses China's nonHan peoples briefly, but focuses primarily on ethnic Chinese or Han peoples who constitute the vast majority of China's population. Topics addressed are ethnicity and identity, scale and complexity, local communities, the local impact of imperial and state institutions, family and kinship, religion and ritual, and gender. Throughout, attention is drawn to the conceptual challenges China poses for the discipline of anthropology.

1. Ethnicity and Identity

China's government recognizes officially 56 *minzu* or 'nationalities,' based on an evolutionary scale of material progress derived from Lewis Henry Morgan and Friedrich Engels. Some groups, notably Tibetans and Uighurs of Western China, and Mongols in the north, have historical claims to large geographical areas, and aspirations for political autonomy. Other groups (for example the 'Miao,' 'Zhuang,' and 'Yi') have been dispersed among Han and other *minzu* over many provinces in South, Central, and Southwestern China. Official recognition as a nationality confers certain legal privileges (most famously, exemption from the 'one-child' policy of population control), but also implies backwardness and legitimates paternalistic treatment from the government. In this respect, China's current government continues a self-consciously 'civilizing' mission with respect to its non-Han populations that dates to imperial times (Harrell 1995).

China's 'Han' peoples are by no means culturally homogeneous, but scholars are divided as to the degree to which Han Chinese can be said to share a common culture. For example, only about half of Han peoples are native speakers of 'Mandarin' or 'the common language' (*putonghua*). The rest speak one of about a dozen major 'dialects' (related languages, but often mutually unintelligible). Broadly speaking, the provinces of Southern and Southeastern China manifest the greatest linguistic diversity among Han Chinese. This diversity reflects the fact these areas were incorporated into the Chinese empire somewhat later than North and Central China. In addition, the preservation of regional cultures in the South and Southeast results from the fact that these areas have been relatively less frequently beset by dramatic population displacements caused by dynastic crises, droughts, floods, and other disasters than have areas in the North and West.

Mitigating regional and linguistic diversity is the fact that Han Chinese of all provinces share a common written language, elite traditions, and a long history of political unification under a succession of dynasties and into the era of nationalist and, now, communist governments. Moreover, although there is no clear consensus as to the precise defining characteristics of Chinese culture, many Chinese communities are marked by similar family institutions, popular religious customs, class relations, forms of corporate association, and broadly Confucian values emphasizing, most importantly, filial piety. Yet the issue of

China's cultural unity, or lack thereof, has long vexed anthropologists, and is increasingly becoming one of political moment in the Sinocentric world. Among China's national minorities, for example, there are movements among Tibetans and Uighurs for independence. By the same token, regional and dialect-based communalism is strong among Han Chinese in the Southeast.

At the time of writing, the potentially most volatile locus of separatist sentiment is Taiwan. Separated politically from the mainland during 50 years of Japanese colonial rule (1895–1945) and subsequently governed by an exile nationalist government, Taiwan's majority Han population—including speakers of the Southern Min dialect (*minnanhua*) shared with southern Fujian province, and of Hakka, another dialect widely dispersed in Southern China—increasingly asserts its political and, in some cases, cultural separation from China. These assertions are anathema to China's government, which considers Taiwan a renegade province. Given such circumstances, the issue of cultural unity and diversity has a political significance that extends well beyond the concerns of anthropologists.

2. Scale and Complexity

China's vast scale and complexity pose particular problems for anthropology because the discipline's crucial organizing concepts—culture and society—have developed historically in the study of small-scale societies. Anthropology's traditional claim to illuminate social-cum-cultural systems holistically—most explicitly in the functionalist traditions of Bronislaw Malinowski and A. R. Radcliffe-Brown—is more easily accomplished in ethnographic descriptions in which overarching institutions and consciousness of common identity do not reach much above the village or tribal level. Given such limits, the interpenetration of kinship, political, religious, and economic institutions is described and analyzed more easily than in China, where economic, cultural, religious, and political ties link metropolitan centers to distant rural locales. An additional complicating consideration is the historical depth of supra-local social organization: China's history of economic, political, and cultural integration at local, regional, and empire-/nationwide levels has exerted and continues to exert a strong influence on local life and institutions. China's significance for the discipline of anthropology lies most of all in the challenge this complexity poses for adapting and modifying conceptual and theoretical tools developed in analyses of societies of much more limited scale.

To this end, the path-breaking work of G. William Skinner, growing out of 'central-place theory,' is particularly significant (Skinner 1964–5, Skinner 1977). Skinner has developed a spatial-cum-temporal model of market-, town-, and city-centered regions in China in late imperial times that form an eight-tiered nested hierarchy culminating in nine 'macro-regions.' Ascendance in the central-place hierarchy (for example, from villages to market towns, to higher-level central places) is characterized by increasing specialization of economic function, social complexity, and cultural sophistication. By the same token, macro-regions are divided into more densely populated and economically concentrated cores and more sparsely populated, and less productive, peripheries. These distinctions are reflected in class characteristics, kinship and religious organization, and other social differences.

Interpenetrating the hierarchy of economic local and regional systems is a hierarchy of political administration. Although there exists a rough articulation of administrative and economic regional organization (for example, many district capitals are also important economic centers), these correspondences are far from perfect (for example, consumers often have access to more than one higher-level economic center, whereas every administrative district is discrete, with a single capital at the next higher level). The ramifications of regional analysis for more conventional styles of ethnographic work are fundamental. Put simply, Skinner's work obviates imagining China as being crudely dividable into distinctions such as 'rural' and 'urban,' or 'elite' and 'folk': From the vantage point of village-based ethnographic studies, it is necessary to situate a locale with reference to its place in both administrative and economic systems if one is to comprehend its place with reference to China as a whole. This caveat applies across the board of social relations and culture—kinship, religious and ritual organization, social class, gender relations, and demographic processes. The potential implications of regional analysis for Chinese anthropology are well recognized, although yet to be thoroughly assimilated. The existence of China's essentially 'global' scale of civilization antedating the emergence of the Western-centered 'capitalist world system' also poses a fundamental conceptual challenge to the recent growth of academic interest in processes of 'globalization.' At the very least, China should provide a comparative reference point to discussions that all too often imagine 'globalization' to be unique to Western history and/or capitalism.

3. Local Communities

Historically, China's population has been overwhelmingly rural (until recently about 85 percent could broadly be characterized as rural), although some of China's cities were probably the world's largest during the European Middle Ages. But, as noted above, 'rural' is a designation too crude to capture the cultural and social distinctions between farming villages located in close proximity to large urban centers (with consequent access to urban markets and culture), and those located in distant peripheries. In brief, more centrally located rural locales tend to conform to more orthodox forms of social organization (for example, with leadership in the hands of Confucian literati), and more peripheral ones tend to be more variable and less orthodox (leadership often exercised by local 'strongmen'). Villages in many parts of China are 'nucleated' (dwellings grouped close together), although some areas (the Sichuan basin, for example) lack nucleated villages, with the population being dispersed. Typically, groups of villages are linked to a market town economically and culturally, and this may also serve as a focus for important local ritual activities, higher-level kin-based groups (e.g., lineage corporations), and other voluntary associations. Most classic ethnographic studies have focused on villages with some references to villagers' participation in market-town-focused activities.

The general picture that emerges from village-based ethnographies is one of considerable variation, but some significant commonalities are also discernible. Single-surname villages and strong corporate patrilineages seem to be relatively more common in the more productive and prosperous regional cores and in the South. Such villages are more likely to find ritual solidarity in lineage-based activities. In contrast, temples to local gods are the more frequent ritual focus of multi-surname villages. The contrast should not be overdrawn, however. Ancestor worship at domestic altars, although discouraged during the high tides of communist reform, seems to have been nearly ubiquitous among Han Chinese, and may be making a comeback in areas where it was repressed during the 1960s and 1970s. By the same token, some deities (Guanyin, for example) are worshipped nearly universally, and most locales produced some local gods closely associated with local lore and history.

Although some village-based ethnographies have a penchant for treating the village as a self-contained community, Skinner argues forcefully that the standard-marketing community was until recently the most important unit of rural social life (Skinner 1964–5). In frequent, sometimes daily, trips to markets, farmers had access to the cultural amenities of the town, interacted with traders, landlords, and other local dignitaries, and found occasion to worship and attend festivals at temples. Higher-level lineage corporations often built lineage halls in market towns, and voluntary associations with market-system-wide memberships also concentrated their activities there. Improved transport and economic development have to some degree eclipsed the traditional 'standard market towns,' thus expanding the horizons of China's rural population, and (at least in some areas) resulted in the emergence of what Skinner terms 'modern trading centers.' During the Maoist era, many of the

functions of 'standard-marketing communities' were assumed by communes (often territorially isomorphic with them), but in the reform era, local markets are re-emerging rapidly (Skinner 1985).

4. The Local Impact of Imperial and State Institutions

In imperial times, the impact of the state on local life was mediated largely by local elites; imperial administration extended to the county level, but the maintenance of social stability depended on local leaders and institutions (Ch'u 1962). The imperial state managed to maintain its hegemony largely because local elites were thoroughly committed to the Confucian ideology upon which the legitimacy of both the state and literati leadership rested. This commitment, in turn, was sustained in part by the imperial examination system. Aspirants in the highly competitive examinations were required to master Confucian classics. Success came in the form of academic degrees and appointment to administrative office. The symbolic and material rewards for successful candidates redounded to the benefit of their kin and communities. Consequently, local wealth and institutional effort were invested in the production of successful examination candidates (for example, lineage corporations often established schools for its sons), on the one hand, and successful candidates were able to use their official positions to return wealth and prestige to their communities. Although the prospects for advancement through the theoretically meritocratic examination system were distant or unrealistic for all but the relatively wealthy (Ho 1962), its values exercised a strong hold on popular imagination in all of China's social classes.

Beyond the pervasive impact of the imperial examination system on China's class system and consciousness, state power affected localities primarily through taxation and social control. In these functions, too, county magistrates often relied on the mediating services of local elites, with whom they shared a similar class background and Confucian education.

The mediating role of local elites and institutions in integrating localities and the state began to unravel in late imperial times, and reached a crisis during the Republican era, when government policy tended to undermine local authority (Duara 1988). The momentum during the post-1949 era was to establish greater central control by binding local cadres and officials more firmly to the policies of the center, often undermining local leadership and institutions. The period of economic reforms beginning in the late 1970s has seen a general loosening of central control over individuals (as, for example, in the initiation of the famous 'household responsibility system') and, to some degree, over local governments. As a result, some of the forms of traditional communalism (for example, territorial cults worshipping local gods) are re-emerging in some parts of China (Dean 1993, Jing 1996).

5. Family and Kinship

Patrilineal descent, virilocal residence, and equal inheritance among sons characterize the standard model of Han Chinese kinship. It is a standard model less in a statistical sense than in the fact that it serves as an ideal type; even families whose own organization does not conform are likely to acknowledge this ideal type as how things ought to be. In principle, a bride should leave her natal household and take up residence in the natal household of her groom—including his parents, unmarried siblings, married brothers, and their wives and children. Prior to 1949, 'five generations living in a single household' was widely held to be both an admirable and enviable achievement. But it was an achievement also recognized to be difficult to attain. Domestic strife, economic misfortune, mortality, or infertility could intervene to prevent the achievement of such a 'grand family.'

The characteristic ethos of Chinese family life is one of the dimensions of Chinese culture that has been examined most closely by ethnographers. The picture that emerges of the Chinese domestic cycle includes tensions between daughters-in-law and their mothers-in-law, stemming in part from their divergent interests with respect to maintaining a large, unified family structure. Daughters-in-law often desire to escape the authority of their mothers-in-law, and agitate for a family division; mothers-in-law exercise their often strong influence over their sons in the interest of keeping the extended family united (Fei 1939, Wolf 1968, 1972, Cohen 1976). By the same token, sons owe filial allegiance to their fathers, but they also owe their children as good a start in life as they can provide. These circumstances can set brothers' interests against each other (Freedman 1966). In the end, competing interests and domestic tensions can result in agreement to divide an estate. For many rural families, the most tangible and immediate manifestation of division was the setting up of separate cooking stoves. Members of the formerly united family continued to reside in the same building, but the separate stoves indicate separate budgets and, symbolically, a parting of ways.

As one might expect, by no means all families were of ideal-typical form. We have already noted some of the factors that might prevent achievement of the ideal of a 'five-generation' household. In addition, we now know that both uxorilocal marriages and 'little daughter-in-law' marriages were quite common in some parts of China (Wolf and Huang 1980). Uxorilocal marriages seem to have occurred most commonly as a strategy in families lacking a male heir. In such circumstances, a son-in-law might agree to marry into his wife's family. Because a married-in son-in-law was

looked down upon (having at least partially abandoned his filial commitments to his own patriline), they typically were men of relatively lower socioeconomic status and background. Because such marriages self-consciously deviated from the ideal type, arrangements for inheritance, descent of children, and so forth would be stipulated in a formal marriage contract. (For example, children might be divided between the patrilines of both the husband and the wife; the groom might agree to change his own surname and become his father-in-law's adopted son; the groom might agree only to support the father-in-law in his dotage.)

'Little daughter-in-law' marriage involves adopting an infant or girl with the intention that she marry her foster brother when she comes of age. No longer widely practiced (they are now illegal), such marriages were common in some locales through the first half of the twentieth century. They were said to save the expense and trouble of a wedding, but Wolf and Huang contend that their real advantage lay most of all in the fact that mothers-in-law were able thereby to develop more amiable relations with their daughters-in-law, having raised them essentially as daughters. Wolf and Huang also argue that improvement of mother/daughter-in-law relations were won at the expense of conjugal ones; divorce rates and infidelity were higher among 'minor marriages' in northern Taiwan, and fertility was lower (Wolf and Huang 1980).

Contracts typically drawn at family division might stipulate that some portion of the estate remain undivided in the form of a corporation in memory of an honored ancestor (often the father of the sons dividing the estate). The income of the corporation typically might be shared among the descendents, used to build an ancestral hall, or to fund annual banquets in memory of shared ancestors. Corporations formed in this fashion are often referred to as lineages (Freedman 1958, 1966). However, lineage corporations could also be formed when a group of patrilineally related men decided to invest in shares and to purchase some common property. By the same token, unrelated parties might form similar corporations to help put the maintenance of a temple or any other enterprise on a stable financial footing. In short, although many lineages in China were organized as shareholding corporations with both ritual and (in some cases) entrepreneurial goals, similar corporations were also founded on bases other than kinship (Sangren 1984).

Lineage corporations, as noted above, tended to be more numerous in prosperous, core areas, especially in the Southeast. However, even in the absence of lineage corporations, patrilineal kinship ties were considered to be important. Consequently, some ambiguity attends to Chinese terms for 'lineage' (*congzu, zu*) because they might refer to a formal corporation or merely to those related to one patrilineally.

The nature and quality of affinal ties seems to have varied considerably by region and social class. Women sought to maintain ties with their natal families, and in some areas such ties were important in the development of the social connectedness (*guanxi*) so important to Chinese social relations. However, in terms of customary law, women retained few rights in their natal lines. Except for gifts bestowed upon them at marriage, women did not inherit. Moreover, after her death a women could be worshipped as an ancestor only in the patriline of her sons.

6. Religion and Ritual

Considered as philosophical or liturgical traditions, Confucianism, Daoism, and Buddhism have exercised an important historical influence on Chinese religion. However, these influences are not clearly distinguishable at the level of popular belief and practice. For example, because of its emphasis on 'filial piety,' ancestor worship is often considered to be in some sense 'Confucian.' However, ideas having to do with the afterlife of the soul, the nature of supernatural spirits, geomancy (the operation of unseen forces in the landscape), and communication with supernatural powers all play an important role in ancestor worship, just as they do in the worship of the local deities (often termed 'Daoist') central to territorial cults, and in the popular worship of Buddhist deities (Guanyin, for example). In other words, Buddhism, Daoism, and Confucianism are relatively distinguishable only in the contexts of monastic Buddhist institutions, the texts and practices of the ordained Daoist priesthood, and (arguably) the self-consciously Confucian writings of the official elite.

'Popular,' 'folk,' or 'local' religion is, as C. K. Yang argued influentially in his definitive treatise (Yang 1961), 'diffused' throughout the institutions of social life. Ancestor worship, for example, can be considered the religious dimension of domestic life. Similarly, territorial cults give form to local communities at levels ranging from neighborhood 'Place God' (*Tudi Gong*) shrines, village-level temples, market-based temples, upward to the City God temples found in administrative capitals (Sangren 1987). City Gods also played a role in the official rites of the imperial state. District magistrates were not only governors; they also officiated as priests in the state cult which culminated in the sacrifices to heaven performed by the emperor himself (Feuchtwang 1977).

Fundamental to popular religion is a belief in the power of supernatural spirits (*ling*); from the point of view of the majority of worshippers, it matters less whether a god or goddess is Buddhist or Daoist, heterodox or orthodox (from the point of view of the Daoist priesthood or Buddhist clergy), than whether it has a reputation for answering prayers and performing

miracles. Individuals pray to gods for blessings for themselves and their families; community leaders organize ritual celebrations to the same gods in the hope of ensuring prosperity on behalf of the community. Indeed, such celebrations constitute one of the main entertainments of local life, punctuating the annual calendar.

The majority of Chinese gods are viewed as deified historical personages; their accumulated legends of posthumous divine intervention on behalf of individuals and communities play a crucial role in the dissemination of their cults. The cults of some gods are of strictly local provenance, while the cults of others (such as those of Guanyin, the 'Goddess of Mercy,' and Guandi, the 'God of War') are popular throughout China. In imperial times, successful local cults might grow to the point where they received imperial recognition, with the emperor claiming the authority to promote and demote such deities. Pilgrimages from local temples to distant centers tied local communities into wider ritual spheres and provided welcome opportunities to travel and see the world outside an individual's own locale.

Chinese polytheism is widely conceived in terms of a celestial bureaucracy that roughly mirrored the imperial state; many gods are viewed as supernatural governors of their assigned districts. Alongside such celestial officials, however, Chinese people worshipped a variety of mother goddesses, tricksterish imps, and even demonic figures.

At death the soul is imagined to journey through the underworld where it is judged and (if found guilty) punished for its deeds. One of the obligations of descendants is to perform rituals on behalf of the deceased to bribe these underworld officials and their demonic henchmen, thereby winning the soul's release. Both Daoist priests and Buddhist clergy may be employed to perform such funerary rites. Lonely ghosts (souls of those who die in tragic circumstances or who have no descendents to worship them as ancestors) are pitied and, in some cases, feared for the mischief they may bring down upon the living. Communities commonly propitiate such spirits during the seventh lunar month.

Communication with unseen powers is established by a variety of techniques. Individual worshippers can often cast 'moon blocks' or draw lots at temple altars in an attempt to discern a deity's response to their queries. 'Spirit writing' via an apparatus believed to be possessed by a god or spirit is another common technique (Jordan and Overmeyer 1986). Spirit-mediums possessed by gods speak directly in the gods' voices (Elliott 1955), and revelation through such mediums has played an important role in the production of hagiographies (Seaman 1987, Kleeman 1994).

There has been a significant growth of Western academic interest in Chinese popular religion in recent years. One of the reasons for this growth is the close association between local social organization and collective ritual activity. Moreover, as Paul Katz argues, China's closest analog to Western 'civic society' or a 'public sphere' is most likely to be found in local temples and their rituals (Katz 1995).

7. Gender

The feminist movement in academia has inspired a large body of research and writing about women in China. In anthropology, much of this work has focused on domestic life. Among the most important conclusions is that, despite the ideological emphasis on patriarchy, women exercise a good deal of practical influence (Wolf 1972). Much of this influence is linked to mothers' close emotional relations with their children, especially their sons. Whereas Confucian ideology emphasizes the fundamental importance of father–son ties, 'filial piety' manifested in popular myth, entertainment, and ritual more often emphasizes children's affection for their mothers. Some analysts (e.g., Martin 1988) believe that women's views on life differ so radically from those of men that a distinctive female ideology exists, one that often contradicts the male, or official, ideology. Alternatively, differences in men's and women's views can be conceived as generated within the family system considered holistically as a productive process.

One of the problems confronting sinological anthropologists at the time of writing is to assess, on the one hand, the degree to which changes in gender ideology (the government now officially advocates gender equality) have improved women's lives—very little, according to some (Wolf 1985)—and, on the other hand, the degree to which changes in family organization (for example, those consequent on the 'one-child family' policy) have altered gender ideology.

See also: Area and International Studies: Development in Southeast Asia; East Asia, Religions of; East Asian Studies: Culture; East Asian Studies: Gender; East Asian Studies: Politics; East Asian Studies: Society; Historiography and Historical Thought: East Asia; International Migration by Ethnic Chinese; Kinship in Anthropology; Nationalism, Historical Aspects of: East Asia

Bibliography

Ch'u T Y 1962 *Local Government in China Under the Ch'ing*. Harvard University Press, Cambridge, MA
Cohen M L 1976 *House United, House Divided: The Chinese Family in Taiwan*. Columbia University Press, New York, NY
Dean K 1993 *Taoist Ritual and Popular Cults of Southeast China*. Princeton University Press, Princeton, NJ
Duara P 1988 *Culture, Power, and the State: Rural North China, 1900–1942*. Stanford University Press, Stanford, CA
Elliott A J A 1955 *Chinese Spirit-medium Cults in Singapore*. Department of Anthropology, London School of Economics and Political Science, London
Fei H T 1939 *Peasant Life in China: A Field Study of Country Life in the Yangtze Valley*. Kegan Paul, Trench, Trubner, London
Feuchtwang S 1977 School-temple and city god. In: Skinner G W (ed.) *The City in Late Imperial China*. Stanford University Press, Stanford, CA
Freedman M 1958 *Lineage Organization in Southeastern China*. Athlone, London
Freedman M 1966 *Chinese Lineage and Society: Fukien and Kwangtung*. Athlone, London
Harrell S 1995 Introduction. In: Harrel S (ed.) *Cultural Encounters on China's Ethnic Frontiers*. University of Washington Press, Seattle, WA
Ho P T 1962 *The Ladder of Success in Imperial China: Aspects of Social Mobility, 1368–1911*. Columbia University Press, New York
Jing J 1996 *The Temple of Memories: History, Power, and Morality in a Chinese Village*. Stanford University Press, Stanford, CA
Jordan D K, Overmyer D L 1986 *The Flying Phoenix: Aspects of Chinese Sectarianism in Taiwan*. Princeton University Press, Princeton, NJ
Katz P R 1995 *Demon Hordes and Burning Boats: The Cult of Marshal Wen in Late Imperial China*. State University of New York Press, Albany, NY
Kleeman T F 1994 *A God's Own Tale: The Book of Transformations of Wenchang, the Divine Lord of Zitong*. State University of New York Press, Albany, NY
Martin E 1988 Gender and ideological differences in representations of life and death. In: Watson J L, Rawski E S (eds.) *Death Ritual in Late Imperial and Modern China*. University of California Press, Berkeley, CA
Sangren P S 1984 Traditional Chinese corporations: Beyond kinship. *Journal of Asian Studies* 43: 391–415
Sangren P S 1987 *History and Magical Power in a Chinese Community*. Stanford University Press, Stanford, CA
Seaman G 1987 *Journey to the North: An Ethnohistorical Analysis and Annotated Translation of the Chinese Folk Novel Pei-yu Chi*. University of California Press, Berkeley, CA
Skinner G W 1964–5 Marketing and social structure in rural China, Parts I, II, and III. *Journal of Asian Studies* 24: 3–43, 195–228, 363–99
Skinner G W 1977 Cities and the hierarchy of local systems. In: Skinner G W (ed.) *The City in Late Imperial China*. Stanford University Press, Stanford, CA
Skinner G W 1985 Rural marketing in China: repression and revival. *The China Quarterly* (September): 393–413
Wolf M 1968 *The House of Lim: A Study of a Chinese Farm Family*. Appleton-Century-Crofts, New York
Wolf M 1972 *Women and Family in Rural Taiwan*. Stanford University Press, Stanford, CA
Wolf M 1985 *Revolution Postponed: Women in Contemporary China*. Stanford University Press, Stanford, CA
Wolf A P, Huang C S 1980 *Marriage and Adoption in China, 1845–1945*. Stanford University Press, Stanford, CA
Yang C K 1961 *Religion and Ritual in Chinese Society: A Study of Contemporary Social Functions of Religion and Some of Their Historical Factors*. University of California Press, Berkeley, CA

P. S. Sangren

Chinese Law

China's modern legal institutions reflect powerful political, economic, and social forces that have struggled to shape them since the latter part of the nineteenth century. For thousands of years, before the last dynasty fell, cultural values in the world's oldest continuous empire were inhospitable to ideals of 'rule of law' that evolved slowly in the West. In the Republic (1911–49) formal legal institutions were only superficially borrowed from abroad. From 1949 to 1979 the Maoist party-state reduced law to the merest tool of totalitarian politics. Mao's successors launched economic reforms in 1979 that have led to the creation of the most significant legal institutions in Chinese history, but at the end of the twentieth century traditional values endured, the ideology and the apparatus of the party-state remained in place, governmental institutions were disorderly, and the economy in flux. The new institutions can grow in strength and legitimacy only if they receive sustained and powerful political support from China's leadership and greater recognition in the legal culture of China's officials and its populace.

1. The Chinese Legal Tradition

Contemporary Chinese institutions should be viewed in light of profound differences between Chinese and Western legal history. Imperial China blended law and morality in contrast to Western Europe, where secular and sacred authority were separated early. The dominant cult and philosophy of Confucianism emphasized governance by men who acquired moral authority by emulating ancient sages in setting virtuous examples of benevolence and social rightness for their subjects to follow. Law was regarded as a set of inferior norms that supplemented more basic principles, especially rules of propriety (*li*) that differentiated individuals according to their status as determined by age and rank in family and society. Confucianism was briefly rivaled by the early philosophical school of Legalism, which stressed the need for harsh penalties using positive law (*fa*) to deter wrongdoing, but both schools shared a vision of society in which proper behavior derived from an individual's status in the hierarchies in which he or she lived.

Law was first codified in the Qin Dynasty (third century BC) and recodified and augmented by a complex body of regulations in subsequent dynasties, notably in the Tang and Ming. Principally penal, it unambiguously reinforced ideas of hierarchy and subordination and was addressed to officials, not to the populace. It was enforced by local county magistrates without legal training or expertise, as part of their general duties to govern on behalf of the emperor. Specialized institutions for adjudication like the centralized judicial systems that developed over centuries in the West were absent, although there were unofficial legal specialists at provincial and central levels. The outcomes of cases had to be substantively correct according to both law and Confucian morality. The concerns for procedural justice and uniformity of results that have come to mark Anglo-American law were absent.

The Chinese state exercised its rule mostly in an indirect manner, through local elites—landowners, family heads, and village elders—which enforced local customs. The concept of personal rights did not develop because the basic units of society were not individuals but rather the collectivities of family, clan, village, and guild. Economic transactions arose and were enforced largely in the context of custom-governed relationships. The official philosophy exerted strong social pressure in favor of mediation and compromise. Litigation before the magistrates was time-consuming, degrading, and costly. Civil disputes were common, nonetheless, but most were settled extra-judicially. Unlike the West, where lawyers emerged, any tendency for legal specialists to act as intermediaries between individuals and the state was actively discouraged, although in the late Qing men who facilitated litigation, albeit tarred as 'litigation tricksters,' did flourish.

From the mid-nineteenth century until 1949, when the People's Republic of China (PRC) was established, sporadic and inconsistent attempts were made to transplant foreign legal institutions. These failed to take root since they were often too complex as well as being irrelevant to Chinese conditions. China established its first professional bar during the Republican period, but lawyers' training and qualifications were uneven and their standards of professional behavior low. Judges were both few and poorly educated, and judicial professionalism and independence were weakened by corruption and favoritism. The authoritarian Nationalist Party undercut the spirit of the new legal reforms.

2. The People's Republic of China

2.1 Maoism, 1949–79

Under Mao Zedong the Chinese Communist Party (CCP) mounted extensive programs of economic reconstruction and social change, relying on both previous experience in ruling large areas before 1949 and on Soviet models, which entwined state institutions with the Party. Law was used as a political tool, along with mass organizations and propaganda media, to mobilize the populace to carry out policies. The criminal process was declared an instrument to exercise 'dictatorship' over members of the former exploiting classes, and sanctions frequently varied according to political 'campaigns' and policies of the moment. Systematized codes of criminal law or criminal procedure were lacking, and the courts merely formalized findings of guilt by the police and the procuracy, which was a prosecutorial agency. The police could impose sentences of as long as four years without any judicial involvement.

The collectivization of almost all private property left little scope for noncriminal law. In the planned economy, disputes between state-owned enterprises were resolved informally through flexible, highly pragmatic attempts to adjust problems without fixing legal blame. Disputes among individuals were usually dealt with through mediation. Mediation committees that formed part of a totalitarian control apparatus which penetrated deeply into Chinese society were charged with attaining politically correct results that would benefit socialist construction and strengthen the party-state's control over 'bad elements.' Politicization was not total, of course; traditional attitudes among mediators and the populace persisted.

Mao and other leaders, determined to speed continued revolution and social change, refused to regularize law and administration. The Cultural Revolution (1966–76), further reduced the relevance of legal institutions that had already been politicized. After the overthrow of the 'Gang of Four' in 1976, the lawlessness of the Cultural Revolution moved their successors, led by Deng Xiaoping, to advocate adoption of orderly legal institutions. An era of reform began, and since then law has risen to greater prominence than ever before in Chinese history.

2.2 Reform Since 1979

Legal reform has been driven by the economic reforms that began in 1979 and have unfolded irregularly but irreversibly. A growing and increasingly differentiated non-state sector has been created and modernization has been aimed at constructing a 'socialist market economy,' including a legal system. China's departure from previous Maoist disregard for formal legislation has led to one of the greatest outpourings of legislation in history.

The structure of the Chinese state has been defined in a Constitution and in 'organic' laws dealing with key state institutions such as the courts and central and local legislative bodies; the General Principles of Civil Law, a partial civil code intended to mature into a comprehensive one; 'basic' laws such as codes of criminal law and criminal procedure; and enactments by the central government, subnational units, and by central ministries and their local branches. These define newly recognized economic relationships and participants in expanding markets and address regulatory problems generated by economic reform. Much

legislation, however, has been incomplete and *ad hoc* as new economic policies appeared, reflecting the difficulties that the leadership has had in defining the direction of economic reform. There is a continuing struggle between concepts of law as a framework for economic activity by autonomous actors and as an administrative instrument.

Extensive legislation also signals China's participation in a global economic community. Direct foreign investment has been addressed by legislation on various investment vehicles and their operation, as well as on such matters as intellectual property, labor, customs, foreign exchange, bank lending and guaranties, and export and import licenses. A taxation system has been established. China has acceded to an extensive range of international agreements, such as the UN Convention on the International Sale of Goods, whose rules have become part of Chinese law.

2.2.1 Building a judicial system. The courts, formerly scorned as 'rightist' institutions at the end of the 1950s and as 'bourgeois' during the Cultural Revolution, have been rebuilt in a four-level hierarchy. The number of civil and economic disputes brought to the courts rose from 2.4 million cases in 1990 to 5.7 million in 1999, while the number of disputes brought to mediation committees declined from 7.4 million in 1990 to 5.1 million in 1999. Growing reliance on contracts and the increase in litigation suggests increasing acceptance of concepts of law-based rights.

The Chinese judicial system presents many problems at the beginning of the twenty-first century. Judges are poorly trained, and most still lack a complete legal education despite efforts to raise their educational qualifications. Over half of the cases brought to the courts are resolved through judicial mediation rather than adjudication of competing claims and rights. Judges often prefer to resolve cases by mediation to avoid reversal by a higher court; lower courts, fearful of being reversed, sometimes request instructions from a higher court before they issue a judgment, thereby rendering meaningless the right of unsuccessful parties to appeal. The finality of judgments is impaired by legislation permitting non-criminal decisions to be reopened within two years after they become effective. Sometimes, too, higher courts reviewing the quality of the work of lower courts reopen decisions even though they have already taken legal effect. The role of judges has been defined only ambiguously, and adjudication has not been significantly differentiated from decision making by administrative agencies in the course of implementing policies.

The independence, powers, and effectiveness of the courts have been constrained by the requirement that they follow CCP policies. In 2000, over 70 percent of judges were members of the CCP and the principal affairs of the courts, including personnel matters, were directed by Party organizations. Judges are appointed and their salaries paid by the local governments in the jurisdictions in which they serve, leading to 'local protectionism' that frequently influences the outcomes of litigation. In addition, *guanxi* (relationships), corruption, and bribery are often employed to influence outcomes that on many occasions pervert justice.

2.2.2 The legal profession. The bar was formally re-established in 1980 following a twenty-year hiatus after a brief experiment with a Soviet-style bar was ended, and legal education was revived. There were over 120,000 lawyers in 2000, but the educational level of many older lawyers is low and legal education remains highly formalistic. By 2000 China had over 8,000 law firms, most of which were state-run, but the number of 'cooperative' firms was growing. The sudden expansion of the legal profession created enormous temptations for lawyers, judges, and officials to engage in bribery and other corrupt practices. The state continued to regulate and scrutinize lawyers' activities, and a major unresolved contradiction existed between the concept of a professional bar and CCP opposition to autonomous organizations and professions.

2.2.3 The criminal process. The criminal process continues to be a tool for the politicized administration of law, as when political leaders focus it on activities deemed to 'endanger the security of the state,' or on other particular types of criminal activity. The formal rationality of the criminal process has been slowly increased in a criminal code and code of criminal procedure, but the extensive power of the police and the CCP over the criminal process have been only ineffectually restrained, and the police-administered system of sanctions begun under Mao remained in place in 2000.

2.2.4 Administrative law. The Chinese leadership began in the 1990s to address the need to create legal institutions that might curb bureaucratic arbitrariness. A series of laws gave affected persons or organizations the right to sue agencies that have acted unlawfully, defined the wide assortment of punishments that may be imposed by administrative agencies, and recognized situations in which governmental agencies may be liable for injurious consequences of their acts. However, the jurisdiction of the courts and their power to restrain arbitrariness remained limited. Chinese laws and administrative rules have generally given agencies very broad discretion, while judicial control of administrative action has been limited by

a reluctance to allow courts to review the validity of general rules issued by administrative agencies or to decide that they had improperly used their discretion. The courts were at best only at the same level of authority as the other institutions of the state apparatus; their limited reach reflected the subordination of law to the bureaucracy.

2.3 The Future

The development, shape and meaningfulness of Chinese legal institutions will depend upon critical factors that lie outside the law.

2.3.1 Policy. As long as the CCP rules China, its policy will have to overcome its ambivalence toward the role—and rule—of law. The Chinese Constitution, amended in 1999 to declare that 'The People's Republic of China shall be governed according to law and shall be built into a socialist country based on the rule of law,' also affirmed 'the leadership of the Chinese Communist Party, Marxism-Leninism and Mao Zedong Thought, and "Deng Xiaoping Theory"' as 'guiding principles.' The leadership has tended to equate law with discipline and to treat it as an instrument to maintain the dominant role of the CCP in Chinese society. At the same time, it has also recognized that law can further rationalize decision making and implementation of policy, while increasing legitimacy at home and abroad.

2.3.2 Structural problems. At the beginning of the twenty-first century institutions for law making heavily reflect the imprint of pre-reform doctrine and practice. Three principal law-making agencies share the central government's legislative power under the Constitution adopted in 1982—the National People's Congress, its Standing Committee and the State Council—but their respective powers were only very generally defined and subject in practice to informal negotiations. The State Council, at the head of the executive branch of the central government, together with the ministries, commissions, and bureaus that are subordinate to it, possesses broad power to generate rules superior to all local enactments.

Although subnational units and more than 20 functional bureaucracies of the central government issue regulations, distinctions among the rules that they issue, and between rule making and implementation, are blurred. No effective mechanism has existed to measure legal norms for consistency with higher-level norms, and the Constitution is not justiciable. Chinese administrative agencies have exercised the power both to issue and interpret their own rules, and to require the courts to enforce them. The lower courts are formally denied power to interpret laws, although in practice the Supreme People's Court has asserted a strong role in the interpretation and clarification of laws. These problems are aggravated by the frequently provisional nature and tentative style of legislation.

Although the dramatic Chinese economic reform at the end of the twentieth century was greatly promoted by increasing the power of local governments, it also facilitated extensive interpenetration of government and business. It was carried out without carefully defining property rights, and local governments took advantage of the uncertainty to form alliances with private enterprises. Local government involvement in enterprises varied from disguised ownership to acceptance of payoffs and bribes. Overall, in the year 2000, marketization was often not synonymous with privatization, and some Western scholars perceived the emergence of corporatist relationships that closely linked non-governmental actors to local governments. Also, the growth of local power increased local deviations from central state policies, and undermined uniformity in the application of legal rules and the reach of the central government generally.

Legal development remains tied to economic reform; its vigor will in turn not only on the strength of the economy and the consolidation of reforms already accomplished, but also on whether solutions are fashioned to deal with basic problems that have been difficult to surmount. The state sector of the economy has been governed by rules and practices to which legal rules are essentially irrelevant. Although reform has long been a goal of the leadership, it has been unable to chart a clear course between privatization and continued dedication to state ownership, or to create mechanisms to deal with the large-scale unemployment and associated social distress that further industrial reform would generate. The establishment of enforceable rules on the governance of formerly state-owned firms that have been converted remains problematic. Financial system reform began in the last years of the twentieth century but was incomplete and faced serious obstacles; and both creation and regulation of capital markets were still in early stages.

2.3.3 The crisis of values.
Reform dramatically relaxed state control over the lives of many Chinese in noticeable ways, but it also created severe social dislocations including income disparity and an impoverished 'floating population' of as many as 100 million peasants who have flocked to China's cities seeking employment. Discontent has risen, among peasants angry at their exploitation by local cadres and among unemployed workers at state-owned enterprises that have closed down. Crime, violent and otherwise, has risen, provoking widespread concern about social order.

The profound political and economic changes of the last two decades of the twentieth century unsettled both traditional and Communist values. The Party's ideology became hollow and its legitimacy increasingly questioned, while the opening of China to the rest of the world exposed the Chinese people to new values and ideas, including Western concepts of legality. The weakening of the totalitarian grip on individual lives and the continuing flux of economic reform have fostered the re-emergence of an emphasis on personal relationships and clientelism. Corruption has grown despite continued efforts by the leadership to check and punish its many manifestations, and has aroused alienation and cynicism among many Chinese.

2.3.4 Chinese legal culture: continuity and change.
Chinese legal culture continues to reflect competing currents. Traditional values remain strong. Many Chinese remain unwilling to take their disputes to courts, choosing to rely on personal relationships or to defer to authority. In the courts, concern for procedural justice is weak. Bureaucrats continue to want to enjoy broad discretion. At the same time, the extensive social and economic changes sparked by reform have promoted consciousness of legal rights and willingness to use legal processes to assert such rights. Lawsuits against government agencies are increasing, although they remain relatively small in number, and peasant and worker protests often invoke published laws and policies to resist official behavior that they consider to be unjust. Some Chinese legal scholars, officials and intellectuals have called for a legal system with a national and autonomous judiciary that applies standards of procedural fairness. Some economic actors in the non-state sector desire stronger protection of their transactions by rules enforced meaningfully and consistently by the power of the Chinese state. Despite the resistance of the CCP to the growth of civil society, the continuing development of non-state economic activity, the strength of communal traditions and the tenacity of some nongovernmental organizations in Chinese society could combine to advance the development of legal consciousness.

3. Conclusion: Perspectives

It should not be assumed that legal development will lead to Western-type institutions or to liberal democracy. The domain considered 'legal' and the boundaries between it and other areas of Chinese state, society, and economy will not necessarily converge with Western concepts, and rights may remain 'soft.' Nor should Western observers overstate the supposed virtues for China of Western concepts and institutions, themselves imperfect and under question.

Twenty years of reform efforts began a journey toward greater legality, and further efforts are underway at the beginning of the twenty-first century to advance judicial reform, add coherence to Chinese law making, and develop administrative law further. The accession of China to the World Trade Organization would impose on China international obligations to increase the transparency of government and the reach of legal institutions. The General Agreement on Tariffs and Trade and other agreements that are implemented by the WTO require all member nations to adopt and implement their laws relating to trade in a manner consistent with the rule of law as it is understood in the West, and China will have to adjust its legal institutions to comply with WTO standards. The deepening of legal reform most depends, however, on political reform. Legal institutions will be hobbled by political constraints as long as any Chinese leadership, Communist or post-Communist, maintains an instrumental view of law, remains ambivalent about the rule of law, and inhibits the growth of an active civil society. For law to grow more meaningful, leadership policy and official ideology must enlarge the domain of the law, end or greatly dilute one-party domination, and remedy institutional weaknesses in the structure of the Chinese state. Even the strongest political commitment will require considerable time to implement further reform, overcome the serious limits on state capacity that make the governance of China difficult under any circumstances, and inspire popular confidence in institutions. The processes of institutional change that have begun can only work slowly at best.

See also: China: Sociocultural Aspects; East Asian Studies: Economics; East Asian Studies: Politics; East Asian Studies: Society; Globalization: Legal Aspects; Law and Society: Sociolegal Studies; Law as an Instrument of Social Change; Legal Culture and Legal Consciousness; Mediation, Arbitration, and Alternative Dispute Resolution (ADR)

Bibliography

Bodde D, Morris C 1967 *Law in Imperial China*. Harvard University Press, Cambridge, MA

Chen J 1999 *Chinese Law: Toward an Understanding of Chinese Law, Its Nature and Development*. Kluwer Law International, The Hague, The Netherlands

Corne P H 1996 *Foreign Investment in China: The Administrative Legal System*. Hong Kong University Press, Hong Kong

He W 1995 Tongguo sifa shixian shehui zhengyi: dui zhongguo faguan xianzhuang de yige toushi [The realization of social justice through judicature: a look at the current situation of Chinese judges]. In: Xia Y (ed.) *Zou xiang quanli de shidai: Zhongguo gongmin quanli fazhan yanjiu [Toward a Time of Rights: A Perspective of the Civil Rights Development in China]*. China University of Politics and Law Press, Beijing, People's Republic of China, pp. 209–84

Huang P C 1996 *Civil Justice in China: Representation and Practice in the Qing*. Stanford University Press, Stanford, CA

Keller P 1994 Sources of order in Chinese law. *American Journal of Comparative Law* **42**: 711–59

Lawyers Committee for Human Rights 1996 *Opening to Reform?: An Analysis of China's Revised Criminal Procedure Law*. Lawyers Committee for Human Rights, New York

Lawyers Committee for Human Rights 1998a *Wrongs and Rights: A Human Rights Analysis of China's Revised Criminal Law*. Lawyers Committee for Human Rights, New York

Lawyers Committee for Human Rights 1998b *Lawyers in China: Obstacles to Independence and the Defense of Rights*. Lawyers Committee for Human Rights, New York

Lubman S (ed.) 1997 *China's Legal Reforms*. Oxford University Press, Oxford, UK

Lubman S 1999 *Bird in a Cage: Legal Reform in China After Mao*. Stanford University Press, Stanford, CA

Turner K G, Feinerman J V, Guy R K (eds.) 2000 *The Limits of the Rule of Law in China*. University of Washington, Seattle, DC

Van der Sprenkel S 1962 *Legal Institutions in Manchu China: A Sociological Analysis*. Athlone, London

Xia Y (ed.) 1995 *Zouxiang quanli de shidai: Zhongguo gongmin quanli fazhan yanjiu [Toward a Time of Rights: A Perspective of the Civil Rights Development in China]*. China University of Politics and Law Press, Beijing, People's Republic of China

S. B. Lubman

Chinese Revolutions: Twentieth Century

In the 1800s, a leading Sinologist claimed the Chinese were the 'most rebellious' but 'least revolutionary' of peoples and Karl Marx, along with other Western social theorists, argued that peasants would never be the driving force in radical movements for change. The twentieth century would prove both the Sinologist and the theorists wrong—many times over. Nearly every decade of it saw a revolutionary event of one kind or another break out in China. In many of these, peasants played central roles.

1. Key Events

The first quarter of the twentieth century witnessed a series of inter-related insurrections that toppled the Qing Dynasty (1644–1911). Known collectively as the 1911 Revolution, these paved the way for the establishment of the Republic of China (ROC) on January 1, 1912, which was also when a revolutionary activist, Sun Yat-sen (1866–1925), was inaugurated as this new country's first President. A path breaking student-led mass struggle also took place in the century's first quarter. This was the May 4th Movement of 1919, which ended with the dismissal from office of three high-ranking officials. In addition, two revolutionary organizations were formed in this period: the Nationalist Party or Guomingdang (GMD), which was led initially by Sun and then after his death by Chiang Kai-shek (1887–1975); and the Chinese Communist Party (CCP) of Mao Zedong (1893–1976) and Deng Xiaoping (1904–1997).

The second quarter of the century began with the GMD and CCP working together in a United Front

(1924–1927) orchestrated by Sun and his Soviet advisor Borodin. The alliance's goal was to defeat warlordism and imperialism and thus get the *Geming* (a Chinese term for revolution whose shades of meaning are returned to below) back on track. In 1927, however, Chiang turned on his erstwhile allies, who had just helped him reunify the country through the military campaigns and mass movements known as the Northern Expedition. He launched a White Terror against members of the CCP and left-wing rivals within the GMD. Seven years later, after persistent GMD extermination campaigns, the CCP set out on its epic Long March (1934–1935) to safety in isolated northern base areas. The two organizations, each tightly disciplined and Leninist in structure, allied again from 1937 to 1945 in a Second United Front against Japan. The 1925–1950 period concluded, however, with a Civil War (1945–1949). This ended with the GMD's retreat to Taiwan and Mao's proclamation, on October 1, 1949, of the establishment of a new People's Republic of China (PRC)—something that this son of a relatively well-to-do farmer was only able to do because his party had won so much peasant support. The CCP then launched a series of radical initiatives, including a partially successful effort to gain adherence to a new Marriage Law (1950) that gave women equal rights in family matters and strove to minimize the power of patriarchal kin-groups.

The century's third quarter began with Mao taking the lead in further campaigns, some of which caused enormous misery. The most notorious included the 'Anti-Rightist Campaign' (a Red Terror directed largely against intellectuals) and the 'Great Leap Forward' (a bizarre experiment in irrational utopianism that contributed to a famine of horrendous proportions). Later in this quarter-century, Mao, angered by his post-Great Leap marginalization within the CCP hierarchy, rallied young loyalists (Red Guards) to challenge the Party bureaucracy. Thus began the Cultural Revolution (1966–1976). Mao's charge, soon echoed by the Gang of Four (a clique that included Jiang Qing, his wife), was that high officials had lost their revolutionary zeal and become corrupt.

The Cultural Revolution spiraled into a chaotic war of all against all that continued into the first year of the century's final quarter. This period also witnessed the abortive revolution of 1989, during which giant demonstrations took place in Beijing and other cities. In the ROC (as Taiwan was re-baptized in 1949), a major breakthrough came with the lifting of a decades old policy of martial law. This laid the groundwork for an East Asian variation of the 'Velvet Revolutions' of Central Europe: the nonviolent transfer of power from the GMD to an opposition party early in the year 2000.

By the time the 1900s ended, so many aspects of Chinese politics and society had been transformed or challenged by insurgents that it now seems strange that the first edition of this Encyclopedia included an entry on 'The Chinese Problem' but not 'The Chinese Revolution.' The rise of the CCP and the Cultural Revolution still lay in the future, but there were clear signs that the twentieth century would be a revolutionary one for China. One indication of just *how* revolutionary is that, by the 1990s, many Chinese were living lives that would have been unrecognizable to their great-grandparents or even their parents. Moreover, the words 'China' and 'revolution' were by then inextricably linked in the minds of many people.

This linkage was particularly strong in the PRC where the term *Geming* continues to have a sacred patriotic meaning. This is of strategic significance to the CCP, which is still struggling, as this entry is being written, to ride out an ongoing legitimacy crisis. The regime continues to find it useful to play the revolutionary legacy card periodically. It did so, for example, in 1999 when American bombs mistakenly killed three Chinese journalists in Belgrade. The victims were quickly dubbed 'revolutionary martyrs' and the official media linked these new deaths to those of patriotic participants in hallowed historic events of the 1910s–1950s.

In addition, even though Westerners often view the words 'reform' and 'revolution' as contrastive, in China *gaige* (reform) is often presented as a method for carrying forward the *Geming*. The policy of opening the PRC to international trade and moving away from a command economy that Deng and his successors have followed since 1979 is typically presented in English language works as a pragmatic 'Reform Program' and a step away from state socialism. Its PRC proponents, however, describe it as an effort to 'build socialism with Chinese characteristics' and an effort to keep the Revolution from ossifying.

It is not just in the PRC that the words 'China' and 'revolution' go together naturally. Most of the few Chinese names and faces recognized by foreigners are those of insurgents—from Mao to the anonymous 'man-who-stopped-the-tanks' in 1989. And many ROC residents grew up learning history from schoolbooks that treated the story of the 1900s as an unending revolutionary struggle, which encountered a terrible setback in 1949 but did not die.

2. Categories and Definitions

This brings us to a question too rarely addressed: did China experience one Revolution or several? Many official PRC histories (as well as some Marxist ones in other languages and standard GMD accounts) refer to a single ongoing Revolution with many stages. Western social theorists (such as Theda Skocpol) and comparative historians (such as Crane Brinton) sometimes prefer to think of a single great event that began in 1911 and ended in 1949. They then fit this almost 40-year long event into a Great Social Revolution model that is also used to interpret more compact phenomena such as the French upheavals of 1789–1799. Many non-Marxist Sinologists, meanwhile, speak of three relatively discrete revolutions: a Republican one in 1911, a National one in the 1920s, and a Communist one.

2.1 The Term 'Geming'

Complicating these questions is the term *Geming*, the meaning of which at times overlaps with, at others diverges from its Western equivalents. *Geming* literally means 'stripping the mandate,' that is, the successful carrying out of an upheaval that demonstrates, through its ability to overturn a ruling house and establish a new dynasty, that heaven now sides with a new regime. It was only from the 1890s on, in part because of new senses the characters had acquired in Japan, that *Geming* began to be linked to the creation of a new political system, not just completion of a dynastic cycle. *Geming*'s original linkage to dynastic cycles makes it curiously like its English and French counterparts, in which visions of return and of forward movement alike can be found. In 1789, the Janus-faced aspect of revolution was signaled by the use of classical goddesses to portray new political virtues. In the 1910s, it was signaled by anti-Qing leaders alternating between presenting themselves as avenging the legacy of the Ming (1368–1644), the ethnically Chinese ruling group the Manchus had displaced, and as struggling to create a new system.

If there are overlaps between the terms 'revolution' and *Geming*, however, there is also a difference: it is never clear whether the sense of the Chinese word is singular or plural, lower or upper case, whether a text is referring to The Revolution or one of many. This is more than merely a linguistic issue: to compare events, we need to know when they began and ended. With France, for example, there is a consensus that the revolution began in 1789 and lasted about a decade, though other supplemental revolutions occurred later (1830, 1848, and 1871). With China, there are more options, including the three alluded to above.

2.2 Problems with Standard Categorization Schemes

There are, however, limitations to each. The continuous Revolution vision focuses too tightly on the achievements of a particular organization. It distorts the shape of twentieth-century history by downplaying struggles not guided by the particular Leninist party—the CCP or GMD—being celebrated.

The 1911–1949 vision is problematic for use in comparison—even though comparativists champion it. Skocpol, for example, does not explain why, if the 'Great Social Revolutions' are essentially alike in

structural terms, the Chinese one took so much longer to play out. Brinton's 'anatomy of revolution' model becomes problematic because 'terrors' occurred at different points in the Chinese *Geming*. In other revolutions, he claims, this 'fever' hit the patient just once, then broke.

A tripartite schema, finally, leaves too little room for radical developments that do not move in lockstep with the rise of governments. 1911, the late 1920s, and 1949 were key turning points in the political story but not necessarily the social and cultural ones.

3. Overlapping Revolutions

A more satisfying approach divides China's recent past, for heuristic purposes, into four overlapping revolutions, each following its own timetable: one political, one cultural/intellectual, one diplomatic, and one socioeconomic. Let us consider each briefly.

3.1 Politics

The political revolution has the clearest starting date: October 10, 1911. GMD official historians present the events that followed the Wuchang Uprising of that day (really a military mutiny) as adhering to a master plan crafted by Sun Yat-sen and carried out by members of his Revolutionary Alliance, the organization that evolved into the Nationalist Party. But many participants had no contact with the Alliance and knew little of Sun or his ideas. Only some were committed to republican ideals. Others were motivated by distrust of the Qing 'barbarians,' anger at particular officials, or a desire to be on the winning side of a Mandate shift.

Still, the 1911 Revolution extinguished not just a dynasty but a system, hence it deserves to be thought of as politically revolutionary. The National Assembly and other republican institutions quickly proved ineffectual. But the complete failure of attempts by Yuan and later another warlord to found new dynasties demonstrated that the rules of political life had changed.

3.2 Cultural and Intellectual Change

Attempts by Chinese revolutionaries to transform traditional belief structures and patterns of behavior began after the Opium War (1839–1842). The military defeat suffered then by China led some within the dominant scholar-official class to begin questioning longstanding assumptions about the inferiority of foreign cultures. The first generations of intellectuals to rethink these issues, while interested in specific things the West had to offer (*yong* or techniques), were seldom revolutionary in their approach to questions of fundamentals (*ti* or essences). Their belief in the superiority of traditional moral codes remained unshaken; they merely sought efficacious ways to combine Confucian *ti* with Western gunboats and other sorts of foreign *yong*.

The *ti/yong* distinction remained at the heart of the debate for decades, until the iconoclastic New Culture Movement (1915–1923) led by intellectuals who had gone abroad, usually to Japan, or been exposed to foreign ideas at one of China's recently formed Western-style schools. They disagreed about many things but shared three convictions. China's weakness was due to the enduring power of entrenched 'Confucian' and 'feudal' beliefs (such as the veneration of age) and practices (such as arranged marriages). Chinese should welcome the best the West had to offer: ideas and methods of inquiry included. And intellectuals needed to educate and mobilize others.

Much New Culture Movement energy was directed toward the publication of new periodicals, which were filled with articles on Social Darwinism, Pragmatism, Anarchism, Marxism, and other imported ideologies. These periodicals also attempted to serve another purpose: their articles, written in a 'plain speech' as opposed to a 'classical' style, were supposed to inform and inspire the masses. This literary move to break down the barriers between intellectuals and non-intellectuals was reinforced by public speaking campaigns on issues ranging from medicine to international affairs.

An important new turn came with the May 4th Movement, when student activists with ties to the New Culture Movement actively appealed to members of other classes to join them in protesting terms of the Treaty of Versailles that transferred control of former German territories in China to Japan. After sympathy strikes by workers and merchants, the students achieved their main domestic goals: the dismissal of three corrupt officials and the release of all those arrested for protesting. But their inability to stop the Treaty of Versailles from taking effect illustrated the need for a diplomatic revolution.

3.3 Diplomatic Change

No diplomatic revolution could take place until the rise of a strong central regime committed to overturning the unequal treaties forced upon the Qing by foreign powers. The Northern Expedition brought this about. After reunifying the nation, however, Chiang claimed that the spread of communism was more dangerous than the continuation of imperialism. Unlike some of his warlord predecessors, Chiang was an outspoken critic of the unequal treaties, but he insisted that China could only regain its place in the world once its house was in order.

World War II precipitated a sea change, as China's position as one of the Allies gave its leader new leverage in pushing for an end to unequal relations with the West. And, in 1943, the Allies renounced all claims to special privileges within Shanghai and other 'treaty-port' cities. This decision and Japan's withdrawal in 1945 made China freer of foreign influence than it had been for a century.

CCP historians argue, however, that the diplomatic revolution was still not complete—and they have a point. The GMD regime remained economically and diplomatically dependent on the USA. If credit for starting the diplomatic revolution rightly goes to Chiang, it remains true that China did not fully regain its status as an independent country until after 1949.

3.4 Socioeconomic Change

The socioeconomic revolution also began long before the Communists came to power. Most notably, the late Qing and Republican (1912–1949) eras saw dramatic shifts in the types of people in control of the government and witnessed the rise within the social hierarchy of merchants. But the development of new alignments near the top, though important, did not have much effect upon the lives of the vast majority of Chinese who continued to reside in villages and work small plots of land. For them, a socioeconomic revolution did not take place until the CCP's land reform campaigns. This socioeconomic revolution (like the others) did not hit all parts of the country at the same time but rather played itself out according to regionally distinctive timetables. By the early 1950s, however, it had affected most of China's villages.

3.5 Unfinished Revolutions

If China's twentieth century is envisioned as a time of multiple revolutions, we need to keep in mind that most were incomplete—and that struggles for change in other spheres were pursued sporadically but never fully carried through. One important unfinished *Geming*, linked to but not quite the same as any of those just described, was the revolution for women. Aspects of sexual politics changed throughout the 1900s, but the dream of complete equality promoted by revolutionaries in various decades never became a reality. Much the same can be said for the democratic revolution: calls for democratization were heard often but oligarchy and one-party authoritarianism tended to prevail.

Ironically, though China's twentieth century was filled with transformations, its final two decades were strikingly similar to its first three. In Taiwan, moves to institute a system of free elections recall experiments made around 1911. On the mainland, there were May

4th era parallels for the calls in 1989 for an end to corruption. And in the automatic weapon fire that accompanied the massacres, there were echoes of killings of the 1920s that were justified as necessary efforts to maintain order and/or protect the *Geming*.

4. Lessons From the Chinese Case

China's twentieth-century experience suggests the need for social scientists to pay more attention in the future to a few factors. One, already mentioned, is the revolutionary potential of villagers. Another is scale. Revolutions have often been treated as purely 'national' events. Recent work on China shows that local dynamics are often crucial—even in upheavals driven by nationalism. So, too, are transnational flows of people (key participants in 1911 were overseas Chinese) and ideas. This suggests that, in future, models used for comparing revolutions will need to make more room not just for revolutions of widely varying lengths but also revolutions that were influenced by local, national, and transnational impulses and actors.

However, China's recent history reinforces some important insights in the comparative and theoretical literature on revolutions. It shows that Alexis de Tocqueville was right to insist that nothing does more to inspire revolutionary activism than an inefficient authoritarian regime's introduction of a reform program that offers too little and comes too late. The 1911 Revolution (which was preceded by unsuccessful Qing reforms) and even, in a way, the mainland's abortive revolution of 1989 and the recent fall of the GMD in Taiwan illustrate the power of Tocqueville's insight. These cases also illustrates the value of stressing, as Marx and Skocpol among others have, the revolutionary potential of groups at the fringe of the governing elite who have rising expectations and are frustrated by being kept away from real power. In addition, Chinese events of the third quarter of the twentieth century in particular underscore the validity of the claim made by both Tocqueville and Skocpol, again among others, that revolutions, while attempting to do other things, often end up strengthening the power of central governments. Finally, the Chinese case shows just how much truth there is in the tragic maxim that revolutions all too frequently and all too regrettably end up devouring their own children.

See also: China: Sociocultural Aspects; Communism; Communist Parties; East Asian Studies: Economics; East Asian Studies: Politics; East Asian Studies: Society; Maoism; Revolutions, Sociology of; Revolutions, Theories of

Bibliography

Bergère M C 1998 [English translation by Lloyd J] *Sun Yat-sen*. Stanford University Press, Stanford, CA
Bianco L 1971 [English translation by Bell M] *Origins of the Chinese Revolution, 1915–1949*. Stanford University Press, Stanford, CA
Brinton C 1965 *Anatomy of Revolution*. Vintage, New York
Dirlik A 1989 *The Origins of Chinese Communism*. Oxford University Press, New York
Duara P 1988 *Culture, Power and the State: Rural North China, 1900–1942*. Stanford University Press, Stanford, CA
Fairbank J K, Goldman M 1998 *China: A New History*, enlarged edn. Belknap Press of Harvard University Press, Cambridge, MA
Fitzgerald J 1996 *Awakening China: Politics, Culture, and Class in the Nationalist Revolution*. Stanford University Press, Stanford, CA
Friedman E, Pickowicz P G, Selden M 1991 *Chinese Village, Socialist State*. Yale University Press, New Haven, CT
Goldstone J A (ed.) 1994 *Revolutions: Theoretical, Comparative, and Historical Studies*, 2nd edn. Harcourt, Fort Worth, CA
Hartford K, Goldstein S (eds.) 1987 *Single Sparks: China's Rural Revolutions*. Sharpe, Armonk, New York
Ono K 1989 [English translation by Fogel J (ed.)] *Chinese Women in a Century of Revolution, 1850–1950*. Stanford University Press, Stanford, CA
Perry E J, Selden M (eds.) 2000 *Chinese Society: Change, Conflict and Resistance*. Routledge, London
Skocpol T 1979 *States and Social Revolutions*. Cambridge University Press, Cambridge, UK
Spence J D 1982 *The Gate of Heavenly Peace*. Penguin Books, New York
Tang T 2000 Interpreting the Revolution in China: Macrohistory and micromechanisms. *Modern China* **26**(2): 205–38
Wakeman F Jr. 1975 *The Fall of Imperial China*. Free Press, New York
Wang Z 1999 *Women in the Chinese Enlightenment: Oral and Textual Histories*. University of California Press, Berkeley, CA
Wong R B 1997 *China Transformed: Historical Change and the Limits of the European Experience*. Cornell University Press, Ithaca, NY
Wright M C (eds.) 1968 *China in Revolution: The First Phase, 1900–1913*. Yale University Press, New Haven, CT
Yue D, Wakeman C 1985 *To The Storm: The Odyssey of a Chinese Revolutionary Woman*. University of California Press, Berkeley, CA

J. N. Wasserstrom

Christian Liturgy

The Greek word *leitourgos* means, literally, 'work of the people' and was associated in ancient Greece both with the payment of civic dues and the performance of ritual duties. In the Christian context, by contrast, it had at first a more specific connotation, concerning the performance of the Eucharistic action—although this apparent narrowing of reference in fact indicated that this action was itself the supreme collective obligation and source of collective unity. Only much later did the term come to denote the entirety of Christian ritual practice. At first, in the seventeenth century, it was used as a neutral term, covering both the Catholic 'Mass' and Protestant 'Communion';

later, Catholic writers such as Dom Odo Casel worried about the degeneration in meaning if *cultus* tended to substitute 'liturgy' as a word describing the whole outward and inward *opus* of Christian piety.

To comprehend the history of the latter, therefore, one must attend also to the evolution in meaning of other terms: 'mystery,' 'cult,' 'rite,' and 'sacrament.' In the antique world there existed, broadly speaking, a contrast between public 'liturgies,' connected to the regular order of the city and its upholding, on the one hand, and private 'mysteries,' 'cults,' or 'rites,' sometimes connected with a certain dissension from civic order, on the other. Public liturgy included animal sacrifice, and was concerned primarily with a symbolic apportioning of different parts of the beast to gods and different classes of men. It was at once a mimesis and a reinstitution of civic order. Private cults, by contrast, also involved deviant sacrifice. Sometimes this was a deviation upwards, as with the Pythagoreans, who modified or refused animal sacrifice, and associated less bloody offerings not with a feeding of the gods but with the transit of their own souls to a higher realm. Alternatively, there were deviations downwards, as with the Eleusinian mysteries, which were essentially older, alien, more agrarian rites involving chthonic gods, reinterpreted in an urban context. Here initiates identified themselves with the perpetual dying and rising to life again of a god, who had been originally a god of fertility. By participating in the god's own self-salvation, the *mystes* hoped to regenerate their lives.

Christianity fused together public liturgy and private rite, with momentous consequences. From early times, it interpreted worship, *latreia*, as meaning, after the incarnation, the entire offering of the whole person to God in charity, which included charity toward one's neighbor. In this way, the whole span of human life was reconceived as 'liturgical,' since the new 'city' was an eternal city which also embraced true human life in time. On the other hand, the language of 'mystery' and 'initiation' was also embraced. In the case of St. Paul's use of the term *mysterion*, it is true, the background is very unlikely to be that of the pagan mystery cult, as was once thought. Instead, the background is Jewish apocalyptic: thus Paul speaks of a primordial 'mystery' now disclosed to us in Christ, a mystery anticipated in the Jewish Passover, which involves a passage through destruction to renewal. Nevertheless, this meant that, at its heart, Christianity involved the mystery of the death and rising again of God, a mystery that was made present again in the rituals of baptism and the Eucharist. Later, Patristic authors expanded this notion in terms that owed something to pagan notions of initiation into secret knowledge: the Syrian fathers spoke of *Raza*, an originally Persian term (*Raz*) denoting secrets of state within the imperial court; one can note here that in this more oriental context, the 'secret' and the 'public' were already identified before Christianity, although neither was yet democratically available to all. This 'orientalism' was also present more in Rome than in Greece, for, in the case of Rome, the plebs were admitted or 'initiated' only gradually into the rites of *connubium* (sacred marriage). The Greek fathers spoke of *mysterion* in ways that fused Jewish apocalyptic expectation and exaltation with a Greek sense of participating in a hidden drama that yields understanding. Nevertheless, the association with mystery religions was viewed typologically, and distance as well as proximity was emphasized. One can note in particular the extent to which the pagan mysteries' involvement of the reslaying of a god was exaggerated in the interests equally of resemblance with and contrast to the (voluntary) death of Christ. Unlike the pagan mysteries, the mystery of Christ involved a once and for all death and an unshakeable resurrection which saved not a god but mortals.

It remains the case, however, that now, in a more 'oriental' (and also more Roman) mode, the most public emerged from the most secret, a rite into which one first had to be initiated as a catechumen. Unlike the ancient Orient, furthermore, (although pagan Rome had already evolved in this direction), *all* could potentially be initiated into the *Raza*, or inner court secret. This was to break with the ancient Greek and Roman association of the aristocratic with the eternal and transcendent reserved for a few, on the one hand, and the democratic, associated with the immanent, open, 'positive,' unmysterious, and available to the many, on the other. Plato, in the *Laws*, had already begun to de-eroticize the transcendent, or, alternatively, to eroticize the democratic, since one must express this both ways around. Now, however, not just in a theoretical text, but in actual practice, the secret was publicized, and, equally, the most public—the Eucharist which engenders the *ecclesia*, the corporate identity—was rendered secret (and permanently mysterious, even for the catechized). Once, either some were to ascend, or all were to remain on an immanent plane; now all were to ascend, continuously.

In accordance with this new conjoining of liturgy and cult, the sacrifice of the Eucharist was public, yet involved no unequal apportionings. All now ingested all that was offered, and yet in eating the totality, the elements and those whom they fed were offered in their entirety back to God. In addition, all 'sacrificial economy' was broken with; nothing was any longer expected from God in return for one's giving. The new sacrifice was one of pure gratitude to the God who, in any case, gives. As with the Pythagoreans, sacrifice involves mainly *human* elevation. This elevation, however, also now includes humans' own free giving in charity to others. In this fashion, elevation no longer abandons the city. Indeed, for Augustine in the *City of God*, it is the whole city which is offered, which is elevated—since the city exists through elevation.

Because of this new, nonsacrificial economy, Augustine refused most of the pagan terms for ritual or worship, espousing only the Greek term *latreia* (CD VI 3). Nevertheless, he spoke of a true *Cultus* as involving a participation in the one true offering made by Christ (CD VII 30). This was an 'inner' *cultus*, not in the sense that outer signs are inefficacious, but in the sense that they must be truly intended. Indeed, participation in the mystery of Christ through the Eucharist and the annual liturgical calendar is now so intense that christians inner life must be understood also in cultic terms: their heart is not mainly 'ltheins,' but rather an altar upon which they sacrifice to God (CD X 3; Ep. 140 *Ad Honoratum*, 18, 45).

Thomas Aquinas reiterated and expounded Augustine's understanding of *latreia* and *cultus*. He stresses that cult does not have God as its *object* but as its *end*, since the aim is not to please God, but to be united with Him, and this is not brought about *through* the work of worship; rather, God brings it about Himself by meeting humans in liturgical acts of worship (S.T. III, Q. 81 a 5; Q. 24 a 5).

Up until the twelfth and thirteenth centuries, this understanding of cult was in the most part preserved. It worked against any notion that the essence of liturgy is a matter of 'correct procedure,' or that the liturgical sphere is a special domain standing over the practical and theoretical aspects of life. Even in Gratian's *Decretals*, the aim of the canonist is to allow proper scope to the force of local custom, so long as this is not inconsistent with the custom and understanding of the church in general, following Augustine of Canterbury's precept that 'place does not approve a custom, custom approves a place' (*Decretals*, 12. C 10).

Nonetheless, the later Middle Ages witnessed an increased notion of juridical thinking in the liturgical sphere, resulting in some separation of private piety from public ritual: in this way, the Christian logic of 'the public secret' started to come undone. The Reformation then protested against a mechanistic formalism which tended to suggest that the following of certain procedures secured salvation. In response, the Council of Trent sought diligently to reconnect the outer and the inner, and to reassert the notion of a *sacramentum* as an outward sign of an inner reality whose exteriority could not be dispensed with, since the fullness of this reality was only to be eschatologically disclosed, and then would transcend the inward/outward contrast. However, the implementation of the Tridentine decrees involved more and more a dry insistence upon outward observance, as sacramental practice came to be viewed as a series of instituted motions with formally consistent entailments ensuing automatically. Such an outlook at once harmonized with Enlightenment rationalism, and was itself part of what the Enlightenment rejected.

By contrast, the spirit of the most ancient tradition was renewed and rethought by Cardinal Bérulle, who insisted that the whole of Christian life, outer and inward, was a participation in, and, in a sense, a re-enactment of the incarnation: only the divine man who utterly gave Himself showed, by giving beyond humanity, true humanity. Ultimately, the French School which he founded helped to sustain some unbroken tradition of Christian liturgy as encompassing all of Christian life, since it was a sharing in the mystery of Christ. The centrality of 'mystery,' and so of the notion of a public secret (or a secret publicness) was emphatically renewed in the nineteenth century by Dom Odo Casel who (though he overstressed the influence of Greek mystery religion) was a decisive influence on Catholic liturgical renewal in the twentieth century.

In many ways, Vatican II restored the theological centrality of liturgical mystery, although it is questionable whether its practical liturgical recommendations were entirely in keeping with this understanding. It misinterpreted a particular ancient local practice at Rome as indicating that originally the priest stood behind the altar to celebrate the liturgy, whereas the design of even the most ancient basilicas suggests this could not have been the case. Most scholars now reject this conclusion, but the adopted new practice of the priest facing the congregation tends to reduce both the sense of approaching eschatological mystery, and of an equal approach by the entire public, both priest and people. Likewise, Vatican II mistook documents of broad direction for liturgical enactments, such as that of Hippolytus and Justin Martyr, as indications of original 'simple' liturgies, organized more formally and without supposedly 'messy' repetitions. In this way, another dimension of public mystery was lost in practice: the endlessly 'stammering' recommencement of an approach to an altar where one can truly worship—an approach that cannot be completed in time. Thereby both eschatological and apophatic aspects were diminished in practice, even though the reformers had stressed these in theory. Equally, the new Latin liturgy and its vernacular translations tended to lose metaphoric richness, typological resonance, and a sense of language as an epiphanic vehicle.

For these reasons, efforts in the tradition of Bérulle and Casel to restore the centrality of Christological mystery and public secrecy to Christian practice remain only partially accomplished.

See also: Pilgrimage; Ritual; Sacrifice; Symbolism in Anthropology; Symbolism (Religious) and Icon

Bibliography

Aquinas T 1964–81 *Summa Theologia*. Eyre and Spottiswood, London

Augustine of Hippo 1984 *Civitas Dei* Bettenson H. Penguin, Harmondworth, UK

Beard M, North J, Price S 1998 *Religions of Rome*. Cambridge University Press, Cambridge, UK, 2 Vols.

Bouyer L 1968 *Life and Liturgy*. Sheed and Ward, London

Bouyer L 1986 *Mysterion: Du Mystère à la Mystique*. Aubier, Paris

Bremmer J 1994 *Greek Religion*, Greece and Rome new surveys. Oxford University Press, Oxford, UK

Bremmond H 1932 *Histoire Litteraire du Sentiment Religieuse en France t. 9: La Vie Chrétienne sous L'Ancien Régime*. Aubier, Paris

Bugnini A 1990 *The Reform of the Liturgy 1948–1975* (trans. M J O'Connwell). liturgical Press, Collegeville, MN

Burkert W 1985 *Greek Religion. Archaic and Classical* [trans. Raffan J]. Blackwell, Oxford, UK

Burkert W 1987 *Ancient Mystery Cults*. Harvard University Press, Cambridge, MA

Casel O 1942 *Das Christliche Kultmysterium*. Munich, Ratisbonne

de Certeau M 1975 *L'Écriture de l'histoire*. P.U.F, Paris

Congar Y 1947 Le Christ, image de Dieu invisible. *La Maison-Dieu: Revue de Pastorale Liturgique* **59**: 132–61

Congar Y 1967 L'Ecclesia ou communicante Chrétienne, sujet integral de l'action liturgique. In: Jossua J-P, Congar Y (eds.) *La Liturgie après Vatican II*. Aubier, Paris, pp. 246–82

Dalmais I H 1990 *Raza* et sacrament. In: de Clerck P, Palazzo E (eds.) *Rituels: Mélanges offerts au Père Gy*. Editions du Cerf, Paris, pp. 173–82

Duval A 1985 *De Sacraments au Concile de Trente*. Paris

Elich T 1991 Using liturgical texts in the Middle Ages. In: Austin G (ed.) *Fountain of Life*. Pastoral Press, Washington, DC, pp. 69–83

Gratian 1995 *The Treatise on Laws* [trans. Thompson A]. Catholic University Press of America, Washington, DC

Harrison T 2001 *Greek Religion: Belief and Experience*. Duckworth, London

Lyonnet S 1967 La Nature du culte dans le N.T. *La Liturgie après Vatican II* Aubier, Paris

Milbank J 1998 The politics of time: Community, gift and liturgy. *Telos* **113** (Fall): 41–69

Mohrmann C 1965 *Sacramentum* dans les plus anciens textes Chrétiens. In: (eds.) *Études sur le Latin des Chrétiens*. , Rome

Pickstock C 1998 *After Writing: On the Liturgical Consummation of Philosophy*. Blackwell, Oxford, UK

Price S 1999 *Religions of the Ancient Greeks*. Cambridge University Press, Cambridge, UK

Riedwig C 1987 *Mysterienterminologie bei Platon, Philon et Klemens von Alexandrien*. Berlin

de Roten P 1992 Le vocabulaire mystagogique de saint Jean Chrysostome. In: Triacca A M, Pistoia A (eds.) *Mystagogie: Pensée Liturgique d'aujourdhui et liturgie ancienne*. Edizioni Liturgiche, Rome

Rotureau G 1944 *Le Cardinal de Bérulle, Opuscules de Pieté*. Aubier, Paris

Zaidman L B, Pantel P S 1992 *Religion in the Ancient Greek City* [trans. Cartledge P]. Cambridge University Press, Cambridge, UK

C. Pickstock

Christian Parties: European

Christian (or Christian democratic) parties have been among the most successful political movements in Europe. Together with their Social democratic counterparts, they have dominated European politics.

They have been leading members of governmental coalitions in such countries as Italy, Germany, Austria, Belgium, and The Netherlands; they currently form (together with their conservative allies) the largest group in the European Parliament.

Christian democratic parties are not just parties that use this label (some do not). As a matter of fact, Christian democratic parties are hardly Christian. They are secular parties operating in highly secularized societies. Today they seem almost indistinguishable from conservative or liberal parties. However, they have a distinct history that both accounts for their particular nature and helps explain their major contribution to politics. This contribution can be articulated around two paradoxical outcomes: although they were formed initially to challenge the emerging European liberal democratic order, these parties eventually became pillars of secularism, liberalism, and democracy in Europe. Christian democratic politicians also pioneered the process of European integration, and although they fought hard against socialism, they ended up building vast welfare states. Their evolution is a stunning illustration of how democratization can be the contingent outcome of political strategies rather than result directly from the dissemination of democratic ideas and principles.

1. Origins

Contemporary Christian democratic parties evolved from the confessional parties that were created in the second part of the nineteenth century and were an expression of political Catholicism. These Catholic parties grew out of the largely antiliberal and ultramontane mass Catholic movement that challenged the ascendancy of liberalism in Europe from a 'fundamentalist' and theocratic perspective (as codified in the 1864 papal encyclical *Syllabus of Errors*). Indeed, Christian democracy was a concept coined in opposition to liberal democracy. Though spearheaded by the Catholic Church which feared for the loss of its privileges, especially in the field of education, Catholic movements won their independence from the church through their transformation into Catholic parties. The Catholic Church resisted this process, which robbed it from its monopolistic control over its flock, as much as it could; but it failed to thwart this development because democracy provided Catholic activists with a powerful source of power and legitimation. Although initially strongly opposed to democracy on ideological grounds, these activists quickly realized that their interests lay in its consolidation and further expansion (Kalyvas 1996).

The process through which confessional parties were formed had two important, though contradictory, consequences: first, it turned religion into the foundational element of confessional parties, the core of their identity; yet religion proved more of a hindrance than an advantage; second, the religious appeal produced a highly heterogeneous sort of party, composed of interest groups which had been united only by their adherence to the message of religious defense; yet this social heterogeneity increased the salience of class within these parties.

2. Religion

Confessional parties, albeit friendly to religion, wanted to disassociate themselves from too close a relationship with the church. Religion restricted their appeal as well as their autonomy. Likewise, the church could only protect its universalistic identity by moving away from these parties. However, the confessional character of these parties could not be shed because religion had become the cement that kept their heterogeneous social basis together. This quandary was solved in an ingenious yet momentous way. Confessional parties redefined religion into a nebulous humanitarian and moral concept that allowed them to be simultaneously Christian and secular. Vague formulations such as 'religious inspiration,' or 'values of Christian civilization' remain the only references to religion one finds in the official discourse of these parties. This led to a situation whereby it is perfectly possible to be simultaneously a Christian democrat and an atheist. In fact, this is not even perceived as a contradiction.

Hence, Christian democratic parties contributed in a fundamental way to the 'desacralization' and secularization of their countries' politics. Paradoxically then, the politicization of religion contributed to the secularization of politics. In a perverse fashion, Christianity was drained of its religious content even while being legitimated as a political identity—and this feat was accomplished by its proponents rather than its opponents. The secularization of confessional parties was, thus, endogenous to these parties and took place well before World War II, rather than being a delayed adaptation to external societal developments as often thought. Besides consolidating democracy, this development further enhanced the position of Christian democratic parties by laying the path, after World War II, for interdominationalism, thus turning Christian democracy into a dominant party in confessionally mixed societies such as Germany.

3. Class

The social basis of confessional parties was made of numerous and often-conflicting interests: social heterogeneity was these parties' hallmark from the outset. In this sense, Christian democratic parties were catch-all parties *avant la lettre* (van Kersbergen 1994). This heterogeneity was the direct result of their ideological profile that emphasized religion at the expense of class. However, external 'nonclassism' produced internal 'classism.' Powerful Catholic Workers' and Peasants' associations had to be incorporated into the new parties which eventually adopted a peculiar confederate structure based on organizations defined in terms of class (*standen* or *lager*). The ensuing conflicts gave rise to intensely accommodationist and compromising practices that were necessary for ensuring the parties' unity and cohesion.

Hence, mediation between these assertive and divergent interest groups became imperative. As a result, Christian democratic parties became particularly skilled in the exercise of the politics of mediation (van Kersbergen 1994), something their opponents have derided as opportunism and a belief 'that the ends justify the means.' The principle of subsidiarity (higher authorities, such as the state, should intervene only where individuals or smaller communities are not competent), a central concept in the process of European integration, can also be traced back to these developments.

Herewith (rather than in papal encyclicals, such as the 1893 encyclical *Rerum Novarum*) lies the source of Christian democracy's strong social component that distinguishes it from mainstream conservative or liberal parties. Indeed, a number of studies have found that Christian democratic strength is positively associated with high levels of welfare expenditure and high levels of unionization. Van Kersbergen (1995) has identified a distinctively Christian democratic core of social policies, which he calls social capitalism. This policy core differs significantly and systematically from both the liberal and social democratic conceptions of social citizenship. The Christian democratic welfare state is as large, in terms of expenditures and size, as its Social democratic counterpart; but it is quite different. It privileges families rather than individuals, cash benefits rather than social services, and seeks to preserve rather than subvert labor market outcomes. Following the end of World War II, social capitalism (along with political anticommunism), rather than religion, provided the foundation on which Christian democratic parties stood—and from which they ruled. Social capitalism was, thus, not only the outcome, but also the means of Christian democratic mobilization.

In the course of the 1990s, Christian democratic parties entered into a protracted and deep crisis. They have experienced steep electoral decline (Austria, Belgium, The Netherlands) or even total collapse (Italy); they have been implicated in major financial scandals (Belgium, Italy, Germany, Austria); and they have failed to expand, as expected, in Eastern Europe. Although the end of the Cold War can be partially credited for some of these developments, this crisis goes far deeper. The imperatives of global economic competition have undermined the social capitalist arrangements that had guaranteed both the parties' cohesion and their electoral appeal. In other words, this is a crisis of Christian democracy rather than a crisis of Christian democratic parties. Christian democratic parties will have to reinvent themselves if they want to remain a relevant force in European politics. Yet if they look back, they will find that their often forgotten history holds a vast repertoire of frequently unintended but nonetheless ingenious practices of adaptation and reinvention.

See also: Church and State: Political Science Aspects; Consumption, History of; Party Systems; Religion and Economic Life; Religion: Mobilization and Power; Religion, Sociology of; Religious Stratification; Socialization: Political; Western European Studies: Religion; Western European Studies: Society

Bibliography

Buchanan T, Conway M 1996 *Political Catholicism in Europe, 1918–1965*. Clarendon Press, Oxford, UK

Irving R E M 1979 *The Christian Democratic Parties of Western Europe*. Allen and Unwin, London

Kalyvas S N 1996 *The Rise of Christian Democracy in Europe*. Cornell University Press, Ithaca and London

Kalyvas S N 1998 From pulpit to party: Party formation and the Christian Democratic phenomenon. *Comparative Politics* **30**: 293–312

van Kersbergen K 1994 The distinctiveness of Christian Democracy. In: Hanley D (ed.) *Christian Democracy in Europe: A Comparative Perspective*. Pinter, London and New York

van Kersbergen K 1995 *Social Capitalism: A Study of Christian Democracy and the Welfare State*. Routledge, London and New York

S. N. Kalyvas

Christianity: Evangelical, Revivalist, and Pentecostal

While 'globalization' as a concept arose as a fiscal planning tool in the 1950s, its extension as an explanatory concept for the sort of territory previously covered by such frameworks as 'world systems theory' dates from the 1970s. At the time of writing, Roland Robertson and Peter Beyer are the key writers in the area as it relates to religion. Indeed, Robertson's pioneering framework arises out of the conundrum which religion presents for standard modernization theory. The rise of Islamic and other forms of religious fundamentalism denies the linear rationalist assumptions of modernization theory and such offspring as secularization theory, which suggest that regional difference and religious conviction should be passing away in the face of rational technical systems and the homogenization of culture. Robertson has since then further articulated the theory through the concept of

'globalization,' which allows for simultaneous global homogenization of culture and local reassertions of difference. Robertson's theory that cultural forces move faster than political and economic forces has received considerable support from historians and analysts of Christian missions, which have noted that the indigenization of Christianity has historically been faster and deeper in Asia and Africa than the movement of formal missionary and colonial structures. In South America, by contrast, there is a body of opinion which states that the combination of state apparatus and church extension actually retarded the extension of Christianity. It is clear, then, that globalization theory is vital for the understanding of the expansion of Christianity generally, just as the study of the expansion of Christianity is vital for understanding the processes of globalization.

While a slow starter to get into missions, evangelical Christianity began to articulate an increasingly sophisticated global vision from the late 1600s, with the rise of the Pietist movement. As Lewis has noted, Pietism restored a sense of personal call to Protestant orthodoxy which, through agencies such as the University of Halle and Moravian missions, expressed itself in a growing internationalism. The correspondence of Zinzendorf, the migration of Moravians, and missionary outreach to Russia, Greenland, and India, created networks and examples of successful missions which informed the expanding networks of new settler societies and expanding capitalism. It was on a trip to the New World that John Wesley, for instance, first ran into Moravians, who, through the influence of Peter Böhler, provided the synthesizing principle to Wesleyan eclectic theology and practice which in turn made it a vibrant missionary force. It was likewise among Scots-Irish and Dutch settlers in the New World that religious revival produced the combination of Protestant theology and religious experience which has become known as 'Evangelical Christianity.' Definitions differ, usually with personal affiliation, but a standard definition of Evangelicalism offered by David Bebbington locates the movement in a quadrilateral of theology and praxis involving activism, cross-centeredness, Bible-centeredness, and conversionism. The fact that nothing like the French Revolution occurred in England helped legitimize the movement as a source of social and cultural stability. The inner energies of the movement, combining a universalizing crucicentrism and biblicism, with conversion-oriented activism, meant that the tens of thousands of converts to the Evangelical Awakening on both sides of the Atlantic provided a vast pool of willing support to the evangelical program to change globalizing British society. The leaders of the movement—in particular William Wilberforce, Lord Shaftesbury, the Clapham sect, and Selina, Countess of Huntingdon—were able to draw upon these networks of support in a dynamic program of social activism over the century 1750–1850. This activism arguably provided important impulse force to the processes of globalization, just as globalizing Western economies provided important resources and opportunities for evangelical expansion and change.

Protestants from Luther's time were faced with an expanding globe in tension with an increasingly outmoded ecclesiology. While, during Luther's own lifetime, Diaz rounded the Cape of Good Hope (1488), Columbus was driven west in pursuit of a millennial vision to land on the shores of America (1492), and other parts of the world were opened to Western influence by da Gama, Cabot, Cortes, Magellan, and Pizarro, Protestants were combining with increasingly nationalistic ruling classes (the nobility in Germany, bourgeoisie in Switzerland and The Netherlands) to reinstitute the 'Christendom' ideal within the national churches of rising nation states. While Catholic empires ruled the seas, Protestant missions were restricted to Europe. While the theology became increasingly arid and formalized, the impact of these churches was to reinforce the nexus between nationalism and capitalism. Capitalism expanded during the period through royal chartered companies, combining national expansion and capitalist enterprise. Halle Pietism specifically used this link to expand into Russia, just as Puritans used the chartered company to establish themselves in Massachusetts Bay. The CMS first fought with and later used the East India Company in Asia, while the Claphamites moved into West Africa on the tails of colonization companies. While Weber's 'spirit of Protestantism' has been revised and attacked in some quarters, it is nonetheless a useful heuristic when viewing the interaction of shipping, chartered, and colonization companies on the one hand, and missionary agencies on the other.

Protestantism provided an 'inner fascination with the world,' and evangelicalism adopted the same fascination and extended it. There has been considerable work done, for instance, on the link between enlightenment and Evangelicalism, indicating that Evangelicalism, through its commercial and missionary emphases, was a major carrier of rationalizing Western concepts of time and space into the rest of the world during the late nineteenth and early twentieth centuries. Not only did Wesley proceed on the assumption of an 'inner enlightenment,' using both the vocabulary and technologies of enlightenment to further the evangelical cause (he was, for instance, an assiduous publisher), but Puritan and evangelical input into the sciences from the sixteenth to the nineteenth centuries was immense. Clergy were not only involved in agencies such as the Royal Society, but were key suppliers of information to enlightenment projects such as the social sciences. (Malcolm Prentis, for example, has demonstrated the link between clerical collection and the construction of an international culture of research in anthropology.) The logical place to look for the globalizing influence of evangelicalism is through the agency of

missions. The marginality of missions at the beginning of the nineteenth century demonstrates the close association of evangelical expansion with Western expansion. By 1800, North America was subject to European settlement, but only on the eastern half and the western rim of the continent, and though there was no real challenge to Hispanic hegemony in South America, Christianization had not really pierced deeply below the surface of the indigenous and emerging plantation cultures. The impact of missions in the Indic, wider Asian, and Muslim worlds was negligible. Obviously, then, developments in the nineteenth century were critical for the development of global Christianity in our own period. Europe at the time was weak and divided religiously. The industrial revolution encouraged both concentration of the sort of wealth which could capture foreign markets and provided the scientific curiosity and the speed of travel to take advantage of new opportunities. While most European expansion in the eighteenth century had been mercantilist in nature—with small colonies of isolated Europeans trading with Asian nations in sealed cantons such as Shanghai, Macau, and Hong Kong—the nineteenth century saw a shift toward extensive settlement and active domination of local politics. At least in part, this was because it was now technically possible, with advances in communication and military hardware, to dominate other less advanced cultures. So Britain absorbed India, Burma, and Ceylon into a new Empire, France annexed Indo-China, and The Netherlands finalized its annexation of Indonesia. Other European powers founded colonies, such as the German colonies in PNG, and annexed parts of Africa, such as Togoland, Southwestern Africa, and the like. At least for the British, Stanley argues that there was a consistent imperial impulse to British society, but no plan of conquest, most acquisitions having been gained in order to protect trading rights. Formal control was never exercised when the much cheaper form of informal control could be used, and it was the increasing need for formal control, driven by the intensified competition of European powers for global resources, which drove Britain to acquire and then defend India as the keystone in its defense of the East.

In terms of the other global religious cultures, evangelicalism also faced weakened opposition. One advantage of the time was that Islam was in retreat—in 1821 Greece was retaken, and from the 1830s European powers began dividing up Islamic parts of Northern Africa such as Morocco, Algeria, and Tunisia. Roman Catholicism at the beginning of the nineteenth century was under siege from the forces of modernization. With the eclipse of Portugal and Spain as imperial powers, increasingly the push for missions in the Catholic world came from France, Belgium, and (significantly for Australia) Ireland. While the Orthodox churches did not pursue much in the way of missions, despite the spread of the Russian Empire during this period, the Protestants, energized by the Evangelical revival, certainly did, both within and outside the English speaking world. Stanley suggests that, while there were agencies such as the Society for the Propagation of the Gospel with a missionary element to them, before the Evangelical awakening there was no consistent acceptance of the burden of foreign missions by either Anglican or Dissenting Protestants. Europe was the same. In 1810, for instance, a revival known as the Reveil spread out of Geneva and affected the French Protestant world deeply, leading to considerable missionary endeavor overseas. Norwegian revivals, most notably commenced by Hans Nielsen Hauge, a lay reader preaching in a way which was not legalized until 20 years after his death, energized Scandinavian missions to North America and later to South America. German missionaries, in the tradition of Halle and the Moravians, traveled all over the world. The interaction of these revival movements and missions can be seen in their common adherence to interdenominational agencies such as the Evangelical Alliance, which was founded in 1847, and held conferences in France, Belgium, Switzerland, Germany, Canada, Sweden, and the United States.

The model provided by the Alliance of a voluntary society was to become the classic form for Protestant missions. Many were formed at the prompting of chaplains and clergy travelling with army, trading company or political representatives. The first of them was the Baptist Missionary Society (1792), inspired by William Carey, who in turn had been inspired to mission by the accounts of the travels of such explorers as Captain James Cook in the Pacific. It was followed by the London Missionary Society (1795), the British and Foreign Bible Society (1804), the Wesleyan Methodist Missionary Society (1813), and many others. Because the Church of Scotland refused the requests of its Evangelical party to form their own missionary agency, most Scots siphoned off into other agencies, such as the LMS. In 1810, preceded by many small bodies dedicated to evangelizing First Nations' peoples, the first American foreign agency was founded in the American Board of Commissioners for Foreign Missions.

The extension of evangelical missions had a number of major interactions with the growth of global society. The first was that, with increased need for personnel, the missions started their own Bible training institutions. These in turn legitimized the long-standing 'old dissenting' academies, supported religious emancipation and social reform, and acted to break down the exclusivism of the established church-linked universities. European states, at slower or faster rates, responded to this broadening of the religious franchise (among other secularizing tendencies) by stepping back from the official sanctioning of one form of religious truth or another. By the end of the century, most European states had become generally 'Christian' countries without confessional attachments, and many, in their colonies (particularly in Canada and Australia) were actively encouraging liberal democratic states. Not only did missions change the education of the increasingly vital professional class at home, but in exporting the Western educational model, also exported Western professional values into the nation states which began to arise in Asia, Africa, and the Pacific from the late nineteenth century. In exporting values such as professional disinterestedness, the importance of technical expertise, and basic human rights, a common culture was established which facilitated not only the spread of global society, but also (through preservation and re-skilling of Fourth World peoples) the means for local opposition to global homogenization. The specter of evangelical African bishops nay-saying advanced liberal proposals at a Lambeth conference, or Aboriginal evangelicals controlling the balance of power in the national assemblies of the United churches of Canada and Australia, have demonstrated the interactivity between evangelical missions and mediation of global culture.

The establishment of comity arrangements between evangelical missions in foreign countries highlights the second major interaction. The movement of religious traditions outside their national boundaries produced a relativization of their content and form, creating movements toward ecumenism based on 'common gospel' assumptions, diminishing the importance of liturgical and cultural tradition, and homogenizing the culture of international Christianity. This was imported back into the West as de-denominalization, and into Third World countries as 'alliance Christianity,' enabling Christianity to be described as a unitary object in contact with other world religions. This sense of relativization of form sparked concerns about relativization of truth, concerns expressed most markedly in the fundamentalism/modernism debates of the 1920s onwards.

Fundamentalism self-consciously identifies itself as a countermodernist movement, particularly in terms of theological modernism. Evangelicalism maintains something of this thrust, at the end of the twentieth century increasingly identifying itself as a counter-postmodernist movement. On another level, however, these debates can be seen as localized resistance to homogenizing forces at the global level, resistance seen most markedly in the general opposition of national evangelicals to agencies such as the World Council of Churches. In some cases, this meant the localization of evangelicalism into extreme nationalist forms. In most cases, however, especially after the rise of the National Association of Evangelicals in the USA and the Billy Graham Organization, the centrality of missions and a self-identity partly defined by contention for the faith caused evangelicals after World War II to take the same globalizing path that the WCC had already taken. This is reflected in the formation of agencies such as the Lausanne Committee, the World Evangelical Fellowship, and worldwide denominational fellowships such as the World Alliance of Reformed Churches. Particularly after World War II, these agencies provided the basis for expansion of English and, with increasing hegemony, American evangelicalism onto the world stage. By the 1990s, it was clear that denominations had become almost irrelevant to the self-definition of most evangelicals, and that localized megachurches were more important for agenda setting.

Likewise, evangelical missions had shifted from being denominationally and agency based to increasing integration with global movements in migration, occupation, and tourism. Short-term mission, and mission originating from countries in the 'South,' contribute nearly as much to the total Christian missionary workforce as do traditional, First World, agency based missions, and is likely soon to outstrip it.

Within these tendencies in evangelicalism in the nineteenth century arose the issue of 'revivalism.' Revivalism is a technical accommodation between the experience of revival, as formalized during and after the First Great Awakening by Calvinists such as Jonathan Edwards, and the utilitarianism implicit in early nineteenth century postenlightenment thought. The emphasis of Edwards and Wesley in defending the use of 'means' for the furtherance of religious revival were codified and extended during frontier revivals in New York State and the expanding American frontier. Not least among the codifiers was Charles Grandison Finney, whose *Lectures on Revival* became the great 'how to' book of the nineteenth century. Revivalism as it expanded from the USA to England, and then around the world (by way of church and migrant diasporas) developed an array of techniques to maintain the association between Christian mass evangelism and spiritual response. It became the tool of choice for many evangelicals as Western societies seemed to be slipping away from their commitments to national religious frameworks, a set of ideas crystallized in the premillennial theology of archetypal evangelistic movements such as the Brethren, Baptists, and Methodists. As a technical accommodation to utilitarianism, revivalism was a natural client and promoter of globalization, which was very largely fueled by the technical innovation of high modernist capitalism. So revivalism quickly spread by the development of Methodist itineracy into the big campaign evangelism of D. L. Moody, Alexander Somerville, Gypsy Smith, and the like. Such itineracy became global, as shipping, then automobiles, and then airplanes, brought other parts of the globe within reach. As communications technologies also improved—through telegraphed newspaper reports, international postage, radioed accounts, and finally television coverage (culminating in the global campaign by satellite of Billy Graham in 1996)—evangelicalism spread with revivalism to all parts of the globe. It is important to note in this regard the high degree of evangelical participation in modern technological enterprises, from Back to the Bible Radio, to the massive media empire of the Universal Church of the Kingdom of God in Brazil. This has been seen as a paradox by some commentators—it is less obviously so when revivalism's accommodation to technological utilitarianism is taken into account. Though revivalism is not limited to evangelicalism (Catholic revivalism, for instance, or the adoption of revivalistic techniques by Hindu and Buddhist promoters in South and Southeast Asia), and not all evangelicalism is revivalistic, it is clear that the two are blood relations and natural partners in many cultures around the world. At the same time, the fact that revivalism is a distillation of 'revival tradition' into a technological form which can thereby cross cultural boundaries makes it eminently transportable. For this reason, Edith Blumhofer has called the major global form of modern revivalism, pentecostalism, 'world evangelicalism,' because of its facility with communications technologies. The ability of pentecostalism to 'cast' itself as a communal form of thought through the abstracting processes of print media and CITs makes it a prime globalizing force. On the one hand, this makes for global expansion of evangelicalism through its revivalist and Pentecostal forms. On the other hand, the same process homogenizes its distinctives and causes it to adapt new local distinctives as it moves across cultures. The lack of a single center (unlike either Islam or Catholicism) is thus a great facilitator of growth, but is also the prime cause of internal dissension and fragmentation as various local evangelical cultures seek to adopt or invent normative centers which enable local communities and protect them from the effects of fragmentation. Neo-fundamentalism, Calvinist renewal movements in the Southern Baptist Convention, the Toronto and Brownsville revivals—each of these may be seen as the creation of new centers, which feed from the energies of globalization, and attempt to create islands of order amidst the chaos of global society.

In particular, evangelicalism as it stands at the beginning of the twenty-first century is clearly largely a two-thirds world phenomenon. As Piggin, Reed, and others have shown, revival is the inculturation of Christianity into local cultures. It is not too much to say, therefore, that the theology of revival, particularly as evidenced in Pentecostal revivalism since the 1950s, is a mainstream legitimating structure for the indigenization of Protestant evangelicalism. This is particularly evident in revivalistic outbreaks such as the East Africa Revival in the 1930s, the blossoming of Pentecostalism in Brazil and later in Argentina, and the Aboriginal revival commencing at Galiwin'ku in Australia's Northern Territory from 1978. In each case, evangelicalism struck new roots and found new accommodations with existing religious cultures which have in turn been exported into the global religious network.

While the East Africa revival had comparatively little experience of charismatic manifestations, Brazil and the Aboriginal revival have been highly charismatic in their combination of local and general characteristics. As Freston notes, the massive expansion of evangelicalism in that showcase of evangelical inculturation, Brazil, is likewise largely Pentecostal in nature. As he noted in 1998, a 'survey of evangelical institutions in Greater Rio de Janeiro discovered that, of the 52 largest denominations, 37 were of Brazilian origin, virtually all Pentecostal. While only 61 percent of all evangelical churches were Pentecostal, 91 percent of those founded in the previous three years were' (Freston 1998, p. 74). Of the 450 million 'evangelicals' and 750 million 'Great Commission Christians' estimated by David Barrett to exist in 1990, some 350 million could be counted within the Pentecostal or charismatic camp. It is clear that at the end of the twentieth century, evangelicalism's expanding edge was clearly Pentecostal/charismatic in nature, leaving the national traditions of the First World heartlands significant challenges of reinvention in their struggle to survive the disappearance of their defining ethnic and national boundaries.

See also: Globalization and World Culture; Globalization, Anthropology of; Historiography and Historical Thought: Christian Tradition; Religion: Evolution and Development; Religion, Sociology of

Bibliography

Bebbington D W 1992 *Evangelicalism in Modern Britain: A History from the 1730s to the 1980s.* Baker Book House, Grand Rapids, MI

Beyer P 1994 *Religion and Globalization.* Sage Publications, Thousand Oaks, CA

Blumhofer E L 1993 *Restoring the Faith: the Assemblies of God, Pentecostalism, and American Culture.* University of Illinois Press, Urbana, IL

Blumhofer E L, Spittler R P, Wacker G A (eds.) 1999 *Pentecostal Currents in American Protestantism.* University of Illinois Press, Urbana, IL

Carwardine R 1978 *Transatlantic Revivalism: Popular Evangelicalism in Britain and America, 1790–1865.* Greenwood Press, Westport, CT

Featherstone M, Lash S, Robertson R (eds.) 1995 *Global Modernities.* Sage Publications, Thousand Oaks, CA

Freston P 1998 Latin American perspectives. In: Hutchinson M, Kalu O (eds.) *A Global Faith: Essays on Evangelicalism and Globalization.* CSAC, Sydney

Marsden G M 1980 *Fundamentalism and American Culture: the Shaping of Twentieth Century Evangelicalism, 1870–1925.* Oxford University Press, New York

McGrath A 1995 *Evangelicalism and the Future of Christianity.* InterVarsity Press, Downers Grove, IL

Noll M A, Bebbington D W, Rawlyk G A (eds.) 1994 *Evangelicalism: Comparative Studies of Popular Protestantism in North America, the British Isles, and Beyond, 1700–1990.* Oxford University Press, New York

Poewe K (ed.) 1994 *Charismatic Christianity as a Global Culture.* University of South Carolina Press, Columbia, SC

Pollak-Eltz A, Salas Y (eds.) 1998 *El pentecostalismo en América Latina entre tradición y globalización.* Ediciones Abya-Yala, Quito, Ecuador

Robertson R 1992 *Globalization: Social Theory and Global Culture.* Sage, London

Robertson R, Garrett W R (eds.) 1991 *Religion and Global Order.* Paragon House, New York

Smith T L 1980 *Revivalism and Social Reform: American Protestantism on the Eve of the Civil War.* Johns Hopkins University Press, Baltimore, MD

Synan V 1997 *The Holiness-Pentecostal Tradition: Charismatic Movements in the Twentieth Century,* 2nd edn. W. B. Eerdmans, Grand Rapids, MI

Thomas G M 1989 *Revivalism and Cultural Change: Christianity, Nation Building, and the Market in Nineteenth-Century United States.* University of Chicago Press, Chicago

M. Hutchinson

Christianity in Anglo-America and Australasia

Historically, the major religious traditions for Anglo-America and Australasia are similar, even though the social contexts in which they are located vary considerably. That they all function, more or less, as cultural establishments within their countries provides a substantial basis for looking at them as a unified religious bloc. The countries making up this large bloc extending across continents—that is, Canada, the United States, Australia, and New Zealand—share origins as English colonies and, thus, are relatively young as nations and bound by Anglo legacies of language and culture. While the countries themselves are relatively young, in another sense the Protestant cultural establishments within them are increasingly viewed by many people as old and faltering—yet another reason for looking at them as of one piece. For all these reasons, comparative analysis of religious trends and dynamics is both possible and desirable, despite some obvious differences in size, polity, and demographics for the various countries.

1. Historical Considerations

From the outset, we should not underestimate the extent to which Anglo religious life continues to be fundamentally shaped by two historical realities, first, a Protestant background, and thus a theological heritage of resistance to religious authority and, second, a common experience and trajectory in the encounter of religion and modernity in the West. Obviously the two are closely related. The Protestant

Reformation unleashed religious energies previously contained in medieval Catholicism and loosened the hold of ascriptive loyalties, thereby giving rise to greater autonomy of the individual in matters of faith and morals. Greater religious choice was accompanied by an elaboration of religious forms and styles, or a further working out generally of what is often referred to as the 'voluntary principle' within Protestantism. This principle is most pronounced in the United States, but elsewhere with Anglo influence, even in England itself, religious establishments have functioned in the modern period in an environment of considerable individual freedom. Protestantism has both given shape to, and been shaped by, high levels of individual freedom. In fact, three quite distinct historical waves of Protestant dissent legitimizing greater individual autonomy may be identified: first, the Calvinist movements; second, the Methodist revivals; and more recently, the Pentecostals. As David Martin observes (1978), the three religious waves correspond to shifting, ever-widening spheres of social influence. Unlike the Calvinists who were limited mainly to social elites, the Methodists empowered working-class and middle-income populations, and the Pentecostals reached still lower social strata, and did so–and still does–in places and contexts often beyond the reach of the other two. For all three, the emphasis on the individual, on education and hard work, and on taking charge of one's life and making the most of it resulted in upward mobility, and with that, a re-focusing of theology and moral principles giving greater weight to the role of an individual's choice and conscience.

The encounter with modernity in the West led to a wide array of consequences, but most notably, to a loosening of the binding character of tradition and memory and an increased awareness of religious pluralism. Both of these mesh well with the mounting importance of individual autonomy and reliance upon personal choice as articulated religiously. With all this came foundational shifts, or what Peter Berger (1979) describes as a 'loss of ontological certainty.' Broadly speaking, the challenges to religious authority and increased pluralism ushered in an era of greater negotiation in matters of faith and commitment in the face of a widening array of choices. As the term 'secularization' is often used, it is much too encompassing and glosses over the nuances of religion's encounter with modernity to adequately describe what happens in this situation, but suffice it to say that the latter as a historical and increasingly global process, creates ruptures in shared religious views and forces upon ordinary people a posture of cognitive bargaining. Organized religion's monopoly over religious and spiritual questions is easily undermined. Religion's presence in the public arena undergoes a qualitative shift. For our purposes here, what is important is not just the parallels between Protestant influence and religion's encounter with the Enlightenment but the fact that, as Berger and many other commentators

point out, Protestantism has confronted the modern situation longer and to a greater extent probably than any other religious tradition. That of course is rapidly changing in the contemporary world where no religious tradition can insulate itself from the pluralizing and individualizing trends. Yet for this very reason, the mainline Protestant experience is important and indeed paradigmatic of what other religions are now facing. Indeed, the fate of Protestantism in the modern West is what people of other faith traditions are quick to notice and worry about as perhaps their own. What they see are deep internal strains within the tradition and disputes between liberal progressives, on the one hand, and conservative traditionalists, on the other, over moral and religious principles and how to forge responsible religious styles in the contemporary world.

Having said all this, it is not necessarily the case that 'Protestant' translates to 'Anglo' and certainly not that Anglo faith traditions can claim any superiority in their responses to modern life. The spiritual malaise that has currently fallen upon the historic, so-called 'mainline' Protestant institutions throughout much of Anglo-America and Australasia augurs against any such claim of superiority. Nor is there any necessary presumption that other faith traditions must inevitably follow the Protestant trajectory in its confrontation with modernity; there are multiple passages and courses of development. Even to argue that the Protestant experience, given its strong Anglo connections, is paradigmatic for other religious traditions is to risk the charge that this is still another, albeit subtle claim to hegemony—alongside a history of racism, sexism, and capitalist exploitation. But we need not draw this latter inference, especially considering the visible, widespread examples of 'Protestantization' within other faith traditions, presumably the choice of conscious believers from within those traditions. Rather, we should look to the various countries described in this article as case studies in which to describe Anglo religious trends, and to examine how these old Protestant establishments view themselves and extent to which they still define and shape religious life within their environments. Writing some 30 years ago, sociologist Charles H. Anderson 1970 observed that 'The decline of the white Protestant majority and of white Protestant hegemony in twentieth century America has encouraged the growth of self-conscious Protestant community' (1970, p. 3). It is an observation about religious identity which applies, in varying degrees, to Anglo-Saxon populations in all the daughter societies of England, and thus a good reason why we should take a close look at these societies.

2. United States

We look first at the United States. It is the prime example of a country with a strong Protestant legacy where the religious norms of individualism are now widely diffused and where the historic, so-called mainline Protestant denominations are mired in a deep spiritual malaise. Some would argue that the United States is the society that has undergone the greatest impact with modernity, that in many respects its beliefs and values are highly secular, or more precisely, that religion in this country is secularized 'from within,' and thus a model of sorts of what to expect in the modern world. Yet, as is commonly observed, by almost any standard of comparison the United States remains distinctive among modern nations given its high levels of church-going and religious membership. Despite significant shifts in religious styles, levels of religious participation for the country as a whole have not greatly changed over the past four decades. Protestant values encouraging the responsible practice of faith on the part of ordinary believers, and not just by religious elites or by politicians seeking votes, remains deeply ingrained in its public life.

It is widely accepted that the religious distinctiveness of the United States is explained by 'supply-side' thinking, that is, by a history of separation of church and state (the heritage of 'voluntarism') and a culture encouraging innovative, competitive religious leaders to gather followers around them and to organize new churches. Innovation in recruitment methods, in developing new organizations, and in the framing of religious messages coincides with a culture that stresses rational choices on the part of individuals. The fact that so many Americans 'switch' religious affiliations and move in and out of religious organizations frequently underscores a high level of choice and social accommodation. Indeed, there is much to support the rational-choice perspective on individuals and their religious affiliations and styles. In religion, as with the mass marketing of goods and services of all kinds, Americans respond to skillful packaging and presentation of the product. 'Selling God' is taken for granted in an economically-driven culture as the selling of anything else, despite the fact that preachers, priests, and rabbis often resist any notion that theirs is a message that in any way would or should be sold.

But there are other considerations involved in accounting for religious trends and dynamics in the United States. An important example is the downward spiral of the 'oldline' Protestant churches, some of them with histories dating to colonial times. It is much too massive a restructuring of American religious life to explain simply by the rise of televangelism or the use of any other innovative techniques for recruiting. Episcopalians, Presbyterians, the United Church of Christ (formerly, the Congregationalists), the Disciples of Christ, and the United Methodists all began to lose members in the mid-1960s and have continued to do so in the intervening years. The declines appear to be slowing down and may possibly be bottoming out, but the fact is that this switch in fate for these culturally established churches—made up largely of white, middle-class, Anglo types—came so suddenly and involved religious organizations so strikingly different in theological heritage and polity could only signal something deeply troubling in the culture at large. To begin with, the low and declining birth rates (well below the replacement level) finally caught up with these churches. The birth rates were already lower than for other traditions, but after the birth-control pill became available to the public the rates dropped even further—indeed, so low that many of these churches in the late 1960s and 1970s had so few teenagers they could not provide very effective programming. A 'generation gap' emerged as large numbers of the post-World War II generation effectively dropped out of active involvement. In fact, the best predictor of declines in these churches were the diminished church school enrollments 10 years earlier: fewer children were brought up in the churches, beginning in the early 1960s, which later translated into significant declines in worship attendance and financial contributions. The decade of the 1960s was itself an important turning point in a broader cultural sense. John F. Kennedy was elected the first Roman Catholic president, an event significant symbolically to a Protestant sensibility and its fears of losing power and influence. The antiestablishment ethos of that period brought on by the struggles over civil rights, the Vietnam War, and gender role and family changes likewise made for a distinct change of mood and outlook, working against those religious institutions that had long been closely identified with the mainstream values.

It is sometimes said that these old Anglo institutions have depleted their theological resources, that the problem is one of 'tired blood.' Certainly the institutions do suffer from a loss of energy and direction and for a long time have ridden on inherited cultural capital. The shift in demographics was itself not inconsequential: the size of the Protestant majority steadily decreased in the twentieth century, as did the ethnic consciousness and identity underlying many of the Protestant communities. Anglo populations and cultures generally feel the squeeze resulting from growing Hispanic and non-Christian faiths. Yet despite the erosions of consciousness and institutions, in a very real sense these churches triumphed to a degree within the culture: many of their goals arising out of the Social Gospel movement were achieved and, more to a theological point, the Protestant principle about believing for yourself and taking responsibility for your actions long inculcated within these traditions now emerged in, admittedly, a far more radical and liberated form. In the 1960s and 1970s, young people—many of them nominally Protestant—turned inward and explored religious alternatives; they sought after experiential faith in a more direct, intimate sense than they had usually found in the dry rituals of the established churches; they felt free to create their own personal collages of belief drawing from a variety of sources and traditions, and worried less about theological consistency and more about the deeper meanings of whatever beliefs they held. Words like 'soul' and 'spiritual' which in the 1950s had all but disappeared in public discourse now returned with excitement. In this and so many other ways, signs pointed to a spiritual ferment which in its early phases that was not so much opposed to religion as alienated from existing bourgeois religious forms, and increasingly so for many college-educated, middle-class youth.

With the declines of the older religious institutions came other developments that point to major restructuring of American religion. One is the deep cleavage between liberals and conservatives, the latter having been rejuvenated in its crusades to restore a Christian society along the lines as defined by evangelicals and fundamentalists. Since the 1970s the latter have grown often picking up dropouts and dissidents from the oldline Protestant churches, and not without subtle appeals often—in the most conservative sectors—to reclaim an older, Anglo-based moral and religious order. While the thesis of a 'culture war' is easily overstated, there is much tension and occasionally overt conflict over unresolved issues like abortion, homosexuality, and prayer in public schools. Such disputes arise out of seriously conflicting, indeed incommensurate, notions of moral and religious authority—whether out of humanistic conceptions of the self and metaphorical views about truth in search of personal truth and happiness or literal interpretations of Biblical authority and a monarchical view of a transcendent God who commands people to obedience.

A second and related development is the rise of a full-blown spiritual quest culture that now permeates much of the nation's population—among mainline Protestants who find their own rituals and worship services in need of rejuvenation, among many 'seeker-minded' evangelicals who know very little about Christian tradition but are eager to adapt faith to their needs and concerns, and among secularists who turn to New Age religions (or more broadly, the 'New Spirituality') in search of inner truth and enlightenment (Roof 1999). This quest culture drives some Protestants to rediscover and reclaim their heritages; for the great majority, it seems to raise their levels of spiritual sensitivity more than their actual commitments to institutions. At present, there is considerable exploration not just of what was once called 'alternative religions' but of psychological teachings and inspirational literature, often of a rather generic quality; much influence of popular television programs and films that address spiritual themes directly, and many new entrepreneurs operating in the religious marketplace offering their versions of spiritual wisdom, holistic thinking, and mind-cure. In fact, many people who are interested in the New Spirituality have no difficulties acknowledging a Protestant past, which means that large numbers of Americans today combine old religious identities and new spiritual sensitivities with great ease, and in ways that appear to be personally rejuvenating but which to their grandparents would no doubt be incomprehensible.

3. Canada

Similar patterns of post-World War II Protestant decline are evident in Canada, despite the fact that the religious situation is very different in that country. Canada is historically less pluralistic, though that is now rapidly changing, and much more shaped historically by the presence of two large religious constituencies, Catholic and Protestant, each vying with one another for power and influence. Catholics have long been numerous in Lower Canada and the Protestants, especially Anglicans and Scotch Presbyterians, are sizable in Upper Canada. For the country as a whole, Protestants for a long time numbered more than Roman Catholics. But as of the national census in 1991, Roman Catholics, benefitting from a higher birth rate, edged above them with roughly 12,500,000 members, concentrated largely in Quebec. The United Church of Christ (a merger in 1925 of Congregationalists, Methodists, and some Presbyterians) is the next largest at approximately 2,000,000 members, concentrated in Ontario and Prairies; the Anglicans (plus the Orthodox) have substantial numbers, around one million. Baptists, Presbyterians, Lutherans, Pentecostals, and assorted other conservative Protestants are the next largest groups, most of them below a million members each. Birth rates for Mormons, the Salvation Army, and for conservative Protestant groups generally are higher than for the more established Protestant denominations.

But the fate of Protestantism in Canada differs in some important respects compared with the United States. Mainline Protestants have suffered membership declines there, losing both to the conservative churches and to Roman Catholic parishes. Proportionately they have lost more to Catholicism than is probably the case in the United States where just the opposite pattern appears to be more prominent—that is, somewhat greater losses to the religious conservatives. Statistically this is what one would expect: the larger the competing population, the greater the likelihood of mainline Protestants switching in, as a result of marriage or by religious choice. The conservative religious presence in Canada is neither as well-institutionalized nor as publicly visible as in its neighbor to the South. Sociologist Reginald W. Bibby (1993) argues in fact that the alleged recent growth of conservative Protestantism in Canada is largely a misperception, more really a 'circulation of the saints,' or movement from one evangelical church to another, than a case really of active and successful recruitment from other churches. Protestants on the whole, and conservative Protestants in particular, tend to be converted over and over again—as a result of social and geographic mobility, marriage, divorce, friendship patterns, preference for religious leaders, and congregational activities. Bibby's research suggests some slight increase in the recruitment of outsiders into the conservative fold over the past two decades, but even with these increases the actual number of converts remains small.

Overall, levels of religious participation in Canada are moderate—higher than those of most European countries but lower than found in the United States. Conservative Protestants have higher levels of weekly worship attendance than other Protestants and Roman Catholics, but because of their relatively small size proportionately and tendency to circulate among themselves their impact is not as widely felt as in the United States. The liberal–conservative cleavage within Protestantism is certainly evident, but the 'culture-war' infrastructure in Canada is weaker than in the United States, and therefore less of structural feature within the society. The conservative-moralist flavor of evangelical Protestantism never had sway over Canadians in the way historically it did, and to some extent still does, in the United States. Of greater significance is the influence of the New Spirituality which functions less as a separate enclave than to permeate religious communities of all kinds, and especially the more moderate-to-liberal communities. Again, to quote Bibby, Canadians are very much into 'religion a la carte.' Or, as he explains, 'New Age religion seems to follow the pattern of most new entries into the Canadian religion market, offering consumers optional item that can be added to more conventional religious beliefs and practices' (Bibby 1993, p. 52). It is not clear whether this is more true in Canada than in the United States; in both countries great numbers of people interested in New Age and metaphysical thought continue to identify, to a considerable extent, with an inherited faith tradition—as Protestant or Roman Catholic. This represents a major convergence for the two countries in the adaptation of religion to modernity. In both of these highly individualized settings, religion is not so much abandoned in some strict sense as it is privatized and modified to fit into people's life-situations at any given time.

4. Australasia

The very term 'Australasia' signals a confrontation and mixing of cultures, of East and West, a term quite fitting to both of our remaining countries, Australia and New Zealand. Both countries have a heritage of European settlements and Anglo dominance over aboriginal cultures, with the practices and structures of that heritage reflected in their social institutions.

Both countries know the tensions arising out of an expanding religious pluralism, brought on largely by successive waves of new migrants. Both are often described as increasingly secular societies, especially in political and civic life.

Yet there are significant differences. Australia has seen fewer new religions or even new versions of older religions than has New Zealand. Religious history for the former is more a telling of stories about a European past unlike for the latter where such stories are shaped more by local conditions and cultural and religious admixtures. Even Anglican church history differs. In Australia, the Anglican Church began as a convict church served by chaplains for whites, whereas in New Zealand, the Anglican Church was at first, and for a long time afterwards, a Maori aboriginal church served by missionaries. It was not until the mid-1800s that the Pakeha, or white Anglicans, began to outnumber the Maoris. The Maori Ratana and Ringatu faiths are two examples of New Zealand's popular mixing of religious and cultural themes, combining aboriginal and Christian elements. This difference between the two countries need not be exaggerated, but it does register in religious and spiritual styles.

Australia's religious profile today is as follows: Roman Catholics, 27 percent; Anglicans, 22 percent; Presbyterians, Methodists, and Uniting Church, 13 percent; other Christian, 11 percent; other Religions, 3 percent; no religion or not stated, 23 percent. The Catholic ascendency over Anglicans emerged about 50 years ago. The old, well-established religious communities—the Anglicans, the Uniting Church, the Presbyterians, and Lutherans—have all suffered declines in absolute numbers during the past two decades. The Christian or Christian-derived groups growing include the Pentecostals, Oriental Christian, Jehovah's Witnesses, and Mormons. Non-Christian groups rapidly increasing but still relatively small proportionately are Buddhists, Hindus, and Muslims, representing the latest of migrating populations into Australia. The greatest change in religious identification since World War II, and particularly among those who were born in this period, is the increase in people having 'no religion' or choosing not to state a religion in the national census. Since the 1970s this population has doubled. Likewise, religious attendance has declined in most of the churches while, somewhat paradoxically, stated interest in spiritual well-being appears to have increased.

In New Zealand, the Anglicans remain the largest single constituency considering that both the Pakeha and the Maoris are included. Roman Catholics are the next largest population, followed by Presbyterians with a continuing, strong Scottish heritage. About 50 percent of the population identify with one of the major Christian churches; by contrast, the evangelicals and Pentecostals appear not to have had as much success in recruiting in New Zealand as they have in Australia. Recent migrant religious communities are growing but are infinitesimal in size compared with all others. There have been substantial declines in religious affiliation and congregational involvement since World War II, especially for major churches, and mostly as a result of trends among younger whites. A third of the population currently report having 'no religion' or object to stating what it is. That the white and non-white populations are on somewhat different religious trajectories is apparent, evident most in the Anglo trends toward reduced organizational involvement; for the Maoris with their folk traditions and close spiritual attachments to the environment, organizational participation was never held up as a religious norm in quite the same way it was for Anglos.

Both Australia and New Zealand have experienced enormous changes in the past half-century, as they evolved from being made up predominately of villages and tribes to becoming more urban and multicultural in character. Religion has lost much of its power to integrate life experiences and has become one among many life-worlds in which people may or may not participate. Anglo religious traditions have suffered in the process. There, as elsewhere in modern societies, we observe greater eclecticism and pragmatism. However, compared with Canada, and even more so with the United States, two things stand out making the religious responses to modernity in Australasia different: one is that fundamentalism seems to attract fewer people and offers less of a viable alternative, and the second is there is less movement generally from one faith tradition to another, the more common movement being simply to leave organized religion in favor of 'no religion.'

See also: American Studies: Religion; Catholicism; Christianity in Asia; Christianity in Central and South America; Christianity Origins: Primitive and 'Western' History; Church and State: Political Science Aspects; Nationalism: General; Religion and Politics: United States; Religion: Definition and Explanation; Religion: Nationalism and Identity; Secularization

Bibliography

Anderson C H 1970 *White Protestant Americans: From National Origins to Religious Group*. Prentice-Hall, Englewood Cliffs, NJ

Berger P L 1979 *The Heretical Imperative: Contemporary Possibilities of Religious Affirmation*. Anchor Press, Garden City, NY

Bibby R W 1993 *Unknown Gods: The Ongoing Story of Religion in Canada*. Stoddart, Toronto, Canada

Bouma G D 1992 *Religion: Meaning, Transcendence and Community in Australia*. Longman Cheshire, Melbourne, Australia.

Martin D 1978 *The Dilemmas of Contemporary Religion*. St. Martin's Press, New York.

Roof W C 1999 *Spiritual Marketplace: Baby Boomers and the Remaking of American Religion*. Princeton University Press, Princeton, NJ

Wuthnow R 1988 *The Restructuring of American Religion: Society and Faith Since World War II*. Princeton University Press, Princeton NJ

W. C. Roof

Christianity in Asia

Christianity in Asia has an ancient history though it remains a minority religion. There are approximately 85 million Christians in Asia but more than 40 percent of them live in just two countries, the Philippines and South Korea. The minority status of Christianity in Asia gives it a distinctive sociological character in relation to Christianity in other regions of the world. For many Asian theologians this distinctive sociological context has meant that the particular focus of their articulation of the Christ of Asia is that of dialogue with the dominant religious and cultural traditions of Asia. In the postcolonial era a strong element of Christian social militancy was observable in many Asian countries. This militancy was associated with the ecumenical Christian Council of Asia, and especially its sponsorship of Urban Rural Mission in a number of countries. The Catholic Federation of Asian Bishops Conference is also an organization which has confronted frequently social and political controversies in particular Asian countries. Postcolonial Asian Christian social protest has focused on various concerns including the continuing social power of caste in India, workers' rights in South Korea and Southeast Asia, and democratic reform of authoritarian political regimes which characterise government in much of the region. A more recent form of militancy in Asian Christianity is associated with the rise of charismatic/Pentecostal and fundamentalist/evangelical groups which have arisen within and beyond the denominational boundaries and institutions established during the colonial era. Adherents of the new charismatic and evangelical forms of Asian church regard Christian worship, spirituality, and personal evangelism, rather than social transformation in the wider society, as the essential vocation of Asian Christians. This more transcendental and salvific emphasis represents a clear rejection of the social protest of earlier forms of postcolonial Asian Christianity. The new militancy is more focused on claims to spiritual power for the new forms of Asian Christian spiritual and congregational life, and the rights of all Asian Christians to freedom of worship, and to proselytise their neighbors. Just as the earlier ecumenical and socially radical militancy was the occasion for formal State resistance in South Korea in the 1970s, and in Singapore, Malaysia, and

Hong Kong in the 1980s, so Asian Christians now find their claimed freedoms to worship and evangelize occasion increased social scrutiny and resistance amongst majority religious and cultural groups and their political leaders.

1. South Asia

There is evidence of Christian activity in South India and Sri Lanka from the sixth century. Kerala is the region where most activity was concentrated, and Christians are still strong there, comprising 20 percent of the population. Christians also comprise a significant proportion of the population of Tamil Nadu. Portuguese colonisers saw a connection between trade and religion and, with the aid of the Jesuit order, encouraged the majority of the population of their settlement in Goa to convert to Christianity by the end of the sixteenth century. Under British rule the East India Company resisted the deployment of missionaries, judging that their presence would exacerbate existing religious tensions between Hindus and Muslims. But in the nineteenth century missionaries were allowed into most of British India. Converts were few and most were from marginal tribal groups, or from untouchables who have much to gain by abandoning Hinduism for Christianity. Since the 1980s a vocal Dalit (untouchable) movement has emerged which is radically anticaste and draws on Latin American-style liberation theology for its inspiration. With the rise of religious politics in India since the Premiership of Mrs Gandhi, religious conflict has become endemic in many parts of India and this has had an increasing impact on Christians. In Sri Lanka Christians are most prominent in the West and make up 30 percent of Colombo's population.

2. Christianity in China

Christianity in China goes back to the migration of Nestorian Christians from Iraq to China along the trade routes in the seventh century CE. The Jesuits arrived in China in the sixteenth century under the leadership of Matteo Ricci who experimented with a radical indigenisation of Christianity to Chinese culture. His efforts at cultural translation were controversial in Rome and the Pope insisted on a reversion to Roman rituals and traditions in 1744. After the opium wars and the Nanking treaty of 1842, Catholic and Protestant missionaries settled in many parts of China. The association between Christianity and Imperialism was strong and conversions were few until the failure of the Boxer rebellion at the end of the nineteenth century when many, especially young, Chinese turned to Christianity as a potential source of social and spiritual restoration. With the advent of Communist government in 1949 all foreign missionaries were removed from China and churches closed. Ironically the exclusion of foreign missionaries allowed Chinese Christianity to flourish in a way it had not before and the Christian presence in China today is much greater than it was at the time of the Communist revolution. Most of the officially recognized churches in China, whether Catholic or Protestant in origin, are known as 'three-self' churches, which means that they are not dependent on extra-Chinese ecclesiastical authority, nor do they rely on funds from overseas. There are also a large number of unofficial churches and congregations in China whose leaders try to circumvent controls on officially recognized churches, and in particular controls on proselytism. Evangelistic and worship meetings are held in secret, in apartments, or in open spaces away from city or town centres. The mass migration of many tens of millions of rural migrants into towns and cities in China since the 1980s, the largest contemporary movement of people on the planet, has occasioned conversions to new religions, including Christianity, as migrants seek to find a substitute for village-folk religion. Churches in urban areas, and especially in southern China, are currently growing very fast, fuelled by the spiritual and ritual vacuum occasioned by the Cultural Revolution and the enforced break-up of traditional Chinese religions, and by intellectual and popular dissatisfaction with secular Communist ideology.

3. Hong Kong, Taiwan, Japan, and Korea

One fifth of the population of Hong Kong are Christian and just under half are Catholics. The principal Protestant and Catholic traditions are represented and there are also a large number of independent and Pentecostal churches which have become established since the 1970s. The majority of Christians in Taiwan are Presbyterian, reflecting a missionary drive in the nineteenth century. Many new Christian groups emerged after the emigration of supporters of the government of Chian Kai-sheck to Taiwan from mainland China. The Jesuit missionary Francis Xavier introduced Christianity to Japan in 1549, after his initial mission to India who converted the Japanese court to Christianity. More than 300,000 Japanese followed their rulers and converted by the end of that century. However, Christianity was later proscribed, though small pockets of Christian activity remained. In the twentieth century Japan has been characterized by remarkable religious innovation, and many New Religious Movements have emerged, particularly since the Second World War. Parallel developments have occurred in Japanese Christianity. New indigenous styles of Christianity have emerged, and Pentecostal groups have also proliferated.

The Catholic Church has roots in Korea as far back as the sixteenth century but Protestantism has taken root in Korea in a manner it has nowhere else in Asia. Forty-one percent of the population are now Christian, and the majority belong to indigenous Korean and Protestant churches. The beginning of the twentieth century saw a particularly rapid influx of Koreans into the Protestant churches, and many Protestant churches have also experienced considerable growth since the Second World War. Seoul has some of the largest church buildings, and the largest congregations, anywhere in the world. Explanations for the strength of Protestantism in Korea are various. One theory is that there is a uniquely individualist strain to Korean Confucianism and that Protestantism individualism, with its more progressive conception of the role of the individual in the fast changing world of the twentieth century, proved particularly attractive to Koreans who were dissatisfied with Confucianism.

4. Southeast Asia

As a consequence of more than three centuries of settlement by the Spanish, and after the Spanish American war, by the United States, Christianity is the principal religion of the Philippines. Virtually the whole country was converted to Roman Catholicism under Spanish rule, though a Muslim minority remained, primarily in Mindanao. The Roman Catholic Church, however, was organized and run exclusively by foreign clergy and resentment at this resulted in an internal revolution whose outcome was the Philippine Independent Church which broke away from Catholicism after 1860. Protestant missionaries arrived with the Americans, including Episcopalians who set out to convert the mountain peoples in North Luzon as they had not been reached by the Catholics.

Roman Catholic missions were active in Vietnam, Cambodia, and Laos in the seventeenth and eighteenth centuries, and established churches in all three countries. Cambodia now has very few Christians indeed. After Year Zero Christians were totally purged from Cambodia. In Laos the Catholic Church has had most converts amongst tribal peoples on the border with Thailand but remains an insignificant presence elsewhere in the country. In Vietnam Christians, the great majority of whom are Catholic, constitute 7 percent of the population. The church was indigenized much more effectively in the North, whereas in the South local leadership was discouraged and there are far fewer adherents. Catholics have been close to political leadership in both North and South Vietnam and the Catholic Church in Rome and in Vietnam was a strong supporter of moves for peace during the war, and of subsequent North–South reconciliation efforts after the war.

Uniquely in Southeast Asia, Thailand has never been colonized by a foreign power and Thai Buddhism is particularly resistant to foreign, including Christian, influence. Strong Chinese communities in the large cities, and especially in Bangkok, are the main locus of Christian adherents. Myanmar Buddhists are also highly resistant to Christianity. Christians are most numerous amongst the Karen tribal group in the forests of the Northwest who are not Buddhist, and do not regard themselves as Burmese.

Christianity was introduced into the Indonesian archipelago by the Dutch in the sixteenth century. Christians are most numerous in Northern Sumatra where the non-Muslim Batak people converted to Christianity in large numbers. There are also churches in most areas of Java, and on some of the other islands. Indonesian Christianity has been subject to the State religious doctrine of Panchasilla which requires that all religious groups express loyalty to the state and tolerance of other religions. Indonesian Christians were active in the struggle for independence from the Dutch after the Second World War and their partnership in the birth of the new independent nation may partly explain why, almost uniquely in the Muslim world, there have in the past been a number of religious conversions. However, a peaceful inter-religious climate characterized by neighborliness and dialogue between the religions recently has turned to conflict as the Suharto and Habibi governments have stirred up religious conflict as a way of maintaining a hold on the votes of the predominantly Muslim population.

Christians in Malaysia number around 7 percent of the population, and 15 percent in Singapore. Dating back to the Portugese settlement of Malacca in the fifteenth century, Malaysian Christianity has taken up a range of influences including Portugese Catholic, Dutch Presbyterian, American Methodist, Anglican, and Pentecostal. Christians are confined to Chinese and Indian minorities on the whole, though tribal peoples in East Malaysia have converted to Christianity in large numbers. The fastest growing forms of Christianity in both Singapore and Malaysia today are Pentecostal or Charismatic. This modern style of Christianity has spawned many independent churches and has also been very influential in mainstream Catholic and Protestant congregations. Both countries have experienced a surge in religious interest and affiliation in recent years, sparked in part by Islamic resurgence among the Malays. This is reflected in a range of religious innovations both within Islam, Buddhism, and Hinduism, as well as in Christianity.

See also: Catholicism; Christianity: Evangelical, Revivalist, and Pentecostal; East Asia, Religions of; India, Religions of; Religion: Evolution and Development; Religion, Sociology of

Bibliography

Ackerman S E, Lee R 1988 *Heaven in Transition*. University of Hawaii Press, Honolulu, HI

Barrett D B (ed.) 1982 *World Christian Encyclopedia: A Comparative Study of Churches and Religions in the Modern World AD 1900–2000.* Oxford University Press, Nairobi, Zimbabwe

Digan P 1984 *Churches in Contestation: Asian Christian Social Protest.* Orbis Books, Maryknoll, NY

von der Mehden F R 1986 *Religion and Modernization in Southeast Asia.* Syracuse University Press, Syracuse, NY

Neill S C 1985 *History of Christianity in India, 1707–1858.* Cambridge University Press, Cambridge, UK

Palmer S J 1967 *Korea and Christianity: The Problem of Identification with Tradition.* Hollym Corp, Seoul, South Korea

M. Northcott

Christianity in Central and South America

Throughout the pre-Hispanic, colonial, and contemporary periods, the history of religion in Central and South America has been inextricably linked to political structures, rituals that ordered everyday life, and movements of rebellion, with Catholicism having played a central role for almost four centuries. After the break up of the monopoly exercised by the Catholic church and the rapid growth of Evangelical churches there is growth, but also fragmentation; creativity as well as uncertainty; individualism, but also the constitution of new communities; freedom, along with the authoritarianism of the leaders of the base communities or of the Pentecostal churches; political quietism side by side with right-wing activism. There are even churches that reversing the traditional direction have established branches outside Latin America.

1. Religion Before the Conquest

As is generally the case in the preindustrial world, in which ideological claims are advanced in mythological terms and reinforced through ritual means, in the area now known as Latin America the social order was religiously legitimized. A proper discussion of the various ways in which this religious legitimization took place would require considering the range of societies found in Meso and South America, from kinship-based groups, found for instance in the Amazonian area, to chiefdoms, to states. Since such an examination cannot be undertaken here, it may suffice to say that societies organized as chiefdoms tend to be theocratic, their political life being heavily ritualized; this also applies to early states, such as the Inca and the Aztec, in which the rulers were sacralized and were considered as the pivot of their society. Thus, in the Andean world the Inca dynasty, originally based in the area of Cuzco in southeastern Peru, claimed descent from Inti, the Sun.

More generally, religious legitimation meant that social distinctions, obligation to work, and access to resources were regarded as being regulated by an order that encompassed the social and the physical world. In order to maintain this order it was necessary to structure time and space, as well as the relations between age groups and the sexes. The organization of time was accomplished at several levels: at the individual level, this involved rites of passage; at the macrosocial levels, on the other hand, the structuring required the use of liturgical calendars which were related to the seasons and, above all, to agricultural work. Similarly, space was structured by establishing mythologically based distinctions among neighborhoods and, at a more extended level, by dividing a territory by means of shrines along imaginary lines, an example of which is the *ceque* system centered in Cuzco, the Inca capital.

2. Conquest, Resistance, Accommodation

The fact that the political, religious, and economic spheres were less differentiated in the Aztec and Inca states than in sixteenth-century Western Europe may have contributed to the speed of the victory of the Spanish and Portuguese adventurers. The 'modernity' of the conquerors should not be exaggerated, however, for the Iberian discovery and conquest of America took place immediately after the defeat of the Muslim kingdom of Granada, and the expulsion of the Jews who had refused to convert to Christianity. It can be said, therefore, that the conquest itself took place as a kind of crusade at a time of politico-religious triumphalism. Moreover, attention should be paid to the fact that Columbus seems to have endowed his enterprise with a millenarian aura, hoping that a portion of the wealth found in the Indies would be used in the conquest of Jerusalem. This millenarian component can also be found at work in the self-understanding of some of the members of the religious orders involved in the process of conversion of the vanquished.

In any event, while the crusading spirit validated the conquest, the transcendentalization of religion and the concomitant separation between the roles of priests and those of soldiers and administrators allowed some clerics to denounce the abuses of conquerors, without, however, condemning the conquest itself. During the colonization of Latin America, therefore, Christianity fulfilled the double role traditionally accomplished by religion: that of validating a social order, beginning with the justification of the conquest itself, while also providing the justification for judging that same order.

Religions' double function can also be seen at work among the indigenous population, for whom Christianity served as a vehicle of accommodation as well as of protest. The first aspect involved what is generally known as syncretism, that is, the amalgamation of Christianity and indigenous religions. Thus, the Christian god incorporated elements of Andean divinities such as Wirakocha and Pachacamac, while the Virgin Mary, as the Virgin of Guadalupe, subsumed the Aztec goddess Tonantzin, 'Our Mother'; Quetzalcóatl, on the other hand, was assimilated to the apostle Thomas. The fact that the physical appearance of some of the inhabitants of the Christian pantheon was said to resemble that of the Indian population, rather than that of the conquerors, indicates on the one hand the extent to which the subjugated population had assimilated the new religion, and on the other, the intimate connection between religion and ethnic identification.

In some cases, conquered elites sought the protection of some of the most bellicose inhabitants of the Christian pantheon, expecting to profit from the power these supernatural beings had shown on the Spanish side; thus, the apostle Santiago, patron of Spain, became syncretized with the Andean Illapa (Lightning), and already in the sixteenth century the Virgin of Copacabana was enlisted in intradynastic struggles. Christianity also played a role in the indigenous rebellions against Spanish domination. This can be seen already on the sixteenth-century Taki Onqoy, and more clearly in the late eighteenth-century Tupac Amaru rebellion, in which the rebels regarded themselves as better Christians than the Spaniards.

3. Religion in the New Republics

The accommodation between indigenous religions and Christianity should not obscure the fact that from the beginning of the conquest, in order to forestall challenges from within, Spanish authorities sought to destroy the indigenous religions, undertaking 'extirpation of idolatries' campaigns; similarly, in order to protect Catholic orthodoxy from external threats, Spanish authorities tried to isolate the colonies from Protestantism, Judaism, and liberalism: Christianity—the Baroque Christianity of the Counter Reformation—served as one of the bastions of Spanish power during the three centuries of colonial rule. The role played by religion in the wars of independence of the early nineteenth century was ambiguous. Whereas the lower clergy tended to side with those who wanted to achieve independence from Spain, the prelates, many of whom had been born in the Iberian peninsula, were generally in favor of maintaining the colonial regime. Once independence was achieved in the nineteenth century, the Creole elites kept in place the church's prerogatives, while at the same time seeking to control it, just as the kings of Spain had done. After the governments of the new republics and the Vatican signed concordats regulating the status of the church, Roman Catholicism generally enjoyed a privileged position, one that was enshrined in the republics' constitutions.

The situation, however, was not always as favorable as clerical groups would have wanted. As in Spain itself, the very hegemony of the church contributed to an atmosphere of anticlericalism which led to attempts to curtail that institution's privileges; this anticlerical attitude was intensified by the influence of liberal and positivist currents. The most radical measures against Roman Catholicism were taken in Mexico, a country that re-established relations with the Vatican only in 1992. In general, however, Latin American governments have regarded the church as an ideological ally, one which played a crucial role in the legitimization of the social order.

4. Religion and Everyday Life

Encompassing domestic devotions and public anticlericalism, individual rites of passage and official liturgies, Catholicism has been an omnipresent reality in the life of Latin Americans. But, as one would expect, Catholicism has been lived differently by men and by women, by members of upper and lower classes, in urban and rural milieus. As in southern Europe, in Latin America everyday religion in its private and public forms has been the domain of women; thus, except for special occasions such as Lent and Christmas, women have constituted the majority of the faithful in Sunday services. Similarly, it is the mothers who traditionally have been in charge of introducing children to the rituals and the moral injunctions of Catholicism. It is in the process of religious socialization that social class plays an important role, as children of the middle and upper classes are generally subject to religious indoctrination in schools directed by members of religious orders, whereas those who attend state schools are subject to minimal religious education.

One of the consequences of this religious indoctrination is that Catholic revival movements such as Catholic Action, or political parties linked to Catholicism, such as Christian Democracy, involve mainly middle and upper class persons. In large cities, public religious activity is usually restricted to Sunday masses and to occasional processions, in some of which participate government dignitaries. The legitimizing role of Catholicism as the state religion can be seen at work in the solemn liturgies with which church and state commemorate independence day, and even more so in the consecration of entire countries to Jesus or the Virgin Mary.

4.1 Popular Religion

The counterpart of official Catholicism is represented by what is known as 'popular religion'—that is, those symbolic practices that seem to want to escape, and even to oppose, the control of religious elites. Ambivalence is at the core of popular religion, since in order to express opposition it is necessary to make use, against the grain, of the symbolic resources of the institutions which one opposes. Popular religion is part and parcel of a complex system of assimilation and rejection, through which subordinate groups sometimes negotiate and others struggle over access to cultural and in the last instance material goods. Latin American popular religion comprises the syncretic processes referred to above, in which elements of the symbolic world of the Spanish conquerors were incorporated into that of the Andean, Mesoamerican, and other conquered groups, as well as contemporary ritual practices in urban and rural milieus, such as processions and pilgrimages, which represent the counterparts of the liturgical functions choreographed by the official Church.

Despite the current academic infatuation with symbolic resistance, however, it must be said that the parodic, carnivalesque, rituals of popular religion generally have not constituted serious threats to the hegemony of Catholicism or of the state. In fact, the expenditures required by the ritual calendar of indigenous communities instead of leveling economic disparities may increase them.

4.2 Millenarian Movements

In general, in order for popular religious practices to turn into insurrections it has been necessary that the state attempt to suppress in a violent manner groups that have sought to isolate themselves from a changing society in order to live according to the teachings of the Gospel under the guidance of a charismatic leader. This happened, among other places, in northeastern Brazil from 1893 to 1897, in the millenarian movement of Canudos; it happened again in southern Brazil from 1912 to 1916 in the Contestado rebellion. Both the Canudos and Contestado movements constituted reactions against the secular, positivistic values of the Brazilian republic—and in the case of the Contestado rebellion it is clear that it was triggered by the dislocations brought about by capitalism. Like millenarian and messianic movements in general, those that have taken place in Latin America have involved marginal regions in transitional periods, and have been led by marginal, literate individuals, such as Antonio Conselheiro, leader of Canudos, and Miguel Lucena Boaventura, known as José Maria, leader of Contestado.

5. Liberation Theology

At the elite level, the privileged status of Catholicism in Latin America has not gone unchallenged either. In the nineteenth century, anticlerical groups, influenced by positivism, had already decried the church's influence; similarly, in the twentieth century politically progressive groups opposed the alliance between oligarchic governments and conservative church. It was, however, during the early 1960s, prompted first by the triumph of the Cuban revolution and then by the Second Vatican Council, that the traditional equation between church and conservative politics was broken. The Cuban revolution, combined with the Council's attempts to re-examine the relation between the church and the world, forced some members of the Latin American clergy to question the role the church had played in the maintenance of an unjust social order. That questioning led to the emergence of a 'prophetic' understanding of Christianity known as the Theology of Liberation. Influenced by the social sciences as much as by traditional methods of theological exegesis, the liberation theologians removed concepts such as sin and salvation from the mere personal and spiritual realms to one that took into account the structures of the societies within which sins were committed and salvation was sought. This theological approach was attacked by conservative Catholics, clerical and lay alike, who accused its proponents of forsaking Christianity and falling prey to Marxism. It cannot be emphasized enough, however, that despite its apparent threat to Catholicism, the theology of liberation constituted an attempt to save Latin America's dominant religion by enlisting it in the task of reforming society. That ultimately, attacked by the local churches and neutralized by Rome, the theology of liberation gave up its distinctive use of sociological categories and retreated into traditional spirituality, was to be expected, given that the liberation theologians were, after all, theologians.

6. Alternatives to Catholicism

But Rome's victory was a hollow one, for the presuppositions shared by both conservative and revolutionary clerics—that Latin America is and will remain Roman Catholic—proved to be illusory. As the conflicts between Rome and the radical theologians were taking place, a far more important development was unfolding, namely the spread of Protestantism—or, to be more correct, of Evangelical forms of Christianity. Nevertheless, despite the fact that the triumph of Protestantism may have demonstrated the ultimate irrelevance of the confrontation between Rome and the theology of liberation, there is a strong affinity between this theology, which could be considered as a Protestant Catholicism, and the evangelical churches. In both cases we find a puritan faith centered upon the Word, suspicious of the rituals of official Catholicism as well as of those that constitute popular religion. It is as if both movements away from a sacramental, hierarchical, agrarian-based vision of the world had developed as a response to the weakening of the agrarian economy with its rituals and mythologies in order to come to terms with a predominantly urban world ruled by the market.

But, instead of the 'disenchantment' of the world, to use Weber's term, we find two religiously ambiguous, half-enchanted formations, the Evangelical and the Catholic, whose task it is to mediate between the two worlds. In both versions of Christianity there is still the attempt to preserve, if only though the Word, the presence of the transcendent, while at the same time deritualizing everyday activities. The causes and consequences of this deritualization have been explained in terms of a rationalization of economic activities, involving, for instance, the avoidance of the burden represented by wasteful ritual expenditures, and in more general terms turning away from the pressure exercised by community and tradition. The result is a world of ever widening economic disparities which must be confronted in an instrumental manner by the individual as individual, rather than as a member of a community. But, rather than repressing emotion, individualism and instrumental reason seem to exacerbate it. Thus, as in the tense coexistence of Pietism and Enlightenment found in eighteenth-century northern Europe, we find that the strongest forms of Latin American non-Catholic Christianity are Pentecostal; this has led to the emergence of charismatic forms of Catholicism—one more example of the proliferation of religious offerings in the religious market that emerged after the break up of monopolistic Catholicism.

In this context reference should be made to the growth of New Age religions among the middle and upper classes, as well as of religions of African origin among groups which are not of African descent, and in countries, such as Argentina, which do not have a significant black population.

While the early spread of Protestantism was caused by the activities of North American missionaries, the subsequent growth of evangelical churches is now largely fueled by local ferment. In some countries, such as Puerto Rico, El Salvador, Guatemala, Chile, and Brazil, evangelicals constitute a significant proportion of the population, whereas in others, such as Venezuela and Colombia, that presence is much smaller. Considering, however, the continuous growth of non-Catholic forms of Christianity, it can be said without reservation that the equation between Latin American religion and Catholicism, presupposed, among others, by the advocates of liberation theology, is a thing of the past. It is true that the Catholic church can still exercise pressure upon governments and legislatures on matters related to the control of female sexuality, but even in these cases, despite the fact that abortion is still illegal in Latin America, birth control campaigns are not uncommon, as the birth rate has decreased in the last several decades, a fact which shows that the influence of the church on the everyday life of ordinary people has diminished substantially.

6.1 Conservative Trends in Catholicism

A development that will likely contribute to the further loss of popularity of the Catholic church among the lower classes, while perhaps increasing it among high-income groups, is the growing importance of conservative Catholic groups such as the Opus Dei, a secretive organization supported by the Vatican. But even in the case of the Opus Dei, one can see its promotion as an attempt on the part of the church to accommodate itself to a changing world. In effect, despite its traditionalism and authoritarianism, the values promoted by this organization are consonant with the demands of a capitalist order, and in more general terms with the demands of modernity.

See also: Catholicism; Christianity: Evangelical, Revivalist, and Pentecostal; Latin American Studies: Religion; Latin American Studies: Society; Religion, Sociology of

Bibliography

Annis S 1987 *God and Production in a Guatemalan Town*. University of Texas Press, Austin, TX
Bastian J-P 1997 *La mutación religiosa de América Latina. Para una sociología del cambio social en la modernidad periférica*. Fondo de Cultura Económica, Mexico City
Burga M 1988 *Nacimiento de una utopía. Muerte y resurrección de los incas*. Instituto de Apoyo Agrario, Lima, Peru
Diacon T A 1991 *Millenarian Vision, Capitalist Reality: Brazil's Contestado Rebellion, 1912–1916*. Duke University Press, Durham, NC
Duviols P 1971 *La lutte contre les religions autochtones dans le Pérou colonial (L'extirpation de l'idolatrie entre 1532 et 1660)*. Institut Francais d'Études andines, Lima [1977 *La destrucción de las religiones andinas (durante la conquista y la colonia)*. UNAM, Mexico City]
Flores Galindo A 1988 *Buscando un Inca: identidad y utopía en los Andes*. Editorial Horizonte, Lima, Peru
Garrard-Burnett V, Stoll D (eds.) 1993 *Rethinking Protestantism in Latin America*. Temple University Press, Philadelphia, PA
Krickeberg W, Trimborn H, Müller W, Zerries O 1961 *Die Religionen des alten Amerika*. Kohlhammer, Stuttgart [1968 *Pre-Columbian American Religions*. Weidenfeld & Nicolson, London/Holt, Rinehart and Winston, New York]
Lafaye J 1984 *Mesías, cruzadas, utopías. El judeo-cristianismo en las sociedades iberoamericanas*. Fondo de Cultura Económica, Mexico City
Levine R 1992 *Vale of Tears: Revisiting the Canudos Massacre in Northeastern Brazil, 1893–1897*. University of California Press, Berkeley
Martin D 1990 *Tongues of Fire: The Explosion of Protestantism in Latin America*. Blackwell, Oxford-Cambridge, UK
Mecham J L 1966 *Church and State in Latin America*. University of North Carolina Press, Chapel Hill, NC
Prien H-J 1978 *Die Geschichte des Christentums in Lateinamerika*. Vandenhoeck & Ruprecht, Göttingen
Stoll D 1990 *Is Latin America turning Protestant? The Politics of Evangelical Growth*. University of California Press, Berkeley

G. Benavides

Christianity: Liberal

'Liberal' is the designation given to a broad trajectory in Christianity by sympathisers and critics alike. In some of its manifestations it is also referred to as 'modernism.' Both terms draw attention to a defining characteristic: a dissatisfaction with earlier forms of religion and a concern to replace them with less restrictive alternatives more open to the spirit of the age. Whilst it has rarely led to the establishment of new churches, liberalism has had a significant impact within all the mainline Christian denominations in the West.

Understood in this broad sense, liberal Christianity can be seen to date back even before the Renaissance to the fifteenth century, when the term 'modern' was first invoked in relation to reforming movements in theology and spirituality like the '*Via Moderna*' and the '*Devotio Moderna.*' Since then Western Christianity has been challenged repeatedly by individuals and movements who have championed the freedom of the individual Christian over against the authority of institutional religion. Yet it is in the modern period that liberal Christianity has become most prominent and has played its most important role in shaping modernity itself.

By the end of the twentieth century something of a consensus had developed amongst sociologists of religion that liberal Christianity was in inexorable decline. This consensus coincided with a period when theological liberalism had fallen out of fashion. It will be challenged in what follows on three grounds: (a) it overlooks the internal variety of liberal Christianity, (b) it ignores evidence of its continuing vitality on the ground, and (c) it fails to recognize that liberal Christianity remains well adapted to many of the socio-economic formations and cultural trends of the modern world.

1. Varieties of Liberalism

1.1 Rationalist

One of the most important ways in which liberal Christianity is implicated with the rise of modernity is through its central role in the Enlightenment of the mid-seventeenth to mid-eighteenth centuries. In their different ways such figures as the Deists, Thomas Jefferson, Tom Paine, René Descartes, John Locke, and Immanuel Kant were all concerned with the liberal reform of religion. They helped shape a liberal Christianity which was characterized by (a) hostility to 'traditional' religion, conceived as superstitious, heteronomous, and divisive, (b) confidence in human reason and the primacy of the sovereign individual, (c) activist optimism about the possibilities of human and social improvement, (d) belief in the harmonious unity of all true ('natural') religion, and (e) high valuation of freedom. Rationalist liberalism tended to be primarily an intellectual movement, though it was often related closely to political radicalism. At the institutional level it gave rise to the Unitarian and Universalist churches.

1.2 Romantic

Whilst many sociologists identify liberal Christianity with its rationalist forms, there are other important varieties. By the late eighteenth century, for example, a Romantic liberalism had begun to exercise an important cultural and religious influence. In America this was best represented by Transcendentalism, and in Germany by the theology of Friedrich Schleiermacher. Romantic liberalism inherited rationalist liberalism's belief that the individual rather than the institution was the locus of true religion ('my mind is my church,' as Tom Paine had put it), but stressed the authority of feeling, imagination, experience, and self-consciousness rather than reason. This stress on the importance of individual experience of God has been carried through into the twentieth century in the work of theologians like Rudolph Bultmann and Paul Tillich.

1.3 Ethical and Social

Kant had located religious authority in moral reason. This 'ethicisation' of the Christian religion was taken further in Germany by theologians like Albrecht Ritschl, Wilhelm Hermann, and Adolf von Harnack, and in America by theologians like Horace Bushnell and Walter Rauschenbusch. The latter, the leader of the Social Gospel movement, was responsible for interpreting Christianity as a force for social reform in industrial society.

1.4 Liberation and Feminist

In the twentieth century the influence of liberal Christianity continues to be felt in new reform movements within the churches and theology, most notably in some important varieties of Liberation theology (a product of Latin America) and Feminist Theology (a product of North America and Western Europe). In both we find a characteristic emphasis on human liberation and the authority of experience, combined with a thoroughgoing criticism of existing structures of power and domination in both the churches and wider society, and a bias towards the oppressed and marginal.

2. The Development of Modern Liberalism

Liberalism has had the greatest impact within mainline Protestant churches, and has been particularly influential in countries where Protestantism has been dominant. Most commentators consider its heyday to have been from the mid-nineteenth century through the 1920s. Liberalism flourished because it was able to meet the new challenges posed by the forces of modernisation. Its critical stance towards Christian tradition enabled it to assimilate the rise of historical method and its application to the Bible. Equally, its long-held belief in progress and the capacity of human reason to fathom the mysteries of God and the world helped it embrace the discoveries of modern science, including evolution. What is more, its libertarianism and individualism enabled it to support the interests of the new middle classes and to play a legitimating role in relation to democracy and the modern state. Far from being threatened by rapid modernisation in the nineteenth century, liberal Christianity tended to view itself as the religious and moral engine of social progress. Nowhere was this truer than in the USA. In Catholic countries the picture was very different. There, led by an increasingly defensive Rome, the church explicitly repudiated the errors of 'modernism' (which included political and religious liberalism), and allied itself with the forces of reaction. In 1907 Pope Pius X condemned those Catholic 'modernists' who had embraced aspects of theological liberalism, and introduced an anti-Modernist oath for the clergy which effectively brought to an end all attempts to develop a liberal Catholicism. It was not until the Second Vatican Council of 1962–5 that a moderate liberalism gained official sanction. Since then there has been an explosion of liberal thought in the Catholic church, despite Pope John Paul II's attempts to curb its influence. The work of theologians like Hans Küng, as well as the rise of Liberation Theology and Feminist Theology has been particularly notable.

The twentieth century has brought unprecedented challenges for Liberal Christianity. These include the rise of conservative evangelical and fundamentalist Christianity and, at the theological level, the rise of Neo-orthodoxy. At the same time many elements of the liberal creed—including belief in progress, reason, 'humanity,' and the ideal of religious unity—have been shaken both inside and outside the churches. This together with shrinking attendance in the mainline Protestant churches most influenced by liberalism has led many commentators to conclude that it is in terminal decline. What this conclusion overlooks, however, is that the mainline denominations still account for the vast majority of Christians (especially if one includes the Catholic church), and that many within these denominations (including the Catholic churches) continue to embrace some version of liberal Christianity (see below). What is more, liberalism remains extremely well adapted to societies that show no real sign of diminishing their commitment to freedom, equality, democracy, and a liberal individualism reinforced by the institutions of a free-market economy.

3. Liberalism on the Ground

Dean Kelley's book *Why the Conservative Churches are Growing* (1972) captured a new mood in the sociology of religion. Where secularisation theory had previously encouraged the conclusion that the more traditional and antimodern forms of religion would be those which would decline most rapidly, the growth of conservative and sectarian bodies alongside evidence of the decline of more liberal denominations led to a change of mind after the 1960s. As noted below, sociological theory was quickly mobilized to explain this change, and to reinforce the prediction of further liberal decline.

Much of the case for liberal decline focuses on the American example. It is clear from census data in the US, like the General Social Survey (GSS), that the three denominations it classifies as 'liberal' (Presbyterian, Episcopal, and United Church of Christ) did indeed decline after 1970. So too did the three denominations it labels as 'moderate' (United Methodist, Lutheran, and Disciples of Christ), together with the Roman Catholic church. By contrast more conservative denominations like the Southern Baptist Convention and the Seventh-day Adventists grew in numbers. There is some evidence, however, that numbers in the liberal denominations may now be stabilising (Roof and McKinney 1987), and it may therefore be premature to pronounce on the relative success or failure of liberal and conservative Christianity in modern times.

It is also necessary to exercise caution when relying on data relating to levels of denominational attendance and affiliation alone in assessing the state of liberal Christianity in the churches. The main problem with this method is that it is blind to complex patterns of belief and commitment within churches and denominations. For example, most mainline churches today—both Catholic and Protestant—contain both liberals and conservatives within their congregations, and it is increasingly hard to label whole denominations 'liberal' or 'conservative.' What is more, there is some important evidence that even more conservative forms of Catholic and evangelical Christianity are increasingly permeable to the influence of liberalism. Thus James Davison Hunter's extensive research among college-age Evangelicals in American uncovered evidence of an increasing liberalisation of their belief, values, and practice (Hunter 1987).

The best way to assess the relative strength of liberalism in the contemporary churches would seem to be through intensive and widespread congregational study. The most important work of this kind is that undertaken by Ammerman (1997) who studied 23 representative congregations across the USA and surveyed almost 2,000 individuals. Her discovery was that respondents fell into three categories: liberal or 'Golden Rule' Christians (51 percent), evangelicals (29 percent), and social activists (19 percent). On the basis of her research Ammerman challenges the assumption that religious liberalism is a spent force, and that liberal religiosity is a paler reflection of conservative Christianity. The Golden Rule Christianity she describes is characterized by an emphasis on the primacy of good deeds motivated by love, care, and compassion, and by a belief in the importance of religious tolerance.

It may be that Ammerman has discovered a fifth variety of Christian liberalism—one which might be labelled 'relational,' and whose significance on the ground in the second part of the twentieth century has been largely overlooked.

4. Sociological Interpretations

At least three clusters of explanations have been offered by sociologists of religion to account for the rise of liberal Christianity in modern times. It has been explained as (a) an accommodation or even a capitulation to modernity (Peter Berger), (b) a natural outgrowth of Protestantism and, in particular, of the latter's emphasis on personal subjective conviction (Ernst Troeltsch), and (c) a means by which the clergy, their social status undermined by modernity, have attempted to protest and regain a social role (Jeffrey Hadden). Woodhead and Heelas (2000) have also drawn attention to liberal Christianity's compatibility with modern socio-economic formations and wider cultural trends such as the turn to the self.

Sociologists have also developed theories to account for liberal Christianity's apparent decline. Kelley explained this by drawing a contrast with conservative religion. Where the latter was 'strict' and 'challenging,' the latter was the opposite. As such, he argued, it was unable to generate or sustain commitment, consensus or strong community. Peter Berger offered a more rigorous version of this explanation by arguing that plausibility is a function of unanimity. The strong, unified communities that characterize conservative religion are better able to sustain plausibility than are the more diffuse and less disciplined communities of liberalism. Meanwhile sociologists like Talcott Parsons and David Martin have also argued that liberalism is a victim of its own success: because its beliefs and values are so close to those of the wider culture it is no longer able to sustain a distinctive identity nor to hold or attract adherents.

Much of this theoretical work depends on a contrast drawn between liberal and conservative Christianity. It is also important to note another boundary: that be-

tween liberal Christianity and radical or 'alternative' forms of spirituality. For whilst the fate of liberal Christianity is bound up with that of conservative Christianity, it is also bound up with that of new forms of religiosity like the New Age. In some ways the latter seems to represent an intensification of key liberal themes like individualism and freedom, but without liberal Christianity's continuing commitment to some form of institutional church. It remains to be seen whether the apparent growth of such religiosity will in the end have the effect of strengthening or of weakening liberalism.

See also: American Studies: Religion; Christian Liturgy; Civil Religion; Feminist Theology; Liberalism; Liberalism: Historical Aspects; Protestantism and Gender; Rationalism; Rationality in Society; Reformation and Confessionalization; Religion and Politics: United States; Religion: Evolution and Development; Religion, Sociology of; Religiosity: Modern

Bibliography

Ammerman N T 1997 *Congregation and Community*. Rutgers University Press, New Brunswick, NJ
Hunter J D 1987 *Evangelicalism. The Coming Generation*. University of Chicago Press, Chicago
Hutchison W R (ed.) 1968 *American Protestant Thought in the Liberal Era*. University Press of America, Lanham, MD
Hutchison W R 1976 *The Modernist Impulse in American Protestantism*. Harvard University Press, Cambridge, MA
Kelley D M 1972 *Why Conservative Churches are Growing*. Harper & Row, New York
Michaelsen R S, Roof W C (eds.) 1986 *Liberal Protestantism: Realities and Possibilities*. Pilgrim Press, New York
Miller D E 1981 *The Case for Liberal Christianity*, 1st edn. Harper & Row, San Francisco
Reardon B M (ed.) 1968 *Liberal Protestantism*. Stanford University Press, Stanford, CA
Roof W C 1978 *Community and Commitment. Religious Plausibility in a Liberal Protestant Church*. Elsevier, New York
Roof W C, McKinney W 1987 *American Mainline Religion. Its Changing Shape and Future*. Rutgers University Press, New Brunswick, NJ
Woodhead L J P, Heelas P L 2000 *Religion in Modern Times*. Blackwell, Malden, MA

L. Woodhead

Christianity Origins: Primitive and 'Western' History

This article considers Christianity in the first 300 years of its existence, before it achieved a close alliance with the Roman state. It pays particular attention to the social forms of early Christianity and their relation to wider society.

1. The Jesus Movement

The movement that centered around Jesus of Nazareth in his own lifetime seems an unlikely candidate for the eventual transformation of Western society. It appears to have been one of many such movements in early first century Palestine led by a charismatic Jewish teacher appealing to a poor and mainly rural audience (Theissen 1978). Jesus's message, which is only comprehensible within a framework of contemporary Jewish beliefs and expectations, centered round the proclamation of the imminent reign of God. From this expectation arose the urgent and sovereign demands to repent and believe in the gospel. All other concerns were secondary—including on occasion those of Jewish law and custom. Yet this message was presented as 'good news': what Jesus offered his followers was the most intimate relationship with a God not of wrath and judgment but of love and mercy—a 'father' who cares with loving tenderness for each one of his children. This God places no barriers on relationship with him—all are welcomed into his kingdom irrespective of their moral, social, or religious status.

2. The Pauline Revolution

Whilst Jesus' mission was primarily to the Jews, the unrestricted address of his message gave it a universalist momentum which would make possible the later spread of Christianity beyond Israel. As a universal religion, Christianity provided an alternative to the national or civic religions, both Roman and Jewish, of the time. It appears to have been the apostle Paul, whose letters are preserved in the New Testament, who played the decisive role in drawing out these universalist implications and giving theological justification to a 'mission to the gentiles.'

A Jew as well as a Roman citizen, Paul was converted by a vision of the risen Jesus. The faith whose spokesman he subsequently became was centered on this risen, cosmic Christ rather than on the historical Jesus of Nazareth. There were important sociological implications in this shift. As Troeltsch (1931) noted, Jesus's original message was 'individualistic' in the sense that it was focused on intimate relation between the individual and God. Whilst its universalist and egalitarian message fostered a broad sense of community between all those called to love God and neighbor, it neither fostered new communities nor made any attempt to influence wider society. It remained a reforming faction within Judaism (Sanders 1985, Elliott 1995).

Paul's reinterpretation of Christianity altered these dynamics of the early Jesus movement very significantly. As Schweitzer (1931) argued, Paul developed a 'Christ-mysticism' in which the believer is incorporated through faith into the 'body of Christ.' Though this mysticism also has an individualist emphasis, incorporation into the body of Christ is corporate—those who have faith are united not only with Christ but with one another. This corporate Christ-mysticism undergirded the development from the mid-first century of a church (ekklesia), which took the form of local communities linked together in a 'catholic' (universal) alliance by their common possession of the Spirit of Christ.

3. The Emergence of Catholic Christianity

Until at least the second century these early Christian communities were charismatic communities (communities of the Spirit), in which social authority was not institutionalized, but conferred by the Spirit. There seems to have been no clear hierarchy of authority, with different functions (such as apostle, teacher, prophet, and miracle-worker) being regarded as mutually constitutive of the body of Christ. In a development that Troeltsch (1931) categorizes as the emergence of 'catholic' and 'sacramental' Christianity, however, the spirit gradually became institutionalized in the sacraments, particularly those of baptism and the eucharist. Here the presence of Spirit is, as it were, guaranteed. The sacraments are material signs of the freely given grace of God and the efficacious tokens of salvation.

The development of a sacramental Christianity allowed for the development of stable and enduring communities not based on the unpredictable outpourings of the spirit. It went hand in hand with the emergence of a clergy whose authority was bound up with their exclusive authorisation to handle and distribute the sacraments. Their status was not based on personal charisma, superior religious achievement, or inheritance. Rather, they were the authorised representatives of the wider Christian community. Early documents defending a sacramental priesthood reveal that this development was not uncontroversial. On the one hand it made possible catholicity and order. On the other it led to exclusions, most notably the exclusion of women from positions of authority in the church.

The development of catholic Christianity also involved the definition and maintenance of uniformity in belief and liturgical practice. This achievement was also a difficult and remarkable one given that 'early Christianity' was never as unified as that title implies. Despite the idealized backward glance of a later era (such as that of the fourth-century church historian, Eusebius), Christianity came into being as a diverse set of largely autonomous communities spread around the Mediterranean basin and in Syria and Asia Minor. Many were centered around a particular apostle and a particular gospel (whether in oral or written form), and developed distinctive forms of belief and practice.

If we compare the four gospels contained in the New Testament (probably the products of such communities), we get some idea of the range of beliefs they held and of their very different understandings of Jesus.

In the face of this diversity, the establishment of an authorised scriptural, creedal, and rhetorical tradition was as important as that of a universal sacramental priesthood (Cameron 1991). By the second century we find early representatives of catholic Christianity listing the documents which should be treated by Christians as authoritative, and which would eventually come to form the New Testament. These were then bound up with the first authoritative Christian scripture, the Jewish Bible or 'Old Testament'. The formation of this scriptural 'canon' went hand in hand with the development of a 'canon of faith.' Both were later debated and defined by the councils and creeds which would become such a distinctive feature of Christianity. Together authorized scripture and doctrine came to define the boundaries of 'orthodoxy.' Again, this process involved exclusions, including that of a large number of gospels, lives, and acts of Jesus, the apostles and saints which are now classified as 'apocryphal,' together with a large body of philosophical–theological literature influenced by Christian, Jewish, Platonic, and Persian sources, which is often classified together as 'gnostic.'

Against the spiritualizing tendencies of the gnostics (a tendency which took further the Pauline spiritualization of Christ), the emerging catholic church developed an emphasis which may be characterised as 'materialist.' The authority of the clergy, e.g., was said to rest on an 'apostolic succession' which consisted of a historical and physical continuity established through the 'laying on of hands' by Christ and the apostles down to the present generation. Likewise, the church was the visible community of men and women gathered together to receive these sacraments rather than an invisible body of the elect, and the authorized means of salvation were the visible and tangible sacraments. In many cases too Christian hope continued to be focused on a physical resurrection, rather than on the release of an immaterial soul from the body. A more hostile attitude to the body and material life would, however, become a feature of some of the asceticism and monasticism that developed within Christian circles from the end of the third century onwards.

Despite this materialist emphasis, however, early Christianity was not involved in any direct attempt to reform the society within which it found itself. Jesus had directed his followers' energies to 'the one thing needful'—love of God and neighbor—rather than to social reform, and this emphasis continued in early catholic Christianity. To the extent that Jesus commanded his followers to love all, including the Roman soldier and the tax collector, it could even be argued that the Jesus movement had a broader social reach than the Pauline and post-Pauline communities whose energies were focused on love of 'the brethren.' Their duty was to 'build up the body of Christ' rather than to change 'the world'—the latter being a category which derived from this mentality.

The result, as Troeltsch (1931) argued, was that the early Christian communities did not develop a 'social teaching.' The Christian response to social problems such as poverty was to advocate individual acts of charity rather than social reform. Ownership of property was neither abolished nor condemned, but possessions were to be used to help the Christian community. Similarly, in relation to class and social position, the early church initiated a revolution within its own walls—slave and free, male, and female were equal before Christ and in relation to salvation—which left wider patterns of social inequality (including slavery and the position of women) virtually untouched. The state, even when persecuting Christians, was regarded by most early Christians as the wielder of a proper and God-given authority that should call forth respect and obedience rather than attempts at reform.

4. Alliance of Church and State

Despite its failure to develop a social teaching, it is clear that early Christianity had a significant impact on its wider social context. It appears to have initiated an inner revolution within the Roman Empire whose effect was felt in a number of ways—not least through the new educational and welfare opportunities it offered, and through the model of an inclusive society which it provided. Whilst it is impossible to reconstruct the nature and extent of the growth of Christianity in the first three centuries of its existence, it is estimated that by the beginning of the fourth century it may have accounted for up to 10 percent of the population of the Empire. Its success appears to have been due to its ability to form 'a compact, even massive, constellation of commitments' (Brown 1997). Morality, philosophy, and ritual, which formally had formed separate spheres of activity in the 'pagan' world, were brought together by the church, and fused into a universal religion.

It was these new characteristics and potencies which eventually enabled Christianity to serve as a unifying and legitimating force for an empire which had once persecuted it. Constantine formalized the process whereby church and state grew into alliance with one another after AD 312, and church leaders rapidly exploited the new opportunities that this opened. In this way a decisive alteration in Christianity's relation to the social order took place, one which would have the most far-reaching consequences not only for the evolution of the church, but for the social and political ordering of Christianity's territories in the East as well as in what—under Christian influence—would eventually become Western Europe.

See also: Classical Archaeology; Historiography and Historical Thought: Christian Tradition; Historiography and Historical Thought: Islamic Tradition; Judaism; Near Middle East/North African Studies: Religion

Bibliography

Brown P 1997 *The Rise of Western Christendom. Triumph and Diversity AD 200-1000*. Blackwell, Malden, MA and Oxford, UK

Cameron A 1991 *Christianity and the Rhetoric of Empire. The Development of Christian Discourse*. Berkeley, CA, Los Angeles, Oxford, UK

Elliott J H 1995 The Jewish Messianic movement: from faction to sect. In: Esler P F (ed.) *Modelling Early Christianity: Social-Scientific Studies of the New Testament in its Context*. Routledge, London and New York

Hazlett I 1991 ed. *Early Christianity. Origins and Evolution to AD 600*. SPCK, London

Meeks W A 1983 *The First Urban Christians: The Social World of the Apostle Paul*. Yale University Press, New Haven, CT

Sanders E P 1985 *Jesus and Judaism*. Fortress Press, Philadelphia

Schweitzer A 1931 *The Mysticism of Paul the Apostle*. A & C Black, London

Theissen G 1978 *Sociology of Early Palestinian Christianity*. 1st American edn. Fortress Press, Philadelphia

Troeltsch E 1931 *The Social Teachings of the Christian Churches* (trans. Wyon O). George Allen and Unwin, London, MacMillan, New York, Vol. 1

L. Woodhead

Chronic Illness, Psychosocial Coping with

1. Background

Improvements in health care technologies and treatments have resulted in increased life expectancies and improved disease management for individuals with chronic illnesses. To a great degree, quality of life for many individuals with these illnesses may be determined by the ways they deal with the illness. Thus, identifying effective and ineffective ways of coping with these diseases may lead to the development of more efficacious interventions for these individuals.

Since 1980 there has been a substantial amount of research devoted to understanding the relation between coping with chronic illnesses and psychological adaptation. Although there have been some consistent findings regarding coping and its impact on psycho-logical outcomes, particularly in the area of coping with pain, the enthusiasm for the empirical study of coping in general has dampened significantly over the course of the past several years. Indeed, recent reviews of coping research have harshly criticized the literature, particularly assessment methodologies (see Coyne and Racioppo 2000). Thus, much of the initial promise for coping research to enhance clinical practice has not been realized.

2. Historical Perspective and Current Concepts of Coping

The psychological study of coping dates back to Sigmund Freud (1896/1966), who put forth the concept of defense mechanisms, defined as mental operations that kept painful thoughts and feelings out of awareness. The next major shift in the study of coping was brought about as a result of cognitive theories. The focus on intrapsychic processes that intervene between events and responses to events increased with the introduction of other cognitive theories such as Beck (1976). According to cognitive theories, cognitive coping mediated between stressful events and psychological and physical responses to stressful events. It was hypothesized that, by examining individual coping differences, a greater understanding of why people react differently to the same events would be achieved.

Research on stress and coping exploded with the work of Lazarus and Folkman (1984), who put forth the transactional stress and coping paradigm. According to Lazarus, coping refers to cognitive and behavioral efforts to manage disruptive events that tax the person's ability to adjust (Lazarus 1981, p. 2). Chronic illness can pose a number of life stressors including loss of physical and social functioning, alterations in body image, managing difficult and complex medical regimens, and chronic pain. According to Lazarus and Folkman (1984) coping responses are a dynamic series of transactions between the individual and the environment, the purpose of which is to regulate internal states and/or alter person-environment relations. The theory postulates that stressful emotions and coping are due to cognitions associated with the way a person appraises or perceives his or her relationship with the environment. There are several components of the coping process. First, appraisals of the harm or loss posed by the stressor (Lazarus 1981) are thought to be important determinants of coping. Second, appraisal of the degree of controllability of the stressor is a determinant of coping strategies selected. A third component is the person's evaluation of the outcome of their coping efforts and their expectations for future success in coping with the stressor. These evaluative judgements will lead to changes in the types of coping employed, as well as play a role in determining psychological adaptation. Two main dimensions of coping are proposed, problem-focused and emotion-focused coping. Problem-focused coping is efforts aimed at altering the problematic situation. These coping efforts include information seeking and problem solving. Emotion-focused coping are efforts aimed at managing emotional responses to stressors. Such coping efforts include cognitive reappraisal of the stressor and minimizing the problem.

How the elements of coping unfold over time is a key theoretical issue involved in studies of coping processes. Despite the fact that the theory is dynamic in nature, most of the research utilizing the stress and coping paradigm put forth by Lazarus (1981) has relied on retrospective assessments of coping and has been cross-sectional. However, a team of researchers, including Affleck, Tennen, and Keefe (e.g., Keefe et al. 1997) has utilized a daily diary approach to assessing coping with pain, a methodology that can examine the proposed dynamic nature of coping.

Towards the end of the twentieth century there has been also been an expansion in theoretical perspectives on cognitive coping. The literature on cognitive processing of traumatic life events has provided a new direction for coping research and broadened theoretical perspectives on cognitive methods of coping with chronic illness. According to cognitive processing theory, traumatic events can challenge people's core assumptions about them and their world (Janoff-Bulman 1992). The unpredictable nature of many chronic illnesses, as well as the numerous social and occupational losses, causes many individuals to question beliefs they hold about themselves. For example, the diagnosis of chronic obstructive pulmonary disease (COPD) can challenge a person's core beliefs about personal invulnerability. To the extent that a chronic illness challenges core beliefs, integrating the illness experience into their pre-existing beliefs should promote psychological adjustment. Cognitive processing has been used as the phrase to define cognitive activities that help people view undesirable events in personally meaningful ways and find ways of understanding the negative aspects of the experience, and ultimately reach a state of acceptance. Attempts to find meaning or benefit in a negative experience are ways patients may be able to accept the losses they experience. Focusing on the positive implications of the illness or finding personal significance of a situation are two ways of finding meaning in the illness. When considering meaning-making coping, one must distinguish coping activities that help individuals to find redeeming features in an event from the successful outcome of these attempts. For example, people who have a serious illness may report that as a result they have found a new appreciation for life or that they place greater value on relationships. Patients may also develop an explanation for the illness that is more benign (e.g., attributing it to God's will). While

cognitive processing theory constructs have been applied to adjustment to losses such as bereavement (e.g., Davis et al. 1998), these constructs have received relatively little attention from researchers examining coping with chronic illness.

Another coping process that falls under the rubric of cognitive coping is social comparison. Social comparison (SC) is a common cognitive process whereby individuals compare themselves to others in order to obtain information about them (Gibbons and Gerrard 1991). According to SC theory, health problems increase uncertainty; uncertainty increases the desire for information and creates the need for comparison. Studies of coping with chronic illness have included social comparison as a focus. A certain type of SC, downward comparison, has been the focus of empirical study among patients with chronic illnesses such as rheumatoid arthritis (RA) (Tennen and Affleck 1997). Wills (1981) has suggested that people experiencing a loss can experience an improvement in mood if they learn about others who are worse off. Indeed, there is evidence to suggest that SC increases as a result of experiencing health problems (Kulik and Mahler 1997). One proposed mechanism for SC is that downward comparison impacts cognitive appraisal by reducing perceived threat. When another person's situation appears significantly worse, then the appraisal of one's own illness may be reduced (Aspinwall and Taylor 1993).

3. Assessment of Coping

3.1 General Coping Checklists

Folkman and Lazarus' Ways of Coping Checklist (WOC, Folkman and Lazarus 1980) has been one of the most widely used instruments to assess coping efforts. This instrument contains two major subscales, problem-focused and emotion-focused coping, as well as a number of subscales including wishful thinking, cognitive restructuring, information seeking, seeking support, self-blame, and minimization. Instructions typically ask the individual to rate how he or she manages the stressor (Manne and Zautra 1989).

Another measure that has been used is the Coping Strategies Inventory (CSI, Tobin et al. 1989). The CSI distinguishes two dimensions of coping, engagement/disengagement strategies and focusing on the problem/focusing on emotions about the stressor. Problem-focused engagement is composed of problem-solving and cognitive restructuring; problem-focused disengagement is composed of problem avoidance and wishful thinking. Emotion-focused engagement is composed of social support and expressed emotion; emotion-focused disengagement is composed of social withdrawal and self-criticism.

Measuring meaning-making coping and other methods of cognitive processing has been done utilizing existing measures. Some aspects of meaning-making coping can be assessed using the cognitive reappraisal subscales of the COPE (Carver et al. 1989) and the Ways of Coping Checklist (Lazarus and Folkman 1984). Other means of measuring the process of meaning-making involve using measures of cognitive processing. For example, the Impact of Events scale (Horowitz et al. 1979) measures attempts to integrate a traumatic event with current schemas. Other studies have utilized questions tailored specifically for their population.

3.2 Illness-specific Checklists

The majority of illness-specific coping instruments have been designed to assess coping with pain associated with chronic illnesses such as rheumatoid arthritis (RA) and osteoarthritis (OA). Two instruments, the Vanderbilt Pain Management Inventory (VPMI) and the Coping Strategies Questionnaire (CSQ) have been the most widely used instruments. Both measures assess the degree to which patients employ a variety of cognitive and behavioral mechanisms to reduce the impact of painful episodes. Brown and Nicassio (1987) developed the VPMI to assess cognitive and behavioral pain-coping strategies. The 18-item VPMI has two subdimensions, active and passive pain coping. The CSQ comprises seven subscales measuring distinct coping strategies. Factor analyses of the CSQ in both RA and OA samples provide evidence for a two-factor solution, Coping Attempts and Pain Control and Rational Thinking (Keefe et al. 1987).

The Coping with Rheumatic Stressors (CORS, Lankveld et al. 1994) was specifically designed to measure stressor-specific coping in RA. This measure is unique in that it measures coping separately with three stressors, pain, limitations, and dependence. The three coping with pain scales are comforting cognitions, decreasing activity, and diverting attention. The three coping with limitation scales are optimism, pacing, and creative solution seeking. The two coping with dependence scales are making an effort to accept dependence and showing consideration.

3.3 Daily Diary Instruments

Only one instrument, the Daily Coping Inventory (Stone and Neal 1984), has been developed to assess daily coping. This inventory has been adapted for chronic pain coping by Affleck et al. (1992). Patients are asked whether or not they utilize each of seven categories of coping: (a) pain reduction attempt; (b) relaxation; (c) distraction; (d) redefinition; (e) vent emotions; (f) seek spiritual comfort; and (g) seek emotional support. These coping categories have been reduced using factor analyses to two factors, labeled emotion-focused and problem-focused coping (Affleck et al. 1999).

4. Studies Using the Stress and Coping Paradigm

4.1 Cross-sectional Studies

Early studies of coping using the stress and coping paradigm were cross-sectional and utilized retrospective checklists such as the WOC. The earliest studies divided coping into the general categories of problem- and emotion-focused strategies, and focused mostly on psychological outcomes, rather than pain and functional status outcomes.

Later studies have investigated specific types of coping. For example, Felton et al. (1984) examined two types of coping, wish-fulfilling fantasy, and information seeking, using a revision of the Ways of Coping Checklist. Wish-fulfilling fantasy was a more consistent predictor of psychological adjustment than information seeking. While information seeking was associated with higher levels of positive affect, its effects on negative affect were modest, accounting for only 4 percent of the variance. In a second study, Felton and Revenson (1984) examined coping of patients with arthritis, cancer, diabetes, and hypertension. Wish-fulfilling fantasy, emotional expression, and self-blame were associated with poorer adjustment, while threat minimization was associated with better adjustment. Scharloo et al. (1998) conducted a cross-sectional study of individuals with COPD, RA, or psoriasis. Unlike the majority of studies, illness-related variables such as time since diagnosis and the severity of the patient's medical condition were entered first into the equation predicting role and social functioning. Overall, coping was not strongly related to social and role functioning. Among patients with COPD, passive coping predicted poorer physical functioning. Among patients with RA, higher levels of passive coping predicted poorer social functioning.

Very few studies have examined coping with other chronic illnesses. Several studies have investigated the association between coping and distress among individuals with MS. Pakenham et al. (1997) categorized coping as either emotion- or problem-focused, and found that emotion-focused coping was related to poorer adjustment, while problem-focused coping was associated with better adjustment. In contrast, Wineman and Durand (1994) found that emotion- and problem-focused coping were unrelated to distress. Mohr et al. (1997) found that problem solving and cognitive reframing strategies are associated with lower levels of depression, whereas avoidant strategies are associated with higher levels of depression.

As previously noted, most studies have used instructions that ask participants how they coped with the illness in general, rather than asking participants how they coped with specific stressors associated with their illness. Van Lankveld et al. (1994) assessed how RA patients cope with the most important stressors associated with RA (pain, functional limitation, and dependence). When coping with pain was considered, patients with similar degrees of pain who used comforting cognitions and diverted their attention from the pain reported higher well-being. Limiting one's activity was associated with lower well-being. When coping with functional limitation was examined, patients who used pacing of their activity reported lower levels of well-being, and use of optimism was associated with higher well-being after functional capacity was controlled for in the equation. Finally, when coping with dependence was examined, only showing consideration was associated with higher well-being after functional capacity was controlled for in the equation.

4.2 Longitudinal Studies

Unfortunately, there have been relatively few studies that have employed longitudinal designs. Overall, passive coping strategies such as avoidance, wishful thinking, and withdrawal, as well as self-blame, have been shown to be associated with poorer psychological adjustment (e.g., Scharloo et al. 1999), and problem-focused coping efforts such as information seeking have been found to be associated with better adjustment (e.g., Pakenham 1999).

5. Studies of Coping with Chronic Pain

The majority of these studies have utilized longitudinal designs. For example, Brown and Nicassio (1987) studied pain-coping strategies among RA patients and found that patients who engaged in more passive coping when experiencing more pain became more depressed six months later than patients who engaged in these strategies less frequently. Keefe et al. (1989) conducted a six-month longitudinal study of the relationship between catastrophizing and depression in RA patients. Those patients who reported high levels of catastrophizing had greater pain, disability, and depression six months later. Other investigators (Parker et al. 1989) have reported similar findings. Overall, studies have suggested that self-blame, wishful thinking, praying, catastrophizing, and restricting activities are associated with more distress, while information seeking, cognitive restructuring, and active planning are associated with less distress.

As previously mentioned, several recent studies have employed prospective daily study designs in which participants complete a 30-day diary for reporting each day's pain, mood, and pain-coping strategies using the Daily Coping Inventory (Stone and Neale 1984). These studies, which have been conducted with RA and OA patients, have shown that emotion-focused strategies, such as attempting to redefine pain to make it more bearable, and expressing distressing emotions about the pain, predict increases in negative mood the day after the diary report. The daily design is a promising new method of evaluating the link between coping strategies and mood. More importantly, these studies can elucidate coping processes over time. For example, Tennen et al. (2000) found that the two functions of coping, problem- and emotion-focused, evolve in response to the outcome of the coping efforts. An increase in pain from one day to the next increased the likelihood that emotion-focused coping would follow problem-focused coping. It appeared that, when efforts to directly influence pain were not successful, participants tried to alter their cognitions and adjust rather than influence the pain.

6. Challenges to the Study of Coping with Chronic Illness

Recently, the general literature on coping has received a great deal of criticism from researchers (e.g., Coyne and Racioppo 2000). The main concern voiced in reviews regards the gap between the elegant, process-oriented stress and coping theory and the cross-sectional, retrospective methodologies that have been used to evaluate the theory. Although the theory postulates causal relations among stress, coping, and adaptation, the correlational nature of most empirical work has been unsuitable to test causal relations. In addition, retrospective methods require people to recall how they coped with an experience, and thus are likely to be influenced by both systematic and non-systematic sources of recall error. Coping efforts as well as psychological outcomes such as distress are best measured close to when they occur. Recent studies have used an approach that addresses these concerns. These studies have employed a microanalytic, process-oriented approach using daily diary assessments (e.g., Affleck et al. 1999). These time-intensive study designs allow for the tracking of changes in coping and distress close to their real-time occurrence and moments of change, are less subject to recall error, and capture coping processes as they unfold over time. The daily assessment approach also can evaluate how coping changes as the individual learns more about what coping responses are effective in reducing distress and/or altering the stressor. These advances may help investigators to more fully examine whether the methods used to cope with stressors encountered in the day-to-day experience of living with a chronic disease predict long-term adaptation. Unfortunately, this approach has only been utilized among individuals with arthritis and has not been applied to individuals dealing with other chronic illnesses.

Another key problem with coping checklists that has been noted in a number of reviews of the coping with chronic illness literature is the instructional format. The typical instructions used (e.g., 'How do you cope with RA?') are so general that it is not clear what aspect of the stressor the participant is referring to when answering questions. Thus, the source of the stress may differ across study participants. There are problems even when the participant is allowed to define the stressor prior to rating the coping strategies used. The self-defined stressor may differ across participants, and thus the analyses will be conducted with different stressors being rated.

A third assessment problem regards the definition of coping. While Lazarus and Folkman (1984) regard only effortful, conscious strategies as coping, other investigators have argued that 'automatic' coping methods also fall under the definition of coping (Wills 1997). Indeed, some coping responses may not be perceived by the individual as choices, but rather automatic responses to stressful events. For example, wishful thinking or other types of avoidant types of coping such as sleeping or alcohol use may be categorized by researchers as a coping strategy, but not categorized as such by the individual completing the questionnaire because the individual did not engage in this as an effortful coping strategy. A related and interesting issue regards the categorization of unconscious defense mechanisms. Cramer (2000), in a recent review of defense mechanisms, distinguishes between defenses that are not conscious and unintentional and coping processes that are conscious and intentional. However, there has been an interest in repressive coping, suggesting that some researchers regard defensive strategies such as denial and repression under the rubric of coping. More clarity and consistency between investigators in the definition of coping, particularly when unintentional strategies are being evaluated, would provide more clarity for research.

A fourth assessment issue regards the distinction between 'problem-focused' and 'emotion focused' coping efforts. While researchers may categorize a particular coping strategy as problem-focused coping, the participant's intention may not be to alter the situation, but rather to manage an emotional reaction. For example, people may seek information about an illness as a way of coping with anxiety and to alter their appraisal of a situation, rather than to engineer a change in the situation. The lack of an association between emotion-focused coping and psychological outcomes may, in part, be due to a categorization strategy that does not account for the intention of the coping. Studies utilizing these two categories to dis-

tinguish coping dimensions may wish to evaluate coping intention.

There are a number of additional methodological and conceptual challenges that are specifically relevant to studies of coping with chronic illness. First, relatively few studies control for disease severity in statistical analyses. Extreme pain or disability can result in both more coping attempts and more distress. Studies that do not take into account these variables may conclude mistakenly that more coping is associated with more distress. In addition, little attention has been paid to the effects of progressive impairment on the selection of coping strategies, and in the perceived effectiveness of those strategies. Chronic progressive illnesses may be expected to increase feelings of hopelessness. For example, Revenson and Felton (1989) studied changes in coping and adjustment over a six-month period and found that lower acceptance, more wishful thinking, and more negative affect accompanied increases in disability.

Another issue is the lack of longitudinal studies. Clearly, longitudinal studies would help the literature in a number of ways. First, this type of design might help clarify whether coping influences distress or whether coping is merely a symptom of distress, a criticism frequently raised in critiques of coping (e.g., Coyne and Racioppo 2000). Second, longitudinal studies may clarify the role of personality factors in coping. While some investigators suggest that personality factors play a limited role in predicting coping, other investigators argue that coping is a personality process that reflects dispositional differences during stressful events.

Although the lack of progress in the area of coping is frequently attributed to methods of assessment and design, the relatively narrow focus on distress outcomes may also account for some of the problem, particularly when coping with chronic illness is being evaluated. Chronic illness does not ultimately lead to psychological distress for the majority of patients. Indeed, many individuals report psychological growth in the face of chronic illness, and are able to find personal significance in terms of changes in views of themselves, their relationships with others, and a changed philosophy of life (Tennen et al. 1992). While positive affect is included as an adaptational outcome in some studies (e.g., Bendtson and Hornquist 1991), the majority of studies do not include positive outcomes. Positive affect will be a particularly important outcome to evaluate when positive coping processes such as cognitive reappraisal and finding meaning in the experience are examined, as these types of coping may play a stronger role in generating and maintaining positive mood than in lowering negative mood.

Finally, relatively few studies have focused solely on coping and distress and have not taken into account potential moderators such as level of pain, appraisals of controllability, gender, and personality. A careful evaluation of potential moderators will provide both researchers and clinicians with information about which circumstances particular coping strategies are most effective.

7. Conclusions

As Lazarus points out in his commentary in *American Psychologist*, 'A premise that occurs again and again ... is that for quite a few years research has disappointed many who had high hopes it would achieve both fundamental and practical knowledge about the coping process and its adaptational consequences. I am now heartened by positive signs that there is a growing number of sophisticated, resourceful, and vigorous researchers who are dedicated to the study of coping' (Lazarus 2000). It is clear that, despite the multiple methodological problems that this area of research has faced in the past, a heightened awareness of these limitations has led to the application of sophisticated methods that might assist this field in fulfilling the high hopes for this field of research. If investigators in the field of coping with chronic illnesses can adapt daily-diary methods to their populations, focus on specific stressors related to the illness when instructing participants to answer coping questions, include coping appraisals and the perceived efficacy of coping efforts, and carefully delineate illness-related, contextual, and dispositional moderators, the findings may lead to the development of effective interventions for clinicians hoping to improve the quality of life for these individuals.

See also: Chronic Illness: Quality of Life; Chronic Pain: Models and Treatment Approaches; Coping across the Lifespan; Coping Assessment; Coronary Heart Disease (CHD), Coping with; Illness Behavior and Care Seeking; Illness: Dyadic and Collective Coping; Pain, Health Psychology of; Pain, Management of; Rheumatoid Arthritis: Psychosocial Aspects; Social Support and Health; Stress and Coping Theories; Well-being and Health: Proactive Coping

Bibliography

Affleck G, Tennen H, Keefe F J, Lefebre J C, Kashikar-Zuck S, Wright K, Starr K, Caldwell D 1999 Everyday life with osteoarthritis or rheumatoid arthritis: independent effects of disease and gender on daily pain, mood, and coping. *Pain* **83**: 601–9

Affleck G, Urrows S, Tennen H, Higgins P 1992 Daily coping with pain from rheumatoid arthritis-patterns and correlates. *Pain* **51**: 221–9

Aspinwall L G, Taylor S E 1993 Effects of social comparison direction, threat and self-esteem on affect, self-evaluation and expected success. *Journal of Personality and Social Psychology* **64**: 708–22

Beck A T 1976 *Cognitive therapy and the emotional disorders.* International Universities Press, New York

Bendtsen P, Hornquist J O 1994 Rheumatoid arthritis, coping and well-being-cross-comparisons and correlational analyies. *Scandinavian Journal of Social Medicine* **22**: 97–106

Brown G, Nicassio P 1987 Development of a questionnaire for the assessment of active and passive coping strategies in chronic pain patients. *Pain* **3**: 53–84

Carver C S, Scheier M F, Weintraub J K 1989 Assessing coping strategies: A theoretically-based approach. *Journal of Personality and Social Psychology* **56**: 267–83

Coyne J C, Racioppo M W 2000 Never the twain shall meet? Closing the gap between coping research and clinical intervention research. *American Psychologist* **55**: 655–64

Cramer P 2000 Defense mechanisms in psychology. *Psychological Review* **3**: 357–70

Davis C G, Nolen-Hoeksema S, Larson J 1998 Making sense of loss and benefiting from the experience: Two constructs of meaning. *Journal of Personality and Social Psychology* **75**: 561–74

Felton B, Revenson T 1984 Coping with chronic illness: A study of illness controllability and the influence of coping strategies on psychological adjustment. *Journal of Consulting and Clinical Psychology* **52**: 343–53

Felton B J, Revenson T A, Hinrichsen G 1984 Stress and coping in the explanation of psychological adjustment among chronically ill adults. *Social Science and Medicine* **10**: 889–98

Folkman S, Lazarus R S 1980 An analysis of coping in a middle-aged community sample. *Journal of Health and Social Behavior* **21**: 219–39

Freud S 1966 Further remarks on the neuro-psychoses of defense. In: Strachey J (ed.) *The Standard Edition of the Complete Psychological Works of Sigmund Freud.* Hogarth Press, London (Original work published 1896), Vol. 3, pp. 141–58

Gibbons F X, Gerrard M 1991 Downward comparison and coping with threat. In: Suls J, Wills T A (eds.) *Social Comparison: Contemporary Theory and Research.* Erlbaum, Hillsdale, NJ, pp. 317–46

Horowitz M, Wilner N, Alvarez W 1979 Impact of event scale: A measure of subjective distress. *Psychosomatic Medicine* **41**: 209–18

Janoff-Bulman R 1992 *Shattered Assumptions: Towards a New Psychology of Trauma.* Free Press, New York

Keefe F J, Affleck G, Lefebvre J, Starr K, Caldwell D, Tennen H 1997 Pain coping strategies and coping efficacy in rheumatoid arthritis: a daily process analysis. *Pain* **69**: 35–42

Keefe F J, Brown G K, Wallston K A, Caldwell D S 1989 Coping with rheumatoid arthritis pain: Catastrophizing as a maladaptive strategy. *Pain* **37**: 51–6

Keefe F J, Caldwell D S, Queen K T, Gil K, Martinez S, Crisson J 1987 Pain coping strategies in osteoarthritis patients. *Journal of Consulting and Clinical Psychology* **55**: 208–12

Kulik J, Mahler H 1997 Social comparison, affiliation, and coping with acute medical threats. In: Buunk B P, Gibbons F X (eds.) *Health, Coping and Well-Being: Perspectives from Social Comparison Theory.* Erlbaum, Mahwah, NJ, pp. 227–61

Lazarus R S 1981 The stress and coping paradigm. In: Eisdorfer C, Cohen D, Kleinman A, Maxim P (eds.) *Models for Clinical Psychopathology.* Spectrum, New York, pp. 177–214

Lazarus R S 2000 Toward better research on stress and coping. *American Psychologist* **55**: 665–73

Lazarus R S, Folkman S 1984 *Stress, Appraisal, and Coping.* Springer, New York

Manne S L, Zautra A J 1989 Spouse criticism and support: Their association with coping and psychological adjustment among women with rheumatoid arthritis. *Journal of Personality and Social Psychology* **56**: 608–17

Mohr D C, Goodkin D E, Gatto N, Van Der Wende J 1997 Depression, coping, and level of neurological impairment in multiple sclerosis. *Multiple Sclerosis* **3**: 254–8

Pakenham K I 1999 Adjustment to multiple sclerosis: Application of a stress and coping model. *Health Psychology* **18**: 383–92

Pakenham K I, Stewart C A, Rogers A 1997 The role of coping in adjustment to multiple sclerosis-related adaptive demands. *Psycholog Health and Medicine* **2**: 197–211

Parker J, Smarr K, Buescher K, Phillips L R, Frank R, Beck N C 1989 Pain control and rational thinking: Implications for rheumatoid arthritis. *Arthritis and Rheumatism* **32**: 984–90

Revenson T, Felton B 1989 Disability and coping as predictors of psychological adjustment to rheumatoid arthritis. *Journal of Consulting and Clinical Psychology* **57**: 344–8

Scharloo M, Kaptein A A, Weinman J A, Hazes J M W, Breedveld F, Anderson S K, Walker S E, Rooijmans H G M 1999 Predicting functional status in patients with rheumatoid arthritis. *Journal of Rheumatology* **26**: 1686–93

Scharloo M, Kaptein A A, Weinman J A, Hazes J M W, Willems L L N A, Bergman W, Rooijmans H G M 1998 Illness perceptions, coping and functioning in patients with rheumatoid arthritis, chronic obstructive pulmonary disease and psoriasis. *Journal of Psychosomatic Research* **44**: 573–85

Stone A A, Neale J M 1984 A new measure of daily coping-development and preliminary results. *Journal of Personality and Social Psychology* **46**: 892–906

Tennen H, Affleck G 1997 Social comparisons and occupational stress: The identification-contrast model In: Buunk B P, Gibbons F X (eds.) *Health, Coping and Well-Being: Perspectives from Social Comparison Theory.* Erlbaum, Mahwah, NJ, pp. 262–98

Tennen H, Affleck G, Armeli S, Carney M 2000 A daily process approach to coping: Linking theory, research and practice. *American Psychologist* **55**: 626–36

Tennen H, Affleck G, Urrows S, Higgins P, Mendola R 1992 Perceiving control, construing benefits and daily processes in rheumatoid arthritis. *Canadian Journal of Behavioral Science* **24**: 186–203

Tobin D L, Holroyd K A, Reynolds R V, Wigal J K 1989 The hierarchical factor structure of the Coping Strategies Inventory. *Cognitive Therapy and Research* **13**: 343–61

van Lankveld W, van de Bosch P V, van Putte L, Naring G, van der Staak C 1994 Disease-specific stressors in rheumatoid arthritis: Coping and well-being. *British Journal of Rheumatology* **33**: 1067–73

Wills T A 1981 Downward comparison principles in social psychology. *Psychological Bulletin* **90**: 245–71

Wills T 1997 Modes and families of coping. In: Buunk B, Gibbons F X (eds.) *Health, Coping and Well-being: Perspectives from Social Comparison Theory.* Erlbaum, Mahwah, NJ, pp. 167–93

Wineman N M, Durand E J, McCulloch B J 1994 Examination of the factor structure of the ways of coping questionnaire with clinical populations. *Nursing Research* **43**: 266–73

S. Manne

Chronic Illness: Quality of Life

1. Background

Increased longevity and the development of sophisticated health care technologies and treatments mean that people today live with chronic health conditions over extended periods of their lives. Quality of life (QOL) has become an important goal of treatment and marker of success in health care interventions in chronic illness generally. In many disorders, e.g., osteoarthritis, health interventions will have little impact on mortality statistics but great potential for reducing disability and increasing QOL.

QOL research first developed in cancer settings where the balance of quality and duration of life became a key concern in decisions to use novel treatments with very serious side effects and only partial efficacy. However, over the past 20 years there has been a burgeoning of research activity in every major chronic illness category. This is evident for different diseases at various structural levels. For instance, the US research funding agency, the National Heart Lung and Blood Institute, require almost all clinical trials and many epidemiological studies they fund to have a QOL component. In rheumatology, there is an international, professionally endorsed cooperative called OMERACT (Outcome Measures in Rheumatoid Arthritis Clinical Trials). They seek to improve QOL outcome measurement through data-driven interactive consensus. In cancer, the European Organisation for Research on the Treatment of Cancer (EORTC) has been established by interested professionals. They have developed a core QOL measure and disease-specific modules for various types of cancer. To the extent that QOL assessment reflects consideration of aspects of these diseases beyond the biomedical, QOL assessment reflects the increasingly biopsychosocial perspective in modern health care.

2. Uses of Quality of Life Assessment in Chronic Illness

QOL research in chronic illness has policy, treatment evaluation, descriptive, and individual clinical uses. There is now a vast literature on, and compendia of, instruments for this very wide set of circumstances and health conditions (e.g., Bowling 1997). At a policy level, initiatives to develop QOL assessment are concerned with means to identify those components of the healthcare system which are most effective in achieving good health outcomes. The Medical Outcomes Study is the major example of this approach. As part of a two-year prospective study to identify the association of reimbursement aspects of a health funding system with health outcomes in the US, a health-related QOL (HRQOL) was devised. The most widely used version, the short-form 36-item questionnaire (SF-36) was developed as a generic HRQOL instrument which could be used with the general population as well as patient groups (Stewart et al. 1989). The SF-36 has eight dimensions: physical functioning; role limitations because of physical health problems; bodily pain; social functioning; general mental health; role limitations because of emotional problems; vitality, energy, or fatigue; and general health perception. Items on each dimension are weighted so that each scale adds to 100 points, with higher scores indicating better health. Thus health profiles across the eight dimensions can be easily compared in graphic form across different disease or treatment groups. For SF-36, individuals rate their own health status. A different approach has been tried at the general population level in the State of Oregon, USA, to assist the public in prioritizing medical treatments for inclusion in publicly funded health care. Here, people were asked to rate the hypothetical impact of various levels of symptoms and restrictions as a way to create a hierarchy of levels of challenge to QOL. However, it has not proven possible to date to develop a system whereby the public are willing to withhold certain treatments from patients on the basis of lesser clinical or QOL benefit.

Much of the work using QOL instruments in chronic illness has been to evaluate the QOL impact of differing types of treatment, e.g., comparing medications. In this formulation, QOL is seen as a dependent variable. Treatment comparisons are usually made on a combination of generic and disease-specific QOL instruments (see *Quality of Life: Assessment in Health Settings*) to cover the range of dimensions in which one intervention may differ from another in impact. In priority terms, QOL is seen on a continuum. It is positioned after efficacy and safety of the treatment and before or after cost-effectiveness, depending on the costs and condition under consideration. One merit of this approach has been to illustrate the sometimes very differing perspectives of professionals and patients. For instance, innovative limb-sparing treatment for cancer was found to result in poorer QOL for patients than the traditional amputation option (Sugarbaker et al. 1982). This finding was subsequently used to refine treatment such that initial difficulties with the limb-sparing approach could be removed and it was then subsequently offered as the better QOL option.

QOL research has provided a large descriptive body of research outlining the experience of various health conditions. This work is of benefit to professionals, patients, and the public understanding the typical HRQOL challenges in different health conditions; e.g., the SF-36 has been used to provide a HRQOL profile of nine common chronic medical conditions (Stewart et al. 1989). From this we can see that cardiac conditions such as myocardial infarction and congestive heart failure have a greater overall impact on HRQOL than do others such as diabetes.

A final use of QOL assessment is to facilitate decision making for the individual patient. While some instruments such as the Dartmouth Primary Care Cooperative Information Project (COOP) charts have been developed with clinical settings and ease of administration and interpretation as a priority, the evidence is that there is little formal QOL assessment in this format at present. This is so despite significant professional support for the broad concept of QOL assessment in clinical practice.

3. Differing Perspectives on Quality of Life: Needs Versus Wants

Quality of life has been generically defined as the capacity of an individual to achieve their life plans or the difference, at a particular point in time, between the hopes and expectations of an individual and their present situation. In Calman's (1984) definition, a small difference or 'gap' is commensurate with a good QOL. He proposes that the gap is widened by experiences such as illness and that it can be reduced by improving the present situation or by reducing the person's hopes and expectations to a more 'realistic' level. The World Health Organization (WHO) definition acknowledges possible cultural, as well as individual, differences in the understanding of the concept of QOL (see *Quality of Life: Assessment in Health Settings*). The WHOQOL instrument is based on a set of five domains: physical function; emotional function; social relationships; levels of independence; and environment. While core domains have been demonstrated to be relevant across cultures, the individual facets and items to assess these domains are developed within cultures. Thus while the domain of independence will feature in both British and Indian versions of the instrument, the particular items to best reflect that domain may differ. The WHOQOL instrument also illustrates the multifaceted nature of QOL; working capacity and vitality/fatigue might relate to work life from the physical function domain while working environment and transport would relate to work from the environment domain. QOL has also been defined more narrowly in a health-related context (HRQOL) (see *Quality of Life: Assessment in Health Settings*). HRQOL provides more focus on those specific aspects of life function likely to be influenced by illness although there is debate about how to differentiate health-related and non-health-related aspects of QOL.

Underlying most definitions of QOL, although usually not articulated, is one of two philosophical perspectives—the 'needs' or the 'wants' approach to QOL (Browne et al. 1997). The needs approach views QOL as the extent to which universal human needs are met. Many HRQOL instruments conform to the needs approach: the themes, questions, and question weightings used are standard and established independent of the person being assessed. The wants approach allows for a definition of QOL using themes, questions, or question weightings determined by the individual being evaluated. The methodologies used to achieve the wants approach are very varied and include content analysis and repertory grid (see *Quality of Life: Assessment in Health Settings* regarding individual QOL methods). These measures typically do not limit the focus of enquiry to health and it is with these assessments (which usually focus more on perception than function) that there are findings of high levels of QOL in groups with major chronic illness as discussed in the next section.

4. Challenges to QOL Assessment in Chronic Illness

One major challenge relates to the comparison of professional and patient perspectives on patient QOL. As reviewed by Sprangers and Aaronson (1992), professionals are poor judges of patient QOL. Moreover, professionals consistently rate patient QOL as poorer than do patients. Where family members are involved in ratings, their views are intermediate. There is little understanding of the processes that facilitate patients to develop or maintain a reasonable QOL in the face of what others define more negatively.

A second complementary challenge arises from comparative QOL assessment where instrument use allows comparison with the general population. Many of these studies find little difference in QOL between 'healthy' individuals and those with serious health conditions; both groups reporting high QOL (Allison et al. 1997). Such study comparisons differ depending on the wants versus needs approach taken to assessing QOL as discussed in the previous section. Interesting work in the cancer area shows how patients with serious cancers, when compared with orthopedic patients and matched healthy controls, focus away from health issues in order to maintain a good level of life satisfaction (Kreitler et al. 1993).

One way to address both of the challenges outlined is to see QOL as having a trait or homeostatic dimension such that individuals 'reset' their evaluative framework in adversity to recreate an appropriate QOL level for themselves. Diener (2000) discusses psychological perspectives on adaptation and goal setting relevant to this issue. The practical challenge when developing this understanding is how to use the knowledge to promote psychological growth in the context of a chronic health condition.

5. Conclusions and Outlook

To date, social and behavioral scientists have made major contributions to QOL assessment in chronic illness on a scale of cooperation with the medical sciences that is probably unique. They have done so in ways that reflect the needs/wants dichotomy of approaches. Many have provided psychometric skills within a largely biomedical framework to address challenges such as increasing responsiveness to change in evaluative research instruments (e.g., McGee et al. 1999) or in developing markers to identify clinical as distinct from statistical significance with HRQOL instruments (e.g., Juniper et al. 1994). The aim of the latter is to be able to use HRQOL scores in much the same manner as one would use blood pressure or body temperature readings to determine what course of action to take and when to do so. Others have been concerned with methods of documenting the salient and dynamic features of QOL for individuals; this has involved both qualitative and quantitative methods from a more phenomenological perspective. The challenge for the coming decades is to find some reconciliation between these two perspectives. In this way QOL assessment can be better used to direct services at individual and societal levels while expanding our understanding of how QOL is developed, maintained and altered as necessary through the course of chronic illness and its treatment.

See also: Chronic Illness, Psychosocial Coping with; Chronic Pain: Models and Treatment Approaches; Coping across the Lifespan; Quality of Life: Assessment in Health Settings; Stress and Coping Theories; Welfare: Philosophical Aspects; Well-being (Subjective), Psychology of

Bibliography

Allison P J, Locker D, Feine J S 1997 Quality of life: a dynamic construct. *Social Science Med.* **45**: 221–30

Bowling A 1997 *Measuring Health: A Review of Quality of Life Scales*, 2nd edn. Open University Press, Birmingham, UK

Browne J P, McGee H M, O'Boyle C A 1997 Conceptual approaches to the assessment of quality of life. *Psychology and Health* **12**: 737–51

Calman K C 1984 Quality of life in cancer patients—an hypothesis. *Journal of Medical Ethics* **10**: 124–7

Diener E 2000 Subjective well-being. The science of happiness and a proposal for a national index. *American Psychologist* **55**: 34–43

Juniper E F, Guyatt G H, Willan A, Griffith L E 1994 Determining a minimal important change in a disease-specific quality of life questionnaire. *Journal of Clinical Epidemiology* **47**: 81–7

Kreitler S, Chaitchuk S, Rapport Y, Kreitler H, Algor R 1993 Life satisfaction and health in cancer patients, orthopaedic patients and healthy individuals. *Social Science Med.* **36**: 547–56

McGee H M, Hevey D, Horgan J H 1999 Psychosocial outcome assessments for use in cardiac rehabilitation service evaluation: a 10-year systematic review. *Social Science and Medicine.* **48**: 1373–93

Sprangers M A G, Aaronson N K 1992 The role of health care providers and significant others in evaluating the quality of life of patients with chronic disease: a review. *Journal of Clinical Epidemiology* **45**: 743–60

Stewart A L, Greenfield S, Hays R D, Wells R D, Rogers W H, Berry S D, McGlynn E A, Ware J E 1989 Functional status and well-being of patients with chronic conditions: Results from the Medical Outcomes Study. *JAMA—Journal of the American Medical Association* **262**: 907–13

Sugarbaker P H, Barofsky I, Rosenberg S A, Gianola P J 1982 Quality of life assessment of patients in extremity sarcoma clinical trials. *Surgery* **91**: 17–23

H. M. McGee

Chronic Pain: Models and Treatment Approaches

1. Introduction

Pain is one of the most common reasons for seeking medical care (Hart et al. 1995, Gureje et al. 1998). For many, pain is an adaptive response warning of the potential for bodily harm. This signal helps to prevent further injury and tissue damage. However, research as well as common experience suggests that pain is much more than a mere barometer of the amount of tissue damage. Despite the universal experience of pain, it is a difficult phenomenon to define precisely. We have all seen instances where two people report radically different amounts of pain despite an equivalent injury. Clinicians have also noted that soldiers report little or no pain after a combat injury until after they are removed from the battlefield. The wide variations in how people communicate their pain further complicate matters. Some may express pain by crying or groaning, whereas others are more stoic and handle their pain by gritting their teeth and suffering silently.

It is important to distinguish pain from nociception. Nociception is a physiological process by which transduction of sensory information is activated in specialized nerve endings that convey information about tissue damage (e.g., location, descriptive features) to the central nervous system. Pain, on the other hand, is an integrated perceptual process. The International Association for the Study of Pain (IASP) recognizes the complexity of pain and treats it as a phenomenological experience unique to each person. According to the IASP definition, pain is 'an unpleasant sensory and emotional experience normally associated with tissue damage or described in terms of such damage' (Merskey 1986). In addition to this global definition, many commonly used pain terms and related phenomena have been described (Turk and Okifuji 2001). For example, pain may be acute and a response to an identifiable trauma or disease, or it may be episodic and occur intermittently as in the case of migraine headache. Pain may also be relatively constant, extending for years. Unlike those with acute or recurrent pain, people with chronic pain may suffer 24 hours a day, 365 days a year. Table 1 includes a list of four classes of pain based upon timing and clinical implications.

In this article an overview is provided of the current understanding of pain and its management. First the conceptualizations that have dominated views of pain historically are reviewed. The current conceptualizations that integrate multifactorial aspects of pain are described. The article also focuses on psychosocial factors that have been shown to contribute to the subjective experience of pain as well as adaptation and response to treatment. Following the discussion of model of pain, a historical overview of the most common perspectives and treatments of pain is presented. The importance of a multidisciplinary approach to understanding and treating complex chronic pain syndromes is stressed. Finally, the psychosocial stra-

Table 1
Four types of pain

Transient Pain: Pain elicited by activation of nociceptive process but no significant injury is present and pain stops as soon as the activation ends. This type of pain is ubiquitous in everyday life and rarely is a reason to seek heath care. EXAMPLES: pain associated with injection for immunization

Acute Pain: Pain elicited by nociceptive activation at the site of injury or disease. This type of pain is often a reason to seek medical care. EXAMPLES: post-surgical pain, pain associated with muscle sprain

Recurrent Pain: Episodic or intermittent pain. Each pain episode is relatively short lasting but recurs across an extended period of time. EXAMPLES: migraine headaches, tic douloureux, sickle cell crisis

Chronic Pain: Usually elicited by an injury but lasting for a long period of time after the original damage has been healed. At the chronic stage, no objective pathology may be present that can explain the presence of pain. EXAMPLES: chronic low back pain, fibromyalgia

Source: Turk & Okifuji 2001

tegies that incorporate behavioral and cognitive–behavioral perspectives with the goals of improving pain and functioning of people suffering from pain are emphasized. It is not meant to be suggested, however, that pain is purely psychological or that physical factors are unimportant. Rather emphasis is put on psychosocial factors, as they have previously been less integrated into conventional thinking about chronic pain. The psychological approaches described are almost always employed within the multidisciplinary treatment program (Flor et al. 1992).

2. Historical Conceptualizations of Pain

Over the centuries, many prominent scholars have attempted to uncover the mechanisms underlying pain. Perhaps among the most influential was the seventeenth century French philosopher, René Descartes. Descartes conceptualized pain as the result of representation of a painful stimulus traveling along the nervous system starting at the periphery (the flame depicted in Figure 1 that will travel along the nerve from the periphery to the spinal cord eventually reaching the brain where it acknowledged as 'pain'). Descartes's approach formed the basis for the mind–body dualism that plays a prominent role in the understanding and treatment of pain.

Figure 1
L'homme de René Descartes (reproduced by permission of René Descartes Paris: Charles Angot, 1664)

2.1 Biomedical (*pain = physical pathology*) Model

The traditional biomedical view that continues to dominate is reductionistic. This perspective assumes that every report of pain must be associated with a specific physical cause (e.g., pain caused by the flame in Figure 1). As a consequence, the extent of pain reported should be directly proportional to the amount of tissue damage. The expectation is that once the physical cause has been identified, appropriate treatment will follow and positive outcomes will be attained. Treatment typically focuses on removing the putative cause of the pain, or by chemically or surgically disrupting the pain pathways (cutting or blocking the transmission of signals from the periphery to the brain). According to this model, once the cause of the pain is removed or the pain pathways are blocked, pain should be eliminated.

There are, however, several perplexing features of pain that do not fit neatly into the biomedical model with its suggestion of a one-to-one relationship between tissue pathology and symptoms. Most notably, not all pain accompanies observable pathology. For example, in over 85 percent of the cases of back pain, one of the most common pain conditions in Western countries, the cause of the pain is unknown (Deyo 1986). Conversely, physical pathology does not necessarily cause pain. Diagnostic imaging studies identify significant pathology in up to 35 percent of people who are pain-free (Jensen et al. 1994). Thus, a paradox exists. On one hand there are people without significant pathology who report severe pain and on the other hand there are people with objectively determined physical pathology who do not report the presence of any pain.

2.2 Psychogenic ('*It's All in Your Head*') Model

According to this model, pain, in the absence of physical pathology, is a result of the patient's inherent personality traits or psychological problems. The psychogenic view is posed as the flip side of the coin from the physical or biomedical model. From this perspective, if the report of pain occurs in the absence of, or is disproportionate to, objective physical pathology, then, *ipso facto*, the pain reports must have a psychological etiology. Thus, a dichotomy is posed, pain is either somatagenic or psychogenic.

2.3 Motivational (*Secondary Gain*) Model

A related conceptualization to the psychogenic one described specifically focuses upon motivation. From this perspective, reports of pain in the absence of physical pathology are attributed to the desire of the person complaining to obtain some benefit such as attention, time off from undesirable activities, or financial (disability) compensation (i.e., secondary gain). Unlike the psychogenic model, in the motivational model, the assumption is that the person is consciously attempting to acquire a desirable outcome based on the complaint of pain. Thus, the complaint of pain in the absence of pathology is taken to be fraudulent. Simply put, the person who reports pain in the absence of objective pathology is lying in order to obtain a desired outcome.

2.4 Operant (Social Reinforcement) Model

The operant or social reinforcement model is based upon the behavioral learning paradigm in which the probability of exhibiting a specific behavior depends on the consequences that follow the behavior. Behaviors are most likely to recur when they are reinforced by desirable consequences (e.g., attention, sympathy), by removal of something aversive (e.g., participating in undesirable tasks, work activity), or avoidance of some undesirable consequence. Fordyce (1976) suggested that certain behaviors associated with pain (e.g., limping, grimacing) could be reinforced to the point where the behaviors recur without the original nociceptive stimuli. Pain behaviors that are consistent with acute pain and that may be reflexive responses to noxious stimulation, may become chronic pain behaviors even when there is no physiological basis for exhibiting those behaviors. Thus, in this model, chronic pain is considered a manifestation of learned behaviors that need to be extinguished, whereas well behaviors, such as activity, need to be increased. The laws of operant learning are viewed as playing a central role in the maintenance of chronic pain behaviors. The role of other factors, such as physiology, emotions, the persons' attitudes and beliefs, play very little role in the operant model.

3. Multidimensional Conceptualization of Pain

The unidimensional models described fail to explain individual and situational variation in pain experiences. The article will now focus on more contemporary models of pain with multifactorial bases.

3.1 Gate Control Theory

Melzack and Wall (1965) developed the gate control theory that integrated physical and psychological factors regarding pain experience. Briefly, the gate control theory proposes that a mechanism in the dorsal horn of the spinal cord acts as a 'gate' that can inhibit or facilitate transmission of nerve impulses from the periphery to the brain. Melzack and Wall postulated that not only injury sites at the periphery

influence the gating mechanism but also by people's psychological states. They suggested that the reticular formation in the brain functions as a central biasing mechanism inhibiting the transmission of pain signals. Psychological factors that affect the reticular formation may modulate the pain experience.

Melzack and Wall emphasized the modulation of inputs in the dorsal horn of the spinal cord and on the dynamic role of the brain in pain processes and perception. As a result, the gate control theory integrates psychological variables such as past experience, attention, and other cognitive activities into current research on and therapy for pain. Prior to this formulation, psychological processes largely were dismissed as merely reactions to pain. This new model suggested that severing nerves, the putative pain pathways, was inadequate as a host of other factors modulated the input. Perhaps the major contribution of the gate control theory was that it highlighted the central nervous system as playing an essential role in the perception and interpretation of nociceptive stimuli associated with the experience of pain.

The physiological details of the gate control model have been challenged and it has been suggested that the model is incomplete. As additional knowledge has been gathered since the original formulation of the gate control model, specific points have been disputed and physiological details of the model have been refined. The conceptual aspects of the gate control theory have, however, proved remarkably resilient and flexible in the face of accumulating scientific evidence. The gate control model still provides a powerful summary of the phenomena observed in the spinal cord and brain, and has the capacity to explain many of the most puzzling problems encountered in the clinic. The gate control theory has had enormous heuristic value in stimulating further research in the basic science of pain mechanisms and in spurring new approaches to treatment.

3.2 Cognitive–Behavioral Model

The focus of the cognitive–behavioral model is on the person's own subjective perspectives (e.g., attitudes, believes, expectations) and feelings about their plight (Turk et al. 1983). The model assumes that although nociceptive stimuli precede pain, how the person perceives the nociceptive event forms a total pain experience by interacting with the sensory event. For example, negative and pessimistic views by people about their pain condition (e.g., 'It's hopeless and it will never get better.') and their capabilities for managing pain and stress (e.g., 'There is absolutely nothing I can do about my pain.') are likely to exacerbate their emotional distress and sense of disability. Similarly, if one views pain as inevitable (e.g., 'I was injured, that is why I hurt.'), attention to sensory events may become pronounced, and as a consequence, relatively subtle sensory information may be interpreted as being painful.

The cognitive–behavioral model also acknowledges the effects of physiological factors and the environment on behaviors and of behaviors on thoughts and feelings. Reporting of symptoms to family and health care providers is influenced by how people view their pain problem and, of course, physical pathology.

The basic assumption of the cognitive–behavioral model is that people are not passive entities who simply react reflexively to nociception or social reinforcement, but actively engaging themselves in defining the experience. Based upon past learning and medical history, people develop subjective representations of illness and symptoms—'schemas.' These schema becomes the filters through which people process new sensory stimulus (Cioffi 1991).

Beliefs about the meaning of pain and one's ability to function despite pain are important aspects of pain schema. When confronted with pain, people draw causal, covariational, and consequential inferences about their symptoms based upon their own schematic references. For example, if the schema includes a strong belief that all physical activities must be ceased when experiencing pain and that pain is an acceptable justification for neglecting domestic and occupational responsibilities, poor adaptation and coping are likely to result (Williams and Thorn 1989).

4. Treatments

As has been discussed previously, pain is a complex phenomenon and diverse in its nature and degrees of associated impairment. It is therefore important to know the objectives of treatments for pain. Many pain states are expected to remit over time with little intervention required. Some types of acute pain may require surgical or pharmacological therapy to treat underlying pathology or to block noxious sensory information. A more comprehensive plan is required for treating people with chronic pain. Many people with chronic pain live with their pain for years, and the adverse effects of pain may be generalized across all aspects of their lives, familial, social, occupational, as well as physical. Given the multilayered problems associated with pain, treatment goals become more global. Rather than treating pain, it becomes necessary to treat people with chronic pain.

4.1 Historical Approaches to Treatment

The earliest approach to treating pain was aligned closely with unimodal views; particularly those based on the biomedical model. Pain was thought of as reflecting a physical problem. Early treatment approaches focused on the idea that something had to be removed or signals had to be interrupted to bring about relief from pain. The earliest reference to medication is referred to in an ancient Egyptian text dating back to 1550 BC where the god Isis recommended the use of opium to relieve Ra's headache (Bonica 1953). Ancient pain treatments have included crocodile dung, oils derived from ants, earthworms and spiders, spermatic fluid from frogs, and moss scraped from the skull of a victim of a violent death. A quick surf of the Internet will reveal that many equally esoteric preparations are endorsed readily even today.

The most common contemporary treatment approaches continue to be based primarily on the biomedical model of pain involving pharmacotherapy (with new drugs touted on an almost weekly basis) or surgery performed along nearly every site of the nervous system including the periphery (sympathectomy), the spinal cord (percutaneous cordotomy, destructive neural blockade), and the brain (thalamatomy, prefrontal lobotomy). Although current methods are more sophisticated than the ancient ones, the basic principles remain the same—alteration of an alleged physical cause should result in symptomatic improvement. Some modalities are quite helpful and a great many people suffering from acute and cancer pain have benefited from those advances in pain medicine and surgery. However, surgery and pharmacotherapy are not panaceas and do not result in adequate control of pain in all cases.

In contrast, some primitive treatment methods focused on the cause of pain being purely psychogenic. The assumption was that if no physical cause could be detected then the pain must be caused by emotional disturbance that required treatment and once psychological problems were resolved the pain would resolve. Such a psychogenic bias can be seen in the current Diagnostic and Statistical Manual (American Psychiatric Association 1994) for mental disorder. Two types of pain disorders are listed as mental disorders: Pain Disorder Associated with Psychological Factors and Pain Disorder Associated with Both Psychological Factors and a general medical condition. In both cases, pain is the primary complaint, with psychological factors being considered important in the onset, severity, exacerbation, or maintenance of the pain. A somewhat presumptuous assumption underlying these disorders is that the 'appropriate' physical etiology of chronic pain must be identifiable (e.g., free from psychological factor) or patients are suffering from a psychiatric disorder. The assumption ignores the current consensus that pain is not a pure sensory experience but is inherently a biopsychosocial phenomenon resulting in an intense, subjective experience of discomfort.

4.2 Comprehensive Approaches to the Treatment of the Person with Chronic Pain

The recognition of pain, particularly chronic pain, as a major healthcare issue, has resulted in the development of growing number of specialists and specialized facilities offering treatments for pain over the last few decades. In the United States alone, over 3300 pain specialists and treatment facilities have been identified (Marketdata Enterprises 1995).

Comprehensive, multidisciplinary treatments involving teams of professionals (physicians, psychologists, physical therapists, occupational therapists, vocational therapists, and nurses) have been developed to treatment patients with the most recalcitrant problems. Flor et al. (1992) summarized the major characteristics of these patients as those with seven years of pain history and at least one failed surgery. These patients are likely to be unemployed, receiving disability payments, and present an array of psychosocial and motivational issues. In addition to the suffering associated with chronic pain, these patients present socioeconomic difficulties for society due to loss of productivity and costs associated with disability payments and medical care.

Focus will be on the pain management approaches that have been developed based upon the psychological models described earlier. Although these interventions can be used separately, with few exceptions (e.g., biofeedback for tension-type headache) unimodal approaches are less effective than comprehensive rehabilitation programs. Typically, the psychological approaches are part of more comprehensive rehabilitation program in which psychologists work together with therapist from other disciplines (e.g., physicians and physical therapists).

The multidisciplinary rehabilitation programs are philosophically distinct from unimodal medical and surgical treatments. The first and most critical distinction is that the major goals of the multidisciplinary treatment programs extend beyond pain relief. Rather, they focus on physical and psychological functioning, as well.

Overall, rehabilitation programs that incorporate a significant psychosocial component are most effective in improving patient functioning, returning patients to work, reducing use of analgesics, reducing health care utilization, and reducing disability costs (Okifuji et al. 1998). 'Cure' of pain (e.g., total relief from pain) is, unfortunately, rarely attained. Reduction of pain is usually only moderate but comparable to that observed with usual medical and surgical approaches that are more invasive and have increased likelihood of iatrogenic consequences.

4.2.1 Treatment based on the operant model. As noted previously, the operant model of pain focuses upon pain-related behaviors believed to be maintained by social reinforcement. Such behaviors are considered to be maladaptive and thus need to be eliminated. As discussed, reinforcers are the consequences of behaviors that increase the likelihood that

behaviors will be repeated. Thus, treatment involves eliminating the rewarding consequences of pain behaviors and increasing the positive responses for activity and other well behaviors. In these programs, moaning, grimacing, and other pain behaviors are ignored. Usual activities of daily living and functional exercises are prescribed and positively reinforced. Medications are made time-contingent, rather than prescribed on an 'as needed' (prn) basis that is believed to reinforce positively the pain behaviors. Simultaneous with the attempts to extinguish pain behaviors, operant treatments are designed to help patients acquire a set of new, more adaptive, behaviors. Quota-based exercise programs with gradually increasing functional activities form the core of operant treatment.

Although operant factors may play an important role in the maintenance of disability, the model has been criticized at two levels. First, it fails to integrate factors other than reinforcement, such as sensory, emotional, and cognitive factors in the overall pain experience. Second, the assumption that pain behaviors are acquired, maintained, and extinguished solely through environmental reinforcement contingencies is questioned. For example, physical signs, patients' self-efficacy beliefs, and depression are also reportedly related to pain behaviors (Buckelew et al. 1953).

Pain behaviors have been considered to be maladaptive manifestations of pain, guided by an incentive for attention or avoidance of physical activity. However, pain behaviors may be functional if indeed the behaviors protect patients from further injury or exacerbation of pain. Determination of whether an overt pain behavior in a given patient is functional or maladaptive needs to be based upon careful assessment of various factors associated with his or her pain conditions not just the reinforcement contingencies. Despite the criticisms, operant-based treatments generally are successful in reducing overt pain behaviors, increasing well-behaviors, and decreasing analgesic medication.

4.2.2 Treatments based on the cognitive–behavioral model. As noted earlier, the cognitive–behavioral model of pain acknowledges the importance of cognitive variables interacting with sensory, affective, behavioral ones to establish, maintain, and exacerbate the pain experience. The nature of specific techniques may vary from program to program, however, the primary goals of the cognitive–behavioral approach are relatively uniform (i.e., enhancement of patients' sense of control over their symptoms, increased use of adaptive skills to cope with pain and stress). Cognitive–behavioral therapy is designed to assist patients to identify, evaluate, and correct maladaptive conceptualizations and dysfunctional

Table 2
Common examples of cognitive errors

Overgeneralization: Extrapolation from the occurrence of a specific event
  or situation to a large range of possible situations. 'This coping strategy didn't work;
  nothing will ever work for me'

Catastrophyzing: Focusing exclusively on the worst possibility regardless of its
  likelihood of occurrence. 'My back pain means my body is degenerating and falling apart'

All-or-none Thinking: Considering only the extreme 'best' or 'worst' interpretation
  of a situation without regard to the full range of alternatives. 'If pain is not completely gone,
  I cannot do anything right'

Jumping to Conclusions: Accepting an arbitrary interpretation without a rational
  evaluation of its likelihood. 'The doctor didn't return my call today. He thinks I am a hopeless case'

Selective Attention: Selectively attending to negative aspects of a situation while
  ignoring any positive factors. 'Physical exercises only make my pain worse'

Negative Predictions: Assuming the worst. 'I know I will not get better even
  with all these therapies and everyone will dislike me for that'

Mind Reading: Make arbitrary assumptions about others without finding out what others
  are thinking. 'My husband does not talk to me about my pain because he doesn't care about me'

---

beliefs about themselves and their predicament. Additionally, patients are taught to recognize the connections linking cognition, affect, and behavior along with their joint consequences. Patients are encouraged to become aware of and to monitor the impact those maladaptive thoughts may have in the maintenance and exacerbation of maladaptive behaviors (see Table 2 for common maladaptive thoughts).

The cognitive–behavioral approach consists of four interrelated phases. These include (a) reconceptualization, (b) acquisition of coping skills and self-management strategies, (c) skill consolidation, and (d) generalization and maintenance. The first phase, reconceptualization, uses cognitive restructuring, a method that encourages people to identify and change maladaptive thoughts and feelings that are associated with the experience of pain. The crucial element in successful treatment is bringing about a shift in the patient's thought processes, away from well-established, habitual, and automatic but maladaptive thoughts toward more hopeful and rational ones. Cognitive restructuring helps foster the reconceptualization by helping patients to become aware of the role thoughts and emotions play in potentiating and maintaining stress and pain. The aim of this phase is to combat the sense of demoralization that many with chronic pain experience. Generally, the process of cognitive restructuring begins with a presentation of a situation or event that provoked a pain-related response. The situation is dissected to identify key thoughts and feelings that precede, accompany, and follow an episode or exacerbation of ongoing pain and pain-related problems. Then patients are encouraged

to challenge the legitimacy of the thoughts—was it true? Was it reasonable? Was it the only way to respond? What alternatives are available? and so on. Patients are instructed to gather evidence for or against their own maladaptive automatic thoughts. Alternatives are discussed, with the suggestion that different ways of thinking can affect mood, behavior (e.g., reducing physical activity leading to greater disability) and even physiological activity (e.g., increase muscle tension and thereby exacerbating pain).

The second phase is the acquisition of self-management skills. A wide variety of techniques have been shown to be effective for reducing suffering and disability. Some of these strategies are self-regulatory skills (e.g., relaxation, controlled breathing, and attention diversion) that allow pain sufferers to regulate their own physiological responses that may be involved in the maintenance and exacerbation of pain. Other self-management strategies include stress-reduction skills (e.g., problem-solving, behavioral rehearsals) that allow people with chronic pain to effectively manage the stress-inducing thoughts, behaviors, and emotions that trigger pain, emotional distress, and other maladaptive responses. Instead of being a passive recipient of a medical intervention (e.g., medication, anesthetic nerve block), patients now learn to use self-management strategies to play an active role in managing the myriad of problems created by the presence of persistent pain. Research has suggested that there is no one specific coping skill that best manages pain and disability (Fernandez and Turk 1992). It is recommended generally that chronic pain patients should be taught various types of coping skills to help them acquire a range of options.

Phase 3 is skill consolidation. During the skill-consolidation phase, patients practice and rehearse the skills that they have learned during the acquisition phase and apply them outside the hospital or clinic. Practice may start with the mental rehearsal, during which patients imagine using the skills in different situations. Therapists can make use of role-playing, in which patients rehearse learned skills in situations that mirror their home environments. Therapists may start with a relatively easy examples and then introduce scenarios that are progressively more realistic. The importance of skill consolidation through home-practice cannot be overstated. When patients practice skills at home, it is useful for them to record their experiences including any difficulties that arise. Once problems associated with using the newly acquired skills are identified, these become targets for further discussion.

The final stage is phase 4; the preparation for generalization and maintenance. To maximize the likelihood of maintenance and generalization of treatment gains, therapists focus upon the cognitive activity of patients as they confront problems throughout treatment (e.g., failure to achieve goals, plateaus in progress, recurrent stress). These circumstances are used as opportunities to assist patients to learn how to handle setbacks and lapses because they are probably inevitable parts of life and will occur after the termination of the treatment. In the final phase of treatment, discussion focuses on ways of predicting and dealing with symptoms and related problems following treatment termination. Patients are encouraged to anticipate future problems, stress, and symptom-exacerbating events during treatment and to plan how to respond and cope with these problems.

Since self-initiating pain management is a key factor in pain rehabilitation. Some type of cognitive–behavioral approach generally is included in a multi-disciplinary pain program.

Cognitive–behavioral approaches have been demonstrated to be effective with a wide range of debilitating pain syndromes including low back pain (Lanes et al. 1995), arthritis (Parker et al. 1995), and fibromyalgia (Turk et al. 1998). Moreover, these methods have been shown to be effective with children (Walco et al. 1992) and geriatric samples (Calfas et al. 1992).

5. Summary

This chapter reviewed the definition of pain and the historical context within which pain has been conceptualized, made a distinction between nociception (a sensory process) and pain (a perception), and described the most common conceptualizations based the unidimensional and multidimensional models of pain. It was noted that treatment strategies have closely followed the conceptualizations of pain and have included unidimensional modalities (i.e. biomedical, psychogenic) and progressed to multidimensional modalities.

Although pain generally is considered a physical phenomenon, pain involves various cognitive, affective, and behavioral features. These psychological factors are important not only in determining the perception of pain, but also defining disability and patients' general well being. It should be clear from the review that pain has three main components: physical, psychosocial, and behavioral, that interact to define the unique pain experience. Because the pain experience is subjective and idiosyncratic, it cannot be understood without evaluating how patients perceive and appraise their conditions. A complete clinical picture involves consideration of how patients view their plight. By understanding the phenomenology of chronic pain and disability, effective treatment can be planned to alleviate persistent and debilitating pain, improve physical and psychological functioning, thereby reducing the disability that accompanies chronic pain.

See also: Chronic Illness, Psychosocial Coping with; Chronic Illness: Quality of Life; Pain, Health Psychology of; Pain, Management of; Pain, Neural Basis of.

Bibliography

American Psychiatric Association, 1994, Diagnostic and Statistical Manual of Mental Disorders: DSM-IV, American Psychiatric Association, Washington, DC

Anonymous 1995 Chronic pain management programs: a market analysis, Marketdata Enterprises, Tampa, FL

Bonica J J 1993 *The Management of Pain.* Lea & Febiger, Philadelphia

Buckelew S P, Murray S E, Hewett J E, Johnson J, Huyser B 1953 Self-efficacy, pain, and physical activity among fibromyalgia subjects. *Arthritis Care Research* **8**: 43–50

Calfas K, Kaplan R, Ingram R 1992 One-year evaluation of cognitive–behavioral intervention in osteoarthritis. *Arthritis Care Research* **5**: 202–9

Cioffi D 1991 Beyond attentional strategies: cognitive-perceptual model of somatic interpretation. *Psychological Bulletin* **109**: 25–41

Deyo R A 1986 Early diagnostic evaluation of low back pain. *Journal of General Internal Medicine* **1**: 328–38

Fernandez E, Turk D C 1992 Sensory and affective components of pain: separation and synthesis. *Psychological Bulletin* **112**: 205–17

Flor H, Fydrich T, Turk D C 1992 Efficacy of multidisciplinary pain treatment centers: a meta-analytic review. *Pain* **49**: 221–30

Fordyce W E 1976 *Behavioral Methods in Chronic Pain and Illness.* Mosby, St. Louis

Gureje O, Von Korff M, Simon G E, Gater R 1998 Persistent pain and well-being: a World Health Organization study in primary care. *JAMA* **280**: 147–51

Hart L G, Deyo R A, Cherkin D C 1995 Physician office visits for low back pain. Frequency, clinical evaluation, and treatment patterns from a U.S. national survey. *Spine* **20**: 11–19

Jensen M C, Brant-Zawadzki M N, Obuchowski N, Modic M, Malkasian D, Ross J 1994 Magnetic resonance imaging of the lumbar spine in people without back pain. *New England Journal of Medicine* **331**: 69–73

Lanes T C, Gauron E F, Spratt K F, Wernimont T, Found E, Weinstein J 1995 Long-term follow-up of patients with chronic back pain treated in a multidisciplinary rehabilitation program. *Spine* **20**: 801–6

Melzack R, Wall P D 1965 Pain mechanisms: a new theory. *Science* **150**: 971–9

Merskey H 1986 Classification of chronic pain. Descriptions of chronic pain syndromes and definitions of pain terms. *Pain –Supplement* **3**: S1–226

Okifuji A, Turk D, Kalauokalani D 1998 Clinical outcome and economic evaluation of multidisciplinary pain centers. In: Block A R, Kremer E F, Fernandez E (eds.) *Handbook of Pain Syndromes: Biopsychosocial Perspectives*, Erlbaum, Mahwah, NJ

Parker J C, Smarr K L, Buckelew S P, Stucky-Ropp R, Hewett J, Johnson J, Wright G, Irvin W, Walker S 1995 Effects of stress management on clinical outcomes in rheumatoid arthritis. *Arthritisis and Rheumatism* **38**: 1807–18

Turk D C, Meichenbaum D, Genest M 1983 *Pain and Behavioral Medicine: A Cognitive–Behavioral Perspective.* Guilford, New York

Turk D C, Okifuji A 2001 Pain terms and taxonomies of pain. In: Loeser J D, Butler S H, Chapman C R, Turk D C (eds.) *Management of Pain.* 3rd edn. Lippincott Williams & Wilkins, Philadelphia

Turk D C, Okifuji A, Sinclair J D, Starz T 1998 Interdisciplinary treatment for fibromyalgia syndrome: clinical and statistical significance, *Arthritis Care and Research* **11**: 186–95

Walco G A, Varni J W, Ilowite N T 1992 Cognitive–behavioral pain management in children with juvenile rheumatoid arthritis. *Pediatrics* **89**: 1075–79

Williams D A, Thorn B E 1989 An empirical assessment of pain beliefs. *Pain* **36**: 351–58

D. C. Turk

Chronology, Stratigraphy, and Dating Methods in Archaeology

1. Introduction: Estimating Age in the Archaeological Record

Of the twenty or so dating methods employed in twenty-first-century archaeology, the US Congressional Office of Technology Assessment (OTA) report on *Technologies for Prehistoric and Historic Preservation* (US Congress, OTA 1986) listed only seven and highlighted two radiocarbon and archaeomagnetic techniques; see Taylor 2000, pp. 75–60. In many

Table 1
Datable materials and appropriate dating methods in common use in early twenty-first century

	Magnetism	Hydration	Amino Acid	E.S.R.	Luminescence	Fission Track	Uranium Series	K-Ar; ^{40}Ar/^{39}Ar	Radiocarbon	Dendrochronology
obsidian	4	4				4		4		
other volcanic rocks	4			4	4	4	4	4		
glass					4					
unburned sediment	4				4					
burned sedimentary stone				4	4					
slag				4	4				4	
pottery, baked earth	4			4	4				4	
shell			4	4			4		4	
tooth enamel				4			4		4	
bone, antler, ivory, teeth				4			4		4	
wood/charcoal									4	4
plant fragments									4	

regions of the world, radiocarbon, dendrochronology, obsidian hydration, and archaeomagnetism are the most common physical dating methods used, presumably in that order, but often together as a group providing redundant checks on one of the most important goals of archaeology—providing a framework of time, a chronology, upon which a rational reconstruction of the past can be built. Regardless of an archaeologist's theoretical or political perspectives, the first goal is to order regional prehistoric or historic sites, a single site, or a portion of the site into meaningful cultural and chronological segments. Chronology is a primary goal, but should not be confused with the intent of reconstructing the past, regardless of what an archaeologist's definition of the ultimate purpose may be.

During the formative cultural historic perspective in archaeology in the first half of the twentieth century, constructing regional and site-oriented chronologies became the primary goal of archaeology, particularly in North America and the UK (Trigger 1989). A dissatisfaction with this rather unilineal explanation of the past stirred archaeologists to look beyond simply constructing chronologies and to begin to understand process and social relationships in the past. Dating methods and the construction of cultural chronologies, however, have remained the basement upon which archaeologists build their understanding of social process through time.

While it would be optimal to discuss all the potential dating methods available to archaeologists, this is not possible in a short synopsis. The most commonly used

```
============ = Numerical Age = ============_____
              _____ ======= Calibrated Age ======= _____
                          _____ ======= Relative Age ======== _____
                                      _____ = Correlated Age =
```

TYPE OF METHOD

Sidereal	Isotopic	Radiogenic	Chemical and Biological	Geomorphic	Correlation
Historical records	*^{14}C	Fission-track	Amino acid racemization	Soil-profile development	Lithostratigraphy
*Dendrochronology	K-Ar and ^{39}Ar-^{40}Ar	_____	*Obsidian and tephra hydration	Rock and mineral weathering	Tephrochronology
Varve chronology	Uranium-series	Thermolumines-cense	Lichenometry	Progressive landscape modification	Paleomagnetism
	_____	Electron-spin resonance	Soil chemistry	*Rate of deposition	*Archaeomagnetism
	Uranium-trend		Rock varnish chemistry	Rate of deformation	*Fossils and artifacts
	Cosmogenic isotopes (^{210}Pb, ^{10}Be, ^{36}Cl, etc.)			*Geomorphic position	Stable isotopes
					Orbital variations
					Tectites and microtectites

Figure 1
Commonly used dating methods in archaeology. Those marked with (*) are discussed in some detail in this entry
Source: adapted from Waters 1992

methods, and those showing promise, will be covered here (see Table 1 and Fig. 1). Refer to the publications in the bibliography for more detailed treatments.

2. Archaeological Stratigraphy

Stratigraphic relations have always been the primary method to infer the relative age of artifacts within a site. Stratigraphy is defined here as the study of the spatial and temporal relationships between the sediments and the soil (Waters 1992, pp. 60–1). Much of this section's discussion can be more robustly understood by referring to the entry *Geoarchaeology*; an awareness of the geological processes of archaeological site formation is crucial to an understanding of dating archeological sediments. Indeed, the methods used by Quaternary geologists to date sediments include most of the methods used by archaeologists and discussed here (see Fig. 1). Stratigraphic studies of archaeological sites are designed to define objectively and categorize the sediments and soils, the contact units between them, and the amount of time they represent, as well as their relationship to the surrounding sediment history.

Archaeological stratigraphy is based on the geological concepts of the law of superposition, which states that older sediments are emplaced at a lower level than more recent sediments. Therefore, sites, features, and artifacts residing in lower levels are, by definition, older than those in upper levels. This conceptual framework in archaeology appears to have

begun with John Frere in 1797 attempting to understand the relationship between stone axes in a sedimentary sequence in England: 'The manner in which…[the hand axes] lie would lead to the persuasion that it was a place of their manufacture and not of their accidental deposit…It may be suggested that the different strata were formed by inundations happening at distant periods' (Frere in Rapp and Hill 1998, p. 5).

This idea that features or artifacts found within a site in the same stratigraphic level are contemporaneous forms the foundation upon which archaeological stratigraphy is based. In early twenty-first century archaeology, the various relative and absolute dating methods such as radiocarbon or archaeomagnetic dating are used to verify this assumption and produce a site chronology (see Fig. 2). Fig. 2 shows a simple stratigraphic profile of a single excavation unit with the relative positions of natural and cultural features, and the position of radiocarbon dates recovered from the various levels. Note that the radiocarbon dates indicate that, in general, the stratigraphy is intact in that the oldest dates are at the bottom and the latest dates at the top, except for one date (CAMS 43177) at 3690 ± 50 BP which seems to be out of sequence and suggests 'small-scale' disturbance probably caused by the digging of the pit structure during the later ceramic period (Shackley et al. 2000).

Time-sensitive artifacts, such as previously dated pottery or projectile point types, can be used as *index fossils* within the stratigraphic column to create a relative chronology within the site. The stratigraphic

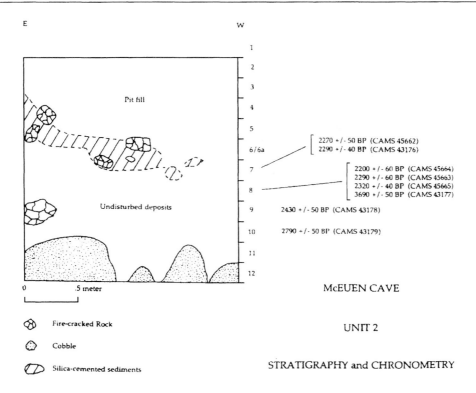

E   W

Pit fill

Undisturbed deposits

2270 +/- 50 BP (CAMS 45662)
2290 +/- 40 BP (CAMS 43176)

2200 +/- 60 BP (CAMS 45664)
2290 +/- 60 BP (CAMS 45663)
2320 +/- 40 BP (CAMS 45665)
3690 +/- 50 BP (CAMS 43177)

2430 +/- 50 BP (CAMS 43178)

2790 +/- 50 BP (CAMS 43179)

0   .5 meter

Fire-cracked Rock

Cobble

Silica-cemented sediments

McEUEN CAVE

UNIT 2

STRATIGRAPHY and CHRONOMETRY

Figure 2
Simple stratigraphic wall profile of a unit at McEuen Cave (AZ W:13:6 ASM) showing position of bedrock, undisturbed strata, pit fill structure, and the position of recovered radiocarbon dates. Source: Shackley et al. 2000

example discussed above also used index fossils, in this case projectile point types, to add another chronological piece of information. In Level 8, where the early radiocarbon date as well as some more recent radiocarbon dates were recovered, Middle Archaic as well as Late Archaic projectile point forms were recovered; both confirming the time range suggested by the radiocarbon date ranges (Fig. 2, Shackley et al. 2000). In this instance the stratigraphy, radiocarbon dates, and index fossils all contributed to an understanding of the site chronology and the integrity of the archaeological deposit.

2.1 Constructing Stratigraphic Chronologies: Competing Ideas

It is important to note, however, that there is considerable recent controversy over the proper method to employ in the interpretation of archaeological stratigraphy (Farrand 1984, Harris et al. 1993, Stein 1987, Waters 1992). Archaeological stratigraphic codes similar to geological stratigraphic codes and methodologies have been proposed but not generally

adopted, since many geoarchaeologists are convinced that the existing geological code is adequate for archaeological research (see Stein 1987). More recently, Harris has proposed an 'archaeological tool' to understand archaeological stratigraphy called the 'Harris Matrix,' essentially a simple postexcavation way in which to understand the relationships between stratigraphic units in a single diagram as reflected on paper, or more recently in digital form (see Harris et al. 1993). Farrand (1984) and others, mainly geologists, have questioned Harris's assumption that archaeological stratigraphy is primarily culturally conditioned rather than geologically determined. In a Harris Matrix analysis the relationship between stratigraphic units is based mainly on index fossils, for example the relationship between artifacts and features, rather than geological features or context—essentially emphasizing content rather than structure. Despite criticism from many geoarchaeologists, the Harris Matrix analysis has become increasingly popular with archaeologists working in varieties of geological and cultural contexts worldwide, particularly in Europe. The growing popularity of the Harris Matrix approach will probably continue, particularly in small site settings where a larger geological view is difficult to obtain or not necessarily relevant.

3. Sidereal Dating Methods

Sidereal dating methods include historical records, glacial varve dating, and dendrochronology. While only dendrochronology will be discussed here, glacial varve dating is quite useful in the upper latitudes, and in some cases may be quite precise. Historical records are a basic dating tool in historic and ethnohistoric archaeology, in addition to the social information they may contain.

3.1 Dendrochronology

The science that uses annual tree rings for dating past events and reconstructing past environmental conditions has undergone explosive growth in recent decades (Dean 1997). While dendrochronology as an archaeological dating tool enjoyed tremendous expansion in the 1990s, particularly in western North America, Europe, Siberia, and the eastern Mediterranean, it is used wherever appropriate trees occur and a sequence has been established. Most importantly, directly dated tree rings have been instrumental in the calibration of the radiocarbon timescale discussed below. This process indicated that the radiocarbon chronology underestimates the true ages of materials older than 2,000 years and that ^{14}C dates must be corrected.

The technique is based on the concept that each year (four seasons) a tree will accumulate one growth ring, and that that ring's attributes reflect the specific climatic regime of that year. Since each year is essentially a unique climatic record, the attributes of the tree ring (thickness of inner and outer bands) are correspondingly unique. In trees, particularly fast-growing conifers, the progression of rings from pith to circumference presents an 'unalterable temporal order, and the production of but one ring per year provides the incremental regularity necessary to establish a fixed [and absolute] time scale' (Dean 1997, p. 34). More than 180 tree and shrub species worldwide possess the attributes required for successful dendrochronological studies: visible and unambiguous ring definition, production of a set number of rings (generally only one) per year, mainly climate-controlled growth, and the presence of useable morphological features that allow for ring comparison. Cross-dating, matching patterns of ring variation among trees, is the necessary principle of dendrochronology. A sequence within a region is derived from overlap between cut trees as well as archaeological specimens, sometimes with great time depth into the thousands of years. While this process is apparently simple, the application necessarily requires

precision. At the turn of the twenty-first century, image analysis technology was being used to develop electronic workstations, including image databases in laptop computers, perform routine comparisons between the database and archaeological wood samples similar to techniques used in obsidian hydration analysis.

Today, in a number of regions of the world (upper altitudes in the North American Southwest, Western Europe, the Eastern Mediterranean) dendrochronology forms the backbone of chronometric dating. When available, dendrochronology provides an absolute chronology that anchors other dating techniques.

4. Isotopic Dating Methods

Perhaps the one area of dating that has seen the greatest advances recently are techniques based on radioactive decay: ^{14}C, K-Ar, and ^{40}Ar/^{39}Ar. Advances in accelerator mass spectrometry and laser fusion have propelled these techniques into the forefront of the arsenal of methods used to deal with time in the archaeological record. Importantly, ^{14}C is generally restricted to dating the last 50,000 years and ^{40}Ar/^{39}Ar, previously restricted to time periods near and over one million years, are now nearly overlapping with ^{40}Ar/^{39}Ar using the laser fusion method and yielding younger and younger ages. These methods do have limitations, but the organic and mineral restrictions are being transcended almost daily.

4.1 Radiocarbon Dating (^{14}C)

Given that the greatest level of human activity occurred after the evolution of modern Homo sapiens, in the last 45,000 years or so, radiocarbon dating has become the most commonly relied upon dating method in archaeology (Taylor in Taylor and Aitken 1997). Radiocarbon dating, now in its fifth decade of general use, is a primary tool used by archaeologists and Quaternary geologists to date the past.

4.1.1 The radiocarbon method.
There are three principal isotopes of carbon which occur naturally: ^{12}C, ^{13}C (both stable), and ^{14}C (unstable or radioactive). The radiocarbon method is based on the rate of decay of the radioactive or unstable carbon isotope 14 (^{14}C), which is formed in the upper atmosphere through the effect of cosmic ray neutrons upon nitrogen 14. The reaction is: ^{14}N + n $\Rightarrow$ ^{14}C + p (where n is a neutron and p is a proton).

The ^{14}C formed is rapidly oxidized to ^{14}CO$_2$ and enters the Earth's plant and animal lifeways through

Table 2
Recent pre-3000 BP (RCY) maize and cucurbit AMS ^{14}C dates from the American Southwest showing reporting conventions

Site	Site type/ context	Lab number	Radiocarbon age BP (1σ)	Dendrocalibrated 2σ age ranges BP [1]
McEuen Cave, AZ	rock shelter	CAMS 43177	3690 ± 50	4151 (4056--3934) 3835
Los Posos, AZ [2]	overbank alluv.	CAMS 34923	4050 ± 50	4792 (4517--4442) 4411
Three Fir Shelter, AZ	rock shelter	BETA 26275	3610 ± 170	4417 (3885) 3457
Tornillo Shelter, NM	rock shelter	GX 12720	3225 ± 240	4076 (3439--3408) 2784
Cerro Juanaqueña, CHIH[3]	trincheras	INSTARR 3985	3310 ± 60	3685 (3548--3479) 3364
Lukachukai, AZ	pit house	AA 9317	3445 ± 45	3829(3684--3543)3508
Lukachukai, AZ	pit house	AA 9321	3050 ± 50	3379(3315--3212)3004
Lukachukai, AZ	pit house	AA 9319	3135 ± 45	3443(3375--3357)3209
Bat Cave, NM	rock shelter	A 4167	3010 ± 150	3550 (3205--3083) 2778
Bat Cave, NM	rock shelter	A 4189	3060 ± 110	3473 (3317--3214) 2894

Source: Shackley *et al.* 2000
1 The 2σ dendrocalibrated minimums (intercepts) and maximums are based on a bidecadal correction in calendar years BP, rounded to the nearest decade, from Stuiver and Reimer (1993, version 3.0.3c, Method A). The maize dates are not corrected for C4 carbon uptake and can actually be up to 240 years older than reported here assuming −10 0/00. 2 This date and context is somewhat suspect, but was associated with a similar charcoal date at Los Pozos in the Tucson Basin (Freeman 1997, see also Gregory 1999). 3 This date on a *Cucurbita sp.* is probably from a wild species. However, three specimens of maize were dated to over 2800 RCY BP (Hard and Roney 1998, p. 1661).

photosynthesis and the food chain. Plants and animals which utilize carbon in biological food chains take up ^{14}C during their lifetimes. They exist in equilibrium with the ^{14}C concentration of the atmosphere; that is, the number of ^{14}C atoms and nonradioactive carbon atoms stays approximately the same over time. As soon as a plant or animal dies, they cease the metabolic function of carbon uptake; there is no replenishment of radioactive carbon, only decay.

Libby, Anderson, and Arnold (Taylor and Aitken 1997) first discovered that this decay occurs at a constant rate. They found that after 5,568 years half the ^{14}C in the original sample will have decayed, and that after another 5,568 years half of that remaining material will have decayed, and so on. The half-life ($t_{1/2}$) is the name given to this value, which Libby measured at 5568 ± 30 years. This became known as the Libby half-life. After 10 half-lives, there is a very

small amount of radioactive carbon present in a sample. At about 50,000 to 60,000 years, then, the limit of the technique is reached (beyond this time, other radiometric techniques must be used for dating, such as $^{40}Ar/^{39}Ar$, as discussed above). By measuring the ^{14}C concentration or residual radioactivity of a sample whose age is not known, it is possible to obtain the number of decay events per gram of carbon. By comparing this with modern levels of activity (1890 wood corrected for decay to AD 1950) and using the measured half-life, it becomes possible to calculate a date for the death of the sample.

It follows from this that any material which is composed of carbon may be dated. Herein lies the true advantage of the radiocarbon method—it is able to be uniformly applied throughout the world. A list of the tremendous quantity of organic material that can be dated by radiocarbon is available at the University of

Waikato's radiocarbon Web site, a standard for understanding the technique: http://c14.sci.waikato.ac.nz/webinfo/int.html.

4.1.2 Calibration and radiocarbon dating. As mentioned above, there are a number of effects that can cause errors in the measurement of radiocarbon dates. For example, shell, in constant contact with more recent atmospheric carbon, will generally yield young dates; conversely a shell artifact deposited in older limestone sediments will obtain a much older date than its actual death. These reservoir effects are in part mitigated by the use of various calibration algorithms, such as the CALIB (2001) and OxCal (2001) programs, both available on-line.

When a radiocarbon lab returns a date from a sample such as 5568 BP, it does not mean that it dates to 3619 BC, because the true half-life of radiocarbon is 5730 years, and, more importantly, the proportion of radiocarbon in the atmosphere has varied through time, as discussed above. So the calibration utilities are written to allow for differential in the absorption of ^{14}C by different materials (i.e., marine shell versus wood charcoal), and to allow for different atmospheric effects. Using the CALIB 4.2 calibration, a radiocarbon assay of 5568 BP with a 1 standard deviation of 55 years on wood charcoal yields a date of:

68.3 (1 Σ)cal 4454–4416 BC

probability distribution 0.409

4408–4354 BC 0.591

Note that there are two dates with ranges of a number of years. The range includes the one standard deviation, and the two dates are due to multiple intercepts on the calibration curve. We can be 68.3 percent certain that the dates fall either from 4454 to 4416 BC or from 4408 to 4354 BC. There are multiple possible dates because the radiocarbon date of 5568 BP intercepts the calibration curve at more than one point. Due to the perturbations in the absorption of radiocarbon over the millennia, the variance is sometimes full of 'wiggles' on the curve, so placement can occur at two or more points.

Radiocarbon dates are reported in a standardized method, as shown in Table 2. The convention calls for reporting the provenience of the sample, the laboratory number, the radiocarbon age, and then the calibrated (in this case dendrocalibrated) age at one or two standard deviations (note that most of these dates yielded multiple intercepts). The calibration method used and any further contextual information should also be supplied.

4.1.3 Accelerator mass spectrometry (AMS) and radiocarbon. From the inception of radiocarbon dating, ^{14}C ages of samples were calculated by decay counting in mainly scintillation counters. This requires a relatively large sample, depending on the amount of carbon remaining in that sample. By the late 1970s a number of researchers discovered that when accelerating sample atoms in the form of ions to much higher energies in particle accelerators, a much smaller sample was required to derive confident dates—in most cases only milligrams instead of tens of grams for scintillation counting. Both cyclotron and tandem accelerator mass spectrometers have been used to accomplish this, with tandem accelerators becoming the most popular. One additional advantage of acceleration is that the 'stripping process' disassociates all molecular species with the result that carbon isotopes can be isolated, and contamination minimized. AMS ^{14}C dating theoretically may push the time frame back to 100,000, effectively overlapping $^{40}Ar/^{39}Ar$ laser fusion dating (Taylor and Aitken 1997).

5. Radiation Dating Methods

As with most of the other types of dating methods, radiation dating methods have undergone tremendous advances in the last decade, although many of these methods remain somewhat controversial in their applications. Electron spin resonance (ESR) and thermoluminescence (both based on the accumulation of trapped electrons in minerals), and fission track dating (produced when alpha particles are created by spontaneous fission of ^{238}U leaving a damage trail), have all had their detractors, but have recently gained recognition as techniques that are useful in dating materials not readily possible with the more accepted technology, for example glass, tooth enamel, and pigments (see Table 1). Archaeomagnetic dating has gained wide acceptance in many regions of the world and deserves some discussion.

5.1 Archaeomagnetic Dating

Archaeomagnetic and paleomagnetic dating both rely on the phenomenon of the frequent and predictable shifts in the Earth's magnetic polarity in space and time. The premise for the method states that the Earth's magnetic poles wander (show secular variation) or flip (reverse direction), and that these variations provide a temporal fingerprint that can be detected in rock and sediments. Iron dipoles in minerals in soft sediments align themselves parallel with the Earth's magnetic field at the time of deposition until the sediment solidifies, for example as baked clay in a hearth. This creates detrital remnant magnetism whose direction and intensity precisely reflects the Earth's magnetic field at the time of deposition; and by matching their magnetic orientation to a master record, it is possible to derive a relatively accurate date. This master curve has been derived for the last 10,000 years. Archaeomagnetism is useful in dating material, as appropriate, when other useful dating material, appropriate for other techniques is absent.

6. Chemical, Temperature, and Water Affected Dating Methods

Some of the more controversial dating methods are those that are based upon changes in chemicals, temperature, and/or water for calibration. Amino acid racemization held great promise for dating organic materials, but is not generally reliable, while obsidian hydration dating, which was also promising, has become equally problematic.

6.1 Obsidian Hydration Dating

Obsidian, a quenched rhyolite glass is common along plate boundaries and volcanic arcs where crustal remelting has occurred. A glassy brittle rock with remarkable cutting properties, it has been used throughout human history in the production of stone tools (Shackley 1998). Obsidian is a noncrystalline glass, and therefore a disordered substance, and moves toward an ordered state by crystallization or, more precisely, perlitization (Friedman et al. 1997, Stevenson et al. 1998). This is accomplished by the absorption of water and a breaking of silicon and aluminum bonds, ultimately devitrifying the glass and forming perlite. As the process proceeds, an absorption front and hydration rim forms that theoretically occurs at a regular, linear rate through time. Measuring this rim with a petrographic microscope in microns theoretically yields an absolute date. On the surface, this would seem to be a remarkable method, resolving a number of dating issues in archaeological contexts in which organic datable material does not occur, but obsidian artifacts are abundant. More recently, the intervening negative effects of variable temperature and humidity through time have been found to influence the rate at which glass will hydrate. Due to this a number of researchers have rejected the method *in toto* (see Morgenstein et al. 1999, Ridding 1996). Still, a number of researchers have continued to utilize the method, and it has a number of devoted followers, even in the face of discrepancies between radiocarbon dates and obsidian hydration dates in the same stratigraphic position. Stevenson, and others have attempted to derive intrinsic hydration models based on the premise that each single obsidian nodule contains a different proportion of water than any other, and this will produce ages compatible with other dating methods (see Stevenson et al. 1998). Most do agree that obsidian hydration is a useful relative dating method which can be used to determine the extent of mixing in a stratigraphic column; given the model, one expects to see larger rim measurements at the bottom of a site than at the top. If this is not the case, then stratigraphic mixing is indicated. Obsidian hydration holds great promise, but most archaeologists are hesitant to include it in the arsenal of absolute dating methods.

See also: Geoarchaeology

Bibliography

CALIB Radiocarbon Calibration Software (2001) http://depts. washington.edu/qil/calib/
Carver M O H 1990 Digging for data: Archaeological approaches to data definition, acquisition and analysis. In: Francovich R, Manacorda D (eds.) *Lo scavo archaeologica: della diagnosi all'edizione*. Edizioni all'Insegna del Giglio, Firenze, Italy, pp. 45–120
Colcutt S N 1987 Archaeostratigraphy: A geoarchaeologist's viewpoint. *Stratigraphica Archaeologica* **2**: 11–18
Dean J S 1997 Dendrochronology. In: Taylor R E, Aitken M J (eds.) *Chronometric Dating in Archaeology*. Kluwer/Plenum Publishers, New York, pp. 31–64
Farrand W R 1984 Stratigraphic classification: Living within the law. *Quarterly Review of Archaeology* **5**: 1–5
Freeman A K L 1997 Middle to Late Holocene stream dynamics of the Santa Cruz River, Tucson, Arizona: Implications for human settlement, the transition to agriculture and archaeological site preservation. Ph.D. thesis, University of Arizona, Tucson, AZ
Friedman I, Trembour F W, Hughes R E 1997 Obsidian hydration dating. In: Taylor R E, Aitken M J (eds.) *Chronometric Dating in Archaeology*. Kluwer/Plenum Publishers, New York, pp. 297–322
Göksu H Y, Oberhofer M, Regulla D 1991 *Scientific Dating Methods*. Kluwer Academic Publishers, Dordrecht, The Netherlands
Gregory D A, Adams J L (eds.) 1999 *Excavations in the Santa Cruz River Floodplain: The Middle Archaic Component at Los Pozos*. Center for Desert Archaeology, Tucson, AZ
Hard R J, Roney J R 1998 A massive terraced village complex in Chihuahua, Mexico, 3000 years before present. *Science* **279**: 1661–4
Harris E C, Brown M R III, Brown G J (eds.) 1993 *Practices of Archaeological Stratigraphy*. Academic Press, London
Herz N, Garrison E G 1998 *Geological Methods for Archaeology*. Oxford University Press, Oxford, UK
Morgenstein M E, Wicket C L, Barkatt A 1999 Considerations of hydration-rind dating of glass artefacts: Alteration morphologies and experimental evidence of hydrogeochemical soil-zone pore water content. *Journal of Archaeological Science* **26**: 1193–210
OxCal Radiocarbon Calibration Software (2001) http://units. ox.ac.uk/departments/rlaha/orau/06_frm.htm
Rapp G Jr., Hill C L 1998 *Geoarchaeology: The Earth Science Approach to Archaeological Interpretation*. Yale University Press, New Haven, CT
Ridding R 1996 Where in world does obsidian hydration work? *American Antiquity* **61**: 136–48
Shackley M S (ed.) 1998 *Archaeological Obsidian Studies: Method and Theory*. Kluwer Academic/Plenum Publishing, New York
Shackley M S, Huckell B B, Huckell L W 2000 Late Preceramic farmer/foragers at the foot of the Mogollon Rim: The McEuen Cave Archaeological Project Testing Report (AZ

W:13:6 ASM). Report prepared for the Bureau of Land Management, Safford Area, AZ, US Department of Interior

Stein J K 1987 Deposits for archaeologists. *Advances in Archaeological Method and Theory* **11**: 337–95

Stevenson C M, Mazer J J, Scheetz B E 1998 Laboratory obsidian hydration rates: Theory, method, and application. In: Shackley M S (ed.) *Archaeological Obsidian Studies: Method and Theory*. Kluwer Academic/Plenum Press, New York, pp. 181–204

Stuiver M, Reimer P J 1993 Extended ¹⁴C data base and revised CALIB 3.0 ¹¹C age calibration program. *Radiocarbon* **35**: 215–30

Taylor R E 2000 Science-based dating methods in historic preservation. In: Williamson R A, Nickens P R (eds.) *Science and Technology in Historic Preservation*. Kluwer Academic/Plenum Press Publishers, New York, pp. 75–96

Taylor R E, Aitken M J (eds.) 1997 *Chronometric Dating in Archaeology*. Kluwer Academic/Plenum Publishers, New York

Trigger B G 1989 *A History of Archaeological Thought*. Cambridge University Press, Cambridge, UK

US Congress, Office of Technology Assessment 1986 *Technologies for Prehistoric and Historic Preservation*, OTA-E-319. US Government Printing Office, Washington, DC

Waters M R 1992 *Principles of Geoarchaeology: A North American Perspective*. University of Arizona Press, Tucson, AZ

S. Shackley

Church and State: Political Science Aspects

The umbrella term Church and State is conventionally used to refer to a range of topics within political science which concern the relationships between religious organizations, institutions, and authorities on the one hand and the polity on the other. Across the world religion has from the earliest times been centrally concerned with the shaping and authoritative allocation of values with which political science in its broadest signification is concerned. In the West churches in their proper sense represent only one type of religious collectivity—albeit historically the most important—whose relationship with the state has been the subject of intense and prolonged controversy; sects, denominations, and cults, each with their distinctive characteristics and drives, have also given rise in their orientation to political authorities, and vice versa, to difficult issues of recognition, regulation, and control. Within the other world religions the term church has no analogue, although the Buddhist *sangha* is often thought to share some features. In the other monotheistic religions, such as Islam and Judaism, and in Hinduism the location of religious authority and the degree of its independence from political authority suggest quite different patterns from those typical of church–state relations in the West. The establishment since 1948 through various international charters and conventions on human rights of foundational claims to religious freedom presents the challenge of institutionalizing ostensibly universal claims in this field within culturally diverse contexts.

1. Church and State in the Perspective of Political Development

In the developmentalist, or modernization, perspective traditional religiopolitical systems were typically understood to combine religious and political functions within a single structure of authority. In certain, particularly oriental, cultures this took the form of institutions of divine kingship or theocratic rule, while in Christian cultures, where the church was from early on conceived as a distinct institution, rulers usually claimed and often successfully asserted over against the church some species of sacral authority. From the time of Constantine, the emergent system of church establishment shifted from epoch to epoch between imperial authority over the church and Papal or Patriarchal authority over the emperors and other temporal authorities, a tension which was only partially resolved into contrasting patterns prevalent in different parts of the Christian world at the times of the East–West Schism in the eleventh century and the Reformation/Counter-Reformation in the sixteenth. In the high Middle Ages the Popes attempted to assert theocratic authority over the kings, princes, and emperors of Western Europe, while in the Orthodox East the Caesaropapist pattern of harmony between a dominant emperor and a subservient patriarch predominated. After the Reformation the authority of secular princes vis-à-vis the church was promoted both in the Protestant north and in the Roman Catholic south as the contest was prosecuted by and between the sponsors of the respective confessions.

Within Islam the institutional differentiation between religious and secular authority did not develop as Medina under Muhammad was considered to provide an unimprovable model for the life of the community of believers. The Prophet himself recognized the sovereignty of God alone; accordingly, it has not been open to his successors (the caliphs) or, more recently, the people and their representatives to claim sovereign authority in their own right. Within this restrictive view it has been the duty of all who exercise authority on behalf of the community faithfully to implement the rules encapsulated in the *Qur'an* and the traditions of the Prophet as interpreted by legal scholars, the jurisconsults. Similarly, within Judaism, the authority of divine law, as interpreted by rabbinical scholars, was held to be supreme within the *diaspora*. The recent reassertion of theocratic claims such as these has helped to undermine the plausibility of the developmentalist perspective with its implication of a unilinear secularization process.

2. Religion and the Rise of the Modern State in the West

The rise of the modern state with its characteristic claim to exclusive authority within a particular territory can be seen as part cause, part consequence of the Renaissance and Reformation crises in Western Europe which divided it between a Protestant north and a Roman Catholic south. It was the religious wars of the sixteenth and seventeenth centuries, brought to an end by the Peace of Westphalia of 1648, which institutionalized, over the protests of the Pope, the right of sovereign authorities to decide *inter alia* on the religious constitution of their territories. In northern Europe, typically, Protestant national monarchies reinforced their developing authority (and their resource base) by taking the church over and introducing more or less Erastian (i.e., unilateral secular) patterns of control; in the south the typical pattern which resulted was an alliance between royal absolutism and national Catholic hierarchies until the French Revolution led to a similar assault on the church's property and independent authority. The subsequent decline of dynastic rule throughout Europe in the nineteenth century and the emergence of nationalist and liberal democratic mass politics saw a further weakening of church authority north and south, east and west. Institutional secularization was furthermore accompanied by a decline in levels of orthodox religious belief and practice as urbanization and industrialization transformed social and economic structures, although revivalism of various sorts meant that the trend was not unilinear. In the USA the first amendment to the Constitution introduced for the first time a relatively thoroughgoing separation of church and state, which barred Congress from making any law 'respecting an establishment of religion or prohibiting the free exercise thereof.' A feature of the pattern which emerged in this context has been that, far from following the general secularising trend seen in Europe' a 'churching of America' occurred as the proportion of members and attenders in the population tended to increase. Few other political systems, even among the liberal democracies, have, however, followed the example of constitutionally mandated disestablishment and even where they have, as for example in the case of France in 1905, the principle of separation has not been upheld with the judicial rigor characteristic of the American case in recent decades.

3. Religious Cleavages and the Development of Party Systems

With the development of mass electoral politics in the nineteenth century the emergent party systems tended to reflect divergent systems of religious—in addition to social, economic, and other—cleavages; indeed, the relative prominence of religious or religion-related cleavages during the formative period up to the 1920s accounts for the survival, by inertia, of patterns of confessional politics which otherwise might well have disappeared. In northern Europe the existence of state–church systems had led over time to the emergence of movements of religious protest and dissent, which typically aligned themselves with other reforming elements in left or liberal movements. In the Counter-Reformation south on the other hand, where religious dissent had been more or less successfully repressed by the historic alliance of throne and altar, reforming and revolutionary movements tended to be militantly secularist, with the effect that the connection between religion and the political right was consolidated. A third pattern developed in the band of mixed-religion territories, which spanned Europe from Ireland to Transylvania, where the liberalization of political systems, when it occurred, ushered in patterns of confessional politics which, in nonmajoritarian settings, took the form of consociationalism.

Beyond Europe, developing party systems tended only marginally or incidentally to be affected by religious cleavages as such; religious connections were usually outgrowths of ethnic or community identities, whether on the part of immigrant populations as in the USA, South Africa, or Australia, or on the part of anticolonial movements committed to seizing independence on behalf of indigenous populations. In the latter case independence movements varied in terms of the religious structure of the populations affected, with the formerly united Indian subcontinent divided between Hindu, Islamic, and (in the case of Sri Lanka) Buddhist leaderships heading up parties which, on independence, became dominant in their respective systems. In more recent decades the often secular leaderships of the movements which successfully claimed independence have been challenged by movements of religious insurgency, driven in part by disappointment with the fruits of independence. Some authors have even identified in these developments a global revival of the influence of religion in politics.

4. The Political Resurgence of the Religious Factor

The late twentieth century has certainly seen a recrudescence of the religious factor in politics which would have surprised (and dismayed) the more naive modernization theorists. In 1979–80 the religious-led Iranian revolution, the prominence in the United States Presidential election of an emergent new Christian right, the overthrow of Nicaraguan dictator Somoza, and the emergence after the visit of Pope John Paul II to his home country Poland of the church-supported Solidarity, indicated that the phenomenon was not restricted to any one corner of the world. Each case could be seen as involving reactions to what were regarded by the 'fundamentalist' militants and activists involved as trends toward secularization or obstacles of entrenched corruption. Prominent among the issues involved were respect for religious authority, the maintenance of religion-related rules governing morality in all its guises (including in the West abortion, pornography, and contraception), and the re-introduction as normative for the political community of core religious values whether Christian, Islamic, Judaic, Buddhist, or Hindu. The liberal rule that the state should be neutral as between different religions and between the religious and nonreligious was most often regarded as either illusory or misguided: illusory, because the all-embracing nature of religious belief- and value-systems left no neutral space to be legitimately marked out, or misguided, because political authority in particular ought not to be exempted from the authoritative purview of religious values.

5. The Contemporary Challenge to State Religious Neutrality

In few, if any, cases has the ideal of state religious neutrality been realized, as the concept itself has progressively become problematized by significant voices claiming that the term has often been made to cover for the artificial and prejudicial exclusion from public debate of religious claims. Until the 1950s in the USA 'mainline' Protestant religion remained as a sort of informal establishment, recognized, albeit without the confessional label, in certain Supreme Court judgments, but since the early 1960s the separation rule has been applied to exclude religious symbol and activities from public institutions such as schools. In a number of cases of continuing church establishment, evenhandedness has been approached by the extension of the list of recognized religions and other 'communities of belief' (as in Belgium, where the state pays the salaries and pensions of religious officials of six recognized confessions) or the effective diminution of the privileges of establishment (as in the UK). Since the end of the Cold War official hostility to religion as such (amounting in the case of Albania to the attempted suppression of religion for over 20 years after 1967) has greatly diminished, although it has not disappeared; thus, China and North Korea, for example, continue to exercise heavy-handed control of religious bodies and activities. Within the world of Islam meantime there has been a significant growth in the number of states, which are either organized as theocratic regimes dedicated to the implementation under clerical leadership of religious law, the *shari'a* (e.g. Iran and Sudan), or which harbor important movements that aim to introduce such a regime (e.g. Pakistan and Algeria).

In the West in particular, the increasing religious diversity of populations occasioned by the emergence of new religious movements, both independently and within existing traditions, and the growth of immigrant communities with distinct confessional profiles has given rise in recent decades to a range of new problems, or the re-emergence of old ones. Thus in connection with Scientology and Transcendental Meditation, questions of recognition have arisen in several countries: are they to be regarded as religions and so accorded attendant tax or other advantages, or not? More established religious traditions, in particular Islam, have called for their values to receive the protection of the law, so that what is judged to be blasphemy should be punishable through the civil courts. In the field of education, historically one of the most contentious in church–state relations, several issues continue to present themselves: should independent schools provided for the education of children of particular religious communities receive recognition, tax advantages, or direct state aid? What provision, if any, should public schools make for collective worship or religious instruction and how should any such arrangements take account of the new religious pluralism? Should public schools allow the display of distinctive religious symbols either on the walls, as in the case of crucifixes, traditional in Catholic communities, or on the pupils themselves, as in the case of Islamic girls' headscarves? Many of these issues continue to agitate public debate episodically but none so much as the traditionally religion-related issues, such as abortion, where religious conservatives of the most varied religious persuasion continue to prosecute a bitter struggle against what is typically seen as an outgrowth of secular humanism.

See also: Civil Religion; Political Culture; Political Sociology; Reformation and Confessionalization; Religion and Politics: United States; Religion, History of; Religion: Mobilization and Power; Religion: Nationalism and Identity; Religion: Peace, War, and Violence; Religious Nationalism and the Secular State: Cultural Concerns

Bibliography

Boyle K, Sheen J (eds.) 1997 *Freedom of Religion and Belief. A World Report.* Routledge, London

Monsma S V, Soper J C 1997 *The Challenge of Pluralism. Church and State in Five Democracies.* Rowman Littlefield, Lanhom, MD

Robbers G (ed.) 1996 *State and Church in the European Union.* Nomos

Robbins T, Robertson R (eds.) 1987 *Church–State Relations: Tensions and Transitions.* Transaction Books, New Brunswick, NJ

Weber P 1990 *Understanding the First Amendment Religion Clauses.* Greenwood Press

Witte J 1999 *Church and State: The American Constitutional Experiment.* Westview Press, Greenwood, CT

J. T. S. Madeley

Cingulate Cortex

Cingulate Cortex

The cingulate cortex is located in the medial wall of the cerebral hemispheres and has extensive reciprocal connections with various limbic structures as well as motor and premotor areas. In studies with rodents and studies of brain activation in humans, the cingulate cortex is implicated in the processes of selective attention and response selection. This article explores the essential areas of convergence of the two bodies of literature, and offers a common mnemonic/associative interpretation of cingulate cortical function.

1. Anatomy of the Cingulate Cortex

The cingulate cortex is a part of the limbic cortex, a term referring to the cortical areas that receive axonal fibers from neurons in the anterior group of thalamic nuclei. By modern convention, cingulate cortex constitutes Brodman's areas 24 and 29 in small animals such as rabbits and rats, and also an additional area, 23, in primates and humans. Brodman's areas 24 and 29 are often referred to, respectively, as anterior and posterior cingulate cortex. A cytoarchitectural map illustrating these areas is shown in Fig. 1.

Both the anterior and posterior cingulate cortices receive afferent fibers from the anterior medial (AM), midline, and intralaminar thalamic nuclei. However, the anterior cingulate cortex is also innervated by the medial dorsal (MD) and parafasicular thalamic nuclei, while the posterior cingulate cortex receives projections from the remaining members of the anterior group of thalamic nuclei: the anterior ventral (AV), anterior dorsal (AD), and lateral dorsal (LD) thalamic nuclei. In addition, neurons of the lateral dorsal and ventral anterior thalamic nuclei project to the posterior cingulate cortex.

Cingulate cortical neurons are richly innervated by pontine and midbrain fibers that fairly uniformly distribute norepinephrine and serotonin but restrictively distribute dopamine to the anterior cingulate cortex. Many additional afferent systems project to the cingulate cortex, including fibers from the visual cortex, hippocampus, subiculum, entorhinal cortex, and amygdala.

Cingulate cortical neurons send efferent fibers to most of the aforementioned thalamic areas, the subiculum, entorhinal cortex, pons, and many areas of the striatal motor system including the caudate nucleus, nucleus accumbens, and zona incerta. Cingulate cortical neurons have also been found to project to multiple areas of the motor and premotor cortex, suggesting that numerous parallel pathways exist whereby cingulate neurons can modulate motor output systems of the brain. In primates there exist direct reciprocal projections of cingulate neurons to lateral

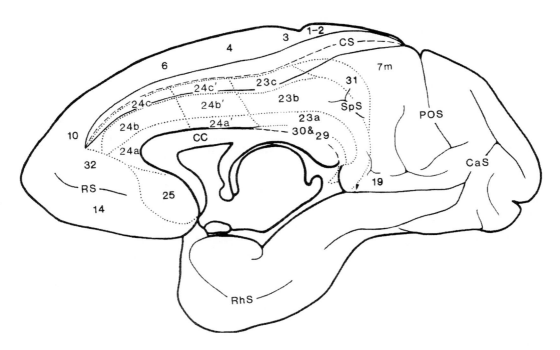

Figure 1
Cytoarchitectural map of the limbic cortex in the rhesus monkey based on Brodman's divisions

prefrontal and parietal cortex, areas believed to be critical for higher-order perceptual and mnemonic functions (Goldman-Rakic 1988).

2. The Role of the Cingulate Cortex in Attention

2.1 Associative Attention: Cingulate Cortical Neuronal Activity

Research in behavioral neuroscience with rabbits and rats indicates that the cingulate cortex mediates selective attention, or attention focused on particular stimuli. The stimuli that are selectively processed by cingulate cortical neurons are associatively significant stimuli, i.e., stimuli that signal important events such as reward or aversion, and call for action on the part of the subject. Since the selective processing of the significant stimuli is a learned, associative process, an apt characterization of the cingulate cortex is that it mediates associative attention to significant stimuli.

Support for the hypothesis that the cingulate cortex mediates associative attention to significant stimuli is shown by results of numerous studies on the activity of cingulate cortical neurons during Pavlovian and instrumental conditioning in animals. For example, extensive research has documented the responses of cingulate cortical neurons during discriminative instrumental learning in rabbits (Gabriel 1993, 2001). In these studies, rabbits occupying a large rotating wheel apparatus learned to step in response to a tone cue (CS +) to prevent a foot-shock delivered five seconds later, and they learned to ignore a different tone (CS −) not followed by shock. Neuronal activity in multiple areas of the cingulate cortex exhibited the development, during training, of massive discriminative neuronal activity, defined as significantly greater firing frequencies in response to the CS + than to the CS − (see Fig. 2). Discriminative activity also developed during acquisition of a discriminative approach response, in which rabbits learned to make oral contact with a drinking spout to obtain a water reward following the CS + and to inhibit contact following the CS −, which did not predict a water reward (Freeman et al. 1996).

Discriminative neuronal activity in the cingulate cortex has also been reported during classical Pavlovian conditioning of heart rate and eyeblink responses in rabbits (Powell et al. 1990). In addition, studies in rats have demonstrated the occurrence of neuronal responses in the anterior and posterior cingulate cortex that are specific to stimuli that predict reinforcement during appetitive conditioning (Segal and Olds 1972, Takenouchi et al. 1999). The activity of cingulate cortical neurons in all these studies may be viewed as a neuronal code for the associative significance of cues since the neurons developed selective responses to stimuli that predicted the occurrence of significant events.

Cingulate cortical neurons have also been shown to exhibit salience compensation, a phenomenon that is supportive of a cingulate cortical involvement in mediating associative attention (Gabriel 1993, Gabriel and Taylor 1998). When rabbits are trained with nonsalient cues such as a brief duration (200 ms) CS + and CS −, greater brief-latency cingulate cortical discriminative neuronal responses are observed than when training is carried out with more enduring (e.g., 500 ms) CSs. The enhanced neuronal encoding of the brief stimuli, or salience compensation, has been interpreted as an attentional process that amplifies the neural representation of nonsalient yet associatively significant stimuli in order to maximize the resources available for processing those cues.

The importance of the attentional processing in the cingulate cortex is demonstrated by studies showing that bilateral, combined lesions of the anterior and posterior cingulate cortices severely impair discriminative avoidance and approach learning in rabbits (Gabriel 1993). In addition, adult rabbits exposed to cocaine *in utero*, an exposure which induced morphological and biochemical abnormalities in the anterior cingulate cortex, exhibited attenuated anterior cingulate discriminative neuronal activity and learning deficits when nonsalient CSs were used during discriminative avoidance learning and Pavlovian conditioning of eyeblink responses (Gabriel and Taylor 1998, Romano and Harvey 1998). The results of these studies illustrate that deficits due to cingulate cortical damage emerge when a high demand is placed on attentional processing.

2.2 Executive Attention: Anterior Cingulate Cortex

The application of neuroimaging and electrical recording techniques, such as positron emission tomography (PET), functional magnetic resonance imaging (fMRI), and high-density electroencephalography (EEG), has led to a large volume of data that implicate the cingulate cortex in cognitive processing. In convergence with results from animal studies, many cognitive experiments in humans have supported the idea that the anterior cingulate cortex is involved in processes subserving attention. These studies show that the anterior cingulate cortex is engaged during tasks in which routine or automatic processing is insufficient, as when novel or conflict-laden situations are encountered. This type of attentional processing has been termed *executive attention* (Posner and DiGirolamo 1998). Situations likely to require executive attention are: a) planning and decision making; b) error detection; c) novel and early stages of learning; d) difficult and threatening situations; and e) overcoming habitual behavior.

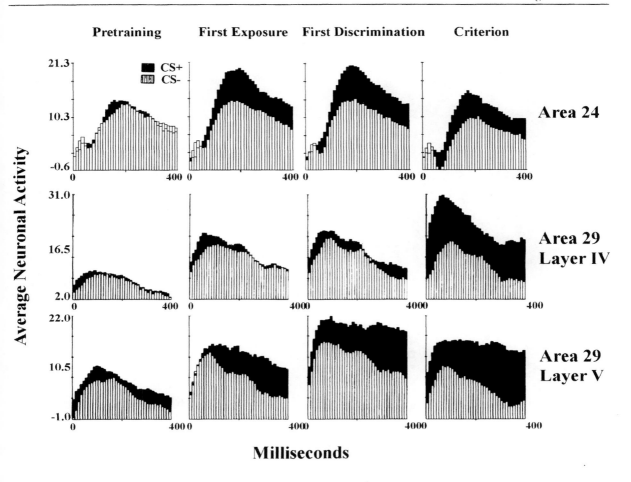

Figure 2
Average anterior (Area 24) and posterior (Area 29, cellular layers IV & V) cingulate cortical integrated unit activity elicited by CS + and CS − in rabbits during pretraining, first exposure session, first significant behavioral discrimination, and criterial behavioral discrimination in a discriminative avoidance task. The neuronal activity for Area 24 is plotted in the form of standard scores normalized with respect to the pre-CS baseline for 40 consecutive intervals following CS onset. Area 29 data are plotted starting 100 ms after tone onset

The role of the anterior cingulate cortex in executive attention is supported by numerous imaging studies that have shown activation in the anterior cingulate cortex during tasks that engender conflict (Posner and DiGirolamo 1998). An example would be a task that requires the selection of a particular response from multiple competing responses. Most of these studies employ a subtraction technique whereby the brain activation found in a neutral or control condition is subtracted from the activation produced by an experimental condition. For example, activation has been found in the anterior cingulate cortex during the generate-uses task, which requires subjects to state uses commonly associated with visually or acoustically presented words (e.g., generating the response 'drive'

to the stimulus word 'car'). The subtracted control condition for this task involves merely reading and pronouncing the words. It is argued that executive attention (and thus anterior cingulate cortical activation) is brought into play as a result of the conflict created by the multiple uses that are potentially relevant to a given stimulus. The activation in the anterior cingulate cortex in this task declines as the subjects are repeatedly exposed to the same words and the generation of uses becomes more routine and less dependent on executive control.

Additional evidence for the contribution of the anterior cingulate cortex to executive attention comes from the results of multiple experiments using the Stroop task, a task that requires subjects to name the

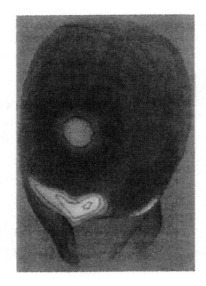

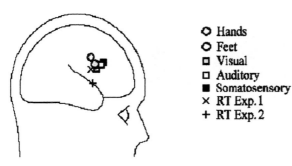

○ Hands
○ Feet
□ Visual
□ Auditory
■ Somatosensory
× RT Exp. 1
+ RT Exp. 2

Figure 3
A 3-D and sagittal view of the human brain illustrating
the source of error-related negativity (ERN) found
after brain electric source analysis (BESA) of event-
related brain potentials. The bottom/right figure
summarizes the results of several ERN studies that
have demonstrated that the source of the ERN is not
affected by response modality (subjects responding with
their feet or hands) or error feedback modality (visual,
auditory, somatosensory). Also shown is the ERN
source for two reaction time experiments, one involving
a decision of whether a number was 'smaller
than/larger than' (RT Exp.1) and another involving a
classification of words into semantic categories (RT
Exp. 2)

ink color of visually presented words in a congruent
condition (e.g., the word 'red' printed in red ink), an
incongruent condition (e.g., the word 'green' printed
in red ink), or a neutral condition (e.g., the word 'door'
printed in red ink) (Posner and DiGirolamo 1998).
The anterior cingulate cortex has been found active in
both the incongruent and congruent conditions when
compared to the neutral condition. It has been
suggested that both the congruent and the incongruent
conditions involve conflict because subjects must
respond to the ink color while inhibiting a response to
the word's meaning. Some studies have found more
activation in the incongruent condition than in the
congruent condition, in line with the expectation that
the incongruent condition creates more conflict and
thus recruits more executive attention in the anterior
cingulate cortex.

Studies employing high-density scalp recordings of
EEG have pointed to an involvement of the anterior
cingulate cortex in error detection, another aspect of
executive attention (Dahaene et al. 1994, Holroyd et
al. 1998, Gehring et al. 1993). These experiments have
demonstrated a marked electrical negativity at mid
frontal regions of the scalp. The negativity peaks
about 100 milliseconds after subjects make an incorrect response, such as an erroneous key press in a
reaction time task. Brain electrical source analyses
(BESA) carried out independently by separate investigators consistently localize the error-related negativity
(ERN) to the anterior cingulate cortex. These results
support the role of the anterior cingulate cortex in
executive attention invoked during error-related processing (see Fig. 3).

3. Movement-related Processing: Response Selection by the Cingulate Cortex

Considering the ample connections of the cingulate
cortex with motor and premotor cortex as well as
areas of the striatal motor system, it is not surprising
that the cingulate cortex has been linked to processes
such as response selection. Several studies have
documented the existence of a topographic organization of the cingulate cortex with respect to particular response modalities. For example, different
areas of the anterior cingulate cortex are active
depending on whether subjects perform in tasks
involving oculomotor, manual, or spoken responses
(Paus et al. 1993).

A case study of patient D.L., who sustained a
circumscribed right hemisphere lesion of the anterior
cingulate cortex after surgery to remove a tumor, adds
further support for cingulate cortical involvement in
movement-related processing (Turken and Swick
1999). Interestingly, D.L. exhibited entirely normal
performance in Stroop-like and divided attention tasks
when responses were orally reported; however, D.L.
showed a dramatic deficit in the same tasks when
manual responses were required. These results were
interpreted as favoring the idea that command signals
are sent to motor output areas through the anterior
cingulate cortex. The authors characterize the role of
the anterior cingulate cortex as confirming the appropriateness of the selected response, thus to facilitate

correct responding while suppressing incorrect responding.

Premotor neuronal activity in cingulate cortex has been demonstrated in several studies of the single-unit correlates of learning and performance. In one such study, approximately half of all single neurons in anterior and posterior cingulate cortex in rabbits exhibited premotor firing ramps that consisted of progressive increases in firing frequency preceding the onset of the behavioral (locomotory) avoidance responses (Kubota et al. 1996). Also, neuronal firing in ventral portions of the anterior cingulate cortex was correlated with the onset of licking behavior during appetititve conditioning of rats (Takenouchi et al. 1999). Thus, cingulate cortical neurons become active preceding the initiation of learned motor responses.

The involvement of the anterior cingulate cortex in response selection does not negate the role of the cingulate cortex in associative and executive attention. Appropriate response selection for a given situation can only occur if attention is devoted to the significant associative stimuli and if conflict among competing motor responses is resolved.

4. Emotion and the Affective Dimension of Pain

Traditionally, the cingulate cortex has been viewed as part of a brain circuit that is involved in the experience and expression of emotion (Papez 1937, Maclean 1975). Although more recent evidence has suggested an important role for the cingulate cortex in processes such as attention and response selection, the role of the cingulate cortex in emotion remains unchallenged.

Activations of the anterior cingulate cortex, in particular, have been found to accompany the experience of emotion in numerous neuroimaging studies. For example, when cerebral blood flow (CBF) was measured using PET while subjects viewed emotional film clips and recalled emotional situations, the anterior cingulate cortex was the only structure to exhibit CBF changes correlated with subjects' scores on the Levels of Emotional Awareness Scale (LEAS), a test that measures the capacity to perceive and differentiate complex emotions in oneself and others (Lane et al. 1998). The results suggested that individual differences in emotional awareness could be related to the degree of activation in the anterior cingulate cortex.

Evidence has also been presented in support of a role for the anterior cingulate cortex in mediating the emotional response to pain in humans (Price 2000). Pain is thought to involve two components, a sensory component and an affective component. The affective component reflects the unpleasantness associated with pain and its long-term consequences. The anterior cingulate cortex receives direct input from spinal pain pathways and other input from areas (e.g., the prefrontal cortex) that are involved in cognitive aspects of pain processing, such as evaluating the immediate threat of the pain and its potential interference with daily activities. The anterior cingulate cortex is thus positioned to integrate these two types of pain-related information in order to select appropriate coping responses such as escape or avoidance.

5. Learning and Memory

5.1 Distinct Roles of the Anterior and Posterior Cingulate Cortex

Compelling evidence suggests an important role for the cingulate cortex in the mediation of learning and memory processes. Available data indicate that the contributions of the anterior and posterior cingulate cortices are functionally distinct. A contribution of the anterior and posterior cingulate cortices to early and late stages of learning, respectively, has been documented in discriminative avoidance learning in rabbits as well as in conditioned visual discrimination in rats (Gabriel 1993, Bussey et al. 1997). In rabbits, discriminative neuronal activity (see Sect. 2.1) in the anterior cingulate cortex develops after fewer training trials than in the posterior cingulate cortex. The observations of neuronal activity coincide nicely with restricted lesion studies showing that lesions confined to the anterior cingulate cortex result in a deficit of behavioral performance in the early stages of learning, whereas lesions confined to the posterior cingulate cortex result in a loss of performance at later stages of learning.

5.2 Context-specific Retrieval Patterns and Spatial Processing: Posterior Cingulate Cortex and the Anterior Thalamus

Although the evidence clearly indicates an involvement of the cingulate cortex in the learning-based coding of associatively significant stimuli, further evidence indicates that this coding subserves the retrieval of learned, context-appropriate responses. Evidence in support of this idea is shown by the existence of unique topographical distributions of CS+-related neuronal activity in different cell layers of the posterior cingulate cortex and in various anterior thalamic nuclei in rabbits, during discriminative instrumental learning. Some layers are activated maximally by the CS+ in the initial stages of training, others in intermediate training stages, and others as the rabbits attain asymptotic discriminative performance. The distribution of the activations changed not only across time (the stage in training) but also with respect to the spatial context. For instance, the same set of cues elicited different patterns of activation depending on whether the rabbits were engaged in a moderately learned discriminative avoidance task or (in a separate training apparatus) a well-learned discriminative approach task. These context-specific patterns of CS + -elicited activity could be associated with the learned responses that are appropriate to a given situation or context. Thus, when a given context specific pattern is elicited on cue presentation, the learned response is retrieved. This mechanism could subserve pattern separation, i.e., the ability to defeat proactive and retroactive interference when multiple similar cues are associated with different memories or responses, as when one tries to recall the names of several recently met individuals. The retrieval hypothesis is consistent with the finding that the brief-latency cue-elicited context-specific patterns in the posterior cingulate cortex are followed by premotor firing, i.e., firing which precedes the onset of the learned behavioral response (see Sect. 2.3).

Additional evidence suggests that the context-specific patterns in the posterior cingulate cortex depend on the integrity of hippocampal connections, which may supply information concerning the operative spatial context to the cingulate cortex. Fornix lesions which disconnect the hippocampal formation from the anterior thalamus disrupt the training-stage-related patterns in the posterior cingulate cortex and these lesions impair concurrent performance in two different discriminative learning tasks that employ very similar cues (Smith et al. 2000).

Posterior cingulate cortical neurons also have functional properties that are similar to those found in neurons of the hippocampus and parietal cortex during spatial processing. For instance, rodent hippocampal neurons are selectively active when subjects occupy a particular location in space, while other neurons code information about directional heading, independently of spatial location or ongoing behavior. Direction-coding neurons have also been documented in the posterior cingulate cortex and related thalamic nuclei, and these neurons, together with those of the hippocampal formation, are thought to contribute to the sense of direction and place in spatial learning situations. Interestingly, in primates, hippocampal neurons are selectively active when the subject is viewing (rather than occupying) a particular space in the environment. The posterior cingulate cortex of primates contains neurons that discharge with eye movement and eye position, a tuning property also found among neurons in the frontal and parietal cortical areas (Olson et al. 1996). The eye direction-coding neurons in primate cingulate cortex are hypothesized to participate in the spatial interpretation of retinal images.

6. Concluding Comment

Studies carried out by behavioral neuroscientists using rats and rabbits as subjects have shown that the cingulate cortex is a critical substrate of learned

responses to predictive stimuli. Cingulate cortical neurons in these animals code associatively significant stimuli and exhibit context-specific topographic patterns that could mediate cued retrieval of context-appropriate learned behavior. These functions occur as a result of intimate interactions of the hippocampal and cingulothalamic brain regions. Studies of cognitive neuroscientists concerning brain activation during cognitive task performance in human subjects have yielded results that are fundamentally in agreement with the studies with rats and rabbits. For example, there is clear agreement that the anterior cingulate cortex subserves an attentional role as its neurons are recruited in situations of high cognitive conflict, e.g., when stimuli acquire new meanings at the outset of learning, or when a decision among multiple-response alternatives must be reached. The involvement in behavioral learning and the associative and memory-bearing characteristics of cingulate cortical neuronal activity have also led behavioral neuroscientists to speak of cingulate cortical attention as associative in character, i.e., a learned form of attention. Cognitive neuroscientists have, on the other hand, discussed the cingulate cortex as involved in attentional processes without reference to memory. Given the findings of behavioral neuroscience and the very close neuro-anatomical association of the cingulate cortex with other structures (e.g., the hippocampus) that are acknowledged components of the brain's memory system, it is very likely that early in the twenty-first century there will be an even greater convergence of behavioral and cognitive neuroscience upon a common mnemonic interpretation of cingulate cortical function.

See also: Attention, Neural Basis of; Emotion, Neural Basis of; Learning and Memory, Neural Basis of; Neural Representations of Direction (Head Direction Cells); Pain, Neural Basis of

Bibliography

Bussey T J, Muir J L, Everitt B J, Robbins T W 1997 Triple dissociation of anterior cingulate, posterior cingulate, and medial frontal cortices on visual discrimination tasks using a touchscreen testing procedure for the rat. *Behavioral Neuroscience* 111(5): 920–36

Dahaene S, Posner M I, Tucker D M 1994 Localization of a neural system for error detection and compensation. *Psychological Science* 5: 303–5

Freeman J H, Cuppernell C, Flannery K, Gabriel M 1996 Limbic thalamic, cingulated cortical and hippocampal neuronal corellates of discriminative approach learning in rabbits. *Behavioral Brain Research* 80: 123–36

Gabriel M 1993 Discriminative avoidance learning: A model system. In: Vogt B A, Gabriel M (eds.) *Neurobiology of Cingulate Cortex and Limbic Thalamus*. Birkhauser, Toronto, Canada

Gabriel M, Talk A 2001 A tale of two paradigms: Lessons learned from parallel studies of discriminative instrumental learning and classical eyeblink conditioning. In: Steinnetz A,

Gluck M, Solomon P (eds.) *Model Systems and the Neurobiology of Associative Learning: A Festschift in Honor of Richard F. Thompson.* Laurence Erlbaum Associates, NJ

Gabriel M, Taylor C 1998 Prenatal exposure to cocaine impairs neuronal encoding of attention and discriminative learning. In: Harvey J A, Kosofsky B E (eds.) *Cocaine: Effects on the Developing Brain.* New York Academy of Sciences, New York

Gehring W J, Gross B, Coles M G H, Meyer D E, Donchin E 1993 A neural system for error detection and compensation. *Psychological Science.* **4**: 385–90

Goldman-Rakic P S 1988 Topography of cognition: Parallel distributed networks in primate association cortex. *Annual Review of Neuroscience* **11**: 137–56

Holroyd C B, Dien J, Coles M G 1998 Error-related scalp potentials elicited by hand and foot movement: Evidence for an output-independent error-processing system in humans. *Neuroscience Letters* **242**: 65–8

Kubota Y, Wolske M, Poremba A, Gabriel M 1996 Stimulus-related and movement-related single-unit activity in rabbit cingulate cortex and limbic thalamus during performance of discriminative avoidance behavior. *Brain Research* **72**: 22–38

Lane R D, Reiman E M, Axelrod B, Yun L S, Holmes A, Schwartz G E 1998 Neural correlates of levels of emotional awareness: Evidence of an interaction between emotion and attention in the anterior cingulate cortex. *Journal of Cognitive Neuroscience* **10**(4): 525–35

MacLean P D 1975 Sensory and perceptive factors in emotional functions of the triune brain. In: Levi L (ed.) *Emotions: Their Parameters and Measurement.* Raven Press, New York

Olson C R, Musil S Y, Goldberg M E 1996 Single neurons in posterior cingulate cortex of behaving macaque: Eye movement signals. *Journal of Neurophysiology* **76**(5): 3285–300

Papez J W 1937 A proposed mechanism of emotion. *Archives of Neurology and Psychiatry* **38**: 725–43

Paus T, Petrides M, Evans A C, Meyer E 1993 Role of the human anterior cingulate cortex in the control of oculomotor, manual, and speech responses. *Journal of Neurophysiology* **70**: 453–69

Posner M I, DiGirolamo G J 1998 Executive attention: Conflict, target detection, and cognitive control. In: Parasuraman R (ed.) *The Attentive Brain.* MIT Press, Cambridge, MA

Powell D A, Buchanan S L, Gibbs C M 1990 Role of the prefrontal-thalamic axis in classical conditioning. In: Uylings H B M, Van Eden C G, De Bruin J P C, Corner M A, Feenstra M G P (eds.) *The Prefrontal Cortex: Its Structure, Function and Pathology* (vol. 85). Elsevier Science, Amsterdam

Price D D 2000 Psychological and neural mechanisms of the affective dimension of pain. *Science* **288**(5472): 1769–72

Romano A G, Harvey J A 1998 Prenatal cocaine exposure: Long-term deficits in learning and motor performance. In: Harvey J A, Kosofsky B E (eds.) *Cocaine: Effects on the Developing Brain.* New York Academy of Sciences, New York

Segal M, Olds J 1972 Behavior of units in hippocampal circuit of the rat during learning. *Journal of Neurophysiology* **35**(5): 680–90

Smith D M, Patel J, Gabriel M 2000 Hippocampal-cingulo-thalamic interactions supporting concurrent discriminative approach and avoidance learning in rabbits. *Society for Neuroscience Abstracts* **26**: 198

Takenouchi K, Nishijo H, Uwano T, Tamura R, Takigawa M, Ono T 1999 Emotional and behavioral correlates of the anterior cingulate cortex during associative learning in rats. *Neuroscience* **93**(4): 1271–87

Taylor C, Freeman J H, Holt W, Gabriel M 1999 Impairment of cingulothalamic learning-related neuronal coding in rabbits exposed to cocaine *in utero*: General and sex-specific effects. *Behavioral Neuroscience* **113**: 62–77

Turken A U, Swick D 1999 Response selection in the human anterior cingulate cortex. *Nature Neuroscience* **2**(10): 920–4

L. Burhans, A. Talk, and M. Gabriel

Circadian Rhythms

This article reviews the nature of biological rhythms in mammals, how they develop, and their eventual deterioration. It discusses the suprachiasmatic nuclei (SCN), the major pacemaker in the brain, and recent advances in understanding the molecular mechanisms of this unique timing system. It also discusses the adaptive value of having an endogenous clock in the brain and its implications for administering therapeutic agents.

1. What Are Circadian Rhythms?

All our behavioral, physiological, and endocrinological functions are controlled by an endogenous clock that measures time in approximately 24-hour intervals. The rhythms the clock generates are known as circadian rhythms (from the Latin, *circa*, about, and *dies*, day). The 'about' is very important. Living systems do not merely respond to cyclic changes in their environment in some phase-locked fashion. Leaves of plants that open during the day and close at night still open and close when the plants are kept in constant darkness. Humans and other animals maintain a period of about 24 hours in bodily functions when they are in environments without time cues. Noise, temperature, and social stimuli can also synchronize, or entrain, the clock, but the strongest entraining signal is the light/dark (LD) cycle.

2. What Are Their Properties?

Figure 1 illustrates two important properties of circadian rhythms in the wheel-running activity of a nocturnal mammal, the white-footed mouse (*Peromyscus leucopus*), that has been placed in a 24-hour LD photoperiod consisting of one hour of light and 23 hours of darkness. It takes the mouse about a week for its activity to become entrained by the LD cycle, after which it begins running immediately after the lights go off. It runs for about 10 hours and then becomes inactive. After 60 days the animal is released into constant darkness. There its activity free-runs with a period of 23.6 hours, that is, it begins to run 24 minutes earlier each day.

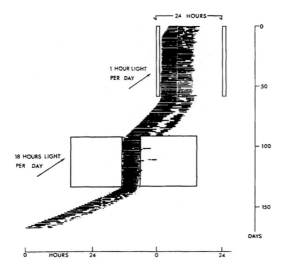

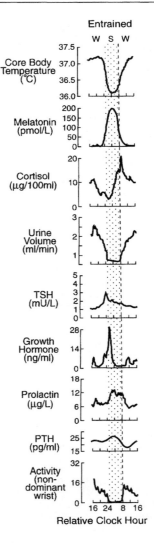

Figure 1
Entrained and freerunning rhythms of wheel-running activity in *Peromyscus leucopus*. The animal uses a running wheel during its nightly activity period which lasts about 10 hours and is recorded as a heavy black lime. Successive days are plotted beneath each other. On the 10th day of the experiment the animal had locked on to (was entrained by) the daily light pulse (one hour duration). On the 60th day, the light was discontinued. The rhythm persisted with a circadian period of 23.6 hours. On the 90th day, it was again entrained by a 24-hour LD cycle in which the light pulse lasted 18 hours. On the 140th day the light was discontinued, and the rhythm again free ran, but with a period of 23.0 hours (from Pittendrigh 1974)

After two weeks in the dark, the mouse is put into a 24-hour LD cycle consisting of 18 hours of light and six hours of darkness. It immediately becomes entrained to the new photoperiod and its activity is tightly confined to the dark period. When it is released back into constant dark, two aspects of its activity are different from the previous stay in the same condition. First, the amount of its activity is lessened. Second, the period of its free-running rhythm is shorter—23 instead of 23.6 hours (Pittendrigh 1974). This indicates that the clock remembers the previous LD cycle and this influences both the amplitude and period of the free-running rhythm. A 'memory' of the preceding daylength is even encoded in the electrophysiological activity of an isolated slice of brain containing the SCN (Mrugala et al. 2000).

Rhythms have different phase relations to the LD cycle. Figure 2 shows entrained rhythms in several physiological parameters in a human subject in a 16:8 LD cycle. Body temperature is high during the day and falls at night, when the subject is asleep. Cortisol is highest at the end of the dark period. Growth hormone

Figure 2
Entrained rhythms of colonic temperature, plasma levels of cortisol, urine volume, and plasma levels of thyroid stimulating hormone, growth hormone, prolactin and parathyroid hormone, and activity in a human monitored in a 16:8 LD cycle. W = waking; S = sleeping (from Czeisler and Khalsa 2000)

is low during the day and shows a sharp peak at the beginning of the dark period, during sleep. Immune system components also have circadian frequencies, and this can be very important in determining both responses to antigens and the timing of treatments such as chemotherapy in cancer. Ideally, one would want to administer a therapeutic agent at a time when it would produce the fewest unwanted side effects and yet be most effective in attacking the dividing cell.

3. Why Do We Need Circadian Rhythms?

There is a distinct advantage in timing various behaviors and metabolic processes to the appropriate time of day. Organisms have to sleep, and they generally do so either in the day or at night. One would want potential mates and food to be available when one is active. But a simple hourglass mechanism, timing precise 24-hour periods, would be inadequate because of seasonal changes in day length. A circadian clock, sensitive to external conditions, can be reset each day, making the clock conform to the environment. Furthermore, an internal clock allows organisms not only to respond to changes in the environment but also to anticipate them. Lizards gain heat by basking in the sun. When they are in their burrows, still with low body temperatures, they crawl to the opening of the burrow and stick their heads above the desert floor before the sun comes up. This way they are in a position to gain enough heat to become active as soon as possible. The early bird *does* catch the worm, and its internal clock wakes it up before dawn. The body temperature of humans falls in the evening, while we are still awake, and begins to rise in the early morning, while we are still asleep. Even in the same entrained environment, people have different phase relations with the LD cycle; some are larks and some are owls.

4. What Controls Circadian Rhythms?

Almost all known plants and animals exhibit circadian rhythms. For instance, the microscopic single-celled aquatic plant, *Gonyaulax polyedra*, is phosphorescent, lighting up at night, and dimming in the day. In 1958, Hastings and Sweeney demonstrated that *Gonyaulax* showed peaks and troughs of luminescence even in constant darkness, but the peak time of luminescence shifted a little later each day. If the plant was exposed to brief pulses of light, the peak of luminescence could be shifted to almost any time of day, depending on when the light pulse was given. Thus, light reset the *Gonyaulax* clock.

In 1972, Moore and Lenn placed a radioactive label into the eyes of rats and found that there was a direct pathway from the retina to two tiny nuclei in the hypothalamus. These nuclei lie behind the eyes right above the location in the brain where fibers from the left and right retinas cross, the optic chiasm, and therefore the nuclei are named the SCN. In that same year, Stephan and Zucker showed that lesions of the SCN could permanently eliminate or weaken circadian patterns of behavior (for a review, see Rusak and Zucker 1979). In a series of papers beginning in 1987, Lehman and his colleagues demonstrated that locomotor activity rhythmicity can be restored in hamsters with SCN lesions by transplants of fetal SCN tissue. There is now no doubt that, for most rhythms, the SCN is the main clock in the mammalian brain. Each morning, light from the eye sends electrical signals to the SCN and resets it. The SCN, in turn, synchronizes the rest of the brain and sets the pace for all daily activity patterns, just as a conductor synchronizes all the instruments in an orchestra.

The analogy of the SCN to an orchestra conductor is inadequate, however, because the cells of the SCN do not act as a single multioscillator unit. Welsh et al. (1995) demonstrated that SCN cells grown in culture oscillate at different rates: this means that each single SCN neuron functions as an independent circadian clock.

5. Are Clocks Similar Throughout the Animal Kingdom?

Clocks are being dissected rapidly through genetic analysis. Clock genes have been identified in cyanobacteria (blue–green algae), the fungus *Neurospora*, and the fruit fly *Drosophila*. In 1988, Ralph and Menaker (1988) identified a *tau* mutation in Syrian hamsters. Hamsters homozygous for the mutation had free-running activity rhythms of about 20 hours, compared to the wild type hamster's rhythm of about 24 hours. In 1994, Takahashi's laboratory discovered the first mouse circadian mutant, *Clock*, which was arrhythmic (Vitaterna et al. 1994). The *Drosophila* clock is proving highly amenable to molecular analysis and there are close connections to the mouse mutation. Many clock genes are highly conserved: some of the same molecules are present in fruit flies and mice, and it is possible that common molecular clock mechanisms from bacteria to humans will be found in the not-too-distant future (see Young 2000, for a review).

6. How Do Circadian Rhythms Develop and Age?

Using ^{14}C-labeled deoxyglucose to monitor metabolic activity in the SCN, Reppert and Schwartz (1986) found that there was a distinct day–night oscillation of metabolic activity in both rat and primate SCN. But fetuses do not process light. They found in rats that the maternal circadian system coordinated the timing of the fetal rhythms. It takes about a month after birth for strong circadian rhythms to develop. In most, but not all individuals, the robustness of the rhythms declines with age. Thus, rats that normally sleep mostly in the light, and eat and drink mainly in the dark, distribute all these activities about equally in the light and the dark when they get old. The mean amount of sleep, food eaten, and water drunk, etc., stays the same: only the pattern changes. These changes are correlated with aberrant SCN firing patterns in SCN slices taken from old rats. This implies that aging could either disrupt coupling between SCN pacemaker cells or their output, or cause deterioration of the pacemaking properties of the individual cells (Satinoff et al. 1993). A better understanding of clock mechanisms should lead to more efficacious clinical treatments for alleviating disorders in the elderly, such as sleep disturbances, that are associated with changes in the clock itself. But aside from pathologies in aging, a more complete understanding of clocks and how they are entrained by light will be useful in helping to ameliorate the discomfort and disability that comes from conditions as disparate as jet lag, sleep disorders in shift workers and blind people, and depression and manic-depressive disorder.

See also: Childhood Health; Sleep and Health; Sleep Disorders: Psychiatric Aspects; Sleep Disorders: Psychological Aspects; Sleep: Neural Systems; Suprachiasmatic Nucleus

Bibliography

Czeisler C, Khalsa S 2000 The human circadian timing system and sleep-wake regulation. In: Kryger M, Roth T, Dement W (eds.) *Principles and Practice of Sleep Medicine*. W.B. Saunders, Philadelphia, PA

Hastings J W, Sweeney B M 1958 A persistent diurnal rhythm of luminescence in *Gonyaulax polyedra*. *Biological Bulletin* **115**: 440–58

Lehman M, Silver R, Gladstone W, Kahn R, Gibson M, Bittman E 1987 Circadian rhythmicity restored by neural transplant. Immunocytochemical characterization of the graft and its integration with the host brain. *Journal of Neuroscience* **7**: 1626–38

Moore R Y, Lenn N J 1972 A retinohypothalamic projection in the rat. *Journal of Comparative Neurology* **146**: 1–14

Mrugala M, Zlomanczuk P, Jagota A, Schwartz W 2000 Rhythmic multiunit neural activity in slices of hamster suprachiasmatic nucleus reflect prior photoperiod. *American Journal of Physiology-Regulatory Integrative and Comparative Physiology* **278**: R987–94

Pittendrigh C 1974 Circadian oscillations in cells and the circadian organization of multicellular systems. In: Schmitt F, Worden F (eds.) *The Neurosciences: Third Study Program*. MIT Press, Cambridge, MA

Ralph M, Menaker M 1988 A mutation of the circadian system in golden hamsters. *Science* **241**: 1225–7

Reppert S, Schwartz W 1986 Maternal suprachiasmatic nuclei are necessary for maternal coordination of the developing circadian system. *Journal of Neuroscience* **9**: 2724–29

Rusak B, Zucker I 1979 Neural regulation of circadian rhythms. *Physiological Reviews* **59**: 449–526

Satinoff E, Li H, Liu C, McArthur A, Medanic M, Tcheng T, Gillette M 1993 Do the suprachiasmatic nuclei oscillate in old rats as they do in young ones? *American Journal of Physiology-Regulatory Integrative and Comparative Physiology* **265**: R1216–22

Vitaterna M H, King D P, Chang A M, Kornhauser J M, Lowrey P L, McDonald J D, Dove W F, Pinto L H, Turek F W, Takahashi J S 1994 *Science* **264**: 719–25

Welsh D, Logothetis D, Meister M, Reppert S 1995 Individual neurons dissociated from rat suprachiasmatic nucleus express independently phased circadian firing rhythms. *Neuron* **14**: 697–706

Young M 2000 Circadian rhythms. Marking time for a kingdom. *Science* **288**: 451–3

E. Satinoff

Cities: Capital, Global, and World

1. The Global City: Introducing a Concept and its History

Each phase in the long history of the world economy raises specific questions about the particular conditions that make it possible. One of the key properties of the current phase is the ascendance of information technologies and the associated increase in the mobility and liquidity of capital. There have long been cross-border economic processes—flows of capital, labor, goods, raw materials. Over the last century, these took place largely within the interstate system, where the key articulators were national states and colonial empires. The international economic system was ensconced largely in this interstate system. This has changed rather dramatically during the 1990s as a result of privatization, deregulation, the opening up of national economies to foreign firms, and the growing participation of national economic actors in global markets.

It is in this context that we see a rescaling of what are the strategic territories that articulate the new system. With the partial unbundling or at least weakening of the national as a spatial unit due to privatization and deregulation and the associated strengthening of globalization, come conditions for the ascendance of other spatial units or scales. Among these are the subnational, notably cities and regions; cross-border regions encompassing two or more subnational entities; and supranational entities, such as global electronic markets and free-trade blocs. The dynamics and processes that get territorialized at these diverse scales can in principle be regional, national, or global.

We can locate the emergence of global cities in this context and against this range of instantiations of strategic scales and spatial units. In the case of global cities, the dynamics and processes that get territorialized are global. This article examines first some of the key theoretical and empirical elements of the global city model, followed by a brief history of the evolution of the literature on cities in the global economy. Section three is a more in-depth discussion of the organizing hypotheses of the global city model.

Sections four and five discuss two specific features: the question of place in a global economy and the question of city-to-city networks in domains other than the economic.

2. Elements in a New Conceptual Architecture

The globalization of economic activity entails a new type of organizational structure. To capture this theoretically and empirically requires, correspondingly, a new type of conceptual architecture. Constructs such as the global city and the global-city region are, in my reading, important elements in this new conceptual architecture. Arrighi's (1994) analysis is of interest here in that it posits the recurrence of certain organizational patterns in different phases of the capitalist world economy, but at gradually higher orders of complexity and expanded scope, and timed to follow or precede particular configurations of the world economy.

There are today several closely linked terms used to capture a particular intersection between global processes and cities (see Stren 1996 and Savitch 1996 for overviews). The most common is world cities, a term attributed to Goethe and then relaunched in the work of Peter Hall (1966) and more recently respecified by John Friedmann (Friedmann and Goetz 1982). Other related terms are 'supervilles' (Braudel 1984), informational city (Castells 1989). Choosing how to name a configuration has its own substantive rationality. The decision to formulate the term 'global city' (Sassen 1984) stemmed out of a recognition of the specificity of the current period. The term world city has precisely the opposite attribute: it refers to a type of city which we have seen over the centuries (Braudel 1984, Hall 1966, King 1990), and most probably also in much earlier periods in Asia than in the West. In this regard it could be said that most of today's major global cities are also world cities, but that there may well be some global cities that are not world cities in the full, rich sense of that term. This is partly an empirical question; further, as the global economy expands and incorporates additional cities into various cross-border networks, it is quite possible that the answer to that particular question will vary over time. Thus the fact that Miami has developed global city functions beginning in the late 1980s does not make it a world city in that older sense of the term (Nijman 1996). (See generally Abu-Lughod 1999, Short and Kim 1999.)

3. The Elements of a New Theoretical Framework

By the early 1980s a number of scholars had begun to study cities in the context of globalization (Walton 1982, Ross and Trachte 1983, Sassen 1982, Rodriguez and Feagin 1986). But it is one article in particular, 'The World City Hypothesis' by Friedmann and Goetz (1982) on which attention centered. This article took a variety of elements that were emerging in the research literature on cities, on the global economy, on immigration, and a number of other subjects, and sought to formalize these into several propositions about the role of cities in the global economy. The key elements in this framework were the emergence of several cities as basing points for global capital, a hierarchy (albeit a shifting one) of such cities, and the social and political consequences for these cities of being such basing points.

With the books by Castells (1989), King (1990), and Sassen (1991/2001), what had been a hypothesis in the early 1980s became a full-fledged theorization and empirical specification. These three books add important and distinct propositions to the general framework: Castells' proposition that globalization as constituted today has engendered a space of flows that reconfigures economic and political power; King's enlargement of the frame of reference to show that the highest levels of internationalization had taken place in the cities of colonial empires rather than in the center of the world economy; Sassen's proposition that it is not simply a matter of global coordination but one of the production of global control capacities and that an examination along these lines allows us to understand the role of global cities as production sites.

It is important to distinguish what is different about this literature from a broader, earlier literature on world cities prominently represented by the work of Peter Hall already in the 1960s, and a new literature on megacities especially focused on Latin America and Asia. These literatures do not have the fact of globalization and the centrality of crossborder networks connecting cities as crucial variables. The earlier literature on world cities is closer to the notion of capitals of empires: one city at the top of the power hierarchy.

In the current literature on global cities the determining factor is a cross-border, global network of cities that function as strategic sites for the management and specialized servicing of global economic operations. There is no such entity as a single global city, as there is with the capital of an empire; by definition, the global city is part of a network of cities. Similarly, an older literature focused on past world cities, as in the work of Braudel (1984), and earlier studies of major centers of world commerce and banking, as well as more recent work on urban hierarchies in the world system (Chase-Dunn 1984), are to be differentiated from the current literature if we historicize the world economy and specify what is distinct today. Finally, we need to distinguish between a narrowly specified literature on global and world cities today and various literatures that directly or indirectly contribute to our understanding of these cities, notably the research on producer services.

By the mid-1990s the subject had clearly emerged as a rather large field for research among scholars in many different disciplines and countries. We can see this in the variety of authors and themes in several state-of-the-art collections, notably by Fainstein et al. (1993), Knox and Taylor (1995), Noller et al. (1995), Lo and Yeung (1996), and several others that elaborate, critique, expand the empirical base, and generally advance this theoretical and methodological project. We can also see it in several new important books that set the stage for highly focused research on particular variables, notably Meyer (1991), Thrift and Leyshon (1994), Keil (1993), Eade (1996) among others. We also see the creation of several book series by various publishers in different countries: the series on World Cities edited by Knox for Belhaven Press, the series edited by Milton Santos and his colleagues in Sao Paulo for Hucitec, the series edited by Martin Wentz for Campus Verlag, are just some.

It is not only the growth of the research literature but also the growth of a body of critical responses and analyses that signals the strength and vigor of this field of inquiry. There is only space here for the briefest mention, a sort of guide to criticisms: Logan and Swanstrom's (1990) critique of the excessive weight given to global structural processes in comparing internal vs. external factors that shape a city's economic development; Hammet's (1996) critique of Sassen's proposition that globalization has contributed to social and economic polarization in global cities; Markusen and Gwiasda's (1994) critique of the notion that New York is at the top of the US urban hierarchy and how a comparison with Washington shows that the latter has a higher level of specialization than New York in many advanced specialized services, notably in legal services; critiques of the literature for its neglect of grassroots transnationalism and the new kinds of politics and identitiy formation that this entails; Beauregard's (1991) critique of the explanatory variables for changes in the built environment and the real estate industry; Simon's (1995) critique of the neglect of the periphery, notably Africa; the debate in *Urban Affairs* (March 1998) on the concept of the global city and a similar one in *Urban Studies* (Summer 2001); the special issue on 'Segregations Urbaines' of *Societes Contemporaines* in 1995; the special issue of *Urban Studies* in 1996, and many others.

There are two types of scholarly literature that intersect with this body of research on cities and the global economy, and indeed often invoke or use it to develop their arguments. They are on the one hand a literature of anthropological and cultural studies on transnationality, globalization, and identity formation (Holston 1996, Low 1999). The other is the scholarship by regional economic geographers on the global economy, who have also focused on cities (e.g., Moulaert and Scott 1997, Gravestijn et al. 1999). In the last few years there has been a new interest in this subject by geographers (Veltz 1996, Scott 2001, Storper 1997).

In terms of method, a number of strategies have been developed. Even where there are data on intercity flows, it will take a lot of work to constitute the requisite data sets. In this regard, an ambitious initiative by the National Academy of Sciences of the US examines how we can construct better data sets at the scale of the city (NAS 2000).

Among the quantitative methodological and data formation strategies are the efforts by Smith and Timberlake (2002) and by Taylor et al. (2002). Smith and Timberlake (2002) conceptualize urban areas as central nodes in multiplex networks of economic, social, demographic and information flows. They use the methodological logic of network analysis, using particularly two measures: one of these is structural or relational equivalence between actors (i.e., cities) in a network; the second measure is centrality. Both of these measures relate to a number of propositions developed in the literature on cities in the global economy.

Taylor et al. (2002) have developed a new and pioneering data set that makes it possible to map the global networks of offices of the leading firms worldwide in several specialized corporate services, such as accounting, law, advertising, and finance. These networks of offices can be used to classify cities in terms of their participation in cross-border networks. The data can be analyzed using a variety of hypotheses and statistical as well as other methods.

There are several other efforts, but space dictates singling out just a few. David Meyer (1991) has developed ways of analyzing international networks through which a variety of exchanges of capital take place. Castells (1989) and Sassen (1991/2001) have developed several techniques of analysis which range from methods to understand the place of cities in global markets to expanding the representation of the global. In *The Informational City* and *The Global City* the authors sought to establish rather broadly what is the array of data sets that can be brought into an analysis of this subject—from international flows of capital and information to very localized social effects. This was an effort to resist the simplification in mainstream accounts which emphasize the global dispersal of activities and telecommunications and exclude most social issues.

Techniques for data analysis traditionally used by economic geographers can also be helpful. For instance Wheeler's (1986) examination of the dispersion of higher-order financial services throughout the US urban hierarchy—which he found had proceeded at a much slower rate than the dispersion of headquarters of other large corporations—can also be used for cross-border hierarchies. Wheeler found that corporations tend to proceed up the urban hierarchy for their advanced service and banking needs.

Elliott (1999) developed a test for the socioeconomic polarization hypothesis in global cities.

4. The Global City Model: Organizing Hypotheses

There are seven core hypotheses that organize the data and the theorization of the global city model. There follows a brief discussion of each as a way of producing a more precise representation of the model. (See Sassen 1991/2001.)

First, the geographic dispersal of economic activities that marks globalization, along with the simultaneous integration of such geographically dispersed activities, is a key factor feeding the growth and importance of central corporate functions. The more dispersed a firm's operations across different countries, the more complex and strategic its central functions—that is, the work of managing, coordinating, servicing, financing a firm's network of operations.

Second, these central functions become so complex that increasingly the headquarters of large global firms outsource them: they buy a share of their central functions from highly specialized service firms: accounting, legal, public relations, programming, telecommunications, and other such services. Thus while even ten years ago the key site for the production of these central headquarter functions was the headquarters of a firm, today there is a second key site: the specialized service firms contracted by headquarters to produce some of these central functions or components of them. This is especially the case with firms involved in global markets and non-routine operations. But increasingly the headquarters of all large firms are buying more of such inputs rather than producing them in-house.

Third, those specialized service firms engaged in the most complex and globalized markets are subject to agglomeration economies. The complexity of the services they need to produce, the uncertainty of the markets they are involved with either directly or through the headquarters for which they are producing the services, and the growing importance of speed in all these transactions, is a mix of conditions that constitutes a new agglomeration dynamic. The mix of firms, talents, expertise from a broad range of specialized fields makes a certain type of urban environment function as an information center. Being in a city becomes synonymous with being in an extremely intense and dense information loop. This is a type of information loop that as of now still cannot be replicated fully in electronic space, and has as one of its value-added features the fact of unforeseen and unplanned mixes of information, expertise, and talent; these can produce a higher order of information. This does not hold for routinized activities which are not as

subject to uncertainty and non-standardized forms of complexity. Global cities are, in this regard, production sites for the leading information industries of our time.

A fourth hypothesis, derived from the preceding one, is that the more headquarters outsource their most complex, unstandardized functions particularly those subject to uncertain and changing markets and to speed, the freer they are to opt for any location because the more the work actually done in the headquarters is not subject to agglomeration economies. This further underlines that the key sector specifying the distinctive production advantages of global cities is the highly specialized and networked services sector. In developing this hypothesis I was responding to a very common notion that the number of headquarters is what specifies a global city. Empirically it may still be the case in many countries that the leading business center is also the leading concentration of headquarters, but this may well be because there is an absence of alternative locational options. But in countries with a well developed infrastructure outside the leading business center, there are likely to be multiple locational options for such headquarters.

Fifth, these specialized service firms need to provide a global service which has meant a global network of affiliates or some other form of partnership, and as a result we have seen a strengthening of cross-border city-to-city transactions and networks. At the limit this may well be the beginning of the formation of transnational urban systems. The growth of global markets for finance and specialized services, the need for transnational servicing networks due to sharp increases in international investment, the reduced role of the government in the regulation of international economic activity, and the corresponding ascendance of other institutional arenas, notably global markets and corporate headquarters—all these point to the existence of a series of transnational networks of cities. One implication of this, and a related hypothesis for research is that the economic fortunes of these cities become increasingly disconnected from their broader hinterlands or even their national economies. We can see here the formation, at least incipient, of transnational urban systems. To a large extent it seems to me that the major business centers in the world today draw their importance from these transnational networks.

A sixth hypothesis, is that the growing numbers of high level professionals and high-profit making specialized service firms have the effect of raising the degree of spatial and socioeconomic inequality evident in these cities. The strategic role of these specialized services as inputs raises the value of top level professionals and their numbers. Further, the fact that talent can matter enormously for the quality of these strategic outputs and, given the importance of speed, proven talent is an added value, the structure of rewards is likely to experience rapid increases. Types of activities and of workers lacking these attributes, notably in manufacturing and industrial services, are likely to get caught in the opposite cycle.

A seventh hypothesis, is that one result of the dynamics decribed in hypothesis six, is the growing informalization of a range of economic activities which find their effective demand in these cities yet have profit rates that do not allow them to compete for various resources with the high-profit making firms at the top of the system. Informalizing part or all production and distribution activities, including of services, is one way of surviving under these conditions.

The first four hypotheses qualify what has emerged as a dominant discourse on globalization, technology, and cities, which posits the end of cities as important economic units or scales. There is a tendency in that account to take the existence of a global economic system as a given, a function of the power of transnational corporations and global communications. According to the global city model, the capabilities for global operation, coordination, and control contained in the new information technologies and in the power of transnational corporations need to be produced. By focusing on the production of these capabilities we add a neglected dimension to the familiar issue of the power of large corporations and the capacity of the new technologies to neutralize distance and place. A focus on the production of these capabilities shifts the emphasis to the practices that constitute what we call economic globalization and global control.

A focus on practices draws the categories of place and work process into the analysis of economic globalization. These are two categories easily overlooked in accounts centered on the hypermobility of capital and the power of transnationals. Developing categories such as place and work process does not negate the centrality of hypermobility and power. Rather, it brings to the fore the fact that many of the resources necessary for global economic activities are not hypermobile and are, indeed, deeply embedded in place, notably places such as global cities, global-city regions, and export processing zones.

This entails a whole infrastructure of activities, firms, and jobs necessary to run the advanced corporate economy. These industries are typically conceptualized in terms of the hypermobility of their outputs and the high levels of expertise of their professionals rather than in terms of the production or work process involved and the requisite infrastructure of facilities and non-expert jobs that are also part of these industries. This in turn brings with it an emphasis on economic and spatial polarization because of the disproportionate concentration of very high and very low income jobs in the city compared with what would be the case at a larger scale such as the region or the country. A focus on regions, in contrast will lead to an emphasis on broad urbanization patterns, a more encompassing economic base, more middle sectors of both households and firms. Emphasizing place, infrastructure, and non-expert jobs matters precisely because so much of the focus has been on the neutralization of geography and place made possible by the new technologies.

Dealing with place brings with it the problem of boundaries. These are at least of two sorts, the boundary of the territorial scale as such and the boundary of the spread of globalization in the organizational structure of industries, institutional orders, places, and so on. In the case of the global city it is possible to opt for an analytic strategy that emphasizes core dynamics rather than the unit of the city as a container—the latter being one that requires territorial boundary specification. Emphasizing core dynamics and their spatialization (in both actual and digital space) does not completely solve the boundary problem, but it does allow for a fairly clear trade-off between emphasizing the core or center of these dynamics and their spread institutionally and spatially.

Finally, the detailed examination of three particular cities (Sassen 1991/2001) brought to the fore the extent to which these cities collaborate through their very specific advantages rather than simply competing with each other. In focusing on global finance in the 1980s and 1990s it becomes clear that the growth of the major centers was partly derived from the growing network of financial centers. In looking at the broader network it also becomes clear to what extent it was and remains characterized by a pronounced hierarchy among the growing number of centers that make up the network.

The growth of networked cross-border dynamics among global cities includes a broad range of domains—political, cultural, social, criminal. There are cross-border transactions among immigrant communities and communities of origin and a greater intensity in the use of these networks once they become established, including for economic activities that had been unlikely until now. We also see greater cross-border networks for cultural purposes, as in the growth of international markets for art and a transnational class of art curators; and for non-formal political purposes, as in the growth of transnational networks of activists around environmental causes, human rights, and so on. These are largely city-to-city cross-border networks, or, at least, it appears at this time to be simpler to capture the existence and modalities of these networks at the city level. The same can be said for the new cross-border criminal networks.

In brief, recapturing the geography of places represented by the network of global cities allows us to recapture people, workers, communities, and more specifically, the many different work cultures, besides the corporate culture, involved in the work of globalization. It also brings with it an enormous research agenda, one that goes beyond the by now familiar focus on cross-border flows of goods, capital and information.

Further, by emphasizing the fact that global processes are at least partly embedded in national territories, such a focus introduces new variables in current conceptions about economic globalization and the shrinking regulatory role of the state. That is to say, the space economy for major new transnational economic processes diverges in significant ways from the duality global/national presupposed in much analysis of the global economy. The duality national vs. global suggests two mutually exclusive spaces— where one begins the other ends. One of the outcomes of a global city analysis is that it makes evident that the global materializes by necessity in specific places and institutional arrangements a good number of which, if not most, are located in national territories.

The two final sections examine two particular aspects that illustrate some of these issues concerning place in a global economy and city-to-city networks in realms other than the economic.

5. New Forms of Centrality

Several of the organizing hypotheses in the global city model concern the conditions for the continuity of centrality in advanced economic systems in the face of major new organizational forms and technologies that maximize the possibility for geographic dispersal. Historically, centrality has largely been embedded in the central city. Have the new technologies and organizational forms altered the spatial correlates of centrality?

Today there is no longer a simple straightforward relation between centrality and such geographic entities as the downtown, or the central business district. In the past, and up to quite recently in fact, the center was synonymous with the downtown or the CBD. The spatial correlate of the center can assume several geographic forms. It can be the CBD, as it still is largely in New York City, or it can extend into a metropolitan area in the form of a grid of nodes of intense business activity, as we see for instance in Frankfurt and Zurich. The center has been profoundly altered by telecommunications and the growth of a global economy, both inextricably linked; they have contributed to a new geography of centrality (and marginality). Simplifying we can identify four forms assumed by centrality today.

First, while centrality can assume multiple spatial correlates, the CBD in major international business centers remains a strategic site for the leading industries. But it is one profoundly reconfigured by technological and economic change (Graham and Marvin 1996). Further, there are often sharp differences in the patterns assumed by this reconfiguring of the central city in different parts of the world, notably the United States and Western Europe (Veltz 1996, Kunzmann 1994).

In the United States, major cities such as New York and Chicago have large centers that have been rebuilt many times, given the brutal neglect suffered by much urban infrastructure and the imposed obsolescence so characteristic of US cities. This neglect and accelerated obsolescence produce vast spaces for rebuilding the center according to the requirements of whatever regime of urban accumulation or pattern of spatial organization of the urban economy prevails at a given time. In Europe, urban centers are far more protected and they rarely contain significant stretches of abandoned space; the expansion of workplaces and the need for intelligent buildings necessarily will have to take place partly outside the old centers. One of the most extreme cases is the complex of La Defense, the massive, state-of-the-art office complex developed right outside Paris to avoid harming the built environment inside the city. This is an explicit instance of government policy and planning aimed at addressing the growing demand for central office space of prime quality. Yet another variant of this expansion of the 'center' onto hitherto peripheral land can be seen in London's Docklands. Similar projects for recentralizing peripheral areas were launched in several major cities in Europe, North America, and Japan during the 1980s. (See Marcuse and van Kempen 2000.)

Second, the center can extend into a metropolitan area in the form of a grid of nodes of intense business activity. One might ask whether a spatial organization characterized by dense strategic nodes spread over a broader region does in fact constitute a new form of organizing the territory of the 'center,' rather than, as in the more conventional view, an instance of suburbanization or geographic dispersal. Insofar as these various nodes are articulated through digital networks, they represent a new geographic correlate of the most advanced type of 'center.' This is a partly deterritorialized space of centrality. Indeed much of the actual geographic territory within which these nodes exist falls outside the new grid of digital networks, and is in that sense partly peripheralized.

This regional grid of nodes represents a reconstitution of the concept of region. Far from neutralizing geography the regional grid is likely to be embedded in conventional forms of communication infrastructure, notably rapid rail and highways connecting to airports. Ironically perhaps, conventional infrastructure is likely to maximize the economic benefits derived from telematics. This is an important issue that has been lost somewhat in discussions about the neutralization of geography through telecommunications.

Third, we are seeing the formation of a transterritorial 'center' constituted, partly in digital space, via intense economic transactions in the network of global cities. These networks of major international business centers constitute new geographies of centrality. The most powerful of these new geographies of centrality at the global level binds the major international financial and business centers: New York, London, Tokyo, Paris, Frankfurt, Zurich, Amsterdam, Los Angeles, Sydney, Hong Kong, among others. But this geography now also includes cities such as Bangkok, Seoul, Taipei, Sao Paulo, Mexico City. The intensity of transactions among these cities, particularly through the financial markets, trade in services, and investment, has increased sharply, and so have the orders of magnitude involved. At the same time, there has been a sharpening inequality in the concentration of strategic resources and activities between each of these cities and others in the same country, a condition that further underlines the extent to which this is a cross-border space of centrality.

The pronounced orientation to the world markets evident in such cities raises questions about the articulation with their nation-states, their regions, and the larger economic and social structure in such cities. Cities have typically been deeply embedded in the economies of their region, indeed often reflecting the characteristics of the latter; and they still do. But cities that are strategic sites in the global economy tend, in part, to disconnect from their region. This conflicts with a key proposition in traditional scholarship about urban systems, namely, that these systems promote the territorial integration of regional and national economies.

In the case of a complex landscape such as Europe's we see several geographies of centrality, one global, others continental and regional. A central urban hierarchy connects major cities, many of which in turn play central roles in the wider global system of cities: Paris, London, Frankfurt, Amsterdam, Zurich. These cities are also part of a wider network of European financial/cultural/service capitals, some with only one, others with several of these functions, which articulate the European region and are somewhat less oriented to the global economy than Paris, Frankfurt, or London. And then there are several geographies of marginality: the East–West divide and the North–South divide across Europe as well as newer divisions. In Eastern Europe, certain cities and regions, notably Budapest, are rather attractive for purposes of investment, both European and non-European, while others will increasingly fall behind, notably in Rumania, Yugoslavia, and Albania. We see a similar differentiation in the south of Europe: Madrid, Barcelona, and Milan are gaining in the new European hierarchy; Naples, Rome, and Marseilles are not quite.

Fourth, new forms of centrality are being constituted in electronically generated spaces. For instance, strategic components of the financial industry operate in such spaces. The relation between digital and actual space is complex and varies among different types of economic sectors. But it is increasingly becoming evident that the highly complex configurations for economic activity located in digital space contain points of coordination and centralization.

6. The Global City as a Nexus For New Politico-cultural Alignments

The incorporation of cities into a new cross-border geography of centrality also signals the emergence of a parallel political geography. Major cities have emerged as strategic sites not only for global capital, but also for the transnationalization of labor and the formation of translocal communities and identities (Smith 1997). In this regard cities are sites for new types of political operations and for a whole range of new 'cultural' and subjective operations (Watson and Bridges 1999, Allen et al. 1999). The centrality of place in a context of global processes makes possible a transnational economic and political opening for the formation of new claims and hence for the constitution of entitlements, notably rights to place. At the limit, this could be an opening for new forms of 'citizenship' (Isin 2000, Holston 1996).

The emphasis on the transnational and hypermobile character of capital has contributed to a sense of powerlessness among local actors, a sense of the futility of resistance. But an analysis that emphasizes place suggests that the new global grid of strategic sites is a terrain for politics and engagement. The loss of power at the national level produces the possibility for new forms of power and politics at the subnational level. Further, insofar as the national as container of social process and power is cracked (Brenner 1998, Taylor 1995) it opens up possibilities for a geography of politics that links subnational spaces across borders. Cities are foremost in this new geography. One question this engenders is how and whether we are seeing the formation of a new type of transnational politics that localizes in these cities.

Immigration, for instance, is one major process through which a new transnational political economy and translocal household strategies are being constituted (Portes 1997, Skeldon 1997). It is one largely embedded in major cities insofar as most immigrants, certainly in the developed world, whether in the US, Japan, or Western Europe, are concentrated in major cities. It is, in many regards, one of the constitutive processes of globalization today, even though not recognized or represented as such in mainstream accounts of the global economy. This configuration contains unifying capacities across national boundaries and sharpening conflicts within cities. Global capital and the new immigrant workforce are two major instances of transnationalized actors that have unifying properties across borders, and thus internally to each, and find themselves in contestation with each other inside cities. Researching and theorizing these issues will require approaches that diverge from the more traditional studies of political elites, local party politics, neighborhood associations, immigrant communities, and so on through which the political landscape of cities and metropolitan regions has been conceptualized in urban studies.

One way of thinking about the political implications of this strategic transnational space anchored in global cities is in terms of the formation of new claims on that space. The city has indeed emerged as a site for new claims: by global capital which uses the city as an 'organizational commodity,' but also by disadvantaged sectors of the urban population, frequently as internationalized a presence in large cities as capital. The 'de-nationalizing' of urban space and the formation of new claims by transnational actors, raise the question 'Whose city is it?'

This is a space that is both place-centered in that it is embedded in particular and strategic locations; and it is transterritorial because it connects sites that are not geographically proximate yet are intensely connected to each other. If we consider that large cities concentrate both the leading sectors of global capital and a growing share of disadvantaged populations—immigrants, many of the disadvantaged women, people of color generally, and, in the megacities of developing countries, masses of shanty dwellers—then we can see that cities have become a strategic terrain for a whole series of conflicts and contradictions (Allen et al. 1999, Tardanico and Lungo 1995). We can then think of cities also as one of the sites for the contradictions of the globalization of capital, even though the city cannot be reduced to this dynamic.

7. Conclusion

An examination of globalization through the concept of the global city introduces a strong emphasis on strategic components of the global economy rather than the broader and more diffuse homogenizing dynamics we associate with the globalization of consumer markets. As a consequence, this also brings an emphasis on questions of power and inequality. And it brings an emphasis on the actual work of managing, servicing, and financing a global economy. Second, a focus on the city in studying globalization will tend to bring to the fore the growing inequalities between highly provisioned and profoundly disadvantaged sectors and spaces of the city, and hence such a focus introduces yet another formulation of questions of power and inequality.

Third, the concept of the global city brings a strong emphasis on the networked economy because of the nature of the industries that tend to be located there: finance and specialized services, the new multimedia sectors, and telecommunications services. These industries are characterized by cross-border networks and specialized divisions of functions among cities rather than international competition *per se*. In the case of global finance and the leading specialized services catering to global firms and markets—law, accounting, credit rating, telecommunications—it is clear that we are dealing with a cross-border system, one that is embedded in a series of cities, each possibly part of a different country. It is a *de facto* global system.

Fifth, a focus on networked cross-border dynamics among global cities also allows us to capture more readily the growing intensity of such transactions in other domains—political, cultural, social, criminal.

Global cities around the world are the terrain where a multiplicity of globalization processes assume concrete, localized forms. These localized forms are, in good part, what globalization is about. Recovering place means recovering the multiplicity of presences in this landscape. The large city of today has emerged as a strategic site for a whole range of new types of operations—political, economic, 'cultural,' subjective. It is one of the nexus where the formation of new claims, by both the powerful and the disadvantaged, materializes and assumes concrete forms.

See also: Cultural Studies: Cultural Concerns; Culture, Sociology of; Globalization and World Culture; Globalization, Anthropology of; Globalization: Geographical Aspects; Globalization, Subsuming Pluralism, Transnational Organizations, Diaspora, and Postmodernity; Information Society; Information Society, Geography of; Information Technology; International Communication: History; Internet: Psychological Perspectives; Science and Technology: Internationalization

Bibliography

Abu-Lughod J L 1999 *New York, Los Angeles, Chicago: America's Global Cities*. University of Minnesota Press, MN

Allen J, Massey D, Pryke M (eds.) 1999 *Unsettling Cities*. Routledge, London

Arrighi G 1994 *The Long Twentieth Century. Money, Power, and the Origins of Our Times*. Verso, London

Beauregard R 1991 Capital restructuring and the new built environment of global cities: New York and Los Angeles. *International Journal of Urban and Regional Research* **15**(1): 90–105

Braudel F 1984 *The Perspective of The World*. Collins, London, Vol. 3

Brenner N 1998 Global cities, global states: Global city formation and state territorial restructuring in contemporary Europe. *Review of International Political Economy* **5**(1): 1–37

Castells M 1989 *The Informational City*. Blackwell, London

Chase-Dunn C 1984 Urbanization in the world system: New directions for research. In: Smith M P (ed.) *Cities in Transformation*. Sage, Beverly Hills, CA

Eade J (ed.) 1996 *Living the Global City: Globalization as a Local Process*. Routledge, London

Elliott J R 1999 Putting 'global cities' in their place: Urban hierarchy and low-income employment during the post-war era. *Urban Geography* **20**(2): 95–115

Fainstein S, Gordon I, Harloe M 1993 *Divided City: Economic*

Restructuring and Social Change in London and New York. Blackwell, New York

Friedmann J, Goetz W 1982 World city formation: An agenda for research and action. *International Journal of Urban and Regional Research* **6**: 309 44

Graham S, Marvin S 1996 *Telecommunications and the City: Electronic Spaces, Urban Places.* Routledge, London

Gravesteijn S G E, van Griensven S, de Smidt M C (eds.) 1998 Timing global cities. *Nederlandse Geografische Studies* **241**

Hall P 1966 *The World Cities.* McGraw-Hill, New York

Hamnett C 1996 Why Sassen is wrong: A response to Burgers. *Urban Studies* **33**(1): 107 10

Holston J (ed.) 1996 Cities and citizenship. *Public Culture* **8**(2)(Winter)

Isin E (ed.) 2000 *Democracy, Citizenship and the Global City.* Routledge, London

Keil R 1993 *Weltstadt- Stadt der Welt: Internationalisierung und lokale Politik in Los Angeles.* Westfaelisches Dampfboot, Munster, Germany

King A D 1990 *Global Cities: Post-Imperialism and the Internationalization of London.* Routledge, London

Knox P L, Taylor P J (eds.) 1995 *World Cities in a World-System.* Cambridge University Press, Cambridge, UK

Kunzmann K R 1994 Berlin im Zentrum europäischer Städtnetze. In: Werner S (ed.) *Hauptstadt Berlin. Band 1: Nationale Hauptstadt Europaeische Metropole.* Berlin Verlag, Berlin, pp. 233–46

Lo F, Yeung Y (eds.) 1996 *Emerging World Cities in Pacific Asia.* United Nations University, Tokyo

Logan J R, Swanstrom T (eds.) 1990 *Beyond the City Limits: Urban Policy and Economic Restructuring in Comparative Perspective.* Temple University Press, Philadelphia

Low S M 1999 Theorizing the city. In: Low S M (ed.) *Theorizing the City.* Rutgers University Press, New Brunswick, NJ, pp. 1–33

Markusen A, Gwiasda V 1994 Multipolarity and the layering of functions in the world cities: New York city's struggle to stay on top. *International Journal of Urban and Regional Research* **18**: 167–93

Machimura T 1998 Symbolic use of globalization in urban politics in Tokyo. *International Journal of Urban and Regional Research* **22**(2): 183–94

Marcuse P, van Kempen R 2000 *Globalizing Cities. A New Spatial Order.* Blackwell, Oxford, UK

Meyer D R 1991 Change in the world system of metropolises: The role of business intermediaries. *Urban Geography* **12**(5): 393–416

Moulaert F, Scott A J 1997 *Cities, Enterprises and Society on the Eve of the 21st Century.* Pinter, New York

National Academy of Sciences (NAS) 2000 *Panel on Urban Data Sets.* Committee on Population, NAS, Washington, DC

Nijman J 1996 Breaking the rules: Miami in the urban hierarchy. *Urban Geography* **17**(1): 5–22

Noller P, Prigge W, Ronneberger K (eds.) 1994 *Stadt-Welt.* Campus Verlag, Frankfurt, Germany

Portes A (ed.) 1995 *The Economic Sociology of Immigration.* The Russell Sage Foundation, New York

Rodriguez N P, Feagin J R 1986 Urban specialization in the world system. *Urban Affairs Quarterly* **22**(2): 187–220

Ross R, Trachte K 1983 Global cities and global classes: The peripheralization of labor in New York City. *Review* **6**(3): 393–431

Santos M, Souze M A A, Silveira M L (eds.) 1994 *Territorio Globalizacao e Fragmentacao.* Editorial Hucitec, Sao Paulo, Brazil

Sassen S 1982 Recomposition and peripheralization at the core. *Contemporary Marxism* **5**: 88–100

Sassen S 1984 The new labor demand in global cities. In: Smith M P (ed.) *Cities in Transformation.* Sage, CA

Sassen S 1991/2000 *The Global City: New York, London, Tokyo.* Princeton University Press, NJ

Savitch H V 1996 Cities in a global era: A new paradigm for the next millenium. In: Cohen M A, Blair J, Ruble J, Tulchin S, Garland A M (eds.) *Preparing for the Urban Future. Global Pressures and Local Forces.* Woodrow Wilson Center Press, Washington, DC, pp. 39–65

Scott A J 2001 *Global City-Regions.* Oxford University Press, Oxford, UK

Short J R, Kim Y 1999 *Globalization and the City.* Longman, Essex

Simon D 1995 The world city hypothesis: Reflections from the periphery. In: Knox P L, Taylor P J (eds.) 1995 *World Cities in a World-System.* Cambridge University Press, Cambridge, UK, pp. 132–55

Skeldon R 1997 Hong Kong: Colonial city to global city to provincial city? *Cities* **14**(5): 265–71

Smith R C 1997 Transnational migration, assimilation and political community. In: Crahan M, Vourvoulias-Bush A (eds.) *The City and the World.* Council of Foreign Relations, NY

Smith D, Timberlake M 2002 Cross-border air traffic patterned networks. In: Sassen S (ed.) *Global Networks/Linked Cities.* Routledge, London

Smith M P, Feagin J R (eds.) 1995 *The Bubbling Cauldron: Race, Ethnicity, and The Urban Crisis.* University of Minnesota Press, Minneapolis

Storper M 1997 *The Regional World: Territorial Development in a Global Economy.* Guilford Press, New York

Stren R 1996 The studies of cities: Popular perceptions, academic disciplines, and emerging agendas. In: Cohen M A, Blair A, Ruble J, Tulchin S, Garland A M (eds.) *Preparing for the Urban Future. Global Pressures and Local Forces.* Woodrow Wilson Center Press, Washington, DC, pp. 392–420

Tardanico R, Lungo M 1995 Local dimensions of global restructuring in urban Costa Rica. *International Journal of Urban and Regional Research* **19**(2): 223–49

Taylor P J 1995 World cities and territorial states: The rise and fall of their mutuality. In: Knox P L, Taylor P J (eds.) 1995 *World Cities in a World-System.* Cambridge University Press, Cambridge, UK, pp. 48–62

Taylor P J, Beaverstock J V, Walker D R F 2002 Introducing GaWC: Researching world city network formation. In: Sassen S (ed.) *Global Networks/Linked Cities.* Routledge, London

Thrift N, Leyshon A 1994 A phantom state? The de-traditionalization of money, the international financial system and international financial centres. *Political Geography* **13**(4): 299–327

Veltz P 1996 *Mondialisation Villes et Territoires: L'Economie d'Archipel.* Presses Universitaires de France, Paris

Walton J 1982 The international economy and peripheral urbanization. In: Norman I, Fainstein S (eds.) *Urban Policy under Capitalism.* Sage, CA, pp. 119–35

Watson S, Bridges G (eds.) 1999 *Spaces of Culture.* Sage, London

Wheeler J O 1986 Corporate spatial links with financial institutions: The role of the metropolitan hierarchy. *Annals of the Association of American Geographers* **76**(2): 262–74

S. Sassen

Cities: Cultural Types

Urban forms and structures vary from one region of the world to the other. For better understanding of such variations the notion of culture realm is helpful.

1. The Intermediate Level of Looking at Cities

From the global point of view cities are local concentrations of population sharing certain features such as site and location factors, form (streets, houses), functions, and land uses. These features are common to all cities around the globe.

At the opposite end of the scale there is the individual city. From the ideographic point of view each city is unique as to its historical development and design.

At an intermediate level and mainly on cosmographic, religious, mercantile, or military grounds, the cities in a specific region of the world have developed certain peculiar traits common only to them and distinguishing them from the cities of other regions. These traits derived from ideas and thoughts of their inhabitants about their way of life and the desire to shape their settlements accordingly. Cities are, to a certain degree, a mirror of the intentions of their founders and of all successive generations over the centuries.

This aspect has been somewhat neglected, even to the present day. Prior to the 1950s, professional geographers were occupied mainly with location and growth factors, and urban functions. During the first quarter of the twentieth century a few German geographers made urban morphology their research topic, and it was in this period that a few cultural–genetic studies appeared. The Austrian Oberhummer participated in the Transcontinental Excursion of 1912 across the United States and published a comparative study on American and German cities in a memorial volume (Oberhummer 1915). Fleure (1920) wrote an article on various types of European cities for the 1920 *Geographical Review*, while in 1928 Passarge convened a symposium on urban issues in various countries and two years later published the results in his book *Stadtlandschaften der Erde* (Townscapes of the World) (Passarge 1930).

Interest in cross-cultural research arose again after 1950 when urban land uses and urban structure became major research topics. Simultaneously, the British geographer Smailes (1955) drew the attention of the English-speaking scientific community to urban morphology with his paper on townscapes. These attempts were, however, very soon superimposed by the so-called 'quantitative revolution' and the rise of *urban social geography*.

This is why the cultural–genetic approach was given rather little attention in standard textbooks. Of course, a few cross-cultural studies appeared, by Scargill (1979), Brunn and Williams (1983), and Agnew et al. (1984). The models of some cultural types of cities are discussed in Ehlers (1992). But separate chapters devoted to cultural types of cities are only found in the urban geography textbooks by Beaujeu-Garnier and Chabot (1963), Hofmeister (1999), and Rugg (1972). A vast amount of material on cultural types of cities will, however, be available in the near future when the series 'Urbanization of the Earth' started by Tietze in 1977 is completed.

It is postulated that urbanization processes are the same all over the world. However, they encounter different cultures and consequently generate different urban forms and structures in various parts of the world.

These regional differences may be seen against the background of culture realms. In the present author's opinion one may distinguish between twelve culture realms in the world and twelve cultural types of cities, respectively. These are the European, Russian, Chinese, Japanese, Southeast Asian, Indian, Oriental (Middle Eastern), Central African, South African, Australian, Anglo-American, and Latin American types.

We should, however, be aware of the fact that the notion of culture realm implies a rather high degree of generalization. As we attempt to go further into details we shall soon realize, for example, that Anglo-American cities are far from alike. The mere existence of the two political entities of the United States and Canada has had some bearing upon urban developments, so that US cities will look somewhat different from Canadian cities (see Goldberg and Mercer 1986). In an attempt to do justice to such variations Holzner et al. (1967) derived 34 sub-types of cities.

Even within the confines of the Dominion of Canada, cities are different to a certain degree as we compare the cities in the predominantly French-settled Province of Quebec with the cities of the Province of Ontario so that we may at least distinguish between a French-Canadian type and an Anglo-Canadian type of city (see Hecht 1977). A further breakdown might lead to even more regional subtypes.

2. Cultural Types of Cities in their Culture Realms

The following paragraphs will restrict themselves to these twelve cultural types of cities corresponding to the twelve great culture realms of the world, and to a few selected cultural traits.

2.1 The European City

Europe's cities originated from processes that started in the eighth century with the consolidation of political power and economic development. The ruler's power, be it clerical or secular, found its manifestation in cathedrals, monasteries, and castles. To the present day, churches and castles have remained focal points of European cities.

Usually the early European town was a dual settlement: besides the ruler's court, merchants' quarters developed as the second point of origin. The town was a closed entity, separated visually from its hinterland by a wall, its residents living under special jurisdiction and enjoying the right of trading. The market place and town hall became the focal point of the city. The heritage of these essentials of early European urbanism are still obvious in present-day townscapes.

There are, however, regional variations. For example, Southern Europe's towns were usually built on hills corresponding to the acropolis of Athens, with the effect of many streets actually being stairway. The hilltop location gave them a certain amount of safety not only against enemies but also against the torrential floods of the seasonally inundating Mediterranean rivers. The numerous squares were integrated intensively into the daily lives of their residents.

In contrast to the Continent, British towns show a less compact building fabric due to much earlier dismantling of their fortifications and a strong desire of people for single family dwellings, these traits making them look more like Anglo-American than European cities.

2.2 The Russian City

Many old Russian towns developed on the western bluffs of rivers with the kremlin as their core while the settlement was less compact on the eastern bank. The second core was the *posad* or merchants' quarters. Small suburban settlements called *slobody* developed as living quarters of other population groups, while still farther away often fortified monasteries were founded. The kremlin eventually lost its strategic function and mutated to become the city's administrative and cultural center.

In the colonial period grid-pattern quarters were added to many historic towns. Especially in the Islamic towns of Central Asia, the modern Russian quarters made for a conspicuous contrast to the cul-de-sac layout of the historic town center.

During the Soviet era, socialist principles were applied to town planning. The concept of microrayon corresponded with the American neighborhood principle inasmuch as entities of 6,000 to 25,000 residents with basic service functions were conceived. Three to four microrayons were called a district, and there were two more levels in the intra-urban hierarchy.

The post-Soviet changes of the 1990s brought foreign investments, mainly into hotels and office buildings, the privatization of *kolkhoz* markets and

some residential quarters, and a somewhat greater mixture of social status groups.

2.3 The Chinese City

The widespread regular grid pattern supposedly originated in military camps on the dangerous northern margin of the later Chinese Empire. Geomantics played a decisive part in the layout of towns. The rectangular system was related to yin, representing the Earth, in contrast to the circular yang, representing Heaven. The ruler's palace always faced south. A fixed number of streets ran north–south, crossing the east–west streets at right angles. However, some streets were a little displaced in order to prevent evil spirits from getting through.

During the nineteenth century many towns along the east coast and the rivers expanded by so-called 'concessions,' i.e., foreign missions, industrial, port and trading facilities, and living quarters established by Europeans and Americans.

In the present People's Republic there is a hierarchical structure of urban residents with a certain number of households forming a residents' group, several groups a residents' committee, and several committees a town. Residents are usually assigned dwelling units and social services by production complexes, these *danweis* being highly autonomous entities. The planning of great modern industrial parks since 1958 gave rise to a number of satellite cities that are supposed to relieve the metropolises from uncontrolled expansion as well as eventually abolishing the urban–rural dichotomy.

2.4 The Japanese City

The rectangular *cho*-pattern copied from China and the observing of geomantic rules made for similarities to the Chinese cities. Around 1950 one half of Japan's cities originated from the castle town or *joka-machi* of the fifteenth and sixteenth centuries. The castle district is located in a strategic hillside position, protected by a system of walls and ditches and divided into the palace area of the *daimyo* in the center and the quarters of the higher and lower *samurai* (warriors). Beyond the wall there were the quarters of the craftsmen, merchants, and priests. During the reforms of 1868 the *daimyo* lost their privileges. The castle district mutated to become a civic center in those castle towns that were able to acquire manufacturing and administrative functions. The other half of Japan's cities are port cities, market places, shrines or spas.

During the twentieth century many small shopping streets grew to the size of large shopping centers, although without any societal and cultural functions. Huge underground centers at the railroad stations became keen competitors for the traditional shopping streets of the temple districts.

A number of walled industrial parks with dormitories for single workers and multi-storey tenements for married workers' families called *danchi* were established. The third trend was land reclamation beyond the former coastlines for large modern industrial plants with their own port facilities and infrastructure of dwelling units, supermarkets, and social institutions.

2.5 The Southeast Asian City

Geomantic and anthropomorphic rules were observed in their layout. The port was considered the 'heart' of the city, while the seat of the clerical power on the south side was its 'soul.' The north was identified with the body's head and was supposed to accommodate the representative functions. The east was compared with the right or working hand and assigned to the craftsmen, the west with brain work and mental culture, and assigned to the officials and guardians of the palace.

Since the Age of Discoveries, European urban patterns and buildings have been introduced, Jakarta's Dutch origin becoming obvious by its *grachten* and Manila's Spanish origin by its *plaza mayor*. As in many colonial cities there was an intermediate status group between the indigenous people and the colonial elite. In Southeast Asia this group is made up of the Chinese, who dominate trade and commerce.

A conspicuous element of many towns is their fishing villages where boat people, often referred to as 'sea gypsies,' spend most of their lifetime on boats or sampans.

Great percentages of Indonesia's urban population are found in settlements referred to as 'kampungs,' these settlements having a functional mixture of dwellings, crafts, and trade, and originating in villages still lacking most urban amenities. Some authors consider them squatter settlements. In recent times many kampungs have been integrated into the building fabric of the growing metropolises, while only those at the urban fringe have maintained their village-like appearance.

2.6 The Indian City

Hindu urban culture is based on meditation images and symbols such as mandalas with a regular street pattern arranged around temples devoted to one of the deities. The regular Indian grid is centered on an intersection of two major axes with a temple nearby, while the palace is integrated into the wall. Ritual and secular uses of streets have been highly interwoven.

The caste system played a decisive role in Hindu culture. The four major castes originated in various parts of the deity Vishnu's body, specific quarters of the city being allocated to each of them. Priests used to live together with the ruler and the members of his court in the central temple and palace district or in the northern sector of town. The officials privileged by their position as supervisors of the ruler's water and land resources lived in the eastern sector, the merchants in the south, and the peasants in the west.

Over the centuries more than 3,000 subcastes have developed due to secessions, political quarrels, and the growing division of labor. These *jatis*, characterized by hereditary professions and high rates of endogamy have made for a very low degree of mobility and a high degree of segregation.

In North India the irregular Indian grid influenced by Islamic culture is characterized partly by winding streets of changing width and crooked byroads.

A completely new element was added to these towns by the Anglo-Indian stations of the British comprising the 'cantonment' or military quarters, the 'civil lines' or quarters of the officials of the Indian Civil Service, private entrepreneurs, and the 'railway colony.' A number of shops were lined up along the Mall while the so-called *sadr bazaar* served those troops recruited from the indigenous people for whom the Hindu town was off limits. Even a new house type was created: the bungalow, with its rectangular shape, pyramid-like roof thatched or covered with bricks, one storey high with porches on each side, and put on stilts for better ventilation and protection against floods.

2.7 The Oriental or Islamic City

There has been a long-lasting controversy as to whether the cities from Morocco to Pakistan should be termed Oriental or Islamic. Adherents to the latter opinion consider the Friday mosque and the bazaar the two dominating elements, while their opponents argue that the suq, the caravansary, and the *hammam* or bathhouse can be traced back to the Roman colonnades, basilica, and thermae of pre-Islamic times, respectively.

One of the most conspicuous traits of the medina or historic town center is its cul-de-sac pattern, while the few thoroughfares are exceptions. One explanation for this phenomenon is the juxtaposition of clans of different origins as to their ethnicity, religion and language, and their desire to live segregated from other residents. Second, in contrast to the Roman carriages, camels and mules were used for transportation. The third reason is the legal status of the cul-de-sacs: they are not public spaces, but rather are owned by their neighbors.

Much real estate of the medina is in *waqfs*, i.e., foundations donated by rulers, officials, or merchants for religious and beneficial purposes or the use of their children, and administered by trustees. Neither these nor the users are interested in investments, so that these foundations prevent urban renewal, leading to the decay of buildings and the emigration of the wealthier people.

The bazaar is structured in a way that the most valuable goods such as jewelry, books, or perfumes are traded in the most centrally located and covered lanes. Spices, shoes, and carpets are found some distance from the center, while pottery, leather goods, auto parts, and other manufactured and bulky goods are found in a still more peripheral location. In recent years this pattern has been weakened. Simple stalls have been replaced by shops with shop windows, and the whole bazaar has faced competition from the development of a central business district (CBD) and modern suburban shopping centers.

2.8 The Central African City

There has been a controversy as to whether the Yoruba towns of southern Nigeria were urban settlements in the strict sense of the word. The Hausa developed a special kind of segregation, since no strangers were allowed into their town, those people founding settlements of their own outside the gates: *sabon-gari* which in Hausa means 'new town.' The British colonial administration adopted the *sabon-gari* system for ethnic and hygienic reasons.

Although the numbers of European soldiers, administrators, and business managers remained small, their settlements were spacious in contrast to the crowded areas of the indigenous people. There were intermediate groups between them and the European elite: the Levantines in West Africa and the Indians in East Africa. They were mainly in trade, transport, and lower ranks of the administration. The Indians especially had their own temples, schools, clubs, and bazaars with *dukas*, i.e., open shops with verandahs closed with wooden shutters at night. In recent times modern shopping centers have developed beside the duka-style bazaars. A slow transformation has occurred from a society composed of the European upper class, the Indian middle class, and the African lower class toward a society structured along socioeconomic lines.

In many towns the indigenous population is divided into a dominating tribal group and several minority groups from different tribes, each of them stressing their own tribal traditions, a phenomenon referred to as 'retribalization' or 'peasantization.'

2.9 The South African City

The early towns of the Cape Province and the towns in Orange Free State and Transvaal were founded by the Afrikaners, and all others by the British. Within a few decades they went full circle from the colonial town through the apartheid town, and a transition period to the post-apartheid town. As early as 1913 the Native Land Act prohibited Africans from acquiring land outside their reservations, or later homelands. They lived either as servants in their employers' households or were forced to stay in 'locations' and hostels.

The central city was reserved for white citizens and, as an exception, for some colored groups, by the Group Areas Act of 1948. Even white people lived more or less segregated as to their Afrikaner, British, or Portuguese origin. The Natives Resettlement Act of 1954 initiated comprehensive relocation. Often railroad tracks, highways, or canals served as barriers between the quarters of racial groups, while each racial quarter was assigned a considerable number of places of employment in order to keep commuting through other racial quarters to a minimum.

However, complete segregation was never achieved. Since 1986, non-white enterprises have been admitted to so-called 'free trade areas' while 'grey areas' have been legalized, and even 'free settlement areas' open to all racial groups have been established. The repeal of the racial laws in 1991 brought about considerable mobility and squatting.

2.10 The Latin American City

The Spaniards founded their overseas towns around the *plaza mayor* with the *cabildo*, cathedral, and courthouse. They had a central–peripheral social gradient with the upper-class people living in the *cuadras* (blocks) nearest to the plaza.

This social structure has persisted to the present partly because centrally located residences are still considered a privilege. Part of the city center mutated into the CBD, with some storeys being added to old patio houses and *edificios* or high-rise office buildings being constructed. Behind the fashionable *paseos*, overcrowded multi-storey tenements or *conventillos* had developed, which received many rural migrants who eventually further migrated to the shantytowns at the urban fringe.

Since the 1930s a sectoral pattern has been superimposed on the traditional zonal structure by the development of manufacturing plants and worker's quarters along railroad lines, and by the centrifugal expansion of upper-class quarters.

At the urban fringe a more or less high percentage of people live in shantytowns called *villas miserias* in Argentina or *favelas* in Brazil. Most of their occupations are in the so-called 'informal sector' of the economy. As a measure of relief, *poblaciones* or public housing estates in combination with site-and-service projects have been built by the governments of various South American states.

2.11 The Anglo-American City

While the grid pattern had already been introduced to colonial North America the grid was applied rigorously to most towns beyond the Appalachian Mountains after the release of the Land Ordinance in 1785.

The United States was the pacemaker in skyscraper construction. Competition from huge suburban shopping centers and the loss of purchasing power of the clientele of downtown shops brought decay to the downtown areas of US cities. Since the 1950s, revitalization programs have been carried out with malls and shopping *gallerías* often in combination with skyways, downtown motels, and modern cultural centers with concert halls, convention centers, and exhibition halls. Historical foundations have purchased and resold many historic buildings by means of revolving funds.

Since in large areas the founding of towns and the construction of railroads occurred simultaneously, railroad tracks often cut right through the town center with level crossings, while large manufacturing areas developed right outside the CBD along the tracks. The inner residential areas decayed, because most of the building stock was made of timber and prone to swift degradation, and the improved-value system of taxation was no incentive for investments, so that tax delinquency and vacancy rates increased rapidly. Moreover, since the 1830s low-status groups of immigrants concentrated in these inner quarters where they were close to their fellow countrymen and to manufacturing jobs. In recent years many such areas have been upgraded by 'urban homesteading' and gentrification.

For many decades suburbia has been dominated by single-family homes and duplexes. Especially, young families moved to the suburbs seeking better schools for their children. Other reasons were investments in high-quality real estate and the chance to live close to neighbors sharing the same lifestyle ('lifestyle suburbs'). The metropolises became completely fragmented by dozens of huge shopping centers, these functioning as catalyzers for modern office and business parks, and the growth of 'urban villages' termed 'edge cities' by Garreau (1991).

2.12 The Australian City

In general, Australia's cities very much resemble the Anglo-American type. There are, however, certain differences. The CBD has never experienced such a high concentration of skyscrapers with all their disadvantages. The inner suburbs of the nineteenth century have not experienced a decay similar to that of US cities due to more favorable conditions: the long rows of terrace houses are rather solid buildings made of brick or natural stone (with the exception of the Queenslander house made of timber and set on stilts), the site-value system of taxation, the much smaller concentration of non-British minority groups, most of these immigrants only arriving after 1950 in a country with a booming economy and high wages enabling them to become home owners in some suburban areas within a few years, and the high degree of gentrification.

Urban sprawl has been even greater than in the United States and made for approximately 70 percent home ownership. Despite this and a high rate of car ownership there are amazingly few urban expressways (with the exception of Perth). A widely accepted planning concept is the development of a limited number of growth corridors along railroad lines and major highways with designated district centers around suburban railroad stations.

See also: Cities: Internal Structure; Cultural Diversity, Human Development, and Education; Cultural Geography; Cultural Landscape in Environmental Studies; Cultural Landscape in Geography; Cultural Resource Management (CRM): Conservation of Cultural Heritage; Ecology, Cultural; Urban Activity Patterns; Urban Growth Models; Urban History

Bibliography

Agnew J A, Mercer J, Sopher D E (eds.) 1984 *The City in Cultural Context*. Allen & Unwin, New York

Beaujeu-Garnier J, Chabot G 1963 *Traité de géographie urbaine*. A. Colin, Paris

Brunn S D, Williams J F (eds.) 1983 *Cities of the World. World Regional Urban Development*. Harper & Row, New York

Ehlers E (ed.) 1992 Modelling the city: Cross-cultural perspectives. *Colloquium Geographicum* 22, Bonn

Fleure H J 1920 Some types of cities in temperate Europe. *Geographical Review* 10: 357–74

Garreau J 1991 *Edge City. Life on the New Frontier*. Doubleday, New York

Goldberg M A, Mercer J 1986 *The Myth of the North American City*. University of British Columbia Press Vancouver, BC

Hecht A 1977 *Die anglo- und frankokanadische Stadt. Trierer Geographische Studien Sonderheft 1*. Trier, Germany, pp. 87–11

Hofmeister B 1999 *Stadtgeographie*, 7th edn. G. Westermann Brunswick, Germany

Holzner D Dommisse E J Mueller J E 1967 Toward a theory of cultural–genetic city classification. *Annals of the Association of American Geographers*: 367–81

Oberhummer E 1915 *Amerikanische und europäische Städte. Memorial Volume of the Transcontinental Excursion of 1912*. New York

Passarge S (ed.) 1930 *Stadtlandschaften der Erde*. Breslau, Germany

Rugg D S 1972 *Spatial Foundations of Urbanism*. W C Brown Co, Dubuque, IO

Scargill D I 1979 *The form of cities*. St. Martin's Press, New York

Smailes A E 1955 Some reflections on the geographical description and analysis of townscapes. *Transactions of the Institute of British Geographers*: 99–115

Tietze W (ed.) 1977 *Urbanization of the Earth/Urbanisierung der Erde*. Berlin

B. Hofmeister

Cities, Images of

Community appearance matters to people. This article reviews scientific findings on the visual features of cities that convey a strong and desirable image to people who experience them. The article defines the concepts, reviews the research, and discusses methodological questions and future research and use of the findings.

1. City Form: A Scientific Approach

City form is shaped by and affects many people. Research shows that appearance is central in human responses to their surroundings (cf. Nasar 1994, 1997). City form 'should be guided by a "visual" plan: a set of recommendations and controls' for its appearance (Lynch 1960). US legislation and the courts grant governments the authority to control appearances (Mandelker 1996) and most American cities do so (Lightner 1993). To work, appearance controls must consider people's image of places. This article centers on the two key aspects of the image: imageability and linkability. Imageability refers to the probability that an environment will evoke a strong image from observers (Lynch 1960); and linkability refers to the probability that an environment will evoke a strong favorable response from observers (Nasar 1997).

For most of its history, urban design—the practice of shaping urban form—has followed a philosophical approach. Theorists speculated on what ought to be, but did not arrive at or test their speculations scientifically. Lynch (1960) suggested and tested a scientific approach. He assumed that people would more likely know, and so use, an environment that was easy to read or legible. This made legibility a valid purpose for research and design.

Lynch described the environmental image as having three parts: *identity, structure,* and *meaning.* This means humans recognize or identify objects (identity), they see a recognizable pattern of relationships between objects (structure), and they draw emotional value (or have feelings) about the objects and structure (meaning). The meaning of a place may take a denotative or a connotative form. Denotative meanings are the same as identity; they refer to judgments of what the place is. Connotative meanings refer to inferences about the quality and character of the place or its users. People often think of such connotative meanings as a question of aesthetics. This article avoids the term 'aesthetics,' because of its connection to art, where a statement may take priority over pleasure, and because many people view aesthetics as something one cannot quantify. Aesthetics also has its roots in philosophy and normative theory. Philosophers question the degree to which aesthetic experience arises from psychical distance or phenomenological involvement; and designers offer top-down speculations about the correct aesthetic for the design of places.

Fechner (1876) introduced the bottom-up approach to the study of aesthetics (meanings). He studied human evaluations of attributes of simple stimuli, such as rectangles and polygons. Almost a hundred years later, Berlyne (1971) revived this scientific approach, called empirical aesthetics; and at a time when psychologists sought real-world relevance, Wohlwill (1976) extended the ideas and approach of Berlyne to the study of real places. Although evaluative responses, such as preference, may vary across individuals (cf. Little 1987), the theories of Berlyne (1971) and Wohlwill (1976) held that certain kinds of physical features would likely have hedonic value. More recently, some theories suggest an evolutionary basis for certain shared environmental preferences (Kaplan and Kaplan 1989, Orians 1986, Ulrich 1993). Theories differ in their interpretation of the importance and interdependency of the individual and the environment in response. Research, however, confirms that beauty rests more in the features of the place evaluated than in the head of the evaluator (Stamps 1995).

Although Lynch recognized the importance of meaning, he felt one could not easily manipulate it through changes in urban form. He accepted the conventional wisdom that preference is highly variable across individuals. He judged meaning as impractical to study, and concentrated on form—identity and structure—separate from meaning.

2. Components of City Imageability

Lynch interviewed residents in three cities to see what they recalled about their cities; he found strong consensus across respondents. They converged on five elements that enhance a city's imageability: landmarks, paths, districts, edges, and nodes. *Landmarks* are visible reference points, such as towers or mountains. *Paths* are channels for movement, such as streets or walkways. *Districts* are large sections of a city that have some recognizable, common perceived identity distinguishing them from other areas. *Edges* are barriers, such as shorelines, rivers, or railroad cuts. *Nodes* are focal points of intensive human activity. Research confirms the stability of these elements for many populations and cities around the world (cf. Nasar 1997). Although the images and prominence of elements may vary across populations and places (Rapoport 1977), the correct arrangement of the elements can heighten the imageability of a city. Research that grew from Lynch's seminal work has yielded much information about mental maps, distance perception, and wayfinding (cf. Evans 1980).

To shape urban form, imageability is not enough. One must consider people's evaluation of the city, the meanings they see, or their evaluative image.

3. Components of the Evaluative Image of the City

Communities might not need a scientific understanding of the bases for evaluative responses if the designers, design review boards, and other experts who shape places produced designs that pleased people. Regrettably, research shows that they often do not (cf. Nasar 1994, 1997).

To find the evaluative image, one must consider both the evaluative responses important to people and the features of the environment that people notice and evaluate. Research has found three important aspects of human evaluative response to places (Russell and Snodgrass 1989). Preference is a purely evaluative dimension. Mixes of pleasure and arousal produce excitement and relaxation. Exciting places feel more pleasant and arousing than boring ones; and relaxing places feel more pleasant but less arousing than stressful ones.

Evaluative response to places may arise from two formal and symbolic variables (cf. Kaplan and Kaplan 1989, Nasar 1994). Formal variables have to do with the structure of form and include such things as shape, proportion, scale, complexity, incongruity, novelty, and order. Symbolic or content variables have to do with the connotative meanings associated with the forms. Several kinds of theories discuss the relationship between these variables and response. One set of theories view preference as dependent on arousal (Berlyne 1971, Mandler 1984, Wohlwill 1976). Of the many variables these theories cite as affecting arousal, complexity and novelty (atypicality) have garnered the most research attention. In theory, complexity and novelty increase arousal, interest, and excitement; but preference has an inverted U-shaped relationship to arousal. Preference would increase with increases in complexity or novelty up to a point, after which increases in complexity or novelty would produce a downturn in preference. Another theory offers an evolutionary model in which human survival depended on preference for involvement and making sense, and as a result, humans now prefer places that offer involvement and either make sense or promise to make sense (Kaplan and Kaplan 1989). This theory posits complexity and mystery (the promise of new information ahead, as in a deflected vista) as creating involvement; and it posits coherence and legibility as helping people make sense of things. People should like a mix of complexity, mystery, coherence, and legibility.

Research shows seven environmental features as prominent in human perception and evaluation of places: naturalness, order, complexity, novelty (atypicality), upkeep, openness, and historical significance (cf. Nasar 1994, 1997). People recognize variation from natural (vegetation) to human-made. Research shows that humans prefer vegetation, that preference increases with the addition of vegetation, decreases with the increase in human-made elements, and that people dislike obtrusive signs, utility poles, overhead wires, and billboards, traffic, and intense land uses. Commuters drive out of their way to use a parkway rather than a less natural expressway; and research suggests that exposure to vegetation may have restorative or healing effects.

Research shows that people notice and prefer order. Preference for order has emerged for many kinds of urban settings and for various ordering variables, including legibility, coherence, identifiability, clarity, compatibility, and congruity. People also prefer well-kept to dilapidated areas. Dilapidation and disorder such as vandalism, boarded up buildings, and litter, which researchers refer to as physical incivilities, also contribute to a perception of the breakdown of social controls, fear of crime, and crime.

Complexity relates to the number of different elements and the distinctiveness between those elements in a scene. Research shows that people notice variations in complexity, and that interest, excitement, and viewing time increase with complexity, but that preference tends to be highest for moderate levels of complexity. Though some research points to contradictory findings, those findings suffer from method biases. Research shows that novelty and atypicality also increase excitement and interest. People prefer moderate to low levels of novelty or atypicality. Though some studies show contradictory results, the discrepancies arise from flaws in measuring novelty and familiarity.

People readily notice changes in spaciousness. Preference increases with openness, but people also like some spatial definition. People also like mystery (in the form of deflected vistas), but for uncertain conditions such as urban areas deflected vistas and uncertainty about information ahead heightens fear.

Places may have historical significance or just look historical. In either case, they evoke favorable response. People also prefer popular styles to the high-style designs. The preference for historical significance and certain popular styles over high styles may arise from connotative meanings associated with them or from the mix of complexity and order in them.

Naturalness, upkeep, and historical significance appear to be symbolic variables, while the others appear to be formal variables, but each one may work for formal or symbolic reasons. In addition, people may like some of these variables for their contribution to order or for their associations with status. Naturalness, upkeep, open views, order (compatibility), and historical significance enhance order, but these same features may look like feature that wealthier persons can afford. People notice status, make accurate judgments of social status from environmental cues, and prefer high-status to low-status areas.

For integrative reviews on perception and preference of these features, see Kaplan and Kaplan (1989), Nasar (1988a, 1988b, 1989, 1994, 1997) and Wohlwill (1976); for vegetation see Kaplan (1995), Ulrich (1983, 1993), and Wohlwill (1983); for disorder incivilities, see Taylor (1989); for atypicality, see Mandler (1984), Purcell and Nasar (1992), and Whitfield (1993); for fear and mystery, see Nasar and Jones (1997).

4. Methodological Issues

Visual quality research makes choices in selecting respondents, environmental stimuli, measures of environmental features, and measures of evaluative response. The choices involve trade-offs between what is practical, what allows experimental control, and what will generalize to the real situation. For a full review of the methodological issues see Nasar (1997, 1999). One thing that differentiates visual quality research from other social science inquiries is the need to get response to the appearance of places (Marans and Stokols 1993). For this, many studies use color photographs and slides. Research shows that responses to such stimuli, even though they lack movement and sound, accurately reflect on-site response (Stamps 1990).

5. Future Directions

Future research needs to better define the linkage between the judged and actual physical attributes. It should examine movement through environments. It should apply scientific methods to historical data to examine longitudinal aspects of evaluative response. It should use meta analysis to integrate findings of previous studies statistically. It should supplement verbal responses with psychophysiological measures and observation of behavior.

To derive specific guidelines for special situations, one can also use visual quality programming. This involves applied research to develop information for a visual quality plan or guidelines. Nasar (1997, 1999) demonstrates examples of this for various applications. This can lead to improvements in the visual quality of communities for residents and visitors.

See also: Memory for Meaning and Surface Memory; Mental Imagery, Psychology of; Mental Representations, Psychology of; Multi-attribute Decision Making in Urban Studies; Space: Linguistic Expression; Spatial Analysis in Geography; Spatial Cognition

Bibliography

Berlyne D E 1971 *Aesthetics and Psychobiology*. Appleton-Century-Crofts, New York

Evans G 1980 Environmental cognition. *Psychological Bulletin* **88**: 259–87

Fechner G 1876 *Vorschule der Asthetik*. Breitopf and Hartel, Leipzig, Germany

Kaplan R, Kaplan S 1989 *The Experience of Nature: A Psychological Perspective*. Cambridge University Press, New York

Kaplan S 1995 The restorative benefits of nature: Towards an integrative framework. *Journal of Environmental Psychology* **15**: 169–82

Lightner B 1993 *A Survey of Design Review Practice in Local Government*. (Monograph) MEMO: Planning Advisory Service (PAS). American Planning Association, Chicago

Little B R 1987 Personality and the environment. In: Stokols D, Altman I (eds.) *Handbook of Environmental Psychology, Vol. 1*. Wiley, New York, pp. 205–44

Lynch K 1960 *The Image of the City*. MIT Press, Cambridge, MA

Mandelker D R 1998 *Land Use Law*. Mische, Charlottesville, VA

Mandler J M 1984 *Stories, Scripts, and Scenes: Aspects of Schema Theory*. Erlbaum, Hillsdale, NJ

Marans R W, Stokols D 1993 *Environmental Simulation: Research and Policy Issues*. Plenum, New York

Nasar J L 1988a *Environmental Aesthetics: Theory, Research, and Applications*. Cambridge University Press, New York

Nasar J L 1988b Perception and evaluation of residential street-scenes. In: Nasar J L (ed.) *Environmental Aesthetics: Theory, Research, and Applications*. Cambridge University Press, New York, pp. 275–89

Nasar J L 1989 Perception, cognition and evaluation of urban places. In: Altman I, Zube E (eds.) *Human Behavior and Environment: Public Spaces*, Plenum, New York, pp. 31–56

Nasar J L 1994 Urban design aesthetics: The evaluative quality of building exteriors. *Environment and Behavior* **26**: 377–401

Nasar J L 1997 *The Evaluative Image of the City*. Sage, Thousand Oaks, CA

Nasar J L 1999 *Design by Competition: Making Design Competition Work*. Cambridge University Press, New York

Nasar J L, Jones K 1997 Landscapes of fear and stress. *Environment and Behavior* **29**: 291–323

Orians G H 1986 An ecological and evolutionary approach to landscape aesthetics. In: Penning-Rowsell E C, Lownthal D (eds.) *Landscape Means and Values*. Allen and Unwin, London, pp. 3–25

Purcell A T, Nasar J L 1992 Experiencing other peoples houses: A model of similarities and differences in environmental experience. *Journal of Environmental Psychology* **12**: 199–211

Rapoport A 1977 *Human Aspects of Urban Form*. Pergamon Press, Oxford, UK

Russell J A, Snodgrass J 1989 Emotion and environment. In: Stokols D, Altman I (eds.) *Handbook of Environmental Psychology, Vol. 1*. Wiley, New York, pp. 245–80

Stamps A E 1990 Use of photographs to simulate environments. A meta-analysis. *Perceptual and Motor Skills* **71**: 907–13

Stamps A E 1995 Stimulus and respondent factors in environmental preference. *Perceptual and Motor Skills* **80**: 668–70

Taylor R B 1989 Toward an environmental psychology of disorder: Delinquency, crime and fear of crime. In: Stokols D, Altman I (eds.) *Handbook of Environmental Psychology, Vol. 2*. Wiley, New York, pp. 951–86

Ulrich R S 1983 Aesthetic and affective response to natural environment. In: Altman I, Wohlwill J F (eds.) *Behavior and the Natural Environment: Human Behavior and Environment, Advances in Theory and Research, Vol. 6*. Plenum, New York, pp. 85–125

Ulrich R S 1993 Biophilia and the conservation ethic. In: Kellert S R, Wilson E O (eds.) *The Biophilia Hypothesis*. Island Press, Washington, DC, pp. 73–137

Whitfield T W A 1983 Predicting preference for everyday objects: An experimental confrontation between two theories of aesthetic behavior. *Journal of Environmental Psychology* 3: 221–37

Wohlwill J F 1976 Environmental aesthetics: The environment as a source of affect. In: Altman I, Wohlwill J F (eds.) *Human Behavior and the Environment: Advances in Theory and Research, Vol. 1*. Plenum, New York, pp. 37–86

Wohlwill J F 1983 The concept of nature: A psychologist's view. In: Altman I, Wohlwill J F (eds.) *Behavior and the Natural Environment*. Plenum, New York, pp. 5–37

J. L. Nasar

Cities, Internal Organization of

Economic activities, land uses, and socioeconomic status of population seldom distribute evenly or randomly in an urban area. They typically differentiate into internally homogeneous clusters. It is difficult not to conceive that this differentiation is governed by some underlying principles of spatial organization. And urban form affects the economic efficiency, social equity, environmental quality, and sense of place. Therefore, understanding theories of urban spatial organization helps advance knowledge and shape better futures for urban areas.

Contemporary urban development has long spread beyond the political boundaries of a city. A typical urban landscape in an advanced economy is a contiguous urbanized area that consists of multiple cities and their suburbs. Hence, urban spatial organization must be analyzed in the context of an urban region.

Most studies in urban spatial organization have been conducted in North America where an advanced capitalist market economy prevails. Their generalizations may not be completely applicable to cities that have evolved in different economic modes, such as those where the public sector dictates urban development or communal institutions control property rights. Furthermore, North American urban places are different from the rapidly growing mega-cities (having populations of more than 15 million people) in Asia and Latin America.

1. Urbanization and Suburbanization

During the nineteenth century, North America rapidly industrialized and urbanized. For example, between 1820 and 1920, the number of US cities with populations of 5,000 persons or more exploded from 39 to 1,467. During this period, these cities were also under transformation. Originally evolved from a focal point of employment, these cities were relatively small and compact because contemporary transportation systems limited their expansion. Technological advances led to successive transportation systems: streetcar, suburban rail, and subway. Each new system helped to push the urbanized area further.

Similarly, in the early twentieth century, the use of trucks, automobiles, and telephones vastly expanded the urban horizon and dispersed wholesale and manufacturing uses to the suburbs. Meanwhile, new building technologies such as elevators and skyscrapers helped rebuild city centers into central business districts (CBDs)—containing blocks having concentrations of high-rise buildings of offices and retail.

While the urban share of the US population first reached 50 percent in 1920, the most striking change that would sweep America, suburbanization, was delayed by the Great Depression and World War Two. In the postwar period, three interrelated processes restructured the urban landscape. High rates of family formation and the 'baby boom' (a surge of births between 1946 and 1964) created extreme housing shortages that the existing urban fabric could not accommodate. Concurrently, huge federal and state expressway-building programs opened up new residential suburbs while urban renewal efforts accelerated the outward movement of blacks from segregated ghettoes into nearby predominantly white neighborhoods. Throughout the 1950s and the 1960s, these last two processes resulted in the so-called 'white flight' or 'flight-from-blight' phenomena (Mieszkowski and Mills 1993). These processes accelerated an already existing decentralizing trend and led to further dispersal of economic activities. As suburban centers captured jobs, housing, and stores, the central cities lost their dominance in metropolitan population and employment. The result was the growth of sprawling urban regions. These trends continued through the late twentieth century as urbanized areas gradually become polycentric.

By 2000, the US demographic character was firmly established. For example, 80 percent of its population was classified as urban, up from 56 percent fifty years earlier. Furthermore, suburbanization gained momentum. In 2000, the share of the urban population living in the suburbs was 60 percent, a complete reversal from the 40 percent of 1950. Suburbanization is not unique to the US; other nations of advanced economies are undergoing similar changes (Ingram 1998).

2. Patterns of Spatial Organization

Evaluating urban spatial organization encompasses several patterns, including land use differentiation, population distribution, household characteristics, income and racial segregation, employment distribution, changing building densities, and the rise of subcenters and polycentric urban forms.

Urban land uses are highly differentiated. Land uses can be compatible or incompatible with one another. Compatible uses generate mutual benefits or positive externalities. Incompatible uses create harmful consequences or negative externalities. Compatible uses usually coexist with one another while incompatible uses show rigid segregation. It is debatable whether public land use control or voluntary market forces contribute to this segregation.

Theoretically, land uses display a number of geometric forms: concentric rings, sectors or wedges, multiple nuclei or small clusters, or a linear formation from a narrow strip to an arc or a corridor. The Burgess model (1925) posits that land uses fall into concentric zones extending outward from the CBD. Two alternative formulations complementing this schema are the sectoral model, arguing that wedges of similar activities radiate from the CBD along transportation corridors, and the multi-nuclei model asserting that secondary CBDs and suburban economic centers emerge to accommodate second-order activities. It appears that these three forms of land-use arrangements can coexist in a single urban area. For example, concentric rings and corridor-type of uses are evident in a polycentric Los Angeles.

The way that population is distributed displays some regularities as well. Urban population densities tend to be higher around the CBD and lower at the edges. Alonso (1964) developed a monocentric model to reflect this pattern and calculated a density decay function, $D(\mu) = D.exp(-b\mu)$, where the average density, D, starts at the fringe of the CBD and declines at a rate, b, per unit distance, μ, away from the center. This function flattens as time changes, i.e., densities at the fringe will marginally increase or the limit of a city continues to expand. Over time, population densities have decreased around the core, reflecting the depopulation of most of the central cities since the 1950s. The monocentric model is limited because its approximation of densities is specific to a specific scale of observation. The gross population density, a commonly used measure, tends to underrepresent the net density in the periphery because it factors unpopulated and nonresidential areas into the analysis. Comparing neighborhood by neighborhood, the net residential density in the outer suburbs may not be too different from that in the inner suburbs.

The spatial distribution of household characteristics is not uniform. Households of small size, female-headed, or with no children are more concentrated in the core. Families and larger size households are more dispersed in the periphery where larger lots and detached housing are more abundant. The differences in preference also reflect the impact of family cycles in housing choice. Families tend to be more sensitive to house size and school quality.

Income segregation is the most noticeable feature of American urban spatial organization. Broadly speaking, higher income groups reside in the suburbs while the low-income groups stay in the core. This general pattern is skewed by the high concentration of poverty in the core and also interrupted by other irregularities. Small high-income precincts are commonly found in the urban core (e.g., Coral Cables in Miami, Georgetown in Washington DC, and Pacific Heights in San Francisco). Similarly, not all suburban households are high-income because many suburban development projects target the middle class. Unlike population density, changes of income level rarely move smoothly away from the CBD. Neighborhoods with large income differences are often separated by such physical barriers as rivers, highways, or even manmade barriers.

Employment distribution exhibits more dispersal than residential distribution. Manufacturing activities started to move out from the center in the 1900s as trucks replaced rail freight movement. By mid century, as air transportation become important, manufacturing and distribution centers gravitated toward airports. Expressway expansion has provided ubiquitous access within urban areas and diminished the locational advantages of their cores. Today, manufacturing and wholesale activities tend to cluster around freeway interchanges in the suburbs. Lower-order retailing activities have also moved to the suburbs as purchasing power has shifted in that direction. Suburban malls were first developed in the late 1950s and within decades modern and bigger malls were built in the newer suburbs, leaving CBD and old suburban retail centers to falter. Despite that the average CBD's share of metropolitan employment has fallen to less than ten percent, CBDs have not completely lost their role because most of them still represent the biggest single concentration of specialized services and government activities.

Building and development densities also exhibit a distance decay relationship with the CBD but their gradients are much steeper and often disrupted by surges of density in secondary CBDs and suburban centers. In general, high-rise development and multi-family housing cluster in the primary and the secondary centers more than in other part of the urban region.

The rise of subcenters and polycentric urban form is a direct result of continuous urban expansion and shifts in population and employment distribution. As population and employment disperse, they gravitate to suburban centers and transform the old monocentric urban structures into polycentric ones. These centers have a propensity to cluster or distribute loosely in a sectoral form. These centers evolve from older settlement points or they create their own set of activities and population concentration. Garreau (1991) characterized the rise of these centers as 'Edge Cities,' recently developed places with a sizeable office and retail space attracting large numbers of commuters. Today, these centers are increasingly self-contained and making suburbs independent of the cores of their metropolitan regions. Recent studies reveal that office and professional service activities are continuing to scatter. As a result, more than half of the commuting traffic is among these centers.

3. Searching for the Principles of Spatial Organization

Explaining the organizing principle(s) of spatial organization requires sophisticated understanding of the social, economic, technological, cultural, and other phenomena influencing urban form and structure. Spatial organization is derived from observable patterns specific to the scale of observation. Also, the paradigm adopted by a researcher generally shapes the findings. This section identifies and discusses common determinants of urban spatial organization.

3.1 Factors that Influence Urban Form and Structure

Second to topography, the urban morphology, the built environment and the associated property rights, is the most important constraint to urban development. The 'urban capital stock,' i.e., lots, buildings, streets, road grids, rail tracks, and expressways are relatively inelastic to changes. Since modifications of urban morphology involve very costly land assembly, older areas in the core are likely to be left derelict. Similarly, streets and freeways usually form impasses of a land use or boundaries to a neighborhood. Infrastructure, such as transportation facilities and transshipment centers and their ancillary uses resist changes. Their obsolescence or closure causes dereliction and blight. Though building structure is malleable and conversion of uses is possible, these transitions are lengthy and sometimes costly, especially in the absence of market demand and public intervention. In contrast, development in the fringe is less risky, subject to less uncertainty and cheaper. As real estate activities tends to be cyclical, construction occurs in waves. Investment converges on certain locations for a short duration and then wanes. Sometimes, these activities create an impressive mark on urban form—power centers, corridors of strip malls, and sprawling gated communities. Successive urban expansions have reflected the impetuous and speculative nature of the development process.

Technological changes greatly affect spatial organization. The prime factor behind persistent decentralization has been advances in transportation technology. For example, expressway systems have radically extended urbanized areas. Contemporary sprawl typically hops along newly developed transportation corridors. Similarly, the development of remote and difficult terrains is possible because of technological changes to such infrastructure systems as water supply, power grid, and sewerage and drainage. Finally, the advent of modern telecommunications incorporating personal computers, facsimiles, and cellular telephones is producing new locational requirements for firms (Graham and Marvin 1996). While some speculate that the revolution in information technology will cause the 'death of distance' and the reintegration of home and workplace, evidence indicates that it merely expands choices of human interaction and does not reduce commuting (Kotkin 2000). Its impact on urban structure is still not clear, as it has generated both centralization and decentralization of economic activities.

Income, wealth, and preferences have a great influence on population distribution. Income and wealth affect consumer preferences and the ability to live in specific locations. Research on housing choice has consistently shown the importance of such attractive attributes as neighborhood amenities, school quality, personal safety, and quality of life. As the spatial distribution of these attractive attributes is highly differentiated, higher income groups tend to outbid lower income groups in all localities in the price competition for these attributes. Therefore, high-income group clusters are not confined to the suburbs. Both 'middle-class flight' and 'gentrification' reflect how higher income groups are sensitive to the perceived changes of neighborhood quality. Furthermore, preferences in choosing neighbors along racial or ethnic lines are translated into such discriminatory practices as selective real estate information, fiscal zoning and other restrictive land use regulations. These practices challenge the argument that income and racial segregation is voluntary. Evidence that minority inner-city residents have greater difficulties in dispersing to the suburbs in comparison to other groups of similar income level indicates that racial preference has prevented smooth and market-driven neighborhood transition.

Economic restructuring destabilizes the old order of industrial location. Traditionally, manufacturing firms were sensitive to transportation costs reflected in the distance toward market or raw material. However, in today's postindustrial era, minimization of transportation costs has become less important as their share in total production costs has declined. Such factors as labor costs and quality, business climate, economies of scale, and quality of life are new considerations. In addition, the agglomeration effects where inter-industry and inter-firm linkages allow sharing of innovations and access to large labor pools and networks of suppliers and purchasers are important. The postindustrial era has also witnessed the employment dispersal that, together with residential decentralization, has developed into a multi-point and multi-directional commuting pattern. Under the new economy, knowledge-based industries require the new set of locational considerations discussed above (Wheeler et al. 2000). Finally, under globalization, urban regions have developed more external links and expanded their hinterlands. While at the same time, the economic functions of inner-city neighborhoods have changed. In some instances, the increase flow of capital, information, products, and people has given rise to specialized districts such as ethnic quarters for immigrants and clusters of import and export firms. In others, especially where in economically isolated neighborhoods, high rates of unemployment have led to severe distress.

Although the private sector leads urban development, the public sector plays an important role as the major undertaker of infrastructure projects and provider of such services as public schools, law and order, waste collection and disposal, parks and recreation, and land use regulation. Infrastructure steers future development and the level of public services directly affects the quality of life. In addition, local tax levels and the efficiency and attitude of local government shape the business climate that most private businesses rely on in making investment decisions. American urban areas commonly contain a large number of small municipalities. This fragmentation has resulted in great variations in the quality of services and business climate. Labeled as the Tiebout effect, these variations induce businesses and residents to move among places, leading localities to compete with one another to attract investment and middle-class residents. This competition is often unequal because some municipalities have fewer resources, and suffer from eroding tax bases and the desertion of the middle class. Such unequal competition reinforces segregated and fragmented spatial organization.

3.2 Interpretations of Spatial Organization

The study of the spatial organization of urban places can take many approaches. Each casts a different image and each adopts a particular set of methods and paradigms. Here are the major approaches.

The ecological approach developed at the University of Chicago was the earliest systematic study of urban form (Park 1925). It viewed the city as a composite of multiple ecological colonies segregated by income, class, and ethnicity. Its organization principle was that the succession and invasion of one colony into another yielded a specific urban form of concentric zones. It suggested a distribution of colonies where the transients, low-income groups, and recent immigrants clustered around the CBD. The working class and more stable immigrant groups were

further out. Single-family dwellings came next and commuters occupied the outmost urban zone. This approach stimulated generations of urban studies. It highlighted the competition and conflict over space among socioeconomic groups. It treated spatial form as a manifestation of a dynamic process of commanding space.

The utility maximization model has been the most dominant approach used to analyze spatial organization in the latter half of the twentieth century. Based on Alonso's seminal monocentric model that assumed that firms and individuals made tradeoffs between transportation costs and locational rent, it stimulated numerous studies focusing on land use and transportation modeling (Ottensmann 1975). The subsequent work commonly adopted neoclassical economic principles as the underlying organizing theme and treated an urban area as one aggregate unit of optimization where each agent settled in the location that maximized its utility and profit. This work was generally mathematical and followed a set of deductive methods that required vigorous formulation of premises. Although the resulting findings followed strong reasoning, they were contingent on the assumptions stated in the model. This work has been employed for the simulation of outcomes of one variable when other variables were under careful control.

An emerging interdisciplinary field, urban morphology, examines the physical form of cities, stresses the historical effects of the built environment and property rights, and studies the interaction of elements of the physical structure at various scales (Vance 1990). A related approach, space syntax, correlates human activities and attributes with physical configurations and linkages of buildings and street blocks. Architects and urban designers have adopted these techniques to examine the evolution of building forms and styles, street layouts, and the massing of buildings throughout history (Kostof 1992). They have extended beyond principles of design to interpretations of historical and institutional constraints and behavioral interactions with space.

The systems approach attempts to understand spatial organization in its entirety (Bourne 1982). It views the city as a human body where its internal environment interplays with its external environment. It tries to understand spatial organization holistically by studying the form, interrelationships, behavior, and evolution of activities of an urbanized area. It considers urban structure an undefined reflection of the historical and organizational principles of society, which, in turn, are the products of current and previous operating rules of culture, technology, economy, and social behavior. Since this approach refuses to isolate these elements, it has had to devise an overarching analytical framework to incorporate various organizing principles. The difficulties in developing paradigmatic coherence have prevented this attempt to flourish.

The most recent effort to understand spatial organization, the postmodern approach, has been adopted across such disciplines as geography, sociology, anthropology, cultural studies, and urban studies (Dear 2000, Soja 1989). Sometimes containing neo-Marxist doctrines, it examines urban development in the context of the rapid transformation of society under globalization and economic restructuring. It is sensitive to the worldviews held by groups differentiated by gender, class, ethnicity, and race. While it does not specifically examine spatial organization *per se*, it provides insights onto how space is perceived, battled over, and controlled. It legitimizes the use of qualitative methods to study the complex urban process. It considers the city not as one economic unit or a production center but a place with multiple functions. It also stresses the interaction of countervailing internal, regional, and global forces in polarizing and tearing apart the traditional connections of urban spaces.

See also: Spatial Interaction Model; Urban Sprawl; Spatial Organization Models; Spatial Pattern, Analysis of; Urban History/Towns and Cities in History; Urban Geography; Urban Sociology; Urban Studies, General; Income Distribution; Wealth Distribution

Bibliography

Alonso W 1964 *Location and Land Use*. Harvard University Press, Cambridge, MA
Anas A, Arnott R, Small K A 1998 Urban spatial structure. *Journal of Economic Literature* **36**: 1426–64
Berry B J L 1965 Internal structure of the city. *Law and Contemporary Problems* **30**(1): 111–19
Bourne L S (ed.) 1982 *Internal Structure of the City*. Oxford University Press, New York
Burgess E W 1925 The growth of the city. In: Park R E, Burgess E, McKenzie R (eds.) *The City*. Chicago University Press, Chicago
Dear J M 2000 *The Postmodern Urban Condition*. Blackwell, Malden, MA
Garreau J 1991 *Edge City: Life on the New Frontier*. Doubleday, New York
Graham S, Marvin S 1996 *Telecommunications and the City: Electronic Spaces, Urban Places*. Routledge, London
Harris R, Lewis R 1998 Constructing a fault(y) zone: Misrepresentations of American cities and suburbs, 1900–1950. *Annals of the Association of American Geographers* **88**(4): 622–39
Ingram G K 1998 Patterns of metropolitan development: What have we learned? *Urban Studies* **35**(7): 1019–35
Kostof S 1992 *The City Assembled: The Elements of Urban Form Through History*. Bulfinch, Boston
Kotkin J 2000 *The New Geography: How the Digital Revolution Is Reshaping the American Landscape*. Random House, New York
Mieszkowski P, Mills E S 1993 The causes of metropolitan suburbanization *Journal of Economic Perspectives* **7**(3): 135–47
Ottensmann J R 1975 *The Changing Spatial Structure of American Cities*. Lexington Books, Lexington, MA
Park R E, Burgess E, McKenzie R (eds.) 1925 *The City*. University of Chicago Press, Chicago
Queen S A, Thomas L F 1939 *The City: A Study of Urbanism in the United States*. McGraw-Hill, New York
Soja E 1989 *Postmodern Geographies: The Reassertion of Space in Critical Social Theory*. Verso, New York
Vance J E Jr. 1990 *The Continuing City: Urban Morphology in Western Civilization*. Johns Hopkins University Press, Baltimore
Webber M M, Dyckman J W, Foley D L (eds.) 1964 *Explorations into Urban Structure*. University of Pennsylvania Press, Philadelphia
Wheeler J O, Aoyama Y, Warf B (eds.) 2000 *Cities in the Telecommunications Age: The Fracturing of Geographies*. Routledge, New York
Yeates M 1998 *The North American City*, 5th edn. Harper and Row, New York

S. Wong

Cities: Internal Structure

Urban research has always focused on big cities. Big cities are concentrates of the cultural and economic potential of mankind. They are centers of innovation as well as hotbeds of social and ecological problems. Moreover, they have long outgrown the limits of perception. Not only do planners plead for a return to human dimensions, but all those engaged in urban research seek to delimit manageable segments, either by subject matter or by spatial criteria.

1. General Principles

1.1 Accessibility and Transport Technology

The city is a centered system based on the twofold premise that the city center is the engine of development and the place easiest to access. Accessibility of both the center and the entire city area is determined by its opening up for development and by transport technology (see Fig. 1).

A city of pedestrians and coaches tended to be circular. When streetcars came into use in Europe, they started mostly at the town gates. This made for star-shaped growth, with the interstitial areas lagging behind in development. Where public transport is predominant, the city center remains the easiest place to access. The *métropole concentrée* of Paris is an example. The absolute predominance of private transport reduces access to the center; under a liberal political system and with land abundantly available, a

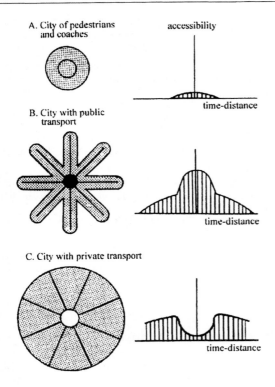

Figure 1
The accessibility of the city center

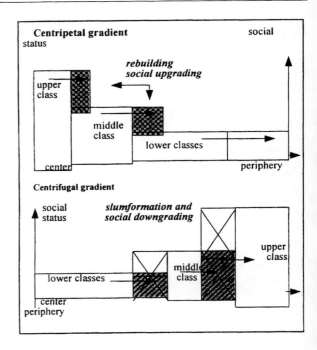

Figure 2
Centrifugal and centripetal social gradients
(*Stadtgeographie* (*Urban Geography*) 1998, p. 110)

city or metropolitan region designed for car traffic emerges in several steps. Los Angeles offers a prototype of this.

1.2 Distance Decay

There are two theoretical approaches for analyzing gradients from the center to the periphery:

1.2.1 Social gradients. The central peripheral organization of urban society may be described by means of centrifugal and centripetal social gradients. These gradients permit the following diagnosis regarding urban growth. Wherever the city center is also the social center and a centripetal social gradient is in evidence, the demand for space of the upper classes extends outward from the center. This causes residential and social upgrading of the adjacent middle-class districts. In the middle zone, former lower-class quarters are turned into middle-class districts. The Founders Period growth of Berlin, Budapest, Copenhagen, Paris, Prague, and Vienna was of this kind. This type of upgrading must not be confused with

the recent phenomenon of gentrification in North American cities. Here, middle and upper income urbanites move centripetally into rundown central districts (see Fig. 2).

Wherever a centrifugal social gradient predominates, as in US cities, a filtering down takes place: with the deterioration of the building fabric in the center, lower-class people move outward into adjacent middle and upper-class districts. This social downgrading of high quality living quarters is hard to stop and presented a major problem for British town planners. Having accomplished the redevelopment of rundown early industrial terrace houses next to the old town centers, they were faced with the daunting task of redeveloping devastated mid- and late nineteenth century terrace house districts (while the necessary renovation of early twentieth century council housing was partly effected by privatization under Thatcher).

1.2.2 Land values gradient. According to the theory of urban land markets (Alonso 1964), urban land use mirrors transport cost as well as the rent of land. Regularly, in socio-economically intact city centers, there is a center-periphery gradient with several consecutive zones of use outward from the central business district (CBD). Replacement of historical city-models by the new model of suburbia together with the re-

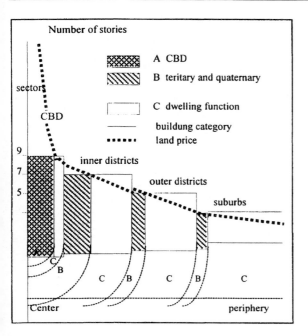

Figure 3
Land values gradient and zoning

duction in accessibility have made for an abandonment of central areas, resulting in 'craters' of land prices and visible decay of inner cities in the USA and parts of Western Europe. In the centers, the gradient now falls in the opposite direction. The Alonso model excludes restrictions on planning land use and vertical development. With zoning laws, building categories, and other legal regulations, the gradient of real estate prices is altered. Each category or zone is divided in two, with the inner zone obviously better suited for business purposes and office space than the outer zone that is used for dwelling as it is more profitable (see Fig. 3).

1.3 Hierarchical Structures

Hierarchical order is one of the basic types of systemic organization. When organizing the physical space of urban areas, a hierarchical order has been attempted wherever planned development was feasible and land in abundant supply. Examples run from 17C Sicily (Granmichele) via Howard's New Town idea (1902), with city center and garden suburbs in a cluster city, to major planning projects for urban peripheries in Europe at present. The hierarchy is constructed from the bottom upwards. The basic units are electoral wards, which in many European countries and in North America double up as statistical units: their dimensions are derived from the traditional 'pedestrian ideology' of 1 km (i.e., 15 minutes walking

distance) as standard size. Comprehensive hierarchical urban structures have been realized only in the former socialist countries of Eastern Europe, above all the USSR. In the rest of Europe, hierarchical organization of urban space is the exception rather than the rule. However, it is frequently found in traditional Oriental cities. There, a spatial hierarchy of family, clan, and local quarters is based on family, religious, and ethnic affiliations. The hierarchical organization of living quarters and sub-centers is paralleled in the hierarchy of semi-private, semi-public, and public links as well as markets.

2. The Impact of Political Systems

2.1 Social-ecological City Models

In their paper, *The Nature of Cities* (1945), Harris and Ullman tried to model internal patterns within cities. The triad of models presented makes use of diverse development phenomena:

(a) invasion and succession of social groups in Burgess' zonal model,

(b) transport-induced ribbon-developments along traffic lines in Hoyt's sector model, and

(c) collective preferences as to the allocation of workplaces in the Harris-Ullman multiple-nuclei model.

However, three important underlying assumptions have not yet been made explicit:

(a) the political system of liberalism,

(b) the historical 'one-dimensionality' of urban development, and

(c) the concept of the city center as CBD.

The models mentioned represent ideal types of North American cities of the interwar period (see Fig. 4).

2.2 Historical-political Systems and the Concept of the City Center

Changes in the political system alter the conceptions of the city and urban society. The function of the city center is changed. European urban development may be defined as a succession of four types of political systems and the respective types of cities. Their concepts of the city center were markedly different: (a) in the burghers' city of medieval, feudal, territorial state the marketplace was the social center; (b) which shifted to the ruler's residence in the residence city of the absolutist state. Thus, a social gradient falling from the center toward the periphery is the general rule in pre-industrial cities. (c) In the age of liberalism, Great Britain created the prototype of the industrial city. A social gradient rising from the center toward the periphery predominated, a development later paralleled in North American cities. (d) Again, Great

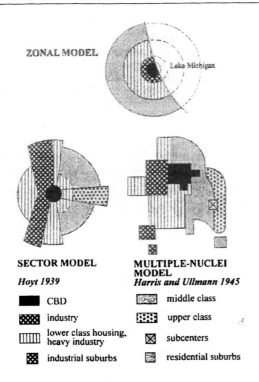

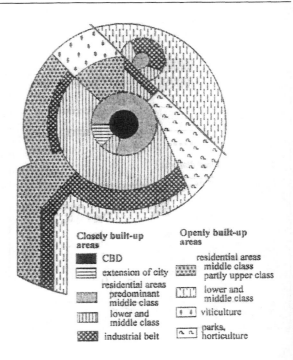

Figure 5
The social ecological model of a continental European city—Vienna (*Geoforum* 1970, **4**: 61)

Figure 4
Social ecological models of US cities during the inter-war-period

Britain set the rules for the New Town idea, the attempt at structuring the amorphous masses of big industrialized cities on a human scale, with the city divided into parts with different functions. From the outset, spatial segregation of inhabitants was barred from the design of New Towns—a fact that is still influential in urban planning today. European city development is most complex; various superpositions and, to different degrees, the persistence of historical structures caused the diversification of socioeconomic patterns and different social gradients.

Vienna in the 1960s offers the model for the traditional continental European city:

(a) Social status is still highest in the core and declines toward the periphery. Depending on site preferences individual districts deviate from this rule.

(b) The CBD has maintained some residential functions and is not surrounded by slums, but by middle and upper class residential districts, encircled by lower class quarters.

(c) The wide belt of multistory blocks is followed on its outside by Founders Period industrial quarters, followed in their turn by loosely built-up districts.

(d) The fringe zone is not defined by an extensive speculation area of 'vacant land' as in North America, but by sectors of intensive agricultural land use (in keeping with the von Thünen model) such as truck farming and viticulture, as well as of allotment gardens and weekend homes (see Fig. 5).

2.3 The Impact of State Socialism

Under state socialism, municipal governments were the local planning authorities, responsible for the mass of multistory housing that was unprofitable because of 'social' low rents. They lost all chances of capital accumulation from real estate property, and became dependent on financial endowments from the central government and on central planning. The consequences were:

The big cities' increasing demand for space was met by extensive incorporations.

Public construction (by state, municipal and other collective institutions) took absolute precedence over private construction.

Architectural design followed totalitarian principles, stressing elements of over wide avenues and huge squares, both imposing and strategically important.

Massive anti-segregation strategies were pursued.

City centers were usually put under monument protection.

City enlargement was effected via New Cities in the shape of hierarchically structured giant multistory blocks.

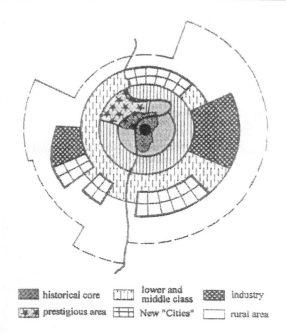

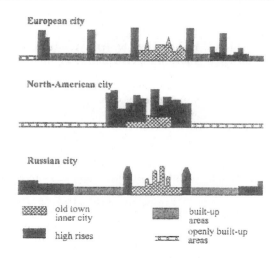

Figure 7
Skylines of European, North-American, and Russian
million-cities (*Stadtgeographie* (*Urban Geography*)
1998, p. 198)

historical core | lower and middle class | industry
prestigious area | New "Cities" | rural area

Figure 6
The model of a socialist city: Prague (*Vienna. Bridge
between Cultures*, 1993, p. 102)

In compliance with the Charter of Athens, industrial
and dwelling zones were strictly separated.

Commuting requirements were taken care of by
subway construction.

Forced industrialization created extensive industrial
zones with plants located close to railway lines and
super-highways.

Extensive leisure zones were created on the fringes,
with both collective recreation facilities and private
second homes (see Fig. 6).

2.4 City Growth and Political Systems

Cities are growing systems, with increasing populations, and/or with increasing demand for space for
diverse urban functions (housing, work, education,
leisure, traffic, etc.) in a setting of economic growth
and technical innovation.

The diverging political-economic effects of central
planning and of a free enterprise economy cause
significant differences in the physical growth of cities
in the respective systems. Cities grow in two directions:
laterally and vertically.

2.4.1 The third dimension. Vertical growth means
high-rise construction. Up to the 1970s, when some
cities changed their laws, European cities could not
expand vertically because of strict zoning laws, but
were forced to grow laterally. This necessitated the
conversion of dwelling space into office space, e.g.,
in Paris and Vienna. High-rise construction in European cities started relatively late (see Fig. 7). Its location within the city—frequently subject to special
permission—is different from that in North America.
There, the vertical structure of urban skylines shows
that land prices peak in the center while in European
cities 'monument protection' bars high-rises from the
centers. Thus, the new landmarks of banks, insurance firms, corporation headquarters, and hotels
keep a polite distance from the old landmarks of
churches, town halls, and castles.

For the sake of access to the various supply and
disposal mains, high-rises are preferably located along
urban 'scars': at the interfaces of traditional zones
where former boundaries still show in open space or
low physical objects. Frequently, new high-rises accent
not only the edge of traditional inner cities but,
centripetally, also major points of access to older outer
cities and suburbs. High-rises also mark the front of
growth of the CBD, busy commuter train stations, as
well as 'satellite' districts. They are also instrumental
in slum clearing.

2.4.2 Urban fringe development. Development of
urban fringes differs materially according to whether
it takes place under private capitalism, in welfare
states or, in retrospect, under state capitalism.

(a) Under US private capitalism, cities grow as
profits from land speculation and rising land prices are

invested in land development and in technical improvements. This starts an upward spiral of development and rising prices. North American cities show two wide zones of speculation. The inner one, around the CBD, is marked by decay and slum areas at present. Far more impressive, at least because of its extent, is the peripheral zone of vacant land around core cities and suburbs, which, even in the 1950s amounted to 20 to 60 percent of the core areas (Bartholomew 1955). Anglo-American urban geography textbooks completely ignore those huge tracts of vacant land—implying that non-utilization of these spaces is taken for granted rather than considered a problem.

(b) In continental Europe, too, urban fringes attracted speculation. During World War I, they were occupied by so-called 'emergency gardening plots,' later turned into allotment gardens. Frequently, these became temporary settlements, partly forerunners of a second-home periphery. All over post-World-War I continental Europe, spontaneous settlements typically marked city fringes—a consequence of fundamental political changes. The absence of government checks on land use made for temporary settlements, among them the pavilions of 'chaotic urbanization' in France as well as the often illegal occupation of land around big central European cities (Belgrade, Budapest, Bukarest, Sofia, Vienna, and Warsaw). This shows that the succession states were less powerful than the Austro-Hungarian monarchy in repelling indigent illegal immigrants. Those postwar squatters were comparable to today's squatter settlements on the fringes of Third World cities beyond the reach of state or municipal authorities.

(c) As to planning and regulating the growth of agglomerations, Great Britain set the standard in the early twentieth century, with the two important concepts of the New Town (referred to above) and the Green Belt. The creation of a Green Belt presupposes government control of land use, replacing the market mechanism of the liberal age. Originating in London, Green Belts have also become constituent features of zoning plans in other cities of the former British Empire. The urban development plan of Ottawa shows a Green Belt several miles wide. Persistent urban sprawl caused a characteristic overspill. In the USA, too, Green Belt concepts were introduced into various urban development plans, but because of the enormous extent of suburbanization they have not been realized along the edges of core cities. At present, there is little interest in creating public green spaces and leisure areas there.

(d) The opposite is true for the former socialist countries where extensive public recreation areas and large private second-home districts exist. (Neither of these important elements of the periphery of urban regions is to be found in the USA.) The public recreation area of Moscow goes back to a Green Belt idea already incorporated in the city development plan

of 1935. It is 20 to 40 km wide and includes major sports and cultural facilities. In most of the big cities of the former USSR, the Green Belt was an integral part of development planning.

3. On the Nature of Cities: the Immanent Question

With current suburbanization and counter-urbanization tendencies, the model of the city as a centered system is becoming obsolete. Scenarios have been developed which anticipate the existence of cities as 'non-places.' But there were also new models developed for the American 'urbanlike system.' During the period 1950–2000, this rapidly growing new system of suburbia created a sort of extensive—though not ubiquitous—network, in part destroying former central place hierarchies, and in part developing the surroundings of metropolitan areas. It also frequently stopped the process of restructuring central cities by means of downtown redevelopment and gentrification. Core cities of mega-metropolises such as Chicago got another chance of redevelopment as new (air) traffic junctions, centers of business, finance, and the quaternary public sector, as well as cultural centers. The dichotomy of the ideal types of 'urbanlike' structures and new mega structures seems to correspond to postindustrial America's abandoning and simply 'forgetting' the areas of urban desertification of earlier industrial city development.

See also: Cities: Cultural Types; Cities, Internal Organization of; Development and Urbanization; Ecology, Political; Fertility Transition: Economic Explanations; Spatial Interaction; Sustainable Development; Sustainable Transportation; Transportation Geography; Urban Activity Patterns; Urban Geography; Urban Growth Models; Urban Life and Health; Urban Poverty in Neighborhoods; Urban System in Geography

Bibliography

Alonso W 1964 *Location and Land Use. Towards a General Theory of Land Rent.* Cambridge, MA
Bartholomew H 1955 *Land Uses in American Cities.* Cambridge, MA
Carter H 1997 *The Study of Urban Geography*, 4th edn. Arnold, London
Heinritz G, Lichtenberger L (eds.) 1986 *The Take-off of Suburbia and the Crisis of the Central City.* Erdkundliches Wissen 76, Steiner, Wiesbaden, Germany
Herbert D T, Thomas C J 1997 *Cities in Space: City as Place*, 3rd edn. Fulton, London
Knox P L 1995 *Urban Social Geography: An Introduction*, 3rd edn. Longman, Singapore

Lichtenberger E 1993 *Wien-Prag*. Metropolenforschung, Böhlau, Vienna

Lichtenberger E 1994 The future of the European city in the West and the East. *European Review* 3(2): 182–93

Lichtenberger E 1998 *Stadtgeographie (Urban Geography)*, 3rd edn. Teubner, Stuttgart, Germany. Italian translation, Geografia dello spazio urbano, 1st edn., Unicopli, Milano, Italy

Lichtenberger L 1970 The Nature of European Urbanism. *Geoforum* **4**: 45–62

Lichtenberger L 1976 The Changing Nature of European Urbanization. *Urban Affairs Annual Reviews* **11**: 81–107

Lichtenberger L 1992 Political Systems and City Development in Western Societies. A Hermeneutic Approach. *Colloquium Geographicum* **22**: 24–40

Lichtenberger L 1993 *Vienna. Bridge between Cultures*. Wiley

Short J R 1996 *The Urban Order: An Introduction to Cities, Culture and Power*. Oxford, MA

E. Lichtenberger

Cities: Post-socialist

1. Issues of Definition

Socialist governments were formed at different times in different parts of the world: in Europe (USSR, eastern Europe), Asia (China, Cambodia, Vietnam), Africa (16 claimed to be socialist, but only Angola, Ethiopia, Mozambique qualified as Afro-Marxist regimes), and the Americas (Cuba). The term socialist is confined to a short historical period: the Soviet Union apart, it refers to the 40-year period after 1948. For the countries in the 'South' the period is even shorter, in the case of Cambodia from 1975 until 1989. It is doubtful that we can talk of a 'generic socialism,' beyond the fact that each country was characterized by the abolition of private ownership and the concentration of economic resources in the hands of the state and by the monopolization of political power in the hands of a 'vanguard party.' (In 1994 still only 15 percent of the population of Ethiopia lived in towns.) The term post-socialist is used to describe urban areas in societies which, until the breaching of the Berlin Wall in 1989, had been known as 'socialist.' At present no government, with the possible exception of China and Cuba, describes itself as 'socialist,' therefore socialist cities no longer exist.

1.1 Socialist Cities?

At a formal level, if it is accepted that these were 'real existing socialist societies,' then their cities were by definition socialist cities—the position adopted in the Soviet Union in 1931. The more difficult question is whether or not the socialist city is qualitatively different from the city in capitalist society. Despite dissenters, the consensus is that a distinction existed (French and Hamilton 1979, Pensley 1998, Smith 1996, Szelenyi 1996). Arguably an *a fortiori* case exists for believing that these characteristics might be found in Russia. As the first socialist country it had the longest period in which to experiment and put its ideological principles into practice. Additionally, it compelled its first satellites in eastern Europe to adopt its model of industrial and urban development. From this point of view it would be possible to gain insights into the essence of the socialist and post-socialist city by studying the experience of the former socialist countries in Europe.

Addis Ababa is a post-socialist city as are Berlin, Beijing, Budapest, Phnom Penh, and Moscow. The capital city in both post-socialist and socialist societies is the distillery of the society's contradictions and conflicts; it contains in hypertrophied form what is found to a much lesser extent in all other cities. The transformation of societies from being socialist to post-socialist is not a unilinear process (Grabher and Stark 1997). Neither does the transition from socialist to post-socialist city follow a clear pattern (e.g., Harloe 1996 Phe and Nishimura 1992). However, generalizations can be made about these cities in terms of their external, representational, and material form, their economic functions, and the social relationships amongst their populations.

2. Urban Form

2.1 The Symbolic, Representational Environment

The aesthetic of the socialist city in the Soviet Union before 1939 represented a triumphant proletariat in a hostile but not yet belligerent world. After 1945 that aesthetic had to include the victory in war against fascism. Thus, to the mausoleum and ubiquitous monuments to the heroes of the Great October Socialist Revolution, in particular Lenin, Marx, and Engels, were added grave, granite memorials to those who died in the titanic struggle against national socialism.

The aesthetic and symbolic representation of the post-socialist city is much more difficult to identify. Just as Soviet leaders, especially, but not only, Stalin and Khrushchev, demolished churches and did much to remove all vestiges of the tsarist past, post-socialist leaders are rebuilding cathedrals—the most classic being the Cathedral of Christ the Saviour near the Kremlin in Moscow—and removing statues to the now fallen heroes of socialism. China, too, destroyed much of the civilizational grandeur of the Imperial City in Beijing, while Cuba allowed Havana to wither (Segre et al. 1997).

Berlin, Budapest and Moscow encapsulate the characteristics of the post-socialist city. During the *belle époque* their architectures expressed their countries' imperial status and cosmopolitan air. Subsequently, architecture came to symbolize inter-war authoritarianism, the defeat of fascism, a divided world—epitomized in the divided Berlin. In contrast to the socialist city, the post-socialist city has no state decreed prototype. The socialist city, as conceived during the 1920s and 1930s based on planning and reason, would, using the most up-to-date construction materials and building technologies to erect multistorey blocks of flats, be the acme of modernism. From 1949 this was the blueprint for all socialist societies.

Now coarse granite blocks that characterised government buildings of the socialist city have been replaced by leafy atriums encased in glass, symbolically representing transparency, the current metaphor for democracy. The architectural preferences of the *nouveau riche* group tend to fall into two categories: either a sentimental veneration of the past and national styles, or an international orientation expressed in a pastiche and rococo post-modernism.

Changing architectural styles and usages of town squares are sound barometers of historical periods. The memorial and monument, which became popular at the turn of the twentieth century, embellished and blemished the streets, squares, and parks of towns and villages after the end of World War I, especially in the newly created, states. Ljubljana European even before the war had begun to substitute a Slovene for its German façade (Jezernik 1998). This process reached its apogee in the socialist city where a baroque Marian column, for example, was 'relocated' in a less visible place, while obelisks were erected to the Red Army and marble memorials were built to partisan leaders.

In many post-socialist cities, these heroes of 40 years have been, if not destroyed, decapitated or mutilated, then banished from public view, in some instances to museums so that they may be reminders of the images of dictators and criminals. These acts highlight the transience not just of heroes, but also of the myths about the inhabitants' past and who they wish or think themselves to be. The erection and removal of monuments are potent symbolic acts, which create and sustain myths and then denigrate and depose them. In the post-socialist city new buildings are themselves monuments, but less to people or events than to the new-found ideology and to the power of money. The architecture of new government buildings represents visions of the meaning and exercise of political power.

The post-socialist city celebrates three myths. The first is a ritualistic pageantry of the past, so easily portrayed in a coat of arms and the insignia of local governance that are deemed to dignify the present. Second, in keeping with contemporary Western planning theory and practice, the squares are pedestrianized and garlanded with new lamps, benches, and cafes. They are again public spaces for everyday events, not just for formal celebrations of socialist power. This is the myth of the harmonious, integrated community where everyone interacts as a free person; where the exotic and bizarre in appearance are silently applauded for their non-conformity as though these ostensible forms are a defence for everyone against socialist conformity. The third myth is that this square, which is really a circus, a place for entertainment and the consumption of material goods and pleasure, is a symbol of Europeanization or Westernization. The civic leaders of the post-socialist city bask in the sunshine of their enthusiasm for what its citizens regard as an abandonment of grayness.

The post-socialist city is cosmopolitan in theory and localist in spirit, and latently nationalist in practice. It is an arena where people learn the laws governing contracts, and the rules protecting and regulating private property. At the same time it massages into life an enemy, which for inhabitants of the socialist city was defined in terms of 'class' and property relations, a mode of analysis no longer acceptable. In the postsocialist city 'the enemy' is the alien, the stranger, the immigrant.

Berlin is distinctive from other cities in many ways, but its singular claim to uniqueness is that its postsocialist incarnation, in combining its socialist and capitalist faces in one city, should be the most visible healing of the painful rupture experienced by European nations. Ironically, however, this particular postsocialist city reveals in concentrated form the contradictions that are endemic in many of the most populous capitalist cities and which the socialist city was to have overcome. A skyline of cranes tells of a booming economy, while unemployment is at a high level; a thriving cultural and political boundary-testing artistic scene co-exists with a growing intolerance of immigrants.

2.2 The Material Environment

2.2.1 The economy.
The keystone of the new global consensus amongst governments is the privatization of public assets and of government functions and the establishment of new property rights. This policy, which is already influencing the structure and functioning of post-socialist cities, is hampered or aided by deeply ingrained regional, cultural traditions.

The economic dimension of cities most distinguishes the socialist from the post-socialist city. The socialist city was unique in that economic wealth, which the privileged enjoyed, could not be conspicuous. Second, the post-socialist city is not just shaped by the wealth of an indigenous bourgeoisie, but also by foreign capital invested in real estate. This critical difference between the socialist and post-socialist city is already visible in three processes; the gentrification of parts of the central city, the creation of a central business district and more luxurious shopping centers, and an influx and visible presence of foreign migrants.

Cities are shaped by movements of capital. In the main, the protective walls which surrounded socialist cities have been pulled down. Previously, in theory but also to a certain extent in practice, cities had planned economic relations with one another as part of a regional, national, and international division of labor. Post-socialist cities are in competition with each other and increasingly subjected to global competition. One aspect of globalization is the attraction of tourists. Only a small proportion of post-socialist cities have a real potential to make this a source of local economic development. More importantly, globalization accelerates attempts to commodify a city's history and culture, which is achievable largely through its sanitization and its conceptual Warholization and material McDonaldization. Globalization has also helped to accelerate the growth of the criminal economy, which is shaping the urban morphology, most visibly (especially in capital cities) in private financial institutions and shopping malls. A number of post-socialist cities, mainly, but not only, capitals (Moscow, Almaty, Berlin, Sofia, Shanghai, Phnom Penh) have become centers for the consumption and transhipment of heroin and other drugs, for trade in illegal immigrants and prostitutes, and for smuggling.

Organized crime and corruption are pervasive but particularly evident in the largest cities. In some countries there is virtually no sphere of revenue-generating activity (including charities) which has not been visited by extortionists ('insurance brokers'). In the space of a decade gangs of extortionists have evolved into 'enforcement partners.' Before signing business contracts, companies acquire information about each other's enforcement partners. Only if the enforcement partners have recognized each other and given mutual guarantees will the contract with all its formal juridical and business attributes be signed.

Whereas the socialist city was characterized by a manufacturing profile with a grossly underdeveloped service sector, the post-socialist city is dominated, at both extremes of the class spectrum, by trading and the provision of services. Both the indigenous and foreign élites have generated a demand for casinos, restaurants, night clubs, and other leisure facilities. This stimulates the local economy, creates new forms of labor market stratification and, with the commodification of land, speculation in real estate. In Cambodia the overnight transfer of state housing into private ownership in 1989 presented local government officials with a golden opportunity, of which they availed themselves, to sell off public land.

2.2.2 Land reform. Land nationalization was central to the twentieth century socialist (agrarian) revolu-

tions. Guided by an idea of social justice it addressed issues of exploitative landlord–peasant relationships, rural poverty and land hunger and the contrast between the housing standards of rich and poor city dwellers. The state allocated land to publicly owned enterprises and institutions, free of charge and for use in perpetuity. No value was imputed to the location of the land. Since in most cases land was not in short supply, organizations applying to the state for plots asked for and received more than they required. The bundle of *de jure* use rights enjoyed by individuals and juridical entities varied from country to country, but in no case were they able to dispose of land, even of that which was surplus to their requirements. Yet, at the same time, land users behaved as though they were powerful, private owners, with the result that detailed building and zoning regulations were frequently neglected or ignored.

The land reforms that have accompanied change at the end of the century have been guided by no such ideal of justice, but are regarded as an obligatory component in the process of privatization and the establishment of a market economy. While one of the defining features of the socialist city was the state expropriation and nationalization of land, the defining feature of the post-socialist society is the returning of land and property to private ownership. This includes the return to the former owners all forms of property, including agricultural land and urban real estate. This process of restitution constitutes one of the thorniest of problems faced by governments and societies. Countries have approached both the general policy of privatization and the specificity of restitution differently (Strong et al. 1996)

In the first case, Belarus, Kyrgyzstan, Uzbekistan, and China are among the firmly against land privatization, while in Russia a minority of the population favors the unrestricted buying and selling of land. And, even in countries where it is legal this has not necessarily meant the formation of a functioning land market. These policies are coming under pressure from external sources, with the European Union in 1999 declaring its opposition to requests from prospective membership candidates (such as the Czech Republic and Hungary) to continue their restrictions on foreign ownership of land. Through the selling of restituted buildings to banks and private companies and the conversion of more substantial houses into luxury flats, shops, and restaurants, restitution plays a distinct role in the stratification and shaping of post-socialist cities.

2.2.3 Housing. The interplay of a variety of factors, primarily the ideological imperative to develop industry rapidly, bequeathed highly polluted and degraded environments to post-socialist cities. The use of less polluting fuels and the introduction of further legislation enforcing air quality control in the 1980s and then the dramatic fall in industrial output in the 1990s combined to reduce stationary sources of air pollution. On the other land, air pollution has increased as a result of the rapid rise in private car ownership and the poor quality of fuel available (Shahgedanova et al. 1999). Thus, there has been a compensatory rise in vehicular pollution, especially carbon monoxide discharge, which is most marked in the economically successful post-socialist cities. Thus, while the sources of pollution are changing, the general level remains the same.

Although the housing stock in socialist societies varied considerably in terms of ownership and physical structure, socialist housing policy rested on two principles: that no-one should draw an unearned income from renting space and that households should not enjoy the use of housing space above a certain, administratively defined norm. Larger properties belonging to more affluent citizens were taken into public ownership and then subdivided and leased at low rents. In most countries state agencies commissioned and financed new building, which they then allocated.

In 1988 the governments of the two largest socialist systems, China and the USSR, introduced legislation designed to transform housing policy. They signalled that rents in the public sector would have to rise and encouraged sitting tenants to buy their homes. In doing so they prepared the ground for the post-socialist city, one of whose defining features is the absolute right of the owner-occupier to dispose of property. The system of targeted housing allowances and the gradual introduction of market-level (or at least cost-covering) rents that is being introduced, is intended over time to make owner-occupation more appealing. This is unlikely to happen until there have been substantial increases in real incomes. The availability of construction materials on the market has meant an expansion in self-build. This not only augments the supply of housing but can also be used to generate income through (sub-)letting. Generally, however, social housing will, in one form or another, play an important role for the foreseeable future (Wang and Murie 1999).

Such has been the importance attached by some governments to the commercial housing sector as a powerful motor to drive the economy and urban development that, in China for instance, many of the 'private' developers are either outright public organizations or government–private partnerships. In many post-socialist societies, the decline in the role and authority of the central state has been accomplished by a growth in local government bureaucracies. But the parvenu princelings in the cities and provinces, who now have greater tax-raising powers, nonetheless lack the financial capacity to fulfil the functions devolved to them, which has meant a much-reduced expenditure on the technical and social infrastructure.

2.2.4 Real estate markets. One of the most defining and visible features of the post-socialist city has been the property boom and the proliferation of real estate agents, unknown in the socialist city. Requiring a minimum of knowledge and finance to be established, real estate agencies have proliferated in most post-socialist cities (and provided another lucrative source of income for organized crime). The immediate force driving the urban economy and responsible for transforming the class structure has been the buying, selling, renting, and construction of real estate. Its development is hampered by the fact that, after a decade of scandals associated with pyramid and other 'banking' schemes, individuals are wary of investing savings in private banks so that a mortgaging system is either totally absent or only in its infancy.

While much of the apparatus of town planning and building, with its institutional rhythms, careers, and entrenched interests, remains intact and ensures that the movement away from high-rise construction, based on the use of prefabricated units and the mass production of standardized parts, will take time, corruptible politicians and impotent and impoverished officials oversee the making of visual urban chaos.

Currently, a challenge is being mounted (from within the European Union) against the decade-long hegemony of the USA in the debate over the role of markets in housing and land (as expressed in Stryuk 1996 (Urban Institute, Washington), Bertaud and Rehaud 1997 (World Bank).

3. Social Relations in the Post-socialist City

3.1 Population

The war-ravaged societies, principally in the 'South,' have created demographically imbalanced cities. In Phnom Penh, 29 percent of households are headed by women. In Moscow, too, because of higher male mortality rates, women predominate. The average age is considerably higher in the cities of some countries, while in others the urban population is much younger. One visible sign of the gender imbalance is the greater presence on the streets of women engaging in petty trading or begging.

Radical transformations of society are accompanied by population movements and new residential configurations. The Soviet Union used an internal passport (*propiska*) system to regulate population flows into metropolitan and other large cities and to control their demographic and ethnic composition. After 1945 this method of control was exported as part of its 'administration package' to countries which adopted the Marxist model of development. Some post-socialist cities, notably Moscow, illegally retain it as an instrument of social control. Urban residents' associations in Ethiopia continue to regulate movement into their territories.

3.2 The Wealthy

Post-socialist societies have created a class of *nouveau riche*, who differ from élites under the previous system by an ostentatious display of their wealth status, especially through the universal symbols of home and private car, both of which make their mark on the shape of, and life in, the post-socialist city. Accommodation for élites under socialism was distinguished by the following features. First, élites lived in the city not out of town and had access to (but did not own) a country villa. Second, they did not live in socially exclusive enclaves, neither, third, did they live close to foreigners. This is in direct contrast to élite districts in post-socialist cities. Members of the new, privileged indigenous élite live in close proximity to foreigners often on small estates consisting of low-rise, detached housing surrounded by walls or fences covered by closed circuit television.

Views differ on the extent to which social segregation could be found in socialist cities (Szelenyi 1996; Prawelska-Skrzypek 1988; Dangschat 1987, Hamilton 1993, Weclawowicz 1992). The market economy of the post-socialist city intensifies any existing tendencies to segregation through the processes of gentrification and suburbanization. In the first case, a location in or near the city center, in buildings erected for prosperous families prior to the country's socialist revolution, is attractive to a variety of social groups. Alongside the modernization of old buildings is the construction of prestige housing and of retail and office space.

The arrival of international organizations has created an additional demand for higher quality housing to rent and purchase. The subsequent rise in the price of housing sometimes leads to the displacement of the local population and a reduction in density as pre-socialist residential buildings in Phnom Penh and Prague changed from multifamily to single-family occupation.

Suburbanization was described and denigrated as an anarchic, capitalist-driven sprawl associated with low-rise, single-family dwellings. Now, from Berlin to Moscow to Almaty to Beijing the flight of the rich to suburban and ex-urban settlements, usually along the main arterial routes, has begun in earnest. This development has been greatly assisted by the growth in car ownership. Both processes put pressure on protective green belts and invade parkland within cities.

3.3 Marginal Groups

In socialist cities apart from gypsies against whom sanctions were not strictly applied or were ineffectual, begging was unknown. Work was available for the able-bodied: for the elderly there were pensions which could be supplemented by other legal activities and the state provided for other 'vulnerable' groups, such as orphans and handicapped people. In the 1960s existing anti-parasite legislation was strengthened to deal with begging and vagrancy, described as anti-social(ist) behavior. As soon as the socialist city transmogrified into the post-socialist city begging, street children, and homelessness appeared as features of the urban landscape (Andrusz 1998, Lugalla and Mbwambo 1999). However, it is doubtful that in cities of less developed countries (such as Dar-es-Salaam and Phnom Penh) where—as South, post-socialist cities, public hygiene, especially the disposal of sewage and solid waste generally, and the provision of clean drinking and washing water remain the key issues—such groups are a wholly new phenomenon, although their numbers have increased. In the 'South,' the vast majority of street children come from the countryside, have inhabited the streets for a longer period, and have received no education at all. Their families of origin are much larger and very frequently polygamous and the mothers illiterate.

Socialist cities had their quotas of materially deprived and vulnerable groups, alcoholics, vagrants, and homeless people. But, unlike in post-socialist cities, they were rarely seen or talked about and did not form pressure groups or demonstrate.

Since, ideologically, such groups could not exist, neither did the organizations to help them; when they did appear the agents of social control dealt with them under the appropriate anti-parasite legislation. Today the visible presence of large numbers of dispossessed people has led to the establishment of a statutory and non governmental framework to address the situation of these individuals. However, even where statutory regulations exist, they are frequently not implemented. The institutional and ideological legacy has ensured that the law enforcement agencies continue to pursue a policy of harassment, intimidation, and abuse of position towards members of these groups. With the help of intergovernmental aid agencies and Western philanthropy, indigenous voluntary organizations are advocating that a more humane and positive approach be taken. But, in societies where most people are, or perceive themselves to be, suffering a deterioration in their standard of living, there is little public sympathy for beggars and special pleading indigents.

Another visible feature of the post-socialist city is that of the completed, but uninhabited luxury housing development, where supply has exceeded demand both because of the high asking price and because either the purchaser does not have the right to acquire the freehold or the period of the lease is too short. At the other end of the housing spectrum are the equally new phenomena of squatting and homelessness. The transition from socialist to post-socialist was quintessentially represented for a brief moment during *perestroika* when part of the space between the Hotel Rossiya and Red Square in Moscow was squatted by homeless people. The unplanned use of land reaches it apogee with squatter settlements in and around Asian and African post-socialist cities. In 1994, up to 15 percent of the population in Phnom Penh was living in such settlements.

Uninhabited, privately constructed, luxury housing on the one hand, and homelessness and squatting on the other, are features of post-socialist cities that were unknown in socialist cities.

4. Conclusion

The post-socialist city is a transparent city. Prostitution and poverty existed in St. Petersburg, Budapest, Beijing, and Havana. The ideology of socialism drew down a curtain on the urban stage concealing and reducing, but not eradicating social phenomena which the system decreed should not exist. It also banished the prosperous and powerful behind grey urban facades or to sylvan retreats. One of the imperatives of capitalism is that the homeless should be seen, disadvantaged groups should be allowed to express and demonstratively broadcast the inequities of their status, and the rich should parade their wealth.

See also: Cities: Cultural Types; Democratic Transitions; Development and Urbanization; Economic Transformation: From Central Planning to Market Economy; Socialism; Socialist Societies: Anthropological Aspects; Transition, Economics of; Urban Activity Patterns; Urban Geography; Urban Growth Models; Urban History; Urban Places, Planning for the Use of: Design Guide; Urban Planning: Central City Revitalization; Urban Studies: Overview

Bibliography

Andrusz G 1998 Housing and class structuration in Russia. In: van Weesep J (ed.) *Proceedings of the Conference Transformation Processes in Easter Europe. Housing and Labour Markers*. The Netherlands Organisation for Scientific Research, The Hague, Part 1 pp. 27–41

Andrusz G, Harloe M, Szelenyi I (eds.) 1996 *Cities after Socialism. Urban and Regional Change and Conflict in Post-Socialist Societies*. Blackwell, Oxford, UK

Bertaud A, Renaud B 1997 Socialist cites without land markets. *Journal of Urban Economics* 41: 137–51

Dangschat J 1987 Sociospatial disparities in a 'socialist' city: the case of Warsaw at the end of the 1970s. *International Journal of Urban and Regional Research* 11(1): 37–96

French R A, Hamiliton R E I (eds.) 1979 *The Socialist City. Spatial Structure and Urban Policy*. John Wiley, New York

Grabher G, Stark D (eds.) 1997 *Restructuring Networks in Postsocialism, Legacies, Linkages and Localities*. Oxford University Press, Oxford, UK

Hamilton E 1993 Social areas under state socialism: the case of Moscow. In: Solomon S (ed.) *Beyond Sovietology: Essays on Politics and History*. M E Sharpe, New York

Harloe M 1996 Cities in the transition. In: Andrusz G, Harloe M, Szelenyi I (eds.) *Cities After Socialism. Urban and Regional Change and Conflict in Post-Socialist Societies*. Blackwell, Oxford, UK

Jezernik B 1998 Monuments in the winds of change. *International Journal of Urban and Regional Research* 22(4): 582–8

Lugalla L, Mbwambo J 1999 Street children and street life in urban Tanzania: the culture of surviving and its implications for children's health. *International Journal of Urban and Regional Research* 23(2): 329–44

Pensley D S 1998 The socialist city? A critical analysis of Neubaugebiet Hellersdorf. *Journal of Urban History* 5: 563–602

Phe H H, Nishimura Y 1992 Housing in Hanoi. *HABITAT INTL* 15(1/2): 101–26

Prawelska-Skrzypek G 1988 Social differentiation in old central city neighbourhoods in Poland. *Area* 20(3): 221–32

Segre R, Coyula M, Scarpaci L 1997 *Havana. Two Faces of the Antillean Metropolis*. John Wiley, Chichester, UK

Shahgedanova M, Burt T P, Davies T D 1999 Carbon monoxide and nitrogen oxides pollution in Moscow. *Water, Air and Soil Pollution* 112: 107–31

Smith D M 1996 The socialist city. In: Andrusz G, Harloe M, Szelenyi I (eds.) *Cities after Socialism. Urban and Regional Change and Conflict in Post-Socialist Societies*. Blackwell, Oxford, UK, pp. 70–99

Strong A, Reiner T, Szyrmer J 1996 *Transitions in Land and Housing. Bulgaria, The Czech and Poland*. St. Martin's Press, New York

Stryuk R (ed.) 1996 *Economic Restructuring of the Former Soviet Block. The Case of Housing*. Urban Institute Press, Washington, DC

Szelenyi I 1996 Cities under Socialism—and: After. In: Andrusz G, Harloe M, Szelenyi I (eds.) *Cities after Socialism. Urban and Regional Change and Conflict in Post-Socialist Societies*. Blackwell, Oxford, UK, pp. 286–317

Wang Y P, Murie A 1999 Commercial housing development in urban China. *Urban Studies* 36(9): 1475–94

Weclawowicz G 1992 The socio-spatial structure of the socialist cities of East-Central Europe. In: Lando F. (ed.) *Urban and Rural Geography*. Cafoscarina, Venice, pp. 129–40

Wu V 1998 The Pudong development zone and China's economic reforms. *Planning Perspectives* 13: 133–65

Wu W P 1999 Shanghai. *Cities* 16(3): 207–16

G. Andrusz

Citizen Participation

'Citizen participation' refers generally to citizen involvement in public decision making. In planning and related fields, the term also has a specialized meaning, designating efforts to facilitate participation of citizens who would normally be unable or disinclined to take part.

1. The Emergence of an Ambiguous Definition

Alexis de Tocqueville, the chronicler of American habits in the mid-nineteenth century, remarked on widespread popular participation in the country's civic life. Americans seemed ready to form groups to address any problem. When mass immigration swelled cities at century's end, citizen activists spearheaded wide-ranging progressive reforms in sanitation, land use, and government organization. American city planning was a direct outgrowth of this citizen movement. Planning commissions were one means of institutionalizing public influence over decisions.

Nevertheless, the 1960s heard an explosion of talk about 'citizen participation' in planning, Community Action and the War on Poverty, and Model Cities. Part of the explanation is that citizens turned away from public life in the quiescent 1950s, but the primary reason is that the Johnson administration policy agenda focused on citizens who had never participated much in public decision making: the poor and blacks. Community Action would involve them in unprecedented ways.

The traditional approach to citizen participation in planning was represented by the federal Housing Act of 1954, which called for citizen advisory committees in urban renewal and other local projects. A 1966 Department of Housing and Urban Development Program Guide suggested categories to be represented, including business groups, civic clubs, churches, schools, government agencies, social service organizations, the mass media, neighborhood organizations, and 'ethnic or racial groups.' The examples and custom made it likely that, with the possible exceptions of neighborhood and racial representatives, most advisory committee members would come from an educational and economic elite.

The Economic Opportunity Act of 1964, the hallmark of the War on Poverty, declared a new approach: 'The term 'community action program' means a program ... which is developed, conducted, and administered with the maximum feasible participation of residents of the areas and members of the groups served.' Two years later, Model Cities began with a consonant call for 'widespread citizen participation.' One sign of a new departure was the Office of Economic Opportunity's investment in community organizing as part of Community Action and its technical assistance to community organizations in Model Cities. The War on Poverty aimed to activate the urban poor, particularly blacks.

'Citizen' participation and 'community' action or participation differ in an important way. A citizen is an individual, whereas a community is a collectivity. Citizens are members of the state, with certain rights, but they do not necessarily have intervening attachments. Communities are groups with membership norms (ranging from residence in a territory to conformity to rules of behavior); social relations, and loyalties. Participation of individual citizens is a quantitative matter: it can be counted, and more is arguably better than less.

In contrast, participation of communities is a qualitative matter. Communities do not take action en masse, but, rather, individuals act in the name of communities. This situation introduces questions of representation: What is a community, who are its members, and to what degree do participants represent members' interests? Partly a matter of calculation, this is largely a matter of judgment, which community members can render and about which many have strong convictions. Thus federal and local officials who encouraged or coped with citizen participation faced community activists who challenged them and forced consideration of what would be representative participation of citizens who are community members.

In addition, community activists, stimulated by the language of the War on Poverty, raised issues of power: could participation of residents in developing, conducting, and administering programs mean anything other than community control? And, if so, what should residents have control over, and how much control was significant? Answers to these questions were complicated by ambiguities in definitions of community and representation: who would have to exercise power over what in order for a community to be represented in making decisions?

In the early 1970s, the Nixon Administration narrowed the meaning of citizen participation in two respects. 'Citizens' became individuals again, rather than community members. 'Participation' less often meant activism or power than opportunities to speak at formal hearings conducted by others, who would make decisions. Over the years, federal planning, housing, community development, and environmental legislation has come to include provisions for citizen participation, and local practice has followed suit. In general, the balance of these practices has taken the narrower view of citizen participation.

Planning in Europe and Australia has adopted language of citizen participation, with variations in practice similar to those in the United States. United Nations and World Bank policies speak of 'community participation' in aid projects. In this context 'community' refers to the locus or target of intervention more than an expectation that an entire community participate in planning and implementation. Practice encounters similar issues about representation and power to American and European planning.

2. What 'Citizen Participation' Could Include But Often Does Not; A Broader Definition

Because 'citizen participation' originally referred to involving people in government-initiated programs, common usage often does not include autonomous citizen activities, even though they are acts of involvement in the society and may aim to influence government. This broader 'citizen participation' includes three types of activity commonly associated with 'community organization.'

'Locality development,' or 'community development,' involves the organization of residents of an area to create the capacity to improve their situation. Projects may address various needs, such as health, housing, education, and infrastructure. Activities may include popular education to understand local conditions.

'Social planning' involves citizens in working with technical data to solve substantive problems. These activities aim to prepare plans for programs to address needs, which may be in many areas. Participants might focus on a single issue, or a community might develop a multifaceted plan.

'Social action' involves the organization of a population to press actors in the larger society, usually institutions and often government, to change policies or practices, redistribute economic or social resources, or yield power over these things. Disadvantaged populations may favor this approach, but many issue-oriented groups (such as the environmental movement and consumer groups) may choose it. Activities include mass mobilization and advocacy.

It is reasonable to consider these activities part of a broad definition of 'citizen participation' as efforts by citizens (including, but not only, the poor and minorities) to influence the policies and practices of government, basic social institutions, or their own neighborhood or community. However, in this context the conventional emphasis on efforts to involve citizens in government-initiated activity produces theoretical ambiguity. In addition, those who hold the narrower view may find conflicts in practice when encountering citizens or communities who hold the broader view.

3. Arguments for Citizen Participation; Practical Benefits

Different views of citizen participation are associated with different arguments for it and claims regarding its benefits. A basic distinction can be drawn between a focus on the benefits to government and other service providers and a focus on the benefits to citizens and communities. The first view emphasizes the ways citizens contribute knowledge and, especially, authority, such that program operators can be more confident citizens will use and benefit from services. The second view emphasizes the ways citizens get more power and economic and social resources that promote their development. The first view is more likely to be associated with the narrower view of citizen participation, and the second with the broader view, but the two may overlap and the correspondence is imprecise. Four types of benefits can be identified.

The first emphasizes *individual development*. Citizen participation has been seen as therapy for the alienated and powerless; involvement in political activity may contribute to self-esteem, a sense of potency, and growth. Inherently, participation in public life makes someone a citizen. Collaboration helps individuals become part of networks that provide social supports. Instrumentally, participation can bring power, knowl-

edge, the ability to solve problems, and improvements in living conditions, including services.

The latter benefits involve sharing in outcomes of collective action, in *community development*. When members of a community articulate and promote their interests with one another, they can resolve conflicts and discover shared community interests. They will develop relationships they can use in acting together on behalf of those interests. As a result, they may gain knowledge, power, resources, and relationships that enable them to influence institutions and other actors and make decisions that change conditions and solve problems. This may mean having more power over societal resources, becoming more self-sufficient, or both. In general, a community whose members deliberate and make decisions together is likely to have a sense of vitality and potency and attract members' loyalty.

Organizational development is a third benefit of citizen participation. When citizens contribute knowledge about their needs, service providers are more likely to design and deliver services that meet those needs, solve problems, and are used. When citizens participate in planning programs, they are more likely to develop relationships with organizations, consider programs legitimate, and use or accept them. In general, voluntary organizations, including community associations, need participation because citizens provide three resources essential to organizational operation and development: work, money, and legitimacy.

Finally, citizen participation contributes to *societal development*. Active citizenship in a democratic framework can be considered inherently good for society. When activists openly discuss their interests, they can resolve conflicts among private interests and discover common, public interests. They can build relationships and learn together about shared conditions. As in communities, citizen participation offers society the possibility of articulating and solving problems knowledgeably and legitimately, with the result that collective actions, including programs, serve more people well.

Some proponents of citizen participation portray it as a means to various ends, whereas others, particularly those concerned with societal development, present it as an end in itself. It can be both, and the delineation of means and ends varies with focus on individuals, communities, organizations, or society.

4. Specific Purposes of Participation Activities; The Issue of Power

The discussion of benefits from citizen participation identifies many possible purposes for activities in which citizens participate in public life. These can be classified as follows:

(a) Communicating information (including perceptions, beliefs, opinions, hopes, expectations, and intentions);

(b) Developing relationships (creating new ones and strengthening existing ones);

(c) Developing the capacity to act and organizing action (including organizing coalitions, planning, strategizing, and creating and exercising power);

(d) Preserving or changing selves and/or others (including policies, practices, conditions, and relationships).

These categories may be seen hierarchically, in that communicating information builds relationships, which in turn develop a capacity to act, which may effect change in some or all parties. However, in practice and in the abstract, the categories overlap: for example, communication may contribute to developing relationships, the creation of which is change and which have the capacity to bring about other change, such as further communication.

In short, citizen participation can enable citizens and others who participate with them to learn and can empower them to act together in ways that would have been impossible otherwise. However, when citizens or those they interact with believe they have conflicting interests, they may participate with other purposes. They may seek to prevent the communication of information, the development of relationships, action by others, and any change in their own practices. Under these conditions, when government officials or funders, for example, organize citizen participation, they may involve citizens but limit their influence.

Sherry Arnstein (1969) analyzed this central question of citizens' power in terms of 'a ladder of citizen participation,' ranging from low to high power:

Nonparticipation

(a) Manipulation: placing citizens on powerless advisory committees for the purpose of 'educating' them or gaining their support for others' positions;

(b) Therapy: trying to change citizens' beliefs, attitudes, or values as a diversion from analyzing and changing social conditions;

Degrees of tokenism

(c) Informing: giving information to citizens but not requesting or listening to their points-of-view;

(d) Consultation: asking citizens' opinions but not making a commitment to act on them;

(e) Placation: placing a few citizens on committees or boards that have limited influence over policies and practices;

Degrees of citizen power

(f) Partnership: sharing decision making power with citizens;

(g) Delegated power: delegating some decision making power to citizens;

(h) Citizen control: citizens have considerable independent power over decisions.

This hierarchy focuses on power over overt decisions, such as policies or programs that address problems. This is the most familiar of three 'levels' of power. Beneath it are decisions about the issues or problems that go onto the agenda for action. It is possible for citizens to have considerable power in selecting from among alternatives on the table without having influence in determining the array of possibilities. Still one level lower are decisions, frequently tacit, about which social conditions are defined as issues or problems and even considered for the agenda. Citizens may have influence in choosing among recognized issues for a group or organization's agenda but have little power to draw public attention to certain conditions that trouble them greatly. The purposes of citizen participation may pertain to each of these levels of power.

5. Means of Citizen Participation

The means of citizen participation are related to its purposes. Some means serve single purposes, but most may serve several purposes. Means can be grouped in five general categories.

Groups, Organizations, Committees, Boards, Councils, and Other Institutions are entities that offer arenas where members and others can deliberate, make decisions, and otherwise act. Examples are community organizations and planning councils, agencies that deliver services or administer programs, planning commissions and other boards that guide or regulate public action, citizen review boards, and task forces. All are concerned about and intervene in public life. They vary in the degree to which they involve citizens in activities characterized by purposes high on Arnstein's ladder.

These entities conduct *meetings* where participants can communicate information, develop relationships, develop the capacity to act, and act in ways that preserve or change people or things. Meetings may be formal or informal, regularly scheduled or *ad hoc*, generally oriented toward organizational affairs or focused on specific issues or problems. Meetings may have single or multiple purposes, such as discussion, planning, or decision making. Some organizations restrict citizens to discussion, whereas others may involve them in planning or decision making as well.

These entities can sponsor *inquiries*, events, or services for one-directional communication of information. Information centers allow citizens to ask for information. Activities in which citizens provide information include public hearings, surveys, focus groups, various structured group activities, referenda, and elections. Organizations vary in their interest in giving information to citizens or receiving it from them.

These entities can sponsor such other *action* as organizing people and developing and implementing interventions. Examples include place- or issue-based organizing, housing development, school reform, and health care provision. Line departments in state and local government, community organizations, and community development corporations typically sponsor these activities. They vary in the extent to which they require or can accommodate lay citizens, rather than experts. Organizations vary in efforts to involve citizens in these activities.

These entities or others can sponsor *technical assistance* to increase citizens' ability to join the entities, participate in meetings, make effective inquiries, and take part in action. Technical assistance includes classes or workshops, as well as *ad hoc* or ongoing consultation or mentoring. 'Advocate planners' work with or represent citizen groups in planning. Topics for assistance include means of participating in organizations such as using parliamentary procedure, engaging in public discussion, making decisions, and exercising leadership; technical and analytic tasks such as budgeting, scheduling, and grant-writing; managerial tasks such as running and organization and planning; and knowledge about substantive fields.

6. Participation and Representation

6.1 Meanings of Representation

When 'citizen participation' refers to individual citizens, each person can be said to represent him- or herself, and participation and representation are equivalent. Both can be measured quantitatively, in terms of how many people or what percentage of members of some unit, such as a geographic neighborhood, participate.

In contrast, when 'citizen participation' refers to a collectivity, such as a community or a racial or cultural group, representation is more complicated and, while related to participation, separate from it. Representation might be measured as a ratio of participants to total members, but to do so would not take into account the characteristics that define the identity of the group, distinguish subgroups from one another, and demarcate various interests. One common shortcut is to identify certain demographic characteristics of the whole—such as race, sex, income, and age—and seek participants who resemble the overall population in these respects. However, this approach assumes that all blacks, women, poor people, or elderly are similar and that what matters about and to them is a simple product of their race, sex, income, and/or age.

There is no single correct way to define or measure representation. Rather, it is useful to consider in a particular instance what aspects of the people involved matter and how they might be represented. For example, in a neighborhood with bad housing, groups may form around distinct positions on improving conditions; their views may be unrelated to race or income, and associated mainly with whether households own or rent and whether they have children. Representation could be defined primarily in terms of positions on issues and secondarily in terms of housing tenure and family composition. Determination of what interests, positions, or characteristics should be represented is consequential because it affects not only which individuals participate, but also which positions are given voice.

6.2 Differences in Ability to Participate

Nevertheless, even if there is agreement about how many and which participants might represent an overall population, some groups can much more easily participate than others. Citizen participation depends on motive, opportunity, and means. The three are related.

A common motive, particularly with regard to participation in activities sponsored by government or other large institutions, is the possibility of influencing conditions, for the benefit of a private or a public interest. A strong motive, that often leads citizens to create or activate an organization, is the desire to resist an action seen as a threat, such as urban renewal, highway construction, or massive development.

When participation opportunities arise, individuals may take part for the pleasure of interacting with others—either specific persons or a group in general. At the same time, they may assess whether these are opportunities to exercise power or accomplish meaningful ends. Government activities, for example, may be linked to formal power but lie beyond local citizens' influence; a community organization may offer individuals considerable opportunity for neighborhood influence but have little control over important outside forces.

Citizens vary in their ability to take advantage of these opportunities. Time is a basic resource and constraint. Those who work full time, parents, and, in particular, single parents have little time for meetings. Middle-class citizens, especially those who have a flexible schedule, do not work full-time, or are supported by a spouse, and particularly those without children at home, are most likely to have time to participate in public life.

Thus citizens' motivations rest on a calculation of the returns on an investment of time. Different citizens are likely to figure the possibilities for influence differently, based on their experience, relationships, skills, and confidence. The means at their disposal affect their ability to take advantage of opportunities. Participation is aided by a cognitive style that allows seeing how the particulars of a moment fit into a big picture—geographically, socially, and temporally. Planning depends on imagining a medium- to long-term future and having confidence in one's ability to affect it. Substantive knowledge matters, both for making informed decisions and for having the confidence to take part. Procedural expertise is crucial, including knowing how to organize people, run a productive meeting, resolve conflicts, and direct discussion toward agreement. Social relations are an important source of work, influence, and knowledge—about issues and participation opportunities.

The conditions of middle-class life are particularly likely to give citizens these means and motivate them to see and take advantage of opportunities for participation. Extended formal education, professional work, intricate social networks, and general success in influencing the world prepare middle-class citizens to participate in ways that elude many who are poorer.

These conditions encouraged the creation of remedial 'citizen participation' activities. Extensive, effective participation of low-income citizens depends on overcoming these obstacles. Time is a difficult constraint to change, but linking civic events with activities in which people already participate is important, as is child care. Training and experience can give people skills and confidence to organize and take an active part in public affairs. Crucially, low-income citizens, as any citizens, are more likely to participate when they see real opportunities for power.

7. Evaluating Citizen Participation Activities

Does citizen participation work? Do some kinds of citizen participation work better than others? How does narrowly defined 'citizen participation' compare with the rest of broadly defined citizen participation? Is citizen participation worth the effort—for citizens, for the government, for anyone else?

These are good, crucial questions. Yet they are difficult to answer. First, terms must be defined. Second, little of the relevant empirical evidence is collected in writing. Hence available data offer only specimens of answers from a larger undetermined universe of possibilities. Third, in any case, the most precise answers are contingent: it depends.

7.1 Defining the Questions

Whether citizen participation 'works' depends on expectations. Most generally, citizen participation is a strategy for solving a problem. Commonly, problems are defined substantively: for example, the poor are unemployed, low-income city residents lack affordable food shopping, or public health programs do not reach low-income children. Alternatively, some problems may be defined procedurally, and many substantive problems, in fact, have procedural roots: for example, the city health department, local hospitals, the state Medicaid division, and low-income health advocates cannot agree on an approach for taking care of indigent children.

One might ask whether citizen participation in planning for such problems contributed to better solutions than would have been likely otherwise.

However, because there cannot be a contrasting case where everything was the same except for citizen participation, it is impossible to answer that question. Moreover, the purpose, or at least the effect, of citizen participation may be to redefine the problem. In particular, in the case of procedural problems defined by the exclusion of citizens, citizen involvement in itself may provide a solution. Hence it is reasonable simply to study events to assess the influence of particular actions by specific people.

Still, citizens may participate in activities that solve problems without themselves having influence over the results. Tensions between the narrow and broad notions of 'citizen participation,' as well as conflicts over substantive and procedural issues, will lead others to try to limit the power of certain citizens. To evaluate the effects of citizen participation, it is necessary to examine the roles and influence of particular groups of citizens at each level of power.

Finally, citizens may participate powerfully in solving problems, but those who take part may not represent a larger group in whose name they speak. An elite may deliberately try to corner power for themselves. Alternatively, a small group of activists who have the skills, time, and connections to participate in wide-ranging activities may, with the most generous of intentions, take leadership, work closely together, succeed in advancing projects, develop proprietary feelings for them, and continue along the easy path of standing for a larger group. They may succeed in solving problems for members of their larger community, who can be said to be represented by the outcomes, but not in the process.

Thus the question of whether citizen participation works, complexly combines issues of effectiveness in solving problems, power, and representation. Still, answers to the question do not affect the normative position that citizen participation in public affairs is a democratic right.

7.2 The Haphazardly Collected Empirical Data

Few citizens record their participatory experiences, probably because few have both the interest and time. Perhaps those who consider themselves successful are most likely to document their activities or draw the attention of observers who will do so. For these reasons there is no way of knowing what universe reported cases represent.

Moreover, it is unclear what should be considered a sufficient account of a case. While many case studies focus on specific 'citizen participation' activities, their context shapes their effects. Hence it would be informative to see the entirety of influences on citizen participation in a case, but it may be uncertain at what distance from the 'main action' to draw boundaries around the case. Within those boundaries there is the question of what the unit of analysis should be—what should be taken as the unit of citizen participation that is to be measured for its effects. It might be an incident, an individual or collective actor, a relationship, a strategy, a tactic, another action, or a combination of these things. Further, it is unclear what characteristics of these elements might matter. For example, when might citizens' age, education, family composition, housing tenure, income, length of residence, occupation, place of residence, race, religion, or sex, be pertinent to their participation in public affairs and the effects of their activities? And how would the context of the case affect the influence of the unit of citizen participation?

These questions are conceptual but also empirical, dependent on data collection and analysis. Little available material is robust enough to address all these questions, and, as a result, it is difficult to compare the effects of citizen participation in different contexts. These questions should direct the recording of cases. For now, the available data should be interpreted as complexly as possible. They offer specimens—examples of what citizen participation may accomplish—which could become the basis for generalizations.

One can find examples of success and failure. There are instances where organized citizens planned and developed programs. There are instances where organized citizens stopped projects they opposed. In these cases, citizens have benefited from such resources as organization, money, effort, skill, knowledge, planning, strategy, alliances, time, and commitment. These findings are consistent with political science research.

See also: Citizenship and Public Policy; Civil Society, Concept and History of; Community Power Structure; Community, Social Contexts of; Community Sociology; Neighborhood Revitalization and Community Development; Participation: Political; Political Representation; Poverty Policy; Poverty, Sociology of; Urban Poverty in Neighborhoods

Bibliography

Arnstein S R 1969 A ladder of citizen participation. *Journal of American Institute of Planners* 35: 216–24
Baum H S 1997 *The Organization of Hope*. SUNY Press, Albany, NY
Checkoway B 1995 Six strategies of community change. *Community Development Journal* 30: 2–20
Checkoway B, Pothukuchi K, Finn J 1995 Youth participation in community planning: What are the benefits? *Journal of Planning Education and Research* 14: 134–9
Fisher R 1984 *Let the People Decide*. Twayne, Boston
Forester J 1989 *Planning in the Face of Power*. University of California Press, Berkeley, CA
Frieden B J, Kaplan M 1975 *The Politics of Neglect*. MIT Press, Cambridge, MA
Glass J J 1979 Citizen participation in planning: the relationship between objectives and techniques. *Journal of the American Planning Association* 45: 180–9
Heskin A D 1991 *The Struggle for Community*. Westview Press, Boulder, CO
Hinsdale M A, Lewis H M, Waller S M 1995 *It Comes from the People*. Temple University Press, Philadelphia
Marris P, Rein M 1982 *Dilemmas of Social Reform*, 2nd edn. University of Chicago Press, Chicago
Medoff P, Sklar H 1994 *Streets of Hope*. South End Press, Boston
Midgley J, Hall A, Hardiman M, Narine D 1986 *Community Participation, Social Development and the State*. Methuen, London
Mogulof M B 1970 *Citizen Participation: A Review and Commentary on Federal Policies and Practices*. Urban Institute, Washington, DC
Moynihan D P 1970 *Maximum Feasible Misunderstanding*. Free Press, New York
Narayan D, Ebbe K 1997 *Design of Social Funds; Participation, Demand Orientation, and Local Organizational Capacity*. World Bank Discussion Paper No. 375. World Bank, Washington, DC
Oakley P, Marsden D 1984 *Approaches to Participation in Rural Development*. International Labour Office, Geneva, Switzerland
Rosener J B 1975 A cafeteria of techniques and critiques. *Public Management* 57: 16–19
Rothman J, Tropman J E 1987 Models of community organization and macro practice perspectives: Their mixing and phasing. In: Cox F M, Erlich J L, Rothman J, Tropman J E (eds.) *Strategies of Community Organization*, 4th edn. Peacock Publishers, Itasca, IL
Spiegel H B C 1968 *Citizen Participation in Urban Development*; Vol. I *Concepts and Issues*. NTL Institute for Applied Behavioral Science, Washington, DC
Stoecker R 1984 *Defending Community*. Temple University Press, Philadelphia, PA

H. S. Baum

Citizenship and Public Policy

The conceptualization of the relationships between citizenship and public policy depends critically on how these terms are defined, and in turn on the sociopolitical context in which they were developed and are located. In the social sciences, these concepts are the products of different histories and significance within Europe and North America. In the European context, public policy is directly connected with social citizenship in the historical context of the emergence of the welfare state and industrial capitalism. Social citizenship can only be understood in the broader historical context of social class relations, the modern capitalist economy and the nation state (Turner 1986). For radical sociologists, citizenship and public policy were state strategies to secure the political compliance of the urban working class (Mann 1987). In the USA, citizenship was originally defined in political terms by reference to the individual rights that followed from the War of Independence and the framing of the Constitution. American citizenship was essentially about nation-building, that is, about the creation of a 'people' in relation to the aspiration of political leaders

(Shklar 1991). In the formation of the American people, political leaders created diverse 'civic ideals' (Smith 1997) that blended liberal, democratic republican, and inegalitarian ascriptive elements. In the late twentieth century, following the civil rights movements and intensive waves of immigration, social citizenship is related to government policies towards naturalization, ethnic integration, and multiculturalism. It is difficult to think of American citizenship without thinking of the 'American dilemma' of race relations (Myrdal 1944). Because the historical development of the welfare states in Europe and America is fundamentally different, the terms of debate have different meanings, functions, and significance. However, with globalization there is some convergence between these different traditions as nation states confront cultural hybridity, a global labor market, and the partial erosion of national sovereignty.

Conventional forms of citizenship were associated with the modernization of society and with the development of the administrative framework of the modern states. In the nineteenth century, for example in the public policies of Bismarck, there emerged a close relationship between nationalism, social insurance, and state formation. The formation of national identity, political integration, and citizenship were aspects of the modernization of state administrations, and citizenship came to form a basis for the convergence of national and masculine identity (Nelson 1998). Nineteenth-century nationalism meant that under the orchestration of the nation state, public policy was also cultural policy. However, with globalization, the sovereignty of the state has been compromised, and the modern debate about policy and citizenship has to be set within the political constraints of a global economy.

The concept of citizenship in British social theory has passed through several stages, from the idealism of T. H. Green to the welfare theories of T. H. Marshall and Richard Titmuss. Marshall's *Citizenship and Social Class and Other Essays* (1950) and *Social Policy in the Twentieth Century* (1967) have dominated recent debate about social citizenship. The principal question in this tradition has concerned how far a comprehensive welfare policy can be effectively implemented in a capitalist system without either destroying the profitability of capitalist enterprises through excessive taxation or compromising the principles of redistributive justice (Loney et al. 1983). Skeptics of the Marshallian approach have claimed that welfare benefits contributed more to the wellbeing of the middle class than the working class. The contemporary British welfare debate has concentrated on the question of European union, the effects of a centralized bureaucracy, and the possibility of the implementing a social wage.

These policy debates can be contrasted with the American tradition. One might argue controversially that, while the European policy debate has been about the possibility of equality in a capitalist economy, the American legacy, drawing on the work of both Alexis de Tocqueville (1966) and John Dewey (1963), has been concerned with electoral democracy and political access. The Tocquevillian position has been to emphasize the contribution of churches, voluntary associations, and community initiative in the delivery of public policy. However, the distinctively American contribution to public policy has been from pragmatism which, from John Dewey to Richard Rorty (1998), has placed its policy aspirations in the role of education for access and participation (Diggins 1994). It is also important to recognise that philanthropy has played a much larger role in policy development and delivery in America than in Europe (Wuthnow 1996).

In general, citizenship establishes the broad legal and social parameters within which public policy is set, but public policy creates the administrative and legislative framework within which citizens can effectively enjoy their rights. Historically, institutionally, and analytically, citizenship and public policy are interconnected and interdependent. Citizenship is a collection of rights and obligations that gives individuals a formal juridicial identity. Social citizenship involves social membership, a distribution of rewards, the formation of identities, and a set of virtues relating to obligation and responsibility. It is constituted by social institutions such as the jury system, parliament, and welfare states. Whereas the history of political institutions identifies the origins of citizenship with the Greek *polis*, social citizenship, as the outcome of the American and French Revolutions, is an essentially modern conception. It is analytically a product of modern liberal theory, specifically de Tocqueville's theory of democratic association.

The social rights of social citizenship are very different in their consequences in contrast with legal and political rights. Social rights require the provision of social services and transfer payments, and as a result involve the state in public expenditure. They also require some administrative structure to deliver these services, and hence further involve the state in fiscal management. Recognition of this fiscal role of the state gave rise to the famous division of welfare by Titmuss (1958) into social welfare (education, health, and social services); fiscal welfare (allowances and relief from taxation); and occupational welfare (benefits received by employees through employment). This provision of social rights clearly illustrates the tensions and contradictions between the state and the market. Radical sociologists like Jürgen Habermas (1976) predicted a 'legitimation crisis,' because the growth of state expenditure in response to electoral pressure would necessarily undermine capitalist profitability. One can argue therefore that the neoliberal policies of the governments of Ronald Reagan and Margaret Thatcher involved 'rolling back the state,' the privatization of welfare, and a return to third-sector involvement through charities, philanthropic institutions, and the voluntary associations. These strategies sought to restore profitability through deregulation, subsidiarity, and community initiatives, but also emphasized the importance of individual and family responsibility for welfare delivery. Conservative critics of bureaucratic welfare argued that welfare benefits undermined the family through payments to single parents, who as a result had no necessary incentive to work and clear incentives not to marry. In the late twentieth century, so-called 'third-sector strategies,' which encouraged local initiative, community development, and voluntary sector delivery, became fashionable, not only in North American and Europe but also in Australia and New Zealand (Brown et al. 2000).

The notion of 'public policy' also requires some preliminary clarification. It is a general term to describe the efforts of governments to coordinate the provision of a variety of governmental services and utilities. Public policy expresses the political intentions and choices of government, and creates the framework within which social planning takes place. 'Public policy' is often referred to as 'social policy,' typically when a broader philosophical dimension is involved. Social policy is often distinguished from public policy by its broad welfare dimension; it attempts to regulate the provision of five social services: housing, education, health, social security, and personal social services. The connection between policy and citizenship was overtly expressed by Marshall, who claimed that social policy includes the general policy of governments with regard to action having a direct and explicit impact on the welfare of citizens by providing them with services or income. Social Administration is the science of the provision of such services through social policy, and in Britain it was established as a discipline at the London School of Economics in 1912. In Europe in the 1840s, the growth of social medicine expressed the idea that the health of individuals should involve the state in the policing of society. Public policy and social citizenship have to be understood as aspects of the growth of state administration designed to bring about social order in a world of expanding capitalism.

For detailed treatment of these and related fields see *Health Policy*; *Immigration: Public Policy*; *Industrial Policy*; *Policy History: Regimes*; *Poverty Policy*; *Public Health*; *Social Insurance: Legal Aspects*.

1. Citizenship and the Rise of Public Policy

Both citizenship and public policy are modern institutions. Neither social citizenship nor public policy could exist without the nineteenth-century expansion of public administration and law. In pre-modern times, it is clear that the church responded to the satisfaction of need through principles of reciprocity and redistribution. Ecclesiastical responses to poverty and need in the Middle Ages were located within a theological debate about economic exchange in which low wages were interpreted through a moral discourse on justice. The church developed various institutional responses to poverty and created the modern framework of charity (Troeltsch 1912). Before the development of the capitalist market system, the poor could rely on custom and communal organizations for subsistence. In the medieval period, guilds and fraternal associations in the towns provided welfare benefits to members and their dependants. These guilds often evolved into mutual societies and the principles of mutuality often survived the growth of capitalism. In traditional societies, it was the church, the patriarchal family, or the landlord who determined the conditions of survival, rather than the labor contract.

We can see the origins of public policy as a social struggle over the conditions by which markets function. In his classic study of *The Three Worlds of Welfare Capitalism*, Esping-Andersen (1990, p. 35) claimed that 'the mainsprings of modern social policy lie in the process by which both human needs and labor power became commodities and, hence, our wellbeing came to depend on our relation to the cash nexus.' However, the impact of the market is modified or moderated by the growth of social citizenship which provides, through public policy initiatives, a variety of safety nets to protect the individual from the full vagaries of unemployment, sickness, and disability. With the decline of traditional patterns of social reciprocity, citizenship expressed through public policy reduces the contingencies of dependence on the market.

The historical controversy in the social sciences has been around the capacity of public policy and citizenship to bring about an effective redistribution of resources. There are broadly two views about the historical role of welfare states. Radical critics of capitalism (O'Connor 1973, Piven and Cloward 1972) have argued that public policy aimed at creating social citizenship is primarily concerned with legitimating governments and protecting them from political instability arising from social conflicts, specifically from a revolutionary working class. Liberal theories of welfare (Lipset 1960) argue that welfare policies reduce the material causes of class conflict, incorporate the working class and enhance democratic access to the state. For sociologists like Frank Parkin (1979), social welfare transforms class conflict into status competition. In broad terms, one can conclude that the production of inflationary pressure of welfare benefits from public policy initiatives has been regarded by the state and its elites as more tolerable than civil conflict and revolutionary protest. Whether or not public policies to institutionalize social citizenship have a real effect on social equality will depend on what type of welfare state (if any) is created by government actions, and how these policies have emerged historically in relation to different forms of capitalism.

In recent scholarship, the radical or Marxist paradigms have been less influential, and debate about public policy and government agency has been influenced by the work of Michel Foucault. Social scientists have in particular recognized the importance of Foucault's concept of 'governmentality' as a paradigm for understanding the microprocesses of administration and control within which self regulation and social regulation are united (Foucault 1991).The concept of 'governmentality' provides an integrating theme that is concerned with the sociopolitical practices or technologies by which the self is constructed. 'Governance' or 'governmentality' refers to the administrative structures of the state , the patterns of self-government of individuals and the regulatory principles of modern society. Foucault argued that governmentality has become the common foundation of all forms of modern political rationality, that is, the administrative systems of the state have been extended in order to maximize the state's productive control over demographic processes. This extension of administrative rationality was first concerned with demographic processes of birth, morbidity, and death, and later with the psychological health of the population. 'Governmentality' can be seen as an administrative rationality that produces the modern self as a consequence of social services. This perspective has been valuable in understanding the growth, for example, of social gerontology as a science, a component of public policy, and as the basis for new professions to discipline the elderly (Katz 1996).

Foucault's historical inquiries gave rise to a distinctive notion of power, in which he emphasized the importance of its local or micro manifestations, the role of professional knowledge and expertise in the legitimation of such power relationships, and the productive rather than negative characteristics of the effects of power. His approach can be contrasted usefully with the concept of power in traditional Marxist sociology, where power is visible in terms of the police and army, concentrated in the state, and ultimately explained by the ownership of the economic means of production. In the Marxist perspective, power is typically negative and signifies a system of institutions that contain, prohibit, and control. Foucault's view of power is more subtle, with an emphasis on the importance of knowledge and information in modern means of surveillance.

'Governmentality' is the generic term for these power relations. It was defined as 'the ensemble formed by the institutions, procedures, analyses and reflections, the calculations and tactics, that allow the exercise of this very specific albeit complex form of power, which has as its target populations'(Foucault 1991, p. 102). The importance of this definition is that the power of the state in the modern period has been less concerned with sovereignty over things (land and wealth) and more concerned with maximizing the productive power of administration over population and reproduction. Furthermore, Foucault interpreted the exercise of administrative power in productive terms, that is enhancing population potential through, for example, state support for the family. For example, the state's involvement in—and regulation of—reproductive technology is an important example of governmentality in which the desire of couples to reproduce is enhanced through the state's support of new technologies. The existence of a demand for fertility is supported by a profamilial ideology that regards the normal household as a reproductive social space. These Foucauldian perspectives have been useful in providing an historical understanding of the relationships between family, state, and public policy. Feminist criticism of neoliberal policy to protect the family has noted that these policy initiatives implicitly or explicitly ignore the presence of married women in the labor force (Wilson 1977).

2. The Dimensions of Citizenship

In historical terms, social citizenship and public policy have been shaped by the relationship between state and market. Public policy attempts to promote a set of general social conditions through which effective entitlement to social resources can be sustained. Welfare has, in practice, never been an unconditional right; entitlements have, in reality, been tied to contribution. The entitlement to benefits in liberal welfare systems have typically been through work, war, and reproduction.

Work was fundamental to the conception of citizenship in the welfare state as described in W. H. Beveridge's *Social Insurance and Allied Services* (1942) and *Full Employment in a Free Society* (1944). Individuals could achieve effective entitlements through the production of goods and services, namely through gainful employment, which was essential for the provision of adequate pensions and superannuation. These entitlements also typically included work care, insurance cover, retirement benefits, and healthcare.

Citizenship for male workers characteristically evolved out of economic conflicts over conditions of employment, remuneration, and retirement .Service to the state through warfare generates a range of entitlements for the soldier–citizen. Wartime service typically leads to special pension rights, health provisions, housing, and education for returning servicemen and their families. War service has been important, as we have seen, in the development of the evolution of social security entitlements (Titmuss 1962).

Finally, people achieve entitlements through the the formation of households and families, which become the mechanisms for the reproduction of society through the birth, maintenance, and socialization of children. These services increasingly include care for the aging and elderly as generational obligations continue to be satisfied through the private sphere (Finch 1989). These services to society through the family provide entitlements to both men and women as parents, that is as reproducers of the nation. These familial entitlements become the basis of family security systems, various forms of support for mothers, and health and educational provision for children. Although the sexual activity of adults in wedlock is regarded in law as a private activity, the state and church have clearly taken a profound interest in the conditions for and consequences of lawful (and more particularly unlawful) sexual activity. Following Foucault, we can argue that heterosexual reproduction has been a principal feature of the regulatory activity of the modern state. It is evident that the values and norms of a household constituted by a married heterosexual couple provides the dominant ideal of British social life , despite the fact that 49 percent of live births in 1998 occurred outside marriage and that among the majority of one-family households 30 percent had no children. In fact, the moral force of the idea of marriage and domesticity is so compulsive in contemporary society that in America a number of states are considering legislation that would enable gay couples to form 'civil unions,' entitling them to about 300 rights and benefits currently available under state law to married heterosexual couples.

3. Regulatory Regimes and Public Policy

This liberal pattern of public policy for social citizenship has been eroded because the three foundations of effective entitlement have been transformed by economic, military, and social changes. It may sound perverse to suggest that in contemporary Britain the decline of economic participation has brought about an erosion of citizenship, when participation in the labor force has been rising continuously since the early 1990s. Increasing economic activity has been especially important for women; between 1971 and 1999, the proportion of the adult female population being economically active increased from 56 to 72 percent. However, high levels of economic participation mask a real change in the nature of the economy and obscure a transition from old to new welfare regimes. The new economic regime is based on monetary stability, fiscal control, and a reduction in government regulation of the economy. In this new economic environment, one version of the 'Third Way strategy' involves not protecting individuals from the uncertainties of the market that had dominated welfare strategies between 1930 and 1970, but helping people to participate successfully in the market through education (lifelong learning schemes), flexible employment (family-friendly employment strategies), and tax incentives (Myles and Quadagno 2000). However, while increasing rates of economic activity have been a positive aspect of economic liberalization, much of this in-

crease in economic participation has required the casualization of the labor force. While the number of men in part-time employment doubled between 1984 and 1999, radical changes in the labor market (job sharing, casualization, flexibility, downsizing, and new management strategies) have disrupted work as a career. While for employers functional and numerical flexibility has broken down rigidities in the workplace, these strategies have compromised job security (Abercrombie and Warde 2000, p. 81).

Sociological studies of social class suggest that, while levels of unemployment have been falling in association with the long American economic boom of the 1990s, the contemporary class structure has new components—an 'underclass' of the permanently unemployable (typically single-parent welfare claimants), a declining middle class associated with the decline of middle management, and the 'working poor' whose skill levels do not permit upward mobility (Sennett 1998). There is some academic consensus that features of the class structure do not encourage active citizenship through economic entitlement, but these changes in the nature of employment are perhaps insignificant when compared to the graying of the population and the social problem of retirement. It is clear that the stereotype of the elderly as a dependent and passive population in disengagement theory is false, but it is also true that the aging of the population has important implications for the shape of the working population and for employment as a basis for entitlement. Intergenerational conflict in the struggle over resources is likely to become an important element in social divisions in this century.

Public policy and social citizenship were aspects of modern state administration that developed in the nineteenth century. We can interpret this administrative complex as a response to social class conflicts in the development of modern capitalism. Social rights were granted as political mechanisms to secure an acceptable level of social solidarity. Walter Bagehot (1963) in his *The English Constitution* warned in 1867 of the dangers of working class combination, which would result in the 'supremacy of ignorance,' and encouraged the 'higher classes' to exercise wisdom and foresight. An extension of social rights was a prudent response to the dangers of combination among the 'lower classes' and social citizenship has remained a valuable public policy option to avoid civil war. However, social citizenship and capitalism have remained in a state of permanent tensions—as Marshall recognized in his concept of 'hyphernated society' in *The Right to Welfare and Other Essays* (Marshall 1981). There is a permanent tension between the liberal rights of individual freedom in a capitalist marketplace and principles of equity and justice that require state interventions to protect social rights.

Public policy and welfare systems oscillate between different regulatory environments. A regulatory regime may be defined as 'a historically specific configuration of policies and institutions which structures the relationship between social interests, the state, and economic actors in multiple sectors of the economy' (Eisner 1993, p. 1). These regimes fluctuate between interventionist welfare systems and deregulated privatized systems. For example, in retrospect, we can see that American public policy passed through different regulatory regimes in the Progressive Era, the New Deal, postwar reconstruction, and the contemporary period. Following the depression, President Roosevelt and his advisors introduced a legislative programme aimed at social and economic recovery. The National Industrial Recovery Act was characteristic of the new policy regime, but the Progressive Era still depended on market forces. The New Deal and postwar reconstruction required an alliance between the state and capital to conduct a global war and then to achieve an economic recovery. In wartime Britain, the social policies of John Maynard Keynes, as expressed in *The General Theory of Interest, Employment and Money* (1936), were adopted to finance the war. Social Keynesianism also formed the basis for postwar reconstruction where the policy of supporting public works, such as direct investment in infrastructure projects, promoted the recovery of employment. These public policies were in direct opposition to the 'Treasury view,' which advocated fiscal constraint and limited government intervention. In the late twentieth century, there was a departure from interventionist policies; environmental controls and workers' safety are not primary objectives, and were seen to conflict with corporate profitability. In both the USA and UK, there has been a similar history involving a rapid departure from the principles of the New Deal, Social Keynesianism, and the postwar consensus in favour of policies that do not assume, for example, full employment or universal criteria in the provision of pensions.

4. Conclusion: Public Policy and Globalization

This historical pattern of policy options changed significantly in the last two decades of the twentieth century with the emergence of a global economy. Although it would be an exaggeration to claim that globalization has resulted in the decline of national sovereignty (Hirst and Thompson 1996), it is the case that global economic processes constrain the capacity of national governments to make independent decisions about national public policy. For example, volatile financial markets responding to global information systems can undercut national public policy through the collapse of local currencies. The Asian financial crisis of the late 1990s was a dramatic illustration of how global uncertainty can destabilize currencies and prevent governments from adhering to public policies that have inflationary consequences. Volatile markets, the fragmentation of public policy

by constant restructuring of government agencies and the economy, an emphasis on individual responsibility and subsidiarity, and the recommodification of services through neoliberalism have encouraged some social scientists to argue that public policy has become postmodern (Petersen et al. 1999). A new policy environment may involve the globalization of delivery through global enterprises that provide services for governments under 'outsourcing' arrangements. The growth of private prisons, managed by global enterprises, to replace or supplement state prison services would be one example. Social experiments in policy delivery in a global context may not be postmodern, but they will certainly be increasingly translocal. As a consequence, the conventional mixture of state, market, and voluntary sector as the framework of public policy will change radically to reflect the changing circumstances of social citizenship in a global economy.

See also: Civil Society, Concept and History of; Civil Society/Public Sphere, History of the Concept; Citizenship, Historical Development of; Citizenship: Political; Citizenship: Sociological Aspects; State and Society; Welfare State

Bibliography

Abercrombie N, Ward A 2000 *Contemporary British Society*. Polity Press, Cambridge, UK
Bagehot W 1963 *The English Constitution*. Collins, London
Barbalet J M 1988 *Citizenship*. Open University Press, Milton Keynes, UK
Beveridge W H 1942 *Social Insurance and Allied Services*. HMSO, London
Beveridge W H 1944 *Full Employment in a Free Society*. Allen & Unwin, London
Brown K, Kenny S, Turner B S 2000 *Rhetorics of Welfare*. Macmillan, Basingstoke, UK
de Tocqueville A 1966 *Democracy in America*. Doubleday, New York
Dewey J 1963 *Freedom and Culture*. Capricorn, New York
Diggins J P 1994 *The Promise of Pragmatism. Modernism and the Crisis of Knowledge and Authority*. University of Chicago Press, Chicago
Eisner M A 1993 *Regulatory Politics in Transition*. The John Hopkins University Press, Baltimore
Esping-Andersen G 1990 *The Three Worlds of Welfare Capitalism*. Polity Press, Cambridge, UK
Finch J 1989 *Family Obligations and Social Change*. Polity Press, Cambridge, UK
Foucault M 1991 'Governmentality'. In: Burchell G, Gordon C, Miller P (eds.) *The Foucault Effect. Studies in Governmentality*. Harvester, London, pp. 87–104
Habermas J 1976 *Legitimation Crisis*. Heinemann, London
Hirst P, Thompson G 1996 *Globalization in Question*. Polity Press, Cambridge, UK
Katz S 1996 *Disciplining Old Age. The Formation of Gerontological Knowledge*. University of Virginia Press, Charlottesville, WV
Keynes J M 1936 *The General Theory of Interest, Employment and Money*. Macmillan, London

Lipset S M 1960 *Political Man. The Social Bases of Politics.* Doubleday, Garden City, NY

Loney M, Bosell D, Clarke J (eds.) 1983 *Social Policy and Social Welfare.* Open University Press, Milton Keynes, UK

Mann M 1987 'Ruling class strategies and citizenship'. *Sociology* 21(3): 339–54

Marshall T H 1950 *Citizenship and Social Class and Other Essays.* Cambridge University Press, Cambridge, UK

Marshall T H 1967 *Social Policy in the Twentieth Century.* Hutchinson, London

Marshall T H 1981 *The Right to Welfare and Other Essays.* Heinemann, London

Myles J, Quadagno J 2000 'Envisioning a Third Way.' *Contemporary Sociology* 29(1): 156–67

Myrdal G 1944 *The American Dilemma.* Harper, New York

Nelson D D 1998 *National Manhood. Capitalist Citizenship and the Imagined Fraternity of White Men.* Duke University Press, Durham, NC

O'Connor J 1973 *The Fiscal Crisis of the State.* St Martin's Press, New York

Parkin F 1979 *Marxism and Class Theory. A Bourgeois Critique.* Tavistock, London

Petersen A, Barns I, Dudley A, Harris P 1999 *Poststructuralism, Citizenship and Social Policy.* Routledge, London

Piven F, Cloward R A 1972 *Regulating the Poor.* Tavistock, London

Rorty R 1997 *Achieving Our Country. Leftist Thought in Twentieth-Century America.* Harvard University Press, Cambridge, MA

Sennett R 1998 *The Corrosion of Character. The Personal Consequences of Work in the New Capitalism.* W W Norton, New York

Shklar J N 1991 *American Citizenship. The Quest for Inclusion.* Harvard University Press, New York

Smith R 1997 *Civic Ideals. Conflicting Visions of Citizenship in US History.* Yale University Press, New Haven, CT

Titmuss R 1958 *Essays on the Welfare State.* Allen & Unwin, London

Titmuss R 1962 *Income Distribution and Social Change. A Case Study in Criticism.* Allen and Union, London

Titmuss R 1968 *Commitment to Welfare.* Allen & Unwin, London

Troeltsch E 1912 *The Social Teaching of the Christian Churches.* University of Chicago Press, Chicago

Turner B S (ed.) 1993 *Citizenship and Social Theory.* Sage, London

Turner B S 1986 *Citizenship and Capitalism. The Debate over Reformism.* Allen & Unwin, London

Wilson E 1977 *Women and the Welfare State.* Tavistock, London

Wuthnow R 1996 *Poor Richard's Principle. Recovering the American Dream through the Moral Dimension of Work, Business and Money.* Princeton University Press, Princeton, NJ

B. S. Turner

Citizenship, Historical Development of

Citizenship means membership in a political community. As *membership*, citizenship confers the status of equality among all citizens with respect to the rights and duties that the status implies. Citizenship also signifies a form of active *behavior* towards the community, which constitutes the good and responsible citizen. These two basic meanings of citizenship apply to all of the historical phases that the formation of citizenship as subject and concept has undergone. The politico-legal status and the ideal of civic virtue constitute the two aspects of a historical concept that has taken on a variety of further meanings and functions over time.

It has shifted between membership in ancient communities and legal membership in the modern state, between a concrete legal status and a wide-ranging concept within political theory. It has been used to describe substantive rights and obligations as well as to sketch a normative ideal of politics. While the theoretical claims of citizenship often tend to be universal, their meaning varies according to historical and national context. The concept of citizenship is rooted in social ethics and institutionalized by law. As such, it is an object of political theory. To analyze the historical development of citizenship means to combine the development of norms of conduct regarding good civic behavior with the legal institutionalization of citizen status and its theoretical conceptualization. It also means tracing the trajectory from a status of the city-state community to a key concept of modern democracy and global political theory.

1. Citizenship as a Historical Subject

Every human group has developed institutions by which to define its members and procedures for making new members. The Greeks, however, were the first society to combine the legal provisions of membership with a political theory of membership virtues and institutions in order to perpetuate their idea of citizenship. The legal status of citizenship established equality among Athenian citizens in terms of their rights and obligations. The status of equal membership marked privilege vis-à-vis nonmembers. The overall legal status of Athenian citizenship was defined by sharp boundaries, which distinguished Athenians from foreigners, resident aliens, and slaves. The minority of full citizens faced a majority of non-privileged noncitizens whose rights were severely circumscribed. Apart from the legal framework, the concept of Athenian citizenship included a set of citizen values, behaviors, and communal attitudes. 'Passive' legal citizenship was not necessarily, but ideally and practically, linked to democracy by the civic virtues of an 'active' citizen, which permitted him to 'share in the polis,' a politically active and autonomous community (Manville 1990). Greek city-state citizenship and its dual construction as legal framework and civic ideal was conceptualized in the political philosophy of Aristotle as a model of 'ruling and being ruled in turn.' It became the model of citizenship as such.

Roman citizenship was more complex, expansive, and legalistic than its Greek counterpart. The history of Roman citizenship over eight centuries, from the end of the monarchy to the decline of the Roman Empire, reveals the stages of its development from an instrument for defining the city-state community to one for the legal integration of an extensive world empire. The Twelve Tables established the quality of Roman citizenship as a legal benefit and attractive political and social status. In the fourth century BC, with the territorial expansion of Roman rule over Latium, Roman citizenship was conferred upon annexed enemies and (Italian) allies alike as an instrument for promoting loyalty and political integration. By the first century BC, citizenship of the Roman Republic had reached its greatest 'density': the highest level of participatory rights in the government of the republic and equality before the law accompanied a golden age of civic education and virtues. This construction lost its balance in the Roman Empire. The largest territorial expansion of Roman citizenship, its conferral upon nearly all men within the confines of the Empire except for slaves, meant the erosion of its quality as a privilege and a proof of superior morality. With the decline of the Empire, the diminution in standards of citizenship corresponded to the degeneration of civic educational standards. Although the concept of citizenship did not necessarily depend on democracy, its development was most favored by the political conditions of a strongly participatory, republican order. A centralized, differentiated legal order within the city or state had, at least, proved to be the indispensable precondition for the development of citizenship. With the loss of a central, universal legal structure at the end of the Roman Empire, citizenship became obsolete as a political concept.

Christianity rejected the model of political order to which ancient philosophy, especially Aristotle and Cicero, had contributed. It developed a complete alternative system of social and moral values, which helped to establish a new institutional political order. The rise of Christian corporatism and its unlimited commitment to the Kingdom of God produced a dichotomous organization of the body politic. A dual system arose of metaphysically based allegiance to the Church and personal allegiance to the monarch. A system of multifaceted loyalty replaced the concentration of the citizen's loyalty upon the state. The notion of citizenship was transferred to a spiritual 'City of God' (Augustine). Thus, the institutional point of reference for the ancient model of citizenship disappeared. In the Middle Ages, the term 'citizenship' (French: *citoyenneté*) did not describe an Englishman's (or Frenchman's) relationship with his country. In keeping with its immediate etymological origins ('city'), it referred solely to the rights and duties of a free city- or town-dweller, i.e., to a local, urban community.

The lack of a centralizing and nationalizing state power in parts of medieval Europe left room for the growth of a strong, urban citizenship, particularly in the city-states of northern and central Italy. Along with the weakness of the monarchy, a certain continuity of Roman law and civic responsibility formed the backdrop for the upsurge of a politically active municipal life with a high participation of the citizenry in decision-making. A vigorous philosophical revival of the Aristotelian concept of citizenship paved the way for a resurgence of the classical concept of citizenship during the Renaissance. The founding of universities, which promoted the development of Roman law, a vital communal life, and a rich theoretical literature on a rational and egalitarian order (particularly the work of Niccolo Macchiavelli) made the city-state world of Upper Italy a birthplace of modern citizenship.

The theory and political order of state sovereignty in European absolutism with its concentration of central state power and its unambiguous claim to loyalty prepared the ground for a national rather than local concept of modern citizenship. The personal and territorial delimitation of sovereign states and the ordering of their international relations increased the problem of defining membership in and allegiance to the state. The call for (individual) rights of religious freedom and self-government, strengthened by religious opponents of the state, and revolutionary efforts at founding government upon popular sovereignty, for example in England, were the predecessors to active citizenship. The institutional foundations for such participatory claims and rights remained narrow, however. They were often confined to the level of local government or socially privileged groups. The contrast between a basically oligarchic and a democratic political citizenship (Heater 1990) became evident.

The eighteenth century brought the breakthrough of citizenship on a central level of political theory and institutions. The word 'citizen'—and its French equivalent *citoyen*—became a key concept in the legitimation of the political struggle against the feudal *ancien régime* (Gosewinkel 2001), as well as in the struggle for equality before the law, freedom from religious discrimination and arbitrary arrest, the extension of political rights and popular democracy. The decisive step from a political and educational program to a legal guarantee was taken by American constitutionalism, however. The revolution of the American colonies against the ties and obligations of subjecthood to the English Crown was accompanied by a decisive change in legal terminology. Within the decade before the enactment of the Federal Constitution (1787), the term 'citizen' came to replace previously related words such as 'subject' and 'inhabitant' in constitutional texts. The republican concepts of 'citizen' and 'citizenship' marked a political and terminological break with the feudal age. From this point onward citizen and citizenship became core terms of a state order based on democracy and constitutionalism. The American constitution introduced a revolutionary new type of legal instrument that firmly rooted any state power in the law, while simultaneously subjecting it to legal control. The constitutionalization of state power represented a fundamental development in early modern Western history: the subjection of social and political relationships to legal norms (*Verrechtlichung*). With the constitutionalization of membership status in a republican state order, the concept of citizenship gained new importance. It unified the claims to equality and political participation inherent in the classical concept of city-state citizenship, transferred it to the state level and gave it a new quality of legal efficacy. The constitutionalization of citizenship with its classical connotation of civil idealism and civic virtue represented a strong and permanent challenge to inequality and exclusion from rights in political practice. At the same time, the shift in scale from the small local community to the level of the abstract state risked attenuation in the practices and understandings of citizenship. The need for a new, expansive legitimation of citizenship to the state arose.

The French Revolution made citizenship (*citoyenneté*) one of its key concepts (Waldinger et al. 1993). This new citizenship combined four traits that were to become essential for the development of citizenship throughout the nineteenth and twentieth centuries: its *egalitarian*, antifeudal impetus, its confirmation as a key concept of the *legal constitution*, its association with extensive *individual rights*, and finally its *nationalization*. The modern concept of citizenship arose together with the concept of the nation-state (Bendix 1964) and became one of its central legal institutions. The age of revolution and constitutionalism in the Western world was also an age of an increasing delimitation of national citizenries. Extended citizenship law came to define membership in the nation-state as well as the rules of naturalisation policy. Whether they were based on an inclusionary, territorial model (USA, France) or an exclusionary, descent-based model (Central and Eastern Europe), citizenship and citizenship law became key instruments for defining national identity and controlling migration in a modern world characterized by increasing transnational mobility (Brubaker 1992). The central function of citizenship in defining membership in the sense of nationality was supplemented by a second main function: that of conferring upon the citizen individual rights vis-à-vis the state. In the nineteenth and early twentieth century, Western constitutional states extended the range of civil, political, and, increasingly, social rights which were reserved mainly for their own citizens. The nationalization of citizenship as a membership status corresponded to a nationalization of citizens' rights. Citizenship became an institution for distributing 'life opportunities' in a world of nation-states.

As the importance of citizenship as a legal entitlement increased, its extension to new members became more and more contested within the national citizenry. The struggle for inclusion, for example in American constitutional law, dominates the history of citizenship to this day. The gradual extension of equal civil rights to groups resident on American soil who had been denied citizenship rights and subjected to discrimination on the basis of ethnic or national origin, religious beliefs, social status, or gender determined the direction that citizenship was to take. The claims of discriminated groups to equality became the motor for full inclusion in the community defined by citizenship.

With the decline of liberal democracy, and the rise of radical nationalism, racism, and totalitarian dictatorship in the constitutional states of Europe and Asia, the period between the two world wars represented an interruption in the development of modern citizenship. The dominance of ascriptive national, ethnic, or racial criteria in admission to citizenship, the splintering of the citizenry through hierarchical classes of rights, the withdrawal of civil rights and massive expatriation of millions, destroyed the core of equality within the concept of citizenship. The rise of an army of stateless people deprived of rights and protection (Arendt 1951) revealed how dependent citizenship was on the liberal legal structures of the nation-state.

Developments after the Second World War were characterized by a dual tendency. On the one hand, the restoration of liberal democracy saw a reconstruction of citizenship. This was reinforced and extended to the global arena after 1989 with the end of ideological block confrontations and the adoption of democratic and constitutional patterns by most of the formerly communist states. On the other hand, there is also evidence of a tendency towards a certain 'devaluation' of citizenship. The weakening of nation-state structures, the trend towards transnational political unions, global standards and guarantees of civil rights as human rights have all diminished the importance of (national) citizenship for the conferral of individual rights. While formal citizenship is still crucial on the level of the right to full participation in the political arena, this no longer applies to economic and social rights. Citizenship as national membership status is of decreasing importance for the exercise of these increasingly relevant rights (Soysal 1994).

The historical development of citizenship from its beginning in the Greek city-states has been characterized by a multiple process of expansion. Citizenship expanded from a membership status in a local community to a central membership in the territorial nation-state. Citizenship as entitlement to individual rights was transferred from the level of the nation-state to that of supranational communities. From its inception in the Greek city-communities, the concept and ideal of citizenship has spread all over the world to states based on the principle of constitutional democracy. The substantive program of citizenship as a set of individual rights has expanded from political and civil to encompass social and economic rights, and ultimately cultural and environmental rights as well.

2. The Historical Conceptualization of Citizenship

Two main features mark the conceptualization of citizenship. The first consists of the twofold structure of a legally defined status of membership and rights on the one hand and a philosophical and normative ideal of 'good' civic behavior on the other. The second feature depends on the basic structure of equality within citizenship. Its conceptual development may be interpreted as a claim for recognition as equal and a struggle for inclusion. In the classical age of citizenship, its inclusive function consisted of either defining a ruling oligarchy with precisely delineated privileges or expanding a low standard of rights to an extensive group for the purposes of political integration. The linkage between a substantively high standard of citizenship rights and its extension to a broad group of persons was the result of a change in politics and theory that began in the early modern period. Between the sixteenth and eighteenth centuries, the concept of citizenship lost its coherence and republican ethos (Riesenberg 1992). The classical idea of citizenship survived as a historical concept in education and political literature, however. It corresponded doubly with the era's need for a break with old categories and concepts. First, the vision of an 'active' citizen fit well with the notion of a modern, visionary, and enterprising 'polytechnic man' as outlined in the political theories of Thomas Hobbes and John Locke. Second, the concept of citizenship was enlarged by bringing the terms 'citizen' and 'subject of the monarch' closer together, and indeed mingling them. The era's most elaborate conceptualization of citizenship, undertaken by Jean Bodin, transferred citizenship from the local to the state level. According to Bodin, the citizen was a superior subject of the sovereign monarch. Citizenship denoted a direct, personal link between the individual and his sovereign. This conceptual transfer opened the way for a revolutionary, egalitarian view: from the perspective of the sovereign all citizens were equal *qua* subjection to the monarch's sovereign authority. It was not until the eighteenth century that this kind of passive equality was transformed by the subject-citizen into a new, revolutionary call for active citizenship, i.e., for participation in sovereignty.

The concept that paved the way for this fundamental change of perspective was the revolutionary idea of 'civil society.' It emerged in the later seventeenth and eighteenth centuries as a result of a crisis both in the reality and idea of social order. In an age marked by an unprecedented commercialization of human relations, the growth of market economies and political revolution, the regulatory idea of the social order was no longer derived from a deity external to the temporal world, but from within it and its ethical values. The vision of an all-encompassing 'society' of human beings, equal, autonomous, and rational by nature, who defined their own political order, and challenged the traditional norms of monarchical order, ecclesiastical claims, and social hierarchy. Beginning with John Locke and the philosophers of the Scottish Enlightenment, and passing on to Kant, Hegel, and eventually Marx, the idea of 'civil society' (in German: 'bürgerliche Gesellschaft') laid the groundwork for a new idea of citizenship. Although not always developed systematically, the concept of the citizen and citizenship constituted the normative core of civil society (Haltern 1985). Out of Locke's view of civil society as a system of individual rights and duties, Kant's definition of the public arena in civil society as a sphere of juridical equality among citizens, and Hegel's (Riedel 1972) and Marx's vision of civil society as a field of conflicting particular interests, elements of a new understanding of citizenship emerged. It now referred to the central state, not the local community, and was based on individual autonomy, not obedience and subjection. It was legally constituted and based on the principle of legal equality, not oligarchic privilege. Finally, it was inclusive with regard to the principles of property and achievement. This new citizenship represented an ideal and became a key concept in the language of American and European revolutions at the end of the eighteenth century. It was not, however, the product of political revolution. Its achievement was the result not only of the conceptualization of 'civil society,' but also of its realization as a new formation of social and political order throughout the Western world. This process marked such a major *caesura* in the historical development of citizenship that it may be considered the rise of a 'second citizenship' (Riesenberg 1992).

In contrast to the universal and egalitarian concept of 'civil society,' the development of citizenship in the nineteenth century ran up against three fundamental obstacles to its realization in political practice. The first obstacle was nationality. Citizenship was conceptualized as membership in the nation-state. While the rights conferred upon citizens by the liberal constitutions of the nineteenth century grew in number and substance, they were increasingly confined to nationals. The universalist pathos of human rights, which was still inherent in the revolutionary declarations of the American and French Revolutions (e.g., The Declaration of the Rights of Man and Citizen), was increasingly reduced to national entitlements and interpreted in this light by legal scholars. The pre- and transnational origins and impetus of 'civil society' gave way to a nationally restricted concept of constitutional citizenship, which had lost its universalist ethos of civic values.

The second obstacle was gender inequality. Citizenship was conceptualized in a seemingly gender-neutral manner, although both membership status and the civic ideal of an 'active citizen' were based on rights and activities that were largely reserved for men. The construction of the state as a 'male state' was a challenge to the principle of equality by law which was proclaimed by the American and French revolutions. From its beginning, the revolutionary principle of citizenship did not imply equal rights for women. The traditional concept of citizenship of the nineteenth and first half of the twentieth century was deeply gendered. Thus it became a central issue of deconstruction in feminist critiques (Pateman 1988).

The third obstacle to democratic citizenship was criticized by Karl Marx in the 1840s. He demonstrated that the provision of equality in civil and political citizenship rights was merely a formal, legal one: it left untouched the practical inequalities in people's abilities to exercise the rights or legal capacities that constituted citizen status. Moreover, even the exercise of the rights of membership could not influence the basic conditions of class inequality because of the purely formal nature of these rights. Marx interpreted bourgeois citizenship as an instrument of class rule, and thus as an institution of industrial society, which was particularly driven by class. Citizenship as a phenomenon of the modern industrializing world thus corresponded to the interest of the new social sciences. It was sociologists, beginning with Max Weber, who analyzed the origins and growing importance of citizenship in the modern social order. Because citizenship was imbedded in the 'Western' model of modernization and industrialization, it came to be identified as a specifically Western concept of political and social order.

During the first half of the twentieth century, though, intellectual interest in the concept of citizenship was mainly historical. As a political ideal it suffered both from Marx's cutting critique and the crisis of the liberal-democratic idea between the world wars. Thus, only the restoration of a democratic political order after the Second World War and the significant success of the welfare states established at that time paved the way for the revival of citizenship as a key concept in both social analysis and politics. It was against this background that the 1950 article on 'Citizenship and social class' by the English sociologist T. H. Marshall attained its path-breaking influence over the entire debate on citizenship in the second half of the twentieth century. Marshall took up the interpretation of citizenship as a set of rights and analyzed its historical development as a successive creation of civil, political, and social rights. Marshall particularly stressed two conclusions that were crucial to the revaluation of citizenship as both an analytical instrument and a political ideal: his emphasis on the gradual expansion of rights and the ultimate undermining of class conflict by the achievement of social

rights weakened the Marxist critique. At the same time, Marshall asserted that by challenging existing inequities and calling for their abolition as an individual right, equality (as the conceptual core of citizenship) was a dynamic principle that continued to exercise an emancipatory and inclusive influence.

By doing so, Marshall's concept of citizenship attained the force of a universal claim to equality that was applicable to a virtually unlimited range of subject matters. Despite continuing Marxist skepticism, social citizenship was interpreted as a call for the stabilization and expansion of social welfare rights (Turner 1986). The lack of civil and political rights strengthened the call for citizenship as a key concept of opposition to dictatorships in the Soviet block. The idea of civil society was rediscovered in Central and Eastern Europe as a basis for citizenship rights and translated into a political program for restructuring post-Soviet societies after 1989.

This expansive conceptualization has had a dual effect. After the downfall of the Soviet block and the global expansion of democratic constitutionalism, citizenship was adopted globally as a constitutive element of the democratic order (Thompson 1970). New states in Asia, Africa, and South America used citizenship to integrate into the society of world democracy. At the same time, social conflict and cultural change within the states with citizenship traditions were often conceptualized as calls for equality and recognition expressed in terms of citizenship. Massive transnational migration and attempts to take account of 'multiculturalism' (Kymlicka 1995), the enforcement of gender equality and sexual rights (Lister 1997), the debates within liberalism and communitarianism surrounding the foundation and values of a 'good' civic life—all of these issues have been interpreted as struggles over citizenship rights. Ultimately, citizenship has become increasingly detached from its association with the nation-state and conceptualized instead as 'transnational citizenship' (Bauböck 1994), culminating in the vision of 'world citizenship' (Heater 1996).

The global success and expansion of the term 'citizenship' has not, however, necessarily stabilized the underlying concept. As a political ideal, citizenship has been transplanted to states that lack the historical foundation of a 'civil society.' It may, therefore, prove inadequate for the social and cultural traditions of non-Western states. Historically, citizenship's efficacy as a claim for rights was always based on political sovereignty—be it monarchical or popular. This was a prerequisite both for addressing individual claims and enforcing the corresponding civil duties. With the pluralist expansion of citizenship rights in a situation of declining nation-state sovereignty and a nascent world state order, citizenship as it currently exists may lack the requisite unifying force. As Roman history demonstrates, the global expansion of citizenship does not necessarily lead to its global achievement.

See also: Citizen Participation; Citizenship: Political; Citizenship: Sociological Aspects; Civic Culture; Civil Society, Concept and History of; Civil Society/Public Sphere, History of the Concept; Democracy; Democracy, History of; Democratic Theory; Freedom/Liberty: Impact on the Social Sciences; Freedom: Political; French Revolution, The; Human Rights, History of; Liberalism: Historical Aspects; Marshall, Thomas Humphrey (1893–1981); Public Sphere: Nineteenth- and Twentieth-century History; Rights; State, History of

Bibliography

Arendt H 1951 *The Origins of Totalitarianism*. Harcourt Brace Jovanovich, New York

Barbalet J M 0000 *Citizenship. Rights, Struggle and Class Inequality*. University of Minnesota Press, Minneapolis, MN

Bauböck R 1994 *Transnational Citizenship. Membership and Rights in International Migration*. Edward Elgar Publishing, Aldershot, UK

Beiner R 1995 *Theorizing Citizenship*. State University of New York Press, Albany, NY

Bendix R 1964 *Nation-Building and Citizenship*. University of California Press, Berkeley, Los Angeles, London

Brubaker R 1992 *Citizenship and Nationhood in France and Germany*. Harvard University Press, Cambridge, MA

Gosewinkel D 2001 Citizenship, subjecthood, nationality: concepts of belonging in the age of modern nation states. In: Eder K, Giesen B (eds.) *European Citizenship Between National Legacies and Postnational Projects*. Oxford University Press, Oxford, UK, pp. 17–35

Hallern U 1985 *Bürgerliche Gesellschaft*. Wissenschaftliches Buchgesellschaft, Darmstadt

Heater D 1990 *Citizenship. The Civic Ideal in World History, Politics and Education*. Longman, London

Heater D 1996 *World Citizenship and Government. Cosmopolitan Idea in the History of Western Political Thought*. Macmillan Press, Basingstoke, UK

Hufton O H 1992 *Women and the Limits of Citizenship in the French Revolution*. University of Toronto Press, Toronto

Kymlicka W 1995 *Multicultural Citizenship. A Liberal Theory of Minority Rights*. Clarendon Press, Oxford, UK

Kymlicka W, Norman W 1995 Return of the citizen: A survey of recent works on citizenship theory. In: Beiner R (ed.) *Theorizing Citizenship*. State University of New York Press, Albany, NY

Lister R 1997 *Citizenship. Feminist Perspectives*. Macmillan Press, Basingstoke, UK

Manville P B 1990 *The Origins of Citizenship in Ancient Athens*. Princeton University Press, Princeton, NJ

Marshall T H 1950 *Citizenship and Social Class—and other Essays*. Cambridge University Press, Cambridge, UK

Pateman C 1988 *The Sexual Contract*. Stanford University Press, Stanford, CA

Riedel M 1972 Artikel Bürger, Staatsbürger, Bürgertum. In: Brunner O, Conze W, Koselleck R (eds.) *Geschichtliche Grundbegriffe*. Ernst Klett Verlag, Stuttgart, Vol. 1, pp. 672–725

Riesenberg P 1992 *Citizenship in the Western Tradition*. The University of Carolina Press, Chapel Hill, NC

Soysal Y 1994 *Limits of Citizenship*. University of Chicago Press, Chicago

Thompson D 1970 *The Democratic Citizen*. Cambridge University Press, New York

Turner B S 1986 *Citizenship and Capitalism: The Debate over Reformism*. Allen and Unwin, London

Waldinger R, Dawson P, Woloch I 1993 *The French Revolution and the Meaning of Citizenship*. Greenwood Press, Westport, CT

Walzer M 1970 The problem of citizenship. In: Walzer *Obligations*. Harvard Unversity Press, Cambridge, MA

D. Gosewinkel

Citizenship: Political

It may seem superfluous to subtitle a discussion of citizenship as 'political.' The term is at core ineradicably political: its oldest, most basic, and most prevalent meaning is a certain sort of membership in a political community. There are nonetheless good reasons to underline just how deeply political citizenship is, as this essay strives to do. The chief reason is that, precisely because citizenship is so profoundly political a term, there are recurrent pressures to depoliticize both its meaning and its accompanying practice. These pressures, and the understandings of citizenship they propagate, are best seen as confirmations of the political character of citizenship, not as alternative, apolitical conceptions.

1. Four Meanings of Citizenship

Perhaps the most familiar meaning of citizenship is in fact the seminal one. In both ancient and modern republics and democracies, a citizen has been a person with political rights to participate in processes of popular self-governance. Yet we also commonly speak of citizenship as a more purely legal status. Citizens are people who are recognized legally as members of a particular political community and who, therefore, possess some basic rights to be protected by that community's government, whether or not those rights include rights of political participation. During the last century, moreover, many have come to use citizen as a way of referring to those who belong to almost any human association, whether a political community or some other group. I can be said metaphorically to be a citizen of my neighborhood, my fitness club, and my university as well as my broader political community. Finally, we often use citizenship to signify not just membership but certain standards of proper conduct, implying that only 'good' citizens are truly citizens in the full meaning of the term.

The word citizen derives from the Latin *civis*, meaning a member of an ancient city-state, preeminently the Roman republic; but *civis* was a Latin rendering of the Greek term *polites*, a member of a Greek *polis*. Innumerable scholars have told how a renowned resident of the Athenian *polis*, Aristotle, defined a *polites* or citizen as someone who rules and is ruled in turn, making citizenship conceptually inseparable from political governance (Aristotle 1968, p. 1275a23). Aristotle doubtless pleased many Athenians by arguing that such a status and activity, properly performed, represented the highest form of life available to most men. Yet this life was not available to Aristotle himself; he was not an Athenian citizen but a metic, a resident alien. He also suggested that the philosophic life he could and did pursue was in the end the highest of all; and the fact that he chose to pursue this life in a city that denied him citizenship may call into question how valuable he really thought citizenship to be.

His fulsome praise of the citizenship his Athenian hosts had created thus suggests how greatly definitions of citizenship have always been shaped by the political structures of power within which they have been offered. It clearly would not have been prudent for Aristotle to denigrate Athenian citizenship. The fact that neither Aristotle nor most of other residents of Athens, including aliens, women and slaves, were eligible for citizenship also underlines how citizenship originated not only as a way of structuring membership, but also as a way of distributing power within a particular political regime. That distribution disempowered far more Athenians than it enfranchised. Even so, the ideal of citizenship as self-governance that Athens and Aristotle established has often served since as an inspiration and instrument for political efforts to achieve greater inclusion and engagement in political life.

As such, this ancient idea of citizenship has often seemed politically threatening to many rulers, who have abolished or redefined the category. It was for this sort of political reason—because the regimes that had created citizenship succumbed to conquest by Alexander the Great's monarchical empire—that ancient Greek citizenship disappeared. And it was for a similar political reason—because the Roman republic gave way to imperial rule generated from within—that Roman citizenship came to have a different meaning than the one Aristotle articulated. In principle, Roman citizenship always carried with it the right to sit in the popular legislative assembly that had been the hallmark of Athenian citizenship. But as participation in that assembly became increasingly meaningless as well as impractical for most imperial inhabitants, Roman citizenship became essentially a legal status comparable to modern nationality (Pocock 1995). It provided rights to legal protection by Roman soldiers and judges in return for allegiance to Rome. That status was less 'political' in the sense that it no longer evoked recurrent engagement in practices of self-governance, but it was quite plainly a politically crafted status that represented a new distribution of power of enormous political significance.

Citizenship was then eclipsed in the West by the various feudal and religious statuses of the medieval Christian world, but it did not vanish entirely. 'Burghers' or the *bourgeoisie* were citizens of municipalities that often had some special if restricted rights of self-governance within feudal hierarchies. Such burghers remained, however, fundamentally subjects of some ruling prince or lord, with their citizenship chiefly providing legal rights of protection in the manner of Roman imperial citizenship. In contrast, during the Renaissance some Italian cities achieved both independence and a meaningful measure of popular self-governance. They invoked ancient 'republican' ideals of participatory citizenship to define and defend their regimes. Their experiences in turn fed into the antimonarchical revolutions that created the first modern republics, including the short-lived seventeenth century English Commonwealth and late eighteenth-century French Republic, as well as the still-enduring United States (Pocock 1975).

In complex fashion, those revolutions inaugurated transformations 'from subjectship to citizenship' across much of the globe that are still ongoing today, when most of the world's governments proclaim themselves to be 'republics' of some sort populated by citizens. It is in that context that we have come to use citizen ubiquitously for almost every kind of membership in every kind of organization, and to equate genuine citizenship with being a good, contributing member of those organizations. These pervasive popularizations of the term reflect, however, political developments that have in some respects diminished the significance of citizenship even as the term has spread.

2. The Politics of Apolitical Citizenship

Men created the early modern republics in an international realm that had been organized by the 1648 Treaty of Westphalia into a system of mutual recognition among overwhelmingly monarchical nation–states. In gaining acceptance within that system, the new republics defined their citizens as having the same international status as national monarchical subjects. For international purposes, these citizens, too, were simply persons who owed allegiance to and could claim protection from particular governments. Thus, Westphalian international law treated modern republican citizenship as akin to the legalistic, protection-oriented version of Roman citizenship.

Furthermore, Americans especially forged their republic amid racial and gender hierarchies that few leaders sought to challenge. Hence they felt compelled to argue that, though free blacks and women might be citizens, citizenship did not in fact inherently entail rights of political participation. It guaranteed, once again, only more limited rights to certain judicial and executive protections (Smith 1997). For long stretches of time, then, both international and domestic politics worked to strengthen legalistic as opposed to the more participatory conceptions of citizenship despite the rise of modern republicanism.

Yet even though courts made the narrower, protection-centered view of citizenship legally authoritative, the notion that genuine citizenship involved rights of political participation remained a resonant rhetorical tool of legislative and constitutional reformers. Eventually both domestic protest movements and international pressures, including the need for broad support in wartime, converged to work for the expansion of the franchise to all adult citizens in the US and most of the western world. In America, blacks won both citizenship and voting rights after the Civil War, even though most came to be effectively disfranchised in the 'Jim Crow' segregation era; and women gained the franchise after World War I. In both cases, arguments appealing to their public service, especially in wartime, and to the idea that true citizenship must include the franchise, played key roles in their successes (Foner 1988, Flexner 1973).

In Britain and to some degree in other western European nations that had been politically configured essentially by feudal and industrial class systems, modern citizenship was wrought out via somewhat different struggles. As Marshall famously argued, first middle and then working class political pressures resulted in the expansion of civil rights of property and protection, then in near-universal rights of political participation, and finally and incompletely, in 'social rights' for all national citizens that included income, housing, medical, and educational guarantees (Marshall 1950). But even as the franchise has broadened in the US, Europe, and elsewhere, the notion of citizenship as active participation in meaningful self-governance has become more remote to many modern citizens. In part the logistics of large-scale modern societies make effective democratic participation very difficult. In part the economic and cultural developments that have led to a focus on 'social citizenship' make political activism seem less important. Engagement in one's social and economic organizations can appear more pressing. Perhaps, then, the term citizenship has become common in such contexts because it is there that people find the memberships that mean the most and in which they can most actively participate. If so, then the inevitable corollary is that citizenship understood as political self-governance has become quite secondary to many modern citizens. Yet this, too, is a signal political development. It is probable that like their predecessors in other regimes, many who wield power in modern republics are content when those they govern think of citizenship chiefly in terms of subnational, often nongovernmental associations, and in terms of the 'good citizen's' civic service rather than vigorous political participation. Certainly few policies within modern republics do much to enhance the feasibility and potency of such participation.

3. The Prospect of Postnational Citizenships

Though some scholars and democratic activists lament this current circumstance, others stress that the heightened transnational economic, transportation, and communication systems that we call globalization are in any case making traditional notions of national citizenship obsolete (Soysal 1994). Regional associations, international legal institutions, and transnational economic, cultural, and political organizations are all said to be more likely to shape humanity's future than existing national regimes. Hence membership in such bodies will represent the most important forms of citizenship in the twenty-first century.

That such globalizing trends exist is undeniable, though often national governmental actors remain major players even in transnational or international organizations and institutions. Despite advances in communication and transportation, moreover, meaningful participation in the governance of such populous and geographically far-flung entities seems even more chimerical for most people, deepening the eclipse of citizenship's oldest meaning. Thus there is a real prospect that the idea of citizenship increasingly will be severed not only from engagement in traditional forms of self-governance, but even from membership in some titularly sovereign political community. It may become a term for membership and participation in a wide variety of human groups, often simultaneously.

There are, however, reasons to doubt this scenario. History suggests that the leaders of political communities rarely give up power willingly. Therefore, it is not surprising that efforts to resist globalizing trends and reinvigorate loyalties to existing nations and regimes are also visible players in modern 'citizenship politics,' particularly in regard to immigration policies. A truly all-encompassing global government, moreover, still seems a fantasy, so that memberships in particular political communities are likely to remain important features of human life, even if those communities come to be constituted in new ways. Under at least some conditions, moreover, many people may feel great concern over the decline in forms of citizenship through which they can exercise some genuine control over their collective lives. The fact that political and social reform movements have often gained wide support by insisting that citizenship means sharing in governance shows that such feelings can be politically powerful fuel driving quite important changes.

Thus, we cannot rule out the possibility that older notions of participatory citizenship may continue to play a role in the recrafting of political institutions and communities that the twenty-first century will inevitably see. But whatever forms of citizenship result, they will almost certainly be the products of political contests that result in distributions of powers and memberships to some people and not others, distributions that will convey to them certain rights and protections, and not others. Hence, citizenship will remain what it has always been, a fundamentally political status through which human beings partly order both their individual and their collective lives.

See also: Citizen Participation; Citizenship and Public Policy; Citizenship, Historical Development of; Citizenship: Sociological Aspects; Civic Culture; Participation: Political; Political Culture

Bibliography

Aristotle 1968 *The Politics of Aristotle*. Clarendon Press, Oxford

Flexner E 1973 *Century of Struggle: The Woman's Rights Movement in the United States*. Atheneum, New York

Foner E 1988 *Reconstruction: America's Unfinished Revolution, 1863–1877*. Harper & Row, New York

Marshall T H 1950 *Citizenship and Social Class and Other Essays*. Cambridge University Press, Cambridge, UK

Pocock J G A 1975 *The Machiavellian Moment: Florentine Political Thought and the Atlantic Republican Tradition*. Princeton University Press, Princeton, NJ

Pocock J G A 1995 The ideal of citizenship since classical times. In: Beiner R S (ed.) *Theorizing Citizenship*. State University Press of New York, Albany, NY

Smith R M 1997 *Civic Ideals: Conflicting Visions of Citizenship in U.S. History*. Yale University Press, New Haven, CT

Soysal Y N 1994 *Limits of Citizenship: Migrants and Post-national Membership in Europe*. University of Chicago Press, Chicago

R. M. Smith

Citizenship: Sociological Aspects

Classical sociological theory was especially interested in the social mechanisms ensuring social solidarity, and in the sources of conflicts that challenge the social structure. It underlined roles, functions or dysfunctions, the networks of sociability which bring the actors together, etc. In general, the founders of the discipline were not very concerned with politics and hardly dealt with the question of citizenship, which marks the integration of actors within their nation. Consequently, until very recently, the question of citizenship had its origins within political theory, having abandoned its social dimensions for a long period.

From Aristotle to Locke and Rousseau, many philosophers have reflected on the nature of the social link, the commitment of individuals within the public space, the formation of the social contract and general willingness. People are conceived here as rational beings: By their entrance into the political community, they have access to the status of citizen which alone gives meaning to its own history. In the contemporary era, from Sheldon Wolin (1993) to Carole Pateman (1970), this reflection of political philosophy on the foundations of a democracy of citizens is illustrated by an immense literature, of which Benjamin Barber (1984) and his 'strong democracy' or Selya Benhabib (1996) are good representatives.

The revival of the political theory on citizenship has, however, found its origins: Hannah Arendt sought within the Greek *polis* the foundations of a *via activa* which would give life to citizens who were indifferent to the social, determined only by their reason, to enter into public space. After Arendt, it was Jürgen Habermas who took it upon himself to seek the origin of modern public space as a place of deliberation and discussion. According to him, public opinion formed by all citizens was born in the seventeenth and eighteenth centuries, in France and in England. Viewing capitalism as a system that alienates actors and destroys their exchanges, he only found reason within contemporary 'communicational behavior'; the use of modern information techniques would therefore give life to a democracy of citizens capable of communicating among themselves. Arendt and Habermas played an immense role in the revival of a political theory on citizenship capable of leading to a community which is undiluted by citizens who are little concerned by their particular historical identity, or their cultural identity, either social or even less biological.

A reflection upon the sociological foundations of citizenship should consequently find food for its debates elsewhere. Thus, it can be claimed that during the nineteenth century, de Tocqueville was one of the few thinkers to extend the eighteenth century tradition by giving it a more sociological context. He clearly poses the question of the commitment of ordinary citizens. Tocqueville asks himself questions about how to avoid the isolation and apathy of individuals, which favors, in France, for example, an indifference propitious to all forms of authoritarianism; in his opinion, the forms of local self-government established by US democracy limit these dangers. For Tocqueville, public space is doomed to silence and to state domination if the associations and social groups that bring individuals together with specific identical interests do not intervene within the elaboration of public politics. Citizens find themselves, from the beginning, plunged into the social. Whereas Marx thrusts aside the coming of citizenship for the birth of a society that has rejected capitalism and sees only alienation in present society, thus silencing the purely political role of determined citizens by their place in production relationships, Tocqueville was already interested in the sociological aspects of citizenship.

Strangely enough, between Tocqueville and T. H. Marshall, the predominance of the social was so important that it was necessary to wait until the end of World War II for the concept of citizenship to return to the heart of the debates: However, this time, it was not the perspective of Rousseau that prevailed but more that of Tocqueville. During his famous conference in 1949, Marshall retraced the evolution which led from legal citizenship, created during the eighteenth century with the obtaining of civil rights, to political citizenship, obtained during the nineteenth century with the exercising of political rights, and then finally to social citizenship which is granted to all, in the twentieth century, with the triumph of the Welfare State and social rights (minimum salary, health provision, etc.) (Marshall 1977).

For Marshall, the triumph of capitalism does not prevent the implementation of citizenship, this time, full and entire: From then onwards, for the first time, citizenship openly bears an essential sociological dimension, as social redistribution considers the diversity of social situations this time beyond the common role of the citizen. If the civil and political dimensions concerned all citizens in their actual state, independently from their specific social identity, the economical dimension aims at correcting the inequalities amongst citizens. Marshall himself does not underline this modification on the principle of citizenship that thrusts it into the social domain, and hardly interferes with its universalistic dimension. He does not consider either—and was later criticized for this—the persistence of so many social inequalities which remain, even in the age of the Welfare State, and occasionally even worsen, actually threatening the citizenship of the most deprived. In this way, Ralph Dahrendorf stresses 'all those who are rejected by citizenship': 'the noncitizens' who are the immigrants; 'those who are no longer entirely citizens,' i.e., the elderly; and finally 'those who are not yet citizens,' i.e., youth. The erosion of citizenship questions the image of the 'good citizen' equipped with all the necessary attributes for entering into public space. The explosion of the 'underclass' breaks the image of a citizenship which is full and entire, which all people would benefit from in an identical manner in the developed world (Heissler 1994).

From then onwards, a fairly important turnaround of perspective occurred. It no longer involved considering, in a traditional manner, that 'in the Nation State each citizen stands in a direct relation to the sovereign authority of the country' (Bendic 1977). It did not reflect on the conditions of admission to citizenship which separate the 'insiders' from the 'outsiders' (Gunsteren 1988). Neither did it extend this type of reflection which uses citizenship as its foundations for the territory of the nation state by dealing with the case of a postnational citizenship which would take place, for example, in the new public European space where all citizens who have become 'cosmopolitan' would benefit from formal identical rights based upon an intangible constitutional principle, that of 'constitutional patriotism' dear to Habermas, hoping for the emergence of collective mobilizations destined to accentuate the democratic dimension (Cesarini and Fulbrook 1996, Delanty 1997). Instead, the systematic research of elements of a 'differentiated citizenship' was undertaken, taking into account the multiple sociological dimensions peculiar to each citizen, whether it be economical, cultural, or a matter of genus.

For Kymlicka, 'the members of certain groups are incorporated into the political community not only as individuals but also through the group. I have sometimes described these rights as forms of differentiated citizenship' (Kymlicka 1995, p. 174). If many sociologists dealt with the consequences of these socioeconomical inequalities on political participation and the exercise of the profession of the citizen, it is even more the dimensions, diagrammatically coming under culture, that increasingly attract attention. In a context of growing crisis within the nation state that greatly effects citizenship in Weber's sense, or even in Marshall's or Bendix's sense, it was suggested that the theory of integration, for example that of Marshall, 'does not necessarily work for culturally distinct immigrants or for various other groups which have been historically excluded from full participation in the national culture—such as blacks, women, religious minorities, gays and lesbians. Some members of these groups still feel excluded from the "common culture," despite possessing the common rights of citizenship' (Kymlicka 1995, p. 180).

Stemming from such a perspective, citizenship finds itself this time plunged into the social with the risk of losing its original meaning: As a result, public space becomes diversified to an infinite extent as citizens preserve their identity there and democracy itself changes its meaning. As Amy Gutmann asks 'What does it mean for citizens with different cultural identities, often based on ethnicity, race, gender or religion, to recognize ourselves as equals in the way we are treated in politics?' (Guttman 1992, p. 3). The democracy of citizens in fact finds itself greatly modified in the same way as the political game, the strategy of parties and of pressure groups who use such identitarian groups as the basis for their actions. Affirmative action, a policy openly destined to smooth out socioidentitarian inequalities by privileging the members of deprived 'ethnic groups,' is the clear outcome which implies a differential management of citizenship and sets down an infinite number of problems of justice and of equality. From the moment that we consider that individuals possess a 'thick self,' it becomes difficult to claim the recovering of these differences by a 'veil of ignorance' (Rawls [1971] 1987), differences which are deep-rooted within these community memberships considered from now on as being essential.

A considerable literature grew up in the area of multiculturalism, which constantly further reduces the importance of the classical theory of citizenship. By moving onward from the fact that it is unfair to ignore the identity of citizens, the tendency is to reinstate their culture with the risk of slipping toward a deep relativism. In this way, the rediscovery of the identity shared by citizens relegitimizes the particular national cultures, the 'ethnic' feelings and also the nationalistic ideologies (Birnbaum 1996) which consider these neglected ethnic groups to be the foundations of their action in aid of the new citizens who are members of these particular homogenous cultural groups.

Plunged into a growing communitarism, citizenship therefore leads to a nationalistic revival. On an internal level of society, he justifies the 'tribalization' of society into many specific homogenous groups separate from each other: with the image of the working class of yesteryear which constituted a countersociety of which they claimed to be the active citizens, immigrants are supposed to conserve their culture, their language, and their own customs by benefiting from the right to vote, of local citizenship when they have not been naturalized. Women or homosexuals, like all social and cultural minorities, are also invited to join together in a particular manner.

The first among the feminist critics severely emphasized the great indifference of the classical theoreticians of citizenship toward the feminine gender: the French Revolution, which was geared towards the universalism of citizens, did, however, force women to return to the only private space (Landes 1988, Hunt 1992). In a more general way, the woman citizen demands consideration for her body and her own values in the exercise of this role within the public space (Young 1990). In this way, it is in fact the classical theories of deliberative democracy and also the models of the integration of the social system, for example, in their systematic Parsonian presentation, which find themselves questioned (Birnbaum 1996). To take into consideration the sociological variables of citizenship is, therefore, in one way or another, to give an advantage to the 'thick self' to the detriment of the 'thin' self upon which the classical theories of citizenship were formerly built (Walzer 1994, Kymlicka and Norman 1994).

See also: Citizenship and Public Policy; Citizenship, Historical Development of; Citizenship: Political; Democracy; Democracy, History of; Marshall, Thomas Humphrey (1893–1981); Nations and Nation-states in History; State Formation; State, History of; State, Sociology of the; Tocqueville, Alexis de (1805–59); Women's Suffrage

Bibliography

Barber B 1989 *Strong Democracy*. University of California Press, Berkeley, CA

Bendic R 1977 *Nation-building and Citizenship*. University of California Press, Berkeley, CA

Benhabib S (ed.) 1996 *Democracy and Difference*. Princeton University Press, Princeton, NJ

Birnbaum P 1996a From multiculturalism to nationalism. *Political Theory* **24**(1)

Birnbaum P 1996b Sur la citoyenneté. *L'Année sociologique* **46**(1)

Cesarini D, Fulbrook M (eds.) 1996 *Citizenship, Nationality and Migration in Europe*. Routledge, London

Delanty G 1997 Models of citizenship: Defining European identity and citizenship. *Citizenship Studies* **1**(3)

Gunsteren H 1988 Admission to citizenship. *Ethics* July

Guttman A 1992 Introduction. In: Taylor C (ed.) *Multiculturalism and the Politics of Recognition*. Princeton University Press, Princeton, NJ

Heissler B 1994 A comparative perspective on the underclass: Questions of urban poverty, race and citizenship. In: Turner B, Hamilton P (eds.) *Citizenship, Critical Concepts*. Routledge, London

Hunt L 1992 *The Family Romance of the French Revolution*. University of California Press, Berkeley, CA

Kymlicka W 1995 *Multicultural Citizenship*. Clarendon Press, Oxford, UK

Kymlicka W, Norman W 1994 Return of the citizen: A survey of recent work on Citizenship Theory. *Ethics* January

Landes J 1988 *Women and the Public Sphere in the Age of the French Revolution*. Cornell University Press, Ithaca, NY

Marshall T H 1977 Citizenship and social class. In: Marshall T H (ed.) *Class, Citizenship and Social Development*. Chicago University Press, Chicago

Pateman C 1970 *Participation and Democratic Theory*. Cambridge University Press, Cambridge, UK

Rawls J [1971] 1987 *A Theory of Justice*. Harvard University Press, Cambridge, MA

Shklar J 1991 *American Citizenship*. Harvard University Press, Cambridge, MA

Young I M 1990 *Justice and the Politics of Difference*. Princeton University Press, Princeton, NJ

Walzer M 1994 *Thick and Thin. Moral Argument at Home and* ..... University of Notre Dame Press, Notre Dame, IN

Wolin S 1993 Democracy, difference and re-cognition. *Political Theory* **21**(3)

P. Birnbaum

Civic Culture

Civic Culture theory asserts that democracy is stable or consolidated when specifically democratic attitudes and practices combine and function in equilibrium with certain non-democratic ones. It was formulated and tested in empirical research in the late 1950s and early 1960s, years still reverberating with the memories of the rise of Communism and Fascism, the collapse of democracy and the catastrophes of World War II. It drew from a contemporary social science literature similarly influenced by the interwar history of the stalemated Third French Republic, the deeply flawed Weimar Germany, the Austrian and Spanish civil wars, and the breakdown of the Fourth French Republic.

It could point to the long tradition in political theory of 'mixed government,' from Plato and Aristotle through to Montesquieu, which supported this anti-populism and prudentialism. Among the post World War II social science influences were works of Joseph Schumpeter, Paul Lazarsfeld and Bernard Berelson, Edward Shils, Robert A. Dahl, and Harry Eckstein, among others.

Schumpeter rejected the 'classic democratic' assumption of the necessity of an informed, activist, rational public for a genuine democracy, and proposed in its place, an 'elites competing for votes' theory (Schumpeter 1947, Chaps. 21 and 22). This minimalist theory could be reconciled with more realistic assumptions of a relatively ignorant and indifferent demos.

Paul Lazarsfeld and Bernard Berelson, theorizing from their 'panel' voting studies of the 1940s similarly saw democracy as associated with a set of cultural and social conditions having the effect of limiting the intensity of social conflict. These included relative economic and social stability, a pluralistic social organization, a basic value consensus. and what we would now call a 'civil society.' They described a democratic equilibrium as involving mixes of involvement and indifference, stability and flexibility, consensus and cleavage (Berelson et al. 1954).

Edward Shils, on the democratic prospects of the new nations, emphasized the importance of a 'widely dispersed civility.' By this he meant a moderate sense of nationality, a degree of interest in public affairs, a consensus on values, institutions, and practices, and a recognition of individual rights and obligations. He wrote ' ... These qualities should not be intense, and they need not be either equally or universally shared.' (Shils 1960, pp. 387ff.)

Robert Dahl's theory of polyarchy, elaborated in 1956 in a full-length contrast with populistic and Madisonian democracy, belongs among these early social science influences on the civic culture. His early characterization of the American political system as providing ' ... a high probability that any active and legitimate group will make itself heard effectively at some stage in the process of decision ... ' (Dahl 1956, p. 145; see also Dahl 1970; Dahl 1989) reflected the minimalist mood that Dahl shared with the generation that emerged out of the great depression and World War II. At the time that *The Civic Culture* was being

written, Dahl's concept of polyarchy already had introduced an empirically grounded and quantitative set of concepts into democratic theorizing. Democracy was not an essence. In its full sense it did not exist, and probably could not exist. Hence the concept *polyarchy* was developed to refer to real political entities which attained measured performance levels on specified empirical dimensions.

Harry Eckstein was the first to emphasize the 'mixed' or paradoxical side of democracy, recognizing the necessity for a democracy not only to represent and formulate the will of the public, but to govern it authoritatively. In his *Theory of Stable Democracy* he describes some of the qualities which enable democracies to reconcile responsible authority and democratic responsiveness. Such reconciliation is facilitated by balances among contrasting qualities; participant behavior is balanced by deference to authority, dogmatism by pragmatism, and the like. Institutionally he attributes democratic stability to the degree to which social authority patterns coincide or are 'congruent' with political ones.

Civic culture theory had the advantage of being formulated in the context of a major empirical investigation informed by this historical experience, and benefiting from this prior research and scholarship. Its results were reported in book form in 1963, in paperback form in 1965; and were reprinted in 1989 (Almond and Verba, 1963, 1965, 1989) and remains in print as of this publication. It was widely reviewed in social science periodicals and in 1980 a retrospective volume was published with critiques of the theory and the findings (Almond and Verba 1980).

The data were made available in the Interuniversity Consortium for Political and Social Research at the University of Michigan, and have been utilized in many secondary studies.

Four of the five countries that it investigated were chosen because they exemplified democratic stability and instability in the first half of the twentieth century—the United Kingdom and the United States exemplifying stability on the one hand—Germany and Italy exemplifying democratic instability and breakdown on the other. The fifth, Mexico, was a target of opportunity, selected with the thought that it might provide some insight into problems of democratization outside the North American-European area. The method used in the study, of combining structured and open-ended questions administered to probability samples of national populations, provided a richer set of data specifically responsive to questions arising out of this historical experience and body of speculative theory.

The conception of stable democratic political culture as a 'mixed' political culture received a fuller elaboration than it had been given in the earlier work of Berelson and Lazarsfeld and Eckstein. The mix of democratic political culture was based on political role theory. People in stable democracies were both citizens and subjects, and they needed to accommodate their non-political, private, and parochial roles. A thriving, stable democracy consists not only of voters, demonstrators, petition signers, and politician button-holers; but of taxpayers, jurors, and military conscripts; as well as parents, mates, work-persons, voluntary association-members, vacationers, and private, self-involved individuals.

It is this mix of roles—participant as well as subject, non-political as well as political—that democratic citizens of a stable democracy must balance and accommodate; and which their institutions must choreograph in a process of converting demands and supports into outputs and outcomes. To shift metaphors, civic culture theory was an equilibrium theory in which political buyers and sellers reach prices at which the political market is cleared. Civic culture theory specified what conditions had to be present in order to clear these markets.

These mixes and balances were located empirically in the British and American cases in the late 1950s and early 1960s—this combination of influentialism and deferentialism, involvement and indifference, conflictual and consensual attitudes, principled and instrumental ones. The relative absence of these balances in the German and Italian cases was noticeable. There was more deferentialism and less participationism in the British case than in the American. A 'reserve of influence' was also noted in the American and British cases, based on the finding that Americans and the British acknowledged the obligation to participate far more frequently than they reported actually participating. This discrepancy between performance and obligation could be viewed as a kind of 'default' mode, a reserve supply of participatory energy available for crises. The civic culture would run cool normally and at a moderate speed, but it had a reserve of influence to draw upon in the twists and turns of democratic politics, as the concerns and interests of different groups of voters were engaged.

By the time the retrospective volume, *The Civic Culture Revisited* was published in 1980 it was evident that British and American civic culture were in trouble (Almond and Verba 1980, Chaps. 5 and 6).

The balance of consensus and conflict had moved toward conflict; pride in nation and confidence in government were down. Participationism had declined. In contrast Germany showed dramatic gains in social trustfulness, confidence in government, and civic competence (Almond and Verba 1980, Chap. 7). In Italy political alienation and extreme partisan antagonism continued largely unchanged. In Mexico the political culture of ambivalent belief in the legitimacy of the democratic revolution, and the corruption of politicians and office-holders, also still survived (Almond and Verba 1980, Chap. 9).

That patterns of political culture would change in response to changes in economy, demography, politics and public policy, communications technology, and

popular education should not have occasioned surprise. That the exemplars of the civic culture of the 1950s—Britain and the United States—should be showing signs of wear and tear in the 1970s and 1980s; and that the problem child of democracy—Germany—was showing strong signs of an emerging civic culture, were not causes for rejecting civic culture theory. The question was whether the changes observed in the two decades after the civic culture study, were in a direction which sustained or disproved the theory. The evidence was moderately supportive of the theory. Thus, for example, the withdrawal of Johnson from the 1968 presidential race, despite the fact that political tradition would have legitimized another term of office, and the resignation of Nixon from the presidency in the 1970s were clear evidences of American instability; and the political disorders of the 1960s and 1970s were clear evidences of cultural disequilibria of one kind or another—conflict had undermined consensus, the legitimacy of government had declined, the modes of participation had radicalized. In contrast Germany had had several decades of experience of effective political leadership and remarkable economic growth appearing to produce a moderating *koalition-fähig* partisanship, growing popular trust in government, civic obligation, and the like.

The place of civic culture theory in the contemporary theory of democracy is in some doubt. In the continuing theoretic polemic about the nature of democracy anything settling for less than perfection partakes of sin. It was precisely to avoid this commingling of the sacred and the secular that led Robert Dahl to invent the concept of polyarchy and to place the concept of *democracy* somewhat, but not completely, off limits. However Dahl's Polyarchy III (which is the closest to ultimate democracy that he gets) is achieved through increasing the depth and extent of attentive publics within the larger mass public, corresponding to the significant issues confronting the polity and policy elites. Modern information technology makes it possible that this gap between policy elites and the mass public might be significantly reduced (Dahl 1989, pp. 338 ff.).

The state of the polemic regarding the competence, rationality, and potential effectiveness of mass publics in contemporary polyarchies is well argued in a symposium held during the 1990s. The merits of the various options—elitism, inventive utilization of information technology, or reducing the scope of politics—are among the issues debated (Friedman 1999).

Civic Culture theory might have enriched this discussion somewhat by affirming the legitimacy of other than political claims upon humankind. If one views the full range of role demands on the time and resources of humans, how do we choose among them? How do these choices interact? What are the tradeoffs, synergies, and opportunity costs? How do we weight the claims of the civic world against the demands of profession, family, edification, and pleasure?

See also: Democracy; Democracy: Normative Theory; Democratic Theory; International Relations, History of; Lazarsfeld, Paul Felix (1901–76); Participation: Political; Schumpeter, Joseph A (1883–1950); Trust, Sociology of

Bibliography

Almond G A, Verba S 1963 *The Civic Culture: Political Attitudes and Democracy in Five Nations*. Princeton University Press Princeton, NJ. Reprinted in 1965 by Boston, Little Brown & Co., and in 1989 by Sage Publications, Newbury Park, CA

Almond G A, Verba S (eds.) 1980 *The Civic Culture Revisited*. Little Brown & Co., Boston. Reprinted in 1989 Sage Publications Newbury Park, CA

Berelson B, Lazarsfeld P, McPhee W 1954 *Voting: A Study of Opinion Formation in a Political Campaign*. University of Chicago Press, Chicago, Chap.14

Dahl R A 1956 *A Preface to Democratic Theory*. University of Chicago Press, Chicago, p. 145

Dahl R A 1970 *Polyarchy: Participation and Opposition*. New Haven, CT

Dahl R A 1989 *Democracy and Its Critics*. Yale University Press New Haven, CT, pp. 338 ff

Friedman J (ed.) 1999 Special Issue: Public ignorance and democratic theory. *Critical Review; An Interdisciplinary Journal of Poliltics and Society* **12**(4)

Schumpeter J A 1947 *Capitalism, Socialism, and Democracy*. Harper and Brothers, New York, Chap. 21 and 22

Shils E 1960 *Political Development in The New States*. Mouton, The Hague, The Netherlands, pp. 387 ff.

G. A. Almond

Civil Law

1. Structural Aspects

In the comparative study of law, legal systems are often seen as belonging to 'legal families.' These may be religious-based legal systems, they may be geographically defined, or they may be distinct because of their structure and methodology. The principal, or characteristic difference between the families of the common law and of the civil law lies in the last of these. This is true despite the fact that both legal families have their roots in the Corpus Iuris Civilis of Justinian (AD 534) and that the common law has preserved some of these traditions to this day, while the civil law has moved closer to the common law in some areas.

With respect to both families, it is dangerous to generalize; there can indeed be marked differences between legal systems belonging to the same 'family.' Thus, the use of codes (for example, the Uniform Commercial Code), the existence of a large body of statutory law, and the adoption of the influential *Restatements* may make the legal system of the United States appear closer to the civil law than to its English roots (see Farnsworth 1996, p. 227). Such a conclusion, however, would misconceive the role and function of statutory law and of the methodology in its application in the civil law, on the one hand, and in common law legal systems, on the other hand.

Codes and statutes consist of rules in all legal systems. These may be very specific or they may be stated with some degree of generality. In some areas, common law codes and other legal texts display extraordinary detail, attempting to anticipate every eventuality. The common law judge, as a consequence, will begin with the factual circumstances of the case and after examining, comparing, and weighing the factual elements of the case, will attempt to find a rule that fits it. This rule may be one of statutory law or derive from prior decisional law. The civilian judge sees the case as a problem to be solved within the legal *structure* of the legal system. First, the problem at hand must be fitted into a legal category. Next, subcategories and sub-subcategories must be identified until 'legal rule' or 'concept' and the problem at hand match. Civilians proceed by *deductive reasoning*, while the common law approach employs an *inductive methodology*.

Categorization, as a structural characteristic of the civil law, also results in the drawing of sharp distinctions between different areas of the law. Private law deals with legal problems that arise between natural persons or between natural and legal persons (such as corporations), while public law (for instance, constitutional law, administrative law, but also criminal law) addresses the relationship between citizen and state. In some civil law systems, this results in the establishment of special courts to deal with these different areas of the law. In Germany, for instance, there are 'ordinary' courts with competence for private law and criminal law, and separate court systems with competence for questions of administrative law, labor law, and social law, each system has its own 'Supreme Court.' Since many cases will obviously involve 'mixed questions' (e.g., of labor and private contract or tort law), there may be contradictory rules of law, with no unifying 'Supreme Court.' In France, the *Conseil d'Etat* stands beside the *Cour de Cassation*, with exclusive competence in certain public fields of law. The exclusivity of the *Conseil's* competence avoids some of the German problems. Germany and Italy have Constitutional Courts, other civil law countries do not. While the divisions are more pronounced in Germany than elsewhere, categorization of fields of law and the establishment of specialized courts unavoidably leads to a high degree of specialization within the legal profession, both among lawyers as well as judges. These lines are much more fluid in common law.

The central role of the *legal rule* in civil law legal systems also explains why precedent (that is, the binding effect of a prior court decision on a different, but similar subsequent case) is quite different from what it is in the common law. The civilian judge applies the law but is not bound (obviously with some exceptions) by earlier decisions of a higher court. In common law, in contrast, it is the decision of the highest court that ultimately is the law and therefore binds inferior courts. Subsequent discussion will return to these points.

2. History

Roman law had no comprehensive codification before Justinian's Corpus Iuris Civilis. Law, such as it was, was divided into *ius civile* and *ius gentium*. The former applied among Roman citizens, the latter applied to legal relationships among others (Romans and foreigners, foreigners among themselves, and slaves). Judicial functions were exercised by *praetores*. The *praetor prereginus* administered the *ius gentium* and conceived and developed legal concepts unknown to the strict Roman *ius civilis*. In a different context, of course, the English chancellor—at the beginning of the equity-jurisprudence—performed equally creative functions. Similar ideas—for equity and judicial creativity—underlie the 'general clauses' of the civil law (see *vide infra*).

With population growth and increasing urbanization, a new profession—that of the jurisconsult—arose. They were legal advisors who prepared written opinions for cases. As the number of opinions grew, principles could be derived from them which could be taught to students and serve as a basis for advice to judges. The development of principles fosters more abstract ways of thinking. Categories are conceived and problems are classified for assignment to various categories. Under Emperor Justinian, opinions, decisions, and other materials were gathered and the Corpus Iuris Civilis was prepared.

The Corpus Iuris stands at the beginning of what Roman law means today. This Code evolved in subsequent times as a result of the work of the Glossators and Commentators. All taken together constituted the 'Ius Commune,' the common law of Europe before, in subsequent centuries, countries and areas began to grow in different ways and today's 'different families' began to take shape. In Europe, England gave rise to the common law (although, especially in the early period, with many Roman law elements). The Scandinavian countries, France, and Germany had a leading role in developing civil law. Once again, 'civil law' is not homogeneous. There are differences among civil law countries, and these differences are also reflected in the legal systems of those countries that modeled their codes or statutes after earlier rules of others. Two codifications in particular replaced the earlier 'ius commune' and proved very influential: the French *code civil* of 1804 and the German *Bürgerliches Gesetzbuch* of 1896 (see also the Austrian *Allgemeine Bürgerliche Gesetzbuch* of 1811). The French Code influenced the development of legal systems not only in many European (especially the Latin and Eastern); countries, it also spread to the Near East, Central and South America, and even to parts of North America (e.g., Louisiana). The German Code affected the law of Eastern and Southern Europe (e.g., Hungary, the Czech Republic, and Slovakia, Yugoslavia, the Baltic States, and Greece) as well as of Japan and China (see Zweigert and Kötz 1998, 159, 160). Roman Law still exists in Southern Africa as Roman-Dutch law, an admixture of Roman law and old Dutch customary law which has interacted with English common law (see Zweigert and Kötz 1998). Codification extended, in these and in other countries, not only to private law and private-law relationships but encompassed criminal law, commercial law, and both civil (private) and criminal procedure.

3. Sources of Law

3.1 Primary Sources

Civil law systems draw a sharp distinction between primary and secondary sources. Primary sources are enacted law, custom, and 'general principles of law.' Of these, the main source is the enacted (statutory) law; it predominates in civil law systems.

A code in a civil law system consists of general principles, arranged in order of importance. At the beginning there may be general rules regulating basic problems that need to be addressed before the particular problem can be analyzed. For example: if a plaintiff seeks damages for breach of contract, preliminary analysis must determine whether the contract was validly concluded. Provisions dealing with invalidity and avoidance of contracts usually are found in the general part of a civil code. Such a general part may be followed by particular parts dealing with individual fields of law, such as torts, contracts, property, or the law of succession. The main or basic codes are supplemented in increasing number by special statutes or codes of limited coverage with which the legal system reacts to new societal problems, for instance, in areas such as consumer protection, telecommunication, and new media.

Custom is also a primary source of law, but tends to be less important in practice because it is often difficult to prove its pervasive observance in society. Customs are nonwritten rules, developed and observed over years and now part of social and economic thinking.

'General principles of the law' are what the term expresses: basic principles of the legal system which are pervasive of it and derive from norms of positive law. Civil law judges resort to 'general principles of the law' as guidelines in the interpretation of statutory norms both for the purpose of defining their interrelation and for the purpose of their application. This is of particular importance when dealing with statutory norms that are rather abstract in their formulation. It is tempting to consider this process to be not very different from the case law methodology of the common law. There is an important difference, however. The common lawyer derives the appropriate interpretation by reliance on precedent. The civilian judge is not so restricted but derives the interpretation considered to be appropriate from the structure of the legal system and the general principles of law that pervade it; nor will the decision in the present case have a necessary effect on later cases. This is not to say that later cases may not reach the same conclusion: at the point of what French lawyers call *jurisprudence constante* and German lawyers *ständige Rechtsprechung*, such decisional law may itself be regarded as having risen to the position of 'general principles of law.'

3.2 Secondary Sources

Secondary sources consist of case law and the legal literature. The legal literature consists of monographs and contributions to the legal periodical literature as well as commentaries. The last are particularly important in civil law countries that follow or are close to the Germanic legal tradition. Commentaries are detailed annotations of each provision of a particular code, consisting of an analysis that brings together all case law dealing with this provision, opinions of others as expressed in the periodical literature, and the commentator's own evaluation and summary.

Case law by itself, as already mentioned in other contexts, does not have the same central importance in a civil law system as it does in a common law system. It is indeed a secondary source, for the judge is bound only by the enacted law, except in the few cases in which—as discussed—the decisional law has reached the level of *jurisprudence constante* or in systems (for instance, Germany) in which a 'constitutional court' has power to bind other courts. To repeat, however, such cases are rare.

Judges will read commentaries and the legal literature in general, just as lawyers do. The process of 'law finding' and its application, however, does not restrict the court to these sources.

4. Developing the Law

If 'law' is a norm in the form of a statutory codification or a 'general principle' derived from such statutory norms, how can a judge decide a case for which no norm or general principles exist and, in the absence of legislative action, how can law develop further? (For comparative discussion see Capalli 1998, p. 87, Adriaansen 1998, p. 107, Baudenbacher 1999, p. 333).

Legislative action is of course the classic instrument for legal change. But the process, from drafting a bill until its ultimate passage and entry into force, can be long. A commission for the revision of the German law of obligations, for instance, has worked on this project for more than a decade. The final report of the commission was published in 1992. Nevertheless, it was not until 2001 that a bill was introduced in Parliament. Thus, problems may need to be addressed that existing legal norms do not cover. The Swiss Civil Code is unique in its candid grant of discretion to the judge to fill the gap. It provides in Art. 1, § 2: 'if the Code does not furnish an applicable provision, the judge shall decide in accordance with customary law, and failing that, according to rule which he would establish as legislator.' The assumption must be, of course, that even with such a grant of authority, the judge will try to fashion a result that conforms to the general structure and tradition of the legal system. The result will not contravene existing conceptions of what the law should be, but rather will fill the gap, and thereby contribute to the evolution of the law. One way of doing this is to work by analogy, that is, to compare the present problem with other problems that similarly require a weighing of the interests of the parties in the dispute. The analogy then extends the balance struck with respect to other problems of the present case. An example is the treatment of leasing in German law. The German Civil Code contains provisions on leases and for sales, but not for leasing. Since leasing is regarded as possessing elements from both fields of law, case law and literature now derive rules from both fields and apply them to the phenomenon of leasing.

The Swiss provision just quoted confers discretion. Yet it was suggested that no court will exercise unfettered discretion but will seek to follow the structure and to implement the values of the particular legal system. This has very much been the experience in other civil law legal systems, for instance, the German. The German Civil Code, as do others, contains provisions of enormous breadth and, consequently, lack of specificity. These are 'general clauses,' of which § 242 of the German Civil Code is perhaps the best example. It requires parties to a contract to perform their obligations in 'good faith.' Section 242 has become the source of an extensive body of case law and of legal concepts not addressed specifically in the civil code. When the economic upheavals of the 1930s threatened parties to contracts with economic ruin, the German Supreme Court invoked Section 242 to develop a doctrine of 'frustration of contract' (*Wegfall der Geschäftsgrundlage*). This doctrine, interestingly never accepted to that extent in the United States (despite the greater freedom of common law courts to fashion law through decisions), permits courts in appropriate cases to adjust the obligations of the parties. The French *Conseil d'Etat*—but not the *Cour de Cassation*—developed a similar remedy, the doctrine of *imprévision* (see De Laubadère 1984, § 637). Good faith, so the German court states, requires the protection of both parties: cancellation of the contract (by analogizing the situation to one of impossibility) would be unfair to one party; enforcing it in full (against the background of totally different and unexpected circumstances) would be similarly unfair to the other party.

The obligations of parties to a contract begin with its conclusion. However, expectations will have been created earlier and their disappointment may cause damage. In certain circumstances, such a situation could be dealt with under the law of *Delikt* (tort), but sometimes the preconditions for a remedy in tort will be lacking. Again, the extension of an existing provision may provide relief. Section 276 of the German Civil Code provides for liability for damage caused intentionally and negligently. For liability to arise, there must be some relationship, some duty owed to the other party. Such a relationship, so states the case law, is created by contract negotiations. Parties thus have a *precontractual* duty of care to each other and may have a remedy for its breach. This is the doctrine of *culpa in contrahendo*.

The civilian judge, despite the different theoretical structure and focus of the legal system, thus can and does display the same creativity as do common law judges, with the principal—perhaps only—distinction that the decision in the individual case does not 'make law.' That new concepts can become part of the law, through repeated practice, is shown by the two examples just given. At that point, sources and methodology may differ, the practical result no longer does.

The basic conceptual difference between common law and civil law finds reflection in still another area: the role of a judge and the conduct of a case. In common law jurisdictions, particularly the United States, litigation is 'fact driven.' The facts need to be established and the applicable precedent must then be found. With such an emphasis on the facts of a case, the role of the lawyers is a particularly active one. The judge functions as a neutral arbiter; judges of courts of appeal ultimately decide questions of law. In a civil law court, the judge starts with the rule of law, as outlined, and searches for the facts that he or she needs for the further categorization of the case. The judge's role thus is much more active. Facts are elicited by the judge; lay judges may participate as members of the court (particularly in commercial matters), but there is never a lay jury in private law matters. The judge also ascertains the applicable law and, if the applicable rule of law happens to be foreign law because of the international aspect of the case, may even have to ascertain the content of the foreign rule of law *ex officio*. As a result, decisions of civil law appellate

courts will read quite differently from those of appellate courts of common law countries. Attention to factual detail will be very slight (this is particularly true of high French courts) and the emphasis will be on legal norms, rather than the other way round.

5. Legal Education and the Legal Profession

In the United States of the eighteenth and nineteenth centuries, the young person could become a lawyer by 'reading law in the chambers of a lawyer,' in other words by serving as a clerk. In the civil law countries of Continental Europe, legal education has been the monopoly of the universities for centuries. With 'doctrine'—not case law—the heart of the legal system, law faculties not only served as the only way of entry to the profession, but its faculty members equaled in stature the position of the high judges in common law systems (see Dawson 1978). (For the practice of '*Aktenversendung*' in Germany in the earlier centuries, see Rheinstein 1938.) German appellate and supreme courts routinely sent case files to the prominent law faculties, virtually for final decision on doctrinal grounds. The influence of law professors on the development of legal doctrine thus has a long tradition and continues to this day.) The course of study reflected, at least until recent times, both the strict categorization of the legal system into specific fields of law and the high level of abstraction that characterizes the deductive analytic method of the civil law. Practical training of the young lawyer was left to a period of time required to be spent in an official training program (such as the *Referendariat* in Germany) or as a junior lawyer under the direction of a licensed lawyer, combined with additional training (such as in France). Full admission to the practice of law then occurs with the completion of these additional requirements. The mindset of the young lawyer had been formed, of course, by the time the university studies were completed, nor would it be changed by the acquisition of practical skills.

In more recent times, law curricula increasingly reflect the offering or requirement of election of interdisciplinary subjects. There is also increasing instruction in the use of new technologies, for instance, how to access and use legal databases. However, to the extent that these offerings represent 'skills training,' they may not be expected to change the structure of the legal system.

6. Outlook

Civil law systems differ among themselves, as noted initially. This also holds true for the course of study and practical training required to become a lawyer. As a result, a lawyer—as in the case of other professionals—may face impediments in attempting to establish a practice in another country or even to render occasional services there. In the European Union, the 1988 so-called 'Diploma Directive' was one of the first steps to implement the European Community's freedom-of-establishment and free-supply-of-services provisions. The 1998 'Establishment Directive' requires foreign lawyers who want to work permanently to pass an aptitude test or to have three years of practical experience in the state where they want to work. The Council of Bars and Law Societies of the European Community (CCBE) is an organization which includes the national associations of lawyers of the member states of the EC. It is the author of the 'Code of Conduct for Lawyers of the European Community.'

In the European Union, civil law meets common law in a shared organizational structure. Efforts to facilitate the transborder practice of law have been accompanied by many legislative acts by the Community that go beyond regulatory economic action but also affect private law. Legal scholars are documenting the doctrinal commonalities in various fields of law—under such titles as 'European-wide tort law' (see Von Bar 1996), or 'Property law in Europe' (Von Bar is currently working on this project)—and there has been discussion concerning the feasibility of a European Civil Code (see Kötz 1996, Lando 1999). If there is, then, some movement toward a new *ius commune* in Europe—which, however, will ultimately extend to a significant additional number of countries as a result of the enlargement of the European Union—many other civil law countries around the world will not participate directly in these developments. But the 'new European law' does not only seek to bridge differences among the civil law countries and between them and the common law; it will also effect reforms and innovations within the civil law. These may well serve as models for other civil law countries, for instance, for those of South America that grow together through similar processes of economic cooperation and integration.

See also: Common Law; Law: Overview; Legal Education; Legal Reasoning and Argumentation; Legal Scholarship; Lex Mercatoria; Supreme Courts

Bibliography

Adriaansen R 1998 Open forum: At the edges of law: Civil law v. common law. A response to Professor Richard B Capalli. *Temple International and Comparative Law Journal* **12**: 107
Baudenbacher C 1999 Some remarks on the method of civil law. *Texas International Law Journal* **34**: 333
Capalli R B 1998 Open forum: At the point of decision: The common law's advantage over the civil law. *Temple International and Comparative Law Journal* **12**: 87
Dawson J P 1978 reprint 1986 *Oracles of the Law*. University of Michigan Law School, Ann Arbor
De Laubadère A 1984 *Moderne & Devolvé, 1 Traité des contrats administratifs*, § 637, 2nd edn. L.G.D.J., Paris
Farnsworth E A 1996 A common lawyer's view of his civilian colleagues. *Louisiana Law Review* **57**: 227
Kötz H 1996 *Europäisches Vertragsrecht*. Mohr, Tübingen, Germany
Lando O (ed.) 1999 *Principles of European Contract Law Parts I and II*. Kluwer International, Dordrecht, The Netherlands
Rheinstein M 1938 Law faculties and law schools: A comparison of legal education in the United States and Germany. *Wisconsin Law Review* **5**: 42
Von Bar C 1996 *Gemeineuropäisches Deliktsrecht*. Beck Publishing Company, Munich, Germany
Zweigert Kötz 1987 *An Introduction to Comparative Law* 3rd edn. Clarendon Press, Oxford, pp. 109–15, 154, 231

P. Hay

Civil Liberties and Human Rights

'Civil liberties' and 'human rights' are closely related terms that embrace the basic freedoms and claims to which individuals are entitled, either as citizens of a particular state or by virtue of being human. The very ideas of civil liberty and human rights presuppose two intertwined convictions: that individuals or groups in civil society have moral status independent of the organized power of society (e.g., the state), and that this power must respect the rights that accrue to this status. Though they arose as a response to political and normative claims in the West, at the beginning of the twenty-first century civil liberties and human rights are at least officially endorsed by virtually all countries and the community of international law. The content and scope of these concepts are contested on philosophical and political grounds. Accordingly, the concepts provide a good method of examining the ways in which important philosophical and legal concepts interact with political and historical forces.

1. Basic Historical Background

The idea of a moral status independent of the state is tied in multifarious ways to notions of higher (or natural) or universal law, democracy, individual conscience, and limited government. These notions have echoes in history as far back as ancient Athens and Rome, and in medieval Christian thought. The modern turn toward individual 'rights' (as opposed to natural 'law') was the product of a complex historical process that included: Renaissance and humanist emphases on human achievement and creativity; the Protestant Reformation's stress on individual religious conscience and religious pluralism; the Enlightenment's belief in the power of reason and the individual, the growth of markets, and—most importantly—the rise of democracy (see *Law and Democracy*). The specifically liberal tradition of limited government and natural rights arose in the political and intellectual history of several European countries, notably England, Scotland, France, and the Netherlands, and in the United States, in the seventeenth and eighteenth centuries.

Social contract theory in the seventeenth and eighteenth centuries envisioned 'social contracts' between the government and the citizenry based on the consent of the governed and the protection of natural rights. Building on the theory of Thomas Hobbes, John Locke (1988) maintained in his influential *Second Treatise on Government* (a work defending the Glorious Revolution in England in 1688, and the 1689 English Bill of Rights) that government's primary purpose is the protection of the rights of individuals found in the state of nature, specifically rights to life, liberty, and property. The American Declaration of Independence (1776) and the French Declaration of Man and the Rights of Citizens (1789) carried these ideas further, declaring the primacy of civil and political liberties.

2. Basic Aspects of Civil Liberty and Human Rights

2.1 Definitions

Though the distinction between 'positive' and 'negative' rights (first articulated by philosopher Isaiah Berlin (1969) is often blurred or overstated, civil 'liberties' are often considered negative rights, in that they serve as shields that protect the liberty and rights of individuals and members of civil society from state oppression. They represent claims against state action. Classic civil liberties include freedom of speech, the press, and assembly, freedom of religion, due process and fairness in legal proceedings (especially criminal process), privacy, and freedom from illegitimate discrimination (see *Censorship and Secrecy: Legal Perspectives; Discrimination*).

Civil liberties should be distinguished from civil rights. Civil 'rights' are often construed as more 'positive' rights, in that they entail the state bestowing a power to do something affirmative, or taking action to protect fundamental interests or claims against private (nongovernmental) actions. For example, the right to use privately owned public accommodations or facilities, or the right not to be discriminated against in private employment, can be construed as civil rights. More broadly defined positive rights may include such claims as the right to a job, to obtain adequate housing, and to share in more equal distribution of resources. More aggressive state action is needed to effectuate such rights (see *Civil Rights; Fundamental Rights and Constitutional Guarantees*).

Civil liberties and rights are generally claims tied to citizenship; in particular, legal orders. 'Human rights' are more universal in nature; they exist simply because one is a human being. These include the civil liberties discussed above, as well as freedom from torture, slavery, and degrading treatment; freedom of the family; and basic self-determination. Debate swirls around whether such rights include basic economic, social, and cultural rights and needs, or broader collective goods.

Though human rights claims can be derived from specific domestic or international legal sources, their claims are distinctively moral. As political theorist Jack Donnelley (1989) remarks, 'Human rights claims are essentially extralegal; their principle aim is to challenge or change existing institutions, practices or norms, especially legal institutions.' Accordingly, Donnelley emphasizes the 'possession paradox': Having a right is most important when 'enjoyment of the object of the right is threatened or denied.' Thus, human rights claims typically arise when a particular claim is not afforded legal protection by a particular country, such as homosexual conduct in some states in the United States, or religious conscience in China.

The distinct concept of 'human' rights arose in the aftermath of World War II, with the widespread condemnation of the atrocities the Nazis committed against Jews and other minorities. After having declined in the wake of skepticism and new political movements in the nineteenth and twentieth centuries (e.g., utilitarianism, emotivism, nationalism, and Marxism), notions associated with natural rights and natural law enjoyed a revival in the aftermath of the war, as democratic theorists regained respect for more objective moral principles that provide standards by which to evaluate the practices of states. Such theorists as Leo Strauss (1950) and Edward Purcell (1973) have written about a postwar 'crisis' in democratic theory along these lines. The term 'human' rights avoided the intellectual and political baggage associated with 'natural' law and rights, while at the same time pointing to universally-held moral principles. In the unprecedented Nuremberg trials held after the war, Allied prosecutors convicted Nazi leaders of crimes against peace and humanity. Also, in the wake of World War II, the new United Nations made human rights an important part of its agenda, and Japan and West Germany, under the aegis of occupying forces, adopted constitutions that protect basic civil liberties and rights.

2.2 Relationship to the State

The concept of individual or natural rights is historically and pragmatically related—both positively and negatively—to the emergence of the modern nation states from feudalism between the thirteenth and seventeenth centuries. In 1648, the Peace of Westphalia, which ended the murderous Thirty Years'

War in Europe between Catholic and Protestant states, constituted the first formal international recognition of the nation state's autonomy from religious authority. It also established the first official tolerance of religious pluralism, a crucial move in the rise of civil liberty and human rights. Yet the Westphalian model of international law left no room for the international enforcement of individual rights, as its main objective was the recognition of the principle of territorial sovereignty (domestic jurisdiction) of strong states.

Yet the rise of strong nation states made individual rights more important than they had been in the past, spawning new theories about the obligations of states to citizens. Indeed, another paradox (which also involves the endemic jurisprudential debate between legal positivism and forms of legal analysis based on natural law) concerns the relationship between rights claims and their enforcement or recognition (see *Natural Law*). Though many theorists persuasively contend that rights claims exist independently of legal protection, rights claims (positive and negative) have to be recognized and enforced by those in power in order to be effective. The Nuremberg trials present a classic example of this fact. (Some have called the verdicts 'victors justice.') As James Madison wrote, following the logic of Hobbes and Locke, liberal freedom can exist only when the state is strong enough to protect its citizens, but also limited enough so as not to oppress them. Writing in the aftermath of World War II, Hannah Arendt (1951) chillingly portrayed how vulnerable stateless people are to abuse of their humanity. Legal theorists Stephen Holmes (1995) puts the matter succinctly: 'Weak-state pluralism is a recipe not for liberalism, but for a proliferation of rival and coercive mafias, clans, gangs, and cults ... Liberal government ... is meant to solve the problem of anarchy *and* the problem of tyranny within a single and coherent system of rules (pp. 270–1).

3. *Some Basic Issues*

Important questions have been raised about the content and intellectual foundation of human rights and civil liberties. What is the scope of rights? Are such rights derived from political or legal agreement, or are they postulates of theological or philosophical inquiry? Do we grasp them by intuition or reason? Which claims are fundamental, and which less fundamental, and how can we make this determination? Should the list of fundamental claims include only basic political and civil liberties, or should it also include social and economic rights? Are rights claims culturally determined or relative, as the American Anthropological Association officially declared in 1947, or are there general principles that make certain claims universal?

Some thinkers, such as Christian Bay (1982), maintain that human rights stem from human 'needs,' which include shelter, food, and livelihood; other emphasize human beings' distinctive moral nature, stressing human dignity, self-respect, and citizenship. The debate concerns those who define human nature in largely materialistic or naturalistic terms, and those who define human nature in terms of such qualities as rationality, moral capacity, or spirituality.

Writers such as Henry Shue (1980), distinguish basic from less basic rights. A right is basic if its enjoyment is 'essential to the enjoyment of all rights.' These rights include physical security, economic security or subsistence, and liberty to participate in the economic and political life of the community. Still others, such as Donnelley, argue that this list is insufficient because a fully developed life requires more opportunities and attributes than these minimums. However, history shows that 'negative' civil liberties are necessary to protect us from the state, so these should always be on the short list of basic rights. If we decide to include more rights as basic, we must do so without sacrificing basic civil liberties. And we must understand that the longer the list of basic rights, the greater the potential for conflict among rights and social policies designed to promote them.

Theorists such as French jurist Karel Vasak (1982) posit 'generations' of rights based on historical development. The first generation consists of political and civil liberties, while the second generation embraces egalitarian social and economic rights. The so-called third generation rights involve humanity as a whole, including cultural self-determination, environmental health, solidarity, and peace.

The founding movements and documents in the rise of liberal democracy accentuated civil and political liberties. Yet the rise of socialism, Marxism, and the working class in the nineteenth century spawned the advocacy of social and economic rights in addition to (or instead of) civil and political rights. In the twenty-first century, such rights are found in the constitutions or fundamental laws of communist (and former communist) states and many developing or Third World States (see *Socialist Law*; *Postcolonial Law*). Though developed liberal states are mainly dedicated to political and civil rights, social and economic rights often comprise parts of their social and legislative policy. In the late 1990s, such internationalist groups as the Lawyers Committee for Human Rights and the Fair Labor Association contend that corporations' use of factories in developing countries has made the protection of economic and social rights in those countries a primary concern.

Human Rights covenants in the United Nations reflect these debates (see *International Law and Treaties*). In 1946, the Economic and Social Council of the UN established the Commission on Human Rights, which led to the Universal Declaration of Human Rights in 1948, a foundational document that has achieved the status of customary international law. In 1966, the International Covenant on Civil and

Political Rights (ICCPR) and the International Covenant in Economic, Social, and Cultural Rights (ICESCR) were signed by most states, taking effect in 1976 (see *Torture: Legal Perspectives*). The ICCPR protects such basic civil liberties as freedom from arbitrary punishment, forced servitude, and unfair criminal process; freedom of thought, conscience, and religion; personal liberty and security; freedom of the family; freedom to participate in fair elections; and equal suffrage. An Optional Protocol of the ICCPR commits ratifying states to allow a special committee of experts to examine claims by individuals against them.

The ICESCR covers such rights as the right to work under good conditions; the right to an adequate standard of living, and the right to social security, food, clothing, shelter, and basic health. The ICESCR is less stringent in its wording than the ICCPR. Signatories established no rank ordering of these rights, and enforcement is more a matter of exposure and persuasion than force.

4. Civil Liberties in Practice

The protection of civil liberties varies (in legal provisions and applications of these provisions) in different countries due to cultural and political factors (see *Fundamental Rights and Constitutional Guarantees; Constitutionalism, Comparative*). We can cite just a few of many examples. For instance, free speech doctrine and practice in the United States protect the advocacy of illegal action, including racist rhetoric, that falls short of directly triggering a disturbance of the peace or inciting violence. Canada, Israel, Germany, France and many other countries, on the other hand, prohibit speech that advocates racism (racist rhetoric), regardless of the likelihood of illegal action. In Germany it is illegal to belong to the Nazi party or to wear a Nazi uniform, while courts in the United States have expressly protected such actions.

Though virtually all countries have basic legal protections for criminal suspects, standards vary widely, especially when we look at practice rather than the letter of the law. In Russia, where legal institutions are poorly developed, preventive detention and criminal procedure rights of criminal suspects are poorly enforced despite legal protections to the contrary; France does not recognize the privilege against self-incrimination. In the area of religion, the United States maintains an exceptionally strict separation of church and state, while such democracies as Ireland, Italy, and Germany allow more accommodation between state and religion. In India, 'personal laws' linked to the major religions (Hindu, Muslim, Christian, and Parsi) are distinguished from normal civil law, thereby accommodating culturally-based discrimination against women in such areas as marriage, divorce, and inheritance. And communist China has persecuted such religious groups as Christians and the Falun Gong because their views are allegedly contrary to state ideology.

Social scientists and legal scholars cite several factors that influence the extent to which countries will support civil liberties and rights on a sustainable basis. Commitment to civil liberty has historically been accompanied by social pluralism, legal institutions based on rule of law, and the differentiation of the state from civil society (see *Rule of Law; Law and Development*). More specific explanations include such factors as the existence of a bill of rights and judicial independence, judicial leadership and control of cases dockets, and a culture of rights consciousness that encourages citizens to think in terms of rights (see *Judicial Review in Law; Legal Culture and Legal Consciousness; Rights: Legal Aspects*).

More recent explanations point to the presence of political and social movements that engender legal change (e.g., the Civil Rights Movement in the United States; the freedom movement of South Africa led by Nelson Mandela). Recently Charles Epp (1998) has pinpointed sustained pressure exerted by a 'support structure for legal mobilization,' which consists of rights-advocacy organizations and lawyers, and sufficient funding from private and (especially) public sources. Rights revolutions succeeded in the United States and Canada in recent decades because of the presence of these factors, while India's rights movement was thwarted despite a favorable Supreme Court because such factors were absent (see *Law as an Instrument of Social Change*).

5. Human Rights in International Practice

Until recently, the international system remained committed to the Westphalian model's strong presumption in favor of the 'domestic jurisdiction' of states. But this situation slowly began to change with the growth of consciousness of human rights, the democratic ethic, and globalization (see *Globalization: Legal Aspects*). The most important events before the end of World War II and the Nuremberg trials include: the abolition of slavery in the British empire in the 1830s and 1840s, culminating in the League of Nations' Slavery Convention of 1926; the policy of 'humanitarian invention' by Western states to protect Christian citizens abroad in the nineteenth century; and several conventions and treaties protecting the rights of soldiers in war promulgated in nineteenth and twentieth centuries.

In the wake of World War II and the humiliating failures of the League of Nations, the world community established the United Nations, which promulgated the UN Charter. Whereas the Westphalian model is premised on the freedom of states over their domestic jurisdictions, the 'UN Charter' or 'new international law' model embraces the Kantian model of international relations and law, which emphasizes universal peace and human dignity. In reality, the models coexist in the contemporary world, posing sometimes vexing questions about where to draw the line between state sovereignty and international human rights norms. Yet the conferees who established the Charter rejected a proposal to authorize intervention to protect rights, and a clause in the Charter expressly prohibits intervention in 'matters which are essentially within the domestic jurisdiction of states.'

In recent decades, many international treaties and forums have been established under the aegis of the UN or other regional and international organizations to promote recognition of human rights (see *International Law and Treaties*). States have signed treaties in conventions against torture, genocide, racial and gender discrimination, and treaties protecting refugees and children. Again, social and political movements have been indispensable to the promotion of human rights logic and practice. In addition to hundreds of regional and intergovernmental organizations ('IO's, such as the Organization of American States, the Organization of African Unity, etc.), such non-governmental organizations (NGOs) as Amnesty International, Human Rights Watch, and the International Committee of the Red Cross have played major roles in raising awareness, linking international organizations, and even bringing cases for enforcement in relevant jurisdictions.

States have drafted regional agreements to protect rights on all continents except Asia. In Europe, the European Convention of Human Rights and Fundamental Freedoms (based on the ICCPR) formed the European Court of Human Rights, which takes cases after they have been heard by the relevant domestic courts (see *European Union Law*). Member states have agreed to accept all of the court's rulings, leading, for example, to changes in Britain's law of criminal procedure (most notably in the area of pretrial detention) and changes in several states' laws concerning the rights of children born out of wedlock.

Not surprisingly, politics has affected the application of the ICCPR and ICESCR covenants. During the Cold War era, Western countries championed the ICCPR, while communist countries supported the ICESCR. Third World countries have advocated rights of self-determination, cultural rights, and collective rights concerning resources (debates over law of the seas, etc.). Cultural relativism remains an issue. In 1993, Asian countries challenged claims about the universality of political and civil rights during the UN World Conference on Human Rights, arguing that such rights can be counterproductive, even dangerous, in the context of economic underdevelopment, fragmented nationalism, and fragile state institutions. Theorists such as Donnelley counter by pointing out that these arguments ignore the actual plights of

persecuted minorities in these countries, thereby serving the interests of entrenched elites or tyrants.

Enforcement of human rights at the international level has remained problematic because of the continued normative and prudential reluctance to intervene in the domestic jurisdiction of states. Hobbes and Locke would have predicted such a result in the absence of an international sovereign with sufficient power to enforce protections of rights. As a result, the main support for human rights has been in the form of moral persuasion (far from meaningless, if not always efficacious), exposure of violations through research and publication, and the deployment of such measures as economic sanctions. UN organizations have investigated several countries, including Chile, Rwanda, Somalia, Zaire, several Latin American countries, Iran, Iraq, and South Africa.

6. Victories and Defeats: The Continuing Dilemma of Rights and the State

The decline of Cold War politics in the UN Security Council has enabled the UN to be somewhat more aggressive, sponsoring peacekeeping and actual interventions to protect human rights in Somalia, Iraq, and Bosnia in the early 1990s. Yet the efforts in Somalia and Iraq have proved short-lived, and Bosnia's fate was quite uncertain as of 1999. And in 1994, the world stood by while massive genocide took place in Rwanda. In 1999, Cuba, China, and Sudan championed the norm of the territorial sovereignty of states in order to shield their abuses of human rights from international intervention, even though these states are themselves members of the United Nations Human Rights Commission.

To be sure, Yugoslav President Slobodon Milosevic was defeated in his attempt to take over Kosovo in 1999, yet this victory was won by the military commitment and might of the North Atlantic Treaty Organization under the leadership of the United States and Britain; victory came only after Serbian forces had already carried out massive ethnic cleansing. During the war, the war-crimes tribunal in the Hague indicted Milosovic for war crimes; earlier (1995) it had indicted Serbian leader Radovan Karadzic and his top military officer, General Ratko Mladic. Yet no political body is in charge of bringing such indictments, and the United States and leading European countries have not managed to arrest these Serbian leaders, preferring instead to target lesser figures as of this writing.

After Kosovo, Czech President Vaclav Havel wrote in 'Kosovo and the End of the Nation-state' that the nation state would end in the next century, giving away to an international community governed 'by universal or global respect for human rights, by universal civic equality and the rule of law, and by a global civil society'. Writer Leon Wieseltier (1999) replied that no oppressed soul had ever been saved by the forces of 'global civil society.' Kosovo was delivered from Milosovic by the willful acts of allied nation states. Though the nation state is a source of evil, 'it is also the nation-state from which we may demand rescue from such evils. The ethical content of a particular sovereignty is what finally matters.'

See also: Censorship and Secrecy: Legal Perspectives; Civil Rights; Civil Rights Movement, The; Constitutionalism, Comparative; Discrimination; European Union Law; Freedom/Liberty: Impact on the Social Sciences; Freedom: Political; Fundamental Rights and Constitutional Guarantees; Globalization: Legal Aspects; Human Rights, Anthropology of; Human Rights, History of; Human Rights in Intercultural Discourse: Cultural Concerns; Human Rights: Political Aspects; International Law and Treaties; Judicial Review in Law; Law and Democracy; Law and Development; Law as an Instrument of Social Change; Legal Culture and Legal Consciousness; Legal Positivism; Natural Law; Rights: Legal Aspects; Rule of Law; Socialist Law; Torture: Legal Perspectives

Bibliography

Arendt H 1951 *The Origins of Totalitarianism.* Harcourt, New York
Bay C 1982 Self respect as a human right: Thoughts on the dialectic of wants and needs in the struggle for human community. *Human Rights Quarterly* **4**: 53–75
Berline I 1969 Two concepts of liberty. In *Four Essays on Liberty.* Oxford University Press, London
Cassese A 1986 *International Law in a Divided World.* Clarendon Press, Oxford
Conot R E 1983 *Justice at Nuremberg.* Harper & Row, New York
Donnelley J 1989 *Universal Human Rights in Theory and Practice.* Cornell University Press, Ithaca, NY
Epp C R 1998 *The Rights Revolution: Lawyers, Activists, and Supreme Courts in Comparative Perspective.* University of Chicago Press, Chicago, IL
Henkin L 1990 *The Age of Rights.* Columbia University Press, New York
Holmes S 1995 *Passions and Constraints: On the Theory of Liberal Democracy.* University of Chicago Press, Chicago, IL
Lawson E (ed.) 1991 *Encyclopedia of Human Rights.* Taylor and Francis, New York
Locke J 1998 *Two Treatises of Government* [ed. Laslett P]. Cambridge University Press, Cambridge, UK
Purcell E A Jr 1973 *The Crisis of Democratic Theory: Scientific Naturalism and the Problem of Value.* University Press of Kentucky, Lexington, KY
Shue H 1980 *Basic Rights: Subsistence, Affluence, and US Foreign Policy.* Princeton University Press, Princeton, NJ
Steiner H J, Alston P (eds.) 1996 *International Human Rights in Context: Law, Politics, Morals.* Clarendon Press, Oxford, UK
Strauss L 1950 *Natural Right and History.* University of Chicago Press, Chicago, IL
Vasak K (ed.) 1982 *The International Dimensions of Human Rights.* Greenwood Press, Westport, CT
Wieseltier L 1999 Winning ugly. *The New Republic* June 28: 27–33

D. A. Downs

Civil Religion

In a seminal thesis published in the Winter, 1967, issue of *Daedalus*, and in later revisions of his argument, Bellah 1967 claimed to have discerned two kinds of civil religion in the USA. One was fairly traditional: a composite of biblical themes that were compatible with the natural law tradition mediated by the church. This legacy saw in the history of the US a version of God's election of ancient Israel. That is why Bellah referred to it as a 'special civil religion' that was compounded of prophetic warnings and commands to a chosen nation burdened with particular rights and responsibilities. The other civil religion was utilitarian rather than traditional, and it was based primarily on the thought, interests, and experiences of the American people themselves. Describing it as 'the lowest common denominator of church religions,' Bellah argued that it paid more attention to the interests than to the responsibilities of the people. Interpreted in terms of the social contract rather than of the covenant, it owed far more to John Locke than to the Bible (Bellah 1976a, p. 57).

Bellah alternated between arguing that the civil religion was vital and enduring and issuing warnings that the civil religion was in a precarious state. Bellah at first seemed to be sure that the civil religion was alive and well: far from dead, it would show its vitality during the American Bicentennial of 1976 (Bellah 1973). However, in reflecting on that celebration and also on the latest Presidential campaign addresses, Bellah was quite clear that Americans had largely forgotten about a past that they had never clearly understood.

Bellah himself alternated between thinking that his article coincided with the debut of the civil religion on the American scene and with its decline. On the one hand, he suggested that the civil religion had only come into being through his publication of the 1967 article and appeared confident in its continued existence (Bellah 1973). On the other hand, disappointed in the results of the Bicentennial, he regretted that it was only an 'empty and broken shell' (Bellah 1975).

Some religious leaders have condemned American civil religion as authoritarian, dangerous, and idolatrous. They are joined in this criticism by some leading politicians who see a civil religion as idolatrous. Some critics, therefore, argued that Bellah was engaged in an attempt to revitalize the nation itself by infusing its political institutions with religious meaning. Bellah merely wished, through exhortation, and admonition to recall the nation to its higher purpose (Crouter 1990). To others it was quite clear that Bellah was trying to resuscitate Protestant beliefs and public influence at a time when both seemed to be losing credibility and support. At the very least he was trying to invoke the legacy of the Protestant establishment of the late nineteenth century. 'Bellah introduced theological principles that he presumed overarched the state and the religions it protected' (Hammond et al. 1994 pp. 8–9). These criticisms persisted, despite Bellah's disclaimer that the civil religion was merely another way of talking about a world view (Hammond et al. 1994, p. 2).

Bellah's claim to have identified a civil religion that endures regardless of those who believe in it or who can verify its existence has elicited criticism or comments from those who see his work not as sociology but as political theology or ideology. Indeed, some noted that his interpretation of American religious and political ideals found its justification in theological propositions (Hammond et al. 1994, pp. 8–9). Perhaps in response to these critics, Bellah has argued that the civil religion needed no help from himself or from anyone else; it could endure on its own terms. On one occasion Bellah insisted that the civil religion had never been a majority viewpoint but continued to exist enshrined in certain texts, particularly Lincoln's Gettysburg address. It, therefore, did not matter how many people believed in the civil religion or whether evidence could be found for it through the use of questionnaires. The civil religion was there, Bellah (1976b, pp. 153–4) argued: a matter of 'faith in certain abstract propositions which derive ultimately from God. If the "larger society" does not conform to them, so much the worse for it' (Bellah 1976b, pp. 153–4).

Bellah himself has pointed out that his case for the American civil religion is quite in keeping with a Durkheimian approach to social life. Societies do express their identity and define themselves in religious terms; indeed any enduring form of social life may well become serious about its foundations, standards, boundaries, and destiny. The sacred is a pervasive aspect of social order. No wonder, then, that for Bellah (1989), while the concept of the civil religion may be dispensable, it nonetheless points to an enduring problem concerning the relation of the political to the religious aspects of any society. (Marty 1974).

To sum up Bellah's many and quite variant readings of the civil religion and of his own arguments, it is helpful to distinguish two sets of axioms. These are shared among sociologists who study religion and are not idiosyncratic to Bellah alone, but Bellah does provide an example of how they may operate in the thought of a single sociologist. On the one hand, Bellah identified himself as working within a set of assumptions that he would attribute to Durkheim. On the other hand, Bellah would also acknowledge the validity of a Weberian viewpoint, that thinks of charisma as being somewhat ephemeral or evanescent and always distorted by any attempt to make it part of a routine or rational social order. Religion, on this view, is disruptive to institutions and is, therefore, most evident during times of crisis or chaos. Bellah would therefore not be surprised that that some sociologists, therefore, have found in the civil religion an episodic phenomenon that is most visible in times of crisis and is only gradually rooted in enduring institutions or ways of life (Marty 1974).

The debate on civil religion thus reflected a wide range of assumptions about the relation of religion to complex societies. Bellah, in keeping with his Durkheimian assumptions, saw the US as largely individualistic and utilitarian as a result of a break with the Biblical tradition. In his view the Constitution owed more to Locke and to notions of interest than to covenantal theology; for Bellah, that break represented a considerable decline in the moral vision of the nation.

On the other hand, also in keeping with a Durkheimian interest in a religion of humanity, Bellah and his associate, Philip Hammond, saw more universal possibilities for the civil religion. All societies express their political unity in civil religious terms. Their critics, however, accused them of expressing an American notion of manifest destiny under the guise of the civil religion (Weddle 1983).

Despite the protest by Hammond et al. (1994, p. 2) that Bellah did not have in mind an 'idolatrous worship' of the American nation–state, Bellah argued that American culture has within it the potential of becoming the basis for a global civil religion. It was a point in keeping with his Durkheimian interest in a religion of humanity, and others have found some support for his thesis. There is some evidence, for instance, that the US space program transformed astronauts from American celebrities into representatives of a global civil religion (Wilson 1984). Furthermore, the US is apparently not peculiar in its use of national heroes as exponents of a civil religion; similar processes appear to be at work in Yugoslavia (Flere 1994).

Subsequent studies have suggested that religion may still be engaged with the political system, but far less at the national than at the local level. Rather than influencing a broad range of social values, religion is now more likely to be engaged in interest-group and single-issue politics. Instead of a steady pull on the direction of social change, religion therefore increasingly exerts a temporary, however intense, influence during spurts of social mobilization on the part of particular communities and constituencies (Demerath and Williams 1992).

Some have argued that the civil religion is no longer a national conscience but a set of partial ideologies. It is, therefore, merely 'a confusion of tongues speaking from different traditions and offering different visions of what America can and should be' (Wuthnow 1998).

That is perhaps why Bellah's more universal claim for the civil religion has aroused another set of criticisms to the effect that the civil religion, at least as Bellah conceived it, ignored the presence and claims of minorities and smacked of 'cultural imperialism' (Moseley 1994, p. 18).

Beyond the context of the US, however, scholars have found the notion of a civil religion to be a particularly suggestive concept. Despite—or because of—Bellah's 'broad and diffuse use of the term,' civil religion, and the 'theoretical instability' of Bellah's model, there has been a proliferation of studies of civil religion in a wide range of national contexts (Crouter 1990, p. 161).

Drawing on Dobbelaere's (1986) discussion of the civil religion, it would be possible to distinguish four conditions under which religion would have different relationships to a national political system. Where religion is still an enduring and vital institution, and where it is still central to the nation–state, one would expect to find such traditional forms of civil religion as Islam and Eastern Orthodoxy. However, where traditional religion has been eroded or transformed, one might expect to find more secularized cultural systems like Soviet Marxism or Nazism. More ephemeral or episodic forms of religion might persist and remain central to a nation–state; consider the notion of a civil religion that is episodic and not widely known but still central to the history, traditions, and identity of the US.

Dynamic relationships between the center and the periphery, however, will change the meaning and location of civil religious beliefs and symbols. In Japan, since the nineteenth century, Shinto has moved from the center, where it was the civil religion of an aristocratic and military elite, to the villages and clans, where it has strengthened national resistance to Western influence. Whereas under the Meiji, Shinto had been central and enduring as a national civil religion, under occupation by the US Shinto was no less enduring, however marginal it had become to the public ideology of the nation (Takayama 1988, p. 328).

Although Japan's national culture was transformed into one that was largely secular and democratic, Shinto remained vital to the ability of Japan to recover from the war and to rebuild its economy while preserving a sense of continuity with the past. However, as Shinto has been adopted by the corporations and the nation–state as a means of mobilizing the loyalty of workers and citizens, it has become more secular and arguably less significant to the mobilization and motivation of Japanese citizens and workers (Dobbelaere 1986).

The beliefs and symbols of the civil religion may therefore become the source of legitimacy for the nation–state or the target of cultural opposition. On the one hand, an ideal of an ethnically pure nation–state may legitimate the most brutal forms of ethnic cleansing. As in the case of Yugoslavia, it would be a mistake to underestimate 'the power of a system of reified, prescriptive culture to disrupt the (contradictory) patterns of social life' (Hayden 1996, p.784). Similarly, in Chile a form of the civil religion reinforced by the church and articulated by the Pinochet regime sought to give religious legitimacy to a repressive military elite and regime (Christi and Dawson 1996). Such attempts, however, associate civil religion with a regime rather than with a nation–state as a whole and, therefore, place it in a more marginal location. The same observation applies to attempts by the dominant regime in Malaysia to use Islamic beliefs and practices to reinforce social discipline and to legitimate the political and economic goals of the state (Regan 1976, p. 103).

As nations become increasingly secularized, the civil religion, to the extent that it survives, will become marginal to the culture and politics of the nation–state and put in only episodic appearances during periods of social mobilization around specific issues. For instance, in Celtic heroes and symbols were central to the resistance of France, Belgium, and the Netherlands against Germany in the nineteenth century. Recently, however, France and Spain have met with resistance from Celtic communal groups on their own peripheries. The symbols and identity of the Celtic periphery are thus being co-opted by the European Union in an attempt to assert a Pan-European communal culture (Dietler 1994).

As the cases of Northern Ireland and Wales demonstrate, there is no necessary connection between strong 'nationalist doctrines' on the periphery and an equally strong 'nationalist politics' (Beuilly 1985, p. 74). In the US, marginal groups that wished to define themselves in opposition to the national center that seemed to them to be insufficiently legitimate have established their own alternative versions of the civil religion: the Seventh Day Adventists being one example (Bull 1989, p. 181).

Some have, therefore, argued that the civil religion is an essential arena for the contest among opposing communal and interest groups and between the center and the periphery, (Willaime 1993, p. 573). There is an intimate connection between civil religious protest on the periphery and oppositional politics toward the center. Indeed, it would appear that civil religion comes into being as a way of arbitrating the protest of local or communal groups against the state. Mexican–Americans, for instance, have joined elements of Catholic liturgy with traditional folk celebrations to mobilize and discipline farm-workers for an agricultural union movement in the United States. The movement used traditional religious symbols that had been central to Mexican culture for the purpose of opposing a dominant class and its institutions in the US (Bennett 1988). Indeed, highly sectarian forms of the civil religion have been developed in order to protest the secularization of the civil religion at the political center; the Unification Church would be a prime example of this authoritarian tendency (Robbins et al. 1976). Similarly, representatives of Native American communities have attacked a politicized civil religion at the center as being inimical to the Indian traditions (Deloria 1992).

As Bryan Wilson and others have argued, there are strong secularizing tendencies in the Christian faith, and these have been deployed on various occasions against civil religion. In Sri Lanka the role of the King has been crucial in maintaining social and cosmic harmony; even the British took the role of the King in the most important ritual of Sri Lankan civil religion, until protest from missionaries forced them to cease their involvement. As a result, the ceremony has been degraded into a festival of Sri Lankan cultural arts, and the society as a whole has lacked the means of legitimating the center to the periphery, (Seneviratne 1984).

There is some evidence that the decay or removal of the civil religion from public discourse in some countries has created space for a secular civil society to emerge. In Norway, civil religious symbols have been used by conservative and Christian elites to legitimate the monarchy, but there is a general tendency to keep religion on the margins of public life; even during times of crisis civil religious symbols may be notable by their absence from public discourse. As they remain on the periphery, however, the symbols of civil religion may be deeply, if not widely held. In Norway, although public discourse is secular and political legitimacy is derived from the legal system, the Christian communities of the south-west still maintain a hope that Norway may become a Christian nation (Furseth 1994 pp. 46, 50–1). Although Canada lacks a civil religion, religious symbols and beliefs remain vital to regional and local communities (Reimer 1995).

On the other hand, some have argued that it is the very secularization of the center that raises fears that the society as a whole may disintegrate; these fears are the source of demands for a revitalized civil religion (Willaime 1993, p. 571). As Martin (1997, pp. 28–35) has pointed out, for a society to survive it must have continuity, to achieve which it must maintain a certain identity. That identity, furthermore, always implies a difference between the society in question and all others. By having a cultural as well as political center, a society forecloses other possible bases for integration. The full range of possibilities, and the uncertainty of making choices among alternative identities, is not open to any society that wishes to maintain its identity, and therefore also its difference from other societies, over time.

Once this is understood, Martin (1997, pp. 29–35) argues, it is no longer problematical that religion may become one of the markers of identity or difference. Whether religion becomes an exclusive marker or becomes associated with other forms of the sacred in a particular society depends on a wide range of circumstances that are both historical and geopolitical. Thus, it is not unusual that traditional forms should be co-opted by chauvinism or become a source of peripheral resistance to the center.

In the course of trying to clarify the civil religion thesis, various proponents have argued that there are a wide range of types based either on the content of the ideology or its social constituency. Martin, however, has pointed out the free-floating nature of the sacred and its contingent relation to religion and politics. Rather than developing complex typologies to encompass these relations, what is needed, therefore, is a series of statements of the 'If … then …' variety that stipulate the conditions under which civil religion may be more or less central, marginal, traditional, secularized, popularized, or politicized. It is appropriate to ask to what extent religion is 'locked into the core processes of cohesion, power, and control' and to investigate the extent to which religion and its dominant institutions maintain their traditional 'relation to territory and history, to national belonging and death' (Martin 1997, p. 104). One must also ask whether the religious community in question has a voluntaristic or ethnoreligious base and whether its symbolic options are more generic or particular. The answers to these questions will then help one interpret each community's or nation's construction of 'the world' as relatively open or closed, hostile or indifferent (Martin 1997 p. 56).

Further work, therefore, remains to be done on civil religion as an expression or outgrowth of conflict within and between civilizations. On this level, it remains to interpret civil religions as cultural developments of civilizations translated from their centers to new peripheries. Following Martin, it would be possible to view the American civil religion as a continuation and residue of the English civil war over a century earlier, just as conflicts between the North American center and its Central or Latin American periphery are continuations of the struggle between Northern and Southern Europe. On the basis of Martin's argument one could interpret the American civil religion as the response of one periphery to the English center: a response composed partly of a tradition of establishment and partly of voluntaristic and ethnoreligious dissent (Martin 1997, p. 57). Similarly, one could investigate Japanese Shinto and Sri Lankan civil religion as the development of Buddhism on Asian peripheries.

If arguments concerning the civil religion are to contribute to mainstream social scientific discussions of nationalism however, further work remains to be done on civil religions as the result of the 'civilizing process' as religion is transplanted from the center to periphery. Relatively few scholars interested in civil religion have focussed on the work of Anderson (1983), who has traced the interaction of Western Christianity with a wide range of societies in both hemispheres. In Anderson's view, Roman Christianity, carried by the Church throughout Europe, had integrated a wide range of local cultures and religions within a common civilization and by means of a *lingua franca* (Latin). In developing local vernaculars into which the Bible and liturgy were then translated, however, the Church succeeded in encouraging indigenous elites to develop a national culture resistant to the imperial center. These smaller and more cohesive entities thus represented a limited and secular reduction of the religious civilization that created them. Thus civil religions, by this argument, are secularized remnants of a trans-national religious civilization.

See also: Citizenship: Sociological Aspects; Civic Culture; Religion and Politics: United States; Religion: Mobilization and Power; Religion: Nationalism and Identity; Religion: Peace, War, and Violence

Bibliography

Anderson B 1983 *Imagined Communities, Reflections on the Origin and Spread of Nationalism*. Verso, London
Bellah R N 1967 Civil religion in America. *Daedalus, Journal of the American Academy of Arts and Sciences* **96**: 1000–21
Bellah R N 1973 American civil religion in the 1970s. *Anglican Theological Review*, Supplemental Series **1**: 8–20
Bellah R N 1975 *The Broken Covenant*. Seabury, New York, pp. 142–158
Bellah R N 1976a The revolution and the civil religion. In: Bauer J C (ed.) *Religion and the American Revolution*. Fortress Press, Philadelphia
Bellah R N 1976b Response to the panel on civil religion. *Sociological Analysis* **37**(2): 153–9
Bellah R N 1978 Religion and legitimation in the American republic. *Society* **15**(4): 16–23
Bellah R N 1980 The five religions of modern Italy. In: Bellah R, Hammond P (eds.) *Varieties of Civil Religion*. Harper & Row San Francisco
Bellah R N 1989 Comment. *Sociological Analysis* **50**(2): 129–46
Bennett S 1988 Civil religion in a new context: The Mexican–American faith of Cesar Chavez. In: Benavides G, Daly M W (eds.) *Religion and Political Power*. State University of New York Press, Albany, NY
Beuilly J 1985 Reflections on nationalism. *Philosophy of the Social Sciences* **15**: 65–75
Bull M 1989 The Seventh-day Adventists: Heretics of American civil religion. *Sociological Analysis* **50**(2): 177–87
Christi M, Dawson L 1996 Civil religion in comparative perspective: Chile under Pinochet (1973–1989). *Social Compass* **43**(3): 319–38
Crouter R 1990 Beyond Bellah: American civil religion and the Australian experience. *The Australian Journal of Politics and History* **36**(2): 155–65
David D H 1998 Editorial: Civil religion as judicial doctrine. *Journal of Church and State* **40**(1): 7–24
Deloria V 1992 Secularism, civil religion, and the religious freedom of American Indians. *American Indian Culture and Research Journal* **16**(2): 9–20
Demerath N J, Williams R H 1992 *A Bridging of Faiths: Religion and Politics in a New England City*. Princeton University Press, Princeton, NJ
Dietler M 1994 'Our ancestors the Gauls': Archeology, ethnic nationalism, and the manipulation of Celtic identity in modern Europe. *American Anthropologist* **96**(3): 584 605
Dobbelaere K 1986 Civil religion and the integration of society: A theoretical reflection and an application. *Japanese Journal of Religious Studies* **13**(2–3): 127–45
Flere S 1994 Le Développement de la sociologie de la religion en Yougoslavie après la deuxième guerre modiale (Jusqu'a son démembrement). *Social Compass* **41**(3): 367 77
Furseth I 1994 Civil religion in a low key: The case of Norway. *Acta Sociologica* **37**: 39–54
Hammond P E, Porterfield A, Moseley J G, Sarna J D 1994 Forum: American civil religion revisited *Religion and American Culture. A Journal of Interpretation* **1**: 1 7
Hayden R M 1996 Imagined communities and real victims: Self-determination and ethnic cleansing in Yugoslavia. *American Ethnologist* **23**(4): 783–801
Martin D 1990 *Tongues of Fire, The Explosion of Protestantism in Latin America*. Blackwell, Oxford, UK
Martin D 1997 *Does Christianity Cause War?* Clarendon Press, Oxford, UK
Marty M 1974 Two kinds of civil religion. In: Richey R, Jones D (eds.) *American Civil Religion* 1st edn. Harper & Row, New York
Moseley J 1994 In: Hammond P E, Porterfield A, Moseley J G, Sarna J D (eds.) *Forum: American Civil Religion Revisited. Religion and American Culture, A Journal of Interpretation* Winter **4**(1): 13–18.
Neuhaus R J 1986 From civil religion to public philosophy. In: Rouner L S (ed.) *Civil Religion and Political Theology*. University of Notre Dame Press, Notre Dame, IN, pp. 98–110
Regan D 1976 Islam, intellectuals and civil religion in Malaysia. *Sociological Analysis* **37**(2): 95–110
Reimer S H 1995 A look at cultural effects on religiosity: A comparison between the United States and Canada. *Journal for the Scientific Study of Religion* **34**(4): 445–57
Richey R, Jones D (eds.) 1974 *American Civil Religion*. Harper & Row, New York
Robbins T, Anthony D, Doucas M, Curtis T 1976 The last civil religion: Reverend Moon and the Unification Church. *Sociological Analysis* **37**(2): 111–26
Seneviratne H L 1984 Continuity of civil religion in Sri Lanka. *Religion* **14**: 1–14
Takayama K P 1988 Revitalization movement of modern Japanese civil religion. *Sociological Analysis* **48**(4): 328
Weddle D L 1983 Review of varieties of civil religion. *Journal of the American Academy of Religion*. **LI**(3): 198–9
Willaime J 1993 La religion civile à la française et ses métamorphoses. *Social Compass* **40**(4): 571–80
Wilson C R 1984 American heavens: Apollo and the civil religion. *Journal of Church and State* **26**(2): 209–26
Wuthnow R 1998 *The Restructuring of American Religion: Society and Faith since World War II*. Princeton University Press, Princeton, NJ, p. 244

R. K. Fenn

Civil Rights

Civil rights legally protect individuals or groups from certain forms of oppression. While civil rights are commonly associated with the 1960s movement in the USA to establish equality for people of African descent and—more generally—with the US Bill of Rights, by the end of the twentieth century their reach and recognition was global. In modern political, academic, and public usage, civil rights embody, and provide legal support for, basic concepts of human dignity and respect for individuals in their diverse cultures and ways. Recognition and enforcement of civil rights, or some assortment of the most fundamental civil rights, is widely understood as a necessary element of freedom, democracy, and equality.

Civil rights are usually established in a written constitution, statute, or treaty. However, they have been based on unwritten constitutions and have occasionally arisen from the pronouncements of monarchs and conquerors, perhaps most famously Napoleon. These sources of civil rights protections are not self-executing: some countries have strongly worded civil rights provisions in written constitutions that are not enforced; the meaning and interpretation of civil rights provisions are usually controversial; and despite the prevalence of civil-rights aspirations and rhetoric, no country has as yet found a reliable method for systematic, consistent protection of civil rights.

1. Origins

The origins of some civil rights go back almost a thousand years to the earliest limitations on governments, which at least indirectly protected individuals. Civil rights as such emerged in the seventeenth and eighteenth centuries, as social development and political and philosophical thought emphasized the individual and, later, based national sovereignty and legitimacy on democratic forms of government. However, systematic legal enforcement, and even widespread aspirational recognition, of civil rights did not occur until after World War II. They quickly achieved global acceptance in the last half of the twentieth century; the laws of almost all countries, and several widely adopted international pacts, at least purport to protect some array of fundamental rights of individuals.

Approached historically and contextually, the various civil rights can be traced to practices by governments or by powerful individuals or institutions that came to be viewed as oppressive. Thus, the Fourth Amendment to the US Constitution limiting police searches was a response to the dreaded house-to-house general searches by British authorities in the colonial period. However, such origins are often obscured, because civil rights—like other basic legal precepts—are usually analyzed and clothed with the rhetoric of foundational principles and tend to take on, in law as well as in politics and fiction, an abstract, timeless quality that transcends history, experience, and human

agency. This has occurred in the USA with freedom of speech, which has acquired a major place in the national origin story, although its most significant features developed in the mid-twentieth century by common forms of social change (Kairys 1982, Levy 1985).

2. Scope

The most common civil rights are: prohibition of discrimination based on race, ethnicity, religion, and gender; the right to personal security, including protections for persons accused or suspected of crimes; the right to vote and to participate in democratic political processes; and freedom of expression, association, and religion. Privacy, which in the US system encompasses personal security and autonomy, as well as control over personal information, is of growing concern throughout much of the world.

Personal security was the first, and remains the primary, civil right. It was a major focus of leading Anglo–American legal authorities, from William Blackstone (1769/1992) and St. George Tucker (1803) to Thomas Cooley (1874). The pathbreaking civil rights text by Thomas Emerson and David Haber (1952) considers the right to personal security first and describes its significance in the introduction: 'In a society based upon human dignity and the development of the individual personality, clearly all members are entitled to security of the person— protection from bodily harm, involuntary servitude, and the fear of physical restraint.' Although the rights of criminal defendants in the USA are commonly thought to originate in 1960s Supreme Court rulings, the US Bill of Rights has as its major subject and most numerous protections a series of limits on the government's power to punish individuals criminally.

International bodies, treaties, and courts—and many countries—prefer the term 'human rights,' which usually encompasses a broader array of rights and places different priorities on some particular rights than does US civil rights law (see *Law: Defense of Insanity*). The United Nations Charter, the *Universal Declaration of Human Rights* (1948), and many other human-rights treaties and covenants protect social, economic, and cultural rights as well as political and civil rights. These rights place affirmative obligations on governments to provide all their people with minimal nutrition, healthcare, housing, and education. Eleanor Roosevelt, criticizing the US reluctance to include economic and social rights, put it best: 'You can't talk civil rights to people who are hungry.'

Internationally, the content of human rights also often exceeds specific US civil rights protections, including, for example, prohibition of the execution of children and mentally disturbed adults and protections against domestic abuse. Other nations may also place different relative importance on various rights, such as rejecting absolutist free-speech rights and emphasizing equality rights. While the USA has adopted most of the human rights treaties and covenants (although often with specific reservations), US courts have not consistently enforced them. The USA is also unusual among the nations of the world in its renewed embrace of capital punishment and in the retrenchment of procedural and fair trial rights to expedite executions.

In most countries, civil rights protect individuals from their governments, but protection for groups and from other individuals have also been recognized. Prohibitions of slavery around the world limit individuals, as well as governments. Equal rights for women have included limits on individually inflicted violence against women and recognition of the rights of women as a group.

3. Universal, Absolute, and Conflicting Rights

Civil rights lose their meaning and importance if they are not extended to all people. However, the universality of civil rights, both within a particular country and across national borders, and the common notion that extension of civil rights to those previously denied them has no affect on others, are problematic.

Typically, recognition of civil rights disturbs a status quo in which privileges and hierarchies were entrenched. If previously silenced speakers or voters gain the rights to speak and vote, the effectiveness of the voices and votes of the previously privileged is diminished. Abolishing racial discrimination in employment or college admissions diminishes the prospects of the previously privileged. Abolishing racial discrimination in public accommodations diminishes the freedom of association of those who wish to exclude racially. Recognition of the rights of people who have been oppressed involves a determination that the interests, expectations, tastes, and sometimes civil rights of others constituted an illegitimate or disproportionate privilege which came only at the expense of that oppression, and to which they should not have been, and no longer are, entitled. The failure to acknowledge the interconnectedness of rights, interests, privileges, and expectations has probably made acceptance of civil rights advances more difficult than it has to be. This has been a substantial problem in the USA, where interconnectedness is only acknowledged for affirmative action and where civil rights tend to be articulated in absolutist terms.

Absolutist conceptions of civil rights usually rest on the same thinking, memorably critiqued by Justice Oliver Wendell Holmes' famous example of shouting 'fire' in a crowded theater. Words have effects, otherwise we might not be so fond of them, and in some circumstances those effects outweigh the value of speech. Such occasions are rare, but they do exist—for example, where one person's speech is interfering with or drowning out another's or all others. Nevertheless, the US Supreme Court has protected electoral campaign finances as speech in absolutist terms that make even minimal regulation difficult or impossible (Buckley vs. Valeo 1976). The Court characterized money as speech and refused to recognize as significant or legitimate countervailing concerns the importance of fair elections to society and other individuals or the speech rights of those whose voices cannot be heard in money-driven elections.

Absolutist conceptions of this sort, though often articulated by staunch advocates of individual rights, are reminiscent of the 'Lochner era' in the USA, in which the civil right to due process was used by the Supreme Court to invalidate a series of economic reforms aimed at protecting working and poor people. The combination of an absolutist formulation and a civil right based on unrestrained free enterprise yielded one of the most notorious eras in US constitutional law. These rights that people around the world seek and rely on for protection from powerful individuals, groups, and institutions, often at considerable personal sacrifice, can become another instrument for the powerful.

There is also a fundamental sense in which all civil rights protect individuals by limiting others—either all others collectively, because civil rights prohibit certain actions by majorities and governments, or individually, in the situations in which civil rights protect against private as well as governmental actions. Thus, civil rights both bestow and limit freedom. They limit the ability of even democratically constituted governments, for example, to discriminate against a racial minority or to ban an opposition political party, by placing the individual's rights above collective power. Civil rights are, in this sense, both a limit on and a necessary feature of democracy.

These tensions permeate heated controversies about the universality of civil rights across national borders. The conventions on the rights of women referred to above have been the subject of an unusual array of national reservations, usually on the ground that they clash with cultures and religions, which also can claim civil rights protection. For example, female genital mutilation violates several of the most fundamental and generally accepted civil and human rights, but it is also central to some cultures and religions.

4. Formulation and Enforcement: the US Model

The US tradition of extensive judicial power, which includes judicial innovation beyond the specific language of a constitution, statute, or treaty, is gaining some acceptance internationally. This expanded acceptance is in part due to its reputed tendency to protect civil rights, although the role of courts in civil rights matters (and more generally) is controversial in the USA. Many other countries have tended to rely on international human rights treaties or legislation. Courts lack the democratic legitimacy of legislatures, while their very distance from democratic processes could enhance the potential for protection of individual rights against even mobilized majorities. Protection of individuals and groups from majoritarian oppression is the hallmark of meaningful civil rights and provides the best measure of a particular society's civil rights record. A closer look at the history and record of a particular country—the USA, because of its historical role and wide recognition as a leader and model for civil rights—demonstrates both the potential and the difficulty of sustained, systematic protection of civil rights.

The role of courts in the civil rights victories of the 1960s and throughout US history is often exaggerated. The integration of public schools (Brown vs. Bd. of Educ. 1954) was a milestone, but most aspects of equality for African Americans in the twentieth century were established by the US Congress. In the 1960s these included banning racial discrimination in voting, housing, employment, and public accommodations. The major civil rights advances of the nineteenth century were achieved by constitutional amendment and legislation.

The history of US courts reveals them to be more often an obstacle to civil rights than a protector of them. For example, the US Supreme Court ruled in 1857 that African Americans have 'no rights which the white man is bound to respect' and are not fully citizens or human beings (Dred Scott vs. Sanford), which destroyed the Missouri Compromise on slavery and was a contributing cause of the Civil War; approved segregation even after the Civil War amendments to the Constitution (Plessy vs. Ferguson 1896); negated the 'privileges and immunities' clause of the Fourteenth Amendment (Slaughterhouse Cases 1873), which applied civil rights protections against the states; refused to protect even the most basic free speech rights until the 1930s (Davis vs. Massachusetts 1897; Kairys 1982); and approved the imprisonment of all persons of Japanese ancestry on the west coast during World War II without any charges or proof of individual guilt (Korematsu vs. US 1944). Generally, throughout US history, oppressed minorities and individuals facing repression by government or organized majorities—including in modern times the repressive McCarthyism of the 1950s and the approval of state criminalization of gay sexual activity continuing into the new millennium—have not been significantly protected by the courts.

There are only two periods in US history characterized by systematic or sustained judicial protection of civil rights, from about 1937 to 1944 and from about 1961 to 1973. Both these periods occurred in the context of mass popular support and successful legislative initiatives for civil rights. During these periods, the Supreme Court established: a system of limited government and protection of individual rights available to people of ordinary means probably unrivaled in world history, including strenuous protection of speech, association, and privacy; procedural and substantive rights of persons accused or suspected of crime; the rights of women; voting and participatory rights; and prohibitions of discrimination (Kairys 1993, 1998; W. Va. Bd. of Educ. vs. Barnette 1943).

The main judicial vehicle for protecting civil rights in these two periods was the 'strict scrutiny' standard of judicial review, by which any government action that infringed or restricted these rights was strictly scrutinized and presumptively invalid, surviving only if supported by a 'compelling' government interest that could not be furthered by 'less restrictive' means. While these decisions seldom articulated absolute rights (although absolutist rhetorical flourishes were common), in practice strict scrutiny meant near-certain invalidity.

Starting in the mid-1970s, as the national political mood and the composition of the justices changed, the Supreme Court repudiated or significantly diluted almost all of the major civil rights advances of the post-World-War-II period. This retrenchment was led in the political arena by President Ronald Reagan and a conservative movement that emphasized limiting government and espoused the sometimes extreme distrust of government evident in many periods of US history (Wills 1999).

The thrust was to empower the people by limiting the courts—in the popular phrase, 'judicial restraint'—which, paradoxically, strengthens government and weakens individual rights. Thus, this conservative judicial restraint trend reviled the 1965 case establishing a civil right to privacy (Griswold vs. Conn.), a decision that protected the individual and the people generally from a state law that banned all use of birth control. A judicially based system of protection of civil (or any other) rights requires the courts to intervene when government is infringing on protected rights, and conservative justices have not hesitated to intervene to protect civil rights they value (e.g., Buckley vs. Valeo 1976; Shaw vs. Reno 1993). Historically, the pattern in the USA has been advocacy of judicial restraint by those whose values and approaches are being rejected by the courts. Perhaps the most vehement and successful advocate of judicial restraint was liberal President Franklin Roosevelt, whose reforms were struck down by a Supreme Court intent on imposing unrestricted laissez-faire economics (Kairys 1998).

In this retrenchment, the rights to exercise nonmainstream religion and against establishment of religion were substantially undercut, including the refusal to protect a Native American religious ceremony that pre-dates Christianity (Empl. Div. vs. Smith 1990). Speech rights available to people of ordinary means were retrenched (for example, the public areas and circumstances available for protest were substantially narrowed), while speech rights available to corporations and wealthy individuals were enhanced, including recognition of corporate free speech rights. The equality rights of minorities were undercut by adoption of virtually insurmountable burdens of proof, resulting in denials of relief for some egregious practices left over from segregation. The equality rights of the white majority have been enhanced, resulting in successful challenges to electoral reapportionment and affirmative action, even where they are good faith remedial efforts to end discrimination against African Americans and other minorities. As a result, almost all the winning parties in racial equality cases decided by the Supreme Court in the last two decades of the twentieth century were white. The US attempt to end centuries of discrimination that included slavery and forced segregation was short and mostly limited to erasing de jure discrimination; the mass of African Americans live in the same segregated poverty they endured under de jure segregation (Kairys 1993, 1994, 1996; Memphis vs. Greene 1981, Richmond vs. Croson 1989, Shaw vs. Reno, 1993).

This retreat was accomplished by a range of judicial means. In some areas, such as exercise of religion and some aspects of privacy, the Court withdrew strict scrutiny protection. In others, such as equality, establishment of religion, and some aspects of free speech, a range of new rules made it near impossible to prove a violation—such as the requirement for proving that government not only violated a civil right but did so purposely, with the specific motivation to violate the right.

None of these new rules is required by the language of the US Constitution or by rules of legal reasoning or analysis; nor is the strict scrutiny standard that was used to protect civil rights. This is characteristic of the judicial model, which in the USA yielded cyclic protection of civil rights in some (not all) periods in which support for those rights had strong, sustained, and politically mobilized support.

By the end of the twentieth century, the lead in civil rights passed from the USA to other nations and to international human rights tribunals and agreements. The Constitutional Court of South Africa led a worldwide trend to ban or limit the death penalty (State vs. Makwanyane 1995); the European Court of Human Rights, unlike the Supreme Court of the USA (Bowers vs. Hardwick 1986), protected the rights of gay men and lesbians (Dudgeon vs. United Kingdom 1981); and the rights of racial minorities and women were advanced principally by international human rights agreements. Progress in this direction has come mostly as a result of international human rights agreements and the growing sense they represent that oppression and repression, though they have hardly ceased, are no longer internationally acceptable.

5. Prospects for Civil Rights

Since civil rights can encompass a variety of possible limits on government to protect individuals and groups (and some limits on other individuals and affirmative obligations of governments), the details of their substance, context, and history are necessary for an understanding of their social meaning and importance. In this sense, it is hard to say that any of us is 'for civil rights,' and perhaps harder to say we are 'against civil rights' (which might mean government without limits), without specifying whose rights, which rights, and the context. For some, government is most oppressive when it limits gun ownership or attempts to overcome the effects of past discrimination; for others, it is most oppressive when it limits exercise of religion, abortion rights, or the rights of historically oppressed minorities. In the post-World-War-II period, the USA set an international standard for protection of minorities and the enforcement of a range of civil rights that protect the individual from oppression by government and powerful majorities; but US history also demonstrates the fragility of civil rights, and the use of civil rights to insulate the powerful from popular reforms aimed at protecting working and poor people.

Civil rights have played an important role in the advancement of human dignity, respect for the ways of diverse cultures and individuals, and democratic forms of government. In a relatively short time in the last half of the twentieth century, racism moved from acceptable or trivial to wrong, and a deep sense of civil rights and fair play became an international intellectual and moral standard. However, this has not stopped—by any reasonable measure—racial, ethnic, religious, and national oppression or violence, or the routine denial of the range of basic civil rights. There is a substantial and troubling divide between our words, aspirations, and moral precepts on the one hand, and our actions on the other. We may be a species whose gift of reason and empathy has outpaced its habits of survival, which still reside—as if helpless to listen to our own pleas—in deepseated (perhaps significantly genetic) tribalism. If this is so, the struggle for civil rights and human dignity will be long, indeed, but all the more compelling.

No single source or enforcement mechanism for civil rights has proved consistently superior to others. Establishment and enforcement seem most effective when accomplished by the most popular and participatory means available, and popular understanding of the importance and history of civil rights is probably the most significant factor in their continued vitality.

See also: Bill of Rights; Civil Liberties and Human Rights; Civil Rights Movement, The; Discrimination; Discrimination: Racial; Fundamental Rights and Constitutional Guarantees; Human Rights, Anthropology of; Human Rights, History of; Human Rights in Intercultural Discourse: Cultural Concerns; Human

Rights: Political Aspects; Race and the Law; Rights; Rights: Legal Aspects

Cases:
Bowers vs. Hardwick, 478 US 186 (1986).
Brown vs. Board of Education, 347 US 483 (1954).
Buckley vs. Valeo, 424 US 1 (1976).
Davis vs. Massachusetts, 167 US 43 (1897).
Dred Scot vs. Sanford, 60 US (19 How.) 393 (1857).
Dudgeon vs. United Kingdom, 45 European Ct. of Human Rights (ser.A), 4 E.H.R.R. 149 (1981).
Employment Division vs. Smith, 494 US 872 (1990).
Griswold vs. Connecticut, 381 US 479 (1965).
Korematsu vs. United States, 323 US 214 (1944).
Lochner vs. New York, 198 US 45 (1905).
Miller vs. Johnson, 115 S.Ct. 2475 (1995).
Memphis vs. Greene, 451 US 100 (1981).
Plessy vs. Ferguson, 163 US 537 (1896).
Richmond vs. Croson, 488 US 469 (1989).
Shaw vs. Reno, 509 US 630 (1993).
Slaughterhouse Cases, 83 US (16 Wall.) 36 (1873).
State vs. Makwanyane, 1995(3) South Africa Law Reports 391 (1995)
West Virginia State Board of Education vs. Barnette, 319 U.S. 624 (1943).

Bibliography

Blackstone W 1992 *Commentaries on the Laws of England.* Hein, New York
Convention of Discrimination Against Women 1992 Recommendation No. 19, Violence Against Women
Cooley T 1874 *Constitutional Limitations.* Little, Brown, Boston
Copelon R 1998 The indivisible framework of international human rights: Bringing it home. In: Kairys D (ed.) *The Politics of Law*, 3rd edn. Basic Books, New York, Chap. 9, pp. 216–39
Cover R 1975 *Justice Accused.* Yale University Press, New Haven, CT
Emerson T, Haber D 1952 *Political and Civil Rights in the United States.* Dennis, Buffalo, NY
Henkin L 1990 *The Age of Rights.* Columbia University Press, New York
Henkin L, Neuman G, Orentlicher D, Leebron D 1999 *Human Rights.* Foundation Press, New York
Janis M, Kay R 1990 *European Human Rights.* University of Connecticut Law School Foundation Press, Hartford, CT
Kairys D (ed.) 1982 *The Politics of Law.* Pantheon Books, New York
Kairys D 1993 *With Liberty and Justice for Some.* New Press, New York
Kairys D 1994 Race trilogy. *Temple Law Review* 71: 1–12
Kairys D 1996 Unexplainable on grounds other than race. *American University Law Review* 45: 729–49
Kairys D (ed.) 1998 *The Politics of Law*, 3rd edn. Basic Books, New York
Levy L 1985 *Emergence of a Free Press.* Oxford University Press, New York
Locke J 1771 *Two Treatises on Civil Government.* Whiston, London
Paine T 1992 *The Rights of Man.* Hackett, Indianapolis, IN
Rousseau J–J 1901 *On the Social Contract.* Tudor, New York
Tribe L 1988 *American Constitutional Law*, 2nd edn. Foundation Press, New York
Tucker St. G 1969 *Blackstone's Commentaries, with Notes of Reference to the Constitution and Laws of the Federal Government of the United States and of the Commonwealth of Virginia.* Rothman, South Hackensack, NJ
Universal Declaration of Human Rights. 1948 G.A. Res. 217A, U.N. Doc. A/810
Wills G 1999 *A Necessary Evil, A History of American Distrust of Government.* Simon and Schuster, New York
Winant H 2001 *The World is a Ghetto.* Basic Books, New York

D. Kairys

Civil Rights Movement, The

The modern American Civil Rights Movement was one of the pivotal freedom struggles of the twentieth century. This article will discuss the historic oppression of African Americans and how the Civil Rights Movement fought to liberate that population. It will also analyze the origins of that movement as well as its national and international achievements.

1. Black Oppression

Even as late as the middle of the twentieth century, millions of Black citizens in the USA were socially oppressed, economically exploited, and disenfranchised politically. These conditions of subjugation endured in a nation viewed as the world's leading democracy. This view of the USA was projected nationally and internationally by White US leaders. The US image of democracy contrasted sharply with the actual treatment of African Americans. Unlike European immigrants, Black Africans were forcibly transported to America as slaves. As captives of the institution of slavery for over two centuries, Blacks supplied the free slave labor that assisted the USA in becoming an economic superpower. Slavery denied Blacks the basic rights that constitute the foundation of a democracy. Indeed, during slavery, African Americans were officially defined as chattel, not human beings.

The American Civil War (1861–5) was the force that overthrew the slave regime. With the triumph of Union forces in 1865, Black equality became a real possibility. For a brief period following the Civil War it appeared that the former slaves would be granted their democratic rights. During the Reconstruction period, Blacks gained expanded citizenship rights including freedom of movement, restricted male access to the franchise, and access to employment. This was a promising beginning but it would not endure for long.

By the turn of the twentieth century the Reconstruction period had come to an end. In the early

1900s, a formal system of racial segregation known as Jim Crow was firmly established. The new form of racial oppression required that Blacks and Whites be segregated on the basis of race. Thus, legally the two races were not allowed to attend the same movie theaters, drink from the same water fountain, sit on the same side of a courtroom, or be sworn in with the same Bible. Blacks and whites were prohibited from occupying the same space on a public bus or train. In short, Blacks were denied equal access to public accommodations. Moreover, Blacks were excluded from the political process. Toward the close of the nineteenth century the emerging Jim Crow regime received backing from the highest court of the nation. Thus an 1896 Supreme Court Ruling, *Plessy vs. Ferguson*, declared that racial segregation was constitutional. It ruled that it was constitutionally legal for the two races to use separate-but-equal facilities. With this ruling the Jim Crow regime became national in scope although it was more rigorously enforced in the South.

By the middle of the twentieth century the majority of Blacks were disenfranchised. In the South, Blacks held no significant political offices and they were constant victims of terror and violence including lynchings. In the labor market Blacks were restricted to low-paying undesirable jobs. As a result, economic exploitation of Blacks was widespread. Beyond material subjugation, African Americans experienced daily personal humiliation because racial segregation marginalized them as a people and labeled them as an inferior race. Human dignity was stripped from African Americans: simple titles of respect such as 'Mr.' or 'Mrs.' were withheld, and even White youngsters held symbolic authority over all Blacks, however elderly or eminent.

2. The Movement's Origin

African Americans consistently attacked the Jim Crow regime. Black protests began during slavery and remained evident during the Jim Crow period. At times, resistance was collective and public, while at other times it remained covert and limited in scope. By the 1950s African Americans had produced a long, rich tradition of social protest. The modern Civil Rights Movement drew upon this tradition and embedded itself deeply within the historic struggle for Black liberation.

The Civil Rights Movement took deep root in the south in the mid-1950s. Thus, this movement emerged where Black oppression was most intense and where racial segregation was firmly entrenched. Given the scope of oppression and the power of the White opposition, the birth of a powerful resistance movement was unanticipated, especially by Whites who thought that segregation had become part of the natural order.

The movement took off during this period for several reasons. First, by the 1950s large numbers of African Americans had migrated to southern cities where they developed tightly knit urban communities and dense, effective communication networks. These resources made it possible for mass mobilization to occur. Second, by the 1950s the National Association for the Advancement of Colored People (NAACP) had won successful legal rulings against the Jim Crow system, especially in the 1954 Supreme Court decision, *Brown vs. Board of Education*, which reversed the 1896 *Plessy vs. Ferguson* decision. The Brown ruling stated that separate schooling based on race was unconstitutional. The implications of this ruling went far beyond this case for it delegitimized the entire system of racial segregation and encouraged struggles to implement the court orders.

Additionally, changing international relations were important to the birth of the movement. By the middle of the twentieth century African and Third World countries were gaining independence through anti-colonial struggles. African Americans identified with those struggles, which intensified their own thirst for freedom. Moreover, the context of decolonization and Cold War rivalry rendered the US Federal Government susceptible to pressure from an oppressed Black population because the USA sought to persuade these new Third World nations to model themselves after US democracy, not the Soviet alternative. However, US racial oppression stood as a barrier to harmonious relations between the USA and new Third World nations. The proliferation of television and communication satellites made it possible for Black oppression to become visible worldwide. America's participation in the two world wars and the Korean War also rendered it vulnerable to Black protest because in those wars the USA championed egalitarian values. In this context, Black soldiers were radicalized while fighting for democracy on distant shores. Thus, the federal government came under increased and sustained international and domestic pressure to support efforts to overthrow institutionalized racial segregation.

2.1 Strategies, Tactics, and Goals

These factors created the fertile soil from which the Civil Rights Movement emerged. By employing the strategy of mass, nonviolent, direct action, this movement mobilized widespread social protest. For such a strategy to succeed, White communities, businesses, and institutions had to be disrupted and prevented from doing business as usual. To this end, civil rights leaders and organizers mobilized thousands of African Americans to confront the Jim Crow regime through social protest.

The Civil Rights Movement succeeded in mobilizing massive nonviolent social protest. Innovative tactics included economic boycotts (beginning with the year-long boycott of a bus company in Montgomery, Alabama, sparked by the arrest of Rosa Parks, in December 1955 and led by Martin Luther King Jr.); sit-in demonstrations intensified in February 1960 by Black college students at a lunch counter in Greensboro, North Carolina; dramatic confrontations in the streets of Birmingham, Alabama in 1963; and mass marches (including a massive mobilization of Whites and Blacks in the August 1963 March on Washington, which culminated in King's 'I have a dream' speech, and protest marches led by King that met with police violence in Selma, Alabama, in January 1965).

The goal of these protests was to overthrow racial segregation and empower African Americans by seizing the franchise. Southern officials utilized their institutional power and the resistance of the larger White community in an intense, and often violent, effort to defeat the movement and to maintain legally enforced racial segregation. Movement participants—many of them women, children, and college students—were often beaten and brutalized by southern law enforcement officials, and thousands were arrested and jailed for their protest activities. Some leaders and participants—such as Medgar Evers, of the Mississippi NAACP in 1963, and three civil rights workers in Mississippi in 1964—were murdered.

Nevertheless, the widespread and highly visible confrontations in the streets, which contrasted the brutality and the inhumanity of the White segregationists with the dignity and resolve of Black protestors, made the cause of Black equality the major issue in the USA for over a decade during the 1950s and 1960s. The nation and its leaders were forced to decide publicly whether to grant African Americans their citizenship rights or to side with White segregationists who advocated racial superiority and the undemocratic subjugation of African Americans.

3. National Achievements

The movement could not be dismissed. Eloquent leaders and their massive followings sustained the pressure on local elites and the federal government. Countless heroic figures inspired and organized a massive following. Among them were Rosa Parks, a dignified older woman and local NAACP activist, who sparked the Montgomery bus boycott when she defied an order to move to the back; Martin Luther King, Jr., who emerged from the Montgomery bus boycott and the Southern Christian Leadership Conference (SCLC) to assume a position of preeminent moral leadership and national influence; James Forman, executive secretary of the more militant Student Nonviolent Coordinating Committee (SNCC), who was to challenge SCLC's and King's strategy; SNCC's leader, Stokely Carmichael (now Kwame Toure), who introduced the slogan 'Black power'; James Farmer and Floyd McKissick who led the Congress of Racial

Inequality (CORE); and Fannie Lou Hamer, who went to a voter registration meeting run by SNCC, was arrested at the courthouse in Indianola, Mississippi, when she tried to register to vote, and then was viciously beaten in prison. Hamer personified the thousands of women who played important roles in organizing and leading the movement.

These leading figures and thousands of movement participants articulated Black suffering and the democratic aspirations of African Americans of every generation and circumstance. In addition, thousands of Whites (students, ministers, lawyers, and other civil rights workers) were inspired to join the Movement. They participated in lunch-counter sit-ins, mass demonstrations, and campaigns such as the 1964 Mississippi Freedom Summer Project, a campaign that involved hundreds of volunteers in voter registration drives and the creation of 'freedom schools.' Some, like Andrew Goodman and Michael Schwerner, who were involved in the Freedom Summer campaign, and Viola Liuzzo, a Michigan homemaker shot by Klansmen after a rally in support of the march from Selma to Montgomery, lost their lives in the Movement and, in turn, helped inspire others.

Differences regarding ideology, leadership style, and goals emerged within the movement as the SCLC, NAACP, SNCC, CORE, and other organizations reached different judgments about the value of nonviolent action, racial integration and separatism, the role of Whites in the movement, and the influence of Black nationalism. Despite these controversies, the moral challenge and the widespread social disruption caused by the economic boycotts, the marches, the sit-ins, and other forms of nonviolent direct action, coupled with the international pressure, created an impasse in the nation that had to be resolved.

As a result, the Civil Rights Movement achieved important legislative victories in Congress. The landmark Civil Rights Act of 1964 outlawed discrimination in public accommodations on the basis of race, color, religion, or national origin and it identified the legal measures to be used to achieve racial integration. Moreover, it barred discrimination in employment practices on grounds of race, color, religion, national origin, or sex. The passage of the 1965 Voting Rights Act was another major achievement, for it suspended the use of literacy tests, authorized the attorney general to challenge the constitutionality of poll taxes, and introduced procedures that provided for the appointment of examiners to ensure that all restrictions on Black voter registration be ended. In short, the Voting Rights Act enfranchised the southern Black population, making it possible for a historic Black elected political class to emerge.

3.1 International Achievements

The significance of the Civil Rights Movement extends far beyond its historic overthrow of the Jim Crow regime. This Movement has affected US politics in fundamental ways. It demonstrated to the oppressed Black community how such protest could be successful, and it made social protest respectable. The Civil Rights Movement also proved that social protest is capable of generating significant change. Hence, the movement broadened the scope of US politics and inspired diverse movements for citizenship rights and social justice in the USA and abroad. Before the Movement, many groups in the USA—women, Hispanics, Native Americans, farm workers, the physically disabled, gays and lesbians, etc.—were oppressed but unaware of how to resist or galvanize support. The Civil Rights Movement provided a model of successful social protest and produced a host of new tactics and social change organizations. Moreover, this Movement had an influence on freedom struggles around the world. Participants in freedom struggles in Africa, Eastern Europe, the Middle East, Latin America, and China have made it clear that they were deeply influenced by the US Civil Rights Movement.

4. Continuing Challenges

For all its success and influences, however, the Civil Rights Movement did not solve all of America's racial problems. At the start of the twenty-first century, African Americans and many other non-White groups are still at the bottom of the social and economic order. These current conditions are exacerbated by a social climate in which the disadvantaged are often blamed for their own predicament. Thanks to the Civil Rights Movement, a relatively large Black middle class has emerged. Yet, over a third of the Black community remains trapped in poverty. Black Americans are disproportionately the victims of police brutality and housed in the rapidly growing prison industry. Thus, during the infancy of the new millennium, some Blacks are the recipients of middle-class comforts while millions of others are victims of poverty and degradation. Poverty and inequality are also widespread outside the Black community. It may be that protest remains the only viable means to achieve greater empowerment. If this is the case, the Civil Rights Movement has left a rich legacy to inspire and inform future struggles. The sparking of a renewed interest in the academic study of social protest is an unnoticed legacy of the Civil Rights Movement. Through such studies it is possible that new mechanisms of social change will come to light.

See also: Civil Liberties and Human Rights; Civil Rights; Conflict Sociology; Integration: Social; Minorities; Nonviolence: Protective Factors; Race and Gender Intersections; Race Identity; Racial Relations; Racism, History of; Racism, Sociology of; Slavery as Social Institution; Slaves/Slavery, History of; Social Movements: Resource Mobilization Theory; Social Movements, Sociology of

Bibliography

Branch T 1988 *Parting the Waters: America in The King Years 1954–63*. Simon and Schuster, New York
Carson C 1981 *In Struggle: SNCC and the Black Awakening of the 1960's*. Cambridge University Press, Cambridge, UK
Garrow D 1986 *Bearing the Cross: Martin Luther King, Jr., and the Southern Christian Leadership Conference*. William Morrow, New York
Klinker P A, Smith R M 1999 *The Unsteady March: The Rise and Decline of Racial Equality in America*. University of Chicago Press, Chicago
Layton A S 2000 *International Politics and Civil Rights Policies in the United States 1941–1960*. Cambridge University Press, Cambridge, UK
McAdam D 1988 *Freedom Summer*. Oxford University Press, New York
Morris A D 1984 *Origins of the Civil Rights Movement: Black Communities Organizing for Change*. Free Press, New York
Morris A D 1999 A retrospective on the Civil Rights Movement: Political and intellectual landmarks. *Annual Review of Sociology*
Robnett B 1997 *How Long? How Long?* Oxford University Press, New York

A. Morris

Civil Service

The civil service is the generic name given in English to the administrative apparatus of the state. The term was first introduced in the British administration in India and then in the UK (1854), and has become almost universally synonymous with civilian (i.e., non-military and nonjudicial) administrators employed by central governments. The civil service is also referred to by different terms (e.g., 'public bureaucracy'), and it differs from other bureaucracies by virtue of its public missions, however defined. It has a collective justification, namely, doing something otherwise unattainable for a certain pubic end, and therefore, civil servants have been entrusted with the task of being the guardians, or at least the interpreters, of the common good. The modern civil service is above all a 'state institution' and this article will focus on the changing relationship between the state and its specialized bureaucratic institution—the civil service.

1. History

There were bureaucratic administrators long before they were known as 'civil servants.' Historical antecedents can be found mainly in centralized States and empires where public bureaucracies were developed to serve the rulers, or the dynasty. Despite their subservience to the emperors and kings, however, these bureaucracies became 'professional,' that is, they manifested some conception of themselves as servants of the 'state,' the polity, or even the community (Eisenstadt 1965). Such embryonic civil service institutions existed in different forms first in the Egypt and China empires, and later, for instance, in the Byzantine, Sassanid, Abbasid, and Ottoman empires. Sculptures of the ancient Egyptian scribes date back to the Old Kingdom (ca. 2600 BC). They belonged to a body of officials who served the Kingdom, as did their Assyrian and Babylonian counterparts. Even more professional were the ancient Chinese functionaries employed in the rather developed court machinery. These officials—whose rank was conspicuously exhibited by the shape and color of the buttons worn on their caps—became much later known in the West as 'mandarins.' The term is often used pejoratively to indicate the aloofness of civil servants, the official jargon and the sheltered life of their long careers.

Broadly speaking, the history of public administration testifies that there has always been a need to link state (or ruler) goals, with the official expertise of a centralized bureaucracy. These bureaucratic entities were engaged in three main types of activities: technical services such as land registration or water allocation; social and political regulation such as administrating justice or collecting taxes; and above all—managing war-related affairs (Finer 1997, Vol. 1, pp. 59–72).

The European patterns of the civil service have emerged gradually from the Greek and especially the Roman law and administrative traditions, of, for example, public construction, food supply regulation, and population census. They were later influenced by the medieval feudal system of financial and judicial administration. Yet, the most strenuous collective effort has always been related to mobilizing money, soldiers, and equipment for the military. Accordingly, throughout the history of most countries, organizational practices, public and private, have been influenced directly by the most readily available example—the military model. This model was further developed to encompass the colonial expansion of some European countries, which required new organizational expertise, both in content and in scope. The influence of the military is most readily seen through such administrative concepts as 'chain of command,' or 'line and staff,' so much so that recent attempts to debureaucratize the civil service are essentially an attempt to break away from the dominance of the military bureaucratic model.

2. The Modern Civil Service

The emergence of the modern civil service is connected directly to the crystallization of the European style state, first in France and Prussia and later in all the 200 or so states that populate the globe in the early twenty-first century. As an institution the civil service dates back to the middle seventeenth century with the inauguration of competence entrance examinations in Prussia under Friedrich Wilhelm I, analogous to the old Chinese practice. Equally important, the German Cameralists were the first modern scholars–practitioners to study public administration and to offer a set of principles for the 'management of the state' (Gross 1964, Vol. I, p. 108). The next stages in the development of the civil service were diffused, but a few milestones can be presented, all of them related to the attempt to create an institutional instrument with acquired experience in running state affairs. The dissimilar features should also be noted as each civil service is also a product of its particular environment, and the human composition of each of them reflects recurring attempts of social groups to enter the ruling elites of their respective states.

2.1 The Napoleonic Reforms Early Nineteenth Century

The Napoleonic Reforms converted the previous French royal service into a State public service. France, and before that Prussia, created the continental model of a professional, tenured and in-house trained civil servant. More than in other countries, continental civil servants embody the state, and the continuity of state affairs, and operate within a specific legal framework of administrative law (Crozier 1964, Suleiman 1974).

2.2 The Northcote–Trevelyan Report 1854

This report introduced competitive examinations into the British civil service and uniform methods of recruitment and promotion across departments. It eventually succeeded in eliminating patronage. Making it a professional life career attracted the educated to enter the senior administrative class, which was given the task of shaping public policy and advising politically elected ministers. Below them were the executive and clerical classes, which were given managerial and routine responsibilities. The UK was the first to establish a civil service commission to oversee the entire operation of the civil service. Politically neutral and very secretive, the British senior home civil service acquired a reputation of integrity and impartiality, and of being guardians of crown affairs, as distinct from the governments of the day.

2.3 The Pendelton Act 1883

The Pendelton Act in the USA marked the beginning of federal civil service reform, aimed at abolishing the previous 'spoils system' in the central government.

Patronage in the federal government was closely related to electoral turnovers in the Presidency and Congress. Unlike the UK, the American system has never achieved the same degree of uniformity, political neutrality, or continuity. In the USA, however, the civil service has been much more open, with recruitment to the senior positions, less dependent on social class and on elite education systems. Consequently, the civil service has never had the aura of 'officialism' as in Europe, and has not acquired the prestige and the consequent status of being a permanent agent of the federal state.

2.4 Nondemocratic Regimes

In nondemocratic regimes the position of the civil service institution is related directly to the scope of the state's monopoly of the different spheres of life. The stronger the state, the more dominant is the public bureaucracy—operating sometimes from the ruler's palace, the military barracks, or the party's headquarters. In such regimes, the civil service hardly exists as a differentiated professional institution. In the Soviet Union, for example, the lines between state and party bureaucracies, and indeed between political and administrative decisions, were practically nonexistent. In this respect, the most troubling phenomenon appeared with the total submission of the highly developed German civil service (including the military and the judicial) to Nazi leaders. This raises the question: Can there be safeguards against turning professional competence –and loyalty—into a sharp tool in the hands of evil political masters?

2.5 New States

In the New States the civil service is a mixture of colonial heritage and unique local elements. In India, and in some other former British colonies, the civil service is a strong institution, and it helps to keep the country going, despite recurring crises and accusations that it impedes development. In many other new countries, particularly where the military took over, the civil service hardly functions. It cannot maintain law and order, let alone carry the task of providing social services. The weaker the state grows, the more helpless is the civil service institution, and the weaker the civil service, the less the ability to sustain stability and encourage positive changes.

3. The Rational Model

Max Weber (1864–1920), one of the most prominent students of bureaucracy, delineated three 'ideal-types' of legitimate authority—the legal-rational, the traditional, and the charismatic, and suggested that the first one requires the existence of a 'rational' administrative staff. Strongly influenced by the Prussian example, Weber drew a list of the characteristics of a modern bureaucracy and the conditions that contributed to its emergence and growth, particularly in capitalist market economies (Weber 1947). His ideas reflected, and to some extent strengthened, the heavy reliance—both in continental Europe and in the USA—of civil service institutions upon administrative law: legal codes, rules, regulations, and precedents. To this very day the notable exception is the UK which (unlike Canada, Australia and its other former dominions) does not have a civil service act of Parliament and does not require legislation to change its public administration system.

The rational ('Weberian') model of the civil service as a permanent institution also includes the following common features, which are assumed to exist in the public bureaucracies of the developed states: the centralization of authority; formal modes of operation; a central commission or agency in charge of civil service affairs; established procedures for recruitment, tenure, promotion, compensation, job evaluation, discipline, and the right to associate and strike; and arrangements for securing political neutrality. In addition, civil servants must adhere to a special code of conduct which specifies their obligations, and constitutes the ethos (or perhaps the myth) of impersonality, neutrality, and guardianship of state secrets.

The important point about the rational model of the civil service is that there is a connection between the development of the modern state and this new form of bureaucratic organization. Indeed, in the twentieth century the civil service and the entire public sector expanded rapidly in response to growing roles of the state, particularly with the growth of the welfare state.

Governments and their civil service apparatus have been asked to provide more services and to find answers to new problems such as environmental degradation. But at the same time, the 'administrative' or 'bureaucratic' state has also come under attack, in terms of the size, structure, and functions of the civil service. New post-Weberian questions have been floated: to whom should the civil service be responsive and accountable: to the state, the law, the government of the day, the multicultured conglomeration of sectors and groups, or perhaps to the individual customers of its services?

4. What do Civil Servants Do?

Civil servants are in charge of a rich menu of government activities ranging from artificially 'seeding clouds' in the sky to induce rainfall, to operating schools, or administrating programs for the increasing number of aged people. In between, civil servants, as in ancient times, continue to collect taxes and perform state functions that cannot be trusted to, or done by, social (voluntary) or private market institutions. These various activities can be grouped under the following headings: shaping and implementing public policy decisions; providing services to individuals, groups and organizations; and administrating regulatory schemes in areas such as aviation, drugs, and election financing.

The main structural entities for carrying out these activities could be divided roughly into three (a) the regular civil service departments and agencies—responsible for the generic governmental functions; (b) the special statutory agencies, authorities, commissions, etc.—responsible for specific tasks removed from the regular civil service, (e.g., the USA Securities and Exchange Commission); and (c) government corporations entrusted with running utilities and other commercial enterprises regarded as natural monopolies or in some other way related to national interests (e.g., postal services, public broadcasting, electricity companies, and regional development projects). The combinations of the various types of activities and the different structures reflect the myriad and ever-changing scope of civil service responsibilities.

It is impossible to prescribe the right number of civil servants per capita, given the differences in their functions, and in the number of intra-state governmental levels in different states. In economically developed states, the tendency is to cut down the scope of civil service activities (and consequently its size too) through privatization, outsourcing, etc. In new states the pressure still exists on the civil service to do much more for their hard-pressed societies.

5. Studying the Civil Service

Woodrow Wilson (1887) was among the pioneers who attempted to create 'a practical science of administration,' aimed at improving not only the personnel, but also the organization and methods of government offices. He saw the field of administration as a field of business which should be outside the sphere of politics. Hence his famous dictum: separate policy-making from administrative execution. But there were other scholarly currents as well. From the 'scientific management' movement in the USA (ca. 1900s) came the notion of 'efficiency,' aimed at increasing workers' productivity through detailed time and motion studies, standardization of tools, and careful attention to training. From the 'human relations' school (ca. 1930s) came the message that in all organizations, individual and group motivations are the most important factors. A little later, and more directly applied to public administration, attempts were made to develop prescriptive principles. For instance, establish one top executive; fit people to organizational structures; ensure unity of command; use specialized staff; maintain homogeneity in organizational subdivisions;

delegate authority; match responsibility with authority; and limit span of control (Gulick and Urwick 1937).

A change came with Herbert Simon's (1946) attack on these principles which he regarded as being no more than 'proverbs of administration.' Simon's concept of 'bounded rationality' that governs the life of all organizations, was an important step away from prescriptions towards observations, and from practical advice on how to run organizations, to laying the foundation of public administration theory and of a comparative perspective. First came the formal studies of the civil service as an institution within the executive branch, or in the context of administrative law. Later, mainly as a result of the impact of studies in political science, the context as well as the horizon were expanded, away from the previous formalism. For example: power, group theory, and communication were introduced into the vocabulary of public administration research. More recently, the related area of public policy has emerged with new emphasis on economic models and game theory, as well as on the redefinition of values, public goods, and the role of politics in decision-making (Majone 1989). New foci were introduced such as implementation, social regulation, and comparative policy analysis in areas such as welfare, health, and environment (Goodin and Klindermann 1996, pp. 551–641).

The most challenging and inadequately researched new area has remained the role of the civil service institution in democracies. This is a practical issue as well: how to reform the civil service within a new democratic framework in the era of state weakening (Silberman 1993).

6. Blurring the Boundaries of the Civil Service

The modern version of the state is changing rapidly, and if there is going to be a 'skeleton state,' there will be a skeleton civil service as well. This process has been gradually occurring both because of internal changes such as the weakening of pubic trust in political institutions, and under the impact of globalization. In the early 2000s there are states still struggling to build a British-type civil service (which does not exist in the UK anymore); other states in which few changes have taken place in their public bureaucracies; and economically-rich states in which the role of the civil service is visibly contracting. There are also new supra-state bureaucracies, not only in international organizations such as the European Union, but also in inter-state agencies and in joint public management of regional projects. These developments have shattered many of the old features of the classical Weberian-type civil service.

Examples:

(a) Civil service monopoly on official information is no longer feasible and government secrecy has yielded to freedom of information acts enacted in most democratic states (Galnoor 1989).

(b) With modern information technology and multi-channel communication, civil servants' anonymity (and perhaps discretion too) has been gradually disappearing.

(c) The previous civil service—interest groups network, has been replaced by a much more intricate and uncontrollable system of organization in the mushrooming 'third sector' (nongovernmental, nonprofit) of public interest groups, NGO's, and philanthropic funds.

(d) The civil service is under great pressure to be more 'representative' in its membership, or at least to assist in achieving equal opportunity through 'affirmative action' and other measures.

(e) Direct accountability of the civil service to the public is demolishing the last walls of insulation. One example is the spread of the Swedish Ombudsman institution. Another is the authority given to special investigation commissions to probe the decision-making discretion of public officials.

These developments were followed by important changes in some of the traditional features of the civil service. For example, in many states the civil service is no longer a life career and new opportunities for entrance to (and exit from) senior positions have been introduced. The emphasis on management skills has downgraded the policy-advice roles of civil servants. The results-oriented business approach has diverted attention to the quality of service aspect, including the idea that civil servants should be rewarded according to their standing in customers' satisfaction surveys.

In states where New Public Management (NPM) reforms were was introduced, a new post-public bureaucracy model is slowly emerging. It requires questioning many assumptions about the civil service—both in scholarship and in practice (Peters and Wright 1996). The most important change in this respect is in the blurring of the old boundaries between the public and private sectors, and between politics and administration.

The first blurred boundary was pointed out long ago by Merriam (1944): the civil service has constituencies, and in many countries corporations exert a great deal of influence on public policy. However, with increased regulation, the private sector became even more involved, and hence the phenomenon of excessive clientelism (Nadel and Rourke 1975). Moreover, as part of the process of 'reshaping the state,' the size, structure, and functions of the civil service are under attack. Independent public and private entities and agencies are performing what used to be civil service tasks such as postal services. Other functions have been 'privatized,' 'marketed,' or 'outsourced' to the private sector: running prisons, computer services, or even recruitment to the civil service itself.

As for the politics–administration dichotomy, for many years it disappeared from public administration

textbooks. Everybody knew that civil servants exercise state power both formally (law application) and informally (policy shaping). However, starting in the 1980s the distinction returned as part of NPM. The new textbooks dealing with the civil service are now called 'introduction to public sector management,' and the civil service is conceived to be market-oriented, customer-driven, deregulated, decentralized, etc. Thus the old Wilsonian dichotomy has returned through the back door: an institutional separation within the civil service between the 'departments' in charge of policy and the 'performance-based organizations' or 'executive agencies' responsible for delivering services to customers.

See also: Administration in Organizations; Administrative Law; Bounded Rationality; Bureaucracy and Bureaucratization; Bureaucratization and Bureaucracy, History of; Decision-making Systems: Personal and Collective; Delegation of Power: Agency Theory; Executive Branch, Government; Governments; Public Administration: Organizational Aspects; Public Administration, Politics of; Public Bureaucracies; Public Management, New; Weber, Max (1864–1920)

Bibliography

Aberbach J D, Putnam R D, Rockman B A 1981 *Bureaucrats and Politicians in Western Democracies.* Harvard University Press, Cambridge, MA

Barnard C 1938. *The Functions of the Executive.* Harvard University Press, Cambridge, MA

Crozier M 1964 *The Bureaucratic Phenomenon.* University of Chicago Press, Chicago

Dror Y 1971 *Design for Policy Sciences.* Elsevier, New York

Eisenstadt S N 1965 *Essays in Comparative Institution.* Wiley, New York

Finer S E 1997 *The History of Government From the Earliest Times.* Oxford University Press, Oxford, UK

Heady F 1979 *Public Administration: A Comparative Perspective,* 2nd edn. Marcel Dekker, New York

Hood C 1999 *Regulation Inside Government.* Oxford University Press, Oxford, UK

Galnoor I 1989 Government Secrecy. In: *International Encyclopedia of Communications.* Oxford University Press, Oxford, UK, pp. 34–7

Goodin R E, Klingemann H-D (eds.) 1996 Public policy and administration. In *A New Handbook of Political Science.* Oxford University Press, Oxford, UK, pp. 551–641

Gross B M 1964 *The Managing of Organizations.* The Free Press, New York

Gulick L, Urwick L (eds.) 1937 *Papers on the Science of Administration.* Institute of Public Administration, New York

Majone G 1989 *Evidence, Argument and Persuasion in the Policy Process.* Yale University Press, New Haven, CT

Merriam C E 1944 *Public and Private Government.* Yale University Press, New Haven, CT

Nadel M V, Rourke F E 1975 Bureaucracies. In: Greenstein F I, Polsby N W (eds.) *Handbook of Political Science.* Addison-Wesley, Reading, MA, **5**: 373–440

O'Donnell G 1973 *Modernization and Bureaucratic Authoritarianism: Studies in South American Politics.* University of California Press, Berkeley, CA

Peters B G, Wright V 1996 Public policy and administration: Old and new. In: Goodin R E, Klingemann H-D (eds.) *A New Handbook of Political Science.* Oxford University Press, Oxford, UK, pp. 628–41

Pressman J L, Wildavsky A 1984 *Implementation,* 3rd edn. University of California Press, Berkeley, CA

Silberman B 1993 *Cages of Reason: The Rise of the Rational State in France, Japan, the United States and Great Britain.* University of Chicago Press, Chicago

Simon H A 1946 The proverbs of administration. *Public Administration Review* **6**: 53–67

Simon H A 1957 *Administrative Behavior: A Study of Decision-Making Processes in Administrative Organizations,* 2nd edn. Macmillan, New York

Suleiman E N 1974 *Politics, Power and Bureaucracy in France.* Princeton University Press, Princeton, NJ

Weber M 1947 *The Theory of Social and Economic Organization.* Oxford University Press, New York

Wildavsky A 1987 *Speaking Truth to Power.* Transaction, New Brunswick, NJ

Wilson J O 1989 *Bureaucracy.* Basic Books, New York

Wilson W 1887 The study of administration. *Political Science Quarterly* **2**: 197–222

I. Galnoor

Civil Society, Concept and History of

Historically, the idea of civil society takes two very different forms. In the first, civil society is 'political community' (*societas civilis* or *koinonia politike*) encompassing a state undifferentiated from society (Ellis 2000). Here, civil society is coterminous with the state: that is power relations ordered through law and institutions with the objective of ensuring social harmony. In the second, civil society is a self-regulating, self-governing body outside and often in opposition to the state, represented both as the nexus of societal associations expected to generate civility, social cohesion and morality, and as the site of reciprocal economic relations among individuals engaged in market exchange activity.

1. Koinonia Politike *and its Historical Modulations*

In Greek and Roman political thought the notion of civil society as political community was not limited to the legal category of citizenship. Central to Aristotle's (384–22 BC) conception of political community was the recognition that people lived in different social spheres and their status varied in terms of property, skills, and abilities. The art of politics was the use of laws and institutions to organize activities within these different spheres with the objective of attaining a harmonious or 'just' social environment. Aristotle regarded the citizen as one who shared in the admin-

istration of justice and held office to this end (Aristotle 1965). In this sense, citizenship in the Athenian city-state was as much a moral as a legal category (Ehrenberg 1999). The household was not excluded from Aristotle's moral scheme. Household subsistence production was 'natural,' while production for commercial exchange and profit was 'unnatural' and subversive of the moral order. The exercise of justice presupposed constraints on commercial activity.

For Cicero (106–43 BC) and the Roman lawyers, civil society (*societas civilis*) was the equivalent of *res publica* (commonwealth), or 'an assemblage of people in large numbers associated in an agreement with respect to justice and a partnership for the common good' (Cicero 1988). Cicero viewed justice as rooted in man's natural 'social spirit' which was informed by reason and induced individuals to forego a measure of self-interest in the interest of common good (Ehrenberg 1999). Cicero was writing when Rome had ceased to be a harmonious 'commonwealth' run by its citizens and their subsistence producing households, but had become an imperial city in which landowners, financiers, and merchants coexisted uneasily with a vast and hungry population of peasants and slaves. Cicero saw the realization of justice as the 'even balancing of rights, duties and functions' within the state (Cicero 1988). *Societas civilis* thus represented groups and individuals united by laws and institutions, which organized their activities and sought to achieve a flexible equilibrium among them.

Until the end of the eighteenth century, the various societies of western Eurasia generally conformed to the Aristotelian model of a politically constituted moral community. In western Europe, however, the idea of *koinonia politike* virtually disappeared during the Middle Ages when extreme political fragmentation led to the Church assuming a central role in government and social life.

On the other hand, in the Byzantine Empire, the idea of a politically constituted community persisted and the Church was subordinated to the political and moral authority of the emperor. The Ottoman Empire succeeded to this mode of political discourse, but added ideas of bureaucratic and hierarchical organization derived from the political traditions of the agrarian empires farther east, notably Persia. This synthesis, which predated the Ottomans, was formalized in the ninth and tenth centuries by Islamic philosophers well-versed in the works of Plato and Aristotle, as well as by the bureaucratic elites of the Islamic states who were educated in the Persian tradition. It was resisted by some sections of the Islamic establishment on the grounds of the equality of all before God. The ensuing power struggles did not, however, result in an autonomous 'Islamic Church,' but rather the religious establishment was subsumed within the political hierarchy.

In the Ottoman Empire, *koinonia politike* was epitomized by the figure of the just ruler, whose ability to establish 'good order,' or *shariah* in the Islamic sense, predicated upon an absence of social strife, constituted justice. Exercise of justice involved laws and institutions accommodating different interest groups in order to sustain the conditions for household subsistence production and to achieve equitable distribution of resources among power holders. Thus laws and institutions represented negotiated settlements between the ruler and different interest groups.

In western Europe, the idea of community created by God and comprising all mankind (i.e., all Christians) was a challenge to the notion of differentiated community constituted through politics to achieve social harmony and justice. St Augustine's *City of God* (*De Civitate Dei*, 413–26), where men were equal before God and united in the universal church, stood in contrast to the Greek and Roman *polis* of differentiated spheres of life. The Church and the temporal rulers responsible for its government derived their right to rule from God and stood outside the community.

However, struggles between the Church and temporal rulers, coinciding with the rise of monarchies, resulted in the division of social activities into spiritual and temporal spheres governed, respectively, by the Church and the kings. The concept of *koinonia politike* found a new foothold in the institution of monarchy. Between the fourteenth and seventeenth centuries, European monarchs, endowed with divine right and with absolute powers, nevertheless engaged in constant negotiations with different interest groups. Political society rested on the exchange of entitlements to different groups and individuals in return for their obedience and/or services they rendered.

2. Koinonia Politike *Transformed*

In the sixteenth and the seventeenth centuries, following a period of religiously-driven civil wars, the idea of a Christian *koinonia politike* was replaced by the concept of the overriding sovereignty of the secular ruler who subordinated religious claims and restored peace. This was the Hobbesian moment in which the modern state rose to define, limit, and enforce moral alternatives to God's order (Maier 1987). Competition among European monarchies, warfare, civil war, and peasant uprisings all contributed to centralization of political power. By the end of the seventeenth century, this was reflected in the institution of the sovereign monarch as a site of bureaucratic administration and regulation. Commercial expansion in the seventeenth and eighteenth centuries meant that economic activity became a primary target of state regulation. The administrative, regulatory state was represented in discourses on economic administration that combined cameralism, mercantilism, political arithmetic, and bullionism.

Thus political or civil society was no longer the politically constituted community characterized by a diffusion of political power. Instead, political society referred to the sphere of absolute sovereignty. Social harmony, which remained the legitimizing objective of rule, was the product of bureaucratic regulations and no longer the outcome of reciprocal exchanges or negotiated settlements between the ruler and the different sectors of society.

Attempts to formalize the sovereign state also had the effect of pointing to the existence of a sphere outside the political domain. In the latter part of the eighteenth century, a new conception of civil society as the site of self-regulation developed, referring to voluntary associations freed from the corporate grip of the Church and urban institutions and to the sphere of economic activity. This concept of a self-regulatory, self-governing society was often in opposition to the regulatory, political domain of the state.

The dichotomous conception of state and civil society, was, however, preceded by the distinction in Natural Law theory between *status civilis* and *status naturalis* (Tribe 1988). The latter was the sphere of discord which the English philosopher Thomas Hobbes (1588–1674) described as *bellum omnium contra omnes*—barter society in which individuals contracted with and against one another (Hobbes 1949), and to which his countryman John Locke (1632–1704) assigned the contentious process of the formation of private property. For Hobbes, the state of nature ended when it submitted to the 'civil union' 'called state or civil society.' For the Prussian Cameralists of the same period, organization of economic activity in political society, or its regulation, ensured the security and prosperity of the commonwealth, including providing the population with subsistence and productive employment. For the English mercantilist, James Steuart (1712–90), self-interest had to be restrained and directed by the 'reason of state' if it were not to damage public good, which he defined in terms of England's increasing commercial success.

Concentration of political power in administrative monarchies had resulted in a decline in the importance of the corporate bodies and deliberative institutions that had earlier served to mediate power. Groups that were excluded from the political process, as well as new bureaucratic elites and commercial classes, sought inclusion through societal associations and political institutions that could provide them with a voice against absolutism. In France, Britain, and Germany respectively, Montesquieu (1689–1755), Ferguson (1723–1816), and Kant (1724–1804) proposed conceptions of civil society focused on delineation of associational spaces, of environments for societal negotiations, of civility, and of publicity (Jacob 1991).

Responding to the despotism of the eighteenth-century French ancient regime, Montesquieu saw in civil society (*l'état civil*) a context for the societal negotiation of the absolute power of the monarch that was not a domain separate from the monarchy. His concept of division of powers addressed a situation in which the monarchy had severed itself from the network of power relations within the political society and had appropriated for itself a separate sphere of power (*l'état politique*). It sought to reintroduce the monarch into the *l'état civil* by means of institutions that would check the absolute authority of the ruler and balance it against the authority of the landed aristocracy, their advocates in the judiciary, and commercial interests (Richter 1998).

Kant first employed the notion of civil society, or *bürgerliche Gesellschaft*, in the sense of political society inseparable from the Prussian absolutism of Frederick the Great (1712–1786), which he considered indispensable for social stability. Secondly, *bürgerliche Gesellschaft* referred to the public sphere or a domain of literate citizenry that was separate from the arena of political power and action. Kant regarded the political arena as the reserve of the state, or the ruler. *Bürgerliche Gesellschaft* referred to a sphere 'beyond the political order,' 'beyond the particularistic concerns of political action' where practical issues of governance could be debated on the basis of universal principles of reason. For Kant, the critical practice of exposing actual state policies to the light of universal reason could act to restrain the absolute power of the ruler as well as legitimizing his power (Ellis 2000). Kant's *bürgerliche Gesellschaft* was composed of individuals from the Prussian bureaucratic and bourgeois elites, educated and trained in state schools and administrative offices, as well as members of social clubs and associations, who could by dint of reason rise beyond the trappings of class or official status.

The thinkers of the Scottish Enlightenment who addressed the issue of civil society did not limit themselves to the issue of restraints to centralized state authority. Adam Ferguson pointed to the corrosion of civic spirit in political society, where the successful commercial classes became servile to the administrative state, which provided them with a 'rule of law' but deprived them of their traditional rights (Keane 1988, Ferguson 1995). He conceived of civil society as networks of self-governing and self-regulating voluntary associations, such as self-help groups and 'friendly' or charitable societies, which had expanded rapidly in the eighteenth century and, in Britain, played an important part in poverty relief efforts. Ferguson pointed to the potential of voluntary associations for engendering civility beyond the special interests of state administration and the commercial classes. The central question facing Ferguson and other eighteenth century European thinkers was how society increasingly differentiated administratively and economically, could remain integrated and harmonious. For Ferguson, as for his compatriot, David Hume (1711–1776), civility was the basis for social cohesion, and he saw it as rooted in sociability or moral and emotional communication among persons 'that fostered social bonds and friendships and cultivated manners and moral tastes' (Trentmann 2000).

Ferguson did not place civil society in opposition to the state; rather, civil society constituted a protective shield from the uncertainties of social and political life.

3. Civil Society as a Separate Domain

For Adam Smith (1723–1790), also a thinker of the Scottish Enlightenment, civilized society consisted in self-regulating and interdependent networks of economic relations among individuals and groups, originating in the decisions of individuals competing in markets for goods, labor and capital. Economic activities of self-interested individuals were guided by the universal, natural laws of supply and demand. For Smith, the civilizing of economic society and the harmonizing of individual interests presupposed a mode of sociability and reciprocal sympathies among individuals (Trentmann 2000).

Smith proposed a separation between the civilized society of economic activity and the political sphere of the state and insisted on the liberation of labor, capital (including land), and goods from the network of relations of political society. The doctrine of *laissez faire, laissez passez*, first introduced by the eighteenth-century French Physiocrats and taken up by Smith, was a plea for the removal of regulations that privileged the landed classes through restrictions on the grain trade, merchants through grants of monopolies, and the 'poor' through grain subsidies provided by the Poor Laws. Smith was an advocate for the new industrial order and opposed to regulations that represented interventions by the state in the economic process, including the free exchange of labor, capital (including land), and of goods.

Smith argued that if individuals, unimpeded by privilege and state regulation, could act in accordance with their self-interest, markets could be trusted to allocate resources equitably in the form of wages, rents, and profits. This, for Smith, was the key to progress, economic growth, and national prosperity (Smith 1974). On the other hand, he was not entirely indifferent to the dislocations generated by markets and he assigned the civil state the duties of administering justice and providing security, including the protection of private property and correction of severe inequalities created by market forces.

Smith's civilized society, like Ferguson's civil society, Kant's *bürgerliche Gesellschaft*, and Montesquieu's *l'état civil*, represented positive images of civil society, which, in the course of encounters with hitherto unknown regions of Asia and the Americas during the seventeenth and eighteenth centuries, became part of Europe's definition of itself as the domain of the 'civilized' (Kocka 2000). The discourse of civilized Europe created its opposite in images of an uncivilized non-Europe, notably the East, which was perceived as the domain of despotism *pace* Montesquieu, of chafing regulations over economic activity *pace* Smith, and of the absence of private property *pace* Marx. Following the last decade of the eighteenth century, with the onset of revolutionary upheavals against absolutist regimes, the terms *bürgerliche Gesellschaft* and civil society were increasingly equated with bourgeois society and acquired a negative connotation as 'the reign of dissoluteness, misery and physical and ethical corruption' (Hegel 1967, Kocka 2000). The European idea of itself as 'civilized' was effectively distanced from understandings of civil society as bourgeois society . No matter how 'barbaric' Europe became in Europe, it would remain 'civilized' vis-à-vis non-Europe, its optimistic image of itself having been fixed in a vocabulary of domination.

Hegel (1770–1831) responded to this situation with the idea of the universal state that was to end the separation between the political and the economic. He subscribed to the political economists' notion of civil society as a nexus of economic interests and relationships that continuously reproduce themselves. He did not, however, share Smith's utopian faith in the mechanistic operations of the market. Revolutionary upheavals had revealed a discrepancy between models of an orderly economy subject to universal laws of nature and the chaotic reality of contemporary society. Conceptualizations of civil society as an autonomous domain capable of generating order and progress through its own dynamics now appeared dubious.

Hegel's civil society was not the civilized society of Smith, but bourgeois society which manifested extremes of wealth and poverty that threatened to destroy the productivity of individuals pursuing their self-interest (Reidel 1984). The destructive potential of civil society, he felt, could be restrained through redirecting individual self-interest by administrative means, including justice, police, and moral measures.

Marx (1818–1883) subscribed to Hegel's critique of political economy and his conception of civil society as an arena of self-interest and divisiveness with a potential for self-destruction (Bottomore 1983). But unlike Hegel, Marx was not concerned with the containment of bourgeois society's destructive potential. Instead he focused on the revolutionary transformation of economic relations in civil society, which he believed was possible through the mobilization of conflicts between different interest groups. For Marx, the state, distinct from civil society or *bürgerliche Gesellschaft*, is largely limited to formalistic and negative activities since in his view, civil society both preceded and determined the state. Civil society required no regulation but was ruled through the contingencies of class struggle.

4. Civil Society and the Liberal State

Political and academic debates of the nineteenth century addressed the question of how to achieve social stability in market societies where the logic of economic activity overrode moral and political concerns regarding equity. Civil, or liberal, society was perceived as a domain shaped by or reformed through the practices of a central state representing the public interest. This constitutes a major departure from eighteenth century thinking. On the one hand, civil society, its actors, its activities, and the economic relations that characterized it, were viewed as inseparable from their legal and administrative formulations. This resulted in the creation of legal entities including trade unions, corporations, and family, and of voluntary and charitable associations, which, while autonomous from the state, remained within the bounds of its administrative–legal vision (Neocleous 1996). On the other hand, the state, 'objectified' in its administrative and legal practices, was understood to stand apart from civil society and to mediate divergent interests and needs.

From the perspective of the English utilitarians, most notably Jeremy Bentham (1748–1832), and of the German social economist Lorenz von Stein (1815–1890), civil society, or the market economy of the political economists, needed to be actively constituted. It was not enough simply to remove the obstacles of obsolete privilege and restrictive policies of mercantilism of the *ancien régime*. For Bentham, the new economic order required positive state intervention, and government was inseparable from an 'art of directing the national industry to purposes to which it may be directed with greatest advantage.' Von Stein, agreeing with Hegel's perception of civil society as a site of conflict and oppression, identified the 'social problem' as the main obstacle to economic progress. Progress required a market economy, or civil society; however, the injustices and inequalities it generated must be ameliorated through the state's administrative activity. The creation of social citizenship and the active participation of the citizen in the state's decision making were central to this process (Pasquino 1981). Thus, civil society represented an outcome of collective struggles and clashes among divergent interests that were mediated through the state's administrative practices, so that for von Stein, as for Bentham, the state was not the *Rechtsstaat* ('rule of law' state) that stood outside civil society, but the *Sozialstaat* (social state) representing a process whereby society was continuously formed and reformed.

Not all observers of nineteenth century Europe saw the centralized administrative state as the liberator of civil society. Conservative Romantics rejected the notion of the state or politics shaping society and assigned self-policing power to society and church. Alexis de Tocqueville (1805–1859) in his *De la democratie en Amerique* (1835–1840) saw the real danger to modern society in the new despotism of the all-pervasive state administrations rather than in class conflicts. Anticipating his fellow Frenchman, Michel Foucault (1926–84), de Tocqueville pointed to the administrative suffocation of civil society as evidenced in the state's monopoly of public education, health care, and social services to the poor and unemployed that subjected all aspects of citizens' lives to state scrutiny (Keane 1988). De Tocqueville stressed the importance of voluntary associations in placing checks on administrative despotism by providing the services that people expected from government, thus pre-empting government intervention in civil society. Recalling the ideas of the Scottish Enlightenment, de Tocqueville saw voluntary associations as generating and expressing community civic values.

Civil society all but disappeared from political and academic debates in the late nineteenth century and the period following World War I, a time of slackening economic growth, rising working-class activism, imperial rivalries, and wars, which witnessed the displacement of political power from state administrations to major organized groups in society. The European welfare states, heirs to the liberal states, increasingly became sites for centralized and bureaucratic bargaining among political parties, labor unions, and business cartels vying for economic and political power and blurring the distinction between state and civil society, public and private (Maier 1987).

Antonio Gramsci (1891–1937), leader of the Italian Communist Party, represented a notable exception to the lack of interest in the notion of civil society in the post-World War I era. He reformulated the Marxist–Hegelian understanding of civil society in terms of the corporatist Zeitgeist of Italy in the 1920s. For Gramsci, civil society was not merely the sphere of individual needs but also of organizations where the hegemony of the ruling class and consent to that rule was negotiated. In this sense, civil society comprised not only all material (economic) but also political and cultural relations. While Marx insisted on separation between state and society, Gramsci held the two were interrelated. Hegemony, which was basic to Gramsci's notion of civil society, presupposed 'interpretations' of the economic structure; that is, the political and cultural mediation of different interests (Bobbio 1988). In that sense, Gramsci had a kindred spirit in Hegel rather than Marx.

5. Late Twentieth Century Understandings of Civil Society

After World War II, the European political and economic order focused politics on the state with welfare states subsuming civil society to state regulation. As in the late nineteenth century and the post-World War I era, economic growth, distribution, and security represented the core themes of politics. However, now these themes were generalized to regions outside Western Europe, including Eastern Europe and post-colonial societies in the so-called Third World. The different regions varied greatly in terms of how growth was attained and sustained, and the efficiency of realizing their economic and social goals. They also varied in terms of their political institutions and modes of resolution of social and political conflict. From the late 1940s to the mid-1970s sustained economic growth in the capitalist economies of Western Europe and North America made challenges to economic redistribution less urgent, and the internationalization of the security problem (e.g., the formation of NATO) led to a consensus regarding security. Capital transfers from a booming United States economy, including military and economic aid, helped to sustain the developing states of the Third World, while the statist socialist regimes relied on the ideological and political disciplining of their populations to generate surpluses centrally distributed by the state.

During the 1950s and 1960s, some social scientists in Western Europe and the United States predicted that under conditions of long-term growth, political problems could be largely transformed into noncontroversial administrative routines resolvable by experts. Socialist regimes perfected this functionalist perception of politics where government excluded all competing forms of political organization, including political parties, trade unions, and collective bargaining. However, this perspective precluded discussion of civil society. Socialist ideologues identified civil society with bourgeois society and held it was superseded by the advent of socialism.

In the mid-1970s, slowing economic growth in the advanced capitalist societies resulted in constraints on the ability of the state to tax business and distribute assistance to the working class in the form of social welfare benefits. The fiscal crisis was further aggravated by rising costs of welfare provisions, and called into question the validity of ideas that subsumed society to state regulation. Since the 1970s, social and political debates have largely focused on the critique of social statism and the differentiation of civil society from the state.

From a neo-conservative stance, over-politicization of the state and the fusion of political and non-political spheres of social life has eroded political authority, weakened governability, and destroyed the autonomy and authority of non-political spheres, including family, religion, and the market. Neo-conservatives proposed the boundaries between state and civil society be redrawn. Civil society, in opposition to the state, represented the depoliticized sphere of market activity and all else, including religion and family. It should be reintegrated through a cultural model that cohered the exchange activities of self-interested individuals. This is a model of the self-regulating civil society of non-profit voluntary associations reminiscent of the eighteenth-century

Scottish Enlightenment. During the 1980s and 1990s, social science paradigms based on individual self-interest and rational expectations, presented models for social programming that would render a politicized civil society unnecessary. In the neoconservative view, the state is a lean structure characterized by effective authoritarian forms of action, approximated by its Thatcherite interpretation in 1980s Britain.

For proponents of the voluntary social movements paradigm, statism had disastrous environmental, political, and social consequences. They proposed an understanding of civil society as an autonomous politicized sphere independent of regulation and constraint by bureaucratic political institutions. Social movements such as the environmentalist, anti-nuclear, and women's and gay movements of the 1970s, were politically motivated by concerns about the environment and quality of life, and issues of equity, authenticity, and participation. Their agendas required 'spontaneous' organization and not 'officially' sanctioned institutions of political parties and trade unions. Here, civil society referred to an intermediate institutional space between private (personal) and public (the object of official political institutions and actors).

Jurgen Habermas' (1929) idea of public sphere parallels this understanding of civil society in the context of ideas and communications; it includes the organization of civic or bourgeois opinion as represented by associations and media. Public sphere is a space where communication about collective values takes place. In advanced capitalist societies where political and economic domains merge, the state became a major actor in the market economy and thus no longer able to advance the common good. This, for Habermas, signals the legitimation crisis of advanced capitalist societies and raises the issue of the formulation of a public discourse outside of the spheres of market economy and the welfare state and in doing so, (in the spirit of Kant) subjects both spheres to the critical scrutiny of communicative rationality.

In the mid-1970s, the crises in socialist states, initially Poland, provoked Central and Eastern European intellectuals to address the issue of the politicization of civil society. After failed revolutions in Hungary (1956) and Czechoslovakia (1968), the new evolutionism of Adam Michnik and Jacek Kuron proposed the bottom-up construction of a civil society to repulse state intrusions into social life. For other dissident socialist intellectuals in the region, most notably Vaclav Havel, civil society represented the domain of anti-politics; it was a vision of society not simply independent of the state but opposed to it.

During the 1980s and 1990s in many parts of the world, including the former socialist states of Central and Eastern Europe, the expansion of the market system, including privatization programs, led to two divergent perceptions of civil society. The first represented civil society in opposition to global capitalism

and to the state as the implementor of market reforms. The second emphasizes the centrality in civil society of religion, family, and voluntary associations for generating moral, economic, and cognitive norms.

See also: Civic Culture; Civil Society/Public Sphere, History of the Concept; Communication and Democracy; Democracy: Normative Theory; Democratic Theory; Hegel, Georg Wilhelm Friedrich (1770–1831); Hobbes, Thomas (1588–1679); Kant, Immanuel (1724–1804); Liberalism: Historical Aspects; Montesquieu, Charles, the Second Baron of (1689–1755); Participation: Political; Smith, Adam (1723–90)

Bibliography

Aristotle 1965 In: Barker E (ed.) *The Politics*. Oxford University Press, New York

Bobbio N 1988 Gramsci and the concept of civil society. In: Keane J (ed.) *Civil Society and the State: New European Perspectives*. Verso, London

Bottomore T (ed.) 1983 *Civil Society. A Dictionary of Marxist Thought*. Blackwell, Oxford, UK

Calhoun C (ed.) 1992 *Habermas and the Public Sphere*. MIT Press, Cambridge, MA

Cicero 1988 *The Republic*. Cambridge University Press, Cambridge, UK

Cohen J L, Arato A 1992 *Civil Society and Political Theory*. MIT Press, Cambridge, MA

Donzelot J 1984 *L'Invention du social*. Fayard, Paris

Ehrenberg John 1999 *Civil Society: The Critical History of an Idea*. New York University Press, New York

Ellis E 2000 Immanuel Kant's two theories of civil society. In: Trentmann F (ed.) *Paradoxes of Civil Society: New Perspectives on Modern German and British History*. Bergham, New York

Gierke O 1958 *Political Theories of the Middle Age*. Beacon, Boston

Ferguson A 1995 *An Essay on the History of Civil Society*. Transaction, New Brunswick, NJ

Havel V 1988 Anti-political politics. In: Keane J (ed.) *Civil Society and the State: New European Perspectives*. Verso, London

Hegel G W 1967 (Knox T M, English translation) *The Philosophy of Right*. Oxford University Press, London

Hobbes T 1949 (Lamprecht S P, English translation) *De Cive or The Citizen*. Greenwood, New York

Jacob C M 1991 The enlightenment redefined: The formation of modern civil society. *Social Research* **58**(2): 475–95

Kant I 1963 What is enlightenment? Beck L W (ed.) *On History*. The Bobbs-Merrill Company, Indianapolis, IN

Keane J (ed.) 1988 *Civil Society and the State: New European Perspectives*. Verso, London

Kocka J 2000 Zivilgesellschaft als historisches Problem und Versprechen. In: Hildermeier M, Kocka J, Conrad C (eds.) *Europäische Zivilgesellschaft in Ost und West: Begriff, Geschichte, Chancen*. Campus Verlag, Frankfurt/Main, Germany

Maier C (ed.) 1987 *Changing Boundaries of the Political: Essays on the Evolving Balance between State and Society. Public and Private in Europe*. Cambridge University Press, Cambridge, UK

Neocleous M 1996 *Administering Civil Society: Towards a Theory of State Power.* MacMillan, London

Offe C 1987 Challenging the boundaries of institutional politics: Social movements since the 1960s. In: Maier C (ed.) *Changing Boundaries of the Political: Essays on the Evolving Balance Between State and Society, Public and Private in Europe.* Cambridge University Press, Cambridge, UK

Pasquino P 1981 Introduction to Lorenz von Stein. *Economy and Society* **10**(1): 1–6

Reidel M 1984 *Between Tradition and Evolution: The Hegelian Transformation of Political Philosophy.* Cambridge University Press, Cambridge, UK

Richter M 1998 Montesquieu and the concept of civil society. *The European Legacy* **3**(66): 33 41

Rosanvallon P 1988 The decline of social visibility. In: Keane J (ed.) *Civil Society and the State: New European Perspectives.* Verso, London

Smith A 1974 *The Wealth of Nations.* Penguin, Harmondsworth, UK

Trentmann F (ed.) 2000 *Paradoxes of Civil Society: New Perspectives on Modern German and British History.* Bergham, New York

Tribe K 1988 *Governing Economy: The Reformation of German Economic Discourse, 1750–1840.* Cambridge University Press, Cambridge, UK

H. Islamoglu

Civil Society/Public Sphere: History of the Concept

The closely related concepts of civil society and public sphere developed in the early modern era to refer to capacities for social self-organization and influence over the state. Civil society usually refers to the institutions and relationships that organize social life at a level between the state and the family. Public sphere is one of several linked terms (including 'public space,' simply 'public,' and the German *Öffentlichkeit*, or publicness) that denote an institutional setting distinguished by openness of communication and a focus on the public good rather than simply compromises among private goods. Located in civil society, communication in the public sphere may address the state or may seek to influence civil society and even private life directly. Key questions concern the extent to which it will be guided by critical reason, and how boundaries between public and private are mediated.

1. Civil Society and Self-organization

The distinction of 'civil society' from the state took its modern form in the seventeenth and eighteenth centuries. Prior to this separation, political and social realms were seldom clearly distinguished. When they were, the social was exemplified by the family and often subordinated as the realm of necessity or mere reproduction to the broader public character and possibilities for active creation that lay in the state.

The Greek conception of the *polis*, for example, usually referred to both, but when a distinction was made, it clearly favored the state.

Roman law contributed the idea of *civitas* and a stronger sense of relations among persons that were neither narrowly familial nor specifically about constituting the political society through the state. Medieval political and legal theory developed this theme, especially in relation to the freedoms claimed by medieval cities but also in relation to the Church. Some strands juxtaposed the notion of legitimacy ascending from 'the people' to the eventually dominant idea of divine right of kings, with its notion of legitimacy descending from God. Also influential was the distinction of civil from criminal law (in which the former governs relations formed voluntarily among individuals and the latter the claims of the whole society against malefactors). Nonetheless, it was only in the course of early modern reflection on the sources of social order that civil society came to be seen as a distinct sphere.

A crucial step in this process was the 'affirmation of ordinary life' (Taylor 1989). Whereas the Greek philosophers had treated the private realm—including economic activity—as clearly inferior to the public realm associated with affairs of state, many moderns placed a new positive value on family and economic pursuits. They argued that both privacy and civil society needed to be defended against encroachments by the state. In this context, it was also possible to conceive of a public sphere that was not coterminous with the state but rather located in civil society and based on its voluntary relations. In this communicative space citizens could address each other openly, and in ways that both established common notions of the public good and influenced the state.

Social contract and natural law theories—especially as joined in the work of John Locke—contributed to this shift by suggesting ways in which the creation of society conceptually preceded the creation of government. From this it was only a short step to say that the legitimacy of government depended on its serving the needs of civil society (or of 'the people'). Thomas Paine and other advocates of freedom from unjust rule advanced an image of the freedoms of Englishmen which was influential not only in England and America, but in France, notably in Montesquieu's account of the 'spirit' of laws which combined an appreciation of English division of powers with an older tradition of republican (and aristocratic) virtue. From Rousseau through Tocqueville, Comte, and Durkheim, this French tradition developed an ever-stronger account of the autonomy of the social (resisting not only the claims of the state but the Cartesian postulate of the primacy of the individual subject).

A crucial innovation was to understand society as at least potentially self-organizing rather than organized only by rulers. If there was a single pivotal intellectual source for this, it lay with the Scottish moralists. In

Adam Smith's (1776) notion of the invisible hand, the market exemplified this self-organizing capacity but did not exhaust it. In his *Essay on the History of Civil Society* (1767), Adam Ferguson presented human history as a series of social transformations leading to modern society. This prompted Hegel (1821) to treat civil society as a field in which the universal and particular contended; their reconciliation depended on the state. The idea of civil society also shaped classical political economy and ideas of social evolution, and informed Marx's account of the stages of historical development as combinations of productive capacity and (conflict-ridden) social relations. Marx also challenged the notion that markets were neutrally self-organizing, emphasizing the role of historical accumulations of power.

Though the actual analyses differed, what had been established was the notion of society as a distinct object of analysis, not reducible to either state or individual. People formed society impersonally as actors in markets, more personally as parties to contracts. The idea of civil society hearkened back to the sort of social life that emerged among the free citizens of medieval cities because this was largely self-regulated—as distinct from direct rule by ecclesiastical or military authorities. It also suggested 'civility' in interpersonal relations. This meant not just good manners, but a normative order facilitating amicable or at least reliable and nonthreatening relationships among strangers and in general all those who were not bound together by deep private relations like kinship. Equally important, the idea of civil society included—in some versions—the notion that communication among members might be the basis for self-conscious decisions about how to pursue the common good. This notion is basic to the modern idea of public sphere.

2. The Idea of a Public Sphere

Rousseau (1762) famously sought to understand how social unity could result from free will rather than external constraint. This depended, he argued, on transcending the particular wills of many people with a general will that was universal. Kant admired Rousseau's pursuit of unity in freedom as distinct from mere social instinct (as in Aristotle's notion of a political animal) or imposition of divine authority. He relied implicitly on the idea of a collective conversation through which individual citizens reach common understandings. Likewise the development of representative institutions in eighteenth century England informed and anchored a public discourse directed at bringing the will and wisdom of citizens to bear on affairs of state. Finally, the idea of the people as acting subject came to the fore in the American and French revolutions. The idea of a public sphere anchored democratic and republican thought in the capacity of citizens in civil society to achieve unity and freedom through their discourse with each other.

Kant, like many eighteenth-century philosophers, lacked a strong notion of the social. This Hegel (1821) supplied, rejecting social contract theory because even in Rousseau's notion of a general will it suggested that the union achieved in the state depended not on its own absolute universality but on a development out of individual wills. Nationalism also shaped ideas of society and political community in holistic ways well matched to unitary states (Calhoun 1999). Marx's (1843, 1927) critique of politics based on bourgeois individual rights further challenged the adequacy of civil society as a realm of freedom and unity. Where Hegel thought that the state in itself might overcome the tension between necessity and freedom and the clash of particular wills, Marx held that only a transformation of material conditions including the abolition of private property could make this possible. As a result, theories stressing stronger ideas of the social were apt to offer weaker notions of public life. The Marxist tradition denigrated 'mere democracy' as an inadequate means of achieving either freedom or unity.

The ideas of public sphere and civil society developed primarily in liberal theory. These were not always seen in the manner of Hegel as merely 'educative' on the way to a more perfect latter unity. Nor was political unity necessarily left to the workings of an invisible hand or other unchosen system, but freedom was treated commonly as a matter of individual rather than collective action. This accompanied the rise of relatively asocial understandings of the market (Polanyi 1944). In addition, the emerging notion of the public sphere was not clearly distinct from other usages of 'public.' State activity, for example, was sometimes described as public without regard to its relationship to democracy or its openness to the gaze or participation of citizens. This usage survives in reference to state-owned firms as 'public' regardless of the kind of state or the specifics of their operation.

More important was the overlapping concept of 'public opinion' (see *Public Opinion: Political Aspects*). The dominant eighteenth-century usage emphasized open expression and debate, contrasting free public opinion to absolutist repression. At the same time, it generally treated public opinion as a consensus formed on the basis of reasoned judgment. 'Opinion' was something less than knowledge, but especially where it had been tested in public discourse, it was not simply sentiment and it gained truth-value from reflexive examination. Various euphemisms like 'informed opinion' and 'responsible opinion,' however, reflected both a bias in favor of the opinions of elites and an anxiety about the possibly disruptive opinions of the masses. During the nineteenth century, this anxiety came increasingly to the fore. Tocqueville (1840) and Mill (1859), thus, both contrasted public opinion to reasoned knowledge; Mill especially worried about 'collective mediocrity' in which the opinion of debased masses would triumph over scientific reason. While advocates of the public sphere saw rational-critical discourse producing unity, critics saw mass opinion reflecting psychosocial pressures for conformity. Implicitly, they associated reason with individuals rather than any collective process. The distinction between 'public' and 'crowd' or 'mass' was lost in such views (Splichal 2000). Early positivist research into public opinion approached it as explicable on the basis of social psychology rather than as a species of reasoned argument. Toennies (1922) sought a way to discern when each approach ought to apply.

Conversely, in the late nineteenth and twentieth centuries, a new field of public opinion research developed that approached public opinion as an aggregation of individual opinions. The shift was based largely on the development of empirical polling methods. It brought a renewal of attention to differences within public opinion, and thus to the distinction between public and crowd (Blumer 1948, Key 1961). It also focused attention on patterns of communication among members of the public rather than the more generalized notions of imitation or emotional contagion. New media—first newspapers, and then broadcast—figured prominently in efforts to understand public communication. While Lippman (1960) and a variety of social psychologists worried that the new media would produce the descent to a lowest common denominator of public opinion that liberals had long feared, Dewey (1927) and other pragmatists defended the capacity for reason in large-scale communication. In this, they hearkened back to the eighteenth-century hopes of Kant and Rousseau.

Even before the apotheosis of the opinion poll, Cooley (1909) had argued emphatically that public opinion ought to be conceived as 'no mere aggregate of individual opinions, but a genuine social product, a result of communication and reciprocal influence.' A key question was whether this communication and reciprocal influence amounted to the exercise of reason. Peirce (1878) had argued that among scientists the formation of consensus on the basis of openness and debate was the best guarantee of truth. Could this view be extended into less specialized domains of public discourse? This has been an enduring focus for Jurgen Habermas, the most influential theorist of the public sphere.

3. Habermas

In the context of some cynicism about democratic institutions, Habermas (1962) set out to show the unrealized potential of the public sphere as a category of bourgeois society. He challenged most directly the tendencies in Marxism and critical theory to belittle democratic institutions—and also the collapsing of public into state characteristic not only of Hegel but of actually existing socialism. Habermas celebrated the emancipatory potential of a collective discourse about the nature of the public good and the directions of state action. This could be free insofar as it was rational—based on the success of argument and critique rather than the force of either status or coercion—and could achieve unity by disregarding particular interests—like particular statuses—in favor of the general good. The best version of the public sphere was based on 'a kind of social intercourse that, far from presupposing the equality of status, disregarded status altogether.' It worked by a 'mutual willingness to accept the given roles and simultaneously to suspend their reality' (Habermas 1962, p. 131).

The basic question guiding Habermas' exploration of the public sphere was: to what extent can the wills or opinions guiding political action be formed on the basis of rational-critical discourse? This is a salient issue primarily where economic and other differences give actors discordant identities and conflicting interests. For the most part, Habermas took it as given that the crucial differences among actors were those of class and largely political-economic status; in any case, he treated them as rooted in private life and brought from there to the public. He focused on how the nature, organization, and opportunities for discourse on politically significant topics might be structured so that class and status inequalities were not an insuperable barrier to political participation. The first issue, of course, was access to the discourse. This was not so simple as the mere willingness to listen to another's speech, but also involved matters like the distribution of the sorts of education that empowered speakers to present recognizably 'good' arguments. Beyond this, there was the importance of an ideological commitment to setting aside status differences in the temporary egalitarianism of an intellectual argument.

The public sphere joined civil society to the state by focusing on a notion of public good as distinct from private interest. It was however clearly rooted in civil society and indeed in the distinctive kind of privacy it allowed and valued.

The bourgeois public sphere may be conceived above all as the sphere of private people coming together as a public; they soon claimed the public sphere regulated from above against the public authorities themselves, to engage them in a debate over the general rules governing relations in the basically privatized but publicly relevant sphere of commodity exchange and social labor. The medium of this political confrontation was peculiar and without historical precedent: people's public use of their reason (Habermas 1962, p. 27).

This public use of reason depended on civil society. Businesses from newspapers to coffee shops, for example, provided settings for public debate. Social institutions (like private property) empowered individuals to participate independently in the public sphere;

forms of private life (notably that of the family) prepared individuals to act as autonomous, rational-critical subjects in the public sphere. But the eighteenth-century public sphere was also distinguished by its normative emphases on openness and rational political discourse. Habermas' concern focused on the way later social change brought these two dimensions into conflict with each other.

The idea of publicness as openness underwrote a progressive expansion of access to the public sphere. Property and other qualifications were eliminated and more and more people participated. The result was a decline in the quality of rational-critical discourse. As Habermas later summed up:

> Kant still counted on the transparency of a surveyable public sphere shaped by literary means and open to arguments and which is sustained by a public composed of a relatively small stratum of educated citizens. He could not foresee the structural transformation of this bourgeois public sphere into a semantically degenerated public sphere dominated by the electronic mass media and pervaded by images and virtual realities (Habermas 1998, p. 176).

While Habermas' account of the continuing value of the category of public sphere evoked by the eighteenth-century ideal set him apart from Horkheimer and Adorno (1944) and their pessimistic turn in critical theory, he largely incorporated their critique of 'mass society' as 'administered society' into his survey of twentieth-century developments and with it many of the fears of nineteenth-century liberals. He held that the public sphere was transformed not only by simple increase of numbers but by the success of various new powers at re-establishing in new form the power to 'manage' public opinion or steer it from above. Public relations agents and public opinion polls replaced rational-critical debate; electronic media allowed openness but not the give and take conversation of the eighteenth-century coffee houses. At the same time, rising corporate power and state penetration of civil society undermined the distinction of public and private, producing a 'refeudalization' of society.

4. Arendt

Hannah Arendt also focused on the problem of collapsing distinctions between public and private. Arendt emphasized the capacity of action in public to create the world that citizens share in common. The term 'public,' she wrote, 'signifies two closely interrelated but not altogether identical phenomena: It means, first, that everything that appears in public can be seen and heard by everybody and has the widest possible publicity. ... Second, the term "public" signifies the world itself, in so far as it is common to all of us and distinguished from our privately owned place in it' (Arendt 1958, pp. 50, 52). Public action, moreover, is the crucial terrain of the humanly created as distinct from the natural world, of appearance and memory, and of talk and recognition. Such action both requires and helps to constitute public spaces—spaces held in common among people within which they may present themselves in speech and recognize others. Public action is thus a realm of freedom from the necessity—notably of material reproduction—that dominates private life.

Arendt's usual term, 'public space,' leaves the 'shape' of public life more open than the phrase public sphere. Public action can create institutions, as in the founding of the American Republic, but as action it is unpredictable. Its publicness comes from its performance in a space between people, a space of appearances, but it is in the nature of public action to be always forming and reforming that space and arguably the people themselves. This conceptualization offers clear advantages for thinking about the place of plurality in the public sphere. As Arendt wrote of America, 'since the country is too big for all of us to come together and determine our fate, we need a number of public spaces within it' (1972, p. 232).

Arendt saw this plurality threatened not just by mass conformity but by the reduction of public concerns to material matters. A focus on sex as much as on the economy threatens the public–private distinction. It not only intrudes on intimacy and private life but impoverishes public discourse. Arendt (1951) saw this problem as basic to totalitarianism, which could allow citizens neither privacy nor free public discourse. Totalitarianism is distinguished from mere tyranny by the fact that it works directly on private life as well as limiting public life. This is not just a matter of contrasting intentions, but of distinctively modern capacity. Modern sociological conditions offer rulers the possibility to reach deeply into the family in particular and personal life in general, to engineer human life in ways never before imagined.

This potential for collapsing the public and private realms is linked to Arendt's unusually negative view of civil society. 'Society,' she writes, is 'that curious and somewhat hybrid realm which the modern age interjected between the older and more genuine realms of the public or political on one side and the private on the other' (1990, p. 122). Civil society is first and foremost a realm of freedom *from* politics. But public freedom is freedom *in* politics. This calls for action that creates new forms of life, rather than merely attempting to advance interests or accommodate to existing conditions. This distinguishes Arendt's view, and republicanism generally, from much liberal thought: 'Thus it has become almost axiomatic even in political theory to understand by political freedom not a political phenomenon, but on the contrary, the more or less free range of nonpolitical activities which a given body politic will permit and guarantee to those who constitute it' (1990, p. 30).

The founding of the United States was a favorite example of such action for Arendt. The American

Founders imagined and created a new kind of society, a new set of institutions. This relied on citizens' public commitments to each other rather than assumptions about human nature or mere external application of law. The Founders 'knew that whatever men might be in their singularity, they could bind themselves into a community which, even though it was composed of "sinners," need not necessarily reflect this "sinful" side of human nature' (1990, p. 174). Arendt's vision of public life as central to a moral community shares much with a republican tradition that deplores the modern decline of the public sphere—generally associated with the rise of particular interests at the expense of concern for the general good, the deterioration of rational public discourse about public affairs, or outright disengagement of citizens from politics (see *Public Sphere: Nineteenth- and Twentieth-century History*). Republican accounts of the public sphere place a strong emphasis on the moral obligations of the good citizen; recent scholarship has often questioned whether citizens lived up to significantly higher standards in earlier eras (Schudson 1998).

5. Differentiation in the Public Sphere and Civil Society

Habermas' account of the public sphere has been enduringly influential (see Calhoun 1992). Its delayed translation into English in 1989 ironically contributed to an invigorating new reading shaped by both the fall of communism and widespread projects of privatization in the West. Critics within communist societies had revived the notion of civil society (as distinct from simply 'society') in order to speak of the realm outside state control and its relative absence in communist societies. Likewise, transitions away from right-wing dictatorships were often treated in terms of a 'return of civil society' (Perez-Diaz 1993). In the US, the idea of civil society was linked not only to democracy but to reliance on voluntary organizations and philanthropy (Powell and Clemens 1998, Putnam 2000).

What civil society signifies in contemporary political analysis is the organization of social life on the basis of interpersonal relationships, group formation, and systems of exchange linking people beyond the range of intimate family relations and without reliance on direction by the government. As a number of scholars of Africa have noted, it incorporates an unfortunate understanding of family privacy that underestimates the positive and supraprivate social roles that African kin organizations can play (see essays in Harbeson et al. 1994). Even more basically, references to civil society often fail to distinguish adequately between systemic capitalist economic organization and much more voluntary creation of social organization through the formation of civic associations, interest groups, and the like—a distinction Habermas has

sought to stress. This has sometimes been a source of confusion in use of the public sphere concept to analyze distinctive institutional developments in diverse political and cultural settings (Calhoun 1993).

Civil society has been important to defenders of free market economics because it suggests the virtues of an economy in which participants' choices are regulated by their interests rather than their official statuses. In principle, such an economy is able to effectively produce and circulate goods on the basis of prices rather than government direction. Civil society has been equally important to advocates of democracy because it signifies the capacity of citizens to create amongst themselves the associations necessary to bring new issues to the public agenda, to defend both civil and human rights, and to provide for an effective collective voice in the political process. This involves both a free press and political mobilization on the basis of parties and interest groups (see Cohen and Arato 1992 for the most detailed review; also Chandhoke 1995, Seligman 1992, Alexander 1998, Keane 1999). Habermas (1992, p. 367) summarizes the recent usage: 'civil society is composed of those more or less spontaneously emergent associations, organizations, and movements that, attuned to how societal problems resonate in the private life spheres, distill and transmit such reactions in amplified form to the public sphere. The core of civil society comprises a network of associations that institutionalizes problem-solving discourses on questions of general interest inside the framework of organized public spheres.' Habermas' work more generally, however, reveals this to be a minimally theorized as well as optimistic usage. It highlights one aspect of civil society but does not make clear the most basic issue.

While part of the heritage of the idea of civil society has been the effort to organize society through public discourse, an equally influential part has been the claim to privacy, the right to be left alone, the opportunity to enter into social relations free from governance by the state or even the public. The idea of business corporations as autonomous creatures of private contract and private property thus reflects the heritage of civil society arguments as much as the idea of a public sphere in which citizens joined in rational-critical argument to determine the nature of their lives together. Civil society refers to the domains in which social life is self-organizing, that is, in which it is not subject to direction by the state. But this self-organization can be a matter of system function or of conscious collective choice through the public sphere (Calhoun 2001).

Habermas' account of the public sphere drew a variety of important critical responses. One of the first focused on the extent to which he focused on the bourgeois public sphere and correspondingly neglected nonbourgeois public life and failed to clarify some of the conditions built into the bourgeois ideal. Negt and Kluge (1972) responded with an account of the proletarian public sphere. Clearly, workers have at many points built their own institutions, media, and networks of communication, and entered into contention with bourgeois elites and other groups over the collective good. But if this is a discursive competition—that is, if workers and bourgeois argue over what constitutes the collective good rather than only fighting about it—then this implies an encompassing public sphere, albeit an internally differentiated one.

Nancy Fraser (1992) has influentially emphasized the importance of 'subaltern counterpublics' such as those framed by race, class, or gender. Some publics—even very partial ones—may claim to represent the whole; others oppose dominant discursive patterns and still others are neutral. Not all publics that are distinguished from the putative whole are subaltern. As Michael Warner (2001) has suggested, the deployment of claims on an unmarked public as *the* public sphere is also a strategy, generally a strategy of the powerful. Yet, it is important to keep in mind both that the existence of counterpublics as such presupposes a mutual engagement in some larger public sphere and that the segmentation of a distinct public from the unmarked larger public may be a result of exclusion, not choice. Feminist scholars especially have drawn attention to both the gender biases within family life that disempower women and the historically strong gender division between public and private realms on which male political freedom has generally rested (Elshtain 1993, Young 2000).

6. Conclusion

Theories of civil society focus on the capacity for self-organization of social relations, outside the control of the state and usually beyond the realm of family. The basic question posed by theories of the public sphere is to what extent collective discourse can determine the conditions of this social life. Contemporary research on civil society and the public sphere turns on the breadth of political participation, the extent to which capitalist markets limit other dimensions of self-organization in civil society, the existence of multiple or overlapping public spheres, the impact of new communications media, and the quality of rational-critical discourse and its relationship to culture-forming activities. These issues also inform discussions about international civil society and its public sphere.

The concepts of civil society and public sphere took on their primary modern dimensions in the late eighteenth and early nineteenth centuries in Western Europe and to a lesser extent the United States. They have become important in a variety of other settings, including in conceptualizing social autonomy in relationship to communist and authoritarian states. They inform democratic projects as well as academic research in a variety of settings and are in turn themselves informed by cultural creativity and social action.

See also: Citizenship and Public Policy; Civil Society, Concept and History of; Democracy; Individual/ Society: History of the Concept; Public Good, The: Cultural Concerns; Public Sphere: Nineteenth- and Twentieth-century History; State, History of

Bibliography

Alexander J C 1998 *Real Civil Societies: Dilemmas of Institutionalization*. Sage, Thousand Oaks, CA
Arendt H 1951 *The Origins of Totalitarianism*. Harcourt Brace, New York
Arendt H 1958 *The Human Condition*. University of Chicago Press, Chicago
Arendt H 1972 *Crises of the Republic*. Harcourt Brace Jovanovich, New York
Arendt H 1990 *On Revolution*. Penguin, New York
Blumer H 1948 Public opinion and public opinion polling. *American Sociological Review* 13: 542–54
Calhoun C (ed.) 1992 *Habermas and the Public Sphere*. MIT Press, Cambridge, MA
Calhoun C 1993 Civil society and public sphere. *Public Culture* 5: 267–80
Calhoun C 1999 Nationalism, political community, and the representation of society: Or, why feeling at home is not a substitute for public space. *European Journal of Social Theory* 2(2): 217–31
Calhoun C 2001 Constitutional patriotism and the public sphere: Interests, identity, and solidarity in the integration of Europe. In: De Greiff P, Cronin P (eds.) *Transnational Politics*. MIT Press, Cambridge, MA
Chandhoke N 1995 *State and Civil Society: Explorations in Political Theory*. Sage, New Delhi
Cohen J, Arato A 1992 *The Political Theory of Civil Society*. MIT Press, Cambridge, MA
Cooley C H 1909 *Social Organization: A Study of the Larger Mind*. Scribner, New York
Dewey J 1927 *The Public and its Problems*. Ohio State University Press, Columbus, OH
Elshtain J B 1993 *Private Man, Public Woman*. Princeton University Press, Princeton, NJ
Ferguson A 1767 *Essay on the History of Civil Society*. Transaction Publishers, New Brunswick, NJ
Fraser N 1992 Rethinking the public sphere: a contribution to the critique of actually existing democracy. In: Calhoun C (ed.) *Habermas and the Public Sphere*. MIT Press, Cambridge, MA, pp. 109–42
Habermas J 1962/1991 *The Structural Transformation of the Bourgeois Public Sphere: An Inquiry into a Category of Bourgeois Society* [trans. Burger T]. MIT Press, Cambridge, MA
Habermas J 1992 *Between Facts and Norms*. MIT Press, Cambridge, MA
Habermas J 1998 In: Cronin C, De Greiff P (eds.) *The Inclusion of the Other*. MIT Press, Cambridge, MA
Harbeson J W, Rothchild D, Chazan N (eds.) 1994 *Civil Society and the State*. Lynne Rienner, Boulder, CO
Horkheimer M, Adorno T W 1944/1972 *Dialectic of Enlightenment*. Herder and Herder, New York
Hegel G W F 1821 *The Philosophy of Right* [trans. Knox T M]
Keane J 1999 *Civil Society*. Stanford University Press, Stanford, CA
Key V O 1961 *Public Opinion and American Democracy*. Knopf, New York

Lippman W 1960 *Public Opinion*. Macmillan, New York

Marx K 1843/1975 On the Jewish question. *Marx–Engels Collected Works*. Lawrence and Wishart, London, Vol. 3, pp. 146–74

Marx K 1927/1975 Critique of Hegel's philosophy of law. *Marx–Engels Collected Work*. Lawrence and Wishart, London, Vol. 3, pp. 1–129

Mill J S 1859 *On Liberty*. Penguin, London

Negt O, Kluge A 1972/1993 *The Public Sphere and Experience*. University of Minnesota Press, Minneapolis, MN

Peirce C S 1878/1992 *The Essential Peirce: Selected Philosophical Writings, 1867–1893*. Indiana University Press, Bloomington, IN

Pérez-Díaz V M 1993 *The Return of Civil Society: The Emergence of Democratic Spain*. Harvard University Press, Cambridge, MA

Polanyi K 1944 *The Great Transformation: the Political and Economics Origins of Our Time*. Beacon, Boston

Powell W, Clemens E (eds.) 1998 *Private Action and the Public Good*. Yale University Press, New Haven, CT

Putnam R 2000 *Bowling Alone*. Simon and Schuster, New York

Rasmussen T 2000 *Social Theory and Communication Technology*. Ashgate, London

Rousseau J-J 1762 *The Social Contract*. Everyman Paperback Classics, London

Schudson M 1998 *The Good Citizen: A History of American Civic Life*. Free Press, New York

Seligman A 1992 *Civil Society*. Free Press, New York

Sennet R 1977 *The Fall of Public Man*. Knopf, New York

Smith A 1776 *On the Wealth of Nations*. Penguin, Harmondsworth, UK

Splichal S 2000 Defining public opinion in history. In: Hardt H, Splichal S (eds.) *Ferdinand Toennies on Public Opinion*. Rowman and Littlefield, London, pp. 11–48

Taylor C 1989 *Sources of the Self*. Harvard University Press, Cambridge, MA

Tocqueville A de 1840/1844/1961 *Democracy in America*. Schocken, New York, Vol. 2

Toennies F 1922/2000 *Kritik der öffentlichen Meinung*; selections translated. In: Hardt H, Splichal S (eds.) *Ferdinand Toennies on Public Opinion*. Rowman and Littlefield, London, pp. 117–210

Warner M 2001 *Public and Counterpublics*. Zone Books, Cambridge, MA

Young I M 2000 *Inclusion and Democracy*. Oxford University Press, Oxford, UK

C. Calhoun

Civilization, Concept and History of

The concept of civilization is inextricably connected with the conditions of its emergence, most notably with the rise of historical consciousness in Europe in the eighteenth and nineteenth centuries, as well as the globalisation of this form of historical understanding and correlative forms of intellectual practice. The concept is complex and imprecise in its definition, but ubiquitous in its uses, and inextricably imbricated with other categories by which historical materials are organized, such as culture, nation, and race. Apart from designating certain morphological features of human society, particularly with reference to urbanism and urbanity, civilization has been a schema for historical categorization and for the organization of historical materials. Here it has generally taken two forms, the universalist evolutionist, and the romantic particularist. The latter was tending to regain, in the ascendant context of identity politics, a certain hegemonic primacy worldwide at the close of the twentieth century. In all, the concept of civilization forms a crucial chapter in the conceptual, social, and political history of history; it, or its equivalents are presupposed, implicitly or explicitly, in the construal and writing of almost all histories.

1. Pre-History

1.1 The Past Continuous

The mental and social conditions for speaking about civilization in a manner recognizable in the year 2000 were not available before the middle of the eighteenth century. Hitherto, in Europe as elsewhere, large-scale and long-term historical phenomena, which later came to be designated as civilizations, had been categorized in a static manner that precluded the consciousness of directional or vectorial historicity as distinct from the mere register of vicarious change.

Hitherto, the succession of large-scale historical phenomena, such as Romanity or Islam, had been regarded (a) typologically, most specifically in the salvation-historical perspective of monotheistic religious discourse, in which successive events are taken for prefigurations and accomplishments of each other; (b) in terms of the regnal succession of world-empires; (c) in the genre of regnal succession, which started with the Babylonian king-lists and the earliest stages of Chinese historical writing, and culminated in medieval Arabic historical writing. Not even the schema of state cycles evolved by the celebrated Ibn Khaldun (d. 1406), where civilization ('umrân) was quasi-sociologically identified with various organizational forms of human habitation and sociality, could meaningfully escape from this finite repertoire of possible historical conceptions.

In the perspective of typology, the continuity of historical phenomena was expressed in the repetition of prophecies successively reaffirming divine intent and inaugurating a final form of order whose *telos* would be the end of time. Thus the Jewish prophets repeat each other and are all figures for Abraham; Jesus is at once the repetition and termination of this unique cycle of terrestrial time and is prefigured in Jewish prophecies; Muhammad is the final accomplishment and the consummation of earlier prophetic revelations, prefigured in Jewish and Christian scriptures; his era inaugurates the consummation of time with the Apocalypse. The structure of time in the Talmud, in the Christian writings of Eusebius (d. 339), of Augustine's Spanish pupil Orosius (fl. 418), of Bernard de Clairvaux (1153), as in Muslim writings such as Muhammad's biography by Ibn Isḥâq (d. after 761) or the universal histories of Tabarî (d. 923) and Ibn Kathîr (d. 1373), is homologous.

All but Jewish typology is independent of ethnic origin or geographical location, and construes historically significant units as religious communities of ecumenical description. This yields the second mode of organizing historical phenomena, the regnal. Thus, the regnal categorization of long-term historical phenomena of broad extent was expressed in terms of the succession of four ecumenical world-empires, succeeding one another as the central actors in world history: the Assyrio-Babylonian, the Median-Persian, the Alexandrian-Macedonian, and the Roman. This perspective was shared by the Book of Daniel and by ecclesiastical works, especially Syrian and Byzantine apocalypses influenced by it, albeit with minor variations, as in Orosius' substitution of the Carthaginian world-empire for the Median-Persian. Muslim caliphs considered their own ecumenical world empire to be the fifth and final order of world history, a conception shared by Muslim apocalypticism and, with many complications and nuances, by universal histories written in Arabic, all of which regarded dynastic succession as both prophetic inheritance and as the renewal of ecumenical imperial ambition, transferred from one line to another.

Analogously, medieval Christian polities, Byzantine as well as Frankish, subscribed to the same theory of *translatio imperii* by regarding themselves as being in a direct line of typological continuity with Rome, variously through Byzantium, the 'New Rome,' or through the Holy Roman Empire. In both, Romanity was the worldly cement of Christianity. This was a conception developed by Eusebius for his contemporary overlord Constantine, and was to remain effective until the dawn of modern times. In all cases, the past was understood to have been completed at its inception, with subsequent polities re-enacting the foundational event.

Finally, mention must be made of the disjunction between these meta-historical and transcendental realms of typological continuity, and the all-too-human chaos of particular histories. No movement or qualitative change is discernible in the context of these, only the predictable succession of wars, rapine, pestilence, and occasionally of praiseworthy acts, without connection with an order of reality that might transcend the events themselves and render sense unto them.

1.2 The Past Estranged

Two roughly contemporary events heralded a new conception of history that made the modern notion of civilization conceivable. Both were specifically European, but their conceptual consequences were globalized in the course of the nineteenth and twentieth centuries. The first was Humanism, particularly in Italy, which for the first time broke the spell of Roman continuity by construing the immediate past as an age of darkness, and by confining Roman grandeur to the republican and early imperial ages. Thus Petrarch's (d. 1374) project of classicism counterposed to living tradition, Flavio Biondo's (d. 1463) anticipation of division of history into the classical, the medieval, and the modern, and Lorenzo Valla's (d. 1457) refutation of medieval documentary forgeries such as the *Donation Constantini*, based on an argument from anachronism: Together, these laid the ground for a view of history as the domain of change rather than of repetition.

Needless to say, the notion of *translatio imperii* was no longer tenable in this context. It is at this point that Humanism converged with the other event foundational of the modern historical consciousness, namely, the Reformation. Criticism of the Church by Wycliff (d. 1384) and Luther, and the historiographic expression of this anti-Traditionalist fundamentalism in John Foxe's *Acts and Monuments* (1563), were in crucial ways congruent in their conception of the past with Humanism. The identification of the Pope with the Antichrist, the designation of the greater part of the history of Christianity as a history of falsehood, and the devalorization of the immediate past as abiding Tradition and its construal as degeneration, also led to the rejection of the notion of *translatio imperii*, and the substitution of notions of Reformation and renovation to that of transfer in continuity.

Thus the ground was prepared for notions of rise, decline, and fall—most notably the decline and fall of Rome and the reclamation of Roman republicanist models in a spirit of revivalism—that were finally to mature in the eighteenth century, with Gibbon and Montesquieu among others, spurred along with the development and ultimately, in the late eighteenth and during the nineteenth centuries, the institutional transformation of philology and antiquarianism into history as a topic of research detached from rhetoric. This was far beyond the late flowering of medievalizing typology with Bossuet (d. 1704), and it made the past tangible in its having-been (*Vergangenheit*), most graphically represented in the establishment of museums during the eighteenth century in many European capital cities.

With Voltaire and other eighteenth-century figures like Volney and Chardin, another notion crucial for speaking of civilization was developed. The notion of qualitative societal and cultural difference (*les moeurs*)—quite apart from the dynastic and the religious—was now available in the eighteenth century, as Europe was accounting for her differences from the Ottomans, the Persians, the Chinese, and tribal peoples in the Americas.

Whereas previously the notion of historical senescence may have been used in a tragical and rhetorical sense, the new notion of decadence required the correlative notion of progress and amelioration. These notions are the very conditions of possibility for conceiving of civilization, as the accomplishment of a continuous line of historical development in which origins and beginnings are transcended rather than repeated.

2. Word and Concept

2.1 Civilization and Culture

The terms civilization and culture are intimately related in their reference, and in many instances are used almost interchangeably, according to national and linguistic conventions. Both are terms of ancient vintage which underwent a gradual lexical expansion until, in the eighteenth century, they came to designate meanings that are recognizable in 2001.

In the course of the seventeenth and eighteenth centuries, the meaning of the term culture expanded, in English, French, and German (as *Kultur*) from a medieval sense indicating the cultivation of land and of the religious cult, figuratively to denote the maintenance and cultivation of arts and letters. This figurative sense was further extended in the course of the eighteenth century to encompass the non-material life of human societies in a very broad sense encompassing the refinement of manners no less than intellectual and artistic accomplishments associated with the Enlightenment—the former sense still persists in terms such as *haute couture* and *Kulturbeutel* (vanity case).

The term was used both locally and in contrast to societies adjudged still living in a state of nature, though in German the accent had been on an aesthetic of the lofty and the sublime as distinct from the crassly material, in association with a correlative emphasis on cultivation, *Bildung*, both individual and collective. In this way, the term was opened up to impregnation by the emergent notion of progress, the progress of individual societies as of humanity in general regarded both as a process natural to human society and as a principle of normative ranking among societies.

Not dissimilarly, and in imitation of 'culture,' in the eighteenth century the term civilization underwent—most especially in France and somewhat later in England—a figurative expansion in its lexical reference from the Latin *civilis*, life under reputable forms of government, to the broader designation of order, civil, and governmental. This order befitted developed societies that might regard themselves as civilized in contradistinction to other, barbarian or savage, yet to be civilized societies. The contrastive connotations of 'civilization' were far more accentuated than those of 'culture,' which was more commonly used in Germany, a land then with little or no experience of the world outside Europe. 'Culture' also came to be used in France and more saliently in England, as in Germany, decidedly to signal social distance and social distinctions within particular countries.

In all cases, these two terms increasingly came to be associated with a developmental perspective on history: not only the linear and cumulative course traversed by historical phenomena in time, but also of languages, geological layers, plant and animal species, and human societies generally (and later, races), towards greater differentiation, complexity and accomplishment. Correlatively, the meanings conveyed by these terms were implied by other terms or by none at all, as for example with Rousseau and Voltaire.

The nineteenth century witnessed a complicated relationship between 'culture' and 'civilization' whose fields of connotation and denotation shade into each other in a manner that has not helped the distinctive clarity and definition of either. The crucial player here was Germany, where *Kultur* took a decidedly romantic-nationalist turn in the early nineteenth century, dwelling on national uniqueness and individuality, and buttressed by the emergence of *Kulturwissenschaft* as a discipline and by studies of folklore.

The further developments of this politico-cultural impulse towards the end of the nineteenth century led not only to the profuse discourses on decadence, *Entartung*, ('disnaturation') but to the extension to France of this particularitic understanding of culture—and of civilization—under the influence of de Joseph de Maistre and the Catholic Counter-Enlightenment. As a result of Franco-German conflicts and of the severe stresses within France, a battle was waged between the advocates of 'culture,' upholders of national particularism, and of 'civilization,' champions of Enlightenment universalism accused by their detractors of crass materialism, a battle that reached its apogee during the first World War in the polemics between Romain Rolland and Thomas Mann.

Yet 'civilization' itself had been increasingly more receptive to particularism and nationalism, most specifically in historical writing. Books on the civilization of France, Germany, Europe, Italy, and England, emerged from the second quarter of the nineteenth century, and in certain ways the very currency of the term made it open to divergent uses. Towards the end of that century, the term came to be used under the influence of the German notion of *Kultur*, a term often rendered as 'civilization' in French translations of German works. One additional but decisive factor was English anthropology, with the appearance in 1871 of Edward Tylor's *Primitive Culture* (1958), and the subsequent predominance of the term 'culture' to designate a condition, on a ladder leading from savagery to barbarism and finally to civilization, in Anglo-Saxon anthropology. With the discovery and mystique of classical Greece towards the end of the eighteenth century, of the unity of the 'West' from Greece, through Rome, on to the Romano-Germanic peoples in the Middle Ages, culminating in modern European civilization, was to become the *locus classicus* of this notion of civilization.

In the latter part of the nineteenth and throughout the twentieth century, both the terms and conceptions outlined were subsequently taken over and became crucial instruments of historical categorization in India, China, and the Arab countries and elsewhere. In Arabic *thaqafa*, an equivalent to the German *Bildung*, came to stand for culture, normally taken to designate intellectual and artistic life in a manner strongly elitist in character, and *hadara* was used for civilization, taken as a more general concept indicating the entire life of society including material life.

2.2 Continuities: Relativism

Linear developmentalism had, in general, underlain the entire body of diverse discourses on civilization and of its sister concept of culture. This developmentalism bifurcated along lines that may be characterized broadly as German and French in original inspiration.

Of the two, the former had been the more intimately associated with romantic national and, later, with civilizational particularism, producing a natural history of human groups regarded in analogy to organic species. These human groups were thus conceived as self-subsistent, continuous over time, largely impermeable, essentially intransitive, and according to many representatives of this view, almost congenitally given to conflict and war.

Originating in conservative reactions to the Enlightenment, with a strong anti-Gallic political impulse, this theory of historical and social development was associated with figures such as Johann Gottfried Herder in Germany and Edmund Burke in England, though it did have a strong representation in France among royalist, Catholic, and other anti-revolutionary (1789, 1848, 1871) currents represented by figures such as de Maistre, Gobineau, and Gustave Le Bon. The principal conceptual feature of this anti-mechanistic concept of history was insistence on individuality in the histories of different nations, races, and civilizations—terms often conflated in various combinations, in analogy with biological organisms, and perhaps best captured in the capacious semantic field of the German word *Volk*. In this sense, one may speak of continuity with pre-Enlightenment concepts of a social organism modeled upon the integrated somatic unity of the human body, as had been previously thought in medieval Arabic historico-political writings and in medieval European conceptions from the time of John of Salisbury (d. 1180). The fear of decline and decadence, conceived as a breakdown of a natural order, was the specific point at which continuity with medieval organismic concepts of the historico-political order made itself evident and conceptually formative. This was at a time when the idea of progress—and in contrast to it—had become a genuinely historical category, involving a consequential conception of change, of evolutionism, of the temporality specific to events (*Verzeitlichung*), and of a distanciation correct between human and natural histories.

The course of a particular history was seen to reside in a number of essential features, which Herder termed *Kräfte*, resulting in a history which, increasingly elevated and evolutive in the course of time as it may be, was still governed by principles which were, in essence, changeless, principles which imparted individuality upon these intransitive histories.

Whereas the Enlightenment provided, and the nineteenth century elaborated, a notion of genetic development along an axis of cumulative time to which civilizations and other historical masses are subject, the organismic, particularist notion conceived a civilization as bound to a self-enclosure inherent in its origins. Although this did not necessarily lead to an historical cyclism, it constituted its conceptual condition of possibility, and facilitated culturalist notions of nationalism that spoke in terms of 'revival.'

It was a cyclical notion of the history of cultural and civilizational circles, *Kulturkreise* according to Ernst Troeltsch (1920) which was made conceivable by the manifold discourses on decadence, malfunction, and historical pathology, notions which implicitly involve a measure against a more consummate state of organic health and well-being implicit in the foundations of each. It was the systematic elaboration of the decadence/normalcy structure that led to great schemas of world-history, divided into intransitive civilizations, of Oswald Spengler's *Untergang des Abendlandes* (Spengler 1922) and of the Spenglerian heresy represented by Arnold Toynbee's *A Study of History* (Toynbee 1934–1959).

Described by Claude Chaunu (1984 as 'a samsara of historical forms,' these vitalist theories of the rise and inevitable decline of civilizations constitute a naturalistic morphology of historical becoming. From this perspective, civilizations were seen as historical phenomena that are perpetually in conflict with one another, each endowed with a particular ethos or animating principle. Such were Spengler's (1922) Magian culture (the Perso-Islamic) and Promethean culture (the European). Such were also Toynbee's (1934–59) Syriac and other civilizations, though with this latter author the inner definition of civilizations was less clearly predetermined, and founded on a firmer and far more scrupulous empirical foundation than with Spengler. Nevertheless, Toynbee does characterize civilizations in terms of particularistic impulses, such as the aestheticism of Greek civilization, the religious spirit of the Indian, and the mechanistic ethos of the West. Each of these is an integrated pattern of daily life, on attitude towards the holy, a style of jurisprudence, a manner of government, an artistic style, and much more.

With both authors, the historical phenomena respectively designated as 'cultures' and 'societies,' obey an iron law of rise and decline, of glory and sensecent atrophy, the terminal phases of which Spengler, in keeping with German usage of the day, derisively termed 'civilization.' It is noteworthy that this morphology of historical masses, be they called civilizations, cultures or societies, that this monocausal description in terms of basic traits such as the Promethean or the aesthetic, was congruent with certain developments in anthropology, particularly in American anthropology in the first half of the twentieth century (Franz Boas, Alfred Kroeber, Ruth Benedict, and Edward Sapir) which identified separate societies according to self-consistent and intransitive personality profiles they ostensibly gave rise to. This had a decisive influence upon the introduction of organismic thinking into the human sciences in general. After a long period of disrepute, the 'culturalized' notions of human collectivities, of self-enclosure, of continuity, have come back to center stage at the close of the twentieth century, correlatively with the politics of identity worldwide.

The organismic and vitalist notion of civilization was, and still is, extremely effective in the writing of history and in the late twentieth century has had a certain political salience in terms of Samuel Huntington's 'war of civilizations' and the mirror-image riposte in terms of the 'dialogue of civilizations.' It denies the possibility of a general human history, which it regards, in the words of Ernst Troeltsch (1920), as being 'violently monistic,' and construes the task of a history of civilizations as separate histories of Europe, China, India, Islam, Byzantium, Russia, Latin, and Protestant Europe, and others, in various possible permutations and successions, as separate cultural and moral spheres which are merely contiguous in space. Correlatively, this constituted the conceptual armature of certain forms of violently particularistic history that was mirrored or endogenously paralleled, among others in India for instance (Savarkar 1969), or in the writings of radical Muslim ideologues.

2.3 Novelties: Universalism

The deficit in historicity evident in romantic and vitalist historism, with its emphasis on organic continuity, was to a great extent made up in the more consistently evolutionist accounts of historicism. It was this conception of history, at once evaluative, evolutive, and vectorial, which bore the burden of the universalist notion of civilization. Whereas in historism the bearers of civilization—or rather of 'culture'— were particular peoples or individual historical

itineraries, such as the West or Islam, the whole of humanity partook of the development of civilization which, in the historicist perspective was universal and continuous.

Several versions of this were in evidence, of which two are of particular note due to their wide conceptual incidence and to the social and political influence they exercised through worldwide social movements, both revolutionary and gradualist, inspired by the Enlightenment. According to this conception of a universal civilization, human societies pass through a uniform series of progressive developments which result in intellectual and moral elevation. They also result in superior social, economic, and political levels of development, marked by a higher and wider order of rationality, social differentiation, and control over nature whose instrument is science.

The more consistently universalist of these versions—exemplified, among others, by Jean Marquis de Condorcet, Auguste Comte, and Herbert Spencer, and in the evolutionist anthropology of Tylor (1958)—saw the whole of humanity as being predisposed to this upward movement. Nevertheless, according to this view some peoples may still subsist in a condition that others (Europe) had already surpassed, being still captive to superstition, to a weak organization of society and the economy, and to undeveloped political institutes (despotism, as in the case of Orientals, or otherwise various forms of acephalic organization, as is the case with primitive societies). The only caveat here is that many theorists of the evolution of human societies did not see human improvement as uniform in developed societies themselves, but that developed societies were not only internally differentiated in the levels of accomplishment attained by different social groups, but were also liable to fall far below the moral ideals that development makes possible. Nevertheless, much writing on the history of universal civilization, especially in countries influenced by Marxism, such as the Soviet Union or the People's Republic of China, saw the historical itineraries they led as crucial and exemplary steps in the development of humanity at large. In this way, the histories of Russia and China come to recuperate and tap world history at large by acting as the vanguard and exemplar of its future consummation.

Correlatively, the other conception of universalism, and this is one of profound conceptual and political importance, recognized the past contributions of various civilizations—the Mesopotamian, Egyptian, and Islamic, and in some instances the Indian and the Chinese as well—to the course of human civilization, which eventually lodged itself in Europe, defined as the abode of Romano–Germanic history, or even in small parts of Europe, such as France or Prussia. This writing of universal history, much in evidence in the plethoric literature of universal histories both popular and learned, was expressed in what is perhaps its most accomplished general formulation by Georg Hegel (1956) in the nineteenth century, and by Karl Jaspers (1949) in the twentieth—the latter is little-read today, but he is one who nevertheless captures this notion with special clarity.

Not infrequently, this second type of universalist history is allied to an important element derived from the romantic theory of the history of civilizations treated in Sect. 2.2, namely the presumption of very long-term individual continuity. Thus the point is habitually made, with varying shades of emphasis and nuance, that universal civilization made Europe its eventual home because some abiding characteristics possessed *ab initio* by 'the West,' such as rationality, the spirit of freedom, vigor and dynamism. This changeless West is counterposed to an eternal East, such as Mesopotamia, Egypt, and Islam which, their relative erstwhile merits apart, constitute, in a categorical degradation, a mere prehistory to fully developed civilization. East and West—not to speak of Islam, the name of a religion transmuted into an atopic location—are metageographical notions which do not allow, except with anachronistic violence, for projection into the antique and late antique worlds. However, this does not disturb the ideological coherence of this notion of civilization.

3. Beyond Totality

Writing about civilization according to the manners outlined contained both large-scale abstraction and a great deal of precise empirical historiography. Under the influence of Marxism, acknowledged as such as well as implicit, historical scholarship, and most specifically social and economic history in the traditions of Max Weber and of the Annales school, produced specifications regarding material and other aspects of civilization that allayed, to a considerable degree, the rhetorical force of thinking civilizations in terms of purely moral and ideological continuities, betokening exclusive socio-historical groups. The notion of a Judæo-Christian civilization, as distinct from textual typology within the Bible, is an excellent illustration of this, having been born and expanded in specific circumstances following the second World War.

In this way, civilizations for contemporary historical writing have come to comprise the total historical conditions that exist in a specific place and time: functional and organizational forms of the state, the *longue durée* of demographic, agricultural, economic, social, urban, ecological, climatic, and other forces underwritten by geographical structures and relations, and non-material culture, such as arts, letters, cognitive structures, and religions. The possibilities of a total history of a civilization is, it must be stressed, an expansion of a previous and more limited form of the cultural history of a particular epoch, exemplified by

Jakob Burckhardt's studies of Constantine and Renaissance Italy (Burckhardt 1955, Vols. 1 and 3).

As a result, since about 1950 it has become possible historically to specify the material elements that constitute the history of a civilization, however its temporal and geographical boundaries may be defined. Correlatively, it has become possible to conceive the specific differences between histories—China and Europe for instance, as in the work of Jacques Gernet (1988)—beyond a discourse on immobility and other immanent characteristics ascribed to this history or that, and to think of specificity in proper historical terms, such as the relative weight of various elements of the rural economy, the relation between state and the economy, the impact of metallurgy, and much more.

In this context, civilizational continuities came to be reconsidered in terms of historically determinant factors of a predominantly geographical nature, not so much in the spirit of geographical determinism as described by the German school of Friedrich Ratzel (1895), but with a greater degree of temporal specification, mediated by Lucien Febvre's (1925) consideration of historical geography and culminating in Fernand Braudel's study of the Mediterranean (1972–73). By the same token, it has become possible squarely to face the nominalist caution required in thinking about civilizations, and to think of their constitution, specification, and collapse in terms of the concrete historical investigation of demography, economy, and society without recourse to the metaphysical rhetoric of decline (Tainter 1988).

These specifications apart, it remains true that the construal of civilizational intransitivity, with Braudel as with others, still needs to resort to a new redaction of the rhetoric of permanence, most particularly with regard to non-material culture, now underscored and almost overdetermined by considerations of relief, soil, water supply, and means of transport—all of which are undeniable factors, albeit ones that modern technology and economy, most poignantly the postmodern economy, have rendered questionable.

Nevertheless, recent historical research has made it concretely possible to tap the genial formulations made by Marcel Mauss in 1930 (Febvre et al 1930) concerning the categorization of historical masses: of civilizations as a 'hyper-social systems of social systems,' as trans-societal and extra-national units of historical perception and categorization. These are conceived in opposition to specific social phenomena, and this conception of civilization valorises the distinction between civilization, society, and culture, freeing the first of the deterministic and totalizing rhetorical glosses of metahistory, and making possible a veritable history of civilizations. Civilization may thus be considered as at once a particular instance of historical becoming, and a specific ideological redaction of the past whose relation to historical reality can be questioned and rendered historical. In this context, the historian may also be able to valorise the extremely expansive *longue durée* implied by such theories as Dumézil's (1958) Indo-European tri-functionalism without recourse to organismic and totalizing figures of particularity and continuity (Le Goff 1965). An historian may be similarly able to valorise recent studies that stress the occurrence and communicability of recurrent phenomena of the imaginary order across vast spaces, cultures, histories, and times, as instanced by Carlo Ginzburg's study of the European witch-hunts (Ginzburg 1990). Finally, given the accent on complexity, one might be able to take the precise and nuanced study of levels and modes of socio-economic, political, institutional, ideational, and other instances of complexity—rather than criteria of simple continuity—as crucial to the delimitation of historical phenomena that one designates as 'civilizations.'

See also: Civilizational Analysis, History of; Civilizations; Cultural Landscape in Geography; Enlightenment; Global History: Universal and World; History: Overview; Modernization and Modernity in History; Societies, Types of; Society/People: History of the Concept; State and Society; State, History of; Time, Chronology, and Periodization in History

Bibliography

Auerbach E 1984 Figura. In: Auerbach E *Scenes from the Drama of European Literature*. University of Minnesota Press, MN

Bénéton P 1975 *Histoire des Mots: Culture et Civilisation*. Fondation Nationale des Sciences Politiques, Paris

Braudel F 1972–73 *The Mediterranean and the Mediterranean World in the Age of Philip II*. Reynolds S (trans). 2 Vols. Collins, London

Braudel F 1993 *Grammaire des Civilisations*. Flammarion, Paris

Burckhardt J 1955 *Renaissance Italy*. Gesemmete Werke. Vols 1 and 3. Schwab, Basle, Switzerland

Chaunu P 1981 *Histoire et Décadence*. Librairie academique Perrin, Paris

Collingwood R G 1946 *The Idea of History*. Clarendon Press, Oxford, UK

Dumézil G 1958 *L'idéologie Tripartie des Indo-Européens*. Collection Latours, Bruxelles, Belgium

Enciclopedia Einaudi 1977–84. G. Einaudi, Torino (s.v. 'Cultura materiale', 'Civiltà')

Encyclopædia Universalis 1968 Encyclopædia Universalis France, Paris (s.v. 'Civilization', 'Culture et civilization')

Encyclopedia of Religion and Ethics 1980 T and T Clark, Edinburgh, UK (s.v. 'Civilisation')

Febvre L 1925 *A Geographical Introduction to History*. Kegan Paul, Trench, Trubner & Co., London

Febvre L, Mauss M, Tonnelat E, Nicophoro A 1930 *Civilisation. Le Mot et l'Idée*. Renaissance du Livre, Paris (*Première Semaine internationale de Synthèse*, Fascicule 2)

Fehl E (ed.) 1971 *Chinese and World History*. The Chinese University of Hong Kong, Hong Kong

Gernet J 1988 *A History of Chinese Civilization*. Forster J R (trans.). Cambridge University Press, Cambridge, UK

Ginzburg C 1990 *Ecstasies: Deciphering the Witches' Sabbath*. Hutchinson, London

Hegel G W F 1956 *Philosophy of History*. Sibree G (trans.). Dover, New York

Herder J G von 1968 *Reflections on the Philosophy of History of Mankind*. Abridged by Manuel F. University of Chicago Press, Chicago and London

Herder J G von 1969 *JG Herder on Social and Political Culture*. F M Barnard (ed. and trans.). Cambridge University Press, Cambridge, UK

Ibn Khaldun 1958 *The Muqaddimah: An Introduction to History*. Rosenthal F (trans.). Pantheon Books, New York

Jaspers K 1949 *Vom Ursprung und Ziel der Geschichte*. Artemis Verlag, Zürich, Switzerland

Kemp A 1991 *The Estrangement of the Past. A Study in the Origin of Modern Historical Consciousness*. Oxford University Press, Oxford and New York

Kosellek R, Widmer P (eds.) 1980 *Niedergang. Studien zu einem geschichtlichen Thema*. Klett-Cotta, Stuttgart, Germany

Kroeber A L 1963 *An Anthropologist Looks at History*. University of California Press, Berkeley and Los Angeles

Kroeber A L, Kluckhohn C 1952 *Culture: A Critical Review of Concepts and Definitions*. The Peabody Museum, Cambridge, MA

Le Goff J 1965 *La Civilisation au l'occident médiéval*. Arthaud, Paris

Lewis M W, Wigen K E 1997 *The Myth of Continents. A Critique of Metageography*. University of California Press, Berkeley and Los Angeles

Marrou H I 1938 Culture, civilization, décadence. *Revue de Synthèse*, **December**: 133

Ratzel F 1895 *Anthropogeographische Beitrage*. Duncker und Humblot, Leipzig, Germany

Rüsen J, Gottlob M, Mittag A (eds.) 1998 *Die Vielfalt der Kulturen. Erinnerung, Geschichte, Identität, 4*. Suhrkamp, Frankfurt am Main, Germany

Savarkar V D 1969 *Hindutva: Who is a Hindu?* 5th edn. Veer Savarkar Parakashan, Bombay, India

Schlanger J E 1971 *Les Métaphores de l'Organisme*. Vrin, Paris

Spengler O 1922 *Der Untergang des Abendlandes*. 2 Vols. W. Braumüller, Vienna and Leipzig

Tainter J A (ed.) 1988 *The Collapse of Complex Societies*. Cambridge University Press, Cambridge, UK

Toynbee A 1934–1959 *A Study of History*. 12 Vols. Oxford University Press, London

Troeltsch E 1920 Der Aufbau der europäischen Kulturgeschichte. *Schmollers Jahrbuch für Gesetzgebung, Verwaltung, und Volkswirtschaft im Deutschen Reiche* **44**(3): 1–48

Tylor E B 1958 *Primitive Culture*. 2 Vols. Harper, New York

Zureiq K 1969 *Nahnu wa't-tarikh*. Dar al- Ilm lil-Malayin, Beirut, Lebanon

A. Al-Azmeh

Civilizational Analysis, History of

The term 'civilizational analysis' is used here to describe a whole cluster of traditions, rather than a specific theoretical perspective. The shared theme is a plurality of fundamental and comprehensive socio-cultural patterns, seen as sufficiently different from each other to justify the idea of civilizations in the plural, and in contradistinction to civilization in the singular. This is the conceptual framework preferred by some of the most seminal theorists in the field. This is predominant in contemporary debates, although authors who opted for a different terminology must be included in the present survey.

1. Origins and Directions of Civilizational Analysis

1.1 General Characteristics

In the context of a broader history of social thought, the civilizational approach emerges as a counterpoint and a potential corrective to mainstream modes of theorizing. It is only in the most recent phase that one can speak of progress towards it becoming a fully-fledged alternative. The most obvious contrast has to do with visions of history: civilizational lines of interpretation stress the plurality of historical trajectories and contest the claims of general evolutionistic theories. For the same reason, the emphasis on original and mutually irreducible cultural configurations runs counter to functionalist postulates of universal constraints or imperatives. This need not mean an outright rejection of any common frame of reference, but its explanatory scope is at best limited.

Civilizational analysis deals with units of larger dimensions and longer duration than the single societies that they encompass, and this focus of interest leads it to question the self-contained image of society (and the underlying fixation on the nation state) that has been central to the sociological tradition. The large-scale and long-term patterns in question can be conceptualized in various ways, and different approaches may be reflected in more or less developed typologies of civilizational formations. In some cases, the organic metaphors commonly linked to functionalist images of society reappear on the civilizational level, but they should not be mistaken for a defining characteristic of civilizational thought.

If civilizational analysis is defined in these broad terms, it does not emphasize any particular type of intercivilizational relations at the expense of others. The historical experience to be analyzed includes closures, encounters, and conflicts. In different situations, some of these patterns of interaction become more salient. Different theoretical approaches may entail correspondingly selective views of the inter-civilizational field. For example, debates on this topic have been marked by a disproportionate emphasis on civilizational conflict.

Finally, the civilizational perspective may serve to highlight macrohistorical continuities as well as major ruptures. Overall, contemporary historians have been more sensitive to civilizations as phenomena of the *longue durée* (Braudel is the prime example), but comparative sociologists (such as S. N. Eisenstadt) have been no less interested in the civilizational dynamics set in motion by major cultural break-throughs.

1.2 Early Developments and Nineteenth-century Reversals

The explicit idea of civilizations in the plural seems to have grown out of the same historical developments as that of civilization in the singular (Starobinski 1983), although it took longer for the plural to be codified for official usage. Both are eighteenth-century responses to internal transformations of the West as well as to encounters with non-Western societies and traditions. However, the pluralistic view was much less clearly articulated and became more marginal as the new phase of Western expansion from the early nineteenth century onwards seemed to herald a triumph of civilization in the singular.

In retrospect, elements or anticipations of civilizational analysis can be found in the writings of earlier authors. Giambattista Vico's *New Science* (definitive Italian edition, 1744; for an English translation, see Vico 1968) is perhaps the most frequently invoked example. Those who regard Vico as a pioneer stress his interest in 'the *differences* as well as the similarities in the patterns and paces of social and cultural processes and structures *across histories*' (Nelson 1976, p. 875). But it can be objected that the latent civilizational perspective remains subordinate to an exclusive focus on European cycles of rise and decline, seen against the background of Greek, Roman, and Jewish sources. The most systematic recent interpretation of Vico's work (Lilla 1993) suggests that the whole comparative inquiry is only a sideline to a traditionalist critique of modernity.

Another ambiguous precursor is Montesquieu, whose *Spirit of the Laws* (first published, 1748; for an English translation, see Montesquieu 1989) linked the analysis of legal and political regimes to 'customs' and drew on new knowledge of Asian civilizations (especially China). But the project as a whole is still centered on the traditional problematic of political philosophy and its implications for a reformist response to absolutism.

Eighteenth-century encounters with Asia were widely and variously reflected in European thought and literature. The attitude of the educated public was less prejudiced than it later became, and the 'intuition about the equal value of cultures,' which Charles Taylor (1990) has identified as a persistent but often subordinate theme in Western thought, was more in evidence. A shift to markedly more Eurocentric approaches took place around 1800 (Osterhammel 1998). The potential openings to civilizational analysis, which we can attribute to the Enlightenment in retrospect, were thus blocked by contrary trends before they could translate into more lasting results.

If some progress was made towards the articulation of a more pluralistic approach, it was more directly linked to the concept of culture than to the ideas of civilizations in the plural. In Herder's *Ideas for a Philosophy of the History of Mankind* (first published, 1784–91; for an English translation, see Herder 1968), there is no reference to cultures in the plural, and culture in the singular remains closely associated with progress and enlightenment. But the emphasis on the singularity of each people gives a pluralizing twist to the model. Cultural particularities are, however, thematized in a way which proved much more important to the history of nationalist thought than for the civilizational approach to human diversity.

The mainstream of nineteenth-century social thought was uncongenial to civilizational analysis. This was the case for the theories drawing on the legacy of German idealism as well as the positivistic conceptions of general social evolution, reinforced by (but not derived from) the Darwinian discovery of biological evolution. The Marxist tradition may be seen as a meeting ground for ideas from these two sources. On both sides, a unilinear vision of history and a universalistic model of development set strict limits to the recognition of cultural plurality.

Contrary to some recent suggestions, it does not seem justified to include Hegel among the pioneers of civilizational analysis. His plurality of collective spirits is only a derivative aspect of the progress of the world spirit throughout universal history, although he undeniably made a certain effort to grasp the individuality of the cultures (including China and India) that he consigned to lower levels of the unfolding design. Similarly, Marx's scattered comments on the Asiatic world and its deviation from the Western pattern of development do not go beyond a general contrast between progress and stagnation (explained in terms of fundamental economic structures). But his well-known analysis of India under British rule reflects some interest in the characteristics of a markedly alien civilization.

2. The Classics of Civilizational Analysis: Sociologists and Metahistorians

Major contributions to civilizational analysis—on theoretical as well as substantive levels—were made during the most formative period of modern sociological thought (roughly between 1890 and 1920). But the new perspectives were not developed to the same degree as the ideas that became more central to sociological theory. In the absence of systematic sociological inquiry, the comparative study of civilizations was pursued along very different lines by writers who defied the conventional academic division of labor.

2.1 Durkheim, Mauss, Weber: The Sociological Discovery of Civilizations

A clearly defined sociological concept of civilizations in the plural appears for the first time in a short text by Durkheim and Mauss, little noticed at the time and long neglected by the most influential interpreters of the Durkheimian tradition, but more recently rediscovered by theorists who have tried to reactivate the civilizational perspective. The *Note on the notion of civilization* was first published in 1913 (for an English translation with a commentary by Benjamin Nelson, see Durkheim and Mauss 1971) and is obviously related to arguments developed in other writings during the last phase of Durkheim's work, such as the *Elementary Forms of the Religious Life*. The common theme is a perceived need to go beyond the concept of society formulated in earlier works (now seen as too close to the idea of a given system of structures and functions) and to explore various ways of doing so.

The particular insight provided by the notion of civilizations in the plural has to do with large-scale units and long-term processes which encompass multiple societies. Civilizations 'reach beyond the national territory' and 'develop over periods of time that exceed the history of a single society'; they constitute 'a moral milieu encompassing a certain number of nations' or 'a plurality of interrelated political bodies acting upon one another' (Durkheim and Mauss 1971, pp. 810–11). The emphasis is on the cultural unity of civilizational complexes ('moral milieu' is obviously to be understood in a broad sense), and political plurality appears as a normal rather than a problematic condition. But there is no *a priori* classification of unifying and fragmenting factors: Durkheim and Mauss call for a comparative study of the civilizational potential inherent in various categories of social phenomena: 'the unequal coefficient of expansion and internationalization (Durkheim and Mauss 1971, p. 811). Although the connection is never made explicit, this variety can also be seen as a matter of the forms and degrees of social creativity, and thus related to a theme which figures prominently in other texts.

Mauss returned to the problematic of civilizations in a later debate with Lucien Febvre and others. A specific civilization is, as he put it, a 'family of societies' or a 'hyper-social system of social systems' (Mauss 1930, p. 89; the term 'system' is evidently not used in a very rigid sense). He proposed a more advanced conceptual framework than in the earlier text: the elements of civilizations—the unequally unified ideas, practices, and products characteristic of a civilizational complex—are distinguished from their forms, i.e., the patterns that grow out of complex combinations of such elements. In addition, the comparative study of civilizations would deal with the characteristics of the areas or regions over which they expand, as well as the interconnections of the societies that belong to them. With regard to the last point,

Mauss adds a passing but potentially far-reaching comment: societies may 'singularize' themselves and enhance their individual features against a broader civilizational background. The varying outcomes and possible implications of such processes are also a matter for comparative analysis.

Mauss went on to draw an important theoretical conclusion. The plurality of civilizations is the most striking case of a characteristic common to all forms of social life: their arbitrariness, or—in other words—the formative role of collective choices embodied in more or less coherent patterns (Mauss 1930, p. 97). Once again, the civilizational perspective brings out the theme of social creativity.

Mauss seemed to have thought of this interpretive model as equally applicable to 'primitive' and 'civilized' societies (if anything, the anthropologists had been quicker to recognize civilizational phenomena than the sociologists). However, it is clearly more attuned to the latter case (the reference to 'families of societies' with shared cultural horizons and historical traditions is easier to understand in that context). The idea of civilizations in the plural is thus reconnected to civilization in the singular, and the prime objects of comparative analysis would be the advanced civilizational complexes (Hochkulturen) whose dynamics have shaped the course of world history. Neither Durkheim nor Mauss made any significant moves in that direction, and later attempts linked to the Durkheim school (especially Marcel Granet's work on China) did not do much to concretize the theoretical project outlined above.

The most important substantive contribution of classical sociology is to be found in Max Weber's analyses of the contrasts between patterns of development in Western and non-Western civilizational settings. But the absence of explicit conceptual foundations and the lack of a clearly defined research program made it difficult to distinguish the civilizational perspective from more narrowly focused parts of Weber's work. The idea of culture as a distinctive way of lending meaning and significance to the world—outlined in Weber's earlier methodological writings—is never put to systematic or comparative use. Although the major civilizational studies variously refer to 'cultural centers,' 'cultural areas,' and 'cultural worlds,' cultural patterns and contexts are never theorized as such.

The resultant ambiguity of Weber's argument is reflected in later controversies around his work. Forms of rationality and dynamics of rationalization were the main foci of his comparative analyses, and he repeatedly stressed that they were always embedded in specific settings. But when it comes to details, the constitutive frameworks—from overall civilizational configurations to specific sociocultural spheres that crystallize within them in varying ways—are overshadowed by a seemingly uniform—but unequally developed—rationality in progress. Those who set out

to reconstruct Weber's problematic have therefore been tempted to ground it in more or less differentiated universal models of rationality, rather than to start with a plurality of cultural patterns and their formative imprints on civilizational complexes.

The civilizational aspect of Weber's project neither was given from the outset nor equally present in all parts of his work. His original and most abiding concern was the combination of multiple and successive developments which had set the Western trajectory apart from all others. The interest in other civilizations developed in this connection and did not lead to totalizing interpretations of non-Western traditions in their own terms or attempts to reorient the comparative strategy from their points of view. None of Weber's comparative studies aspires to do what Louis Dumont later proposed to do through a new interpretation of India. On the other hand, closer consideration of non-Western cases raises questions which go beyond the initial issues, reveals new interconnections and opens up new perspectives on the Western experience.

This shift towards a more comprehensive framework was still in progress in Weber's last writings, but the results varied—both in kind and in degree—from case to case. Weber's most extensive work on the ancient world focuses on socioeconomic structures. The analysis of ancient Judaism is primarily concerned with a religious breakthrough and its long-term rationalizing potential. The studies of China and India (Weber 1920–21, pp. 1–2) deal most extensively with complex and long-term interrelations of cultural traditions and institutional contexts, and are therefore closest to the model of civilizational analysis as defined by Durkheim and Mauss.

2.2 The Other Tradition: from Spengler to Toynbee and Beyond

As shown above, the sociological classics left civilizational analysis in a very inconclusive and fragmentary state: there was no connection between the Durkheimian sketch of a theoretical framework and the Weberian exploration of historical testing grounds, and neither of the two overtures was followed by further work. For several decades after Weber's death, the idea of a comparative study of civilizations was mainly associated with metahistorical projects of the kind exemplified by Oswald Spengler's *Decline of the West* (1923) (for an English translation, see Spengler 1926–28) and Arnold Toynbee's *Study of History* (Toynbee 1934–61). Among later attempts to deal with questions raised by Spengler and Toynbee, Franz Borkenau's posthumously published fragments (Borkenau 1981) deserve special mention.

In general terms, this tradition should be given credit for preserving the insight that the dynamics of world history involve units of greater size and longer duration than the single (or artificially singled-out) societies more familiar to mainstream scholarship, and that the patterns of formation, flowering and decline of such macro units call for closer examination. Moreover, analyses in this vein have sometimes thrown new light on inter-civilizational relations, despite a tendency to stress the separate and self-contained history of each civilizational domain. Spengler's notion of 'pseudomorphosis' is a case in point. It refers to the impact of dominant cultures in latent decline on those emerging within their orbit; the original example was the transformation of the Near East in the shadow of the Roman Empire, culminating in the rise of Islam, but plausible attempts have been made to generalize the concept.

On the other hand, the Spengler–Toynbee tradition has been beset by major problems. Apart from a general tendency to indulge in speculation far beyond the limits of historical evidence, more specific weaknesses are inherent in the overall pattern. Spengler, Toynbee, and those who followed their lead were —notwithstanding differences in emphasis—inclined to exaggerate the cultural or societal closure of civilizational units. Nevertheless, at the same time, they took a cross-civilizational identity of developmental patterns for granted: a uniform, more or less consistently cyclical model was applied across otherwise rigid boundaries.

When it came to concrete analysis and demarcation of civilizational domains, this line of thought led to a dilemma. If the self-contained units in question are defined based on unique cultural features, claims to cross-cultural understanding and theorizing are thereby undermined. To avoid this self-defeating turn, exemplified by Spengler's work, Toynbee shifted the focus towards civilizations as 'societies,' distinct and durable frameworks of interaction, but found it very difficult to specify the characteristics of a civilizational society. At an advanced stage of his project, he sought to defuse the problem by relegating civilizations to the prehistory of universal religions.

3. The Renaissance of Civilizational Analysis

Since the 1970s, several developments have led to a revival of interest in civilizational analysis. The plurality of civilizations has resurfaced as a key theme in the work of prominent historians (Braudel 1994). Projects drawing on anthropological and sociological traditions have moved towards a civilizational perspective; here Louis Dumont's work on India is of particular importance (Dumont 1967). Occasional attempts have been made to bring the problematic legacy of Spengler and Toynbee into the orbit of a historical sociology of civilizations. Various approaches to a shared problematic are represented in the International Society for the Comparative Study of Civilizations, which publishes *Comparative Civilizations Review*. However, when it comes to innovative theoretical conceptions, two projects seem to deserve a somewhat more detailed account.

3.1 Benjamin Nelson: Orientations and Encounters

Benjamin Nelson's programmatic outline of a civilizational theory, presented in a series of essays (Nelson 1981) but never developed in a systematic fashion, is inseparable from a reinterpretation of Max Weber's work. As Nelson argued (in the 1960s and 1970s, when more restrictive readings of Weber dominated the field), the agenda most succinctly summarized in the 'Author's Introduction' to the *Protestant Ethic*, centered on the comparative study of civilizational patterns and their historical trajectories. At the same time, Nelson went beyond Weber in thematizing the cultural cores of civilizational complexes. The different clusters of cultural orientations, also equated with 'structures of consciousness,' gave rise to correspondingly different frameworks for the rationality of conduct, social coexistence, and reflexive thought. Nelson took a particular interest in the rationalizing efforts which led to the overcoming of traditional dualisms, such as those of the religious and the mundane life or the insider and the alien, and this enabled him to reinterpret the triangular comparison of China, India, and the West in more focused terms than Weber had done.

But the emphasis on breakthroughs to more inclusive and interactive forms of social life did not lead Nelson to neglect the other side of civilizational dynamics: some of his essays stress the productive potential of internal conflicts at the level of the most basic cultural premises (he refers to them as 'civil wars within the structures of consciousness'). His favorite example was the highly articulate tension between faith and reason in the course of the eleventh- and twelfth-century transformation of Western Christendom.

This crucial phase of European history, much more important for Nelson's genealogy of modernity than it had been for Weber, also exemplifies the decisive role of intercivilizational encounters: the interaction with the Byzantine and Islamic worlds had an epoch making impact on Western ways of life and thought, not least through an unprecedented revival of interest in classical sources. Nelson discussed other encounters, such as the contacts between China and the West, and although his treatment of this problem was in some ways inconclusive, he did more than anybody else to integrate it into the domain of civilizational theory.

3.2 S. N. Eisenstadt: Breakthroughs and Dynamics

In contemporary social theory, S. N. Eisenstadt's work stands out as the most sustained exploration of civilizational themes. His interest in this field grew out of several research projects, but they converged in a critique of the conventional distinction between tradition and modernity. The diversity of modern societies could not be explained without reference to the ongoing formative role of traditions, and the most important factors of that kind have to do with enduring civilizational legacies. A comparative study of empires, designed to distinguish their complex social and political structures from stereotypes of traditional society, raised questions about civilizational backgrounds and their influence on imperial formations. Most importantly, a comparative analysis of modern revolutions (Eisenstadt 1978) took an explicitly civilizational turn: the 'great revolutions' that had come to be seen as paradigms of radical change were based on a more fundamental cultural shift which opened the constitutive visions of social order to dissent, protest, and innovation. The revolutionary cultural foundations of modernity mark it as a new civilization.

After discovering the civilizational dimension from these different angles, Eisenstadt's next step was a closer examination of the historical cases that seemed to have brought it to the fore in the most revealing way. The epoch already described by some earlier authors as an 'Axial Age,' covering a few centuries around the middle of the last millennium BC, was—as Eisenstadt argued—the prime example of a civilizational breakthrough. In some major cultural centers (ancient Greece, ancient Israel, India, and China), radical changes to cultural ontologies gave rise to new images of social order: ideas of a fundamental contrast between transcendental and mundane realities, unknown to more archaic cultures, translated into orderbuilding visions and strategies.

Nevertheless, the expanded scope for imagination, in the interpretive as well as the institutional domain, was also conducive to higher levels of interpretive conflict and ideological rivalry; the elites and coalitions that mobilized the new cultural resources had to confront more or less structured currents of heterodoxy and dissent. Eisenstadt's analyses have highlighted the variety and dynamism of social formations that develop within this framework, although the Axial constellation—defined in the most general sense —seems to have a uniform structure (for a theoretical discussion, accompanied by case studies of major civilizations, see Eisenstadt 1986). Among the offshoots of the Axial transformation, European civilization—shaped by recurrent combinations of diverse sources—became the main center of another civilizational mutation: the transition to modernity. But other civilizational backgrounds left their traces on the specific patterns of modernity that emerged within their orbit.

Both the analysis of Axial civilizations and the general interpretive framework growing out of it are still in progress. The results so far achieved suggest that this is a particularly promising line of inquiry.

4. Alternative Views

Among the few constructive responses to the metahistorical tradition discussed in Sect. 2.2, Jaroslav Krejci's work is noteworthy for its scope and ambition (Krejci 1982, 1993). The starting point is a critique of inconsistencies and loose ends in Toynbee's theory. In particular, the incomplete analysis of creative elites as civilization builders and the unclear status of universal religions as supracivilizational units are singled out for reconsideration from a more sociological angle. As Krejci sees it, 'protagonist groups and changing relationships between them (such as the shifting balance between Brahmins and kshatryas in India) play a key role in the construction of civilizations.' But they operate through specific core institutions (empires, states, churches, or ideological communities of various kinds) and are inspired by distinctive—more or less overtly religious—visions of the human condition. Religious traditions are thus reintegrated into the civilizational frame of reference, and their formative role is analyzed in terms of interpretive patterns that lend meaning to life and death.

Krejci distinguishes various 'paradigms of the human predicament,' ranging from the theocentric invented in ancient Mesopotamia to the utilitarian version of the anthropocentric in the modern West. This key to civilizational theory provides an alternative to the more common typologies of social formations, based on the division of labor, and to the a-theoretical use of geographic or historical criteria to demarcate civilizations. However, once the defining anthropological premises have been identified, geographical and historical perspectives can be given their due; it becomes possible to distinguish civilizational areas and sequences.

Arguments developed by Johann P. Arnason (1988, 2001) draw more directly on classical sources. The ideas put forward by Durkheim and Mauss on one side and Weber on the other are seen as incomplete insights to be synthesized, but this would require a closer connection between the Weberian theme of world interpretation and the Durkheimian notion of collective representations. The idea of imaginary significations—introduced by Cornelius Castoriadis—appears as the most suitable basis for such a rapprochement.

Imaginary significations are horizons of meaning, irreducible to experiential foundations as well as to functional constraints or rational principles. Specific clusters of such significations are at the core of different social worlds and structure their relations to nonsocial domains of reality as well as their internal forms of differentiation and integration. On this view, civilizational patterns can be analyzed as the most comprehensive and distinctive constellations of imaginary significations. In that capacity, they give rise to specific ways of being in the world and corresponding types of relationships between the main spheres of social life. These constitutive frameworks make it possible for civilizations to encompass groups of societies and maintain their identity throughout successive historical phases (for Durkheim and Mauss, integrative capacities manifested in space and time were the defining feature of civilizations). At the most visible level, civilizational formations take the shape of regional configurations, central to the agenda of comparative history.

To speak of civilizations in this sense is not to prejudge the levels of coherence, unity, and consistency. The approach just outlined can allow for significant variations in all these respects. In particular, it may be argued that some civilizations are more markedly characterized by conflicting cultural orientations than others (among the major non-Western traditions, interpretations of India have laid more emphasis on this theme than those of China). Comparative analyses of such differences—and other related ones—would be the most effective antidote against the identitarian and overintegrated models which continue to obstruct the progress of civilizational studies.

See also: Civilization, Concept and History of; Civilizations; Primitive Society; States and Civilizations, Archaeology of

Bibliography

Arnason J P 1988 Social theory and the concept of civilization. *Thesis Eleven* **20**: 87–105
Arnason J P *Civilization and Difference*. Sage, London
Borkenau F 1981 *End and Beginning: On the Generations of Cultures and the Origins of the West*. Columbia University Press, New York
Braudel F 1994 *A History of Civilizations*. Penguin, Harmondsworth, UK
Dumont L 1967 *Homo hierarchicus: essai sur le système des castes*. Gallimard, Paris
Durkheim E, Mauss M 1971 Note on the notion of civilization. *Social Research* **38**(4): 808–13
Eisenstadt S N 1978 *Revolution and the Transformation of Societies: A Comparative Study of Civilizations*. Free Press, New York
Eisenstadt S N (ed.) 1986 *The Origins and Diversity of Axial Civilizations*. SUNY Press, Albany, NY
Herder J G 1968 *Reflections on the Philosophy of the History of Mankind*. Chicago University Press, Chicago
Krejci J 1982 Civilization and religion. *Religion* **12**: 29–47
Krejci J 1993 *The Human Predicament: Its Changing Image: A Study in Comparative Religion and History*. St. Martin's Press, New York
Lilla M 1993 *G.B. Vico: The Making of an Anti-modern*. Harvard University Press, Cambridge, MA
Mauss M 1930 Les civilisations: Elements et formes. In: Febvre L et al. (eds.) *Civilisation: Le mot et l'idee*. La Renaissance du Livre, Paris
Montesquieu C 1989 *The Spirit of the Laws*. Cambridge University Press, Cambridge, UK
Nelson B 1976 Vico and comparative historical civilizational sociology. *Social Research* **43**(4): 874–81
Nelson B 1981 *On the Roads to Modernity: Conscience, Science and Civilizations*. Rowman and Littlefield, Totowa
Osterhammel J 1998 *Die Entzauberung Asiens: Europa und die asiatischen Reiche im 18*. Beck Verlag, München, Germany
Spengler O 1926–28 *The Decline of the West*. Knopf, New York, Vols. 1–2
Starobinski J 1983 Le mot 'civilisation.' *Le temps de la réflexion* **4**: 13–52
Taylor C 1990 Comparison, history, truth. In: Reynolds F, Tracey D (eds.) *Myth and Philosophy*. SUNY Press, Albany, NY
Toynbee A J 1934–61 *A Study of History*. Oxford University Press, Oxford, UK, Vols. 1–12
Vico G B 1968 *The New Science of Giambattista Vico*. Cornell University Press, Ithaca, NY
Weber M 1920–21 *Gesammelte Aufsätze zur Religionssoziologie*, Bd. 1–3. Mohr Verlag, Tübingen, Germany

J. P. Arnason

Civilizations

1. Introduction

The term 'civilization' has been used in modern social science and historical literature in several different ways. One such way, developed above all in Germany from about the end of the nineteenth century through the period up to World War II and perhaps best represented by scholars like Alfred Weber (and taken over to a certain extent in the English-speaking world by R. M. McIver), designated 'civilization'—as distinct from 'society' and above all from 'culture'—as encompassing above all the technological, material factors and to some extent organizational aspects of social life as against the deeper, more 'spiritual' cultural and aesthetic ones.

Another designation of the term, made famous by Norbert Elias in his *Über den Prozess der Zivilisation* (1939) focused on the 'socializing' process through which the image of the civilized person, as constructed in the courtly and also early bourgeois society in Europe, was promulgated and institutionalized. This designation of civilization was related to an earlier one rooted in the French Enlightenment, in which civilization was seen as the opposite of barbarism. However, in later works by Elias's followers, for instance Goudsblom, this view of civilization was extended to cover many other societies and historical periods, going back even to the impact of the presumably first domestication of fire.

The third and most extensive designation of civilization was promulgated by scholars such as Max Weber,

Emile Durkheim, Oswald Spengler, Pitirim Sorokin, Arnold Toynbee, A.L. Kroeber, Carroll Quigley, Cristopher Dawson, Fernand Braudel, William H. McNeill, Adda Bozeman, or Immanuel Wallerstein, and lately very forcefully by Samuel Huntington. However great the differences in perspective, methodology, focus, and concepts that pervade the works of these scholars, they share the use of the term civilizations as distinct societal-cultural units which share some very important, above all cultural, characteristics. Here we shall use the term civilization in a way very close to, but also distinct from, such a designation.

> Civilization as combination of ontological or cosmological visions, of conceptions of trans-mundane and mundane reality, with the definition, construction, and regulation of the major arenas of social life and interaction

The central analytical core of the term civilization as employed here—as distinct from such social formations as political regimes, different forms of political economy or collectivities like 'tribes,' ethnic groups or nations, and from religion or cultural traditions—is the combination of ontological or cosmological visions, of visions of trans-mundane and mundane reality, with the definition, construction, and regulation of the major arenas of social life and interaction.

The central core of civilizations is the symbolic and institutional inter-relation between the formulation, promulgation, articulation, and continuous reinterpretation of the basic ontological visions prevalent in a society, its basic ideological premises and core symbols on the one hand, and the definition and regulation of major arenas of institutional life on the other. Such definitions and regulations construct the broad contours, boundaries, and meanings of the major institutional formations and their legitimization, and greatly influence their organization and dynamics.

The impact of such ontological visions and premises on institutional formation is effected through the processes of interaction and control that develop in a society. Such processes of control—and the opposition to them—are not limited to the exercise of power in the 'narrow' political sense. Rather, they are activated by major elites in a society. The most important such elite groups are the political, the cultural, and the economic ones and those which construct the solidarity and collective images of the major groups, all of which have different cultural visions and represent different interests.

The structure of such elite groups is closely related, on the one hand, to the basic cultural orientations prevalent in a society; that is, different types of elite groups bear different orientations or visions. On the other hand, and in connection with the types of cultural orientations and their respective transform-ation into basic premises of the social order, these elite groups tend to exercise different modes of control over the allocation of basic resources.

Such combination of ontological visions and of structuration of institutional formations and collective identities constitutes an inherent component of the formation of any society, and is always closely interwoven with the more organizational aspect of any institutional formation—political, economic, or family and kinship.

The very implementation or institutionalization of such premises and the concomitant formation of institutional patterns through processes of control, symbolic and organizational alike, also generate tendencies to conflict and change. The crystallization of these potentialities of change usually takes place through the activities of secondary elite groups who attempt to mobilize various groups and resources to change aspects of the social order.

The full development of the distinct ideological and institutional dimensions, and of some awareness of their distinctiveness, has emerged in some very specific historical settings—namely, the so-called Axial Civilizations—even if some very important kernels thereof can be identified in some archaic civilizations such as those of ancient Egypt, Assyria, or Mesoamerica.

2. Axial Age Civilizations: the Reconstruction of the World and the Crystallization of Distinct Civilizational Complexes

By Axial Age civilizations (to use Karl Jaspers' nomenclature), we mean those civilizations that crystallized during the thousand years from 500 BC to the first century of the Christian era, within which new types of ontological visions, of conceptions of a basic tension between the transcendental and mundane orders, emerged and were institutionalized in many parts of the world. Examples of this include ancient Israel; later in Second-Commonwealth Judaism and Christianity; Ancient Greece; possibly Zoroastrianism in Iran; early imperial China; Hinduism and Buddhism; and, beyond the Axial Age proper, Islam.

The crystallization of these Axial civilizations constitutes a series of some of the greatest revolutionary breakthroughs in human history, which have shaped contours of human history in the last two to three millennia. The central aspect of these breakthroughs was the emergence and institutionalization of new ontological metaphysical conceptions of a chasm between the transcendental and mundane orders.

The development and institutionalization of these ontological conceptions entailed the perception of the given mundane order as incomplete, inferior—oftentimes as evil and polluted. It gave rise in all these civilizations to attempts to reconstruct the mundane world, from the human personality to the sociopolitical and economic order, according to the appropriate 'higher' transcendental vision.

The revolutionary conceptions, which first developed among small groups of autonomous, relatively unattached 'intellectuals' (a new social element at the time), were ultimately transformed into the basic 'hegemonic' premises of their respective civilizations, and were subsequently institutionalized. That is, they became the predominant orientations of both the ruling elites and of many secondary elites, fully embodied in the centers or subcenters of their respective societies.

One of the most important manifestations of such attempts in all these civilizations was the strong tendency to construct societal centers to serve as the major autonomous and symbolically distinct embodiments of respective ontological visions, as the major loci of the charismatic dimension of human existence. But at the same time the 'givenness' of the centers could not necessarily be taken for granted. The construction and characteristics of the center tended to become central issues under the gaze of the increasing reflexivity which focused above all on the relations between the transcendental and mundane orders. The political dimension of such reflexivity was rooted in the transformed conceptions of the political arena and of the accountability of rulers. The political order as one of the central loci of the mundane order had to be restructured according to the precepts of the transcendental visions. The rulers were usually held responsible for organizing the political order according to such precepts.

At the same time the nature of rulers became greatly transformed. The king-god, embodiment of the cosmic and earthly order alike, disappeared, and a secular even if often semisacral ruler appeared. Thus there emerged the conception of the accountability of rulers and community to a higher authority, God, Divine Law, or a metaphysical vision. Accordingly, the possibility of calling a ruler to judgement appeared. One such dramatic appearance of this conception occurred in ancient Israel, in the priestly and prophetic pronunciations. 'Secular' conceptions of such accountability to the community and its laws appeared in both the northern shores of the eastern Mediterranean, in ancient Greece, as well as in the Chinese conception of the Mandate of Heaven.

Concomitantly with the emergence of these conceptions of accountability of rulers, autonomous spheres of law began to develop as somewhat distinct from purely customary law. Such developments could also entail some beginnings of a conception of rights even if the scope of these spheres of law and rights varied greatly. Of special importance from the point of view of our analysis is the fact that one of the most important manifestations of the attempts to reconstruct the social order was the strong tendency to define certain collectivities and institutional arenas as

most appropriate for the implementation of transcendental visions.

3. Autonomous Elites as Bearers of Civilizational Visions: Change, Protest, and Heterodoxies

The development of new ontological metaphysical conceptions in the Axial civilization was closely connected with the emergence of a new type of elite, carriers of models of cultural and social order. These were often autonomous intellectuals, such as the ancient Israelite prophets and priests, and later on the Jewish sages, the Greek philosophers and sophists, the Chinese literati, the Hindu Brahmins, the Buddhist Sangha, the Islamic Ulema. Initial small nuclei of such groups of cultural elites developed the new ontologies, the new transcendental visions and conceptions, and were of crucial importance in the construction of the new 'civilizational' collectivities.

The new type of elites differed greatly from the ritual, magical, and sacral specialists in the pre-Axial Age civilizations. They were recruited and legitimized according to autonomous criteria, and were organized in settings distinct from those of the basic ascriptive political units of the society. The acquired a potentially countrywide and also trans-country status of their own. They also tended to become potentially independent of other categories of elites, social groups, and sectors.

At the same time a far-reaching transformation of other elites, such as political elites, took place. All these elites saw themselves not only as performing specific technical activities—be they those of scribes, ritual specialists, and the like—but also as potentially autonomous carriers of a distinct order related to the prevalent transcendental vision. They saw themselves as the autonomous articulators of the new order, and rival elites as both accountable to them and as essentially inferior. Moreover, each of these groups of elites was not homogeneous, and within each of them a multiplicity of secondary influentials developed.

These new groups became transformed into relatively autonomous partners in the major ruling coalitions. They also constituted the most active elements in the movements of protest and processes of change that developed in these societies and which evinced some very distinct characteristics at both symbolic and organizational levels.

First, there was a growing symbolic articulation and ideologization of the perennial themes of protest found in any human society, such as rebellion against the constraints of division of labor, authority, and hierarchy, and of the structuring of time dimension, the quest for solidarity and equality, and for overcoming human mortality.

Second, utopian orientations were incorporated into the rituals of rebellion and the double image of society. It was this incorporation that generated alternative conceptions of social order and new ways of bridging the distance between the existing and the 'true' resolution of the transcendental tension.

Third, new types of protest movements appeared. The most important were intellectual heterodoxies, sects, or movements which upheld the different conceptions of the resolution of the tension between the transcendental and the mundane order, and of the proper way to institutionalize such concepts. Since then, continuous confrontation between orthodoxy on the one hand, and schism and heterodoxy on the other, has been a crucial component in the history of mankind.

Fourth, and closely related to the former, was the possibility of the development of autonomous political movements and ideologies usually oriented against an existing political but possibly also religious center.

All these developments ushered into the arena of human history the possibility of the conscious ordering of society, and also the continuous tension that this possibility generated. The new dynamics of civilization transformed group conflicts into potential class and ideological conflicts, cult conflicts into struggles between the orthodox and the heterodox. Conflicts between tribes and societies could become missionary crusades. The zeal for reorganization informed by each civilization's transcendental vision made the entire world at least potentially subject to cultural-political reconstruction.

4. The Expansion of Axial Civilizations

Concomitantly with the institutionalization of Axial civilizations, a new type of intersocietal and intercivilizational world history emerged. To be sure, political and economic interconnection have existed between societies throughout human history. Some conceptions of a universal kingdom emerged in many post-Axial civilizations, like that of Genghis Khan, and many cultural interconnections developed between them, but only with the institutionalization of Axial civilizations did a more distinctive ideological and reflexive mode of expansion develop, with potentially strong semimissionary orientations.

It was indeed in close connection with the Axial civilizations' tendency to expansion that there developed new 'civilizational' collectivities, distinct from political and from 'primordial' ones, yet impinging on them, continuously challenging them, and provoking continual reconstruction of their respective collective identities. Such processes were effected by the interaction between the new autonomous cultural elites and the various carriers of solidarity and political elites of the different continually reconstructed 'local' and political communities.

In the continuous encounter of Axial civilizations with non-Axial or pre-Axial civilizations it was usually the Axial that came out victorious, without however necessarily obliterating many of the symbolic and institutional features of the non-Axial. The most important case of an encounter of non-Axial with Axial civilization in which the former absorbed the latter has been Japan.

5. The Multiplicity of Axial Civilizations and World Histories

The general tendency to reconstruct the world and to expand was common to all the post-Axial age civilizations. But the concrete implementation varied greatly. There emerged a multiplicity of different, divergent, yet mutually impinging world civilizations, each attempting to reconstruct the world in its own mode, and either to absorb the others or to segregate itself from them.

Two sets of conditions were of special importance in shaping these different modes of institutional creativity and expansion. One such set are variations in the basic cultural orientations. The other is the concrete structure of the social arenas in which these institutional tendencies can be played out.

Among the different cultural orientations the most important have been differences in the very definition of the tension between the transcendental and mundane orders and the modes of resolving this tension. There is the distinction between the definition of this tension in relatively secular terms (as in Confucianism and classical Chinese belief systems and, in a somewhat different way, in the Greek and Roman worlds) and those cases in which the tension was conceived in terms of a religious hiatus (as in the great monotheistic religions and Hinduism and Buddhism).

A second distinction is that between the monotheistic religions in which there was a concept of God standing outside the Universe and potentially guiding it, and those systems, like Hinduism and Buddhism, in which the transcendental, cosmic system was conceived in impersonal, almost metaphysical terms, and in a state of continuous existential tension with the mundane system. The 'secular' conception of this tension was connected, as in China and to some degree in the ancient world, with an almost wholly this-worldly conception of salvation.

A third major distinction refers to the focus of the resolution of the transcendental tensions. Here the contrast is between purely this-worldly, purely other-worldly, and mixed this- and other-worldly conceptions of salvation. The metaphysical nondeistic conception of this tension, as in Hinduism and Buddhism, tends towards an other-worldly conception of salvation, while the great monotheistic religions emphasize different combinations of this- and other-worldly conceptions of the transcendental vision.

Another set of cultural orientations which influenced the expansion of the various Axial civilizations was the extent to which the access to their centers and major attributes of the sacred within them was open to all members of the community or was mediated by specific institutions.

In addition, there are differences in the way in which relations between the attributes of cosmic and social order of civilizational collectivities and those of the major primordial ascriptive collectivities are conceived—the extent to which there is a disjunction between the two, to which these respective attributes are mutually relevant, each serving as a referent of the other.

But the concrete working out of all such tendencies depends on the second set of conditions—namely the arenas for their concretization. These conditions included, first, the respective concrete economic political-ecological settings, whether they were small or great societies, whether they were societies with continuous compact boundaries, or with cross-cutting and flexible ones. Second was the specific historical experience of these civilizations—especially in terms of mutual penetration, conquest, or colonization.

6. *Internal Transformation of the Axial Civilization: Secondary Breakthroughs and the Crystallization of Modern Civilization*

One of the most important aspects of the dynamics of Axial civilizations was the possibility of development within them of internal transformation, of what has been designated as secondary breakthroughs, the most important illustrations of which have been Second Temple Judaism and Christianity; later Islam, Buddhism, and to a lesser extent Neo-Confucianism, all of which developed out of heterodox potentialities inherent in the respective 'original' Axial civilizations.

But the most dramatic transformation from within one of the Axial civilizations has probably been that of modernity as it first emerged in Western Europe and as it expanded—encompassing most parts of the world, giving rise to development of multiple, continually changing modernities.

The cultural and political program of modernity constituted in many ways a sectarian heterodox breakthrough in the West and Central European Christian Axial civilization. Such transformation took place through the Reformation and in the Great Revolutions, in which there developed very strong emphasis on the bringing together of the City of God and the City of Man. It was in these revolutions that sectarian activities were taken out from marginal or segregated sectors of society and became interwoven not only with rebellions, popular uprisings, movements of protest but also with the political struggle at the center, and were transposed into the general political movements and the centers thereof.

It was above all in the French Revolution that the fully secular transformation of the sectarian antinomian orientation with strong Gnostic components

took place. It was epitomized in the Jacobin orientations which became a central component of the modern political program—to reappear yet again forcefully, as Alain Besançon has shown, in the Russian Revolution, and later in the Chinese and Vietnamese revolutions.

The strong sectarian roots of modernity and of the tensions between totalist Jacobin and pluralistic orientations which developed in Europe find very strong resonance in the utopian sectarian traditions of the Axial civilizations. It is also the religious roots of the modern political program that explain the specific modern characteristics of what may be seen as the most antimodern contemporary movements—namely the various fundamentalist movements which, contrary to the view which defines them as traditional, constitute a new type of Jacobin movement constructing tradition as a totalistic ideology.

7. *The Cultural and Political Program of Modernity: Premises and Antinomies*

The cultural and political program of modernity, as it crystallized first in Western Europe from around the seventeenth century, was rooted in the premises of the European civilization and European historical experience and bore these imprints—but at the same time it was presented and perceived as being of universal validity and bearing.

The radical innovation of this cultural program as it developed in Europe lay first in the 'naturalization' of man, society, and nature; second in the promulgation of the autonomy and potential supremacy of reason in the exploration and even shaping of the world; and third the emphasis on the autonomy of man, of his reason and/or will.

In connection with these orientations there took place far-reaching transformations of the symbolism and structure of modern political centers, as compared with their predecessors in Europe or with the centers of other civilizations. The crux of this transformation was first the charismatization of the political centers as the bearers of the transcendental vision of the cultural program of modernity; second the development of continual tendencies to permeation of the peripheries by the centers and of the impingement of the peripheries on the centers, of the concomitant blurring of the distinctions between center and periphery; and third was the incorporation of themes of protest as basic, legitimate components of the premises of these centers. These themes became central components of the project of emancipation—a project which sought to combine equality and freedom, justice and autonomy, solidarity and identity of modern political discourse and practice. The program also entailed a distinctive mode of the construction of the boundaries of collective identities. Such identities were not taken as preordained by some transcendental authority, but continually constructed and continually problematized, becoming also foci of political struggle by national and ethnic movements.

The civilization of modernity as it developed in the West was from its very beginning beset by internal contradictions, giving rise to critical discourse which focused on the tensions and contradictions between its premises, and between these premises and institutional development. The most important such tensions in this program were first that between totalizing and more pluralistic conceptions of its major components—of the very conception of reason and its place in human life and society, and of the construction of nature, of human society and its history; second, between reflexivity and active construction of nature and society; third, those between different evaluations of major dimensions of human experience; and fourth between control and autonomy.

These basic tensions, contradictions, and antinomies inherent in the cultural program of modernity were continually played and worked out in major institutional arenas.

8. Continually Changing Multiple Modernities

It was out of the conjunction of these cultural orientations with the development of market, commercial, and industrial economies; with the crystallization of a new political and state order; and with military and imperialist expansion, that the civilization of modernity emerged. Its crystallization and expansion were not unlike those of the expansion of all historical civilizations. What was new was first that the great technological advances and the dynamics of modern economic and political forces made this expansion, the changes and developments attendant on them and their impact on the societies to which it expanded much more intensive. The expansion, through the use of military, political, and economic forces, of modern civilization which took place first in Europe and then beyond it continually combined economic, political, and ideological aspects and forces, and its impact on the societies to which it expanded was much more intense than in most historical cases. It spawned a tendency—rather new and practically unique in the history of mankind—to the development of universal, worldwide institutional, cultural, and ideological frameworks and systems. Yet all of these frameworks were multicentered and heterogeneous, each generating its own dynamics.

Of special importance in this context was the relative place of the non-Western societies in the various—economic, political, ideological—international systems which differed greatly from that of the Western ones. It was not only that it was Western societies which were the 'originators' of this new civilization. Beyond this and above all was the fact that the expansion of these systems, especially insofar as it took place through colonialization and imperialist expansion, gave to the Western institutions the hegemonic place in these systems. Yet it was in the nature of these international systems that they generated a dynamics which gave rise both to political and ideological challenges to existing hegemonies, as well as to continual shifts in the loci of hegemony within Europe, from Europe to the United States, then also to Japan and East Asia.

But it was not only the economic, military-political, and ideological expansion of modernity from the West throughout the world that was important in this process. Of no lesser significance was the fact that this expansion has given rise to continual confrontation between the cultural and institutional premises of Western modernity and those of other civilizations. Thus, while the spread or expansion of modernity has indeed taken place throughout most of the world, it did not give rise to just one civilization, one pattern of ideological and institutional response, but to at least several basic variants—and to continual refracting thereof.

Consequently, multiple modernities have emerged. These civilizations, which share many common components and which continually constitute mutual reference points, have been continually unfolding, giving rise to new problematiques and reinterpretations of the basic premises of modernity. All these attest to the growing diversification of the visions and understanding of modernity, of the basic cultural agendas of different sectors of modern societies—far beyond the hegemonic vision of modernity that was prevalent before. The fundamentalist—and the new communal-national—movements constitute one of such new developments, in the unfolding of the potentialities and antinomies of modernity.

Such developments may indeed also give rise to highly confrontational stances—especially to the West—but these stances are promulgated in changing modern idioms, and they may entail a continual transformation of the cultural programs of modernity. At the same time the new diversity was closely connected—perhaps paradoxically—with the development of new multiple common reference points, and with a globalization of cultural networks and channels of communication far beyond what existed before.

See also: Civilization, Concept and History of; Civilizational Analysis, History of; Cultural History; Cultural Psychology; Elias, Norbert (1897–1990); Elites: Sociological Aspects; Hegemony: Cultural; National Character; Societies, Types of

Bibliography

Breuer B 1994 Kulturen der Achsenzeit. Leistung und Grenzen eines geschichtsphilosophischen Konzepts. *Saeculu* **45**: 1–33

Durkheim E, Mauss M 1971 Note on the notion of civilization. *Social Researc* **38**: 808–13

Elias E 1939 *Über den Prozess der Zivilisation.* Haus zum Falken, Basel

Eisenstadt S N 1973 *Tradition, Change and Modernity.* John Wiley & Sons, New York

Eisenstadt S N 1982 The axial age: the emergence of transcendental visions and rise of clerics. *European Sociology* **23**(2): 294–314

Eisenstadt S N (ed.) 1986 *The Origins and Diversity of Axial Age Civilizations.* State University of New York Press, Albany, New York

Eisenstadt S N 1982 Heterodoxies and dynamics of civilizations. *Diogene* **120**: 3–25

Eisenstadt S N, Achlama R 1992 *Kulturen der Achsenzeit II, ihre institutionelle und kulturelle Dynamik.* Suhrkamp, Frankfurt am Main, 3 Vols.

Eisenstadt S N 1996 *Japanese Civilization: A Comparative View.* University of Chicago Press, Chicago

Eisenstadt S N 1999 *Fundamentalism, Sectarianism and Revolution. The Jacobin Dimension of Modernity.* Cambridge University Press, Cambridge, UK

Huntington S P 1996 *The Clash of Civilizations and the Remaking of World Order.* Simon and Schuster, New York

Kroeber A L, Kluckhohn C 1952 *Culture: A Critical Review of Concepts and Definitions.* The Museum, Cambridge, MA

MacIver R M 1931 *Society: Its Structure and Changes.* R. Long & R. R. Smith, Inc. New York

Melko M 1969 *The Nature of Civilizations.* Porter Sargent, Boston

Nelson B 1981 *On the Roads to Modernity.* Rowman and Littlefield, Totowa, NY

Ogburn W F 1922 *Social Change: With Respect to Culture and Original Nature.* Huebsch, New York

Schluchter W 1979 *Die Entwicklung des okzidentalen Rationalismus—Eine Analyse von Max Webers Gesellschaftsgeschichte.* Mohr, Tubingen

Schluchter W 1981 (1985) *The Rise of Western Rationalism, Max Weber's Developmental History.* University of California Press, Berkeley

Schluchter W 1989 *Rationalism, Religion and Domination. A Weberian Perspective.* University of California Press, Berkeley

Weber A 1921 Prinzipielles zur Kultursoziologie. *Archiv für Sozialwissenschaft und Sozialpoliti* **XL**(VII): 1–49, J-C-B. Mohr, Tubingen

Weber A 1931 Kultursoziologie. In: Enke F (ed.) *Handwörterbuch der Soziologie.* Alfred Vierkandt, Stuttgart, pp. 284–94

Weber M 1922–3 *Gesammelte Aufsätze zur Religionssoziologie.* Mohr, Tübingen

S. N. Eisenstadt

Clan

The modern, now widely accepted, definition of the clan, as a group of persons who believe themselves to be related by unilineal descent but who are unable to trace genealogical connections linking all members of the group, has emerged out of a complex intellectual history stretching back to the Enlightenment. Many social theorists of the eighteenth and nineteenth centuries who were concerned to understand the origins of the state and democracy favored evolutionist explanations. Some viewed the family as the original form of society which, over the course of human history, had aggregated into progressively larger and more complex kinship-based groupings of clans and tribes, which were transformed eventually into the territorially-based political formation of the state. Drawing on the work of Barthold Niebuhr (1828), George Grote (1851) and other historians of Greece and Rome, social theorists such as Sir Henry Maine, Numa Fustel de Coulanges, and Lewis Henry Morgan used the ancient Greek and Roman kinship groups, the *genos* and the *gens*, as models upon which they based their understanding of early stages of social evolution.

Maine's (1861) analysis of the evolution of legal systems, using the example of the Roman *gens* and the concept of agnation—that is, kinship traced through exclusively male links—posited a primitive stage of social development in which membership in patriarchal kinship groups defined a person's social status. Maine emphasized that the *gens* was a corporate group which had a legal personality that endured beyond the lives of its individual members, an insight which has been very influential in subsequent work on clans and other forms of descent grouping.

In contrast to Maine's theory of primitive patriarchy, John Ferguson McLennan (1865) and Lewis Henry Morgan (1877) argued that the early stage of social evolution was characterized by group marriage, which meant that paternity was uncertain, and kinship was traced in the maternal line. For some authors favoring the theory of primitive matriliny, the term 'clan' was applied exclusively to matrilineal descent groups, while *gens* referred to patrilineal groups, a terminological distinction that has fallen out of use in the modern literature. Morgan, whose own research among the Iroquois in New York State had been influenced by Grote's analysis of the ancient Greek *genos*, saw descent group organization, which he termed the 'gentile' system, as characteristic of much of early human social history. McLennan, basing his reasoning on contemporary reports of female infanticide in India, claimed that primitive societies were obliged, in their struggles for survival, to engage in this population-limiting practice, which in turn led kin groups to procure wives by capture from outside their own group. McLennan termed this marriage outside the group 'exogamy,' which came to be seen, by many nineteenth and early twentieth century social theorists, as another characteristic attribute of clanship.

McLennan was also influential in developing the theory of totemism, which built on E. B. Tylor's notion that primitive religion was based on animism, the worship of inanimate objects or fetishes which were believed to be the abodes of spirits. Along with his follower W. Robertson Smith and Smith's student Sir

James Fraser, McLennan defined totemism as a system that originally combined animistic religious beliefs with matrilineal descent and exogamy. According to this view, through their ignorance of paternity caused by group marriage and their belief in animism, primitive societies posited links to original animal or plant ancestors. These natural species, which were treated as sacred emblems or 'totems' of different clans, were worshipped periodically by clan members in totemic rituals.

Emile Durkheim (1912), in his work on the social origins of religion which drew extensively on early ethnographic reports of aboriginal Australian societies, reproduced many of these classic arguments concerning totemism, particularly emphasizing the concept of a sacred social solidarity based on a belief in a shared substance between clan members and their ancestral totemic species. Claude Lévi-Strauss' (1962) subsequent general critique of theories of totemism, which emphasized the lack of a necessary coincidence between totemic species as emblems, exogamous clans, and religious sacrifice, served to unhitch the clanship concept from the pseudo-historical hypotheses of nineteenth century evolutionism while, at the same time, helping to clarify the classificatory logic operative in cultural categories such as the clan.

The work of the British structural-functionalist A. R. Radcliffe-Brown (1950) and his followers E. E. Evans-Pritchard, Meyer Fortes (Fortes and Evans-Pritchard 1940), and others between the two world wars, did much to put the study of unilineal descent systems on a firmer ethnographic footing, while refining the conceptual framework for their study. The model of the segmentary lineage, consisting of a nested set of increasingly inclusive corporate unilineal descent groups linked by a comprehensive genealogical structure, is the most well-known outgrowth of their work, with the term 'clan' often being used by these authors to label a particular segmentary level within a lineage system. Although Radcliffe-Brown's (1950, pp. 39–40) definition of the clan, given in the first sentence of this article, has come to be widely used, this application of the term to characterize one of the levels in a segmentary lineage system is not always appropriate. It reflects a continuing influence of earlier understandings of totemism, in which descent group exogamy and totemic taboos were taken to be defining attributes of clanship.

Although a definitional contrast between clan and lineage is thus still not always made clearly in the more modern literature, there is analytical value in maintaining a definite distinction, since the organizational implications of the two forms of descent grouping are different. Members of a lineage know, or claim to know, the genealogical connections interlinking all members of the group, and these links, viewed in terms of generation and relative birth order, often provide a basis for calculating relations of seniority or degrees of relatedness between individuals and segments within a lineage. Lineage genealogy can also be the basis for internal segmentation of groups, according to the segmentary lineage model. In contrast, lacking such a comprehensive internal genealogical armature, relations of clanship are categorical in character and typically nonhierarchical within the clan. Persons are members of a clan because of being the offspring of their fathers or mothers, with the terms 'patriclan' and 'matriclan' often being used to indicate a clan's mode of recruitment of its members. Although ascending descent links beyond the grandparental or great-grandparental generation are normally of little or no organizational significance, clan members in many societies do nonetheless recognize a founding clan ancestor, who is often of mythical or nonhuman status. Thus, when clans do segment according to putative genealogical links, this is typically 'from the top', with reference to the founding ancestor and his or her children, producing a set of sub-clan categories that also lack comprehensive internal genealogical structures.

Terminological confusion is also possible in the case of the descent group known as the conical clan, or ranked lineage, which combines characteristic features of both lineages and clans. Such descent groups are differentiated internally into a high ranked, lineage-like, chiefly or noble descent line, and a lower ranked and internally undifferentiated clan-like category of commoners (Kirchhoff 1959, Friedman 1979). Chiefly rank in a conical clan typically is based on relative birth order in present and ancestral generations, so that senior sons or daughters of senior ranking ancestors keep careful track of their pedigrees to validate their noble status. Junior offspring of junior ancestors, on the other hand, have little motivation in remembering their genealogies, and their affiliation to the group is more categorical in character. Numerous ethnographers have drawn attention to the structural potential of conical clanship, particularly as a transitional formation between uncentralized and centralized political systems. Conical clan structures are relatively common in Polynesian societies, such as the Maori, and in south-east and central Asian societies, such as the Mongols.

The clans of the Scottish Highlands also displayed such internal ranking (Dodgshon 1998). The Scottish clan chief and his close relatives enjoyed high status due to their close patrilineal connection to the founding clan ancestor. The commoner members of the clan, on the other hand, could not necessarily demonstrate such genealogical links, but were bound to their clan chief by diverse social ties including land tenancy or marriage alliance, as well as real or fictive kinship expressed by a common surname.

Systems of clanship occur in many parts of the world, and their diversity of form can be understood in relation to several key variables. Of prime importance is their capacity for organized collective action as corporate groups, which frequently is limited or absent due to the spatial dispersal of clan memberships. Particularly in territorially extensive societies with large populations, a clan's members often reside in many different locations, and there are limited possibilities for the full membership of a clan to meet as a total group. In such circumstances, clans may act collectively on only a few occasions, such as during annual rituals like the aboriginal Australian *corroboree* ceremonies, which clans celebrated to ensure the continued fertility of their totemic species. In other cases of spatially dispersed clan membership, a clan may never meet as a totality, but simply act as a named category from which localized sets of clan members may be mobilized to pursue collective action if necessary or advantageous.

In addition to their variable capacities for organizing group action, numerous authors have also drawn attention to the potential of clanship systems to serve a social networking function. For example, in West Africa among speakers of the Mande family of languages (Jackson 1974), a limited set of clan names is found throughout this large zone, and a clan member making a long journey can feel confident of finding members of his or her clan who will provide assistance at the distant destination.

Even in cases where the set of clan names changes from one society to an adjacent one, conventional equivalences are often established between clan names to facilitate the extension of such networks of mutual aid. Similar clan networks have also been noted among North American Amerindian and aboriginal Australian societies.

Although ethnographic analysts of clanship frequently have conflated it with lineage structure, as mentioned above, the logic of clanship is often more a matter of 'sub-ethnicity' rather than 'super-lineage.' Many cultures' understandings of clanship, which are often rooted in myth, posit a primordial clan identity which is seen as immutable, much like many cultures' conceptualizations of ethnicity. It is this theme that Lévi-Strauss (1962) explored in his work on totemism, in which the classificatory logic of clans as social species is seen as homologous to cultural classifications of animal and plant species. In such cases, the total number of clans in a society may be quite small and be viewed as unchanging, with the various clanship categories standing in long-term interrelationships of marriage alliance, ritual cooperation or other modes of mutual exchange or solidarity. In societies where the total number of clan categories is only two, these groupings are conventionally referred to as 'moieties.'

In contrast, some societies have systems of proliferating clans in which it is evident to the analyst, from the presence of large numbers of clans with relatively small memberships in the context of overall population growth, that clans are undergoing segmentation, although this is not acknowledged by clan members themselves. Such systems of proliferating clanship tend to be found in politically uncentralized societies with high rates of spatial mobility, where local groups frequently split as a mode of dispute settlement. In such cases it may be posited that, following an episode of intraclan dispute which has been resolved by group fission and spatial displacement, the members of the resultant new segments have an active interest in denying knowledge of former genealogical interlinkage. Such systems of proliferating clanship, characterized by many small clans that are widely dispersed spatially, are not conducive to the maintenance of the patterns of long-term interclan alliance mentioned above.

In some cases, the term 'clan' has also been applied to territorial groups which are recruited both on the basis of unilineal descent and long-term co-residence. Such a usage is common in New Guinea. Here, immigrant strangers hailing from other clans may initially be welcomed in order to strengthen a localized clan grouping.

Over time, cultural theories of personal identity may posit, for example, that through continued consumption of foodstuffs cultivated on the clan's land, the physical nature of such incomers becomes transformed into that of true clansmen, thus converting co-residence into shared unilineal descent. In effect, as argued by the American kinship specialist, George P. Murdock (1949), such a 'compromise kin group' reflects the difficulty of constituting a large-scale, residentially unified and collectively functional kinship grouping on the basis of unilineal descent alone.

Finally, it should be recognized that, in common parlance, the term 'clan' is often used in a metaphorical way to refer to any group of persons who act toward each other in a particularly close and mutually supportive way. Thus, criminal organizations such as the Mafia may be referred to as 'clans,' in recognition of the ideology of kinlike solidarity that binds their members together.

See also: Chiefdoms, Archaeology of; Kinship in Anthropology; Matrifocality; Tribe

Bibliography

Dodgshon R 1998 *From Chiefs to Landlords*. Edinburgh University Press, Edinburgh, UK

Durkheim E 1912 *Les Formes Elémentaires de la Vie Religieuse*. Alcan, Paris [1915 *The Elementary Forms of the Religious Life*. Allen & Unwin, London]

Fortes M, Evans-Pritchard E E (eds.) 1940 *African Political Systems*. Oxford University Press for the International African Institute, London

Friedman J 1979 *System, Structure and Contradiction in the Evolution of 'Asiatic' Social Formations*. National Museum of Denmark, Copenhagen, Denmark

Fustel de Coulanges N 1876 *La Cité Antique*. Hachette, Paris [1980 *The Ancient City*. Johns Hopkins University Press, Baltimore]

Grote G 1851 *A History of Greece*, 3rd edn. John Murray, London

Jackson M 1974 The structure and significance of Kuranko clanship. *Africa* **44**(4): 397 415

Kirchhoff P 1959 The principles of clanship in human society. In: Fried M (ed.) *Readings in Anthropology*. Crowell, New York, Vol. II

Kuper A 1988 *The Invention of Primitive Society*. Routledge, London

Lévi-Strauss C 1962 *Le Totemisme Aujourd'hui*. Presses Universitaires de France, Paris [1969 *Totemism*. Penguin, Harmondsworth, UK]

Maine H 1861 *Ancient Law*. John Murray, London

McLennan J F 1865 *Primitive Marriage*. Adam & Charles Black, Edinburgh, UK

Morgan L H 1877 *Ancient Society*. Henry Holt, New York

Murdock G P 1949 *Social Structure*. Macmillan, New York

Niebuhr B 1828 *The History of Rome*. Taylor, Cambridge, UK

Radcliffe-Brown A R 1950 Introduction. In: Radcliffe-Brown A R, Forde D (eds.) *African Systems of Kinship and Marriage*. Oxford University Press for the International African Institute, London

P. Burnham

Class Actions: Legal

A class action is a procedure whereby one or more claimants, called the class representative, may bring suit (or, more rarely, be designated as a defendant class) to obtain a remedy responsive to the legal interest of all members of the class (Lindblom 1996). The remedy may be an injunction, for example prohibiting racial discrimination in public schools, or compensatory damages and, in some instances, punitive damages, for example in claims of mass consumer fraud. The suit may seek both an injunction and monetary redress for or against a class. The procedure facilitates assertion of similar claims on behalf of a large number of allegedly injured parties, including claims that could not, as a practical matter, otherwise be asserted on account of the cost of litigation. A suit against a defendant class typically would seek imposition of an identical remedy against all of them, for example, against stockholders or creditors of a corporation. By the same token, because the procedure aggregates claims, it can impose very heavy liability and hence can become a weapon of 'legal blackmail.' The procedure is governed by Rule 23 of the Federal Rules of Civil Procedure in federal courts and by similar rules in state courts. Class suits are very controversial but they are an important component in the American use of litigation to address public issues of compensatory and distributive justice.

1. History

English courts recognized litigation on behalf of groups from no later than the fifteenth century and perhaps earlier. The concept of a class suit evolved in the Court of Chancery in the sixteenth and eighteenth centuries, in such cases as rights to fish in a river, rights of creditors against an insolvent debtor, rights of shareholders to enforce duties of corporate directors and obligations of parishioners to pay church titles (Yeazell 1987). By the end of the eighteenth century the basic formula for a class suit had been established, in these terms: 'Plaintiff, suing on behalf of himself and all others similar situated, alleges as follows: ...'

In the United States the class suit procedure was elaborated by Justice Joseph Story in his treatise on Equity and was recognized in the federal courts, notably in the case of *Smith v. Swormstedt*, (57 US [16 How] 288 [1853]). In the nineteenth century the class suit evolved in state court procedure, particularly in litigation by city taxpayers complaining about improper municipal expenditures and in proceedings to reorganize insurance companies that had overextended themselves. The 'taxpayers' suit' has since evolved into a standard procedure for obtaining judicial review of action by municipal and state government. The insurance reorganization proceedings have since evolved, in one direction into bankruptcy procedure and in another offshoot into procedures for reorganization of insurance companies and banks (Hazard et al. 1998). The class suit procedure was used only infrequently until the litigation involving desegregation of the public schools in the 1960s and 1970s, in which the procedure was a standard technique.

The class suit procedure was given greater status and more precise definition in the Federal Rules of Civil Procedure, adopted in 1938. Federal Rule 23 permitted class suits for injunctions, damages and multiple claims against a limited fund. In 1966 Federal Rule 23 was elaborately amended to provide clearer criteria for when class suits maybe maintained and greater protection for class members, particularly those who were not the designated representative parties.

The validity of class suit procedure has been recurrently questioned in terms of due process. The issue is essentially whether, and in what circumstances, a judgment in a class suit can validly determine the rights of members of class who do not actively participate in the litigation. The courts have upheld the concept of the class suit but have given ambiguous pronouncements about its effect on absent class members. Leading Supreme Court cases addressing that issue include *Hansberry v. Lee* (311 US 32 [1938]) disapproving a class suit where the representative has a conflict of interest; *Phillips Petroleum Co. vs. Shutts* (472 US 797, [1985]) approving a class suit in state court determining rights of residents of other states; and *Amchem Products, Inc. vs. Windsor* (521 US 591, [1997]), and *Ortiz vs. Fibreboard Corp.* (527 US 815 [1999]) disapproving class suit settlements covering potential claimants who could not be given notice of the suit.

2. Requirements for a Class Suit

The requirements for a class suit in federal court are set forth in Federal Rule 23. Essentially similar requirements prevail in state court procedures.

The class suit complaint must be set forth, first, that plaintiff is a party injured in the manner detailed in the complaint's subsequent allegations and, second, that the plaintiff maintains the action on behalf of all members of the described class, for example, all Black children seeking admission to the defendant public school or all consumers who borrowed money from the defendant lending institution. The first of these allegations establishes 'standing' to sue and the second asserts plaintiff's assumption of a representative capacity in the litigation. The remedy must be sought for all members of the class. The complaint must describe the wrong in accordance with the usual pleading rules. It must also allege that the members of the group are too numerous to sue separately; that there are common questions presented in the claims for the class; and that the representative party will be an adequate representative of the entire class. It must also be shown that common relief for all class members is necessary or at least convenient and that the procedure will be efficient as a means of resolving the many claims involved.

The terminology in Federal Rule 23(b) differentiates three types of class suits: 23(b)(1), involving a course of conduct by defendant that affects all class members; 23(b)(2), in which an injunction is sought against conduct affecting all members of the class; 23(b)(3), in which similar injury has allegedly been inflicted on all class members, for which damages are sought. These distinctions are not mutually exclusive. For example, a proper class suit can seek both an injunction against future wrong and damages for past conduct. However, other provisions of Rule 23 impose different procedural requirements on the basis of this typology, particularly a requirement that all members of a '(b)(3)'class be given individual notice of the pendency of the suit. This discrepancy as well as redundancy in other terminology in Rule 23 have resulted in much confusion in administrating class suits. There is a large and complex procedural jurisprudence concerning these requirements (Wright et al. 1986).

However, there are two essential questions. The first is whether, all things considered, the litigation may be maintained on a group basis, or may not be so maintained. This is the 'certification' issue, so-called because the court must certify the suit as a proper class proceeding if it is to proceed as such. The second critical question is whether individual notice to all class members will be required.

3. Certification

A class suit may be maintained as such only with the approval of the court, that is, certification that the suit is proper. An initiative by the plaintiff to proceed with a class suit is ordinarily necessary, except in unusual situations where a defendant class is established. However, a plaintiff initiative is not sufficient without the court's approval. Usually the question of certification is a major preliminary issue, strenuously contested with legal and factual argument. A great deal depends on resolution of this issue. If certification is denied, the lawsuit lapses into a claim by one or a few parties, rather than on behalf of a large group. Reduction of the size of the case to the claims of the individual representatives usually makes further pursuit of the litigation by the plaintiff unattractive or impractical. On the other hand, if certification is granted, the lawsuit may immediately assume major proportion for the defendant, often creating a compulsion to reach expensive settlement.

Despite extensive procedural jurisprudence, and intensive professional and academic debate, the issue of certification in a specific case remains relatively open ended and hence very much a matter of judicial judgment and discretion (Newberg and Conte 1992). For many years the question of certification was held to be an interlocutory determination and hence not subject to appellate review until final resolution after determination of the merits of the class members claims. See *Eisen v. Carlisle & Jacquelin* (417 US 156 [1974]). This made the certification issue in the trial court all the more crucial. Denial of certification was termed the 'death knell' of a class suit, while grant of certification usually resulted in defendant feeling obliged to negotiate a settlement with the class. In 1999, Rule 23 was amended to permit immediate appeal of a grant or denial of certification. Immediate appeal of the trials courts' certification decision has been permitted under class suit procedure in most states.

4. Initiative to Prosecute Class Suits

A class suit can be initiated by a pre-existing group, such as a labor union or trade association; by a political action organization wishing to press a legal contention, such as the NAACP's litigation to end school desegregation; or by a group recognizing itself to have a common interest in making claims, such as disaffected shareholders of a corporation. Initiation of such efforts requires assistance of a lawyer willing to prosecute the case. In modern practice such an initiative is often by lawyers specializing in class suit litigation. Because class suits typically involve large stakes so far as defendant is concerned, most class suits are strongly contested. That prospect in turn requires that the organizer, whether an action group or the lawyer, have financial resources and staying power to sustain costly and protracted litigation. Legal grievances that can be framed as class suits hence ordinarily result in escalation of a dispute into litigation of major proportion.

The initiator of a class suit, whether a claimant action group or a lawyer, defines the grievant group by the description of the class in the complaint. The class is defined in terms of common characteristics and usually a specified time interval, for example, 'female employees of defendant corporation in the period January, 1998 through December, 1999.' The time interval refers to the period in which the alleged injuries occurred and is called the 'class period.' A larger class may be subdivided into subclasses having different specific characteristics, either by the plaintiff or by order of the court.

Some class suits are almost entirely the result of lawyer initiative. A lawyer envisions that a wrong has been committed against many people, locates someone fitting the description to serve as class representative, and then manages the lawsuit. The lawyer's incentive in such a case includes the prospect of large fees upon obtaining a judgment or, much more likely, a settlement. Some analysts differentiate between 'cause' class suits, such those asserting civil rights, and 'money' class suits, where large damages are sought. 'Money' class suits are typified by cases where inventive lawyers frame class damage claims out of transactions too small to be worth individual prosecution but affecting thousands of alleged victims. A classic illustration is a California case seeking restitution from a taxi company that allegedly fixed its meters to record fares at a rate higher than legally permitted. See *Daar vs. Yellow Cab Co.* (67 Cal. 2d 695 [1967]): Claims on behalf of corporate stockholders, alleging misrepresentation in the corporation's financial projections, are a common type of modern class suits. Many class suits involve both politically significantly issues and large financial stakes. In any event the class permits isolated individual legal grievances to be amalgamated into large scale claims.

5. Uses and Abuses of Class Actions

The typical class suit defendant is a business corporation or a government bureau. The class suit procedure is an important device for commutative and distributive justice on behalf of individuals who have suffered legal wrong at the hands of powerful actors in modern mass society. At the same time, the class suit procedure is a menacing device by which self-constituted protagonists, chiefly lawyers, can exploit relatively minor legal mistakes to reap large recoveries from 'target' defendants. Officials of such a defendant typically consider that they cannot afford the risk to their organization's continuity of a big judgment—the risk, in common parlance, of 'betting the ranch.'

A class suit also presents opportunity for the plaintiff's lawyer to exploit the class, often through connivance of the defendant. A class suit settlement typically calls for defendant to pay the plaintiff's lawyer a substantial fee. A defendant is typically indifferent whether settlement money goes to the lawyer or to the class members. A settlement could pay could pay $1 million to the lawyer and $9 million to the class, or $2 million to the lawyer and $6 million to the class. The terms of a settlement injunction can be similarly manipulated. The class members typically are dispersed and not organized, hence in a weak position to contest the terms of settlement (Coffee 2000).

6. Use and Abuse of Class Suits

Most class suits are resolved by settlement, typically after a period of intensive discovery and extensive motion practice. Hence, although class suit litigation typically is expensive, there are few cases where an adjudication has determined the merits. Most of the controversy over class suits is founded on dispute about the fairness of settlements.

Control against blackmail of a defendant or exploitation of absent class members is afforded through exercise of responsibility by class counsel and by court supervision. Most class counsel are faithful to their responsibilities, notwithstanding that class suit defendants typically assert that they are being oppressed. But some class counsel have been flagrantly exploitive. The quality of court supervision varies greatly. Some judges conduct searching inquiries into the basis and terms of a proposed settlement, particularly the attorney fees. Some judges make only a perfunctory review. Close supervision is in any event difficult because there is no reference point as to the merits of the claim and both sides are at high risk in a trial on the merits—plaintiff through possible loss of its investment in the litigation, defendant through possible loss on the merits (Hensler et al. 2000).

Both the opportunity to achieve justice for individuals suffering common wrongs and the danger to defendants of 'betting the ranch' could be improved if clearer definition could be drawn of claims appropriate for class suits. Efforts in this direction have been without much success. Congress adopted special provisions concerning securities class suits in federal court but their effect has been avoided by bringing suits in state courts. Proposed legislation would extend federal court jurisdiction to class suits involving interstate transactions, but encountered intense criticism that they would stifle proper class suits and inappropriately burden the federal courts. Revisions in Rule 23, in addition to making certification orders immediately appealable, have been proposed but probably would have modest effects.

Much of the controversy over class suits implicates other aspects of American civil procedure, including broad discovery, the right of jury trial of issues of fact, and the American rule concerning court costs (Yeazell

1987). Class suits typically involve extensive discovery which, under broad American discovery practice, can extend to thousands of documents and dozens of witness depositions. The right of jury trial imposes inherent risks to a 'deep pocket' defendant and, perhaps more important, precludes decisions by the judge of issues of fact that might narrow the controversy or resolve it altogether. The American cost rule, whereby the winner of litigation generally is not entitled to recover its litigation costs, means that a class suit plaintiff has no 'down side' risk of becoming liable for a defendant's costs. Moreover, many class suits claims are based on statutes that provide recovery of litigation costs to winning plaintiffs but not to defendants. A commonly voiced criticism of these statutes is that they contemplated individual suits, where litigation costs would make enforcement of rights practically impossible, whereas the class suit is another approach to enforcement of individual rights through a 'private attorney general.'

See also: Legal Process and Social Science: United States; Liability: Legal; Litigation; Parties: Litigants and Claimants; Procedure: Legal Aspects; Rules in the Legal Process

Bibliography

Coffee J 2000 Class action accountability: Reconciling exist, voice, and loyalty in representative litigation. *Columbia Law Review* **100**: 370
Hazard G, Gedid J, Sowle S 1998 An historical analysis of the binding effects of class suits. *University of Pennsylvania Law Review* **146**: 1849
Hensler D R, Pace N M, Dombey-Moore B, Giddens B, Gross J, Moller E K 2000 *Class Action Dilemmas: Pursuing Public Goals for Private Gain*. RAND, Santa Monica, CA
Lindblom P H 1996 *Group Actions and the Role of the Courts: A European Perspective*. Kluwer, The Hague, Netherlands
Newberg H, Conte A 1992 *Newberg on Class Actions*, 3rd edn. McGraw-Hill, New York
Vos W de 1996 Reflection on the introduction of a class action in South Africa. *Tydskrif vir die Suid-Afrikaanse Reg* **4**: 639–57
Wright C, Miller A, Kane M 1986 *Federal Practice and Procedure*. West, St Paul, MN, Vols. 7A–7C
Yeazell S 1987 *From Medieval Group Litigation to the Modern Class Action*. Yale University Press, Haven, CT

G. C. Hazard, Jr.

Class and Law

1. Basic Marxist Assumptions

The basic assumptions in a Marxist explanation of the origin, the development, and the function of law include the following: Productive labor is the basis and thus the focus of social ascriptions, i.e., of a collectively sharped pattern of social identity (not gender, ethnicity, and the like). On a certain level of productivity a surplus can be produced. The mode of production and appropriation of a surplus changes historically. Classes evolve out of unequal property relations to the means of production. Owners and non-owners of the means of production form the dominating vs. the dominated, exploited classes. (In non-Marxist approaches, e.g., in Max Weber, classes are defined not only according to their market position or possession but also according to their relation to the mode of production and appropriation; Weber 1964, p. 688.) Classes are not only structural, anonymous entities. Classes operate as collective actors vested with class consciousness (*Klasse für sich*) and class interests. The interests of the economically dominating class are backed by the state as an instrument of suppression. (In contrast, Max Weber suggests that the legal order has an impact on the power order of a society (Weber 1964, p. 678), which is determined by, among other things, the economic *Klassenlage*, insofar as the legal order protects the free disposition of the owners of the means of production (Weber 1964, p. 682).

At the same time, law disguises class domination behind a veil of ideological justification. The legal ideology of the formal equality of autonomous market subjects legitimates both the economic and the political order. Instead of mere force, a system of alleged universal legitimized domination, and thus the step from might to right, is institutionalized. Therefore, not only class interests but also general (class-independent) conditions of a society are secured by state and law. By its intellectual sublimation and doctrinal systematization, law gains a relative autonomy. Law is no longer the pure expression of the economic basis or state power. There exists a feedback of legal regulations on the economic basis including the class structure.

According to the basic assumptions of Marxist historical materialism, the systematic relationship between the class basis and the legal superstructure evolves in historical stages: In ancient 'primitive,' 'classless' societies, which do not produce a surplus, there is no need for state and law. In hierarchical societies that are economically based on slavery or a feudal system, state and law play a dominant role. In the tradition of Marxist legal theory, this characterization was denied by Eugen Pašukanis (1924). According to his approach, law exists only in capitalist (market) societies with antagonistic interests of the owners of commodities. Preceding social formations are marked by lawless domination. The stage of the dictatorship of the proletariat is, according to Marx/Engels and Lenin, signified by the use of law as an instrument of overt state domination, even of terror. After that, law is used as an instrument to build up and to secure a socialist society. The future of state and law in a communist society was an open question. The answers range from the notion of the withering away of law and state, to a 'state of the whole people' in which law still serves administrative purposes.

In the following systematic presentation the concept of law is used either in the sense of legislative acts, or the activities of the legal staff, or the legally relevant activities, opinions, and beliefs of the citizens in general.

2. Class Legislation

In Marx's base–superstructure scheme (Marx 1859, pp. 8–9), law (as an element of the superstructure) is conceived of as an expression of the economic base. In the writings of Marx and Engels, the instrumental view comes in via the notion of *Rückwirkung* (feedback) of the superstructure onto the economic base. This instrumental view was dominant from the time that the communists gained power; for example, in the writings of Stalin. In the instrumentalist view, law is conceived of as an instrument used by the ruling class(es) in order to realize a socialist order. The theoretical background of Marxist legal theory can be characterized by this oscillation between law as an expression of the given class structure and law as an instrument of class domination.

But what are the concrete mechanisms by which a link between social classes and legislation, between the dominant class(es) and the legislative majority, can be achieved (as soon as there are distinct political bodies)? What is the logic of 'class legislation' (Mill 1861, Chap. 10)?

On a primitive level, members of the dominating class(es) are *in persona* members of the legislative body. With growing differentiation 'class representation' becomes important: parliamentary representatives are to a large extent nominated or elected by members of the dominant class; the legislative power of the dominant class can be secured by special arrangements (e.g., Prussian *Dreiklassenwahlrecht* (1849–1918) by which the representatives were elected according to the amount of taxes paid by groups of voters). This becomes a problem with the introduction of equal, universal suffrage. Class influence then can be maintained by a combination of economic and political positions, by regulations concerning access to Members of Parliament and government, by lobbying and corruption. Alternatively, input-orientation–output-orientation becomes more relevant; i.e., via threats and sanctions, capitalists can use their economic power (reduction, relocation, export of jobs, and investments, flight from taxation, etc.) to make the legislator issue certain regulations. The legislator has to take into account the consequences threatened by the employers. The subtlest form—often found in the critique of the bourgeois ideology of formal law—is the use of general, universal norms, the application of which confirms economically privileged positions. The construct of formal equality in civil law among allegedly free autonomous persons veils substantial inequality in market positions (e.g., in the labor market between employers and workers, in the housing market between landlords and tenants). But this normative pattern is relativized by special, protective regulations in these fields, when the weaker position of one group is acknowledged and becomes legally relevant.

3. Class Justice

It is a truism that courts cannot act neutrally in a class society and in a class state. If class justice is the justice of the class state that is organized according to the interests of the dominating class, how is it organized? What mechanisms ensure that the courts will act in the interest of the ruling class? To which class do judges belong? How are the interests of the dominating class transferred into the courts? (See *Judges*.)

The easiest example is, of course, where members of the economically and politically dominating class themselves have jurisdiction. The *Landesherr*, for example, is in charge of the administration of justice in his region. But with the professionalization of the judiciary, and a rudimentary separation of powers, the problem arises as to how the interests of the dominating class can be promoted by persons who are not themselves members of this class but rather act as class representatives. A number of factors help to promote the interests of the dominant class.

The first factor that promotes the interests of the dominant class is socialization. Judges tend to come from a similar background (Griffith 1981). Family background, and especially the occupation of the father, helps to explain the class bias in the administration of justice. And the high costs of education, in particular the costs of academic legal education, make the legal professions accessible only to members of families with a high income.

The second factor promoting the interests of the dominant class is the process of professionalization. That all judges share a common academic background and training is likely to have an impact on the attitude of law students, reinforcing a *status quo* orientation. Furthermore, judges must adhere to a set of professional standards; if they do not, they may suffer political consequences, or be subjected to professional discipline. Thus, in almost every state—be it a dictatorship, an apartheid regime, or a democracy—organizational means are successfully employed to secure the conformity of the legal profession to the political regime, and to the dominant political ideology.

Illuminating examples of the operation of these mechanisms can be found in Karl Liebknecht's critique of the class justice during the German Reich and in Prussia before the First World War: 'If we look at where our judges come from it is obvious out of which milieu, from which point of view they regularly will decide. Naturally the judges will be recruited only from the possessing classes simply because of the high costs of education, because of the low income at the beginning of their career, by which the need for an adequate way of life, that still exists, cannot be satisfied.' (Liebknecht 1910, pp. 26–7) During this period the criterion of political reliability was overtly and restrictively used by the court administration to regulate the access to the judiciary. There are also brief remarks on the English system by Max Weber (1964, p. 1049) on the recruitment of judges from the advocacy who served the capitalistic interests of their clients (For England see Griffith (1981) and the recent analysis of Abel (1998): the access to the judiciary is politically controlled by the Lord Chancellor and there still exist strong financial barriers.) (See *Judicial Selection.*)

Although according to Marxist theory, state and law are always 'class state' and 'class law,' in socialist countries the term 'class justice' was not used as a self-description of their courts, but solely in a pejorative sense against 'bourgeois justice', etc.

Is there still—as it was evident for Karl Liebknecht in cases where workers were involved (as an accused or, in civil cases, with an employer on the other side)—a class bias in the administration of justice? What about civil cases in which the parties come both from the same class, i.e., from the class of the owners of the means of production, or from the proletariat— and here possibly as blue-collar workers versus white-collar workers? What if conflicting parties avoid court litigation? And in penal cases, how do we compare legally similar cases in which the judgment differs solely because of the different class affiliation of the accused? The appropriate field of study of class justice seems to be labor courts with employers and employees as parties, i.e., where class conflict is transformed into legal conflict (cf. Rottleuthner 1984).

There is substantial evidence documenting discrimination in penal courts with a high selectivity against the poor, from police arrest, through state prosecution, to disparities in sentencing and imprisonment. Assessing the extent to which capital punishment (see *Death Penalty*) is discriminatory in the US is methodologically complicated because of the correlation of crimes rates with social status, race and even gender (see *Gender and the Law*). Further, statistical correlations between race or gender and the law are hard to interpret because it is still an open question how these factors become operative within legal argumentation. The overrepresentation of lower class people in the penal system could be explained to a certain degree by legal standards, because there are correlations between legally relevant variables like observability of a crime, recidivism, confession, way of life, and sociologically relevant variables like (lower) class (see *Crime and Class*). The use of purely external variables that do not take into account legal argumentation raises several problems. The 'background approach' (i.e., the use of variables like father's occupation, religion, ethnicity, party, and other group affiliations) in judicial research did not lead to clear results. Does there still exist a homogeneous working class culture with distinct socialization patterns? Does legal education and role expectations on the job neutralize a possible impact of the social background? What about lay judges who have almost no legal training? When a jury is selected, lawyers consider the composition of race and gender (see *Juries*). There is strong evidence that neither the background or education of judges, nor their more recently achieved attributes like group or party affiliations, have an impact on the outcome of judicial decisions (particularly for labor courts; cf. Rottleuthner 1984). The focus of research into the outcomes of litigation has therefore shifted from the personality of judges to features of the parties to a court conflict (cf. Galanter 1974). Success in a civil court litigation can be explained by the experience of repeat players—in general bigger firms which tend to come out ahead of private one-shotters.

The focus of sociolegal research has furthermore shifted away from the courts to what happens out of court: to different legal needs (of the rich and poor), to unequal access to courts and other legal or extralegal remedies (see *Justice, Access to: Legal Representation of the Poor*), in general to the selectivity of legal procedures (see *Law, Mobilization of*). The problem of access to courts has been adressed by Max Weber (1964, p. 719) in the case of the English system: monetary barriers for the poor lead to denial of the administration of justice.

4. Class Consciousness and Law

There are no empirical studies that contrast the attitudes of workers (or of the proletariat) to legal norms and legal institutions with those of employers (or of capitalists). Empirical research into knowledge and opinion about law uses simple indicators of social status (preferably income or occupation), but no class variables in a strict sense. Georg Lukács (1920) dealt theoretically with the attitutde of the proletariat towards legality and illegality and towards the bourgeois law and state in general. In order to establish successfully a proletarian state, the proletariat has to acquire a sober, purely tactical attitude toward law and state. The state has to be seen solely as an element of power, as an empirical entity without any normative obligatory force. Legality or illegality are not matters of principle but of utility. This instrumental attitude towards law and state can also be found among the members of Communist parties. After their experiences with bourgeois legislation and class justice, they, having gained power, used law as an instrument of suppression and of strengthening the socialist state. The doctrine of the withering away of law and state was discarded; and law was not understood as a limit on state power.

5. Abiding Marxian Concepts

The replacement of the Marxian concept of class with constructs like status and milieu, and with indicators such as income, education, and occupation can itself be explained by substantial social changes. Labor is no longer the focus of social ascriptions. The forms of property or ownership (of the means of production) have changed and have become objectively blurred by the development of big companies (see *Property: Legal Aspects*). Other forms of social inequality became important like gender, race, ethnicity, nationality, age, etc. Of course, hierarchical stratification still exists: the haves and have-nots (the distinction between *Besitzenden* and the *Besitzlosen* constituted the *Klassenlage* in Weber 1964, p. 679), rich and poor, the legally included and excluded, that share or do not share the benefits and compensations of the welfare state, the politically dominating and dominated, etc. Instead of property, the notion of access becomes more important. Scholars are interested in the access to the means of production, but also the access to money, to the labor market, to information, knowledge, education (cultural capital), access to medical care, to other social benefits and rewards, to legal services and remedies, to leisure time options, to political power, etc. It is important to look at correlations and congruence between these varieties of access. There are no longer collectively conscious actors like classes. Some authors deny the existence of collectivities altogether under the heading of individualization; others speak of social movements (Eder 1993). Finally, the role of law has changed. Law is no longer conceived of as a general structure of society, whether based on social contractual consensus or on class domination or an anonymous economic base. Law serves as a political instrument, among others, used in order to achieve certain goals. Law, in particular welfare and labor law, is applied in order to compensate for the shortcomings of formal equality. Law is constitutive of state and social activities (see *Law as Constitutive*); and law can work to limit political power.

Basic Marxian concepts are used today only metaphorically. Everything, including culture and law, becomes a matter of production. The notion of capital is converted into social capital and cultural capital (Bourdieu 1986). Class becomes an empty shell signifying every form of inequality. Lenski (1966), for example, speaks of various class systems according to different principles of stratification. There is not only a 'power class,' but also a 'sexual' class system, (on class in general, see Milner 1999). Marxist legal theory could be understood as an economic analysis of law. But what today is labelled as 'economic analysis of law,' the individualistic, utilitarian approach of the Chicago school, would have become the target of Marx' sarcasm.

Class has been used as an explanatory variable, namely as a background variable, in order to explain the behavior of legislators or judges, or as a variable attributed to the accused or to the parties involved in a legal conflict. But it has regularly been used in a non-Marxian sense; in empirical research, indicators other than the property relationship to the means of production are often used. Thus the concept of class has been dissolved into notions like status, stratum, milieu, etc., and indicators like income, occupation, and level of education have taken the place of the theoretical construct of class. In sociology, as in sociolegal studies, class has become a vague notion relevant to social stratification or to social movements.

The critical heritage implied in analyses of class legislation, class justice, and legal class consciousness lies in the disclosure of inequality that is veiled behind formally equal legal rules. Marxian and Marxist analysis like Critical Legal Studies (see *Critical Legal Studies*) teach us about the 'dialectic' of formal and material equality. Formal equality in law means that there are legal rules framed in neutral language with no overt discrimination. But the application of these rules has a discriminatory impact on those who do not, in practice, have the options that are imputed to allegedly autonomous persons. The strategy of argumentation is fundamental for the discourse of inequality in general (see *Discrimination*.) insofar as it holds not only for class discrimination but also for unequal treatment in the cases of gender, race, color, ethnicity, nationality, etc. Also the attempts to overcome the contradiction between formal and material inequality, legally and/or politically, are similar in the various domains. Should one adopt compensatory legal measures, such as protective regulations? Should one opt for positive discrimination? (See *Affirmative Action: Comparative Policies and Controversies*; *Affirmative Action: Empirical Work on its Effectiveness*.) Or should one dispose of law generally because of its class character as Marx did in his critique of the Gotha program: law is by necessity a law of inequality (*Recht der Ungleichheit*) that cannot cope with the variety of individuals. (A similar argument can be found in radical feminism against the intrinsic male character of law. See *Feminist Legal Theory*.)

A negative heritage of the Marxist juxtaposition of class and law lies in the conception of law either as the expression of a basic anonymous class structure or as an instrument of the dominant class(es) as conscious actors. What has been systematically neglected is the ubiquitous constitutive role of law (already in the fundamental property relationships) and the functioning of law as a possible limit to political power; in short, the intrinsic value of legal normativity for a social order.

Bibliography

Abel R L 1998 *The Legal Profession in England and Wales.* Blackwell, London

Bourdieu P 1986 Forms of capital. In: Richardson J G (ed.) *Handbook of Theory and Research for the Sociology of Education.* Greenwood, Westport, CT, pp. 241–58

Eder K 1993 *The New Politics of Class. Social Movements and Cultural Dynamics in Advanced Societies.* Sage, London

Galanter M 1974 Why the 'haves' come out ahead: Speculations on the limits of legal change. *Law Society Review* **9**: 95–160

Griffith J A G 1981 *The Politics of the Judiciary*, 2nd edn. Fontana, London

Institut gosudarstva i prava AN SSSR (ed.) 1970 *Marksistko-leninskaja obščaja teorija gosudarstva i prava* (Marxist–Leninist general theory of state and law). Moscow

Lenski G 1966 *Power and Priviledge: A theory of Social Stratification.* Mcgraw-Hill, New York

Liebknecht K 1910 Gegen die preußische Klassenjustiz (Against the Prussian class justice). In: *Gesammelte Reden und Schriften*, Vol. III. 1960 Dietz, Berlin, pp. 3–55

Lukács G 1920 1971 Legality and illegality. In: *History and Class Consciousness: studies in Marxist Dialectics.* MIT Press, Cambridge, MA

Marx K 1859 Zur Kritik der politischen Ökonomie. Vorwort (On the critique of political economy. Preface). In: *Marx-Engels-Werke*, Dietz, Berlin 1975, Vol. 13, pp. 7–11

Mill J S 1861 1962 *Considerations on Representative Government.* Reprint Regnery, Chicago

Milner A 1999 *Class.* Sage, London

Pašukanis E 1924 1980 General theory of law and Marxism. In: Beirne P, Sharlet R (eds.) *Selected Writings on Marxism and Law.* Academic Press, London

Rottleuthner H (ed.) 1984 *Rechtssoziologische Studien zur Arbeitsgerichtsbarkeit* (Socio-legal studies on labor courts). Nomos Verlagsgesellschaft, Baden-Baden

Weber M 1964 *Wirtschaft und Gesellschaft* (Economy and society). Kiepenheuer and Witsch, Berlin

H. Rottleuthner

Class Consciousness

1. A Key Concept of Marxist Theory

In Marx's work the concept of class consciousness is based on his theory of social classes and the distinction he makes between existing social classes and politically active ones. It is not sufficient for a large number of individuals merely to be living under similar social conditions for them to constitute a class. In *The Eighteenth Brumaire of Louis Bonaparte* (1852), Marx describes the living conditions of peasant families. He sees them as having few connections with each other and even less with the rest of society. For this reason, these families do not form a social class. Only groups of individuals engaged in common activities, mainly relations of production and exchange, constitute a social class.

In the struggle that necessarily opposes the owners of the means of production and the workers, who possess only their labor power, all the conditions are fulfilled for the proletariat to constitute a true social class. The workers are all equally dependent upon their employers. They are forced to sell their labor and must also resist the stronghold of capital whose demands continually threaten their livelihood. This situation of dependence and resistance, this class struggle, which accompanies the beginnings of capitalist relations, becomes particularly intense due to the system's growing contradictions. As observed by Marx from 1845 onward, this is the context in which the issue of class consciousness arises. In other words, it is the situation through which workers become conscious of their shared socioeconomic conditions, of their fundamentally antagonistic relationship with the capitalists, and hence of the need for political struggle. This awareness signals a new change within the working class itself, leading it from the condition of class 'in itself' to one of class 'for itself.'

In *The Poverty of Philosophy* (1847), Marx analyzes the economic transformation of the working class and the ensuing changes in its subjective position. Since workers have been brought together, 'agglomerated,' in the same workplaces, they experience similar labor conditions. They face the same demands from their employers, and are therefore led to organize strikes together and to form 'coalitions,' which persist beyond the period of strike. Such struggles and communal activities bring the entire working class above the level of local conflicts and heighten its awareness of its political role. This rise in consciousness represents more than simply the awareness of a particular situation. For Marx, proletarian consciousness is simultaneously the discovery by the laborers of their extreme alienation and of their need to overcome such alienation through a form of action aimed at destroying the capitalist mode of production. Class consciousness is considered to be the *sine qua non* of social revolution.

Such a concept, which is both an element of Marxist philosophy of history and a theory of social change, comes from two major sources: one theoretical, the other empirical. Hegel, in *The Phenomenology of Mind* (1807), describes 'self-consciousness' as a moment in the mind's evolution by means of which the subject reaches a heightened level of awareness and a new potential for action. Yet it is essentially the changes in working conditions in the UK and France that inspired Marx to formulate such a concept. As E. P. Thompson (1963) shows in his study, *The Making of the English Working Class*, the years 1820–40 witnessed a decline in the traditional organization of the various trades, a re-enforcement of the process of proletarianization of the English working class, and the beginnings of chartism. In France, during the 1840s an increasing number of scientific and journalistic writings emphasized the unification of the working class, who thereby transcended divisions between the trades and traditional organizations. Newspapers appeared, written by workers, in which they asserted their need to express their own claims and their hopes for a new form of social organization. Some of these reiterated the appeal formulated by Saint-Simon as early as 1820, calling for class consciousness as the fundamental condition necessary for political activity by the agents of production.

2. A Political Debate

In 1865, Proudhon, one of the founders of anarchism, developed a theory similar to that of Marx. In his work, *De la capacité politique des classes ouvrières* (On the political potential of the working classes), he poses the question of the conditions necessary for a social class to unite in political action. He formulates three conditions: the achieving of self-consciousness, the formulation of a political program, and the capacity to carry out such a program. He believes that the working class has fulfilled the first two conditions since 1848, but that it has yet to reach the third condition. He emphasizes, even more than does Marx, the dynamics of the social movement and also the problems it faces as it attempts to achieve its goals.

This theory of class consciousness led to divergent and far-reaching interpretations. One could indeed conclude from it that the function of a labor party should be only to encourage class consciousness, without aiming to control or direct it. On the contrary, Lenin, in his 1902 publication *What is to be Done*, states that the class consciousness of the workers has led spontaneously within the context of capitalism to purely economic claims. He considers that it is not the working class, but rather intellectuals of bourgeois origin, who produced the theory of social revolution. He therefore concludes that the political leadership of the movement must not be handed over to representatives of the working class (who tend towards reformism and anarchism), but rather to professional revolutionaries, united by strong party discipline. These sociopolitical arguments provoked critical reactions on the part of Marxist theoreticians (Rosa Luxembourg, Georg Lukacs, Antonio Gramsci), who feared the consequences of replacing class consciousness by an authoritarian party.

3. Four Sociological Criteria

After World War II, certain works suggested that such a theory should be made sociologically relevant. To this end Mann (1973) distinguished four principles which together would constitute class consciousness: (a) identity—the definition of oneself as a member of the working class; (b) opposition—the designation of an opposing class; (c) totality—the vision of society as a whole; (d) alternative—an alternative vision of society based on different principles of organization and aimed at replacing the established order. These four conditions give rise to many different questions which numerous studies have attempted to answer.

Many studies lean toward a positive answer to the first principle, or condition, concerning the awareness of an identity. Richard Hoggart's work (1957) asks whether it is pertinent to emphasize the originality of working-class culture. Using the perspective of cultural anthropology, the study undertaken by Hoggart in England in the 1950s illustrates the uniqueness of the attitudes, the habits and the representations of the lower classes. Hoggart underlines the permanence of a strong identity among members of this milieu and their heightened awareness of the social distance existing between themselves and other social classes. The opposition between 'us' and 'them' lies at the heart of their entire social representation.

The world of the 'others' is a vague congregation of employers of the private sector and civil servants. However, such a feeling of membership does not necessarily lead to the consciousness that there exists an inevitable conflict. Moreover, class consciousness is limited essentially to those who work in industry. One might add that studies which adopt the perspective of social stratification bring nuances to this notion of identity. The works by W. L. Warner, published in the USA in 1949, suggest that the social structure differentiates between multiple levels of social status. Three of them—the lower-middle class, the upper-lower class, and the lower-lower class—together make up the working class. To this is added the distinction between ethnic groups, characterized by differing feelings of membership.

The principle of the opposition to, and the designation of, an adversarial class may be regarded both from the perspective of representation and from that of action. Many studies indicate that it is not among the most disadvantaged workers that one finds the most entrenched adversarial stances. Material difficulties, unemployment, insecurity, and lack of qualification generate a consciousness of the opposition between 'us' and 'them,' but not a polarization against an adversarial class. It is mainly in professions such as mining and among dock workers, where attachment to one's job and loyalty between members of the working group are very strong, that one finds the most adamant expressions of general opposition to authority (Touraine 1966). In industry, among skilled workers, attitudes are less radical. In their research, J. H. Goldthorpe and his collaborators (1969) formulated the general hypothesis that prosperous 'affluent' workers, who have a more functional relationship to their work, seek to obtain job stability and a higher salary, and are more interested in consumption than conflict. Patterns of strike participation confirm the main points of this thesis. In industry, strikes have wide participation, while in the service sector (banking, administration), where the organizing unions are concerned more with obtaining satisfaction for particular claims (raises, better working conditions, shorter working hours), they tend to result in negotiations.

The theory of class consciousness presupposes that the working class, due to its subordinate position, will eventually come to have a global image of society, as opposed to those who own wealth and whose horizons are limited by their personal interests (Lukács 1971). Studies of the 'images' which workers hold of the social system help to shed light on such assumptions (Bulmer 1975). These studies show that workers' representations are not as homogenous as Marxist theory might lead one to assume. Depending on whether the people questioned interpret the social system in terms of power, of prestige, or of property, they are more or less likely to perceive the social system in terms of conflict. The most adversarial perception of society is expressed by those whose perceptions are linked to power. Yet such a representation is not the most frequent one. W. L. Warner's studies of US workers already suggest that differences exist depending on the type of workplace, the degree of urbanization, and the level of qualification. The attitude of the 'affluent workers,' because they tend toward representations related to possession, suggest the generalization of an image of society in which the majority is made up of a middle class, subdivided according to wealth, income, and consumption habits.

These studies cast doubt upon the argument that claims that the working class is driven by a will for political change and by a capacity to support an alternative program. During the 1960s, these observations led to the proposal that such a political potential for change was no longer to be found among unqualified workers, but instead in a 'new working class' made up of technicians and more qualified workers from cutting-edge industries such as computers, communications, and petrochemical industries (Mallet 1963). This idea, which places emphasis on new skills, has not been confirmed. It assumes that these highly qualified technicians and workers will call upon their unions to adopt radical political stances. Yet the low level of union membership among workers in general, and in particular among such technicians, tends to indicate that they have different types of demands. They ask their unions to negotiate to safeguard their own interests, while expecting political parties to defend national interests. In this sense they reproduce the traditional divisions found in public opinion rather than following the model of political awareness supposedly characteristic of the working class.

See also: Bourgeoisie/Middle Classes, History of; Class: Social; Labor Movements, History of; Marx, Karl (1818–89); Mobility: Social; Poverty, Culture of; Social Class and Gender; Social Mobility, History of; Social Movements, Sociology of; Social Stratification; Working Classes, History of

Bibliography

Bulmer M (ed.) 1975 *Working Class Images of Society*. Routledge & Kegan Paul, London
Dahrendorf R 1959 *Class and Class Conflicts in Industrial Society*. Routledge & Kegan Paul, London
Goldthorpe J H, Lockwood D, Bechhofer F, Plat J 1969 *The Affluent Worker in the Class Structure*. Cambridge University Press, Cambridge, UK
Hoggart R 1957 *The Uses of Literacy. Aspects of Working-Class Life with Special References to Publications and Entertainments*. Chatto & Windus, London
Lockwood D 1958 *The Blackcoated Worker. A Study in Class Consciousness*. George Allen and Unwin, London
Lukács G 1971 [trans. Livingstone R] *History and Class Consciousness: Studies in Marxist Dialectics*. Merlin Press, London
Mallet S 1963 *La nouvelle classe ouvrière*. Editions du Seuil, Paris
Mann M 1973 *Consciousness and Action among the Western Working Class*. Macmillan, London
Thompson E P 1963 *The Making of the English Working Class*. Gollancz, London
Touraine A 1966 *La conscience ouvrière*. Editions du Seuil, Paris
Warner W L, Meeker M, Eells K 1960 *Social Class in America. A Manual of Procedure for the Measurement of Social Status*. Harper & Row, New York

P. Ansart

Class: Social

Class is a key concept in sociological theory, but its precise meaning and definition is highly contested. It is also a core explanatory variable in much empirical research, yet there is enormous diversity in the ways in which it is operationalized and measured. Most sociologists agree that social class refers to how people make a living, and that there are relatively stable patterns of inequality between different classes—but there the consensus ends. Indeed, some sociologists now argue that the concept of social class has outlived its usefulness and should be abandoned altogether.

1. Marx's Class Theory

The concept of 'class' was central to Marx's theory of how societies are constituted and how they change, although Marx himself never produced a definitive statement of how class was to be conceptualized. The treatment of class in his different works is not always consistent, but five basic themes emerge.

First, although different classes generally have different levels of income and different life-styles, it is not their income or life-style *per se* that distinguishes them. The crucial determinant of class is ownership (or nonownership) of productive property. Because people either own, or do not own, the basic means of production in a society, it follows that there can be only two principal classes in any mode of production. Under capitalism, these are the bourgeoisie and the proletariat.

Second, class is not a 'position' which we occupy in society, but a relationship which one group in society has to another. This relationship is one of exploitation, for those who own the means of production add to their wealth by using the labor power of those who own nothing. Because class relations are always exploitative, they are always antagonistic. Class struggle is an inherent feature of all class societies, and this perpetual battle between classes is the motor driving human history.

Third, class is more than just a concept developed by social scientists to help them make sense of the world. Classes exist, and they have real effects. Even where the members of a given class do not recognize their class identity (a situation which Engels labeled 'false consciousness'), class is still an objective reality shaping their lives.

Fourth, class struggle is a feature of every society since the development of settled agriculture. Even where divisions seem to reflect factors other than property ownership (e.g., in caste systems where status at birth counts more than wealth), the 'real' force structuring social relations is still class. Class relations shape every aspect of social life. Politics, law, art, and philosophy are the 'superstructural' expressions of a more 'basic' relation between owners and nonowners of the means of production. Class relations impose their stamp on every aspect of life.

Fifth, Marx claimed that the class relation between bourgeoisie and proletariat was becoming increasingly sharp. Capitalist societies were polarizing between a small number of large capitalists and a large number of propertyless proletarians. He predicted that the condition of the proletarians would become increasingly miserable, and that sooner or later, there would be a revolution which would replace the capitalist system with a socialist one in which there would be no classes because all productive property would be owned in common.

2. The Marxist Tradition of Class Analysis

Later Marxists have wrestled with some major problems left unresolved by Marx's analysis.

2.1 How Many Classes?

One of the most intractable problems arises out of Marx's insistence that class is structured around the relationship between owners and nonowners of the means of production. Logically, this implies that there are only ever two classes, yet in *Capital* he identifies *three* classes in modern capitalism (landowners, wage laborers, and capitalists), and, analyzing the 1848 events in Paris, he finds as many as *nine* (proletarians, financiers, industrialists, the middle class, the petty bourgeoisie, the lumpenproletariat, intellectuals, the clergy, and the peasantry).

Later Marxists have sought to resolve this confusion in two ways. First, they have distinguished 'classes' and 'class fractions.' Owners of capital, for example, are a single class, but different 'fractions' of this class squabble when their interests diverge. Thus, landowners seek to extract high rents, but this conflicts with the interests of industrialists who want to keep their overhead costs down. Industrialists and landowners share a common class interest in the maintenance of the capitalist system, but their different interests in respect of profits and rents creates different fractions within the bourgeoisie.

Second, Marxist theorists have distinguished between a pure 'mode of production' (where there are only ever two classes) and actual 'social formations' (which may contain elements of more than one mode of production, and thus more than two classes). For example, France and the UK are structured around a capitalist mode of production (with two classes, bourgeoisie and proletariat), but they also contain elements of an earlier, feudal, mode of production (the surviving elements of a peasant class in France, and an aristocratic class in the UK).

2.2 Theorizing the Middle Class

A common feature of modern capitalism in all parts of the world is the growth of managerial, administrative, and professional occupations. This 'middle class' cannot easily be explained as either a 'fraction' of one of the two 'main' classes, or a remnant of an earlier mode of production. Braverman (1974) suggested that large sections of it are 'really' part of the proletariat because they are increasingly subject to typically 'proletarian' conditions of labor such as job insecurity and deskilling, but this interpretation has been challenged, and higher up the hierarchy it is clear that managers and professionals are in quite a different situation from manual workers as regards remuneration, security of employment, career prospects, and workplace autonomy.

Recognition of these differences has resulted in various attempts to develop Marx's theory to take account of the distinctiveness of the 'new middle class.' Carchedi (1975) theorized it as employees who simultaneously contribute to the functions of 'collective worker' (e.g., by coordinating the labor process) and of capital (e.g., by controlling their fellow workers). Poulantzas (1975) distinguished it on 'political' (supervisory functions) and 'ideological' (mental labor), as well as 'economic' (nonproductive activity) criteria. And Wright (1985), while emphasizing the division between owners and nonowners of capital assets as fundamental, differentiated nonowners according to their ability to 'exploit' skills and organizational assets (a class of 'expert managers,' for example, exploits both skills and organizational assets, while proletarians can exploit neither).

All of these formulations have been influential. Their weakness, however, is their complexity (Wright's schema, for example, generates a total of 12 different classes). The more Marxist theorists have tried to develop a descriptively adequate account of the contemporary class structure, the more they have had to sacrifice the theoretical sharpness of Marx's original approach.

3. Weber's Concept of Class

Weber contradicts almost every element in Marx's approach. Where Marx insists that classes arise out of the organization of production, Weber treats them as distributional categories. For him, 'economic classes' can be identified wherever individuals share a common *market situation*, either in property markets (where those who are 'positively privileged' can live off revenues from assets) or in labor markets (where those who are 'positively privileged' can command high salaries in return for their scarce skills and qualifications). 'Social classes' are simply clusters of economic classes between which inter- or intragenerational mobility is 'easy and typical.'

In this approach, social classes are not defined in relation to each other, as they are for Marx, but are mapped positionally in a hierarchy according to their market capacity. Weber therefore has no problem identifying a 'middle class'; indeed, logically, there are two middle classes (a petty bourgeoisie of small property owners with a relatively weak labor-market position, and an intelligentsia who own few assets but who command high returns in the labor market because of their education and training). They sit between an upper class (positively privileged in property and skills) and a working class (negatively privileged on both, and therefore relatively poorly remunerated).

'Class' is not 'real' for Weber as it is for Marx—it is simply an analytical construct, a label to refer to clusters of individuals. Sometimes people express a common class identity and act accordingly—but a failure to think and act in class terms does not constitute a 'false consciousness' as it does for Engels.

It is also clear that Weber does not see class as pervasive and enduring in the way that Marx does. For him, class (market power) is only one dimension of power in society. In the modern period, it is often the most important dimension, but in other periods, the 'social power' of status groups (such as the old European aristocracy or the high castes in India), or the 'political power' of parties, mobilizing to turn state authority to their own advantage, has outweighed that of classes. Even today, status and political power can cut across class lines. There is no assumption in Weber, as there is in Marx, that the dominant economic classes are also the dominant social and political force in any society.

4. The Weberian Tradition

4.1 Class Location and Social Action

Weber's approach to class analysis was essentially concerned with classification—social classes are ideal types. This has made things easier for later theorists, for unlike Marx's approach, Weber's work can readily be adapted and developed to take account of changed conditions (such as the growth and increased complexity of the middle classes).

What is lacking in Weber's approach, however, is a causal theory. For Marx, classes *act*—they drive history through struggle. For Weber, however, classes are simply categories into which people can be classified, and the role played by these categories in the explanation of social phenomena is left open. Class may help explain some of the things that people do, but it may be irrelevant to others—the usefulness of the concept is left to empirical research to determine.

This is both a strength and a weakness of the Weberian legacy. Its strength is that it has enabled the development of class typologies which appear both valid (they adequately capture some of the key sources of differentiation in contemporary societies) and reliable (they predict fairly accurately different patterns of social behavior and attitudes). Its weakness is that Weberian class analysis has often been limited to mapping differences between classes rather than explaining them. It generates useful depictions of the 'class structure' but seems to lack a theory of 'class action' (why and how a person's location in the structure influences social action).

4.2 Work, Market, and Status Situations

One influential attempt to link people's class position to their attitudes and behavior was David Lockwood's (1958) study of clerical workers in Britain. He defined class position by people's 'work situation' (i.e., the degree of autonomy they enjoy and the authority invested in them or exercised over them) and 'status situation' (i.e., their occupational prestige) as well as their 'market situation' (i.e., their income, job security, and career prospects), and he showed that on all three criteria, clerical employees differed radically from manual workers. These differences were then reflected in their behaviors and attitudes, such as willingness to join a trade union.

Lockwood and his colleagues utilized much the same approach in a later study of the British working class (Goldthorpe et al. 1969). The research refuted the *embourgeoisement* thesis –the idea that affluence was blurring the boundary between the working class and the middle class—by identifying clear differences in the work, market and status situations of well-paid manual workers as compared with white-collar workers. These differences were then held to explain the different patterns of consciousness found in each group. Lockwood (1966) also analyzed differences *within* the working class, arguing that different work and 'community' situations could account for the different 'images of society' characteristic of traditional proletarian workers (e.g., miners), traditional deferential workers (e.g., farm laborers), and privatized workers (such as those employed in modern, high-wage industries).

Since then, John Goldthorpe (1987) has used differences in the 'work situation' (authority relations) and 'market situation' (income, security, and prospects) of different occupational groups to develop a new, 11-category model of the class structure. Developed initially as a framework for the study of social mobility in Britain, this typology became the basis for a major international study of mobility rates (Erikson and Goldthorpe 1992), and it has also been used to investigate issues such as the class basis of voting behavior (Heath et al. 1985). In comparison with other schema, it has been found to have a stronger predictive power and clearer internal consistency (Marshall et al. 1988, Breen and Rottman 1995), and it has won widespread acceptance in much of Western sociology.

4.3 Class Structuration and Social Closure

Lockwood's concern with linking people's experience, at work and in the locality, with their sense of class identity was later elaborated in Giddens's theory of class structuration. He explicitly addressed the problem of how a shared economic location becomes important for collective social action.

Weber's answer to this question emphasized patterns of social mobility and closure—social classes are clusters of individuals occupying market situations between which mobility is readily possible. Giddens (1973) refers to this as the 'mediate' structuration of social classes. He argues that market situations in modern capitalism typically cluster into three cate-

gories based around ownership of property, possession of qualifications, and possession of manual labor power, and that movement between these three is typically limited. These are the three social classes of the modern period, but Giddens then goes on to identify the factors ('proximate structuration') which keep them apart and help promote distinctive class identities. Here he echoes Lockwood's work by emphasizing the importance of differences in the workplace (e.g., in authority relations) and in the locality (e.g., residential segregation). He argues that proximate structuration always leads to some degree of 'class awareness,' though not necessarily to 'class consciousness' in a Marxist sense.

The problem of linking the 'class position' that people occupy to their values, beliefs, and actions was tackled very differently by Frank Parkin (1979), who resurrected Weber's neglected concept of 'social closure.' Closure refers to the way groups try to improve or maintain their privileges by restricting the access of others, and Parkin identified two main strategies. 'Exclusion' operates downwards and involves protection of privileges by dominant groups; 'usurpation' operates upwards and represents the attempt by subordinate groups to claim more privileges for themselves.

Exclusion typically seeks to defend privileges associated with property rights or qualifications (e.g., professional closure). Parkin defines the dominant class as those whose resources (revenues or salaries/fees) derive mainly from the exercise of exclusion. Usurpation, by contrast, is typified by forms of solidaristic action such as trade-union organization, and it is the defining feature of the subordinate class. Those in white-collar occupations, who frequently claim rewards on the basis of their individual qualifications (exclusion) and through membership of the organized labor movement (usurpation), constitute an 'intermediate class' between these two.

Defining classes by their action (mode of closure), rather than by their location in a structure of positions, Parkin claims to have sidestepped the recurring problem of how to link class positions to behavior. In his view, the 'class structure' derives from collective forms of action, rather than the other way around, and there is no structure of positions independent of the way people act.

5. Measurement of Class

Theoretical debates over whether and how to divide the population into discrete class categories are reflected in the different ways the class concept has been operationalized in empirical research.

5.1 Class as a System of Categories

Class has often been operationalized in quite crude and untheorized ways. Many studies have simply distinguished 'manual' and 'nonmanual' occupational groups, and some have used the marketing industry's sixfold system of classification based on spending power, but neither of these approaches corresponds to any sociological concept of class. In the UK, research has often used the government's five (later six) class schema, but the criteria underpinning this system shifted over time from occupational prestige to skill levels creating confusion over what the classes designate.

In recent years, there has been a growing consensus around the use of systems of classification based on the Goldthorpe schema, and even the UK government's system of classification has now been revised to bring it more into line with the neo-Weberian emphasis on work and market situation (Rose and O'Reilly 1997). However, there is still intense disagreement among researchers over whether it makes sense to measure class in terms of *categories* at all, irrespective of how they are derived.

5.2 Class as a Continuous Scale

In the USA, there is a long tradition of measuring class differences on a continuous scale rather than a categorical system of classification. The best known example is the 96-point scale developed by Blau and Duncan (1967) for their study of social mobility. They justified using a continuous scale rather than discrete categories on the grounds that there are no clear cutoff points between occupations on any of the pertinent criteria that might differentiate them. In other words, classes shade off into one another.

Their approach attracted widespread criticism. Despite reporting high correlations (> 0.9) between occupational prestige and income, and education levels, they were accused of measuring status differences rather than differences in market power, and they were attacked for their 'conservative' assumption that there is a consensus over the prevailing system of occupational rewards (Horan 1978). Partly in order to counter such criticisms, Stewart et al. (1980) developed a scale which ranks occupations according to the 'social distance' that separates them, and which does not therefore depend on any assumption of value consensus over the worth of different positions. In practice, this scale looks very similar to those based on prestige rankings and correlates highly with them, which suggests that the problem of 'ideological contamination' of occupational prestige scales has probably been exaggerated.

The advantage of continuous scales over categorical schema (such as Goldthorpe's) is that they avoid the problem of drawing artificial class 'boundaries' (Kelley 1990). There is, however, no reason why we should not use both in empirical research.

6. The Future of Class Analysis

Controversy continues today, not only over how to measure class, but also over whether the concept remains useful.

6.1 Women and Class

Feminists have criticized the failure of class analysis adequately to encompass the position of women. Like students, retired people, and the unemployed, married women who do not have full-time jobs are usually classified according to the occupation of their husbands, and even women who do have jobs may be allocated to their male partner's social class where that is 'higher' than theirs. Goldthorpe defends this on the grounds that the 'life chances' of a lower-class woman married to a higher-class man are shaped more by his market situation than by hers, but this issue still generates considerable disagreement. Very different pictures of the class structure emerge depending on whether women are allocated to their own, or to their husband's, class location.

6.2 Nonclass Identities

Feminists have also criticized class analysis for the assumption that 'class location' is more important than gender in determining life chances and influencing values and behavior. Their argument is complemented by those (notably in the USA) who emphasize the primary importance of race and ethnicity rather than class. There has also been some debate over whether people's 'consumption location' (e.g., as home owners or renters) outweighs their class location, and postmodernists insist that clear class divisions have now fragmented into a multitude of different interests and identities.

Class analysts have tended to respond to such criticisms by appealing to evidence that class identity is still primary (Marshall et al. 1988). They point out that class effects may be crosscut by gender, race, or other identities without class itself losing its significance.

6.3 The Relevance of Class

Some critics (Pahl 1989, Clark and Lipset 1991) argue that class is a concept that has outlived its usefulness. People no longer think of themselves in class terms, movement between class locations is common, boundaries between classes have blurred, and class analysis has failed to explain the causal link between class locations and social outcomes.

Responding to this, Breen and Rottman (1995) accept that class is a weak source of identity for many people, but they argue that people's 'objective' class location is still crucial in explaining many aspects of their lives. Recent work on class differences in health and morbidity (Wilkinson 1996) are one striking example. It is probably fair to conclude that class does still correlate significantly with many of the phenomena studied in social science, but we often lack a clear explanation of the mechanism which translates 'class position' into social outcomes.

See also: Class Consciousness; Consumption, Sociology of; Equality of Opportunity; Income Distribution; Inequality; Inequality: Comparative Aspects; Marx, Karl (1818–89); Mobility: Social; Social Class and Gender; Social Mobility, History of; Status and Role: Structural Aspects; Underclass; Wealth Distribution; Weber, Max (1864–1920)

Bibliography

Blau P M, Duncan O D 1967 *The American Occupational Structure*. Wiley, New York
Braverman H 1974 *Labor and Monopoly Capital*. Monthly Review Press, New York
Breen R, Rottman D B 1995 *Class Stratification: Comparative Perspective*. Harvester Wheatsheaf, New York
Carchedi G 1975 Economic identification of the new middle class. *Economy and Society* 4: 1–86
Clark T N, Lipset S M 1991 Are social classes dying? *International Sociology* 6: 397 410
Erikson R, Goldthorpe J H 1992 *The Constant Flux: A Study of Class Mobility in Industrial Societies*. Clarendon Press, Oxford, UK
Giddens A 1973 *The Class Structure of the Advanced Societies*. Hutchinson, London
Goldthorpe J H 1987 *Social Mobility and Class Structure in Modern Britain*, 2nd edn. Clarendon Press, Oxford, UK
Goldthorpe J, Lockwood D, Becchoffer F, Platt J 1969 *The Affluent Worker in the Class Structure*. Cambridge University Press, London
Heath A, Jowell R, Curtice J 1985 *How Britain Votes* 1st edn. Pergamon Press, Oxford, UK
Horan P M 1978 Is status attainment research a theoretical? *American Sociological Review* 43: 534–41
Kelley J 1990 The failure of a paradigm: Log-linear models of social mobility. In: Clark J, Modgil C, Modgil S (eds.) *John H Goldthorpe: Consensus and Controversy*. Falmer Press, London
Lockwood D 1958 *The Blackcoated Worker*. Allen and Unwin, London
Lockwood D 1966 Sources of variation in working class images of society. *Sociological Review* 14: 249–67
Marshall G, Newby H, Rose D, Vogler C 1988 *Social Class in Modern Britain*. Unwin Hyman, London
Marx K, Engels F 1968 *Collected Works in One Volume*. Lawrence and Wishart, London
Pahl R E 1989 Is the emperor naked? *International Journal of Urban and Regional Research* 13: 709–20
Parkin F 1979 *Marxism and Class Theory: A Bourgeois Critique*. Columbia University Press, New York
Poulantzas N 1975 *Classes in Contemporary Capitalism*. New Left Books, London
Rose D, O'Reilly K 1997 *Constructing Classes: Towards a New Social Classification for the UK*. ESRC and ONS, Swindon, UK
Stewart A, Prandy K, Blackburn R M 1980 *Social Stratification and Occupations*. MacMillan, London
Weber M 1968 *Economy and Society*. Bedminster Press, New York
Wilkinson R 1996 *Unhealthy Societies: The Afflictions of Inequality*. Routledge, London
Wright E 1985 *Classes*. Verso, London

P. Saunders

Classical Archaeology

The notion of 'classical archaeology' is of relatively recent origins in the vocabulary of the humanities. Its common usage dates to the second half of the nineteenth century, when archaeology, a newly formed university discipline, sought its place within the broader intellectual framework of the sciences of antiquity, the *Altertumswissenschaft* of German scholarship. For knowledge of antiquity to be scientific, it had to encompass all the creations of human genius. Thus, just as philology had emancipated itself from theology, so was archaeology to free itself from philology in order to constitute, together with the latter and with ancient history, the third pillar of *Altertumswissenschaft*. This disciplinary triangle effectively constitutes the foundations of the modern conception of the classical past—that is, the past of the Greco-Roman world.

1. The Definition of Classical Archaeology

Such a definition of classicism is quite evidently arbitrary. It rests on a very specific and thoroughly European experience of antiquity, in which Greco-Roman literature and its concepts are overwhelmingly privileged. In specifying the chronological and geographical boundaries of the classical world, nineteenth century historians and archaeologists have confirmed a spatio–temporal distinction already initiated during antiquity, and notably in the Alexandrian golden age of the third and second centuries BC. Following this definition, the classical world effectively begins with the dispersal of the Greeks in the Mediterranean during the eighth century BC, and ends with the fall of the occidental Roman empire in 476 AD. In terms of its geographical extension, the classical world reaches as far as the farthest expansion of the Roman empire, at the end of the first century AD.

As can be seen, this mode of historical representation clearly focuses on the Mediterranean as the zone of contact between Europe, Africa and Asia. But where does this Mediterranean space actually ends? Is it somewhere in the vast European plains? On the shores of the Black Sea? At the foot of the mountain ranges bordering Anatolia or Africa? According to their readings of both the classical sources and the surrounding landscapes, experts have drawn different boundaries to the classical world. Given this diversity of opinions, German archaeologists have proposed the notion of *Randkulturen* to designate all those civilizations known to have been in contact with the classical world without fully merging with it: Scythians, Parthians, Germans, Phoenicians, Egyptians, and many others.

Chronology is not much better established. When the Archaic epoch was first identified, archaeologists knew nothing of the Minoan world and the palace civilizations of Greek antiquity, civilizations which later on would end being called preclassical. At the other end of the scale, the date commonly chosen to signal the conclusion of Greco-Roman history—the fall of the occidental Roman empire in 476 AD—proves to be equally problematic: it takes no account of the persistence of the oriental Roman empire until the fall of Constantinopolis in 1453.

2. The History of Classical Archaeology

With its uncertain chronological and geographical boundaries (a problem admittedly shared with protohistory), classical archaeology stands somewhat apart from other, more global, strands of archaeology. It is both the oldest among these archaeologies, and the one most influenced by tradition: the ancient Greek word *archaiologia* retains within it all its meaning as a discourse on antiquity. It was, after all, in fifth century Greece that the historical genre first appeared, the reasoned discourse on the past to which the Greeks gave the name of *historia* (enquiry). And since Varron in the first century BC, the title of antiquary has been given to the man who seeks to interpret and classify ancient objects or monuments. In Greece as well as in Rome, these antiquaries contributed to elucidate the past; they assembled series of objects and monuments, collected inscriptions, and then put them in order and sought to understand them.

In this respect, the collapse of the Occidental Roman Empire was not without consequence, for with it a whole social class of knowledge- producers and users came to disappear. Secular men of letters were gradually replaced by clerics, whose function was to educate the masses and the elite in the Christian faith. To be sure, there were among these clerics some antiquarians who undertook to collect and investigate the monuments of antiquity. But one has to wait until the end of the Middle Ages to find an antiquarian movement comparable to that of Greco-Roman times.

It was in Renaissance Italy that a new passion for antiquity emanated which was also a means for reinventing the contemporary world. Collections of Greek and Roman manuscripts arose passions, ancient coins were coveted, monuments begun to be excavated for the sculptures and architectural remains they may have contained. The past that was sought after and revived was that of Greece and Rome, if only because a reference to this world was seen as a means to do away with a present seen as barbarous, illiterate and indeed 'gothic.'

For Renaissance scholars, antiquity was quintessentially Greco-Roman: the literary works, sculptures and architecture of these periods were seen as unsurpassable productions, to be studied and emulated by the best contemporary artists. This classical focus dominated scholarly and artistic production until the end of the eighteenth century, and it explains that 'barbarian' antiquities received only marginal interest. The Renaissance has thus contributed to conflating the knowledge of the past with the investigation and understanding of the Greco-Roman heritage—the part of universal culture believed to be 'classic' by virtue of being the veritable pedestal of humanist scholarship. There were some scholars who manifested considerable interest for the oriental world, Egypt or even Mesopotamia, and others, particularly in Scandinavia, Britain and Germany, who paid attention to local antiquities, but the model for the organization of knowledge derived directly from the prestigious Greco-Roman tradition.

Renaissance scholars and their Enlightenment successors assembled together coins, inscriptions, sculptures, and sometimes even ceramics or other objects of daily life. These collections were displayed in 'cabinets of curiosity' and eventually came to adorn the first public museums, such as the Venetian collections and the Ashmolean Museum in Oxford (from 1683). However, since no careful observations were made regarding the place of discovery and the mode of manufacture of these collected works and monuments, it was only with the greatest difficulty that scholars were able to classify them in terms of their dates and provenance. In fact, it was only the antiquarians of the eighteenth century who were first able to lay the grounds of a critical analysis of archaeological monuments.

These advances occurred at different paces, and they were due both to discoveries in the field and to new attitudes towards finds and their study. In this respect, the fortuitous discovery of the buried cities of Pompeii and Herculaneum at the beginning of the eighteenth century did much to awaken the interest of the elite in the Greco-Roman world. What was being unearthed there by the excavating teams of the King of Naples were no longer usual ruins, but entire cities, covered by volcanic eruptions and thus miraculously preserved from the ravages of destruction. Closely guarded by the Neapolitan government, the exploration of Pompeii gave rise to an unprecedented craze for the painting, architecture and implements of daily life of the time. Given the context of their discoveries, these items could also for the first time be attributed a secure chronological position. Naples thus played the role of an antiquarian capital, and gradually came to compete with Rome in the esteem of travelers and connoisseurs.

Without interpretation, however, discovery is nothing. In the second part of the eighteenth century, two men revolutionized the understanding of antiquity. The first of these was Johannes Winckelmann (1717–68), a German scholar from a small Prussian town who achieved tremendous influence with his work. His *History of Art in Antiquity*, published in Leipzig in 1764, offered to amateurs of Greco-Roman art the first ever systematic and chronological treatise on the subject. Aided by a thorough familiarity with textual sources, Winckelmann depicted and commented on antique objects scattered throughout European collections. Drawing on his personal study of the most important Roman collections, he could propose to his readers a remarkable history of plastic forms in antiquity. The style of this work, the quality of its descriptions, and the philosophical spirit which animated it, all explain its unprecedented success: with it, the occident could at last discover the sources of Renaissance art in the classical world. Winckelmann, otherwise an enemy of the aristocracy and determined critic of the ancient regime, received his highest acclaim from the courts of kings and princes, among those who sought antiquity for the aesthetic pleasure it procured them.

One of the most notable aristocrats in the court of France, the Comte de Caylus (1692–1765), was instrumental in drawing the attention of his contemporaries to another aspect of the study of the past. For Caylus, what justified the quest for antiquity is not the aesthetic, but the technical achievements of the past. He therefore developed an approach to the study of past techniques in which can be recognized our current concerns with artifact morphology and archaeometry. Each in his way, Winckelmann for the appreciation of art and Caylus for the understanding of techniques, laid down the bases for a history of the *oeuvres* of antiquity, a research programme developed and followed throughout the nineteenth century.

3. The Rules of Classical Archaeology

The exploration of antiquity thus gradually transformed itself into a new discipline of archaeology. Under this framework, nineteenth century scientists elaborated and imposed new rules for the extraction, analysis and publication of evidence from the past. Archaeology distanced itself from collections and from the social milieu of collecting, and advocated instead the necessity of observing finds in the field, and of recognizing them as coherent wholes open to

rigorous analysis. While the antiquarian channeled his passion for the past to the collection of objects, the archaeologist aimed to valorise these objects and monuments in the context of their discovery. This approach found its most systematic expression in Germany with the research programme of E. Gerhard (1795–1867), who effectively fought for an autonomous archaeology, free from collectors, philologists and artists. Archaeologists must take the place of connoisseurs with their various intermediaries, and themselves seek for the evidence on the ground.

They must also distance themselves from philologists, and challenge the primacy of written over nonwritten sources. Finally, they must take leave of aesthetic considerations, and study ancient productions in all their material and technical dimensions. Building on advances in historical studies, this positivist program also drew on developments in geology and natural history to forge for itself its specific scientific instruments.

Three complementary pillars came then to form then backbone of archaeology. One, *stratigraphy*, consists of observing the conditions of deposition of objects and monuments in the ground. The second, *typology*, seeks to identity in the objects themselves some evidence regarding the time and place of their manufacture. The third, *technology*, deals with the modes of production, the raw materials, the procedures of fabrication. It was in fact only by the end of the nineteenth century, when these three strands were mastered and marshaled together, that archaeology became a fully-fledged discipline able to undertake the reliable and methodical investigation of the past. The body of doctrines and institutions which accompanied this development contributed to giving archaeology, and specifically to classical archaeology, its distinctive identity. In this respect E. Gerhard created a novel kind of institution which prefigures in many ways those of today: the *Instituto di corrispondenza archeologica*, established in 1829 in Rome through the activities of aristocrats and scholars from across Europe, took it as its aim to collect, excavate and publish as thoroughly as possible all the antiquities of the Mediterranean world.

By drawing archaeologists to the field, by elaborating a modern strategy of publication based on detailed sections and descriptions, the *Instituto* virtually launched the new discipline that was embodied in this dedicated research institution located in Rome, one of the capitals of the classical world.

Until the middle of the nineteenth century, the exploration of the Greco-Roman world had been a matter of individual enterprise with occasional royal support. From then on, archaeology would become what the discoverer of Greek Asia Minor T. Wiegand (1864–1936) has called a *Grosswissenschaft*, a state-sponsored science. The leading European powers established then various institutes or schools in Rome and Athens, and these encouraged archaeological expeditions throughout the main urban sites of the Mediterranean. The enormous success encountered by the private initiatives of the German businessman Heinrich Schliemann (1822–90) at Mycenae and Troy fueled a veritable scramble for new excavating territories among the countries of Europe and even America. This competition contributed notably to the growth of collections in the main European and American museums. The rise of such museums as the British Museum, the Louvre, the Berlin museums and even the Metropolitan Museum in New York, all catering for an ever-increasing public, corresponded with the ascendancy of a classical archaeology closely entwined with the economic developments of capitalism and colonialism. The conquest of the past was effectively an instrument of foreign policy in the hands of all main powers, beginning with the core area of the Greco-Roman world and reaching towards the Orient, Africa, and the globe as whole.

Archaeological schools, museums and, of course, universities were all part of this expansion, from which they have benefited. Whereas in the mid nineteenth century only Germany was endowed with a network of university Chairs in classical archaeology, by 1914 all European nations as well as the United States had established university curricula in classical archaeology. This three-pronged movement, involving the development of museum collections, the systematic excavation of sites, and the setting of an academic theoretical and educational framework, effectively gave to classical archaeology its modern appearance.

4. The Paths of Classical Archaeology

Set out during the second half of the nineteenth century, this disciplinary model witnessed during the first half of the twentieth century a considerable expansion and consolidation in both qualitative and quantitative terms. Alongside a marked increase in the number of excavations carried out, the main archaeological institutions followed the German model by systematically publishing catalogues of finds and collections according to specific descriptive protocols. This increased and refined considerably the existing knowledge on artistic and artisanal productions: sculptures, architecture, ceramics were all researched, and so were numismatics and glyptics. Thus classical archaeology forged itself a vast corpus of systematic reference, bearing equally on chronology, typology and technology.

Some criticisms and contradictions emerged, however, during the second half of the twentieth century. The implicit supremacy of Greco-Roman culture came under challenge; the comparative study of cultures raised questions over the Hellenocentrism characteristic of most Classical archaeologists, while advances in the study of mentalities promoted a critique

of Eurocentrism. The Greek and Roman worlds are now understood as melting-pots rather than *hochkulturen*. Under the influence of economic history, scholarly interest has shifted from a history of art in the narrow sense towards a wider history of productions. The better chronological grasp allowed by typological studies has served to advance studies on colonization, on long distance contacts and trade. Studies of the relations between centre and periphery, between Greeks, Roman and 'barbarians' have benefited from developments in the field of protohistory. It may indeed be said that the research program of classical archaeology has undergone a wide-reaching redefinition during the 1960s.

No longer considered as the elder of the sciences of antiquity, it is now one discipline among others, sharing resources and addressing issues similar to other strands of archaeology. In this context, such topics as the history of the landscape, or that of the movements of populations and the exchanges of goods and ideas, all open up new perspectives which contribute to extricate classical archaeology from its somewhat marginal position.

At the same time, advances in the iconography and the sociology of representations make it possible to cast a new light and reach a more satisfying understanding of otherwise well-known bodies of evidence. Thus, building on the strength of its centuries-long traditions as a science dedicated to Ancient art, Classical archaeology is developing now into to a human science in the full sense of the term.

See also: Christianity Origins: Primitive and 'Western' History; Chronology, Stratigraphy, and Dating Methods in Archaeology; Historiography and Historical Thought: Classical Period (Especially Greece and Rome)

Bibliography

Bérard C, Vernant J-P 1989 *A City of Images. Iconography and Society in Ancient Greece*. Princeton University Press, Princeton, NJ

Bordein A, Hölscher T, Zanker P (eds.) 2000 *Klassiche Archaeologie, eine Einführung*. Dieter Reimer Verlag, Berlin, Germany

Elsner J A 1955 *Art and the Roman Viewer, the Transformation of Art from the Pagan World to Christianity*. Cambridge University Press, Cambridge, UK

Goldhill S, Osborne R (eds.) 1994 *Art and Text in Ancient Greek Culture*. Cambridge University Press, Cambridge, UK

Marchand S L 1996 *Down from Olympus. Archaeology and Philhellenism in Germany*. Princeton University Press, Princeton, NJ

Morris I (ed.) 1994 *Classical Greece, Ancient Histories and Modern Archaeologies*. Cambridge University Press, Cambridge, UK

Parslow C C 1998 *Rediscovering Antiquity, Karl Weber and the Excavations of Herculaneum, Pompeii and Stabiae*. Cambridge University Press, Cambridge, UK

Schnapp A 1997 *The Discovery of the Past*. Harry Abrams, New York

Thomson de Grummond N (ed.) 1996 *An Encyclopedia of the History of Classical Archaeology*. Greenwood Press, Westport, CT

A. Schnapp

Classical Conditioning and Clinical Psychology

Classical conditioning occurs when neutral stimuli are associated with a psychologically significant event. The main result is that the stimuli come to evoke a set of responses or emotions that may contribute to many clinical disorders, including (but not limited to) anxiety disorders and drug dependence. Research on conditioning has uncovered many surprising details about the underlying learning process, as well as methods for eliminating emotional and behavioral problems.

1. Historical Background

Classical conditioning was first studied systematically at the turn of the twentieth century by the Russian physiologist, Ivan Pavlov (Pavlov 1927). In the usual description of his best-known experiment, Pavlov rang a bell and then gave a dog some food. After a few pairings of bell and food, the dog began to salivate to the bell, and thus anticipated the presentation of food. The classical conditioning phenomenon quickly attracted psychologists who applied it to clinical issues. Before most of Pavlov's work was available in English, John Watson showed that human emotions are also influenced by classical conditioning (Watson and Rayner 1920). Watson showed an infant boy a stimulus (which happened to be a laboratory rat) and then made a frightening noise. After a few pairings of the rat and the noise, the child became afraid whenever the rat was presented. This fear generalized to a rabbit, a dog, and a fur coat. Watson saw conditioning as a means by which emotions could be elicited by an expanding range of cues.

The application of conditioning to clinical issues became central to the behavior therapy movement that began in the 1950s and 1960s (e.g., Wolpe 1958, see also *Behavior Therapy: Psychological Perspectives*). The idea was that psychiatric disorders could be understood and treated using scientifically established principles of learning. The view that anxiety disorders result from classical conditioning was later criticized (e.g., Rachman 1977). However, many of the criticisms were directed at an obsolete view of conditioning, the science of which continued to advance after behavior therapy began (see below).

2. Behavioral Consequences of Classical Conditioning

The events in Pavlov's experiment are often described using terms designed to make the experiment applicable to any situation. The food is the 'unconditional stimulus,' or US, because it unconditionally elicits salivation before the experiment begins. The bell is known as the 'conditional stimulus,' or CS, because it only elicits the salivary response conditional on the bell–food pairings. The new response to the bell is correspondingly called the 'conditional response' (CR), while the natural response to the food itself is the 'unconditional response' (UR).

Culture has created the impression that conditioning is a rigid affair in which a fixed event comes to elicit a fixed response. In fact, conditioning is more complex and dynamic than that. For example, signals for food may evoke a large set of responses that prepare the organism to digest food: They can elicit secretion of gastric acid, pancreatic enzymes, and insulin in addition to the famous salivary response. The CS can also elicit approach behavior, an increase in body temperature, and a state of arousal and excitement. When a signal for food is presented to a quiescent, food-replete animal, the animal may get up and eat more food. Signals for food evoke a whole 'behavior system' that is functionally organized to deal with the meal (Timberlake 1994).

Classical conditioning is also involved in other aspects of eating. Through conditioning, humans may learn to like or dislike different foods. In infrahuman animals, flavors associated with nutrients (sugars, starches, calories, proteins, or fats) come to be preferred. Flavors associated with sweet tastes are also preferred, while flavors associated with bitter tastes are avoided. At least as important, flavors associated with illness become disliked, as illustrated by the person who gets sick drinking tequila and consequently learns to hate the flavor. The fact that flavor CSs can be associated with such a range of biological consequences (USs) is important for omnivorous animals that need to learn about new foods. And it has clinical implications. For example, chemotherapy can make cancer patients sick, and can therefore cause the conditioning of an aversion to a food that was eaten recently (or to the clinic itself). And conditioning can enable external cues to trigger food consumption and craving, a potential influence on overeating and obesity.

Classical conditioning also occurs when we ingest drugs. Whenever a drug is taken, it constitutes a US, and it may be associated with potential CSs that are present at the time (rooms, odors, injection rituals, etc.). CSs that are associated with drug USs can have an interesting property: They often elicit a conditioned response that seems opposite to the unconditional effect of the drug (Siegel 1989). For example, although morphine causes a rat to feel less pain, a CS associated with morphine elicits an opposite increase, not a decrease, in pain sensitivity. Similarly, although alcohol can cause a drop in body temperature, a conditioned response to a CS associated with alcohol is typically an increase in body temperature. In these cases, the conditioned response is said to be 'compensatory' because it counteracts the drug effect. Compensatory responses are another example of how classical conditioning helps organisms prepare for a biologically significant US.

Compensatory conditioned responses have implications for drug abuse. First, they can cause drug tolerance, in which repeated administration of a drug reduces its effectiveness. As a drug and a CS are repeatedly paired, the compensatory response to the CS becomes stronger and more effective at counteracting the effect of the drug. The drug therefore has less impact. One implication is that tolerance will be lost if the drug is taken without being signaled by the usual CS. Consistent with this idea, administering a drug in a new environment can cause a loss of drug tolerance and make drug overdose more likely (see Siegel 1989). A second implication stems from the fact that compensatory responses may be unpleasant. A CS associated with an opiate may elicit several compensatory responses—it may cause the drug user to be more sensitive to pain, undergo a change in body temperature, and perhaps become hyperactive (the opposite of another unconditional morphine effect). The unpleasantness of these responses may motivate the user to take the drug again to get rid of them. Compensatory responses may often resemble withdrawal effects (Siegel 1989). The idea is that the urge to take drugs may be strongest in the presence of CSs that have been associated with the drug. The hypothesis is consistent with self-reports of abusers who, after a period of abstinence, are tempted to take the drug again when they are re-exposed to drug-associated cues.

Classical conditioning is also involved in anxiety disorders, as Watson originally envisioned. We now know that CSs associated with frightening USs can elicit a whole system of conditioned fear responses, again broadly designed to help the organism cope. In animals, cues associated with frightening events elicit a set of natural defensive reactions that have evolved to prevent attack by predators. They also elicit changes in respiration, heart rate, and blood pressure, and even a (compensatory) decrease in sensitivity to pain. Brief CSs that occur close to the US in time can also elicit adaptively timed protective reflexes. For example, the rabbit blinks to a brief signal that predicts a mild electric shock near the eye. The same CS, when lengthened in duration and paired with the same US, elicits mainly fear responses. And fear elicited by a CS

may potentiate the conditioned eyeblink response elicited by another CS or a startle response to a sudden noise. Once again, CSs do not merely elicit a simple reflex, but evoke a complex and interactive set of responses.

Classical fear conditioning can contribute to phobias (where specific objects may be associated with a traumatic US) as well as other anxiety disorders. For example, in panic disorder, people who have unexpected panic attacks can become anxious about having another one (see *Panic Disorder*). In this case, the panic attack (the US or UR) may condition anxiety to the external situation in which it occurs (e.g., a crowded bus) and also internal ('interoceptive') CSs created by early symptoms of the attack (e.g., dizziness or a sudden pounding of the heart). These CSs may then come to evoke anxiety or panic responses. Panic disorder may begin because external cues associated with panic can arouse anxiety, which may then exacerbate the next unconditional panic attack and/or panic response elicited by an interoceptive CS (Bouton et al. 2001). Interestingly, the emotional reactions elicited by CSs may not require conscious awareness for their occurrence or development. Indeed, fear conditioning may be independent of conscious awareness (e.g., LeDoux 1996).

In addition to eliciting conditioned responses, CSs also motivate ongoing behavior. For example, presenting a CS that elicits anxiety can increase the vigor of instrumental or operant behaviors that have been learned to avoid or escape the frightening US. Thus, an individual with panic disorder will be more likely to express avoidance in the presence of anxiety cues. Similar effects may occur with CSs that predict other USs (such as drugs or food)—as already mentioned, a drug-associated CS may motivate the drug abuser to take more drugs. The potential influence of classical conditioning on behavior is thus extensive and ubiquitous.

3. The Learning Process in Classical Conditioning

Modern research has revealed some important details about the learning process that underlies classical conditioning (Rescorla 1988). For example, conditioning is not an inevitable consequence of pairing a CS with a US. Such pairings will not cause conditioning if there is a second CS present that already predicts the US (Kamin 1969). This sort of finding ('blocking') suggests that a CS must provide new information about the US if learning is to occur. Many theorists now suppose that conditioning is determined by the discrepancy between (a) the US predicted by all CSs present on a trial and (b) the US that actually happens on the trial (Rescorla and Wagner 1972). One implication is that, depending on the size and direction of the discrepancy, the pairing of a CS and traumatic

US, for example, can cause an increase in fear conditioning, no change in conditioning, or even a decrease in conditioning.

The latter implication is interesting. A new CS can acquire a negative value if the US is smaller than that which other CSs present predict. Casually speaking, the new CS predicts 'less US than expected.' Such negative signals are called 'conditioned inhibitors' because they inhibit performance elicited by other CSs. They are clinically relevant because they may hold pathological CRs like anxiety at bay. A loss of the inhibition would allow the anxiety response to emerge.

Classical conditioning is most robust if the CS and US are intense or salient. It is also best if the CS and US are novel. For example, in 'latent inhibition,' repeated exposure to the CS alone before conditioning can diminish its ability to elicit responding when it is paired with the US. In the 'US pre-exposure effect,' repeated exposure to the US before conditioning can likewise decrease the conditioning that later occurs when a CS and the US are paired. One idea is that the CS and the US must be 'surprising' at the time of their pairing for learning to occur. Thus, the effects of pairing a CS with trauma or drug USs may depend in subtle ways on the individual's prior experience with the CS and US.

There are important variants of classical conditioning. In 'sensory preconditioning,' two stimuli (A and B) are first paired, and then one of them (A) is later paired with the US. Stimulus A evokes conditioned responding, of course, but so does stimulus B—indirectly, through its association with A. One implication is that exposure to a potent US like a panic attack may influence our reactions to stimuli that have never been paired with the US directly; the sudden anxiety response to stimulus B might seem spontaneous and mysterious. A related finding is 'second-order conditioning.' Here, A is paired with a US first and then subsequently paired with stimulus B. Once again, both A and B will evoke responding. Sensory preconditioning and second-order conditioning increase the range of stimuli that can control conditioned responses.

Emotional responses can also be conditioned through observation. For example, a monkey that merely observes another monkey being frightened by a snake can learn to be afraid of the snake itself (Mineka 1992). The observer learns to associate the snake (CS) with its own emotional reaction (US/UR) to the other monkey being afraid. Although monkeys readily learn to fear snakes, they are less likely to associate other salient cues (such as colorful flowers) with fear in the same way. This is an example of 'preparedness' in classical conditioning—some stimuli are especially effective signals for some USs because evolution has made them that way. (Another example is the fact that tastes are easily associated with illness but not shock, whereas auditory and visual cues are easily associated with shock but not illness.) Preparedness may explain why human phobias tend to be for certain objects (snakes or spiders) and not others (knives or electric sockets) that may as often be paired with pain or trauma.

4. 'Unlearning' in Classical Conditioning

Once one accepts a role for conditioning in behavioral and emotional disorders, the question becomes how to eliminate it. Pavlov studied 'extinction': conditioned responding decreases if the CS is presented repeatedly without the US after conditioning. Extinction is the basis of many therapies that reduce pathological conditioned responding through repeated exposure to the CS. Another elimination procedure is 'counterconditioning,' in which the CS is paired with a very different US/UR. Counterconditioning was the inspiration for 'systematic desensitization,' a behavior therapy technique in which frightening CSs are deliberately associated with relaxation during therapy (Wolpe 1958).

Although extinction and counterconditioning reduce unwanted conditioned responses, they do not destroy the original learning, which remains in the brain, ready to return to behavior under the right circumstances. For example, conditioned responses that have been eliminated by extinction or counterconditioning can recover if time passes before the CS is presented again ('spontaneous recovery'). Conditioned responses can also recover if the patient returns to the original context of conditioning (the general situation, mood, or state in which conditioning occurred), or if the current context is associated with the US (Bouton 2000). All of these phenomena are potential mechanisms for relapse. Techniques that may minimize relapse include conducting therapy in the contexts where the disorder is a problem, conducting therapy in multiple contexts, or providing the client with retrieval cues or retrieval strategies that help recall therapy (Bouton 2000). In the long run, contemporary research on extinction and counterconditioning may suggest ways to optimize their clinical effectiveness.

5. Challenges

The idea that classical conditioning is a basis of behavior disorders, particularly anxiety disorders, has not gone unchallenged. However, most challenges have been directed at early versions of conditioning theory that did not recognize factors such as information value, latent inhibition, preparedness, or context. For instance, Rachman (1977) noted that London air raids during World War II did not cause an increase in anxiety disorders despite their emotional impact. We now know that air raids might not have caused conditioning if the potential CSs were familiar rather than novel, if the raids were experienced in the presence of safety cues that inhibited fear (e.g., relatives, bomb shelters), or if the raids were signaled by other cues (e.g., sirens) that could have 'blocked' conditioning of potential CSs (Kamin 1969). Another criticism was that fears in the general population are disproportionately directed toward things like snakes, a fact that is consistent with the preparedness principle (above). As a final example, critics of conditioning explanations of panic disorder have asked why a CS like a pounding heart does not elicit panic in the context (say) of athletic exercise, or why extinction exposure to the CS without panic during exercise does not eliminate its ability to cause panic in other situations. The answer may be that the loss of responding that occurs in extinction is especially specific to the context in which it is learned (Bouton et al. 2001). Thus, although fear may extinguish in the context of exercise, that extinction will not abolish the CS's ability to elicit fear in other contexts, such as a crowded bus or a shopping mall. The fact that conditioned responses generalize more across contexts than extinction does may be a reason why many disorders are so persistent.

6. Future Directions

Basic research on classical conditioning will continue to investigate the circumstances that allow (and prevent) conditioning to occur, how conditioning is represented in memory and the brain, and how it ultimately influences cognitions, emotions, and behavior. Research will also address how extinction and other behavior-elimination procedures work and can be improved. That research may eventually explain why conditioning processes like extinction seem more context-specific than conditioning itself. And it will also eventually provide a more complete account of the factors that determine the nature and form of conditioned responses, and how the many responses that CSs can evoke can also interact and interrelate.

As our understanding of classical conditioning continues to deepen and expand, so will our insight into its possible role in various clinical disorders. Understanding the role of conditioning in causing a disorder, however, will probably also require prospective studies in which clinical investigators observe conditioning trials as they naturally occur in the world and then measure their effects as the disorder actually develops. It will also benefit from a better appreciation of how conditioning processes interact with biological factors (such as genetically linked vulnerabilities) that may also play a role. And it will benefit from a better understanding of how conditioning interacts with cognitive factors such as thoughts, beliefs, and awareness. Although biological and cognitive factors are sometimes viewed as alternatives to simple learning

processes like classical and operant conditioning, a complete appreciation of any disorder will probably require a more integrative perspective on how these factors work in combination.

In the meantime, classical conditioning remains a surprisingly rich scientific phenomenon that can be expected to come into play whenever people experience significant emotional and biological events and can associate them with other events in their world.

See also: Autonomic Classical and Operant Conditioning; Behavior Therapy: Psychological Perspectives; Classical Conditioning, Neural Basis of; Clinical Psychology: Animal Models; Fear Conditioning; Operant Conditioning and Clinical Psychology; Panic Disorder; Pavlov, Ivan Petrovich (1849–1936); Watson, John Broadus (1878–1958)

Bibliography

Bouton M E 2000 A learning theory perspective on lapse, relapse, and the maintenance of behavior change. *Health Psychology* **19** (Suppl.): 57–63

Bouton M E, Mineka S, Barlow D H 2001 A modern learning theory perspective on the etiology of panic disorder. *Psychological Review* **108**: 4–32

Kamin L J 1969 Predictability, surprise, attention, and conditioning. In: Campbell B A, Church R M (eds.) *Punishment and Aversive Behavior*. Appleton-Century-Crofts, New York, pp. 279–96

LeDoux J 1996 *The Emotional Brain*. Simon and Schuster, New York

Mineka S 1992 Evolutionary memories, emotional processing and the emotional disorders. *The Psychology of Learning and Motivation* **28**: 161–206

Pavlov I P 1927 *Conditioned Reflexes*. Oxford University Press, Oxford, UK

Rachman S 1977 The conditioning theory of fear-acquisition: A critical examination. *Behavior Research and Therapy* **15**: 375–87

Rescorla R A 1988 Pavlovian conditioning: It's not what you think it is. *American Psychologist* **43**: 151–60

Rescorla R A, Wagner A R 1972 A theory of Pavlovian conditioning: Variations in the effectiveness of reinforcement and nonreinforcement. In: Black A H, Prokasy W F (eds.) *Classical Conditioning II*. Appleton-Century-Crofts, New York, pp. 64–99

Siegel S 1989 Pharmacological conditioning and drug effects. In: Goudie A J, Emmett-Oglesby M W (eds.) *Psychoactive Drugs*. Humana Press, Clifton, NY pp. 115–80

Timberlake W 1994 Behavior systems, associationism, and Pavlovian conditioning. *Psychonomic Bulletin and Review* **1**: 405–20

Watson J B, Rayner R 1920 Conditioned emotional reactions. *Journal of Experimental Psychology* **3**: 1–14

Wolpe J 1958 *Psychotherapy by Reciprocal Inhibition*. Stanford University Press, Stanford, CA

M. E. Bouton

Classical Conditioning, Neural Basis of

Classical conditioning, a phenomenon described by Pavlov around 1900, is an elementary form of associative learning that is considered to be an essential building block for complex learning. This article will present some essential characteristics of classical conditioning that permit this learning to be a model system *par excellence* for understanding the neurobiology of how the brain encodes, stores and retrieves memory.

1. Introduction and Historical Background

Classical or Pavlovian conditioning is the simplest form of associative learning by which animals, including humans, learn relations among events in the world so that their future behaviors are better adapted to their environments (Rescorla 1988). Generally, classical conditioning ensues when an initially neutral stimulus (conditional stimulus, CS) is paired in close temporal proximity with a biologically significant stimulus (unconditional stimulus, US) that elicits an unlearned, reflexive behavior (unconditional response, UR). Through CS–US association formation, the animal learns to exhibit a learned behavior (conditional response, CR) to the CS that generally (a) resembles the UR (but not always), (b) precedes the US in time, and (c) reaches a maximum at about the time of US onset. A typical classical conditioning arrangement is represented in Fig. 1. [It should be noted that the contingent (informational), rather than contiguous (temporal), relationship between CS and US is essential in classical conditioning. For detailed treatment of this see Kamin 1968, Rescorla, 1968, Wagner et al. 1968.]

Classical conditioning was first characterized by Ivan P. Pavlov, a Russian physiologist. [The English translation of Pavlov's book *Conditioned Reflexes* was first published in 1927. Classical conditioning was also independently discovered by an American Psychologist, Edwin B. Twitmyer.] Having already conducted prominent work on the digestive system, for which he received a Nobel Prize in 1904, Pavlov employed a salivary-conditioning procedure in dogs to systematically characterize some of the fundamental principles of classical conditioning. In brief, Pavlov's dogs were presented with a discrete CS (e.g., the beat of a metronome) just prior to the delivery of a US (e.g., meat powder). Initially, the subjects did not respond to the CS but salivated profusely (UR) to the US. With repeated CS–US pairings, Pavlov's dogs exhibited salivation (CR) to the CS that both preceded US onset and occurred in the absence of the US.

2. Behavioral Principles of Classical Conditioning

Since Pavlov, various types of classical conditioning procedures have been developed, ranging from a potently fast (one-trial) taste aversion conditioning

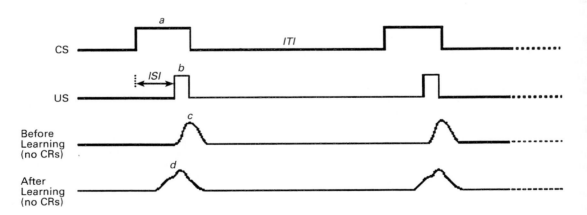

Figure 1

A typical classical conditioning procedure requires that the CS and the US are paired in close temporal proximity. Presentation of CS and US may be scheduled according to two different temporal arrangements: (i) In delay conditioning, CS onset procedes US onset, such that the two stimuli overlap and terminate together; (ii) In trace conditioning, the CS and the US are separated by some 'empty' interval in which neither stimuli is present. The top two traces indicate presentation of the CS and the US in a delay conditioning arrangement. The bottom two traces depict behavioral responses before learning and after learning. (*a*), CS duration; (*b*), US duration; (*c*), UR; (*d*), CR + UR; *ISI* (Inter-stimulus Interval), the time between the CS onset and the US onset; *ITI* (Inter-trial Interval), the time between the termination of one CS–US pairing and the beginning of the next CS–US pairing (e.g., Garcia et al. 1974) to a relatively slow and incremental eyeblink conditioning (e.g., Gormezano et al. 1983), and a wide variety of organisms have been used, ranging from invertebrates (e.g., *Aplysia*) to primates (e.g., humans). These different types of classical conditioning, however, all share certain common factors that influence the formation of CS–US associations which can be classified into three general categories: *contiguity* (or temporal) constraints, *sensory* constraints, and *contingency* (or informational) constraints (Table 1). Clearly, these constraints must be considered when employing classical conditioning in learning and memory research.

In addition to simple CS–US pairings (also called first order conditioning), there are many other training protocols within classical conditioning that can serve as effective tools for investigating the theoretical and biological mechanisms of learning and memory. Some of these are presented in Fig. 2.

1st order conditioning :	CS^O	+	US^R	$\longrightarrow$	CS^R
Extinction :	CS^R alone			$\longrightarrow$	CS^O
Compound conditioning :	CS_1^O/CS_2^O	+	US^R	$\longrightarrow$	$CS_1^R ; CS_2^R$
2nd order conditioning : (i)	CS_1^O	+	US^R	$\longrightarrow$	CS_1^R
(ii)	CS_2^O	+	CS_1^R	$\longrightarrow$	CS_2^R
Overshadowing :	CS_1^O/CS_2^O	+	US^R	$\longrightarrow$	$CS_1^R ; CS_2^O$
Blocking : (i)	CS_1^O	+	US^R	$\longrightarrow$	CS_1^R
(ii)	CS_1^R/CS_2^O	+	US^R	$\longrightarrow$	$CS_1^R ; CS_2^O$

Time $\longrightarrow$

Figure 2
Various classical conditioning phenomena. CS^O = no or small magnitude CR to CS; CS^R = CR to CS; US^R = UR to US; CS_1/CS_2 = simultaneous presentations of the two CSs; in Overshadowing, CS_1 is more salient than CS_2; 2nd order conditioning is often elusory and transient when it does appear

3. Classical Conditioning as a Model System for Studying the Neurobiology of Learning and Memory

Current views recognize that, in mammals, there are multiple forms or aspects of learning and memory (e.g., habituation, sensitization, classical conditioning, priming, procedural learning, episodic, semantic) that are subserved by different structures in the central nervous system (e.g., reflex pathways, cerebellum, amygdala, striatum, diencephalon, medial temporal lobe, neocortex) (Squire 1987). Considerable progress has been made in the understanding of these different learning and memory systems through the use of various experimental techniques (e.g., lesions, reversible inactivation, drug administration, neural recordings, genetic manipulations, brain imaging). The success of this work is due in large part to the use of classical conditioning as a model system, since it provides an important advantage over other, more complex, forms of learning in that the stimuli involved

Table 1
Behavioral principles of classical conditioning

Contiguity constraints	**Sensory constraints**	**Informational constraints**
ISI function. Conditioning occurs when the CS and the US are paired within a well-defined temporal window. The optimum conditionable ISI can range anywhere from a fraction of a second in eyeblink conditioning to hours in taste aversion conditioning.	**Repetition.** The magnitude of conditioning is proportional to to the number of times the CS–US pairings are presented.	**Contingency.** Organisms learn not only about the temporal relationship between stimuli but also about the predictive relationship between the stimuli. In general, if the CS is positively correlated with the US, excitatory conditioning will occur. In contrast, if the CS is negatively correlated with the US, then inhibitory conditioning will follow.
Timing. The peak onset of the CR generally corresponds to the time at which the US is presented. This temporal process allows the organism to anticipate and respond adaptively to the occurrence of the US.	**Familiarity.** The more familiar the CS and/or the US are to the organism, the slower the rate of conditioning (CS pre-exposure and US pre-exposure effects). The asymptote of conditioning, however, remains the same.	**Genetic predisposition.** Conditioning is robust when the CS and the US are relevant to each other. Some CS–US associations do not readily occur.
ITI function. For a fixed ISI, conditioning appears to be more efficient with longer ITIs. As the ITI lengthens, the possibility of the ISI and ITI interacting and thus interfering with the CS–US temporal processing decreases.	**Intensity.** Generally, the more intense (or salient) the CS and/or the US, the stronger the conditioning. The use of a more intense US will result in a faster rate as well as a higher asymptotic conditioning. The use of a more salient CS will also result in a faster rate of conditioning but the asymptote of conditioning will be the same.	

(CS and US) are well defined and can be precisely controlled, and the behavioral output is discrete and may be accurately assessed.

3.1 Localization of Brain Substrates of Classical Conditioning: Rationale

The identification of the locus of learning and memory storage in the brain is a prerequisite to an understanding of the neurochemical, cellular and molecular mechanisms by which organisms acquire and retain information. For many years the task of localizing memory storage (the *engram*) has been the paramount challenge facing investigators of memory mechanisms in mammalian systems. Classical conditioning is especially attractive as a model system for use in these types of investigations since only two stimuli are involved, and thus the learning or association of CS and US must occur at the brain site(s) where the two pieces of information converge. For instance, in classical eyeblink conditioning, where animals (such as mice, rats, rabbits or humans) learn to exhibit eyeblink responses to a CS (e.g., tone) that has been paired with a US (e.g., air-puff to the eye), one can trace the pathways from the peripheral sensory receptors in the ear (for CS) and around the eye (for US) to the brain and examine those brain regions where the CS and US pathways converge. It is only in the past 20 years, however, that technology has permitted this type of analysis, and only then at the gross structural level.

The convergence of CS and US information, however, is not a sufficient condition for identifying the locus of learning. In order for a particular region of the brain to be considered a viable candidate as a learning and memory site, it must demonstrate the following criteria:

(a) permanent lesions of the putative site prior to CS–US training should completely and permanently abolish the acquisition of the CR;

(b) permanent lesions made after training should completely abolish the expression of the CR, and the CR should not be reacquired with further CS–US pairings;

(c) reversible inactivation during CS–US training should block the development of the CR such that when the structure is activated again the CR should develop comparably to that of a naïve animal (i.e., no evidence of *savings*);

(d) reversible inactivation following training should temporarily impair the expression of the CR;

(e) learning-related neural activities should occur that correspond with and immediately precede the behavioral CR;

(f) electrical stimulation of the CS and the US input pathways to the putative site should effectively substitute for the peripheral stimuli and support conditioning; and

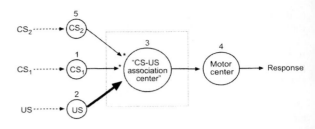

Figure 3
A highly schematized diagram of a hypothetical learning site in classical conditioning. The shaded box represents the locus of conditioning. * denotes modifiable connections underlying learning

(g) electrical stimulation of the putative site should evoke the CR.

If there is a single locus of learning that supports classical conditioning, then these seven criteria must be demonstrable within that specific learning site; whereas if there are multiple structures that encode CS–US association, then these seven criteria must be satisfied collectively by these structures. Figure 3 illustrates how these different criteria can be applied to a putative locus of CS–US association.

In Fig. 3, the afferent CS and US information is relayed via *hypothetical* structures 1 (and 5 for different CSs) and 2 (for US), respectively, to the learning site 3. The outputs (efferents) from structure 3 activate the motor center 4 that in turn controls the CR. Permanent lesions of structures 1, 2, 3 or 4 prior to conditioning will block the acquisition and/or expression of the CR. Thus, the permanent lesion technique (e.g., electrical, chemical, radio-frequency, aspiration, ischemia) is limited in that it does not allow for dissociation of the site of learning from the sites of input or from motor centers. In contrast, the reversible inactivation (pharmacological, cooling) technique, which temporarily inactivates the neurons within a structure, is not so constrained. For example, reversible inactivation of structures 1, 2 or 3 during conditioning will block acquisition of the CR to CS_1. In subsequent CS–US training when the inactivation has been reversed, the animal should learn as though it is naïve. By contrast, reversible inactivation of structure 4 at the time of CS–US training will block the expression of the CR, but once the inactivation is removed, the animal will immediately exhibit CRs to the CS because the CS–US association center was not affected during conditioning.

Thus structure 4 must be efferent to the site of learning. Structures 1, 2 and 3 can be further dissociated by examining the effects of reversible inactivation to CSs of different sensory modalities. Whereas inactivation of structure 2 and 3 will block conditioning to all CS modalities (e.g., CS_1 and CS_2), inactivation of structure 1 will block conditioning to CS_1 but not CS_2. Thus structure 1 must be afferent to the site of learning. Finally, structures 2 and 3 can be dissociated by examining the reversible inactivation effects following conditioning: once the animal has acquired the CR, inactivating structure 3 should abolish the expression of CR, whereas inactivation of structure 2 should not interfere with the expression of the CR because the CS inputs to the CS–US association center remain intact. Interestingly, with continued CS–US training, inactivation of structure 2 will lead to extinction of the CR because the CS–US association center will, as a result, receive only the CS information (just as in CS-alone extinction training). If structures 1 and 2 relay information about the CS and the US, then electrical stimulation of the CS and US pathways should also support conditioning. Lastly, recordings from structure 3 (the site of learning) should reveal learning-related changes in neural activity that model the behavioral CR, whereas recordings from CS and US input structures should show stimulus-evoked neural activities.

The neural circuitry of the brain is almost infinitely complex and thus no single experimental technique is in itself sufficient to identify the site of learning. It is also important to note that different types of classical conditioning (e.g., eyeblink versus fear conditioning) are subserved by different neural circuits. Through the utilization of various techniques, however, the structures and mechanisms involved in this type of learning can be reasonably delineated and systematically analyzed for its validity.

3.2 Putative Cellular Mechanisms of Classical Conditioning

Once the learning and memory storage site has been identified, a logical next step is to determine what neural changes take place that allow a CS that previously did not elicit a CR (before conditioning) to now evoke a CR (after conditioning). It is generally assumed that an initially weak connection between a CS relaying structure and a CS–US association structure becomes strengthened as a function of CS–US paired training, such that the CS becomes able to effectively activate the CS–US association structure, which in turn activates the CR pathway. It is further hypothesized that changes in synaptic efficacy (that is, the efficacy with which a neuron is able to communicate with another neuron) underlie this type of strengthening of the CS relay-to-CS–US association connection (e.g., Hebb's postulate (Hebb 1949)). Two forms of experimentally-induced synaptic plasticity, long-term potentiation (LTP) and long-term depression (LTD), have received close scrutiny as the most promising cellular mnemonic mechanisms (Bliss and Collingridge 1993; Ito 1989). LTP and LTD refer to sustained increase and decrease of synaptic transmission, respectively, following different stimulation patterns of afferent fibers. In brief, LTP is charac-

terized by its rapid inducibility and longevity (lasting of the order of hours *in vitro* to weeks *in vivo*), as well as its being strengthened by repetition and demonstrating specificity and associativity. LTD displays similar characteristics desirable of an information storage mechanism. Both LTP and LTD have been demonstrated in various brain structures, including those that are hypothesized to be critical for learning and memory.

One can easily imagine how LTP and LTD might be applicable to classical conditioning. For example, suppose that the CS pathway to the site of learning (pathway between steps 1–3 in Fig. 3) is initially weak and that, as a result, the CS alone cannot sufficiently activate the CS–US association center to produce a CR. Following CS–US pairings, if this pathway is strengthened via LTP (or LTP-like changes), then the CS alone will be able to activate the CS–US association center to elicit a CR. Similarly LTD or LTD-like changes may support conditioning by weakening the inputs to a structure that normally inhibits the CS–US association center (as is postulated to occur in eyeblink conditioning circuit). It is likely that combinations of LTP- and LTD-like forms of synaptic plasticity (and perhaps other unknown cellular changes), involving a network of synapses, are important in classical conditioning.

3.3 Neuronal Substrates of Eyeblink Conditioning

Classical eyeblink conditioning in rabbits has been used extensively to investigate brain mechanisms underlying learning and memory. Converging lines of evidence from lesion, recording, stimulation, reversible inactivation, and brain imaging studies indicate that the cerebellum mediates the formation of the CS–US association for eyeblink conditioning (Thompson 1990). In brief, selective lesions of the cerebellum (i.e., the interpositus nucleus) block the acquisition and retention of eyeblink CRs; the lesion is limited to the CR since the UR (reflexive eyeblink) to the US is not affected. (An important feature of eyeblink conditioning is that the CR and the UR can be dissociated and, thus, effects of various manipulations on memory versus performance can be carefully addressed.) Correspondingly, recording studies indicate that cells in specific regions of the cerebellum undergo plastic changes during eyeblink conditioning; for example, cells in the interpositus nucleus increase their activity (postulated to occur via LTP-like changes), while Purkinje cells in the cortex, which send inhibitory projections to the interpositus nucleus, decrease their activity (postulated to occur via LTD-like changes).

The involvement of the cerebellum in eyeblink conditioning is also evidenced by stimulation studies which show that direct stimulation of the two major afferents to the cerebellum, the mossy fibers from the pontine nucleus and the climbing fibers from the inferior olive, can substitute for the peripheral CS and US, respectively. Since limited lesions of the pontine nucleus (i.e., the lateral region) abolish CRs to a tone CS but not to a light CS, and lesions of the inferior olive in animals that already acquired CRs result in behavioral extinction with continued CS–US-paired training, it is not likely that these afferent structures are the site of learning and memory storage. Reversible inactivation studies further support the conclusion that the cerebellum, and not its efferent structures, is the locus of CS–US association. Moreover, recent human brain-imaging studies reveal eyeblink conditioning-related activity changes in the cerebellum. Collectively, these findings strongly suggest that the cerebellum is essential for eyeblink conditioning. Although the cerebellum seems to be critical, the relative importance of the cerebellar cortex and the interpositus nucleus in supporting eyeblink conditioning is not clear and has been disputed (see Kim and Thompson 1997 for detailed treatment of this topics and a putative eyeblink conditioning circuit). The fact that the critical CS–US association in eyeblink conditioning occurs within the cerebellum, however, permits research at the molecular level of analysis.

3.4 Neuronal Substrates of Fear Conditioning

In fear conditioning, CSs such as tones, lights or experimental chambers are typically paired with aversive US such as electric shock. Following CS–US pairings, the CS can elicit numerous fear CRs, such as an increase in blood pressure, reduction in pain sensitivity (analgesia), fear-potentiated startle, and/or defensive freezing. Several lines of evidence point to the amygdala, one of the principle structures of the limbic system that seems to be situated such that it has access to both sensory inputs and response outputs, as a critical neural substrate for this type of emotional learning (LeDoux 1996). In brief, the critical role of the amygdala in fear conditioning is supported by observations that:

(a) amygdalar lesions (permanent and reversible) abolish various fear CRs as well as innate fear responses;

(b) selective lesions of structures afferent to the amygdala affect conditioning to specific CSs (e.g., medial geniculate nucleus of the thalamus for tones, and the hippocampus for contexts);

(c) selective lesions of structures efferent to the amygdala abolish specific CRs (e.g., the lateral hypothalamus for blood pressure CR, and the ventral region of the periaqueductal gray matter for freezing CR);

(d) recording studies reveal that neurons in the amygdala respond to both CS and US and undergo plastic changes during fear conditioning (e.g., LTP-like changes);

(e) electrical stimulation of the amygdala elicits fear responses; and

(f) drugs that block LTP also prevent fear conditioning.

However, there is also evidence that the amygdala may not necessarily be involved in fear learning and memory, and that other brain structures (e.g., insular cortex) may mediate fear conditioning (McGaugh et al. 1996). Thus, additional studies are required to firmly establish the role of the amygdala in fear conditioning.

4. Conclusion

Although classical conditioning is well understood at a behavioral level and the neuroanatomical circuits that underlie it are beginning to be unveiled, there is much left to learn. However, this most basic form of associative learning offers a useful means to investigate the synaptic and molecular mechanisms underlying learning and memory and may help reveal common biological mechanisms shared by all learning and memory systems.

See also: Autonomic Classical and Operant Conditioning; Behavioral Assessment; Cardiovascular Conditioning: Neural Substrates; Conditioning and Habit Formation, Psychology of; Eyelid Classical Conditioning; Fear Conditioning; Learning and Memory, Neural Basis of; Long-term Depression (Hippocampus); Long-term Potentiation and Depression (Cortex); Long-term Potentiation (Hippocampus); Memory, Consolidation of; Pavlov, Ivan Petrovich (1849–1936)

Bibliography

Garcia J, Hankins W G, Rusiniak K W 1974 Behavioral regulation of the milieu interne in man and rat. *Science* **185**: 824–31

Gormezano I, Kehoe E J, Marshall B S 1983 Twenty years of classical conditioning research with the rabbit. In: Sprague J M, Epstein A N (eds.) *Progress in Psychobiology and Physiological Psychology*. Academic Press, New York

Hebb D O 1949 *The Organization of Behavior: A Neuropsychological Theory*. John Wiley and Sons, New York

Ito M 1989 Long-term depression. *Annual Review of Neuroscience* **12**: 85–102

Kamin L J 1968 Attention-like processes in classical conditioning. In: Jones M R (ed.) *Miami Symposium on the Prediction of Behavior: Aversive Stimulation*. University of Miami Press, Miami, FL, pp. 9–32

Kim J J, Thompson R F 1997 Cerebellar circuits and synaptic mechanisms involved in classical eyeblink conditioning. *Trends in Neurosciences* **20**: 177–181

LeDoux J 1996 *The Emotional Brain*. Simon ans Schuster, New York

McGaugh J L, Cahill L, Roozendaal B 1996 Involvement of the amygdala in memory storage: Interaction with other brain systems. *Proceedings of the National Academy of Sciences of the United States of America* **93**: 13508–14

Pavlov I P 1927 *Conditioned Reflexes*. Oxford University Press, London

Rescorla R A 1968 Probability of shock in the presence and absence of CS in fear conditioning. *Journal of Comparative and Physiological Psychology* **66**: 1–3

Rescorla R A 1988 Behavioral studies of Pavlovian conditioning. *Annual Review of Neuroscience* **11**: 329–52

Squire L R 1987 *Memory and Brain*. Oxford University Press, NY

Thompson R F 1990 Neural mechanisms of classical conditioning in mammals. *Philosophical Transactions of the Royal Society of London Series B-Biological Sciences* **329**: 161–70

Wagner A R, Logan F A, Haberlandt K, Price T 1968 Stimulus selection in animal discrimination learning. *Journal of Experimental Psychology* **76**: 171 80

J. J. Kim

Classical Mechanics and Motor Control

In order to control the execution of limb movements, the central nervous system must solve complex problems of mechanics. A substantial body of evidence supports the view that, in solving these problems the nervous system develops internal representations of the mechanics of the body coupled with its environment. Thus, through the process of motor learning (see *Motor Control*) the brain becomes implicitly an 'expert' in classical mechanics. After discussing the problems of kinematics and dynamics associated with the control of movement, this article introduces the formal definitions and the empirical evidence that constitute the underpinnings of the theory of internal representations in motor control.

1. Dynamics

According to the laws of Newtonian physics, if one wants to impress a motion upon an object with mass m, one must apply a force, F, that is directly proportional to the desired acceleration, a. This is Newton's equation:

$$F = ma$$

A desired motion may be expressed as a sequence of positions, x, that one wishes the object to occupy at subsequent instants of time, t. Such a sequence is called a trajectory and is mathematically represented as a function, $x = x(t)$. To use Newton's equation for

deriving the needed time-sequence of forces, one must calculate the first temporal derivative of the trajectory, the velocity, and then the second temporal derivative, the acceleration. Finally, one obtains the desired force from this acceleration. The above calculation is an example of an inverse dynamic problem. The direct dynamic problem is that of computing the trajectory resulting from the application of a force, $F(t)$. Direct problems are a common challenge for physicists who are concerned, for example, with predicting the motion of a comet from the known pattern of gravitational forces. Unlike physicists, the brain deals most often with inverse problems: we routinely recognize objects and people from their visual images—an 'inverse optical problem'—and we find out effortlessly how to distribute the forces exerted by several muscles to move our limb in the desired way: an inverse dynamics problem.

One of the central questions in motor control (see *Motor Control*) is how the central nervous system may solve the inverse dynamics problem and generate the motor commands that guide our limbs (Hollerbach and Flash 1982). In the biological context, however, the inverse dynamic problem assumes a somewhat more complex form than the one described above. A system of second-order nonlinear differential equations is generally considered to be an adequate representation for the passive dynamics of a limb. A compact expression for such a system is:

$$D(q, \dot{q}, \ddot{q}) = \tau \qquad (1)$$

where q, $\dot{q}$, and $\ddot{q}$ represent the limb configuration vector—for example the vector of joint angles—and its first and second time derivatives. D is a non-linear vector, valued mapping from the current state and its rate of change to the vector of joint torques, τ. In practice, the expression for D may have a few terms for a two-joint planar arm, or it may take several pages for more realistic models of the arm's multi-joint geometry. The inverse dynamics approach to the control of multi-joint limbs consists in solving explicitly for a torque trajectory, $\tau(t)$, given a desired trajectory of the limb, $q_D(t)$. This is done by replacing $q_D(t)$ for the variable q on the left side of Eqn. (1):

$$\tau(t) = D(q_D(t), \dot{q}_D(t), \ddot{q}_D(t)) \qquad (2)$$

2. Kinematics, Statics, and Coordinate Systems

A significant computational challenge comes from the need to perform changes of representation—or, more technically, coordinate transformations—between the description of a task and the specification of the body motions. Tasks, such as 'hitting a ball with a racket,' are described most efficiently and parsimoniously with respect to some fixed reference points in the environment. In this example, the racket is the site at which one interacts with the environment. Borrowing some terminology from robotics, such a site is called an 'endpoint.' The position of the racket is fully determined by six coordinates. These coordinates may be measured with respect to three orthogonal axes originating, for example, from the shoulder. Then, a position in endpoint coordinates may be specified as a point $p = (x, y, z, \theta_x, \theta_y, \theta_z)$. The coordinates, x, y, and z determine a translation with respect to the orthogonal axes. The angular coordinates, θ_x, θ_y, and θ_z determine an orientation with respect to the same axes. Consistent with this notation, a force in endpoint coordinates is a vector with three linear and three angular components, $F = (F_x, F_y, F_z, \tau_x, \tau_y, \tau_z)$.

A different way of describing the position of an arm is to provide the set of joint angles that define the orientation of each skeletal segment either with respect to fixed axes in space or with respect to the neighboring segments. Joint angles are a particular instance of generalized coordinates. According to the standard definitions of analytical mechanics, generalized coordinates are independent variables, which are suitable for describing the dynamics of a system (see for example Goldstein 1980).

Once we have defined a set of generalized coordinates we may also define a set of corresponding generalized forces. For example, if we use joint angles as generalized coordinates, the corresponding generalized forces are the torques measured at each joint. The dynamics of any mechanical system with N generalized coordinates are described by N second order differential equations relating the generalized coordinate to their first and second time derivatives and to the generalized forces. The dynamics Eqn. (1) is an example of formulation in generalized coordinates.

Movements are executed by the central nervous system activating of a multitude of muscles. Muscle coordinates afford the most direct representation for the motor output of the central nervous system. A position in this coordinate system is described by a collection of muscle lengths, $l = (l_1, l_2, ..., l_M)$. Accordingly, a force is a collection of muscle tensions, $f = (f_1, f_2, ..., f_M)$.

Both the transformations from generalized coordinates to endpoint coordinates, and from generalized coordinates to actuator coordinates are nonlinear mappings. In the case of the arm, the transformation from joint to endpoint coordinates is a nonlinear function:

$$p = L(q) \tag{3}$$

The transformation from joint to muscle coordinates is another nonlinear mapping:

$$l = M(q) \tag{4}$$

Some experimental studies (see Flash and Hogan 1985, Morasso 1981) have suggested that actions are planned by the brain in terms of endpoint coordinates.

For example, one can mentally formulate (and execute) commands such as 'move the hand 10 cm to the right' without being concerned with the set of muscle commands that are involved with this action. However, once one has decided a plan of action one must somehow choose which muscles to activate and in what temporal order. In carrying out this task the brain must faces the challenges associated with kinematic redundancy: the imbalance between the number of joints that may participate in a movement, the number of degrees of freedom of the hand, and the number of independently controlled muscles acting upon the joints. There are typically fewer hand coordinates than joint angles and fewer joint angles than muscles. Such imbalance renders both transformations (3) and (4) non-invertible.

3. Internal Models of Limb Dynamics

The ability to generate a variety of complex behaviors cannot be attained by just storing somewhere the control signals for each action and recalling these signals when subsequently needed. Simple considerations about the geometrical space of meaningful behaviors are sufficient to establish that this approach would be inadequate (see Bizzi and Mussa-Ivaldi 1998). To achieve its typical competence, the motor system must take advantage of experience for going beyond experience itself, by constructing internal representations of the controlled dynamics. These representations allow us to generate new behaviors and to handle situations that have not yet been encountered (see *Motor Control Models: Learning and Performance*). A vivid illustration of how explicit representations of dynamics, also called internal models, may facilitate motor learning is offered by work of Atkeson and Schaal (1997, Schaal 1999) who studied the task of balancing an inverted pendulum on the hand of a robotic arm. They found that robots learn to carry out this task successfully when they can build an internal model of the dynamics associated with the balancing act. Such a model may be constructed using data derived from the observation of humans engaging competently in the same task.

The term 'internal model' refers to two distinct mathematical transformations: (a) the transformation from a motor command to the consequent behavior; and, (b) the transformation from a desired behavior to the corresponding motor command (see Kawato and Wolpert 1998). A model of the first kind is called a 'forward model.' Forward models provide the control system with the means not only to predict the outcome of a command, but also to estimate the current state in the presence of feedback delay. A representation of the mapping from planned actions to motor commands is called an 'inverse model.' Strong experimental evidence for the biological and behavioral relevance of internal models has been offered by experiments that involved the adaptation of arm movements to a perturbing force field generated by an instrumented manipulandum (Sabes et al. 1998, Shadmehr and Mussa-Ivaldi 1994). The major findings of these studies are as follows: (a) when exposed to a complex but deterministic field of velocity-dependent forces, arm movements are first distorted and, after repeated practice, the initial kinematics are recovered; (b) if, after adaptation, the field is suddenly removed, after effects are clearly visible as mirror images of the initial perturbations; (c) adaptation is achieved by the motor system through the formation of a local map that associates the states (positions and velocities) visited during the training period with the corresponding forces; and, (d) after adaptation this map—that is the internal model of the field -undergoes a process of consolidation (see Brashers-Krug et al. 1996).

4. The Neurobiological 'Building Blocks' of Internal Models

Once it has been established that the motor system creates internal representations of complex multi-joint dynamics, it remains to determine how these representations may come about. As pointed out by David Marr (1982), any mathematical transformation may be carried out in different ways depending upon which building blocks or 'primitives' are employed (see *Computational Neuroscience*). Electrophysiological studies involving the stimulation of muscles and of the spinal cord in frogs (Bizzi et al. 1991) indicated: (a) that the stimulation of a site in the lumbar spinal cord results in the activation of multiple muscles acting on the leg on the same side of the stimulation; (b) that concomitant or 'synergistic' muscle recruitment generates a field of viscoelastic forces over a broad region of the leg workspace; and, (c) that the simultaneous activation of multiple spinal sites leads to the vectorial summation of the corresponding force fields. These and similar findings suggest that motor commands reaching the spinal cord from higher brain centers are not directed at controlling the forces of individual muscles or single joint torques. Instead, the descending motor commands modulate the viscoelastic force fields produced by specific sets of muscles. These force fields have influence over broad regions of the limb state space as each active muscle within a synergy contribute a significant force over a large range of positions and velocities.

From a mathematical standpoint, the force fields generated by neural modules in the spinal cord are nonlinear functions of limb position and velocity and of time: $\varphi_i(q, \dot{q}, t)$. Consistent with the finding of vector summation, the net force field induced by a pattern of K motor commands may be represented as a linear combination:

$$\sum_{i=1}^{K} u_i \varphi_i(q, \dot{q}, t) \qquad (5)$$

In this expression, each spinal field is a force that depends upon the state of motion of the limb, $(q, \dot{q})$ and upon time, t, in a fixed stereotyped way. The descending commands, $(u_1, u_2, ..., u_K)$, act as coefficients that modulate the degree with which each spinal field participates in the combination. These commands can just select the modules by determining how much each one contributes to the net control policy. The linear combination (5) generates the torque that drives the limb inertia. Substituting it for $\tau(t)$ in Eqn. (1) one obtains:

$$D(q, \dot{q}, \ddot{q}) = \sum_{i=1}^{K} u_i \varphi_i(q, \dot{q}, t) \qquad (6)$$

Least squares approximation can efficiently determine an optimal set of tuning coefficients given a desired trajectory, $q_D(t)$:

$$u_i = \sum_{j=1}^{K} [\Phi]_{i,j}^{-1} \Lambda_j \qquad (7)$$

with

$$\begin{cases} \Phi_{l, m} = \int \varphi_l(q_D(t), \dot{q}_D(t), t) \bullet \varphi_m(q_D(t), \dot{q}_D(t), t) \, dt \\ \Lambda_j = \int \varphi_j(q_D(t), \dot{q}_D(t), t) \bullet D(q_D(t), \dot{q}_D(t), \ddot{q}(t)) \, dt \end{cases} \qquad (8)$$

The symbol $\bullet$ indicates the ordinary inner product.

While spinal force fields offer a practical way to generate movement, they also provide the central nervous system with a movement's representation (see *Neural Representations of Intended Movement in Motor Cortex*). This representation is geometrically similar to the representation of space by a set of Cartesian coordinates. In the latter case, we may take three directions—represented by three independent vectors—and then project any point in space along these directions. As a result, an arbitrary point in space is represented by three numbers, the coordinates x, y, and z. The movements of a limb can be considered as 'points' in an abstract geometrical space. In this abstract geometrical space, the force fields produced by a set of modules play a role equivalent to that of Cartesian axes and the selection parameters that generate a particular movement may be regarded as generalized projections of this movement along the module's fields.

4.1 A Computational Approach to Motor Adaptation

If the dynamics change while the modules remain unchanged, then the representation of the movement must change accordingly. This is shown by the following argument. Suppose that a trajectory, $q(t)$, is represented by a selection vector $c = (c_1, c_2, ..., c_K)$ for a limb with the dynamics of Eqn. (6). Now, suppose that the limb dynamics are suddenly modified by an additional load, $E(q, \dot{q}, \ddot{q})$. Leaving the representation and the fields unchanged we have now a new differential equation

$$D(q, \dot{q}, \ddot{q}) + E(q, \dot{q}, \ddot{q}) = \sum_{m=1}^{K} c_m \cdot \phi_m(q, \dot{q}, t) \qquad (9)$$

whose solution is a trajectory $\tilde{q}(t)$, generally different from the original $q(t)$. The original set of coefficients, c_m, now generates the trajectory $\tilde{q}(t)$ and can, accordingly, be considered as its representation within the modified environment, $D + E$. The old trajectory is recovered by changing the selection coefficients to a new set, $c' = c + e$ with

$$E(q(t), \dot{q}(t), \ddot{q}(t)) = \sum_{m=1}^{K} e_m \cdot \phi_m(q(t), \dot{q}(t), t) \qquad (10)$$

With these new coefficients, the new dynamics become equivalent to the old dynamics along the original trajectory.

The modified coefficients c' offer a new representation of the old movement $q(t)$ in the altered dynamics. This procedure for forming a new representation and for recovering the original movement is consistent with the empirical observation of aftereffects in load adaptation (see Shadmehr and Mussa-Ivaldi 1994). If the load is removed after the new representation is formed, the dynamics become

$$D(q, \dot{q}, \ddot{q}) = \sum_{m=1}^{K} (c_m + e_m) \cdot \phi_m(q, \dot{q}, t) \qquad (11)$$

that can be rewritten as

$$D(q, \dot{q}, \ddot{q}) - \sum_{m=1}^{K} e_m \cdot \phi_m(q, \dot{q}, t) = \sum_{m=1}^{K} c_m \cdot \phi_m(q, \dot{q}, t) \qquad (12)$$

Therefore, removing the load with the new representation corresponds approximately to applying the opposite load with the old representation.

Is it necessary for the motor system to modify a movement's representation each time the limb dynamics changes? Or is there a way for restoring the previously existing representations? From a computational point of view, whenever a dynamical change becomes permanent—as when we undergo growth or damage—it would seem convenient for the central nervous system to have the ability to restore the previously learned motor skills (that is, the previously learned movement representations) without need to relearn them all. It is possible for the adaptive system to restore, at least partially, the motor representations that preexist a change in dynamics by modifying the modules and their force fields. A specific modification is obtained when we may express the coefficients $e =$

$(e_1, e_2, ..., e_K)$ as a linear transformation of the original coefficients $c = (c_1, c_2, ..., c_K)$:

$$e = Wc$$

This transformation is a coordinate transformation of the selection vector and may be implemented by a linear associative network (see *Neural Networks: Biological Models and Applications*). With a minimum of algebra one sees that

$$\begin{aligned}
D(q, \dot{q}, \ddot{q}) + E(q, \dot{q}, \ddot{q}) &= \sum_{m=1}^{K} c'_m \cdot \phi_m(q, \dot{q}, t) \\
&= \sum_{m=1}^{K} (c_m + e_m) \cdot \phi_m(q, \dot{q}, t) \\
&= \sum_{m=1}^{K} c_m \cdot \bar{\phi}_m(q, \dot{q}, t)
\end{aligned}$$

$$(13)$$

where the old fields ϕ_m have been replaced by the new fields

$$\bar{\phi}_m = \sum_{l=1}^{K} (\delta_{l,m} + W_{l,m}) \cdot \phi_l \quad \delta_{l,m} = \begin{cases} 1 & \text{if } l = m \\ 0 & \text{otherwise} \end{cases}$$

$$(14)$$

This is, again, a coordinate transformation of the original fields that may be implemented by a neural network intervening between the descending commands and the original fields. By means of such coordinate transformations, one obtains the important result that the movement representation—that is the selection vector c—can be maintained invariant after a change in limb dynamics.

In conclusion, the system of motor primitives induced by independent modules within the spinal cord—as well as within higher structures of the nervous system—provides us with an alphabet for representing the mechanics of the body and for modifying this representation as required by changes in limb and environmental dynamics.

See also: Motor Control; Motor Control Models: Learning and Performance; Motor Cortex; Motor Skills, Psychology of; Neural Representations of Intended Movement in Motor Cortex

Bibliography

Atkeson C, Schaal S 1997 Robot learning from demonstration. In: Fisher D (ed.) *Machine Learning: Proceedings of the Fourteenth International Conference (ICML 97)*. Morgan Kaufman, San Francisco

Bizzi E, Mussa-Ivaldi F A 1998 The acquisition of motor behavior. *Daedalus* **127**: 217–32

Bizzi E, Mussa-Ivaldi F A, Giszter S 1991 Computations underlying the execution of movement: A biological perspective. *Science* **253**: 287–91

Brashers-Krug T, Shadmehr R, Bizzi E 1996 Consolidation in human motor memory. *Nature* **382**: 252–5

Flash T, Hogan N 1985 The coordination of arm movements: An experimentally confirmed mathematical model. *Journal of Neuroscience* **5**: 1688–703

Goldstein H 1980 *Classical Mechanics*. Addison–Wesley, Reading, MA

Hollerbach J M, Flash T 1982 Dynamic interactions between limb segments during planar arm movement. *Biological Cybernetics* **44**: 67–77

Kawato M, Wolpert D 1998 Internal models for motor control. *Novartis Foundation Symposium* **218**: 291–307

Marr D 1982 *Vision: A Computational Investigation into the Human Representation and Processing of Visual Information*. W H Freeman and Co, San Francisco, CA

Morasso P 1981 Spatial control of arm movements. *Experimental Brain Research* **42**: 223 7

Sabes P N, Jordan M I, Wolpert D M 1998 The role of inertial sensitivity in motor planning. *Journal of Neuroscience* **18**: 5948–57

Schaal S 1999 Is imitation learning the route to humanoid robots? *Trends in Cognitive Sciences* **3**: 233–42

Shadmehr R, Mussa-Ivaldi F A 1994 Adaptive representation of dynamics during learning of a motor task. *Journal of Neuroscience* **14**: 3208–24

S. Mussa-Ivaldi

Classical (Psychometric) Test Theory

1. Introduction

One of the most striking and challenging phenomena in the Social Sciences is the unreliability of its measurements: Measuring the same attribute twice often yields two different results. If the same measurement instrument is applied twice, such a difference may sometimes be due to a change in the measured attribute itself. Sometimes these changes in the measured attribute are due to the mere fact of measuring. For example, people learn when solving tasks and they change their attitude when they reflect on statements in an attitude questionnaire. In other cases the change of the measured attribute is due to developmental phenomena, or it might be due to learning between occasions of measurement. However, if change of the attribute can be excluded two different results in measuring the same attribute can be explained only by 'measurement error.'

Classical (Psychometric) Test Theory (CTT) aims at studying the reliability of a (real-valued) test score variable (measurement, test) that maps a crucial aspect of qualitative or quantitative observations into the set of real numbers. Aside from determining the reliability of a test score variable itself, CTT allows answering questions such as:

(a) How do two random variables correlate once the measurement error is filtered out (correction for attenuation)?

(b) How dependable is a measurement in characterizing an attribute of an individual unit, i.e., which is the confidence interval for the true score of that individual with respect to the measurement considered?

(c) How reliable is an aggregated measurement consisting of the average (or sum) of several measurements of the same unit or object (Spearman–Brown formula for test length)?

(d) How reliable is a difference, e.g., between a pretest and post-test?

2. Basic Concepts of Classical Test Theory

2.1 Primitives

In the framework of CTT, each measurement (test score) is considered being a value of a random variable Y consisting of two components: a 'true score' and an 'error score.' Two levels, or more precisely, two random experiments may be distinguished: (a) sampling an observational unit (e.g., a person) and (b) sampling a score within a given unit. Within a given unit, the true score is a parameter, i.e., a given but unknown number characterizing the attribute of the unit, whereas the error is a random variable with an unknown distribution. The true score of the unit is defined to be the expectation of this intraindividual distribution.

Taking the across units perspective, i.e., joining the two random experiments, the true score is itself considered to be a value of a random variable (the 'true score variable'). The 'error variable' is again a random variable, the distribution of which is a mixture of the individual units' error distributions. Most theorems of CTT (e.g., Lord and Novick, 1968) are formulated from this across units' perspective allowing talking about the correlation of true scores with other variables, for instance.

More formally, CTT refers to a (joint) random experiment of (a) sampling an observational unit u (such as a person) from a set Ω_t of units (called the population), and (b) registering one or more observations out of a set Ω_o of possible observations. The set of possible outcomes of the random experiment is the set product: $\Omega = \Omega_t \times \Omega_o$. The elements of Ω_o, the observations, might be qualitative (such as 'answering in category a of item 1 and in category b of item 2'), quantitative (such as reaction time and alcohol concentration in the blood), or consisting of both qualitative and quantitative components. In Psychology, the measurements are often defined by test scoring rules prescribing how the observations are transformed into test scores. (Hence, these measurement are also often called 'tests' or 'test score variables.') These scoring rules may just consist of summing initial scores of items (defining a psychological scale) or

Table 1
Basic Concepts of Classical Test Theory

Primitives	
The set of possible events of the random experiment	$\Omega = \Omega_r \times \Omega_o$
Test Score Variables	$Y_i : \Omega \to \mathbb{R}$
Projection	$U : \Omega \to \Omega_r$
Definition of the Theoretical Variables	
True Score Variable	$\tau_i := E(Y_i \| U)$
Measurement Error Variable	$\varepsilon_i := Y_i - \tau_i$

might be more sophisticated representations of observable attributes of the units. CTT does not prescribe the definition of the test score variables. It just additively decomposes them into true score variables and error variables. Substantive theory and empirical validation studies are necessary in order to decide whether or not a given test score variable is meaningful. CTT only helps disentangling the variances of its true score and error components.

Referring to the joint random experiment described above the mapping $U : \Omega \to \Omega_r$, $U(\omega) = u$, (the unit or person projection) may be considered a qualitative random variable having a joint distribution with the test scores variables Y_i. Most theorems of CTT deal with two or more test score variables (tests) Y_i and the relationship between their true score and error components. (The index i refer to one of several tests considered.)

2.2 The core concepts: True score and error variables

Using the primitives introduced above, the true score variable $\tau_i := E(Y_i|U)$ is defined by the conditional expectation of the test Y_i given the variable U. The values of the 'true score variable' τ_i are the conditional expected values $E(Y_i|U=u)$ of Y_i given the unit u. They are also called the 'true scores' of the unit u with respect to Y_i. Hence, these true scores are the expected values of the intraindividual distributions of the Y_i. The 'measurement error variables' ε_i are simply defined by the difference $\varepsilon_i := Y_i - \tau_i$. Table 1 summarizes the primitives and definitions of the basic concepts of CTT.

3. Properties of True Score and Error Variables

Once the true score variables and error variables are defined a number of properties (see Table 2) can be derived, some of which are known as the 'axioms of CTT.' However, since the work done by Novick (1966) and Zimmerman (1975, 1976) it is well known that all these properties already follow from the definition of true score and error variables. They are not new and independent assumptions as has been originally proposed (e.g., Gulliksen 1950). All equations in Table 2 are no assumptions. They are inherent properties of

true scores and errors. Hence, trying to test or falsify these properties empirically would be meaningless in just the same way, as it is meaningless to test whether or not a bachelor is really unmarried. The property of being unmarried is an inherent part or logical consequence of the concept of a bachelor.

Only one of the 'axioms of CTT' does not follow from the definition of true score and error variables: 'uncorrelatedness of errors variables' among each other. Hence, uncorrelatedness of errors has another epistemological status as the properties displayed in Table 2 (the other 'axioms'). Uncorrelatedness of errors is certainly a desirable and useful property; but it might be wrong in specific empirical applications (e.g., Zimmerman and Williams 1977). In fact it is an assumption and it plays a crucial rule in defining models of CTT.

Equation 1 of Table 2 is a simple rearrangement of the definition of the error variable. Equation. 2 shows that the variance of a test score variable, too, has two additive components: the 'variance of the true score variable' and the 'variance of the error variable.' This second property follows from Eqn. 3 according to which a true score variable is uncorrelated with a measurement error variable, even if they pertain to different test score variables Y_i and Y_j. Equation 4 states that the expected value of an error variable is zero, whereas Eqn. 5 implies that the expected value of an error variable is zero within each individual observational unit u. Finally, according to Eqn. 6 the conditional expectation of an error variable is also zero for each mapping of U. This basically means that the expected value of an error variable is zero in each subpopulation of observational units.

3.1 Additional Concepts: Reliability, Unconditional and Conditional Error Variances

Although the true score and error variables defined above are the core concepts of CTT, in empirical applications, the true scores can only be estimated. What is also possible, is to estimate the 'variances' of the true score and error variables in a random sample (consisting of repeating many times the random experiment described earlier). The variance $Var(\varepsilon_i)$ of the measurement error may be considered a gross parameter representing the degree of unreliability. A normed parameter of unreliability is $Var(\varepsilon_i)/Var(Y_i)$, the proportion of the variance of Y_i due to measurement error. Its counterpart is $1 - Var(\varepsilon_i)/Var(Y_i)$, i.e.,

$$Rel(Y_i) := Var(\tau_i)/Var(Y_i) \qquad (1)$$

the 'reliability' of Y_i. This coefficient varies between zero and one. In fact, most theorems and most empirical research deal with this 'coefficient of reliability.' The reliability coefficient is a convenient information about the dependability of the measurement 'in one single number.'

Table 2
Properties of True Score and Error Variables Implied by Their Definition

Decomposition of the Variables	$Y_i = \tau_i + \varepsilon_i$	(1)
Decomposition of the Variances	$Var(Y_i) = Var(\tau_i) + Var(\varepsilon_i)$	(2)
Other Properties of True Score and	$Cov(\tau_i, \varepsilon_i) = 0$	(3)
Error Variables implied by their definition	$E(\varepsilon_i) = 0$	(4)
	$E(\varepsilon_i|U) = 0$	(5)
for each (measurable) mapping of U:	$E[\varepsilon_i|f(U)] = 0$	(6)

In early papers on CTT, reliability of a test has been defined by its correlation with itself (e.g., Thurstone 1931, p. 3). However, this definition is only metaphoric, because a variable always correlates perfectly with itself. What is meant is to define reliability by the correlation of 'parallel tests' (see below). The assumptions defining parallel tests in fact imply that the correlation between two test score variables is the reliability. Note that the definition of 'reliability' via Eqn. (1) does not rest on any assumption other than $0 < Var(Y_i) < \infty$.

'Reliability' is useful to compare different instruments to each other if they are applied in the same population. Used in this way, reliability in fact helps evaluating the quality of measurement instruments. However, it may not be useful under all circumstances to infer the dependability of measures of an individual unit. For the latter purpose one might rather look at the 'conditional error variance' $Var(\varepsilon_i|U = u)$ given a specific observational unit u or at the 'conditional error variances' $Var(\varepsilon_i|\tau_i = t\,)$ given the subpopulation with true score $\tau_i = t$.

4. Models of Classical Test Theory

The definitions of true score and error variables have to be supplemented by assumptions defining a model if the theoretical parameters such as the reliability are to be computed by empirically estimable parameters such as the means, variances, covariance, or correlation of the test score variables. Table 3 displays the most important of these assumptions and the most important models defined by combining some of these assumptions.

The assumption (a_1) to (a_3) specify in different ways the assumption that two tests Y_i and Y_j measure the same attribute. Such an assumption is crucial for inferring the degree of reliability from the discrepancy between two measurements of the same attribute of the same person. Perfect identity or 'τ-equivalence' of the two true score variables is assumed with (a_1). With (a_2) this assumption is relaxed: the two true score variables may differ by an additive constant. Two balances, for instance, will follow this assumption if one of them yields a weight that is always one pound larger than the weight indicated by the other balance, irrespective of the object to be weighed. According to Assumption (a_3), the two tests measure the same attribute in the sense that their true score variables are linear functions of each other.

The other two assumptions deal with properties of the measurement errors. With (b) one assumes measurement errors pertaining to different test score variables to be uncorrelated. In (c) 'equal error variances are assumed,' i.e., these tests are assumed to measure equally well.

4.1 Parallel Tests

4.1.1 Definition. The most simple and convenient set of assumptions is the model of 'parallel tests.' Two tests Y_i and Y_j are defined to be parallel if they are τ-equivalent, if their error variables are uncorrelated, and if they have identical error variances. Note that Assumption (a_1) implies that there is a uniquely defined latent variable being identical to each of the true score variables. Hence, one may drop the

Table 3
Assumptions and Some Models of CTT

Assumption used to define some models of CTT	
(a_1) τ-equivalence	$\tau_i = \tau_j$,
(a_2) essential τ-equivalence	$\tau_i = \tau_j + \lambda_{ij}$, $\lambda_{ij} \in \mathbb{R}$,
(a_3) τ-congenerity	$\tau_i = \lambda_{ij0} + \lambda_{ij1}\tau_j$, $\lambda_{ij0}, \lambda_{ij1} \in \mathbb{R}$, $\lambda_{ij1} > 0$
(b) uncorrelated errors	$Cov(\varepsilon_i, \varepsilon_j) = 0$, $i \neq j$
(c) equal error variances	$Var(\varepsilon_i) = Var(\varepsilon_j)$.

Models defined by combining these assumptions
Parallel tests are defined by Assumptions (a_1), (b) and (c).
Essentially τ-equivalent tests are defined by Assumptions (a_2) and (b).
Congeneric tests are defined by Assumptions (a_3) and (b).

Note: The equations refer to each pair of tests Y_i and Y_j of a set of tests $Y_1, ..., Y_m$, their true score variables, and their error variables, respectively.

Table 4
The Model of Parallel Tests

Definition	Assumptions (a₁), (b) and (c) of Table 3
Identification	$E(\eta) = E(Y_i)$
	$Var(\eta) = Cov(Y_i, Y_j), i \neq j$
	$Var(\varepsilon_i) = Var(Y_i) - Cov(Y_i, Y_j), i \neq j$
	$Rel(Y_i) = Corr(Y_i, Y_j), i \neq j$
Testability	
in the total population	$E(Y_i) = \mu$
	$Var(Y_i) = \sigma_Y^2$
	$Cov(Y_i, Y_j) = \sigma_\eta^2$
within each subpopulation s	$E^{(s)}(Y_i) = \mu_s$

Note: The indices i and j refer to tests and the superscripts s to a subpopulation. The equations are true for each test Y_i of a set of parallel tests $Y_1, ..., Y_m$ or for each pair of two such tests, their true score variables, and their error variables, respectively.

index i and denote this latent variable by η. The assumption of τ-equivalence may equivalently be written $Y_i = \eta + \varepsilon_i$, where $\varepsilon_i := Y_i - E(Y_i|U)$.

4.1.2 Identification. For parallel tests the theoretical parameters may be computed from the parameters characterizing the distribution of at least two test score variables, i.e., the theoretical parameters are identified in this model if $m \geqslant 2$. According to Table 4 the expected value of η is equal to the expected value of each of the tests, whereas the variance of η can be computed from the covariance of two different tests. The variance $Var(\varepsilon_i)$ of the measurement error variables may be computed by the difference $Var(Y_i) - Cov(Y_i, Y_j)$, $i \neq j$. Finally, the reliability $Rel(Y_i)$ is equal to the correlation $Corr(Y_i, Y_j)$ of two different test score variables.

4.1.3 Testability. The model of parallel tests implies several consequences that may be tested empirically. First, all parallel tests Y_i have equal expectations $E(Y_i)$, equal variances $Var(Y_i)$, and equal covariances $Cov(Y_i, Y_j)$ in the total population. Second, parallel tests also have equal expectations within each subpopulation (see Table 4).

Note that these hypotheses may be tested separately and/or simultaneously as a single multidimensional hypothesis in the framework of 'simultaneous equation models' via AMOS (Arbuckle 1997), EQS (Bentler 1995), LISREL 8 (Jöreskog and Söerbom 1998), MPLUS (Muthén and Muthén 1998), MX (Neale 1997), RAMONA (Browne and Mels 1998), SEPATH (Steiger 1995), and others. Such a simultaneous test may even include the hypotheses about the parameters in several subpopulations (see Table 4). What is not implied by the assumptions of parallel tests is the equality of the variances and the covariances of the test score variables in subpopulations.

For parallel tests $Y_1 + \cdots + Y_m$ as defined in Table 4, the reliability of the sum score $S := Y_1 + \cdots + Y_m$ may

be computed by the 'Spearman-Brown formula for lengthened tests:'

$$Rel(S) = Rel(S/m) = \frac{m \cdot Rel(Y_i)}{1 + (m-1) \cdot Rel(Y_i)}$$

Using this formula the reliability of an aggregated measurement consisting of the sum (or average) of m parallel measurements of the same unit can be computed. For $m = 2$, each with $Rel(Y_i) = 0.80$, for instance

$$Rel(S) = 2 \cdot 0.80/1 + (2-1) \cdot 0.80 \approx 0.89$$

The Spearman–Brown formula may also be used to answer the opposite question. Suppose there is a test being the sum of m parallel tests and this test has reliability $Rel(S)$. What would be the reliability $Rel(Y_i)$ of the m parallel tests? For example, if $m = 2$, what would be the reliability of a test half?

4.2 Essentially τ-equivalent Tests

4.2.1 Definition. The model of essentially τ-equivalent tests is less restrictive than the model of parallel tests. Two tests Y_i and Y_j are defined to be 'essentially τ-equivalent' if their true score variables differ only by an additive constant (Assumption a_2 in Table 3) and if their error variables are uncorrelated (Assumption b in Table 3). Assumption (a_2) implies that there is a latent variable η that is a translation of each of the true score variables, i.e.,

$$\eta = \tau_i + \lambda_i, \lambda_i \in \mathbb{R}, \text{ such that } Y_i = \eta + \lambda_i + \varepsilon_i$$
$$\text{where } \varepsilon_i := Y_i - E(Y_i|U) \text{ and } \lambda_i \in \mathbb{R}$$

Also note that the latent variable η is uniquely defined up to a translation. Hence, it is necessary to fix the scale of the latent variable η. This can be done by fixing one of the coefficients λ_i (e.g., $\lambda_1 = 0$) or by fixing the expected value of η [e.g., $E(\eta) = 0$].

Table 5
The Model of Essentially τ-Equivalent Tests

Definition	Assumptions (a$_2$) and (b) of Table 3
Fixing the scale of η	$E(\eta) = 0$
Identification	$Var(\eta) = Cov(Y_i, Y_j), i \neq j$
	$Var(\varepsilon_i) = Var(Y_i) - Cov(Y_i, Y_j), i \neq j$
	$Rel(Y_i) = Cov(Y_i, Y_j)/Var(Y_i), i \neq j$

Table 5 summarizes the assumptions defining the model and the consequences for identification and testability. In this model, the reliability cannot be identified any more by the correlation between two tests. Instead the reliability is identified by

$$Rel(Y_i) = Cov(Y_i, Y_j)/Var(Y_i), \quad i \neq j.$$

Furthermore, the expected values of different tests are not identical any more within each subpopulation. Instead, the differences between the expected values $E^{(s)}(Y_i) - E^{(s)}(Y_j)$ of two essentially τ-equivalent tests Y_i and Y_j are the same in each and every subpopulation. All other properties are the same as in the model of parallel tests. Again, all these hypotheses may be tested via structural equation modeling.

For essentially τ-equivalent tests $Y_1, ..., Y_m$, the reliability of the sum score $S: = Y_1 + \cdots + Y_m$ may be computed by the 'Cronbach's coefficient α:'

$$\alpha = \frac{m}{m-1}\left(1 - \frac{\sum_{i=1}^{m} Var(Y_i)}{Var(S)}\right). \tag{2}$$

This coefficient is a lower bound for the reliability of S if only uncorrelated errors are assumed.

4.3 τ-Congeneric Tests

4.3.1 Definition. The model of τ-congeneric tests is defined by the Assumptions (a$_3$) and (b) in Table 3.

Hence, two tests Y_i and Y_j are called τ-congeneric if their true score variables are positive linear functions of each other and if their error variables are uncorrelated. Assumption a$_3$ implies that there is a latent variable η such that each true score variable is a positive linear function of it, i.e.,

$$\tau_i = \lambda_{i0} + \lambda_{i1}\eta, \; \lambda_{i0}, \; \lambda_{i1} \in \mathbb{R}, \; \lambda_{i1} > 0,$$

or equivalently:

$$Y_i = \lambda_{i0} + \lambda_{i1}\eta + \varepsilon_i,$$

where $\varepsilon_i: = Y_i - E(Y_i|U)$.

The latent variable η is uniquely defined up to positive linear functions. Hence, in this model, too, it is necessary to fix the scale of η. This can be done by fixing a pair of the coefficients (e.g., $\lambda_{i0} = 0$ and $\lambda_{i1} = 1$) or by fixing the expected value and the variance of η [e.g., $E(\eta) = 0$ and $Var(\eta) = 1$].

Table 6 summarizes the assumptions defining the model and the consequences for identification and testability assuming $E(\eta) = 0$ and $Var(\eta) = 1$. Other ways of fixing the scale of η would imply different formula. As can be seen from the formula in Table 6, the model of τ-congeneric variables and all its parameters are identified if there are at least three different tests for which Assumptions a$_3$ and b hold. The covariance structure in the total population implied by the model may be tested empirically if there are at least four test score variables. Only in this case the model has fewer theoretical parameters determining the covariance matrix of the test score variables than there elements in this covariance matrix. The implications for the mean structure are testable already for three test score variables provided the means of the test score variables are available in at least four subpopulations.

4.4 Other Models of CTT

The models treated previously are not the only ones that can be used to determine the theoretical para-

Table 6
The model of τ-Congeneric Tests

Definition	Assumptions (a$_3$) amd (b) of Table 3
Fixing the scale of η	$E(\eta) = 0$ and $Var(\eta) = 1$
Identification	$\lambda_{i1} = \sqrt{\frac{Cov(Y_i, Y_j)\, Cov(Y_i, Y_k)}{Cov(Y_j, Y_k)}}, \; i \neq j, i \neq k, j \neq k$
	{eqn6.eps}
	$Var(\varepsilon_i) = Var(Y_i) - \lambda_{i1}^2$
	$Rel(Y_i) = \lambda_{i1}^2/Var(Y_i)$
Testability	
in the total population	$\frac{Cov(Y_i, Y_k)}{Cov(Y_j, Y_k)} = \frac{Cov(Y_i, Y_l)}{Cov(Y_j, Y_l)}, \; i \neq k, i \neq l, j \neq k, j \neq l$
	{eqn7.eps}
between subpopulations	$\frac{E^{(1)}(Y_i) - E^{(2)}(Y_i)}{E^{(1)}(Y_j) - E^{(2)}(Y_j)} = \frac{E^{(3)}(Y_i) - E^{(1)}(Y_i)}{E^{(3)}(Y_j) - E^{(1)}(Y_j)}$
	{eqn8.eps}

Note: The indices i and j refer to tests and the superscripts to one of four subpopulations.

meters of CTT such as reliability, true score variance, and error variance. In fact, the models dealt with are limited to unidimensional models. However, true score variables may also be decomposed into several latent variables. 'Confirmatory factor analysis' provides a powerful methodology to construct, estimate, and test models with multidimensional decompositions of true score variables. Note, however, that not each factor model is based on CTT. For instance, there are one-factor models that are not models of τ-congeneric variables in terms of CTT. A model with one common factor and several specific but uncorrelated factors is a counter example. The common factor is not necessarily a linear function of the true score variables and the specific factors are not necessarily the measurement error variables as defined in CTT.

4.5 Some Practical Issues

Once a measurement or test score has been obtained for a specific individual, one might want to know how dependable that individual measurement is. If the reliability of the measurement is known and if one assumes a normal distribution of the measurement errors which is homogeneous for all individuals, the 95 percent-confidence interval for the true score of that individual with respect to the measurement Y_i can be computed by:

$$Y_i \pm 1.96 \cdot \sqrt{Var(Y_i) \cdot (1 - Rel(Y_i))}. \tag{3}$$

Another result deals with the correlation between two true score variables. If the reliabilities for two test score variables Y_1 and Y_2 are known, and assuming uncorrelated measurement errors, one may compute

$$Corr(\tau_1, \tau_2) = \frac{Corr(Y_1, Y_2)}{\sqrt{Rel(Y_1)} \cdot \sqrt{Rel(Y_2)}}. \tag{4}$$

This eqn. is known as the 'correction for attenuation.'

Another important issue deals with the 'reliability of a difference variable,' for example, a difference between a pretest Y_1 and a posttest Y_2. Assuming equal true score and error variances between pre- and posttest implies identical reliabilities, i.e., $Rel(Y_1) = Rel(Y_2) = Rel(Y)$. If additionally uncorrelated measurement errors are assumed, the reliability $Rel(Y_1 - Y_2) := Var(E(Y_1 - Y_2 | U)/Var(Y_1 - Y_2)$ of the difference $Y_1 - Y_2$ may be computed by:

$$Rel(Y_1 - Y_2) = \frac{Rel(Y) - Corr(Y_1, Y_2)}{1 - Corr(Y_1, Y_2)} \tag{5}$$

According to this formula, the reliability of a difference between pre- and posttest is always smaller than the reliability of the pre- and posttest, provided the assumptions mentioned above hold. In the extreme case in which there is no differential change, i.e., $\tau_2 = \tau_1 + constant$, the reliability coefficient $Rel(Y_1 - Y_2)$ will be zero. Obviously, this does not mean that the change is not dependable. It only means that there is no variance in the change, since each individual changes by the same amount. This phenomenon has lead to much confusion about the usefulness of measuring change (e.g., Cronbach and Furby 1970, Harris 1963, Rogosa 1995). Most of these problems are now solved by structural equation modeling (allowing the include latent change variables such as in growth curve models (e.g., McArdle and Epstein 1987, Willet and Sayer 1996) or, more directly, in true change models (Steyer, Eid, and Schwenkmezger 1997, Steyer, Partchev, and Shanahan, 2000). Models of this kind are no longer hampered by reliability problems and allow the explanation of inter-individual differences in intraindividual change.

5. Discussion

It should be noted that CTT refers to the population level, i.e., to the random experiment of sampling a single observational unit and assessing some of its behavior (see Table 1). CTT does not refer to sampling models that consist of repeating this random experiment many times. Hence, no questions of statistical estimation and hypothesis testing are dealt with. Of course, the population models of CTT have to be supplemented by sampling models when it comes to applying statistical analyses, e.g., via structural equation modeling.

Aside from this more technical aspect, what are the limitations of CTT? First, CTT and its models are not really adequate for modeling answers to individual items in a questionnaire. This purpose is more adequately met by models of item response theory (IRT) which specify how the probability of answering in a specific category of an item depends on the attribute to be measured, i.e., on the value of a latent variable.

A second limitation of CTT is the exclusive focus on measurement errors. 'Generalizability theory' presented by Cronbach et al. (1972) (see also Shavelson and Webb 1991) generalized CTT to include other factors determining test scores.

Inspired by Generalizability Theory Tack (1980), Steyer et al. (1989) presented a generalization of CTT, called 'Latent State-Trait Theory,' which explicitly takes into account the situation factor, introduced formal definitions of states and traits, and presented models allowing to disentangle person, as well as situation and/or interaction effects and from measurement error. More recent presentations are Steyer et al. (1992) as well as Steyer, et al. (1999). Eid (1995, 1996) extended this approach to the normal ogive model for analyses on the item level.

The parameters of CTT are often said to be 'population dependent,' i.e., meaningful only with respect to a given population. This is true for the variance of the true score variable and the reliability coefficient. The reliability (coefficient) of an intelligence test is different in the population of students than the general population. This is a simple consequence of the restriction of the (true score) variance of intelligence in the population of the students. However, such a restriction neither exists for the true score estimates neither of individual persons nor for the item parameters λ_i of the model of 'essentially τ-equivalent tests,' for instance. Proponents of IRT models have often forwarded the population dependence critique. They contrast it with the 'population independence' of the person and the item parameters of IRT models. However, 'population independence' also holds for the person and the item parameters of the model of essentially τ-equivalent tests, for instance.

In applications of CTT it is often assumed that the error variances are the same for each individual, irrespective of the true score of that individual. This assumption may indeed be wrong in many applications. In IRT models no such assumption is made. However, it is possible to assume different error variances for different (categories of) persons in CTT models as well. In this case, the unconditional error variance and the reliability coefficient are not the best available information for inferring the dependability of individual true score estimates. In this case one should seek to obtain estimates of conditional measurement error variances for specific classes of persons. It is to be expected that persons with high true scores have a higher measurement error variance than those with medium true scores and that those with low true scores have a higher error variance again. (This would be due to 'floor and ceiling effects.') Other patterns of the error variance depending on the size of the true score may occur as well.

Such phenomena do not mean that 'true scores' and 'error scores' would be correlated; only the 'error variances' would depend on the true scores. None of the properties listed in Table 2 would be violated. As mentioned before, the properties listed in Table 2 cannot be wrong in empirical applications. What could be wrong, however, is the true score interpretation of the latent variable in a concrete structural equation model. Misinterpretations of this sort can be most effectively prevented by empirical tests of the hypotheses listed in the testability sections of Tables 4 to 6.

The most challenging critique of many applications of CTT is that they are based on rather arbitrarily defined test score variables. If these test score variables are not well chosen any model based on them is also not well founded. Are there really good reasons to base models on sum scores across items in questionnaires? Why take the sum of the items as test score variables Y_i and not another way of aggregation such as a weighted sum, or a product, or a sum of logarithms? And why aggregate and not look at the items themselves?

There is no doubt that IRT models are more informative than CTT models if samples are big enough to allow their application, if the items obey the laws defining the models, and if detailed information about the items (and even about the categories of 'polytomous items,' such as in 'ratings scales') is sought. In most applications, the decision how to define the test score variables Y_i on which models of CTT are built is arbitrary, to some degree. It should be noted, however, that arbitrariness in the choice of the test score variables cannot be avoided altogether. Even if models are based on the item level, such as in IRT models, one may ask 'Why these items and not other ones?' Whether or not a good choice has been made will only prove in model tests and in validation studies. This is true for models of CTT as well as for models of alternative theories of psychometric tests.

See also: Dimensionality of Tests: Methodology; Factor Analysis and Latent Structure; IRT and Rasch Models; Generalizability Theory; Psychometrics; Reliability: Measurement; Test Theory: Applied Probabilistic Measurement Structures

Bibliography

Arbuckle J L 1997 *Amos User's Guide: Version 3.6.* SPSS, Chicago, IL

Bentler P M 1995 *EQS. Structural Equation Program Manual.* Multivariate Software, Encino

Browne M W, Mels G 1998 Path analysis (RAMONA). In: SYSTAT 8.0 -Statistics. SPSS, Inc., Chicago

Cronbach L J, Furby L 1970 How should we measure 'change'—or should we? *Psychological Bulletin* **74**: 68–80

Cronbach L J, Gleser G C, Nanda H, Rajaratnam N 1972 *The Dependability of Behavioral Measurements: Theory of Generalizability of Scores and Profiles.* Wiley, New York

du Toit M, du Toit S 2001 Interactive LISREL: User's Guide. Scientific Software International, Chicago

Eid M 1995 *Modelle der Messung von Personen in Situationen* [Models of measuring persons in situations]. Psychologie Verlags Union, Weinheim, Germany

Eid M 1996 Longitudinal confirmatory factor analysis for polytomous item responses: model definition and model selection on the basis of stochastic measurement theory [online]. *http://www.ppm.ipn.uni-kiel.de/mpr/issue1/art4/eid.pdf*: 1999-7-5

Fischer G H, Molenaar I W 1995 *Rasch Models.* Springer, New York

Gulliksen H 1950 *Theory of Mental Tests.* Wiley, New York

Jöreskog K G, Sörbom D 1998 *LISREL 8. Users Reference Guide.* Scientific Software, Chicago

Lord F M, Novick M R 1968 *Statistical Theories of Mental Test Scores.* Addison Wesley, Reading, MA

Muthén L, Muthén B 1998 *Mplus User's Guide.* Muthén & Muthén, Los Angeles

Neale M C 1997 MX: Statistical Modeling, 4th edn. Department of Psychiatry, Richmond, VA

Novick M R 1966 The axioms and principal results of classical test theory. *Journal of Mathematical Psychology* **3**: 1–18

Rogosa D 1995 Myths and methods: 'Myths about longitudinal

research' plus supplemental questions. In: Gottman J M (ed.) *The Analysis of Change*. Lawrence Erlbaum, Mahwah, NJ

Shavelson R J, Webb N M 1991 *Generalizability Theory. A Primer*. Sage, Newbury Park

Steiger J H 1995 Structural equation modeling. In: STATISTICA 5—Statistics II. StatSoft Inc., Tulsa, OK

Steyer R, Ferring D, Schmitt M J 1992 States and traits in psychological assessment. *European Journal of Psychological Assessment* **8**: 79–98

Steyer R, Majcen A-M, Schwenkmezger P, Buchner A 1989 A latent state-trait anxiety model and its application to determine consistency and specificity coefficients. *Anxiety Research* **1**: 281–99

Steyer R, Partchev I, Shanahan M 2000 Modeling true intra-individual change in structural equation models: the case of poverty and children's psychosocial adjustment. In: Little T D, Schnabel K U, Baumert J (eds.) *Modeling Longitudinal and Multiple-Group Data: Practical Issues, Applied Approaches, and Specific Examples*. Erlbaum, Hillsdale, NJ, pp. 109–26

Steyer R, Schmitt M, Eid M 1999 Latent state-trait theory and research in personality and individual differences. *European Journal of Personality*

Tack W H 1980 Zur Theorie psychometrischer Verfahren: Formalisierung der Erfassung von Situationsabhängigkeit und Veränderung [On the theory of psychometric procedures: formalizing the assessment of situational dependency and change]. *Zeitschrift für Differentielle und Diagnostische Psychologie* **1**: 87–106

Thurstone L L 1931 *The Reliability and Validity of Tests*. Edwards Brothers, Ann Arbor

Zimmerman D W 1975 Probability spaces, hilbert spaces, and the axioms of test theory. *Psychometrika* **40**: 395–412

Zimmerman D W 1976 Test theory with minimal assumptions. *Educational and Psychological Measurement* **36**: 85–96

Zimmerman D W, Williams R H 1977 The theory of test validity and correlated errors of measurement. *Journal of Mathematical Psychology* **16**: 135–52

R. Steyer

Classification and Typology (Archaeological Systematics)

Classification is the initial means through which we impose a degree of order on the enormously diverse remains of the human past. As such, it is probably the single most basic analytical procedure employed by the archaeologist. Excavation yields an enormous diversity of materials that are not self-labeling; they must be endowed with identity and meaning by the excavator or the analyst. This is done in the first instance through classification.

1. Classification and Typology

Archaeologists often use the terms classification and typology interchangeably, but in this article a distinction will be made. A classification is any set of formal categories into which a particular field of data is partitioned, while a typology is a particular type of rigorous classification, in which a field of data is divided up into categories that are all defined according to the same set of criteria, and that are mutually exclusive. As will be shown later, most archaeological classifications of artifacts are typologies, while most classifications of cultures are not.

1.1 Archaeological Classification and Culture

The basic organizing concept for most prehistorians, as for most other anthropologists, is the concept of culture, but it is somewhat differently defined in the two cases. The cultural anthropologist conceives of the world as divided into a set of distinct peoples— tribes, nations, or ethnic groups—each of which has its own unique set of behavior patterns and beliefs, very often including its own language, which together constitute a culture. The prehistorian thinks of the ancient world as similarly partitioned, but the various long-vanished peoples can now be recognized only by the distinct kinds of artifact types they left behind. In place of forgotten languages and behavior patterns, every artifact type is treated as tantamount to a deliberate cultural expression—a culture trait. An archaeologically defined 'culture' is then a unique combination of artifact, house, and burial types, which are assumed, because of their cultural commonality, to be the remains left by a distinct, self-recognizing people. Those commonalities are recognized above all through processes of classification.

1.2 Kinds of Archaeological Classification

Obviously, any of the different kinds of material remains that archaeologists find can be classified, and there are in fact many different kinds of archaeological classifications and typologies. In the broadest sense, all of them fall into two categories, which may be called analytic and synthetic. Analytic classifications are classifications of one particular kind of object, in which all of the regularly recurring variants are recognized, defined, and named. The things most often classified are those that show a high degree of culturally patterned variability, including various kinds of stone tools and weapons; pottery; beads and other ornaments; house types; and grave types. Classifications of these things are usually typologies; that is, they partition the entire field of variability into a comprehensive set of mutually exclusive categories, because they are very commonly used for sorting and counting the objects found.

Artifact typologies can be made in a wide variety of ways, depending on what criteria of identity are considered important. This in turn will depend on the purpose for which the classification is made. Among the many kinds of artifact classifications it is possible to recognize purely morphological typologies, based on the overall form of objects; stylistic typologies, which specially emphasize stylistic features; functional classifications, in which objects are classified according to their presumed use; 'emic' classifications, in which objects are classified according to criteria believed to have been important to the makers; and distributional typologies, in which objects are classified according to their distribution in time and space.

In addition to the analytic classifications of particular object types, there are also synthetic classifications, in which recurring combinations of different artifact, house, and grave types are taken together to define 'cultures.' These classifications are quite different from artifact classifications, in that they are not typologies. That is, they are not used to divide up material into discrete, mutually exclusive units. The boundaries between units are not always sharp, and the criteria of identity are not always uniform. Some 'cultures' have been identified primarily on the basis of pottery types, others by stone tool types, and still others by house types. Archaeological 'cultures' are above all historical constructs; they are the prehistorian's basic way of mapping the prehistoric world, by dividing it into units of study which can be thought of as equivalent to peoples.

Culture classifications generally have a chronological as well as a spatial dimension. That is, the classification includes cultures that existed in different areas, but also that existed in different periods of time in the same area. Very often a generalized regional culture, like Anasazi, is divided into a sequence of developmental stages, which in the case of Anasazi are designated as Pueblo I, II, III, IV, and V. Like biological classifications, then, culture classifications often have a genetic component, when later cultures are recognized as 'descended from' earlier ones.

2. Historical Background

Although the excavation of ancient sites, for antiquarian purposes, had its beginnings in the Renaissance, the scientific investigation of prehistory began only in the nineteenth century, above all in Scandinavia. It was Danish archaeologists who developed the first 'culture classification'—the division of all European prehistory into Stone, Bronze, and Iron Ages—and they also developed the specific artifact typologies on which the 'Three-Age System' was based. In the later nineteenth century, especially in France, prehistorians carried the same basic approach much further, dividing up the Stone Age into a whole succession of phases, or cultures, defined by distinctive tool types. In this work, artifact classification was conceived above all as an aid to dating; that is, to the placing of prehistoric remains in their proper chronological order.

In the Americas there was a general belief that prehistoric Indian remains were not more than two or three millennia old, and consequently there was not much interest in sorting out their chronology. American prehistorians were much more struck by the spatial than by the chronological variability of the indigenous cultures, as they began to recognize the very wide diversity of pottery types, tool types, and house types that had been used in different parts of the continent. Beginning in the early twentieth century, they set about defining and naming a whole panoply of localized cultures and subcultures on the basis of these variable traits. As their work intensified and their methods improved, however, they also became aware of temporal differences among the remains they studied, again based on typological features. In 1927 A. V. Kidder and his associates proposed the 'Pecos Chronology,' in which prehistoric and historic Southwestern remains were assigned to seven developmental phases, designated as Basket Maker II and III, and Pueblo I–V, each with its defining typological characteristics. Within a decade, similar chronological schemes had been devised in many other parts of North and Middle America.

Once they were drawn into the classificatory enterprise, prehistorians both in the Old and the New Worlds devoted much of their energies to the development of what have been called 'time–space grids,' which were to become the basic map of prehistory. The prehistoric world was divided into a set of cultures, and most cultures were further divided into developmental phases, strictly on typological grounds. To a very large extent, the schemes that were developed remain in use down to the present day.

By the middle of the twentieth century the 'time–space' grids were mostly in place, at least over North America and Europe, and archaeologists began making classifications for new purposes. As a result at that time of a strong influence from functionalist anthropology, it was argued that classifications should emphasize what the objects were used for, or what they meant to the makers and users, rather than simply what was useful to the archaeologist for purposes of identity and dating. The functionalist paradigm lasted for about a generation, and then was replaced by what may be called the nomothetic paradigm. It was argued, in the 1960s and 1970s, that scientific archaeology should devote itself not to historical issues of cultural development but to the testing of general, causal hypothesis about culture processes, and classifications should be developed that would aid in that process. In reality very few of them ever were; the nomothetic paradigm, as applied to classification, was much more a lofty ideal than a practical reality.

A subsequent revolution, or at least an anticipated revolution, came about with the introduction of computers. The practical problem in making typologies was always that of limiting the attributes to be considered to a finite number, without at the same time introducing the bias of human judgment. It was believed, however, that if all the possible attributes of a group of objects were fed into a computer, the machine itself could determine, on a purely quantitative basis, which were and were not important. Thus was born the concept of 'numerical taxonomy,' in which computers would designate types, and differentiate them from other types, purely on the basis of the numbers of shared traits, regardless of what the traits were. The goal was 'automatic classification,' in which human judgment would be altogether eliminated.

After two decades of experimentation, however, this goal was found to be illusory. Unless there was some preselection of attributes to be coded, based on human judgmental decisions, the classifications produced by computers were far too cumbersome and particularized to have any practical utility. Every partitioning scheme that was tried produced hundreds of types. Moreover, the 'types' they produced could not be shown to have meaning with reference to any specific purpose. As a result, most of the typologies that are in use today are still those that were developed in the earlier part of the century, in the heyday of 'time–space partitioning.'

3. Artifact Classifications and Types

Basic to all artifact classifications is the concept of 'type.' Whatever kind of material is being classified—pottery or stone tools, for example—it is partitioned into a set of mutually exclusive categories that are usually called types. The type concept is actually a good deal more complex than it at first appears, and it has been the subject of various controversies that will be considered later. A type consists in the first instance of a body of objects having common features that set them apart from other objects. However, the type concept also includes our ideas about the things and what they have in common, and the words and sometimes the pictures that we use to describe them. Every type, in short, has members (actual objects), a description, a definition, and a name.

It is important to notice that these things may be modified independently of one another; we may refine our notions about what defines a particular type, based on the finding of additional material, but we may also find better ways of defining and describing the type, even if no new material is found. We may find that some characteristics are important that we had formerly ignored. Useful type concepts are always and necessarily mutable: they evolve continually as more material is found, but also as we develop new ideas about what is and is not important.

Within any typological system, the types must have two characteristics: identity and meaning. A type which cannot be recognized by any objective measure has obviously no practical utility. It would be possible, in theory, to conceive of a type including all of the pottery made at Pueblo Bonito between 1100 and 1125 CE, and such a type would have enormous interpretive utility if it could be recognized. In fact, it cannot: there

is no way of differentiating the pottery made at Pueblo Bonito from that made at other nearby sites. On the other hand, it is also possible to designate types that are readily recognizable—for example, all vessels having scratch marks on one side—but that have no evident significance for any purpose.

3.1 The Criterion of Identity

The basic criterion of identity for artifact types have been designated as variables, and attributes. To make the distinction in the simplest terms, 'color' is a variable, while 'red' is one of the attributes of the color variable. Artifact types are never designated on the basis of *all* their visible attributes. To do so would result in a typology in which every single object was a separate type, since no two things are ever absolutely identical. Rather, certain variables are selected out as a basis for the differentiation of types, while others are ignored. To cite one example, color is usually treated as a significant variable in the case of pottery types, because it is something produced deliberately by the vessel makers, whereas it is nearly always ignored in classifications of stone tools, because it is an accidental property of the lithic material selected. Some qualities are ignored simply because they do not vary: they are common to all of the types in a typology.

Every variable has a specified set of attributes, and these also are selected in accordance with the needs of the typologist. How much distinction is made between attributes of the same variable—colors, for example—will depend partly on their identifiability, but also on how much hair-splitting is necessary for the typologist's purposes. Pottery vessels made in the prehistoric American Southwest may exhibit a very wide variety of surface colors, but typologists have generally been content to assign them to five color categories: white wares, yellow wares, buff wares, orange wares, and red wares.

3.2 The Question of Purpose

Above all, it is the typologist's purpose that determines which variables and which attributes are selected in making a classification. Artifact classifications can in practice be made for a very wide variety of purposes, and classifications that yield meaningful results for one purpose may not do so for another.

The various purposes that may be served by artifact classifications can for convenience be characterized as basic, ancillary, and instrumental. Basic purposes are served when we classify objects in such a way as to learn or to express something important about the objects themselves. Pottery vessels, for example, may be classified on the basis of their constituent clays and tempers, which indicate where they were made, or they may be classified on the basis of vessel shapes, which may indicate what they were used for, or they may be classified on the basis of decorative designs, which will say something about the cultural preferences of the makers and users.

Objects, however, may also be classified for ancillary purposes: not because we want to learn or say something about the material itself, but because we want to use it as a guide to other understandings. Pottery types and certain stone tool types have long been treated as 'index fossils' or horizon markers, to identify a particular culture or a particular period in time. Their presence in a site may enable us to date that site within a century or even a generation, or to say that it was inhabited by a particular people and not by another, contemporary people. Some rather elaborate and highly particularized pottery classifications have been developed primarily as an aid to dating sites. Classifications made for this purpose will place special emphasis on whatever features show the most recognizable variability in time and space, whether or not any functional significance can be attached to them. Other kinds of ancillary classifications have been developed in order to yield information about manufacturing technologies, about resource acquisition, and for other purposes.

Some classifications are also made purely in the interest of practical convenience; for example, economy of description. Editors will usually not allow the archaeologist an unlimited number of pages in which to describe a mass of finds, such as beads or cutting tools. For economy of space they must be described in groups rather than individually. Some classifications are also made for the same reason that library books are classified: there must be a coherent way of dividing up the material into groups, for purposes of storage.

3.3 Frequency Seriation

When artifact types are used as a basis for the dating of sites, this is often done through the technique of frequency seriation. We recognize that cultures do not evolve in time through a series of instantaneous leaps, in which old artifact types are suddenly and totally replaced by new ones. Rather, there is a gradual process of transformation and replacement, in which some new types are becoming increasingly common at the same time that older ones are becoming less common. Consequently, sites may be assigned to a particular developmental phase, such as Pueblo II or Pueblo III, not on the basis of types absolutely present or absent, but on the percentages of particular types present or absent.

Obviously, frequency seriation requires quantification: the actual counting of the numbers of each artifact type present. It is for this reason that artifact typologies must be different from other kinds of classifications, such as culture classifications. A typology is a sorting and counting system, and as a result it must have a degree of rigor not necessarily found in

other classifications. The complete typology must be a comprehensive set of categories (types), such that there is one and only one type for each object found. The types must all be defined on the basis of the same set of criteria, and they must be mutually exclusive.

By way of summation, it may be said that a typology is a conceptual system made by partitioning a specified field of entities into a comprehensive set of mutually exclusive categories (types), according to a uniform set of criteria dictated by the purposes of the typologist. Within any typology, each type is a category created by typologists, into which they can place discrete objects having specific identifying characteristics, to distinguish them from objects having other characteristics, in a way that is meaningful to the purposes of the typology.

4. Problems and Controversies: the 'Typological Debate'

Everyone recognizes that archaeological types are not self-labeled; it is the classifiers who give them names and definition. There has nevertheless been a very long-running debate over whether our types are 'natural' or 'artificial.' Are we merely 'finding the joints in nature,' as one proponent has it, or are we imposing our own artificial order on nature? In reality, both things are true: nearly all artifact types are partly natural and partly artificial. They are natural in that the differences between one object and another have objective reality; they were not created by us. On the other hand it is we, the typologists, who decide which distinguishing characteristics we will focus on, and which we will ignore, in making a typology. There may often be varying degrees of 'naturalness' between types in the same typology. Some types will stand out very sharply in a great many respects, while we may decide to differentiate other types only because of minor stylistic differences that are nevertheless important for dating purposes.

A related question is whether types should be created by object clustering or by attribute clustering. Should we begin our typology by dividing up a collection of objects into groups that look intuitively similar to one another, or should we first decide which variables and attributes will be important, and then decide that all unique combinations of those attributes will automatically constitute a type? Again, the practical reality lies between the two positions. Virtually all useful typologies develop dialectically through a feedback between object clustering and attribute clustering. We begin, necessarily, with a collection of objects, and make some initial observations about what seem to be the most obvious differences, on the basis of which we divide them into types. As more material accumulates, however, our ideas about what is and is not important change, and we may add some new criteria of differentiation while eliminating others.

Often we will find that we have split hairs too finely in the differentiation of some types, and not finely enough in other cases.

Types, we say, must be defined by a combination of 'internal cohesion and external isolation.' They must have features that are common to all of their members, but they must also lack features that are possessed by the members of other types. Archaeologists, however, have differed in their emphasis on one or another of these characteristics. Some have argued that types must be defined by central tendencies, without a strict definition of their boundaries; other have insisted that if typologies are to be used as sorting systems, every type must have clear boundaries. There is no one correct solution to this problem; it will depend to a considerable extent on the purpose for which the typology is to be used. The sharper the type boundaries, the more useful is the typology for sorting purposes. It must be recognized, however, that in practice there are very few artifact types that do not exhibit some fuzziness at the boundaries. The sorter will often, like a baseball umpire, have to make purely arbitrary decisions in borderline cases.

Although the theoretical literature on archaeological classification is voluminous, much of it bears little relation to what really happens in practice. There are two reasons for this disjunction. First, most of the literature refers to closed classifications, intended to classify only material already in hand. Such classifications can be as rigidly formal and immutable as the classifier wishes. In practice, however, the vast majority of artifact classifications are open systems, intended for the processing of future finds as well as for material already in hand. Such systems must necessarily by mutable: capable of continual adjustment as more material comes to hand.

Second, too many authors have ignored the fact that types must have not only identity, but also meaning relevant to some specific purpose or purposes. As we have seen above, a great many legitimate purposes may be served by archaeological classifications, and the nature of the classifications will vary accordingly.

See also: Archaeology and Philosophy of Science; Ceramics in Archaeology; Classification: Conceptions in the Social Sciences; Culture as Explanation: Cultural Concerns

Bibliography

Adams W Y, Adams E W 1991 *Archaeological Typology And Practical Reality*. Cambridge University Press, Cambridge, UK

Cormack R M 1971 A review of classification. *Journal of the Royal Statistical Society*, Series A, **134**: 321–53

Doran J E, Hodson F R 1975 *Mathematics and Computers in Archaeology*. Harvard University Press, Cambridge, MA

Dunnell R C 1971 *Systematics in Prehistory*. Free Press, New York

Dunnell R C 1986 Methodological issues in Americanist artifact classification. *Advances in Archaeological Method and Theory* **9**: 149–207

Ford J A 1954 The type concept revisited. *American Anthropologist* **56**: 42–54

Gardin J-C 1962 *Archaeological Constructs*. Cambridge University Press, Cambridge, UK

Kaplan A 1984 Philosophy of science in anthropology. *Annual Review of Anthropology* **13**: 25–39

Klejn L 1982 *Archaeological Typology*, trans. Dole P. BAR International Series **153**

Krieger A D 1944 The typological concept. *American Antiquity* **9**: 271–88

Marquardt W H 1978 Advances in archaeological seriation. *Advances in Archaeological Method and Theory* **1**: 257–314

McKern W C 1939 The Midwestern Taxonomic Method as an aid to archaeological culture study. *American Antiquity* **4**: 301–13

Rouse I 1960 The classification of artifacts in archaeology. *American Antiquity* **25**: 313–23

Rouse I 1967 Seriation in archaeology. In: Riley C L, Taylor W W (eds.) *American Historical Anthropology*. Southern Illinois University Press, Carbondale, IL pp. 153–96

Sokal R R, Sneath P H A 1963 *Principles of Numerical Taxonomy*. W. H. Freeman & Co, San Francisco, LA

Spaulding A G 1960 Statistical description and comparison in artifact assemblages. In: Heizer R F, Cook S F (eds.) *The Application of Quantitative Methods in Archaeology*. Viking Fund Publications in Anthropology **28**: 60–83

Whallon R, Brown J A (eds.) 1982 *Essays on Archaeological Typology*. Center for American Archaeology Press, Evanston, IL

W. Y. Adams

Classification: Conceptions in the Social Sciences

Classification is the assignment of objects to classes. For example, an educational researcher might want to establish a taxonomy of teaching styles that covers all possible approaches to teaching. A psychologist studying personality might be interested in whether children can be grouped into categories according to their patterns, or profiles, of personality traits. A sociologist might be interested in whether certain combinations of characteristics of urban areas (average socioeconomic status, crime rate, building types, etc.) occur much more often than other combinations. A biologist might want to study whether animals showing a particular phenotype have specific combinations, or patterns, of genetic codes. In all these cases, objects (teachers, children, urban areas, animals) are classified based on their patterns of some observable characteristics (teaching behaviors, personality traits, city characteristics, genes).

The task of classifying objects poses several problems. The objects to be classified, the properties based on which they are classified, and the way of assessing similarities among objects have to be specified. The aim is to identify individual classes, to decide how many classes are warranted, and to establish procedures for identifying which class each object should be assigned to. Eventually, the success of the classification system must be evaluated. There are problems associated with each of these steps, and different solutions have been suggested for each problem.

In a sense, this paper recreates the process of establishing and testing a classificatory system. First, we define the topic more precisely, clarify the terminology, and provide some examples. Then, we present an outline of the first steps in a classification process and discuss one of the most debated issues: What is the concept of a class? After this, we deal briefly with procedures for assigning objects to classes and with the—frequently neglected—question of how to evaluate the resulting classification system.

1. Definition of the Topic

1.1 Terminology

Depending on the research tradition, the objects to be classified into a system are called elements, cases, units, exemplars, specimens or items. They are the sources or 'carriers' of properties, characteristics or variables. These properties may be dichotomous or polytomous, qualitative or quantitative. A property can only be useful in a classification, if it varies within the set of objects, that is, if at least two different values (categories, states, labels) on the respective property occur in the sample. When more than one property is used to characterize an object, the object can be described as a vector of values, a profile, a set of symptoms, or a pattern of features.

Sometimes, the data do not consist of objects and their properties, but of measures of relations between objects, such as their similarity, likeness, or belonging together. For example, a researcher might ask participants to rate the similarity between different politicians. The similarity ratings can then be used to classify politicians into groups. Based on this classification, the researcher can then study on which features people's perceptions of similarities between politicians are based.

The crucial assumption underlying classification is that objects are elements of a class, of a set, of a partition or—in biology—of a taxon. In other terminologies, the terms 'category' or 'cluster' are also used. Classification is the process of finding classes and of assigning entities to these classes. The end-product of this order-creating process, however, is often also referred to as 'classification.' To stress this distinction, the term 'classification system' can be used for the end-product, although in clinical psychology and biology the word 'taxonomy' is more common. Identification is the assignment of a specific case or object to (usually only one) of the classes.

1.2 Limits of Discussion

In studying classification in the behavioral and social sciences, we have to distinguish between two questions. (a) What theory and empirical evidence are available about how people classify objects? (b) What theories and methods are used to create classification systems? The first question will not be dealt with here (see *Concept Learning and Representation: Models*). The second question refers to the formal and empirical procedures used for defining classes and the rules that have evolved for assigning cases to classes. This second question is what concerns us here; it will be discussed from a conceptual rather than a statistical point of view. For more statistically-oriented discussions of classification methods see, for example, *Statistical Clustering*; *Mixture Models in Statistics*; *Configurational Analysis*.

One commercially 'booming' application of classification that this paper does not refer to is in biometric authentification. The aim of these methods is to use combinations of characteristics of individuals to uniquely identify each individual. Thus, conceptually, the task is to assign one of very many cases into a class, when there might be as many cases as classes. In this process, an observed pattern of features, or even an observed set of such patterns, is matched against a stored list of patterns. For example, DNA is used in this way in forensic criminology, as are records of the past *modus operandi* of individual criminals in detective work. This is, however a fairly unique example of classification, because the number of classes is intended to be equal to the number of cases, which is rarely the case in the social and behavioral sciences.

1.3 Purposes of Classification

The fundamental purpose of classification is to find structure. Typically, a large number of objects is reduced to a much smaller set of classes without too much loss of information about the objects. The data thus summarized allow objects to be identified, at least in part, through the class to which they belong. Specifying the boundaries describing a class has several advantages. One is that limits to generalization can be established, and another is that it becomes possible to generate predictions about how different classes are composed and how class membership relates to other variables.

2. Some Examples of Classifications

The most well-known examples of classifications are from the natural sciences, rather than the social sciences. A well known, still used, and expanding classification is Mendelejew's *Table of Elements*. It can be viewed as a prototype of all taxonomies in that it satisfies the following evaluative criteria: (a) Theoretical foundation: A theory determines the classes and their order. (b) Objectivity: The elements can be observed and classified by anybody familiar with the table of elements. (c) Completeness: All elements find a unique place in the system, and the system implies a list of all possible elements. (d) Simplicity: Only a small amount of information is used to establish the system and identify an object. (e) Predictions: The values of variables not used for classification can be predicted (number of electrons and atomic weight), as well as the existence of relations and of objects hitherto unobserved. Thus, the validity of the classification system itself becomes testable.

Another successful classification system is biological taxonomy. Indeed, most attempts to formalize classification have some intellectual roots in this tradition (Sokal and Sneath 1963). The result of such classification is frequently depicted as a 'phylogenetic tree,' today often the result of comparative genomics. In biological taxonomy, however, theory is not so strong as to warrant completeness, as in the *Table of Elements* (e.g., how should one deal with archaebacteria?). Moreover, the identification of a specimen requires information from morphology and sometimes from behavioral observation. In addition, the system abounds with nested criteria. And, compared with physics, predictions of future developments or of 'missing links' in biological taxonomy are vague. However, the classes of the phylogenetic system are still useful because, at the very least, they indicate boundaries to generalization.

In the behavioral and social sciences, hundreds of classifications are published every year. Noteworthy examples are Bloom's taxonomy of educational objectives (Krathwohl et al. 1964), as well as the *DSM* (*Diagnostic and Statistical Manual of Mental Disorders*) and *ICD* (*International Classification of Diseases*) classification systems used in psychology and psychiatry. None of these systems have been formally derived, however. Instead, they were generated based on 'experience.' The resulting classes are so heterogeneous that they acknowledge many exceptions. Also, a phenomenon called 'comorbidity' shows that these classification systems are not optimal yet. It refers to the simultaneous existence of two or more disturbances in the same patient. If comorbidity is the rule rather than the exception, then the classification system loses plausibility and practicability.

3. Preparing the Basis of a Classification

3.1 Selecting the Cases

In the beginning of the process of developing a classification, two main questions arise. (a) Which elements are to be differentiated in a classification? One searches for a (complete, if possible) list of cases to be classified. This list is called the 'extension' of a classification. (b) Which properties characterize the cases? The list of these properties is called the 'intension' of the classification. The answers to these questions already determine, in part, the results of the classification. To quote Hartigan (1982, p. 2): 'Clearly, the selection of variables to measure will determine the final classification. Some informal classification is necessary before data collection: deciding what to call an object, deciding how to classify measurements from different objects as being of the same variable, deciding that a variable on different objects has the same value.' Sometimes, no well-defined population of objects is available from which to sample, and a preliminary selection has to be made intuitively. In such cases, future applications of the classification system may result in more or different classes from those originally obtained.

3.2 Specifying the Properties

The question of feature selection (selection of the properties on which the classification will be based) arises at two points in the process of classifying. First, as mentioned above, it arises at the very beginning of the process. The second opportunity to select properties comes when an established procedure is tested for identification. This problem is very similar to one in regression analysis: Which variables should be retained because they discriminate best, between the classes (see Pankhurst 1991). Even if computational problems do not play a role, use of too many properties can still be problematic, if measuring these variables is expensive or dangerous. In both instances of selecting properties, reliability is a very important issue. With decreasing reliability of the measurement of the properties, the identification of classes becomes more difficult.

Another important question is whether the values of the properties should be transformed before searching for classes. The results of most classification procedures will be influenced by transformations. If differences in variability between the variables are of substantive importance, no transformations that equate variability across variables should be used. The use of transformations is also called 'a priori weighting.' 'A posteriori weighting' refers to cases in which different variables are given different emphasis in the identification process.

Especially in routine applications, a good strategy for selecting properties to be retained in the final classification might be to find a minimal set of variables sufficient to discriminate between all the classes. Relative to the set of all variables, the minimal set may not be unique. If this is the case, one will often prefer a set with few practical problems, and replace properties and take other aspects, such as minimization of costs, into account (see Pankhurst 1991 for an algorithm).

3.3 Determining the Similarity

After the objects to be classified and their relevant properties have been selected, the similarity between objects is determined. Similarity is a key concept in classification. As was mentioned earlier, there are two basic ways to obtain similarity measures: The researcher can either collect similarity judgments from participants, or derive similarity measures from the empirical co-occurrence of properties. Methods for obtaining similarity judgments in the context of the first approach—similarity 'in the eyes of the participants'—are discussed in the context of data theory (Coombs 1964). 'Proximity' measures can also be derived from confusion or generalization data, association probabilities, substitutability ratings, sorting procedures, and so on. The second case—'similarity in the mind of researchers'—amounts to comparing the feature patterns of objects and describing the similarity between objects using *similarity coefficients*. A large, and still growing, number of these coefficients exist, and monographs on classification devote a lot of space to them. Therefore, the choice of one particular coefficient should be explicitly justified. An analysis of the metric properties of coefficients is given by Gower and Legendre (1986). To choose a coefficient, one may refer to their axiomatic foundation (Baulieau 1999).

Another important distinction in the selection of similarity coefficients refers to 'negative matching,' i.e., deciding whether to include observations stating that two objects agree that a property is absent rather than present that is, whether similarity between two objects in the absence, rather than the presence, of a property should be included in the similarity measure. Jaccard's (1908) coefficient excludes negative matchings.

Although most classification methods make use of similarity information, clustering models exist that do not refer to similarity. Another aspect that might be taken into account is the concept of similarity used: Why only use pairwise co-occurrences, and not higher order contingencies (Daws 1996)?

4. Establishing a Classification

After a measure of similarity has been selected, the next step is the actual classification of the objects based on the similarities between them. Formally (e.g., Biggs 1999), classes can be thought equivalent to (a) partitioning a set into subsets, (b) classifying a set of objects, and (c) distributing a set of objects into a set of 'boxes.' These various perspectives differ markedly in their implications for classification. For example, in most mathematical conceptualizations, an element is classified into exactly one class. Some clustering procedures, however, allow for residual elements, which are not considered clusterable.

Depending on the approach to classification that a researcher has chosen, certain considerations and precautions are necessary. For example, similarity judgment data may not fulfill some necessary assumptions: Generally, related objects are to be located in the same class. The relationship xRx when 'x is related to x' has the properties of reflexivity: xRx, symmetry: $xRy \Rightarrow yRx$, and transitivity: xRy and $yRz \Rightarrow xRz$. These are the properties of an equivalence relation. If the empirical data are similarity judgments, they do not necessarily fulfill this relation. Some properties of this relation can be tested statistically. Another important consideration applies if the objects are classified by using rules referring to features. In such cases, these rules need to be free of contradictions (for a test, see Feger 1994).

Only a few substantive theories in the behavioral and social sciences allow one to deduce the number and kind of classes needed to describe a given range of phenomena. Therefore in many cases inductive procedures have to be used to generate classes. For this, one needs a concept of what constitutes a class. Many researchers apply inductive classification methods without ever considering explicitly the class concept that their method implies. The following part of the paper gives a brief discussion of the class concepts implied in frequently used methods for finding classes. The list is not complete, and the 'cluster analysis proper' dominates all other approaches, because of the frequency of its use.

Before discussing class concepts in detail, one more general distinction needs to be made. If classes are defined by properties of objects, two levels of definition can be distinguished. A general definition specifies the relationship between the properties and the classes. Specific definitions provide detailed translations of the general definition into formal operations for assigning the objects to the classes. Obviously there can be many different specific definitions. General definitions can be ordered by the kind and amount of variability they allow among objects within the class. There are two general positions with respect to within-class variability. The 'monothetic' position (Sutcliffe 1993) assumes that a class is defined by one or a few necessary properties. The 'polythetic' counter-position (Gyllenberg and Koski 1996) assumes that some properties of a specified total set, not necessarily the same for every object, are sufficient. According to this position, a property is shared by most, but not necessarily all objects of a given class. Proponents of the monothetic camp tend to stress that some properties are more important than others, and that these properties should be used to establish the classification. The opposite position assumes equal importance of all properties. As a third type of general definition, one may add definitions referring to a 'prototype,' that is, the most typical example of a class or a hypothetical mean object. In this last case, 'closeness' or similarity decides about class membership, and the prototype may be defined with or without allowing for variation in its properties.

Given properties as the base for a classification, the actual observations often are represented as a data matrix containing, for example, the objects as the columns and their properties as the rows. The cells of the matrix contain either the values '0' or '1' to indicate the absence or presence of properties, or they contain frequencies, durations, intensities, or symbols (in the case of qualitative polytomous items) that indicate the type or degree of the respective property in the respective object. As this enumeration shows, the procedure can accommodate data of all scale types. The goal now is to find a 'feature by classes' matrix, called—corresponding to its purpose—the reference or identification matrix, or simply 'a classification.'

4.1 Concepts of Classes

Cluster analysis proper. When authors (e.g., Everitt 1993) illustrate the concept of a cluster, they often use two-dimensional graphs to show the clusters as clouds of points (representing the objects). The clouds can have various forms; generally there are 'gaps' between the clusters that contain no data points, so that the clusters are isolated from one another. While such explanations of the cluster concept seem intriguing as they invoke classical 'gestalt' concepts, it is important to remember that the properties of (good) figures are defined by several 'laws,' not just one or two axioms or rules, as in cluster concepts.

Helpful as visualizations are, the more general definition of a cluster does not refer to any particular conception of space, be it dimensional, metric or Euclidean. Set theory defines a cluster as the maximal subset of elements for which proximities within this subset are larger than between any elements of the subset and elements not contained within it. As was discussed above, proximities are information about the extent to which objects 'belong together,' and could be expressed in many different ways, for example, as similarities, distances, ranks, or binary information about set membership. More than one subset may exist; subsets may be disjointed or overlapping; and they may or may not be hierarchically ordered. Given this very broad conceptualization, social scientists have access to a large number of clustering procedures. The large number of options reveals that no 'one and only' definition of a cluster can be found. Presumably, the availability of so many approaches is one reason for the paucity of comparative studies on methods of clustering.

Clustering procedures can be classified as 'leading to a structure that is either hierarchical or non-hierarchical.' The most frequently applied classification procedures are hierarchical, disjointed, and provide exactly one class for each object. The best known hierarchical procedures are agglomerative, that is, in a series of partitions they successively and with increasing dissimilarity, fuse the objects into classes. Each step provides a set of classes, from which the researcher has to make his choice. Once a fusion is made, it is irrevocable, so the early fusions should be very reliable. *Additive clustering* (Shepard and Arabie 1979) is a hierarchical partitioning allowing membership of objects in any number of classes. Here, the classes might be interpreted as properties (Lee 1999).

The cluster concept treated thus far is based on similarity as formally represented either in a space or by set theory. A close relative is prototype theory, popular in cognitive research. A prototype can be defined as a vector of values of selected properties; usually a list of cases as exemplars of this prototype is also available. One fundamental assumption of the prototype-oriented approach can be formulated as follows: If there is high similarity among a set of patterns, these patterns are also similar to an—observed or inferred—prototypical pattern. An inferred pattern could, for example, be the vector of mean values. This pattern has high or maximal similarity to every other pattern. The idea of inferring the prototypical pattern from the data forms a bridge to the similarity-based conception. But the researcher has to be more active in abstracting and defining a specific instance as the prototype.

Contingencies of higher order than similarities between the properties are exploited in some other generalizations of the concept of similarity-based clustering, such as Configural Frequency Analysis (Krauth and Lienert 1973) and Pattern-Analytic Clustering (McQuitty 1987). For example, Configural Frequency Analysis identifies combinations of properties that occur more often than expected from some specified base model.

A recent trend, increasing in strength, is to use mixture models for clustering. The original purpose of these methods was to base classification on a model that allows for inference-statistical treatment. But they have since found wider purposes. The basic idea of mixture models can be illustrated using the following example: Assume that a sample of measurements of body height is drawn from a human population. While it is known that all the cases are male or female, gender is not recorded for individual respondents. It is, however, possible, based on the distribution of heights in the total sample, to estimate the coefficients of the separate height distributions for men and women. This is done by interpreting each measurement as a sum of weighted height measurements for women and for men. These weights are the probabilities for each measurement to be from a man and from a woman. 'Thus the density function of height has been expressed as a superposition of two conditional density functions; it is known as a finite mixture density.' (Everitt 1993, p. 110).

Mixture models are based on a 'space' concept rather than a 'similarity' concept; clusters are regions of relative point densities in this space. The assumptions for mixture models are comparable with those of the general linear model: cardinal scale level and multivariate normal (or similar) distributions of the data. A comparatively common mixture model for categorical data is latent class analysis (De Soete 1993).

To conclude this classification of class concepts, one further concept needs to be mentioned. This conception, models for block structure, is close to the raw data matrix and the Aristotelian tradition. A block is a maximal rectangular submatrix combining some objects and some properties with the same (or similar) values in the cells of the data matrix. The scale level of the values is not fixed; and the similarity concept is not invoked in the analytical procedure. In a block, the set of partially similar objects corresponds to the extension of a concept or class. The set of partially similar properties corresponds to the intension. The symmetry in the definitions of intension and extension is fully exploited and preserved (see Feger and De Boeck 1993).

4.2 Evaluation of a Clustering Result

Although model evaluation is only a part of the overall evaluation of a classification (see Sect. 5), it is an important one. As Dunn and Everitt (1982, p. 94) state: 'Since clustering techniques will generate a set of clusters even when applied to random, unclustered data, the question of validating and evaluating becomes of great importance.' Jain and Dubes (1988) classify the criteria of validation as follows:

> *External criteria* measure performance by matching a clustering structure to a priori information.... *Internal criteria* assess the fit between the structure and the data, using only the data themselves.... *Relative criteria* decide which of two structures is better in some sense, such as being more stable or appropriate for the data.

Considerable progress has been made in internal statistical cluster evaluation. Statistical procedures exist for testing the existence of 'natural' clusters, for testing the adequacy of computed classifications, and for the determination of a suitable number of clusters (see, e.g., Bock 1996). A very plausible way to evaluate any solution, independent of the clustering approach used, is to reproduce, or 'derive,' from the solution all information that the solution gives about raw data that would fit with the solution, and then to compare this information with the actual raw data.

4.3 Procedures to Assign Cases to Classes

Procedures to assign single cases to classes are needed for two purposes. One purpose is to assign newly observed cases to the classes of an already existing classification. The other purpose is to evaluate a classification by taking 'old' cases from the original sample on which the classification was based, and

checking which class they would be assigned to. In both cases, the question is: Into which class should the case be placed? In practice, experts (e.g., physicians) are often consulted for the answer this question. In other cases, numerical procedures ('automatic classification') are used. Here, the properties may be used, either sequentially, as in a diagnostic key, or simultaneously by some type of matching between the case and the existing classes (see Dunn and Everitt 1982, especially on diagnostic keys). Quite often, as identification with certainty is impossible 'either because too many characters are variable within taxa or because all assessments of character states are subject to error, probabilistic identification methods are often used' (Dunn and Everitt 1982, p. 112). Of the probabilistic procedures, the Bayes approach (see *Decision Theory: Bayesian*) and discriminatory analysis (see *Multivariate Analysis: Classification and Discrimination*) are especially well known.

Other placement rules can be used if they are transparent, unambiguous, and do not lead to contradictions. For example, the principle of 'nearest neighbor' computes the distances of a new pattern to all existing classes. It assigns the new case to the class to which the distance is shortest (for details and other rules, see Looney 1997). Rules may also include options such as rejecting a case as 'not classifiable' or postponing a decision until more information is available. Most rules currently applied are compensatory, but rules could also be disjunctive or conjunctive, requiring at least one value to reach a high amount, or all values to surpass a given minimum (Coombs 1964).

Different rules lead to different results, especially if the classes vary in their *a priori* probability, if the distributions and covariances of the variables are very different, and if the number of observations is small. The single most important criterion for evaluating an assignment procedure is the number of correct classifications. But this 'apparent error rate' is optimistically biased, because it does not take into account the probability of correct assignments by chance. If base rates of class membership are known, the predictions have to perform better than the base rate (Pires and Branco 1997).

5. Evaluating a Classification

While every step of the classification process can be evaluated (Milligan 1996), two stages have received special attention: the evaluation of class definitions and of the identification procedure. Both have been mentioned previously. There also exist procedures to evaluate the overall performance of a classification system. The main method is 'cross validation,' using a new sample of data comparable to the old one, or splitting the original sample randomly into two halves and using one half to evaluate the classification obtained in the other half.

Another way of evaluating the results of a classification process is by comparing the results of using different classification procedures. Usually the researcher has several choices in the classification process, and is not forced by theory to select just one option. Examples include multiple options about the selection of cases and variables, of similarity coefficients, of clustering models and of identification rules. With computers, it is easy to try several combinations of such choices. Confidence that the classification captures substantial information in the data grows with the amount of agreement in the results from different combinations of choice options (for the evaluation and comparison of solutions, see Everitt 1993). To aid the interpretation of the resulting class structure, Milligan (1996, p. 346) suggests deliberately adding 'ideal types,' that is, characteristic patterns constructed by the researcher, to the data, and to assess what clusters these patterns are assigned to.

Can a classification be wrong? In most cases, a classification is just a systematic description, and as such, may, or may not, be useful. New observations may require changes in the classification. But if there exists a theory about the definitions of the classes, and the theory is strong enough to allow for specific predictions, then these predictions can be falsified and/or lead to revisions of the classification system.

6. Conclusions

More in the past than in the present, opinions fundamentally critical of the possibility of classification in the social sciences have been expressed. For example, Galt and Smith (1976, p. 58) stated: 'Because they usually lack measurable dimensions, social entities are difficult to classify, and any given system of classification will inevitably be arbitrary.' Indeed, numerical classification definitely requires measurement, or more generally, the interpretation of observations as variables. Indeed, every variable is itself a classification, defined as a set of disjointed, exclusive and together sufficient classes, and the 'categories' of variables are referred to as their values. Without variables in this formal sense, one might consider a heuristic equivalent in abstraction from, and ordering of, observations: the 'ideal type,' as introduced by Max Weber.

Variables used to establish a classification may be discrete or continuous. For a classification to be justified, the frequency or density distributions of the properties should not be equal distributions, but show one or several peaks. Then, when the joint distributions of more than one variable are considered, some combinations of values may be more frequent than other combinations, perhaps even more frequent than would be expected based on the marginal distributions. This is one of the fundamental phenomena enabling the formal definition of classes.

While classification is a 'process,' the temporary result is a 'structure.' Dynamic aspects, such as the development of a property and other trends and changes, might be included in the definitions of variables. This does not, however, make a formal classification a process model. In this sense, classification is static. It temporarily fixes the sometimes turbulent—streams of information. Changing a classification means the (re-)interpretation of some substantive area.

See also: Statistical Clustering; Multivariate Analysis: Classification and Discrimination; Mixture Models, in Statistics; Measurement Theory: Conjoint; Person-centered Research; Configurational Analysis

Bibliography

Arabie P, Hubert L-J, De Soete G (eds.) 1996 *Clustering and Classification*. World Scientific, Singapore

Baulieau F B 1999 Two variant axiom systems for presence/absence based dissimilarity coefficients. *Journal of Classification* 14: 159–70

Biggs N L 1999 *Discrete Mathematics*. rev. edn. Clarendon Press, Oxford, UK

Bock H-H 1996 Probability models and hypothesis testing in partitioning cluster analysis. In: Arabie P, Hubert L J, De Soete G (eds.) *Clustering and Classification*. World Scientific Singapore , pp. 377–453

Coombs C H 1964 *A Theory of Data*. Wiley, New York

Daws J T 1996 The analysis of free-sorting data: Beyond pairwise cooccurrences. *Journal of Classification* 13: 57–80

De Soete G 1993 Using latent class analysis in categorization research. In: van Mechelen I, Hampton J, Michalski R S, Theuns P (eds.) *Categories and Concepts*. Academic Press, London, pp. 309–30

Dunn G, Everitt B S 1982 *An Introduction to Mathematical Taxonomy*. Cambridge University Press, Cambridge, UK

Everitt B S 1993 *Cluster Analysis*. 3rd edn. Edward Arnold, London

Feger H 1994 *Structure Analysis of Co-occurrence Data*. Shaker, Aachen, Germany

Feger H, De Boeck P 1993 Categories and concepts: Introduction to data analysis. In: van Mechelen I, Hampton J, Michalski R S, Theuns P (eds.) *Categories and Concepts*. Academic Press, London, pp. 203–23

Galt A H, Smith L J 1976 *Models and the Study of Social Change*. Wiley, New York

Gower J C, Legendre P 1986 Metric and Euclidean properties of dissimilarity coefficients. *Journal of Classification* 3: 5–48

Gyllenberg M, Koski T 1996 Numerical taxonomy and the principle of maximum entropy. *Journal of Classification* 13: 213–29

Hartigan J A 1982 Classification. In: Kotz S, Johnson N L, Read C B (eds.) *Encyclopedia of Statistical Sciences*. Wiley, New York, Vol. 2, pp. 1–10

Jaccard P 1908 Nouvelles recherches sur la distribution florale. *Bulletin de la Société Vaudoise de Science Naturelle* 44: 223–70

Jain A K, Dubes R C 1988 *Algorithms for Clustering Data*. Prentice-Hall, Englewood Cliffs, NJ

Krathwohl D R, Bloom B S, Masia B B 1964 *Taxonomy of Educational Objectives*. Longman, London

Krauth J, Lienert G A 1973 *KFA Die Konfigurationsfrequenzanalyse*. Alber, Freiburg, Germany

Lee M D 1999 An extraction and regularization approach to additive clustering. *Journal of Classification* **16**: 255–81

Looney C G 1997 *Pattern Recognition Using Neural Networks*. Oxford University Press, New York

McQuitty L L 1987 *Pattern-Analytic Clustering: Theory, Method, Research and Configural Findings*. University Press of America, New York

Milligan G W 1996 Clustering validation: Results and implication for applied analyses. In: Arabie P, Hubert L J, De Soete G (eds.) *Clustering and Classification*. World Scientific, Singapore, pp. 341–75

Pankhurst R J 1991 *Practical Taxonomic Computing*. Cambridge University Press, Cambridge, UK

Pires A M, Branco J A 1997 Comparison of multinomial classification rules. *Journal of Classification* **14**: 137–45

Shepard R N, Arabie P 1979 Additive clustering representations of similarities as combinations of discrete overlapping properties. *Psychological Review* **86**: 87–123

Sokal R R, Sneath P H A 1963 *Principles of Numerical Taxonomy*. Freeman, San Francisco

Sutcliffe J P 1993 Concept, class, and category in the tradition of Aristotle. In: van Mechelen I, Hampton J, Michalski R S, Theuns P (eds.) *Categories and Concepts*. Academic Press, London, pp. 35–65

H. Feger

Classifiers, Linguistics of

Classifiers are overt morphemes that constitute morphosyntactic systems which are semantically motivated and subject to discourse-pragmatic conditions of use. Classifier systems are not found in Indo–European languages. They are in essence secondary linguistic systems characterized, on the one hand, by their clear lexical origin and persistent semantic motivation and, on the other, by their functioning as morphosyntactic systems. The better-known systems are the numeral classifier systems of Asian or Amerindian languages, illustrated in Table 1.

Classifier studies became of interest to general linguists in the 1970s, following proposals to capture the universal semantic properties of classifier systems. Adams and Conklin (1973), Denny (1976), Allan

Table 1
Examples of numeral classifier systems

Japanese

enpitsu ni-hon	hon ni-satsu
pencil 2-CL(1D)	book 2-CL(bound volume)
'two pencils'	'two books'

Tzotzil

j-p'ej alaxa	j-ch'ix kantela
1-CL(3D) orange	1-CL(1D) candle
'one orange'	'one candle'

Table 2
Lexical sources of basic classifiers

Classifiers	Lexical origin
1D: long-rigid	tree/trunk
2D: flat-flexible	leaf
3D: round	fruit

(1977) have provided the framework for many of the subsequent descriptions and discussions, and can be considered as classics of the field. Adams and Conklin were the first to wade through much comparative data and claim the existence of some universal semantic properties, based primarily on data from Asian numeral classifier systems. They established the primacy of three basic shapes, which are semantically combinations of one of the major dimensional outlines of objects (1D, 2D, 3D) with a secondary characteristic of consistency and/or size. This combination is directly inherited from the most common lexical sources of a basic set of classifiers, which are the primary elements of the physical world being handled for the survival of human communities (Table 2).

Denny (1976) is the work of a psychologist handling data secondhand. He offers the appealing proposal that the semantic traits of classifiers may be organized into three kinds, those of 'social, physical and functional interaction,' assuming that what classifiers are 'good for' is to signal how humans interact with the world. Under social interaction he places interaction with animate entities of our world, principally fellow human beings, classified by sex, social rank, or other categorization schema, as well as other entities such as divinities and other powers specific to a culture. In the physical interaction realm, objects of the world are classified along certain parameters linked to their nature as manipulable and manipulated objects, principally the parameter of shape. Finally, in the functional interaction realm, entities of the world are classified by the use to which they are put, such as items of clothing, hunting or fishing, transportation, for instance.

Allan (1977) is a first typological of study of so-called classifiers, based on a broad data base of fifty classifier languages. Although the reliability of the data is variable and different types of nominal classification systems are lumped together under the label of 'classifiers,' there is still remarkable overlap between his seven 'categories of classification' (material, shape, consistency, size, location, arrangement, and quanta) and Denny's three. Two of Allan's original statements are of particular interest for later discussions on the nature and purpose of classifier categorization; they are the fact of a total absence of color classifiers, and the constraint that the characteristics denoted by the categories of classification be perceivable by more than one of the senses alone, such as sight and touch,

Table 3
Specific, unique, and repeaters in Jakaltek-Popti'

Type of classifier	CL	Class members
specific:	no'	ALL animals, except dog, AND all products of animals (*no' hos* 'egg,' *no' lech* 'milk,' leather shoes, wool blankets etc ...)
unique:	metx'	ONLY *metx' tx'i* 'dog'
repeater + specific:	tx'otx'	*tx'otx' tx'otx'* 'dirt, ground' AND all objects made of clay (*tx'otx' xih* 'pottery jug' etc ...)
repeater + unique	atz'am	ONLY *atz'am atz'am* 'salt'

where sight means primarily perception of shape. It is worth noting here that to arrive at the kind of statements of universals found in the above mentioned publications meant wading through vast amounts of data from fieldwork often containing large sets of classifiers, and interpreting their semantics through approximate translations, in order to identify those universal characteristics.

Besides varying as to the semantics of the individual classifying elements, systems of classifiers vary greatly as to the number and the specificity of the classes around which the systems seem to be organized. The classes headed by classifiers can vary from very simple to very complex; they can be small or large, homogeneous or extremely heterogeneous. Homogeneous classes are those with transparent semantic motivation, while heterogeneous classes are usually considered to be composed of a core set of prototype elements to which others have been added through various means of extension. Therefore, within the literature on classifier systems one finds different labels to indicate the nature of the classes themselves. One talks, for instance, of specific, general, unique and repeater classifiers. *Specific classifiers* are the most common type. The classes they head are built around prototypical exemplars, with incorporation of other elements by any number of types of extensions of the class. One of the most notorious examples in the literature of a specific classifier heading a very heterogeneous class is the case of the Japanese numeral classifier *hon*, used prototypically for long, thin objects.

General classifiers, as their label indicates, are largely desemanticized and head large heterogeneous classes with no distinct semantic motivation. Large Asian numeral classifier systems are known to have general classifiers. At the opposite end, *unique classifiers* head classes of just one element. One finds in the literature examples of unique classifiers for certain animals, for instance, such as the elephant or the tiger, or even the dog, generally interpreted *a posteriori* as highlighting some cultural item of particular significance. Finally, the term *repeater* refers to classifiers that are homophonous with a noun while being either unique or specific (Table 3). The existence of repeaters is what makes for the openendedness of some classifier systems.

The semantic studies of the 1970s had a tendency to overlook the existence of different types of systems, often lumping together classifier systems with other systems. Towards the end of the twentieth century, attention has been given to the fact that classifier systems are one type of nominal classification system among several others, as argued in Grinevald (2000), in contrast to the position taken by Aikhenvald (1999). The non-lumping position argues that classifier systems are intermediate systems in a continuum of nominal classification systems that range from lexical to morphosyntactic systems. At the lexical end they may be distinguished from two types of systems, the measure terms and class terms systems, with which they are often either confused or consciously lumped. At the grammatical end, they are widely considered as distinct from the gender systems and the noun class systems, which are both essentially grammaticalized concordial systems.

All languages have lexical sets of measure terms, the expression 'measure terms' being used here as a cover term for what are strictly speaking measures and for types of arrangements. Examples of English measure terms include actual measure terms such as a glass of water, a pound of sugar, a slice of bread, a sheet of paper, and arrangements such as a pile of books, a group of children, a line of cars. Class terms are sets of lexical items used in lexicogenesis; they participate in compounding processes of word formation that are functionally equivalent to derivational processes. The English class terms '-berry' (as in strawberry, blueberry, boysenberry, goodberry, loganberry), '-tree' (as in apple tree, banana tree, cherry tree), or even '-man' (as in mailman, policeman, garbage man) are the functional equivalent of French derivational suffixes such as '-*ier*' (as in *pommier* 'apple tree,' *bananier* 'banana tree,' *cerisier* 'cherry tree') or '-*ier*/-*eur*' (as in *facteur* 'mailman,' *policier* 'policeman,' *éboueur* 'garbage man').

Table 4
Class markers in Tswana (Bantu)

a.	le-kau	le	le-leele	le	le-ntsho	le	le	opelang	le-le
	5-boy	5	5-tall	5	5-black	5	5	sing	5-DEM
	'this tall black boy who is singing'								

b.	**Le**-kau	le lapile;	Ke	le	thusitse
	5-boy	5-is tired	I	5	have helped
	'the boy is tired, I have helped him'				

At the grammatical end of the continuum of nominal classification systems are the gender systems found in Indo–European languages and the noun class systems of Bantu languages. Note in the examples inTable 4 the ubiquitous presence of noun class markers (here of class 5) on nouns, adjectives, and demonstratives, and in the verb as pronominal clitics. The different degrees of grammaticalization of gender/noun class systems and classifier systems are generally assessed according to the set of criteria listed in Table 5.

Beyond distinguishing classifier systems from other systems of nominal classification it is important to acknowledge the existence of several subsystems of classifiers, which are usually identified and labeled primarily by their morphosyntactic locus. The best known and documented types are the ones found as elements of the noun phrase itself, such as the numeral classifiers (numeral + CL) used in quantifying expressions; the noun classifiers (CL noun) so-called for appearing with a bare noun, not linked to the expression of quantification or possession; and the genitival or possessive classifiers (poss + CL) that are part of possessive constructions. The verb forms are the locus of two possible systems of classification: the verbal classifiers (verb-CL) which belong to the systems of nominal classification and the lesser known verb classifiers, which actually classify types of verbs rather than nominal arguments.

Noun classifiers; Jakaltek-Popti' (Craig 1986, p. 264)
    xil   naj xuwan no7 lab'a
    saw CL John   CL snake
    '(man) John saw the (animal) snake'
Numeral classifiers; Ponapean (Rehg 1981, p. 130)
    pwihk riemen   'two pigs'
    pig 2 + CL: animate
    tuhke rioapwoat   'two trees'
    tree 2 + CL: long
Genitive classifiers; Ponapean (Rehg 1981, p. 184)
    kene-i mwenge   'my(edible) food'
    CL-GEN.1 food
    were-i pwoht   'my(transport) boat'
    CL-GEN.1 boat
Verbal Classifiers; Cayuga (Mithun 1986, pp. 386–8)
    a. ohon'atatke: ak-hon'at-a:k
         it-potato-rotten past.I-CL-eat 'I
         (potato)ate a rotten potato'

    b. so:wa:s akh-nahskw-ae'
         dog I-CL:domestic.animal-have
         'I have a (pet) dog'
    c. skitu ake'-treh-tae'
         skidoo I-CL: vehicle-have
         'I have a car'
                    Gunwinggu (Oates 1964
                    in Mithun 1986, p. 389)
    d. gugu ga-bo:-mangan
         water it-CL: liquid-fall
         'water is falling'

The major argument to prove the existence of different types of classifiers is the co-occurrence of several independent systems in the same language. These are systems with different inventories of classifier morphemes, different semantics and different morphosyntactic loci, such as the coexisting numeral and possessive classifier systems of Micronesian languages like Ponapean, for instance. Although much remains to be done in terms of the study of the semantics of classifiers, preliminary exploration of a correlation between the major morphosyntactic types of classifiers known and their semantic profiles point to the following alignment (Grinevald 2000).

Shape seems to be the dominant semantic parameter in numeral classifier systems, while function is the major semantic parameter of genitival classifier systems, and material the major one of noun classifier systems, in the following pattern:

  (a) numeral classifiers = physical categories:
      two-ROUND oranges;
      three-LONG RIGID pencils;
      four-FLAT FLEXIBLE blankets
  (b) genitive classifiers = functional categories
      my-EDIBLE food;
      his-DRINKABLE potion;
      their-TRANSPORT canoe
  (c) noun classifiers = material/essence categories
      an ANIMAL deer;
      the ROCK cave;
      MAN musician

The claim that there exist different types of classifiers raises two questions about the function of classifiers: one is the unavoidable one about the common function of classifiers in general in the languages that avail themselves of such systems. The other arises from the identification of different types of classifier systems and concerns the distinct functions that those different

Table 5
Criteria for distinguishing noun classes and classifiers

	Noun classes	Classifiers
a.	classify all nouns	don't classify all nouns
b.	in a small number of classes	in large(r) number
c.	closed system	open system
d.	fused with other grammatical categories (number, case ...)	not fused
e.	can be marked on N	not marked on N itself
f.	in concord/agreement pattern	not part of concord systems
g.	N assigned to one class	can be to assigned to several classes
h.	no speaker variation	possible speaker variation
i.	no register variation	possible formal vs informal use

Source: Dixon 1982

types of classifier fulfill, in view of their different morphosyntactic loci and semantic profiles. It has to be noted that when the issue of the function of classifier systems has been addressed in the literature, it has generally been, admittedly or not, from the perspective of numeral classifiers only, without regard for the variety of classifier types. In this context, (numeral) classifiers have been seen as markers of individuation or unitizing that operate in languages in which the semantics of nouns is taken to be essentially equivalent to that of mass or concept nouns of Indo–European languages.

One proposal dealing with the distinct functions of the various types of classifier systems has been an analysis of noun phrases as layered structures parallel to verbal layered structures in which different types of operators are found. In this framework numeral classifiers were considered to be quantification operators with semantics that appealed to the handling of items to be counted, hence primarily shape and physical characteristics. It was further argued that possessive classifiers were localizing operators, and their semantics linked to the function of the items appropriated, while the noun classifiers were quality operators and as such appealed to the material or essence of the items that appeared as arguments of discourse (Grinevald 2000). Much remains to be done to document the variety of classifier systems well enough to be able to address this issue comprehensively.

One of the major challenges of classifier studies is that the essentially intermediate nature of classifier systems, as secondary linguistic systems halfway between lexicon and grammar, means great variability of the systems. Acknowledging the need to take into account the inherent dynamics of classifier systems makes the descriptive task both more onerous and more productive if comparative and typological work is to proceed properly. The need is felt to include a number of dynamic variables to handle the description of specific classifier systems, by attending to their place in the overall grammar of the language within which

they develop and are used. These variables include:

(a) their degree of grammaticalization: within each subtype of classifier system, one can identify systems at different stages of grammaticalization. For instance, incipient systems of noun classifiers can be found on the Australian continent next to well-established ones, meanwhile the numeral classifiers of the Chibchan languages of Central America are much more grammaticalized than those of Asian languages.

(b) the age of the system: some systems are very old, e.g., the Chinese system of numeral classifiers, while others can be argued to be only several centuries old, like the qʼanjobʼalan-Mayan noun classifiers.

(c) the productivity of a classifier system must be considered too, independently of its age. For instance the Thai numeral classifier system, which is very old, is also very productive: it is open and adapting to the language of modern life, while the noun classifier system of Jakaltek-Poptiʼ, which is not very old, seems frozen and unable to cope with the classification of modern imports and products.

(d) the particular classifier system needs to be assessed in the context of the common phenomenon of areal spread of such systems. The spread can operate either through the actual borrowing of a system, morphology included, as was the case with the expansion of the original Chinese numeral classifier system into its surrounding regions, or through the borrowing of the idea and motivation for the development of such systems, as seems to have taken place between the qʼanjobʼalan languages of Guatemala and their neighboring Mamean languages.

While early propositions of matching classifier systems with morphological types of languages were not enlightening, there is indeed a tendency for different types of nominal classification systems in general, and of different types of classifiers in particular, to distribute themselves in clusters around the world. For instance, gender systems are a widespread phenomenon in Indo–European languages, while noun class systems were originally mostly known from

Bantu languages. In addition, they have been described for languages of Australia and Papua New Guinea, and are perhaps more widespread than previously recognized in Amazonia.

Turning our attention to classifier subtypes, numeral classifiers are best known for their presence in South East Asian languages, but have also been identified in America, in particular Mesoamerica. Noun classifiers appear to be a rare type, mostly identified in Mesoamerica and Australia, while possessive classifiers are the hallmark of Micronesian languages, although they are also found in various parts of America. As for verbal classifiers, they have been documented for North American languages and for signed languages, though it is sometimes difficult to establish how segmentable and identifiable the actual classifier morphemes are in verbal predicates.

Classifier studies raise difficult methodological issues. There is the first-degree challenge of the fieldwork to be done to produce descriptions of these systems. Fieldwork faces the problem of the ethnocentrism of the semantic analysis. This will continue as long as much of this work is done through translation, and is still largely carried out by linguists who are native speakers of languages where the phenomenon does not exist. (Work done on South East Asian languages is to some extent an exception to this problem.) For instance, it is often difficult to say whether the semantics of a classifier is one of the strictly physical characteristic of shape or one of function, since certain shapes naturally lend themselves to certain functions. Are objects hollowed or made to be concave to be considered for their shape, as round hollow objects, or for their function, as recipients and containers? The basic issue is, of course, whether the right questions are being asked of these systems in the first place. There is the further challenge of the fundamental lexico-grammatical nature of such systems, with their common open-endedness and subtle discourse functioning that require extensive studies all too rare in the descriptive tradition. And there is the second-degree challenge facing linguists working on secondhand data of uncertain reliability and common incompleteness, particularly in terms of the pervasive dynamics and complex internal typology of such systems, of the kind introduced in this article.

A number of publications are shaping the field of classifier studies in the context of the wider discipline of nominal classification. Craig (1986) meant to begin to confront various approaches to the study of nominal classification systems and included articles on the acquisition, historical development, discourse function, and semantics of classifier systems. Senft (2000) is a more recent collection (based on a 1993 working conference) where the issues of typology, grammaticalization, and function of classifiers are further elaborated. Aikhenvald (1999) is a substantial monograph which attests to the importance of Amazonian

data, for the richness of its classification systems and the challenges they pose to the proposed typology, and which underlines in general the extreme complexity of the inter-relation of systems in many languages. Sands (1995) is a useful survey of nominal classification systems in Australia which reveals two interesting phenomena: one is the parallel development, in different languages, of concordial noun class systems and noun classifier systems out of the same lexical material of generic nouns; and the other is the documentation of the various stages of the evolution of noun classifier systems from the discourse sensitive use of generic nouns and through the increasingly frequent collocation of generics and nouns in classifier constructions. Bisang (1996, 1999) provides overviews of the grammaticalization dynamics through which the classifier systems of East and South East Asian languages arose, within the areal typological frame called for by the language contact situation of the region.

In terms of an agenda for the development of classifier studies in the twenty-first century, the work is proceeding on two fronts. On the linguistic fieldwork front, there is still an enormous need for more comprehensive descriptions. And, given the fact that many systems worth investigating are to be found in the languages of Amazonia, Australia, and Papua New Guinea, the challenging nature of this fieldwork has to be kept in mind. Work on nominal classification processes in signed languages is also under way; a collective volume on that topic in a cross-linguistic perspective is scheduled to appear following a working conference in 2000 (Emmorey in press).

A better understanding of the general phenomenon of classifiers should also emerge from the confrontation of what is now known of nominal classification systems with the much less known phenomenon of verb classification. This phenomenon has been described for some Australian languages, but has not come fully to the attention of linguists interested in nominal classification. However, the identification of a similar phenomenon in South American languages such as the Barbacoan languages of Ecuador and its ongoing description should facilitate further exploration of the parallels between the organization of nominal and verbal linguistic expressions and the similarity in the function of their operators, in particular that of their respective classifier systems.

On the more theoretical front, various debates are open and in need of further consideration. They include taking a position on the *a priori* lumping or not lumping together of most nominal classification systems. Lumping means subsuming, under the label of classifiers, cases of class terms, measure terms, noun classes, as well as classifiers. This position is defensible in terms of how the new data collected in the field, particularly data on languages until recently never described, appear startling if not overwhelming because of overlapping layers of elements of supposedly various types of systems. Alternatively one can opt to tease apart different types of classification systems using as a reference clear cases of classifier systems with the characteristics given above in Table 5.

To handle the cases of data overlaps one can proceed with a number of tools from a functional-typological approach to the study of language. One is the notion of prototype, with its accompanying concept of fuzzy boundaries; this allows for some systems to be intermediate between two systems, such as noun class and classifier. Another is the notion of the grammaticalization dynamics, inter- and intra-types of nominal classification systems, allowing in particular for variations along this parameter within the same type, which can change an analysis of multiple classifier systems to one of incipient noun class system for instance. A third is the notion that several systems may indeed co-exist, the original system and another one evolved in part from it, resulting in homophonous morphemes belonging to various systems, such as class terms and classifiers.

Another major issue due for more debate in the twenty-first century is the issue about how much the linguistic phenomenon of classifiers is linked to categorization of referents in the world linguistic classification of nouns. This has been best articulated by Lucy (1992), while Foley (1997, Chap. 12) provides a good summary of recent experimental work on the cognitive impact of classifiers in categorization. It is clear that before constructing experimental studies that use classifiers in the search for the nature of the links that hold between language and cognition, an assessment of the degree of grammaticalization of the systems is needed. Ongoing discussions of so-called classifiers in signed languages underline also their fundamental discourse functions of referent identification and referent tracking, and the likelihood that the term 'classifiers,' now well established in the literature, both in its narrower and wider scope, may very well be a misnomer which delays a better grasp of their role in language.

See also: First Language Acquisition: Cross-linguistic; Foreign Language Teaching and Learning; Language Acquisition; Language Development, Neural Basis of

Bibliography

Adams K L, Conklin N F 1973 Towards a theory of natural classification. *Papers from the Regional Meeting of the Chicago Linguistic Society* 9: 1–10
Aikhenvald A 1999 *Classifiers. A Typology of Noun Categorization Devices*. Clarendon Press, Oxford, UK
Allan K 1977 Classifiers. *Language* 53: 285–310
Berlin B 1965 *Tzeltal Numeral Classifiers*. Mouton, The Hague
Bisang W 1996 Areal typology and grammaticalization: Processes of grammaticalization based on nouns and verbs in East and Mainland South East Asian languages. *Studies in Language* 20–3: 519–97
Bisang W 1999 Classifiers in East and Southeast Asian languages: Counting and beyond. In: Gvozdanovic J (ed.) *Numeral Types and Changes Worldwide*. Mouton de Gruyter, Berlin
Craig C G (ed.) 1986 *Noun Classes and Categorization*. John Benjamins, Amsterdam
de León L 1988 Noun and numeral classifiers in Mixtec and Tzotzil: A referential view. Ph.D thesis, University of Sussex, UK
Denny J P 1976 What are noun classifiers good for? *Papers from the Regional Meeting of the Chicago Linguistic Society* 12: 122–32
Dixon R M W 1982 Noun classifiers and noun classes. In: Dixon R M W (ed.) *Where Have all the Adjectives Gone? And Other Essays on Semantics and Syntax*. Mouton, The Hague, pp. 211–33
Dixon R M W 1986 Noun classes and noun classification in typological perspective. In: Craig C G (ed.) *Noun Classification and Categorization*. John Benjamins, Amsterdam, pp. 105–12
Emmorey K (ed.) in press *Perspectives on Classifier Constraints in Sign Languages*. Erlbaum, Mahwah, NJ
Foley W 1997 *Anthropological Linguistics: An Introduction*. Blackwell, Oxford, UK
Greenberg J H 1978 How does a language acquire gender markers? In: Greenberg J H (ed.) *Universals of Human Language, Vol. III*. Stanford University Press, Stanford, CA, pp. 47–82
Grinevald C 2000 A morphosyntactic typology of classifiers. In: Senft (ed.) *Nominal Classification*. Cambridge University Press, Cambridge, UK, pp. 50–92
Lucy J 1992 *Grammatical Categories and Cognition*. Cambridge University Press, Cambridge, UK
Matsumoto Y 1993 Japanese numeral classifiers: A study of semantic categories and lexical organization. *Linguistics* 31: 667–713
Mithun M 1986 The convergence of noun classification systems. In: Craig C G (ed.) *Noun Classification and Categorization*. John Benjamins, Amsterdam, pp. 379–97
Oates L 1964 A tentative description of the Gunwinggu language. *Oceania Linguistic Monographs* 10, University of Sydney, Australia
Rehg K 1981 *Ponapean Reference Grammar*. University Press of H7awaii, Honolulu, HI
Sands K 1995 Nominal classification in Australia. *Anthropological Linguistics* 37: 247–346
Senft G 2000 *Systems of Nominal Classification*. Cambridge University Press, Cambridge, UK

C. Grinevald

Classroom Assessment

Around the end of the 1980s, the traditional conception of teachers' classroom assessment roles began to change. Previously, teachers' classroom assessment responsibilities were narrowly focused on summative decisions narrowly related to grouping, grading, and selecting students. In the late 1980s, close examination of what teachers do and what decisions they are called on to make in their classrooms increased substantially views of teachers' classroom lives, responsibilities, and assessments (Jackson 1990, Wittrock 1986). A synthesis of this research identified three generalizations that provided a useful perspective of the realities of the classroom teachers' classroom.

First, classrooms are both academic and social environments that teachers must master and understand to successfully instruct and interact with their students. Many teacher decisions are dependent on the social and academic knowledge they acquire about their students. Second, classrooms are busy, interactive, and ad hoc settings that call on the teacher to make many and varied decisions. Third, although many nonteachers view classrooms as a unified whole, teachers know that such uniformity is illusionary. In classrooms, teachers continually deal with a range of individual student concerns and issues. Understanding the implications of these three classroom realities produces a broad domain for assessments.

Given the richness and complexity of classrooms, a more realistic description of classroom assessments is the process of collecting, synthesizing, and interpreting information to aid teachers in making classroom decisions. While the overriding purpose is to make decisions, classroom assessment involves many different decisions and contexts. In particular, classroom assessments focus on learning about students at the start of school, planning and delivering instruction to students, and formally assessing student learning. Note that each of these three assessment focuses is dependent on the collection, synthesis, and interpretation of assessment. These three focuses are used to structure the discussion of classroom assessments below.

1. Classroom Assessment at the Start of School

The beginning days of school are important for both teachers and students. In the first few weeks of school the teacher and students must get to know and understand each other so that they can be organized into a classroom learning community. The activities in the early few days of school set the stage for how well students will behave, attend, and learn during the school year (Airasian 2001, Stiggins 1997). In the first early days of school, teachers have their antenna up, observing, listening, mentally recording, and assessing their perceptions of the students. In order to know how to group, teach, motivate, manage, accommodate, and reward students, the teacher must learn their particular characteristics.

Many forms of planned and unplanned, formal and informal, sources of information contribute to teachers' perceptions of their students, e.g., 'on the fly' observations, hearsay from the school grapevine, and prior teachers' comments, as well as information such as school records, formal assessment results, and performance in the classrooms. Two increasingly important areas teachers want to know about are

student disabilities and medication. Note that although cognitive information is important to all teachers, the classroom society requires that affective and psychomotor student characteristics also must be identified.

Integrating the pieces of formal and informal information gathered in the first two or three weeks, the teacher forms a description or perception of each student and the class as a whole. This provides the teacher with the kind of nitty-gritty information needed to make the classroom function effectively (Good and Brophy 1997). Because teachers cannot spend a great deal of time assessing their students at the start of school, the validity and reliability of the initial student assessments are important. Two major validity concerns during start-of-school assessments are labeling students based on stereotypes and treating students' cultural or language differences as if they were student deficits (Oakes and Lipton 1999). The main concern of reliability is that teachers obtain sufficient and recurring information before labeling students. These important initial teacher assessments are often overlooked as an important and influential form of classroom assessment.

2. Classroom Assessment in Planning and Delivering Instruction

Teacher classroom decisions about planning and delivering instruction encompass a variety of issues. There are, for example, many considerations that teachers must recognize and assess in order to successfully plan lessons for their students. Student characteristics vary with student readiness, attention span, prior subject knowledge, attitude toward school, disabilities, and other characteristics that must be considered when planning instruction. Similarly, school and classroom resources range from textbooks to copying machines to sophisticated laboratory apparatus, and can hamper or enhance lesson planning. Time is a critical factor in planing, as every teacher knows. Also, teacher characteristics such as subject matter knowledge, physical limits, and preferred teaching style influence planning. A significant amount of assessment is involved in decision making for valid and viable lesson plans (Wragg 1997).

Once relevant information about the student, the teacher, and the instructional resources are identified, the teacher's task is to synthesize and decide how to construct a set of instructional plans containing educational objectives, instructional materials, teaching strategies, and assessment procedures (Airasian 2001). Different objectives call for different forms of instruction and assessment, and teachers must be able to teach students in more than one way. Objectives indicate the outcomes of student learning. Higher level objectives include cognitive processes such as application, analysis, synthesis, and evaluation. Lower level objectives emphasize rote memorization. Because educational objectives are developed before instruction begins, teachers often must make a decision to adapt objectives, materials, and instructional strategies to suit student readiness and needs. Suitable strategies to accommodate students with disabilities also must be planned. The decisions teachers make to match instruction to objectives and make appropriate instruction for students with disabilities improve the validity of their instruction and assessment.

During teaching, the teacher is concerned with decisions and assessments to determine how well the instruction is progressing. Planning and instructing assessments are integrally related; the processes constantly cycles from planning to delivering to revising to planning and so on. There is a logical, continuous, and natural link between the two processes.

Oral questioning is the most common form of instructional assessment because it best fits the flow of instruction (Airasian 2001). During instruction, teachers ask questions for many reasons, to reinforce important points, to maintain students' attention, to assess student learning, and to promote deeper processing of important information. Teachers use both convergent questions that have a single correct answer and divergent questions that have more than one appropriate answers. Lower level questions tap recall and memorization while higher level questions tap processes more complex than recall. Classroom questioning strategies can be improved by asking questions related to important objectives, avoiding overly general questions, distributing questions among many students, allowing sufficient 'wait time' before calling on students, stating questions clearly to avoid confusion, probing student responses with follow-up questions such as 'why' or 'explain your answer,' and remembering that oral questioning is a social process in which student answers should be treated with respect, regardless of the quality of the answer.

3. Assessments of Formal Learning

3.1 General Aspects of Formal Assessments

Formal assessment is the culmination of planning and delivering instruction. It focuses on the extent to which students have learned from instruction. There is an important difference between good teaching and effective teaching. Good teaching refers to what teachers do during planning and delivering instruction. Effective teaching refers to whether students have learned from their instruction. Formal assessments are concerned with the effectiveness of learning from instruction. Formal assessments are also called summative assessments and commonly include tests, projects, term papers, lab reports, portfolios, performances, products, and final examinations. These are assessments

that can have important consequences for students and therefore are taken seriously by students, parents, and teachers (Black 1998).

A fair and valid formal assessment includes information and skills similar to those presented in instruction. While the type of assessment strategy chosen to assess students depends on the nature of instruction, all types should represent the objectives and instruction presented. Factors such as the age of the students, the subject matter assessed, and the length of time for testing, all impact the length of formal assessments.

Obtaining fair and valid formal assessments involves alignment among objectives, instruction, and assessments, providing students with good instruction, and selecting appropriate strategies to assess learning. Formal assessments gather valid and reliable samples of student performance and use them to make generalizations about general student learning. The most important preparation for formal assessment is a good teacher. Students should also be familiar with the assessment item formats and be given a review session prior to the assessment.

If these factors are not met, invalid assessment results can occur. Other practices that diminish assessment validity are: failure to develop assessments based on objectives and instruction, failure to assess all the important objectives taught, failure to select item types that prevent students from showing their full performance, including topics or objectives not taught, including too few items to obtain adequate assessment reliability, and using tests to punish students. Further, the success of formal assessment can be undone if the test questions are faulty or confusing. Poorly constructed or unclear assessment questions do not provide students a fair chance to show what they have learned from instruction, and consequently, diminish assessment validity.

3.2 Types of Formal Classroom Assessments

There are many types of test items that are used in classrooms assessments. Selection items include multiple-choice, true–false, and matching items to which students respond by selecting an answer from a set of presented items. Supply items include short-answer, completion, and essay items to which students are required to create or supply their own answers. Selection items can cover many items in a short time and can be scored quickly. Supply items can be constructed quickly and permit students to provide their own constructed answers. Selection items are difficult to construct and encourage guessing, while supply items are difficult to score and cover smaller samples of instruction (Gronlund 1998).

Common guidelines for writing and critiquing test items include: (a) assess important objectives; (b) state items clearly, describing the students' task; (c) avoid ambiguous and confusing wording and sentence structure—students should have a clear understanding of what is expected of them; (d) use vocabulary appropriate to the students being assessed; (e) write selection items that have one correct answer; (f) provide information about the nature and form of the desired response, particularly for essay questions; (g) avoid clues to correct answers; and (h) review items before assessing students.

In assembling and preparing items for a formal assessment the following suggestions should be applied: (a) group items of the same type; (b) place selection items first and supply items last; (c) provide directions for each type of test item; and (d) diminish assessment anxiety by giving advanced notice of the assessment, providing a review session before assessment, and most of all, providing students with good instruction. Many students experience anxiety before and during testing. While it is difficult to eliminate test anxiety, these strategies can lower it. Plan accommodations for students with disabilities. Two types of accommodations should be addressed, one for test administration (e.g., having directions read to students, giving extra time) and one for the test itself (e.g., divide the test into small section, provide a sample of each test item, arrange student items from concrete to abstract).

Unfortunately, cheating on classroom assessments is a fairly common occurrence. Forms of cheating range from looking at another's paper, bringing crib sheets into class, to other illicit strategies (Cizek 1999). No matter how or why it is done, cheating is dishonest and unacceptable. When cheaters state or imply that the work they have turned is their own, they are lying, and should be penalized. Useful strategies to discourage cheating on classroom assessments include spreading seating arrangement, careful proctoring, and movement around the classroom during testing.

Ultimately, all formal classroom assessments will be scored, usually by the classroom teacher. Scoring selection items is straightforward, efficient, and objective. Each student's score is compared to a scoring key and an overall score is obtained. Selection items are typically scored objectively, that is, two or more independent scorers would agree on a student's score. Supply and especially essay items tend to be more difficult and time-consuming to score. Because student responses to supply items are more lengthy and varied than those of selection items, the former are more likely to be subjectively scored. That is, scores of two or more independent scorers do not agree on the same or similar student score. Many factors influence essay subjectivity, including handwriting, spelling, neatness, and teacher fatigue. These factors are not central to the essay, but their presence influences the teacher's perception of students' essays and can influence the objectivity of essay scoring.

Two common essay scoring approaches are holistic and analytic. Holistic scoring provides a single score to describe the essay's quality. Analytic scoring breaks the essay down into component parts such as organization, spelling, accuracy, and grammar and gives each component an individual score. Holistic scoring is most used in grading students, while analytic scoring is most used to correct and improve initial drafts of written responses. To ensure objectivity in essay scoring, the following steps should be followed. Define what constitutes a good essay answer before it is administered. Tell students whether handwriting, spelling, grammar, and punctuation will count in scoring the essay. If possible, score students essays anonymously. If multiple essays are in the assessment, score all students' answers to the first essay question before moving on to score the second essay item, and so on. Reread some of the essays a second time to determine the reliability of scoring.

In addition to selection and short-answer items, there are other important types of items that are important in classroom assessments. The most prominent of these item types is performance assessment, also referred to as authentic or alternative assessments (Mehrens et al. 1998). Performance assessments allow students to demonstrate what they know or can do in a real situation. Examples of performance assessments are essays, pronouncing a foreign word, setting up laboratory equipment, catching a ball, reciting a poem, identifying unknown chemicals, generalizing experimental data, working in cooperative groups, obeying school rules, and painting a picture. All of these performances require more than memorization and a one or two word response.

All performance assessments are developed in four steps: (a) identifying the purpose of the performance assessment; (b) stating the observable aspects of the performance, also called performance criteria; (c) selecting a suitable setting to carry out the performance assessment; and (d) scoring the quality of the performance. The key aspect of assessing performance assessments is the identification of the criteria that define a good performance. Performances are normally broken down into specific, observable criteria that can be individually assessed. Criteria should be specific and unambiguous. For example, stating 'information is presented in a logical sequence' is better than stating the more ambiguous 'has organization,' and 'can be heard in all parts of the room' is better than 'speaks correctly.' Statements of clear performance criteria are important for both holistic and analytic scoring approaches.

Multiple approaches to scoring students' performance assessments are available, and all are based on performance criteria. Checklists, rating scales, and scoring rubrics are most commonly used to assess performance assessments. A checklist is a written list of performance criteria that the teacher uses to judge student performance on each of the criteria. Checklists allow only 'yes' or 'no' judgments of each criterion. A rating scale is a written list of performance criteria that permits the teacher more than two choices (e.g., good, fair, poor or excellent, good, fair, poor) to judge student performance of each criterion. A scoring rubric summarizes the overall performance on the criteria into holistic descriptions representing different levels of a student's overall performance. Rubrics describe performance in a summative way, while checklists and rating scales provide specific diagnostic information about each criterion in a formative way (Airasian 2001, Goodrich 1997).

Another important addition to performance assessment is the portfolio. A portfolio is a carefully selected collection of a student's performances that show accomplishments and improvements over time. Portfolios allow students and teachers to revisit and reflect prior work. Like any performance assessment, performance criteria are defined to identify and judge each of the individual pieces and the overall portfolio. As in all classroom assessments, the criteria should be aligned to the teacher's objectives (Arter and Spandel 1992). The purpose of performance assessment is the same as all formal classroom assessments, to determine how well students have learned from the instruction they were provided. To improve the validity and reliability of performance assessments, teachers should select performance criteria that are appropriate for their students, observe and record student performance while it is being performed rather than at some later date, judge student performance in terms of the performance criteria not the personal characteristics of the students and, if possible, observe a student's performance more than once.

Managing and scoring portfolios is a time-consuming activity, and teachers who attempt portfolio assessment are advised to start a portfolio with a single topic with a limited number of entries in the portfolio.

4. Grading

Grading is the formal process of judging the quality of a student's performance. Grades are always based on teacher judgment. However, the helping relationship that teachers have with their students can make it difficult to judge them in a completely objective manner. Further, since there is no uniformly accepted teacher grading strategy, teachers must find a grading approach that they feel is fair to themselves and to the students (Brookhart 1998, Frisbie and Waltman 1992).

All grading approaches are based on comparisons. The most common grading comparisons are norm-referenced and criterion-referenced grading. Norm-referenced grades are determined by comparing how a given student performed compared to the performance of other test takers. Norm-referenced grading is also called grading on the bell curve. Criterion-referenced grades are determined by comparing how a student performed in comparison to pre-established standards. In norm-referenced grading not all students can

attain high scores, while in criterion-referenced grading they can if they all reach the standard. Grading students based on a comparison of student performance to the teacher's estimate of the student's ability is not recommended because estimating ability is difficult to do accurately. Similarly, grading based on student improvement over time is also not recommended. In general, regardless of the grading approach selected, it is strongly advised that grades be based mainly on students' academic performance.

5. Assessment of Ethical Responsibilities

Thus far discussion has focused on the technical aspects of classroom assessment. However, it is important to recognize that teachers' assessments have short-term and long-term consequences for students, thus requiring that teachers have an ethical responsibility to make decisions that are the most valid and reliable as possible. A number of groups in the USA have set standards for teachers' ethical performance (American Federation of Teachers et al. 1990 and National Education Association 1992–3). Among teachers' ethical responsibilities are: to provide students access to varying points of view; not to expose students to embarrassment or ridicule; not to exclude, deny, or grant advantages on the basis of students' race, color, creed, gender, national origin, religion, culture, sexual orientation, or disability; and not to label students with stereotypes.

This article has indicated that classrooms are complex environments that call upon teachers to make many and varied decisions. The bases for these decisions derive from a wide range of formal and informal assessment information. Although it is not expected that every teacher assessment decision will always be correct, it is expected that they can provide defensible assessment evidence to support classroom decisions. This should be expected in a context in which teachers' actions have important consequences for students.

See also: Classroom Climate; Educational Assessment: Major Developments; Instructional Design; Instructional Psychology; Performance Evaluation in Work Settings; Program Evaluation; Teacher Behavior and Student Outcomes; Teacher Expertise; Teaching and Learning in the Classroom; Test Administration: Methodology

Bibliography

Airasian P W 2001 *Classroom Assessment: Concepts and Applications*. McGraw-Hill, Boston
American Federation of Teachers, National Council on Measurement in Education, National Education Association 1990 Standards for teacher competence in educational assessment

of students. *Educational Measurement: Issues and Practice* **9**(4): 30–2

Arter J, Spandel V 1992 Using portfolios of student work in instruction and assessment. *Educational Measurement: Issues and Practice* **11**: 36–44

Black P J 1998 *Testing: Friend or Foe? Theory and Practice of Assessment and Testing.* Falmer Press, London

Brookhart S M 1998 *Teaching about Grading and Communicating Results.* School of Education, Duquesne University, Pittsburgh, PA

Cizek G J 1999 *Cheating on Tests: How to Do it, Detect it, and Prevent it.* Erlbaum Associates, Mahwah, NJ

Frisbie D A, Waltman K K 1992 Developing a personal grading plan. *Educational Measurement: Issues and Practice* **11**(3): 35–42

Good T L, Brophy J E 1997 *Looking in Classrooms*, 7th ed. Longman, New York

Goodrich H 1997 Understanding rubrics. *Educational Leadership* **54**(4): 14–17

Gronlund N E 1998 *Assessment of Student Achievement.* Allyn & Bacon, Boston

Jackson P W 1990 *Life in Classrooms.* Teachers College Press, New York

Mehrens W A, Popham W J, Ryan J M 1998 How to prepare students for performance assessments. *Educational Measurement: Issues and Practice* **17**(1): 18–22

National Education Association 1992–3 Ethical Standards for Teachers' Relations with Pupils. In: *NEA Handbook.* National Education Association, Washington, DC, pp. 366–7

Oakes J, Lipton M 1999 *Teaching to Change the World*, 1st ed. McGraw-Hill, Boston

Stiggins R J 1997 *Student-centered Classroom Assessment*, 2nd edn. Merrill, Uppersaddle River, NJ

Wittrock M C (ed.) 1986 *Handbook of Research on Teaching.* Macmillan, London

Wragg T 1997 *Assessment and Learning.* Routledge, London

P. W. Airasian

Classroom Climate

In the 30 years since the pioneering use of classroom climate assessments in an evaluation of Harvard Project Physics (Walberg and Anderson 1968), the field has undergone remarkable growth, diversification, and internationalization. Literature reviews (Fraser 1994, 1998) place these developments into historical perspective and show that classroom climate assessments have been used as a source of dependent and independent variables in a variety of research applications spanning many countries. The assessment of classroom climate and research applications has involved a variety of quantitative and qualitative methods, and an important accomplishment within the field has been the productive combination of quantitative and qualitative research methods (Tobin and Fraser 1998).

A historical look at the field of classroom climate over the past few decades shows that a striking feature is the availability of a variety of economical, valid, and widely applicable questionnaires that have been developed and used for assessing students' perceptions of classroom climate. This article makes some of these valuable instruments readily available by describing some major questionnaires and their past application in various lines of research.

Although using students' and teachers' perceptions to study classroom climate forms the focus of this article, this method can be contrasted with the external observer's direct observation and systematic coding of classroom communication and events and the techniques of naturalistic inquiry, ethnography, case study, or interpretive research. In the method considered in detail in this article, defining the classroom climate in terms of the shared perceptions of the students and teachers has the dual advantage of characterizing the setting through the eyes of the participants themselves, and capturing data which the observer could miss or consider unimportant.

1. Instruments for Assessing Classroom Climate

Historically, the development of classroom climate instruments commenced three decades ago with the appearance of *Learning Environment Inventory* (LEI) and *Classroom Environment Scale* (CES). The LEI was developed in conjunction with evaluation and research related to Harvard Project Physics (Walberg and Anderson 1968). The respondent expresses degree of agreement with each of 105 statements (seven per scale) using the four response alternatives of strongly disagree, disagree, agree, and strongly agree. The names of some of the scales are cohesiveness, speed, difficulty, goal direction, and disorganization. The CES (Moos and Trickett 1987) grew from a comprehensive program of research involving perceptual measures of a variety of human environments including psychiatric hospitals, prisons, university residences and work milieus (Moos 1974). The final published version contains nine scales with ten items of true–false response format in each scale. Scales include involvement, teacher support, task orientation, and innovation.

Three more contemporary classroom climate instruments are described below: *Science Laboratory Environment Inventory* (SLEI); *Constructivist Learning Environment Survey* (CLES); and *What Is Happening In This Class* (WIHIC) questionnaire.

1.1 Science Laboratory Environment Inventory

Because of the importance of laboratory settings in science education, an instrument specifically suited to assessing the climate of science laboratory classes at the senior high school or higher education levels was developed (McRobbie and Fraser 1993). The SLEI has five scales (student cohesiveness, open-endedness, investigation, rule clarity, and material environment), each with seven items. The five response alternatives are almost never, seldom, sometimes, often, and very often. Typical items are 'I use the theory from my regular science class sessions during laboratory activities' (integration) and 'we know the results that we are supposed to get before we commence a laboratory activity' (open-endedness).

1.2   Constructivist Learning Environment Survey

The CLES (Taylor et al. 1997) was developed to assist researchers and teachers to assess the degree to which a particular classroom's climate is consistent with a constructivist epistemology, and to assist teachers to reflect on their epistemological assumptions and re-shape their teaching practice. The CLES has 36 items with five response alternatives ranging from almost never to almost always. The scales are personal relevance, uncertainty, critical voice, shared control, and student negotiation. Typical items are 'I help the teacher to decide what activities I do' (shared control) and 'other students ask me to explain my ideas' (student negotiation).

1.3   What Is Happening In This Class (WIHIC) Questionnaire

The WIHIC questionnaire brings parsimony to the field of classroom climate by combining modified versions of the most salient scales from a wide range of existing questionnaires with additional scales that accommodate contemporary educational concerns (e.g., equity and constructivism). Whereas an Australian sample of 1,081 students in 50 classes responded to the original English version, a Taiwanese sample of 1,879 students in 50 classes responded to a Chinese version that had undergone careful procedures of translation and back translation (Aldridge et al. 1999). This led to a final form of the WIHIC containing the seven eight-item scales of student cohesiveness, teacher support, involvement, investigation, task orientation, cooperation, and equity.

1.4   Different Forms of Questionnaires

The instruments discussed above have not only a form to measure perceptions of 'actual' or experienced classroom climate, but also another form to measure perceptions of 'preferred' or ideal classroom climate. The preferred forms are concerned with goals and value orientations and measure perceptions of the classroom climate ideally liked or preferred. For example, an item in the actual form such as 'there *is* a clear set of rules for students to follow' would be

changed in the preferred form to 'there *would be* a clear set of rules for students to follow.'

Tobin and Fraser (1998) point out that there is potentially a problem with nearly all existing classroom climate instruments when they are used to identify differences between subgroups within a classroom (e.g., males and females) or in the construction of case studies of individual students. The problem is that items elicit an individual student's perceptions of the class as a whole, as distinct from a student's perceptions of his/her own role within the classroom. For example, items in the traditional class form might seek students' opinions about whether 'the work of the class is difficult' or whether 'the teacher is friendly towards the class.' In contrast, a personal form of the same items would seek opinions about whether 'I find the work of the class difficult' or whether 'the teacher is friendly towards me.' For these reasons, most of the questionnaires discussed above have a personal form.

Comprehensive statistics supporting the validity and reliability of the above questionnaires are provided in Fraser (1998).

2.   Research Involving Classroom Climate Instruments

2.1   Associations Between Student Outcomes and Classroom Climate

The strongest tradition in past classroom climate research has involved investigation of associations between students' cognitive and affective learning outcomes and their perceptions of psychosocial characteristics of their classrooms. Fraser's (1994) tabulation of 40 past studies shows that associations between outcome measures and classroom climate perceptions have been replicated for a variety of cognitive and affective outcome measures, a variety of classroom climate instruments, and a variety of samples (ranging across numerous countries and grade levels). Using the SLEI, associations with students' cognitive and affective outcomes were found for a sample of approximately 80 senior high school chemistry classes in Australia (Fraser and McRobbie 1995 and Fraser 1993), 489 senior high school biology students in Australia (Fisher et al. 1997) and 1592 grade 10 chemistry students in Singapore (Wong and Fraser 1996).

2.2   Evaluation of Educational Innovations

Classroom climate instruments can be used as a source of process criteria in the evaluation of educational innovations. An evaluation of the Australian Science Education Project (ASEP) revealed that, in comparison with a control group, ASEP students perceived their classrooms as being more satisfying and individualized and having a better material environment (Fraser 1979). The significance of this evaluation is that classroom climate variables differentiated revealingly between curricula, even when various outcome measures showed negligible differences. Recently, the incorporation of a classroom climate instrument within an evaluation of the use of a computerized database revealed that students perceived that their classes became more inquiry oriented during the use of the innovation (Maor and Fraser 1996). In an evaluation of an urban systemic reform initiative in the USA, use of the CLES painted a disappointing picture in terms of a lack of success in achieving constructivist oriented reform of science education (Dryden and Fraser 1996).

2.3 Differences Between Student and Teacher Perceptions of Actual and Preferred Climate

An investigation of differences between students and teachers in their perceptions of the same actual classroom climate and of differences between the actual climate and that preferred by students or teachers was reported by Fisher and Fraser (1983) for a sample of 116 classes for the comparisons of student actual with student preferred scores, and a subsample of 56 of the teachers of these classes for contrasting teachers' and students' scores. Students preferred a more positive classroom climate than was actually present for all five climate dimensions. Also, teachers perceived a more positive classroom climate than did their students in the same classrooms on four of the dimensions. These results replicate patterns emerging in other studies in other countries (Fraser 1998).

2.4 Teachers' Attempts to Improve Classroom Climates

Feedback information based on student or teacher perceptions has been employed in a five-step procedure as a basis for reflection upon, discussion of, and systematic attempts to improve classroom climate (Yarrow et al. 1997). First, all students in the class respond to the preferred form of a classroom climate instrument, while the actual form is administered in the same time slot about a week later (assessment). Second, the teacher is provided with feedback information derived from student responses in the form of profiles representing the class means of students' actual and preferred climate scores (feedback). These profiles permit identification of the changes in classroom climate needed to reduce major differences between the nature of the actual climate and that preferred by students. Third, the teacher engages in private reflection and informal discussion about the profiles in order to provide a basis for a decision about

whether an attempt would be made to change the climate in terms of some of the dimensions (reflection and discussion). The main criteria used for selection of dimensions for change are, first, that there should be a sizeable actual-preferred difference on that variable and, second, that the teacher should feel concerned about this difference and want to make an effort to reduce it. Fourth, the teacher introduces an intervention of about two months' duration in an attempt to change the classroom climate (intervention). For example, strategies used to enhance the dimension of teacher support could involve the teacher moving around the class more to mix with students, providing assistance to students, and talking with them more than previously. Fifth, the student actual form of the scales is re-administered at the end of the intervention to see whether students perceive their classroom climate differently from before (reassessment).

Yarrow et al. (1997) reported a study in which 117 preservice education teachers were introduced to the field of classroom climate through being involved in action research aimed at improving their university teacher education classes and their 117 primary school classes during teaching practice. Improvements in classroom climate were observed, and the preservice teachers generally valued both the inclusion of the topic of classroom climate in their preservice programs, and the opportunity to be involved in action research aimed at improving classroom climate.

2.5 Combining Quantitative and Qualitative Methods

Significant progress has been made towards the desirable goal of combining quantitative and qualitative methods within the same study in research on classroom climates (Tobin and Fraser 1998). Fraser's (1999) multilevel study of classroom climate incorporated a teacher-researcher perspective as well as the perspective of six university-based researchers. The research commenced with an interpretive study of a Grade 10 teacher's classroom at a school which provided a challenging classroom learning climate in that many students were from working-class backgrounds, some were experiencing problems at home, and others had English as a second language. Qualitative methods involved several of the researchers visiting this class each time it met over five weeks, using student diaries, and interviewing the teacher-researcher, students, school administrators, and parents. A video camera recorded activities for later analysis. Field notes were written during and soon after each observation, and team meetings took place three times weekly. The qualitative component of the study was complemented by a quantitative component involving the use of a questionnaire which linked three levels: the class in which the interpretive study was undertaken; selected classes from within the school; and classes distributed throughout the same State.

This enabled a judgment to be made about whether this teacher was typical of other teachers at the same school, and whether the school was typical of other schools within the State. Some of the features identified as salient in this teacher's classroom climate were peer pressure and an emphasis on laboratory activities.

2.6 Cross-national Studies

Educational research which crosses national boundaries offers much promise for generating new insights for at least two reasons (Aldridge et al. 1999). First, there usually is greater variation in variables of interest (e.g., teaching methods, student attitudes) in a sample drawn from multiple countries than from a one-country sample. Second, the taken-for-granted familiar educational practices, beliefs, and attitudes in one country can be exposed, made 'strange,' and questioned when research involves two countries. In a recent cross-national study, six Australian and seven Taiwanese researchers worked together on a study of classroom climate. The WIHIC was administered to 50 junior high school science classes in Taiwan (1,879 students) and 50 classes in Australia (1,081 students) (Aldridge et al. 1999). An English version of the questionnaire was translated into Chinese, followed by an independent back translation of the Chinese version into English, again by team members who were not involved in the original translation. Qualitative data, involving interviews with teachers and students and classroom observations, were collected to complement the quantitative information and to clarify reasons for patterns and differences in the means in each country.

Data from the questionnaires guided the collection of qualitative data. Student responses to individual items were used to form an interview schedule to clarify whether items had been interpreted consistently by students and to help to explain differences in questionnaire scale means between countries. Classrooms were selected for observation on the basis of the questionnaire data, and specific scales formed the focus for observations in these classrooms. The qualitative data provided valuable insights into the perceptions of students in each of the countries, helped to explain some of the differences in the means between countries, and highlighted the need for caution when interpreting differences between the questionnaire results from two countries with cultural differences.

2.7 Transition from Primary to High School

There is considerable interest in the effects on early adolescents of the transition from primary school to the larger, less personal climate of the junior high school at this time of life. Midgley et al. (1991) reported a deterioration in the classroom climate when students moved from generally smaller primary schools to larger, departmentally organized lower secondary schools, perhaps because of less positive student relations with teachers and reduced student opportunities for decision making in the classroom. Ferguson and Fraser's (1998) study of 1,040 students from 47 feeder primary schools and 16 linked high schools in Australia also indicated that students perceived their high school classroom climates less favorably than their primary school classroom climates, but the transition experience was different for boys and girls and for different school size 'pathways.'

3. Conclusion

The major purpose of this article has been to make this exciting research tradition involving classroom climate more accessible to wider audiences by portraying several widely applicable instruments for assessing perceptions of classroom climate and by describing several major lines of previous research.

See also: Classroom Assessment; Educational Assessment: Major Developments; Environments for Learning; Group Processes in the Classroom; School as a Social System; Teacher Behavior and Student Outcomes; Teaching and Learning in the Classroom

Bibliography

Aldridge J M, Fraser B J, Huang T-C I 1999 Investigating classroom environments in Taiwan and Australia with multiple research methods. *Journal of Educational Research* **93**: 48–62

Ferguson P D, Fraser B J 1998 Changes in learning environment during the transition from primary to secondary school. *Learning Environments Research* **1**: 369–83

Fisher D L, Fraser B J 1983 A comparison of actual and preferred classroom environment as perceived by science teachers and students. *Journal of Research in Science Teaching* **20**: 55–61

Fraser B J 1979 Evaluation of a science-based curriculum. In: Walberg H J (ed.) *Educational Environments and Effects: Evaluation, Policy, and Productivity.* McCutchan, Berkeley, CA, pp. 218–34

Fraser B J 1994 Research on classroom and school climate. In: Gabel D (ed.) *Handbook of Research on Science Teaching and Learning.* Macmillan, New York, pp. 493–541

Fraser B J 1998 Science learning environments: assessment, effects and determinants. In: Fraser B J, Tobin K G (eds.) *International Handbook of Science Education.* Kluwer, Dordrecht, The Netherlands, pp. 527–64

Fraser B 1999 'Grain sizes' in learning environment research: combining qualitative and quantitative methods. In: Waxman H, Walberg H (eds.) *New Directions for Research on Teaching.* McCutchan, Berkeley, CA, pp. 285–96

Maor D, Fraser B J 1996 Use of classroom environment perceptions in evaluating inquiry-based computer assisted learning. *International Journal of Science Education* **18**: 401–21

Midgley C, Eccles J S, Feldlaufer H 1991 Classroom environment and the transition to junior high school. In: Fraser B J, Walberg H J (eds.) *Educational Environments: Evaluation, Antecedents and Consequences.* Pergamon, London, pp. 113–39

Moos R H 1974 *The Social Climate Scales: An Overview.* Consulting Psychologists Press, Palo Alto, CA

Moos R H, Trickett E J 1987 *Classroom Environment Scale manual*, 2nd edn. Consulting Psychologists Press, Palo Alto, CA

Taylor P C, Fraser B J, Fisher D L 1997 Monitoring constructivist classroom learning environments. *International Journal of Educational Research* **27**: 293–302

Tobin K, Fraser B J 1998 Qualitative and quantitative landscapes of classroom learning environments. In: Fraser B J, Tobin K G (eds.) *International Handbook of Science Education.* Kluwer, Dordrecht, The Netherlands, pp. 623–40

Walberg H J, Anderson G J 1968 Classroom climate and individual learning. *Journal of Educational Psychology* **59**: 414–19

Yarrow A, Millwater J, Fraser B J 1997 Improving university and primary school classroom environments through pre-service teachers' action research. *International Journal of Practical Experiences in Professional Education* 1(1): 68–93

Dryden M,, Fraser B J 1996 *Evaluating Urban Systemic Reform Using Classroom Learning Environment Instruments.* Paper presented at the annual meeting of the American Educational Research Association, New York

Fisher D, Henderson D, Fraser B 1997 Laboratory environments and student outcomes in senior high school biology. *American Biology Teacher* **59**: 214–19

Fraser B J, McRobbie C J 1995 Science laboratory classroom environments at schools and universities: A cross-national study. *Educational Research and Evaluation* **1**: 289–317

McRobbie C J, Fraser B J 1993 Associations between student outcomes and psychosocial scince environment. *Journal of Educational Research* **87**: 78–85

Wong W L F, Fraser B J 1996 Environment-attitude associations in the chemistry laboratory classroom. *Research in Science and Technological Education* **14**: 91–102

B. J. Fraser

Cleavages: Political

'Political cleavages' are political divisions among citizens rooted in the structure of a given social system. However, although cleavages are political divisions, not all political divisions among citizens spring from structural cleavages. For one to talk of 'cleavages' such divisions must be permanent and noncontingent. They must orient people's behavior and sense of belonging stably and constantly. Political cleavages are the partisan expression of an underlying division among the members of a given society (whether national, subnational, or supranational).

1. The Lipset–Rokkan Model

The concept of 'cleavage' has been current in the social sciences for some time, although it was given full development only in the 1960s by Seymour Martin Lipset and Stein Rokkan. Both of them political sociologists by training, Lipset and Rokkan (1967) sought to redefine and specify the 'social bases of politics.' Writing when structural-functionalism was at its height—and, therefore, influenced by the Parsonian theory which assigned to the political parties the function of encapsulating social conflicts and stabilizing the social system—they set out to explain the persistence of party systems in the European democracies. In the 1960s, in fact, those systems still displayed features similar to those that had been institutionalized at the beginning of the century. Not surprisingly, their explanation was called the theory of the 'freezing' of the European party systems.

Their method was primarily historical–sociological in so far as it connected existing political divisions in the European countries with the principal cleavages that had opened up in the course of their development, from the birth of the nation-state in the sixteenth century to its full democratic maturation in the twentieth. The specific political cleavages that gave rise to the modern party systems accordingly were seen to be the result of two great historical processes: the one that had bred national revolutions (and, therefore, the formation of the modern European nation-states), and the one that had engendered the industrial revolution (and, therefore, the formation of modern European capitalist systems).

National revolutions had created two structural divisions: (a) between the center and the periphery, or between the groups and areas that sought to impose a single public authority on a given territory and the groups and areas which asserted their traditional autonomy against such centralizing pressures; (b) between the lay state and the church, or between groups which sought to separate temporal from religious authority and groups intent on preserving the intimate connection between them. The industrial revolution in its turn created two further structural divisions: (a) between agriculture and industry, or between groups and areas whose survival depended on traditional activities and groups and areas which endeavored to remove traditional constraints in order to foster the growth of new activities and production methods; (b) between capital and labor, or between the groups that dominated the new industrial structure and the workers, whose only possession was their capacity to perform labor.

In Europe, only the parties that reflected these cleavages were able to survive, that is, reproduce themselves electorally and institutionally. The institutionalized interaction among these parties gave rise to the modern party systems which, in individual European countries, and in forms that differed from one country to another, still conserved in the mid-twentieth century the cleavages that had arisen in previous ones.

2. Subsequent Debate

The Lipset–Rokkan model heavily influenced the debate conducted during the 1960s on the political parties. The discussion started from the premise that political parties were necessary to make democracy safe (i.e., stable), as Schattschneider (1948) had already argued. However, the model was not endorsed universally, at least in its entirety. In a study of a small Scandinavian democracy, Eckstein (1966) pointed out the existence of multiple political divisions, identifying ones due to specific disagreements on particular public policies, others due to cultural divergences on interpretations of political life, and yet others arising from segmental cleavages caused by objective social differences. Again in 1966, Daalder examined the small democracies of continental Europe and pointed out the existence of political divisions due to factors (for instance, the nature of the political regime or the concept of nationality) other than those envisaged by the Lipset–Rokkan model.

But it was Sartori (1969) who challenged most radically the Lipset–Rokkan model, by reversing its causal logic. For Sartori, it was not social divisions that encouraged the birth of parties; rather, it was the parties that gave visibility and identity to a particular structure of social divisions. In short, Sartori argued, political sociology (and political science) should take the place of sociology of politics if partisan politics in the European democracies were to be understood properly. Lipset (1970) himself acknowledged the ability of parties to exacerbate politically a cleavage that might socially be in decline. Nonetheless, he reiterated that a social basis was necessary for a party to exist. Thus, while for Lipset and Rokkan social cleavages were necessary, though not sufficient, for the formation of parties and of party systems, for Sartori they were neither necessary nor sufficient because politics can only be conducted independently of other social spheres. This autonomy of the parties from society had already been shown by Kirchheimer (1966) in his celebrated study in which he investigated the transition from the 'party of social integration' to the 'catch-all party,' that is, a party able to represent diverse classes and social groups electorally.

From the 1970s onwards, partly due to the development of more sophisticated techniques of social research, the debate moved in a more microempirical and less macrohistorical direction. The decade saw numerous studies of electoral behavior, although their results were equivocal. While early studies like Rose (1974) showed the relative decline of politics based on social cleavages (or 'cleavage politics,' as it came to be called), the magnitude and implications of this decline were given various interpretations by scholars. The 1992 study by Franklin suggested that the decline of cleavage politics was ineluctable, those of Inglehart (1977), Dalton et al. (1984) and subsequent studies until seemingly showed that cleavage politics were evolving in a new direction so that 'cultural' cleavages were now taking the place of fading social cleavages and reorienting electoral and political behavior.

For these authors, the new structure of divisions might indeed have a 'social basis,' but it was manifest in a clash of values: between industrial values (in favor of the quantitative growth of affluence) on the one hand, and postindustrial ones (which gave priority to the quality of life and the protection of the environment) on the other. Associated with each side were socioeconomic groups and geographical areas, but the clash involved distinct (and opposed) cultural conceptions and lifestyles. Of course, there was no lack of criticism of this approach—especially by Bartolini and Mair (1990)—given that it emptied Lipset and Rokkan's original concept of cleavage of much of its meaning. For this reason, Bartolini and Mair proposed the following redefinition of the notion: (a) empirically, a cleavage must be definable in terms of social structure; (b) normatively, a cleavage is a system of values which gives a sense of collective identity to a social group; (c) behaviorally, a cleavage is manifest in the interaction among political actors. Thus redefined, the concept of cleavage is broader in its compass and becomes a means to order social relations.

3. The Freezing of Cleavages

Sociologists and economists also joined the debate. Goldthorpe (1996), for example, found that traditional social divisions were still conditioning political allegiances and electoral choices at the end of the twentieth century. Other studies appeared which, although they extended the concept of social cleavage, continued to frame it in structural terms. Lijphart (1977), in his study of the small consociative democracies of continental Europe, and then in his analyses of the established democracies (Lijphart 1999), showed that ethnic divisions performed the same function in structuring identity and behavior as did the other social divisions of the Lipset–Rokkan model. These divisions, too, sprang from the long historical process that had led to the formation of the nation-state. Thereafter, they had continued to predominate despite the divisions created by the process of industrialization. In the nation-states, the divisions between agriculture and industry, and between capital and labor were absorbed by more basic ethnic-linguistic cleavages. According to Lijphart, the diverse nature of these cleavages lay at the origin of the two principal models of democracy (what he called 'consensual' and 'majoritarian') that developed in the West after the World War II.

The model of consensual democracy based on the inclusion in the executive of all the country's main ethnic groups proved highly effective (in stabilizing democracy). It was accordingly used by authors (starting from Sartori and his studies of party systems in the 1970s) to investigate the workings of national societies connoted by identity divisions, albeit based on ideology rather than ethnicity or language. The reference here is to the postwar European democracies distinguished by the presence of powerful communist parties. Even these democracies were consensual in nature, although their operation was sustained, not by inclusive coalitions in the executive (access to which was barred to communist parties, owing to the geopolitical cleavages created by the Cold War), but by consensual practices in parliament. However, while these ideological cleavages proved unstable with the passage of time, this was not the case of ethnic ones. It seemed, indeed, that the model of consensual democracy had ended up by 'freezing' ethnic allegiances, though managing to cushion their impact.

The reasons why party systems were frozen in the postwar European democracies were expressly investigated by Mair and Bartolini (1990). These two authors examined three different hypotheses with regard to the freezing process. First, it may involve the freezing of social cleavages, that is, the stabilization of the social structure from which the parties draw legitimation for their political action. Second, the freezing may be due to the institutionalization of the political parties, albeit accompanied by the fading of the social divisions that had prompted their formation (here by 'institutionalization' is meant the parties' ability to stand as the only practicable electoral choices). Third, the freezing may be due to the stabilization of the party system as such, or put otherwise, the institutionalization of the system of interactions among the main political actors. Mair and Bartolini seem to suggest that the third of these hypotheses is the most plausible, given that both the hypothesis of the freezing of social cleavages and that of the freezing of political parties must admit to so many exceptions that they are not falsifiable. In short, for both authors a distinction must be drawn between the freezing of party systems and the freezing of individual parties.

The freezing hypothesis has also been discussed in terms of voting behavior. Several surveys have sought—using different indicators—to collect reliable data on the stability and instability of voting choices. Many scholars, from Pederson (1983) to Maguire (1983) and especially Bartolini (2000), have shown that rates of aggregate electoral volatility were relatively low until the 1980s: which corroborated Lipset and Rokkan's original contention that continuity rather than change was the distinguishing feature of partisan politics in Europe. These studies came in for criticism, of course, mainly on the grounds that electoral stability does not necessarily coincide with stable interaction among the political parties, and that stability may conceal processes of dealignment and realignment sufficient to gainsay the logic of the Lipset–Rokkan model.

4. Between Europe and America

The theory of cleavages has been developed on the basis of the experiences of the Western European countries, with no reference to the other great model of democracy: that of the United States. And yet it was precisely in the United States that modern political parties and party systems were invented. Indeed, the myth of American exceptionalism has been fostered by this European neglect; a neglect motivated by the belief that American society, unlike those of European countries, is based on cross-cutting cleavages which—as Lipset maintained as early as 1963—are unable to produce stable divisions among citizens. This absence of cleavage politics, the argument ran, gave rise to the depolarization of partisan conflict in the United States that underpinned the stability of 'American democracy.' In short, the more cleavages multiply and interweave, the more numerous the divisions among citizens become, and the safer democracy grows.

And yet, as Bensel (1987) showed, the situation in the United States was not so clear-cut, for that country, too, displayed, and still does, a stable political cleavage; sectional rather than social and cultural, although it has latterly acquired these features as well. This is the political cleavage between states and regional areas expressed in two radically different conceptions of the balance of powers to be struck between the states and the center of the federation. And it should not be forgotten that this fracture provoked one of the most violent and bloody civil wars of the modern age. It is around this cleavage that the various party systems that have arisen since the foundation of American republic have structured themselves.

In the light of the postnational experience of Europe at the end of the twentieth century, the case of the United States appears less exceptional than it did in the past. This is because the process of European integration has generated a sectional divide among geo-economic areas of the continent which cuts across the traditional (in Europe) party-political axis ranging from right to left. And in this case, too, the new contraposition has taken the form of a different interpretation of the balance of powers that should be established between the European and national institutions. Can European integration be regarded as a further historical cleavage—in addition to those singled out by the Lipset–Rokkan model—destined to produce another political structural cleavage? If so, the cleavage theory might be updated, this time bridging the European and American experiences.

See also: Conflict/Consensus; Conflict Sociology; Ethnic Conflict, Geography of; Ethnic Conflicts; Party Systems; Pluralism; Political Geography; Political Sociology; Race Relations in the United States, Politics of

Bibliography

Bartolini S 2000 *The Class Cleavage: The Political Mobilization of the European Left, 1860–1980*. Cambridge University Press, Cambridge, UK

Bartolini S, Mair P 1990 *Identity, Competition and Electoral Availability*. Cambridge University Press, Cambridge, UK

Bensel R F 1987 *Sectionalism and American Political Development: 1880–1980*. University of Wisconsin Press, Madison, WI

Daalder H 1966 Parties, elites and political development(s) in Western Europe. In: LaPalombara J, Weiner M (eds.) *Political Parties and Political Development*. Princeton University Press, Princeton, NJ

Dalton R J, Flanagan C S, Beck P A 1984 *Electoral Change in Advanced Industrial Democracies: Realignment or Dealignment?* Princeton University Press, Princeton, NJ

Eckstein H 1966 *Division and Cohesion in Democracy: A Study of Norway*. Princeton University Press, Princeton, NJ

Franklin M T, Mackie T, Valen H (eds.) 1992 *Electoral Change: Responses to Social and Attitudinal Structures in Western Countries*. Cambridge University Press, Cambridge, UK

Goldthorpe J H 1996 Class and politics in advanced industrial societies. In: Lee D J, Turner B S (eds.) *Conflict about Class: Debating Inequality in Late Industrialism*. Longman, London

Inglehart R 1977 *The Silent Revolution. Changing Values and Political Styles among Western Publics*. Princeton University Press, Princeton, NJ

Kirchheimer O 1966 The transformation of the Western European Party systems. In: LaPalombara J, Weiner M (eds.) *Political Parties and Political Development*. Princeton University Press, Princeton, NJ

Knutsen O 1988 The impact of structural and ideological party cleavages in Western European democracies: A comparative empirical analysis. *British Journal of Political Science* **18**: 323–52

Lijphart A 1977 *Democracy in Plural Societies: A Comparative Exploration*. Yale University Press, New Haven, CT

Lijphart A 1999 *Patterns of Democracy*. Yale University Press, New Haven, CT

Lipset S M 1963 *Political Man: The Social Bases of Politics*. Johns Hopkins University Press, Baltimore, MD

Lipset S M 1970 *Revolution and Counterrevolution*. Anchor Books, New York

Lipset S M, Rokkan S 1967 Cleavage structures, party systems and voter alignments: An introduction. In: Lipset S M, Rokkan S (eds.) *Party Systems and Voter Alignments*. Free Press, New York

Maguire M 1983 Is there still persistence? Electoral change in Western Europe, 1948–1979. In: Daalder H, Mair P (eds.) *Western European Party Systems Continuity and Change*. Sage, Beverly Hills, CA

Pederson M N 1983 Changing patterns of electoral volatility in European party systems, 1948–1977. In: Daalder H, Mair P (eds.) *Western European Party Systems. Continuity and Change*. Sage, Beverly Hills, CA

Rose R 1974 *Electoral Behaviour: A Comparative Handbook*. Free Press, New York

Sartori G 1969 From sociology of politics to political sociology. In: Lipset S M (ed.) *Politics and the Social Sciences*. Oxford University Press, New York

Sartori G 1976 *Parties and Party Systems*. Cambridge University Press, New York

Schattschneider E E 1948 *The Struggle for Party Government*. University of Maryland, College Park, MD

S. Fabbrini

Climate Change and Health

This article outlines the potential impacts on human health of climate change due to the accumulation of greenhouse gases in the earth's atmosphere. It describes the range of potential mechanisms by which health could be affected and the difficulties of estimating the magnitude of such effects. It concludes with a brief discussion of how, not withstanding the need to prevent climate change as far as possible, humankind will have to adapt to changing climate if the adverse effects are to be minimized.

1. Background

1.1 Climate Change

Human activities, particularly the burning of fossil fuels, but also changes in land use, are leading to the accumulation of greenhouse gases such as carbon dioxide and methane in the earth's atmosphere. The resulting increase in 'radiative forcing' is leading to warming of the earth's surface. The United Nations set up the Intergovernmental Panel on Climate Change (IPCC)—a multidisciplinary body of scientific advisers, which in its third assessment report forecast an increase in the average global temperature of 1.4–5.8 °C between 1990 and 2100 (IPCC 2001). There are a number of sources of uncertainty in projections of future climate, including changes in greenhouse gas emissions and concentrations, the sensitivity of climate to greenhouse gases, and the impact of modulating processes, such as the short-term cooling effects of aerosols as a result of industrial emissions. However, it does appear likely that the rate of climate change over the twenty-first century will be far greater than any natural changes in world climate over the past 10,000 years. There has been substantial warming since 1856, when records began, with particularly rapid increases in temperatures since about 1980. The warmest year on record was 1998, partly as a result of the marked El Niño which occurred over 1997–8. In its second assessment report the IPCC concluded that the balance of evidence suggested that the impact of human

Table 1
Mediating processes and direct and indirect potential effects on health of changes in temperature and weather

Mediating process	Health outcome
Direct effects	
Exposure to thermal extremes	Changed rates of illness and death related to heat and cold
Changed frequency or intensity of other extreme weather events	Deaths, injuries, psychological disorders; damage to public health infrastructure
Indirect effects	
Disturbances of ecological systems: Effect on range and activity of vectors and infective parasites	Changes in geographical ranges and incidence of vector borne disease
Changed local ecology of water borne and food borne infective agents	Changed incidence of diarrheal and other infectious diseases
Changed food productivity (especially crops) through changes in climate and associated pests and diseases	Malnutrition and hunger, and consequent impairment of child growth and development
Sea level rise with population displacement and damage to infrastructure	Increased risk of infectious disease psychological disorders
Biological impact of air pollution changes (including pollens and spores)	Asthma and allergies; other acute and chronic respiratory disorders and deaths
Social, economic, and demographic dislocation through effects on economy, infrastructure, and resource supply	Wide range of public health consequences: mental health and nutritional impairment, infectious diseases, civil strife

Source: McMichael and Haines 1997

activities on global climate was now discernible (IPCC 1996). The subsequent IPCC report pointed to 'new and stronger evidence that most of the warming over the last 30 years was attributable to human activities.'

1.2 Other Global Environmental Changes

Climate change is not occurring in isolation and there are a range of other global changes—stratospheric ozone depletion, loss of biodiversity, changes in land use patterns and depletion of aquifers, all of which may also have effects on human health and society. There are linkages between climate change and some of these other phenomena, for example, the rise in the temperature of the lower atmosphere may increase stratospheric ozone depletion. Deforestation leads to loss of biodiversity, particularly when it involves tropical forests, and also results in a release of substantial amounts of carbon dioxide into the atmosphere. Population growth in developing countries and unsustainable patterns of consumption in industrialized nations are increasing the strain on earth's life support systems and the demand for energy (McMichael and Powles 1999).

2. Potential Impacts on Health

2.1 Range of Effects

Climate change is likely to have substantial effects on human health through a range of pathways (McMichael and Haines 1997, McMichael et al. 1996) (Table 1). The potential effects of climate change on health are sometimes divided into direct and indirect to separate those impacts where the chain of causation is short, such as increased deaths during heatwaves, and those that are mediated through a longer causal chain. The latter include changes in ecosystems which can, for example, effect the distribution of insect vectors of disease. Most of the anticipated effects are likely to be adverse, although some, such as possible reductions in excess winter death rates due to warmer winters in cool-temperate countries, could be beneficial. Quantification of potential impacts is complicated by the many uncertainties involved and any estimates should be taken as indicative.

2.2 Approaches to Assessing Potential Impacts

There are a number of approaches to assessing the potential impacts of climate change on health. These include the study of historical analogues that simulate certain aspects of future climate change. One example is the study of the effects of the El Niño/Southern Oscillation (ENSO), a large irregularly occurring atmosphere–ocean system which results in relatively short-term climate changes over the Pacific region every 2–7 years. The warm event (El Niño) is followed frequently by a cold event (La Niña). The ENSO is also linked by distant connections (teleconnections) to climatic anomalies elsewhere in the world, particularly in countries bordering the Pacific and Indian oceans. Integrated mathematical modeling is also being used increasingly to estimate the future impact on health of climate change. In order to undertake such modeling each component of the sequence of climate, environmental and social change, is represented mathematically.

2.3 Direct Effects of Heat and Cold

The link between heatwaves and increased death rates has been described in many parts of the world. Excess mortality especially is experienced by the elderly, in particular by those who live in disadvantaged areas without adequate air conditioning. Some of the increase in deaths is due to mortality displacement, i.e., short-term shift in the time of death of those who would have died anyway in the near future. The threshold at which increased death rates occur depends on population acclimatization and is, therefore, higher in those cities where the populations are used to high temperatures. The impact of the first heatwave on mortality in a given summer is often greater than the impact of subsequent heatwaves, probably because a disproportionate number of susceptible people die during the first heatwave. Several studies have quantified the impact of climate change on heat-related mortality. For example, one study (Kalkstein and Greene 1997) estimated an annual excess mortality attributable to climate change (assuming acclimatization) of between 500 and 1,000 for New York and 100 and 250 for Detroit by the year 2050.

There is controversy over the degree to which increases in summer mortality will be outweighed by decreases in winter mortality. Although death rates are higher in winter than in summer in the temperate countries, the relationship may not be directly due to low temperatures and increased viral infections may be partly responsible. Some countries with very cold winters, for example, Russia, seem to have low excess winter mortality, probably because of the effective adaptation of the population to cold winters by the use of warm winter clothing and adequate indoor heating (Donaldson et al. 1998). The UK has a particularly high winter excess mortality and this may be due, at least in part, to fuel poverty. Within Europe larger increases in winter mortality may occur with decreasing temperature in warmer locations, e.g., Athens, than in colder locations (Eurowinter Group 1997)

perhaps because populations in countries with generally mild winters fail to wear suitable clothing or their housing is not adapted to low temperatures.

2.4 Studies of the Effects of El Niño/Southern Oscillation

ENSO can affect rainfall, leading to either droughts or floods in parts of the world, as well as causing increases in temperature and changes in the frequency, intensity, and geographical distribution of extreme weather events such as storms.

The ENSO cycle has been associated with substantial changes in the incidence of malaria in countries such as Pakistan, Sri Lanka, Colombia, and Venezuela (reviewed by Kovats et al. 1999). The incidence of dengue fever (a viral disease carried by mosquitoes) is affected by the ENSO cycle in some Pacific Islands (Hales et al. 1996). There are large increases in the numbers of people affected by natural disasters at a global level in El Niño years, and the year following (Bouma et al. 1997). Other health impacts of El Niño include increases in respiratory disorders due to very high levels of air pollution as a result of forest fires that occurred, for example, both in Indonesia and Brazil in association with the 1997/98 event. The ENSO phenomenon is clearly not strictly an analogue for global climate change but does demonstrate that some diseases and health outcomes are sensitive to changes in climate. Recently, there have been suggestions that the frequency of El Niño may increase in the future as a result of climate change (Timmermann et al. 1999). Increasingly, forecasting is being used to give early warning of El Niño in order to improve preparedness and reduce the adverse effects.

2.5 Mathematical Modeling of Malaria

Mathematical modeling has been applied to the assessment of likely changes in the geographical range of vector-borne diseases such as malaria. One estimate, for example, suggests that approximately 45 percent of the world's population live in zones of potential malaria transmission as defined by current climatic circumstances, and this would increase to around 60 percent towards the end of the next century assuming other relevant factors remain constant (Martens et al. 1995). Highly aggregated models such as the one used in this example are, of necessity, unable to take into account complexity of future changes. Nevertheless, they give a broad indication of the potential magnitude and direction of change and are continually being refined. They suggest that changes in distribution of malaria are likely to occur particularly at the edges of the current distribution, including, for example, mountainous regions in the tropics and subtropics. Estimation of numbers of excess cases and deaths in the twenty-first century as a result of climate change is hampered by our lack of knowledge, for example, about the potential advances in the development of an effective vaccine for malaria, the distribution of impregnated bed nets to reduce transmission, and the trends in the development of resistance of the parasites to drugs used in treatment.

A number of empirical studies in Zimbabwe, Rwanda, and Ethiopia have examined how climate variability influences the distribution of malaria. They have indicated that highland malaria can respond to climatic variability, but whether changes in the altitudinal range of malaria which have apparently been observed in a number of sites are due to global climate change, is currently a matter of scientific debate. Only long-term monitoring of climate, vector populations, and the incidence of malaria, as well as potential confounding factors, such as changes in vector control programs and forest cover can finally resolve the controversy.

2.6 Other Vector-borne Diseases

Other vector-borne diseases which may be affected include those carried by ticks such as tick-borne encephalitis (inflammation of the brain) and Lyme disease. The former occurs widely in Central and Eastern Europe and in Scandinavia and the latter occurs in both Europe and the North Eastern US. Other factors which may effect tick-borne diseases include the pattern of forest cover that can influence the distribution of animal hosts on which the ticks can feed and changing patterns of leisure activities which may influence exposure to bites by infected ticks. There are several clinical types of Leishmaniasis, which are transmitted by sandflies in Asia, the Americas, Southern Europe, and Africa. Sandflies are sensitive to changes in temperature and, for example, it was estimated that a 3 °C increase in temperature could increase both the geographic and seasonal distribution of one important species in Southwest Asia (Cross and Hyams 1996). The tsetse fly that transmits sleeping sickness (human African trypanosomiasis) is also climate sensitive. In Latin America, the distribution of Chagas' disease, which is transmitted by the triatomine bug and causes long-term damage to the heart and to the muscle of the gastrointestinal tract, could be affected.

2.7 Extreme Events, Malnutrition, and Sea Level Rise

On average, every year around 120,000 people were killed by natural disasters between 1972 and 1996, with around 60 percent of the deaths occurring in Africa. Over the same period on average nearly 140 million people were affected by such disasters annually, most of these were living in Asia (International Federation of Red Cross and Red Crescent Societies 1998). Drought, famine, and flood are the main categories of disaster responsible for the majority of people affected.

Floods may cause a range of impacts on health including deaths and injuries from trauma or drowning, increased incidence of diarrheal disease and sometimes leptospirosis caused by exposure to infected rats' urine in floodwaters. Malnutrition may increase following flooding in some countries where food security is a problem. The impacts on mental health may be substantial and in some cases long-lasting. An increase in suicides was reported from Poland following floods in 1997 and an increase in behavioral disorders amongst children has been reported. Some parts of the world may experience increased rainfall due to climate change that could lead to larger floods (IPCC 1998).

Climate change could exacerbate periodic and long-term shortages of water especially in the arid and semi-arid parts of the world (IPCC 1998). Droughts tend to effect health particularly by causing a reduction in the availability of food. There may also be an increase in diarrheal diseases because water is short and there may not be sufficient for hygienic purposes. Severe drought may not invariably result in famine or major food shortages. For example, a severe drought in southern Africa in 1992 resulted in crop failure rate approaching 80 percent in some of the most affected areas but famine was averted because of regional cooperation and external assistance which provided grain shipments (Noji 1997). Unfortunately, international assistance to support humanitarian relief has fallen overall, for example, it declined 17 percent in real terms between 1992 and 1996, whereas emergency aid has tended to increase. After remaining steady at under half the United Nations target of 0.7 percent of gross national product (GNP) for more than 20 years, aid as a share of donor's wealth fell to 0.25 percent in 1996, its lowest level ever (International Federation of Red Cross and Red Crescent Societies 1998). If this trend continues, populations in the twenty-first century may be not only more vulnerable to climatic disaster but less likely to receive effective assistance.

There have been many studies to assess potential changes in food production globally and regionally under conditions of climate change. In general, it appears likely that agricultural yields may increase in the twenty-first century in middle to high latitudes depending on crop type, growing season, and changes in temperature and seasonality of precipitation. However, there are concerns that yields may decrease in parts of the tropics and subtropics particularly where dryland, nonirrigated agriculture predominates (IPCC 1998). This could lead to increased hunger, particularly in Africa.

Sea level rise caused by climate change may result in displacement of some populations particularly those living on deltas and low lying islands as well as leading to salination of fresh water and increased vulnerability to extreme events.

2.8 Air Pollution

The weather has a substantial influence on the ambient concentrations of air pollutants, for example, high-pressure systems often create a temperature inversion which traps pollutants in the boundary layer near the earth's surface. Because of increases in anticyclonic conditions in summer in some parts of the world, climate change may increase concentrations of some pollutants. Ozone formation and destruction occurs by means of a complex series of photochemical processes and concentrations in the troposphere may be higher under climate change depending on the emission of precursors. Any increase in forest fires could have substantial effects on human health because of the formation of 'haze' with high concentrations of fine particulates (see earlier discussion on El Niño). Concentrations of aeroallergens (pollen, etc.) could be affected by both temperature and precipitation but other factors are also involved such as changes in land use and farming practices (Emberlin 1994).

3. Adaptation and Vulnerability

The reductions in greenhouse gas emissions resulting from the Kyoto protocol of the UN Framework Convention on Climate Change are likely to have little effect on the projected rises in temperature within the first half of the twenty-first century (Parry et al. 1998). Thus, reducing vulnerability to climate change is an important goal for public health in the twenty-first century. There are a number of factors which influence vulnerability, notably poverty with its associated lack of resources and infrastructure. Although historically the majority of greenhouse gas emissions have come from the industrialized nations, vulnerability to climate change is probably greater in developing countries.

Adaptation may be autonomous, indicating a natural or spontaneous response by individuals, or purposeful, typically by governments or other institutions in response to projected climate change. The latter might include strengthening existing disease surveillance systems for potentially climate sensitive diseases, improving vector control programs, and enhancing disaster preparedness plans.

4. Conclusions

Whilst adaptation to climate change is necessary this does not negate the importance of strategies to mitigate climate change, particularly by reducing fossil fuel use (Haines and McMichael 1997). This could have near term benefits by reducing deaths and other adverse effects on health of air pollution (Working Group on Public Health and Fossil Fuel Combustion 1997). The provision of 'clean energy' is an important contribution to improving health, particularly in developing countries (Haines and Kammen 2000).

See also: Desertification; Globalization and Health; Globalization: Geographical Aspects; Health Policy

Bibliography

Bouma M J, Kovats R S, Goubet S A, Cox J S, Haines A 1997 Global assessment of El Niño's disaster burden. *Lancet* **350**: 1435–38

Emberlin J 1994 The effects of patterns in climate and pollen abundance on allergy: 1994. *Allergy* **49**: 15–20

Cross E R, Hyams K C 1996 The potential effect of global warming on the geographic and seasonal distribution of *Phlebotamus papatasi* in Southwest Asia. *Environmental Health Perspectives* **104**: 724–27

Donaldson G C, Tchernjavskii V E, Ermakov S P, Bucher K, Keatinge W R 1998 Winter mortality and cold stress in Yekaterinberg, Russia: Interview survey. *British Medical Journal* **316**: 514–18

The Eurowinter Group 1997 Cold exposure and winter mortality from Ischaemic heart disease, cerebrovascular disease, respiratory disease, and all causes in warm and cold regions of Europe. *Lancet* **349**: 1341–46

Haines A, McMichael A J 1997 Climate change and health: implications for research, monitoring, and policy. *British Medical Journal* **315**: 870–4

Haines A, Kammen D 2000 Sustainable energy and health. *Global Change and Human Health* **1**: 78–87

Hales S, Weinstein P, Woodward A 1996 Dengue fever epidemics in the South Pacific driven by El Nino southern oscillation? *Lancet* **348**: 1664–5

International Federation of Red Cross and Red Crescent-Societies 1998 *World Disaster Report 1998*. Oxford University Press, New York

Intergovernmental Panel on Climate Change (WGI) Houghton J T, Meira Filho L G, Callander B A, Harris N, Kattenberg A, Maskell K (eds.) 1996 *Climate change, 1995—the science of climate change: Contribution of Working Group 1 to the second assessment report of the Intergovernmental Panel on Climate Change*. Cambridge University Press, New York

Intergovernmental Panel on Climate Change, Watson R T, Zinyowera M C, Moss R H, Dokken D J (eds.) 1998 *The regional impacts of climate change, an assessment of vulnerability*. Cambridge University Press, New York

Intergovernmental Panel on Climate Change Working Group 1 2001 *Third assessment report*. Intergovernmental Panel on Climate Change, www.ipcc.ch

Kalkstein L S, Greene J S 1997 An evaluation of climate/mortality relationships in large US cities and the possible impacts of climate change. *Environmental Health Perspectives* **105**: 84–93

Kovats R S, Bouma M J, Haines A 1999 El Niño and Health, WHO Task Force on Climate and Health, WHO/SDE/PHE/99.4, Geneva

Martens W J M, Jetten T H, Rotmans J, Niessen L W 1995 Climate-change and vector-borne diseases: A global modeling perspective. *Global Environment Change* **5**: 195–209

McMichael A J, Haines A 1997 Global climate change: The potential effects on health. *British Medical Journal* **315**: 805–9

McMichael A J, Haines A, Sloof R, Kovats R S 1996 Climate Change and Human Health WHO, EHG 96/7, Geneva

McMichael A J, Powles J W 1999 Human numbers, environment, sustainability and health. *British Medical Journal* **319**: 977–80

Noji E K (ed.) 1997 *The Public Health Consequences of Disaster.* Oxford University Press, New York

Parry M, Arnell N, Hulme M, Nicholls R, Livermore M 1998 Adapting to the inevitable. *Nature* **395**: 741

Timmermann A, Oberhuber J, Bacher A, Esch M, Latif M, Roeckner E 1999 Increased El Nino frequency in a climate model forced by future greenhouse warming. *Nature* **3989**: 694–7

Working Group on Public Health and Fossil-Fuel Combustion 1997 Short-term improvements in public health from global-climate policies on fossil-fuel combustion: An interim report. Lancet **350**: 1341–8

A. Haines

Climate Change, Economics of

There are two sides to the economics of climate change. The first recognizes the economic costs and potential benefits that can be attributed to the physical and natural impacts of a changing climate—warmer temperatures, changes in precipitation patterns, rising sea level, and so on. These economic impacts include the cost of adapting to change in addition to the economic consequences that remain after such adaptation is effected. They also include the benefits that climate change might bring that would otherwise not have been forthcoming. The second side recognizes the economic costs that would be attributed to policies designed to mitigate climate change. These costs, too, include the cost of adapting to policy in addition to the residual consequences that persist in the wake of this adaptation.

Estimates of the economic impacts on both sides are highly uncertain, given our inability to understand fully the science of climate change and to look many decades into the future with any clarity. Estimates of both are also evolving continuously over time, so any estimate must be read with a sense of what was known at the time that it was published. The coverage offered here will provide some insight into this evolution even as it reports on the latest results that were available at the turn of the twentieth century.

1. The Economic Cost of Climate Change Impacts

Costs associated with the impacts of climate change are generally judged in terms of economic damage that would be avoided if the change did not occur; benefits are similarly estimated in terms of fortuitous impact that otherwise would not have happened. The Intergovernmental Panel on Climate Change (IPCC) reported preliminary estimates of the annual economic impact of a doubling of concentrations of greenhouse gases (~ 550 ppmv) and an associated 2.5 °C increase in global mean temperature (Houghton et al. 1996). The estimates reported by the IPCC for the United States, for example, ranged from a low of \$55.5 billion (1990\$) offered by Nordhaus (1991) to a high of \$139.2 billion (1990\$) authored by Titus (1992). The low and high estimates were calculated to be 1.0 percent and 2.5 percent of anticipated gross domestic product in 2065, respectively. The year 2065 was chosen as a benchmark because that was when the specified doubling of concentrations was anticipated to occur.

All of the estimates reported in 1995 by the IPCC were dominated by declines in agricultural production. Agriculture is, of course, a sector whose current practices would likely be threatened by higher temperatures and less precipitation. Most of the estimates for agriculture and other sectors were, however, the result of vulnerability studies that paid little attention to the ability of humans and their institutions to reduce economic damage and expand economic opportunity by adapting—that is, by changing practices so that they became less vulnerable to the new climate or so that they could take greater advantage of its appearance. Moreover, most of these early studies relied on relatively primitive methods of tracking the different regional consequences of a 2.5 °C warming. Global climate modelers have long expected that some regions would see temperatures increase by more than 2.5 °C while others might actually get cooler. Some areas would get wetter while others get drier. Seas would rise in some places and actually fall more slowly elsewhere (where the coastline is actually rising at present). Finally, few of the early studies were able to consider the effects of changes in humidity, frequency of extreme temperature events, or any of the other more subtle physical ramifications of global warming.

More recent cost estimates have begun to overcome these shortcomings. Table 1 presents regional cost estimates of market impacts published by Mendelsohn et al. (2000) for a 2 °C warming and a 50 cm increase in sea level. Notice that the overall annual effect on world economic activity, a 0.3 percent reduction, is much smaller than in the earlier studies. Effects on agriculture still dominate, but the regional distribution of impacts is striking. Some regions, notably North America and Europe, are now seen to benefit from warming whereas others such as Africa are severely harmed. These results were based on a statistical approach that looked carefully at how various regions cope with their current climates to see how other regions might respond if their climates changed.

Table 2 gives estimates from Tol (1998) for a 1 °C warming in even geographical greater detail. Only

Table 1
Regional market impacts for a 2°C warming (billions 1990$)

Region	Agriculture	Forest	Coast	Energy	Tourism	Total	%GDP
Africa	−11	−6	0	−2	−3	−22	−0.8
Asia	−14	−1	−5	−9	−8	−37	−0.1
Latin America	−7	−5	0	−4	−5	−22	−0.4
Europe	34	16	−4	4	31	82	0.2
North America	21	14	0	0	13	47	0.2
Oceana	−3	−1	0	−1	−1	−7	−0.6
OECD	26	16	−7	2	45	82	0.15
Non-OECD	6	−1	−3	14	−18	−40	−0.1

Source: Mendelsohn et al. (1999, Table 1)

Table 2
Annual impact for a 1°C warming (billions 1990$)

Region	Estimate	Standard deviation	Percent of GDP	Standard deviation
American OECD	175	107	3.4	2.1
European OECD	203	118	3.7	2.2
Pacific OECD	32	35	1.0	1.1
Central Europe & former Soviet Union	57	108	2.0	3.8
Middle East	4	8	1.1	2.2
Latin America	−1	5	−0.1	0.6
Southern and southeast Asia	−14	9	−1.7	1.1
Centrally Planned Asia	9	22	2.1	5.0
Africa	17	9	4.1	2.2

Source: Tol (1998, Table 7)

Latin America and southern and southeast Asia suffer losses in his work, and many regions (including Africa) benefit substantially. Modest warming might, it would seem, be a good thing. Indeed, Mendelsohn et al.'s work also supports this suggestion. Tol's results do, however, offer a warning about leaping to that conclusion too quickly. Two columns in Table 2 report standard deviations for his estimates. The standard deviation is a measure of uncertainty that indicates roughly a 66 percent likelihood that the true impact of a modest 1°C warming would lie within a range of plus or minus the standard deviation from the recorded figure. For example, then, Tol suggests roughly a 66 percent likelihood that the annual impact of a 1°C warming on the Pacific members of the OECD would lie between a 0.1 percent loss (= 1.0–1.1) in gross domestic product (GDP) and a 2.1 percent gain in GDP. Given current understanding of climate and economic systems, therefore, there is roughly a 17 percent chance that GDP would climb by more 2.1 percent and a 17 percent chance that GDP would fall by more than 0.1 percent of GDP. There is also a 17 percent chance that the economic damage suffered by southern and southeast Asia in the wake of a 1°C warming would be larger than 2.8 percent of GDP. The size of the uncertainty within which impact estimates must be contemplated is still enormous, and

the distributional ramifications of this uncertainty can be quite unsettling.

The role of adaptation and learning how to incorporate physical impacts other than temperature is clearly demonstrated in Table 3. Regional estimates offered by four other scholars plus Tol are depicted there for a 2.5°C temperature increase. Some include adaptation—switching crops, adjusting planting dates, adding or eliminating irrigation, adjusting fertilizer practices, and so on; others do not. Some include the fertilizing effect on plant productivity of higher carbon dioxide concentrations in the atmosphere, while others do not. Notice that carbon dioxide fertilization can turn damages into benefits and that adaptation can reduce damage and increase benefits. Indeed, all of Tol's estimates with adaptation represent gains. Be warned, though, that he still reports enormous ranges of uncertainty surrounding them.

Finally, all of these results envision smooth if not predictable climate change. The real concern on the impacts side could, however, be the potentially exaggerated effects of sudden, surprising and perhaps irreversible consequences of warming. Economic systems never cope well with sudden changes in their environment, even if the changes are ultimately beneficial. As a result, the estimates quoted above could be dwarfed if the physical impacts of climate change are

Table 3
Economic impacts on agriculture of a 2.5 °C warming (percent of gross agricultural product)

	Kane et al.	Tsigas et al.		Darwin et al.	Reilly et al.			Tol	
Fertilization?	No	No	Yes	No	No	Yes	Yes	Yes	Yes
Adaptation?	No	No	No	Yes	No	No	Yes	No	Yes
American OECD	0.03	−0.31	0.05	0.10	0.03	0.00	0.00	−0.25	1.30
European OECD	−0.52	−0.73	0.14	−0.41	−0.34	−0.06	−0.02	0.55	2.09
Pacific OECD	−2.08	−1.38	−0.06	0.31	−0.31	−0.04	−0.01	−0.15	0.80
Central Europe/former Soviet Union	−0.02	−1.48	−0.07	0.14	−0.18	−0.25	−0.18	0.94	2.65
Middle East	−0.01	−1.48	−0.07	0.14	−0.18	−0.25	−0.18	−0.44	0.58
Latin America	0.05	−2.18	−0.47	0.10	−0.22	−0.15	−0.16	−0.76	0.55
Southern and southeast Asia	−0.08	−2.26	−0.32	−0.04	−0.91	−0.17	−0.13	−0.66	0.63
Centrally Planned Asia	3.84	−3.97	0.28	0.11	−10.09	0.04	0.53	1.73	3.10
Africa	−0.01	−1.48	−0.07	0.14	−1.18	−0.25	−0.18	−0.23	0.47

Source: Tol (1998, Tables 1 and 2). He references Kane et al. (1992), Tsigas et al. (1996), Darwin et al. (1996), and Reilly et al. (1996)

not smooth. Yohe and Schlesinger (1998) computed the economic cost of sea level rise on the developed coastline of the United States with and without sufficient foresight for markets to response to the threat of inundation. The difference between the two, one estimate under the best of circumstances of the extra cost of surprise, was as large as 100 percent even for sea-level rise trajectories in the middle of its own range of uncertainty.

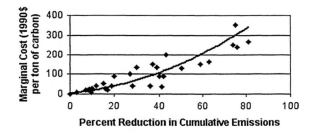

Figure 1
The marginal cost of reducing emissions of carbon dioxide

2. The Economic Cost of Mitigating Climate Change

The scale and pace of climate change can be influenced by policy interventions that slow the emission of greenhouse gases. Many researchers have investigated the cost of this sort of climate change mitigation. They have, in particular, focused their attention on energy consumption and the resulting emission of carbon dioxide. Carbon dioxide is a product of burning fossil fuel, and its emission varies from fuel to fuel. Burning coal, for example, emits 25 percent more carbon per unit energy than burning oil, and burning oil emits 43 percent more than natural gas. Burning hydrogen emits no carbon. Hydroelectric, wind, solar, and nuclear power are similarly carbon-free sources of energy. Mitigation simply involves substituting carbon-free sources of energy for carbon-based fuels *and* low-carbon fossil fuels such as natural gas for high-carbon fuels such as coal. Our ability to effect and to sustain this sort of substitution over the very long run depends upon the availability of new technology and the supply of low-carbon and carbon-free sources of energy.

The most effective means of conveying the cost of mitigation is to track the economic impact of reducing cumulative global emissions through the year 2100 from 'baseline' levels that would have been anticipated

in the absence of any policy intervention. Fig. 1 displays reductions in cumulative emissions from various baselines through the year 2100 against the estimated tax (marginal cost) that would have to be imposed per ton of carbon to achieve those reductions. The points portrayed there indicate selected estimates published by various researchers through the middle of 1998, and the curve summarizes these cost data as a function of percentage emissions reduction. Fig. 1 shows clearly that the marginal cost of emissions reduction increases at an increasing rate even though the taxes estimated for any particular reduction in emissions are disperse. This dispersion is a reflection of the uncertainty with which these costs can be computed—uncertainty caused by assumptions about technology, supplies, and the intensity with which future economic activity would employ energy along the baseline.

2.1 Interventions that Limit Atmospheric Concentrations

The Framework Convention on Climate Change (FCCC) committed the globe in 1992 to holding concentrations of greenhouse gases below levels that would prevent 'dangerous anthropogenic interference with the climate system.' The precise concentration target that corresponds with this imperative has not yet been identified, so many researchers have investigated the economic cost of reducing emissions over the next 100 years so that concentrations do not exceed a range of thresholds. Manne and Richels (1997) estimate that the cost of achieving the most popular threshold, 550 ppmv, could be as high as $3.5 trillion (1990$) or as low as $650 billion (1990$). Estimates from other researchers were comparable; but they differed from one another for the same reasons as mentioned above. Costs for lower thresholds such as 450 ppmv are much higher. However, some possible low-emissions baselines achieve stable concentrations around 750 ppmv without any intervention of any kind.

Cost estimates for meeting concentration thresholds depend critically on the timing and location of each unit of emissions reduction. Wigley et al. (1996) have called the 'where' and 'when' flexibility components of cost. Their 'WRE' results emphasize that costs would be minimized if each ton of emissions reduction were taken from the least costly source regardless of where it is located. Their results also required that emissions should be reduced at any point in time only if the present value of the associated cost is in line with all other reductions at all other times. Compared with emissions reductions suggested by the IPCC (see Houghton et al. 1992), the combined effect of exploiting both types of flexibility allowed the 'WRE' path to cut the cost of achieving the same 550 ppmv threshold from the same middle emissions baseline by more than 80 percent.

The 'WRE' results are controversial because 'when' flexibility implies that early reductions in emissions would be smaller than they would under the IPCC proposal. As a result, the near-term pace of climate change would be larger. Meanwhile, 'where' flexibility has served as an anchor for a wide range of proposals that would allow countries to trade permits to emit greenhouse gases. The idea here is that an emerging market for permits would work to ensure that least cost sources of reductions were always exploited.

It is difficult to contemplate near-term mitigation in the absence of any knowledge about the appropriate concentration target and without any real understanding about whether future baseline emissions will be relatively high or low. Yohe and Wallace (1996) looked as this problem as one of hedging. Policy directed at a low threshold along a high-emissions path would be far more vigorous in the near-term than a policy directed at a high threshold along a low-emissions path. Either would be in error, though, if either the presumed target or the presumed emissions path turned out to be incorrect. As a result, adopting either would impose extra cost on the global economy. Yohe and Wallace reported that least-cost hedging would support focusing on a middle concentration target such as 550 ppm and assuming that emissions would otherwise track slightly higher than commonly accepted 'best-guess' baseline. This sort of hedging would increase the costs of meeting a concentration target, but only modestly under the assumption of maximum geographical and intertemporal flexibility.

2.2 *The Kyoto Emissions Reduction Protocol*

The Third Conference of the Parties of the FCCC agreed in 1997 through the Kyoto Protocol to impose a set of greenhouse gas emissions targets for the world's developed countries (the so-called Annex I or Annex A countries). The targets were different for different countries, but their combined effect would reduce total emissions from Annex I countries by nearly 6 percent relative to their 1990 levels and almost 20 percent from their 1999 levels by 2012. Non-Annex I countries were exempted by the Protocol from any emissions reduction.

Subsequent research has raised a large number of issues in regard to achieving any eventual FCCC concentration limit. Some are technical and deal with accounting procedures for counting emissions reductions. Others are more fundamental. First among these is the observation that full compliance by Annex I by 2012 with fixed total Annex I emissions thereafter will not stabilize concentrations at any level for most baselines. It follows that non-Annex I countries will eventually have to accept limits on their emissions, as well, if the FCCC objective of stable concentrations is to be achieved. Indeed, a 550 ppmv threshold would not be achieved along many baselines even if Annex I eliminated all dependence on fossil fuel by the middle of the twenty-first century.

Second, Annex I compliance with their Kyoto targets by 2012 does not conform with the cost-minimizing pattern of maximal intertemporal flexibility for most baselines and most concentration targets. Passing through the Kyoto benchmark increases the cost of meeting any threshold above 500 ppmv along all but the most energy intensive baselines.

Finally, negotiations about how to arrange for geographic flexibility within the implementation of the Kyoto Protocol are critical. The equity and cost implications of allowing flexibility with Annex I and/or the ability for Annex I countries to be credited for reductions that they underwrite in non-Annex I countries are enormous. McKibben and Wilcoxen (1999) have argued that changes in the so-called 'terms of trade' caused by massive transfers of wealth to non-Annex I countries in exchange for emissions reduction credits could actually lower their economic welfare. In addition, Manne (1999) observed that the partial global coverage of the Protocol could lead to significant 'leakage' so that global emissions might not fall as far as expected. Why? Because restricted emissions in Annex I would cause the prices of fossil fuels to fall and thereby increase emissions across the developing world.

2.3 Optimal Emissions Reductions

Nordhaus (1991) was the first researcher to weigh the present value of the benefits of mitigation policy against the present value of their costs to compute an economically optimal policy trajectory over the long term. His results were based on the anticipation that impacts would be smooth and amount to roughly 1 percent of gross world product if the global mean temperature rose by 2.5°C. Corroborated by his own subsequent work and by others, they support modest early intervention followed by smooth and gradual tightening of emissions restrictions. Indeed, most optimality exercises propose carbon taxes between $10 and $20 around 2000; and most see those taxes increasing over time at ∼ 3 percent per year. None of the results achieve stable atmospheric concentrations along most baselines, and none come close to the restrictions imposed on 2012 emissions by the Kyoto Protocol.

3. Synthesis as the Future Unfolds

Synthesizing the economics of climate change and climate policy is an evolving process that will continue well into the twenty-first century. As researchers learn more about both, the costs associated with both could easily fall. However, they may not, particularly on the climate side of the calculus. The possibility of sudden and, as yet, unanticipated impacts could change the picture dramatically.

See also: Agricultural Change Theory; Agricultural Sciences and Technology; Agriculture, Economics of; Climate Change and Health; Climate Impacts; Climate Policy: International; Desertification; Ecological Economics; Economic Geography; Environmental Adaptation and Adjustments; Environmental and Resource Management; Environmental Challenges in Organizations; Environmental Planning; Environmental Policy; Environmental Vulnerability; Food Security; Globalization: Geographical Aspects

Bibliography

Darwin R F, Tsigas M, Lewandrowski J, Raneses A 1996 *World Agriculture and Climate Change*. US Department of Agriculture Report 703. US Department of Agriculture, Washington, DC

Houghton J T, Callander B A, Varney S K (eds.) 1992 *Climate Change 1992. The Supplementary Report to the IPCC Scientific Assessment*. Cambridge University Press, Cambridge, UK

Houghton J T, Meira Filho L G, Callander B A, Harris N, Kattenberg A, Maskell K (eds.) 1996 *Climate Change 1995: The Science of Climate Change*. Cambridge University Press, Cambridge, UK

Kane S, Reilly J M, Tobey J 1992 An empirical study of the economic effects of climate change on world agriculture. *Climatic Change* 21: 17–35

Manne A 1999 International carbon agreements, trade and leakage. In: *Proceedings of the IEA/EMF/IIASA Energy Modeling Meeting*. Energy Modeling Forum, Stanford, CA

Manne A, Richels R 1997 On stabilizing CO_2 concentrations—cost-effective emission reduction strategies. In: Cameron O K, Fukuwator K, Morita T (eds.) *Proceedings of the IPCC Asia–Pacific Workshop on integrated Assessment Models*. Center for Global Environmental Research, Ibaraki, Japan, pp. 439–59

McKibben W, Wilcoxen P 1999 The theoretical and empirical structure of the G-Cubed model. *Economic Modelling* 16: 123–48

Mendelsohn R, Morrison W, Schlesinger M E, Andronova N G 2000 Country-specific market impacts of climate change. *Climatic Change* 45: 553–69

Nordhaus W D 1991 To slow or not to slow: the economics of the greenhouse effect. *Economic Journal* 101: 920–37

Nordhaus W D 1994 *Managing the Global Commons: The Economics of Climate Change*. MIT Press, Cambridge, MA

Reilly J M, Baethgen W, Chege F E, van de Geijn S C, Lin E, Iglesias A, Kenny G, Patterson D, Rogasik J, Roetter R, Rosenzweig C, Sombroek W, Westbrook J 1996 Agriculture in a changing climate: impacts and adaptation. In: Watson R T, Zinyowera M C, Moss R H (eds.) *Climate Change 1995: Impacts, Adaptations and Mitigation of Climate Change: Scientific–Technical Analysis—Contributions of Working Group II to the Second Assessment Report of the Intergovernmental Panel on Climate Change*. Cambridge University Press, Cambridge, UK, pp. 427–68

Titus J G 1992 The cost of climate change to the United States. In: Majumdar S K, Kalkstein L S, Yarnal B, Miller E W, Rosenfeld L M (eds.) *Global Climate Change: Implications, Challenges and Mitigation Measures*. Pennsylvania Academy of Science, Easton, PA, pp. 217–35

Tol R S J 1998 *New Estimates of the Damage Costs of Climate Change. Part I: Benchmark Estimates*. Institute for Environmental Studies, Vrije Universiteit, Amsterdam

Tsigas M E, Frisvold G B, Kuhn B 1996 Global climate change in agriculture. In: Hertel T W (ed.) *Global Trade Analysis: Modeling and Applications*. Cambridge University Press, Cambridge, UK, pp. 3–15

Wigley T, Richels R, Edmonds J A 1996 Economic and environmental choices in the stabilization of atmospheric CO_2 concentrations. *Nature* 379: 240–43

Yohe G, Schlesinger M E 1998 Sea-level change: the expected economic cost of protection and abandonment in the United States. *Climatic Change* 38: 447–72

Yohe G, Wallace R 1996 Near-term mitigation policy for global change under uncertainty: minimizing the expected cost of meeting unknown concentration thresholds. *Environmental Modeling and Assessment* 2: 47–57

G. W. Yohe

Climate, History of

1. Introduction

Climatologists and climate historians have assembled robust evidence that the world's climate has changed significantly over the past millennium. However, for most historians climate still is an unacknowledged constant. There remain serious intellectual and practical obstacles to understanding and using the new evidence that is now becoming available (Richards 2001). The first section of this article reviews the discussion on the issue. The second section examines the evidence and the approaches used for reconstructing past weather and climate. The third section reviews the main trends of climate variability over the last millennium. In the last section the assessment of climate impacts on premodern societies is considered.

2. The Discussion on 'Climate and History'

Every society develops philosophical and mythical interpretations about the role of the natural environment in human affairs. Enlightenment thinkers concluded that cultures were determined or strongly shaped by climate. Economists and geographers (e.g. Stanley Jevons, Eduard Brückner) assumed that economic life was affected by climatic cycles. Environmental determinism was carried to an extreme by the geographer Ellsworth Huntington in the early twentieth century (Fleming 1998). Sociologist Emile Durkheim summarily rejected efforts to link human performance to climate changes. He postulated that social issues could be explained solely by social factors (Glaeser 1994). The discussion on the social significance of climatic variations was resumed by historians of the French Annales School (e.g., Emmanuel Le Roy Ladurie) after World War II. Ladurie suggested that historical climate should first be reconstructed for its own sake without considering its potential significance for human history. This issue should only be addressed in a second step based on reliable reconstructions of past climate. However, he was skeptical in this respect, postulating that 'the narrowness of the range of secular temperature variations and the autonomy of the human phenomena which coincide with them in time make it impossible for the present to claim that there is any casual link between them' (Le Roy Ladurie 1971, p. 293). The English meteorologist Hubert Lamb (1988), who took an active interest in history, became Le Roy Ladurie's most prominent opponent. Lamb was convinced that weather and climate had affected human affairs in the past and that humankind would do well to examine some of the lessons provided by nature.

From the early 1990s the framework of the discussion changed. On one hand the issue of the increased greenhouse effect was put on the agenda stimulating efforts towards reconstructing past climates. In this respect historical climatology cooperated with scientific disciplines. Remarkable progress was made from mostly isolated attempts at reconstructing local climate histories, to successful attempts at boiling down regional evidence into quasi-homogeneous highly correlated monthly time series of temperature and precipitation indices on the supra-regional scale (Pfister et al. 1999). In the late 1990s historical climatology was moving at the center of the controversial detection debate about anthropogenic climate change, because documentary data is the only evidence for assessing the frequency and clustering of rare but socioeconomically significant disasters such as intense storms, severe floods, and droughts.

On the other hand the mainstream of historians turned away from structural history and the 'longue durée' in favor of discourse analysis. As a consequence the incentive to investigate the impacts of the climatic variability being detected by climate historians declined. In the context of the ongoing debate the issue of the social perception of (reconstructed) climate change may become attractive for historians of ideas.

3. The Reconstruction of Weather and Climate from Natural and Manmade Archives

The global climate of the last millennium is reconstructed using evidence from both natural and manmade archives. Data from natural archives (e.g., tree ring or ice core data) is essential for those periods of history and those regions of the world for which documentary evidence is sparse or nonexistent, such as precolonial North America. However, most reconstructions from natural archives cannot be broken down into sufficiently short units of time (e.g., months or seasons) and into specific parameters (temperature and precipitation) (Bradley 1999) that would be needed for conclusive investigations into the human dimension of climatic change.

Data from manmade archives (i.e., documentary evidence) is well researched in Europe and East Asia. Investigations have hardly begun in Latin America. The evidence for Africa is spotty. In the Islamic world the possibly abundant evidence remains to be explored.

Documentary evidence is classified into descriptive and proxy data. Descriptive data includes chroniclers' narratives of weather patterns characteristic of a particular region. Chinese historians have drawn upon observations found in local gazetteers maintained by local gentry in nearly every district. In order to portray more objectively the character of extreme events, chroniclers referred to the duration of snow cover or the freezing of bodies of water, to the development of crops, and to high and low water levels. In Europe daily weather observations were promoted by the rise of planetary astronomy from the late fifteenth century.

Regular instrumental measurements of weather began in the late seventeenth century. From 1860 national meteorological networks came into being.

Evidence providing an indirect measure of climate is mostly drawn from administrative records. These may yield long, continuous, and quasi-homogeneous series of climate related data that reflect the beginning of agricultural activities (e.g., the vine harvest), agricultural production (e.g., yield of vineyards), or the time of freezing and opening up of waterways (Pfister et al. 1999).

Records of rogations (i.e., standardized religious ceremonies to put an end to a meteorological stress situation) are a promising source for the Spanish-speaking world. In Spain rogations were recorded in the account books of both the municipalities and the church (Martin and Barriendos 1995).

Manmade archives are interpreted by historical climatology, which serves as an interface between climatology and history. It is directed towards three objectives (Pfister et al. 1999):

(a) reconstructing weather and climate as well as natural disasters prior to the creation of meteorological networks;

(b) investigating the vulnerability of past societies to climatic extremes and natural disasters;

(c) exploring past discourses on and social representations of climate.

Usually the evidence available for a given month or season is converted to ordinal indices for temperature and precipitation. The computing of transfer functions with instrumental series allows temperature and precipitation to be assessed for the pre-instrumental period. Series of indices were also included in statistical models to reconstruct monthly mean air pressure at sea level for the eastern North Atlantic-European region (25°W to 30°E, and 35°N to 70°N) back to 1659 (Luterbacher et al. 2000).

4. Climatic Trends and Anomalies Over the Last Millennium

4.1 Three Main Phases

Palaeoclimatologists and climate historians describe three main phases of climatic change over the past millennium: A 'Medieval Warm Period' to 1300 (Hughes and Diaz 1994); a subsequent cool phase lasting to the late nineteenth century that is labeled 'Little Ice Age' because glaciers in most regions of the globe were expanding during that time (Bradley and Jones 1996). The twentieth century is the warmest period of the millennium, partly as a consequence of the increased greenhouse effect. However, such generalizations on the global level mask a broad array of contrasting regional and local trends. Moreover, in order to investigate human vulnerability to climatic stress, the perspective of 'ages' needs to be broken down to regional monthly or seasonal temperature and precipitation patterns. So far, this level of detail is only available for Europe and China.

4.2 Central Europe

After a cold phase in the twelfth century, winters were prevailingly warm from 1180 to 1300. From 1300 to 1900 the winter half-year was colder than today. This is related to more frequent and sustained advection of cold, dry continental air-masses from the (north) east. Severe winters were frequent from 1306 to 1328, 1430 to 1490, 1565 to 1615, 1655 to 1710, 1755 to 1860, and 1880 to 1895. From 1365 to 1400, 1520 to 1560, and from 1610 to 1650 moderate winters prevailed. Springs were extremely cold in the 1690s and in the 1740s.

Summers do not show distinct long-term characteristics. Those in the thirteenth century were prevailingly warm and dry. In the fourteenth century clusters of cold and wet summers occurred repeatedly (e.g., in the 1310s and 1340s). From 1380 to 1430 and again from 1530 to 1565 the summer half-year was as warm as today. Over the last third of the sixteenth century cold spells and long rains in midsummer expanded at the expense of warm anticyclonic weather. This tendency culminated in the 1590s (Pfister et al. 1999). Summers at the beginning and end of the seventeenth century were prevailingly cool while those from 1630 to 1687 were moderate. In the 1700s several warm decades (the 1720s, the 1730s, and the 1780s) stand out in England and in Central Europe, whereas the first half of the nineteenth century, particularly the 1810s, was markedly cooler (Bradley and Jones 1996).

4.3 Russia

Winters became more severe at the end of the sixteenth century, in particular from 1620 to 1680 and in the first half of the nineteenth century.

In the summer half-year droughts were frequent from 1201 to 1230, 1351 to 1380, and 1411 to 1440. A period of comparatively warm conditions in all seasons stands out during the first half of the sixteenth century. Subsequently, cold spells occurred more often from 1590 to 1620 and from 1690 to 1740 with a peak in the 1730s. Droughts occurred frequently from 1640 to 1659 and from 1680 to 1699. The six decades from 1770 to 1830 were warm, and droughts were frequent from 1801 to 1860. Summers from 1890 to 1920 were by far the coldest in the last 500 years. This included an unusually large number of extreme dry and wet seasons (Bradley and Jones 1996).

4.4 China

In South China the thirteenth century was the warmest of the last millennium. Three cold periods—1470 to

1520, 1620 to 1740, and 1840 to 1890—are identified, the 1650s being by far the coldest decade. Rainfall during the seventeenth century was extremely variable. Temperatures during the eighteenth century, unlike in Europe, rarely climbed to twentieth century levels, but precipitation conditions were more favorable. Climate variability increased markedly throughout the nineteenth century to a maximum in the early twentieth century. In North China two cold periods—1500 to 1690 and 1800 to 1860—stand out over the last six centuries. Considering all seasons, the period from 1650 to 1670 was the coldest, but the summer half-year was almost equally cold from 1580 to 1600 (Wang 1991).

4.5 The Mediterranean

After a cold twelfth century the period 1200 to 1400 was very warm in the southwest. Annual precipitation in Morocco was generally lower from the sixteenth to nineteenth centuries (Bradley and Jones 1996). In Catalonia (northeastern Spain) dry spells in the winter half-year were frequent in the mid-sixteenth century, but almost absent from 1580 to 1620. Numerous autumnal floods were reported from 1580 to 1630, from 1770 to 1800, and again from 1840 to 1870 (Martin and Barriendos 1995).

4.6 Latin America

In both Spanish and Portuguese America there seems to have been a trend to greater aridity in the 1700s compared to the 1600s. Dendroclimatic evidence for the Santiago de Chile area indicates higher than average rainfall from 1450 to 1600 whereas droughts became frequent over the subsequent centuries (e.g., 1637 to 1640, 1770 to 1773, 1790s, 1810s). In the Buenos Aires region (Argentina) the 1700s were drier than the previous century. Prolonged droughts are recorded in the 1690s, the 1710s, the 1750s, and 1771 to 1774 (Claxton 1993).

4.7 ENSO

The El-Niño Southern Oscillation (ENSO) is the result of a cyclic warming and cooling of the ocean surface in the central and eastern Pacific that strongly affects rainfall in the areas around the Pacific and the Indian Ocean. Archival data suggests that ENSO episodes from 1600 to 1900 had more intense and global effect than those of the twentieth century. For example, the worst droughts in the colonial history of India (mid 1590s, 1629 to 1633, 1685 to 1688, 1788 to 1793, 1877 to 1878) are related to ENSO connected failures of the monsoon. For the last two events the global dimension of these episodes is demonstrated (Grove and Chappell 2000).

5. The Historical Significance of Climatic Change

The issue of whether climatic change has had a significant impact on history is controversial. It should not be overlooked that both 'climate' and 'history' are blanket terms located on such a high level of abstraction that relationships between them cannot be investigated according to the rules of scientific methodology. In order to become more meaningful, the issue needs to be broken down to lower scales of analysis e.g., by focusing on specific human activities and/or needs in relation to a given set of climatic variables. Regarding preindustrial societies this concerns primarily the availability of biomass (e.g., food, fodder) and energy (e.g., wind, water-power) but also processes of population dynamics (e.g., patterns of disease and epizootics, as well as fertility of men and livestock), and transport and communications as well as military and naval operations. Undoubtedly, beneficial climatic effects tend to enlarge the scope of human action, whereas climatic shocks restrict it or even lead to emergency situations. Which climatic constellations matter for energy availability and population dynamics depend on the environmental, cultural, and historical context.

Models of climatic effects on society are often framed as a chain of causation. Climatic patterns have a first order or biophysical impact on agricultural production or on the outbreak of diseases or epizotics. These may have second order effects on prices of food or raw materials, which may then ramify into the wider economy and society (third order impacts). The farther we move away from first order impacts, the greater the complexity of the factors masking the climatic effect. It is also plain that it is easier to investigate the effects of short-term impacts. In dealing with the effects of multidecadal climate variations we have to account for modifications in the economic, institutional, and environmental setting so great as to vitiate any attempt at strict comparison or measurement (Kates et al. 1985). Most climatic impacts were related to food scarcity or famines.

Crises were triggered by a slump in overall agricultural production. This could be a consequence of climatic shocks or warfare. In Central Europe severe climate induced crises (e.g., 1569–74, 1627–29, 1692–94, 1769–72, 1816–17, 1853–55) were connected to a cumulation of unfavorable weather patterns, which made the traditional risk minimizing strategies ineffective (Richards 2001). Rainfall is the limiting factor in the subtropical and tropical zones; in higher latitudes it is summer warmth. Connections between climatic anomalies and diseases are complex. Some diseases (e.g., cholera) are climate related whereas others (e.g., bubonic plague) are not (Rotberg and Rabb 1983). The theory of pre-industrial trade cycles considers the harvest the critical determinant influencing urban income and rural employment levels. A sharp rise in food prices promoted widespread unemployment, begging, and vagrancy that further propagated infectious diseases and increased crisis mortality (Post 1985).

Crises represented a major challenge for political and social systems. Rather than investigating changes in average values, historical climatology should focus on changes in the frequency and severity of extremes. The evidence is growing that exogenous shocks (including natural disasters) have a tendency to cluster rather than being randomly distributed along the time axis, as is often believed. This allows us to distinguish between periods of high and low climatic stress.

An example is provided by sixteenth-century Europe: there was a sudden increase in the number of cold anomalies after 1565. Over the subsequent decades climate became more significant for food prices than population levels and increases in the money supply. The case is even more obvious for wine production which as a consequence of an almost uninterrupted series of cold summers nearly collapsed from 1585 to 1600 across a large region ranging from Switzerland to Hungary. The slump of vine production had far-reaching consequences for major social groups depending on vine growing. Many peasant communities suffered such a large collective damage from the effects of continuous crop failures that they pressed the authorities to permit witch hunts. Thousands of witches were burnt as scapegoats of climatic change (Behringer 1999).

Based on the new reconstructions that are becoming available, the significance of climatic variability needs to be reassessed in many contexts of economic, social, and environmental history without including deterministic overtones.

See also: Climate Change and Health; Climate Change, Economics of; Climate Impacts; Desertification; Environmental Determinism; Irrigation Societies; Water Resources

Bibliography

Behninger W 1999 Climatic change and witch hunting: The impact of the little ice age an mentalities. In: Pfister C, Brazdil R, Glazer R (eds.) *Climatic Variability in Sixteenth-century Europe and its Social Dimension*. Kluwer, Dordrecht, The Netherlands
Bradley R S 1999 *Palaeoclimatology*. Academic Press, San Diego, CA
Bradley R S, Jones P D (eds.) 1996 *Climate Since AD 1500*. Routledge, London
Claxton R H 1993 The record of drought and its impact in colonial Spanish America. In: Herr R (ed.) *Themes in Rural History of the Western World*. Iowa State University Press, Ames, IA
Dupâquier J 1989 Demographic crises and subsistence crises in France, 1650–1725. In: Walter J, Schofield R (eds.) *Famine, Disease and the Social Order in Early Modern Society*. Cambridge University Press, Cambridge, UK

Fleming J R 1998 *Historical Perspectives on Climate Change*. Oxford University Press, Oxford, UK
Glaeser B 1994 Soziologie der Umwelt. In: Ernste H (ed.) *Pathways to Human Ecology*. Lang, Bern, Switzerland, pp. 115–32
Grove R, Chappell J (eds.) 2000 *El Niño, History and Crisis*. White Horse Press, Knapwell, UK
Hughes M K, Diaz H F 1994 *The Medieval Warm Period*. Kluwer, Dordrecht, The Netherlands
Kates R W, Ausubel J H, Berberian M (eds.) 1985 *Climate Impact Assessment, Studies of the Interaction of Climate and Society*. Wiley, Chichester, UK
Lamb H H 1988 *Weather, Climate & Human Affairs*. Routledge, London
Le Roy Ladurie E 1971 *Times of Feast, Times of Famine: A History of Climate Since the Year 1000*. Doubleday, Garden City, NY
Luterbacher J, Rickli R et al. 2000 Monthly mean pressure reconstruction for the late Maunder minimum period (AD 1675–1715). *Journal of Climatology* 20: 1049–66
Martin V J, Barriendos V M 1995 The use of rogation ceremony records in climatic reconstruction. *Climatic Change* 30: 201–21
Pfister C, Brázdil R, Glaser R (eds.) 1999 *Climatic Variability in Sixteenth Century Europe and its Social Dimension*. Kluwer, Dordrecht, The Netherlands
Post J D 1985 *Food Shortage, Climatic Variability, and Epidemic Disease in Preindustrial Europe*. Cornell University Press, Ithaca, NY
Richards J F 2001 *The Unending Frontier: Environmental History in the Early Modern World*. University of California Press, Berkeley, CA
Rotberg R I, Rabb T K (eds.) 1983 *Hunger and History*. Cambridge University Press, Cambridge, UK
Wang S W 1991 Reconstruction of temperature series of North China from 1380s to 1980s. *Science in China* B 34: 751–9
Wigley T M L, Ingram M J, Farmer G (eds.) 1981 *Climate and History*. Cambridge University Press, Cambridge, UK

C. Pfister

Climate Impacts

1. Introduction

While there is scientific consensus that increased atmospheric concentrations of greenhouse gases will likely raise global temperatures, with associated increases in global precipitation and sea level, there is no consensus on how fast and how much the climate may change, on how regional climates may change, or on how climate variability may change. Climate change impact assessment for a country or region consists of a set of tasks beginning with problem definition and leading through sector analysis to analysis of adaptation methods and response policies.

A broad understanding of the potential future with climate change demands multifaceted analyses, involving study of both biophysical and socioeconomic processes. A wide range of methods for climate change impact analysis has been developed, from simple

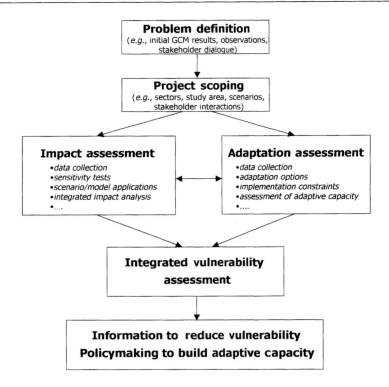

Figure 1
Integrated impacts, adaption, and vulnerability framework
Source: Rosenzweig and Iglesias 2000

regression models to complex integrated systems models. Techniques are becoming ever more complex as more interacting systems and the propagation of uncertainties are included in the analysis. The challenge is to simulate the biophysical and socioeconomic aspects of a system (such as agriculture, human health, urban areas) in a framework appropriate to regional, national, international, and global scales. Spatial analyses and first-order biophysical impacts are important, as well as assessment of vulnerability in the socioeconomic welfare of the different components of the system. Thus, biophysical scientists and social scientists must work together to provide realistic assessments of how climate change might affect a system in the future (see Fig. 1).

Methodological issues to be resolved include how to generalize from the enormous heterogeneity of exposure units and systems and how to address spatial scales and units of analysis from field to region to nation and beyond. Models must be continually tested, calibrated, and validated, and improved for their use to be well-founded. The inclusion of the transient nature of climate change and its associated uncertainties in the modeling techniques is particularly important.

2. Approach

There are several approaches that serve as foundations to climate change impact studies. One approach is based on climate change scenarios, that is, projections of what future climate variables (and the characteristics of future impacts) may be like. Equilibrium climate change scenarios have been most often used in this approach, but recent more realistic studies and projections incorporate dynamic or 'transient' climate change scenarios. The climate change scenarios approach sometimes includes the study of responses of the system to past climatic variations, in order to allow comparison with future projections.

Another approach is threshold-based, and attempts to define the limits of sensitivity of a system as it is currently configured to changes in climatic variables. The first approach addresses the question, 'What will the system be like in a given future changed climate?' while the threshold approach asks, 'What type, magnitude, and rate of climate change would seriously perturb the system as we know it?' This approach most often applies transient scenarios of climate change. Both of the approaches construct a chain of causality from the biophysical responses at a small scale to socioeconomic effects at the regional, national, and international levels.

Several different techniques from the field of economics have been used in climate change impact analysis. One technique is the utilization of economic data to estimate the value of climate to the exposure unit (i.e., farmers) implicitly through regression equations. Linear programming models of the national sector (i.e., agriculture) are also used, as well as linked national and regional models.

Analysis of adaptive responses to climate change is an important part of climate change impacts research. The biophysical approaches described above allow the explicit examination of exposure unit adaptations, while the economic approach deals with adaptation implicitly.

3. Climate Change Scenarios

Climate change scenarios are defined as plausible combinations of climatic conditions that may be used to test possible impacts and to evaluate responses to them. Scenarios may be used to determine how vulnerable a sector is to climate change, to identify thresholds at which impacts become negative or severe, and compare the relative vulnerability among sectors in the same region or among similar sectors in different regions.

It is still difficult, if not impossible, to associate probabilities with any particular scenario of climate change, due to uncertainties in future emissions of radiatively active trace gases and in the response of the climate system to those emissions. Thus, impact studies based on climate change scenarios do not make actual predictions; rather, they are useful in defining for critical biophysical and socioeconomic systems directions of change, relative magnitudes of change, and potential critical thresholds of climate-sensitive processes. By conducting climate change impact analyses, researchers and resource managers are conducting 'practice' exercises, which help to engender flexibility in the systems' responses to potentially changing conditions in the future.

3.1 Arbitrary Scenarios

The simplest scenario is the application of prescriptive changes, such as a 2 °C increase in temperature and/or a 10 percent decrease in precipitation, to observed climate. Tests with such simple changes can help to identify the sensitivities of systems to changes in different variables. One can isolate the effects of one climate variable, for example, temperature, while holding other variables constant. However, such tests do not offer a consistent set of climate variables, since evaporation, precipitation, wind, and other variables are all likely to change with change in temperature. Arbitrary scenarios do, however, provide a set of

responses to which other types of scenarios may be compared.

3.2 Historical Analogs

Another type of climate change scenario is based on the historical record. Observations from cool or warm, wet or dry historical periods are used to construct scenarios for use in modeling studies of climate change impacts. Such periods are also useful for the insights provided by studying the responses of any given system to periods of climatic extremes. The Dust Bowl of the 1930s in the Southern Great Plains is a well-known example (see e.g., Warrick 1984), but past freeze events, aquifer depletion, and lake-level changes have also been used to study societal responses to regional climate change (Glantz 1988).

A difficulty with either of these scenario approaches as proxies for the global warming currently predicted for increasing CO_2 and other trace gases is that the patterns of climate warming may be different depending on the nature of the atmospheric forcing mechanisms.

3.3 GCM-based Scenarios

Climate change scenarios are also derived from global climate model (GCM) experiments with specified forcing mechanisms (e.g., 1 percent annual increase in greenhouse gas concentrations in the atmosphere). Current GCM model experiments are conducted to produce transient climate projections. The advantages of GCM scenarios are their internal consistency and global extent. GCMs estimate how regional and global climates may change in response to increased concentrations of trace gases. Thus, regional and global climate responses are internally consistent. The climate variables are also physically consistent, as heat, moisture, and energy processes are calculated from a consistent set of equations representing physical processes.

At present, GCMs represent current climate at global and zonal (latitudinal) scales, but do not do particularly well at simulating regional current climate. Differences in climate projections among GCMs increase as scale decreases from the global to the regional and gridbox levels. GCM simulation of current temperature regimes is better than simulation of current hydrological regimes. A range of GCM scenarios should be included in the design of impact studies in order to incorporate a range of climate sensitivities to greenhouse gas forcing, and it is very important to consider GCM regional climate change projections as examples of possible future climates, rather than as actual predictions.

Because GCM simulation of current climates is often inaccurate, direct projections of GCM-generated future climates is seldom used. Changes in climate variables in the perturbed simulations relative to the control run are often applied to historical observed weather data to create the climate change scenarios used in impact studies. Absolute model biases are omitted by using the relative changes. Thirty years of current climate data are often used to develop the baseline climate scenario to which the GCM changes are applied. A 30-year period is considered long enough to represent 'normal' climate variability. Recent periods, e.g., 1951–80, or 1961–90, are often selected, representing current climate and having accurate data most easily available. The latter period contains some of the warmest years on record that may have been caused by the enhanced greenhouse effect.

The use of GCM transient scenarios (i.e., time dependent) in climate change impact studies is growing, since they provide a much more realistic picture of the projected warming from current conditions to some point in the future.

4. Integrated Global Change Scenarios

Climate is not the only factor that will be changing as the twenty-first century unfolds. Population growth and changing economic and technological conditions are likely to affect world society and the environment even more than changes in climate. It is important to take such changes into account in climate change impact analyses: first, because climate change will occur not in the present but in the future, and second, because such changes may affect the sensitivity of a system or sector to climate. However, predicting population growth rates and future economic conditions is equally if not more uncertain than predicting the future climate. Therefore, future scenarios need to be designed carefully to address a range of possible conditions. One approach is to contrast 'optimistic' and 'pessimistic' views of the future. In the optimistic scenario, population growth rates are low, economic growth rates and incomes rise, environmental pollution decreases, and land degradation abates. In more pessimistic scenarios, population growth rates are high, economic growth rates and incomes are low, environmental pollution increases, and land degradation accelerates. A scenario of no change (i.e., present conditions) should also be included. The differential effects of climate change on current conditions, and on these two alternative scenarios of the future may then be evaluated.

In order to place possible changes in climate in the context of potential socioeconomic changes, estimates of population, economic growth, and technological change are needed. These estimates will also affect future rates of CO_2 and other greenhouse gas emissions. Economic projections beyond the next 10 to 20 years generally are unreliable. Furthermore, socio-economic factors are not unrelated, since changes in population are likely to affect national and per-capita income. Recent IPCC scenarios include estimates of population and economic growth rates for a set of possible futures (IPCC 2000).

Socioeconomic factors that are often considered in future scenarios include population, income, productivity, and technology levels. Environmental factors may include stratospheric and tropospheric ozone levels and changes in land use. Institutions and legal structures may change as well, but these evolutions are very hard to predict. The World Bank (1994) and the United Nations (1999) have published population estimates by country through 2100 for a range of scenarios. The World Bank (1993) has published estimates of changes in income. Various economic models are used to project such productivity factors as gross domestic product (GDP) into the future. Population and economic growth may bring increases in urbanization, expansion of agriculture and mining of natural resources, and accelerating rates of deforestation, habitat fragmentation, desertification, and water and air pollution (FAO 1993, Dregne and Chou 1992).

4.1 CO_2 and Greenhouse Gas Emission Scenarios

CO_2 and greenhouse gas emission scenarios are needed, especially for agriculture because of the need to estimate crop responses to the CO_2 fertilization effect, as well as projections of sea-level rise. Climate modelers need estimates of future levels of atmospheric CO_2 and other trace gases in order to prepare transient scenarios of future climate. Crop and forest modelers also need such estimates in order to take fertilization effects into account in their impact analyses. Global emissions of CO_2, the most important greenhouse gas, depend primarily on fossil fuel use in three major sectors—electrical generation, industry, and transportation. A growing world economy consists of growth in industrial production, consumption of goods, and travel and concomitant increases in energy use. Deforestation also contributes to CO_2 emissions and is linked to economic growth as land is converted from natural ecosystems to agriculture and other uses.

The IPCC (2000) and others estimate growth rates of world carbon emissions from fossil fuels and deforestation in order to calculate atmospheric CO_2 levels for climate projections. Such calculations are also important in international negotiations that consider limiting CO_2 emissions. Since only a portion (about one-half) of the carbon added to the atmosphere remains, carbon cycle models are used to translate carbon emissions into atmospheric levels of CO_2. Models that include the effects of CO_2 fertilization, feedback from stratospheric ozone depletion, and the radiative effects of sulfate aerosols have been combined to project radiative forcing of climate, changes in global-mean temperature, and sea level (Wigley and Raper 1992). Recent projections have tended to reduce the projected rates of warming and sea-level rise, but they are still four to five times the rates observed over the twentieth century.

5. Modeling Techniques: A Case Study of the Agricultural Sector

Modeling techniques of several kinds are used to study potential impacts and responses of agriculture to changing climate and atmospheric composition. The agricultural sector is chosen to illustrate the range of modeling techniques, because agriculture is a key socioeconomic sector for development in many regions, agricultural land use is a primary driver of land-use change, and agriculture is a sector vulnerable to global environmental change. Choice of technique depends on the sphere of analysis considered and the research questions posed.

5.1 Biophysical Modeling

5.1.1 Crop suitability. Spatial analysis consists of identification of critical environmental limits (primarily climate, soil and water resources) of specific crops or agricultural systems, applications of climate change scenarios, and calculation of resulting spatial shifts in crop or agricultural regions. This agroclimatic method provides an approximation of possible changes in crop areas from a biological perspective, but does not address potential changes in either yield or production.

5.1.2 Potential production. Potential production may be estimated from climatic variables or indices such as length of growing season, precipitation, evapotranspiration, solar radiation, and temperature. A prime example of this technique is found in the Agro-Ecological Zone Project of the FAO (FAO 1978). The FAO Agro-Ecological Zone modeling technique simulates both crop zonation and potential production (Leemans and Solomon 1993, Cramer and Solomon 1993, Fischer et al. 2001).

5.1.3 Statistical regression models. Multiple regression models have been developed from the statistical relationships between historical crop yields and climatic variables in specific locations (i.e., Waggoner 1983). The use of regression models is limited by their lack of explanatory power, since the techniques rely on statistical coefficients rather than on descriptions of the underlying biophysical relationships.

5.1.4 Dynamic crop models. Dynamic crop growth models formulate the principal physiological, morphological, and physical processes involving the transfers of energy and mass within the crop and between the crop and its environment. Such models have been developed for most of the major crops, with the aim of predicting their responses to specified climatic, edaphic, and management factors governing production. Dynamic models capable of simulating the response of crops to climatic variables may be used in conjunction with GCM climate change scenarios to explore the consequences of increased atmospheric CO_2 and climate change on yields and phenology or to determine thresholds of crop growth sensitivity to changing climate variables. They are also useful for testing possible adaptations to climate change, such as altered planting dates, irrigation scheduling, or crop variety (see Rosenzweig and Iglesias (1994) for applications of crop models to climate change impact evaluation).

5.2 Economic Techniques

Economic measures are an important component of the information that policymakers need to evaluate the climate change issue. Economic analyses are concerned with the reciprocal relations between physical and biological changes on the one hand and the economic responses of individuals and institutions on the other. Once crop yield impacts are estimated, it is useful to translate such biophysical responses into economic measures of human welfare. While biophysical analyses focus primarily on the production of agricultural crops, economic analyses consider both producers and consumers of agricultural goods. Economic measures of interest include the responses of input and output market prices to yield changes and the responses in terms of inputs and outputs that affected individuals make to minimize losses or maximize gains, based on the changes in production and consumption opportunities and in price. If climate change causes substantial changes in outputs, price and quality changes can result, which, in turn, can lead to further market-induced output changes. Even if prices remain constant, accurate indications of output changes are needed if production practices and types of outputs may change.

Previous work on the economics of environmental stresses on agriculture has resulted in a number of general findings (Rosenzweig and Hillel 1998). Important points are that both producers and consumers are included in the domain, that economic activities constitute a type of societal adaptation to environmental stresses, leading in the most part to mitigation of negative effects, and that environmental stresses have differential effects on the comparative advantage of regions and countries.

Economic models calculate estimates of the potential impacts of climate change on measurable economic quantities, including production, consumption, income, gross domestic product (GDP), and employment. It is important to remember, however, that these may be only partial indicators of social welfare. Different social systems, households, and individuals may not be represented in models that are based on producer and consumer theory. Furthermore, many of the economic models do not account for climate-change induced alterations in land availability and water for irrigation; these nonmarket aspects of a changing climate may be critical.

As a starting point, the gathering of available information about production, consumption, and policies provides a framework for determining the existence and possible magnitude of economic vulnerability in the agricultural sector (US Country Studies Program 1994). Microeconomic farm-level models are designed to simulate the decision-making process of a representative farmer in regard to methods of production and allocation of capital, labor, and land and infrastructure. Such models are based on the goal of maximizing economic returns to inputs. Some farm-level models include a range of farmer behavior in regard to risk, for example risk-averse or risk-neutral.

Macroeconomic equilibrium models of the agricultural sector include price-responsive behavior for both consumers and producers. Equations for these relationships are developed based on economic principles that consumers will maximize the utility of their food-buying and that producers (farmers) will minimize their costs of production. Such models usually are calibrated for a given reference year; for climate change purposes, the models solve for the reference year given perturbations in crop production and water supply and demand for irrigation derived from biophysical techniques (see e.g., Adams et al. 1990). Population growth and improvements in technology are set exogenously (i.e., not computed dynamically in the model). Model results include equilibrium prices and quantities.

General equilibrium economic models are useful because they measure the potential magnitude of climate change impacts on the economic welfare of both producers and consumers of agricultural goods. They do not, however, provide a detailed picture of how the economy will respond over time. These models may overestimate the adjustment of the agricultural economy to climate change. Results of changes in production and prices from agricultural sectoral models can then be used in general equilibrium models of the larger economy.

Regression models have been developed that test for statistical relationships between climate variables and economic indicators such as farm values. Some recent studies utilize these methods known as the 'Ricardian' approach (e.g., Mendelsohn et al. 1994, Polsky and Easterling 2001). The behavior of consumers is not included in this approach and world food prices, domestic farm output prices, and thus farm revenues that are dependent on changes in agricultural production inside and outside of the US are assumed to be held constant.

6. Integrating across Sectors

Integrated studies link the biophysical and economic realms, and ideally may extend to interactions both within and across sectors such as agriculture and its competing demands for water by irrigators or urban users, or shifting patterns of land use between agricultural and forest (or other natural) ecosystems. This is a more realistic, but more complicated approach, because individual biophysical and socioeconomic sectors will not be affected by climate change in isolation. For example, agricultural responses will be sensitive not only to changes in crop yields, but also to alterations in water supplies, demand for water from other sectors, and to the inundation and salinization of arable land by rising seas. The following are some examples of integration in agricultural impact studies:

(a) Parry et al. (1988) report on integrated agricultural sector studies in high-latitude regions in Canada, Iceland, Finland, USSR, and Japan, that involved teams of meteorologists, agronomists, and economists. The general conclusions of the studies were that warmer temperatures may aid crop production by lengthening the growing season at high latitudes, but that potential for higher evapotranspiration and drought conditions may counteract the positive effects and may even be detrimental to productivity.

(b) Adams et al. (1990) conducted an integrated study for the US, linking models from atmospheric science, plant science, and agricultural economics. While the outcomes for US agriculture in the study depended on the severity of climate change and the compensating effects of carbon dioxide on crop yields, the simulations suggest that irrigated acreage will expand and that regional patterns of US agriculture will shift with predicted global warming. With the more severe climate change scenario tested, the movement of US production into export markets was reduced substantially.

(c) The Missouri, Iowa, Nebraska, and Kansas (MINK) study integrated potential biophysical and economic effects of climate change on agriculture and other sectors (Rosenberg 1993). The study incorporated the physiological effects of CO_2 and adaptation by farmers to the climatic conditions of the 1930s. Even with the relatively mild warming (1.1 °C) of the 1930s and with farmer adaptation and CO_2 effects taken into account, regional production declined by 3.3 percent. Given the estimate of 2.5 °C warming for doubled CO_2 conditions, the results of the MINK study imply agricultural losses of about 10 percent (Cline 1992).

(d) Strzepek et al. (1996) linked climate change impacts in Egypt on agriculture, water, and the coastal zone in an economic model. This integrated study demonstrates that the sectors directly affected by climate change need to be analyzed in concert with the other sectors of the economy in sufficient detail so that feedback can be part of the analysis. Egypt was found to be highly vulnerable to the warming as well as to changes in precipitation and river runoff that are forecast to accompany greenhouse-gas-induced climate change.

In its fullest sense, integrated assessment attempts to close the loop by linking the greenhouse gas emissions caused by human activities, the climatic consequences of the emissions, the impacts of the climate changes on important systems, and the feedback of the impacts back to the generation of greenhouse gas emissions. Modeling frameworks have been devised to integrate the causes, impacts, feedbacks, and policy implications of global climate change (Nordhaus 1992, Manne et al. 1993, Hulme and Raper 1993, Alcamo et al. 1993, Edmonds et al. 1993). An example of a feedback in such models is the pathway leading from energy consumption, to greenhouse gas emissions, to climate warming, to changes in demand for energy (e.g., decreases in demand for energy for heating and increases in demand for energy for air conditioning), and thus back to changes in energy consumption. The models may be used, for example, to explore the effects of policies limiting greenhouse gas emissions, the ensuing reduction in global warming, and the alteration of potential climate change impacts, for example, on agriculture.

7. *Thresholds, Risk, and Surprises*

The identification of thresholds in climate change impacts research involves the analysis of the effects of different levels of climate forcing on a system or activity and the identification of possible discontinuities in response. The determination of critical levels of climate change for any given system may be separated into biophysical and socioeconomic realms. In the biophysical realm, although the thermal regimes and responses of managed and unmanaged ecosystems and water resource availability are complex, critical temperatures (minimum, optimum, and maximum) have been defined for many individual processes. In the socioeconomic realm, defining critical levels of warming is more challenging, due, at least in part, to the interplay of supply, demand and prices, and to the adaptability of the system. Here, determining critical levels of warming involves defining relative impacts on actors from diverse geographic and social groups.

For example, global effects of climate change in agriculture measured with current economic valuation techniques generally are predicted to be small to moderate. This occurs because the economic system is, in general, effective in fostering adaptation to the projected biophysical changes. However, the global perspective masks differences in levels of effects, regionally and socially. Studies done to date concur that there will be significant change in global agricultural patterns. All regions are likely to be affected, but large differences occur among regions. While changes in global production with climate change may be small, the potential remains for regional vulnerability to food deficits due to distributional problems of getting food to specific regions and groups of people. For subsistence farmers and people lacking entitlement to food, lower yields may result not only in measurable economic losses, but possibly malnutrition and starvation. Several studies have addressed vulnerability to food deficits explicitly and found potential increases (e.g., Rosenzweig and Parry 1994, Fischer et al. 2001).

Risk can be evaluated when the probability of occurrence of an event is known, but in impact evaluation, the associated probabilities to a particular scenario are generally not known. Therefore, the inclusion of uncertainty (i.e., when the event is known but the probabilities that it will occur are not known) into climate change impact methods is very important and recent studies are now beginning to include explicit methods to deal with it. Earlier studies have often used 'best estimate' scenarios that represent the mid-point of predictions. The inclusion of a range of scenarios representing upper and lower bounds of the predicted effects is more realistic and allows for the propagation of uncertainty throughout a model system. Further, probability distributions of different events may be defined, with contrasts between low probability catastrophic events (surprises) and higher probability gradual changes in climate trends.

One 'surprise' (i.e., when reality departs qualitatively from expectations) may lead to another in a cascade, since subsystems are connected. Complex systems and chaos theory provide conceptual and analytical tools for anticipating and preparing for surprises. Identification of potential surprises and communication of them to the public and policymakers should allow improvements in environmental and societal resilience to surprise. Surprises related to global climate change may be either scientific or societal in nature. The anticipation of surprises in the science of global climate change may be encouraged by efforts to integrate across disciplines, to support a multiplicity of research approaches, and to focus on outlier outcomes and unconventional views. Beyond the anticipation of scientific surprise, it seems worthwhile to increase the resilience and adaptability of social structures, so that the sensitivity to impacts of unexpected or uncertain perturbations is decreased. Such societal preparedness might include the diversification of economic, productive, and technological systems; the establishment of disaster, coping, and entitlement systems; and the creation of adaptive management systems capable of learning from surprises.

See also: Climate Change and Health; Climate Change, Economics of; Climate Policy: International; Environmental Adaptation and Adjustments; Environmental Challenges in Organizations; Environmental Change and State Response; Environmental Policy: Protection and Regulation; Environmental Risk and Hazards; Environmental Sciences; Environmental Surprise; Environmentalism: Preservation and Conservation; Global Environmental Change: Human Dimensions; Integrative Assessment in Environmental Studies; International and Transboundary Accords, Environmental; Land Use and Cover Change

Bibliography

Adams R M, Rosenzweig C, Pearl R M, Ritchie J T, McCarl B A, Glyer J D, Curry R B, Jones J W, Boote K J, Allen L H Jr 1990 Global climate change and US agriculture. *Nature* **345**: 219–24

Alcamo J, Kreileman G J J, Krol M, Zuidema G 1993 Modelling the global society-biosphere-climate system: Part 1: Model description and testing. *Water, Air and Soil Pollution* **76**: 1–35

Cline W R 1992 *The Economics of Global Warming*. Institute for International Economics, Washington, DC, p. 399

Cramer W P, Solomon A M 1993 Climatic classification and future global redistribution of agricultural land. *Climate Research* **3**: 97–110

Dregne H E, Chou N -T 1992 Global desertification, dimension, and costs. In: Dregne H E (ed.) *Degradation and Restoration of Arid Lands*. Texas Tech University, Lubbock, TX

Edmonds J A, Pitcher H M, Rosenberg N J, Wigley T M L 1993 Design for the Global Change Assessment Model GCAM. Paper presented at the International Workshop on Integrated Assessment of Mitigation, Impacts and Adaptation to Climate Change, 13–15 October 1993. International Institute for Applied Systems Analysis, Laxenburg, Austria, p. 7

Fischer G, Shah M, van Velthuizen H, Nachtergaele F O 2001 *Executive Summary Report: Global Agro-ecological Assessment for Agricultive in the 21st Century*. IIASA, Laxenburg, Austria

Food and Agriculture Organization of the United Nations 1978 *Report on the Agro-Ecological Zones Project*. Vol. 1. Methodology and Results for Africa. FAO, Rome, p. 158

Food and Agriculture Organization of the United Nations 1993 *Agriculture: Towards 2010*. United Nations, Rome

Glantz M H (ed.) 1988 *Societal Responses to Regional Climatic Change*. Westview Press, Boulder, p. 428

Hulme M, Raper S 1993 An integrated framework to address climate change (ESCAPE) and further developments of the global and regional climate modules (MAGICC). Paper presented at the International Workshop on Integrated Assessment of Mitigation, Impacts and Adaptation to Climate Change, 13–15 October 1993. International Institute for Applied Systems Analysis, Laxenburg, Austria, p. 14

IPCC 1995 *IPCC Guidelines for Assessing Impacts and Adaptations under Changing Climate*. Carter T R, Parry M L, Harasawa H, Nishioka S (eds.), University College London and Center for Global Environmental Research, London and Tsukuba, p. 59

IPCC 2001 *Special Report on Emissions Scenarios*. Nakicenovic N, Swart R (eds.) Cambridge University Press, Cambridge, UK

Leemans R, Solomon A M 1993 Modeling the potential change in yield and distribution of the earth's crops under a warmed climate. *Climate Research* **3**: 79–96

Manne A, Mendelsohn R, Richels R 1993 MERGE—A Model for Evaluating Regional and Global Effects of GHG Reduction Policies. Paper presented at the International Workshop on Integrated Assessment of Mitigation, Impacts and Adaptation to Climate Change, 13–15 October 1993. International Institute for Applied Systems Analysis, Laxenburg, Austria, p. 14

Mendelsohn R, Nordhaus W D, Shaw D 1994 The impact of global warming on agriculture: A Ricardian analysis. *The American Economic Review* **84**(4): 753–71

Nordhaus W D 1992 The DICE model: Background and structure of a dynamic integrated climate economy model of the economics of global warming. Cowles Foundation Discussion Paper No. 1009. New Haven, CT

Parry M L, Carter T R, Konijn N T (eds.) 1988 *The Impact of Climatic Variations on Agriculture. Volume 1: Assessments in Cool Temperate and Cold Regions*. Kluwer, Dordrecht, The Netherlands, p. 876

Polsky C, Easterling W E III 2001 Adaptation to climate variabilily and change in the US Great Plains: A multi-scale analysis of Ricardian climate sensitivities. *Agriculture, Ecosystems and Environment* **85**: 133–44

Rosenberg N J (ed.) 1993 *Towards an Integrated Impact Assessment of Climate Change: The MINK Study*. Kluwer, Dordrecht, The Netherlands

Rosenzweig C, Hillel D 1998 *Climate Change and the Global Harvest: Potential Impacts of the Greenhouse Effect on Agriculture*. Oxford University Press, New York, p. 324

Rosenzweig C, Iglesias A (eds.) 1994 *Implications of Climate Change for International Agriculture: Crop Modeling Study*. US Environmental Protection Agency, Washington, DC

Rosenzweig C, Parry M L 1994 Potential impact of climate change on world food supply. *Nature* **367**: 133–8

Strzepek K M, Onyeji S L, Saleh M, Yates D N 1996 An assessment of integrated climate change impacts on Egypt. In: Strzepek K M, Smith J B (eds.) *As Climate Changes: International Impacts and Implications*. Cambridge University Press, Cambridge, UK, pp. 180–200

United Nations 1999 Population Division of the Department of Economic and Social Affairs of the United Nations Secretariat (1999). *Long-range World Population Projections: Based on the 1998 Revision* (ESA/P/WP.153)

US Country Studies Program 1994 *Guidance for Vulnerability and Adaptation Assessments*. Washington, DC

Waggoner P E 1983 Agriculture and a climate changed by more carbon dioxide. In: *Changing Climate*. National Academy of Sciences Press, Washington, DC, pp. 383–418

Warrick R A 1984 The possible impacts on wheat production of a recurrence of the 1930s drought in the U.S. Great Plains. *Climatic Change* **6**: 5–26

Wigley T M L, Raper S C B 1992 Implications for climate and sea level of revised IPCC emissions scenarios. *Nature* **357**: 293–300

World Bank 1993 *Income Projections*. Washington, DC

World Bank 1994 World Population Projections 1994–95: Estimates and Projections with Related Demographic Statistics. Eduard Bos, My T. Vu, Ernest Massiah, and Rodolfo A. Bulatao. 532 pages. Published for the World Bank by The Johns Hopkins University Press, Baltimore, MD

C. Rosenzweig

Climate Policy: International

As early as the closing years of the nineteenth century natural scientists postulated that human activities, particularly burning fossil fuels, could lead to climate change, but it was only late in the twentieth century that the international community began to develop public policies to deal with climate change. The lag resulted from the necessity of developing scientific understanding and public awareness and the immense difficulty of crafting and implementing policies that would be effective. The climate is a classic common good. Policies to deal with it must overcome all of the obstacles to providing common goods.

1. History

Svante Arrhenius, a Swedish chemist and Nobel laureate, first put forth the theory that rising concentrations of carbon dioxide would lead to global warming in 1896. According to his calculations a doubling of carbon dioxide (CO_2) in the atmosphere would result in an increase of 5° Celsius in global average surface temperatures (Arrhenius 1896). Arrhenius's forecast was based on the concept of a greenhouse effect, which was first advanced by Jean-Baptiste Fourier in 1827. Fourier argued that the sun's rays would enter the atmosphere, but not all of them would escape, thus warming the atmosphere. John Tyndall developed this idea by suggesting that particular atmospheric gases—water vapor and carbon dioxide—were responsible for the greenhouse effect. Arrhenius's contribution was to suggest that the strength of the greenhouse effect would increase. His forecast, however, was largely ignored until the second half of the twentieth century. The dominant view was that the climate was essentially constant except for short-term fluctuations.

Starting in the 1950s, scientists, nongovernmental organizations (NGOs), and eventually governments began to pay greater attention to the possibility of climate change. Scientific advances were important. Roger Revelle and Hans Suess of the Scripps Institute of Oceanography developed doubts about the ability of the oceans to absorb the amount of carbon dioxide that was being emitted (Revelle and Suess 1957). The belief that the oceans could absorb all of the carbon dioxide was a principal factor shaping the view that the climate was constant. The increasing availability of data was also important. In 1957 a station to measure atmospheric carbon dioxide was established at the Mauna Loa observatory in Hawaii. By the 1960s this station was reporting a steady increase in carbon dioxide concentrations in the atmosphere. In 1963 the US-based Conservation Foundation sponsored a meeting on climate issues. The report forecast that a doubling of carbon dioxide in the atmosphere would produce a 3.8 °C temperature increase. In 1964–5,

Roger Revelle chaired the Environmental Pollution Panel of the US President's Science Advisory Committee. The panel concluded that projected increases in carbon dioxide concentrations in the atmosphere could produce changes in the climate (USA/PSAC 1965).

Deepening concern with climate change stimulated research. Fourier, Tyndall, and Arrhenius had provided the broad framework for this research. Models could be built using the framework. Testing the models would require collecting and assembling data. Lewis Frye Richardson, a British meteorologist, developed the first numerical weather prediction system in the early years of the twentieth century (Richardson 1922). Although at the time the calculations required were too complex for his system to have any practical use, when computers were developed his system could be applied. It provided the basis for the development of General Circulation Models (GCMs) which simulate the global circulation of the atmosphere. GCMs are basic instruments for weather and climate prediction. To study the climate, GCMs must be coupled with other models, particularly of ocean circulation.

The Mauna Loa observatory continued to provide data documenting an increase of CO_2 concentrations in the atmosphere. The World Meteorological Organization (WMO) established the World Weather Watch (WWW) in 1968. WWW promotes standardized observations and the exchange of data. In 1967 WMO and the International Council of Scientific Unions (ICSU) launched the Global Atmospheric Research Program (GARP). GARP was an international research program that focused on the transient behavior of the atmosphere and the factors that determine statistical properties of the general circulation of the atmosphere. GARP culminated in a 12 months global experiment that began on 1 December 1978, in which the earth's atmosphere and weather were observed and measured.

As scientific knowledge of the climate system increased, scientists issued firmer warnings about the possibility and dangers of climate change. In 1977 a US National Academy of Sciences panel that Roger Revelle chaired concluded that if the use of fossil fuels continued to increase at present rates, average global surface temperature could rise by about 6 °C over the coming 200 years, with potentially ominous consequences for agriculture and fishing (USA/NAS 1977). Public and governmental concern mounted during the 1970s. The possibility of climate change and the effects of this change were discussed at a series of UN-sponsored large-scale conferences on the human environment (1972), food (1974), water (1977), and desertification (1977).

WMO initiated a program on the climate in 1974 and, together with the United Nations Environment Program (UNEP) and the International Council of Scientific Unions, convened the First World Climate Conference in Geneva, Switzerland in February 1979.

The First World Climate Conference brought together experts who focused on the scientific aspects of climate change. Later in 1979, on the basis of the conference's recommendation, WMO established the World Climate Programme (WCP). The WCP consists of the World Climate Research Program (which succeeded GARP), the World Climate Data and Monitoring Program, the World Climate Applications and Services Program, and the World Climate Impact Assessment and Response Strategies Program. The WCP fosters international research, coordinates data and monitoring activity, and facilitates access to information.

Stimulated by a sequence of abnormally hot years, concern about climate change grew stronger during the 1980s. Pressure grew for the adoption of international policies to mitigate climate change. WMO and UNEP sponsored a workshop of climate scientists on Developing Policies for Responding to Climatic Change' in Villach, Austria and Bellagio, Italy in the fall of 1987. In their report on the workshop the scientists concluded that as a consequence of the emission of greenhouse gases (GHG) average global surface temperatures would increase at a rate of 0.3 °C per decade. There would also be changes in precipitation and soil moisture and sea level rise. They called for a treaty to reduce GHG emissions (WMO 1987). In June 1988, the government of Canada organized an expert conference in Toronto on 'The Changing Atmosphere: Implications for Global Security.' The conference called for a reduction in deforestation and a 20 percent cut back in CO_2 emissions from 1988 levels by 2005 with the eventual aim of a 50 percent cut back (WMO et al. 1988). Representatives in many national legislative bodies and other governmental officials called for action.

The Toronto conference brought out sharp differences between the USA and many other countries. These differences have surfaced regularly. Because the USA had the largest greenhouse gas emissions, and because of its place in the global economy and the strength of its scientific establishment, these differences have had a profound impact on the negotiations about the climate change regime.

In 1978 the National Climate Program Act (PL 95-367) established the United States National Climate Program Office in the National Oceanic and Atmospheric Administration which coordinated research efforts on climate change throughout the federal government and US involvement in international programs. US national research efforts were substantial and the USA played an important role in international research efforts. The USA, however, was concerned about the costs of cutting GHG emissions (Brenton 1994, pp. 167–9, Rowlands 1995, pp. 74–6) and sought to organize a mechanism that would have broad legitimacy for obtaining objective scientific advice. The USA was an important leader in the decision in 1988 by the World Meteorological Organi-

zation and the United Nations Environment Program to create the Intergovernmental Panel on Climate Change (IPCC).

IPCC is open to all members of WMO and UNEP. Its mandate is to assess scientific, technical, and socioeconomic information relevant to understanding the risk of human-induced climate change. It has three working groups and a task force. Working Group I assesses the scientific aspects of the climate system and climate change. Working Group II addresses the vulnerability of socioeconomic systems to climate change and options for adapting to it. Working Group III assesses options for mitigating climate change. The Task Force on National Greenhouse Inventories oversees the National Greenhouse Gas Inventories Program. The IPPC does not carry out research. It bases its assessments mainly on published and peer reviewed scientific literature. Governments appoint members of IPCC.

The Intergovernmental Panel on Climate Change issued its first scientific assessment in 1990 (Houghton et al. 1990). The Second World Climate Conference was held later that year. The IPCC report and the Second World Climate Conference laid the scientific foundation for negotiations toward a treaty on climate change. The IPCC stated in its report that it was confident of the existence of a natural greenhouse effect and that emissions resulting from human activities were substantially increasing the atmospheric concentrations of greenhouse gases. It specifically mentioned carbon dioxide, methane, chlorofluorocarbons, and nitrous oxide. Carbon dioxide, chlorofluorocarbons, and nitrous oxide are removed from the atmosphere only slowly. Their sources and sinks in the atmosphere, biosphere, and oceans determine their atmospheric lifetimes, which can last from decades to centuries. The IPCC concluded that global mean surface air temperature had increased by 0.3 °C to 0.6 °C over the past 100 years and the size of this increase was consistent with the predictions of climate models.

Greenhouse gas emissions are essentially a product of the number of people times the level of development. The energy intensity of development and the carbon intensity of energy use modify the effects of the level of development. Under IPCC's business-as-usual scenario, greenhouse gas emissions would increase following historically based trajectories. The IPCC predicted that the consequence of the increased concentration of long-lived gases in the atmosphere would be an increase in the global mean surface temperature of about 0.3° Celsius per decade. This would result in an increase of about 1 °C by 2025.

The IPCC report and the Second World Climate Conference, where the report was discussed and its conclusions reaffirmed, provoked concern and also made it obvious how complicated dealing with climate change would be. Governments responded with what in the history of international diplomacy must be regarded as alacrity. The first session of the Intergovernmental Negotiating Committee for a Framework Convention on Climate Change was held in February 1991.

The goal was to have a treaty ready for signature at the United Nations Conference on Environment and Development, which was held in Rio de Janeiro in June 1992. The Rio Conference was an immense gathering (Brenton 1994, pp. 223–35). Representatives of 178 governments attended including 117 heads of state or government. More than 1,400 NGOs were represented and there were more than 35,000 accredited representatives. The deadline set by the date of the Rio Conference and the publicity associated with the conference put considerable pressure on governments.

Despite this pressure, the USA insisted that it would not sign a treaty that contained binding emissions limitations. Many NGOs and several governments wanted the treaty to include emission limitations. The US administration led by President George H. W. Bush did not believe that at that time the USA could fulfill a commitment to limit emissions, and it doubted the capacity of other countries to do so. Eventually the US position was accepted (Soroos 1997, pp.191–200), and in June 1992 154 states and the European Union (EU)—in legal terms the European Economic Community—signed the United Nations Framework Convention on Climate Change (UNFCCC). The treaty came into effect in March 1994 after 50 states had become parties. As of mid-2000, there were 184 parties to the convention.

2. The United Nations Framework Convention on Climate Change

The UNFCCC is one of the most far-reaching treaties ever negotiated. Since greenhouse gas emissions are the result of so many aspects of modern life, becoming a party to the treaty commits states to subjecting almost all aspects of their economic activities to some form of international scrutiny and supervision. The legal instruments that will be negotiated under the UNFCCC will have profound impacts on national economies.

The objective of the treaty is '... stabilization of greenhouse gas concentrations in the atmosphere at a level that would prevent dangerous anthropogenic interference with the climate system' (Article 2). Greenhouse gases are defined as 'gaseous constituents of the atmosphere, both natural and anthropogenic, that absorb and re-emit infrared radiation.' In its first scientific assessment IPCC concluded that during the decade from 1980 to 1990 carbon dioxide had contributed 55 percent of the greenhouse gases to the change in radiative forcing, chlorofluorocarbons 24 percent, methane 15 percent, and nitrous oxide, 6 percent.

Carbon dioxide emissions result primarily from fossil fuel combustion and land use and land use changes. Agriculture contributes a large share of methane and nitrous oxide emissions.

The production and use of chlorofluorocarbons were controlled under the 1985 Vienna Convention for the Protection of the Ozone Layer and the 1987 Montreal Protocol on Substances that deplete the Ozone Layer and subsequent amendments. These accords phase out the production and use of chlorofluorocarbons.

The first principle of the UNFCCC is that 'The Parties should protect the climate system for the benefit of present and future generations of humankind, on the basis of equity and in accordance with their common but differentiated responsibilities and respective capabilities' (Article 3). Other principles include exhorting the parties to give special consideration for developing countries, take 'precautionary measures,' promote sustainable development, and promote a 'supportive and open international economic system.'

All parties to the treaty undertake commitments (Article 4) to meet the treaty's objective. Though these commitments are stated in general terms in the framework convention, they are to be made more specific through additional legal instruments negotiated later. The UNFCCC defines various categories of countries and establishes differential responsibilities for them. There are three categories of parties to the treaty: developed countries, developed countries with special financial responsibilities, and developing countries.

Developed countries, or Annex I countries, are exhorted to take 'immediate action' to limit greenhouse gas emissions. Annex I includes 38 states, of which 13 were Eastern Europe states in transition to democracy and market economies, and the European Union (in formal legal terms the European Community). Article 4, paragraph 2, explicitly requires Annex I countries 'to adopt national policies and take corresponding measures on the mitigation of climate change' by limiting their anthropogenic emissions of greenhouse gases. The Article further requires them to report on the steps that they take with the aim of 'returning individually or jointly to their 1990 levels these anthropogenic emissions of carbon dioxide and other greenhouse gases not controlled by the Montreal Protocol.'

The countries that are listed in Annex II of the UNFCCC are required 'to provide new and additional financial resources to meet the full agreed costs incurred by developing country Parties in complying with their obligations' to produce national inventories of their 'emissions by sources and removals by sinks of all greenhouse gases not controlled by the Montreal Protocol.' They also have responsibilities for providing financial assistance to the developing countries for other agreed tasks (Article 4, paragraph 3). Annex

II includes Annex I countries except those in transition to democracy and market economies.

The requirements for developing countries are more modest. They are specifically required to submit their inventories to the UNFCCC secretariat. Beyond that they are exhorted to adopt policies and take measures to mitigate climate change and adapt to it.

3. The Kyoto Protocol

The process of negotiating legal instruments under the UNFCCC was launched at the first Conference of the Parties (COP-1) in Berlin in 1995. The IPCC published its second assessment report in 1996 (Houghton et al. 1996, Watson et al. 1996, Bruce et al. 1996). The report confirmed that climate change was occurring because of human actions and analyzed the impacts of climate change and the measures that could be taken to adapt to and mitigate climate change. The report provided a strong stimulus for further action.

An initial agreement to establish legally binding quantified emissions limitations and reduction commitments was reached at COP-3 in Kyoto, Japan on 10 December 1997. Article 3, paragraph 1 of the Kyoto Protocol would require Annex I countries collectively to reduce their overall greenhouse gas emissions 'by at least five percent below their 1990 levels in the commitment period 2008 to 2012.' Specifically the Kyoto Protocol required the USA to reduce its greenhouse gas emissions to 93 percent of the 1990 levels, Japan to 94 percent, and the European Economic Community to 92 percent. Norway, on the other hand, is allowed to increase its emissions to 101 percent of the 1990 level, Australia to 108 percent, and Iceland to 110 percent. The European Community's obligation applied to the Community as a whole. Under arrangements made within the EU some countries, especially Germany and the UK, which had the largest emissions, agreed to reduce their emissions more than 8 percent below the 1990 levels, which would allow others, such as Greece and Portugal, to increase their emissions above the 1990 levels. Greece would be allowed to increase its emissions by 25 percent and Portugal by 27 percent.

The Kyoto Protocol covered six greenhouse gases that were not covered by the Montreal Protocol: carbon dioxide, methane, nitrous oxide, hydrofluorocarbons, perfluorcarbons, and sulphur hexaflouride. The limitations apply to 'net changes in greenhouse gas emissions by sources and removals by sinks resulting from direct human-induced land-use changes and forestry activities, limited to afforestation, reforestation and deforestation since 1990, measured as verifiable changes in carbon stocks in each commitment period' (Article 3, paragraph 3). The emissions from the other five greenhouse gases that were covered in the protocol were measured in terms of their carbon

dioxide equivalents calculated in terms of global warming potential. The methodologies for measuring emissions and calculating global warming potential were those developed by the IPCC.

The Kyoto Protocol included three flexible mechanisms. One was emission trading. Annex I countries would be able to trade emission allowances. For instance, if a party had difficulty meeting its required limitations, it would be able to purchase emission allowances from another party that had emissions that were lower than its limitation. Joint Implementation among Annex I countries was another flexible mechanism. If a party engaged in a project to increase the sinks on another party's territory through reforestation the two parties could share the credit for the increased sinks. The third flexible mechanism was the Clean Development Mechanism. Annex I countries could engage in projects in non-Annex I countries that reduced prospective emissions and share the credit for this. The US government and many economists argued that these flexible mechanisms would make it possible to limit emissions at the least possible cost. The US administration of President William J. Clinton argued that the USA could only meet its commitment in the Kyoto Protocol if it were allowed to use flexible mechanisms.

How well these flexible mechanisms would work was unknown. Emission trading mechanisms were included in US domestic legislation and the 1979 Convention on Long Range Transboundary Air Pollution. Various pilot projects have been undertaken. Whatever the fate of the Kyoto Protocol, flexible mechanisms in some form will likely be part of the climate change regime. Flexible mechanisms will put heavy demands on the capacity of UNFCCC organs and the parties to the convention.

The Kyoto Protocol did not include requirements that specify policies and measures that parties must adopt, although it could have under the terms of the UNFCCC. It did not require that countries impose a carbon tax or ensure that appliances or automobiles meet efficiency standards. Many European states argued that any effort to limit greenhouse gas emissions should require uniform policies and measures. Some US economists also made this argument. The US government preferred that international accords state obligations and that parties should be free to adopt whatever policies and measures they choose to meet their obligations. Policies and measures—whether they are uniform or country-specific—will inevitably be part of the climate change regime. They will also place heavy demands on the capacity of countries that are parties to the UNFCCC.

Of the Annex I countries in the late 1990s only Austria, Germany, Luxembourg, the UK, and the Eastern European countries in transition to democracy and market economies had emissions below 1990 levels (Grubb et al. 1999, p. 82). The UK's emissions fell because of its transition from coal to natural gas and Germany's because of the collapse of East German industries. Industries had also collapsed in the countries in transition.

As of January 2000 84 countries had signed the Kyoto Protocol and 22 had ratified it. None of the Annex 1 countries had ratified the Kyoto Protocol. Prior to COP III the US Senate adopted a resolution by a vote of 95 to 0 stating that the USA would not agree to a treaty limiting emissions unless limitations also applied to developing countries. After COP III adopted the Kyoto Protocol, Senators from both parties stated that the protocol was not ratifiable. Senators and representatives of industry and labor argued that unless developing countries were included in the emission limitation requirement, developing countries would have an economic advantage. Some argued that industry would move from developed to developing countries.

Without US ratification, it would be difficult for the Kyoto Protocol to come into effect. To come into effect 55 states, which together accounted for 55 percent of the 1990 carbon dioxide emissions of Annex I countries, must have become parties to the protocol (Article 25). US emissions accounted for more than a third of the 1990 totals for Annex I countries.

Several factors contributed to the differences between the USA and other countries and to the US reluctance to accept the Kyoto Protocol. Under the US legal system, individual citizens or NGOs can sue the government to force it to comply with an international treaty to which the USA is a party. The USA does not ratify treaties unless the government is confident that it can comply. Other states have different legal systems where suing the government is much more difficult. For other states becoming a party to a treaty is frequently a statement of intention to try to comply. The size and climate of the USA are factors in the US propensity to consume energy. More compact countries with milder climates have more modest energy requirements. Unlike many developed countries, the US population was growing in the late twentieth century and was projected to continue to grow, leading to increased demands for energy and other products that would increase greenhouse gas emissions. At least partly because the USA was a petroleum producer, the US public was addicted to inexpensive energy. Efforts to increase energy prices regularly produced political outcries.

If the Kyoto Protocol did not come into effect, a new agreement would have to be negotiated. If the protocol did enter into force, it would require that additional limitations should be negotiated for subsequent periods—that is, those after 2008–2012—and that these negotiations should begin no later than 2005 (Article 3, paragraph 9). Eventually a global bargain will have to be struck involving all parties, both developed and developing countries. The process of negotiating instruments to implement the UNFCCC will be long-lasting.

Bringing developing countries into the climate change regime will be essential but extraordinarily difficult to achieve. Developing countries accounted for slightly more than 30 percent of greenhouse gas emissions in 1990, and their emissions were growing rapidly. As of 2000 developing countries accounted for just fewer than 80 percent of the world's population. Future population growth was projected to occur primarily in developing countries. Developing country governments desire rapid economic growth. Population and economic growth will increase developing country greenhouse gas emissions. Developing countries will become the dominant source of greenhouse gas emissions in the twenty-first century.

Developing countries are also extremely vulnerable to climate change. The small island states could be submerged by sea-level rise. Sea-level rise could threaten coastal zones where developing country populations are often concentrated. Countries that are heavily dependent on agricultural production could suffer greatly from climate change. Petroleum-producing countries could see their incomes cut if petroleum consumption were to decrease.

Promoting economic growth is arguably one of the most effective steps developing countries could take to deal with climate change. The more developed it is, the more resources a country has to devote to limiting greenhouse gas emissions. Developed countries also can adapt more easily to climate change. Developing countries will never agree to limit their economic growth. To become effective the climate change regime will have to find ways to promote sustainable development.

4. Issues

The climate is a classic common good. Human action anywhere affects the climate and humans everywhere are affected by the climate. Mitigating climate change will require the combined efforts of governments and—in response to government policies—of individuals throughout the world. Article 4 of the United Nations Framework Convention on Climate Change requires that these efforts be based on equity. This acknowledges the common good character of the climate. Parties to the UNFCCC will only act if they feel that the burdens of dealing with climate change are borne equitably. The treaty embodies one concept of equity. The special requirements placed on Annex I and Annex II countries recognize their relative wealth and the fact that because of their historical lead in industrializing they have contributed more to current concentrations of greenhouse gases in the atmosphere. The resolution adopted by the US Senate reflects another concept of equity, the necessity of all states taking at least some action particularly in view of the growing share of greenhouse gases emitted by non-Annex I countries. These different concepts of equity will have to be reconciled for effective action to be taken.

Knowledge is a second issue. Decades of work have greatly improved the natural science of climate change. Climate change models have become more sophisticated and the amount of data has increased. There are roughly two dozen large-scale models that are used in this work. They produce somewhat different results, particularly with respect to forecasts of regional impacts, but the range of differences with respect to the global average mean surface temperature is not different from the range that has existed since the beginning of the twentieth century. Even though work on the economic and social dimensions of climate change started later substantial progress has been made. Sophisticated models have been developed to estimate future emissions of greenhouse gases and the costs of mitigation strategies (Nordhaus 1994, Watson et al. 1996, pp. 263–396).

Estimates produced by these models vary because they are sensitive to assumptions about appropriate model structure and demographic and economic growth and the availability of demand (energy efficiency) and supply-side (alternative sources of supply) energy options. Research has produced better understanding of the mechanisms that promote compliance with international accords. Despite this progress in the natural and social sciences much remained to be done, especially concerning the economic and social dimensions. Efforts to adapt to and mitigate climate change will require modifying human behavior. Understanding how to promote appropriate modifications in behavior is a crucial issue for research.

See also: Climate Change and Health; Climate Change, Economics of; Climate, History of; Climate Impacts; Tropospheric Ozone: Agricultural Implications; United Nations: Political Aspects

Bibliography

Arrhenius S 1896 On the influence of carbonic acid in the air upon the temperature on the ground. *Philosophical Magazine* **41**: 237–76
Brenton T 1994 *The Greening of Machiavelli: The Evolution of International Environmental Politics*. Earthscan, London
Bruce J P, Lee H, Haites E F (eds.) 1996 *Climate Change 1995: Economic and Social Dimensions of Climate Change: Contribution of Working Group III to the Second Assessment Report of the Intergovernmental Panel on Climate Change*. Cambridge University Press, Cambridge, UK
Grubb M, Vrolijk C, Black D 1999 *The Kyoto Protocol: A Guide and Assessment*. Royal Institute of International Affairs, London
Houghton J T, Jenkins G J, Ephraums J J 1990 *Climate Change: The IPPC Scientific Assessment, Report Prepared for IPCC by Working Group I*. Cambridge University Press, Cambridge, UK
Houghton J T, Meira Filho L G, Callander B A, Harris N, Kattenberg A, Maskell K 1996 *Climate Change 1995: The Science of Climate Change: Contribution of Working Group I to the Second Assessment Report of the Intergovernmental Panel on Climate Change*. Cambridge University Press, Cambridge, UK
Nordhaus W D 1994 *Managing the Global Commons: The Economics of Climate Change*. MIT Press, Cambridge, MA
Revelle R, Suess H E 1957 Carbon dioxide exchange between atmosphere and ocean and the question of an increase in atmospheric CO_2 during the past decade. *Tellus* **9**: 18–27
Richardson L F 1922 *Weather Prediction by Numerical Process*. Cambridge University Press, Cambridge, UK
Rowlands I H 1995 *The Politics of Global Atmospheric Change*. Manchester University Press, Manchester, UK
Soroos M 1997 *The Endangered Atmosphere: Preserving a Global Commons*. University of South Carolina, Columbia, SC
United States of America, National Academy of Sciences (USA/NAS) 1977 *Climate, Climatic Change, and Water Supply*. National Academy Press, Washington, DC
United States of America, President's Science Advisory Council (USA/PSAC) 1965 *Restoring the Quality of Our Environment: Report of the Environmental Pollution Panel*. The White House, Washington, DC
Watson R T, Zinyowera M C, Moss R H 1996 *Climate Change 1995: Impacts, Adaptations and Mitigation of Climate Change: Scientific-Technical Analyses: Contribution of Working Group II to the Second Assessment Report of the Intergovernmental Panel on Climate Change*. Cambridge University Press, Cambridge, UK
World Meteorological Organization (WMO) 1987 *Developing Policies for Responding to Climatic Change: A Summary of the Discussion and Recommendations on the Workshop held in Villach, 28 September–2 October 1987 and Bellagio, 9–13 November 1987*, (WMO/TD 225). WMO, Geneva
World Meteorological Organization (WMO), Environment Canada, United Nations Environment Program 1988 *The Changing Atmosphere: Implications for Global Security, Toronto Canada, 27–30 June 1988, Conference Proceedings*. WMO, Geneva

H. K. Jacobson

Clinical Assessment: Interview Methods

The single most common method of assessment in both clinical practice and research is an interview, whereby the clinician speaks directly to a person to obtain the clinical assessment (Widiger and Saylor 1998). Additional methods of assessment, such as self-report inventories, projective instruments, or laboratory tests, are often used to supplement or inform a clinical interview, but only under quite special circumstances would a clinician rely solely upon one of these other techniques, whereas clinicians and researchers will often rely solely upon a clinical interview.

1. Advantages of a Clinical Interview

Many of the advantages of a clinical interview are somewhat obvious, but worth noting for the record nevertheless (Groth-Marnat 1997). First, clinical interviews are substantially more flexible than alternative methods. Interviewers can alter the focus, depth, or even the style of an interview to be optimally responsive to the particular demands, interests, or needs of the respondent or the assessment. Response sets (intentional, habitual, or unconscious tendencies to provide false or misleading responses) can affect the validity of a clinical interview (Rogers 1995), but interviewers can themselves be sensitive and responsive to symptom exaggeration, distortion, or denial during the course of an interview. Interviewers may notice if a respondent is being excessively acquiescent or defensive, if the mood state of a respondent is contributing to excessive self-denigration, or if the responses are inconsistent across the interview. The interviewer can then alter immediately the format, style, or scoring of the interview to make adjustments for the response sets, can conduct follow-up queries to assess for the presence of problematic response sets, or even discuss a response set directly with the respondent in order to decrease its effects.

A disadvantage of other methods of clinical assessment is that they will routinely cover domains of functioning that will not be particularly relevant or necessary for an issue or patient at hand and yet, at the same time, fail to cover in adequate depth the domain of functioning of most interest or relevance to the patient and clinician. For example, most omnibus self-report inventories attempt to cover virtually all domains of psychopathology but must then provide an inadequate assessment for any one of them. An interviewer has the unique advantage of being able virtually to abandon a focus of inquiry during the course of an assessment to spend more time and effort on a particular line of investigation.

Finally, the clinician conducting the interview is usually the person who will ultimately provide the clinical report, and seeing or hearing for oneself is usually much more compelling than being told by something or someone else. The clinician is able to see and experience firsthand the person's behaviors, feelings, statements, and manner of relatedness. The presentation of the patient's psychopathology in his or her speech, affect, and behavior within the clinician's office can provide a powerfully vivid and compelling portrayal.

2. Limitations of Unstructured Clinical Interviews

Many of the benefits and advantages of a clinical interview, however, fail to be realized in routine clinical practice, as the freedom and authority provided by a clinical interview does not come without substantial responsibilities, costs, and limitations. The reliability and validity of a clinical interview depend substantially upon the conscientiousness, skills, and talents of the clinician. Seeing for oneself can be very compelling, but it can be equally illusory and deceiving. Many clinicians may place excessive faith, or at least have excessive confidence, in their own perceptions and judgments, despite the fact that studies have shown repeatedly that unstructured clinical assessments often obtain poor agreement across different interviewers (Dawes 1995, Garb 1998) (see *Clinical Psychology: Validity of Judgment; Clinical versus Actuarial Prediction*). Two clinicians relying upon their own skills, talents, and abilities will often provide different conclusions regarding the same patient. At least one of them will be wrong, but both will believe it is the other clinician. The instrument of the unstructured clinical interview is for the most part the clinician, and there are perhaps few clinicians who truly recognize or adequately appreciate their own limitations, deficits, and flaws.

Many studies have documented that unstructured clinical interviews tend to be unreliable and are highly susceptible to primacy effects, halo effects, false expectations, misleading assumptions, and confirmatory biases (Dawes 1994, Garb 1998, Widiger and Saylor 1998), and this research appears to have had only a marginal effect upon the beliefs or behavior of most individual practitioners (e.g., Westen 1997). The lack of an adequate impact of this research is perhaps due in part to the ability of persons to believe that the research is primarily relevant to persons other than themselves. An advantage of other methods of assessment is that the research indicating, for example, systematic errors within a laboratory instrument, will clearly be relevant to almost any administration of that instrument. Research indicating the systematic errors of a sample of clinicians might not be applicable to a clinician who did not actually participate in that particular study. Clinicians can then argue and believe that the decision-making research is not really applicable to them because they are in fact adequately sensitive and responsive to the issues, errors, biases, or concerns identified in this research.

A major source for the failure of unstructured clinical interviews to provide reliable or valid assessments is the failure to conduct systematic or comprehensive assessments. An innovation of the American Psychiatric Association's (APA) *Diagnostic and Statistical Manual of Mental Disorders* (*DSM-IV*; APA 1994) is the provision of relatively specific and explicit diagnostic criteria for each mental disorder (see *Mental and Behavioral Disorders, Diagnosis and Classification of*). Reliable and valid clinical diagnoses are now readily obtained as long as the interviewer does indeed comprehensively assess every diagnostic criterion in a systematic manner (Nathan and Langenbucher 1999). Many studies, however, have indicated that clinicians will often reach a conclusion after determining the presence of only a small subset of the diagnostic criteria set, and will fail to assess for the presence of additional symptomatology of other possible disorders (Garb 1998, Widiger and Saylor 1998). Zimmerman and Mattia (1999), for example, compared the clinical diagnoses provided for 500 patients who were assessed with unstructured clinical interviews with the diagnoses provided by a semistructured interview that systematically assessed for the presence of the diagnostic criteria for most of the commonly occurring Axis I mental disorders (i.e., mental disorders other than personality disorders or mental retardation). More than 90 percent of the patients receiving the unstructured clinical interview were provided with only one diagnosis, whereas more than a third of the patients assessed with the semistructured interview were discovered to have met the diagnostic criteria for at least three different mental disorders. Comorbidity among mental disorders has substantial significance and importance to clinical treatment, yet it appears to be grossly underrecognized in general clinical practice (Zimmerman and Mattia 1999).

A variety of studies have also indicated that clinicians relying upon unstructured clinical interviews routinely fail to assess for the presence of the specified diagnostic criteria (Widiger and Sanderson 1995). One of the more compelling demonstrations of this failure was provided by Morey and Ochua (1989). Morey and Ochua provided 291 clinicians with the 166 *DSM-III* (APA 1994) personality disorder diagnostic criteria and asked them to indicate which *DSM-III* personality disorder(s) were present in one of their patients and to indicate which of the 166 diagnostic criteria were present. Kappa for the agreement between their diagnoses and the diagnoses that would be given based upon the diagnostic criteria they indicated to be present was very poor, ranging from 0.11 (schizoid) to only 0.58 (borderline). In other words, their clinical diagnoses agreed poorly with their own assessments of the diagnostic criteria for each of the personality disorders. Comparable results have since been reported in many subsequent studies (Widiger and Saylor 1998).

Among the more consistently documented errors in clinical practice are gender and racial biases in the application of diagnostic criteria (Garb 1998). *DSM-IV* diagnostic criteria sets will contain a degree of gender and racial bias (Hartung and Widiger 1998). However, racial and gender biases that have been documented empirically have been due in large part to a failure of clinicians to adhere to the specified diagnostic criteria set for a respective mental disorder (Whaley 1997, Widiger 1998). When clinicians are compelled to follow closely the criteria set for a mood, psychotic, or personality disorder, gender and racial biases are significantly less likely to occur.

3. Advantages of Semistructured Clinical Interviews

Limitations of unstructured clinical interviews can be addressed in part through the administration of more structured interview schedules in which a set of specified questions must be administered, the interpretation and scoring of the responses to which are guided by an accompanying manual. These interview schedules can vary substantially in the extent to which the questions are open-ended, observations of the respondent are included, and the interviewer is allowed to conduct follow-up queries. A fully structured interview would be essentially equivalent to a verbally administered self-report inventory (Widiger and Saylor 1998). Most interview schedules, however, are more accurately described as being semistructured, as they will include subtle and indirect questioning, will require follow-up queries, and will include open-ended questions, the responses to which will require professional judgment and expertise for interpretation and scoring. The only difference between some semistructured interviews and a skilled clinician is that the inclusion of a semistructured interview documents explicitly the obtainment of a reliable, replicable, systematic, objective, and comprehensive assessment of all of the relevant symptomatology.

Semistructured interviews are the preferred method for obtaining clinical assessments in research, but are perhaps rarely used in general clinical practice. Clinicians perceive semistructured interviews as being constraining, impractical, or superficial (Westen 1997). Semistructured interviews are indeed constraining, as they are a means by which to ensure that the findings are reliable, replicable, systematic, comprehensive, and objective by constraining the clinician from failing to assess all of the necessary criteria in a minimally adequate manner (Segal 1997). Most semistructured interviews, however, allow and do in fact encourage clinicians to have a significant impact through the administration of follow-up queries and the reliance upon their professional judgment for the scoring of the responses.

One of the major impediments to the implementation of a semistructured interview in general clinical practice is the amount of time that is required for their complete administration. Researchers will often pay both interviewers and patients for two or three hours of interviewing; no such funding luxury is available in general clinical practice. However, the amount of time required for the administration of a semistructured interview can be reduced substantially by first administering a screening questionnaire to narrow the line of inquiry. Screening questionnaires with a high false positive rate (i.e., err in the direction of identifying too much rather than too little psychopathology) are also useful in alerting the clinician to domains of functioning that might have been otherwise neglected.

Many clinicians will also perceive some of the required questioning to be simplistic or superficial. However, it is important to appreciate that a substantial amount of research has informed the development of a particular line of questioning. Semistructured interviews can in fact be an excellent source for discovering new and effective methods of inquiry. Semistructured interviews, however, will not be as effective as an unstructured interview in establishing rapport. Most clients will appreciate the comprehensive and thorough nature of a semistructured interview, but if the establishment of rapport is a major clinical issue, then a lengthy semistructured interview will at times be problematic.

4. Recommendations for Future Research

A clinical and scientific limitation of many semistructured interviews is the absence of data normally obtained through the course of the development and validation of a psychometric instrument. For example, semistructured interview reliability data are often simply confined to an agreement with respect to the scoring of a previous or concurrent administration of the interview. The poor reliability obtained in general clinical practice is due to inconsistent, incomplete, or idiosyncratic interviewing. It is unclear if some of the semistructured interviews have actually resolved this problem given the absence of studies on the interrater (or test–retest) reliability of independent administrations of the interview (Rogers 1995, Segal 1997, Widiger and Saylor 1998).

There are a variety of different interview schedules to assess the same domains of psychopathology. An advantage of this diversity is the availability of different options to choose from. However, current research suggests that these different interview schedules are providing different findings and it is unclear if the failure to replicate findings across studies is due to idiosyncratic administration of interviews, differences in setting, or differences in the interview schedules. One suggestion has been to confine future research to just one interview schedule (Regier et al. 1998). This confinement would contribute to the obtainment of more uniform results, but at the cost of the failure to appreciate the extent to which the results in fact reflect unique aspects of a particular interview schedule. What is needed are studies comparing directly the concurrent and predictive validity of alternative interview schedules within the same patient sample.

Normative data are also lacking for many of the semistructured interviews. The test manuals that accompany the publication of a semistructured interview are often surprisingly weak in their coverage of reliability and validity data. Diagnoses obtained through the administration of a semistructured interview are used as the criterion by which the validity of other instruments is evaluated, but semistructured interview schedules may rely too heavily for their own derivation on simply face validity. In defense of the validity of semistructured interviews, the most compelling published research concerning the etiology, course, pathology, and treatment responsivity of various mental disorders has relied substantially on the administration of a semistructured interview. The results of this extensive research provide considerable support for the construct validity of the respective semistructured interviews that were used in these studies. In addition, detailed summaries of the reliability and validity of alternative interview schedules are provided in a number of published papers and texts (e.g., Rogers 1995, Segal 1997, Widiger and Sanderson 1995).

5. Conclusions

In sum, the many advantages of semistructured interviews clearly outweigh their limitations and disadvantages. Many are now being used in general clinical practice when the results of the clinical assessment might be subsequently questioned or reviewed (e.g., custody, disability, and forensic assessments). A highly talented clinician can provide a more valid assessment than a semistructured interview, but it is risky to assume that one is indeed that talented clinician. It would at least seem desirable for a talented and insightful clinician to be fully informed by a systematic and comprehensive assessment. Semistructured interviews are used routinely in general clinical research and perhaps will eventually be used routinely in general clinical practice. Individually administered intelligence tests are comparable to a fully structured clinical interview, particularly an assessment of verbal intelligence that involves a series of specified questions, the responses to which are scored according to a test manual. Very few clinicians would attempt to diagnose mental retardation in the absence of the administration of one of these structured interviews. Perhaps in the future no clinician will attempt to diagnose an anxiety, mood, psychotic, dissociative, personality, or other mental disorder without at least considering the results obtained by the administration of a respective semistructured interview.

See also: Clinical Psychology: Validity of Judgment; Clinical versus Actuarial Prediction; Minnesota Multiphasic Personality Inventory (MMPI)

Bibliography

American Psychiatric Association 1994 *Diagnostic and Statistical Manual of Mental Disorders*, 4th edn. American Psychiatric Association, Washington DC
Dawes R M 1994 *House of Cards: Psychology and Psychotherapy Built on Myth*. Free Press, New York
Garb H N 1998 *Studying the Clinician. Judgment Research and Psychological Assessment*. American Psychological Association, Washington, DC
Groth-Marnat G 1997 *Handbook of Psychological Assessment*, 3rd edn. Wiley, New York

Hartung C M, Widiger T A 1998 Gender differences in the diagnosis of mental disorders: Conclusions and controversies of *DSM-IV*. *Psychological Bulletin* **123**: 260–78

Morey L C, Ochua E S 1989 An investigation of adherence to diagnostic criteria: Clinical diagnosis of the *DSM-III* personality disorders. *Journal of Personality Disorders* **3**: 180–92

Nathan P, Langenbucher J W 1999 Psychopathology: Description and classification. *Annual Review of Psychology* **50**: 79–107

Regier D A, Kaelber C T, Rae D S, Farmer M E, Knauper B, Kessler R C, Norquist G S 1998 Limitations of diagnostic criteria and assessment instruments for mental disorders. Implications for research and policy. *Archives of General Psychiatry* **55**: 109–15

Rogers R 1995 *Diagnostic and Structured Interviewing. A Handbook for Psychologists.* Psychological Assessment Resources, Odessa, FL

Segal D L 1997 Structured interviewing and *DSM* classification. In: Turner S M, Hersen M (eds.) *Adult Psychopathology and Diagnosis.* Wiley, New York, pp. 24–57

Westen D 1997 Divergences between clinical and research methods for assessing personality disorders: Implications for research and the evolution of Axis II. *American Journal of Psychiatry* **154**: 895–903

Whaley A L 1997 Ethnicity/race, paranoia, and psychiatric diagnoses: Clinician bias versus sociocultural differences. *Journal of Psychopathology and Behavioral Assessment* **19**: 1–20

Widiger T A 1998 Sex biases in the diagnosis of personality disorders. *Journal of Personality Disorders* **12**: 95–118

Widiger T A, Sanderson C J 1995 Assessing personality disorders. In: Butcher J N (ed.) *Clinical Personality Assessment. Practical Approaches.* Oxford University Press, New York, pp. 380–94

Widiger T A, Saylor K I 1998 Personality assessment. In: Bellack A S, Hersen M (eds.) *Comprehensive Clinical Psychology.* Pergamon, New York, pp. 145–67

Zimmerman M, Mattia J I 1999 Psychiatric diagnosis in clinical practice: Is comorbidity being missed? *Comprehensive Psychiatry* **40**: 182–91

T. A. Widiger

Clinical Psychology: Animal Models

Over the years, considerable debate has surrounded the question of whether psychopathology and its treatment can be studied meaningfully in animals. One side has argued that psychopathological syndromes such as anxiety and depression are uniquely human and cannot be experienced in animals. Another side argues that there are both naturally occurring and experimentally induced psychopathological states in animals that closely parallel those seen in humans. This side also argues that there is so much to be learned from the systematic study in controlled settings of emotional or otherwise disturbed behavior in animals that this more than offsets any problems created by potential species differences. Proponents of this position bring animals into laboratory settings and study them under controlled experimental conditions to help us better understand various aspects of human disorders. The goal in these attempts is to develop an *animal model* of a disorder or its treatment.

1. Historical Background

Although the study of emotions such as fear and sadness in animals dates back at least to Darwin (1872), the experimental study in animals of the neurotic extremes of emotional states and other aspects of psychopathology did not begin until some years later (e.g., Pavlov 1927). Shortly after that time in the United States, where the methods of Pavlov and Thorndike to study learning were enthusiastically embraced, interest in Pavlov's so-called 'neuroses of the experiment' spread during the 1930s and 1940s. Indeed, a number of well-known laboratories were established to study what came to be called *experimental neurosis* (e.g., Liddell, Gantt, Masserman, and N. R. F. Maier). At the time, this work was reasonably influential, partly because other extant models of what causes psychopathology were generally very primitive. By contrast, ideas for studying human psychopathologies through developing animal models seemed remarkably advanced. Indeed, the success of various experimental manipulations in producing disordered behavior and emotions in several different species, was clearly influential in establishing the foundations of behavioral approaches to the etiology and treatment of anxious and depressive disorders.

Unfortunately, this early work on experimental neurosis was fairly unsystematic. Investigators explored the effects of experimental variants on traditional learning paradigms (often discovered accidentally) that seemed to produce disturbed behavior in their animals. However, the next steps were not taken. One would have been to manipulate systematically various aspects of the procedures to determine what the critical (causal) features were. Investigators also needed to demonstrate (but did not) compelling phenotypic (symptomatic) and/or functional similarities between the 'neurotic symptoms' seen in animals and human patients. Instead, somewhat superficial, and often anthropomorphic, assertions of similarity were made. As a consequence of these failures, the study of animal models for psychopathological disorders fell into relative obscurity for several decades (see Mineka and Kihlstrom 1978).

2. Contemporary Use of Animal Models

A resurgence of interest started about 1970, when a number of investigators began to make persuasive arguments that animal models of some disorders could be very useful if certain criteria are adhered to in developing the model. For example, Seligman (1975) and McKinney (1974) both argued that animal models can be useful if one attempts to document similarities and parallels in the symptoms, etiology, therapy, and prevention of the animal and human syndromes. Obviously, at the outset not all of the parallels will be possible to detail because little may be known about some of these factors (e.g., prevention) for either the animal or the human disorder. Nevertheless, herein lies one of the special advantages of developing an animal model. Initially some compelling similarities must be drawn between the human disorder and the animal model. Then, however, the animal model can be used to test hypotheses about other possible parallels (e.g., prevention) that often cannot easily be tested experimentally with humans. Some of the work developing such full-fledged animal models has been quite successful, as discussed below.

Alternatively, others have argued that requiring adherence to all these criteria may be unnecessarily restrictive, given that for most disorders no such complete models have yet been discovered. This is partly because of significant limitations on the range of human symptoms that can be modeled in animals—especially if expression of that symptom is mediated by higher cortical structures in the brain not shared by most species. There are, however, many very interesting and important 'mini-models' which help illuminate different aspects of the symptomatology, *or* etiology, *or* prevention, *or* treatment of these disorders. Mini-models are emotional, behavioral, cognitive, and/or physiological phenomena studied in animals (or humans) that may clarify some of the most prominent features of the origins or treatment of a disorder. The behaviors and emotional responses are manipulated experimentally through either behavioral or physiological experimental manipulations. Although any given mini-model may illuminate only a subset of prominent features of a disorder, in nature such factors would operate in interaction with other factors in the etiology or treatment of a human disorder.

3. Animal Models in Psychopharmacology and Behavioral Pharmacology

Nowhere has the use of animal models been more prominent than in the fields of psychopharmacology and behavioral pharmacology, where researchers develop new medications to treat mental disorders and try to understand how the medications work to ameliorate symptoms. Nearly all medications are initially tested on animals before being approved for use by humans—to determine both their effectiveness and their safety. However, before this can be done, researchers must first develop and validate an animal model of the human disorder (or often just a subset of symptoms of a disorder) before they can test their medications. For example, determining if a new medication serves as an *anxiolytic* (anxiety-reducing) medication, requires knowing how to produce strong symptoms of anxiety in animals (as well as knowing that the measure of anxiety is functionally if not phenotypically, related to human anxiety). The same, of course, applies to treatments of other disorders.

Staying with the anxiety example, at least 30 different animal models have been used to test the effectiveness of anxiolytic drugs. One of the most common uses a conflict/punishment procedure. Rats are first trained to press a bar to obtain food reinforcement on an occasional basis. Later they can still obtain food on some trials but now they also receive an unpleasant electric shock following the food. Not surprisingly, this punishment procedure puts hungry rats in a state of conflict: anxiety about punishment now conflicts with hunger. Typically, rates of responding for the food are diminished substantially unless an effective anxiolytic medication is given (e.g., diazepam from the benzodiazepine category). Having been validated as a model in numerous studies with medications known to reduce anxiety in humans, the model is then used to test potential new anxiolytic compounds.

Researchers must beware, however, that this method produces both false positives and false negatives. Sometimes a medication that seems to work in the animal model, is later shown not to work in humans. Alternatively, a medication that does not seem effective with animal models may nonetheless be effective in humans. In such cases further work is needed to determine the source of the discrepancy. To illustrate, a relatively new anxiolytic compound known as buspirone (not from the benzodiazepine category) did not initially seem effective using the conflict/punishment procedure in rats. However, buspirone operates through different physiological mechanisms, and has a different time course of action, than do traditional benzodiazepine compounds. Animal models incorporating this knowledge do show buspirone to be effective. Thus researchers must beware, when an established animal model does not demonstrate effectiveness of a novel compound, that the new compound should not be dismissed without further work. Such work is needed to avoid the risk of prematurely screening out potentially effective novel medications (e.g., Rodgers 1997).

Another use of pharmacological models involves testing theories of the physiological underpinnings of different disorders, rather than their treatment. Here researchers use various pharmacological agents to induce physiological and behavioral states in animals that resemble those seen in a human disorder. Caution is also needed here. Observing that a drug induces a state in animals resembling that in humans neither justifies the conclusion that the same system is normally involved in the human case, nor speaks to the issue of whether there may be a number of alternative routes to the human disorder (e.g., Weiss and Uhde 1990).

4. Animal Models of Anxiety and Anxiety Disorders

4.1 Specific and Social Phobias

Historically, research on animal models of anxiety—especially fears and phobias—began before models of other disorders. The role of classical conditioning (see *Classical Conditioning and Clinical Psychology*) in the etiology of specific phobias, first proposed by Watson and Rayner (1920) has been the subject of some controversy since about 1970. Some theorists ask how classical conditioning can play an important role both: (a) when some people recall no traumatic conditioning experiences; and (b) and when others who can recall traumatic experiences are not fearful/phobic. They have also wondered why some objects and situations are much more likely to become the objects of fears and phobias than others (e.g., phobias for snakes, spiders, and heights are far more common than for cars, guns, or knives, which may also be associated with trauma).

However, contemporary research with animal models illustrates that Pavlov's and Watson's core ideas about the role of classical conditioning were sound, but need to be expanded to incorporate the broader knowledge now available about the complexities of conditioning (see also *Classical Conditioning and Clinical Psychology*). For example, a primate model showed that conditioning sometimes occurs observationally or vicariously—that is, watching someone behave fearfully with, for example, a snake, may be sufficient to induce a fear of snakes in the observer (without any direct trauma occurring). Moreover, the role of conditioning (vicarious or direct) must be considered in light of various vulnerability and invulnerability factors that influence the outcome of a traumatic conditioning experience (cf. Mineka and Zinbarg 1996). For example, animal research by Pavlov and others laid the foundation for showing how individual differences in personality/temperament (such as levels of trait anxiety) affect conditioning and the likelihood of acquiring fears and phobias. Animal work also illustrates a wide range of experiential differences across individuals that strongly affect the outcome of direct or indirect conditioning experiences (and therefore why many *without* phobias will have such histories that involved putative conditioning events). For example, having extensive previous neutral or positive experiences with a potentially phobic object (e.g., a dog) can prevent the acquisition of dog phobia if the individual is later bitten by a dog.

Moreover, a primate model showed that being reared with a strong sense of mastery and control over one's environment makes one less susceptible to the effects of the stressors that later may be involved in conditioning incidents.

Finally, there are evolutionarily based predispositions to acquire fears and phobias of certain objects or situations (e.g., snakes, water) that once posed a threat to our early ancestors more readily than other objects and situations not present in our early evolutionary history (e.g., guns, knives). Thus animal models have shown us that personality, experiential, and evolutionary factors may serve as diatheses or vulnerability factors for the development of phobias in certain individuals, given appropriate experiential input (cf., Mineka and Zinbarg 1996).

In social phobias, people have strong and persistent fears of various types of social interaction where they fear they may be evaluated and judged unfavorably. Again, traumatic conditioning experiences (direct or vicarious) are thought to play an important role, but with the same caveat as for specific phobias. That is, animal models demonstrate that personality, experiential, and evolutionary variables determine a person's level of vulnerability/invulnerability to developing social phobias. Considerable knowledge in this area stems from animal models of social anxiety (such as occur following defeats in physical fighting, when the animal typically becomes afraid of all dominant conspecifics rather than simply the one involved in the defeat) (cf. Mineka and Zinbarg 1996).

4.2 Panic Disorder with Agoraphobia

Individuals with panic disorder have recurrent unexpected panic attacks, usually associated with persistent anxiety about having another attack (anticipatory anxiety). Many also develop some degree of agoraphobic avoidance, learning to avoid situations in which they fear panicking. A full-fledged animal model of panic disorder remains elusive, although some pharmacological agents that provoke panic attacks in humans with the disorder, do seem to produce a panic-like state in some primates. Nevertheless, animal mini-models of panic and anxiety together have proved important in the development of a new theory of the origins of panic disorder that is largely based on contemporary principles of learning studied in animals (Bouton et al. 2001). The essence of this complex theory is that the occurrence of panic attacks sets the stage for the conditioning of anxiety to both internal and external cues that preceded a panic attack, thus explaining the development of both anticipatory anxiety and anxiety leading to agoraphobic avoidance. In addition, internal cues associated with the beginning of an attack can become conditioned to elicit panic attacks themselves. For example, a few heart palpitations that often occur early during an attack could come to serve as conditional stimuli that trigger full-blown panic attacks (see *Classical Conditioning and Clinical Psychology*).

4.3 Post-traumatic Stress Disorder (PTSD)

This disorder develops in some individuals following exposure to a traumatic event in which the person experienced or witnessed events involving actual or threatened death to themselves or others. Symptoms include persistent re-experiencing of the event (e.g., through nightmares and flashbacks), persistent avoidance of stimuli associated with the trauma, and arousal symptoms such as difficulty concentrating and exaggerated startle responses. Recently, animal models of PTSD have been the focus of much research, providing useful insights into the nature of this disorder as well as its etiology and treatment. Animal models involve exposure to unpredictable and/or uncontrollable stress which initiates the emotional, behavioral, and physiological symptoms resembling those seen in human PTSD. The intense physical stressors used in animal studies resemble those in some forms of human traumatization associated with PTSD, including torture, abuse, and assault. This has in turn drawn attention to the role that perceptions of uncontrollability/unpredictablity play in the development of human PTSD symptoms and has led to studies testing these ideas.

This animal model has also shown the powerful role that various vulnerability and invulnerability factors play in determining who is more or less likely to develop PTSD, given exposure to the same trauma. For example, the animal model has revealed that prior exposure to uncontrollable stressors prior to the relevant trauma sensitizes the animal (or human), making it *more* likely to develop PTSD-like symptoms than animals without prior exposure to the uncontrollable stressors. Conversely, prior exposure to controllable stressors before the relevant trauma leads to an immunization effect, making it *less* likely the animal will develop PTSD-like symptoms. These hypotheses are beginning to be corroborated in human research. Finally, the idea that perceptions of uncontrollability and unpredictability mediate many aspects of PTSD has led to the formulation of hypotheses about the importance of re-instilling a sense of control and predictability as part of treatment. Such hypotheses are currently being tested (see Mineka and Zinbarg 1996).

5. Animal Models of Depression

Clinically significant depression is a surprisingly common condition. There are emotional, motivational, cognitive and somatic symptoms. Some of these can be modeled better in animals than others (the cognitive ones are especially difficult). Since the 1960s, various animal models of depression have produced useful insights into human depression, ranging from new ideas concerning etiology, prevention, and treatment. The models have differed in several ways, perhaps most notably in the methods used for causing 'depression' in the animals.

Some of the earliest and most striking work with primates used a social separation paradigm. Following on earlier work demonstrating that human infants undergoing prolonged separations from their mothers showed a biphasic response to the separation, Harlow and colleagues in the 1960s began to study this phenomenon in infant rhesus monkeys separated from their mothers. Both the monkey and human infants typically go through an initial state of intense agitation and distress (the protest phase—often seen as a prototype of anxiety), followed several days later (if the separation persists) by a phase of despair/depression, characterized by social withdrawal and rejection. Although some have argued this is at best a model of infant depression, others have argued that infant depression is in fact a prototype for adult human depression, with most of the prominent symptoms being functionally quite similar (except the cognitive ones).

By studying social separation in monkeys one can manipulate experimentally numerous variables, both before and during the separation, to test hypotheses about factors promoting minimal versus exaggerated responses to separation—something that obviously cannot be done in human infants. Research using animal models made it clear, for example, that having a sibling or alternate caregiver present during the separation from mother can attenuate (but usually not eliminate) the response to separation. But similar research with different species of monkeys, in which separated infants automatically get adopted by 'aunts,' also showed that reducing behavioral signs of distress is not tantamount to reducing physiological signs of distress and arousal which can remain high (e.g., Coe et al. 1985). Another line of primate work showed the importance of preseparation experiences in determining the outcome of any given separation. For example, infant monkeys of one species (bonnet macaques) whose mothers are relatively permissive, allowing the infants considerable freedom to interact with other adults, cope reasonably well with separations. By contrast, infants of another species (pigtail macaques) whose mothers are quite possessive and restrictive of their infant's freedom, do not cope as well with separations (e.g., Kaufman 1973). Observational follow-up work with human infants has often corroborated the hypotheses developed based on experimental animal models which are better able to pinpoint causal factors (see Mineka and Zinbarg 1991).

Another influential animal model of depression derives from the learned helplessness phenomenon and theory (e.g., Seligman 1975). In the late 1960s, Seligman and his colleagues Maier and Overmier noted that laboratory dogs initially exposed to uncontrollable shocks later showed major deficits in learning to control shock in different situations; indeed, they mostly seemed to accept the shock passively rather than trying to escape it. Yet animals first exposed to equal amounts of controllable shock showed no such deficits. Learned helplessness theory proposed that exposure to uncontrollable events leads one to learn that responses are ineffective in bringing relief, i.e., one is helpless to control important outcomes. The expectation of helplessness leads to: (a) cognitive deficits (difficulty learning to control shock), (b) motivational deficits (reduced incentive to try responding in other situations because of a belief that responses will be ineffective); (c) emotional changes (e.g., feelings of sadness, depression, and anxiety); and (d) physiological changes that occur with uncontrollable but not controllable stress. Seligman (1975) later proposed that the primary symptoms of depression resembled these primary changes seen with learned helplessness quite strongly.

Seligman also proposed etiological similarities. A large percentage of humans experiencing clinical depression have had one or more significant life stressors in the recent past (such as a major loss or unemployment, etc.). His argument was that all such precipitants could be seen as inducing a sense of lack or loss of control over important aspects of one's environment. Thus perceptions of helplessness may be the proximal cause of such cases of depression. Finally, Seligman also developed the corollary hypothesis that re-instilling a sense of control may be a core ingredient in the most effective treatments for depression (see Peterson et al. 1993).

This animal model of depression led to an enormous amount of animal and human research, much of it continuing today. Interestingly, although originally developed as a model of depression, its relevance has expanded to include a role in theories of several anxiety disorders (most notably PTSD, see above). For example, the initial emotional state during and following uncontrollable stress is one of intense and diffuse anxiety, which may lapse later into a depressive state. This idea is highly consistent with neurochemical results, indicating a shift from an intense aroused anxious state to a later depressed state, sometimes called conservation-withdrawal (e.g., Woodson et al. 1998). Interestingly, as noted above, anxious symptoms also precede depressive symptoms during primate and human infant separations, as well as following major losses in adults (Bowlby 1980). In addition, far more people who suffer depression at some point in their lives have suffered from an anxiety disorder first than the reverse (cf. Maser and Cloninger 1990). Thus both animal models of depression discussed here illustrate important features of the sequential relationship between anxious and depressed symptoms that also occurs in humans.

Other animal models of depression have also provided somewhat different but also partially overlapping information about both the symptom picture, and etiological factors in depression. The learned helplessness model has also generated hypotheses about effective treatment and prevention. Pharmaceutical companies make ample use of the most practical animal models to test their antidepressant compounds. Although recent etiological theories of human depression have generally now come to incorporate features that cannot be modeled in animals (such as feelings of hopelessness about the future), many useful insights from the original models remain generally intact.

6. Other Animal Models

Animal models of numerous other disorders have also been studied, including psychopathy, schizophrenia, and addictions. For example, regarding psychopathy, Newman (1997) and his colleagues used the well-known animal syndrome that stems from dysfunction in septo-hippocampal areas of the brain to model various features of psychopathic behavior—most notably the failure to inhibit inappropriate behaviors and inability to delay gratification. Fowles and Missel (1994) also summarized an important series of findings using animal and human mini-models, indicating the centrality of deficits in passive avoidance learning (learning what not to do to avoid punishment) to many important features of psychopathy. Both lines of work have led to new insights on psychopathy.

In schizophrenia, one early example of the use of animal models came when researchers first attempted to discovered how traditional antipsychotic medications work to reduce schizophrenic symptoms in humans. Animal research helped to show the important role that the neurotransmitter dopamine plays in the effects of these medications, and also helped lead to the development of the dopamine hypothesis of schizophrenia (including its etiology). This very influential theory, now known to be overly simplistic, was developed and tested in good part with animal mini-models.

Finally, the use of animal models to study of addictions has proved very important for understanding how addictive substances induce brain and behavioral changes. Using alcohol as an example, initially this work necessitated developing methods through which animals became addicted to alcohol (or other drug of interest). Subsequently, animal research with alcohol has revealed the numerous different neurotransmitter pathways in the brain with which alcohol interacts, leading to numerous alterations in brain function and behavior. Animal research has also facilitated understanding of brain mechanisms involved in maintaining the motivation and desire to drink. In addition, animal research focusing on environmental determinants of alcohol use, such as availability of alternative reinforcers, stress, and ease of access, etc., has provided important information. Some of this work has also focussed on genetic determinants of alcohol preference and alcohol use, and on how genetic factors interact with environmental factors (National Institute on Alcohol Abuse and Alcoholism 1997).

7. Conclusions

As indicated by this necessarily selective review of historical and contemporary research on animal models, such research has made important contributions to our understanding of various forms of human psychopathology and its treatment (see also *Classical Conditioning and Clinical Psychology*). Some of this research has attempted to develop full-fledged models by uncovering parallels between symptoms, etiology, treatment, and prevention in the animal model and the human disorder (e.g., the learned helplessness model of depression). However, an even greater amount of work exemplifies the mini-model approach in which only a subset of cardinal features of a human disorder are studied. An important advantage of studying animal models is that through experimental manipulation one can better determine what the critical causal features are than is generally possible in human research. With this background of success, further research with animal models certainly will continue to provide important new insights and information about many areas of human psychopathology and its treatment.

See also: Animal Rights in Research and Research Application; Anxiety and Anxiety Disorders; Anxiety Disorder in Children; Childhood Depression; Depression; Depression, Clinical Psychology of; Genes and Behavior: Animal Models; Panic Disorder; Pavlov, Ivan Petrovich (1849–1936); Spatial Memory Loss of Normal Aging: Animal Models and Neural Mechanisms

Bibliography

Bouton M, Mineka S, Barlow D H 2001 A modern learning theory perspective on the etiology of panic disorder. *Psychology Review*, **108**: 4–32

Bowlby J 1980 *Attachment and Loss, III: Loss, Sadness and Depression*. Basic Books, New York

Coe C, Wiener S, Rosenberg L, Levine S 1985 Endocrine and immune responses to separation and maternal loss in nonhuman primates. In: Reite M, Field T (eds.) *The Psychobiology of Attachment and Separation*. Academic Press, New York

Darwin C R 1872 *Expression of Emotion in Man and Animals*. John Murray, London

Fowles D C, Missel K A 1994 Electrodermal hyporeactivity, motivation, and psychopathy: Theoretical issues. In: Fowles D C, Sutker P, Goodman S H (eds.) *Progress in Experimental Personality and Psychopathology Research*. Springer, New York

Kaufman I C 1973 Mother–infant separation in monkeys: An experimental model. In: Scott J P, Senay B (eds.) *Separation and Depression: Clinical and Research Aspects*. AAAS, Washington, DC, pp. 33–52

Maser J, Cloninger C (eds.) 1990 *Comorbidity in Anxiety and Mood Disorders*. American Psychiatric Press, Washington, DC

McKinney W T 1974 Animal models in psychiatry. *Perspectives in Biology and Medicine* **17**: 529–41

Mineka S, Kihlstrom J F 1978 Unpredictable and uncontrollable aversive events. *Journal of Abnormal Psychology* **87**: 256–71

Mineka S, Zinbarg R 1991 Animal models of psychopathology. In: Walker C E (ed.) *Clinical Psychology: Historical and Research Foundations*. Plenum Press, New York, pp. 51–86

Mineka S, Zinbarg R 1996 Conditioning and ethological models of anxiety disorders: Stress-in-dynamic-context anxiety models. In: Hope D (ed.) *Perspectives on Anxiety, Panic, and Fear*. 43rd Annual Nebraska Symposium on Motivation. University of Nebraska Press, Lincoln, NE, pp. 135–211

Newman J P 1997 Conceptual models of the nervous system: Implications for antisocial behavior. In: Stoff D M, Breiling J, Maser J D (eds.) *Handbook of Antisocial Behavior*. Wiley, New York, pp. 324–35

National Institute on Alcohol Abuse and Alcoholism (NIAAA) 1997 Ninth special report to the US Congress on *Alcohol and Health*. NIH Publication, Washington No. 97–4017

Pavlov I P 1927 *Conditioned Reflexes*. Oxford University Press, London

Peterson C, Maier S F, Seligman M E P 1993 *Learned Helplessness: A Theory for the Age of Personal Control*. Oxford University Press, New York

Rodgers R J 1997 Animal models of 'anxiety': Where next? *Behavioral Pharmacology* **8**: 477–96

Seligman M E P 1975 *Helplessness: On Depression, Development, and Death*. Freeman, San Francisco

Watson J B, Rayner R 1920 Conditioned emotional reactions. *Journal of Experimental Psychology* **3**: 1–14

Weiss S R, Uhde T W 1990 Animal models of anxiety. In: Ballenger J (ed.) *Neurobiology of Panic Disorder*. Wiley-Liss, New York pp. 3–27

Woodson J C, Minor T R, Job R F S 1998 Inhibition of adenosine deaminase by erythro-9-(2-hydroxy-3-nonyl) adenine (EHNA) mimics the effect of inescapable shock on escape learning in rats. *Behavioral Neuroscience* **112**: 399–409

S. Mineka

Clinical Psychology in Europe, History of

1. Introduction

Europe is characterized by its social, linguistic, and cultural diversity (e.g., Drenth et al. 1990, Poortinga 1996), which is rooted in very different histories and traditions of the 48 or so countries. Even the geographical or political extent of Europe is a matter for some debate, though it is assumed that the growth of the European Union (currently 15 states, all of them in western Europe) will clarify this in future years. Although psychology as a discipline originated with Wundt's laboratory in Leipzig, Germany, in 1879, the profession of clinical psychology was considerably slower to develop in Europe than in the USA (Sexton and Misiak 1976, Eysenck 1990, Sexton and Hogan 1992).

The major influence for the development of clinical psychology in many western European countries was the rebuilding of Europe after World War II in the 1940s and 1950s and the development of mental health facilities by European states, as the challenge of mental problems and mental health presented itself to health authorities (Lunt 2000). In eastern European countries clinical psychology developed much later as these countries emerged in the 1980s from political regimes which were critical of the discipline (e.g., Pawlik 1996). It is only relatively recently that these countries have begun to develop a profession of clinical psychology.

2. The Field of Clinical Psychology

Although there are differences between countries, it is possible to provide a general definition of the field which would be agreeable to all European countries; clinical psychologists may be defined as psychologists who

> apply psychology in a clinical context, usually a hospital, medical or community setting, with people (patients or staff) who consider themselves to be in need of a psychological perspective on their lives. In practice, the majority of clinical psychologists contribute to the assessment and treatment of people who see themselves as having psychological problems, such as those with mental health difficulties, but they also work with the handicapped, families, those with learning difficulties, and, more widely, with staff and organisations (Llewelyn 1994).

There are some differences in the practice of clinical psychology, from countries where the majority are employed by the state such as the United Kingdom where most clinical psychologists work for the National Health Service (NHS) and there is relatively little private practice, to countries such as Switzerland and Germany where many clinical psychologists work in private practice, with charges reimbursed by medical insurance companies. Furthermore, there are differences in the dominant activity of clinical psychologists: in many European countries the main activity is psychotherapy, whereas in others there is a broader role which includes assessment and other forms of intervention, and also a role in training and consulting with other staff. While the dominant paradigm informing clinical psychology in the United Kingdom is

cognitive behavior therapy, other European countries such as France and Italy historically have been more influenced by psychoanalytic ideas. Although all European countries have been influenced by the USA, this influence has been perhaps most striking in the Scandinavian countries which embraced the 'scientist practitioner' approach to practice from an early stage.

2.1 Europe

As mentioned, the political face of Europe is developing and changing rapidly (see Lunt 1998). Many of the central and eastern European countries have applied for membership of the European Union, and are working towards criteria which will enable them to join. This will mean an expanded and changed Europe in the not too distant future, bringing together the early members of the European Union and nonmember states; many of the latter in Eastern Europe and formerly belonging to the Soviet Union. The countries of Europe constitute a very diverse group that may nevertheless be grouped into broad regions with some commonality in their organization and practice of clinical psychology. For these purposes, at a very broad level it is possible to identify a Nordic group of countries with considerable commonalities in their practice (the Scandinavian countries), Great Britain which has much in common with education and training in the USA and other parts of the English-speaking world, the German speaking countries, a southern European group, and an eastern European group. Of course, within these regions, the countries are characterized by their individuality and their diversity, and the different histories that have had a profound influence on the development of clinical psychology.

3. The Early Years of Clinical Psychology

There are a number of models in the field of clinical psychology, a field which emerged in European countries substantially after World War II (see above). It emerged as a recognizable profession at different times in different countries. In the United Kingdom the two World Wars provided a significant impetus to the emergence of this profession, initially through the need to develop psychological tests to recruit suitable personnel, and later in 1948 with the formation of the NHS that provided a considerable impetus to the development of this new profession. In these early days, the role of the clinical psychologist was largely one of laboratory technicians administering psychometric and other tests, usually for medical practitioners (Eysenck 1990). However, in the United Kingdom, the development of behavior therapy, in particular under the influence of Hans Eysenck who established clinical psychology as a profession in England in 1949, led to clinical psychologists developing a therapeutic role, and by the 1960s they had become clinical practitioners in their own right.

In the Nordic countries, also, clinical psychology emerged substantially after World War II, in the 1940s and early 1950s; the Norwegian Psychological Association was founded in 1934, the Danish Psychological Association in 1947, the Swedish Psychological Association in 1955, and the Finnish Union of Psychologists in 1957. The formation of these Psychological Associations reflected the emergence in these countries of a profession of psychology, mainly clinical psychology, which progressed through similar broad major phases as the UK; that is, a phase focusing on diagnostic examination and testing of individual patients, a phase focusing on therapeutic work involving mainly psychotherapy, and a phase focusing on indirect work with other professional groups through techniques such as consultation and training.

In Spain, on the other hand, clinical psychology has had a shorter history (Belloch and Olabarria 1994) and is said to have emerged in the 1970s along with fundamental changes in Spanish society. Similarly in Italy, clinical psychology as a professional application emerged substantially in the 1960s and there remain some tensions over the autonomy and role of clinical psychologists and their relationship with medical practitioners, especially psychiatrists. The Association of Greek Psychologists, founded in 1963, reflects the existence of professional psychology in Greece, although at that time and until very recently, all clinical psychologists received their training overseas, and the profession was very much dominated by the medical profession.

As mentioned above, clinical psychology emerged much later in Eastern European countries, and it was not until the 1980s that psychotherapy was fully recognized as a profession (Pawlik 1996). Until recently, nearly all psychologists were employed in state institutions, though in recent years there has been a growth in demand which has resulted in a growth in private practice.

In all European countries, clinical psychologists represent the largest group of psychologists, and experienced a rapid growth in their number between the 1960s and the 1990s with the expansion of mental health provision and the growing awareness of the contribution of clinical psychology to a wide and diverse range of areas of work (EFPPA 1997). Indeed, the 31 Member Associations of EFPPA (see below) represent 150,000 psychologists, the majority of whom are clinical psychologists.

Since the 1990s, in many European countries the emergence of the specialty of health psychology, with a focus on prevention rather than treatment, and the promotion of health rather than a more therapeutic or curative function, has led to attempts to define and differentiate a new field of psychological activity within the mental health field. This has been supported by the WHO commitment to Health for All by the Year 2000; EFPPA has had three Task Forces, focusing respectively on clinical psychology, health psychology, and psychotherapy, which have drawn up a model defining overlap and separate areas of activity within the health field, with corresponding commonalities and differences in education and training (EFPPA 1997).

4. Training of Clinical Psychologists

Education and training of clinical psychologists varies in European countries though, again, there are major regional groupings. Across Europe, as in other regions of the world, the education and training period has increased, with moves in some European countries for doctorate training for clinical psychologists, and more demanding requirements in all countries for the internship period. In the United Kingdom, there is a strong commitment to a scientist–practitioner model: 'the clinical psychologist is first and foremost an "applied scientist" or "scientist–practitioner" who seeks to use scientific knowledge to a beneficial end' (Marzillier and Hall 1990). This commitment also characterizes the Nordic countries which have been influenced substantially by the USA, and also by the UK. These countries would sign up to the definition that:

> clinical psychologists share several common attributes. They are psychologists because they have been trained to use the guidelines of knowledge of psychology in their professional work. They are clinicians because they attempt to understand people in their natural complexity and in their continuous adaptive transformations ... they are scientists because they utilize the scientific methods to achieve objectivity and precision in their professional work. Finally, they are professionals because they render important human services by helping individuals, social groups, and communities to solve psychological problems and improve the quality of life (Kendall and Norton-Ford 1982, p. 4).

This model is also espoused by Spanish clinical psychology where Belloch and Olabarria (1994) state that clinical psychology training is 'very similar to that proposed in the 1940s, in the famous Boulder Conference, organised by the APA.' In France, where there is a strong clinical psychoanalytic tradition, there is less of a commitment to the 'Boulder' model, and more of a philosophical or hermeneutic tradition in relation to education and practice.

However, since 1957 when the Treaty of Rome provided the foundation for the European Community (later Union), there have been requirements on individual countries ('states') to provide procedures for the mutual recognition of psychologists' qualifications across national boundaries (see McPherson 1988). Wider moves within the European Union such as the Bologna Agreement, which was signed by 29 Ministers in 1999 and commits them to greater convergence in terms of university degree structures, mean that even within Europe there is likely to be greater similarity in terms of structures of education and training for clinical psychologists.

5. Professionalization of Clinical Psychology

The period since the 1950s has seen a greater professionalization of clinical psychology in all European countries, with the development of codes of ethics (Lindsay 1996) and increased regulation and laws for clinical psychologists (Lunt 2000) across European countries. These political and professional developments have been supported by EFPPA which has brought together clinical psychologists from all over Europe to work on the professional aspects of practice at a European level and to support individual European countries seeking to develop their ethical codes, laws protecting the title of psychologist, and education and training in clinical psychology.

6. Organization of Clinical Psychology

It is also possible to trace the history of clinical psychology through its organization in Europe (Gilgen and Gilgen 1987, Lunt 1998). Many European countries founded scientific societies for psychologists in the early twentieth century whose purpose was to foster research and psychological science. At the time of World War II, separate professional associations to meet the needs of professional psychologists, often mainly clinical psychologists, were founded in a number of European countries. These associations had, as a focus, issues concerning professional practice and emerged in some countries as Trade Unions, negotiating salaries and terms and conditions of work for clinical psychologists as well as wider professional issues such as regulation, legislation, and ethical codes. In 1981, at a time when the provisions of the European Community demanded that European member states encourage mobility of professionals across Europe, the European Federation of Professional Psychologists Associations was formed to bring together professional associations in Europe and to collaborate on matters of common professional concern.

EFPPA currently has 31 member associations representing all the countries of the EU, all other countries in western Europe, and a growing number of member associations from central and eastern Europe. The federation provides a unique opportunity for comparison between the practices of different European countries and a forum for discussion and debate of important issues. The formation of EFPPA in 1981, when matters of mobility and mutual recognition were becoming more pressing, was due to a realization by

psychologists and psychology associations of member states that a federation would provide a professionally and politically useful way to move forward and to begin to develop common policies in this area. Clinical psychologists, in particular, were faced with the growing prospects of mobility between countries in the European Union, and the implications of the Treaty of Rome that provided the foundation for the European Community in 1957.

As a federation of Professional Psychology Associations representing around 150,000 professional psychologists in Europe, EFPPA spends most of its efforts on clinical psychology and clinical psychologists, also the largest group of psychologists within Europe (as in the rest of the world). In many countries psychology has become one of, if not the, most popular subjects to study at university. The majority of students studying psychology aspire to become clinical psychologists, and for this reason, in many European countries, there is an oversupply of qualified practitioners. Many countries now operate a so-called *numerus clausus*, either at the start of the psychology study, or during the study. This controls the numbers in training. In the United Kingdom, where specialist training in clinical psychology is funded by the NHS— where the vast majority of clinical psychologists work— the number of 'trainee' posts is strictly limited and is planned according to staffing needs in the different regions of the country. In other countries, where there is a tradition of predominantly private practice in clinical psychology, there are large numbers of qualified psychologists unable to find work. In all European countries, the ratio of female to male students is between 6:1 and 3:1, leaving the profession in danger of becoming an almost feminized profession in the future (Schorr and Saari 1995). There has also been some difficulty in many countries in recruiting students from the range of ethnic groups represented in Europe's increasingly multiethnic population. This clearly has implications for the clinical treatment of different client groups.

7. The Future

As new fields of practice in the health field evolve, in particular health psychology, there are pressures on clinical psychology. For example, in some countries it has been said that there may no longer be a field of clinical psychology, since there are strong moves towards a broader field of health psychology and a greater focus on preventive work. These newer areas, such as health psychology, neuropsychology, and forensic psychology, are leading to greater specialization within and outside clinical psychology. Although European countries differ in the extent and nature of their specialisms within the health field, there is an increasing trend for specialization and demands for higher qualifications. In one respect, psychologists working within the health system could be said to be becoming more generic, while on the other hand there are increasing specializations within this field of work.

8. Summary

The brief 50-year history of clinical psychology in Europe has seen an enormous increase in numbers both of students and of practitioners, such that the majority of psychologists are now clinical psychologists. This rapid professionalization has been accompanied by higher qualifications, greater regulation, the development of ethical codes, and all the characteristics of traditional professions. However, as the number of clinical psychologists increases, and the question of mobility across Europe becomes more pressing, there will be increasing attempts to develop more common frameworks and standards for education and practice; the challenge will be to achieve a balance between allowing individual countries their own autonomy which reflects their differing history and culture ('subsidiarity' as it is called), and developing more common agreed frameworks of practice which reflect a possible future 'federalization' of Europe.

See also: Clinical Psychology in North America, History of; Freud, Sigmund (1856–1939); Psychiatry, History of; Psychoanalysis, History of; Psychoanalysis in Clinical Psychology; Psychotherapy: Ethical Issues; Psychotherapy, History of: Psychiatric Aspects; Training in Clinical Psychology in the United States: Practitioner Model; Training in Clinical Psychology in the United States: Scientist–Practitioner Model

Bibliography

Belloch A, Olabarria B 1994 Clinical psychology: Current status and future prospects. *Applied Psychology: An International Review* **43**(2): 193–211
Drenth P J D, Sergeant J A, Takens R J 1990 *European Perspectives in Psychology*, vol. 2. Wiley, Chichester, UK
EFPPA 1997 Report to the General Assembly of EFPPA of Clinical Psychology Task Force. Available from EFPPA secretariat
Eysenck H 1990 Clinical psychology in Europe and in the US: Development and future. In: Drenth P J D, Sergeant J A, Takens R J (eds.) *European Perspectives in Psychology*. Wiley, Chichester, UK, Vol 2
Gilgen A R, Gilgen C K (eds.) 1987 *International Handbook of Psychology*. Greenwood Press, New York
Kendall P C, Norton-Ford J D 1982 *Clinical Psychology. Scientific and Professional Dimensions*. Wiley, New York
Llewelyn S P 1994 Assessment and therapy in clinical psychology. In: Spurgeon P, Davies R, Chapman A (eds.) *Elements of Applied Psychology*. Harwood Academic Publishers, Chur, Switzerland
Lindsay G 1996 Developing an ethical psychological practice. In: Georgas J, Manthouli M, Besevegis E, Kokkevi A (eds.) *Contemporary Psychology in Europe*. Hogrefe & Huber, Göttingen
Lunt I 1998 Psychology in Europe: challenges and opportunities. *The European Psychologist* **3**(2): 93–101
Lunt I 2000 Psychology as a profession. In: Pawlik K, Rosenzweig M (eds.) *The International Handbook of Psychology*. Sage, London
Marzillier J, Hall J 1990 *What is Clinical Psychology?*, 2nd edn. Oxford University Press, Oxford, UK
McPherson F 1988 Psychologists and the EEC. *The Psychologist* **9**: 353–5
Pawlik J 1996 The situation of the psychologists in Eastern European countries today. In: Georgas J, Manthouli M, Besevegis E, Kokkevi A (eds.) *Contemporary Psychology in Europe*. Hogrefe & Huber, Göttingen
Poortinga Y 1996 Cultural diversity in Europe: Extrapolations from cross-cultural research for professional psychology. In: Georgas J, Manthouli M, Besevegis E, Kokkevi A (eds.) *Contemporary Psychology in Europe*. Hogrefe & Huber, Göttingen
Pilgrim D, Treacher A 1992 *Clinical Psychology Observed*. Routledge, London
Schorr A, Saari S (eds.) 1995 *Psychology in Europe*. Hogrefe, Göttingen
Sexton V S, Hogan J D (eds.) 1992 *International Psychology. Views from around the World*. University of Nebraska Press, Lincoln & London
Sexton V S, Misiak H (eds.) 1976 *Psychology around the World*. Brooks/Cole, Monterey, CA

I. Lunt

Clinical Psychology in North America, History of

Clinical psychology is concerned primarily with the study of psychopathology and with its diagnosis and treatment. It shares this domain with several other mental health disciplines, including psychiatry, social work, nursing, and various types of counseling. Compared to these other disciplines, clinical psychology is distinctive for its training in research and for its expertise in psychometrics and the behavior therapies. North America played an important role in the emergence of clinical psychology. The field usually dates its origin from the founding of the first psychology clinic in 1896 by Lightner Witmer (1867–1956) at the University of Pennsylvania (Routh 1996). Clinical psychology in the English-speaking parts of Canada developed in a pattern similar to that seen in the US (with doctoral training required for independent practice) but somewhat later in time. The field developed in French-speaking Canada and in Mexico in a way more resembling that of European countries, with master's or licenciate-level training required for independent practice. The North American Free Trade Agreement (NAFTA) now exerts pressure on all three countries and their states and provinces to coordinate these differences to a greater degree, to permit more freedom of movement to qualified clinical psychologists.

1. The Prehistory of the Mental Health Field

The need for humans to deal with the problems now called mental illness did not emerge suddenly a century ago. It seems reasonable to assume that such problems have existed in some form in every society through all the millenia of human experience. The ancient literatures of India, Egypt, China, Greece, and Rome contain descriptions of disturbed behavior, often interpreted in religious terms as some type of retribution by magical or divine forces. Legal systems as they developed in all of these civilizations necessarily included provisions for seeing to the management of the affairs and property of persons who were temporarily or permanently unable to manage for themselves (Routh 1998).

2. Greek Ideas Concerning Psychopathology

Western concepts of psychopathology have their roots in those of the ancient Greeks, including the writings attributed to the physician Hippocrates (460–377 BC). These Hippocratic writings include terms such as melancholia, mania, paranoia, and dementia, with meanings not all that different from their present ones, albeit with different explanations. For example, in Greek, the word 'melancholia' simply means 'black bile.' In the Hippocratic theory of the humors, a person suffering from severe mental depression had an overabundance of black bile, a substance thought to be produced by the spleen. Within this system, one aspect of treatment quite reasonably aimed to reduce the amount of black bile by administering a purgative such as hellebore. Another disorder was that of 'phrenitis,' literally meaning an inflammation of the mind. This referred to mental disturbance accompanied by fever, and the approach taken was simply to wait for the fever to abate. Though some of these Hippocratic ideas may seem strange to us now, it is worth reflecting why some of them lasted well into the eighteenth century and beyond.

3. Emergence of Psychiatry

Although according to Herodotus (ca. 484–425 BC), medical specialties existed even in ancient Greece, the one we now call psychiatry did not emerge until the late eighteenth century in Europe. The ancients did not conceptualize mental disorders as a separate category but regarded them as being illnesses like any other. When psychiatry did emerge, with the work of such pioneers as Philippe Pinel (1745–1826), Benjamin Rush (1745–1823), and Vincenzo Chiarugi (1759–1820), it was associated with the development of mental asylums or hospitals as a separate locations for the care of those with mental derangements. The theory of 'moral treatment' that was typical of that time tried to minimize the use of coercive methods such as chaining patients to restrain them and instead insisted that they be treated with kindness and courtesy. It was often found that even some very disturbed patients responded positively to such a regimen.

4. Modern Psychology and the Study of Psychopathology

Long before a formal discipline of psychology existed, people in every society still no doubt reflected upon human experience and behavior. As was the case of Hippocrates in relation to medicine and psychiatry, the influence of ancient Greek philosophers such as Plato (427–347 BC) and Aristotle (384–322 BC) upon our present psychological concepts was pervasive. There is conventional agreement that psychology emerged as a formal academic discipline only in the mid-nineteenth century in Europe. Wilhelm Wundt (1832–1920) of the University of Leipzig is usually named as the founder of the field, and 1879, the year in which he set up his psychology laboratory there, is celebrated as the key event in its origin. Wundt's work and those of the other early psychologists often focused on sensory processes, reaction time, and memory. It is also noteworthy that the study of psychopathology was a possible topic of psychological study even in those days. The eminent psychiatrist Emil Kraepelin (1856–1926) was influenced by Wundt's writings and was interested in psychology. His main motive for becoming a psychiatrist was that this was the only way he could see to make a living while doing psychological research. He later actually studied under Wundt, who encouraged him to keep on with his work combining psychology and psychiatry. Kraepelin set up psychology laboratories at his psychiatric clinics in both Heidelberg and Munich.

Many of the pioneers in psychology in both Europe and the US were trained as medical doctors. In France these included Theodule Ribot (1839–1916), who wrote about diseases of memory and about personality disorders. An important French colleague was Pierre Janet (1859–1947), who studied anxiety, hysteria, and obsessions and developed concepts of dissociation that continue to be influential today. In the US the leading pioneer in psychology, William James (1842–1910) was originally trained in medicine but wrote a psychology textbook that proved to be the most influential of all. In 1896, James gave his Lowell lectures on exceptional mental states, much influenced by the work of Janet. Boston neurologist Morton Prince also became interested in Janet's writings and published a description of a woman with multiple personalities who had been his patient. Prince established the *Journal of Abnormal Psychology* in 1906 and later gave it to the American Psychological Association. Subsequently, in 1926, he established the Harvard Psychological Clinic, which was a research facility rather than one delivering mental health services. The most influential medically trained student of psychology of this time was no doubt Sigmund Freud (1856–1939). Breuer and Freud's book *Studies in Hysteria*, was published in 1895 and Freud's book on the interpretation of dreams in 1900. The first international psychoanalytic meeting was held in Salzburg in 1908. In 1909, Freud came to the US for the first and only time.

5. Lightner Witmer and Clinical Psychology

As the above paragraphs make clear, Witmer was hardly the first to suggest that psychologists study psychopathology. Instead, his main contribution was to go beyond that to advocate that psychologists try to help people as well as study them. Witmer had been an undergraduate at the University of Pennsylvania and then for a time, before going to Leipzig to obtain his Ph.D. under Wundt, served as a school teacher. He had as a student a young man with marked difficulty in reading and was able to help the youngster succeed in school and go on to attend college. This turned out to be a formative experience for Witmer. After Witmer had obtained his Ph.D. and returned to his *alma mater* as a psychology professor, a school teacher named Margaret Maguire asked his advice about one of her pupils with a spelling problem. Witmer reasoned that if psychology was of any practical use, it should be able to be of help in a case of this kind. Thus was the psychological clinic and the field of clinical psychology launched.

Witmer's clinic worked more with children than with adults and tended to concentrate on academic difficulties such as reading, spelling, or general backwardness in school as opposed to emotional or behavioral problems. His historic forebears are thus not Hippocrates and Pinel but rather eighteenth and nineteenth century French physicians and special educators such as Jacob Pereire (1715–1780) (who taught deaf-mutes to speak), J. M. G. Itard (1775–1838) (who worked with the 'wild boy' of Aveyron), and Edouard Seguin (1812–1880) (a physician who devised a 'physiological method' of sensory and motor training in an attempt to remediate mental retardation). Witmer used existing laboratory procedures including the Seguin formboard and sensory/motor procedures adapted from Wundt to evaluate the children referred to him and often tried to teach them simple tasks as a part of his diagnostic efforts. In his treatment activities he often collaborated with school teachers, as well as with physicians, thus serving as more of a consultant than doing anything resembling present-day psychotherapy. As a matter of fact, he was little influenced by the activities of the Boston School of psychotherapy that was contemporary with his work, nor later by Freud and his psychoanalytic movement.

Witmer is not remembered for any noteworthy scientific discoveries but rather for his persistence in enacting this new role of the clinical psychologist. At the University of Pennsylvania's Ph.D. program, he essentially trained most of the first generation of clinical psychologists. He maintained his clinic as a service and training facility and in 1907 began a journal, the *Psychological Clinic*, to publicize these activities (Witmer 1907).

6. The Binet Test

There is still no consensus among psychologists as to precisely how to interpret its findings. Still, Alfred Binet's 'metric scale' of intelligence (Binet and Simon 1905) may be the most noteworthy piece of technology developed by psychology in its first century. Certainly it had a major impact on the new field of clinical psychology. In fact, before World War II, probably the most characteristic activity of the typical clinical psychologist was the administration of the Binet test and other similar measures (Routh 1994). This was true despite the fact that Lightner Witmer, the founder of the field, was quite critical of the Binet test and used it only as one part of his extensive battery of laboratory procedures.

In the light of how influential his test was, it is interesting to note that Alfred Binet himself was not particularly identified with the field of clinical psychology. Originally trained as a lawyer, Binet became part of the circle around the influential neurologist Jean Charcot at the Salpetriere in Paris. Much of his psychology was self-taught, through extensive reading at the *Bibliothèque Nationale*. In France, Binet became known as one of the founders of the entire field of psychology (often characterized worldwide as 'experimental psychology') and edited the influential journal, *Année psychologique*. As is well known, Binet's successful attempts to devise an intelligence test departed from the conventional approach of using relatively 'pure' sensory and motor tasks to use complex worksamples of the kinds of things schoolchildren might be expected to know and do.

For some reason, Binet's new test did not create as much of a stir in his homeland as it did in the US. Psychologist Henry Goddard, who directed the psychology laboratory at the Vineland Training School, in New Jersey, had the Binet test translated and soon confirmed its impressive validity in identifying persons with mental retardation. The use of the Binet spread like wildfire among the early clinical psychologists in the US, beginning with those employed in the field of mental retardation. Goddard founded the first psychology internship in 1908 at Vineland, NJ. Goddard went on to become the first professor of clinical psychology at Ohio State University, like the University of Pennsylvania an important early training center in the field (Routh 1994).

Lewis M. Terman (1877–1956) at Stanford University developed a standardized version of Binet's test, collected normative data for it, and introduced certain refinements such as the ratio IQ score (originally suggested by Wilhelm Stern of Hamburg). The 1916 Stanford–Binet, as it was called, dominated this field for many years. At about the same time, 1915, Robert Yerkes pointed out the unsuitability of the concept of mental age and of this testing format for use with adults and introduced his own 'point scale' as a substitute for it. Yerkes and his colleagues were also responsible for the development of group intelligence tests, the Army Alpha (for those who could read) and Army Beta (for the illiterate), used for mass testing of military recruits during World War I. Another wartime development was Robert S. Woodworth's Personal Data Sheet published in 1917. This was one of the first rationally developed self-report questionnaires intended to detect neurotic tendencies (Routh 1994).

7. The Child Guidance Center Movement

The development of child guidance centers was another factor that influenced early clinical psychologists in the direction of working with children more than with adults. The first child guidance clinic was the Institute of Juvenile Research, established in 1909 by physician William Healy in conjunction with the juvenile court of Chicago. The idea behind such facilities was that careful clinical study of children engaging in antisocial activities could assist in guiding them away from crime. Healy was joined at first by clinical psychologist Grace Fernald and subsequently by her replacement, Augusta Bronner (Healy and Bronner 1926). The child guidance clinic was the origin of the 'clinical team' of psychiatrist, psychologist, and social worker that later spread to other settings. The typical pattern was that the psychiatrist saw the child, the social worker saw the family, and the psychologist did the testing. The child guidance movement was supported by the Harkness family's philanthropy in the form of the Commonwealth Fund and replicated in many US cities and abroad.

8. The First Clinical Psychology Organization

In 1917, in Pittsburgh, a group of eight clinical psychologists organized themselves into what they called the American Association of Clinical Psychologists (AACP) and invited 48 colleagues to join them (Routh 1994). They were led by J. E. W. Wallin

(1876–1969) and Leta Hollingworth (1886–1939). Incidentally, Hollingworth was the first to suggest in 1918 that a person trained in clinical psychology receive a distinctive type of degree, the doctor of psychology. The new organization was viewed by many as divisive and was soon incorporated into the American Psychological Association as its Clinical section. An effort by the same group to introduce procedures for certifying qualified clinical psychologists failed, however.

9. Psychometric Developments

The interwar years were a fertile time for the emergence of various new psychometric procedures, many of which continue to be in use today. For example, in 1921, the Swiss psychiatrist Herman Rorschach (1884–1922) published his well-known inkblot test. It was brought to the US by a child psychiatrist who taught it to a clinical psychology graduate student at Columbia named Samuel Beck (1896–1976). Beck then proceeded to do his dissertation on this new test and eventually to develop his own system for administering and scoring it. Psychologist Bruno Klopfer (1900–1971), a disciple of Carl Jung (1875–1961), also introduced the Rorschach to the US and developed a separate system for administering and scoring it (see *Projective Methods in Psychology*). In 1936 the Thematic Apperception Test was introduced by Henry A. Murray (1893–1988) of the Harvard Psychological Clinic, and a colleague. Also in 1935 Edgar A. Doll (1889–1969), introduced the Vineland Social Maturity Scale, an interview-based method involving informants familiar with the person, for assessing the social competence of individuals suspected of mental retardation. David Wechsler (1896–1981) published the original version of his Wechsler–Bellevue intelligence test for adults. This was but the first of many Wechsler tests of intelligence and memory. It introduced the use of the deviation IQ, a standard score comparing the individual to age-matched normative subjects. In 1943, psychologist Starke R. Hathaway and psychiatrist J. C. McKinley introduced the first edition of the Minnesota Multiphasic Personality Inventory (MMPI). The MMPI had novel 'validity' indicators, and its measures of psychopathology were empirically keyed to psychiatrically defined groups (see *Minnesota Multiphasic Personality Inventory (MMPI)*).

10. Organizational Activities

In 1937 a new organization known as the American Association of Applied Psychology (AAAP) split off from the American Psychological Association (APA) to provide a home for various professionally oriented groups including the clinical psychologists, who at this same time dissolved the Clinical Section of the APA.

The AAAP began to publish the *Journal of Consulting Psychology*, which subsequently developed into a high-prestige clinical psychology journal (Routh 1994).

It was also at this time that some preliminary developments in psychology began in other parts of North America. In 1937, for example, the first psychology curriculum was devised at UNAM, the National Autonomous University of Mexico, in Mexico City. In 1939, the Canadian Psychological Association was founded. It had 38 members to begin with, and it has been estimated that there were only 53 psychologists in all of Canada at the time. Needless to say, there were few prewar developments in Canada or Mexico specifically relating to clinical psychology.

11. The Post-World War II Boom in US Clinical Psychology

Clinical psychology expanded so greatly in the US after World War II that many brief historical accounts of the field even consider its development to have begun at that time. The war effort tended to draw everyone into it, either on the battlefield or on the home front. Many psychologists whose interests prior to the war had been strictly in research and in the academic side of the field found themselves assigned to carry out psychological testing or to help medical staff in treating psychiatric casualties. After the war, it was clear that the Veterans Administration (VA) would have to be vastly expanded to deal with the need for residential care, psychotherapy, or at least vocational counseling of some of those returning from military service.

In 1945, the VA and the newly established National Institute of Mental Health in the US came to the APA to ask it to establish a system for accrediting training programs in clinical psychology. The government intended to pour millions of dollars into training such individuals and needed to know which programs were competent to carry this out. In response, APA created a system of accreditation, and for the first time, it began to be possible to say who was a well trained clinical psychologist and who was not. David Shakow (1901–1981) was the architect of the 1949 conference held in Boulder, Colorado, which ratified what has come to be called the 'scientist–practitioner' model of training clinical psychologists (Raimy 1950) (see *Training in Clinical Psychology in the United States: Scientist–Practitioner Model*).

Postwar clinical psychologists continued in their role as mental testers, but gave more emphasis to the assessment of personality and psychopathology, not just cognitive status. This was the heyday of projective tests, and at least for a time the Rorschach inkblot was an appropriate symbol for the clinical practitioner of psychology. A well known exemplar of the clinical psychologist as projective tester in this era was David Rapaport (1911–1960), chief psychologist at the Menninger Clinic in Kansas. A two volume set of books published at this time by Rapaport and co-workers (Rapaport et al. 1945, 1946) established the Rorschach, the TAT, and the Wechsler test to be a 'full test battery' for almost a half century to come.

The clinical psychologists of this era were also eager to become full-fledged psychotherapists as well as mental testers. Their route to therapeutic training was blocked to some extent by the American Psycho-analytic Association's 1938 policy decision (contrary to Freud's own views) that only psychiatrists were to be trained in psychoanalysis. Clinical psychologists thus became very ingenious in devising ways of becoming therapists. The best known of them was perhaps Carl Rogers (1902–1987), whose original therapy supervisor was the social worker Jessie Taft. Taft, in turn, had received her training from Otto Rank, a psychologist from Vienna who had received orthodox psychoanalytic training there and had been a close colleague of Freud's. Rogers was successfully assertive in other ways. At one point in his career he was director of a child guidance clinic when such administrative positions were supposed to be held only by physicians. Rogers also was determined to combine his psychology training with his role as a therapist. He was among the first to produce recordings of actual psychotherapy sessions, and was a pioneer in doing controlled research on the outcome of psychotherapy. Rogerian therapy ('client centered' or 'person centered,' therapy, as it was later called) is still practiced and studied both in North America and elsewhere (Routh 1994, 1998) (see Person-centered Therapy).

In 1945, the first state law certifying psychologists for independent practice was passed by Connecticut. By 1977, all states in the US had passed such certification or licensing laws regulating the use of the title, 'psychologist' or the practice of psychology (Routh 1994).

12. The Behavior Therapy Movement

Some psychologists were of the opinion that clinical psychologists in their professional activities should not simply try to duplicate the activities of psychiatrists. In 1913, John Watson had boldly proclaimed a behavioristic approach to psychology, which was widely influential at least in academic psychology in the US. In a famous paper reporting research carried out under Watson's supervision, Jones (1924) described the case of 'Peter,' whose fear of rabbits she desensitized. Not even Jones herself realized the wider implications of this study at the time, but in the light of events many years later some considered her to have been 'the mother of behavior therapy' (see *Behavior Therapy: Psychological Perspectives*).

The behavior therapy movement progressed not only by following its own agenda but by attacking its opponents. Psychologist Eysenck (1952) in England thus skeptically reviewed the evidence for the effectiveness of psychotherapy. It was not enough, he noted, to show simply that psychotherapy patients improved. One also needed to consider the rate of spontaneous improvement of patients who did not receive psychotherapy.

In 1962 in Charlottesville, Virginia, a behavior therapy conference was held, sponsored by psychiatrist Joseph Wolpe and psychologists Andrew Salter and Leo Reyna. At the time Wolpe had just published a book on his success in treating patients with phobias using the behavioral method of systematic desensitization. Soon afterward, Lang and Lazovik (1963) published the first controlled study of desensitization, in treating snake phobia. Soon the behavior therapy movement was in full swing, with its own organizations, journals, and many adherents. Sidney Bijou and his colleagues established behavioral treatments based on the research of B. F. Skinner. These came to be known as applied behavior analysis and were especially influential in work with the behavior disorders of children and of those with mental retardation (see *Behavior Analysis, Applied*).

13. Canadian Clinical Psychology

It was in the 1960s that clinical psychology finally came of age in Canada. It was and is the largest applied specialty in psychology numerically in that country, as it is in the rest of the world. In 1965, the Couchiching Conference basically endorsed the 'Boulder model' of scientist–practitioner training for clinical psychology. Some Canadian doctoral programs such as the one at McGill even sought accreditation by the American Psychological Association. There was even something of a boom north of the border. It is said that by 1966, more than half the doctoral psychologists in Canada were either American born or trained in the US. In 1983, the Canadian Psychological Association established its own program of accreditation. The first CPA-accredited doctoral programs in clinical psychology were those at McGill, Concordia, and Simon Fraser Universities. The success of doctoral training in clinical psychology tells only part of the story there, however. In Quebec and some other eastern provinces, the master's degree was accepted as the entry level of training for independent clinical practice. By 1996, Canada had 88 graduate training programs in professional psychology (including clinical): 57 doctoral and 31 terminal masters.

Canadian clinical psychology is noted for particular strength in the area of neuropsychology, which built on Canadian strengths in the neurosciences, including the work of neurosurgeon Wilder Penfield at the Montreal Neurological Institute. In academic psychology, the research and writings of Donald Hebb concerning the CNS (conceptual nervous system) were influential. It was at McGill University that Olds and Milner published their famous 1954 paper on the reinforcement of an animal's behavior by electrical stimulation of its brain. On the clinical side, Ronald Melzack elaborated his theory of gating mechanisms influencing the experience of pain. Brenda Milner explored the role of the hippocampus in semantic memory, including work with her famous patient, 'H.M.' This man developed permanent memory deficits after surgery inadvertently destroyed his hippocampus bilaterally. Doreen Kimura documented the left cerebral hemisphere advantage in dichotic listening.

14. Clinical Psychology in Mexico

In 1997, the Division of Clinical Psychology of the APA held its midwinter board meeting in Mexico City, hosted by Juan Jose Sanchez-Sosa, the director of the school of psychology at UNAM, the National Autonomous University of Mexico. Sanchez-Sosa provided his US colleagues with a tour of this school, itself as large as many an entire college campus in the US. The school offers both Master's and Ph.D. degrees in psychology, but as in much of Europe, these degrees are intended for those headed for academic and research careers. Those who intend to practice psychology, including clinical psychology, in Mexico need only a 'licentiate' or diploma to do so, which is awarded after 6 years of what to persons trained in the US seems to be undergraduate training. But students in such a program spend essentially full time on psychology, without the need for a broad liberal arts distribution of courses. This includes a significant amount of practicum experience. The psychology clinic, one of the practicum facilities used at UNAM, features a variety of clinical activities, including psychological testing, psychodynamic therapy, behavior therapy, group therapy, and even biofeedback. Since there is no certification or licensing system beyond the licentiate degree itself, it is difficult to be sure how many of these graduates are practicing clinical psychology in a way parallel to what would be seen in the US or Canada.

15. Independent Practice of Clinical Psychology

Although Lightner Witmer in his clinical work often collaborated with school teachers, physicians, or others, psychologists working in his clinic were never supervised by members of any other profession. This tradition of independent work has continued within the field of clinical psychology, somewhat in contrast with social work and nursing. The post-World War II expansion of the field in the US was primarily in the public sector, typically VA hospitals, but also child guidance centers and eventually community mental health centers. The large government training grants supporting clinical psychology programs at the time presupposed that the graduates would go to such public sector jobs or teach in colleges and universities. In the 1980s, the Reagan administration made most such training grants a thing of the past (Routh 1994).

David Mitchell, a Ph.D. student of Lightner Witmer, was one of the first individuals to make his living primarily in the private practice of psychology. Eventually, he was joined by many others. After all, the state and provincial laws that developed to regulate psychology after 1945 specified what qualifications were necessary to offer one's services to the public as a psychologist. Many psychologists trained in Boulder-model Ph.D. programs did no research after graduation, and eventually the idea of training psychologists as practitioners rather than scientist–practitioners emerged. Beginning with the University of Illinois in 1966, a number of programs began to offer the doctor of psychology (Psy.D.) degree rather than the Ph.D. The conference in Vail, Colorado in 1973 officially legitimized such practitioner training for the first time. In fact, a number of nonuniversity-affiliated schools of professional psychology sprang up beginning in the 1970s, many of them offering Psy.D. degrees. Often these programs were supported only by student tuition, and many students assumed substantial loans to finance their education (Routh 1994). No such private school of professional psychology has emerged in Canada (nor in Mexico) (see *Training in Clinical Psychology in the United States: Practitioner Model*).

As psychologists in private practice emerged in larger numbers, they also became more active politically. The first practitioner became president of the APA in 1977, and within 20 years the first Psy.D. was elected to this position. The practitioners began to dominate both the APA and the Canadian Psychological Association to a greater and greater extent. In response, many academic psychologists retreated to form national organizations of their own that were more research-oriented. Thus, the American Psychological Society was founded in 1988. Similarly, in 1989, academic and research psychologists in Canada founded the Canadian Society for Brain, Behaviour, and Cognitive Science.

Practicing psychologists both in the US and Canada battled psychiatrists for their share of the mental health 'market.' Thus, they fought to obtain hospital privileges. They supported 'freedom of choice' legislation to become eligible as health providers reimbursable by health insurance companies and Health Maintenance Organizations (HMOs). In 1988, a law suit by clinical psychologist Bryant Welch and others forced the American Psychoanalytic Association to begin to admit psychologists for training at its local institutes (Routh 1994). Most recently, a number of practicing psychologists in the US, led by Patrick DeLeon, have been trying to obtain the right to prescribe medications for mental health conditions, so far without much success.

16. The Continued Commitment of Clinical Psychology to Research

Well before the founding of Witmer's clinic, there was a strong interest on the part of psychology in research on psychopathology, including its diagnosis and treatment. This continues to be the case. In fact, psychologists are far more likely than psychiatrists or those in other fields to be principal investigators on research grants from the National Institute of Mental Health. Such research is international in scope and is a collaborative interdisciplinary enterprise. The turf battles that characterize the marketplace of practice are much less typical in the research arena, where clinical psychologists often cooperate smoothly with experimental psychologists and statisticians as well as with medical colleagues. In research, it is neither possible nor necessary to draw any bright line to show the boundaries between these fields.

The diversity of such research is so great that it would be impossible to cover it in an article as brief as this one. Instead, a few examples must suffice. In 1954, psychologist Evelyn Hooker received her first NIMH grant to study homosexuality. Her work, much of it using the types of projective testing that were typical of clinical psychological work at the time, suggested that homosexuals might be essentially normal psychologically. This research was related to the later decisions to delete homosexuality as a pathological category from the Diagnostic and Statistical Manual of the APA.

In the 1950s, psychologist Leonard Eron began collecting peer-rating data on aggressive behavior in 8-year-old children. The subsequent longitudinal research he and his colleagues did helped establish the fact that aggressive behavior is highly stable well into adulthood. Psychologist Gerald R. Patterson studied aggressive behavior in children using direct behavioral observations, relating it to coercive processes in the parent–child dyad and doing controlled intervention studies showing how it could be reduced.

In the late 1950s, psychologist C. Keith Conners devised a simple teacher rating scale for the assessment of varied types of disordered behavior in school children. Together with child psychiatrist Leon Eisenberg he helped carry out the first controlled studies of the effects of stimulant medications on children's disruptive behavior (Conners and Eisenberg 1963). Such research formed an important basis of present concepts of Attention Deficit Hyperactivity Disorder (ADHD), the most commonly diagnosed type of child psychopathology and one still typically treated with stimulant medications. By the 1970s, Thomas Achenbach and his colleagues had begun to develop the use of parent, teacher, and self-ratings for child behavior into the most widely used forms of assessment by mental health workers.

In 1962, Meehl published a classic paper on 'schizotaxia, schizotypy, and schizophrenia,' elaborating his concepts as to how genetic factors might be involved in the development of this disorder (Meehl 1962). In 1973, psychologist Holzman and co-workers announced their discovery of smooth pursuit eye-movement difficulties in patients with schizophrenia (Holzman et al. 1973). This neurological symptom proved to be an important 'trait' marker in the first degree relatives of schizophrenics as well, whether or not they manifested any overt psychopathology. In Denmark, psychologist Sarnoff A. Mednick carried out a series of studies using the excellent public registers that characterize that country to do longitudinal, epidemiological studies of schizophrenia, implementing the type of research that Meehl had only been able to imagine.

Problems of the dysregulation of affect and emotion are the most ancient in the field of psychopathology, having been with us since Hippocrates. Beginning in the 1960s, psychologist Richard Lazarus elaborated his concepts of stress, appraisal, and coping and demonstrated experimentally how his subjects' use of different coping strategies could dampen or heighten their physiological stress (Lazarus 1966). Beginning in the 1970s, Charles Spielberger and his colleagues began the development and validation of measures of state as well as trait anxiety and later of state and trait anger as well. In the 1970s, Martin E. P. Seligman and his colleagues showed how his studies of learned helplessness in dogs could be used to reconceptualize human depression.

In conclusion, clinical psychology has both international and important North American roots. In its first century, it has developed into a viable science and profession, and there is good reason to suppose that its trajectory will continue in the twenty-first century.

See also: Clinical Psychology in Europe, History of; Psychiatry, History of; Psychoanalysis, History of; Psychotherapy, History of: Psychiatric Aspects; Training in Clinical Psychology in the United States: Practitioner Model; Training in Clinical Psychology in the United States: Scientist–Practitioner Model

Bibliography

Binet A, Simon T 1905 A new method for the diagnosis of intellectual level of abnormal persons. *Annee Psychologique* **11**: 191–244
Conners C K, Eisenberg L 1963 The effects of methylphenidate on symptomatology and learning in disturbed children. *American Journal of Psychiatry* **120**: 458–64
Eysenck H J 1952 The effects of psychotherapy: An evaluation. *Journal of Consulting Psychology* **16**: 319–24
Healy W, Bronner A F 1926 *Delinquents and Criminals: Their Making and Unmaking*. Macmillan, New York
Holzman P S, Proctor L R, Hughes D W 1973 Eye tracking patterns in schizophrenia. *Science* **181**: 179–81
Jones M C 1924 The elimination of children's fears. *Journal of Experimental Psychology* **7**: 382–90
Kraepelin E 1987 *Memoirs*. Springer, Berlin
Lang P J, Lazovik A D 1963 Experimental desensitization of a phobia. *Journal of Abnormal and Social Psychology* **66**: 519–25
Lazarus R S 1966 *Psychological Stress and the Coping Process*. McGraw-Hill, New York
Meehl P E 1962 Schizotaxia, schizotypy, and schizophrenia. *American Psychologist* **17**: 827–38
Raimy V C (ed.) 1950 *Training in Clinical Psychology*. Prentice-Hall, New York
Rapaport D, Gill M M, Shafer R 1945 *Diagnostic Psychological Testing*, Vol. 1. Yearbook, Chicago
Rapaport D, Gill M M, Shafer R 1946 *Diagnostic Psychological Testing*, Vol. 2. Yearbook, Chicago
Routh D K 1994 *Clinical Psychology since 1917: Science Practice and Organization*. Plenum, New York
Routh D K 1996 Lightner Witmer and their first 100 years of clinical psychology. *American Psychologist* **51**: 244–7
Routh D K 1998 Hippocrates meets Democritus: A history of psychiatry and clinical psychology. In: Bellack A S, Hersen M (eds.) *Comprehensive Clinical Psychology*, Vol. 1. Pergamon, New York, pp. 1–48
Witmer L 1907 Clinical psychology. *Psychological Clinic* **1**: 1–9

D. K. Routh

Clinical Psychology: Manual-based Treatment

The practice of psychotherapy has seen dramatic and sweeping changes since the 1950s. One of the most dramatic changes impacting the delivery and dissemination of specific psychotherapeutic service has been the development of detailed explanatory manuals for complex psychological treatments. More recently client 'workbooks' are available that guide the client through therapeutic direction. The main function of these treatment manuals is to, 'outline the procedures, techniques, and strategies which comprise an acceptable implementation of a given [psychotherapeutic approach]' (Luborsky and DeRubeis 1984, p. 7) and to make the process of psychotherapy more accessible to clients and clinicians alike. Typically these manuals describe session-by-session strategies for specific problems such as depression or phobias for therapists to follow.

Many changes in the field have led to the impetus for specific treatment manuals to be developed including the demand for 'good and better research,' in which the therapeutic intervention is specified for all to examine, and the burgeoning of the hegemonic managed behavioral healthcare system. In response to these many demands, the number of manuals has proliferated. Although the psychotherapeutic community has positively received the majority of manuals, some front-line clinicians raise objections to this approach, stating, among other objections, that manuals damage the therapeutic relationship, and that clinical innovation is restricted (Addis et al. 1996). Despite these obstacles, treatment manuals appear entrenched in the forefront of clinical psychology.

1. Developmental History of Treatment Manuals

The initial impetus for the development of treatment manuals came from psychotherapy researchers who in the early 1960s began to test broadly the effectiveness of specific treatments in controlled outcome studies. Looking to demonstrate successfully that psychological interventions could withstand rigorous scientific investigation, similar to that of existing pharmacological treatments (Luborsky and DeRubeis 1984), scientist–practitioners realized that they needed treatment tools that would allow for systematic replication and comparison. Wilson (1996) more specifically pointed out that treatment manuals sought to eliminate any 'error' associated with 'clinical judgment' or intuition that might cause one therapist to behave in a substantially different manner from another. Thus, to study the effectiveness of these therapies, treatments were condensed into manuals that could then be reviewed and used across studies. Many researchers hoped that by utilizing treatment manuals, presented in this fashion, psychological interventions would be able to withstand the methodological constraints of research protocols. More specifically, 'treatment manuals help support the internal validity of a given study by ensuring that a specific set of treatment procedures exists, that procedures are identifiable, and that they can be repeated in other investigations' (Dobson and Shaw 1988, p. 675). This is in contrast to the conduct of treatment outcome research prior to manualization, in which specific therapeutic techniques were often not explained and thus could not be compared to other treatments or be replicated by other investigative groups. As a consequence, the use of a treatment manual is currently a prerequisite to receive federal funding for psychotherapy research in many countries.

Another push to develop specific treatment manuals came from the development of the Agency for Health Care Policy and Research (AHCPR) in the United States in 1989. The sole purpose of this Agency was to facilitate identification of the effectiveness of specific strategies for specific disorders, with the aim of increasing the quality and reducing the cost of healthcare (Barlow 1996). One major mechanism of accomplishing this goal was the creation of clinical practice guidelines that explicitly articulate the optimal strategies for assessing and treating a variety of psychological problems (see *Psychotherapy: Clinical Practice Guidelines*). Treatments recommended in these clinical practice guidelines are typically based on two specific factors: (a) efficacy; or internal validity of the specific treatment, the determination of which is based on the results of a systematic evaluation of the intervention in a controlled setting, and (b) effectiveness; or clinical utility of the treatment, which is based on the feasibility, generalizability, and cost-effectiveness of the intervention actually being delivered in a local setting. Based on these equally important and rigorous bases of evidence, the development of treatment manuals that could produce the necessary evidence was encouraged. As a result, manual-based treatments have been incorporated as one of the major components of evidence-based service delivery (Strosahl 1998).

2. Manualized Treatment in Behavioral Health Care Settings

One of the final steps in the progression of manual-based treatments is their incorporation into managed care treatment settings. Strosahl (1998) points out that these manuals are especially appealing to these settings because they are essentially an easily discernable roadmap for the most appropriate way to implement clinical practice guidelines. Within managed care organizations, where psychotherapy must demonstrate: (a) its overall effectiveness, (b) may be limited to a certain number of sessions, and (c) increasingly is delivered by practitioners with less than doctoral degrees, treatment manuals are embraced for their ability to facilitate the delivery of empirically supported treatments at lower costs. Treatment manuals increasingly are also adopted because they aid in the training of master's level clinicians.

3. Specific Treatment Manuals

The earliest treatment manuals were based on behavioral treatment techniques (Dobson and Shaw 1988). These treatments were the logical outgrowth of behavior therapy's de-emphasis of therapist variables in favor of specific procedures (Parloff 1998). Nonbehavioral varieties of treatment manuals are currently available, although behavioral and cognitive behavioral techniques tend to predominate. The majority of treatment manuals do not adhere to more traditional psychotherapy models, which tend to emphasize a more individualized theory-based understanding of underlying patient problems (Wilson 1996). Rather, most manuals target the specific diagnostic categories specified by *DSM-IV*. For example, specific manuals exist for a wide variety of anxiety disorders including panic disorder, generalized anxiety disorder, obsessive-compulsive disorder, posttraumatic stress disorder, and social phobia. Most of these manuals utilize cognitive and behavioral techniques with an emphasis on identifying and challenging maladaptive cognitions and eliminating behaviors that serve to increase and maintain anxiety. Other manuals with a cognitive behavioral emphasis include treatments for bulimia nervosa, weight reduction, stress reduction, depression addictive behaviors, and sexual dysfunction.

As noted above, other forms of therapy have been manualized into specific books such as interpersonal psychotherapy for depression (IPT), which stresses the alleviation of destructive interpersonal patterns that are maintaining depressive mood, and Dialectical Behavior Therapy (DBT) for borderline personality disorder which draws on cognitive-behavioral techniques and eastern philosophy. More recently, important new treatments for bipolar disorder and schizophrenia, featuring family systems therapy directed at emotional lability in these families, have been developed. All of these treatments have received empirical support and are also incorporated into many aspects of clinical practice guidelines.

4. Pros and Cons of Treatment Manuals

One distinct advantage of treatment manuals is that they have been shown to be effective in controlled treatment outcome studies (Barlow and Hofmann 1997, Nathan and Gorman 1998). Thus, when practitioners implement techniques they can do so with the confidence that they are delivering services that have a high probability of success. Furthermore, manuals guide clinicians to use strategies that are spelled out and are clearly discernable.

Wilson (1996) points out that treatment manuals can reduce the errors that might be associated with unrestrained clinical judgment. 'What is typically overlooked, however, and what research on human judgement so clearly documents, is that individualized clinical judgement can just as easily produce worse results than standardized treatments, by introducing errors and inappropriate strategies that are not part of manual-based treatments' (Wilson 1996, p. 302). Manuals, however, outline specific techniques to be used in each session, which have been created by systematic investigation, rather than relying upon clinical judgment to choose a session topic.

Due to their structure, treatment manuals may also facilitate a more highly focused and efficient therapy. With a limited number of sessions and specific goals and strategies outlined for each of these sessions, Wilson (1998) suggests that this more focused approach may actually lead to a more active engagement in therapy for patients.

Treatment manuals also make it easier to train and supervise therapists in specific clinical techniques and strategies (Calhoun et al. 1998). By providing nascent clinicians and supervisors with specific guidelines and techniques to monitor, treatment manuals streamline the learning process and delineate a specific set of therapeutic skills to be learned. This in turn may lead to a greater aptitude and ability for learning therapeutic techniques in general, and a larger armentarium of clinical skills.

Treatment manuals, as structured interventions, can also help clinicians deliver therapy in a brief and in many cases non-traditional format (Craske et al. 1995). For example, even a very brief and unstructured intervention for patients presenting to an emergency room with panic attacks may be effective if delivered early enough to less severe patients (Swinson et al. 1992). Considering the high prevalence rates of clinical and subclinical mental disorders in primary care settings (Fifer et al. 1994) such interventions are clearly cost effective.

Finally, utilization of treatment manuals can promote innovation in the delivery of clinical services. That is, when highly specified treatments are delivered, and assuming appropriate outcomes measures are collected, clinical administrators can determine when a specific treatment is working and for whom. In the case of failures either individually or systematically, it will then be clear that innovations to the treatment program are needed and should be incorporated and evaluated.

Despite these many advantages, a sizeable segment of practicing clinicians object to the notion of treatment manuals, pointing out the many disadvantages in the delivery of what has been called derisively, robot-like therapy (Parloff 1998). For example, dissenters have argued that randomized controlled trials, utilized to validate most manualized treatments, exclude patients with co-morbid diagnoses, among other constraints, and that the results of these types of research studies inherently have limited applicability to 'real-world' settings (Bologna et al. 1998). These same individuals note that highly structured, manualized psychological interventions used in clinical trials cannot generalize to practice settings where psychotherapy is often applied more flexibly and adapted to meet the needs of the patients, who may present with multiple problems (Barlow 1996). This set of objections is based on the fundamental idea that the scientific method, as it is known, is incapable of proving the effectiveness or ineffectiveness of psychotherapy, and that some alternative methodological approach to psychotherapy research is preferable. These are important criticisms that cannot be ignored. But Wilson (1998) outlines how there are significant and important differences between the use of treatment manuals in therapy protocols and their use in clinical practice, with the latter context allowing for greater flexibility. Furthermore, the beginning of much needed research in this area suggests generalizability of manualized treatments to front line clinical settings despite high co-morbidity and a diverse population base (Barlow et al. 1999).

Other clinicians bemoan that structured treatment manuals will compromise the integrity of the therapeutic relationship and thus interfere with the therapy process (Garfield 1996). For example many of these clinicians fear that manualized therapy may reduce the therapy process to mechanized and robotic delivery of techniques, thereby eliminating the importance of the therapist as a clinical tool. Further, innovation and the development of unique and creative strategies will be stagnated by reliance on prescribed treatment strategies. Parloff (1998) summarized these sentiments by stating that many saw the reliance on actuarial decision making over honed clinical judgment as 'perverse.' Many clinicians also feel hindered by having to adhere to a specific set of goals for a given session, and prefer to rely on their own judgment to guide them. However, Wilson (1996) notes, 'if clinical artistry is taken to connote such necessary therapeutic elements as developing a therapeutic relationship and engaging patients in the change process, then treatment manuals do not obfuscate it—rather they demand it' (p. 305). It can also be assumed that even though the therapist utilizing a treatment manual is encouraged to deliver the techniques outlined, within this delivery they are also encouraged to rely on their own personal skills to convey the therapy to the patient (Dobson and Shaw 1988). Finally, the data indicate that therapists engaged in manualized treatments in clinical practice can form strong alliances (Addis et al. 1996). Simply because the therapist has to spend a segment of time conveying specific therapeutic techniques does not mean that they are not building alliances with their patients. Furthermore, a great deal of time is allotted in manual-based therapies to emphasize alliance building. Examples include such strategies as identifying client and therapist expectations for treatment and eliciting client feedback (Addis et al. 1996).

Criticisms of treatment manuals also encompass the belief that manuals may undermine successful case formulation. That is, many clinicians argue that manual-based treatments will be less effective because these approaches assume that all individuals with a given disorder are uniform and have the same symptoms for the same reasons (Wilson 1996). As such, these techniques will 'miss the boat' for a certain subset of patients and will attempt to treat them with techniques that are not applicable. The fact that manuals do not allow for clinical exploration that might lead to the discovery of what works for patients with dissimilar etiology is a commonly expressed concern that may lead to diminished treatment innovation. In fact, treatment manuals do emphasize the current symptom picture over past development processes and idiosyncratic etiology. But research has yet to suggest that therapeutic attention to past developmental processes contributes in a substantial way to the amelioration of the disorder.

Many of these criticisms of manualized treatment have some validity and will be grist for the research mill. Research on the effectiveness or external validity of therapeutic interventions will be the ground on which these competing ideas will be evaluated and tested.

5. The Future of Structured Treatment Manuals

The science and practice of psychotherapy has undergone comprehensive shifts in the 1990s, none arguably more central than the proliferation of semistructured treatment manuals. In this era of treatment guidelines, best practice algorithms, and behavioral healthcare management organizations, treatment manuals increasingly are being embraced. Despite objections, and lingering doubts, treatment manuals have many merits, with demonstrated efficacy the principal attribute. As psychotherapeutic services become more integrated with other forms of healthcare in the twenty-first century, treatment manuals with demonstrated outcomes may become the preferred method of nondrug interventions, and 'formularies' of effective psychological treatments may begin to appear in mental health services or managed behavioral healthcare organizations. In this context, research will progress to address the reasonable concerns that have arisen regarding the implementation of these strategies.

See also: Psychological Treatments, Empirically Supported; Psychological Treatments: Randomized Controlled Clinical Trials; Psychotherapy: Case Study; Psychotherapy: Clinical Practice Guidelines; Psychotherapy: Ethical Issues; Psychotherapy Process Research

Bibliography

Addis M E, Wade W A, Hatgis C 1999 Barriers to dissemination of evidence based practices: Addressing practitioners' concerns about manual based psychotherapies. *Clinical Psychology: Science and Practice* 6(4): 430–41

Barlow D H 1996 Health-care policy, psychotherapy research, and the future of psychotherapy. *American Psychologist* 51(10): 1050–58

Barlow D H, Hofmann S G 1997 Efficacy and dissemination of psychological treatments. In: Clark D M, Fairburn C G (eds.) *Science and Practice of Cognitive Behaviour Therapy*. Oxford University Press, Oxford, UK, pp. 95–117

Barlow D H, Levitt J T, Bufka L F 1999 The dissemination of empirically supported treatments: A view to the future. *Behaviour Research and Therapy* 37: 5147–62

Calhoun K S, Moras K, Pilkonis P A, Rehm L P 1998 Empirically supported treatments: Implications for training. *Journal of Consulting and Clinical Psychology* 66: 151–62

Craske M G, Maidenberg E, Bystrisky A 1995 Brief cognitive-behavioral versus non-directive therapy for panic disorder. *Journal of Behaviour Therapy and Experimental Psychiatry* 26: 113–20

Dobson K S, Shaw B F 1988 The use of treatment manuals in cognitive therapy: Experience and issues. *Journal of Consulting and Clinical Psychology* **56**(5): 673–80

Fifer S K, Mathias S D, Patrick D L, Mathias S D, Mazonson P D, et al. 1994 Untreated anxiety among adult primary care patients in a health maintenance organization. *Archives of General Psychiatry* **5**: 740 50

Garfield S L 1996 Some problems associated with 'validated' forms of psychotherapy. *Clinical Psychology: Science and Practice* **3**(3): 218–29

Luborsky L, DeRubeis R J 1984 The use of psychotherapy treatment manuals: A small revolution in psychotherapy research style. *Clinical Psychology Review* **4**: 5–14

Nathan P E, Gorman J M 1998 *A Guide to Treatments that Work*. Oxford University Press, New York

Parloff M B 1998 Is psychotherapy more than manual labor? *Clinical Psychology: Science and Practice* **5**(3): 376–81

Strosahl K 1998 The dissemination of manual-based psychotherapies in managed care: Promises, problems, and prospects. *Clinical Psychology: Science and Practice* **5**(3): 382–6

Swinson R P, Soulios C, Cox B J, Kuch K 1992 Brief treatment of emergency room patients with panic attacks. *American Journal of Psychiatry* **149**: 944–6

Wilson G T 1996 Manual-based treatments: The clinical application of research findings. *Behaviour Research and Therapy* **34**(4): 295–314

Wilson G T 1998 Manual-based treatment and clinical practice. *Clinical Psychology: Science and Practice* **5**(3): 363–75

D. H. Barlow and K. A. I. Greene

Clinical Psychology: Validity of Judgment

A large body of research exists on the validity of judgments made by mental health professionals (Garb 1998). Most of the studies have been conducted by clinical psychologists, counseling psychologists, and psychiatrists, but important studies have also been conducted by neuropsychologists, social workers, and sociologists. The studies describe how well mental health professionals perform on a range of tasks, e.g., how well they make diagnoses and treatment decisions.

Research on mental health professionals should be of interest to the general public. Many of the studies can help us to understand important social issues, e.g., the occurrence of race bias, gender bias, and other types of biases. Also, a large number of the studies bear on questions that are important for our justice system. These questions include: should mental health professionals be allowed to testify as expert witnesses? (see *Expert Witness and the Legal System: Psychological Aspects*). Are mental health professionals able to make accurate predictions of violence? Are they able to make accurate decisions regarding child abuse and domestic violence? Do they make appropriate judgments when petitioning to have individuals committed to psychiatric hospitals? Finally,

the empirical findings should also be of particular interest to individuals who devise health care policy and decide what services to reimburse. For example, there is a new and intense controversy over the validity of judgments made by clinicians who use the Rorschach Inkblot Test (Wood et al. 1996) (see *Projective Methods in Psychology*). This controversy is well known within the field of clinical psychology, but is not yet well known by people in other professions.

There is another group that should be interested in the results from studies on mental health professionals. Consumers of mental health services should be especially interested in the results of studies on clinicians. If one includes family members of consumers of mental health services and potential consumers of mental health services, then one can conclude that virtually everyone should be interested in this research.

Overall, a huge number of studies (over 1,000) have been published on the validity of clinical judgments and most of the studies have been well designed. Yet, they are not well known outside of mental health fields. In this article, highlights of the research will be described. Topics include: (a) assessment of personality and psychopathology, (b) diagnosis, (c) case formulation, (d) prediction of behavior, and (e) treatment decisions. In general, mental health professionals are able to make reliable and valid judgments for some tasks, but not for others (Garb 1998).

1. Assessment of Personality and Psychopathology

Mental health professionals almost always evaluate a client's personality traits and psychiatric symptoms. Some clinicians also evaluate a client's defense mechanisms. Personality traits can include characteristics like narcissism and dependence, while psychiatric symptoms can include things like hallucinations or panic attacks. A defense mechanism, as defined by psychoanalytic theory, is an unconscious strategy that protects the ego from anxiety. For example, a client may push impulses and thoughts that are unacceptable to the ego into the unconscious.

Results on reliability and validity vary for the tasks of describing psychiatric symptoms, personality traits, and defense mechanisms. Mental health professionals are often good at describing psychiatric symptoms. This should not be surprising. Clients are often able to report if they have had hallucinations, panic attacks, or other symptoms. On the other hand, inter-rater reliability varies widely for describing personality traits, and it is poor for describing defense mechanisms. Perhaps this is because these tasks require clinicians to make more inferences. Given the poor results for describing defense mechanisms, it is important to point out that many clinicians do not perform this task. Psychodynamic therapists regularly evaluate clients' defense mechanisms, but other clinicians (e.g., cognitive behavior therapists) rarely concern themselves with this task (see *Psychoanalysis in Clinical Psychology*).

2. Diagnosis

Diagnostic classification systems have been constructed to help clinicians make diagnoses. The most commonly used classification system in the United States is the American Psychiatric Association's *Diagnostic and Statistical Manual of Mental Disorders*, 4th edition (1994, generally referred to as *DSM-IV*). This classification system contains specific and explicit criteria for making diagnoses (see *Mental and Behavioral Disorders, Diagnosis and Classification of*).

Clinicians' diagnoses are reliable and moderately valid, but only when they attend to diagnostic criteria. Unfortunately, there is evidence that a significant number of clinicians do not adhere to criteria when making diagnoses. That is, many clinicians may think that they are making diagnoses according to the *DSM-IV* criteria, but they do not refer to the criteria when making a diagnosis, and examination of their diagnoses reveals that they are not made in accordance with the *DSM-IV* criteria. This can lead to different types of problems including race bias, gender bias, age bias, and the underdiagnosis or overdiagnosis of some mental disorders. These problems are described below.

The most widely replicated finding for race bias involves the differential diagnosis of schizophrenia and psychotic affective disorders. African-Americans and Puerto Rican Hispanics with bipolar affective disorder (formerly called manic depression) are more likely than Whites with bipolar affective disorder to be misdiagnosed as having schizophrenia. For this reason, Black patients and Puerto Rican Hispanic patients are more likely than White patients to be overmedicated with neuroleptic medications, and their depressive symptoms are more likely to be untreated.

The most widely replicated finding for gender bias involves the differential diagnosis of histrionic personality disorder and antisocial personality disorder. When different groups of mental health professionals have been given identical case histories except for the designation of gender, clinicians have been more likely to diagnose women as having a histrionic personality disorder and men as having an antisocial personality disorder. Histrionic personality disorder is characterized by overly dramatic, attention seeking behaviors (e.g., uncomfortable when not the center of attention), and antisocial personality disorder is characterized by antisocial behaviors (e.g., habitual lying, having no regard for others, showing no remorse after hurting others) (see *Personality Disorders*).

The most widely replicated finding for age bias involves the differential diagnosis of organic impairment and depressive disorder. Compared to young and middle-aged patients, elderly patients are more likely to be diagnosed as having organic impairment and they are less likely to be diagnosed as having a depressive disorder, even when all of the clients are described by the same case history except for the designation of age. Of course, someone diagnosed as having organic impairment will be less likely to receive psychotherapy and antidepressant medicine.

It should be noted that even when clinicians attend to diagnostic criteria and apply them the same way for different groups of patients (e.g., for African-American and White patients), diagnoses can be biased (Widiger 1998). For example, diagnoses can be biased because diagnostic criteria, not the cognitive processes of clinicians, are biased. Diagnostic criteria are said to be biased if they are more valid for one group than for another (e.g., if diagnostic criteria for a particular disorder are more valid for males than for females). In general, little is known about whether diagnostic criteria are biased.

Research has also described other types of errors. Mental health professionals disagree strongly over whether dissociative identity disorder (formerly called multiple personality disorder) is overdiagnosed or underdiagnosed. There is also a controversy over whether attention-deficit/hyperactivity disorder (ADHD) is overdiagnosed. Diagnoses of ADHD have doubled in frequency in recent years (see *Attention-deficit/Hyperactivity Disorder (ADHD)*), while diagnoses of dissociative identity disorder have increased 10-fold. Finally, research suggests that clinicians underdiagnose mental disorders in the mentally retarded, they also underdiagnose mental disorders (e.g., major depression) in terminally ill patients, they frequently underdiagnose personality disorders, they underdiagnose substance abuse in psychiatric patients, and they underdiagnose mental disorders in individuals admitted to substance abuse treatment programs.

3. Case Formulations

The most difficult task for mental health professionals involves making causal judgments. When making causal judgments, clinicians try to explain the causes of their clients' behaviors and symptoms. Inter-rater reliability and validity for this task is often poor. This has been true when psychodynamic clinicians described clients using psychoanalytic theory and when behavior therapists conducted functional analyses to understand the relations that exist between causal variables and behavior problems. One study on reliability will be described in detail. In this study (DeWitt et al. 1983), case formulations were made by two teams of psychodynamically trained clinicians after viewing videotapes of intake evaluations that lasted from 60 to 90 minutes. Both teams were composed of three clinicians. Descriptions were made by consensus. Each team was to, 'Define the basic neurotic conflict(s) that lie at the core of the patients' difficulties. Include the kind of stress to which the patient is vulnerable' (p. 1124). Each team wrote formulations for 18 adults who sought psychotherapy for pathological grief reactions after the death of a parent. With regard to the results, agreement between the two teams was poor. Typically, they mentioned different symptoms, emphasized different conflictual areas, and formulated different cause–effect explanations.

4. Prediction of Behavior

With regard to predicting behavior, mental health professionals have been able to make reliable and moderately valid judgments. For the prediction of suicide and the prediction of violence, inter-rater reliability has ranged from fair to excellent. However, validity has been poor for the prediction of suicidal behavior (suicidal behavior refers to suicide gestures, suicide attempts, and suicide completions). For example, in one study (Janofsky et al. 1988), mental health professionals on an acute psychiatry in-patient unit interviewed patients and then rated the likelihood of suicidal behavior in the next seven days. They were not able to predict at a level better than chance. In contrast to the prediction of suicidal behavior, predictions of violence have been more accurate than chance. In fact, though the long-term prediction of violence is commonly believed to be a more difficult task than the short-term prediction of violence, both short- and long-term predictions of violence have been moderately valid. Finally, the validity of clinicians' prognostic ratings has rarely been studied, but there is reason to believe that clinicians' prognostic ratings for patients with schizophrenia may be too pessimistic (patients with schizophrenia may do better than many clinicians expect).

5. Treatment Decisions

Perhaps the most important task is to make treatment decisions. Unfortunately, many problems exist with the treatment decisions made by clinicians. Problems that will be described include: poor inter-rater reliability, nonconformance with ethical and legal issues, and the use of controversial techniques.

Inter-rater reliability has been poor for several judgment tasks. Two examples will be given. In one study (Felton and Nelson 1984), six clinical psychologists, all trained in behavioral assessment, were asked to formulate specific treatment plans for three clients. When psychologists conducted interviews, treatment plans were in agreement only 59 percent of the time. When psychologists conducted interviews and also used questionnaires and role-playing sessions to collect additional assessment information, trea-

tment plans were in agreement only 62 percent of the time. Inter-rater reliability has also been poor when psychiatrists have made decisions about whether a patient with major depressive disorder should receive psychotropic medicine, electroconvulsive treatment, and/or psychotherapy (e.g., Keller et al. 1986). Differences in the amount and type of treatment could not be explained by variation in the clinical characteristics of patients. The best predictor of treatment was medical center, indicating that the type of treatment severely depressed patients receive depends largely on which hospital they go to.

For some decision tasks, many mental health professionals make decisions that are not in agreement with legal and ethical principles. For example, several studies have reported that many psychiatrists do not make appropriate judgments about committing a patient to a hospital. For example, in one study (Bagby et al. 1991), 26 percent of the individuals depicted as meeting the criteria for involuntary hospitalization were not recommended for commitment. At the same time, 20 percent of those who did not meet the legal standard for commitment were recommended for involuntary hospitalization.

Another example will also illustrate how many mental health professionals make decisions that are not in agreement with legal principles. Mental health professionals are mandated by law to report child abuse, but a widely replicated finding in clinical judgment research is that large numbers of clinicians do not report child abuse (e.g., Brosig and Kalichman 1992). This may sometimes occur because they are unfamiliar with mandatory reporting laws, and it may sometimes occur because they believe it will interfere with treatment.

Some mental health professionals use treatment interventions that are controversial. For example, one controversy involves the recovery of lost memories. Some clinicians will inform their clients that they believe their emotional problems are due to having been abused. They may say this even when the clients have no memory of having been abused. They may believe the client has been abused because of some of the client's symptoms, e.g., low self-esteem or sexual dysfunction. Clinicians may then use a variety of techniques to help clients 'remember' having been abused. For example, they may tell the clients that they were abused and repeatedly ask them to remember the events. Unfortunately, these interventions may lead a client to 'remember' an episode of abuse that never occurred.

6. Discussion

Though biases and errors sometimes occur, it is important to note that clinicians' judgments are frequently reliable and valid. For example, diagnoses are moderately useful when they are made by clinicians who attend to the *DSM-IV* criteria. When made appropriately, diagnoses can inform us about the nature, course, outcome, and recommended treatment for patients. It is also important to note that many clinicians use treatment interventions that have been supported by empirical research. Empirically validated treatment interventions used by psychologists are listed in the Winter 1995 issue of *The Clinical Psychologist* and in subsequent issues of the journal.

See also: Clinical versus Actuarial Prediction

Bibliography

American Psychiatric Association 1994 *Diagnostic and Statistical Manual of Mental Disorders DSM-IV*, 4th edn. American Psychiatric Association, Washington, DC

Bagby R M, Thompson J S, Dickens S E, Nohara M 1991 Decision-making in psychiatric civil commitment: an experimental analysis. *American Journal of Psychiatry* **148**: 28–33

Brosig C L, Kalichman S C 1992 Clinicians' reporting of suspected child abuse: a review of the empirical literature. *Clinical Psychology Review* **12**: 155–68

DeWitt K N, Kaltreider N B, Weiss D S, Horowitz M J 1983 Judging change in psychotherapy: reliability of clinical formulations. *Archives of General Psychiatry* **40**: 1121–8

Felton J L, Nelson R O 1984 Inter-assessor agreement on hypothesized controlling variables and treatment proposals. *Behavioral Assessment* **6**: 199–208

Garb H N 1998 *Studying the Clinician: Judgment Research and Psychological Assessment*. American Psychological Association, Washington, DC

Janofsky J S, Spears S, Neubauer D N 1988 Psychiatrists' accuracy in predicting violent behavior on an inpatient unit. *Hospital and Community Psychiatry* **39**: 1090–4

Keller M B, Lavori P W, Klerman G L, Andreasen N C, Endicott J, Coryell W, Fawcett J, Rice J P, Hirschfeld R M A 1986 Low levels and lack of predictors of somatotherapy and psychotherapy received by depressed patients. *Archives of General Psychiatry* **43**: 458–66

Widiger T A 1998 Invited essay: Sex biases in the diagnosis of personality disorders. *Journal of Personality Disorders* **12**: 95–118

Wood J M, Nezworski M T, Stejskal W J 1996 The comprehensive system for the Rorschach: A critical examination. *Psychological Science* **7**: 3–10

H. N. Garb

Clinical Treatment Outcome Research: Control and Comparison Groups

The essential paradigm for determining if a treatment is effective is to compare it with something else. However, the issue of what that 'something else'—a control or comparison group—should be in any given clinical trial is quite complicated and has enormous theoretical and practical implications. This article will briefly review the role of control and comparison conditions in clinical treatment outcome research and describe advantages and disadvantages of several different types of control and comparison designs. For readers interested in more detailed review of this important area, the classic texts by Kazdin (1980, 1998) are excellent sources.

1. Background

The randomized controlled trial is the *sine qua non* of treatment efficacy research (see *Psychological Treatments: Randomized Controlled Clinical Trials*). A given treatment cannot be considered 'empirically validated' (see Chambless and Hollon 1998) unless trials purporting to establish its effectiveness have employed at least two fundamental methodological features: (a) a credible control condition, and (b) random assignment to the experimental and control conditions. These critical features offer enormous advantages in evaluating a treatment's efficacy. For example, random assignment of participants to the experimental vs. control condition is essential in ruling out alternate explanations of findings, including regression to the mean, maturation, history, effects of repeated testing, and selection basis (Kazdin 1998). The selection of an appropriate comparison or control group also is essential in determining, all other things being equal, if a treatment is effective for a given disorder, and whether it has benefits relative to other treatments for the disorder, as well as how it may achieve its effects and what its 'active ingredients' may be.

2. What Should Control Groups Control for?

The historical paradigm for control groups in behavioral research is the placebo control for pharmacotherapy efficacy trials. Placebo (*I shall please*) controls provide a means of evaluating a pharmacotherapy's efficacy compared with those 'placebo' or 'nonspecific' effects which may occur simply because participants believe they are receiving a credible treatment (Frank 1961). Placebo effects in pharmacotherapy trials, which may be associated with substantial and durable improvement, may occur because of participants' expectations of improvement, demand characteristics, the instillation of hope, the provision of support and education, and other nonspecific effects that are associated with simply being in treatment. Thus, because (a) the pill (or, sometime, injection) in placebo control conditions is medically inert, and (b) nonspecific elements are assumed to be comparable in the 'active medication' and pill placebo conditions, differences in outcome are assumed to be due to the unique 'active ingredients' of the experimental medication.

However, the issue of what constitutes an appropriate 'placebo' condition (and even if the term 'placebo' is appropriate for control conditions in behavioral research) in psychotherapy efficacy research is much more complex and has been the subject of much controversy for many years (see Critelli and Neumann 1984, O'Leary and Borkovec 1978, Parloff 1986, Wilkins 1986). Soon after Rosenthal and Frank (1956) declared that the only adequate control condition in psychotherapy research was a placebo group, several problems with this strategy were raised. Defining a 'psychologically inert' approach that is an appropriate 'placebo' control for behavioral research raised a number of conceptual, practical, and ethical concerns (O'Leary and Borkovec 1978).

Conceptually, defining an appropriate nonspecific control condition for psychotherapy is difficult because many of the 'nonspecific' elements that are common to many psychotherapies (e.g., formation of a therapeutic alliance, provision of support and education, and the instillation of hope) are not inert, in that they are associated with legitimate psychological processes of change and have been shown to have powerful effects on psychological conditions (O'Leary and Borkovec 1978). Moreover, Parloff (1986) noted that referring to these 'common elements' or 'nonspecific elements' as placebos suggests that these powerful mechanisms of change are somehow spurious.

Practically, it can be difficult to conceive of a psychologically inert approach (e.g., an approach that has no theoretically supported rationale for influencing the behavior in question) that is sufficiently credible to participants (O'Leary and Borkovec 1978). This is particularly difficult in the case of lengthy trials where it is essential to retain participants in those conditions over periods of several weeks or months. Furthermore, there has been little agreement on what constitutes an acceptable 'placebo'; thus, there is no single, widely recognized or standardized placebo condition. This makes comparison of effect sizes (a standardized estimate of the magnitude of the effect of the experimental condition relative to the control) across studies very complex (Parloff 1986). This can pose problems, for example, in meta-analyses aimed at comparing the effect sizes for different types of behavioral approaches for a given disorder.

Ethically, for many treatment-seeking populations it is highly questionable whether providing a placebo—a treatment that is expected to have no effect on the presenting problem—can be justified. Furthermore, many placebo conditions, in presenting a credible rationale but no interventions that are expected to improve the participant's problem, are also inherently deceptive (Kazdin 1980, O'Leary and Borkovec 1978).

Given these issues, a variety of different control conditions have been proposed for psychotherapy research. Several of the most common will be described below.

3. Types of Control Groups

3.1 No-treatment Controls

This strategy compares the experimental approach to no treatment; addressing the question 'Does this treatment work better than no treatment at all?' In this paradigm, participants are assessed, randomized to treatment condition, and reassessed after completion of treatment (or after an equivalent length of time for the no-treatment control group).

3.1.1 Advantages. No-treatment controls are generally seen as the 'minimal' or basic standard for evaluating the effectiveness of an intervention (Chambless and Hollon 1998). No treatment control conditions are sometimes referred to as assessment-only controls, as they control for the effects of the study assessments and the passage of time. Thus, they are useful in evaluating conditions that have a high likelihood of improving without intervention (e.g., spontaneous remission) or when the natural history of a disorder is not well established.

3.1.2 Disadvantages. There are a number of problems with no-treatment control conditions. No-treatment controls do not control for the effects of participant expectancies, 'common elements' or nonspecific effects, or time spent in treatment. Ethical and practical issues arise when no-treatment controls are used with populations seeking treatment for a particular condition, and particularly when the condition is life-threatening or associated with significant medical, psychosocial, or other problems. Furthermore, withholding treatment from individuals who request it raises ethical issues, particularly for those disorders where effective alternative treatments have been demonstrated to exist. No-treatment controls may also raise practical issues, because individuals assigned to the no-treatment condition may seek alternative therapies or become demoralized and drop out of the study, particularly for more lengthy trials. This can lead to problems associated with confounding of conditions or differential attrition.

Some of the practical and ethical concerns associated with no-treatment control conditions can be avoided in designs where the experimental treatment is 'added on' to a standard treatment program and the control group receives the standard treatment only. Thus, all participants would, at minimum, receive the standard treatment. This design addresses the question, 'Does the addition of Intervention X improve outcomes over standard treatment for this disorder' and avoids many ethical and practical problems. However, this strategy still does not control for time spent or nonspecific effects.

3.2 Wait List/Delayed Treatment Controls

This strategy is similar to the no-treatment control approach, but differs in that some form of treatment is offered to those assigned to the no-treatment control condition after completion of study assessments. Thus, after completing all past treatment assessments, participants originally assigned to the delayed-treatment condition may be given the option of no further treatment or receiving the experimental treatment or an alternative approach.

3.2.1 Advantages.
Like the no-treatment control condition, this strategy is one that addresses the question, 'Is Treatment X effective compared with no treatment?' and can help clarify the effects of the experimental intervention with respect to the natural history of the disorder. Provided that participants in the delayed treatment control are adequately monitored and the disorder of interest is one where the likelihood of clinical exacerbation and negative consequences are minimal, this strategy avoids some of the ethical problems associated with withholding treatment from individuals who need or request it. Some prospective participants who might not accept randomization to a no-treatment control condition may be more likely to accept randomization to a delayed treatment control.

3.2.2 Disadvantages.
Like the no-treatment control strategy, delayed treatment controls do not control for differences in nonspecific effects of treatment, including expectancies, demand characteristics, attention, and so forth. Moreover, evaluation of long-term effects of treatments is difficult with delayed treatment controls, as provision of treatment to the participants in the delayed-treatment condition may obfuscate determination of long-term effectiveness of the treatment in follow-up evaluations. This can, of course, be avoided by waiting to provide treatment to the delayed-treatment condition until after the completion of all follow-up assessments, but this may in turn result in the same practical and ethical problems associated with no-treatment controls.

3.3 Attention/Discussion/Minimal Treatment Controls

This strategy most closely resembles what has been referred to as a psychotherapy 'placebo.' In this paradigm, the participants are assigned to a condition that provides some common elements of psychotherapy (e.g., time spent, presentation of a credible rationale for the approach, receiving support and attention), but does not offer the hypothesized 'active ingredients' of the experimental intervention. The specific nature of this type of control group varies widely from trial to trial, but may include interventions such as having the participants meet with a clinician who provides education and support, 'discussion control' groups where several participants meet to provide mutual support or are presented with education materials, 'bibliotherapy' conditions where participants receive written reading or other educational materials such as videotapes, and several more.

3.3.1 Advantages.
Attention-control conditions, by controlling for time spent and providing some common elements of psychotherapy, are typically seen as more stringent control than no-treatment or delayed-treatment control conditions. If well-conceived, carefully implemented and monitored attention controls can provide a test of the hypothesized active ingredients of the experimental condition and may allow for some evaluation of mechanisms of action of the experimental condition, which is not usually feasible with no-treatment or delayed-treatment controls.

3.3.2 Disadvantages.
As noted above, there have been several problems with attention/discussion control conditions. First, it is unclear whether many of these approaches actually adequately control for nonspecific elements of the experimental intervention (Basham 1986). Second, given that a key ingredient of such approaches is the presentation of a convincing rationale, but at the same time the intervention '...should have no currently supported theoretical reason why the placebo would influence the behavior under question' (O'Leary and Borkovec 1978, p. 821), a truly convincing rationale for these conditions is not so easily formulated. If participants are not convinced or do not see themselves as deriving adequate benefit from the approach, they may be more likely to drop out of the condition, leading to problems of differential attrition in the control vs. experimental condition. Furthermore, since the attention/discussion is intended to be 'inert' and not directly affect the disorder or problem, ethical questions regarding the withholding of treatment may be raised for those conditions where effective alternative approaches exist. Finally, as noted above, because there has been little consensus on what such controls should consist of (either within or across different disorders), attention control conditions vary widely from study to study, making cross-study comparisons difficult.

3.4 Active Treatment or Comparative Controls

In this strategy, the experimental intervention is compared with another 'active' intervention, ideally one of demonstrated efficacy for the disorder. Thus, a comparative design directly compares two treatment conditions without conceptualizing either as being a formal control group (Basham 1986). Rather than addressing the issue of 'Does this treatment work?' this strategy addresses questions such as 'Is Treatment A more effective than Treatment B' and 'Does Treatment A offer advantages over standard treatment for this disorder?' It should be noted that for many disorders, the comparison condition may be a psychotherapy or a pharmacotherapy.

3.4.1 Advantages. When well conceived and executed, comparison controls do control for many artifacts and demand characteristics, including time spent in treatment, the provision of a credible rationale, and other common elements or nonspecific effects (although it should be noted that equivalence of nonspecific elements across conditions must be supported by process evaluations). This strategy has the additional advantage of permitting more thorough evaluation of treatment process and mechanisms of action, and it can help identify what treatment is best for a given disorder, as well as what type of treatment is best for what type of individual (Basham 1986, Kazdin 1986, O'Leary and Borkovec 1978). Furthermore, by comparing the experimental intervention to a treatment of demonstrated efficacy for the disorder (e.g., a 'standard' or 'reference' condition), this approach avoids deception and many of the ethical problems discussed earlier.

3.4.2 Disadvantages. Comparison controls, by controlling for nonspecific elements and essentially pitting the hypothesized 'active ingredients' of one approach against those of another, are highly stringent tests of novel interventions. Thus, such studies often lead to small effect sizes and findings of no significant differences between interventions (Luborsky et al. 1975), which in turn may lead to problems in interpretation of the study outcomes. For example, in a trial comparing two active treatments where no significant difference in effectiveness is found, interpretation of the 'absolute' effectiveness of the treatments is problematic. That is, although the treatments compared were not significantly different, it is often hard to gauge the magnitude of the effect of either treatment on the symptoms targeted (Nathan 1997). Kazdin (1986) has also pointed out that comparative designs may overemphasize elements that differentiate the treatments compared (e.g., use of specific techniques) over other important variables that may affect outcome (e.g., characteristics of thera-

pists or participants). Finally, for those disorders where a number of viable comparison approaches are available, but no one clear standard or 'reference' condition that is widely acknowledged as the most effective, choice of the comparison condition is challenging. Kazdin (1986) has provided thoughtful recommendations for the selection and implementation of appropriate active treatment control conditions.

The relative stringency of comparison controls relative to attention/discussion, delayed-treatment, or no-treatment controls has practical implications as well. For example, within a given field, if one type of intervention (Treatment A) routinely uses no-treatment controls in efficacy studies, while another type of intervention (Treatment B) uses discussion control conditions, while trials evaluating Treatment C routinely use active treatment controls, the estimated effect size of Treatment A is likely to be larger than that for Treatment B, which is in turn likely to be larger than for Treatment C, even though all three approaches may be comparably effective. Progressively smaller effect sizes for different types of control conditions (no treatment, placebo, active treatment) has been suggested in several meta-analyses (Basham 1986).

3.5 Dismantling Controls

Also referred to as component control condition, this strategy essentially requires specification of a given treatment or treatment 'package' into its component elements, and then evaluating the effectiveness of the treatment with or without one specific element or technique of interest. For example, a cognitive behavioral approach might be evaluated with and without a relaxation training component.

3.5.1 Advantages. By altering only a single element of a treatment, component control strategies offer an elegant strategy for evaluating well-defined techniques and components. Component control conditions can address issues of particular theoretical or clinical relevance, by isolating the most effective 'ingredients' of complex or multifaceted treatment packages. Furthermore, because the interventions compared differ only with respect to a single element, many of the practical, ethical, and theoretical issues associated with placebo and no-treatment controls can be avoided (O'Leary and Borkovec 1978).

3.5.2 Disadvantages. Before treatments or treatment packages can be dismantled, they must first be demonstrated to be effective. Thus, for a given disorder, there may only be a small number of approaches with sufficient empirical support that would justify their 'dissection' in a dismantling study. Similarly, not all approaches are easily parsed into discrete components. Furthermore, to justify a full dismantling trial, a compelling rationale for the component to be evaluated must be made, e.g., the component might be '... very risky, costly, or theoretically interesting' (Strayhorn 1987).

3.6 Pill Placebo Conditions

Citing the problems noted above with placebo conditions for psychotherapy research, Klein (1997) and others have argued for wider use of pill placebo controls for psychotherapy trials. In this strategy, the experimental psychotherapy would be compared with a pill placebo condition. This strategy was used in the landmark NIMH Treatment of Depression Collaborative Research Program (Elkin et al. 1985), which compared cognitive therapy and interpersonal psychotherapy to a placebo/clinical management condition (with imipramine/clinical management as a reference condition).

3.6.1 Advantages.
The use of pill placebo conditions in psychotherapy research has a number of potential advantages. First, when carefully implemented, pill placebos provide control for participant expectations and many demand characteristics. Klein (1997) also points out that this approach enables researchers to evaluate psychotherapy effects in the context of a pharmacotherapy-responsive population. This approach avoids problems with 'psychotherapy placebo' conditions, as it compares the effects of a given psychotherapy with those nonspecific effects of a pill placebo. This strategy may also allow clearer evaluation of treatment processes and mediation effects (Crits-Christoph 1997).

3.6.2 Disadvantages.
Pill placebo controls require the availability of a widely recognized effective pharmacotherapy for the disorder in question, as the rationale for the pill placebo control requires that participants expect to improve by taking the pill. Thus, a major drawback of this approach is that for many conditions for which psychotherapies may be appropriate, no such reference pharmacotherapy exists. Moreover, because most pharmacotherapies are delivered in conjunction with a minimal supportive psychotherapy condition to foster compliance and enhance retention (conditions which closely resemble placebo psychotherapies), the problems associated with conceiving and implementing minimal or placebo psychotherapies may not be avoided entirely (Carroll 1997).

4. Summary

Just as there is no one 'perfect' clinical trial, there is no one perfect control group. The particular control group selected does determine, however, the nature of the questions that can be addressed by the trial (e.g., 'Does this treatment work' to 'Does this treatment work for the reasons we believe it does' to 'Does this treatment have specific benefits compared with other available treatments?').

Selection of an optimal control condition for a given study thus depends on many factors, including the level of development of the treatment being evaluated, the availability of alternative treatments for the disorder, the severity or natural history of the disorder, and many others (Crits-Christoph 1997). Thus, early in the development of a field, where questions remain about a disorder's natural course, and available treatments are scarce, no-treatment or delayed treatment controls may be appropriate choices. However, as a field becomes more sophisticated and alternative treatments are identified, research questions also become more fully developed and require the use of control groups that can address progressively more complex questions.

See also: Censuses: Demographic Issues; Internal Validity; Psychological Treatments: Randomized Controlled Clinical Trials; Psychological Treatments, Empirically Supported

Bibliography

Basham R B 1986 Scientific and practical advantages of comparative design in psychotherapy outcome research. *Journal of Consulting and Clinical Psychology* **54**: 88–94

Chambless D L, Hollon S D 1998 Defining empirically supported therapies. *Journal of Consulting and Clinical Psychology* **66**: 7–18

Carroll K M 1997 Manual guided psychosocial treatment: A new virtual requirement for pharmacoltherapy trials? *Archives of General Psychiatry*. **54**: 923–8

Critelli J W, Neumann K F 1984 The placebo: Conceptual analysis of a construct in transition. *American Psychologist* **39**: 32–9

Crits-Christoph P 1997 Control groups in psychotherapy research revisited. *Treatment, 1, Comment 1,* posted September 22

Elkin I, Parloff M B, Hadley S W, Autry J H 1985 NIMH treatment of depression collaborative research program: Background and research plan. *Archives of General Psychiatry* **42**: 305–16

Frank J D 1961 *Persuasion and Healing.* Johns Hopkins University Press, Baltimore, MD

Kazdin A E 1980 *Research Design in Clinical Psychology.* Harper and Row, New York

Kazdin A E 1986 Comparative outcome studies of psychotherapy: Methodological issues and strategies. *Journal of Consulting and Clinical Psychology* **54**: 95–105

Klein D F 1997 Control groups in pharmacotherapy and psychotherapy evaluations. *Treatment, 1, Article 1,* posted September 22

Luborsky L, Singer B, Luborsky L 1975 Comparative studies of psychotherapies: Is it true that 'everyone has won and all must have prizes'?*Archives of General Psychiatry* **32**: 995–1007

Nathan P E 1997 Would a pill placebo have redeemed Project MATCH? *Treatment*, 1, *Comment* 3, posted September 22

O'Leary K D, Borkovec T D 1978 Conceptual, methodological, and ethical problems of placebo groups in psychotherapy research. *American Psychologist* **33**: 821–30

Rosenthal D, Frank J D 1956 Psychotherapy and the placebo effect. *Psychological Bulletin* **53**: 294–302

Strayhorn J M 1987 Control groups for psychosocial intervention outcome studies. *American Journal of Psychiatry* **144**: 275–82

Wilkins W 1986 Placebo problems in psychotherapy research: Social-psychological alternative to chemotherapy concepts. *American Psychologist* **241**: 551–6

K. M. Carroll

Clinical versus Actuarial Prediction

Paul Meehl's book *Clinical Versus Statistical Prediction: A Theoretical Analysis and a Review of the Evidence* (Meehl 1954) concluded that the prediction of numerical criterion variables of psychological interest (e.g., faculty ratings of graduate students who had just obtained a Ph.D.) from numerical predictor variables (e.g., scores on the Graduate Record Examination, grade point averages, ratings of letters or recommendation) is better done by a proper linear model than by the clinical intuition of people presumably skilled in such prediction. The point of this article is to review summaries and conclusions subsequent to Meehl's original one and to present evidence that even what can be termed 'improper' linear models (Dawes 1979) often yield predictions superior to human intuition.

1. Type of Statistical Models

A proper linear model is one in which the weights given to the predictor variables are chosen in such a way as to optimize the relationship between the prediction and the criterion. Simple regression analysis, where the predictor variables are weighted in order to maximize the correlation between the subsequent weighted composite and the actual criterion, is the most common example. Discriminant function analysis is another example; weights are given to the predictor variables in such a way that the resulting linear composites maximize the discrepancy between two or more groups. Ridge regression analysis, another example, attempts to assign weights in such a way that the linear composites correlate maximally with the criterion of interest in a new set of data.

2. Review of the Empirical Findings

Meehl was concerned primarily with the statistical vs. clinical methods for *integrating* information; thus, he compared instances in which both types of prediction had been made on the basis of exactly the same data. (He also insisted that the accuracy of the statistical model should not be checked on the same data on which it was derived—or that the sample size be so large that it will not appear superior owing to capitalizing on chance fluctuations.) Twelve years later, Jack Sawyer (1966) published a review of about 45 studies; again, in none was clinical prediction superior. Unlike Meehl, Sawyer also included studies in which the clinician had access to more information than that used in a statistical model—for example, interviews of people about whom the predictions were made, or interviews by experts who had access to the statistical model information prior to the interview. Such interviews did not improve the clinical predictions. In fact, the predictions were better when the opinions of the interviewers were ignored.

A prototypical study by Carroll et al. (1988) supports Sawyer's conclusion. A Pennsylvania parole board considered about 25 percent of the 743 parolees to be failures within one year of being released, for reasons such as being recommitted to prison, absconding, being apprehended on a criminal charge, or committing a technical parole violation. A parole board interviewer's ratings had predicted none of these outcomes; the largest correlation was only 0.06. In contrast, a three-variable model based on the type of offense that had led to imprisonment, the number of past convictions, and the number of noncriminal violations of prison rules did have a modest predictability, correlating about 0.22, a result consistent with earlier findings that actuarial predictions based on prior record predict with a correlation of about 0.30 across a large number of settings. When parolees were convicted of new offenses, the seriousness of their crimes was correlated 0.27 with the interviewers' ratings of assaultive potential, but a simple dichotomous evaluation of past heroin use correlated 0.46. All parole board interviewers had access to all this statistical information, but did worse.

None of these correlations is particularly high; first, the sample is highly select, being limited to those who have been convicted of a crime; second, not all the parolees who committed crimes were caught, and third, these types of behaviors are not as predictable as we believe they are or would like them to be. The difference in the effectiveness of actuarial vs. clinical prediction is, however, clear.

Moreover, this difference is consistent with comparisons of actuarial vs. clinical methods for predicting violence (see, e.g., Werner et al. 1984, Monahan 1997).

An important qualification: the best prediction in general is that neither violence nor criminal behavior will be repeated. Although the general 'base rate' prediction is that people will *not* repeat problems, judges—professional and nonprofessional alike—have a bias to believe that repetition is common. The studies show that judgments about who is more likely than whom to repeat are much better made on an actuarial than on a clinical basis.

After his book had been out about 30 years, Meehl (1986) was able to conclude. 'There is no controversy in social science which shows such a large body of qualitatively diverse studies coming out so uniformly in the same direction as this one.' Since that time, even more evidence has been accumulating in favor of Meehl's generalization and practical conclusion; 110 studies that Dawes et al. (1989) reviewed favored it. Subsequently, Grove and Meehl (1996) published a meta-analysis involving even more studies. Their conclusion (Grove and Meehl (1996 p. 293) was, 'The *clinical method* relies on human judgment that is based on information contemplation and, sometimes, discussion with others (e.g., case conferences). The *mechanical method* involves a formal, algorithmic, objective procedure (e.g., equation) to reach the decision. Empirical comparison of the accuracy of the two methods (136 studies over a wide range of predictors) shows that the mechanical method, is almost invariably equal to or superior to the clinical method.'

There are four logical relationships possible between the information set on which a clinician or expert makes a prediction and information set on which a formal model (e.g., equation) is based. These sets may be identical, which was the original requirement for a comparison in Meehl's 1954 book. Or one information set may be a subset of the other; in the studies reviewed by Sawyer and in almost all subsequent studies having this structure, the set on which the model is based is the subset of the set available through the clinician (who, for example, is allowed to supplement a sparse information set with an interview). In the field of psychology, the model prediction has always been superior. There are, however, exceptions in the field of medicine, in the situations where the clinical physician has access to more information than is used by the model (*not* in situations where the inputs are identical). Even in these, however, the models may be modified on the basis of interviewing the clinicians themselves to 'distill' what they are responding to, so that once again the statistical prediction becomes superior. For example, a predictive system termed APACHE-II did not predict as well as physicians who would survive in emergency wards, yet the modified model termed APACHE-III did in fact predict better than physicians who would survive the first 24 hours (Knaus et al. 1991). Another possible relationship is that the information sets are overlapping, which has not been studied much.

3. Explanation for the Empirical Findings

Why the consistent results? The answer involves an understanding of which factors are favorable to the linear model and which disfavor the intuitive prediction. Whatever additional factors there may be that disfavor the model or favor the clinician are outweighed by the former types of factors in almost all contexts.

First, consider the statistical prediction. Each instance to be predicted is characterized in terms of its aspects that allow its location in a category or along a dimension. These categories and locations have been found in the past to be *in general* predictive. Aspects that have no such predictive power are automatically ignored. The model involves the weighting of the predictive aspects. Moreover, these aspects often are diverse, e.g., an undergraduate grade point average, a number of prison violations, an instance of violence that led to hospitalization (even a rating routinely made on the first day of hospitalization). The statistical model automatically makes the predictive variables comparable, by assigning weights to integrate them.

Now, consider the drawbacks of attempting to make an intuitive integration of the information. Suppose even that we are not interested in making an optimal prediction, just in integrating information from diverse and incomparable dimensions. Suppose, for example, we were deciding between two jobs where the important considerations are pay and enjoyment of the activities involved. It may be very easy, knowing our preferences for different types of activities, to judge which job will be more enjoyable. But now job A pays more than job B, but is less enjoyable. Which should be chosen? We must weight the two dimensions—at least implicitly—if we are to make a choice. What psychologists have found (e.g., Svenson 1992, Langer 1994) is that in such conflicting dimensions situations people generally search for reasons to dismiss one or another of the dimensions as 'not really that important.' Then, there is no conflict between dimensions, and all that must be done is to make an ordinal judgment, again of the form 'more is better.'

Now, consider the additional complications of trying to decide on an intuitive basis which of two instances is more predictive of something. While we might at least have some insight—explicit or implicit—into how we assess differences and how much to care about them, we often have less insight into how to assess differences and to weight them in order to predict. (Feedback observing *all* outcomes without being affected by our judgment—e.g., of success or failure—is necessary, but not sufficient; see Einhorn and Hogarth (1978).)

As noted, statistical integration has the advantage that weighting obviates the problem of conflicting dimensions. The question then arises of whether the weighting system need be optimal in order to maintain the advantage. The answer—based on mathematical considerations, simulations, and empirical investigation—is no. The robust result is that so long as the dimensions are weighted in the correct direction, *ad hoc* weighting (e.g., 'intuitive weighting,' unit weighting, or even weights chosen according to some random sampling scheme) yields results that are close enough to those provided by optimal weighting that the resulting linear composites still outperform clinical intuition, especially when the predictive variables tend to be positively correlated with each other. Composites based on such nonoptimal weights have been termed 'improper linear models' (Dawes 1979). In fact, not only may such models yield predictions similar enough to optimal models that they outperform clinical judgment, but they may even outperform optimal models on cross-validation, because they are not subject to the 'overfitting' problem that plagues many optimal models. For example, the 'robustness' of unit-weighted models on cross-validation has been noted as far back as the 1930s by Wilks (1938). The mathematical rational for this robustness of unit weighting has been provided by Wainer (1976) and Wainer and Thissen (1976).

In fact, improper models such as unit-weighted models may be particularly advantageous in situations where models developed in one context are to be applied in a slightly different context—which many of us (Dawes 1997) believe to be the norm in social science, as opposed to applying a model developed on one sample of a particular population to another sample drawn from this exact same population. ('Cross-validation' actually refers to such a subsequent application to a sample from the exact same population; a far more descriptive term would be simply 'validation,' where what is commonly termed a 'validation' sample should be termed a 'development' sample. The point here is that when we move across contexts that vary to some—perhaps known perhaps unknown—degree, even the estimate based on what is standardly termed 'cross-validation' may be overly optimistic.)

An empirical overview of the success of improper models in general is provided by Dawes (1979). Perhaps the most famous example of an improper model is that provided by Goldberg (1965) to predict a diagnosis of psychosis vs. neurosis by using MMPI profiles. The unit-weighted composite obtained by adding together three scaled scores indicating psychosis (*L*, *Pa*, *Sc*) and subtracting two indicating neurosis (*Hy*, *Pt*) not only 'outperformed all diagnosticians' (Goldberg 1965, p. 24) but was more stable across subsamples than were nonlinear complex scores—and it was not for want of trying enough of the latter.

Later, Dawes and Corrigan (1974) demonstrated that improper weights (in fact two weighting systems chosen on random bases except for the direction of the weights) not only outperformed clinical judgment in the MMPI diagnosis problem and several others, but

did as well as the linear composites based on the diagnostic experts' judgments. Unit weighting was even better.

4. Conclusions and Recommendations

Thus, 'the whole trick is to know what variables to look at and then to know how to add' (Dawes and Corrigan 1974, p. 105). Of course, there are some contexts where configural, multiplicitive, or even more complicated models are more appropriate than are simple additive models; such models may, for example, be found in the area of predator–prey population dynamics. But the decision making discussed here involves a prediction of important human outcomes where—although the human experience may be complex—what can be best distilled from it are simple predictive variables where more (or less) is better (e.g., test scores, indicators of past performance, past criminal or psychiatric record). Not only do we find such simple monotone relationships in our studies, but we search for such relationships and tend to code our social world in terms of variables capturing monotone relationships to what is important to us. (Occasionally, a predictor variable has a single-peaked relationship to the criterion, as when moderate aggression is more desirable in a business person; such a variable is easily transformed into a monotone variable by evaluating distance from the ideal.) When there are strong scientific reasons for hypothesizing a complex model, naturally they should not be ignored. In the absence of such theory or evidence, however, the claim that it is possible to construct a valid nonadditive model 'in our head'—particularly one representing some sort of valid, ineffable intuition—is pure hubris.

In contrast, an understanding of the research reviewed in this article leads to 'an awareness of the modest results that are often achieved by even the best methods, [an awareness which] can help to counter unrealistic faith in our predictive powers and our understanding of human behavior. It may well be worth exchanging inflated beliefs for an unsettling sobriety, if the result is openness to new approaches and variables that ultimately increase our explanatory and predictive powers' (Dawes et al. 1989, p. 1673).

For the most recent survey and analysis, see Swets et al. (2000).

See also: Clinical Psychology: Validity of Judgment

Bibliography

Carroll J S, Werner R L, Coates D, Galegher J, Alibrio J J 1988 Evaluation, diagnosis, and prediction in parole decision making. *Law and Society Review* **17**: 199–228

Dawes R M 1979 The robust beauty of improper linear models in decision making. *American Psychologist* **34**: 571–82

Dawes R M 1997 Qualitative consistency masquerading as quantitative fit. In: Dall Chiara M L, Doets K, Mundici D (eds.) *Structures and Norms in Science*. Kluwer, Dordrecht, The Netherlands, pp. 387–94

Dawes R M, Corrigan B 1974 Linear models in decision making. *Psychological Bulletin* **81**: 95 106

Dawes R M, Faust D, Meehl P E 1989 Clinical versus actuarial judgment. *Science* **243**: 1668 74

Einhorn H J, Hogarth R M 1978 Confidence in judgment: persistence in the illusion of validity. *Psychology Review* **85**: 395–416

Goldberg L R 1965 Diagnosticians vs. diagnostic signs: the diagnosis vs. neurosis from the MMPI. *Psychological Monographs* **79**: 1–28

Grove W M, Meehl P E 1996 Comparative efficiency of informal (subjective, impressionistic) and formal (mechanical, algorithmic) prediction procedures: the clinical–statistical controversy. *Psychology, Public Policy, and Law* **2**: 293–323

Knaus W A, Wagner D P, Lynn J 1991 Short-term mortality predictions for critically ill hospitalized adults: science and ethics. *Science* **254**: 389–94

Langer E 1994 The illusion of calculated decisions. In: Schank R, Langer E (eds.) *Beliefs, Reasoning and Decision Making: Psycho-Logic in Honor of Bob Abelson*. L. Erlbaum, Hillsdale, NJ, pp. 33–53

Meehl P E 1954 *Clinical Versus Statistical Prediction: A Theoretical Analysis and a Review of the Evidence*. University of Minnesota Press, Minneapolis, MN

Meehl P E 1986 Causes and effects of my disturbing little book. *Journal of Personality Assessment* **50**: 370–5

Monahan J 1997 Clinical and actuarial predictions of violence. In: Faigman D, Kaye D, Saks M, Sanders J (eds.) *Modern Scientific Evidence: the Law and Science of Expert Testimony*. West, St. Paul, MN, Vol. 1, pp. 300–18

Sawyer J 1966 Measurement and prediction, clinical and statistical. *Psychological Bulletin* **66**: 178–200

Svenson O 1992 Differentiation and consolidation theory of human decision making: a frame of reference for the study of pre- and post-decision processes. *Acta Psychologica* **80**: 143–68

Swets J A, Dawes R M, Monahan J 2000 Psychological science can improve diagnostic decisions. *Psychological Science in the Public Interest* **1**: 1–26

Wainer H 1976 Estimating coefficients in linear models: it do not make no nevermind. *Psychological Bulletin* **83**: 213–7

Wainer H, Thissen D 1976 Three steps toward robust regression. *Psychometrika* **41**: 9–34

Werner P D, Rose T L, Yesavage J A, Seeman K 1984 Psychiatrists' judgments of dangerousness in patients on an acute care unit. *American Journal of Psychiatry* **141**: 263–6

Wilks S S 1938 Weighting systems for linear functions of correlated variables when there is no dependent variable. *Psychometrika* **8**: 20–6

R. M. Dawes

Clitics, Linguistics of

Clitics straddle the boundary between words and affixes because they have some properties of each. Therefore clitics pose a quandary for the longstanding division of labor in grammar between syntax and morphology. Clitics can be found in nearly every language; however, they may be hard to recognize, because they may be disguised as contracted forms, for instance. Clitics also exhibit some unique properties that have been especially difficult to account for in grammar. For that reason, they help linguists to reformulate hypotheses about the grammatical structure that underlines language (Nevis 2000).

1. Illustration of Clitics

Grammatical analysis offers a basic distinction between words and affixes: words are independent elements used for phrase and sentence formation (see *Word, Linguistics of*), whereas affixes are word-building units that attach to roots and stems (see *Morphology in Linguistics*). Problematic for this division are two sorts of objects: those that form phrases but are not fully independent, and those that help to build words but exhibit a loose attachment that typical affixes do not. Both kinds have been labeled *clitics*, a term derived from Ancient Greek *enklitikón* 'leaning on a previous (word),' which in various guises has been used in grammatical description for two millennia.

As an illustration of clitics, consider English contracted forms, such as *'ve* in *you've*. It lacks the independence of *have*, but otherwise acts like a full verb by helping to form sentences and by showing agreement with the subject. If *'ve* is a verb, then it is a verb pronounced without a vowel (since the *e* is silent here)—can a word in English consist of a single pronounced consonant? While most contractions in English and in other languages qualify as clitics, not all do.

A different sort of example is the English possessive *'s* (see *Possession (Linguistic)*, and Jespersen 1922). Unlike other affixes in English, it attaches to an entire phrase, as in *the King of Morocco's death*, where the *'s* is affixed to the phrase *the King of Morocco* rather than just to the word *Morocco* (that is, this is not Morocco's death). If *'s* is to be treated as an affix, then grammarians will have to adopt an expanded view of affixation that includes such phrasal affixes.

The study of clitics is important because their position on the edge of the word/affix distinction sheds light on the complexities involved in determining how languages are constructed. The passage in Sect. 3 below will survey some of the unique properties attributed to clitics that have forced linguists to accommodate new facts into their theories of grammar.

2. Types of Clitics

Clitics have traditionally been cited according to the way they attach: they may be *enclitics* (attaching leftward onto a host), *proclitics* (attaching rightward), or *endoclitics* (attaching inside the host). In Spanish *me* 'me' illustrates both the enclitic and the proclitic options: when *me* follows its host word, as in *díga-me* 'tell me,' it functions as an enclitic, but when it precedes the host as in *no me díga* 'don't tell me' it is a proclitic. Most scholars assume that clitics attach in a very loose fashion to their hosts, and therefore must occur outside of regular affixes. Following that reasoning, proclitics precede any and all prefixes, and enclitics follow all suffixes. Endoclitics are so rare—if they exist at all—that specialists have examined any putative cases closely to see whether the positing of endoclitics can be avoided altogether.

In technical descriptions of languages, a category 'clitic' remained commonplace throughout the twentieth century, but seldom had it been incorporated into grammatical theories until the 1970s, when the phenomenon was surveyed by Zwicky (1977). Zwicky's early investigations established three types of clitics: simple clitics, special clitics, and bound words. In later work, bound words and special clitics merged, producing two categories: simple and special clitics.

Simple clitics can be substituted for full words. The simple clitic is thus considered a reduced version of an independent word, sharing its meaning and manifesting a similar pronounciation. An example is the pronoun *them* in a sentence like *we like them*, which is often reduced in casual speech to *we like 'em*. The clitic form *'em* is relatable to full form *them* and the clitic's distribution in a sentence is a subset of the distribution of the full word, with the contraction occuring in most places the nonclitic is found, but when the pronoun occurs under emphasis or in isolation, clitic *'em* is not permitted and the full form is used. For example, in response to the question *Who do you like better, us or them?*, the full word *them* is an acceptable answer, but the contraction *'em* is not. Although simple clitics might be related to their free forms, they are not mere reductions due to fast speech: in this regard note that the English simple clitics like *'em* are used in slow speech as well.

Special clitics, on the other hand, either lack a freeform equivalent or show some special syntax (to be discussed in the next section). The English possessive *'s* lacks a nonclitic alternative, therefore it constitutes a special clitic. As illustrated below, the Tagalog pronouns are restricted to the second position of the sentence, so they constitute special clitics in Zwicky's scheme.

3. Unique Properties of Clitics

Accommodating clitics in theories of grammar has proven challenging. Initial investigations into clitics focused on their status in between words and affixes and pondered whether the notion clitic should be viewed as a special unit of grammar (distinct from the affix and the word) or as a sort of deviant affix or deviant word. Although early views opted for separate treatment, the debate persevered through the 1990s, with some scholars arguing for affixal status and others for word status. Positing the clitic as a unit distinct from the word and the affix has led scholars to attribute to it a special set of properties (Zwicky 1977, Spencer 1991, Katamba 1993). Usually the main thrust of this approach is to present a scheme locating and attaching the clitic in the appropriate place in a phrase and attaching the clitic to one of two neighbors.

Unique characteristics such as clitic doubling and special syntax have been claimed to be shared with neither affixes nor words. Such special properties help highlight differences between clitics on the one hand and words or affixes on the other, or to enrich linguists' understanding of the syntactic patterns of pronouns and other word classes. Some unique properties are particular to clitic pronouns, and in the last quarter of the twentieth century many scholars have devoted their efforts to the study of these aspects of clitic pronouns. In particular, the clitic pronouns in Spanish and French have attracted considerable attention because the pronouns may occur in places where regular nouns may not. French and Spanish direct objects follow the verb if they are noun phrases (in French *tu as vu le chien* 'you have seen the dog') whereas they precede the verb if they are pronouns (*tu l'as vu* 'you have seen it,' literally *you it have seen*). There are other differences as well (van Riemsdijk 1999).

Clitic doubling occurs when a pronoun appears in the same clause as the noun phrase to which it refers. For example, in certain South American Spanish varieties, the proclitic pronoun *lo* can be found together with the direct object:

Lo	vimos	a	Juan
Him	saw	to	Juan

'We saw John'

Normally pronouns replace noun phrases rather than repeat them, so this behavior is noteworthy.

Another pattern unique to clitics is *Wackernagel's Law*, which refers to the restriction of elements to a slot immediately after the first unit of a phrase or clause; that initial unit can be a phrase or word (Steele 1977, Nevis et al. 1994). An example of Wackernagel clitics comes from Tagalog. In Tagalog, pronouns and certain adverbs must occur after the first word or phrase of the sentence. Usually this is the verb, but it can also be the negative *hindi* or some other word. The following sentences offer several clitic pronouns and particle clitics (*na* 'already,' *lamang* 'only,' and politeness marker *po*; such 'particle clitics' function as adverbs in Tagalog), which are highlighted to indicate the second position in the sentence.

Nakita	**ko**	**na**	**siya**
Seen	I	already	her/him

I have already seen her/him'

Hindi	**ka**	**niya**	*kapatid*
Not	you	his/her	sibling

'You aren't his/her sibling'

Tatlo	*lamang*	*po*	*sila*
Three	only	POLITE	them

'There are only three of them'

The Tagalog clitics must remain in the second slot in the sentence, no matter what comes before them (verb, negative, or numeral).

4. Clitics vs. Leaners

Studies on clitic elements must establish that the objects under investigation exhibit mixed status between affixes and words. Diagnostic tests can be used to identify properties of clitics, words and affixes (Zwicky 1977). Because the phonological attachment of a clitic to its host cannot be assumed and must be proved, it is important to distinguish clitics from *leaners* (also called *quasiclitics* or *semiclitics*), which are simply unstressed words. Although clitics also usually lack stress, they nevertheless show clear evidence of being part of a word's pronunciation. By contrast, a leaner is merely unstressed and does not become part of another word's pronunciation.

For example, the contraction of English *is* to *'s* entails a change in pronunciation according to the last sound of the word it attaches to. Accordingly it is pronounced *z* at the end of *dog* but *s* after *cat*:

The dog's barking.

The cat's purring.

This is the behavior of the plural suffixes as well, which has two pronunciations, *z* and *s*, under the same conditions as the contracted form of *is*:

The dogs are barking.

The cats are purring.

Thus, contracted *'s*, which is a clitic, and plural *s*, which is a suffix, share a pattern of pronunciation that depends crucially on the last sound of a word. This fact of pronunciation distinguishes clitic *'s* from a word that is merely unstressed, as demonstrated by the pronunciation of the word *who* when used to introduce a relative clause (e.g., *the one who got elected*)—it is usually pronounced with a reduced vowel in casual conversation (that is, more like *huh* and not with full vowel *u*). Here unstressed *who* is considered a leaner rather than a clitic because it does not attach phonologically to a neighboring word as does contracted *'s*.

It is not always easy to decide what is a clitic and what is not. When speakers contract *want to* to *wanna*, investigators determine whether *wanna* can be derived in a principled way from *want* plus *to* using regular rules of grammar. If it can, then *wanna* may contain a clitic form of *to*. However, if additional rules are needed to handle this case in an idiosyncratic way, then the derivation is not considered valid and *wanna* might instead be considered a single indivisible word rather than a composite of *want* and *to*. In English, *wanna* is not just a matter of fast speech reduction because it can convey a difference in meaning from the sequence *want* plus *to*: a sentence like *Tung Chee-hwa I want to succeed* offers two meanings (*I want Tung Chee-hwa to succeed* and *I want to succeed Tung Chee-hwa*), whereas the sentence *Tung Chee-hwa I wanna succeed* is restricted for most speakers to one meaning (*I want to succeed Tung Chee-hwa*) and resists the other interpretation.

5. Clitics as Derived Words and Phrasal Affixes

Many of the scholars researching clitic doubling, and to a certain extent Wackernagel's Law, seem to assume that clitics are wordlike in nature. A number of studies treat clitics as derived words. But even if most clitics are analyzable as derived words, there is nevertheless a small residue of clitics that are better handled as affixes. English possessive *'s* is an example of one such clitic: it is best treated as an affix attaching not to any individual word but to a group of words insofar as it offers no wordlike characteristics beyond phrasal affiliation and clearly patterns with the other inflectional affixes of English in morphology and pronunciation. To the chagrin of theoreticians, both kinds of clitics appear to be required to handle such puzzles as the wordlike contracted auxiliaries of English (e.g., *'ve*) and its phrasal affix possessive.

Clitics can sometimes cluster into longer sequences. These sequences exhibit looser order than affix chains but stricter order than word order is generally capable of. In Tagalog, for example, all pronoun clitics consisting of a single syllable precede all particle clitics, which in turn precede all pronoun clitics consisting of two syllables (e.g., *ko* 'I' precedes *na* 'already,' and *na* precedes *siya* 'her/him.'

Nakita	*ko*	*na*	*siya*
Seen	I	already	her/him

'I have already seen her/him'

But among the two-syllable pronouns order is not restricted; *nila* 'they' and *ako* 'me' may occur in either order:

Hindi	*nila*	*ako*	*nakita* = *Hindi* **ako** **nila** *nakita*
Not	they	me	seen

'They didn't see me'

Similarly, order need not be limited among the particle clitics; *lamang* 'only' and the politeness marker *po* occur in two orders as well.

Tatlo	**lamang**	**po**	*sila* = *Tatlo* **po** **lamang** *sila*
Three	only	POLITE	them

'There are only three of them'

Surprisingly, such clitic sequences have been used to argue for the more wordlike standing of clitics, for the affixal nature of clitics, and for the unique status of clitics. Clearly more work needs to be done in this area.

6. Clitics in Historical Studies

In the 1980s and 1990s the focus was on accommodating clitics into current theories of grammar, but previously to this most investigations of clitics had scrutinized historical change and the development of affixes from separate words. Affixes can arise from several sources historically; one such source is a former word. A word can become less stressed, begin to lean on a neighboring word, and eventually turn into a fully dependent element. This is known as the *agglutination cycle* (see *Grammaticalization*). For instance, the Modern English adjective suffix *ly* developed from a Germanic word that also yielded Modern English *like*. One hypothesis is that full words first cliticize before becoming affixes, as demonstrated in the nearly extinct Balto-Finnic language Livonian, which has a comitative suffix -*ks* meaning 'with' (e.g., *suu-ks* 'with the mouth') that came from a former word *kansa* 'with' (that is, this word would originally have been the phrase **suun kansa*, literally 'mouth with'), which cliticized into -*kas* before becoming suffix -*ks*. However, it is by no means evident that cliticization is a necessary stage in the development of affixes from words.

Another question is whether the agglutination cycle operates in one direction only. Normally a word weakens into a clitic, and then the clitic fuses as an affix into the host. For example, German *dem* 'the' has fused with *zu* 'to' to form *zum* 'to the.' So if the agglutination cycle is limited to one direction of development (that is, it is unidirectional), then affix sequencing might be a good indication of an earlier word order. Since the affixes would have been separate words previously, they could provide a tool for linguistic reconstruction of word order patterns in earlier stages of a language (see *Linguistics: Comparative Method*).

But exceptions to this scenario have been noted. An affix can loosen and can become a clitic, and a clitic can likewise become a separate word. The modern English possessive is a case in point because it is a clitic derived from a regular suffix in old English. Older English exhibited attachment of the possessive to the head noun in a phrase (as is expected of an affix) rather than to the end of the phrase (as a phrasal-affix type clitic):

Earlier: The King's crown of England
Now: The King of England's crown

An illustration of a clitic turning into a word can be found in the Sami languages (formerly called Lappish), where the original abessive ending developed first into a clitic and then in some varieties of Sami into a separate word. The abessive expresses absence (and is translated as 'without'). In Northern Sami, the abessive is an enclitic on a preceding noun (e.g., *airoj-taga* 'without oars'), whereas in the Enontekiö subdialect it has become an independent adverb, standing even without a preceding noun:

Mun báhcen taga
I   go   without
'I do without'

Clitics may play a role in word order change. When verbal clitics are attracted to the second position, the Wackernagel slot, that pattern may be generalized to other, nonclitic verbs. If a language had originally placed verbs at the end of a sentence, generalizing this second position pattern would cause verbs to migrate to second position. That is, a subject–object–verb pattern will become subject–verb–object (see *Word Order*). Although the details of this proposal may not be widely accepted, it demonstrates that the role of clitics should not be ignored in the study of word order change.

7. Conclusion

Most, if not all, languages offer at least one clitic element. However clitics themselves do not seem to form a homogeneous class, as illustrated in English by the rather wordlike contracted auxiliary *'ve* and the more affixal possessive *'s*. Clitics cross-cut most word classes (see also *Word Classes and Parts of Speech*) and may appear as adverbs, pronouns, prepositions, auxiliary verbs, and the like. Apparently, the only word classes inaccessible to clitics are nouns and verbs, as well as adjectives (and this is because putative 'clitic nouns' and 'clitic verbs' would be treated separately as *incorporations*; see *Linguistics: Incorporation*).

Apart from the historical studies, much of the literature on clitics in the first three-quarters of the twentieth century was pretheoretical in nature insofar as investigators struggled to understand the fundamentals of what a clitic is. Subsequent debates were often couched in particular theoretical frameworks or focused exclusively on certain kinds of clitics (especially pronominal clitics). Although numerous generalizations have been established, no real consensus had resulted in a single theory of clitics by the end of the twentieth century—probably because clitic phenomena do not constitute a uniform phenomenon. To supplement such argumentation, future research on clitics will have to incorporate evidence from areas such as psycholinguistic experimentation (see also *Psycholinguistics: Overview*) and language disorders as well as acquisition of language (see also *First Language Acquisition: Cross-linguistic*), and will have to better integrate studies on the historical evolution of clitics. But above all, the study of clitics will continue to assist scholars in defining and delimiting related areas such as Phonology, Morphology, and Syntax).

See also: First Language Acquisition: Cross-linguistic; Grammaticalization; Linguistics: Comparative Method; Linguistics: Incorporation; Morphological Case in Linguistics; Morphology in Linguistics; Phonology; Possession (Linguistic); Syntax; Valency and Argument Structure in Syntax; Word Classes and Parts of Speech; Word, Linguistics of; Word Order

Bibliography

Bauer L 1988 *Introducing Linguistic Morphology*. Edinburgh University Press, Edinburgh, UK

Carstairs A 1981 *Notes on Affixes, Clitics, and Paradigms.* Indiana University Linguistics Club, Bloomington, IN

Jespersen O 1922 *Language, Its Nature, Development and Origin.* Allen and Unwin, London

Katamba F 1993 *Morphology.* St Martin's Press, New York

Nevis J 2000 Clitics. In: Booij G, Lehmann C, Mugdan J, Skopeteas S (eds.) *Morphology: An International Handbook on Inflection and Word Formation.* de Gruyter, Berlin, Article 41

Nevis J A, Joseph B D, Wanner D, Zwicky A 1994 *Clitics: A Comprehensive Bibliography 1892–1991.* Benjamin, Amsterdam

van Riemsdijk H (ed.) 1999 *Clitics in the Languages of Europe.* de Gruyter, Berlin

Spencer A 1991 *Morphological Theory: An Introduction to Word Structure in Generative Grammar.* Blackwell, Oxford, UK

Steele S 1977 On the count of one. In: Juilland A (ed.) *Studies Presented to Joseph Greenberg.* Anma Libri, Saratoga, CA

Zwicky A 1977 *On Clitics.* Distributed by the Indiana University Linguistics Club, Bloomington, IN

J. A. Nevis

Closed and Open Systems: Organizational

Closed and open systems refer to whether organizational entities, such as groups and organizations, are viewed as relatively closed or open to their environment. Such a perspective has a profound influence on how organizations are described and studied. When treated as closed systems, organizations are unaffected by their environment, and attention is directed inward to internal structures and behaviors. As open systems, organizations are interdependent with their environment, and focus is outward to how such interaction is managed.

Knowledge of closed and open systems derives from the broad framework of general systems theory (GST) which seeks to explain the structure and behavior of complex wholes called systems (e.g., von Bertalanffy 1956, Miller 1978). This broad metatheory is based on related research from the physical, biological, and social sciences, and seeks to discover general laws which apply to all levels of systems from single cells to societies.

This article shows how GST applies to organizations. It describes the systemic properties of organizations as closed and open systems, and explains how they are structured and managed.

1. Organizations as Systems

Organizational scholars use GST to describe the general properties of organizational systems. This includes defining their constituent parts and how they are inter related to form a system. It also involves identifying different levels of organizational systems and explaining how they interact with each other.

1.1 Organizational Parts, Relationships, and Wholes

A key premise of GST has to do with the definition of a system and how it forms an organized whole. A system is composed of parts and relationships among them. The system provides the framework or organizing principle for structuring the parts and relationships into an organized whole. This makes systems capable of behaving in ways that are greater than merely the sum of the behaviors of their parts, thus leading to the common adage: 'the whole is greater than the sum of its parts.' Organizational scholars have expended considerable effort in identifying the constituent members or subunits of organizational systems and examining relationships among them. They have sought to discover the organizing principals through which the parts are arranged into a coherent whole. For example, job design researchers have identified different elements of jobs; they have shown how they can be combined to affect employee motivation. Group dynamics scholars have spent considerable time addressing issues of group membership and member interaction. They have discovered different ways of structuring groups to perform tasks that members could not do working alone. They have shown how, under certain conditions, groups can outperform individuals, thus leading to various high-performing group designs, such as self-managing teams, quality circles, and cross-functional teams. Similarly, organization theorists have identified the different components of organizations and examined relations among them. They have found different ways to organize the components and relationships for competitive advantage.

1.2 Levels of Organizational Systems

A second principle of GST has to do with the multilevel nature of systems. Systems exist at different levels; the levels exhibit a hierarchical ordering, with a higher level of system being composed of systems at lower levels. For example, societies are composed of organizations; organizations are composed of groups; groups are composed of individuals; and so on. Higher-level systems provide constraints and opportunities for how a system organizes its parts, and the nature of those parts affects the system's organizing possibilities. Thus, to describe a system at a particular level and explain its behavior, it is necessary to look both upward to the higher level system within which it is embedded and downward to its constituent parts.

This multilevel perspective has led scholars to identify different levels of organizational systems, and to focus on understanding them and how they interact with each other. Considerable attention has been directed at specifying appropriate levels of analysis, both for conceptualizing about organizational systems and for aggregating and disaggregating data that apply to different levels. For example, scholars have developed analytical guides for aggregating data from individuals to devise measures of group and organization functioning. As researchers have developed more comprehensive theories and more powerful analytical methods, they have made finer distinctions among levels of organizational systems, particularly above the organization level. This has led to at least five levels of organizational systems:

(a) individual member, role, or job;

(b) group;

(c) organization;

(d) population of organizations and/or alliance among organizations; and

(e) community of populations and/or community of alliances.

2. Organizations as Closed Systems

Closed systems do not interact with the environment, and consequently their behavior depends largely on the internal dynamics of their parts. They seek to maintain a steady state or equilibrium among their parts while performing goal-directed behaviors. Because the environment is inconsequential for goal achievement, system behavior is highly specified and maximally controlled within the system.

Until the late 1960s, organizational scholars tended to employ a closed-system perspective for studying organizations. Organizational environments were seen as relatively simple and predictable, and thus were not problematic or significant for how organizations behaved. Attention was directed at the internal dynamics of groups and organizations, particularly at how member behavior was controlled to achieve specific objectives and goals. This led to extensive knowledge of organizational control mechanisms and search for the best way to structure organizational systems. For example, at the individual level, job design researchers discovered how to analyze and maximally specify the most efficient way to perform various tasks. At the group level, researchers showed how group structures and processes could contribute to member conformity to group norms. At the organization level, scholars studied a variety of devices for controlling member behavior, such as managerial hierarchy, rules/procedures, and functional design.

3. Organizations as Open Systems

In the late 1960s, organizational scholars began to broaden their focus to external forces affecting organizational systems. This open systems view was fueled by growing applications of GST to the social sciences and by realization that the behavior of organizational systems could not be adequately explained without examining environmental relationships and their effects on the system (e.g., Aldrich 1979, Buckley 1967, Katz and Kahn 1966, Lawrence and Lorsch 1967, Scott 1981, Thompson 1967). It has led to considerable research about organizational environments, their dynamics and effects, and how organizational systems interact with them. An open systems perspective draws attention to how organizations exchange information and resources with their environment, and how the two mutually influence each other. Moreover, it provides a number of useful concepts for understanding how organizations maintain functional autonomy while influencing and adapting to external forces.

3.1 Critical Functions

To survive and prosper, open systems need to perform at least four critical functions:

(a) transformation of inputs of energy and information to produce useful outputs;

(b) transaction with the environment to obtain needed inputs and to dispose of outputs;

(c) regulation of system behavior to achieve stable performance; and

(d) adaptation to changing conditions.

Because these different functions often place conflicting demands and tension on open systems, system viability depends on maintaining a dynamic balance among them. Organizational researchers have devoted considerable time to identifying and explaining how these four functions operate and contribute to organizational survival and effectiveness. This has led to knowledge about how organizations and groups produce products and services through operating and developing different technologies; how they protect their technologies from external disruptions while acquiring raw materials and marketing finished products; how they regulate themselves for stable performance while initiating and implementing innovation and change. This research defines a key role of management in organizational systems as sustaining a dynamic balance among these four functions; one that allows the organization sufficient stability to operate rationally yet requisite flexibility to adapt to changing conditions.

3.2 Information and Resource Flows

As open systems, organizations seek to sustain a cycle of activities aimed at taking in inputs of information and resources from the environment, transforming them into outputs of goods and services, and exporting them back to the environment. This cycle enables organizations to replenish themselves continually, so long as the environment provides sufficient inputs and the organization delivers valued outputs. Considerable research has gone into understanding how organizations manage these information and resource flows. One perspective focuses on how organizations process information to learn how to improve themselves and to relate to their environments. Organizations must be capable of learning from their experiences and of disseminating such knowledge widely if they are to change themselves to respond to emerging conditions. Consequently, research has been directed at organizational learning and knowledge management, particularlyatdiscoveringmechanismstoenhancelearning capability, such as shared databases, groupware, and decision-support systems. Another view concentrates on how organizations compete for resources through managing key resource dependencies. Attention has been directed at how organizations gain access to resources without becoming overly dependent on those who supply them. Still another perspective focuses on how organizations gain legitimacy from environmental institutions, so they can continue to function with external support. Researchers have sought to identify the institutional demands of powerful resource providers, and how organizations respond to them.

3.3 Boundaries

In managing information and resource flows, organizations, like all open systems, seek to establish boundaries around their activities. These organizational boundaries must be sufficiently permeable to permit necessary environmental exchange, yet afford the organization adequate protection from external demands to allow for rational operation. Organizational scholars have devoted considerable attention to understanding the dual nature of organizational boundaries. They have studied various boundary-spanning roles that relate the organization to its environment, such as sales, public relations, and purchasing. They have examined how organizational members perceive and make sense out of environmental input, and how organizational boundaries vary in sensitivity to external influences. Researchers have also identified different strategies for protecting transformation processes from external disruptions while remaining responsive to suppliers and customers.

3.4 Self-regulation

Viewed as open systems, organizations use information about how they are performing to modify future behaviors. Referred to as cybernetics, this information feedback enables organizations to be self-regulating (e.g., Ashby 1956). They can adjust their behavior to respond to deviations in expected performance. To be effective however, organizations must have sufficient diversity of responses to match the variety of disturbances encountered. Thus, as techno-

logies and environments become more complex and uncertain, organizations seek to become more flexible and nimble. They can enhance their adaptive capabilities through such innovations as downsizing, employee empowerment, and re-engineering.

Extensive research has been devoted to understanding how organizations regulate themselves. Using modern information technology, organizations have developed a variety of methods for setting goals, obtaining information on goal achievement, and making necessary changes. For example, database technologies enable organizations to store large batches of information and to logically connect events, actions, and outcomes. Employees can access and revise this information through on-line, common databases.

3.5 Equifinality

As open systems, organizations display the property of equifinality. They can achieve objectives with varying inputs and in different ways. Consequently, there is no one best way to design and manage organizations, but there are a variety of ways to achieve effective performance. This contrasts sharply with a closed system perspective which seeks the one best way to structure and control organizations.

Organizational researchers have devoted considerable attention to identifying different choices for designing and managing organizations. This has led to a virtual revolution in new organizational designs aimed primarily at making organizations leaner, more flexible, and more responsive to human resources. For example, traditional bureaucratic structures that emphasize efficiency and control have increasingly been supplanted with designs that emphasize flexibility and innovation, such as matrix organizations, horizontal organizations, network organizations, and virtual organizations. Moreover, researchers have developed contingency theories which specify under what technological, environmental, and human conditions different organizational designs are likely to be most successful. For example, these newer, more innovative designs are best suited to situations where technologies are complex, environments are unpredictable, and people have high growth needs.

4. Promising Trends

Organizational researchers have recently applied systems concepts to understand how organizations can adapt to rapidly changing, unpredictable environments. They have borrowed heavily from complexity theory which seeks to explain the behaviors and changes that can occur when the parts of complex systems interact (e.g., Holland 1995, Brown and Eisenhardt 1998).

Such systems tend to be self-organizing in response to environmental feedback; they can change in nonlinear and dynamic ways and can invent entirely new responses to external forces. These concepts provide a dynamic, change-oriented perspective on organizations. They help to explain how organizations can restructure themselves continually to keep pace with fast-changing environments.

See also: Bureaucracy and Bureaucratization; Bureaucratization and Bureaucracy, History of; Leadership in Organizations, Psychology of; Leadership in Organizations, Sociology of; Organization: Overview; Organizational Climate; Organizational Decision Making; Organizations and the Law; Organizations, Sociology of

Bibliography

Aldrich H E 1979 *Organizations and Environments*. Prentice-Hall, Englewood Cliffs, NJ
Ashby W R 1956 *An Introduction to Cybernetics*. Wiley, New York
Brown S L, Eisenhardt K M 1998 *Competing on the Edge*. Harvard Business School Press, Boston
Buckley W 1967 *Sociology and Modern Systems Theory*. Prentice-Hall, Englewood Cliffs, NJ
Holland J H 1995 *Hidden Order: How Adaptation Builds Complexity*. Addison-Wesley, Reading, MA
Katz D, Kahn, R L 1966 *The Social Psychology of Organizations*. Wiley, New York
Lawrence P R, Lorsch J W 1967 *Organization and Environment*. Harvard University Press, Boston
Miller J G 1978 *Living Systems*. McGraw-Hill, New York
Scott W R 1981 *Organizations: Rational, Natural, and Open Systems*. Prentice-Hall, Englewood Cliffs, NJ
Thompson J O 1967 *Organizations in Action*. McGraw-Hill, New York
von Bertalanffy L 1956 General systems theory. *General Systems* **1**: 1–10

T. G. Cummings

Co-constructivism in Educational Theory and Practice

Ever since Piaget's dynamically Kantian epistemology, it has been widely accepted as a pervasive assumption that learning is a constructive process. In contrast to the epistemological assumption of empiricism that what we know is a direct reflection of ontological reality, learning is considered as an active construction of knowledge. Learners, as they strive to make sense of their world, do not passively receive stimulus information matching independent physical structures, but genuinely interpret their experience by

(re)organizing their mental structures in increasingly sophisticated ways, while interacting with the physical and symbolic environment. According to Piaget and most of his successors in cognitive, developmental, and educational psychology, this process of adaptive and viable reality construction is enabled and constrained both by biologically grounded structures (the strength and scope of which, however, are not yet well known) and by the already existing preknowledge (concepts, operative schemas, and structures) of the individual.

Even though the constructivist assumption makes some traditional problems in both psychology and education easier to solve, it also raises some new ones. An important problem is how we can think of achieving intersubjectivity. How can individuals who personally construct their knowledge independently of each other come to the same or similar cognitive structures? How can we *share* a knowledge of our culture if people are conceived of as being solo learners, and socially isolated Robinson Crusoe figures?

One striking answer, which at the same time challenges traditional (Western) epistemological constructivism, stems from symbolic interactionist (Mead 1934) and sociocultural theory (Vygotsky 1962). It claims that learning is fundamentally a *social activity*. Learning and enculturation are not bounded by the individual brain or mind but are intrinsically social endeavors, embedded in a society and reflecting its knowledge, perspectives, and beliefs. People construct their knowledge, not only from direct personal experience, but also from being told by others and by being shaped through social experience and interaction. The basis of personal development and enculturation, thus, is not the socially isolated construction of knowledge, but its co-construction in a social and cultural space. Or, as Bruner puts it: 'Most learning in most settings is a communal activity, a sharing of the culture. It is not just that the child must make his knowledge his own, but that he must make it his own in a community of those who share his sense of belonging to a culture' (Bruner 1986, p. 86). Knowledge, from this perspective, is no longer seen as solely residing in the head of each individual, but as being distributed across individuals whose joint interactions and negotiations determine decisions and the solution of problems.

1. Concept and Process of Co-construction

No precise and widely accepted definition of the concept and process of co-construction can be found in psychological or educational literature. What has been provided is very diverse and depends on the theoretical context in which it is embedded. Differences can be found with regard to at least three aspects:

(a) the social type of discourse eligible to be called co-constructive: mother–child dialog, peer interaction, teacher–student interaction, learning in teams, computer-supported collaborative work;

(b) the psychopedagogical processes involved in productive co-constructive activity: productive dialog such as exploratory talk and collective argumentation, collaborative negotiation after sociocognitive conflict or as a process of reciprocal sense-making, joint construction of a shared understanding, elaboration on mutual knowledge and ideas, giving and receiving help, tutoring and scaffolding;

(c) the expected outcomes of collaboration: taken-as-shared individual vs. socially shared cognitions; convergence and intersubjectivity; academic task fulfillment, student motivation, and conceptual development; effects on skills in listening, discussion, disputation, and argumentation.

Common to most theoretical contexts of co-constructivism is the implication of some kind of collaborative activity and, through joint patterns of awareness, of seeking some sort of convergence, synthesis, intersubjectivity, or shared understanding, with language as the central mediator. Theorists, moreover, largely converge in the adopted methodology of microgenetic analysis that has been used to examine the inherently fragile processes of co-construction.

1.1 (Neo-)Piagetian Perspective

In a (neo-)Piagetian framework, true dialog becomes possible and facilitates the individual cognitive construction of operatory structures when children are able to take other persons' points of view into consideration and when they are able to resolve sociocognitive conflict. Although regarded (by the early Piaget) as a developmental factor, social interaction—specifically, peer interaction—remains more of a catalyst for individual cognitive development. According to studies carried out by co-workers of Piaget (e.g., Doise and Mugny 1984, Perret-Clermont et al. 1991), social factors, such as the need to deal with conflicting perspectives, can have a productive impact on cognitive behavior. For example, in a Piagetian conservation task, pupils more easily progressed to a subsequent level of development after having been confronted by contradictory judgments given by an adult or another child.

1.2 (Neo-)Vygotskyan context

In Vygotsky's cultural-historical view of development as a process of meaningful appropriation of culture, the interactive foundation of the cognitive is at the core of the developmental process. In contrast to Piaget's view, however, 'the constructivist principle of the higher mental functions lies outside the in-dividual—in psychological tools (such as 'language') and interpersonal relations' (Kozulin 1998, p. 15). According to Vygotsky's claim that interpersonal interactions on a social plane serve as prototypes for intrapersonal processes, i.e., for functions to be internalized, co-construction can be seen as (asymmetrical) adult–child interaction, or interaction between a child and a more capable peer, in the 'zone of proximal development.' 'What a child can do today in co-operation, tomorrow he will be able to do on his own' (Vygotsky 1962, p. 87). The quality and development of higher order thinking is prepared by the co-constructive patterns and distinctive properties of social interaction. Meaningful new learning emerges by embedding mental functions (like logical argumentation, proof, reflection, or problem solving) into specific forms of goal-directed interaction and dialog, where more knowledgeable individuals tailor a task in such a way that a child can successfully coperform it. The acquisition of a new concept or mental function becomes progressively more skillful as the child learns to respond in gradually more sophisticated and personally more meaningful ways to the co-constructive, sense-mediating context of adult regulations, and eventually takes over responsibility for his or her own learning.

1.3 Perspective of Situated and Socially Shared Cognition

Situated learning theory views human cognition as being embedded in and inseparable from specific sociocultural contexts. The goal of learning is to enter a community of practice and its culture, i.e., to learn, like an apprentice, to use tools as practitioners use them (Brown 1989). As a process, learning takes place through the interaction and transaction between people and their environments. Co-construction, from a situated cognition perspective, can be seen as having two or more individuals collaboratively construct a shared understanding, or a solution to a problem, which neither partner entirely and necessarily possesses beforehand (Chi 1996). In a widely quoted definition proposed by Roschelle and Teasley (1995): 'Collaboration is a coordinated, synchronous activity that is the result of a continued attempt to construct and maintain a shared conception of a problem' (p. 70).

At the heart of this concept of co-construction are two coexisting activities: collaboratively solving the problem, and constructing and maintaining a *joint problem space*. Both activities require constant negotiations and recreations of meaning, i.e., trying to find out what can reasonably be said about the task in hand, and occur in structured forms of conversation and discourse utilizing language and physical actions as their most important mediators and resources. With the use of symbolic tools, it becomes possible for the conversants to express and objectify meanings, to compare and change them deliberately, to exchange and renegotiate them with others, and to reflect on the organization of judgments and arguments (see van Oers 1996). However, as observational studies show, co-constructive learning is hardly a homogeneous but an inherently fragile process in the service of convergence and mutual intelligibility. The achievement of a shared conceptual structure cannot be reliably predicted, nor does the iterative construction of a joint problem space through cycles of displaying, confirming and repairing occur by simply putting two students together. As Roschelle and Teasley (1995, p. 94) remark:

> Students' engagement with the activity sometimes diverged and later converged. Shared understanding was sometimes unproblematic and but oftentimes troublesome. The introduction of successful ideas was sometimes asymmetric, although it succeeded only through coordinated action. These results point to the conclusion that collaboration does not just happen because individuals are co-present: individuals must make a conscious, continued effort to coordinate their language and activity with respect to shared knowledge.

1.4 Context of Discourse Linguistics: Grounding

From the perspective of communication or conversation analysis, co-constructive or collaborative learning requires individuals to establish, maintain, and update some degree of mutual understanding. The basic process by which this is accomplished between individuals is called *grounding* (Clark and Brennan 1991). Grounding as a basic form of collaboration means the moment-by-moment coordination and synchronization of the content-specific as well as the procedural aspects and steps of co-constructive activity. There is no need, however, to fully ground every aspect of an utterance. Clark and Brennan (1991, p. 148) frame a pragmatic criterion for grounding: The conversants 'mutually believe that they have understood what [they] meant well enough for current purposes.' Thus, the techniques that are used for grounding are shaped by the goal and the medium of communication. That is, the criterion of grounding and the techniques exploited for its maintenance dramatically change according to the purpose of communication (e.g., planning a party, swapping gossip, or gaining deep understanding) and the constraints of its medium (copresence and visibility in face-to-face communication; sequentiality and reviewability in letter communication, e-mail, or computer-supported collaborative work).

1.5 Pedagogical Context of Tutoring

Another aspect of concern for the social nature of learning—and for a crucial way in which it is supported by culture—is instructional dialog or conversation. This term refers to a discursive activity in

classrooms that permits the co-construction of meaning between teachers and students, tutors and tutees, the more and the less experienced. Consistent with Vygotsky's theory of the constructive role played by adults in children's acquisition of knowledge, the teacher's goal of assistance can be seen as trying to get the students to share his or her understanding and knowledge. However, because of the asymmetrical distribution of knowledge between teachers and students, understanding might be expected to be less jointly constructed in instructional conversation than it is observed to be in peer-cooperative dialog. Actions that tutors or teachers can take in order to elicit responses, including some co-constructive behavior from a tutee, are, for example, described in literature on reciprocal teaching and on cognitive apprenticeship (Collins et al. 1989). They can be subsumed under two broad categories: (a) modeling, scaffolding, and fading as content-specific ways of providing hints, strategies, and situational forms of coaching and guidance that are tailored to the needs of individual students; and (b) prompting as a more content-neutral invitation by the tutor to elicit elaborations, reflections, and self-explanations from students (Chi 1996).

2. Pedagogical Facilitation of Co-construction

The question of how best to support co-constructive learning is concerned with the design of effective collaborative learning environments. Much empirical work has addressed the conditions under which productive collaborative interaction is most likely to occur, and a whole range of possible ways to enhance its quality has been provided. Among the input characteristics that exert a complex influence upon the quality of interaction are: the preparation of the students for collaborative learning (including training for cooperation and discourse prior to the collaborative learning event), the establishment of a culture of dialog and of problem-based learning, group characteristics (composition, size, ability and sex), the goal and incentive structure of the task, and the structuring of group interaction (see, for a review, Webb and Palincsar 1996).

2.1 Importance of Dialog

Probably the most important single feature of a culture of collaborative learning is dialog as opposed to, e.g., solo learning and teacher monologs. Emphasis on joint learning and instructional conversation among peers, and between teachers and students, is associated with the internal mediating processes that are essential for an understanding of how co-construction through discourse operates and influences outcomes. The pedagogical cultivation of processes such as negotiation of meaning, reciprocal sense-making, revising one's cognitions in situations of sociocognitive conflict, precise verbalization of reasoning and knowledge, listening to others' lines of argumentation, tuning one's own information to that of a partner, giving and receiving help, or modeling cognitive and metacognitive activities to be internalized by the participating individuals should, thus, be placed at the core of instructional design.

2.2 Support Structures for Collaborative Thinking and Problem Solving

A means of improving the quality of collaborative thinking is explicit process-related and task-related support structures in the learning environment (Pauli and Reusser 2000). *Process-related support structures* refer to the structuring of the interaction through the implementation of scripts for collaboration, such as 'reciprocal teaching', 'scripted cooperation', or 'prompting' for questions and elaborations. These techniques have in common the fact that a set of cognitive and metacognitive strategies which have to be used in a prescribed way is provided. A complementary way of supporting collaborative learning is to provide students with *task-specific support structures* and help. The main goal of task-related assistance, including more or less explicit instructions, domain-specific formats of task representation, and the modeling of strategies, is to scaffold students' domain knowledge construction, understanding, and skill acquisition. What is not yet clear, however, is how much structuring of the interaction is actually beneficial. Ideally, the quality and quantity of guidance and help has to be adjusted to the learners' subjective needs. As Cohen (1994) has pointed out, overstructuring interaction may be counterproductive and have detrimental effects, if it 'prevent[s] students from thinking for themselves and thus gaining the benefits of the interaction' (p. 22).

One promising possibility for making environments more supportive for collaborative learning is to enrich learning situations with technology. Well-designed *computer-based cognitive tools* provide users with both process-related and task-related instruments of thought and communication. As mediational resources and cognitive tools for the representation, negotiation, and modeling of concepts and activities, educational software has the potential—by making conceptual structures and processes visible, accessible, and manipulable on a computer screen—to facilitate processes of sharing understanding and of achieving convergence and intersubjectivity (Reusser 1993).

2.3 Structuring the Role of Teachers

The role of teachers in the co-constructive activities of learners can be described within the didactic framework of 'cognitive apprenticeship' (Collins et al. 1989). According to the ethnographic model in which practices and principles of traditional craftsmanship are applied to cognitive learning activities, teachers, experts, or more capable peers provide guidance and support to learners as they participate as apprentices in authentic and task-related, structured social interactions. As opposed to a transmissionist view of instruction, teachers should provide aid in the intellectual development of students in ways that leave room for negotiation and joint expansion of meaning: (a) as scaffolds and role models for the behavior that students are expected to engage in; (bi) as active participants in learning groups aiming at shaping the group's dialog; (c) as monitors of co-constructive norms in social interactions in which negotiation of taken-as-shared meaning is essential (Webb and Palincsar 1996); (d) as advocates of content-specific standards and of the achievement of convergence and intersubjectivity in understanding and problem solving.

Associated with this shift in the pedagogical orientation of teachers is a shift in the role of learners and the organization of classrooms. In the wake of a view that sees learning essentially as sociocultural interaction, classrooms should develop from aggregations of solo learners to communities engaged in co-constructive learning. That is, individuals should become acculturated members of a culture and community through collaboration and negotiation. Or, as Bruner (1986, p. 123) has put it: culture as 'a *forum* for negotiating and renegotiating meaning and for explicating action ... is constantly in process of being recreated as it is interpreted and renegotiated by its members.'

See also: Cooperative Learning in Schools; Piaget, Jean (1896–1980); Piaget's Theory of Human Development and Education; Situated Cognition: Contemporary Developments; Situated Cognition: Origins; Vygotskij, Lev Semenovic (1896–1934); Vygotskij's Theory of Human Development and New Approaches to Education

Bibliography

Brown J S, Collins A, Duguid P 1989 Situated cognition and the culture of learning. *Education Researcher* **18**(1): 32–42

Bruner J S 1986 *Actual Minds, Possible Worlds*. Harvard University Press, Cambridge, MA

Chi M T H 1996 Constructing self-explananations and scaffolded explanations in tutoring. *Applied Cognitive Psychology* **10**: 10–49

Clark H H, Brennan S E 1991 Grounding in communication. In: Resnick L B, Levine J, Teasley S D (eds.) *Perspectives on Socially Shared Cognition*. American Psychological Association, Washington, DC pp. 127–49

Cohen E G 1994 Restructuring the classrooms: Conditions for productive small groups. *Review of Educational Research* **64**: 1–35

Collins A, Brown J S, Newman S E 1989 Cognitive apprenticeship: Teaching the crafts of reading, writing, and mathematics. In: Resnick L B (ed.) *Knowing, Learning, and In-*

struction: *Essays in the Honor of Robert Glaser*. Erlbaum, Hillsdale, NJ

Doise W, Mugny G 1984 *The Social Development of the Intellect*. Pergamon Press, Oxford

Kozulin A 1998 *Psychological Tools. A Sociocultural Approach to Education*. Harvard University Press, Cambridge, MA

Mead G H 1934 *Mind, Self, and Society*. University of Chicago Press, Chicago

Pauli C, Reusser K 2000 Cultivating students' argumentation and reasoning in solving mathematical text problems through the use of a computer tool: a video-based analysis of dialogues. *Research Report*. University of Zurich Institute of Education (http://www.didac.unizh.ch)

Perret-Clermont A-N, Perret J-F, Bell N 1991 The social construction of meaning and cognitive activity in elementary school children. In: Resnick L B, Levine L, Teasley S D (eds.) *Perspectives on Socially Shared Cognition*. American Psychological Association, Washington, DC pp. 41–62

Reusser K 1993 Tutoring systems and pedagogical theory: Representational tools for understanding, planning, and reflection in problem-solving. In: Lajoie S P, Derry S (eds.) *Computers as Cognitive Tools*. Erlbaum, Hillsdale, NJ pp. 143–78

Roschelle J, Teasley S D 1995 The construction of shared knowledge in collaborative problem solving. In: O'Malley C E (ed.) *Computer-supported Collaborative Learning*. Springer, Berlin pp. 69–97

van Oers B 1996 Learning mathematics as meaningful activity. In: Steffe L P, Nesher P, Cobb P, Goldin G A, Greer B (eds.) *Theories of Mathematical Meaning*. Erlbaum, Mahwah, NJ pp. 91–113

Vygotsky L S 1962 *Thought and Language*. Harvard University Press, Cambridge, MA

Webb N M, Palincsar A S 1996 Group processes in the classroom. In: Berliner D C, Calfee R C (eds.) *Handbook of Educational Psychology*. Macmillan, New York pp. 841–73

K. Reusser

Code switching: Linguistic

Code-switching (CS) refers to the mixing, by bilinguals (or multilinguals), of two or more languages in discourse, often with no change of interlocutor or topic. Such mixing may take place at any level of linguistic structure, but its occurrence within the confines of a single sentence, constituent, or even word, has attracted most linguistic attention. This article surveys the linguistic treatment of such *intrasentential* switching.

In combining languages intrasententially, various problems of incompatibility may arise. The most obvious derive from word order differences: under what conditions, if any, can the boundary between constituents ordered differently in two languages host a switch? Other potential combinatorial difficulties involve mismatches in grammatical categories, sub-categorization patterns, morphology, and idiomatic expressions. Systematic examination of the spontaneous speech of bilinguals resident in a wide range of communities suggests, however, that speakers generally manage to circumvent these difficulties. CS tends not to produce utterances that contain monolingually ungrammatical sentence fragments. Discovery of the mechanisms enabling such 'grammatical' CS is the major goal of current research. Central questions include locating permissible switch sites and ascertaining the nature (hierarchical or linear, variable or categorical) of the constraints on switching.

1. Background

Though CS is apparently a hallmark of bilingual communities world-wide, it has only begun to attract serious scholarly attention in the last few decades. Researchers first dismissed intrasentential code-switching as random and deviant (e.g., Weinreich 1953/1968) but are now unanimous in the conviction that it is grammatically constrained. The basis for this conviction is the empirical observation that bilinguals tend to switch intrasententially at certain (morpho) syntactic boundaries and not at others. Early efforts to explain these preferences proceeded by proscribing certain switch sites, for example, between pronominal subjects and verbs or between conjunctions and their conjuncts. However, these particular sites were soon reported to figure among the regular CS patterns of some bilingual communities.

The first more general account of the distribution of CS stemmed from the observation that CS is favored at the kinds of syntactic boundaries which occur in both languages. The *equivalence constraint* (Poplack 1980) states that switched sentences are made up of concatenated fragments of alternating languages, each of which is grammatical in the language of its provenance (see also Muysken 2000). The boundary between adjacent fragments occurs between two constituents that are ordered in the same way in both languages, ensuring the linear coherence of sentence structure without omitting or duplicating lexical content.

That general principles, rather than atomistic constraints, govern CS is now widely accepted, though there is little consensus as to what they are or how they should be represented. Much current research assumes unquestioningly that the mechanisms for language switching follow directly from general principles of (monolingual) grammar. Theories based on this assumption tend to appeal to such abstract grammatical properties as inter-constituent relationships (e.g., government, case assignment) and/or language-specific features of lexical categories (i.e., subcategorization of grammatical arguments, inherent morphological features).

Since Klavans's (1985) proposal that CS was constrained by structural relations, the formal linguistic theories successively in vogue have each been extended to encompass the data of CS. Di Sciullo et al. (1986), for example, identified the relevant relations as C-command and government: CS cannot occur where a government relation holds. Replacement of the function of government in standard theory by the notion of feature agreement led to a parallel focus on feature matching in CS studies. The *Functional Head Constraint* (Belazi et al. 1994) adds language choice to the features instantiated in functional and lexical categories, prohibiting CS where a mismatch occurs. A more recent Minimalist proposal (MacSwan 1999) restricts CS at structural sites showing cross-language differences in monolingual features.

This distinction between lexical and functional categories is not new to CS research. It is a hallmark of theories invoking the complement structure of individual lexical items to characterize permissible CS sites (e.g., Joshi 1985) and its sequel, the *Null Theory of CS* (Santorini and Mahootian 1995; see also Bentahila and Davies's *Subcategorisation Constraint* 1983). Perhaps the most detailed model involving the contrast between lexical properties and functional (or 'system') morphemes is the *Matrix Language Frame* model (Azuma 1993, Myers-Scotton 1993). Here, structural constraints on CS result from a complex interaction between a dominant matrix language and the prohibition against embedding 'system' morphemes from the 'embedded' language in matrix language structure.

The assumption that bilingual syntax can be explained by general principles inferred from the study of monolingual grammar has not yet been substantiated. While formal theories of grammar may account well for monolingual language structure, including that of the monolingual fragments in CS discourse, there is no evidence to suggest that the *juxtaposition* of two languages can be explained in the same way. Bilingual communities exhibit widely different patterns of adapting monolingual resources in their code-mixing strategies, and these are not predictable through purely linguistic considerations. The equivalence constraint, as formalized by Sankoff (1998), is a production-based explanation of the facts of CS, which incorporates the notions of structural hierarchy and linear order, and accounts for a number of empirical observations in addition to the equivalent word order characterizing most actual switch sites. These include the well-formedness of the monolingual fragments, the conservation of constituent structure, and the essential unpredictability of CS at any potential CS site. The mechanisms of monolingual and bilingual grammars are not assumed *a priori* to be identical.

2. Evaluating CS Theories

There has been remarkably little cross-fertilization among CS theories; indeed, each has been greeted with a host of counter-examples. Testing the fit of competing models against the data of CS should be a straightforward matter since they often make competing predictions. But their disparate assumptions, goals, and domains of application have hindered such efforts. Assessment of the descriptive adequacy of a theory of CS requires that at least two methodological issues be resolved. One involves classification of other-language phenomena, the other, confronting the predictions of the theory with the data of actual bilingual behavior.

It is uncontroversial that CS differs from the other major manifestation of language contact: *lexical borrowing*. Despite etymological identity with the donor language, established loanwords assume the morphological, syntactic, and often, phonological, identity of the recipient language. They tend to be recurrent in the speech of the individual and widespread across the community. The stock of established loanwords is available to monolingual speakers of the recipient language, who access them normally along with the remainder of the recipient-language lexicon. Loanwords further differ from CS in that there is no involvement of the morphology, syntax, or phonology of the lexifier language.

Recent research has shown that borrowing is actually much more productive than implied above (see the papers in Poplack and Meechan 1998). In particular, the social characteristics of recurrence and diffusion are not always satisfied. This results in what has been called, after Weinreich (1953/1968), *nonce borrowing* (Sankoff et al. 1990). Like its established counterpart, the nonce loan tends to involve lone lexical items, generally major-class content words, and to assume the morphological, syntactic, and often, phonological identity of the recipient language. Like CS, on the other hand, nonce borrowing is neither recurrent nor widespread, and necessarily requires a certain level of bilingual competence. Distinguishing nonce borrowings from single-word CS is conceptually easy but methodologically difficult, especially when they surface bare, giving no apparent indication of language membership.

The classification of lone items is at the heart of a fundamental disagreement among CS researchers over (a) whether the distinction between CS and borrowing should be formally recognized in a theory of CS, (b) whether these and other manifestations of language contact can be unambiguously identified in bilingual discourse, and (c) criteria for determining whether a given item was switched or borrowed. Researchers who consider lone other-language items to be CS tend to posit an *asymmetrical* relationship, in which one language dominates and other-language items are inserted (e.g., Joshi 1985, Myers-Scotton 1993). Where the class of CS is (in the first instance) limited to unambiguous *multiword* fragments, both languages are postulated to play a role (Belazi et al. 1994, Sankoff 1998, Woolford 1983). Muysken (2000) admits the possibility of both strategies.

The appropriateness of data is also relevant to evaluating CS theories. The literature on CS largely is characterized by the 'rule-and-exception' paradigm. Despite the onslaught of counter-examples provoked by successive CS theories, very few have in fact been tested systematically against the data of spontaneous bilingual usage. Instead, both the theories and tests of their applicability tend to be based on isolated examples, drawn from judgments, informant elicitation, and linguist introspection. The relation between such data and actual usage is not known; nor do they permit us to distinguish between the recurrent and systematic patterns of everyday interaction and examples which may be judged 'acceptable' in some sense, but which rarely or never occur.

The equivalence constraint has been verified as a general tendency in Spanish-English (Poplack 1980); Finnish-English (Poplack et al. 1987), Arabic-French (Naït M'Barek and Sankoff 1988), Tamil-English (Sankoff et al. 1990), Fongbe-French and Wolof-French (Meechan and Poplack 1995), Igbo-English (Eze 1998), French-English (Turpin 1998) and Ukrainian-English (Budzhak-Jones 1998) bilingual communities. But most of the voluminous literature on CS, especially of the 'insertional' type, is based on data which represents, properly speaking, lexical borrowing. As only the grammar and word order of the recipient language are pertinent to borrowing, attempts to understand the structure of CS based on a mixture of borrowing and true CS (e.g., Myers-Scotton 1993 and many others) appear unwieldy or descriptively inadequate.

3. Identifying the Results of Language Contact

Insofar as CS and borrowing are based on some principled combination of elements of the monolingual (i.e., *unmixed*) vernaculars of the bilingual community, it is important to have as explicit an idea as possible of the nature of these vernaculars before concluding that a code-mixed element is behaving like one or the other. The analysis of code-mixing as a discourse mode requires access to the grammars of the contact languages as they are spoken, and spoken language is characterized by structural variability. In confronting, rather than evading this variability, Sankoff et al. (1990) and Poplack and Meechan (1998) developed a method to compare bilingual structures with the unmixed source languages of the same speakers. Making use of the framework of linguistic variation theory (Labov 1969), the inherent variability of such forms is used to determine their status. If the rate and distribution of, for example, case-marking of the contentious lone other-language items show quantitative parallels to those of their counterparts in the (unmixed) recipient language, while at the same time differing from relevant patterns in the donor language, the lone other-language items are inferred to be *borrowed*, since only the grammar of the recipient language is operative. If they pattern with their counterparts in the (unmixed) donor language, while

at the same time differing from the patterning in the unmixed recipient language, the lone other-language items must result from CS.

Quantitative analysis of language mixing phenomena in typologically distinct language pairs shows that lone other-language items, especially major-class content words, are by far the most important component of mixed discourse. These lone items show the same fine details of quantitative conditioning of phonological, morphological, and syntactic variability as dictionary-attested loanwords, both of which in turn parallel their unmixed counterparts in the recipient language (Poplack and Meechan 1998). This tendency is apparent regardless of the linguistic properties of the language pair. This is evidence that most lone items are borrowed, even if only for the nonce, despite the lack, in some cases, of dictionary attestation or diffusion within the community.

4. Future Directions

Lack of consensus characterizing the discipline is related to a number of methodological problems. Foremost among them is failure to distinguish code-switching from other types of language mixture, which, despite similarities in surface manifestation, are fundamentally different mechanisms for combining languages. The current state of knowledge suggests that borrowing, nonce or established, is the major manifestation of language contact in most bilingual communities. Its linguistic structure is well accounted for in the traditional language contact literature (Weinreich 1953/1968). Intrasentential CS involving multiword fragments of two or more languages is also attested in some communities. Achievement of consensus on an empirically verifiable characterization of the rules for juxtaposing these fragments within the sentence remains an important goal for CS research. Fit between theories and data could be improved by a broader empirical base. This would permit researchers to situate bilingual behavior with respect to the monolingual vernaculars implicated in language mixing, account for the disparate CS strategies that have evolved in different bilingual communities, and distinguish among incommensurable manifestations of bilingual language contact.

See also: Bilingual Education: International Perspectives; Bilingualism and Multilingualism; Bilingualism: Cognitive Aspects; First Language Acquisition: Cross-linguistic; Second Language Acquisition; Sociolinguistics

Bibliography

Azuma S 1993 The frame-content hypothesis in speech production: Evidence from intrasentential code switching. *Linguistics* **31**: 1071–93

Belazi H M, Rubin E J, Toribio A J 1994 Code-switching and X-bar theory: The functional head constraint. *Linguistic Inquiry* 25(2): 221–37

Bentahila A, Davies E E 1983 The syntax of Arabic-French code-switching. *Lingua* 59(4): 301–30

Budzhak-Jones S 1998 Against word-internal code-switching: Evidence from Ukrainian-English bilingualism. *International Journal of Bilingualism* 2(2): 161–82

di Sciullo A-M, Muysken P, Singh R 1986 Government and code-mixing. *Journal of Linguistics* 22(1): 1–24

Eze E 1998 Lending credence to a borrowing analysis: Lone English-origin incorporations in Igbo discourse. *International Journal of Bilingualism* 2(2): 183–201

Joshi A K 1985 Processing of sentences with intrasentential code-switching. In: Dowty D R, Karttunen L, Zwicky A M (eds.) *Natural Language Parsing: Psychological, Computational and Theoretical Perspectives*. Cambridge University Press, Cambridge, UK, pp. 190–204

Klavans J L 1985 The syntax of code-switching: Spanish and English. In: King L D, Maley C A (eds.) *Selected Papers from the XIIIth Linguistic Symposium on Romance Languages*. Benjamins, Amsterdam, pp. 213–21

Labov W 1969 Contraction, deletion, and inherent variability of the English copula. *Language* 45(4): 715–62

MacSwan J 1999 *A Minimalist Approach to Intrasentential Code Switching*. Garland Press, New York

Meechan M, Poplack S 1995 Orphan categories in bilingual discourse: Adjectivization strategies in Wolof-French and Fongbe-French bilingual discourse. *Language Variation and Change* 7(2): 169–94

Muysken P C 2000 *Bilingual Speech: A Typology of Code-mixing*. Cambridge University Press, Cambridge, MA

Myers-Scotton C 1993 *Duelling Languages*. Clarendon Press, Oxford, UK

Naït M'Barek M, Sankoff D 1988 Le discours mixte arabe/français: des emprunts ou des alternances de langue? *Revue Canadienne de Linguistique* 33(2): 143–54

Poplack S 1980 Sometimes I'll start a sentence in Spanish Y TERMINO EN ESPAÑOL: Toward a typology of code-switching. *Linguistics* 18(7/8): 581–618

Poplack S, Meechan M (eds.) 1998 *Instant Loans, Easy Conditions: The Productivity of Bilingual Borrowing; Special Issue of the International Journal of Bilingualism*. Kingston Press, London

Poplack S, Wheeler S, Westwood A 1987 Distinguishing language contact phenomena: Evidence from Finnish-English bilingualism. In: Lilius P, Saari M (eds.) *The Nordic Languages and Modern Linguistics*. University of Helsinki Press, Helsinki, pp. 33–56

Sankoff D 1998 A formal production-based explanation of the facts of code-switching. *Bilingualism: Language and Cognition* 1(1): 39–50

Sankoff D, Poplack S, Vanniarajan S 1990 The case of the nonce loan in Tamil. *Language Variation and Change* 2(1): 71–101

Santorini B, Mahootian S 1995 Code-switching and the syntactic status of adnominal adjectives. *Lingua* 96: 1–27

Turpin D 1998 "Le français c'est le last frontier": The status of English-origin nouns in Acadian French. *International Journal of Bilingualism* 2(2): 221–33

Weinreich U 1953/1968 *Languages in contact*. Mouton, The Hague

Woolford E 1983 Bilingual code-switching and syntactic theory. *Linguistic Inquiry* 14(3): 519–36

S. Poplack

Coeducation and Single-sex Schooling

Coeducation or single-sex schooling does not only refer to an organizational form of separating or mixing girls and boys, but also refers to such questions as: should there be different goals, curricula, rights, and outcomes for the two genders? Equality is not perceived in all countries and not always an important principle for men and women. For a long time, education was oriented to prepare girls and boys for their different spheres in adult life. Today, equality is the goal, but it is not at all clear whether separation or coeducation is the better way to reach this goal.

1. A Brief History of Coeducation

The history of educational systems shows, for most countries, that especially for education beyond elementary levels, single-sex schools have been the preferred form, although coeducation was not unusual. Financial restrictions in mass education forced coeducational schooling, but for ideological reasons, separation was preferred by the authorities. While this is mainly true for Europe, in the United States, soon after establishing public schools, coeducation became the norm. David Tyack and Elisabeth Hansot describe the beginning as 'smuggling in the girls' which led to the adoption of coeducation by gradually moving from 'why to why not' (Tyack and Hansot 1992, p. 47). Even in secondary education, only 12 cities out of 628 reported that they had single-sex high schools at the end of the nineteenth century. The European secondary education was for boys only—especially in Germany; girls received secondary education only on a private basis and were not allowed to attend higher education at all. Prussian universities enrolled women, but not before 1908.

Democratic movements in all countries valued equality of education and therefore pledged for coeducation. The debates emphasized the question of difference or similarity of women and men as human beings. While the assumption of similarity historically was associated with the preference for coeducation, those who postulated differences were divided in advocates and opponents to coeducation. The advocates thought coeducation would ensure that girls and boys themselves would make sure they behaved like girls and boys. The opponents feared that girls and boys together would encourage the loss of their engendered behavior.

In most European countries, the years between 1960 and 1980 brought big educational reforms, and coeducation was one of those (Wilson 1991, p. 203)—although it was more of a side-effect of the reforms, and astonishingly, after the heated discussions in the first half of the twentieth century, a change nearly without debate. Efforts to establish 'schools for all' would not go along with separation. Poland has had equal opportunity programs since 1965; Sweden since the late 1960s, and most other European countries since the beginning 1970s, except for Greece (mid-1970s) and Spain (1980s). Today all European countries have coeducation with the exception of Ireland, and to a lesser degree, in England and Wales. Some countries still have single-sex classes in some subjects, such as Physical Education and Crafts.

In the US, with its long tradition of coeducation, Title IX of the Educational Amendments in 1972 was the major legal tool in implementing equal education by stating that discrimination on the basis of sex is illegal in any educational program receiving federal funding. This already made clear that coeducation does not necessarily guarantee equality and the absence of sexism.

2. New Women's Movement and Coeducation

'Sexism' was the new term to mark inequality for women and men in society. Evaluations of the educational reforms showed differences in attainment between the countries, between social groups and between gender. A close look at processes in the educational system reveals successes as well as failures: women participate much more in higher education but there is under-representation of young women in some educational fields, especially in vocational education and in science. At the same time, women's self-confidence remains at lower levels than men's. The new Women's movement criticized the outcomes of coeducation, and showed that it put women at a disadvantage. Beginning in the 1980s, the critics started a new debate on coeducation. It provided a new research area, although one has to admit that the basis of the literature, even in the late 1990s was still rather thin; the reports are mostly 'anecdotal' (AAUW 1998).

3. Research about Coeducation and Single-sex Schooling

Compilations of research show the advantages and disadvantages of coeducation. The Organization for Economic Co-operation and Development (OECD) published in 1986 a report on 'Girls and Women in Education,' and the American Association of University Women (AAUW) released their report: 'How Schools Shortchange Girls,' in 1992. There are at least two fields in which research found relevant gender inequalities:

(a) Coeducation retains the gender-hierarchical division of the world. It strengthens gender-specific interests and seldom encourages thinking and be-

havior against the traditional gender-stereotypes. The school curriculum serves as a 'hidden curriculum' to ensure those processes.

(b) Classroom interaction processes show unbalanced communication structures. Dominance and forced attention for boys are tolerated, self-effacement by and disregard of girls remain unnoticed.

The central reason for this outcome lies in gender stereotypes and in the gender-division of labor: both are still to such a degree 'normal' that the 'masculine dominance' still remains effective, unquestioned by most people.

The hidden curriculum was a major theme in the OECD report, describing three forms of sex bias:

(a) Picture books, reading schemes and children's literature are characterized by the lack of representation of women and female roles.

(b) The curriculum and textbooks in school tend to be either male-oriented or female-oriented rather than 'bicultural.'

(c) The presentation of men and women in the curriculum shows a picture of the social world that is 'more sexist than reality' (OECD 1986, p. 75).

These results did force many of the political institutions responsible for the educational system to set up new criteria for school books and material. One can admit that there have been some changes, although the situation still has not changed radically.

Quite a lot of mostly qualitative studies deal with the interaction process. Maggie Wilson resumés their results:

> Although teachers often deny that differential treatment of boys and girls exists in classrooms, case studies from Belgium, Spain, Sweden, Greece, West Germany and England and Wales chart the great amount of attention which teachers give young boys, albeit in the form of both praise and censure, and their overtly expressed preference for teaching boys, especially at the upper levels of school and in certain subject areas, such as in Science and Mathematics (Wilson 1991, p. 213).

Research in the USA is very much in line with these findings (Riordan 1990).

Florence Howe, and others, called on the 'myth of coeducation.' She wrote: 'One of the central ideas of coeducation provides a central myth: that if women are admitted to men's education and treated exactly as men are, then all problems of sexual equity will be solved' (Howe 1984, p. X). The valuing of admittance as the only criteria for equality made us forget that there were other qualities in school education that proved to be unequal, e.g., the hidden curriculum and the interaction processes.

Although the AAUW report did not recommend single-sex schooling, it mentioned that research studies would indicate that girls often learn and perform better in same-sex work groups than in mixed-sex groupings (AAUW 1992, p. 130). This, together with many other publications, supported the remaining women colleges in the USA and also helped to keep, and even to start private girls' schools. In Europe, especially in Germany, campaigns to enroll young women in science and technology subjects experimented with the separation of gender.

At the end of 1997, the AAUW organized a round table entitled 'Separated by Sex—a critical look at single-sex education for girls,' in order to resume the outcomes of the debate about coeducation and single-sex education since their 1992 report. The main results are consistent with research from other countries and could therefore be state-of-the-art for coeducation today:

(a) There is neither a significant correlation between the self-concept of students, nor the gender-stereotyping and coeducational or single-sex schooling.

(b) Students in single-sex schools rarely believe that mathematics and science are specifically male subjects, while students in coeducation schools believe this more often.

(c) These beliefs do not lead to differences in capacities between the students from the two types of schooling.

(d) Better results were found in the US single-sex schools only for 'at-risk-students,' especially Spanish-American girls from low socioeconomic families. The results are very small however, and they are due to the academic orientation of these schools.

(e) Sexism could be found everywhere, not the separation of gender or coeducation but mainly the awareness of teachers is responsible for non-sexist environments.

(f) The majority of students wish to attend coeducational schools.

Altogether, the report called for more complexity in the research design as well as in the theorizing of gender. Both could help to deal with educational questions of gender equity more adequately than just criticizing coeducation and valuing separation.

4. Perspectives

Since the beginning of the new debate on coeducation, working with girls was added to working with boys about masculinity (Connell 1995), and, slowly but surely, is changing the coeducational classroom.

The research reports, as well as the practical experiences in different schools, show that single-sex education can help to deal with some of the problems of gender. More especially, those courses dealing with gender stereotypes; physical education programs that let girls and boys have new untypical experiences, can help them gain more self-respect and a better understanding of gender-processes. But it cannot be done just by separating girls and boys, it requires awareness and cautious acting!

Coeducational settings do need more sensitive reflections about what is going on in classrooms.

Barrie Thorne analyzed the 'gender play' in schools and she found: 'Gender boundaries are episodic and ambigious, and the notion of "borderwork" should be coupled with a parallel term—such as "neutralization"—for processes through which girls and boys (and adults who enter into their social relations) neutralize or undermine a sense of gender as division and opposition' (Thorne 1993, p. 84).

Further research, gender studies in programs for teaching credentials as well as teacher training for more awareness of interaction processes dealing with gender questions, would help to make education gender-sensitive and valuable for both girls and boys.

See also: Education and Gender: Historical Perspectives; Education (Higher) and Gender; Education (Primary and Secondary Schools) and Gender; Gender and School Learning: Mathematics and Science; Gender Differences in Personality and Social Behavior; Mathematical Education; Sex-role Development and Education

Bibliography

American Association of University Women Educational Foundation 1992 *How Schools Shortchange Girls. A Study of Major Findings on Girls and Education.* Marlowe, New York

American Association of University Women Educational Foundation 1998 *Separated by Sex—a Critical Look at Single-sex Education for Girls.* Washington, DC

Connell R W 1995 *Masculinities.* University of California Press, Berkeley, CA

Diller A, Houston B, Morgan K P, Ayim M 1996 *The Gender Question in Education.* Westview Press, Boulder, CO

Eder D, Evans C C, Parker S 1995 *School Talk.* Rutgers University Press, New Brunswick, NJ

Faulstich-Wieland H 1991 *Koedukation—enttäuschte Hoffnungen?* [*Coeducation—disappointed hopes?*] Wissenschaftliche Buchgesellschft, Darmstadt, Germany

Faulstich-Wieland H, Horstkemper M 1995 *'Trennt uns bitte, bitte nicht!'. Koedukation aus Mädchen- und Jungensicht.* [*'Please don't separate us!' Coeducation as Girls and Boys see it*]. Leske and Budrich, Opladen, Germany

Howe F 1984 *Myths of Coeducation.* Indiana University Press, Bloomington, IN

OECD 1986 *Girls and Women in Education. A Cross-national Study of Sex Inequalities in Upbringing and in Schools and Colleges.* Paris

Riordan C 1990 *Girls and Boys in School. Together or Separate?* Teachers College, Columbia University, New York

Thorne B 1993 *Gender Play.* Rutgers University Press, New Brunswick, NJ

Tyack D, Hansot E 1992 *Learning Together. A History of Coeducation in American Public Schools.* Russell Sage Foundation, New York

Wilson M (ed.) 1991 *Girls and Young Women in Education. A European Perspective.* Pergamon Press, Oxford, UK

H. Faulstich-Wieland

Cognition, Distributed

Like all other branches of cognitive science, distributed cognition seeks to understand the organization of cognitive systems. Like most of cognitive science, it takes cognitive processes to be those that are involved in memory, decision making, inference, reasoning, learning, and so on. Also following mainstream cognitive science, it characterizes cognitive processes in terms of the propagation and transformation of representations.

What distinguishes distributed cognition from other approaches is the commitment to two related theoretical principles. The first concerns the boundaries of the unit of analysis for cognition. While boundaries are often a matter of tradition in a field, there are some general rules one can follow. Bateson (1972) says one should bound the unit so that things are not left inexplicable. This usually means putting boundaries on units where the traffic is low. The second principle concerns the range of mechanisms that may be assumed to participate in cognitive processes. While mainstream cognitive science looks for cognitive events in the manipulation of symbols (Newell et al. 1989), or more recently, patterns of activation across arrays of processing units (Rumelhart et al. 1986, McClelland et al. 1986) inside individual actors, distributed cognition looks for a broader class of cognitive events and does not expect all such events to be encompassed by the skin or skull of an individual.

When one applies these principles to the observation of human activity 'in the wild,' at least three interesting kinds of distribution of cognitive process become apparent: cognitive processes may be distributed across the members of a social group, cognitive processes may be distributed in the sense that the operation of the cognitive system involves coordination between internal and external (material or environmental) structure, and processes may be distributed through time in such a way that the products of earlier events can transform the nature of later events. The effects of these kinds of distribution of process are extremely important to an understanding of human cognition.

The roots of distributed cognition are deep, but the field came into being under its current name in the mid-1980s. In 1978, Vygotsky's *Mind in Society* was published in English. Minsky published his *Society of Mind* in 1985. At the same time, Parallel Distributed Processing was making a comeback as a model of cognition (Rumelhart et al. 1986). The nearly perfect mirror symmetry of the titles of Vygotsky's and Minsky's books suggests that something special might be happening in systems of distributed processing, whether the processors are neurons, connectionist nodes, areas of a brain, whole persons, groups of persons, or groups of groups of persons.

1. Mind in Society

For many people, distributed cognition means cognitive processes that are distributed across the members of a social group (Salomon 1993). The fundamental question here is how the cognitive processes we normally associate with an individual mind can be implemented in a group of individuals? A wide range of disciplines in the social sciences has explored this question.

Treating memory as a socially distributed cognitive function has a long history in sociology and anthropology. Durkheim, and his students, especially Halbwachs (1925), maintained that memory could not even be coherently discussed as a property of an isolated individual. Roberts (1964) proposed that social organization could be read as a sort of architecture of cognition at the community level. He characterized the cognitive properties of a society (its memory capacity and ability to manage and retrieve information) by looking at what information there is, where it is located, and how it can move in a society. Schwartz (1978) proposed a distributional model of culture that emphasized the distribution of beliefs across the members of a society. Romney et al. (1986) created quantitative models of the patterns of cultural consensus. The identification of patterns raised the question of why such patterns form. Sperber (1985) introduced the idea of an epidemiology of representations. He suggested an analogy in which anthropology is to psychology as epidemiology is to pathology. In the same way that epidemiology addresses the distribution of pathogens in a population, anthropology should treat questions about the distribution of representations in a community. A similar set of developments followed from Dawkins' (1976) discussion of 'memes' as the cultural analog of genes. These ideas have now coalesced in the field of memetics (Blackmore 1999). March and Simon (1958) argued that organizations can be understood as adaptive cognitive systems. Juries are an important class of distributed problem solving organization and they have been intensely studied by social psychologists (Hastie 1993). Of course, in social psychology there is a vast literature on small-group decision making, some of which discusses the properties of aggregates.

Scientific communities have received special attention because the work of science is fundamentally cognitive and distributed. The phenomena that have been explored include how the organization of communication media in a scientific community affect the kinds of things the community can learn (Thagard 1993), how conditions external to the individual scientists can affect their individual choices in ways that lead to different high-level structures to emerge (Kitcher 1990), how the distribution of cognitive activity within social networks and between people and inscriptions accounts for much of the work of science (Latour 1987), and how scientific facts are created by communities in a process that simply could not be fit into the mind of an individual (Fleck 1935).

Economists have been interested in the tension between what is individually rational and what is rational at the aggregate level. This theme has been explored in game theory under the rubric of the Prisoner's Dilemma, the paradox of the commons, and other cases where individual rationality and group rationality diverge (Von Neumann and Morgenstern 1964).

Anthropologists and sociologists studying knowledge and memory, social psychologists studying small-group problem solving and jury decision making, organizational scientists studying organizational learning, philosophers of science studying discovery processes, and economists and political scientists exploring the relations of individual and group rationality, all have taken stances that lead them to a consideration of the cognitive properties of societies of individuals. There is ample evidence that the cognitive properties of a group can differ from the cognitive properties of the members of the group.

2. The Society of Mind

The work described above looks for mind-like properties in social groups. This is the *Mind in Society* reading. The metaphor can be run the other way as is done in Minsky's *Society of Mind* (1985). Rather than using the language of mind to describe what is happening in a social group, the language of social groups can be used to describe what is happening in a mind.

Minsky argued that to explain intelligence we need to consider a large system of experts or agencies that can be assembled together in various configurations to get things done. Minsky also allowed that a high-level agency itself could be composed of low-level agencies. With Papert (Minsky and Papert 1988), he argued that the low-level agencies (the ones that take on 'toy-sized problems') could be implemented as distributed computations in connectionist nets. Minsky said, '... each brain contains hundreds of different types of machines, interconnected in specific ways which predestine that brain to become a large, diverse society of partially specialized agencies' (1988). What this means of course is that the cognition of an individual is distributed cognition too.

A problem that remained unsolved by Minsky's work was 'how such systems could develop managers for deciding, in different circumstances, which of those diverse procedures to use' (1988). That is, how can the relations among the agencies get organized to perform new functional skills? To solve this problem, Minsky and Papert invoked biological maturation. An alternative way to approach this problem is to note that each 'society of mind' resides and develops in a community of similar societies of mind. This means, of course, that both what's in the mind, and what the mind is in are societies. Getting internal agencies into coordination with external structure can provide the organization of the relations between the internal agencies that is required to perform the new functional skill.

Vygotsky developed this idea of the social origins of individual psychological functions in *Society of Mind* (Vygotsky 1978, Wertsch 1985). Vygotsky argued that every high-level cognitive function appears twice: first as an interpsychological process and only later as an intrapsychological process. The new functional system inside the child is brought into existence in the interaction of the child with others (typically adults) and with artifacts. As a consequence of the experience of interactions with others, the child eventually may become able to create the functional system in the absence of the others. This could be seen in Minsky's terms as a mechanism for the propagation of a functional skill from one society of mind to another. From the perspective of distributed cognition, this sort of individual learning is seen as the propagation of a particular sort of pattern through a community. Cultural practices assemble agencies into working assemblages and put the assemblages to work. Some of these assemblages may be entirely contained in an individual, and some may span several individuals and material artifacts. The patterns of activity that are repeatedly created in cultural practices may lead to the consolidation of functional assemblages, the atrophy of agencies that are rarely used, and the hypertrophy of agencies that are frequently employed. The result can be individual learning or organizational learning, or both.

2.1 Interaction as a Source of Novel Structure

An important property of aggregate systems is that they may give rise to forms of organization that cannot develop in the component parts. Freyd (1983) argued that some of the features of language that are identified as linguistic universals could arise out of the necessity of sharing the linguistic code. For instance, the reason that linguistic categories tend to approximate discrete structures may have little to do with the organization of the brain, and everything to do with the problem of pushing a complex representation through a very narrow channel. As Minsky and Papert point out, symbols can be expected to arise where there are bottlenecks in communication. That means we should look for the origins of symbols at places where the information 'traffic' is relatively low—or at the boundaries of our various units of analysis.

The phenomena related to the social distribution of cognition are most often investigated using ethnographic methods. In some cases, however, simulation models may be used to test hypotheses about the behavior of such distributed systems. For example, Hutchins and Hazlehurst (1995) explored Freyd's ideas in a series of simulation models in which individuals (modeled by connectionist networks) interact with one another. They developed a robust procedure in which a shared lexicon emerges from the interactions of individuals. Hazlehurst and Hutchins (1998) demonstrated the emergence of reduced conventional sequences of lexical items—which they take to be the beginnings of syntax. These conventional sequences arise only in the condition of negotiated learning where the representing structures must simultaneously come to accurately represent the world and be shared among individuals, that is, be able to pass the communication bottleneck between individuals. Representations that are learned inside an individual, without the requirement of sharing them with others, come to represent the world, but do not show the reduced conventional code aspects that are the hallmarks of language and syntax.

By simultaneously considering the society of mind and mind in society, the distributed cognition approach provides a new place to look for the origins of complexity. Phenomena that are not predictable from the organization of any individual taken in isolation may arise in the interactions among individuals. Once having developed in this larger system, they may become elements of cultural practices and thereby become available for appropriation by individuals. This sort of scheme may be a partial solution to the paradox of how simple systems can lead to more complex ones.

3. The Material Environment

A second major thread in the fabric of distributed cognition concerns the role of the material environment in cognitive activity. Again, the question of where to bound the unit of analysis arises. The potential of the material environment to support memory is very widely recognized. But the environment can be more than a memory. Cognitive activity is sometimes situated in the material world in such a way that the environment is a computational medium.

Cognitive artifacts are the *Things that Make Us Smart* in the title of Norman's (1993) book. The notion that cognitive artifacts amplify the cognition of the artifact user is fairly commonplace. If one focuses on the products of cognitive activity, cognitive artifacts do seem to amplify human abilities. A calculator seems to amplify one's ability to do arithmetic, writing down something one wants to remember seems to amplify one's memory. Cole and Griffin (1980) point out that this is not quite correct. When I remember something by writing it down and reading it later, my memory has not been amplified. Rather, I am using a different set of functional skills to do the memory task. Cognitive artifacts are involved in a process of organizing functional skills into cognitive functional systems.

Consider an example from the world of ship navigation (Hutchins 1995). Navigators frequently face the problem of computing the ship's speed from distance traveled over a given period of time. If a ship travels 1,500 yards in 3 minutes, what is the speed of the ship in knots? There are many ways to solve this problem. Most readers of this article would probably attempt to use a paper and pencil plus their knowledge of algebra to solve it. That procedure is effective, but not nearly as efficient as the 'so-called' 3-minute rule. An experienced navigator need only see the problem stated to see that the answer is 15 knots. The speed in knots equals the number of hundreds of yards covered in 3 minutes. The use of this rule is a case of situated seeing. The rule itself is an internal cognitive artifact. But suppose the ship covered 4,000 yards in 7 minutes? For that problem a material artifact called the three-scale nomogram is more appropriate. A nomogram has three logarithmic scales: one each for distance, time, and speed. If the values of any two variables in a distance/rate/time problem are known, the other can be determined by laying a straight edge on the nomogram so that it touches the known values. The straight edge will touch the third scale at the value of the answer. It is clear that cognitive work is being done, but it is also clear that the processes inside the person are not, by themselves, sufficient to accomplish the computation. A larger unit of analysis must be considered. The skills of scale reading and interpolation are coordinated with the manipulation of objects to establish a particular state of coordination between the straight edge and the nomogram. This is a very different set of agencies than was involved in doing the problem via algebra and paper and pencil. In fact, the skills that are needed to use the nomogram are the things that humans are good at: pattern matching, manipulation of objects in the world, and mental simulation of simple dynamics (Rumelhart et al. 1986).

A computation was performed via the manipulation of a straight edge and nomogram. The nomogram was designed in such a way that the errors that were possible in algebra are impossible when using the nomogram. It is essential to distinguish the cognitive properties required to manipulate the artifact from the computation that is achieved via the manipulation of the artifact. This is a key point, and the failure to see it clearly has been the source of many difficulties in cognitive science.

4. Distributing Cognition in Time

Simon (1998) offered a parable as a way of emphasizing the importance of the environment for cognition. He argued that, as we watch the complicated movements of an ant on a beach, we might be tempted to attribute to the ant some complicated program for constructing the path taken. In fact, Simon says, that trajectory tells us more about the beach than about the ant. Similarly, in watching people thinking in everyday settings, we may be learning as much about their environment for thinking as about what is inside them. The environments of human thinking are not 'natural' environments. They are artificial through and through. They develop over time. The crystallization of partial solutions to frequently encountered problems in artifacts such as the 3-minute rule and the nomogram is a ubiquitous strategy for the stabilization of knowledge and practice. Humans create their cognitive powers in part by creating the environments in which they exercise those powers.

5. Conclusion

It does not seem possible to account for the cognitive accomplishments of our species by reference to what is inside our heads alone. One must also consider the cognitive roles of the social and material world. But, how shall we understand the relationships of the social and the material to cognitive processes that take place inside individual human actors? This is the problem that distributed cognition attempts to solve.

According to Gardner (1985), a more or less explicit decision was made in cognitive science to leave culture, context, history, and emotion out of the early work. These were recognized as important phenomena, but their inclusion made the problem of understanding cognition too complex. The 'Classical' vision of cognition that emerged was built from the inside out, starting with the idea that the mind is a central logic engine. From that starting point, it followed that memory could be seen as retrieval from a stored symbolic database, that problem solving is a form of logical inference, that the environment is a problem domain, and that the body is an input device (Clark 1996). Attempts to reintegrate culture, context, and history into this model of cognition have proved very frustrating. The distributed cognition perspective aspires to rebuild cognitive science from the outside in, beginning with the social and material organization of cognitive activity.

See also: Cognitive Science: Overview; Situated Cognition: Origins

Bibliography

Bateson G 1972 *Steps to an Ecology of Mind.* Balantine Books, Location

Blackmore S 1999 *The Meme Machine.* Oxford University Press, Oxford

Clark A 1996 *Being There: Putting Brain, Body and World Together Again.* MIT Press, Cambridge, MA

Cole M, Griffin M 1980 Cultural amplifiers reconsidered. In: Olson D (ed.) *The Social Foundations of Language and Thought.* Norton, London

Dawkins R 1976 *The Selfish Gene.* Oxford University Press, Oxford

Fleck L 1979 *The Genesis and Development of a Scientific Fact.* University of Chicago Press, Chicago

Freyd J 1983 Shareability: the social psychology of epistemology. *Cognitive Science* 7: 191–220

Gardner H 1985 *The Mind's New Science.* Basic Books

Halbwachs M 1925 *Les Cadres Sociaux de la Mémoire.* Libraire Felix Alcan, Paris

Hastie R 1993 *Inside the Juror: The Psychology of Juror Decision Making.* Cambridge University Press, Cambridge, UK

Hazlehurst B, Hutchins E 1998 The emergence of propositions from the coordination of talk and action in a shared word. *Language and Cognitive Process* (special issue on Connections Approaches to Language Development edited by Kim Plunkett). **2 & 3** April/May

Hutchins E 1995 *Cognition in the Wild.* MIT Press, Cambridge, MA

Hutchins E, Hazlehurst B 1995 How to invent a lexicon: the development of shared symbols in interaction. In: Gilbert N, Conte R (eds.) *Artificial Societies: The Computer Simulation of Social Life.* UCL Press, London

Kitcher P 1990 The distribution of cognitive labor. *The Journal of Philosophy* **87**(1): 5–22

Latour B 1987 *Science in Action.* Harvard University Press, Cambridge, MA

March J, Simon H 1958 *Organizations.* Wiley, London

McClelland J, Rumerlhart D, PDP research group 1986 *Parallel Distributed Processing: Explorations in the Microstructure of Cognition. Vol 2: Psychological and Biological Models.* MIT Press, Cambridge, MA

Minsky M 1985 *Society of Mind.* Simon and Schuster, Hemel Hempstead, UK

Minsky M, Papert S 1988 *Perceptrons.* MIT Press, Cambridge, MA

Newell A, Rosenbloom P, Laird J 1989 Symbolic architectures for cognition. In: Posner M (ed.) *Foundations of Cognitive Science.* MIT Press, Cambridge, MA

Norman D 1993 *Things that Make Us Smart.* Addison Wesley, Location

Roberts J 1964 The self-management of cultures. In: Goodenough V (ed.) *Explorations in Cultural Anthropology: Essays in honor of George Peter Murdock.* McGraw-Hill

Romney A K, Weller S, Batchelder W 1986 Culture consensus: A theory of culture and informant accuracy. *American Anthropologist* **88**(2): 313–38

Rumelhart D, McClelland J, PDP research group 1986 *Parallel Distributed Processing: explorations in the Microstructure of Cognition. Vol 1: Foundations.* MIT Press, Cambridge, MA

Rumelhart D, Smolensky P, McClelland J, Hinton C 1986 Schemata and sequential thought processes in PDP models. In: McClelland J, Rumelhart D, PDP research group (eds.) *Parallel Distributed Processing: Explorations in the Microstructure of Cognition. Vol 2: Psychological and Biological Models.* MIT Press, Cambridge, MA

Salomon G 1993 *Distributed Cognitions.* MIT Press, Cambridge, MA

Simon H 1998 *The Sciences of the Artificial* 3rd edn. MIT Press, Cambridge, MA

Schwartz T 1978 The size and shape of a culture. In: Barth F (ed.) *Scale and Social Organization.* Universitetesforlaget

Sperber D 1985 Anthropology and psychology: towards an epidemiology of representations. *Man* **20**: 73–89

Thagard P 1993 Societies of minds: Science as distributed computing. *Studies in History and Philosophy of Science* **24**: 49–67
Von Neumann J, Morgenstern O 1964 *Theory of Games and Economic Behavior*. Wiley, Chichester
Vygotsky L 1978 *Mind in Society: The Development of Higher Psychological Processes*. Harvard University Press, Cambridge, MA
Wertsch J 1985 *Vygotsky and the Social Formation of Mind*. Harvard University Press, Cambridge, MA

E. Hutchins

Cognitive Aging

Cognitive aging is concerned with age-related changes in adulthood in the basic processes of learning and memory, as well as the complex higher order processes of language and intellectual competence or executive functioning. Although most of the literature has been concerned with explaining the mechanism of cognitive decline, there is also a substantial interest in issues such as compensation and the role of external support, including collaborative problem solving.

1. Definition of Cognitive Aging

There have been two distinct traditions in the study of cognitive aging. The first grew out of experimental child psychology while the second derives from psychometric roots.

1.1 Experimental Study of Memory Functions and Language

The concern in this literature is to explicate possible causal variables that would explain why many adults suffer memory loss and decline in the complex manipulation of language variables such as text processing. The typical approach here is to design experiments testing for the effects of single variables in carefully controlled laboratory settings requiring only limited numbers of subjects. Because there is often little interest in individual differences, or population parameters, study participants are typically drawn from convenience samples (McKay and Abrams 1996).

1.2 Descriptive Study of Adult Intellectual Development

Descriptive studies of adult intellectual development often stem from the longitudinal follow up of samples first assessed in childhood or adolescence. Other such studies may represent carefully stratified samples from

defined populations, first assessed at a particular life stage, whether in early adulthood or in early old age. Although descriptive studies often begin as cross-sectional inquiries, they are most frequently conducted as longitudinal analyses since the interest is often in individual differences in intraindividual change, or in the elucidation of typologies of individuals who follow different growth trajectories. These are frequently large-sample studies, and the use of correlational or quasi-experimental approaches is typical (Baltes et al. 1999, Schaie 1996b).

2. Methodological Issues

2.1 Age-comparative vs. Age Change Designs

Much of the experimental cognitive aging literature is based on age-comparative studies, which typically contrast a group of young adults (typically college students) with convenience samples of community-dwelling older adults in their sixties and seventies. It should be recognized that such comparisons are fraught by the problem that it is often unreasonable to assume that the two age groups can be adequately matched for other status variables that might provide a rival explanation for any observed age difference on the dependent variable. This creates particular problems for identifying the mechanisms that may be implicated in age-related decline from young adulthood into old age. Age-comparative designs are also inadequate in explaining individual differences in age changes. The latter can only be investigated by means of longitudinal paradigms (Schaie 1965).

2.2 The Role of Response Speed

A number of theorists have argued that changes in the central nervous system are the primary common cause for the observed age-related declines in cognitive performance. In fact, there have been many published analyses that show a substantial reduction in age differences, if some measure or measures of reaction time or perceptual speed is partialled out of the relation between a given cognitive process and chronological age (Salthouse 1999). This issue is of particular concern because it is not clear whether the observed average increase in reaction time (generally assumed to be of the magnitude of approximately 1.6 from the early twenties to the late sixties), while reliably demonstrable in the laboratory, is of significance in many or most tasks of daily living.

3. Basic Findings from the Experimental Literature on Cognitive Aging

Most of this literature is cross-sectional in nature and usually consists of a comparison of convenience samples of young adults (often sophomore psychology students) and of community-dwelling older adults (often participants in adult education programs). The major findings regarding age differences in cognitive performance include the following.

3.1 Memory

It is currently thought that older persons are at a disadvantage in retrieving information from memory when the information to be retrieved is complex and when there are few cues or other environmental support. Hence, age differences are far greater in recall than in recognition of information. It is also thought that the magnitude of age difference in memory is far greater when a task involves effortful processing than when automatic processing is involved. Hence, greater age differences have been found for explicit than implicit memory. Older persons are also thought to have greater difficulty in integrating the context of information they are trying to remember. It is also thought that working memory capacity (i.e., the information kept in immediately accessible store) becomes reduced with increasing age. On the other hand there is little evidence for age differences in long-term storage. Memory deficits occurring with age include nonverbal tasks such as memory for spatial location, memory for faces, and for actions and activities. Studies of prospective memory (i.e., remembering something to be done in the future) suggest that older people do well in remembering simple and event-based tasks, but are at a disadvantage when tasks become complex or are time-based. In sum, it appears that age differences are known to increase in magnitude as a function of the processing requirement of a given task (Salthouse 1999, Smith 1996).

3.2 Language

Age-related differences in language behavior are closely related to the processes of encoding and retrieving verbal materials discussed above. But in addition there appear to be greater age differences in textual tasks that involve recent connections than in those that involve recollection of older connections.

Language production also seems to be adversely affected in older persons under intense time pressure. The interesting tip-of-the-tongue phenomenon involving word-finding difficulty, however, seems to be more likely with infrequently used words. Significant age differences have also been found in language planning, that is, in planning what one intends to say and how to say it during language production. Hence, older persons are more likely to engage in hesitations, false starts, and repetitions. Age-linked deficits in story recall is thought to be more of a general deficit in connection formation than in specific communication ability. Older persons tend to benefit from textual material that provides priming of association because it contains learned semantically linked information (McKay and Abrams 1996).

4. Basic Findings from the Descriptive Literature on Age Changes in Intellectual Competence

Changes in intellectual competence over the adult life span have been studied primarily with either the Wechsler Intelligence Scale or with ability batteries derived from the Thurstonian Primary Mental Ability framework.

Distinctions are made between fluid abilities thought to be innate and crystallized abilities which involve the utilization of culturally acquired knowledge (Cattell 1963). More recently further distinctions have been introduced between the mechanics (or basic processes) of intellectual competence and the pragmatics that involve cultural mediation (Baltes et al. 1984).

What has been found in most longitudinal studies is that the adult life course of mental abilities is not uniform. The so-called fluid abilities (sometimes defined as cognitive mechanics or primitives) peak in early midlife and begin to decline in the early sixties. By contrast, crystallized abilities, or the pragmatics of intellectual competence that represent abilities acquired in a given cultural context (particularly verbal abilities), do not usually peak until the fifties are reached and begin to show significant decline only in the seventies and often show only minimal decline even in the eighties (Schaie 1996a). However, recent work in advanced old age suggests increasing convergence and steeper decline for both aspects of intellectual competence, probably caused by the increasing decline of sensory and central nervous system functions (Baltes and Lindenberger 1997, Baltes and Mayer 1999).

However, at any particular time, a cross-sectional snapshot may yield very different ability profiles because of the fact that subsequent population cohorts reach different asymptotes in midlife. For example, there has been a positive linear cohort trend in the twentieth century for inductive reasoning, the basic component of most problem-solving tasks, while there has been a negative trend in numeric skills. The magnitude of cohort differences in abilities since the 1950s has been comparable to the average age changes observed from young adulthood into the seventies. Hence, many older persons may appear to have declined markedly in comparison to young peers, even though the age difference may be primarily due to what might be called the obsolescence of earlier cohorts (Schaie 1996b).

Studies of individual differences suggest that while most persons have declined on some aspect of intellectual functioning from their own peak as the sixties are reached, that specific patterns of decline may well depend on complex patterns of individual life experience. Most healthy community-dwelling persons are able to maintain a high level of function until advanced old age (but see Baltes and Mayer 1999 for the consequences of sensory dysfunctions). Because most tasks of daily living represent complex combinations of basic cognitive processes, many individuals can maintain their abilities above the minimally necessary threshold level for independent functioning by often rather complex compensatory processes (cf. Baltes et al. 1984, Baltes et al. 1999).

5. Can Cognitive Aging be Slowed or Reversed?

Once the course of adult intellectual development had been described and a number of antecedents of individual differences had been identified, it then became useful for researchers to think about ways in which normal intellectual aging might be slowed or reversed.

In a number of laboratories (primarily in the USA and in Germany) cognitive training programs have been developed that have been applied in the laboratory, and more recently in cooperative multisite intervention trials. In contrast to training young children, where it can be assumed that new skills are conveyed, older adults are likely to have access to the skills being trained, but through disuse have lost their proficiency. Information from longitudinal studies is therefore particularly useful in distinguishing individuals who have declined from those who have remained stable. In the former, training is directed towards remediation of loss, while in the latter the enhancement of previous levels of functioning are sought with the intention of compensating for possibly cohort-based disadvantage of older persons.

Results from such cognitive interventions allow the conclusion that cognitive decline in old age, for many older persons, is likely to be a function of disuse rather than of the deterioration of the physiological or neural substrates of cognitive behavior. For example, a brief five-hour training program for persons over 65 resulted in average training gains of about one half SD on the abilities of spatial orientation and inductive reasoning. Of those for whom significant decrement could be documented over a 14-year period, roughly 40 percent were returned to the level at which they had functioned when first studied. The analyses of structural relationships among the ability measures prior to and after training further allow the conclusion that training does not result in qualitative changes in ability structures, and is thus highly specific to the targeted abilities. A seven-year follow up further demonstrated that those subjects who showed significant decline at initial training do remain at substantial advantage over untrained comparison groups (Willis and Schaie 1994). It should be noted, however, that while cognitive training may improve performance in the elderly and may function to reduce effects of age decrement,

such training will also be effective in enhancing the performance of young adults such that age differences tend to remain robust (cf. Baltes and Kliegl 1992).

6. Other Related Topics in Cognitive Aging

Much of the work on cognitive aging in the past has been concerned with age-related development in the mechanics and basic processes of cognition. It should be recognized that current attention in the study of cognitive aging is turning to the discovery of how these basic processes operate within more complex domains. Of particular interest here are the study of wisdom (e.g., Baltes and Staudinger 1993, Sternberg 1990), the application of the basic processes to social cognition (e.g., Staudinger 1999), the development of expert systems (e.g. Charness and Bosman 1990), and in everyday problem solving (Willis 1996). The extensive literature on these topics is beyond the scope of this article.

See also: Aging and Health in Old Age; Aging, Theories of; Aging Mind: Facets and Levels of Analysis; Brain Aging (Normal): Behavioral, Cognitive, and Personality Consequences; Differential Aging; Ecology of Aging; Lifespan Theories of Cognitive Development; Memory and Aging, Cognitive Psychology of; Memory and Aging, Neural Basis of; Old Age and Centenarians; Social Cognition and Aging; Spatial Memory Loss of Normal Aging: Animal Models and Neural Mechanisms

Bibliography

Baltes P B, Dittmann-Kohli F, Dixon R A 1984 New perspectives on the development of intelligence in adulthood: Toward a dual process conception and a model of selective optimization with compensation. In: Baltes P B, Brim O G Jr (eds.) *Lifespan Development and Behavior*. Academic Press, New York, Vol. 6, pp. 33–76

Baltes P B, Kliegl R 1992 Further testing of limits of cognitive plasticity: Negative age differences in a mnemonic skill are robust. *Developmental Psychology* **28**: 121–5

Baltes P B, Lindenberger U 1997 Emergence of a powerful connection between sensory and cognitive functions across the adult life span: A new window at the study of cognitive aging. *Psychology and Aging* **12**: 12–21

Baltes P B, Mayer K U (eds.) 1999 *The Berlin Aging Study: Aging from 70 to 100*. Cambridge University Press, Cambridge, UK

Baltes P B, Staudinger U M 1993 The search for a psychology of wisdom. *Current Directions in Psychological Science* **2**: 75–80

Baltes P B, Staudinger U M, Lindenberger U 1999 Lifespan psychology: Theory and application to intellectual functioning. *Annual Review of Psychology* **50**: 471–507

Cattell R B 1963 Theory of fluid and crystallized intelligence: A critical experiment. *Journal of Educational Psychology* **54**: 1–22

Charness N, Bosman E A 1990 Expertise and aging: Life in the lab. In: Hess T H (ed.) *Aging and Cognition: Knowledge*

Organization and Utilization. Elsevier, Amsterdam, pp. 343–85

McKay D G, Abrams L 1996 Language, memory, and aging: Distributed deficits and the structure of new-versus-old connections. In: Birren J E, Schaie K W (eds.) *Handbook of the Psychology of Aging*, 4th edn. Academic Press, San Diego, CA, pp. 251–65

Salthouse T 1999 Theories of cognition. In: Bengtson V L, Schaie K W (eds.) *Handbook of Theories of Aging.* Springer, New York, pp. 196–208

Schaie K W 1965 A general model for the study of developmental problems. *Psychological Bulletin* **64**: 92–107

Schaie K W 1996a *Intellectual Development in Adulthood, The Seattle Longitudinal Study.* Cambridge University Press, New York

Schaie K W 1996b Intellectual functioning and aging. In: Birren J E, Schaie K W (eds.) *Handbook of the Psychology of Aging*, 4th edn. Academic Press, San Diego, CA, pp. 266–86

Schaie K W, Willis S L 1999 Theories of everyday competence. In: Bengtson V L, Schaie K W (eds.) *Handbook of Theories of Aging.* Springer, New York, pp. 174–95

Smith A D 1996 Memory. In: Birren J E, Schaie K W (eds.) *Handbook of the Psychology of Aging*, 4th edn. Academic Press, San Diego, CA, pp. 236–50

Staudinger U M 1999 Social cognition and psychological approach to an art of life. In: Blanchard-Fields F, Hess T B (eds.) *Social Cognition, Adult Development and aging.* Academic Press, San Diego, CA, pp. 343–75

Sternberg R J 1990 Wisdom and its relation to intelligence and creativity. In: Sternberg R J (ed.) *Wisdom: Its Nature, Origins, and Development.* Academic Press, New York, pp. 142–9

Willis S L 1996 Everyday problem solving. In: Birren J E, Schaie K W (eds.) *Handbook of the Psychology of Aging*, 4th edn. Academic Press, San Diego, CA, pp. 287–307

Willis S L, Schaie K W 1994 Cognitive training in the normal elderly. In: Forette F, Christen Y, Boller F (eds.) *Plasticité cérébrale et stimulation cognitive.* Fondation Nationale de Gérontologie, Paris, pp. 91–113

K. W. Schaie

Cognitive and Interpersonal Therapy: Psychiatric Aspects

Cognitive and interpersonal therapies are each structured psychological treatments. They differ considerably in their rationale and therapeutic procedures, but both have been subject to research since their inception. In recent years, each has been demonstrated to offer effective symptomatic help for a range of specific mental disorders. This has facilitated their adoption in publicly or insurance funded health services, where major changes have been taking place in the pattern of therapeutic provision and in the training of mental health professionals. In English-speaking countries, where psychiatrists trained in psychological treatments were, even 10 years ago, more likely to offer psychoanalytic psychotherapy than any other kind, provision of cognitive or interpersonal therapy is increasingly common. Cognitive therapy is also provided frequently by clinical psy-

chologists. This article will provide a brief overview of their respective rationales, methods, and current applications. It concludes with some speculations on future developments.

1. Cognitive Psychotherapy

1.1 Overview

All forms of cognitive therapy (CT) work from the premise that common mental disorders are consequent to and/or maintained by faulty thinking (rather than the reverse). Cognitive therapists, therefore, set out to identify cognitions associated with a target problem (such as depressed mood or hypochondriacal behavior) then use this analysis as the basis for an explicit therapeutic plan. Treatments addressing these cognitions can adopt a number of techniques, depending upon the problem addressed, the formulation of an individual case, and the specific form of cognitive psychotherapy favored by individual practitioners.

1.2 Rationale

Although cognitive therapy has only gained currency since 1970, its basic aims are not new. Attempts to restore mental health by arguing sufferers out of their false beliefs underpinned much 'moral therapy' in eighteenth-century asylums. As a modern movement, CT emerged from behavior therapy (qv). This had its theoretical rationale in learning theory (qv), derived from experimental manipulation of contingent responses in laboratory animals. Behavioral treatments had sought behavioral change through functional analysis of target symptoms. Behavioral theory paid little attention to the 'black box' of the mind and any mediating role it played between environmental stimulus and behavioural response. Cognitive therapy developed in reaction to this denial of the importance of thought, but was helped by clinical evidence that thinking could actively obstruct the progress of behavioral treatment unless it was explicitly attended to. The behavioral and cognitive approaches to psychological treatment have retained many common features, including emphasis on explicit formulation, and an empirical and collaborative approach. Behavioral and cognitive techniques may be combined within a treatment, and the close relationship between the two is reflected in the designation of 'cognitive-behavior therapy' or 'CBT' for much work that remains essentially cognitive.

Cognitive therapists have used a variety of models to account for how cognitive processes contribute m psychopathology. While these can be impressive in their orderliness and ingenuity, and can be of great heuristic value in practice, they nearly always derive from clinical experience. At the same time, independent support for such models has been sought from experimental psychology. Few cognitive findings in emotional disorders remain robust when stringently tested, although a good deal of evidence exists that selective preference for negative memories is common in people with depressed mood, and irrational expectations of future danger is more common in people prone to anxiety (Williams et al. 1990).

The development of cognitive therapy has gone through a succession of stages of increasing theoretical complexity. These have accompanied a tendency, shared with other maturing psychotherapies, to follow early successes with relatively straightforward cases by attempts to deal with those that are more resistant to simple measures. While the theoretical ramifications of this are beyond the scope of the present article, it is helpful to distinguish between two kinds of cognition that have been seen as pathogenic—'surface' and 'deep.' Surface cognitions are available to introspection, transient, and situation specific. Deep cognitions are less easy to access, enduring and more global in scope.

The most influential package of models informing therapeutic practice derive from Beck and co-workers (Beck 1989). As applied to common disorders in which the main features are anxiety symptoms or depression, cognitive changes lead to evident differences in appraisal of a 'cognitive triad' of three interlinked areas. These are someone's automatic attitudes concerning their world, themselves, and what is likely to happen. Beck terms surface cognitions of these kinds 'automatic thoughts.' While their content is colored by the particulars of an individual's experience and personal values, some themes have been demonstrated as common to people having a particular kind of emotional disorder. For instance, when anxiety is marked, automatic thoughts about future danger are common; with depression, personal helplessness, and perceived inability to change their personal circumstances; with hostility, thoughts that the world is a bad or very unreliable place. Beck identifies two other kinds of cognitive pathology that accompany these developments. One is a set of ways in which cognitive processes frequently are distorted. These ensure that appraisals based on automatic thinking are likely to be confirmed. Examples include making of arbitrary or personal inferences, selective abstraction and overgeneralization from experience, and all or nothing ('dichotomous') thinking. At the level of deep cognitions, Beck recognizes the presence of 'schemas' as constellations of assumptions and beliefs which, being more latent but enduring cognitions that can be reactivated by events, are associated with predisposition to emotional disorders. The main functional relationships between these elements are summarized in Fig. 1.

While a good deal of reasoning in cognitive therapy represents extensions or amendments to this framework, a significant conceptual departure came with revision of the concept of the 'schema.' Used to refer to a variety of kinds of deep cognition, the term's

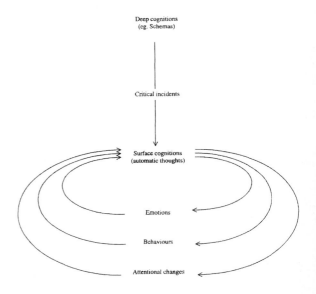

Figure 1
A map of problem cognitions

adoption by Young (1994) to refer to 'early maladaptive schemas' (EMS) has had important practical implications. An EMS is not only latent and enduring, but presumed to result from experiences early in life. It is rigid in restricting the scope of thinking and likely to be associated with very strong affect if challenged. Because of this emotional valence, EMSs can appear to be quasi-autonomous, acting to preserve themselves (schema maintenance). There can be a preference for executive functions that either fail to activate the schema (schema avoidance) or that disguise it behind displays of contrary traits (schema compensation). EMSs resistance to change means they cannot be inferred straightforwardly from behavior or simple enquiries.

1.3 Methods

In general, therapeutic strategies aim to counteract cognitive distortions by teaching patients skills by which they can recognize and revise problematic cognitions, as well as working to challenge specific current cognitions and to establish a more adaptive way of thinking. Essentially, this will involve techniques for the identification of surface and deep cognitions and their sequelae that are not otherwise amenable to simple introspection, and for the modification of beliefs and cognitive distortions so encountered. Although this account will concentrate on interventions directed at cognitions, both of these tasks are carried out in practice through the prescription of behavioral experiments and exercises. For instance, when working with people subject to panic attacks who fear they may die from a heart attack during a panic episode, the assumption that physical symptoms such as dizziness, breathlessness, and awareness of accelerated heartbeat indicate collapse and death are imminent is addressed by a behavioral procedure. In order to break the link between these experiences and expectations, a patient agrees to hyperventilate under controlled conditions until these sensations are induced. The strength of their beliefs concerning the consequences of the hyperventilation exercise would be rated and recorded at its outset and its conclusion, as part of a therapeutic examination of the validity of the expectations in the light of a disconfirmatory experience. This example illustrates the general principle that, even when using a behavioural manipulation, a cognitive therapist would insist it subserves a cognitive goal, and that attention is paid to its cognitive impact throughout.

Measures to identify automatic thoughts include analysis of situations in which a target problem occurs. This is unlikely to be successful through generalized recall: specific instances need to be examined in detail. These might be recounted in the session; lived through between sessions after a patient is instructed on how to maintain a detailed and contemporaneous record of associated negative thoughts; or reconstructed as a patient has a shift of affect in a session. Other techniques such as role-plays or induction of imagery may be employed in sessions to stimulate automatic thoughts. Measures intended to facilitate reattribution expose not only the irrationality of automatic thoughts but their incompatibility with experience. The importance of active testing in modifying them, alongside regular and explicit reappraisal of the validity of the thoughts, has already been referred to. Patients and therapists are likely to collaborate in drawing up a set of alternative explanations whose fit with the facts of experience can then also be tested.

As experience of cognitive techniques has developed, there has been a progressive shift of interest away from factors leading simply to inaccurate appraisal of situations, to those by which faulty cognitions, and problems associated with them, are maintained (Salkovskis 1991). These may be automatic thoughts associated with plans of action that perpetuate a problem by protecting a faulty cognition from challenge (safety behaviors) or attentional shifts that have a similar impact through distraction. Interventions that address these maintaining factors directly can allow cognitive techniques to be effective where attention to errors in appraisal alone would not.

Deep cognitions in the form of schemas are not only more difficult to identify than surface cognitions, but harder to attempt to change therapeutically. Identification needs a more probing and hypothetical approach in the course of guided discovery by use of techniques such as the 'vertical arrow.' This is a reiterative questioning of patients' suppositions about the implications of a negative idea being the case, until

a fundamental and general belief about themselves emerges. Attempts to change schemas would normally only be made when there had been some progress with emotional symptoms. As the previous description of the kinds of concealment and resistance associated with EMSs implies, schema-focused work is likely to be more complicated and prolonged than work with automatic thoughts. Because schemas may embody templates for how someone relates to others, and be associated with manifest relationship problems, therapeutic work with them is likely to resemble psychodynamic psychotherapy (qv) more closely than other forms of cognitive therapy (Safran and Segal 1990).

1.4 Applications

Unlike psychoanalytic psychotherapies, cognitive psychotherapy has developed through its application to conditions in which symptoms or problematic habits are associated with specific patterns of thinking. Its growth since 1970 has been accompanied by progressive developments in psychiatric nosology. The diagnostic and statistical manuals of the American Psychiatric Association chart diagnostic developments which have involved the progressive refinement of diagnoses based on anxiety, depression, psychosis, and distortions of personality, with the effective invention of categories to encompass the so-called somatoform, dissociative, adjustment, and eating disorders (APA 1968, 1980, 1994). These have facilitated understanding of common cognitive patterns associated with these and development of specific treatment techniques. Use of cognitive therapy in depression and anxiety disorders are best established, while diagnostic subclassifications that have clarified the characteristics of bipolar depressive disorder and panic disorder have been followed by specific cognitive techniques for their management. The category of personality disorders has not only been refined through this period, but, with the advent of multiaxial classification, been designated as an independent axis for summary clinical descripton (axis II). Given that the basic difference between disorders of personality from the symptom focused categories of axis I lies in their early onset and relative stability, models of their cognitive pathology have emphasized 'deep' cognitions over surface ones, and more recently the early maladaptive schema model of Young. Efforts to link specific personality types with consistent schema formations continue. A further development of particular significance to psychiatrists has been the application of cognitive therapy to schizophrenia. These have included treatments for specific symptoms (delusions and hallucinations) as well as measures to live with the impact of illness and enhance coping capacities (Chadwick et al. 1996).

The vast majority of cognitive therapy is provided as individual therapy. However, group treatments have been pioneered for specific disorders including depressive, anxiety, and eating disorders. Beck has advocated its use with couples experiencing conflict.

More recently, attempts have been made to differentiate between psychological therapies with reference to the strength of independent evidence concerning their clinical effectiveness. An empirically supported treatment is one which is clearly defined and, for a given clinical problem, is consistently more efficacious than placebo treatments on the evidence of controlled clinical trials. On this basis, cognitive therapies have emerged as empirically supported in adults for anxiety disorders (including panic disorder, generalized anxiety disorder, and social phobia); unipolar depression; anorexia nervosa and bulimia nervosa (Roth and Fonagy 1996).

1.5 Comment

The remarkable growth of cognitive therapy has been facilitated by a number of external developments: the growth of clinical psychology as a profession whose members receive training in cognitive theory and techniques within their core curriculum; compatibility between cognitive models of psychopathology and classifications adopted for diagnosis, care management, and organization of the evidence base; and an intellectual Zeitgeist that favors explanations based on information processing or neurocognitive paradigms. The relative rapidity of the clinical effects of CT has invited comparisons of their efficacy with those of pharmacological treatments, while their longer term impact is not always clear. They enjoy a high level of acceptability that reflects their collaborative and transparent style. However, the emphasis on monitoring, rating, and homework exercises can be seen as excessively demanding by some patients, and the relative lack of attention to the historical origins of difficulties is not to all patients' taste. Practical methods are relatively easily learned and taught, although growing evidence concerning the added value of intensive training and supervision for clinical outcomes suggests this ease is deceptive. Important developments in the theoretical base and practice of cognitive therapies continue to be made. Some of these, in indicating the importance of formative experience, of the relationship with the therapist and patterns of relating, and of increasingly inaccessible ('unconscious') cognitive structures underlying behavior, are narrowing the gap between cognitive and psychodynamic models of psychotherapy in practice.

2. Interpersonal Therapy

2.1 Overview

Interpersonal therapy (IPT) is an increasingly common model of brief psychotherapy that was developed as a specific treatment for depression in the 1970s. Findings from research into the interpersonal precipitants of depression were used in designing an intervention that could bring symptomatic relief through improvements in interpersonal functioning (Klerman et al. 1984). Different therapeutic strategies are used, depending upon which of four basic kinds of interpersonal problem is paramount in an individual case. IPT is now being adapted to other disorders and settings (Klerman and Weissman 1993).

2.2 Rationale

IPTs basic rationale is that depressed mood is usually secondary to deterioration in interpersonal relationships, and can be reversed by deliberate attention to the quality of current relationships. Historically, it was developed in deliberate contrast to psychodynamic therapies, in which the importance of interpersonal relationships within the therapy itself as well as in a patient's life are paramount. A key difference has been that psychodynamic psychotherapies not only pay considerable attention to the formative influence of past relationships, but they focus on (maladaptive) patterns of relating that are seen as characteristic of a person. Interpersonal therapy pays attention to current relationships for their own sake. It does not conceptualise underlying patterns, although it would expect someone's style of relating to improve through reinforcement of positive changes achieved in the relationships targeted in therapy. Although the 'interpersonal psychiatry' of Sullivan (1953) is frequently quoted as an antecedent of IPT, its focus on in-session interactions and on enduring patterns of relating is inconsistent with this new therapy, despite their mutual emphasis on the importance of good interpersonal relationships for personal mental health.

IPT has used theoretical developments in a number of fields, from attachment theory to life events research, to highlight the association of onset of depression with loss through grief or major life changes, conflict, and isolation. Its model identifies whether a person's most pressing need is resolution of grief, role transitions, interpersonal disputes, or interpersonal deficits.

The model was designed to be researchable from the outset, its method being summarized in a manual (Klerman et al. 1984) to promote consistent application in practice. Studies have not only addressed its efficacy for specific conditions (see below) but the impact of process on outcome. An important literature has therefore also developed concerning the impact of training on the practice of psychotherapy (Rounsaville et al. 1988).

2.3 Method

As a time-limited therapy, IPT was pioneered over 12 sessions per treatment, now often 16. A typical treatment is subdivided into initial, treatment, and termination phases. During the initial phase, the patient is educated to see their difficulties as the consequence of having a depressive illness, and to allow themselves to occupy a sick role. (This means they should not feel responsible for this state of affairs, and allow others to take on some of their normal duties so they can concentrate on recovery.) A detailed inventory is drawn up with the therapist summarizing all current relationships, however insignificant. This not only provides a map of potential areas of difficulty, but of sources of potential support and opportunities for the development of relationships in future. Detailed questioning in the first phase allows a treatment focus to be identified which reflect four distinct forms of interpersonal need: grief (where the loss of a significant other through death has not been overcome); role disputes (where conflict in a key relationship, perhaps in the form of an impasse rather than overt fighting, cannot be resolved); role transitions (where adaptation to a different situation, commonly following loss events, is required). In some residual cases, where a patient's interpersonal situation is particularly impoverished through an inability to establish relationships, a fourth category of interpersonal deficits applies.

Different therapeutic techniques are likely to be required in each of these instances, the model being sufficiently flexible to accommodate these. Examples would be assisted mourning with grief, and attention to communication in interpersonal disputes. In all cases, there is careful attention to affect and considerable emphasis on its successful expression throughout treatment.

Therapy concludes with explicit attention to termination, both in anticipating and working through loss of the therapy and in planning for continuing progress along the lines tried out during the therapy.

2.4 Applications

IPTs use in the treatment of major depression was highlighted by a large randomized controlled trial sponsored by the US National Institute of Mental Health (Elkin et al. 1989). This remains one of the largest comparative trials of psychological and pharmacological treatments ever conducted, providing information on the relative benefits from two psychotherapies (CT and IPT), imipramine and a drug placebo. The results were encouraging for IPT, showing it to be as effective as CT in relieving symptoms overall, while having the lowest attrition, and significantly better results than CT among the most severely depressed patients.

Since its original application in studies of clinical depression, IPT's use has been broadened to incorporate depressed populations with special needs; patients with distinct mental disorders and adapta-

tions of the therapeutic process to fit different working contexts (cf. Klerman and Weissman 1990). Depression in adolescents and the elderly, as well as the chronic low grade depression known as dysthymic disorder, have all been shown to benefit from treatment (Markowitz 1998). Modifications of therapeutic technique can be involved, for instance greater involvement of significant others in the treatment process with adolescents, and use of less frequent maintenance sessions after the phase of regular sessions in dysthymia. Adjustment of content is likely to be involved with use of IPT with other disorders. A great deal of exploratory work in the field of substance misuse has so far failed to show significant benefits. An area of greater promise has been in the treatment of bulimia nervosa, where lasting clinical improvements comparable to those from CT have been achieved (Agras et al. 2000).

The principal adaptations to the model to suit different contexts have been its shortening to six brief sessions for use with subclinical populations in primary care settings (cf. Klerman and Weissman 1990). Attempts to develop a group model of IPT for treatment of social phobia are promising but at an early stage.

3. Conclusion

Although cognitive and interpersonal therapeutic packages are relatively new, each has elaborated principles of good psychiatric management—respectively, the importance of a patient's attitude or social relationships to their health and recovery—that are widely recognized. Their rapid growth reflects their proven efficacy for specific disorders, the relative ease with which they can be learned and disseminated, and the promise of brief psychological treatment for clinical conditions that account for a large proportion of psychiatric practice. Both are widely used alongside physical treatments such as psychotropic medication. Developments are likely to include continuing influence of basic research in psychology and the neurosciences on the refinement of therapeutic models and methods, and increasing rapprochement with other therapeutic models as integrative models of treatment are developed for more complex and treatment-resistant conditions.

Bibliography

Agras W S, Walsh B T, Fairburn C G, Wilson G T, Kraemer H C 2000 A multicenter comparison of cognitive-behavioural therapy and interpersonal theapy for bulimia nervosa. *Archives of General Psychiatry* **57**: 459–66

American Psychiatric Association 1968 *Diagnostic and Statistical Manual of Mental Disorders*, 2nd edn. APA, New York

American Psychiatric Association 1980 *Diagnostic and Statistical Manual of Mental Disorders*, 3rd edn. APA, New York

American Psychiatric Association 1994 *Diagnostic and Statistical Manual of Mental Disorders*, 4th edn. APA, New York

Beck A T 1989 *Cognitive Therapy and the Emotional Disorders*. International Universities Press, New York

Chadwick P D J, Birchwood M J, Trower P 1996 *Cognitive Therapy for Hallucinations and Delusions*. Wiley, Chichester, UK

Elkin I, Shea M T, Watkins J T, Imber S D, Sotsky S M, Collins J F, Glass D R, Pilkonis P A, Leber W R, Docherty J P, Fiester S J, Paloh M B 1989 National Institute of Mental Health Treatment of Depression Collaborative Research Programme: General effectiveness of treatment. *Archives of General Psychiatry* **46**: 971 83

Klerman G L, Weissman M M, Rounsaville B J, Chevron E S 1984 *Psychotherapy for Depression*. Basic Books, New York

Klerman G L, Weissman M M (eds.) 1990 *New Applications of Interpersonal Psychotherapy*. American Psychiatric Press, New York

Markowitz J C 1998 *Interpersonal Psychotherapy for Dysthymic Disorder*. American Psychiatric Press, New York

Roth A, Fongagy P 1996 *What Works for Whom?* Guilford Press, New York

Rounsaville B J, O'Malley S, Foley S, Weissman M M 1988 Role of manual-guided training in the conduct and efficacy of interpersonal psychotherapy for depression. *Journal of Consulting and Clinical Psychology* **56**: 681–8

Safran J D, Segal Z V 1990 *Interpersonal Process in Cognitive Therapy*. Basic Books, New York

Salkovskis P M 1991 The importance of behaviour in the maintenance of anxiety and panic: A cognitive account. *Behavioural Psychotherapy* **19**: 6–19

Sullivan H S 1953 *The Interpersonal Theory of Psychiatry*. Norton, New York

Williams J M G, Watts F N, MacLeod L, Matthews A 1990 *Cognitive Psychology and the Emotional Disorders*. Tavistock, London

Young J E 1994 *Cognitive Therapy for Personality Disorders: A Schema Focused Cognitive Therapy*. Professional Resource Exchange, Sarasota, FL

C. J. Mace

Cognitive Anthropology

Cognitive anthropology attempts to link anthropology with the cognitive sciences. Culture, as one of anthropology's central objects of research, has an effect in two respects: on the one hand, in a material sense in the form of cultural phenomena, on the other hand, mentally, in the form of cultural contents. Cultural contents are based on mental representations. While cultural phenomena are public and thus easy to document ethnographically, cultural contents are not directly accessible since mental representations cannot be observed. What actually happens inside people's heads is the object of research of the cognitive sciences. Cognitive sciences see the human experience of reality and human thinking as acts of processing information. In addition to the study of perception, mental representation, and memory, the objective is to make transparent those mental faculties that enable all humans to internalize the social and cultural characteristics of the society into which they are born. But these are also central topics of anthropological research.

1. From Ethnoscience to the Cognitive Sciences

The year of birth of the 'cognitive revolution' in which, apart from social anthropology, various human sciences participated, to some extent independently of each other, is considered to be 1956. That year, at a conference on information theory at the Massachusetts Institute of Technology, Newell and Simon presented a paper on computer programs, Miller presented his famous treatise *The Magical Number Seven*, and the 28-year-old Chomsky read excerpts from his thesis *Three Models of Language*. In the same year, Bruner's book *A Study of Thinking* was published and two anthropologists, Goodenough and Lounsbury, published the first two programmatic articles on cognitive anthropology, *Componential Analysis and the Study of Meaning* and *A Semantic Analysis of the Pawnee Kinship Usage*.

With cognitive anthropology or, more precisely, with the ethnoscience phase of cognitive anthropology, a new field of research came to the fore. Its goal was to describe other cultures in their own conceptualization, that is, in emic terms or from the inside. Different cultures categorize the world differently and apply a different type of logic in dealing with their environment. This difference should be recorded as it reveals different cognitive worlds. The underlying question was an old one: What does the 'order out of chaos' look like? More precisely, the basic questions were 'How do other cultures label the things in their environment, and how are these labels related to each other?' This according to the assumption that with the help of cultural phenomena the cultural contents, and thus the mental representations, could also be documented.

1.1 Three Premises

One can argue that three premises formed the background to this ambitious program:

1.1.1 Premise 1: Culture is common (shared) knowledge.

A highly significant definition of culture was coined by Goodenough: 'A society's culture consists of whatever it is one has to know or believe in order to operate in a manner acceptable to its members, and to do so in any role that they accept for any one of themselves. ... It is the forms of things that people have in mind, their models for perceiving, relating, and otherwise interpreting them. ... Culture does not exist of things, people, behaviour, or emotions, but in the forms or organizations of the things in the minds of people' (Goodenough 1957, pp. 167–8).

Seen in this way, culture is a mental phenomenon.

1.1.2   Premise 2: Knowledge has the form of a cultural grammar. Anthropologists must, on the basis of the statements made by their informants, inductively discover this abstract and shared knowledge as a systematic mental representation. In principle, they can, in order to do so, limit themselves to one person, as applies when learning a foreign language, where at first sight it suffices to have one speaker at one's disposal. The knowledge system of a culture is understood to be a conceptual model which embraces the organizational principles of the culture and the behavior of its members. The model is, so to speak, a cultural grammar.

1.1.3   Premise 3: Language is the best means of access to mental phenomena. With the reduction of chaos, certain phenomena and characteristics are selected from the environment as being significant, named, and given a classificatory meaning. The main (but not the only) proof of the existence of a category is its label.

The equation of culture and knowledge proved to be very fruitful. In the 1960s, ethnoscience experienced rapid success. Innumerable studies were published—which was to be expected –about terminologically densely structured individual fields, such as those on kinship, colors, ethnozoology, ethnobotany, or illness. One succumbed, as it were, to the great theoretical temptation to reduce complex and ostensibly heterogeneous things to a few rules (inclusion, exclusion, and intersection) and to present them as elegant models (taxonomy, paradigm, see below) which were looked upon as mental representations of individuals.

At the beginning of the 1970s, however, only a very few studies appeared, and Keesing (1972, p. 229) was justified in starting a paper with the sentence: 'Tell me, whatever happened to ethnoscience?' Here lies the irony: when, at the end of the 1950s, ethnoscience took over this model from linguistics and it became the focal point in the 1960s, it had already been swept aside in linguistics itself by Chomsky's new generative linguistics.

The result was an opening up and turning towards modern trends in neighboring disciplines. Computer science proved to have particularly strong influence; when the first computer programs appeared which played chess, the question arose, 'If computers can have programs, why can't people, too?' In endeavoring to reproduce human cognitive representations in the model, cognitive anthropology adopted the 'information-processing approach.' In so doing, the assumption (at that time) that cognitive processes

follow the same pattern universally, whether in humans, animals, or the machine (in other words, that the software is the same everywhere, irrespective of the hardware in which it is processed) was, from a philosophical point of view, highly explosive.

1.2   Revised Premises

As a consequence, the three premises of ethnoscience were reconsidered and extended; the emphasis turned to where knowledge is sought and how it is represented.

1.2.1   Revised Premise 1: Turning towards the individual. Attention at the end of the twentieth century was no longer focused on the collective knowledge system as the whole of a culture (as représentation collective in the sense of Durkheim), supposed to be recorded as the ideal type, but on the scattered, variable knowledges acquired, stored (memorized), and applied by individuals in their everyday life. The focus shifted, because it was recognized that inferences cannot be directly drawn from cultural phenomena and linguistic material in order to elaborate individual cognitive processes or representations.

1.2.2   Revised Premise 2: Operationalization instead of categorization. As soon as knowledge is no longer defined as an isolated, static system (that is, simply as grammar) but as something which is evident (verbally or nonverbally) in everyday use by individuals, it becomes clear that many categories and semantic fields have no fixed boundaries, and cannot be defined in the classical sense (fuzzy sets). They are now also grouped according to what a person can do in daily life ('taskonomy' instead of taxonomy) or else according to prototypes (best example from a category). It is everyday cognition that a housewife needs when she shops, a milkman when he distributes dairy products to his customers according to a certain pattern, a Yakan in the Philippines when he wants to enter a house correctly.

1.2.3   Revised Premise 3: Turning away from language as the only instrument to code knowledge. Knowledge is also expressed by means of actions or emotions. Habitual actions in particular can be very 'eloquent' in the sense of tacit knowledge. In 1977, the computer specialist Schank and the sociopsychologist Abelson introduced the significant term 'script' to describe stereotyped sequences of actions in certain situations. Thus, although language remains one of the focal points, it is treated differently;

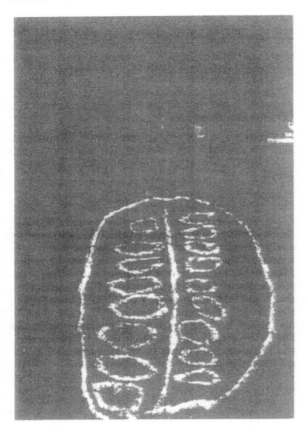

Figure 1
Ndanda, an old Yupno man (Papua New Guinea),
draws a picture of the world.

Figure 2
Gwarane, an old Yupno woman, sorts objects (sorting
task) following a hot/cold schema, after having first
verbally given a taxonomic order which, however, plays
no role in her everyday life.

no longer as a lexicon, but in everyday use as
discourse from which inferences must be drawn as to
the intended message (Hutchins 1980). Beyond
this, the (controversial) idea is that the structure of
knowledge (as stored in the mind as representation) is
not necessarily language-like: 'Knowledge organized
for efficiency in day-to-day practice is not only
nonlinguistic, but also not language-like in that it
does not take a sentential logical form' (Bloch 1991,
pp. 189–190). In addition, the question arises whether
language should not be ignored more frequently
because certain kinds of knowledge cannot be
externalized linguistically, or only with great difficulty
(Wassmann 1993) (Fig. 1 and Fig. 2).

If the individual acting in his or her daily life now
arouses interest, this is a consequence of a paradigmatic change: cognitive anthropology now considers itself more clearly as part of the cognitive
sciences, which, inter alia, leads to the word 'cognition'
being better understood. Cognition is no longer an
expression of a culture as a whole and abstracted from
linguistic material, but understood as the mental
activity of individuals who actively apply knowledge
in different contexts, in that they think, generalize,
draw inferences, perceive, recognize and categorize;
analyze, combine, assess possibilities, solve problems
and make decisions; classify, differentiate and choose;
remember and master new situations. These activities
are performed individually or between individuals
but, nevertheless, take place somehow within the
broad framework of the 'Culture.'

2. The Representation of Knowledge

The most important models to represent knowledge in
cognitive anthropology are briefly described below.

2.1 Taxonomy

The inner order of a semantic field (e.g., 'kinship,'
'colors') depends on a small number of ordering
principles which structure the lexical components

Table 1
Taxonomy

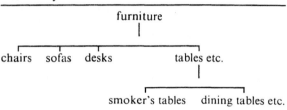

Table 2
Paradigm

		Sex	
		a1	a2
Generation	b1	grandfather	grandmother
	b2	father	mother
	b3	Ego	
	b4	son	daughter
	b5	grandson	granddaughter .

(lexemes) of the field (e.g., 'mother,' 'red'). The ordering principles are inclusion, exclusion (contrast), and intersection. A taxonomy is the description of a semantic field; it lists the categories (lexemes) and shows how they are connected with each other, i.e., according to the principles of inclusion and exclusion in hierarchic order. Categories at the same level exclude each other (exclusion) while categories at the lower level are included in the categories at the higher level (inclusion). The grouping in Table 1 shows that 'dining tables' are different from 'smokers' tables' but that both are a kind of table. And also that chairs are distinguished from tables. It does not say what are the distinguishing characteristics.

2.2 Paradigm

If a semantic field is structured according to the principle of intersection, it is a paradigm. Hierarchy, inclusion, and exclusion are missing; instead the distinctive features (or criterial attributes) are stated which distinguish the different categories. In order to construct such a model, a componential analysis is made (Tyler 1969). A complete lexicon of a semantic field, e.g., 'blood relationship' is established and then those characteristics (components) are looked for according to which of the lexemes differ, e.g., 'male' and 'female' in the dimension 'sex,' as well as the distance from Ego in the dimension 'generation.' Every single lexeme is now defined by a bundle of components. In the graphic representation in Table 2 these components intersect at the defined lexeme.

Taxonomy and paradigm are the classic models of ethnoscience. They are strongly idealized, consistently

Table 3
Prototypes

Prototype	Category
chair	furniture
car	vehicle
orange	fruit
gun etc.	weapon etc.

emic and only to a small degree 'cognitive.' They are understood as the 'mind' of a whole culture and (as we know today) they are not really instruments of thinking.

2.3 Prototype

Within a category of objects, that object is a prototype (for the whole category) which is thought to be the best example or the clearest case. Thus, for example, in the category 'furniture' the 'chair' is a better example than, for instance, 'radio.' Of course one could define 'furniture' as a category of objects having certain semantic characteristics or attributes in common (and whatever does not have these characteristics does not belong). However, this (checklist) definition does not allow any grading such as 'chair' being a better example, more of a prototype of 'furniture' than, for instance, 'radio' (although both belong to 'furniture'). It may happen that there are no criterial attributes common to all parts (i.e., no semantic field, no class according to ethnoscience), but only a large number of characteristics which may 'match' some but by no means all. As a consequence, they have only a 'family resemblance'-structure (a term Rosch adopted from Wittgenstein (Rosch and Merris 1975)). Following Lévi-Strauss, prototypes are particularly good to think (Table 3).

2.4 Script, Schema and Cultural Model

The information theory approach forces the anthropologist to be explicit. Exactly that has to be made explicit which normally remains implicit. This additional information is called 'script.' It is the tacit knowledge enabling us to also understand incomplete descriptions and suggestions: we automatically add what is missing by an inference process. Every situation requires specific knowledge and accordingly there are scripts for 'eating in a restaurant,' 'playing football,' 'attending a birthday party.' But not only our actions are based on scripts, but our language as well, as exemplified briefly in the following; a story told with all the details would be tedious.

I am in New York and somebody asks me the way to Coney Island; I tell him to take the 'N'-train to the terminus. This instruction only makes sense 'if this improperly specified algorithm can be filled out with a great deal of knowledge about how to walk, pay for the subway, get in the train and so on' (Schank and Abelson 1977, p. 20).

If the typical characteristics of a situation are grasped, hence the stereotypical, the standard-like is stressed but raised to a higher level of abstraction; we can talk about schemata and cultural models (which partly replace the older term of the folk model). All the knowledge we acquire, remember, and communicate about this world is neither a simple reflection of this world nor does it consist of a series of categories (as ethnoscience assumed), but it is organized into different situation-relevant, prototypical, simplified sequences of events. We basically think in simplified worlds: '... cultural models are composed of prototypical event sequences set in simplified worlds' (Quinn and Holland 1987, p. 32). What is more, these models are probabilistic and partial; they are actual frames we can use to react to new situations as well. They are world-proposing yet cannot be directly observed, since they are not presented but merely represented by the behavior of the people. They are models *of* the mind and *in* the mind. The organizing principle behind these models seems to be metonymy, a part of the whole, the prototypical, conspicuous part is passed off as the whole, i.e., a whole is represented by one of its parts (cf. the frame theory of Minsky, and story grammar by Rumelhart).

2.5 Mental Images

Knowledge may also be represented by inner images. The image schema consists of schematized, simplified images. These images are able to make comprehensible and imaginable physical objects or logical relationships difficult to conceptualize. The organizing principle behind them appears to be the metaphor; through analogy, information from the physical world is introduced into the nonphysical world, for example, rage can be imagined as a hot liquid in a container, evaporation as rising molecules springing out of the water like popcorn, electricity as a crowd of people (in front of the gate of a stadium at a sports event).

3. How Deep?

The structure of the representations of knowledge as presented here under Sects. 2.3, 2.4, and 2.5 allows us to answer three questions central to cognitive anthropology (Quinn and Holland 1987, pp. 3–4).

(a) It is able to explain the apparent systematicity of cultural contents (knowledge) by pointing to a number of general-purpose models which can repeatedly be integrated into other concrete models which are special-purpose orientated.

(b) Mastering the enormous amount of knowledge every one of us has is possible because we only store what is prototypical, reduced, but are able to actualize

it on demand (in concrete situations), i.e., supplement it with details (instantiation).

(c) It is possible to interpret new experiences because these models not only represent knowledge but also allow us to draw conclusions from them to new situations.

When answering these three questions, modern cognitive anthropology faces three more general problem areas.

3.1 Knowledge and Knowing

Giddens writes 'The vast bulk of the "stocks of knowledge" ... incorporated in encounters is not directly accessible to the consciousness of the actors. Most of such knowledge if practical in character, it is inherent in the capability to 'go on' within the routines of social life' (Giddens 1984, p. 4). Imagine having to describe to somebody how to ride a bicycle; doing so, one has to question the traditional conception of knowledge. It seems to be advantageous to distinguish between knowledge (what is known, as an abstract pool of information, declarative and verbalized) and knowing (how to do something in practice, implicit and hidden, primarily accessed through performance)—the focus being on the latter. We may even reorient our analysis and reverse the process—by starting with knowing and seeing how knowledge is constituted from it (Borofsky 1994).

3.2 Language and Cognition

Does language shape our thinking? This question seems to be receiving attention once more (Gumperz and Levinson 1996). Thus spatial orientation and communicating it certainly belongs to the cognitive and linguistic basic equipment of all people and societies. However, there are different linguistic systems of orientation, and, for us, very basic spatial categories such as 'left,' 'right,' 'in front' or 'behind' cannot be taken for granted. Many languages do not know these terms and instead use a geocentric system based, for example, on the cardinal points and use this not only in navigation but also in everyday life (the glass is not placed to the left of the plate but to the east, for instance). However, these differences of a linguistic and cultural kind (probably) also influence the (cognitive) perception of spatial relationships as well as their storage in memory (Wassmann and Dasen 1998). Here cognitive anthropology contradicts the prevailing school of thought of cognitive linguistics in which the worldwide diversity of languages is only seen as a cultural phenomenon and hence one of surface.

3.3 Universals?

Cognitive processes such as categorizing, classification, memorizing, and perception are the foundations of the contents of knowledge and structure these. In principle they are thought to be universal but can be applied in different ways.

'We found evidence of differences across cultural groups, differences in habitual strategies for classifying and for solving problems, differences in cognitive style, and differences in rates of progression through developmental stages ... These differences, however, are in performance rather than in competence. They are differences in the way basic cognitive processes are applied to particular contexts, rather than in the presence or absence of the processes. Despite these differences, then, there is an underlying universality of cognitive processes' (Segall et al. 1990, p. 184).

It seems, however, that the deep structure might be influenced by culture in a more lasting way than has been assumed. In the cognitive sciences, the fact that a major part of the mental representations and processes studied might be of a cultural nature receives little attention. Frequently universality is simply postulated without taking into consideration the possibility of a cultural cogeneration. To sensitize cognitive scientists to the ambitious question of the range of cultural variability is a task for which no discipline is better suited than anthropology. A promising field of work for both disciplines could be the PDP-models (Parallel Distributed Processing), also called 'connectionistic models' or neuronal networks, which Rumelhart and McClelland (1986) developed as computer models. These are able to construct models of the functioning of schemata: not as loading in a set of instructions, but as gradually building up associative links among repeated or salient aspects of experience. This vagueness and dependency on empirical knowledge from our everyday life, hence of cultural phenomena, make these models attractive to anthropologists as well (Shore 1996, Strauss and Quinn 1997).

See also: Cognitive Modeling: Research Logic in Cognitive Science; Cognitive Science: History; Cognitive Science: Overview; Conceptual Blending; Cultural Studies of Science; Grammatical Relations; Mental Models, Psychology of; Mental Representation of Persons, Psychology of

Bibliography

Bloch M 1991 Language, anthropology and cognitive science. *Man* **26**: 183–98
Borofsky R 1994 On the knowledge and knowing of cultural activities. In: Borofsky R (ed.) *Assessing Cultural Anthropology*. McGraw-Hill, New York, pp. 331–46
Giddens A 1984 *The Constitution of Society: Outline of the Theory of Structuration*. University of California Press, Berkeley, CA
Goodenough W 1957 Cultural anthropology and linguistics. In: Garvin P L (ed.) *Reports of the Seventh Annual Round Table Meeting on Linguistics and Language Study*. Georgetown University Press, Washington, DC, pp. 167–73
Gumperz J, Levinson S C (eds.) 1996 *Rethinking Linguistic Relativity*. Cambridge University Press, Cambridge, UK
Hutchins E 1980 *Culture and Inference*. Harvard University Press, Cambridge, MA
Keesing R M 1972 Paradigms lost: The new ethnography and the new linguistics. *Southwestern Journal of Anthropology* **28**: 299–332
Keesing R M 1987 Models, 'folk' and 'cultural': Paradigms regained? In: Holland D, Quinn N (eds.) *Cultural Models in Language and Thought*. Cambridge University Press, Cambridge, UK, pp. 368–93
Quinn N, Holland D 1987 Culture and cognition. In: Holland D, Quinn N (eds.) *Cultural Models in Language and Thought*. Cambridge University Press, Cambridge, UK
Rosch E, Merris C 1975 Family resemblances: Studies in internal structure of categories. *Cognitive Psychology* **7**: 573–605
Rumelhart D E, McClelland J L (eds.) 1986 *Parallel Distributed Processing: Explorations in the Microstructure of Cognition*. MIT Press, Cambridge, MA
Schank R C, Abelson R P 1977 *Scripts, Plans, Goals and Understanding: An Enquiry into Human Knowledge Structures*. Erlbaum, Hillsdale, NJ
Segall M H, Dasen P, Berry J, Poortinga Y 1990 *Human Behavior in Global Perspective: An Introduction to Cross-cultural Psychology*. Allyn and Bacon, Boston
Shore B 1996 *Culture in Mind: Cognition, Culture, and the Problem of Meaning*. Oxford University Press, New York
Strauss C, Quinn N 1997 *A Cognitive Theory of Cultural Meaning*. Cambridge University Press, Cambridge, UK
Tyler S (ed.) 1969 *Cognitive Anthropology: Readings*. Holt, Rinehart, and Winston, New York
Wassmann J 1993 *Das Ideal des Leicht Gebeugten Menschen. Eine Ethno-Kognitive Analyse der Yupno von Papua Neuguinea*. Reimer Verlag, Berlin
Wassmann J, Dasen P R 1998 Balinese spatial orientation. Some empirical evidence of moderate linguistic relativity. *Journal of the Royal Anthropological Institute* **44**: 689–711

J. Wassmann

Cognitive Archaeology

Cognitive archaeology is an approach to research explicitly emphasizing the central role of cognition and mental phenomena in explanations of the past. It rejects behaviorism, with its emphasis on stimulus–response relationships, and the overriding concern with environmental adaptation which underlies much processual archaeology. The theoretical underpinnings of cognitive archaeology derive instead from post-positivist philosophy of science, cultural anthropology, linguistics, psychology and, more broadly, the cognitive neurosciences. Primary research topics include the origin of art, belief, language, tool use, and the human mind; and the reconstruction of prehistoric religion and ideology. Cognitive archaeologists look to a broad range of empirical data to investigate these interests, including stone tools, settlement patterns, ceramics, and art and iconography. Ethnohistorical data are also commonly employed as a starting point, as many cognitive archaeologists are advocates of the direct-historical approach. While concerns with art and belief and an emphasis on individual cognition and motivation ally cognitive archaeologists with recent postmodernist concerns, typically they maintain a commitment to scientific method, including the testing of hypotheses and the development of scientific knowledge.

1. Definitions

Cognitive archaeology has been defined in various ways. According to Renfrew (1982) it is 'the archaeology of the mind.' Flannery and Marcus (1993, 261) define it as 'a study of all those aspects of ancient culture that are the product of the human mind ... cosmology ... religion ... ideology ... iconography ... and all other forms of human intellectual and symbolic behaviour that survive in the archaeological record.'

These definitions reflect a rejection of a long-held archaeological belief that cognitive phenomena or mental products cannot be observed in the archaeological record, let alone reconstructed from it. Cognitive archaeologists, in contrast, commit a significant part of their effort in reconstructing the past to just this area of concern. While they do not deny the relevance of culture-history, technology, adaptation, subsistence, trade, and other traditional archaeological topics, cognitive archaeologists argue that a holistic interpretation or explanation of the past requires more than these traditional topics alone can provide.

2. Philosophical and Theoretical Foundations

The development of cognitive archaeology as an intellectual trend has involved the rejection of certain key tenets of scientific archaeology as practiced by Anglophone researchers (variously called new, processual or settlement-subsistence archaeology) in the latter half of the twentieth century. One of these tenets is logical positivism as a philosophy of science, with its emphasis on explanatory cover laws, the hard distinction between theory and fact, and a belief in unequivocal singular tests for hypotheses. Another is behaviorism which implicitly serves as the explanatory paradigm for much processual archaeology (Peebles 1992). This emphasizes the importance of stimulus-response relationships in explanation, especially concerning adaptation to the environment, and denies the relevance of mind, intellect, and cognition in human action, along with their byproducts such as belief, ritual, and art. To the processual archaeologist these are epiphenomenal, meaning derivative in origin and secondary in importance, and therefore analytically irrelevant.

Cognitive archaeology has instead adopted ongoing developments in the philosophy of science, including especially post-positivist approaches. Commonly these maintain a commitment to scientific knowledge, albeit acknowledging that over time science only increasingly approximates the 'real' truth, with scientific method based on 'inference to the best hypothesis' rather than singular critical tests (Kelley and Hanen 1988). Implicit in much cognitive archaeology moreover is *embodied scientific realism*. This accepts the existence of a world independent of our understanding of it, as well as the fact that we can have stable knowledge of this world. But it also holds that knowledge is relative to our bodies, minds, and interactions with the environment. This conclusion derives from empirical results of cognitive neurosciences studies which show that certain universal aspects of human conceptual development result from the embodied nature of the mind (Lakoff and Johnson 1999).

These philosophical commitments resolve two fundamental even if largely unrecognized conceptual contradictions in processual archaeology. First, by adopting embodied scientific realism, cognitive archaeology supports a model of humankind and its development that is fully reconcilable with evolutionary principles. Processual archaeology, even when explicitly claiming to be evolutionarily based, instead implicitly invokes a pre-Darwinian model of disembodied reason and mind due to its disavowal of any real relevance for cognitive phenomena. Because cognitive capabilities (which we all share) are ignored, they must be taken as a given; they 'just are' in processual archaeological theory. Ultimately this position then must resort to creationism and divine intervention to explain the totality of the human condition, which must include our ability to think and reason. Second, by insisting that mental phenomena are irrelevant but also conceding that the goal of archaeological science is to create knowledge (a cognitive construct), processual archaeology further requires a difference *in kind* between prehistoric peoples, whose thinking is putatively irrelevant and epiphenomenal, and contemporary westerners, including archaeologists whose professional purpose is to create knowledge. Such a distinction in kind between different peoples precludes the kinds of law-like explanations that processual archaeology has sought as its goal. Cognitive archaeology gives equal weight to the importance of mental phenomena in the lives of both prehistoric and contemporary humans.

Other theoretical aspects of cognitive archaeology derive from its relationship with cultural anthropology. These partly reflect the definition of culture as a cognitive worldview, a system of beliefs and meanings, thereby helping to situate aspects of cognitive archaeological research as a kind of anthropological archaeology in the interpretation of prehistoric culture. Similarly, anthropological studies of the nature of traditional thought and belief systems (e.g., Sperber 1982) have dispelled the notion that these are necessarily irrational and therefore somehow inherently inaccessible to rationalist science. As anthropologist Robin Horton (1982) has instead shown, all cultures share a core of cognitive rationality that involves the development of theory, based on deductive, inductive, and analogical reasoning, used in the explanation, prediction, and control of events. The analysis and interpretation of culture and its expression in symbolism, meaning, and worldview need not then necessarily reduce to particularistic and empathic statements based on some kind of privileged access to the feelings of people in the past, but instead can be based upon empirically grounded generalizations that stand up to empirical analysis.

Perhaps most importantly, linguistic, psychological, and neuropsychological models of the human mind—brain and how it operates have been instrumental in cognitive archaeological studies. And while some of the topics that cognitive archaeologists include in their analyses, such as ritual, belief, symbolism, and meaning, are the same as those that are highlighted in humanist and postmodernist studies and approaches (called 'post-processualism' in archaeology), the models, techniques, and methods that the cognitive archaeologists employ to understand these aspects of the past are quite different from those that postmodernists might allow, as the scientific models used by cognitive archaeologists themselves imply.

3. Analytical Approaches: Linguistic and Psychological Models

A measure of the versatility of cognitive archaeology is seen in the fact that many of its applications have occurred at opposite ends of the archaeological spectrum: Paleolithic or Stone Age archaeology, which involves studies of the earliest human societies (even including in some cases the archaeology of prehuman hominids); and late prehistoric, protohistoric and historical archaeology, where direct cultural and linguistic links tie the archaeological past to recent peoples studied by ethnographers and historians.

Perhaps the first example of an in-depth cognitive archaeological study was provided by Paleolithic archaeologist André Leroi-Gourhan (1967) in his analysis of western European cave paintings dating from about 35,000 to 10,000 years ago. A similar approach was used by historical archaeologist James Deetz (1977) in his study of Euro-American Colonial artifacts. In both cases analysis was based on a structuralist model of mind. Originating in the linguistic theories of Ferdinand de Saussure and Roman Jacobson, structuralism posits a human mind that organizes empirical phenomena and concepts in terms of binary oppositions or dualities: black versus white; male versus female; good versus bad; etc. Structuralist

analysis then concerns not so much the dual objects themselves but the relationships between the pairs. Both Leroi-Gourhan and Deetz showed that such a relational structure could be identified in their respective Paleolithic and Colonial data, thereby significantly amplifying their abilities to make inferences about the symbolic meanings of their archaeological remains.

Psychological models of the human brain–mind have figured prominently in other cognitive archaeological studies. Paleolithic archaeologist Thomas Wynn (1989), for example, has used psychologist Jean Piaget's theories on the development of thought in children and what these imply about spatial abilities to infer kinds of intelligence and levels of cognitive development in *Homo habilis* and *Homo erectus*, based on analyses of the kinds of stone tools that these ancient hominids created. Psychologist William Noble and archaeologist Iain Davidson (e.g., 1996) have collaborated in a series of studies, bringing together archaeological evidence on early symbol-making with theories of perception and communication in order to chart the evolution of the human mind and the appearance of language. Steven Mithen (1996) has invoked neural models of brain modularity along with cognitive scientist Howard Gardner's theory of multiple intelligences in an effort to explain the 'Upper Paleolithic Revolution': the seemingly sudden appearance of art, symbolism, and presumably belief roughly 50,000 years ago, literally tens of thousands of years after the earliest skeletal evidence for anatomically modern humans. In these cases psychological models have not been used to help explain the archaeological record: rather, the archaeological record has been employed in order to make inferences, informed by psychological theories, about prehuman and human intellectual and cognitive evolution.

4. Analytical Approaches: Neuropsychological Models

A subset of the psychological models used in cognitive archaeological studies involves *neuropsychology*: models based on theories of the mind–brain and the nervous system and how the two interact. These have been particularly influential in analyses of hunter-gatherer rock art tied to shamanistic religions where trance or altered states of consciousness (ASC) were considered key kinds of religious experiences. Because all humans share the same neural architecture, the mental, visual, emotional, and bodily reactions of ASC fall within a predictable range, regardless of cause, culture, or time period (Hobson 1994). This fact creates a kind of 'neuropsychological bridge' promoting analytical access to aspects of the ancient mind that involved ASC experiences.

Using the results of clinical studies, Lewis-Williams and Dowson (1988) constructed a model of the effects of ASC on mental imagery—the 'visions' of a shaman's trance. Their model has three components: three progressive stages of ASC; the principles by which mental imagery is perceived at each stage; and the seven most commonly perceived entoptic phenomena, the phosphenes or geometric light images generated in the brain and visual system during the first stage of an ASC. After confirming the validity of their model using corpora of rock art known from ethnographic evidence to have been produced by shamans to depict visionary imagery, these archaeologists then used it to test whether European Paleolithic rock art, which lacks any ethnographic record, was also shamanistic in origin.

Central to their analysis is the use of *analogy*, but in this case analogy based on timeless and unchanging determining structures (human neuropsychology and its effects on ASC imagery), not analogy based on formal similarities. Note too that their concern was the *origin* of Upper Paleolithic art, not its *meaning*. While neuropsychology predicts human reactions to ASC, it does not tell us how such experiences will be interpreted or understood by different peoples or cultures and at different times. Subsequent neuropsychological studies of rock art have also considered the origins of universal aspects of shamanic symbolism, such as 'mystical flight' or 'death and rebirth,' as metaphoric expressions of the bodily and emotional hallucinations of ASC which were used verbally and graphically to describe what otherwise is a largely ineffable experience (Whitley 2000).

5. The Direct Historical Approach

Another analytical strategy, called the direct historical approach, involves the development of interpretive models of aspects of traditional cultures, like religion or ideology, based on ethnographic and ethnohistoric evidence. If derived from directly relevant cultures, these models can be cautiously applied to the prehistoric past to both chart continuity and identify change in cognitive systems. Marcus and Flannery (1994), for example, used sixteenth and seventeenth century Spanish documents to reconstruct Zapotec Indian religion in southern Mexico. Comparisons with archaeological evidence of religion and ritual indicated that the ethnohistorically described religious system first appeared between 200 BC and AD 100. Thomas Huffman (1996) has likewise used African Nguni ethnography concerning settlement structure, religion, and ideology to interpret the site of Great Zimbabwe, dating from the thirteenth to the fifteenth centuries.

Though sometimes criticized for projecting ethnography on to the prehistoric past, careful applications of the direct historical approach need do no such thing. Indeed, Huffman has shown that they can result in a rewriting of aspects of the ethnographic record when the archaeological evidence contributes

subsidiary information not previously documented in writing. Moreover, the applicability of the direct historical approach is enhanced by the fact that religious and belief systems tend to be very conservative and slow to change, as other recent archaeological analyses have shown (e.g., Taçon et al., 1996).

6. Future Trends

Two circumstances favor the continued development and growth of cognitive archaeology. The first is its scientific robustness, based on the fact that many practitioners successfully incorporate different methodologies and kinds of data in their analyses and interpretations. Rock art researchers, for example, have combined the direct historical approach with neuropsychological and physical models, creating convergent scientific theories (e.g., Whitley et al., 1999). These are advantaged because the use of different kinds of data tested with distinct methodologies greatly enhances the degree of confirmation of their hypotheses and ensures that they do not follow from any one set of methodological assumptions. The results are scientific interpretations and explanations that are as empirically grounded and as well-tested as any that archaeology can offer.

Equally importantly, cognitive archaeology increasingly borrows from the cognitive neurosciences, an area of research that has advanced dramatically in the 1990s and which promises to influence greatly, if not change, all disciplines concerned with human behavior. Archaeologists have not yet exploited the range of information that is relevant to their research and that is currently available in the cognitive neurosciences, nor can we yet predict what future advances in this field will imply for archaeology. But what is certain is that, as cognitive neuroscientists improve our understanding of how the contemporary human mind-brain operates, this will contribute further to our understanding of cognitive aspects of the prehistoric past.

See also: Archaeology and Philosophy of Science; Archaeology and the History of Languages; Cognitive Anthropology; Cognitive Neuroscience; Cognitive Science: History; Cognitive Science: Overview; Structuralism

Bibliography

Deetz J J F 1977 *In Small Things Forgotten: The Archaeology of Early American Life*. Anchor Press-Doubleday, New York

Flannery K V and Marcus J 1993 Cognitive archaeology. *Cambridge Archaeological Journal* 3: 260–7

Hobson J A 1994 *The Chemistry of Conscious States: Toward a Unified Model of the Brain and the Mind*. Little, Brown and Company, Boston

Horton R 1982 Tradition and modernity revisited. In: *Rationality and Relativism*, edited by Hollis M and Lukes S, pp. 201–60, MIT Press, Cambridge, MA

Huffman T 1996 *Snakes & Crocodiles: Power and Symbolism in Ancient Zimbabwe*. Witwatersrand University Press, Johannesburg, South Africa

Kelley J H and Hanen M P 1988 *Archaeology and the Methodology of Science*. University of New Mexico Press, Albuquerque, NM

Lakoff G and Johnson M 1999 *Philosophy in the Flesh: The Embodied Mind and Its Challenge to Western Thought*. Basic Books, New York

Leroi-Gourhan A 1967 *Treasures of Prehistoric Art*. Abrams, New York

Lewis-Williams J D and Dowson T A 1988 The signs of all times: entoptic phenomena in Upper Paleolithic art. *Current Anthropology* **29**: 201–45

Marcus J and Flannery K V 1994 Ancient Zapotec ritual and religion: an application of the direct historical approach. In: *The Ancient Mind: Elements of Cognitive Archaeology*, edited by Renfrew C and Zubrow E B W, Cambridge University Press, Cambridge, UK, pp. 55–74

Mithen S 1996 *The Prehistory of the Mind: A Search for the Origins of Art, Religion and Science*. Thames and Hudson, London

Noble W and Davidson I 1996 *Human Evolution, Language and Mind: A Psychological and Archaeological Inquiry*. Cambridge University Press, Cambridge, UK

Peebles C S 1992 Rooting out latent behaviorism in prehistory In: Gardin J-C, Peebles C S (eds.) *Representations in Archaeology*, Indiana University Press, Bloomington, IN, pp. 357–84

Renfrew C 1982 *Towards an Archaeology of Mind*. Cambridge University Press, Cambridge, UK

Sperber D 1982 Apparently irrational thoughts. In: *Rationality and Relativism*, Hollis M, Lukes S (eds.) MIT Press, Cambridge, MA, pp. 149–80

Taçon P S C, Wilson M and Chippindale C 1996 Birth of the Rainbow Serpent in Arnhem: land rock art and oral history. *Archaeology in Oceania* **31**: 103–24

Whitley D S 2000 *The Art of the Shaman: The Rock Art of California*. University of Utah Press, Salt Lake City, UT

Whitley D S, Dorn R I, Simon J M Rechtman R and Whitley T K 1999 Sally's rockshelter and the archaeology of the vision quest. *Cambridge Archaeological Journal* **9**: 221–247

Wynn T 1989 *The Evolution of Spatial Competence*. University of Illinois Press, Urbana, IL

D. S. Whitley

Cognitive Control (Executive Functions): Role of Prefrontal Cortex

Control refers to the ability to direct mental function and behavior in accord with an internally represented set of intentions. This is manifest in higher cognitive function in many forms: the ability to direct attention to a specific stimulus within a large array of other competing, and perhaps more salient stimuli (e.g.,

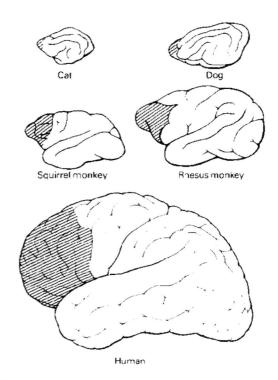

Cross-species comparison of prefrontal cortex

Cat

Dog

Squirrel monkey

Rhesus monkey

Human

Figure 1
Relative size of prefrontal cortex (grayed region) in five species (http://www.psychol.ucl.ac.uk/kate.jeffery/C567/Lecture13_Frontal/overheads/img003.jpg)

finding the face you are looking for within a crowd), maintaining a new and important piece of information in mind against distraction (e.g., remembering a telephone number you just got from directory assistance until you dial, while in a phone booth at a noisy airport terminal), overcoming a compelling but undesirable behavior (e.g., suppressing the urge to scratch a mosquito bite) or pursuing a complex but unfamiliar behavior (e.g., playing a new piano piece) and, perhaps most importantly, the ability to respond flexibly and productively in novel circumstances (e.g., mentally explore the consequences of a complex sequence of moves in a game of chess).

The distinction between controlled and automatic processing is one of the central concepts within modern cognitive psychology. Controlled processing is considered to be effortful, and to rely on a limited capacity system, while automatic processing is assumed to occur independently of this system (Posner and Snyder 1975, Shiffrin and Schneider 1977). This concurs with common experiences, such as the ability to carry on a conversation while driving a car (an automatic process) but not while conducting multi-digit arithmetic in one's head (a process that relies on control). Many contemporary theories posit that there is actually a continuum between controlled and automatic processing (for a review, see Cohen et al. 1990). Nevertheless, virtually all theorists acknowledge the need for some mechanism, or set of mechanisms, responsible for the coordination of processing in a flexible fashion—particularly in novel or demanding tasks. This idea figures centrally in Baddeley's classic theory of working memory (Baddeley 1986), which postulates two critical components: a storage component responsible for the active maintenance of information in a short-term store, and a executive control component responsible for the manipulation and coordinated use of this information. For example, in a multi-digit multiplication problem, the storage component maintains the intermediate products while the executive carries out the arithmetic operations.

The postulation of a central executive closely paralleled theorizing regarding the nature of frontal lobe function (for a review, see Shallice 1982), based on the clinical observation that patients with frontal lesions exhibit a 'dysexecutive syndrome.' The frontal lobes are the area of the brain most highly expanded in humans relative to other species (see Fig. 1). Damage to this area is associated with impairments in characteristically human cognitive functions that are directly dependent upon control (such as planning, or the ability to respond adaptively in novel circumstances), and disturbances of this structure have been implicated consistently in neuropsychiatric diseases such as schizophrenia that also appear to be uniquely human. Indeed, the earliest neurologists, neuroscientists and neuropsychologists recognized the importance of the frontal lobes in the control of behavior. Perhaps this observation was made most dramatically in the classic case of Phineas Gage, the unfortunate railroad foreman who suffered damage to his prefrontal cortex (PFC) when a 1-1/2"-diameter rod penetrated his skull in a construction accident. Originally someone who was considered to be thoughtful, responsible, and of sound judgment, following the accident he was described as 'capricious ... and unable to settle on any of the plans he devised for future action' (Harlow 1848). Such changes have been observed repeatedly in patients with damage to the frontal cortex (for a review, see Stuss and Benson 1986). Furthermore, patients with frontal damage perform poorly in tasks that require even the simplest forms of cognitive control, such as the Wisconsin Card Sort Task (WCST) (Milner 1964), and, most recently, brain imaging studies consistently have revealed increased activity of the prefrontal cortex while subjects are performing tasks that demand cognitive control (for a review, see Miller and Cohen 2001). Although this accumulation of findings has led most investigators to assume that the prefrontal cortex plays a critical role in cognitive control, they have provided little insight into the specific contribution that it makes, or the

mechanisms by which it operates. However, more detailed neurobiological studies have begun to shed light on this question.

Using single unit recording techniques, Fuster and Alexander (1971) and Niki (1974) reported the remarkable finding that some neurons in the prefrontal cortex continue to fire during the delay between a stimulus and a contingent response, even after the stimulus has disappeared. Goldman-Rakic and her colleagues followed up on this finding and, in a series of elegant studies, demonstrated that the firing of such neurons was stimulus-selective, and was critical for performance in delayed-response tasks (Goldman-Rakic 1990).

These findings strongly implicate neuronal activity in PFC as the site of temporary storage of information in working memory. Recent neuroimaging studies of humans have provided strong convergent support for this idea, demonstrating sustained activity in PFC during the performance of simple working memory tasks (for a review, see Smith and Jonides 1999). However, this discovery seemed to pose an interesting puzzle. Most of the neuropsychological data suggested that the PFC housed the central executive which, at least within Baddeley's influential theory of working memory, was clearly distinguished from the storage component thought by most to be housed primarily in more posterior structures. Computational models of cognitive control have offered a different perspective on this problem that may reconcile the role of the PFC in control and storage.

1. Computational Models

Shallice (1982) presented the first account of the role of PFC in cognitive control within an explicitly computational framework. He proposed that the PFC housed a supervisory attentional system (SAS)—a mechanism by which PFC coordinates complex cognitive processes. Shallice's theory was described in terms of a production system architecture. This has appeal, as it relates the executive functions of frontal cortex to the well characterized mechanisms of other production system theories, which include the active representation of goal states to coordinate the sequences of production firings involved in complex behaviors (e.g., Anderson 1983). One feature of goal representations is that they must be maintained actively throughout the course of a sequence of actions to direct behavior effectively. This coincides with the observation that PFC appears to be specialized for the active maintenance of task-relevant information. Thus, it is possible that PFC is specialized for the maintenance of a *particular type* of information, as a means of executing control over performance.

While Shallice's theory was not implemented originally as a functioning model, Kimberg and Farah (1993) proposed a model of frontal function—also using a production system architecture—that simulated performance in a variety of tasks considered to rely on frontal lobe function (including the WCST), and illustrated that damage to this component of the model produced impairments similar to those observed in patients with frontal damage. However, while such models have produced insights into the functional role of PFC in cognitive control, their components do not have a transparent mapping on to specific neurobiological mechanisms. Neurobiological plausibility is not a requirement, *per se*, of a theory that seeks to explain the cognitive functions of PFC. Nevertheless, the question of how goal directed behavior arises from the firing of millions of neurons presents a mystery in its own right. Furthermore, understanding how different forms of cognitive impairment arise from different forms of damage to PFC (e.g., the effects of stroke or injury vs. schizophrenia) provides an important motivation for understanding how cognitive control may arise from the specific neurobiological mechanisms housed within PFC.

Recently, investigators have begun to use neural network models to better understand how PFC may carry out its functions. Such models (also known as connectionist, or parallel distributing processing models) simulate the behavioral performance of human subjects (or animals) in cognitive tasks using neurally-plausible processing mechanisms (e.g., the spread of activity among simple processing units along weighted connections; see Rumelhart and McClelland 1986). The goal of this effort is to identify principles of neural function that are most relevant to behavior. Using this approach, Dehaene and Changeux (1989), Levine and Prueitt (1989), and Cohen and Servan-Schreiber (1992) have all described models of prefrontal function, and used these to simulate the performance of normal and frontally-damaged patients in tasks that are sensitive to PFC damage, such as the WCST and others. All of these models simulate PFC function as the activation of a set of units that represent the 'rules' of the task; that is, units whose activation leads to a task-relevant response, even when this may not be the one most strongly associated with the stimulus. However, in most models, the PFC units themselves are not responsible for generating the response directly. Rather, they influence the activity of other units whose responsibility this is. This is clearly illustrated by a model of the Stroop task developed by Cohen et al. (1990).

In the Stroop task (Stroop 1935), subjects respond to words either by reading them, or by naming the color in which they are displayed. In the critical condition, the word itself conflicts with the color in which it is displayed (e.g., the word GREEN displayed in red). Subjects have no trouble reading such words (e.g., saying 'green'). However, when they are asked to name the color (e.g., say 'red'), they are significantly slower, and sometimes even make errors. This reflects the highly practiced, and therefore prepotent tendency

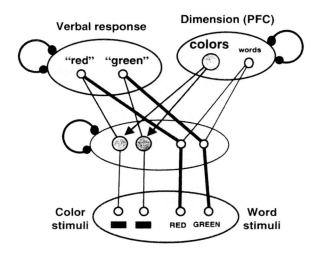

Figure 2
Model of the Stroop Task (adapted from Cohen et al. 1990), showing the pathways for word reading, color naming, and top-down control. Connections between units in different layers are excitatory and within layers are inhibitory (closed circles). Shown with color dimension unit active, biasing color-naming pathway

to read written words, which interferes with the ability to name the color of a Stroop conflict stimulus. The ability to name the color in the face of such interference (that is, to produce the weaker, but task-relevant response) is a simple but clear example of cognitive control.

Cohen et al. (1990) constructed a model of this task, as shown in Fig. 2. The connections among the units in this model defined two processing pathways, one for word reading and another for color naming. The connections in the word-reading pathway were stronger, capturing the assumption that this was the more practiced task. Because of these stronger connections, information flowing along the word pathway interfered with color naming, simulating the interference effects observed when human subjects perform this task. Indeed, the model's ability to produce a response to the color in the face of such interference required the addition of a set of units (labeled 'Dimension' in Fig. 2), which provided additional activation of the units in the color-naming pathway. This additional activation biased processing in favor of this pathway, allowing it to compete more effectively with, and prevail over, activity flowing along the stronger word pathway. This biasing effect corresponds precisely to the role of top-down control in neurophysiological models of attention (such as the Biased Competition Model of Desimone and Duncan 1995), and has been proposed as a mechanism by which PFC exerts control over processing (Cohen and Servan-Schreiber 1992, Miller and Cohen 2001).

Models such as this have been used to simulate the performance of both normal subjects and patients with frontal damage in a wide range of tasks that tap cognitive functions commonly associated with PFC function, such as working memory, attention, behavioral inhibition, planning, and problem solving.

2. Guided Activation as a Method of Control

The Stroop model brings several features of PFC function into focus. First, it emphasizes the view that the role of the PFC in control is modulatory, guiding the flow of activity along pathways in other parts of the brain that are responsible for task performance. For example, activating the color unit does not in itself transmit information about a particular response (red or green). Rather, it simply insures that activity flowing along the color-naming pathway will have a greater influence over the response than activity flowing along the word pathway. In this way, representations within the PFC can function as intentions, rules, or goals (comparable to those in a production system architecture), by setting up the appropriate relationship between a stimulus (or category of stimuli) and an associated response (or set of responses) through the proper guidance of activity along pathways in other parts of the brain. Recent neurophysiological findings regarding the firing properties of neurons in PFC provide strong support for this view (for a review, see Miller and Cohen 2001). Recent neuroimaging studies also provide convergent support, indicating that PFC activity occurs when behavior relies upon explicit knowledge about rules or arbitrarily determined conjunctions of stimulus features (for a review, see Miller and Cohen 2001). Note that this function is not necessarily restricted to mappings from stimuli to responses, but applies equally well to mappings involving internal states (e.g., thoughts, memories, emotions, etc.). Note also that this function is not necessarily unique to PFC. There may also be more local forms of control, responsive to regionally specific needs for the biasing of processing. However, the wide range of anatomic connections that the PFC shares with virtually all associative areas of the brain places it in a strategic position to guide the flow of activity between and among these other regions (for a review, see Miller and Cohen 2001)—a position well suited to its presumed role in the control of higher cognitive processes.

The emphasis of this guided activation model of PFC on its modulation of other brain areas actually responsible for task execution is consistent with the classic pattern of neuropsychological deficits associated with frontal lobe damage: The individual elements of a complex behavior are usually left intact, but the subject is not able to coordinate them in a task-appropriate way (for example, a patient who, when preparing coffee, first stirred and then added cream; Shallice 1982). The guided activation model also captures another critical feature of theories about the role of PFC in executive function: the importance of sustained activity as a critical component of control. For a representation to have a biasing influence, it must be activated. For this influence to endure (e.g., over the course of performing a task), it's activity must be sustained. For example, to continue color naming, the activity of the color unit must be maintained, lest the word begin to dominate processing. Similarly, an increase in the demand for control requires greater or more enduring activity of the corresponding units in PFC. This concurs with accumulating evidence from the neuroimaging literature, that tasks thought to rely on controlled processing consistently engage the PFC (for a review, see Smith and Jonides 1999). It is also consistent with both behavioral and neuroimaging findings regarding the effects of practice on automaticity and the involvement of PFC. Increased practice on a task should strengthen its underlying pathway, reducing its reliance on control. Indeed, consistent practice on a task reduces the amount of PFC activity observed, and PFC damage can impair new learning but spare performance on well-practiced tasks (for a review, see Miller and Cohen 2001).

Finally, this approach helps to unify the role that PFC plays in the variety of cognitive functions with which it has been associated, such as selective attention, behavioral inhibition, and executive function in working memory. These can all be seen as varying reflections, in behavior, of the operation of a single underlying mechanism of cognitive control: the biasing effects of representations in PFC on processing in pathways responsible for task performance. For example, selective attention and behavioral inhibition may be viewed as two sides of the same coin: Attention is the effect of biasing competition in favor of task-relevant information, and inhibition is the consequence that this has for the irrelevant information (cf. the Biased Competition Model of Desimone and Duncan 1995). This assumes that inhibition occurs due to local competition between conflicting representations (e.g., between the two responses in the Stroop model), rather than centrally by the PFC. The 'binding' function of selective attention can also be explained by such a mechanism, by assuming that PFC representations can select the desired combination of stimulus features (over other competing combinations) to be mapped on to a response.

3. Outstanding Questions

The guided activation model provides an integrative, and mechanistically explicit framework for considering the role of PFC in cognitive control. At the same time, it brings into focus a number of important and unanswered questions. For example, despite the longstanding observation of delay-period activity for PFC neurons, and the centrality of this property in neural network models of PFC, little is known about the actual mechanisms by which neuronal activity is sustained. This could reflect a cellular property of PFC neurons (e.g., bistability), or a circuit-level phenomenon (e.g., recirculation of activity within the PFC, or between PFC and other structures). Several models have proposed the latter, assuming that representations are maintained in PFC as attractor states (for a review, see O'Reilly et al. 1999). However, neurobiological studies are needed to confirm this hypothesis. A closely related question concerns the mechanisms by which patterns of activity are updated in PFC. These must be able to satisfy two conflicting demands: On the one hand, they must be responsive to relevant changes in the environment; and on the other, they must be resistant to updating by irrelevant changes. Neurophysiological studies suggest that PFC representations are selectively responsive to task-relevant stimuli and robust to interference from distractors (for a review, see Miller and Cohen 2001). Not surprisingly, two hallmarks of damage to PFC are perseveration (failure to update) and distractibility (inappropriate updating). These observations suggest the operation of mechanisms that insure the appropriate updating of PFC activity in response to behavioral demands.

Recent modeling work has suggested that brainstem dopaminergic systems and the basal ganglia may play an important role both in updating representations in PFC and learning how and when to do so (for a review, see Miller and Cohen 2001). Other work has suggested that the anterior cingulate cortex—a midline structure within the frontal lobes—may play an important role in monitoring task performance, and identifying the need to allocate control (Botvinick et al. 2001). Such theories make important predictions about the neural mechanisms underlying cognitive control that serve as valuable challenges to future neurobiological research in this area.

An equally fundamental question concerns the nature of representations in PFC and how they arise. For example, the Stroop model assumes there are units that represent each of the two dimensions of the stimulus (color and word), with the appropriate connections to the corresponding pathways. However, are there such units in the PFC for every possible combination of stimulus and response of which tasks may be composed? This seems unlikely. Yet, there must be sufficient representational richness to support the flexibility in behavior that the PFC seems to afford. What principles define this set of representations, how they are organized, and how they are learned are important questions at both the computational and neurobiological levels.

A better understanding of the mechanisms underlying active maintenance may also provide insight into one of the most striking and perplexing properties of cognitive control: its severely limited capacity. This has long been recognized in cognitive psychology (Posner and Snyder 1975, Shiffrin and Schneider 1977), and is painfully apparent to anyone who has tried to talk on the phone and read email at the same time. The resource limitation of cognitive control has played an explanatory role in many important models of human cognition. However, to date, no theory has provided an explanation of the limitation *itself*. This is a *sine qua non* of cognitive control, and therefore provides an important benchmark for any theory that seeks to explain its underlying mechanisms.

Finally, it is important to recognize that the PFC is certainly not the only brain structure involved in cognitive control. As noted above, mechanisms similar to those within PFC may operate locally in other parts of the brain. Furthermore, there are certainly other types of mechanism critical to cognitive control. For example, the mechanisms responsible for keeping an immediate goal in mind (e.g., working on a book chapter) are not likely to be the same ones responsible for realizing long-term goals (e.g., getting the book published). While the former may be guided by representations actively maintained in PFC, the latter almost certainly engage mechanisms of long-term storage. Some suggestions have been made about how the PFC may interact with the hippocampus to orchestrate the storage and retrieval of goal representations at appropriate times (O'Reilly et al. 1999), however, this remains another area in need of further research.

4. Conclusion

One of the great mysteries of the brain is how purposeful, goal-directed behavior emerges from the millions of relatively simple processing units that are its basic computational elements. Behavioral, neuropsychological, and neurobiological data converge on the idea that the frontal lobes play a critical role in cognitive control. Neural network models have begun to suggest how this may be carried out, as sustained patterns of activity within PFC modulate, or 'guide' the flow of activity along pathways in other parts of the brain responsible for performing a task. However, many fundamental questions remain to be addressed. The human brain is arguably the most complex device in the known universe, and its capacity for higher cognitive function continues to be one of its deepest mysteries. Unraveling this mystery stands as one of the most exciting challenges in science, and the rapid development of sophisticated new empirical methods (such as functional brain imaging) and theoretical tools (such as neural network modeling) offer hope that this challenge can be met.

See also: Dysexecutive Syndromes; Prefrontal Cortex; Prefrontal Cortex Development and Development of Cognitive Function

Bibliography

Anderson J R 1983 *The Architecture of Cognition*. Harvard University Press, Cambridge, MA

Baddeley A 1986 *Working Memory*. Clarendon Press, Oxford, UK

Botvinick M M, Braver T S, Carter C S, Barch D M, Cohen J D 2001 Conflict monitoring and cognitive control. *Psychological Review*

Cohen J D, Dunbar K, McClelland J L 1990 On the control of automatic processes: A parallel distributed processing account of the Stroop effect. *Psychology Review* 97: 332–61

Cohen J D, Servan-Schreiber D 1992 Context, cortex and dopamine: A connectionist approach to behavior and biology in schizophrenia. *Psychology Review* 99: 45–77

Dehaene S, Changeux J P 1989 A simple model of prefrontal cortex function in delayed-response tasks. *Journal of Cognitive Neuroscience* 1: 244–61

Desimone R, Duncan J 1995 Neural mechanisms of selective visual attention. *Annual Review of Neuroscience* 18: 193–222

Fuster J M, Alexander G E 1971 Neuron activity related to short-term memory. *Science* 173: 652–4

Goldman-Rakic P S 1990 Cellular and circuit basis of working memory in prefrontal cortex of nonhuman primates. *Progress in Brain Research* 85: 325 35

Harlow J M 1848 Passage of an iron rod through the head. *Boston Medical and Surgical Journal* 39: 389–93

Kimberg D Y, Farah M J 1993 A unified account of cognitive impairments following frontal lobe damage: The role of working memory in complex organized behavior. *Journal of Experimental Psychology* 122: 411–28

Levine D S, Prueitt P S 1989 Modeling some effects of frontal lobe damage—novelty and perseveration. *Neural Networks* 2: 103–16

Miller E K, Cohen J D 2001 An integrative theory of prefrontal cortex function. *Annual Review of Neuroscience* 24: 167–202

Milner B 1964 Some effects of frontal lobectomy in man. In: Warren J M, Akert K (eds.) *The Frontal Granual Cortex and Behavior*. McGraw-Hill, New York, pp. 313–31

Niki H 1974 Prefrontal unit activity during delayed alternation in the monkey. 1. Relation to direction of response. *Brain Research* 68: 185–96

O'Reilly R C, Braver T S, Cohen J D 1999 A biologically-based computational model of working memory. In: Miyake A, Shah P (eds.) *Models of Working Memory: Mechanisms of Active Maintenance and Executive Control*. Cambridge University Press, New York

Posner M I, Snyder C R R 1975 Attention and cognitive control. In: Solso R L (ed.) *Information Processing and Cognition*. Erlbaum, Hillsdale, NJ

Rumelhart D E, McClelland J L 1986 *Parallel Distributed Processing: Explorations in the Microstructure of Cognition*. MIT Press, Cambridge, MA

Shallice T 1982 Specific impairments of planning. *Philos. Trans. R. Soc. London Ser. B* 298: 199–209

Shiffrin R M, Schneider W 1977 Controlled and automatic human information processing: II. Perceptual learning automaticity, attending and a general theory. *Psychology Review* 84: 127–90

Smith E E, Jonides J 1999 Storage and executive processes in the frontal lobes. *Science* 283: 1657–61

Stroop J R 1935 Studies of interference in serial verbal reactions. *Journal of Experimental Psychology* 18: 643 62

Stuss D T, Benson D F 1986 *The Frontal Lobes*. Raven, New York

J. D. Cohen

Cognitive Development: Child Education

By the nature of their subject matter, education and cognitive development are closely intertwined. The goal of education, to produce knowledgeable problem solvers, who can apply their knowledge flexibly in real world contexts, and who have the skills and motivation to acquire effectively new knowledge and understanding, is what models of cognition and cognitive development attempt to describe and explain—that is, how we learn, remember and know, and how these processes change and are affected by the interplay of environment and person over development.

This article first presents a brief historical overview and summary of the assumptions underlying psychological and especially cognitive developmental theories and research as they pertain to education, and then considers a set of current issues that highlight the link between the two and the potential for dynamic interaction. 'Education' is clearly a broad term that can encompass learning throughout the lifespan. In this article the central focus will be on education defined as formal instruction during the school years.

1. Historical Overview

Historically, the impact of understanding of cognitive development on educational practice can be traced to the influences of psychology in general. The great movements of functionalism and behaviorism that shaped psychology in the first half of the twentieth century also affected models of education and educational practice. The subsequent 'cognitive revolution' affected education in a variety of ways. Theory and research on cognitive skill development (e.g., strategy acquisition and use) and on conceptual structure (e.g., concept organization and change; logicomathematical reasoning) led to a concern with facilitating reasoning and problem-solving strategies, and with facilitating concept acquisition and retrieval, especially through active, hands-on problem solving.

Although educational practice has been influenced at the most general level by ideas about cognition and cognitive development, a dynamic interplay between cognitive developmental research and educational practice has been neither widespread nor systematic in the typical classroom. This is not surprising, as noted by Olson and Bruner (1996, p. 9): 'Theoretical knowledge of how cognition develops continues to grow but just how to relate this knowledge to the practical contexts ... to educate ... remains almost as mysterious as when such efforts first began.' This is beginning to change as new tools emerge. Over the past decades, cognitive science research has produced detailed analyses of tasks and learners that allow more sophisticated models of the knowledge that a learner brings to the educational setting, and of the component skills necessary for successful performance within specified domains such as mathematics and physics. In addition, there are powerful models of early and late conceptual skill development, and of reasoning processes that emerge within and outside of formal education. These models carry the promise of better specification of the design and implementation processes for successful learning environments.

1.1 Specific Influences

The influence of cognitive developmental theory and research on education has changed as models of cognition, learning, and education have altered. During the heyday of behaviorism, especially in the USA, the explanatory mechanisms underlying both development and education were based on elementary principles of associative learning; educational strategies were based on behavior analysis, association, and reinforcement contingencies; and educational outcome was assessed in quantitative terms. At the beginning of the twenty-first century, although general learning principles inform educational practice (e.g., the relative value of internal vs. external reinforcement, the effectiveness of spaced vs. massed trials, learning and forgetting curves, curricula organized as an accumulation of simple units) a strict learning model approach has largely been restricted to behavioral modification programs and some programmed instruction, most notably for foreign language learning.

The most general result of the cognitive revolution was a new focus on the active, problem-solving child and classroom. Although an oversimplification, two influences were particularly important. One influence is from the broad class of structuralist models, most notably Jean Piaget's genetic epistemology. Most of these models have been based on the assumption that the child is an active participant in the acquisition and organization of knowledge—that is, that there is a dynamic interplay between the knower's current level of understanding and the information and problems presented by the environment. This perspective led to a focus on understanding the child's view of events, on describing the nature and organization of concepts and reasoning structures, and on matching instruction to developmental level. A second influence, arising from the broad array of information-processing

models of cognitive functioning, led to a focus on specifying task structure and problem solving strategies, and on the information processes underlying memory, reasoning, and learning.

2. Cognitive Development

Examples of the specific influences of cognitive development theories and research can be captured by answers to the questions: who is the learner, what is being learned, and how does learning proceed?

2.1 Who Is the Learner?

Probably one of the most revolutionary ideas of scholarly study and research on childhood and education undertaken in the twentieth century was that neither education nor cognitive development can be understood without taking account of the active child/learner. Although this view informed ideas about education from an early point (cf. White 1992), it was strengthened by widespread interest in the theories of Jean Piaget and their adaptation to educational issues, especially mathematics and science education. The central idea is that the child actively assimilates new information on the basis of general reasoning structures, which themselves change in regular ways over the course of development. Recent research on the cognitive abilities of the very young child and infant have complemented this idea to suggest that knowledge and knowledge acquisition in some domains (such as language, arithmetic, and the elementary natural and social worlds) is precocious. One conclusion from this work is that the child brings to the formal educational context a set of robust ideas (or 'theories') about the physical, social, and natural worlds.

The goal of information-processing/cognitive science models is to develop descriptions of learners, tasks, processes, and performance that will allow a detailed specification of the componential skills and processes underlying cognitive activities. From this more information-processing perspective, the learner is seen as a consumer who gathers, stores, organizes, and uses information in problem solving, and who, with development and instruction, becomes increasingly adept at directing, monitoring, and manipulating these skills strategically across a variety of content areas.

2.2 What Is Being Learned?

There is of course no single 'cognitive developmental' answer to the question of what is learned, but rather a family of answers that have in common a focus on knowledge and mental representation as the products of experience and/or education.

The gist of most structuralist viewpoints is that cognitive development consists of qualitative changes in the ways that concepts (i.e., knowledge about the mathematical, material, and social worlds) are organized. These changes enable the child to reason in increasingly complex ways. The description of conceptual structure varies: according to Piagetian models, conceptual structure is described in terms of general and universal logical-mathematical relations; other models refer to causal or semantic structures that may vary across content domains.

The answer to 'what is learned' from an information-processing perspective on cognitive development is skill-based. A large number of cognitive developmental studies have documented changes in the speed and control of processing skills (perception, attention, and memory), and associated increases in cognitive performance, as well as changes in conceptual organization and rule use. Catalyzed by a seminal paper by Flavell (1979) on metacognition and cognitive monitoring, cognitive developmental research focused on the acquisition of cognitive processing strategies, and metacognitive skills and knowledge, as important mechanisms of developmental change in cognitive performance. Teaching these skills to improve general performance across content area (e.g., self-monitoring, strategy retrieval and use) has informed research and practice, as has teaching these skills within a variety of content areas, including reading, writing, mathematics, and science.

2.3 How Does Learning Proceed?: Implications for Education

The central tenet of constructivist models is that cognitive change/learning is a reciprocal process of interpreting information according to current conceptual structure and adapting that structure to task demands. Learning does not proceed by recording received information directly or passively. Learning proceeds at best according to constructivist models, when the learner can experiment actively to discover, invent or infer the solutions to problems. This approach is reflected in active, hands-on classrooms, where a host of strategies attempt to foster active engagement: the discovery method, activity centers, and inquiry-based instruction that focuses on acquiring principles, not just facts (e.g., Hedegaard and Lompscher 1999).

From a cognitive science/information-processing perspective, learning proceeds by acquiring declarative and procedural knowledge within content domains, domain-specific and domain-general rules for operating with that content, strategies and skills for interpreting and attending to new information, and an ability to monitor, access, and control these skills intentionally, including learning how to learn (cf. Bruer 1993, Bransford et al. 1999).

3. Contemporary Issues for Cognitive Development and Education

The following section discusses four complementary areas in cognitive developmental research that have a strong potential to affect educational models and practice: (a) the metaphor of the child as 'universal novice', (b) conceptual change models—the role of naive theories and 'misconceptions', (c) individual differences, (d) cognitive development and education as social phenomena.

3.1 The Development of Novice-to-Expert

The discovery that experts and novices, regardless of age, differ with respect not only to the sheer amount of knowledge they possess, but also with respect to the organization of that knowledge, offers a metaphor for the processes of education in which universal novices become educated experts. Many studies have demonstrated that prior knowledge predicts learning outcomes, and that the knowledge base of novices in any particular domain differs from that of experts in systematic ways (Bransford et al. 1999). This approach has the potential to make a powerful impact on educational practice because it suggests that the acquisition of domain-specific information, not just domain-general skills, is necessary for deep knowledge acquisition. Expert content knowledge can compensate for other skills that predict performance, such as age, aptitude or metacognitive skills. The expert novice distinction and attempts to design curricula to move novices to become experts has become a catchword of general education in math and science, and in specialized curricula such as medicine.

3.2 Intuitive Knowledge and Misconceptions

Studies of reasoning, concept formation, and conceptual understanding in young children have demonstrated convincingly that there is probably no period during development when the child is a 'blank slate.' Rather, even young children show rich knowledge about a variety of concept domains, including number, biological kinds, physics, social phenomena, and the like. Although this knowledge can provide a strong initial base for formal instruction, some early knowledge may clash with information presented in formal learning contexts for mathematical, literary, and scientific domains, because the concepts to be learned in these domains do not match everyday experience. For example, children's difficulties in performing mathematical operations on fractions or negative numbers arise in part from inappropriately generalizing knowledge about natural, whole numbers (Gelman 1994). Similarly, informal knowledge about biological kinds, movement through space, physical causality, and even cosmology, can clash with learning about formal, complex systems in school (e.g., acceleration, force, gravity, and biology). Most clearly demonstrated in math and science, the study of 'misconceptions' has shown the power of children's implicit and everyday concepts. It underscores the importance of basing instruction on a good diagnosis of current understanding, and of devising ways to promote conceptual change through active experimentation and confrontation in rich everyday contexts. There is general agreement that 'a logical extension of the view that new knowledge must be constructed from existing knowledge is that teachers need to pay attention to the incomplete understandings, the false beliefs, and the naive renditions of concepts that learners bring with them to a given subject' (Bransford et al. 1999, p. 10).

3.3 Individual Differences

In its attempts to explain mental growth and change, mainstream cognitive developmental research has focused more on phenomena that are believed to characterize development universally, and less on individual differences. Nonetheless, a number of traditional and emerging areas suggest that systematic differences not only in cognitive style and cognitive strategies, but also in more basic conceptual structure, may provide a means to tailor educational practice more closely to children's specific learning needs.

For example, well documented sex differences in spatial skills that may be tied to differences in representation mode or organization, not just to experiential differences, may be exploited to develop alternative methods of mathematics instruction. Analogously, descriptions of multiple forms of intelligence (cf. Gardner 1993) may offer to the teacher different approaches to a topic and different modes of presenting key concepts (Bransford et al. 1999).

Detailed studies tracing the processes of conceptual change, strategy acquisition and discovery, and the like, also illustrate the large range of individual differences in developmental rate, style, and pattern. Microgenetic studies, i.e., investigations that follow the emergence, development, and consolidation of cognitive skills at an intensive individual level over a period of time, have been applied to a variety of content domains such as language, mathematical skills and problem solving, scientific reasoning, and memory and concept development (cf. Siegler and Crowley 1991, Weinert and Schneider 1999). These studies have illustrated the large variability in skill learning and use, and have shown that average developmental functions do not characterize developmental change at the individual level. Insight into the conditions that facilitate problem solving and that help consolidate newly formed competencies may inform the development of more individualized learning assessment and curricula.

3.4 Cognition in Context

Researchers have recently returned to classic questions concerning the role of culture in cognition, the importance of context and motivation in explaining and understanding cognition in everyday contexts, and the influences of formal and informal learning contexts on cognitive development. Two phenomena have heightened such interest: national differences in cognitive performance, especially in mathematics and science; and research findings showing large discrepancies between cognitive performance in formal educational settings and informal everyday contexts. Both of these perspectives have motivated new research on the types and effects of formal and informal education and have amply illustrated the effects of schooling on a variety of cognitive tasks tapping mathematics, logic, classification, and memory strategies (cf. Rogoff and Chavajay 1995).

A cognitive model that has been highly influential in education is based on the theories of Lev Vygotsky. Vygotsky (1962) characterized cognition as the internalization of external and culturally transmitted structure, rules, and principles that are mediated by language. According to this model, development proceeds most effectively when there is adequate environmental support within the 'zone of proximal development,' a construct to indicate the difference between a child's actual and potential performance. The zone of proximal development is usually measured as the difference between tasks a child can solve working independently, and those a child can solve with assistance from adults, instructors or other competent models. This approach underlies 'reciprocal education' and 'reciprocal teaching', in which the learner acquires strategies from expert models in social settings. The educational goal is to develop supporting social contexts in which a 'community of learners' collaborates in fostering learning outcomes (Brown and Campione 1994).

4. Conclusions

As noted above, mainstream cognitive developmental research and theory have influenced educational practice at only the most general levels. As the relatively new field of multidisciplinary cognitive science has become established and institutionalized, its methods and results are being tested in school contexts (cf. Bruer 1993, Bransford et al. 1999). The fields of cognitive development and education are ripe for forging collaborations that allow the science of learning to inform the practice of education in classroom contexts.

See also: Cognitive Development in Childhood and Adolescence; Cognitive Development: Learning and Instruction; Instructional Technology: Cognitive Science Perspectives; Piaget, Jean (1896–1980);

Piaget's Theory of Human Development and Education; Situated Cognition: Contemporary Developments; Situated Learning: Out of School and in the Classroom; Vygotskij's Theory of Human Development and New Approaches to Education

Bibliography

Bransford J, Brown A L, Cocking R (eds.) 1999 *How People Learn: Brain, Mind, Experience and School.* National Academy Press, Washington, DC
Brown A L, Campione J C 1994 Guided discovery in a community of learners. In: McGilly K (ed.) *Classroom Lessons: Integrating Cognitive Theory and Classroom Practice.* MIT Press, Cambridge, MA
Bruer J T 1993 *Schools for Thought.* MIT Press, Cambridge, MA
Flavell J H 1979 Metacognition and cognitive monitoring: A new area of cognitive-developmental inquiry. *American Psychologist* **43**(10): 906–11
Gardner H 1993 *Frames of Mind.* Basic Books, New York
Gelman R 1994 Constructivism and supporting environments. *Human Development* **6**: 55–82
Hedegaard M, Lompscher J (eds.) 1999 *Learning Activity and Development.* Aarhus University Press, Aarhus, Denmark
Olson D, Bruner J 1996 Folk psychology and folk pedagogy. In: Olson D, Torrance N (eds.) *The Handbook of Education and Human Development.* Blackwell, Cambridge, MA pp. 9–27
Rogoff B, Chavajay P 1995 What's become of research on the cultural basis of cognitive development? *American Psychologist* **50**(10): 859–77
Siegler R S, Crowley K 1991 The microgenetic method: A direct means for studying cognitive development. *American Psychologist* **46**(6): 606–20
Vygotsky L S 1962 *Thought and Language.* MIT Press, Cambridge, MA
Weinert F, Schneider W (eds.) 1999 *Individual Development from 3 to 12: Findings from the Munich Longitudinal Study.* Cambridge University Press, New York
White S H 1992 G. Stanley Hall: From philosophy to developmental psychology. *Developmental Psychology* **28**(1): 25–34

M. Bullock

Cognitive Development in Childhood and Adolescence

In a typical textbook on cognitive development, one would find chapters on representation, memory, language, conceptual development, reasoning, problem solving, and strategy development and use. Currently, no single theory unites the study of all of these areas of cognition. Indeed, little communication exists among them. Not unlike the Indian parable in which six blind men give different answers to 'what is an elephant,' researchers in each area suggest that something different is 'what develops' in cognitive development in childhood and adolescence. In this article the domain of causal reasoning is used to describe general trends in cognitive development. After reviewing age-related developments in causal reasoning, processes that have been implicated as mechanisms of change in causal reasoning specifically and cognitive development more generally (including analogical reasoning, attention, working memory, selection and use of strategies, and domain-specific knowledge) are described. The article closes with a brief review of postnatal neural developments thought to underlie developmental changes in these processes.

1. Causal Reasoning

Whereas no one theory unites the numerous disparate domains of cognitive development, some cognitive operations are common across them. Causal reasoning provides an illustrative example of how several areas of cognition develop in concert to support a higher-level skill. Reasoning can be defined as goal-directed activity that often relies on the use of inferences to reach a conclusion (DeLoache et al. 1998). Causal relations are 'the cement of the universe' (Mackie 1980) in that they provide systematic links between precursors and consequences. Causal reasoning thus allows for identification of the cause–effect relations observed in the world. Inhelder and Piaget (1958, 1964), founders of scholarship in cognitive development, began the tradition of research on causal reasoning in the developing child and set the stage for much of the research done to date. Motivated by the desire to understand how children and adolescents think and reason about events in the world, researchers have examined infants' perceptions of causality, young children's ability to perform causally linked actions in sequential order so as to achieve a goal, and older children's abilities to infer causal mechanisms and to test for cause–effect relations (i.e., to reason scientifically).

For more detailed discussion of the above topics and for additional references see *Transfer of Learning, Cognitive Psychology of; Early Concept Learning in Children; Infant Development: Physical and Social Cognition; Piaget's Theory of Child Development; Scientific Concepts: Development in Children;* and *Problem Solving (Everyday), Psychology of.*

2. Early Developments in Causal Reasoning

2.1 Perception of Causality in Infancy

Within a few months of birth, infants demonstrate sensitivity to causes and their consequents. Oakes and Cohen (1990) showed 7- and 10-month-old infants different events in which one toy traveled across a screen and either (a) made contact with another toy, which immediately moved; (b) made contact with another toy, which moved only after a brief delay; or

(c) stopped before contacting the other toy, which, after a brief delay, moved. Only the first event contained the causal elements of spatial and temporal contiguity. The researchers found that the 10-month-olds were sensitive to the causal structure of the events as demonstrated by longer looking to the events that violated causal principles. Leslie (1984) found that infants as young as six and a half months are sensitive to causal structure when simpler stimuli (e.g., colored blocks) are used.

2.2 Enacting Causal Sequences to Achieve a Goal

By the second half of the first year of life infants not only appear to recognize basic conditions of causality, they also use them to guide their own actions to reach desired goals. In Willatts (1984), nine-month-old infants were presented with a cloth within their reach on which rested a desired toy just outside their reach. The infants needed to remove a barrier in order to pull the cloth and thereby obtain the toy. Compared to infants in a control condition in which the toy rested just off the cloth, infants in the 'causal' condition more often removed the barrier and pulled the cloth. By 12 months of age infants are able to solve a more complex version of this means–ends task: they successfully navigate multiple steps including removing a barrier to reach a cloth, pulling the cloth to reach a string, and reeling in a toy attached to the string. By 18 months, in age-appropriate versions of means–ends tasks, children use a variety of strategies and monitor the effectiveness of their strategies for reaching their goals (see Willatts 1990 for a review).

2.3 Planning a Path from Cause to Effect

Shortly after children show appreciation of existing causal connections, they begin to create their own paths from causes to effects. In Bauer et al. (1999), 21- and 27-month-old children were required to plan a course of action to achieve an effect. The children were shown either the initial state or the goal state of a problem that required a three-step solution. Each of the steps was necessary, but not sufficient, to achieve the goal. For example, for the problem of 'making a rattle' (Step 1: put a block in a cup; Step 2: cover the cup and block with a second cup; Step 3: shake the cups to make a rattling sound), an experimenter modeled either the initial step of putting the block in the cup or the goal step of shaking the rattle. In both cases, the experimenter verbally provided the children with the goal of the activity (i.e., 'make a rattle'). Note that the children were given the same amount of information (one step of the three-step solution) in each of the two conditions. When the children were shown the initial step of the causal sequence, neither the 21- nor the 27- month-olds solved the problem on

more than 8 percent of the trials. In contrast, when provided with the goal step of the solution, 23 percent of the 21-month-olds and 50 percent of the 27-month-olds were able to plan a path to the goal. This study not only demonstrates the primacy of the goal state in aiding children's production of cause–effect sequences, but also shows rapid developments in planning abilities.

2.4 Identifying Causal Relations in the Preschool Years

Whereas in the toddler years, children show facility with planning a course of action to achieve a specific effect, in the preschool years, they reason as effectively about effects, causes, and the steps that unite them. Gelman et al. (1980) trained three- and four-year-old children to read three-picture 'stories' that depicted the initial state of an object, a causal agent, and the object in a transformed state. For example, children were shown an intact coffee cup (initial state), a hammer (causal agent), and a broken coffee cup (transformed state). The children then were presented with a series of stories in which one of the three pictures was missing. They were asked to complete the story by selecting one of three choice cards. The researchers found that both three- and four-year-olds were able to infer the causal agent as well as the initial and transformed states. In related research it has been shown that children understand a number and variety of causal relations, including melting, cutting, and burning (Goswami and Brown 1989).

Just as important as the ability to infer causes, consequences, and causal agents is the ability to recognize that not all cause–effect relations are deterministic. In the real world, causality tends to be probabilistic. For example, if an object is tremendously heavy, pulling the cloth on which it rests might not be sufficient to retrieve it. Kalish (1998) tested three- and five-year-olds and adults' understanding of probabilistic causal relations in the domain of illness. Whereas adults recognize that causes of illness are probabilistic (e.g., coming into contact with a sick person does not inevitably result in getting sick), children treat them as deterministic. This research suggests that the development of sensitivity to probabilistic causality is more protracted, relative to understanding of causal events with definite outcomes. Thus, lack of sensitivity to probabilistic outcomes represents a limitation of the causal understanding of preschool-age children.

3. Later Developments in Causal Reasoning

In addition to demonstrated competencies in reasoning about cause–effect relations, preschool-age children also show early manifestations of scientific reasoning. The goal of scientific reasoning is to test hypotheses in order to identify cause–effect relations. Children as young as four and five years of age will search for the causal mechanism that resulted in an effect even when they do not see it (Bullock 1984). Therefore, even very young children are sensitive to the necessity of a cause. Nevertheless, just as they initially overgeneralize and treat all cause–effect relations as deterministic (i.e., failing to recognize the probabilistic nature of some causal relations), as shown below, in the preschool and early school years, children also overgeneralize one of the strongest cues to causality, namely, contiguity.

Schlottman (1999) presented five-, seven-, and nine-year-old children and adults with a mystery box that could contain one of two mechanisms. Both mechanisms caused a bell to ring when a ball was dropped in one of two holes in the box. One causal mechanism was 'slow' in ringing the bell because the ball had to travel down a runway in order to ring the bell at the opposite end of the box. The other causal mechanism was 'fast' because the ball dropped onto a lever that acted like a seesaw and immediately rang the bell. In the task, a ball was dropped into one of two holes in the box. Seconds later, the second ball was dropped and the bell immediately rang. Participants were asked to identify which of the two balls had caused the bell to ring. When they did not have knowledge of which of the two mechanisms was in the box, participants of all ages attributed causality to the contiguous event. That is, they selected the ball that was dropped immediately before the bell rang. Even after they were informed of which mechanism was in the box, five- and seven-year-olds continued to select the contiguous event, regardless of mechanism. In contrast, when appropriate, the nine-year-olds and adults ignored contiguity and made decisions based on the properties of the mechanism. This research makes clear both the profound influence that prior knowledge and experience have on causal and scientific reasoning and the great strides in treatment of data made by children in the early elementary school years.

Even beyond the early elementary school years, individuals' beliefs influence the ways in which they design experiments and the hypotheses that they test. Schauble (1996) asked fifth and sixth graders and noncollege adults to design experiments to identify the variables that affect the speed of a boat down a canal and the extension of a spring into water when a weight is attached. Both adults and children entered the experiment with beliefs about the objects and the relations about which they were to reason. In general, adults' beliefs were more appropriate than children's beliefs. For example, only 30 percent of the adults compared with 80 percent of the children expressed the belief that 'big things weigh more than small things.' *A priori* beliefs about causal variables influenced the experiments that both the children and the adults designed. Specifically, adults used their experimentation trials to understand the variables for which they did not hold prior beliefs. In contrast, children used their experiments to confirm the beliefs they held prior to investigation. This difference was partially responsible for the overall higher performance of adults in identifying the causal variables.

Schauble's (1996) research also makes clear that children and adults differ in the systematicity with which they approach the experimental space. First, although the children and the adults conducted the same total number of experiments, the children often inadvertently duplicated their experiments (even though they were provided with data cards to record their experimental manipulations). Second, within an experiment, the children were less systematic in the conduct of trials. They were less likely to control variables across two trials and often changed two variables at once in their attempts to test causal hypotheses. Because they based their causal inferences on confounded tests, children showed lower levels of performance relative to adults. These patterns indicate that in addition to domain-specific knowledge (as assessed by prior beliefs), domain-general experimentation strategies influence children's abilities to design experiments and to determine causal mechanisms.

Scientists are required not only to design experiments to test hypotheses, but are also required to draw conclusions on the basis of data obtained by others. In drawing conclusions, scientists must attend to a number of features, including the presence or absence of co-variation, the availability of a plausible causal mechanism, the size of the sample, and the sampling method used. Koslowski et al. (1989) presented sixth and ninth graders and college students with a series of story problems, each of which described the way evidence was gathered (direct intervention or correlation), the sample size (large or small), the causal mechanism (present or absent), and the results (co-variation or no co-variation). Participants were then asked to judge the extent to which they believed the proposed cause was responsible for an observed effect. Whereas all participants were sensitive to the co-variation of cause and effect, developmental changes were apparent in sensitivity to each of the other types of information. Sixth graders continued to give high ratings for the proposed cause when co-variation was present even when there was no causal mechanism provided and when a small sample size was used. Ninth graders provided high ratings for their confidence in the proposed cause with either a small or a large sample size, but only when a causal mechanism was present. College students showed even more refined scientific reasoning. They were less confident in the proposed cause when a causal mechanism was absent (even when co-variation was present) and when a small sample size was used. These findings suggest a developmental progression in scientific reasoning in which co-variation is primary, followed by a sensitivity to the presence of causal mechanism, with a later developing sensitivity to sample size. Notice that absent from the list of features to which college students were sensitive is the nature of the evidence: Koslowski et al.'s participants did not discriminate direct intervention studies from correlational approaches. Thus although, with development, participants evidenced greater awareness of the types of information that scientists use in their evaluation of a potential cause and effect relation, the additional distinction of sampling method is needed to truly 'think like a scientist.'

4. Mechanisms of Cognitive Change

From infancy through adolescence, children's understanding of causality undergoes tremendous refinements. Developments in several cognitive domains support these advances in causal reasoning. The abilities include analogical reasoning, attention, working memory, selection and use of strategies, and domain-specific knowledge. Developments in each domain are described in turn.

Analogical reasoning refers to the process by which knowledge is transferred from one domain to another. It is appropriate when the domains share fundamental or 'deep structure' similarities. Analogical reasoning plays an important role in causal and scientific thinking because it allows for extension of knowledge from a well-known or better known situation to another less well-known domain. Children as young as 16 to 20 months of age show evidence of generalization of knowledge from one domain to another (Bauer and Dow 1994). Goswami and Brown (1989) demonstrated that preschoolers can use their understanding of causal relations to complete analogies wherein the higher order relation between the elements is the causal mechanism (e.g., chocolate is to melted chocolate as a snowman is to a melted snowman). Analogical reasoning also permits transfer of strategies from one task to another. For example, Chen and Klahr (1999) found that fourth graders transferred the strategy of control of variables even after a seven-month period. With development there are changes in the efficiency and proficiency with which analogical transfer is employed (see DeLoache et al. 1998 for a review).

Attention also shows tremendous developments from infancy to adolescence. There are documented developmental differences in the ability to sustain attention on a task, to switch attentional focus between tasks, and within a task, to focus on relevant versus irrelevant features (e.g., Ruff and Lawson 1990). In research on causal reasoning, the tasks presented to young children typically require focus on a limited number of features. The absence of irrelevant features makes it easier for young children to focus on those that are related to the causal structure. As tasks and problems become more complicated and more variables and features are involved, it is necessary to differentiate what is relevant from what is irrelevant,

and to ignore 'distractions.' A comparison of Willatts' (1984) research on means–ends problem solving by nine-month-olds with Schlottman's (1999) research on the use of contiguity to identify causal mechanism by five to nine-year-olds makes clear that the older children are required to attend to many more features to produce or identify the cause–effect relation. In addition, with development, people become better able to attend selectively to the variables at hand. Selective attention may promote the control of variables when designing experiments and assist children in ignoring deceptive surface-feature similarities (Chen and Siegler 2000).

Age-related changes in working memory also play a large part in the development of causal reasoning abilities. Working memory refers to the ability to hold information in mind and simultaneously process it. A major model of working memory proposes that it is comprised of short-term information stores or 'buffers,' access to and use of which is controlled by a central executive function that also retrieves information from long-term memory and controls action planning and goal-directed behaviors (Baddeley 1986). Over the course of development, there are age-related changes in each of these functions. Whether developmental changes are the product of increases in available memory capacity (Halford et al. 1994) or of increasingly efficient use of available capacity (Case 1992) is under debate. Nevertheless, what is clear is that with development, there are increases in the length of time over which information can be held or maintained and the facility and speed with which it can be processed (see Gathercole 1998 for a review). For example, absent sustained, focused attention or rehearsal, auditory information remains persistent in short-term memory for 12 seconds in adults, 10 seconds in 10–12 year olds, and for only eight seconds in six–seven-year-olds (Keller and Cowan 1994). As reviewed in Swanson (1996), there also are age-related increases in working memory span, or the number of items that can be recalled in the context of a concurrent processing task. As demonstrated in Schauble's (1996) research, each of these elements plays a supportive role in causal reasoning. That is, compared with adults, children were more likely to lose sight of their plans for experimentation and were less systematic in their execution of plans. In each case, the presumed source of lower performance was difficulty remembering what already had been tested and what had been found.

Also implicated in developments in causal reasoning are changes in the selection and use of problem-solving strategies. For example, as demonstrated in Schauble (1996), relative to children, adults are more likely to use a control of variables strategy when testing hypotheses. Developmental changes in the selection and use of more and less sophisticated and effective strategies can be characterized as a series of overlapping 'waves' of approaches or solutions to problems (Siegler 1996). Multiple strategies exist in the repertoire simultaneously. They compete with one another both over time and within a given problem resulting in waves of use as some strategies gradually decline and the frequency of others gradually increases. The implication is that strategies such as control of variables likely exist in the repertoires of both children and adults, alongside less advanced strategies of experimentation. Consistent with this suggestion, it has been shown that second graders can be trained to use a control of variables strategy (Chen and Klahr 1999). Nevertheless, the presence of the strategy in the child's repertoire does not guarantee that it will be used when appropriate or that it will be executed successfully when it is deployed.

Finally, analogical reasoning, attention, working memory, and selection and use of strategies all are influenced by the individual's familiarity with the domain. For example, Chi (1977) documented higher levels of reasoning by children in domains in which they had expertise (e.g., chess) than in domains in which they were relative novices. Goswami and Brown (1989) found that analogical reasoning was facilitated by knowledge of the causal mechanisms involved in the transformations that children were asked to judge. Similarly, Schauble (1996) found that both children's and adults' beliefs about causality influenced the hypotheses that they tested. Thus, the influence of domain knowledge is consistent throughout the life span. The facilitative effects of knowledge also extend to the component processes that support problem solving. Specifically, working memory span is greater for familiar words than for nonwords (Hulme et al. 1991). In addition, greater experience within a domain allows participants to guide their attention to the relevant attributes of the problem to be solved, and to disregard those features that are irrelevant to the solution (Goswami and Brown 1989).

5. Neurological Changes Related to Cognitive Development

Although the precise linkages are not clear, it is widely assumed that cognitive developmental changes in processes such as attention and working memory are related to developments in the neural substrates that subserve them. The prefrontal cortex supports planning and working memory and undergoes a protracted course of development (see Nelson et al. 2000 for review). For example, although adult levels of metabolic activity are approximated in the first year of life, development continues into adolescence (Chugani 1994), and frontal pruning of synapses (Huttenlocher 1994) and myelination (Jernigan et al. 1991) continue into adolescence. Thatcher (1992) demonstrated that the coherence of EEG patterns between frontal and posterior lobes increases throughout middle childhood. Case (1992) has shown that the patterns of coherence in EEG mirror the patterns in the development of attention over the same time period (see Case 1998, for a review).

Other neurological developments include brainwide changes such as myelination that results in faster transmission of impulses between neurons. There also are age-related increases in white matter density that are consistent with greater myelination of fiber tracts throughout adolescence (Paus et al. 1999). Increased speed of processing benefits working memory and attention.

6. Summary

The refinements that occur through brain development produce changes in the cognitive processes that support causal understanding. With development, children accrue a greater knowledge base, process information more rapidly, attain greater attentional and strategic resources, and improve in the efficiency with which they utilize resources. These component processes support a range of behaviors that are united by the appreciation of causal mechanisms, from behaviors as basic as infants' perception of causality to adolescents' abilities to design and evaluate experiments to test causal relations. Although we observe qualitative differences in these behaviors through the course of development, what underlies these advances are continuous changes in the brain and the resulting cognitive component processes that develop to support them.

Bibliography

Baddeley A D 1986 *Working Memory*. Oxford University Press, Oxford, UK

Bauer P J, Dow G A A 1994 Episodic memory in 16- and 20-month-old children: Specifics are generalized, but not forgotten. *Developmental Psychology* **30**: 403–17

Bauer P J, Schwade J A, Wewerka S S, Delaney K 1999 Planning ahead: Goal-directed problem solving by 2-year-olds. *Developmental Psychology* **35**: 1321–37

Bullock M 1984 Preschool children's understanding of causal connections. *British Journal of Developmental Psychology* **2**: 139–48

Case R 1992 The role of the frontal lobes in the regulation of cognitive development. *Brain and Cognition* **20**: 51–73

Case R 1998 The development of conceptual structures. In: Kuhn D, Siegler R S, Damon W (eds.) *Handbook of Child Psychology*, 5th edn. John Wiley, New York, Vol. 2, pp. 745–800

Chen Z, Klahr D 1999 All other things being equal: Acquisition and transfer of the control of variables strategy. *Child Development* **70**: 1098–120

Chen Z, Siegler R S 2000 Across the great divide: Bridging the gap between understanding of toddlers' and older children's thinking. *Monographs of the Society for Research in Child Development*, Vol. 65.

Chi M T H 1977 Age differences in memory span. *Journal of Experimental Child Psychology* **23**: 266–81

Chugani H T 1994 Development of regional brain glucose metabolism in relation to behavior and plasticity. In: Dawson G, Fischer K (eds.) *Human Behavior and the Developing Brain*. Guilford Press, New York, pp. 153–75

DeLoache J S, Miller K F, Pierroutsakos S L 1998 Reasoning and problem solving. In: Kuhn D, Siegler R S, Damon W (eds.) *Handbook of Child Psychology*, 5th edn. Wiley, New York, Vol. 2, pp. 801–50

Gathercole S E 1998 The development of memory. *Journal of Child Psychology and Psychiatry* **39**: 3–27

Gelman R, Bullock M, Meck E 1980 Preschoolers' understanding of simple object transformations. *Child Development* **51**: 691–9

Goswami U, Brown A L 1989 Melting chocolate and melting snowmen: Analogical reasoning and causal relations. *Cognition* **35**: 69–95

Halford G S, Maybery M T, O'Hare A W, Grant P 1994 The development of memory and processing capacity. *Child Development* **65**: 1338–56

Hulme C, Maughan S, Brown G D A 1991 Memory for familiar and unfamiliar words: Evidence for a long-term memory contribution to short-term memory span. *Journal of Memory and Language* **30**: 685–701

Huttenlocher P R 1994 Synaptogenesis, synapse elimination, and neural plasticity in human cerebral cortex. In: Nelson C A (ed.) *Minnesota Symposium on Child Psychology: Vol. 27—Threats to Optimal Development: Integrating Biological, Psychological, and Social Risk Factors*. Erlbaum, Hillsdale, NJ, pp. 35–54

Inhelder B, Piaget J 1958 *The growth of Logical Thinking From Childhood to Adolescence*. Basic Books, New York

Inhelder B, Piaget J 1964 *The Early Growth of Logic in the Child*. Harper & Row, New York

Jernigan T L, Trauner D A, Hesselink J R, Tallal P A 1991 Maturation of human cerebrum observed in vivo during adolescence. *Brain* **114**: 2037–49

Kalish C W 1998 Young children's predictions of illness: Failure to recognize probabilistic causation. *Developmental Psychology* **34**: 1046–58

Keller T A, Cowan N 1994 Developmental increase in the duration of memory for tone pitch. *Developmental Psychology* **30**: 855–63

Koslowski B, Okagaki L, Lorenz C, Umbach D 1989 When covariation is not enough: The role of causal mechanism, sampling method, and sample size in causal reasoning. *Child Development* **60**: 1316–27

Leslie A M 1984 Spatiotemporal continuity and the perception of causality in infants. *Perception* **13**: 287–305

Mackie J L 1980 *The Cement of the Universe: A Study of Causation*. Clarendon Press, Oxford, UK

Nelson C A, Monk C S, Lin J, Carver J L, Thomas K M, Truwit C L 2000 Functional neuroanatomy of spatial working memory in children. *Developmental Psychology* **36**: 109–16

Oakes L M, Cohen L B 1990 Infant perception of a causal event. *Cognitive Development* **5**: 193–207

Paus T, Zidgenbos A, Worsley K, Collins D L, Blumenthal J, Giedd J N, Rapoport J L, Evans A C 1999 Structural maturation of neural pathways in children and adolescents: in vivo study. *Science* **283**: 1908–11

Ruff H A, Lawson K R 1990 Development of sustained, focused attention in young children during free play. *Developmental Psychology* **26**: 85–93

Schauble L 1996 The development of scientific reasoning in knowledge-rich contexts. *Developmental Psychology* **32**: 102–19

Schlottman A 1999 Seeing it happen and knowing how it works: How children understand the relation between perceptual causality and underlying mechanism. *Developmental Psychology* **35**: 303–17

Siegler R S 1996 *Emerging Minds: The Process of Change in Children's Thinking*. Oxford University Press, New York

Swanson H L 1996 Individual and age-related differences in children's working memory. *Memory and Cognition* **24**: 70–82

Thatcher R W 1992 Cyclic cortical reorganization during early childhood. *Brain and Cognition* **20**: 24–50

Willatts P 1984 The Stage-IV infants' solution of problems requiring the use of supports. *Infant Behavior and Development* **7**: 125–34

Willatts P 1990 Development of problem-solving strategies in infancy. In: Bjorklund D F (ed.) *Children and Strategies: Contemporary Views of Cognitive Development*. Erlbaum, Hillsdale, NJ, pp. 23–66

P. J. Bauer and M. M. Burch

Cognitive Development in Infancy: Neural Mechanisms

1. Background

Until the past decade the study of cognitive development in human infants has been conducted relatively independently of any consideration of the brain. This relative neglect of biological factors in the study of behavioral development is surprising since the origins of developmental psychology can be traced to biologists. Darwin was one of the first to take a scientific approach to human behavioral development, and to speculate on the relations between phylogenetic and ontogenetic change. Piaget, who was originally trained as a biologist, used then-current theories of embryological development to generate his accounts of human cognitive development. McGraw and Gesell tried to integrate brain development with what was known of behavioral development. While they focused on motor development, they also extended their conclusions to mental and social development (Gesell 1928, McGraw 1943). While both these authors developed sophisticated informal theories that attempted to capture non-linear and dynamic approaches to development, their efforts to relate brain development to behavioral change remained very speculative due to the paucity of knowledge at the time.

From the 1960s to the late 1980s biological approaches to human behavioral development were neglected for a variety of reasons, including the widely held belief among cognitive psychologists during that period that the 'software' of the mind is best studied without reference to the 'hardware' of the brain. However, the recent expansion of knowledge at the end of the twentieth century on brain development makes the task of relating it to behavioral changes considerably more viable than previously. In addition, new molecular and cellular methods, along with theories based on artificial neural networks, have led to great advances in our understanding of how primate brains are constructed during ontogeny. These advances, along with those in functional neuroimaging, have led to the recent emergence of the interdisciplinary science of developmental cognitive neuroscience (see Johnson 1997).

What benefits can accrue from taking a developmental cognitive neuroscience approach to infants? First, considering evidence from brain development may help constrain, or even change, the type of cognitive theories that we consider. Second, being able to relate brain to cognitive development will potentially allow a more complete explanation not only of normal development, but also of developmental disorders resulting from genetic abnormality, and the long-term effects of early brain damage.

2. Human Postnatal Brain Development

A number of lines of evidence indicate that there are substantive changes during postnatal development of the human brain. Perhaps most obviously, the volume of the brain quadruples between birth and adulthood. This increase comes from a number of sources such as more extensive fiber bundles, and nerve fibers becoming myelinated. In addition, there is a dramatic increase in size and complexity of the dendritic tree of many neurons. Less apparent with standard microscopy, but evident with electron microscopy, is a corresponding increase in the density of synapses.

Huttenlocher (1990) and colleagues have reported a steady increase in the density of synapses in several regions of the human cerebral cortex. For example, in parts of the visual cortex, the generation of synapses (synaptogenesis) begins around the time of birth and reaches a peak at around 150 percent of adult levels toward the end of the first year. In the frontal cortex (the anterior portion of cortex, considered by most investigators to be critical for many higher cognitive abilities), the peak of synaptic density occurs later, at around 24 months of age (see Goldman-Rakic et al. 1997). Although there is variation in the timetable, in all regions of cortex studied so far, synaptogenesis begins around the time of birth and increases to a peak level well above that observed in adults.

Somewhat surprisingly, regressive events are commonly observed during the development of nerve cells and their connections in the brain. Due to the paucity of human data, the regional timetable for this decrease is still unclear and there is controversy about whether or not it shows differences between regions. Nevertheless, in humans, most neocortical regions and pathways appear to undergo this 'rise and fall' in synaptic density, with the density stabilizing to adult

levels at different ages during later childhood. The postnatal rise-and-fall developmental sequence can also be seen in other measures of brain physiology and anatomy. For example, using PET, Chugani et al. (1987) observed an adult-like distribution of resting brain activity within and across brain regions by the end of the first year. However, the overall level of glucose uptake reaches a peak during early childhood, which is much higher than that observed in adults. The rates return to adult levels after about 9 years of age for some cortical regions. The extent to which these changes relate to those in synaptic density is currently the topic of further investigation.

A controversial issue in developmental neuroscience concerns the extent to which the differentiation of the cerebral neocortex into areas or regions with particular cognitive, perceptual, or motor functions can be shaped by postnatal interactions with the external world. This issue reflects the debate in cognitive development about whether infants are born with domain-specific 'modules' for particular cognitive functions such as language, or whether the formation of such modules is an activity-dependent process (see Elman et al. 1996, Karmiloff-Smith 1992). Since around 1900 neuropsychology has taught us that the majority of normal adults tend to have similar functions within approximately the same regions of cortex. However, we cannot necessarily infer from this that this pattern of differentiation is intrinsically prespecified (the product of genetic and molecular interactions), because most humans share very similar pre- and postnatal environments. In developmental neurobiology this issue has emerged as a debate about the relative importance of neural activity for cortical differentiation, as opposed to intrinsic molecular and genetic specification of cortical areas. Supporting the importance of the latter processes, Rakic (1988) proposed that the differentiation of the cortex into areas is due to a protomap. The hypothesized protomap either involves prespecification of the tissue that gives rise to the cortex during prenatal life or the presence of intrinsic molecular markers specific to particular areas of cortex. An alternative viewpoint, advanced by O'Leary (1989) among others, is that genetic and molecular factors build an initially undifferentiated 'protocortex,' and that this is then subsequently divided into specialized areas as a result of neural activity. This activity within neural circuits need not necessarily be the result of input from the external world, but may result from intrinsic, spontaneous patterns of firing within sensory organs or subcortical structures that feed into the cortex, or from activity within the cortex itself (e.g., Katz and Shatz 1996).

Although the neurobiological evidence is complex, and probably differs between species and regions of the cortex, overall it tends to support the importance of neural activity-dependent processes (see Johnson 1997 for a review). With several notable exceptions, it seems likely that activity-dependent processes contribute to the differentiation of functional areas of the cortex, especially those involved in higher cognitive functions in humans. During prenatal life, this neural activity may be largely a spontaneous intrinsic process, while in postnatal life it is likely also to be influenced by sensory and motor experience.

3. Methods for Studying Human Postnatal Brain Development

Part of the reason for the recently renewed interest in relating brain development to cognitive change comes from advances in methodology which allow hypotheses to be generated and tested more readily than previously (see also Nelson and Bloom 1997). One set of tools relates to brain imaging. Some of these imaging methods, such as positron emission tomography (PET), are of limited utility for studying transitions in behavioral development in normal infants and children due to their invasive nature and their relatively coarse temporal resolution. However, two other methods may prove more useful.

Since the 1960s, scalp recorded event-related potentials have been used to assess brain function in infants and children for several decades. These recordings can either be of the spontaneous natural rhythms of the brain (EEG), or the electrical activity evoked by the presentation of a stimulus (ERP). Recent developments of the ERP method allow the relatively quick and easy installation of large numbers of sensors, thus making the method easier to use and also improving spatial resolution. Functional MRI allows the noninvasive measurement of cerebral blood flow with fine spatial resolution and temporal resolution on the order of seconds. Although this technique has been applied to children (Casey et al. 1997), the distracting noise and vibration, and the presently unknown possible effects of high magnetic fields on the developing brain, make its usefulness for healthy children under 4 or 5 years of age unclear. However, there has been at least one MRI study of infants initially scanned for clinical reasons (Tzourio et al. 1992), and the advent of 'open' scanners in which the mother can hold the infant may increase possibilities further.

Apart from brain imaging, the neural basis of cognitive development in infants can be examined by administering behavioral 'marker tasks' to infants who have suffered perinatal brain damage or developmental disorders of genetic origin. These marker tasks are adapted from tasks previously linked to a brain region or pathway in adult primates and humans by cognitive neuroscience studies. By testing infants or children with versions of such a task at different ages, the researcher can use the success or otherwise of individuals as indicating the functional development of the relevant regions of the brain. Finally, there is a continuing need for the neuroanatomical study of postmortem tissue. For a variety of reasons such studies are difficult to conduct.

4. Relating Brain to Cognitive Development

A number of different approaches have been taken to relating brain to cognitive development. These different approaches depend on very different sets of assumptions about development.

4.1 Maturational Models

The most common approach to developmental cognitive neuroscience is based on a maturational framework, in which it is assumed that as particular brain regions mature they allow or enable new cognitive functions to come on line. By this view postnatal brain development is assumed to be heavily governed by genetic and molecular factors, and relatively (though not completely) independent of experience. In brief, postnatal brain development is seen as a necessary, but not sufficient, cause of change in cognitive abilities. Two areas in which this approach has been applied concern the transition from subcortical to cortical control over visually guided behavior, and the later onset of frontal and prefrontal cortex control.

In one of the first specific attempts to relate changes in behavior to brain development in infants, Bronson (1974) presented evidence that the subcortical retino-collicular visual pathway primarily controls visually guided action in the newborn human infant. He also showed that it is only by around 3 months of age that visually-guided behavior switches to cortical pathways. More recent research indicates that there is probably some, albeit limited, cortical activity in newborns, and that the onset of cortical control over behavior is a gradual, rather than all-or-none, transition. Johnson (1990) updated Bronson's thesis to incorporate several different cortical pathways now known to underlie visually guided action in adult primates. The logic underlying this model was that changes in visually guided behavior of infants over the first months of life could be attributed to the graded onset of each of several different cortical pathways. Further, which pathways were active could be predicted from the developmental neuroanatomy of the primary visual cortex at that age, since this structure was the gateway to most of these pathways. While this model had reasonable success in accounting for the sequence changes in behavior observed, in the past few years studies involving ERPs, and studies of infants with focal cortical damage, show that frontal cortical regions are active earlier than more posterior regions, a sequence not predicted by the original Johnson (1990) model.

Another prominent maturational model has concerned the onset of prefrontal cortex functioning. In terms of structural neuroanatomy, this part of the cortex shows the most prolonged development of any region of the human brain, with changes in synaptic density detectable even into the teenage years (Huttenlocher 1990). Diamond (1991) has argued that the maturation of prefrontal cortex during the period 6–12 months accounts for a number of transitions observed in the behavior of infants in object permanence and object retrieval tasks. In one such task infants younger than 8 months often fail to accurately retrieve a hidden object after a short delay period if the object's location is changed from one where it was previously successfully retrieved. The basis for Diamond's claims come from the observations that (a) monkeys with lesions to the dorsolateral prefrontal cortex (DLPC) show the same patterns of impairment as young human and monkey infants, and (b) there are neurochemical and neuranatomical changes in the human DLPC at around the age they begin to perform successfully. Diamond (1991) has speculated that the DLPC is critical for performance when (a) information has to be retained or related over time or space, and (b) a prepotent response has to be inhibited. She argues that prior to the maturation of the DLPC, infants do not successfully perform tasks that require both of these abilities.

Further evidence linking success in the object permanence task to frontal cortex maturation in the human infant comes from two sources. The first of these is a series of EEG studies with normal human infants (e.g., Bell and Fox 1992), in which increases in frontal EEG responses correlate with the ability to respond successfully over longer delays in delayed response tasks. The second source is work on cognitive deficits in children with a neurochemical deficit in the prefrontal cortex resulting from Phenylketonuria (PKU). Even when treated, this inborn error of metabolism can have the specific consequence of reducing the levels of a neurotransmitter, dopamine, in the dorsolateral prefrontal cortex. These reductions in dopamine levels in the dorsolateral prefrontal cortex, result in these infants and children being impaired on tasks thought to involve parts of the prefrontal cortex, such as the object permanence task and an object retrieval task, and being relatively normal in tasks thought to depend on other regions of the cortex (Diamond et al. 1997, Welsh et al. 1990).

4.2 Selectionist Models

As discussed earlier, during the postnatal development of the cortex there is a rise and fall in synaptic density. This observation has led to a number of 'selectionist' theories being advanced in which the essential notion is that there is experience related sculpting of neural connectivity. For example, Changuex (1985) proposes that molecular and genetic processes specify the initial overproduction of synaptic

contacts. These initial connections are labile, but either stabilize or regress, depending on the activity in the postsynaptic cell, a process referred to as 'selective stabilization.' Changeux and Dehaene (1989) suggested that this model could be used to bridge from the brain to cognitive and behavioral levels, and that the same process of 'Darwinian' change could occur. Perhaps the best example of this type of change at the behavioral level comes from the work on phonemic discrimination in infants, showing that while they can initially discriminate a very large range of phonetic boundaries used in speech, including those not found in their native language, this ability becomes restricted to those boundaries important for their native language around 12 months of age.

Selectionist models have recently been criticized for the assumption that the initial stage of overproduction is not sensitive to experience (Quartz and Sejnowski 1997), and for focusing too heavily on only one aspect of neural development (Purves 1994). It is also important to remember that neuroanatomical measures of synaptic density are a static measure of dynamic processes. Since there is constant turnover of synapses, it is unlikely that there are clearly distinct phases of growth and pruning. Rather, both stages are likely to be simultaneously occurring within cortical regions.

4.3 Activity-dependent Models

A number of factors suggest that the field needs to move beyond the maturational framework. First, increasing evidence from developmental neuroscience suggests that neuronal activity itself plays a vital role in prenatal brain development, and it would seem reasonable to suggest that the same processes may extend into postnatal life. Second, there is evidence from neuroimaging and the study of infants with focal brain damage to suggest that there are dynamic changes in the timing and pattern of cortical activation in infants relative to adults. These dynamic changes take a number of forms, including changes in the overall spatial extent in cortex-activated ones (localization), changes in the extent to which the activation of a cortical region is stimulus-specific (specialization), and changes in the temporal stage of cortical processing at which specialization can be observed (see Johnson 2000).

Event-related potential experiments with infants have indicated that both for word learning (Neville 1991) and face processing (de Haan et al. submitted) there is increasing localization of processing with age/experience of a stimulus class. That is, more widespread scalp leads show a difference between the words or faces that control stimuli in younger infants than in older ones. In the example of face processing, both the left and the right ventral visual pathways are differentially activated by faces in early infancy, but in many (but not all) adults this further localizes only to the right ventral pathway (de Haan et al. 1998). In the example of word recognition, differences are initially found over widespread cortical areas, but narrow to left temporal leads after further experience with this class of stimulus (Neville 1991). Johnson (2000) presented an 'interactive specialization' framework within which changes in localization are a direct consequence of increases in specialization within and between cortical pathways. He suggests that this framework also provides a way of thinking about the fact that the same behavior can be mediated by different patterns of cortical activation in infants from those observed in adults.

Activity-dependent models can also be extended more broadly to the view that, at a given stage in postnatal development, the human infant may actually seek out the sensory input it needs to enable the further specialization of it its own brain. In other words, the infant is not a passive absorber of experience, but rather an active and selective seeker of it. Thus, the infant changes its 'effective environment' during development. One example of this comes from the development of face processing, where it has been argued that primitive tendencies for the newborn to orient to face-like stimuli ensures that developing cortical circuitry is preferentially exposed to that class of stimulus (see Johnson 1997).

See also: Brain Development, Ontogenetic Neurobiology of; Functional Brain Imaging; Infant Development: Physical and Social Cognition; Neural Plasticity; Prefrontal Cortex; Prefrontal Cortex Development and Development of Cognitive Function; Prenatal and Infant Development: Overview; Sensitive Periods in Development, Neural Basis of

Bibliography

Bell M A, Fox N A 1992 The relations between frontal brain electrical activity and cognitive development during infancy. *Child Development* 63: 1142–63

Bronson G 1974 The postnatal growth of visual capacity. *Child Development* 45: 873–90

Casey B J, Trainor R J, Orendi J L, Schubert A B, Nystrom L E, Giedd J N, Xavier Castellanos J L et al. 1997 A developmental functional MRI study of prefrontal activation during performance of a go-no-go task. *Journal of Cognitive Neuroscience* 9: 835–47

Changeux J P 1985 *Neuronal Man: The Biology of Mind.* Pantheon Books, New York

Changeux J P, Dehaene S 1989 Neuronal models of cognitive functions. *Cognition* 33: 63–109

Chugani H T, Phelps M E, Mazziotta J C 1987 Positron emission tomography study of human brain functional development. *Annals of Neurology* 22: 487–97

de Haan M, Oliver A, Johnson M H 1998 Electrophysiological correlates of face processing by adults and 6-month-old infants. *Journal of Cognitive Neuroscience* 36 Supp. S

de Haan M, Pascauis O, Johnson M H (submitted) Spatial and temporal characteristics of cortical activation in adults and infants viewing faces

Diamond A 1991 Neuropsychological insights into the meaning of object concept development. In: Carey S, Gelman R (eds.) *The Epigenesis of Mind: Essays on Biology and Cognition.* Erlbaum, Hillsdale, NJ, pp. 67–110

Diamond A, Hurwitz W, Lee E Y, Bockes T, Grover W, Minarcik C 1997 Cognitive deficits on frontal cortex tasks in children with early-treated PKU: Results of two years of longitudinal study. *Monographs of the Society for Research in Child development, Monographs* No. 252: 1–207

Elman J L, Bates E, Johnson M H, Karmiloff-Smith A, Parisi D, Plunkett K 1996 *Rethinking Innateness: A Connectionist Perspective on Development.* MIT Press, Cambridge, MA

Gesell A L 1928 *Infancy and Human Growth.* Macmillan, New York

Goldman-Rakic P S, Bourgeois J, Rakic P 1997 Synaptic substrate of cognitive development: Life-span analysis of synaptogenesis in the prefrontal cortex of the nonhuman primate. In: Krasnegor N A, Reid Lyon G, Goldman-Rakic P S (eds.) *Development of the Prefrontal Cortex. Evolution, Neurobiology and Behavior.* Paul H Brookes, Baltimore, MD, pp. 27–48

Huttenlocher P R 1990 Morphometric study of human cerebral cortex development. *Neuropsychologia* 28: 517–27

Johnson M H 1990 Cortical maturation and the development of visual attention in early infancy. *Journal of Cognitive Neuroscience* 2: 81–95

Johnson M H 1997 *Developmental Cognitive Neuroscience: An Introduction.* Blackwell, Oxford, UK

Johnson M H, de Haan M 2001 Developing cortical specialization for visual-cognitive function: The case of face recognition. In: McClelland J L, Siegler R S (eds.) *Mechanisms of Cognitive Development: Behavioral & Neural Perspectives.* Lawrence Erlbaum Associates, Mahwah, NJ

Johnson M H 2000 Functional brain development in infants: elements of an interactive specialization framework. *Child Development* 71(1): 75–81

Karmiloff-Smith A 1992 *Beyond Modularity: A developmental Perspective on Cognitive Science.* MIT Press/Bradford Books, Cambridge, MA

Katz L C, Shatz C J 1996 Synaptic activity and the construction of cortical circuits. *Science* 274: 1133–8

McGraw M B 1943 *The Neuromuscular Maturation of the Human Infant.* Columbia University Press, New York

Nelson C A, Bloom F E 1997 Child Development and Neuroscience. *Child Development* 68: 970–87

Neville H J 1991 Neurobiology of cognitive and language processing: Effects of early experience. In: Gibson K R, Petersen A C (eds.) *Brain Maturation and Cognitive Development: Comparative and cross-cultural Perspectives.* Adaline de Gruyter Press, Hawthorne, NY, pp. 355–80

O'Leary D D 1989 Do cortical areas emerge from a protocortex? *Trends in Neuroscience* 12: 400–6

Purves D 1994 *Neural Activity and the Growth of the Brain.* Academia Nazionale Dei Lincei, Cambridge University Press, Cambridge, UK

Quartz S R, Sejnowski T J 1997 A neural basis of cognitive development: A constructivist manifesto. *Behavioural and Brain Sciences* 20: 537–96

Rakic P 1988 Specification of cerebral cortical areas. *Science* 241: 170–6

Tzourio N, de Schonen S, Mazoyer B, Bore A, Pietrzyk U, Bruck B, Aujard Y, Deruelle C 1992 Regional cerebral blood flow in two-month old alert infants. *Society for Neuroscience Abstracts* **18**: 1121

Welsh M C, Pennington B F, Ozonoff S, Rouse B, McCabe E R 1990 Neuropsychology of early-treated phenylketonuria: Specific executive function deficits. *Child Development* **61**: 1697–713

M. H. Johnson

Cognitive Development: Learning and Instruction

Scientific conceptualizations of the relations between cognitive development and learning on the one side, and learning and instruction on the other side, have always been controversial in psychology and continue to be so. Theoretical standpoints depend on whether they take a universal or differential perspective, whether they are dominated by evolutionary-genetic or environment-oriented approaches, and whether they are biased ideologically toward an optimistic or pessimistic view on education. For these reasons, this entry will (a) present the universal relations between cognitive development, learning, and instruction; (b) analyze differential aspects of these three concepts; (c) describe theoretical approaches to the relation between cognitive development and learning; and (d) present theoretical conceptualizations of the relation between learning and instruction. The final section will contain some conclusions for educational practice.

1. Cognitive Development, Learning, and Instruction from a Universal Perspective

Inspired by evolutionary ideas in general, and the epistemological approach of Jean Piaget (1970) in particular, most classic theories on childhood cognitive development can be characterized by four basic principles. Their theoretical models are:

    (a) universal (valid for all human beings),

    (b) general (valid for all cognitive phenomena),

    (c) structural (valid for all basic changes in the cognitive systems and functions that internally determine the acquisition of knowledge and skills),

    (d) naturalistic-descriptive (stating that developmental changes are caused by the species-specific nature of human beings and may be influenced by environmental variables but not produced by them).

A typical example is Flavell's (1970) theoretical assumption 'that cognitive changes during childhood have a specific set of formal "morphogenetic" properties, that presumably stem from the biological-maturational growth process underlying these changes. Thus, childhood cognitive modifications are largely inevitable, momentous, directional, uniform, and irreversible' (p. 247).

In such a general conception, learning processes and their external conditions take a subordinate role. Instructions may not only promote natural development but also disrupt or impair it, and although cognitive development is also a condition and outcome of education, it is, nonetheless, a particularly important goal when the interest is in maintaining the dynamics and continuity of the developmental process for as long as possible in order to reach the highest possible level of cognitive development (Kohlberg and Mayer 1972).

At the beginning of the twenty-first century, many scientists are skeptical about such purist theories of cognitive development. This applies not only to the role of learning and of external learning opportunities but also to the impact of instruction and schools on cognitive development. For example, Geary (1995) discriminates between primary and secondary biological abilities. He views primary abilities as innate mental dispositions that enable even infants to learn from experience under almost any sociocultural conditions through the assistance of a strong intrinsic motivation. This is how they acquire domain-specific competencies (e.g., a mother tongue; elementary numerical skills; physical, biological, psychological, and social knowledge).

In comparison, secondary skills vary greatly between cultures, subcultural groups, and cohorts. The learning processes needed to acquire secondary competencies (scientific knowledge, higher mathematical skills, metacognitive skills) are cumulative, proceed at a relatively slow pace, require individual effort, and generally call for extrinsic motivation and didactic support. The level of secondary abilities that may be achieved collectively, and is actually achieved individually, depends on the state of cultural development and the availability of schools or equivalent institutions.

Hence, Geary's (1995) model assumes that early cognitive development depends on a large number and variety of necessary, autonomous, and automatically effective learning processes, and that although instructions (models, feedback, reinforcement, indications, availability of learning opportunities, etc.) take an important role, they are not decisive, because the acquisition of primary abilities is universal, genetically predetermined, and intrinsically motivated. In contrast, cognitive development in middle childhood, adolescence, and adulthood is influenced far more strongly by a person's cultural, familial, and individual situation. Instructionally guided and promoted learning is decisive for the course, the contents, and the level of cognitive development. However, there are large interindividual differences—even under similar cultural conditions—in the speed, efficacy, and quality of learning. Such individual differences in cognitive learning and, thus, in cognitive development, cannot be explained completely as consequences of prior learning.

2. Cognitive Development, Learning, and Instruction from a Differential Perspective

Each attained state of cognitive development determines learning, and the outcomes of cumulative learning processes influence the course of cognitive development. This general rule is moderated by the strength and stability of individual differences in intellectual abilities.

Ever since Binet and Simon constructed the first intelligence test in 1905, psychometrically oriented research has assumed that interindividual differences in abilities are relatively stable from middle childhood onward, and that these differences in the speed and quality of cognitive development permit long-term predictions. In a theoretically sophisticated but skeptical review of the available empirical findings, Wohlwill (1980) concluded, 'A reasonable coherent picture of the stability of IQ, over different portions of the age span, and some of the variables affecting it, has emerged from...research' (p. 401). How can we explain this high stability in individual IQ differences? The most plausible answer is to assume the existence of cognitive and social mechanisms with the same effect as the Matthew Principle of 'For unto everyone that hath shall be given.'

Despite numerous theoretical and methodological controversies, the available research on twins leads to the conclusion that one half or slightly more of the variance in IQ in the industrialized nations is determined genetically (which naturally also means that almost one half of this variance is not determined genetically). In contrast to much prejudiced belief, genetic factors and environmental conditions do not impact independently on the individual's cognitive development, but covary to a major degree. As a rule, biological parents are also the most important actors in the young child's social environment. Persons already react differentially in accordance with the infant's genotype, and children become actively involved in selecting preferential segments of the environment at an early age. These covariations help to strengthen and stabilize interindividual differences. Moreover, more intelligent children profit to a larger extent from the same learning opportunities and instructional aids than their less intelligent peers. Those who are more successful as a result of a cumulation of favorable factors develop a higher degree of self-confidence that encourages them to make a greater effort to solve difficult problems. Finally, young persons with greater abilities and higher achievements generally get a better education, which leads to greater career opportunities that are also associated in the long term with more cognitive stimulation and challenge.

Scientists and educators differ greatly in their response to the empirical evidence of stable differences in cognitive development. In the 1960s and 1970s, people thought that an egalitarian leveling out of individual differences in cognitive abilities and achievements was possible and could be achieved through intervention. The concept of mastery learning was viewed as the key for this. The idea was to grant less gifted and unsuccessful students a temporary increase in necessary learning time, while simultaneously adapting instruction to match their learning aptitudes as closely as possible. The educational and, to some extent, ideological aspirations invested in this model of learning have never paid off. Students with low abilities and poor prior knowledge differ greatly in what they can learn during a similar amount of learning time. As a result, large differences in the amount of learning time are required if equal achievements are to be attained in a heterogeneous population (Slavin 1987).

The opposing standpoint is well-characterized by Herrnstein and Murray's (1994) book *The Bell Curve*. According to their research in the USA, the interplay of differences in genetic endowment and sociocultural conditions lead, at a very early stage, to stable interindividual differences in intellectual abilities, motivational tendencies, and patterns of social behavior. The attempts to increase equality through compensatory education in recent decades have led to no long-lasting reduction in intellectual differences. As a result, the authors, strongly recommend discontinuing interventions for disadvantaged children and investing the available financial resources in educating those students whose high mental potential means that they will be responsible for generating the largest part of the gross national product in the years to come.

Both radical positions give a very one-sided interpretation of the current state of research. They overlook the fact that all children have to learn all competencies, and that all students profit from good instruction, while, at the same time, major differences in cognitive abilities and performance cannot be leveled out through intensive developmental interventions and academic instruction.

3. Cognitive Development and Learning: Which Comes First?

Psychology has a long tradition of assuming that learning is the only mechanism for explaining cognitive development. With the expert approach, this assumption has even survived the shift from behaviorist theories to cognitive models. Indeed, the expert approach has even be applied to cognitive development (Carey 1984, Sternberg 1998). For example, Carey (1984) has postulated: 'Children differ from adults only in accumulation of knowledge' (p. 37). As a result: 'Children know less than adults. Children are novices in almost every domain in which adults are experts' (p. 64).

Gagné (1968) had adopted a similar position in this criticism of the structuralist stage theories of cognitive development (e.g., Piaget 1970):

In an oversimplified way, it may be said that the stage of intellectual development depends upon what the learner knows already and how much he has yet to learn order to achieve some particular goals. Stages of development are not related to age, except in the sense that learning takes time. They are not related to logical structures, except in the sense that the combining of prior capabilities into new ones caries its own inherent logic Gagné 1968 (p. 189).

Does learning really determine all of cognitive development during childhood? There is still not enough empirical evidence to answer this question. Nonetheless, the confirmation of domain-specific knowledge in infancy, of the acquisition of demanding (linguistic or numerical) competencies during early childhood without any recognizable signs of a prior acquisition of the necessary cognitive preconditions, and the interindividual similarly in cognitive development despite different learning opportunities, supports the idea that innate predispositions must also be involved in not only specific but also unspecific cognitive learning processes.

As children grow older, the externally controlled acquisition (through learning) of competencies seems to become more important for cognitive development than internally guided learning processes. For example, the information-processing approach has revealed large intraindividual differences in solving structurally similar tasks that nonetheless differ in content. The influence of learned declarative as well as procedural knowledge on the development of cognitive competencies has been confirmed convincingly. Studies on how novices develop into experts in specific contexts have also shown what outstanding levels of performance can be achieved through long-term, deliberate practice (Siegler 1991).

Even though relations between innate and acquired competencies, between ontological and logical restrictions to learning, between domain-specific and domain-unspecific learning opportunities, between explicit and implicit learning modes, between neurobiological and behavioral indicators of learning, are currently a field of intensive research, new methodological paradigms, and numerous theoretical speculations, they have still not been subjected to solid and consistent theory formulation (Richardson 1998).

4. Learning and Instruction: Are Learners Really Their Own Best Instructors?

The role and function of instruction for learning, particularly for academic learning, were already controversial topics in the philosophical tradition of educational science, and this has not changed during the more than 100-year-old history of educational psychology and the scientific study of teaching methods. Some examples of what are, in part, very different conceptions of teaching methods are nondirective instruction as an aid toward self-generated insight in the student (the Socratic method); the adaptation of learning goals, learning conditions, and learning methods to the mental state of the individual learner; the application of psychological laws to initiate learning and make it successful (experimental teaching methods at the beginning of the twentieth century); open but stimulating learning environments to arouse students mentally (the educational reform movement of the twentieth century); the planning, organization, structuring, and evaluation of learning in the classroom through the teacher (direct instruction); or the moderation of the activities of independent and responsible student learners (self-regulated learning approach).

The theoretical (and sometimes ideological) controversies over the role and function of instruction for learning are particularly relevant at the start of the twenty-first century. In a comparison of psychological research on learning and educational research on teaching. Shulman (1982) even believed that he could recognize a potential paradox: 'Although the research on learning has taught us the importance of the active, transforming role of the learner, the research on teaching continues to demonstrate the importance of direct instruction, an approach which seems to suggest a passive view of the learner' (p. 97).

The apparently paradoxical pattern of results from experimental and developmental research on the one hand, and research on classroom instruction on the other hand, is not at all contradictory when one goes beyond the negative stereotype associated with direct instruction and considers the features and operationalizations used in many models of direct instruction. Direct instruction can be characterized by the following points: (a) The teachers classroom management is effective and the rate of student's interruptive behavior is very low; (b) the teacher maintains a strong academic focus and uses instructional time intensively to initiate and facilitate active, constructive, and goal-directed learning activities; (c) the teacher ensures that as many students as possible achieve successful learning processes by carefully chosing appropriate tasks, clearly presenting subject-matter information, continuously diagnosing each student's learning progress and learning difficulties, and providing effective help through remedial instruction.

Many studies have shown that instruction in which the teacher actively supports the learning process of the active and constructive working students is more effective than an educational strategy in which the teacher's only role is to provide for external conditions that made individual learning possible (Weinert and Helmke 1995).

Nonetheless, self-regulated learning has become a broad field of psychological research in recent years as well as a powerful movement for educational reform (Boekaerts 1999). This reveals a broad consensus that self-directed learning is one of the most important goals of education. The only controversy is over whether this goal can be attained exclusively through self-directed learning activities by students, regardless of whether or not these learners possess appropriate learning strategies or how far the contents of learning are close to the individual learner's experience.

5. Conclusions

Although it has been possible to solve or clarify many scientific problems regarding the relation between cognitive development, learning, and instruction during the last century, psychology and educational science are still far from possessing satisfactory theoretical models. Nonetheless, the current state of knowledge reveals a few interesting perspectives and conclusions for future psychological research and current educational practice:

(a) At the present time, neurobiological and psychological research are still unable to work in concert, particularly with babies and young children. There is a need for improvement in the forms of interdisciplinary cooperation and a speeding up of knowledge transfer.

(b) A very important question seems to be what do we have to teach in order to ensure that certain competencies will be in any way acquired and lead to the emergence of the desired special patterns of cognitive development.

(c) As well as examining universal changes in development, there is a need for studies on interindividual differences in cognitive structures and processes to improve the understanding of learning effects and the effectiveness of instruction. Which deficient competencies can be compensated or substituted through learning and through instruction, and which trade-offs can be anticipated?

(d) As well as studying representative samples of children at different stages of development, basic research needs to pay more attention to the developmental course of both gifted and mentally retarded children. Which qualitative differences in ability and development can be found? What consequences do they have for the possibility, speed, and quality of learning? How can instruction be adapted in line with individual differences in intelligence, talent, and learning?

(e) It has proved to be unacceptable theoretically and also dysfunctional in terms of research strategy to study cognitive development in middle age and old age in an (inverted) analogy to childhood development. Developmental processes in the early and late sections of the lifespan differ in fundamental terms.

(f) No universal, unequivocal, and concrete recommendations for educational practice can be derived from the available general theories on development, learning, and instruction.

At the beginning of the twenty-first century, it therefore seems wise for school administrators and teachers not to follow radically one-sided scientific recommendations, but to apply variable combinations of instruction methods to meet different educational goals and comply with the different learning preconditions in their students.

See also: Childhood and Adolescence: Developmental Assets; Cognitive Development: Child Education; Cognitive Development in Childhood and Adolescence; Cognitive Psychology: Overview; Cognitive Styles and Learning Styles; Education: Phenomena, Concepts, and Theories; Educational Learning Theory; Instructional Design; Instructional Psychology; Intelligence, Prior Knowledge, and Learning; Learning and Instruction: Social-cognitive Perspectives; Learning Theories and Educational Paradigms; Piaget's Theory of Human Development and Education; School Achievement: Cognitive and Motivational Determinants

Bibliography

Binet A, Simon R 1905 Application des méthodes nouvelles au diagnostic du niveau intellectuelle chez des enfants normaux et anormaux d'hospice et d'école primaire. *Année Psychologique* **11**: 245–336

Boekaerts M 1999 (ed.) Self-regulated learning: Where we are today. *International Journal of Educational Research* 31: 443–551

Carey S 1984 Cognitive development. The descriptive problem. In: Gazzaniga M S (ed.) *Handbook of Cognitive Neuroscience.* Freeman, New York, pp. 37–66

Flavell J H 1970 Cognitive change in adulthood. In: Goulet R, Baltes P. B. (eds.) *Life-span Developmental Psychology: Research and Theory.* Academic Press, New York, pp. 247–53

Gagné R M 1968 Contributions of learning to human development. *Psychological Review* **75**: 177–91

Geary D C 1995 Reflections of evolution and culture in children's cognition. *American Psychologist* **50**: 24–36

Herrnstein R J, Murray C 1994 *The Bell Curve.* The Free Press, New York

Kohlberg L, Mayer R 1972 Development as the aim of education. *Harvard Educational Review* **49**: 294–303

Piaget J 1970 Piaget's theory. In: Mussen P H (ed.) *Carmichael's Manual of Child Psychology.* Wiley, New York, Vol. 1, pp. 703–32

Richardson K 1998 *Models of Cognitive Development.* Psychology Press, Hove, UK

Shulman L S 1982 Educational psychology returns to school. In: Kraut A G (ed.) *The G Standley Hall Lecture Series.* American Psychological Association, Washington, DC, Vol. 2, pp. 77–117

Siegler R S 1991 *Children's Thinking*, 2nd edn. Prentice-Hall, Englewood Cliffs, NJ

Slavin R E 1987 Mastery learning reconsidered. *Review of Educational Research* **57**: 175–213

Sternberg R S 1998 Abilities are forms of developing expertise. *Educational Researcher* **27**: 11–20

Weinert F E, Helmke A 1995 Learning from wise mother nature or big brother instructor: The wrong choice as seen from an educational perspective. *Educational Psychologist* **30**: 135–42

Wohlwill J F 1980 Cognitive development in childhood. In: Brim O G, Jr., Kagan J (eds.) *Constancy and Change in Human Development*. Harvard University Press, Cambridge, MA, pp. 359–444

F. E. Weinert

Cognitive Dissonance

1. Foundations of Dissonance Theory

The theory of cognitive dissonance is elegantly simple: it states that inconsistency between two cognitions creates an aversive state akin to hunger or thirst that gives rise to a motivation to reduce the inconsistency. According to Leon Festinger (1957), cognitions are elements of knowledge that people have about their behavior, their attitudes, and their environment. As such, a set of cognitions can be unrelated, consonant, or dissonant with each other. Two cognitions are said to be dissonant when one follows from the obverse of the other. The resultant motivation to reduce dissonance is directly proportional to the magnitude and importance of the discrepant cognitions, and inversely proportional to the magnitude and importance of the consistent cognitions. This tension is typically reduced by changing one of the cognitions, or adding new cognitions until mental 'consonance' is achieved. Festinger's original formulation proved to be one of the most robust, influential, and controversial theories in the history of social psychology. Although a number of challenges and revisions have been suggested, the basic behavioral observation remains uncontested and continues to stimulate fresh research.

Application of this theory has yielded many surprising and nonintuitive predictions. For example, conventional wisdom suggests that behavior follows from attitudes; dissonance theory, however, identifies conditions under which just the opposite occurs. An early and often replicated experiment illustrates the power and counterintuitiveness of the theory. In what is now known as the induced compliance effect, Festinger and Carlsmith (1959) asked individuals to perform 30 minutes of a mind-numbingly tedious activity, and then to persuade a waiting participant that the activity was in fact quite interesting. This situation created cognitive dissonance in most individuals—they believed that the task was boring, yet inexplicably found themselves arguing quite the opposite. Half of the participants were given a ready excuse for telling this lie—they were paid $20 to do so—while the other half, paid only $1, had no such excuse. Those with a clear justification for their odd behavior experienced no dissonance and, as one would expect, later reported that the task was rather boring. The other half, however, given insufficient justification for their behavior, experienced dissonance between the knowledge that the task was boring and the reality that they were misleading a fellow participant into believing the opposite. Rather than endure the aversive experience of believing one thing but saying another, these individuals changed their opinion and convinced themselves that the task was actually interesting. In other words, their attitude was shaped by their behavior.

Subsequent studies have confirmed the basic theory of cognitive dissonance and demonstrated its far-reaching impact. For example, cognitive dissonance explains the increased commitment so frequently observed following a severe initiation into a group. The theory also explains why, when faced with a choice among several desirable options, we observe the tendency to highlight positive aspects of the chosen option and negative aspects of the rejected alternatives after (and only after) the choice has been made. In the course of such studies, we have learned much about the boundary conditions associated with the theory and have identified anomalies not easily explained by the original theory. Since the 1960s, a number of theoretical revisions have sought to subsume these limitations under a unifying theory. This article summarizes briefly the leading reformulations of dissonance theory and speculates on future directions.

2. An Early Theoretical Challenge: Self-perception Theory

Dissonance did not come quietly into psychology, nor did controversy begin over the finer points of the underlying process. Rather, the theory challenged the reigning theoretical paradigm of behaviorism of the 1950s by questioning the sovereign utility of basic learning theory. Rather than increased rewards leading to more positive attitudes, Festinger and Carlsmith (1959) had shown quite the opposite: participants who received a smaller reward for counterattitudinal advocacy developed more positive attitudinal responses. The majority of early criticisms, therefore, focused not on the details of the dissonance theory but rather on its fundamental legitimacy. During parts of the next two decades, one of the enduring intellectual feuds in social psychology debated whether dissonance phenomena were the result of complex cognitive processes in the mind of the participant, or whether they were merely the result of complex cognitive processes in the mind of the experimenter. Daryl Bem (1972) took the position that one could derive similar predictions through far more parsimonious behavioral processes. He argued that participants in dissonance experiments were not experiencing negative psychological tension due to inconsistency, but rather were simply inferring their attitudes from their behavior and the situation in which it occurred. In essence, he suggested that people view their own behavior as though they were outside observers, and infer their underlying attitude from an analysis of their behavior. In support of this position, Bem replicated Festinger and Carlsmith (1959) and demonstrated that independent observers, aware of the monetary inducements, attributed attitudes to the participants that were nearly identical to the participants' actual attitudes. The critical test between these theories revolved around the search for physiological arousal. Festinger was quite clear that inconsistent cognitions created an aversive motivational state that could presumably be measured. Bem's self-perception theory, by contrast, predicted neither psychological nor physiological tension. However, Zanna and Cooper (1974) found indirect evidence for physiological arousal by showing that if arousal were misattributed to an irrelevant source, the effects of dissonance disappeared. The debate over dissonance vs. self-perception was finally laid to rest by a series of experiments that identified the precise conditions under which each was operative. Fazio et al. (1977) found that small discrepancies between attitude and behavior (defined as those within a person's latitude of acceptance) tended to elicit self-perception processes, but larger discrepancies (those that fall in the person's latitude of rejection) were more likely to generate dissonance processes. Croyle and Cooper (1983) added direct support for Festinger's original position by showing that engaging in counterattitudinal advocacy, at least outside people's latitude of acceptance, is marked by measurable increases in people's skin conductance responses. Ultimately, the importance of self-perception theory lay in its contributions to identifying boundary conditions of dissonance processes and in provoking research that established physiological arousal as one of the hallmarks of dissonance.

3. Introduction of the Self

It may be that all cognitive inconsistencies are not psychologically equivalent. According to some theorists, inconsistencies that implicate aspects of the self maintain a privileged position. This suspicion led Elliot Aronson (1968) and Claude Steele (1988) to consider the role of self-concept in the dissonance process. Aronson concurred with Festinger's view that dissonance was caused by inconsistencies, but argued that it was a particular inconsistency that mattered most in arousing dissonance, i.e., the discrepancy between a person's general expectations for the self and his or her actual behavior. In other words, the arousal due to dissonance came about when a person's belief that he or she was a good and rational individual was called into question by behavior that was neither good nor rational. Aronson predicted that dissonance arousal would be more frequent and more powerful

among those with high self-esteem—that is, among those whose past history had led them to believe that their high internal standards of behavior were likely to be achieved. By contrast, Aronson predicted that those with low self-esteem, who were accustomed to behaving less competently, would not be surprised or discomfited to find themselves once again behaving in an incompetent manner.

To illustrate his point, Aronson (1968) argued that the dissonance aroused in Festinger and Carlsmith's (1959) experiment was not due to inconsistency between the thoughts 'I believe the task was dull' and 'I told someone the task was interesting.' Instead, Aronson proposed that dissonance was aroused by inconsistency between cognitions about the self (e.g., 'I am a decent and truthful human being') and cognitions about the behavior (e.g., 'I have misled a person ... (and) conned him into believing something that just isn't true,' p. 24). Aronson concluded: 'at the very heart of dissonance theory, where it makes its clearest and neatest prediction, we are not dealing with just any two cognitions; rather we are usually dealing with the self-concept and cognitions about some behavior. If dissonance exists it is because the individual's behavior is inconsistent with his self-concept' (1968, p. 23).

Claude Steele and his colleagues (1988) suggested a different interpretation of the role of the self in creating dissonance. Like Aronson, Steele viewed inconsistent cognitions as a threat to the self; but unlike Aronson's self-consistency model, he suggested that the primary function of dissonance reduction was not to rescue the specific self-cognitions threatened by a behavioral outcome, but instead to restore the completeness of the overarching self-system. The difference, then, was not about the origin of dissonance arousal, but rather about the purpose and mechanism underlying dissonance reduction. Whereas Aronson focused on individual susceptibility to dissonance arousal, Steele's self-affirmation theory focused on individual resilience to dissonance. Interestingly, from Aronson's point of view, it is those individuals who have a positive self-regard that are most likely to experience dissonance arousal. Steele, by contrast, asserted that it is those same individuals—wrapped in their armor of self-resources—who feel immune from the need to reduce dissonance. Based on the data provided by Aronson and Steele, it is probably fair to say that those with high self-esteem are both more susceptible to dissonance arousal and more resistant to its effects because they can focus on their many other strengths. Holding all else constant, high self-esteem serves both as a catalyst that generates dissonance and as a buffer that mitigates the need to reduce dissonance.

4. A New Look at Dissonance

In 1984, Cooper and Fazio provided a comprehensive review of the dissonance literature and challenged the dominant assumption that dissonance was driven by a need for psychological consistency. According to their 'New Look' model, dissonance is aroused when people perceive that their behavior has been responsible for bringing about consequences that are unwanted or aversive. If there are no such consequences, then inconsistent behavior will not produce the state of dissonance. For example, Cooper and Worchel (1970) replicated Festinger and Carlsmith's (1959) study with a condition in which the waiting participant was not convinced by the subject's lie. In this condition, the aversive consequence of misleading a fellow participant was removed along with all evidence of the dissonance process. Cooper and Fazio concluded from this and many other studies that responsibility for an aversive event rather than cognitive inconsistency plays the vital role in producing cognitive dissonance.

5. Future Directions—Self-standards Model of Dissonance

Each of these reformulations of dissonance theory differs with respect to one major issue: what is the role of self-concept in dissonance processes? Is it a problem, a benefit, or completely irrelevant to the arousal and reduction of cognitive dissonance? There are data in favor of each position—data that are not easily reconcilable. However, a recent synthesis discussed by Cooper (1999) and Stone (1999) suggests that dissonance is caused by a discrepancy between the outcome of a behavioral act and the standard to which it is compared. According to the self-standards model, sometimes the standard that people use to measure their behavioral outcomes are personal and idiosyncratic. In such cases, people's views of themselves will play a crucial role. At other times, the assessment of an act is based on broad, normative standards that are shared in the culture. At these times, the self will not play a role in the dissonance process.

In summary, it is still useful to think of dissonance as involving inconsistency among cognitive elements and to conclude that inconsistency produces motivation for change. It is also fair to conclude that the future of dissonance theory will include a role for behavioral consequences, an assessment of the self, and an analysis of the contextual variables that make different standards the basis of judgment for behavioral outcomes. The evolution of cognitive dissonance calls for an integration that will likely include insights from the currently dominant perspectives.

See also: Attitudes and Behavior; Motivation and Actions, Psychology of; Motivation: History of the Concept; Self-monitoring, Psychology of; Social Comparison, Psychology of

Bibliography

Aronson E 1968 Dissonance theory: Progress and problems. In: Ableson R P, Aronson E, McGuire W J, Newcomb T M, Rosenberg M J, Tannenbaum P H (eds.) *Theories of Cognitive Consistency: A Sourcebook*. Rand McNally, Chicago

Bem D J 1972 Self-perception theory. *Advances in Experimental Psychology* **6**: 1–62

Cooper J 1999 Unwanted consequences and the self: In search of the motivation for dissonance reduction. In: Harmon-Jones E, Mills J (eds.) *Cognitive Dissonance: Progress on a Pivotal Theory in Social Psychology*. American Psychological Association, Washington, DC, pp. 149–73

Cooper J, Fazio R H 1984 A new look at dissonance theory. *Advances in Experimental Psychology* **17**: 229–62

Cooper J, Worchel S 1970 Role of undesired consequences in arousing dissonance. *Journal of Personality and Social Psychology* **16**: 199–206

Croyle R, Cooper J 1983 Dissonance arousal: Physiological evidence. *Journal of Personality and Social Psychology* **45**: 782–91

Fazio R H, Zanna M P, Cooper J 1977 Dissonance and self-perception: An integrative view of each theory's proper domain of application. *Journal of Experimental Psychology* **13**: 464–79

Festinger L 1957 *A Theory of Cognitive Dissonance*. Row, Peterson, Evanston, IL

Festinger L, Carlsmith J M 1959 Cognitive consequences of forced compliance. *Journal of Abnormal Social Psychology* **58**: 203–10

Steele C M 1988 The psychology of self-affirmation: Sustaining the integrity of the self. *Advances in Experimental Psychology* **12**: 261–302

Stone J 1999 What exactly have I done? The role of self-attribute accessibility in dissonance. In: Harmon-Jones E, Mills J (eds.) *Cognitive Dissonance: Progress on a Pivotal Theory in Social Psychology*. American Psychological Association, Washington, DC, pp. 175–200

Zanna M P, Cooper J 1974 Dissonance and the pill: An attribution approach to studying the arousal properties of dissonance. *Journal of Personality and Social Psychology* **29**: 703–9

J. Cooper and K. M. Carlsmith

Cognitive Functions (Normal) and Neuropsychological Deficits, Models of

The field of cognitive neuropsychology centers around two coupled goals: to use patterns of cognitive deficits in brain-damaged patients to inform theories and models of how cognitive processes are carried out by the brain, and to apply existing models to explain the specific deficits of individual patients in order to design more effective strategies for remediating these deficits. The roots of this effort can be traced back to the pioneering work of Broca, Wernicke, and Lichtheim in the mid- to late nineteenth century. These neurologists attempted to decompose complex cognitive func-

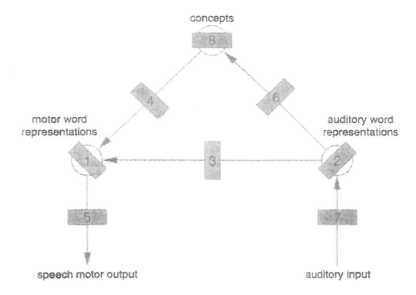

Figure 1

Lichtheim's (1885) model of aphasia. Grey bars indicate lesions to processing centers (circles) or pathways between them (arrows), giving rise to the following classic aphasia syndromes (in modern terminology): (a) Broca's aphasia; (b) Wernicke's aphasia; (c) conduction aphasia; (d) transcortical motor aphasia; (e) dysarthria; (f) transcortical sensory aphasia; (g) pure word deafness; (h) anomic aphasia

tions, such as language, into the joint operation of multiple functional 'centers' with specific patterns of connectivity between them. Damage either to the centers themselves or to the pathways between them were thought to give rise to distinct patterns of cognitive deficits. Indeed, the traditional scheme used today to categorize patterns of language impairment into distinct clinical syndromes—such as Broca's aphasia, Wernicke's aphasia, transcortical sensory or motor aphasia, etc.—derives from the Wernicke–Lichtheim model of the organization of the language system developed in the late nineteenth century (see Fig. 1).

1. Box-and-arrow Modeling

Although the form of explanation offered by these so-called 'diagram makers' was criticized roundly in the early twentieth century, it is echoed in modern-day cognitive neuropsychology in the form of box-and-arrow information processing models (see Fig. 2). While the functions ascribed to the centers or components are far more specific than in the nineteenth century, the same underlying explanatory logic is applied—the patterns of performance of brain-damaged patients are explained by positing one or more 'lesions' to the so-called functional architecture of the cognitive system. Typically, the predictions of the model, both in normal operation and under damage, have consisted of verbal descriptions based

on fairly general notions about how the various modules would operate and interact. While these types of predictions may suffice for capturing the more general characteristics of normal and impaired cognitive functioning, they become increasingly unreliable as the model is elaborated to account for more detailed phenomena.

Two recent trends have increased the usefulness of box-and-arrow theorizing within cognitive neuropsychology. First, with improvements in techniques for structural lesion localization in patients and for functional brain imaging in both patients and normal subjects, there has been a more concerted effort to situate the components and pathways in specific brain regions. This is important because information on neuroanatomic localization places strong constraints on how components participate in various tasks and on how the system must be damaged to account for the performance of specific patients.

The second, and perhaps more important trend has been the development of working computer simulations of cognitive models that can both reproduce the characteristics of normal performance and can exhibit the appropriate deficits when damaged in a manner analogous to brain damage. Computational modeling makes it possible to demonstrate the sufficiency of the underlying theory in accounting for the phenomena by making the behavior of a detailed cognitive model explicit. A working simulation guarantees that the underlying theory is neither vague nor internally inconsistent, and the behavior of the

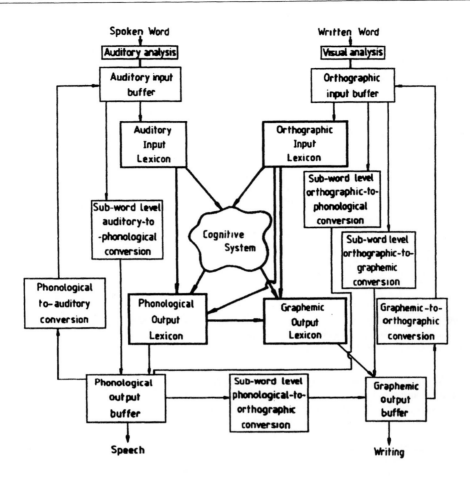

Figure 2
A box-and-arrow model of written and spoken word processing (from Howard and Franklin 1988)

simulation can be used to generate specific predictions of the theory.

One example of computational modeling based on box-and-arrow theorizing is the work of Coltheart and co-workers (Coltheart et al. 1993) in simulating a dual-route model of word reading. In the model, one pathway from print to sound applies grapheme-phoneme correspondence rules (e.g., B at the beginning of a word is pronounced /b/), while the other uses memorized whole-word correspondences. (These are the two pathways in Fig. 2 from the 'Orthographic input buffer' to the 'Phonological output buffer' that bypass the 'Cognitive System.') The rule route is effective for regular words (e.g., MINT) and for pronounceable but meaningless pseudowords (e.g., RINT); however, the lexical route is needed to pronounce exception words (e.g., YACHT, PINT) whose pronunciations violate the rules. In Coltheart and co-workers' implementation, the rule route consists of a collection of template-matching rules that operate left-to-right

on the input string and generate single phonemes at fixed intervals. The lexical route is a version of a highly influential model of word recognition developed by Rumelhart and McClelland (1982), known as the Interactive Activation model, which contains a separate processing unit for each word in the vocabulary. Damage to the lexical route yields a reading pattern in which exception words are regularized (e.g., PINT read to rhyme with MINT), analogous to patients with acquired surface dyslexia (Patterson et al. 1985). Conversely, damage to the rule route causes impaired reading of pseudowords relative to words, corresponding to acquired phonological dyslexia (Beauvois and Derouesné 1979).

2. Connectionist Modeling

Although substantial progress has been made within the framework of box-and-arrow theorizing, many

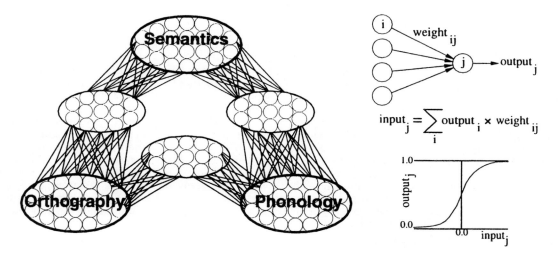

Figure 3
A distributed connectionist framework for lexical processing. The output of each unit is a smooth, nonlinear function of the summed, weighted input from other units (adapted from Plaut 1997)

researchers have come to believe that, in order to capture the full range of cognitive and neuropsychological phenomena, a formalism is needed that is based more closely on the style of computation employed by the brain. One such formalism that is widely used in connectionist modeling (see, e.g., McClelland et al. 1986, McLeod et al. 1998, Rumelhart et al. 1986).

In connectionist models—sometimes called neural networks or parallel distributed processing systems—cognitive processes take the form of cooperative and competitive interactions among large numbers of simple, neuron-like processing units (Fig. 3). Typically, each unit has a real-valued activity level, roughly analogous to the firing rate of a neuron. Unit interactions are governed by weighted connections that encode the long-term knowledge of the system and are learned gradually through experience. The activity of some of the units encodes the input to the system; the resulting activity of other units encodes the system's response to that input. The patterns of activity of the remaining units constitute learned, internal representations that mediate between inputs and outputs. Units and connections generally are not considered to be in one-to-one correspondence with actual neurons and synapses. Rather, connectionist systems attempt to capture the essential computational properties of the vast ensembles of real neuronal elements found in the brain through simulations of smaller networks of units. In this way, the approach is distinct from computational neuroscience (Sejnowski et al. 1988) which aims to model the detailed neurophysiology of relatively small groups of neurons. Although the connectionist approach uses physiological data to

guide the search for underlying principles, it tends to focus more on overall system function or behavior, attempting to determine what principles of brain-style computation give rise to the cognitive phenomena observed in human behavior.

The simplest type of connectionist system is a feedforward network, in which information flows unidirectionally from input units to output units, typically via one or more layers of hidden units (so called because they are not visible to the environment). Such networks are useful in many contexts but have a limited ability to process time-varying information. In such contexts, recurrent networks, that permit any pattern of interconnection among the units, are more appropriate. In one common type of recurrent network, termed an attractor network, unit activities gradually settle to a stable pattern in response to a fixed input. Recurrent networks can also learn to process sequences of inputs and/or to produce sequences of outputs. For example, in a simple recurrent network (Elman 1990), the internal representation generated for each element in a sequence is made available as an additional input to provide context for processing subsequent elements. Critically, the internal representations themselves adapt so as to encode this context information effectively, enabling the system to learn to represent and retain relevant information at multiple time scales.

An issue of central relevance in the study of cognition is the nature of the underlying representation of information. Connectionist models divide roughly into two classes in this regard. In localist models, such as the Interactive Activation model mentioned earlier, each unit corresponds to a distinct,

2117

familiar entity such as a letter, word, concept, or proposition. By contrast, in distributed models, such entities are encoded not by individual units but by alternative patterns of activity over the same group of units, so that each unit participates in representing many entities. Both localist and distributed models are 'connectionist' in the sense that the system's knowledge is encoded in terms of weights on connections between units.

Because localist models specify the form and content of representations, they tend to de-emphasize the role of learning. With a distributed model, by contrast, there is greater emphasis on the ability of the system to learn effective internal representations. Thus, instead of attempting to stipulate the specific form and content of the knowledge required for performance in a domain, the approach instead stipulates the tasks the system must perform, including the nature of the relevant information in the environment, but then leaves it up to learning to develop the necessary internal representations and processes.

Learning in a connectionist system involves modifying the values of weights on connections between units in response to feedback on the behavior of the network. A variety of specific learning procedures are employed in connectionist research; most that have been applied to cognitive domains, such as back-propagation (Rumelhart et al. 1986) take the form of error correction: change each weight in a way that reduces the discrepancy between the correct response to each input and the one actually generated by the system. Although it is unlikely that the brain implements back-propagation in any direct sense, there are more biologically plausible procedures that are computationally equivalent (see, e.g., O'Reilly 1996).

In an early application of error-correcting learning, Rumelhart and McClelland (1986) showed that a single network could learn to generate the past-tense forms of both regular verbs (e.g., BAKE ⇒ 'baked') and irregular verbs (e.g., TAKE ⇒ 'took'), thereby obviating the need for dual rule-based and exception mechanisms (Pinker 1999), analogous to those in the dual-route reading models mentioned earlier. Although aspects of the approach were criticized strongly (Pinker and Prince 1988), many of the specific limitations of the model have been addressed in subsequent simulation work (see, e.g., MacWhinney and Leinbach 1991, Plunkett and Marchman 1993, 1996). Of particular interest is recent work by Joanisse and Seidenberg (1999) showing that damage either to phonological or to semantic representations within single processing system can account for the observation of selective impairments in performance on regular vs. irregular verbs following Parkinson's disease vs. Alzheimer's disease, respectively (Ullman et al. 1997).

A similar line of progress has taken place in the domain of English word reading. An early connectionist model (Seidenberg and McClelland 1989) provided a good account of word reading but was poor at pronouncing word-like pseudowords (e.g., MAVE, Besner et al. 1990). A more recent series of simulations (Plaut et al. 1996) showed that the limitations of this preliminary model stemmed from the model's use of poorly structured orthographic and phonological representations. By contrast, networks with more appropriate representations were able to learn to pronounce both regular and exception words, and yet also pronounce pseudowords as well as skilled readers. Moreover, damage to semantic representations in such networks gave rise to surface dyslexia, in which patients produce regularization errors to exception words. In closely related work (Hinton and Shallice 1991, Plaut and Shallice 1993), damage to the pathway between orthography and phonology, combined with secondary damage to the semantic pathway, yielded the complementary pattern of deep dyslexia—often viewed as a severe form of phonological dyslexia—in which patients are extremely poor at pronouncing pseudowords and make semantic errors in reading words aloud (e.g., misreading RIVER as 'ocean'; see Coltheart et al. 1980). With the additional of an attentional mechanism, fully recurrent networks have also been used to account for the interaction of both perceptual and lexical/semantic factors in the reading errors of neglect dyslexic patients (Mozer and Behrmann 1990). In fact, such networks have been applied to a wide range of neuropsychological phenomena, including selective impairments in face recognition (Farah et al. 1993), visual object recognition (Humphreys et al. 1992), spatial attention (Cohen et al. 1994), semantic memory (Farah and McClelland 1991), anomia and aphasia (Dell et al. 1997), spelling (Brown and Ellis 1994), and executive control (Cohen and Servan-Schreiber 1992).

One of the main attractions of distributed connectionist models is their ability to discover the structure implicit in ensembles of events and experiences. Accomplishing this, however, requires making only very small changes in response to each input so that the resulting weight values reflect the long-term experience of the system. Attempts to teach such networks the idiosyncratic properties of specific events one after the other do not generally succeed since the changes made in learning each new case produce 'catastrophic interference' with what was stored previously in the weights (McCloskey and Cohen 1989). McClelland et al. (1995) observed, however, that catastrophic interference does not occur if continued training of old knowledge is interleaved with the training of new knowledge. They proposed that the brain employs two complementary learning systems: a cortical system for gradual learning using highly overlapping distributed representations, and a sub-cortical, hippocampal-based system for rapid learning using much sparser, less-overlapping representations. On their account, stored instances in the hippocampus provide the training input for past experience that must be inter-leaved with ongoing experience to prevent interference in cortex. The argument was that learning in cortex and in distributed networks are similarly constrained, so that the strengths and limitations of structure-sensitive learning in networks explained *why* the brain employs two complementary learning systems in hippocampus and neocortex.

Although fully recurrent networks are capable of learning to exhibit complex temporal behavior, for reasons of efficiency it is more common to apply simple recurrent networks in temporal domains. For example, Elman (1991) demonstrated that a simple recurrent network could learn the structure of an English-like grammar, involving number agreement and variable verb argument structure across multiple levels of embedding, by repeatedly attempting to predict the next word in processing sentences. St. John and McClelland (1990) also showed how such networks can learn to develop a representation of sentence meaning by attempting to answer queries about thematic role assignments throughout the course of processing a sentence. There have, however, been relatively few attempts at applying simple recurrent networks to neuropsychological phenomena.

3. Future Directions

In many ways, the application of computational modeling to understanding normal and impaired cognition is still in its infancy. Only a small fraction of the relevant behavioral phenomena have been addressed in any detail by existing models. Certainly considerable fruitful work remains in applying existing methods to a broader range of empirical issues. Even so, it seems clear that existing computational frameworks have a number of limitations which hamper their broader application. This is particularly true with regards to the application of connectionist networks to complex temporal domains, such as language, reasoning, and problem solving. While there have been some promising initial steps in these areas, substantial development of the computational methodology itself is likely to be necessary before satisfactory models will be possible.

4. Summary

Researchers interested in human cognitive processes have long used computer simulations to try to identify the principles of cognition. The strategy has been to build computational models that embody a set of principles and then examine how well the models capture human performance in cognitive tasks. A number of formalisms have been used to model cognitive processing in normal individuals. Those based on general principles of neural computation—including connectionist or neural-network models—

have proven most effective at capturing the effects of brain damage on cognition. Considerable work remains, however, in extending such models to address more complex temporal phenomena.

See also: Artificial Intelligence: Connectionist and Symbolic Approaches; Artificial Neural Networks: Neurocomputation; Cognitive Neuropsychology, Methodology of; Computational Neuroscience; Connectionist Approaches; Connectionist Models of Language Processing; Language Acquisition; Language Development, Neural Basis of; Lexical Processes (Word Knowledge): Psychological and Neural Aspects; Neural Networks: Biological Models and Applications; Neuropsychological Functioning, Assessment of; Syntactic Aspects of Language, Neural Basis of; Word Recognition, Cognitive Psychology of

Bibliography

Beauvois M-F, Derouesné J 1979 Phonological alexia: Three dissociations. *Journal of Neurology, Neurosurgery, and Psychiatry* **42**: 1115–24

Besner D, Twilley L, McCann R S, Seergobin K 1990 On the connection between connectionism and data: Are a few words necessary? *Psychological Review* **97**(3): 432–46

Brown G D A, Ellis N C (eds.) 1994 *Handbook of Normal and Disturbed Spelling*. Wiley, New York

Cohen J D, Romero R D, Servan-Schreiber D, Farah M J 1994 Mechanisms of spatial attention: The relation of macrostructure to microstructure in parietal neglect. *Journal of Cognitive Neuroscience* **6**(4): 377–87

Cohen J D, Servan-Schreiber D 1992 Context, cortex, and dopamine: A connectionist approach to behavior and biology in schizophrenia. *Psychological Review* **99**(1): 45–77

Coltheart M, Curtis B, Atkins P, Haller M 1993 Models of reading aloud: Dual-route and parallel-distributed-processing approaches. *Psychological Review* **100**(4): 589–608

Coltheart M, Patterson K, Marshall J C (eds.) 1980 *Deep Dyslexia*. Routledge and Kegan Paul, London

Dell G S, Schwartz M F, Martin N, Saffran E M, Gagnon D A 1997 Lexical access in normal and aphasic speakers. *Psychological Review* **104**: 801–38

Elman J L 1990 Finding structure in time. *Cognitive Science* **14**(2): 179–211

Elman J L 1991 Distributed representations, simple recurrent networks, and grammatical structure. *Machine Learning* **7**: 195–225

Farah M J, McClelland J L 1991 A computational model of semantic memory impairment: Modality-specificity and emergent category-specificity. *Journal of Experimental Psychology: General* **120**(4): 339–57

Farah M J, O'Reilly R C, Vecera S P 1993 Dissociated overt and covert recognition as an emergent property of a lesioned neural network. *Psychological Review* **100**(4): 571–88

Hinton G E, Shallice T 1991 Lesioning an attractor network: Investigations of acquired dyslexia. *Psychological Review* **98**(1): 74–95

Howard D, Franklin S 1988 *Missing the Meaning?* MIT Press, Cambridge, MA

Humphreys G W, Freeman T, Müller H J 1992 Lesioning a connectionist model of visual search: Selective effects on distractor grouping. *Canadian Journal of Psychology* **46**: 417–60

Joanisse M F, Seidenberg M S 1999 Impairments in verb morphology after brain injury: A connectionist model. *Proceedings of the National Academy of Science, USA* **96**: 7592–7

Lichtheim L 1885 On aphasia. *Brain* **7**: 433–84

MacWhinney B, Leinbach J 1991 Implementations are not conceptualizations: Revising the verb learning model. *Cognition* **40**: 121–53

McClelland J L, McNaughton B L, O'Reilly R C 1995 Why there are complementary learning systems in the hippocampus and neocortex: Insights from the successes and failures of connectionist models of learning and memory. *Psychological Review* **102**: 419–57

McClelland J L, Rumelhart D E, PDP Research Group (eds.) 1986 *Parallel Distributed Processing: Explorations in the Microstructure of Cognition. Volume 2: Psychological and Biological Models*. MIT Press, Cambridge, MA

McCloskey M, Cohen N J 1989 Catastrophic interference in connectionist networks: The sequential learning problem. In: Bower G H (ed.) *The Psychology of Learning and Motivation*. Academic Press, New York, Vol. 24, pp. 109–65

McLeod P, Plunkett K, Rolls E T 1998 *Introduction to Connectionist Modelling of Cognitive Processes*. Oxford University Press, Oxford, UK

Mozer M C, Behrmann M 1990 On the interaction of selective attention and lexical knowledge: A connectionist account of neglect dyslexia. *Journal of Cognitive Neuroscience* **2**(2): 96–123

O'Reilly R C 1996 Biologically plausible error-driven learning using local activation differences: The generalized recirculation algorithm. *Neural Computation* **8**(5): 895–938

Patterson K, Coltheart M, Marshall J C (eds.) 1985 *Surface Dyslexia*. Erlbaum, Hillsdale, NJ

Pinker S 1999 *Words and Rules: The Ingredients of Language*. Basic Books, New York

Pinker S, Prince A 1988 On language and connectionism: Analysis of a parallel distributed processing model of language acquisition. *Cognition* **28**: 73–193

Plaut D C 1997 Structure and function in the lexical system: Insights from distributed models of naming and lexical decision. *Language and Cognitive Processes* **12**: 767–808

Plaut D C, McClelland J L, Seidenberg M S, Patterson K 1996 Understanding normal and impaired word reading: Computational principles in quasi-regular domains. *Psychological Review* **103**: 56–115

Plaut D C, Shallice T 1993 Deep dyslexia: A case study of connectionist neuropsychology. *Cognitive Neuropsychology* **10**(5): 377–500

Plunkett K, Marchman V A 1993 From rote learning to system building: Acquiring verb morphology in children and connectionist nets. *Cognition* **48**(1): 21–69

Plunkett K, Marchman V A 1996 Learning from a connectionist model of the acquisition of the English past tense. *Cognition* **61**(3): 299–308

Rumelhart D E, Hinton G E, Williams R J 1986 Learning representations by back-propagating errors. *Nature* **323**(9): 533–6

Rumelhart D E, McClelland J L 1982 An interactive activation model of context effects in letter perception: Part 2. The contextual enhancement effect and some tests and extensions of the model. *Psychological Review* **89**: 60–94

Rumelhart D E, McClelland J L 1986 On learning the past tenses of English verbs. In: McClelland J L, Rumelhart D E, PDP Research Group (eds.) *Parallel Distributed Processing: Explorations in the Microstructure of Cognition. Volume 2: Psychological and Biological Models*. MIT Press, Cambridge, MA, pp. 216–71

Rumelhart D E, McClelland J L, PDP Research Group (eds.) 1986 *Parallel Distributed Processing: Explorations in the Microstructure of Cognition. Volume 1: Foundations*. MIT Press, Cambridge, MA

Seidenberg M S, McClelland J L 1989 A distributed, developmental model of word recognition and naming. *Psychological Review* **96**: 523–68

Sejnowski T J, Koch C, Churchland P S 1988 Computational neuroscience. *Science* **241**: 1299–1306

St. John M F, McClelland J L 1990 Learning and applying contextual constraints in sentence comprehension. *Artificial Intelligence* **46**: 217–57

Ullman M T, Corkin S, Coppola M, Hicock G, Growdon J H, Koroshetz W J, Pinker S 1997 A neural dissociation within language: Evidence that the mental dictionary is part of declarative memory and that grammatical rules are processed by the procedural system. *Journal of Cognitive Neuroscience* **9**: 266–76

D. C. Plaut

Cognitive Maps

1. Introduction

A cognitive map is a representative expression of an individual's cognitive map knowledge, where cognitive map knowledge is an individual's knowledge about the spatial and environmental relations of geographic space. For example, a sketch map drawn to show the route between two locations is a cognitive map—a representative expression of the drawer's knowledge of the route between the two locations. Because a cognitive map represents/demonstrates an individual's geographic knowledge, geographers, psychologists, and others use them as the principle means by which to assess how we learn, process, and store geographic information gained from primary (e.g., walking through an area) and secondary (e.g., reading a map) sources. An understanding of how we undertake these mental tasks is thought to be important because it reveals the fundamental cognitive processes and structures that underlie spatial decision and choice making, and thus spatial behavior—why we choose certain routes, places to visit, locations to live, and so on (see *Spatial Cognition; Behavioral Geography*).

2. Cognitive Mapping

The combined process by which we learn, store, and use information relating to the geographic world is

Table 1
Lynch's classification

Category	Description
Paths	Paths are the channels along which an individual moves. They may include streets, walkways, railways
Edges	Edges are the linear elements not considered as paths. They are the boundaries between two phases, linear breaks in continuity such as shores or walls
Districts	Districts are the medium-to-large scale sections to the city, conceived as having a two-dimensional extent, which the observer mentally enters, and which have some common identifiable character
Nodes	Nodes are points, the strategic spots in the city into which an observer can enter, and which are the intensive foci to and from which (s)he is traveling. They may be primarily junctions, transportation changeovers, a crossing, or convergence of paths
Landmarks	Landmarks are another type of point-reference. They are usually a physical object such as a building, sign, store, or mountain

known as cognitive mapping, and this term is used to define the field of study which investigates this process. Cognitive mapping as a field of enquiry is relatively young. Whilst there are a handful of studies which predate 1960, the vast majority of research has occurred after this date and the publication of Kevin Lynch's seminal work 'The Image of the City'. Ever since Lynch's ground-breaking book, cognitive mapping research has been a multidisciplinary endeavor, undertaken by geographers, psychologists, anthropologists, computer, and information scientists. However, whilst a vast amount of research has been conducted as yet there is only limited consensus as to the fundamental processes of cognitive mapping. As such, there are a number of theories that seek to explain how we construct, process, and store cognitive map knowledge and how this knowledge is used to make spatial decisions and choices. These theories generally have been formulated on the basis of evidence provided by cognitive maps (see Downs and Stea 1977, Gärling and Golledge 1993, Portugali 1996, Golledge and Stimson 1997).

3. Cognitive Maps

Until very recently the bases and processes of human cognitive mapping was exclusively measured and assessed through cognitive (sketch) maps and other external forms of knowledge representation (e.g., estimating distances). More recently these methods of data generation have been supplemented by qualitative and neurological approaches. Moreover, there has been a transference of experimental setting from the laboratory to the natural environment.

Whilst a cognitive map is any 'map' which represents an individual's knowledge of an area, it generally takes the form of a sketch map drawn on a sheet of paper (it could, however, be a drawing in sand or a map constructed out of natural material). In experimental conditions, subjects are given a sheet of paper

and are asked to draw a map of a certain location, area, or route between locations. The scale of the geographic realm to be drawn can vary substantially from the global (e.g., draw a map of the world) to the local (e.g., draw a map of your neighborhood). Variants on this simple sketch mapping exercise include providing respondents with a small portion of the map to provide a scale and reference, and teaching subjects a sketch map language where specific symbols are used to denote particular features. By aggregating together the cognitive maps of several individuals it is possible to determine their shared level of knowledge and which elements of an environment are most salient. This is the technique pioneered by Lynch. He analyzed individuals maps by classifying their elements into five different classes (see Table 1) which he then used to produce a composite map where the symbol size/shading density is proportional to the number of times an element appeared on the individual maps. Using this technique he aggregated together the sketch maps of residents in Boston, Jersey City, and Los Angeles to create composite cognitive maps of these cities (see Fig.1)

The analysis used by Lynch is a content classification. A number of other classification schemes have been used to analyze cognitive maps. For example, there have been classifications that assess map style, structure, and accuracy. In these cases the focus moves beyond what elements an individual draws to assessing the relationship between the elements and their relativity to the real world. In addition, the accuracy of the spatial relations portrayed can be analyzed statistically using spatial statistics. For example, in many studies bidimensional regression has been used to compare the geometry of the cognitive map to a cartographic map. Bidimensional regression is a two-dimensional equivalent of linear regression that quantifiably assesses scale, rotation, and translation differences between the actual and estimated pattern of responses.

Using the technique of sketch mapping to generate data about a person's cognitive map knowledge and

The Boston image as derived from sketch maps

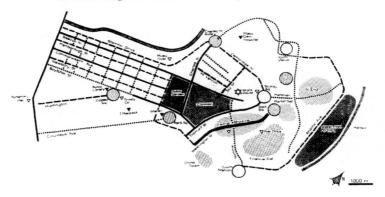

The Jersey City image as derived from sketch maps

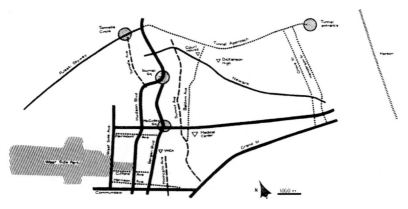

The Los Angeles image as derived from sketch maps

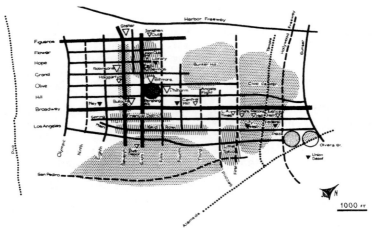

Figure 1
Cognitive maps of Boston, Jersey City and Los Angeles

their ability to use this knowledge is not without criticism. For example, a number of researchers have argued that sketch maps have a number of qualities that make them unreliable and inaccurate measures of spatial knowledge (note not geographic knowledge): they are dependent upon drawing abilities and familiarity with cartographic conventions; they suffer from associational dependence where later additions to the sketch will be influenced by the first few elements that are drawn; their content and style are influenced by the size of paper used for sketching; they are difficult to subjectively score and code; and they often show less information than the respondent knows. As a consequence of these criticisms it is becoming less common for researchers to use sketch mapping as an analytical tool to assess individual and collective cognitive mapping. Instead, researchers are turning to a range of other techniques.

4. Other Ways to Measure Cognitive Map Knowledge

4.1 Other Action Measures

Other forms of action (e.g., drawing) measures can be divided into those that, like sketch mapping, are two-dimensional in nature and those that are unidimensional. Other two-dimensional measures include completion tasks and recognition tasks. Completion tasks require an individual to complete a task that has already been started for them. For example, spatial cued response tests require subjects to place locations in relation to locations that are preplaced. A highly cued version of this are cloze procedure tests that require a subject to 'fill in' a missing space (an aspatial example of which would be, 'a dog barks but a cat ------?' Recognition tasks measure how successful subjects are at identifying spatial relationships. Iconic tests require the respondent to identify correctly features on a map or aerial photograph. Configuration tests require a subject to identify correctly which configuration, out of several, displays the correct spatial relations. Verifiable statement tests require subjects to identify whether a textual description of a spatial relationship is true or false. Spatial cued response data are often analyzed like sketch maps using bidimensional regression.

Cloze procedure and recognition tests are analyzed by constructing an accuracy score that reveals as a percentage the number of correct placements or recognitions.

Unidimensional tests seek to uncover one-dimensional aspects of cognitive map knowledge such as distance and direction. These dimensions are thought to be representative of spatial knowledge in general, but are particularly useful for measuring levels of route (procedural) knowledge. Distance tasks are used to assess an individual's knowledge of the distance between locations. In his review, Montello (1991) identifies five groups of tests designed to measure cognitive distance estimates: ratio scaling, interval and ordinal scaling, mapping, reproduction, and route choice. Ratio scaling adapts traditional psychophysical scaling techniques to a distance context, with subjects estimating the distance to a location as a ratio of some other known distance, such as an arbitrary scale or the length of a ruler. Interval and ordinal scaling are similar to ratio scaling but differ in their level of measurement: paired comparison requires a respondent to decide which one of a pair of distances is longer; ranking requires a respondent to rank various distances in order along the dimension of length; rating requires a respondent to assign the distance between places to a set of predetermined classes that represent relative length; partition scales require a respondent to assign distances to classes of equal-appearing intervals of length. Mapping is the measurement of distances from a sketch map for comparison with the actual distances. Reproduction requires a respondent to provide distance estimates at the scale of the estimated distance. Route choice consists of inferring judgments of cognitive distance from the choice of route an individual makes when asked to take the shortest route between two locations.

Like sketch map data, distance data can be analyzed individually or aggregated beforehand to provide data about a group. A common method to analyze ratio scaling, mapping, and reproduction data is to regress the cognitive distance estimates onto the objective distance values, observing the relationship between the two. Another common strategy, and one also used with interval or ordinal distance data, is to analyze the data using multidimensional scaling techniques (MDS). MDS techniques explore the latent structure of a set of distance estimates by assessing the dimensionality of the data. They do this by constructing a two-dimensional space from one-dimensional data using a series of algorithms. In essence, they construct a 'map' showing the relationship between a number of objects. This 'map' can then be compared to an actual map using techniques such as bidimensional regression.

Direction tasks assess an individual's knowledge of the direction between two locations. The most common direction task is pointing. Pointing involves standing at, or imagining being at, a location and pointing to another location. An alternative technique involves drawing on a compass the direction to a location from another. Direction estimates have been analyzed by comparing the estimates to the actual directions, often through a simple subtraction process. In other cases, a technique of projective convergence has been used to construct a 'map' from estimates by calculating where estimates to the same location but from different sites intersect.

4.2 Qualitative Approaches

In recent years there has been an increase in the use of qualitative methodologies to investigate cognitive map knowledge. In some cases, this has involved a scientific approach and in others an interpretative approach. The scientific approach continues the tradition described above, but rather than externally representing their knowledge through actions (e.g., drawing, pointing) individuals are required to describe verbally routes or layouts in experimental conditions. Like cognitive maps these data can be analyzed for content, style, structure, and accuracy. The interpretative approach, however, is less structured in terms of data collection. It posits that talking to and observing individuals as they interact with an environment reveals information concerning spatial behavior. Such an approach might seek to gain a spatial understanding of an area by adopting a strategy of in-depth interviews, discussing the reasoning behind spatial decision making.

4.3 Neurological Approaches

In contrast to the approaches above, which seek to understand the process of cognitive mapping by examining external measures (action or verbal), neurological approaches measure neural activity within the brain. A set of brain-scan techniques exist, differentiated by their temporal and spatial resolution. Magnetic Electroencephalography (MEG) has a high temporal resolution (0–300 ms) but low spatial resolution (providing only a general indication of neural activity). Positron Emission Tomography (PET) is the converse, with functional Magnetic Resonance Imagery (fMRI) providing a middle ground for both parameters. To reveal information about spatial cognition, scans are taken as the individual undertakes a series of spatial, problem-solving tasks. As such, neurological approaches seek to explain spatial thought and spatial behavior by identifying its neural, physiological bases rather than its psychological basis. To date there has been very little work that has sought to marry the findings of neurological and psychological research to provide a comprehensive, physiological and psychological model of cognitive mapping.

4.4 Naturalistic Settings

Many studies, particularly from psychology, which seek to understand cognitive map knowledge are conducted in controlled laboratory settings. For example, respondents may be required to learn the layout of objects in a experimental laboratory, and then to map the location of objects, or estimate distance and directions between objects. The laboratory is attractive to the researcher because they can control/monitor all the variables that may affect spatial learning and processing. Some researchers, however, question the ecological validity of this approach given that cognitive map knowledge concerns the geographic environment and it is this environment in which spatial behavior occurs. For these reasons they suggest that testing should occur in the natural environment, and increasingly this is becoming more common.

5. Summary

Cognitive maps are representative expressions of spatial knowledge. They are part of a wider set of analytical measures which seek to determine how we learn, store, and process knowledge of the geographic environment. These measures are important because they reveal fundamental aspects of cognition and reveal the cognitive processes that underlie spatial decision and choice making.

See also: Hippocampus and Related Structures; Knowledge (Explicit and Implicit): Philosophical Aspects; Mental Maps, Psychology of; Spatial Thinking in the Social Sciences, History of

Bibliography

Downs R M, Stea D 1977 *Maps in Minds: Reflections on Cognitive Mapping*. Harper & Row, New York
Gärling T, Golledge R G (eds.) 1993 *Behavior and Environment: Psychological and Geographical Approaches*. North Holland, Amsterdam
Golledge R G, Stimson R J 1997 *Spatial Behavior: A Geographic Perspective*. Guildford Press, New York
Lynch K 1960 *The Image of the City*. Technology Press, Cambridge, MA
Montello D R 1991 The measurement of cognitive distance: methods and construct validity. *Journal of Environmental Psychology* 11: 101–22
Portugali J (ed.) 1996 *The Construction of Cognitive Maps*. Kluwer, Dordrecht

R. Kitchin

Cognitive Modeling: Research Logic in Cognitive Science

Cognitive science is a genuinely interdisciplinary field, which owes its existence to the insight that, in different disciplines, interesting research was based on the common assumption that cognition could be regarded as computation (see *Artificial Intelligence in Cognitive Science; Cognitive Science: Overview*). It follows that if cognition is computation, theories of cognition should be specified in terms of representations and the computational steps performed on them. Thus, cognitive modeling follows naturally from the basic tenet of cognitive science.

Cognition has been addressed by philosophy for at least 2,500 years, by psychology since well into the nineteenth century, and by artificial intelligence since the mid-twentieth century –anyone would be ill-advised to mistake cognitive science as the only science of cognition. In fact, it overlaps considerably with cognitive psychology and parts of several other disciplines. Cognitive modeling is a unifying methodology for the whole field of cognitive science.

Cognitive modeling combines research methods of vastly different origin. The first group consists of techniques of formal analysis of tasks and systems, usually from philosophy, logic, theoretical linguistics, mathematics, physics, and the foundations of computer science. The second group consists of the empirical methods used predominantly in experimental psychology and in neuroscience, which are used to test models for cognitive adequacy. Finally, the third group of methods are the programming techniques developed in artificial intelligence, which are used to build working computer models. As a whole, the methodology combines formal and empirical analysis with constructive synthesis.

To identify cognitive modeling with computer simulation would be wrong for two reasons: first, we would ignore that building the computer model is just one, albeit essential, part of the methodology. Second, a computer simulation may be successful if it produces the same kinds of results, such as a commercial chess program, but a cognitive model (e.g., of a human cognitive function) must arrive demonstrably at the same results through the same kinds of computations (see also *Social Simulation: Computational Approaches*).

1. Cognitive Modeling as Second-order Model Construction

1.1 Epistemological Perspective

Cognition comprises sophisticated means of a system's adaptation to its environment, notably planning, which in turn draws on anticipation of the results of actions. Anticipation rests on learning and, in its most advanced forms, on episodic memory. Planning and decision rely on mental representations of the system's environment (world model) and the system as an actor in it (the system's self-model). The construction of these models is constrained by the interaction between system and environment. In the case of organisms, the necessities of evolution have ensured that internal world models are sufficiently realistic to be adaptive and ensure the survival of the species. In technical cognitive systems (e.g., autonomous robots), the need also arises to represent important features of the

environment. Cognition therefore implies modeling the environment, the system itself, and other systems (as in discourse models used in communication).

Science in general aims at constructing models. Cognitive science attempts to model cognition in biological as well as technical systems. And since model building (in the sense discussed ʿbove) is an essential part of cognition, scientific models of cognition are about how cognitive systems construct models of their environment and of themselves. In short, cognitive modeling amounts to second-order modeling (and it is important to keep both levels well apart).

1.2 General Characteristics of Models

A model is a mapping from an empirical domain (a set of elements and certain relations defined between them) to another one, the model domain (often a numerical one, as in measurement). Modeling is constrained on both sides. The empirical domain, as viewed for modeling, is a highly reduced abstraction, and the model domain (a formal system) often includes relations that are not relevant to the model at all.

Scientific models are abstractions in the sense that the empirical domain grasped by the model comprises only part of the objects (elements) and their relations. Which ones to select depends on the epistemological interest, i.e., on the theoretical perspective as well as on intended applications. For instance, a typical driver's map of some region ignores geology, climate, biology, etc., and concentrates exclusively on roads, abstracting even there from most of the details. In cognitive modeling, we usually focus on certain aspects of mental representations (e.g., of a memory trace), and some relation or relations, which may be as different as association (linking two elements) and entailment (the semantic relation of logical implication between two statements).

On the model side, we must be careful to define which of the many known relations in the formal system being used to model the empirical domain is part of the model. This is well known from psychological scaling, where only a few of the relations known to hold among real numbers (if those have been chosen as the model domain) are valid model characteristics. For example, only the relation $\geq$ may be valid for an ordinal scale, while differences and ratios between numbers are meaningless. Likewise, the computer programs typically chosen in cognitive modeling exhibit a wealth of parameters and other details of data structures and control flow, some of which are certainly irrelevant as an aspect of the model. With computer programs, however, it is much more difficult to analyze just which relations are valid parts of the model (see Sect. 5.2).

2. Model Domains for Cognitive Modeling

The traditional framework of cognitive modeling has been defined by Marr (1982) and Newell (1982). They distinguish an abstract level of cognitive theory (the knowledge level) from the level of description typically chosen in cognitive modeling (symbol level, or algorithmic level). The level below that (implementation level) is considered as irrelevant to cognitive modeling. This does not exclude the construction of computational models for specific implementations, however. Such models have been used with much success as mediators between psychological and neurobiological analyses of brain functioning.

2.1 Symbol-processing Approaches

According to Newell and Simon (see *Artificial Intelligence: Connectionist and Symbolic Approaches; Cognitive Science: Overview; Problem Solving and Reasoning, Psychology of*), cognitive processes are symbol transformations on arbitrary complex symbol structures (i.e., mental representations). Accordingly, the classical approach to cognitive modeling aims to construct programs that manipulate symbol structures of compositional semantics by means of algorithms taken from artificial intelligence (e.g., heuristic search). This approach adheres closely to the Turing Machine model of computation.

This approach provides considerable degrees of freedom regarding how to go about constructing models. In practice, most of the work has made use of a production system architecture, or of a declarative knowledge base coupled with an inference algorithm. Therefore, the *if–then* rules of production systems and logical statements (e.g., the Horn clauses used in Prolog) are among the most widely used formalisms for cognitive modeling. Semantic networks, or frames, with inheritance (the *is a* relation) are another well-known example of this approach.

2.2 Connectionist Approaches

These approaches are different with respect to the algorithmic level. Simple elements or 'nodes' (which may be regarded as abstract neurons, see *Artificial Intelligence: Connectionist and Symbolic Approaches; Connectionist Approaches*) are connected in a more or less pre-specified way, the connectionist network's architecture. Each element's output is a function of its inputs integrated over time, and is passed on to other nodes that are connected with it. Two groups of connectionist models can be distinguished according to the semantics of representation employed: parallel distributed processing (PDP) and localist networks. In the latter each node is a representation of something (e.g., a concept), whereas in PDP it is the vector of activation values taken over a number of nodes that

has representative character. This aspect of PDP models has been highlighted as pertaining to a 'subsymbolic' level by Smolensky (1988), who also stresses that artificial neural networks define a computational architecture that is nearer to symbol processing than to biological neural networks.

2.3 Nonlinear Dynamics and Other Approaches

Connectionist models, relying on differential equations rather than logic, paved the way to simulations of nonlinear dynamic systems (imported from physics) as models of cognition (see also *Self-organizing Dynamical Systems*).

Purely descriptive mathematical models have also been used in cognitive science, of course, but they do not take the form of an implemented computer program, and hence cannot be considered to be at the heart of cognitive modeling, but rather to be part of the formal analyses typically executed to arrive at sound specifications for cognitive models (see *Mathematical Models in Philosophy of Science*).

3. Cognitive Modeling and Cognitive Architectures

3.1 Unified and Modular Theories of Cognition

The process of cognitive modeling makes use of computational architectures, as we have seen for symbol processing and connectionist frameworks. As a special case, the framework may be a general theory about the architecture of the human mind, usually called a cognitive architecture.

Relying on a general cognitive architecture is to assume that all cognitive processes instantiate the same principle (e.g., firing a production rule). The present state of cognitive science casts doubt on the reasonableness of this assumption. The functional organization of the human brain is such that cognitive functions may be highly specialized, neuroanatomically focused, not open to introspection, and working in parallel with other cognitive processes (Kolb and Wishaw 1990).

3.2 General Cognitive Architectures

All these architectures take the form of a production system. This computational architecture, developed in the 1960s, comprises knowledge in the form of production rules (*if–then* rules), contained in a permanent memory, plus a working memory of unlimited capacity and a rule interpreter for control. Several lines of development have led to a number of systems that claim to be both a unified theory of human cognition and a program development environment for cognitive modeling, among them SOAR (Laird et al. 1987, Newell 1990), ACT, known best in the versions ACT* (Adaptive Control of Thought; Anderson 1983) and its revision, ACT-R (Atomic Components of Thought; Anderson and Lebiere 1998), and others such as CAPS, EPIC, or PRODIGY. Apart from being production systems at heart, all these architectures differ markedly. For instance, SOAR relies on productions only, whereas ACT* also has a declarative memory (a spreading activation network of unlimited capacity). Both address learning, but differently (see Johnson (1998) for a more extensive comparison of ACT and SOAR). ACT-R (following EPIC there) now also includes a number of perceptual and motor components. This means that at least some of these architectures have grown beyond a uniform approach.

The advantages of modeling within a cognitive architecture are obvious. Much of the work of modeling has already been done, and programmers can use special predefined functions. At least the architectures of long-standing tradition (ACT and SOAR) boast a number of successful empirical tests and applications (see also *Cognitive Theory: ACT*; *Cognitive Theory: SOAR*. Drawbacks are that the modeler is confined to a specific architecture and its means, and that these architectures have grown so big that it becomes difficult to assess an architecture's relevance to some specific small-scale model.

3.3 Alternative Computational Frameworks

Cognitive modeling may be based on almost any computational model. These may be specialized (tailored) processing architectures of artificial intelligence, such as the blackboard architecture (Hayes-Roth 1985), case-based reasoning (see *Problem Solving and Reasoning: Case-based*), or architectures for autonomous social agents (see *Autonomous Agents*). Beyond symbol processing, we find connectionist models of the PDP (see McClelland (1999) for an overview) or the localist orientation (Page 2000). Arbitrary combinations of different approaches (hybrid systems) may also be employed (see also *Artificial Intelligence: Connectionist and Symbolic Approaches*).

It may be advantageous to base one's model of a specific cognitive function on a computational framework that is ideally suited for the task, and do without the massive overhead of the big cognitive architectures. The usual drawback is that one cannot build on the long work of others. COGENT (Cooper and Fox 1998) promises to ease the work of individual model building by providing, in modern object-oriented programming style, a toolkit for cognitive modeling with a user-friendly graphical interface for development.

At present, it is difficult to recommend a particular computational framework for cognitive modeling. What works best, or what is easier to develop, depends heavily on one's own experience, and on the cognitive function one wants to model.

4. Cognitive Modeling Produces Theories

The computer programs resulting from cognitive modeling have the status of a well-formulated theory about cognition. They have the advantage of being explicit (no computer would execute a 'magic' command) and fully specified (for the same reason), which means that theories cannot focus on certain issues while leaving others in the dark—something that is just too easily done on paper. As soon as the program has been implemented successfully on a computer, and produces the expected output, this is proof of the logical consistency of the theory and positive evidence (proof being impossible) for its adequacy.

4.1 Generative Theories as Compared with Scientific Laws

The most important characteristic of cognitive modeling is that it results in generative theories: computer programs that not only explain, but actually *produce*, the cognitive phenomena in question. This is very different from 'natural laws' stating, for example, that in our universe, nothing can travel with a speed beyond that of light.

Models in psychology and other behavioral and social sciences usually take the form of a system of equations for computing the value of some variables given the value of some other variables. These models, however, do not give a detailed explanation (as in an algorithm, i.e., a step-by-step computation without any 'magical' operations) of how the resulting values are arrived at. Being generative is the main advantage of cognitive models.

4.2 Validation Strategies in Cognitive Modeling

Cognitive modeling is more than just constructing a computer program that produces data more or less indistinguishable from 'real data' as gathered in psychological experiments. As a methodology, it includes testing and comparing models. This is where the pitfalls of cognitive modeling lie: they do not render themselves easily to the falsification strategy (Popper 1968) usually recommended in science.

First, anyone who has constructed a model that seems to work well is reluctant to focus on its weaknesses (but this is typical of all science: no one should misinterpret Popper as obliging individual scientists to falsify their own theories; it is sufficient that there are other scientists around to do that.) Second, the programs that are the result of cognitive modeling are often highly complex, and their relation to empirical data cannot been tested exhaustively, but only for specific cases. Third, there is a fundamental problem: it is always the case that many models (each consisting of a representational and an operational, or process, part) may fit the same data.

Criteria for the empirical assessment of models are: good fit to data in essential aspects (e.g., difficulty of tasks is reflected in computational effort in the model; the model produces preferences, or errors, of the kind found in human subjects, etc.), and formal qualities (e.g., the fewer parameters on which the model depends, the better: a variant of Occam's razor). Typically, some empirical studies give rise to the model, and further empirical studies are used to test it.

Formal analyses of the tasks used in the domain (e.g., analyzing the syntactic structure and complexity of sentences in computational psycholinguistics) can and should be used not only to find hints as to how a model could be constructed, but also to exclude classes of models.

4.3 An Evaluation of Cognitive Modeling

Cognitive modeling is the research methodology which follows from the basic tenet of cognitive science that the essential aspect of cognition is that it is a computational process. Its main assets are that it produces theories which are explicit, complete, consistent, and generative. Formal analyses of the domain as well as empirical studies are required both as a prerequisite for the construction of models, and as the means of validating these models, e.g., to test their generalizability. Cognitive science since the 1970s has demonstrated that this is an extremely successful research strategy.

For further information, the reader is referred to Scarborough and Sternberg (1999) for an excellent collection of approaches to cognitive modeling.

See also: Computational Approaches to Model Evaluation; Connectionist Models of Concept Learning; Connectionist Models of Development; Connectionist Models of Language Processing; Knowledge Representation; Network Models of Tasks; Neural Networks: Biological Models and Applications; Scientific Discovery, Computational Models of

Bibliography

Anderson J R 1983 *The Architecture of Cognition*. Harvard University Press, Cambridge, MA

Anderson J R, Lebiere C 1998 *Atomic Components of Thought*. Lawrence Erlbaum Associates, Hillsdale, NJ

Cooper R, Fox J 1998 COGENT: A visual design environment for cognitive modeling. *Behavior Research Methods, Instruments and Computers* **30**: 553–64

Hayes-Roth B 1985 A blackboard architecture for control. *Artificial Intelligence* **26**: 251–321

Johnson T R 1998 A comparison between ACT-R and SOAR. In: Schmid U, Krems J F, Wysotzki F (eds.) *Mind Modelling: a Cognitive Science Approach to Reasoning, Learning and Discovery*. Pabst, Berlin, pp. 17–37

Kolb B, Wishaw I Q 1990 *Fundamentals of Human Neuropsychology*. Freeman, San Francisco

Laird J E, Newell A, Rosenbloom P S 1987 SOAR: An architecture for general intelligence. *Artificial Intelligence* **33**: 1–64

Marr D 1982 *Vision. A Computational Investigation into the Human Representation and Processing of Visual Information*. Freeman, San Francisco

McClelland J L 1999 Cognitive modeling: Connectionist. In: Wilson R A, Keil F C (eds.) *The MIT Encyclopedia of the Cognitive Sciences*. MIT Press, Cambridge, MA, pp. 137–44

Newell A 1982 The knowledge level. *Artificial Intelligence* **18**: 87–127

Newell A 1990 *Unified Theories of Cognition*. Harvard University Press, Cambridge, MA

Page M 2000 Connectionist modelling in psychology: A localist manifesto. *Behavioral and Brain Sciences* **23**: 443–512

Popper K R 1968 *The Logic of Scientific Discovery*, 5th edn. Hutchinson, London

Scarborough D, Sternberg S (eds.) 1999 *Methods, Models, and Conceptual Issues*. MIT Press, Cambridge, MA

Smolensky P 1988 On the proper treatment of connectionism. *Behavioral and Brain Sciences* **11**: 1–74

G. Strube

Cognitive Neuropsychology, Methodology of

Cognitive neuropsychology is the study of what one can learn about the organization of the cognitive system from observing the behavior of neurological patients. Its utility derives from one aspect of the organization of the cerebral cortex, namely the relative localization of function, such that different regions of the cortex are differentially involved in different types of cognitive process. Thus patients can have disorders that are relatively specific to a single cognitive process, and so investigation of their impairments can provide critical information on the nature of the process.

One still controversial example is that of the so-called 'category-specific disorders' in which the patient loses the ability to identify one particular class of item. Thus certain patients with herpes simplex encephalitis can virtually entirely lose the ability to identify animals, plants, and foods, but show a far better preservation of their knowledge of human artifacts (Warrington and Shallice 1984). This is a loss of knowledge and not of early perceptual processes or the lower levels of language. By contrast other patients can be considerably better at identifying the 'animate categories' than human artifacts (Warrington and McCarthy 1983). This double dissociation was originally interpreted in terms of the semantic representations of sensory quality knowledge being stored separately from knowledge about function, the latter being the more critical for identifying artifacts. Such an approach has been elaborated into quite complex models (e.g., Farah and McClelland 1991). Alternative ways of modeling the double dissociation have, however, been produced (e.g., Gonnerman et al. 1997, but see Garrard et al. 1998). Moreover the original results have led to extensive functional-imaging investigations of the regions activated when different types of knowledge are concerned (e.g., Moore and Price 1999).

Very different methodologies have been used when patients are studied experimentally for what they can tell about the organization of cognitive functions. In the early twentieth century, when the nineteenth-century method of rather casual clinical descriptions was rejected for a more scientific approach, patients began to be studied as groups. Initially this took the form of a series of case histories (e.g., Head 1926), but in the 1950s and 1960s it became normal to average behavior over patients with particular characteristics. Groups could be defined by their gross lesion site (e.g., Milner 1958), or in terms of their global syndrome (e.g., in language fluent vs. nonfluent aphasia deriving from the work of Goodglass et al. 1964).

This approach has remained the standard one for those approaching neuropsychology with either a physiological psychology or clinical background. However in the 1960s and 1970s researchers more influenced by cognitive psychology began to use single-case studies increasingly because they were held to capture more satisfactorily from a theoretical perspective the essence of selective disorders corresponding to impairments of single cognitive processes. Indeed, in the 1980s it became popular amongst this group of researchers to argue that only single-case studies could be properly said to produce behavioral findings from neurological patients from which one could draw theoretical conclusions about the organization of the normal cognitive system (Ellis 1987). The position was best articulated by Caramazza (1986), whose argument was essentially that the behavior of the average of a group of subjects was not necessarily equivalent to that of any possible patient in the group. The argument will be discussed in more detail below.

One may now distinguish a variety of different types of experimental methods in regular use in cognitive neuropsychology. However I will begin with the simplest and arguably the most powerful method.

1. The Single-case Study

In this type of study one selects for study a patient whose disorder appears to be in conflict with the implications of an existing theory, or to suggest a novel theoretical possibility. An example of the first type of situation is the study of patient KF (Shallice and Warrington 1970), where it was shown that the patient performed quite normally on a variety of tests of auditory-verbal long-term memory but was grossly impaired on measures of what would now be called the 'phonological buffer' (Baddeley 1986), such as the recency component of the (auditory-verbal) free recall serial position curve. This was in conflict with memory theory of the time, which held that the laying down of information in the long-term (secondary) memory system required that it be retained initially in a short-term (primary) memory system. The study showed that measures of auditory-verbal long-term memory could be normal even if measures of auditory-verbal short-term memory were grossly impaired, and was held to be in conflict with a serial organization of the short- and long-term verbal memory systems.

An example of the second type is the analysis of the writing disorder of patient LB (Caramazza et al. 1987). In this study it was shown that semantic variables did not influence LB's rate of spelling errors, and also that lexical variables had little effect, but that performance was strongly dependent on word length. Moreover the errors could nearly always be interpreted in terms of single or double operations on single letters, such as substitutions, deletions, insertions, and transpositions. The pattern was held to support the existence of a graphemic buffer which held abstract letter-level information while words were being written.

Studies of these sorts should involve either two or three stages following the stage of patient selection. *First, one needs to carry out standard clinical (baseline) tests.* The single-case study methodology differs from that in most other sciences in that replication of any given result is not generally possible for other researchers in the field. If a highly counterintuitive result is obtained with apparently major theoretical consequences, such as the initial observations of category-specific semantic memory dissociations (e.g., Nielson 1946) or the observations of object-based neglect described in patient NG (Caramazza and Hillis 1990), then it is not open to other workers in the field to attempt to replicate it. They generally do not have access to the patient. Therefore it is necessary that as rich a description of the patient's general cognitive characteristics are given so as to provide the raw material for other researchers in the field to produce alternative explanations of any novel experimental findings. This is best provided by giving the patient's performance on standard clinical tests in the particular cognitive domain.

Second, the investigation will involve tests used to examine particular theoretical possibilities for the patient's difficulties. These can be obtained from the experimental psychological or neuropsychological literature or be specifically constructed. It is normally necessary that control data from normal subjects also be provided. Again because of the general impossibility of replicating investigations in findings in single-case studies, all theoretical inferences drawn from the patient's performance should be based on the results of at least two experiments, or on a patient-internal replication of a single experiment. It is inappropriate to draw theoretical inferences from a single unreplicated experimental finding.

The third and optional stage of the procedure is a detailed analysis of the patient's performance in certain tests, rather than just using overall scores. This can include the effects of relevant stimulus variables, of different error types, of consistency of performance on the same items across replications of the same material, and so on.

The theoretical utility of the single-case study needs to be considered in the context of two different types of model. The first are models of the global cognitive architecture in a given domain in which the components are functional subsystems (Posner 1978) that are anatomically isolable and so can be individually damaged by neurological disease. Such models can be characterized as having a *modular functional architecture* where the term 'modular' is used with a less specific referent than in Fodor's (1983) sense. For such models, when a single subsystem is damaged, one will obtain a dissociation between impaired performance on tasks which require the subsystem and intact performance on tasks which do not require it. A standard move in cognitive neuropsychology is to treat the existence of a set of dissociations in a patient between tasks Y_1 to Y_i and task N_1 to N_j as evidence in favor of models where the pattern can arise from damage to one or more subsystems or connections, and against models where no such combination can produce the observed *overall pattern of performance*. This however depends on the following assumptions which are derived in part from those of Caramazza (1986) (see Shallice 1988 for a much more extensive discussion):

(a) Cognitive subsystems are qualitatively and quantitatively similar across individuals, at least by comparison with the effects of neurological disease.

(b) The task procedure, used by the patient, in the sense of the cognitive schemas that are controlling the overall operation of the collection of functional subsystems involved, does not differ markedly from that in use by normal subjects. This implies that the patient is not using a strategy unusual in normals, as, for instance, in letter-by-letter reading, which involves sounding out each letter in turn and then attempting to read by combining them into a word, as is found in the syndrome pure alexia.

(c) Reorganization of function following the lesion has had no more than a secondary effect in task performance. Clearly if the patient's cognitive system is qualitatively different from a normal system in its organization of subsystems, it will not be possible to make inferences from the patient's performance to the organization of the normal system.

(d) The tasks N_1 to N_j, on which performance is impaired, are not more demanding of some critical cognitive resource than tasks Y_1 to Y_i where performance is intact.

The most complex of these is the last, the presupposition that for most behavioral purposes the effects of damage to a subsystem can be ordered on a single dimension—resource. It has been argued by Glymour (1994) that the introduction of this concept makes cognitive neuropsychology a theoretically intractable enterprise, as far as the determination of the modular functional architecture using the observed overall pattern of performance of patients is concerned. Glymour argues that the degrees of freedom open to possible explanations would be greater than the constraints imposed by the observations of task performance. However, that analyses based on the resource concept can in practice be used to differentiate between alternative models has been shown in the concrete case of phonological output buffer disorder by Shallice et al. (2000).

The introduction of the resource concept allows one to infer that if a complementary set of dissociations is observed in a second patient producing a *double dissociation*, in at least one of the two cases, the pattern of Y_1 to Y_i contrasting with N_1 to N_j cannot be explained merely in terms of differential resource demands on a single subsystem being made across the set of tasks (see Shallice 1988, Chap. 10 for extended discussion). It should be noted, however, that these arguments are restricted to modular cognitive architectures. The existence of a double dissociation does not entail that the underlying system is modular; other possibilities include a continuum of processing space, within which different regions are damaged, overlapping processing regions, and systems in which different levels or aspects of operation of a subsystem can be separately damaged, as for instance on-line processing and the capacity to learn (see Shallice 1988, Chap. 11). However one alternative which does seem to be ruled out is an equipotential distributed system (Bullanaria and Chater 1995, but see Plaut 1995).

Inferences in neuropsychology from impaired behavior to mechanism are not, however, restricted to inferences based on the overall pattern of performance and the global organization of a modular functional architecture (see McCloskey 2000). The second type of model is those specifying how particular subsystems operate. More detailed aspects of the patient's performance can give more specific information about the operation of a processing system. Thus, in attentional dyslexia, patients show migrations of letters from one word to another (e.g., 'flip snag' to 'snip flag') (Saffran and Coslett 1996). This is compatible with damage to a mechanism which specifies over which parts of the visual field the results of letter-form level analysis are admitted for higher-level processing (see Mozer 1991 for more detailed discussion of the theoretical implications of the disorder).

2. The Multiple-case Study and the Functional Syndrome

Any individual patient's performance can be influenced by a variety of factors which reduce its relevance for inferences to normal processing. The patient may have an idiosyncratic functional or anatomical organization of their cognitive system, use an unusual strategy in some tests, or the disorder may even be influenced by psychiatric factors, so-called 'functional overlay.' One pragmatic way of partially guarding against these possibilities is to report two or more patients showing the same pattern of symptoms.

Second, if a dispute arises about the interpretation of empirical aspects of the report of an individual case, there is no way it can be resolved, other than by further investigation of the patient's difficulties, or reanalysis of existing findings. In practice these approaches are only rarely undertaken. Therefore, the recourse tends to be to find alternative arguments on the basic theoretical position held, in which case the original findings become redundant. (An example of an unresolvable theoretical question in the *individual patient* is arguments of whether evidence for syllabic structure in graphemic buffer disorder patient LB represents the effects of orthographic or phonological based processes; see Caramazza and Miceli 1990, Jonsdottir et al. 1996).

One way of making the neuropsychological database more solid is to establish *functional syndromes*, or characteristics held in common by all of a group of patients. However, a combination of characteristics can arise because of the anatomical proximity of *different* functional systems, producing so-called associated deficits. The concept of functional syndrome has therefore often been rejected metatheoretically on the grounds that a single counterexample can lead to the collapse of the putative functional syndrome. This is not necessarily the case. The functional syndrome may *fractionate* with both subvarieties being theoretically interpretable; one example is the two varieties of so-called letter-by-letter readers who circumvent the word-reading difficulty induced by their pure alexia. One group uses the names of the letter forms and knowledge of the spelling; the other uses a sounding-out strategy (see Patterson and Kay 1982). Moreover, the overall performance of a single patient can also derive from multiple impairments. This is not therefore an argument against the functional syndrome perspective, given that one restricts functional syndromes to ones in which all patients behave in the same fashion, and treats the subsyndromes resulting from fractionation of an original functional syndrome as each requiring theoretical explanation. The functional syndrome is therefore a concept which has the utility of producing a more solid database on which to assess alternative theories (see, for example, Shallice et al. 2000 for a concrete example of the approach).

Functional syndromes are of relevance for theories other than modular ones. Connectionist models can predict functional syndromes with complex characteristics too (see, for example, Mozer and Behrmann 1990). However, a different type of multiple single-case study is more usually relevant to this type of model. This is the use of a database for confronting theory of all patients showing deficits in a particular processing domain; their behavior is then individually fitted, but using different parameter values within a common underlying model. The prototypic example of this approach is the study of Dell et al. (1997) on naming errors in aphasics (but see Ruml et al. in press for detailed criticism).

3. The Anatomically Based Group Study

A method which is very frequently used is to group patients according to the location of lesion and average the results of each group. A potential problem with this approach is that patients in a given group may vary qualitatively as well as quantitatively. The reason is simple. The defining anatomical region will typically involve subsystems other than that which is the critical theoretical focus of the study. Thus Caramazza's (1986) argument on the functional heterogeneity of the group becomes relevant, in particular that the pattern of performance of the average of the group may not correspond to that of any individual representative of the group.

This possibility should not, however, be thought to invalidate the approach completely. While it presents a theoretical danger, its potency depends upon the nature of the averaged data and the nature of this theory. Thus, for certain types of theories the same problem occurs when the findings of normal subjects are confronted with theory. Second, for certain types of evidence, in particular double dissociations, it requires the conditions, which are *a priori* highly unlikely, for the pattern to arise as an average artifact and *not* be present in individual complementary pairs of subjects within the contrasting groups (see Shallice 1988, Chap. 9). Thus the existence of the double dissociation in the group data virtually always entails it occurring in specific pairs of individual subjects. This means that the situation when making inferences from the *overall pattern of performance* of groups to theory is virtually equivalent to that when making inferences from individual subjects. I know of no actual case where theoretical inferences from an anatomically based group study have been criticized as being vitiated by an averaging artifact.

A further key issue in anatomically based group studies is how to define the relevant region for patient inclusion. Typically, regions are defined *a priori*, such as lesions being confined to or involving a particular lobe. However, approaches are being developed in which determination of group membership is indirectly influenced by statistical procedures for analyzing functional-imaging results, such as statistical parametric mapping (SPM) (Friston 1997). This has resulted in the development of more complex procedures for determining the specification of the anatomical regions most appropriate for most sharply differentiating good and poor performance on a given measure. For instance, Stuss et al. (1998) have used classification and regression test (CART) procedure (Breiman et al. 1984) to assign patients to subgroups.

4. The Functionally Based Group Study Approach

An alternative methodology is to constitute groups according to the functional characteristics, such as when studies contrast Broca's aphasics and Wernicke's aphasics, or amnesics and normal controls. In many respects the methodological issues raised are similar to those of the previous approach. However, a critical problem relates to the criteria used for group definition, and hence the possibility of replication. In studies contrasting amnesic and control groups, for instance, this has often been a critical issue (see Butters and Cermak 1974). However, in aphasia research it has been a key issue since the 1980s. Thus there has been a very long-standing and as yet unresolved controversy on whether the comprehension performance of Broca's aphasics mimics their production problems, in the sense of showing a dissociation between comprehension of active and passive sentences. Some early cases seemed to indicate that in certain patients it did not (see Berndt et al. 1996).

However, Grodzinsky et al. (1999) reject this meta-analysis on the grounds that it applied too loose criteria for patient selection. Some patients included, it was argued, were not Broca's aphasics. Caramazza et al. (2000) have pointed out that Berndt et al.'s findings are still obtained when the more restrictive criteria, endorsed by Grodzinsky et al., are applied.

To be satisfactory, this approach must be based on effective functional syndromes that do not fractionate and on good operational criteria for diagnosing them; Broca's and Wernicke's aphasia probably do not pass the test. The danger of the clinically based group study approach is that if the functional syndrome which is used to define group membership does fractionate, then the critique of Caramazza (1986) will be potentially highly relevant, and only very simple characteristics of the averaged findings will prove inferentially relevant.

See also: Brain Damage: Neuropsychological Rehabilitation; Case Study: Logic; Case Study: Methods and Analysis; Case-oriented Research; Cognitive Functions (Normal) and Neuropsychological Deficits, Models of; Neuropsychological Functioning, Assessment of

Bibliography

Baddeley A D 1986 *Working Memory*. Clarendon Press, Oxford, UK

Berndt R S, Mitchum C C, Haedinges A W 1996 Comprehension of reversible sentences in agrammatism: A meta-analysis. *Cognition* **58**: 289–308

Brieman L, Friedman J H, Olshen R A, Store C J 1984 *Classification and Regression Trees*. Wadworth, Belmont, CA

Bullinaria J A, Chater N 1995 Connectionist modelling: Implications for cognitive neuropsychology. *Language and Cognitive Processes* **10**: 227–64

Butters N, Cermak L S 1974 Some comments on Warrington and Baddeley's report of normal short-term memory in amnesic patients. *Neuropsychologia* **12**: 283–5

Caramazza A 1986 On drawing inferences about the structure of normal cognitive systems from the analysis of patterns of impaired performance: The case for single-patient studies. *Brain and Cognition* **5**: 41–66

Caramazza A, Hillis A E 1990 Spatial representation of words in the brain implied by studies of a unilateral neglect patient. *Nature* **346**: 267–9

Caramazza A, Miceli G 1990 The structure of graphemic representations. *Cognition* **27**: 243–97

Caramazza A, Cappa E F, Ray A, Berndt R S 2001 Agrammatic Broca's aphasia is not associated with a single pattern of comprehension performance. *Brain and Language* **76**: 158–84

Caramazza A, Miceli G, Villa G, Romani C 1987 The role of the graphemic buffer in spelling: Evidence from a case of acquired dysgraphia. *Cognition* **26**: 59–85

Dell G S, Schwartz M F, Martin N, Saffran E M, Gognon D A 1997 Lexical access in normal and aphasic speech. *Psychological Review* **104**: 801–38

Ellis A W 1987 Imitations of modelarity, or, the modularity of mind: Doing cognitive neuropsychology without syndromes. In: Coltheart M, Sartori G, Job R (eds.) *The Cognitive Neuropsychology of Language*. Erlbaum, London

Farah M J, McClelland J L 1991 A computational model of semantic memory impairment: Modality specificity and emergent category specificity. *Journal of Experimental Psychology General* **120**: 339–57

Fodor J A 1983 *The Modularity of Mind*. MIT Press, Cambridge, MA

Friston K 1997 Analysing brain images: Principles and overview. In: Frackowiak R S J et al. (eds.) *Human Brain Function*. Academic Press, San Diego, CA, pp. 25–42

Garrard P, Patterson K, Watson P C, Hodges J R 1998 Category specific semantic loss in dementia of Alzheimer's type. Functional-anatomical correlations from cross-sectional analyses. *Brain* **121**: 633–46

Glymour C 1994 On the methods of cognitive neuropsychology. *British Journal of Philosophy of Science* **45**: 815–35

Gonnerman L, Anderson E S, Devlin J T, Kempler D, Seidenberg M S 1997 Double dissociation of semantic categories in Alzheimer's disease. *Brain and Language* **57**: 254–79

Goodglass H, Quadfasel F A, Timberlake W H 1964 Phrase length and the type and severity of aphasia. *Cortex* **1**: 133–53

Grodzinsky Y, Pinango M M, Zurif E, Drai D 1999 The critical role of group studies in aphasia: Comprehension regularities in Broca's aphasia. *Brain and Language* **67**: 134–47

Head H 1926 *Aphasia and Kindred Disorders of Speech*. Cambridge University Press, Cambridge, UK

Jonsdottir M, Shallice T, Wise R 1996 Language-specific processes in graphemic buffer disorder. *Cognition* **59**: 169–97

McCloskey M 2001 The future of cognitive neuropsychology. In: Rapp B (ed.) *The Handbook of Cognitive Neuropsychology.* Psychology Press, Philadelphia, pp. 593–610

Milner B 1958 Psychological deficits produced by temporal-lobe excision. *Research Publications, Association for Research in Nervous and Mental Disease* **36**: 244–57

Moore C J, Price C J 1999 A functional neuroimaging study of the variables that generate category-specific object processing differences. *Brain* **122**: 943–62

Mozer M C 1991 *The Perception of Multiple Objects.* MIT Press, Cambridge, MA

Mozer M C, Behrmann M 1990 On the interaction of selective attention and lexical knowledge: A connectionist account of neglect dyslexia. *Journal of Cognitive Neuroscience* **2**: 96–123

Nielson J M 1946 *Agnosia, Apraxia, Aphasia: Their Value in Cerebral Localization.* Hoeber, New York

Patterson K E, Kay J 1982 Letter-by-letter reading: Psychological descriptions of a neurological syndrome. *Quarterly Journal of Experimental Psychology, Series A* **34**: 411–41

Plaut D C 1995 Double dissociation without modularity: Evidence from connectionist neuropsychology. *Journal of Clinical and Experimental Psychology* **17**: 291–321

Plaut D C, Shallice T 1993 Deep dyslexia: A case study of connectionist neuropsychology. *Cognitive Neuropsychology* **10**: 377–500

Posner M I 1978 *Chronometric Explorations of Mind.* Erlbaum, Hillsdale, NJ

Ruml W, Caramazza A 2000 An evaluation of a computational model of lexical access: Comment on Dell et al. 1997 *Psychological Review* **107**: 609–34

Saffran E M, Coslett B 1996 Attentional dyslexia in Alzheimer's disease: A case study. *Cognitive Neuropsychlogy* **13**: 205–28

Shallice T 1988 *From Neuropsychology to Mental Structure.* Cambridge University Press, Cambridge, UK

Shallice T, Warrington E K 1970 Independent functioning of the verbal memory stores: A neuropsychological study. *Quarterly Journal of Experimental Psychology* **22**: 261–73

Shallice T, Rumiati R I, Zadini A 2000 The selective impairment of the phonological output buffer. *Cognitive Neuropsychology* **17**: 517–46

Stuss D T, Benson D F 1984 Neuropsychological studies of the frontal lobes. *Psychological Bulletin* **95**: 3–28

Stuss D T, Alexander M P, Hamer L, Palumbo C, Dempster R, Binns M, Levine B, Izuakawa D 1998 The effects of focal anterior and posterior brain lesions on verbal fluency. *Journal of the International Neuropsychological Society* **4**: 265–78

Warrington E K, McCarthy R 1983 Category specific access dysphasia. *Brain* **106**: 859–78

Warrington E K, Shallice T 1984 Category specific semantic memory impairment. *Brain* **107**: 829–54

T. Shallice

Cognitive Neuroscience

The discipline has emerged in the 1990s at the interface between the neural sciences and the cognitive and computational sciences. On one side, it grows out of the traditions of cognitive psychology and neuropsychology, which use behavioral experiments to uncover the processes and mechanisms lying behind human cognitive functions, and of computational approaches within cognitive psychology, which rely on computational models to develop explicit mechanistic accounts of these functions. On the other side, it grows out of the traditions of behavioral, functional, and systems neuroscience, which use neurophysiological and neuroanatomical methods to explore the mechanisms underlying complex functions. It draws on findings and principles of cellular and molecular neuroscience. It joins these approaches with the use of new functional brain imaging methods, such as functional magnetic imaging (fMRI), positron emission tomography (PET), as well as other methods including electroencephalography (EEG) and magnetoencephalography (MEG), and with a growing research tradition in computational neuroscience.

1. The Microstructure of Cognition

1.1 Patterns of Activity Arising in Ensembles of Simple Elements

A starting point for cognitive neuroscience is the idea that a cognitive or mental state consists of a pattern of activity distributed over many neurons. For example, the experience an individual has when holding, sniffing, and viewing a rose is a complex pattern of neural activity, distributed over many brain regions, including the participation of neurons in visual, somatosensory, and olfactory, and possibly extending to language areas participating in representing the sound of the word 'rose' and/or other areas where activity represents the content of an associated memory that may be evoked by the experience.

These patterns of activation arise from excitatory and inhibitory interactions among the participating neurons, mediated by connections called synapses. The inputs neurons receive cause them to 'fire' or emit impulses called spikes or action potentials, which travel down their axons to synaptic terminals where they cause the release of chemicals that then have excitatory or inhibitory influences on the neurons on the other side of the synapse. The combined effect of the incoming signals to each neuron, together with its recent history, determines whether it will fire at a particular moment. Figure 1 indicates something of the fundamental circuitry involved, though it should be noted that only one out of 100 of the neurons in the tiny region shown (about 3×3 mm) are indicated. While the computations performed by individual neurons should not be underestimated (see *Neurons and Dendrites: Integration of Information*), it seems likely that what gives the system its power and complexity is the number of neurons involved (most estimates place the number in the human brain between 10 and 100 billion) and of the density of

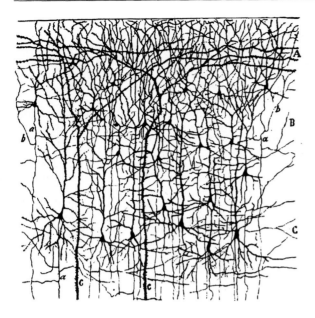

Figure 1
An early camera lucida drawing of the circuitry of the
neocortex, based on the Golgi stain method, which
impregnates just one out of every 100 cortical neurons.
The diagram depicts the rich dendritic branching
structure of the individual neurons present, whose cell
bodies appear as small, pyramid-shaped blobs. The
dendrites (and the little spines visible on the surfaces of
some of the larger dendrites) are the structures on
which the neurons receive most of their inputs from
other neurons

connections among them (typical cortical neurons
receive between 10,000 and 100,000 individual
synapses from other neurons).

1.2 Distributed Representations

A great deal of research has concerned the nature of
the active representations the brain uses for objects of
perception or cognition, such as the rose discussed
above. There is now a great deal of support for the
view that the brain's representations typically consist
of patterns of activity involving fairly large ensembles
of neurons. Individual neurons are often described as
'detectors' for particular stimulus or situational
features or conjunctions of features (e.g., the 'edge
detectors' introduced by Hubel and Weisel 1962 in
their seminal studies in visual cortex), but most such
neurons are fairly broadly tuned, so that they will also
be partially activated by a wide range of stimuli
overlapping in one way or another with the optimal
stimulus, and thus will participate at least partially in
the representation of many different inputs.

A prime example of distributed representation is the
representation of the direction of arm movements in
the motor cortex. It appears that the representation of
a particular direction of reaching is a pattern over a
large population of neurons, each of which responds
maximally to a particular preferred direction, but
responds to a lesser degree to neighboring directions,
and thus participates partially in the representation of
many different directions of reaching (Georgopoulos
et al. 1986). There are other types of distributed
representations used in the brain, in which a neuron
can participate in two different representations, without there being a clear shared feature or other
similarity between the situations that cause the neuron
to fire. For example, in the hippocampus, individual
neurons participate in distributed representations of
the animals' location in external space and other
aspects of the current behavioral situation. Interestingly, the same neurons may participate in different
ways in the representation of different environments,
or even of two distinct representations of the same
environment when the animal in performing different
tasks (Markus et al. 1995).

1.3 Knowledge and Learning in the Strengths of Connections

The particular pattern of activation that arises in
experiencing an input (or in reconstructing a memory
or formulating an imagined experience) is determined
by the connections among the neurons. A key issue,
then, is to understand the processes that lead to the
formation of the specific excitatory and inhibitory
connections that shape the processes of perception,
cognition, and action. Generally, it is thought that
largely activity independent processes establish an
initial skeleton framework of connectivity early in
development, for example, causing connections to
form between neurons in the retina of the eye and
other neurons in the lateral geniculate nucleus, a way
station for visual information on the way to the cortex.
Then, activity-dependent processes selectively refine
and stabilize some of the connections, and perhaps
cause new ones to form, while other connections are
pruned away.

Activity-dependent processes continue throughout
life, at least in many parts of the brain, and appear to
provide the basis of both explicit and implicit learning.
They have been the subject of intense scrutiny in
neuroscience. Donald Hebb, the mid-twentieth century neuropsychologist, proposed that if one neuron
participates in firing another, the connection from the
first to the second will be strengthened (Hebb 1949).
Hebb's idea has been encapsulated in the phrase 'cells
that fire together wire together.' While there is no
direct proof that this is a principle basis of learning in
the brain, the idea has received a great deal of
experimental support in experiments that have been

carried out in slices of brain tissue (see *Neural Plasticity*). It should be understood that there may also be plasticity at the level of the whole neuron (in some specialized brain areas, neurons are continually created and incorporated into circuits while others are continually being lost). There is likely also to be some plasticity at the level of the branches of axons and/or dendrites, which provide the scaffolding underlying the formation and loss of synaptic connections.

2. System-level Organization: The Macrostructure of Cognition in the Brain

2.1 Specialization of Brain Regions

A central and important fact about the organization of cognition in the brain is that individual brain regions are specialized. The cerebral cortex can be partitioned conceptually into primary, secondary, and tertiary cortical zones (Luria 1966). According to this conception, the primary areas contain neurons whose responses can be largely characterized as reflecting relatively simple, local properties of inputs or outputs within a given modality, such as the presence of an oriented line segment at a particular position on the retina of the eye, the presence of acoustic energy in a particular frequency band, or the presence of a tactile stimulus at a particular point on the skin surface. Corresponding motor areas contain neurons whose responses may correspond to the activation of specific muscles or elementary movement elements. Secondary areas contain neurons whose responses represent higher-order stimulus attributes within a given modality, such as conjunctions of features, and the representations in these areas may be relatively invariant over some lower-level properties, such as position of the stimulus containing the feature on the sensory surface (Tanaka 1996). Tertiary areas are responsible for representations that transcend individual modalities, such as representations of the current task context, or representation of one's location in extra-personal space, or representation of semantic content. It should be noted that this picture is only a very crude approximation, and many so-called primary areas appear to participate in the representation of the global structure of a stimulus or response situation, and many areas that are treated as modality specific can be modulated by influences from other modalities (see below). It should also be noted that structures outside the neocortex also play very important roles in cognitive functions. Among these are the diffuse neuromodulatory systems that regulate behavioral/cognitive states such as alertness, wakefulness, and mood; and other systems in the thalamus, lymbic system, and cerebellum.

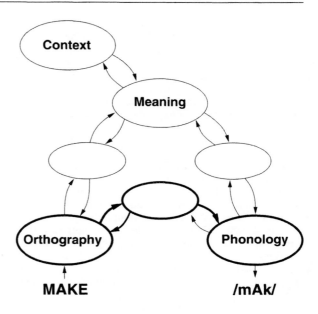

Figure 2
The interactive, distributed framework for modeling individual word reading of Seidenberg and McClelland 1989. All of the relevant processing pathways are assumed to be bidirectional

2.2 Modular vs. Interactive Approaches to the Organization of Function

The above provides only the starting place for the formulation of an understanding of how cognitive processes arise from neural activity. There are two contrasting views: (a) The modular approach, championed by David Marr for vision and Noam Chomsky for language, and systematized as a general approach by Fodor (1983), holds that the brain consists of many separate modules that are informationally encapsulated in that their operation is informed only by a very limited range of constraining sources of information. The modular view also holds that the principles of function are specific to each domain, and that distinct and individualized mechanisms are used to subserve each distinct function. For example, the initial assignment of the basic grammatical structure to a sentence is thought to be based only on the syntactic classification of words and their order and is thought to be governed by the operation of a system of structure sensitive rules. The module that carries out this assignment is thought to be structured specifically so that it will acquire and implement structure-sensitive rules, and to contrast in the principles that it employs internally with other modules that carry out other tasks, including other aspects of language processing, such as the assignment of meanings to the words in a sentence. In Fodor's view, there are many specialized modules (corresponding approximately to primary and secondary cortical areas and their sub-cortical inputs and outputs). These are complemented by a general-purpose cognitive system that is completely open-ended in the computations that it can undertake and in the range of informational sources that it can take into consideration.

The alternative, interactive approach, has its seeds in the ideas of Luria (1966), and has been championed by Mesulam (2000) and by Rumelhart et al. (1986), and overlaps with the ideas of Damasio (1989). On this view, cognitive outcomes such as the assignment of an interpretation to a sentence arise from mutual, bi-directional interactions among neurons in populations representing different types of information. An example of a system addressing the representations and interactions involved in reading individual words aloud is shown in Fig. 2. As the figure suggests, the formation of the sound of a word from a visual input specifying its spelling arises from an interactive process involving orthographic (i.e., letter identity), semantic, phonological, and contextual information. Both the modular and the interactive view are consistent with the idea that neurons in the brain are organized into populations specialized for representing different types of information. Where they differ is in the extent and the role of bidirectional interactions among participating brain areas.

2.3 Evidence of Interactive Processes in the Brain

The debate between modular and interactive approaches is a long-standing one, and can be seen as the modern legacy of a history of diverse views on the localization of functions within the brain (Luria 1966). While the debate is likely to continue to evolve with additional empirical evidence, it may be worth considering a few elements of evidence that support the idea that processing may be interactive. One relevant anatomical point is the fact that connectivity within and between brain areas is generally reciprocal: when there are connections from region A to region B, there are nearly always return connections.

While there is no consensus on the function of reciprocal connections, there is some evidence that they subserve distributed, interactive computations, at least in particular cases. For example, there is evidence that interactive processes influence the activation of individual neurons in primary visual cortex (Area V1). Traditionally, individual neurons in this area have been seen as encoding the presence of segments of oriented edges at particular positions in a visual display. Recent evidence suggests, however, that primary visual cortex participates in a distributed and interactive process that contributes to the representation of global stimulus properties such as figure-ground organization. The firing of neurons in primary visual cortex is strongly affected by temporary inactivation of corresponding portions of secondary

visual cortex, suggesting that reciprocal interactions between these areas shape neuronal responses in V1 (Hup et al. 2001). Although the initial response of neurons in V1 is determined by appropriate oriented line segments at a specific location, by about 80 ms their firing is heavily dependent on the global structure of the display (Lee et al. 1998). Furthermore, neurons in V1 respond to illusory contours that fall in their receptive field. The response occurs at a lag of about 80 ms, suggesting an indirect source, perhaps arising from feedback from higher cortical areas (Lee and Nguyen 2001). There is also considerable evidence of between modality interactions. For example, activity in auditory processing areas associated with speech perception is enhanced by visible speech (Callan et al. 2001). There are many corresponding examples of cross-modal influences in single neuron recording studies in animals.

3. Methods and Approaches in Cognitive Neuroscience

Cognitive neuroscience is a highly interdisciplinary endeavor, and draws on a wide range of research methods and approaches, each with its own history and underlying theoretical frame of reference. One important challenge for the field is to find ways of integrating the insights gained from the different methods to allow the field as a whole to converge on a common theoretical framework. Here the predominant research approaches are briefly described, and some of the prospects for integration are considered.

3.1 Lesion and Behavior Approaches (Cognitive Neuropsychology and Behavioral Neuroscience)

These research approaches within the field have the oldest historical roots, based as they often are in the assessment of the effects of naturally-occurring brain damage on cognitive function. A seminal case study was the report by Broca (1861) of a man with a severe disturbance of language arising from a large brain lesion in the posterior portion of the left frontal lobe. Since Broca's day, neurologists and neuropsychologists have investigated the effects of accidental or therapeutic brain lesions in humans, and many key insights have arisen from these studies (see *Agnosia*; *Amnesia*; *Aphasia*; *Dyslexia (Acquired) and Agraphia*). The subdiscipline of cognitive neuropsychology has arisen specifically around the study of the effects of brain lesions (see *Cognitive Neuropsychology, Methodology of*). A complementary has grown up around the use of brain lesions in animals carried out with specific experimental intent. This tradition is relevant to human cognitive neuroscience in view of the very close homology between many structures in the human brain and corresponding structures in the primate and rodent brains. This work has obvious advantages in that lesions can be carefully targeted to particular brain areas to test specific hypotheses (see *Lesion and Behavior Approaches in Neuroscience*). Many key insights have emerged from this work, including the discovery of complementary processing streams in the visual system (Ungerleider and Mishkin 1982; see *Neural Plasticity*). However, the approach is not without its pitfalls, since a lesion may have unintended and unobserved effects in other brain regions; the refinement and extension of experimental lesion techniques is ongoing.

3.2 Neuronal Recording Studies

Studies relying on microelectrodes to record from neurons in the brains of behaving animals can allow researchers to study the representations that the brain uses to encode information, and the evolution of these representations over time. Several fundamental observations have, some of which have been discussed above. These studies indicate, among other things, that the brain relies on distributed representations, that neurons participate dynamically and interactively in the construction of representations of external inputs, and that the representational significance of the firing of a particular neuron can vary as a function of context. Neuronal recording studies have had a profound impact on our understanding of the nature of representations of extrapersonal space. There are neurons in the brain that encode the location of objects in extrapersonal space simultaneously in relation to many different parts of the body, including the limbs and the head (Duhamel et al. 1991, Graziano and Gross 1993) and other neurons that encode the locations of objects in relation to other objects (Olson and Gettner 1995). Furthermore, recordings from neurons in parietal cortex suggest that when we move our eyes from one location to another, we update our internal representations of the locations of important objects in space, based on where we anticipate they will be after the upcoming eye movement (Duhamel et al. 1992).

An important recent development is the ability to record from up to 100 individual neurons at a time (see *Perception and Cognition, Single-/Multi-neuronal Recording Studies of*). A key finding that has come out of this work is the confirmation in studies with rodents that the simultaneous and successive patterns of activity acquired during behavior may be reactivated in the brain during subsequent sleep (Wilson and McNaughton 1994). Such methods are in their infancy, but their potential to shed light on the moment-by-moment relations between activations of different neurons and between distributed brain representations and specific inputs and outputs makes them essential to the future of cognitive neuroscience.

3.3 Functional Brain Imaging

Cognitive neuroscience has arisen as a separate discipline in tandem with the emergence of functional brain imaging methods (PET and fMRI) as major tools for the analysis of human cognition, and it may be that the prospect of visualizing specifically human cognitive activity has been a major catalyst. First used to analyze cognitive functions by the St. Louis group (Petersen et al. 1988; see *Functional Brain Imaging*), these methods are now coming into widespread use. While these methods currently have low temporal and spatial resolution compared to neuronal recording studies, they still provide our best opportunity to explore the neural mechanisms underlying distinctly human cognitive functions.

To date the observations arising from functional imaging studies have tended to corroborate findings from other methods, and/or to explore commonalities and differences in human and animal organization. As one recent example, it has now been possible to visualize the alternating strips in visual cortex reflecting what are known as ocular dominance stripes. Beyond corroboration, a great deal of new information has also been provided by functional brain imaging studies. For example, in a fairly early PET study, investigators found that an area of the cerebellum became active when subjects were required to generate the action that goes along with a concrete object (e.g., the word HAMMER requires a response such as 'pound'). Subsequent investigation of an individual with damage to this region of the cerebellum indicated that the patient had considerable difficulty with the generation task, confirming the importance of this area in the task.

Brain imaging studies, like lesion studies, have often been used to try to determine the loci in the brain associated with particular cognitive functions. However, in addition to this, brain imaging has begun to reveal a great deal about the plasticity of the brain, since patterns of brain activation can change dramatically with practice (Karni et al. 1998). Imaging is also being used in search of distributed networks in the brain that contribute to particular cognitive functions. For example, Just et al. (1996) have shown that as sentences become more complex, there is an increase in neural activity in an ensemble of brain regions, including Broca's and Wernicke's area on both the left and to a lesser degree the right side of the brain. As another example, investigators have begun to use covariation in neural activity in different brain regions in an effort to determine which brain regions are influencing each other's activation (Maguire et al. 2000) in different task situations.

Imaging methods (including magneto and electro-encephalography, as well as fMRI and PET) are likely to improve dramatically over time, allowing far higher spatial and temporal resolution. The potential for this to bring us closer to the goal of understanding the details of information processing in the human brain will be discussed below.

3.4 Computational and Mathematical Modeling Approaches

While investigations relying on lesion and behavior approaches, neuronal recording studies, and functional brain imaging have provided and will continue to provide the empirical evidence on which to build our understanding of the basis of cognitive functions in the brain, these approaches, even when used in a convergent way, may still fail to provide a complete understanding of how cognitive functions emerge from underlying neural activity. This may require the use of additional tools provided by mathematical modeling and computer simulation. These approaches allow researchers to formulate possible accounts of specific processes in the form of explicit models that can be analyzed mathematically or simulated using computers to determine whether they can account for all of the relevant neural and behavioral evidence.

Three examples of cases in which computational models have already led to new thinking will be briefly considered. First, a number of computational modeling studies have shown that many aspects of the receptive field properties of neurons and their spatial organization in the brain can arise through the operation of very simple activity-dependent processes shaped by experience and a few rather simple additional constraints (Linsker 1986, Miller et al. 1989; see *Neural Development: Mechanisms and Models*). Second, models may aid in the understanding of the pattern of deficits seen in patients with brain lesions. Certain patients with an acquired dyslexic syndrome known as deep dyslexia make a striking form or error known as semantic errors; for example the patient may misread APRICOT as 'peach.' In addition, all such patients also make visual errors, for example, reading SYMPATHY and 'symphony.' Early, noncomputational accounts postulated that there must be two separate lesions, one affecting visual processing and the other affecting semantic processing. However, computational models of the reading process (Hinton and Shallice 1991; see *Cognitive Functions (Normal) and Neuropsychological Deficits, Models of*) have shown that a single lesion affecting either the visual or the semantic part of an interactive neural network will lead to errors of both types. Thus, the coexistence of these errors may be an intrinsic property of the underlying processing architecture rather than a reflection of multiple distinct lesions. A third area where computational models have shed considerable light is in the interpretation of the receptive field properties of individual neurons (Zipser and Andersen 1988). While initial interpretations were based on verbally describable features such as oriented bars or edges, such properties are not always apparent, and even when

they are, a more detailed characterization may be possible in computational terms (Pouget et al. 1999). A further area of fertile research is in the use of computational models to explain and catalog the ways in which neuronal activation changes dynamically in the course of task performance (Moody et al. 1998).

4. Open Issues in Cognitive Neuroscience

Cognitive neuroscience is young, and there is a great deal of work to be done. No aspect of cognition is fully understood, and in general, the more abstract or advanced the cognitive function, the less is known about its neural basis. A few of the most important and interesting issues that remain to be addressed are considered briefly here.

4.1 How Does the Brain Learn?

There is a great deal known about the basic mechanisms of synaptic plasticity, but typically these are studied in highly reduced preparations such as brain slices. The basic processes that are studied in slices surely play a role in the shaping of neural connections in the whole, living brain, but they are also undoubtedly modulated by processes that are usually eliminated in slices. We know that attention and engagement in processing is essential for learning, and there is good reason to believe that learning is gated by various neuromodulatory mechanisms in the brain, but the details of the modulation and gating processes are only beginning to be explored.

4.2 What Makes an Experience Conscious?

Although some considerable progress has been made in characterizing the concomittants of consciousness (see *Consciousness, Neural Basis of*), there is no overall understanding of exactly what it is about the activity of the brain that gives it the attribute of consciousness. It appears likely that consciousness will not be localizable; although it may be highly dependent on specific brain structures (e.g., those that regulate sleep vs. wakefulness, etc.), it may well depend on the intact functioning of many interacting parts of the brain. Exactly why or how consciousness arises from these interactions is not at all understood.

4.3 What is the Basis for the Unique Cognitive Capacities of the Human Brain, Relative to that of Other, Simpler Organisms?

The issue of what sets humans apart from other organisms remains one of the central unresolved questions. The similarity of the human genome to that of closely related species can be taken in different ways. It can suggest to some that a very small number of specific faculties have been added which differentiate the human from, say, the chimpanzee; or it could suggest that rather than new faculties, the human brain really differs only in the expansion and extension of structures already present to a degree in other organisms. The idea that the highest cognitive functions are emergent functions rather than localizable or locally encoded in genes remains an attractive, though elusive possibility.

5. The Future of Cognitive Neuroscience

Nobel laureate Eric Kandel has suggested that cognitive neuroscience will increasingly assume center stage in the neurosciences in the twenty-first century, and it has begun to make dramatic inroads into the field of cognitive psychology, where many leading investigators have redirected their research to exploit ideas and methods from neuroscience. Future research in cognitive neuroscience will address the general issues raised above as well as many other topics. What makes the future of the field so exciting is the prospect of further development of a number of important contributing methodologies. Breakthroughs in functional brain imaging and other related methods are likely to provide far greater spatial and temporal resolution of brain activity. Another, very important area of methodological advance is the ability to create genetically altered brains especially in small mammals and invertebrates, and thereby to explore the consequences of these alterations for function (see *Memory: Genetic Approaches*). These methods have already reached the point where it is possible to allow an organism to develop normally, and then induce a region-specific gene knockout, thereby providing the opportunity to investigate, for example, the effect of the alternation of synaptic plasticity in a specific part of the brain. Breakthroughs should be expected in many other areas of cognitive neuroscience as well, including neuronal recording, functional imaging, and computational modeling approaches. Together, these methods will lead to a deeper understanding of how the highest capabilities of the human mind arise from the underlying physical and chemical processes in the brain.

See also: Animal Cognition; Brain, Evolution of; Cerebral Cortex: Organization and Function; Cognitive Control (Executive Functions): Role of Prefrontal Cortex; Cognitive Neuropsychology, Methodology of; Cognitive Psychology: History; Cognitive Psychology: Overview; Cognitive Science: History; Cognitive Science: Overview; Cognitive Science: Philosophical Aspects; Comparative Neuroscience; Computational Neuroscience; Evolutionary Social Psychology; Human Cognition, Evolution of

Bibliography

Broca P 1861 Remarques sur le siege de la faculte de la parole articulee, suives d'une observation d'aphemie (perte de parole). *Bulletin de la Societe d'Anatomie* **36**: 330–57

Callan D E, Callan A M, Kroos C, Vatikiotis-Bateson E 2000 Multimodal contribution to speech perception. *Cognitive Brain Research*

Damasio A R 1989 Time-locked multiregional retroactivation: A system-level proposal for the neural substrates of recall and recognition. *Cognition* **33**: 25–62

Duhamel J-R, Colby C L, Goldberg M E 1991 Congruent representations of visual and somatosensory space in single neurons of monkey ventral intraparietal cortex (area VIP). In: Paillard J (ed.) *Brain and Space*. Oxford University Press, Oxford, UK, pp. 223–6

Duhamel J-R, Colby C L, Goldberg M E 1992 The updating of the representation of visual space in parietal cortex by intended eye movements. *Science* **255**: 90–2

Fodor J A 1983 *Modularity of Mind: An Essay on Faculty Psychology*. MIT Press, Cambridge, MA

Georgopoulos A P, Schwartz A B, Kettner R E 1986 Neuronal population encoding of movement direction. *Science* **233**: 1416–9

Graziano M S A, Gross C G 1993 A bimodal map of space: Somatosensory receptive fields in the macaque putamen with corresponding visual receptive fields. *Experimental Brain Research* **97**: 96–109

Hebb D O 1949 *The Organization of Behavior*. Wiley, New York

Hinton G E, Shallice T 1991 Lesioning an attractor network: Investigations of acquired dyslexia. *Psychological Review* **98**(1): 74–95

Hubel D H, Weisel T 1962 Receptive fields, binocular orientation and functional architecture in the cat's visual cortex. *Journal of Physiology* **166**: 106–54

Hup J M, James A C, Girard P, Lomber S G, Payne B R, Bullier J 2001 Feedback connections act on the early part of the responses in monkey visual cortex. *Journal of Neurophysiology* **85**: 134–45

Just M A, Carpenter P A, Keller T A, Eddy W F, Thulborn K R 1996 Brain activation modulated by sentence comprehension. *Science* **274**(5284): 114–6

Karni A, Meyer G, Rey-Hipolito C, Jezzard P, Adams M M, Turner R, Ungerleider L G 1998 The acquisition of skilled motor performance: Fast and slow experience-driven changes in primary motor cortex. *Proceedings of the National Academy of Science USA* **95**(3): 861–8

Lee T S, Mumford D, Romero R, Lamme V A F 1998 The role of primary visual cortex in higher level vision. *Vision Research* **38**: 2429–54

Lee T S, Nguyen M 2001 Dynamics of subjective contour formation in early visual cortex. *Proceedings of the National Academy of Science USA*

Linsker R 1986 From basic network principles to neural architecture, I: Emergence of orientation columns. *Proceedings of the National Academy of Sciences USA* **83**: 7508–12

Luria A R 1966 *Higher Cortical Functions in Man*. Basic Books, New York

Maguire E A, Mummery C J, Buchel C 2000 Patterns of hippocampal-cortical interaction dissociate temporal lobe memory subsystems. *Hippocampus* **10**(4): 475–82

Markus E J, Qin Y, Leonard B, Skaggs W E, McNaughton B L, Barnes C A 1995 Interactions between location and task affect the spatial and directional firing of hippocampal neurons. *Journal of Neuroscience* **15**: 7079–94

Mesulam M M 2000 *Principles of Behavioral and Cognitive Neurology.* Oxford University Press, New York

Moody S L, Wise S P, di Pellegrino G, Zipser D 1998 A model that accounts for activity in primate frontal cortex during a delayed matching-to-sample task. *Journal of Neuroscience* **18**(1): 399–410

Olson C R, Gettner N 1995 Object-centered direction selectivity in the supplementary eye field of the macaque monkey. *Science* **269**: 985–8

Petersen S E, Fox P T, Posner M I, Mintun M, Raichle M E 1988 Positron emission tomographic studies of the cortical anatomy of single-word processing. *Nature* **331**: 585–9

Pouget A, Deneve S, Sejnowski T J 1999 Frames of reference in hemineglect: A computational approach. *Progress in Brain Research* **121**: 81–97

Rumelhart D E, McClelland J L, the PDP Research Group 1986 *Parallel Distributed Processing: Explorations in the Microstructure of Cognition. Vol. 1: Foundations.* MIT Press, Cambridge, MA

Seidenberg M S, McClelland J L 1989 A distributed, developmental model of word recognition and naming. *Psychological Review* **96**: 523–68

Tanaka K 1996 Inferotemporal cortex and object vision. *Annual Review Neuroscience* **19**: 109–39

Ungerleider L G, Mishkin M 1982 Two cortical visual systems. In: Ingle D J, Goodale M A, Mansfield R J W (eds.) *Analysis of Visual Behavior.* MIT Press, Cambridge, MA

Wilson M A, McNaughton B L 1994 Reactivation of hippocampal ensemble memories during sleep. *Science* **265**: 676–9

Zipser D, Andersen R A 1988 A back propagation programmed network that simulates response properties of a subset of posterior parietal neurons. *Nature* **331**: 679–84

J. L. McClelland

Cognitive Psychology: History

Since the beginning of experimental psychology in the nineteenth century, there had been interest in the study of higher mental processes. But something discontinuous happened in the late 1950s, something so dramatic that it is now referred to as the 'cognitive revolution,' and the view of mental processes that it spawned is called 'cognitive psychology.' What happened was that American psychologists rejected behaviorism and adopted a model of mind based on the computer. The brief history that follows (adapted in part from Hilgard (1987) and Kessel and Bevan (1985)) chronicles mainstream cognitive psychology from the onset of the cognitive revolution to the beginning of the twenty-first century.

1. Beginnings

From roughly the 1920s through the 1950s, American psychology was dominated by behaviorism. Behavior-ism was concerned primarily with the learning of associations, particularly in nonhuman species, and it constrained theorizing to stimulus–response notions. The overthrow of behaviorism came not so much from ideas within psychology as from three research approaches external to the field.

1.1 Communications Research and the Information Processing Approach

During World War II, new concepts and theories were developed about signal processing and communication, and these ideas had a profound impact on psychologists active during the war years. One important work was Shannon's 1948 paper about *Information Theory*. It proposed that information was communicated by sending a signal through a sequence of stages or transformations. This suggested that human perception and memory might be conceptualized in a similar way: sensory information enters the receptors, then is fed into perceptual analyzers, whose outputs in turn are input to memory systems. This was the start of the 'information processing' approach—the idea that cognition could be understood as a flow of information within the organism, an idea that continues to dominate cognitive psychology.

Perhaps the first major theoretical effort in information processing psychology was Donald Broadbent's *Perception and Communication* (Broadbent 1958). According to Broadbent's model, information output from the perceptual system encountered a filter, which passed only information to which people were attending. Although this notion of an all-or-none filter would prove too strong (Treisman 1960), it offered a mechanistic account of selective attention, a concept that had been banished during behaviorism. Information that passed Broadbent's filter then moved on to a 'limited capacity decision channel,' a system that has some of the properties of short-term memory, and from there on to long-term memory. This last part of Broadbent's model—the transfer of information from short- to long-term memory—became the salient point of the dual-memory models developed in the 1970s.

Another aspect of Information theory that attracted psychologist's interest was a quantitative measure of information in terms of 'bits' (roughly, the logarithm to the base 2 of the number of possible alternatives). In a still widely cited paper, George Miller (1956) showed that the limits of short-term memory had little to do with bits. But along the way, Miller's and others' interest in the technical aspects of information theory and related work had fostered mathematical psychology, a subfield that was being fueled by other sources as well (e.g., Estes and Burke 1953, Luce 1959, Garner 1962). Over the years, mathematical psychology has frequently joined forces with the information processing approach to provide precise claims about memory, attention, and related processes.

1.2 The Computer Modeling Approach

Technical developments during World War II also led to the development of digital computers. Questions soon arose about the comparability of computer and human intelligence (Turing 1950). By 1957, Alan Newell, J. C. Shaw, and Herb Simon had designed a computer program that could solve difficult logic problems, a domain previously thought to be the unique province of humans. Newell and Simon soon followed with programs that displayed general problem-solving skills much like those of humans, and argued that these programs offered detailed models of human problem solving (a classic summary is contained in Newell and Simon (1972)). This work would also help establish the field of artificial intelligence.

Early on, cross-talk developed between the computer modeling and information-processing approaches, which crystallized in the 1960 book *Plans and the Structure of Behavior* (Miller et al. 1960). The book showed that information-processing psychology could use the theoretical language of computer modeling even if it did not actually lead to computer programs. With the 'bit' having failed as a psychological unit, information processing badly needed a rigorous but rich means to represent psychological information (without such representations, what exactly was being processed in the information processing approach?). Computer modeling supplied powerful ideas about representations (as data structures), as well as about processes that operate on these structures. The resultant idea of human information processing as sequences of computational processes operating on mental representations remains the cornerstone of modern cognitive psychology (see e.g., Fodor 1975).

1.3 The Generative Linguistics Approach

A third external influence that lead to the rise of modern cognitive psychology was the development of generative grammar in linguistics by Noam Chomsky. Two of Chomsky's publications in the late 1950s had a profound effect on the nascent cognitive psychology. The first was his 1957 book *Syntactic Structures* (Chomsky 1957). It focused on the mental structures needed to represent the kind of linguistic knowledge that any competent speaker of a language must have. Chomsky argued that associations *per se*, and even phrase structure grammars, could not fully represent our knowledge of syntax (how words are organized into phrases and sentences). What had to be added was a component capable of transforming one syntactic structure into another. These proposals about

transformational grammar would change the intellectual landscape of linguistics, and usher in a new psycholinguistics.

Chomsky's second publication (1959) was a review of *Verbal Behavior*, a book about language learning by the then most respected behaviorist alive, B. F. Skinner (Skinner 1957). Chomsky's review is arguably one of the most significant documents in the history of cognitive psychology. It aimed not merely to devastate Skinner's proposals about language, but to undermine behaviorism as a serious scientific approach to psychology. To some extent, it succeeded on both counts.

1.4 An Approach Intrinsic to Psychology

At least one source of modern cognitive psychology came from within the field. This approach had its roots in Gestalt psychology, and maintained its focus on the higher mental processes. A signal event in this tradition was the 1956 book *A Study of Thinking*, by Bruner, Goodnow, and Austin (Bruner et al. 1956). The work investigated how people learn new concepts and categories, and it emphasized strategies of learning rather than just associative relations. The proposals fit perfectly with the information-processing approach— indeed, they were information processing proposals— and offered still another reason to break from behaviorism.

By the early 1960s all was in place. Behaviorism was on the wane in academic departments all over America (it had never really taken strong root in Europe). Psychologists interested in the information-processing approach were moving into academia, and Harvard University went so far as to establish a Center for Cognitive Studies directed by Jerome Bruner and George Miller. The new view in psychology was information processing. It likened mind to a computer, and emphasized the representations and processes needed to give rise to activities ranging from pattern recognition, attention, categorization, memory, reasoning, decision making, problem solving, and language.

2. The Growth of Cognitive Psychology

The 1960s brought progress in many of the above-mentioned topic areas, some of which are highlighted below.

2.1 Pattern Recognition

One of the first areas to benefit from the cognitive revolution was pattern recognition, the study of how people perceive and recognize objects. The cognitive approach provided a general two-stage view of object recognition: (a) describing the input object in terms of

a. Collins and Quillan Semantic Network

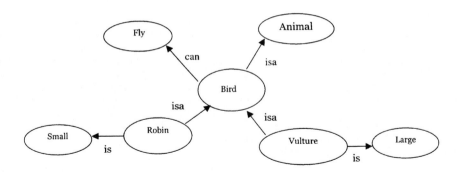

b. Anderson and Bower Propositional Network

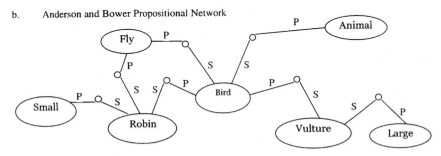

c. Simplified Connectionist Network

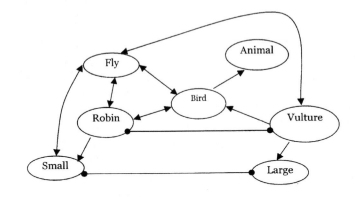

Figure 1
(a) Part of a Collins and Quillian (1969) semantic network. Circles designate concepts and lines (arrows) between circles designate relations between concepts. There are two kinds of relations: subset–superset ('Robin is a bird') and property (e.g., 'Robins can fly'). The network is strictly hierarchical, as properties are stored only at the highest level at which they apply. (b) Part of an Anderson and Bower (1973) propositional network. Circles represent concepts and lines between them labeled relations. All propositions have a subject–predicate structure, and the network is not strictly hierarchical. (c) Part of a simplified connectionist network. Circles represent concepts, or parts of concepts, lines with arrowheads depict excitatory connections, and lines with filled circles designate inhibitory connections; typically numbers are put on the lines indicate the strength of the connections. The network is not strictly hierarchical, and is more interconnected than the preceding networks

relatively primitive features (e.g., 'it has two diagonal lines and one horizontal line connecting them'); and (b) matching this object description to stored object descriptions in visual memory, and selecting the best match as the identity of the input object ('this description best matches the letter A'). This two-stage view was not entirely new to psychology, but expressing it in information-processing terms allowed one to connect empirical studies of object perception to computer models of the process. The psychologist Ulrich Neisser (1964) used a computer model of pattern recognition (Selfridge 1959) to direct his empirical studies and provided dramatic evidence that an object could be matched to multiple visual memories in parallel.

Other research indicated that the processing underlying object perception could persist after the stimulus was removed. For this to happen, there had to be a visual memory of the stimulus. Evidence for such an 'iconic' memory was supplied by Sperling in classic experiments in 1960 (Sperling 1960). Evidence for a comparable brief auditory memory was soon provided as well (e.g., Crowder and Morton 1969). Much of the work on object recognition and sensory memories was integrated in Neisser's influential 1967 book *Cognitive Psychology* (Neisser 1967). The book served as the first comprehensive statement of existing research in cognitive psychology, and it gave the new field its name.

2.2 Memory Models and Findings

Broadbent's model of attention and memory stimulated the formulation of rival models in the 1960s. These models assumed that short-term memory (STM) and long-term memory (LTM) were qualitatively different structures, with information first entering STM and then being transferred to LTM (e.g., Waugh and Norman 1965). The Atkinson and Shiffrin (1968) model proved particularly influential. With its emphases on information flowing between memory stores, control processes regulating that flow, and mathematical descriptions of these processes, the model was a quintessential example of the information-processing approach. The model was related to various findings about memory. For example, when people have to recall a long list of words they do best on the first words presented, a 'primacy' effect, and on the last few words presented, a 'recency' effect. Various experiments indicated that the recency effect reflected retrieval from STM, whereas the primacy effect reflected enhanced retrieval from LTM due to greater rehearsal for the first items presented (e.g., Murdock 1962, Glanzer and Cunitz 1966). At the time these results were seen as very supportive of dual-memory models (although alternative interpretations would soon be proposed—particularly by Craik and Lockhart 1972).

Progress during this period also involved empirically determining the characteristics of encoding, storage, and retrieval processes in STM and LTM. The results indicated that verbal material was encoded and stored in a phonologic code for STM, but a more meaning-based code for LTM (Conrad 1964, Kintsch and Buschke 1969). Other classic studies demonstrated

that forgetting in STM reflected a loss of information from storage due to either decay or interference (e.g., Wickelgren 1965), whereas some apparent losses of information in LTM often reflected a temporary failure in retrieval, (Tulving and Pearlstone 1966).To a large extent, these findings have held up during over 30 years of research, although many of the findings would now be seen as more limited in scope (e.g., the findings about STM are now seen as reflecting only one component of working memory, e.g., Baddeley (1986), and the findings about LTM are seen as characterizing only one of several LTM systems, e.g., Schacter (1987)).

One of the most important innovations of 1960s research was the emphasis on reaction time as a dependent measure. Because the focus was on the flow of information, it made sense to characterize various processes by their temporal extent. In a seminal paper in 1966, Saul Sternberg reported (Sternberg 1966) that the time to retrieve an item from STM increased linearly with the number of items in store, suggesting that retrieval was based on a rapid scan of STM. Sternberg (1969) gave latency measures another boost when he developed the 'additive factors' method, which, given assumptions about serial processing, allowed one to attribute changes in reaction times to specific processing stages involved in the task (e.g., a decrease in the perceptibility of information affected the encoding of information into STM but not its storage and retrieval). These advances in 'mental chronometry' quickly spread to areas other than memory (e.g., Fitts and Posner 1967, see also Schneider and Shiffrin 1977).

2.3 The New Psycholinguistics

Beginning in the early 1960s there was great interest in determining the psychological reality of Chomsky's theories of language (these theories had been formulated with ideal listeners and speakers in mind). Some of these linguistically inspired experiments presented sentences in perception and memory paradigms, and showed that sentences deemed more syntactically complex by transformational grammar were harder to perceive or store (Miller 1962). Subtler experiments tried to show that syntactic units, like phrases, functioned as units in perception, STM, and LTM (Fodor et al. (1974) is the classic review). While many of these results are no longer seen as critical, this research effort created a new subfield of cognitive psychology, a psycholinguistics that demanded sophistication in modern linguistic theory.

Not all psycholinguistic studies focused on syntax. Some dealt with semantics, particularly the representation of the meanings of words, and a few of these studies made use of the newly developed mental chronometry. One experiment that proved seminal was reported by Collins and Quillian (1969). Participants were asked simple questions about the meaning of a word, such as 'Is a robin a bird,' and 'Is a robin an animal?'; the greater the categorical difference between the two terms in a question, the longer it took to answer. These results were taken to support a model of semantic knowledge in which meanings were organized in a hierarchical network, e.g., the concept 'robin' is directly connected to the concept 'bird,' which in turn is directly connected to the concept 'animal,' and information can flow from 'robin' to 'animal' only by going through 'bird' (see the top of Fig. 1). Models like this were to proliferate in the next stage of cognitive psychology.

3. The Rise of Cognitive Science

3.1 Memory and Language

Early in the 1970s the fields of memory and language began to intersect. In 1973 John Anderson and Gordon Bower published *Human Associative Memory* (Anderson and Bower 1973), which presented a model of memory for linguistic materials. The model combined information processing with recent developments in linguistics and artificial intelligence (AI), thereby linking the three major research directions that led to the cognitive revolution. The model used networks similar to that considered above to represent semantic knowledge, and used memory-search processes to interrogate these networks (see the middle of Fig. 1). The Anderson and Bower book was quickly followed by other large-scale theoretical efforts that combined information processing, modern linguistics, and computer models. These efforts included Kintsch (1974), which focused on memory for paragraphs rather than sentences, and Norman, Rumelhart, and the LNR Research Group (1975), Anderson (1976), and Schank and Abelson (1977), which took a more computer-science perspective and focused on stories and other large linguistic units.

As psychologists became aware of related developments in linguistics and artificial intelligence, so researchers in the latter disciplines become aware of pertinent work in psychology. Thus evolved the interdisciplinary movement called 'cognitive science.' In addition to psychology, AI, and linguistics, the fields of cultural anthropology and philosophy of mind also became involved. The movement eventuated in numerous interdisciplinary collaborations (e.g., Rumelhart et al. 1986), as well as in individual psychologists becoming more interdisciplinary.

3.2 Representational Issues

In the 1970s and early 1980s, cognitive science was much concerned with issues about mental representa-

tions. Whereas the memory-for-language models described earlier had assumed representations that were language-like, or propositional, other researchers argued that representations could also be imaginal, like a visual image. Shepard and Cooper (1972) provided evidence that people could mentally rotate their representations of objects, and Kosslyn (1980) surveyed numerous phenomena that further implicated visual imagery. In keeping with the interdisciplinariness of cognitive science, AI researchers and philosophers entered the debate about propositional versus imaginal representations (e.g., Block 1981, Pylyshyn 1981). In addition to questions about the modality of representations, there were concerns about the structure of representations. While it had long been assumed that propositional representations of objects were like definitions, researchers now proposed the representations were *prototypes* of the objects, fitting some examples better than others (Tversky 1977, Mervis and Rosch 1981, Smith and Medin 1981). Again the issues sparked interest in disciplines other than psychology (e.g., Lakoff 1987).

The cognitive science movement affected most areas of cognitive psychology, ranging from object recognition (Marr 1982) to reasoning (e.g., Johnson-Laird 1983) to expertise in problem solving (e.g., Chase and Simon 1973). The movement continues to be influential and increasingly focuses on computational models of cognition. What has changed since its inception in the 1970s is the kind of computational model in favor.

4. Newer Directions: Connectionism and Cognitive Neuroscience

4.1 Connectionist Modeling

The computer models that dominated cognitive psychology from its inception used complex symbols as representations, and processed these representations in a rule-based fashion (for example, in a model of object recognition, the representation for a frog might consist of a conjunction of complex properties, and the rule for recognition might look something like 'If it's green, small, and croaks, it's a frog'). Starting in the early 1980s, an alternative kind of cognitive model started to attract interest, namely 'connectionist' (or 'parallel distributed processing') models. These proposals have the form of neural networks, consisting of nodes (representations) that are densely interconnected, with the connections varying in strength (see the bottom of Fig. 1).

In 1981 Hinton and Anderson published a book surveying then existent connectionist models (Hinton and Anderson 1981), and in the same year McClelland and Rumelhart (1981) presented a connectionist model of word recognition that explained a wide variety of experimental results. The floodgates had been opened, and connectionist models of perception, memory, and language proliferated, to the point where they now dominate computational approaches to cognition. Why the great appeal? One frequently cited reason is *neurological plausibility*: the models are clearly closer to brain function than are traditional rule-based models. A second reason is that connectionist models permit *parallel constraint satisfaction*: different sources of activation can converge simultaneously on the same representations or response. A third reason is that connectionist models manifest *graceful degradation*: when the model is damaged, performance degrades slowly, much as is found in human neurological disorders (Rumelhart et al. 1986).

From a historical viewpoint, there is an ironic aspect about the ascendancy of connectionist models. Such models return to the pure associationism that characterized behaviorism. While connectionist models hardly fit with all behaviorist dictums—their representations are not restricted to stimuli and responses, and they routinely assume massively parallel processing—still their reliance on associations runs counter to Chomsky's arguments that sheer associationism cannot explain language (Chomsky 1957, 1959). This issue has formed part of the basis for critiques of connectionist models (e.g., Fodor and Pylyshyn 1988). Newell (1990), one of the founders of traditional computational models, suggested a plausible resolution: lower-level cognitive processes like object recognition may be well modeled by connectionist models, but higher-level cognitive processes like reasoning and language may require traditional symbolic modeling.

4.2 Cognitive Neuroscience

The other major new direction in cognitive psychology is the growing interest in the neural bases of cognition, a movement referred to as 'cognitive neuroscience.' There had been little interest in biological work in the research that brought about the cognitive revolution. That early work was as much concerned with fighting behaviorism as it was with advancing cognitive psychology, and consequently much of the research focused on higher-level processes and was completely removed from anything going on in the neurobiology of its day. Subsequent generations of cognitive psychologists solidified their commitments to a purely cognitive level of analyses, by arguing that the distinction between cognitive and neural levels of analyses was analogous to that between computer software and hardware, and that cognitive psychology (and cognitive science) was concerned primarily with the software. Since the early 1990s, views about the importance of neural analyses have changed dramatically. There is a growing consensus that the standard information processing analyses of cognition can be substantially enlightened by knowing how cognition is implemented in the brain.

While many factors may have been responsible for the change in view, three will be mentioned here. First, the rise of connectionist models that were loosely inspired by brain function had the side effect of increasing interest in what was known in detail about brain function. Indeed, these two recent movements have become increasingly intertwined as connectionist models have increasingly incorporated findings from cognitive neuroscience. Second, in the 1970s and 1980s there were breakthroughs in systems-level neuroscience that had implications for mainstream cognitive psychology. As one example, research with neurological patients as well as with nonhuman species established that structures in the medial temporal lobe were essential for the formation of memories that could serve as the basis for recall ('explicit memory'), but not for other kinds of 'implicit memories' (e.g., Schacter 1987, Squire 1992). As another example, research with nonhuman primates showed that two distinct systems were involved in the early stages of visual perception: a 'where' system that is responsible for spatial localization, and a 'what' system that is responsible for recognition of the object (e.g., Ungerleider and Mishkin 1982). Both of these discoveries had major implications for the cognitive level of analyses, e.g., computational models of object recognition or memory would do well to divide the labor into separate subsystems.

The third factor responsible for the rise of cognitive neuroscience is methodological: the development of neuroimaging techniques that produce maps of neural activity while the brain is performing some cognitive task. One major technique is positron emission tomography (PET). In 1988, Michael Posner, Marcus Raichle, and colleagues used PET in a groundbreaking experiment to localize neurally different subprocesses of reading—PET images obtained while participants looked at words showed activated regions in the posterior temporal cortex; images obtained while participants read the words revealed additional regions activated in the motor cortex; and images obtained while participants generated constrained associations to the words revealed still additional regions in frontal areas (Posner et al. 1988). PET analyses of object recognition, memory, and language soon followed. A more recent technique is functional magnetic resonance imaging (fMRI). It is now being used to study virtually every domain of human cognition.

5. Conclusion

This article has given short shrift to important contributions that tend to fall off the mainstream of cognitive psychology. One such case is the work done by Dan Kahneman and Amos Tversky (e.g., Kahneman and Tversky 1973, Tversky and Kahneman 1983) on the use of heuristics in decision making, which can result in deviations from rational behavior. Another example is the cognitively inspired study of memory and language deficits in neurological patients (Shallice (1988) provides a review). There are other cases like these which deserve a prominent place in a fuller history of cognitive psychology.

Bibliography

Anderson J R 1976 *Language, Memory, and Thought.* Erlbaum, Hillsdale, NJ

Anderson J R, Bower G H 1973 *Human Associative Memory.* Winston, Washington, DC

Atkinson R C, Shiffrin R M 1968 Human memory: a proposed system and its control processes. In: Spence K, Spence J (eds.) *The Psychology of Learning and Motivation.* Academic Press, San Diego, CA, Vol. 2

Baddeley A D 1986 *Working Memory.* Oxford University Press, Oxford, UK

Block N J 1981 *Imagery.* MIT Press, Cambridge, MA

Broadbent D E 1958 *Perception and Communication.* Pergamon, New York

Bruner J S, Goodnow J J, Austin G A 1956 *A Study of Thinking.* Wiley, New York

Chase W G, Simon H A 1973 Perception in chess. *Cognitive Psychology* 4: 55–81

Chomsky N 1957 *Syntactic Structures.* Mouton, The Hague, The Netherlands

Chomsky N 1959 Review of B F Skinner's *Verbal Behavior. Language* 35: 26–58

Collins A M, Quillian R M 1969 Retrieval time from semantic memory. *Journal of Verbal Learning and Verbal Behavior* 8: 240–7

Conrad R 1964 Acoustic confusions in immediate memory. *British Journal of Psychology* 55: 75–84

Craik F I, Lockhart R S 1972 Levels of processing: a framework for memory research. *Journal of Verbal Learning and Verbal Behavior* 11: 671–84

Crowder R G, Morton J 1969 Precategorical acoustic storage (PAS). *Perception and Psychophysics.* 5: 365–73

Estes W K, Burke C J 1953 A theory of stimulus variability in learning. *Psychological Review* 60: 276–86

Fitts P M, Posner M I 1967 *Human Performance.* Brooks/Cole, Belmont, CA

Fodor J A 1975 *The Language of Thought.* Crowell, New York

Fodor J A, Bever T G, Garrett M F 1974 *The Psychology of Language: an Introduction to Psycholinguistics and Generative Grammar.* McGraw-Hill, New York

Fodor J A, Pylyshyn Z W 1988 Connectionism and cognitive architecture: a critical analysis. *Cognition* 28: 3–71

Garner W R 1962 *Uncertainty and Structure as Psychological Concepts.* Wiley, New York

Glanzer M, Cunitz A R 1966 Two storage mechanisms in free recall. *Journal of Verbal Learning and Verbal Behavior* 5: 351–60

Hilgard E R 1987 *Psychology in America: a Historical Survey.* Harcourt, Brace Jovanovich, San Diego, CA

Hinton G E, Anderson J A 1981 *Parallel Models of Associative Memory.* Erlbaum, Hillsdale, NJ

Johnson-Laird P N 1983 *Mental Models: Towards a Cognitive Science of Language, Inference, and Consciousness.* Cambridge University Press, Cambridge, MA

Kahneman D, Tversky A 1973 Psychology of prediction. *Psychological Review* 80: 237–51

Kessel F S, Bevan W 1985 Notes toward a history of cognitive psychology. In: Buxton C E (ed.) *Points of View in the Modern History of Psychology.* Academic Press, New York

Kintsch W 1974 *The Representation of Meaning in Memory.* Erlbaum, Hillsdale, NJ

Kintsch W, Buschke H 1969 Homophones and synonyms in short-term memory. *Journal of Experimental Psychology* 80: 403–7

Kosslyn S M 1980 *Image and Mind.* Harvard University Press, Cambridge, MA

Lakoff G 1987 *Women, Fire, and Dangerous Things: What Categories Reveal About the Mind.* University of Chicago Press, Chicago

Luce R D 1959 *Individual Choice Behavior: a Theoretical Analysis.* Wiley, New York

Marr D 1982 *Vision: a Computational Investigation into the Human Representation and Processing of Visual Information.* Freeman, San Francisco

McClelland J L, Rumelhart D E 1981 An interactive activation model of context effects in letter perception: I. An account of basic findings. *Psychological Review* 88: 375–407

Miller G A 1956 The magical number seven, plus or minus two: some limits on our capacity for processing information. *Psychological Review* 63: 81–97

Miller G A et al. 1960 *Plans and the Structure of Behavior.* Holt, New York

Miller G A 1962 Some psychological studies of grammar. *American Psychologist* 17: 748–62

Murdock Jr B B 1962 The serial position effect in the recall. *Journal of Experimental Psychology* 64: 482–8

Neisser U 1964 Visual Search. *Scientific American* 210: 94–102

Neisser U 1967 *Cognitive Psychology.* Appleton-Century-Crofts, New York

Neisser U 1968 The processes of vision. *Scientific American* 219: 204–14

Newell A 1990 *Unified Theories of Cognition.* Harvard University Press, Cambridge, MA

Newell A, Shaw J C, Simon H A 1958 Elements of a theory of human problem solving. *Psychological Review* 65: 151–66

Newell A, Simon H A 1972 *Human Problem Solving.* Prentice-Hall, Englewood Cliffs, NJ

Norman D A, Rumelhart D E, and the LNR Research Group 1975 *Explorations in Cognition.* Freeman, San Francisco

Posner M I, Petersen S E, Fox P T, Raichle M E 1988 Localization of cognitive operations in the human brain. *Science* 240: 1627–31

Pylyshyn Z W 1981 The imagery debate: analogue media versus tacit knowledge. *Psychological Review* 88: 16–45

Rosch E, Mervis C B 1981 Categorization of natural objects. *Annual Review of Psychology* 32: 89–115

Rumelhart D E, Hinton G E, Williams R J 1986 Learning representations by back-propagating errors. *Nature* 323: 533–6

Rumelhart D E, McClelland J L, PDP Research Group 1986 *Parallel Distributed Processing: Explorations in the Microstructure of Cognition.* MIT Press, Cambridge, MA

Schacter D L 1987 Implicit memory: history and current status. *Journal of Experimental Psychology: Learning, Memory, and Cognition* 13: 501–18

Schank R C, Abelson R P 1977 *Scripts, Plans, Goals and Understanding: an Inquiry into Human Knowledge Structures.* Erlbaum, Hillsdale, NJ

Schneider W, Shiffrin R M 1977 Controlled and automatic human information processing: I. Detection, search, and attention. *Psychological Review* **84**: 1–66

Selfridge O G 1959 Pandemonium: A Paradigm for Learning. The Mechanization of Thought Processes. Her Majesty's Stationery Office, London

Selfridge O G, Neisser U 1960 Pattern recognition by machine. *Scientific American* **203**: 60–8

Shallice T 1988 *From Neuropsychology to Mental Structure.* Cambridge University Press, Cambridge, UK

Shannon C E 1948 A mathematical theory of communication. *Bells Systems Technical Journal* **27**: 379–423, 623–56

Shannon C E, Weaver W 1949 *The Mathematical Theory of Communication.* University of Illinois Press, Urbana, IL

Shepard R N, Cooper L A 1972 *Mental Images and their Transformations.* MIT Press, Cambridge, MA

Skinner B F 1957 *Verbal Behavior.* Appleton-Century-Crofts, New York

Smith E E, Medin D L 1981 *Categories and Concepts.* Harvard University Press, Cambridge, MA

Sperling G 1960 The information available in brief visual presentations. *Psychological Monographs* **77**(3, no. 478)

Squire L R 1992 Memory and the hippocampus: A synthesis from findings with rats, monkeys, and humans. *Psychological Review* **99**(2): 195–231

Sternberg S 1966 High-speed scanning in human memory. *Science* **153**: 652–4

Sternberg S 1969 The discovery of processing stages: extensions of Donders' method. *Acta Psychologica* **30**: 276–315

Treisman A M 1960 Contextual cues in selective listening. *Quarterly Journal of Experimental Psychology* **12**: 242–8

Tulving E, Pearlstone Z 1966 Availability versus accessibility of information in memory for words. *Journal of Verbal Learning and Verbal Behavior* **5**: 381–91

Turing A M 1950 Computing machinery and intelligence. *Mind* **59**: 433–60

Tversky A 1977 Features of similarity. *Psychological Review* **84**: 327–52

Tversky A, Kahneman D 1983 Extensional versus intuitive reasoning: the conjunction fallacy in probability judgment. *Psychological Review* **90**: 293–315

Ungerleider L G, Mishkin M 1982 Two cortical visual systems. In: Engle D J, Goodale M A, Mansfield R J (eds.) *Analysis of Visual Behavior.* MIT Press, Cambridge, MA, pp. 549–86

Waugh N C, Norman D A 1965 Primary memory. *Psychological Review* **72**: 89–104

Wickelgren W A 1965 Acoustic similarity and intrusion errors in short-term memory. *Journal of Experimental Psychology* **70**: 102–8

E. E. Smith

Cognitive Psychology: Overview

1. Meanings of the Term 'Cognitive Psychology'

Cognitive Psychology has at least three different meanings. First, the term refers to 'a simple *collection of topic areas*,' that is, of behaviorally observable or theoretically proposed phenomena that are studied within the boundaries of the field of Cognitive Psychology. Second, the term alludes to the fact that cognitive psychologists attempt to explain intelligent human behavior by reference to a *cognitive system* that intervenes between environmental input and behavior. The second meaning of Cognitive Psychology thus refers to a set of assumptions governing the operations of the proposed cognitive system. Third, Cognitive Psychology means a particular *methodological* approach to studying, that is, to empirically addressing potential explanations of human behavior. The two latter meanings of Cognitive Psychology are discussed in some depth below, after a very brief consideration of the scope of modern Cognitive Psychology and its historical roots.

2. The Scope of Cognitive Psychology

At present, Cognitive Psychology is a broad field concerned with many different topic areas, such as, for instance, human memory, perception, attention, pattern recognition, consciousness, neuroscience, representation of knowledge, cognitive development, language, and thinking. The common denominator of these phenomena appears to be that all of the phenomena reflect the operation of 'intelligence' in one way or another, at least if intelligence is broadly defined as *skill of an individual to act purposefully, think rationally, and interact efficiently with the environment.* Thus, at a general level, Cognitive Psychology is concerned with explaining the structure and mental operations of intelligence as well as its behavioral manifestations.

3. Historical Roots of Cognitive Psychology

3.1 The Term Cognitive Psychology

The term Cognitive Psychology (latin: *cognoscere*; greek: *gignoskein* = to know, perceive) is rather young. Although we do find the related term 'cognition' mentioned occasionally in the psychologies of the late nineteenth and early twentieth century (e.g., James, Spence, Wundt) where it denoted the basic elements of consciousness and their combinations, the present meanings of the term cognitive psychology owe little to the early theoretical and philosophical considerations of the human mind. Rather, the current modern meanings of the term owe much more to (a) the fact that the study of cognition emerged in opposition to the prevailing behavioristic view in the 1940s and 1950s that was trying to explain human behavior primarily in terms of its antecedent environmental conditions, and to (b) the availability of both new theoretical concepts (e.g., information theory [Shannon], cybernetics [Wiener], systems theory [von Bertalanffy]) and practical computing machines that offered new insights into the potential nature of the mental device intervening between the outside world and human behavior.

Accordingly, the history of Cognitive Psychology can be parsed into four distinct periods: philosophical, early experimental, the cognitive revolution, and modern cognitive psychology. Early philosophy (ancient Egyptians, Greek philosophers, British empiricists) provided a context for understanding the mind and its processes (i.e., associations), and identified many of the major theoretical issues that were later studied empirically (e.g., how does perception work? how are concepts represented?). Early experimental work began, at the latest, during the middle part of the nineteenth century, when Fechner empirically studied the relation between stimulus properties (e.g., weight) and accompanying internal sensations, and when, in 1879, Wilhelm Wundt founded the first department of psychology in Leipzig, Germany. The early experimental phase of Cognitive Psychology was in full swing when, during the early 1900s, Donders and Cattell conducted perception experiments on imageless thought, and Frederic Bartlett investigated memory from a naturalistic viewpoint.

4. Modern Cognitive Psychology

In the mid-1950s and early 1960s, Cognitive Psychology experienced a renaissance. *Cognitive Psychology*, a textbook that systematized the re-emerged science, was written by Neisser and was published in the United States (1967). Neisser's book was central to the solidification of Cognitive Psychology as it gave a label to the field and defined the topical areas. Neisser used the computer metaphor to capture the selection, storage, reception, and manipulation of information in the human cognitive system. In 1966, Hilgard and Boweradded a chapter to their book *Theories of Learning* in which the idea of using computer programs to serve as models of theories of cognition was developed.

The 1970s saw the emergence of professional journals devoted to Cognitive Psychology, such as *Cognitive Psychology, Cognition, Memory & Cognition*, and a series of symposia volumes, including the *Loyola Symposium on Cognition* and the *Carnegie–Mellon Series*. Cognitive laboratories were built, symposia and conferences appeared at both national and international levels, courses in Cognitive Psychology were added to the curricula, textbooks written on the topic, and professors of Cognitive Psychology hired.

In the 1980s and 1990s, serious efforts to discover the neural components that are linked to specific cognitive constructs began, and the field underwent transformations due to major changes in computer technology and brain science. As a result, Cognitive Psychology converged with computer science and

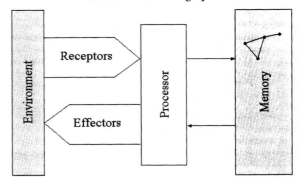

Information – Processing System

Figure 1
A basic information-processing system

neuroscience to create a new discipline called 'Cognitive Science.'

Even more recently, with the advent of new ways to see the brain at work (e.g., functional magnetic resonance imaging fMRI, positron emission tomography PET, electroencephalogram EEG), cognitive psychologists have expanded their operations to neuroscience, in the hope of being able to empirically localize the components of the brain that are involved in specific operations of the cognitive system.

5. The Properties of the Cognitive System: The Computer Metaphor

Currently, the dominant metaphor underlying theoretical and empirical research in Cognitive Psychology is the computer metaphor. According to the computer metaphor, the cognitive system of humans, that is, the device intervening between environmental input and behavior, can be understood best in analogy to an information-processing framework. A basic information-processing system (see Fig. 1) contains two basic components, a memory and a processor, that interact with each other. In addition, the processor interacts with the environment through receptors and effectors. Newell and Simon argue that any physical-symbol system, such as an information-processing system, has the necessary and sufficient means to generate intelligent action (physical symbol systems hypothesis).

In laymen's terms, the information-processing framework formally described by Newell and Simon (1972, pp. 20–21) can be said to be based on seven basic ideas (Lachman et al. 1979): (a) humans are viewed as autonomous, intentional beings who interact with the external world; (b) the cognitive system is a general-purpose, symbol-processing system; (c) there exists a fundamental distinction between processes and data (i.e., memories). Data are acted on by processes that manipulate and transform data; (d) cognitive processes take time, such that predictions about response times can be made if it is assumed that processes occur in sequence and have specifiable complexity; (e) the cognitive system is a limited-capacity processor that has both structural and resource limitations; (f) the cognitive system depends on, but is not entirely constrained by, a neurological substrate; (g) the goal of psychological research is to specify the processes and representations underlying intelligent performance on cognitive tasks.

6. Current Themes of the Computer Metaphor

The idea that a human cognitive system can be viewed as an information-processing device has had a dramatic impact on both theoretical and empirical research on the functioning of the human mind. A few select current themes in Cognitive Psychology reflecting this approach are the following.

6.1 Data-driven or Conceptually Driven Processes?

A data-driven mental process is one that relies almost exclusively on the 'data,' that is, on the stimulus information being presented in the environment. Whereas data-driven processes are assisted very little by already known information, conceptually driven processes are those that rely heavily on such information. Thus, a conceptually driven process uses the information already in memory, and whatever expectations are present in the situation, to perform a task; data-driven processes use only the stimulus information.

The distinction between data-driven and conceptually driven processes has been studied intensely in, among others, the area of pattern recognition. Models of perception attempt to explain, in large part, how patterns are recognized. Early models assumed that this process was primarily data-driven. However, the results of more recent research suggests that pattern recognition is also influenced by top-down conceptual processes.

6.2 Attention

Attention is often assumed to be a critical mental resource that is necessary for the operation of any mental process. Most theories that discuss attention assume that it is a limited mental resource and that the amount of attention that is available determines how many separate processes can be simultaneously performed.

One of the perhaps most interesting problems surrounding the role of attention has been concerned with the question of whether *attentional selection*

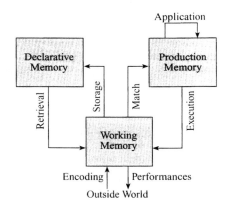

Figure 2
The basic architecture of ACT* (Anderson 1983)

occurs early or late within the cognitive system. Much of the early research on this topic focused on the extent to which unattended stimuli are processed. Early selection models hold that selection occurs at a relatively early level in the cognitive system, that is, before meaning has been extracted. Initial support for this notion came from dichotic listening tasks in which listeners had to verbally repeat information presented to one ear while different (or the same) information was simultaneously presented to the other ear. Results suggested that little of the information presented to the unattended ear was noticed. However, it was soon realized that attentional selection was not an all-or-none phenomenon. Thus, at least under some circumstances unattended information seems to reach higher levels of the cognitive system.

The topic of attentional selection has received rather widespread interest not only in studies with normal adults but also with neuropsychological samples because in some patient populations (e.g., attention-deficit disorder, schizophrenia), the attentional selection system appears to be impaired.

6.3 Separate or Unitary Memory Systems?

The debate over memory types has a long history in Cognitive Psychology. For example, in the 1960s Atkinson and Shiffrin introduced an information-processing model containing sensory, short-term, and long-term memory stores. Craik and Lockheart, a few years later, advanced a unitary view of memory. More recently, distinctions have been made between declarative/explicit (intentionally recollecting earlier experiences) and procedural/implicit (nonintentional influences from earlier exposure) memory systems, that, in turn, have been challenged by the argument that many apparent dissociations can be accommodated when one considers the match between encoding operations and retrieval operations (transfer-appropriate processing). At present, it is unclear how many distinct memory systems exist in the human cognitive system. However, recent studies with amnesic patients and brain-imaging studies seem to suggest that memory may not be unitary.

6.4 The Nature of the Cognitive Architecture

Cognitive architectures specify the permanent properties of the human cognitive system, akin to the hardware of a modern computer. Recent proposals sketch the human cognitive architecture in a much more fine-grained and detailed manner than was apparent in Newell and Simon's earlier proposal of a basic information-processing device.

Fig. 2 depicts the basics of a cognitive architecture, that has been proposed by Anderson (1983), called ACT* (*adaptive control of thought*). In Anderson's architecture, the existence of a long-term declarative memory for basic facts that are connected to each other in a semantic net is assumed. In addition, Anderson proposes a second long-term, procedural, memory that consists of productions. Each production has a set of conditions that test elements of working memory and a set of actions that create new structures in working memory. Strengths are associated with each long-term memory element (both network nodes and productions) as a function of its use. Working memory itself is activation based and contains the activated portion of declarative memory plus declarative structures generated by production firings and perception.

Activation spreads automatically (as a function of node strength) through working memory and from there to other connected nodes in declarative memory. Activation, along with production strength, determines how fast the matching of production proceeds. Selection of productions to fire is a competitive process between productions matching the same data.

New productions are created by compiling the effects of a sequence of production firings and retrievals from declarative memory. Whenever a new element is created in working memory, there is a fixed probability that it will be stored in declarative memory.

Cognitive architectures like ACT* are important not only in their own rights, that is, because they are theories of the structural and processing components of the human cognitive system, but also because they set important constraints for more specific theories that address more local characteristics of the cognitive system.

7. Recent Challenges to the Computer Metaphor

In recent years, an increasing number of theorists have come to reject the view that the human cognitive system operates like a computer. Two new metaphors

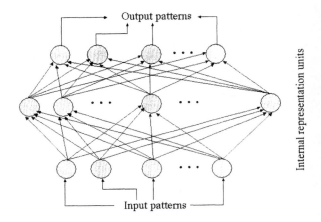

Figure 3
A basic connectionist model

have been proposed. First, some theorists have argued that the human cognitive system might be better understood in terms of a *brain metaphor*, assuming that cognitive systems consist of elementary, neuron-like units that are connected and produce behavior as a whole. Second, at least some areas within Cognitive Psychology have adopted an *ecological*, or *context metaphor*, arguing that cognitive systems need to be understood in terms of organism-environment relations.

7.1 The Brain Metaphor

According to the brain metaphor, human cognition is best understood in terms of the properties of the brain. The brain metaphor, and more specifically, so-called neural-like, connectionist networks as computational implementations of how our brain might work, have become highly popular in recent years and have seriously challenged the premier status of the computer metaphor when it comes to theorizing about the nature of human cognition.

Connectionist networks, neural networks, or parallel distributed processing models as they are variously called, differ from theories based on the computer metaphor in various respects. For example, in theories adhering to the computer metaphor, all processes assumed to underlie human behavior need to be explicitly described. Connectionist networks, on the other hand, can to some extent 'program' themselves in that they can learn to produce specific outputs when certain inputs are given to them. Furthermore, connectionist theorists often reject the use of explicit rules and symbols and use distributed representations, in which concepts are characterized as patterns of activation in a network.

Current connectionist networks typically have the following characteristics:

(a) the network consists of elementary or neuron-like units or nodes that are connected to each other such that a single unit has many links to other units;

(b) units affect other units by exciting or inhibiting them;

(c) the units usually takes the weighted sum of all input links and produces a single output to another unit if the weighted sum exceeds some threshold value;

(d) the network as a whole is characterized by the properties of its units, by the manner in which the units are connected to each other, and by the algorithms or rules used to change the strength of connections among units;

(e) networks can have different structures of layers; they can have a layer of input units, intermediate layers (of so-called 'hidden units'), and a layer of output units;

(f) a representation of a concept is stored in a distributed manner by a pattern of activation throughout the network;

(g) the same network can store many different patterns without them necessarily interfering with each other;

(h) one algorithm or rule used in networks to permit learning to occur is known as backward propagation of errors.

How do individual units act when activation impinges on them? Any given unit can be connected to several other units (see Fig. 3). Each of these other units can send an excitatory or an inhibitory signal to the first unit. This unit generally takes a weighted sum of all these inputs. If the sum exceeds some threshold, then the unit produces an output that may feed into other units.

This type of network can model cognitive behavior without recourse to the kinds of explicit rules found in the domain of the computer metaphor. The networks do so by associating various inputs with certain outputs, and by storing patterns of activation in the network. The networks typically make use of several layers to deal with complex behavior. One layer consists of input units that encode a stimulus as a pattern of activation. Another layer is an output layer that produces some response, again as a pattern of activation. When the network has learned to produce a particular response at the output layer following the presentation of a particular stimulus at the input layer, it can exhibit behavior that very much looks like a rule being applied.

One of the most critical aspects of connectionist networks is the learning rule or algorithm used to form patterns of activation. One algorithm that has been used to permit connectionist networks to learn is called backward propagation. At the beginning of a learning episode, the network is set up with random connection weights among the units. During the early stages of learning, when the input pattern has been presented, the output units often produce a response that is not the required output pattern. Backward propagation compares this imperfect pattern with the known required response, noticing the differences. It then back-propagates activation through the network such that the units are adjusted in such a way that they will tend to produce the required pattern on the next learning cycle. This process is repeated with a particular stimulus pattern until the network produces the required response pattern.

Networks have been used to produce very interesting results. For example, Sejnowski and Rosenberg produced a connectionist network called NETtalk that takes an English text as its input and produces reasonable English speech as its output. Thus, the network appears to have learned the 'rules of English pronunciation' but has done so without requiring explicit rules that combine and encode sounds in various ways.

7.2 The Ecological Metaphor

Ecological psychology focuses specifically on the interdependencies of humans and their environments, which typically are studied under real-world conditions rather than in the laboratory. The approach has given rise to a variety of very different approaches and lines of research, only two of which will be briefly considered. One approach is concerned with explaining and understanding perception, and can be traced to E. Brunswick and more recently, J. J. Gibson; the other approach is concerned with social behavior and appears to go back to K. Lewin and R. Barker. Although the two lines of research share the ecological perspective of examining functional adaptations of organisms to their environment, they are concerned with different issues and employ different methods. The two theoretical lines are much less explicit about the actual properties of the assumed cognitive system that intervenes between perception and action than are the computer and brain metaphors discussed above, and both have much less influence in contemporary Cognitive Psychology as do their two contenders. Nevertheless, they represent a succinctly different understanding of how the cognitive system might function and belong, at least in part, to the realm of Cognitive Psychology.

7.2.1 Gibson's ecological psychology. Following classical ecological theory, Gibson regards organism and environment to be an inseparable pair. A critical feature of this conception is that environment is not defined independently of organisms, nor are organisms defined independently of environments.

Gibson considers the first task of ecological psychology to be an adequate description of the environment. Environment consists of a medium, substances, and surfaces separating substance from medium. In a successful adaptation, organisms need to perceive which aspects of surface, substance, and medium persist and which aspects change in regard to specific environmental events.

The ecological approach to visual perception assumes that senses represent evolved adaptations to an organism's environment. These adaptations develop in relation to environmental factors contributing to an organism's survival. Evolutionary success requires sensory systems that directly and accurately depict the environment. The key stimulus features that contribute to an organism's survival which Gibson termed 'affordances' are invariant. Affordances differ according to situation and species and are perceived directly from the pattern of stimulation arising from them. They do not change as the needs of observers change; affordances have both objective and subjective properties, becoming a fact of the environment and a fact of behavior.

Gibson's approach is sometimes referred to as the theory of direct perception, and has received empirical support from, among others, research by E. J. Gibson, studying the development of perceived invariance in infancy. E. J. Gibson's research, for instance, has demonstrated that one of the properties of perceptual learning and development does appear to be the increasing ability to extract information about the permanent properties of objects.

7.2.2 *Barker's ecological psychology.* According to R. Barker, behavior should be studied without outside manipulation or imposition of structure. Rather than contrive artificial settings, Barker advocated the study of behavioral settings that already exist, using methodology that exerts minimal influence upon the situation.

To collect systematic records of behavior in natural contexts, Barker argued for the establishment of so-called field stations, established organizational units that were to continue over time and whose staff included both continuing and visiting researchers. Barker and co-workers established the Midwest Psychological Field Station in Oskaloosa, Kansas, where for a period of 24 years detailed systematic records were kept of community life. Observers were stationed throughout the town, and recorded everyday activities of children. Barker concluded that the behavior of a child could often be predicted more accurately from knowing the situation the child was in, than from knowing individual characteristics of the child.

Barker's conception of ecological psychology rests on several assumptions, (a) human behavior must be studied at a level that recognizes the complexity of systems of relations linking individuals and groups with their social and physical environments; (b) environment–behavioral systems have properties that develop over long periods of time; (c) change in one part of the system is likely to affect other parts of the system; and (d) the challenge of ecological psychology

is to obtain sufficient understanding to be able to predict and control the effects of planned and unplanned interventions.

Barker's conception of ecological psychology has been extended and refined in recent years (e.g., J. Barker, K. Fox, A. Wicker). For example, Fox has linked it to social accounting theory, showing how data from large-scale inventories of behavior settings can reveal changes in the quality of life in communities.

From the brief desciption of ecological psychology above, it should be clear that despite the fact that the ecological metaphor has more than some intuitive appeal to it, both its level of precision and its scope are far smaller than those of the computer and the brain metaphors. Consequently, the ecological metaphor plays a very minor role in current Cognitive Psychology.

8. Research Methods in Cognitive Psychology

Cognitive psychologists rely heavily on the experimental method, in which independent variables are manipulated and dependent variables are measured to provide insights into the specifics of the underlying cognitive system. To statistically evaluate the results from experiments, Cognitive Psychology relies on standard hypothesis testing, along with inferential statistics (e.g., analyses of variance).

The research methods Cognitive Psychology utilize depend, in part, on the area of study and consist primarily of chronometric methods, memory methods, cross-population studies, case studies, measures of brain activity, and computational modeling.

8.1 Chronometric Methods

Beginning with early work by Donders (1868–1969), cognitive psychologists have used reaction times to measure the speed of mental operations. Donders developed the so-called subtractive method. For example, task A might be assumed to require Process 1, whereas task B might require Processes 1 and 2. Donders assumed that cognitive operations are independent of each other and are processed in a strictly serial manner. Thus, the duration of Process 2 can be estimated by subtracting the response time for task A from the reaction time for task B.

To circumvent some of the restrictive assumptions of the subtractive method, Saul Sternberg introduced an additive factors logic. According to this logic, if a task contains distinct processes, then there should be variables that selectively influence the speed of each process. Thus, if two variables influence different processes, their effects should be statistically additive. By contrast, if two variables affect the same process, their effects should statistically interact.

More recently, researchers have empirically identified for so-called cascaded systems in which neither the assumptions of Donders nor of Sternberg hold because mental processes occur simultaneously at different information-processing levels. New measures have been developed that combine reaction time measurement with the measurement of other properties of the cognitive system (e.g., speed-accuracy tradeoff functions, eye-tracking methods).

8.2 Memory Methods

One of the first to experimentally study human memory was Hermann Ebbinghaus who developed the savings technique to assess retention of nonsense syllables. Retention was measured in terms of the number of trials necessary to relearn a list of syllables relative to the number of trials necessary to learn the list for the first time.

More recently, researchers have begun to distinguish between three different aspects of memory, encoding, retention, and retrieval, and have developed methods to study the three aspects in isolation. For example, one way of investigating encoding processes is to manipulate humans' expectancies by way of intentional vs. incidental learning instructions. By contrast, retrieval processes are often studied in one of two general ways. On an explicit memory test, participants are presented a list of materials and at some later point in time are given a test in which they are asked to retrieve the earlier presented material. Retrieval is measured in terms of recall, recognition, or cued recall. On implicit memory tests, participants are not directly asked to recollect an earlier episode, but rather, are asked to engage in a task where performance might benefit from earlier exposure to the stimulus items. Interestingly, recent research has demonstrated that some neuropsychological populations (e.g., amnesic patients) can be unimpaired on implicit memory tests, but can show considerable impairment in explicit memory tests.

8.3 Case Studies

Although relatively rarely used in Cognitive Psychology, single case studies can provide vital information on how the cognitive system may be structured and which specific processes might be necessary to complete specific tasks. The classic case of HM, who as a consequence of an earlier epilepsy operation, acquired severe memory loss on explicit tasks though not implicit tasks, might serve as a striking example arguing for the dissociation of different memory structures. Case studies can provide rather convincing constraints for cognitive psychologists' understanding of the architecture of human cognition.

8.4 Cross-population Studies

Cognitive Psychology relies heavily on college students as their research participants. Recently, however, there

has been an increasing interest in comparing both the structure and the processes of the cognitive system across distinct populations. For example, studies of cognition from early childhood to older adulthood attempt to trace developmental changes in specific mental operations, such as speed of processing and memory. In addition, studies with special clinical populations are conducted in order to understand breakdowns in mental functioning, such as they occur in Alzheimer's disease, schizophrenia, or amnesia.

8.5 Measures of Brain Activity

In recent years a variety of possibilities to measure some correlates of mental activity in the brain (e.g., evoked potentials, positron emission tomography [PET], functional magnetic resonance imaging [fMRI]) have become available. Evoked potentials measure the electrical activity of systems of neurons; PET measures blood flow. Because the measures differ widely in their invasiveness and in terms of their temporal and spatial resolutions, a combination of these methods, together with behavioral measurements (e.g., reaction time, accuracy) appears to be an extremely promising candidate for increasing understanding of the interaction between Neuropsychology and Cognitive Psychology.

8.6 Computational Modeling

Since the early research of Newell and Simon on the General Problem Solver, theoretical assumptions concerning both the structure of, and the processing within, the cognitive system have been tested by implementing the assumptions in running computer programs. Recently, the modeling has been of two different varieties, connectionist versus symbolic modeling (see above). For example, in order to model the processes underlying human language learning, the symbolic modeling approach assumes that humans acquire a set of rules that specify how language constituents can be combined within a language and can be specified in a running program. Alternatively, the cognitive system might acquire the 'rules of language' without directly specifying these rules as symbols at all, that is, within a distributed representational system (connectionist theory). At present, the controversy surrounding these two alternative modeling accounts is far from settled, and, importantly, reflects a fundamental issue regarding the nature of the human cognitive system that was addressed in more detail above (computer metaphor vs. brain metaphor).

9. The Future of Cognitive Psychology

If the past is a good predictor of the future, then the future of Cognitive Psychology is difficult to predict.

Most likely, however, neither the theoretical scope nor the empirical methods of the field are going to change dramatically. If there will be disagreement among scientists, it will concern the nature of the mental system intervening between environmental input and behavior. The most desirable future scenario is perhaps one in which the three main metaphors (i.e., computer, brain, ecological) will be integrated into a coherent one. Because the three metaphors deal with distinct levels of the human mind, this scenario is perhaps not an unlikely, remote theoretical possibility.

See also: Brain Development, Ontogenetic Neurobiology of; Cognitive Neuroscience; Cognitive Psychology: History; Cognitive Science: History; Cognitive Science: Overview; Cognitive Science: Philosophical Aspects; Experimentation in Psychology, History of; Human Cognition, Evolution of; Information Processing Architectures: Fundamental Issues; Intelligence, Evolution of; Intelligence: Historical and Conceptual Perspectives; Mathematical Psychology; Problem Solving and Reasoning, Psychology of; Psychology: Historical and Cultural Perspectives; Psychology: Overview

Bibliography

Anderson J R 1983 *The Architecture of Cognition*. Harvard University Press, Cambridge, MA
Anderson J R 1995 *Cognitive Psychology and its Implications*. Freeman, New York
Broadbent D E 1958 *Perception and Communication*. Pergamon, New York
Chomsky N 1959 Review of Skinner's verbal behavior. *Language* **35**: 26–58
Fodor J A 1983 *The Modularity of Mind*. MIT Press/Bradford Books, Cambridge, MA
Fodor J A, Pylyshyn Z W 1988 Connectionism and cognitive architecture: A critical analysis. *Cognition* **28**: 3–71
Gardner H 1985 *The Mind's New Science: A History of the Cognitive Revolution*. Basic Books, New York:
Gibson J J 1979 *The Ecological Approach to Visual Perception*. Houghton Mifflin, Boston
Lachman R, Lachman J L, Butterfield E C 1979 *Cognitive Psychology and Information Processing*. Erlbaum, Hillsdale, NJ
McClelland J L, Rumelhart D E (eds.) 1986 *Parallel Distributed Processing: Explorations in the Microstructure of Cognition*, Vol. 2. MIT Press/Bradford Books, Cambridge, MA
Miller G A, Galanter E, Pribram K H 1960 *Plans and the Structure of Behavior*. Holt, Rinehart & Winston, New York
Minsky M 1985 *The Society of Mind*. Simon and Schuster, New York
Neisser U 1967 *Cognitive Psychology*. Appleton-Century-Crofts, New York
Newell A 1980 Physical symbol systems. *Cognitive Science* **4**: 135–83
Newell A 1991 *Unified Theories of Cognition*. Cambridge University Press, Cambridge, MA

Newell A, Simon H A 1972 *Human Problem Solving*. Prentice-Hall, Englewood Cliffs, NJ
Pylyshyn Z W 1984 *Computation and Cognition*. MIT Press, Cambridge, MA
Rumelhart D E, McClelland J L (eds.) 1986 *Parallel Distributed Processing: Explorations in the Microstructure of Cognition*, Vol. 1. MIT Press/Bradford Books, Cambridge, MA
Simon H A 1969 *The Sciences of the Artificial*. MIT Press, Cambridge, MA

P. A. Frensch

Cognitive Science: History

The roots of cognitive science extend back far in intellectual history, but its genesis as a collaborative endeavor of psychology, computer science, neuroscience, linguistics, and related fields lies in the 1950s. Its first major institutions (a journal and society) were established in the late 1970s. This history describes relevant developments within each field and traces collaboration between the fields in the last half of the twentieth century.

A key contributor to the emergence of cognitive science, psychologist George Miller, dates its birth to September 11, 1956, the second day of a Symposium on Information Theory at MIT. Computer scientists Allen Newell and Herbert Simon, linguist Noam Chomsky, and Miller himself presented work that would turn each of their fields in a more cognitive direction. Miller left the symposium 'with a strong conviction, more intuitive than rational, that human experimental psychology, theoretical linguistics, and the computer simulation of cognitive processes were all pieces from a larger whole, and that the future would see a progressive elaboration and coordination of their shared concerns' (Miller 1979).

This early conference illustrates an enduring feature of cognitive science—it is not a discipline in its own right, but a multidisciplinary endeavor. Although a few departments of cognitive science have been created at universities in subsequent decades, most of its practitioners are educated and spend their careers in departments of the contributing disciplines. The relative prominence of these disciplines has varied over the years. Computer science and psychology have played a strong role throughout. Neuroscience initially was strong, but in the years immediately following the 1956 conference its role declined as that of linguistics dramatically increased. By the 1970s, such disciplines as philosophy, sociology, and anthropology were making distinctive contributions. Recently, with the emergence of cognitive neuroscience, neuroscience has once again become a central contributor.

1. Intellectual Ancestors of Cognitive Science

1.1 Artificial Intelligence

One of the central inspirations for cognitive science was the development of computational models of cognitive performance, which bring together two ideas. First, conceiving of thought as computation was an offshoot of the development of modern logic. In his 1854 book, *The Laws of Thought*, the British mathematician George Boole demonstrated that formal operations performed on sets corresponded to logical operators (and, or, not) applied to propositions; Boole proposed that these could serve as laws of thought. Second, conceiving of computers as devices for computation can be traced back to Charles Babbage's plans in the 1840s for an 'analytical engine' and his collaboration with Lady Lovelace (Ada Augusta Byron) in developing ideas for programming the device. These ideas gained new life in the 1930s and 1940s with the development of automata theory (especially the Turing machine), cybernetics (centered on Norbert Weiner's feedback loops), designs for implementing Boolean operations via electric on/off switches (Claude Shannon), and information theory (also Shannon). Implementation became possible with the invention of electrical circuits, vacuum tubes, and transistors and was put on a fast track by World War II (ENIAC was completed at the University of Pennsylvania in 1946). By the mid-1950s, Newell and Simon (at RAND and then Carnegie-Mellon) produced the first functioning program for reasoning, a theorem-prover called Logic Theorist, and the first list-processing language, IPL. Meanwhile, John McCarthy and Marvin Minsky at MIT were developing a broad based agenda for the field they named artificial intelligence (AI) and more specialized endeavors also got underway (e.g., machine translation of languages and chess-playing programs, neither truly successful until the 1990s).

1.2 Psychology

During the same period psychology began emerging from a long domination by behaviorism, especially in North America. Behaviorism had the lasting impact of focusing experimental psychology on explaining behavior and relying on behavior as its primary source of evidence. Radical behaviorists, such as B. F. Skinner, actively opposed positing internal processes and focused on what was observable: describing how behavioral responses changed with contingencies of reinforcement. Other behaviorists, such as Clark Hull, were willing to posit variables intervening between stimulus and response, such as drive, but emphasized doing so in the context of developing a mathematico-deductive theory accounting for behavior. Edward Tolman, an atypical behaviorist, went so far as to propose that rats navigate their environments by constructing cognitive maps. Most psychologists, however, took learning rather than cognition as their domain of concern. The sentiment was well captured by George Mandler, looking back on his graduate student days at Yale: '... cognition was a dirty word for us ... because cognitive psychologists were seen as fuzzy, hand-waving, imprecise people who never really did anything that was testable' (quoted in Baars 1986).

Although behaviorism cast a broad shadow in the US, alternatives which later influenced cognitive science thrived elsewhere: Continental Europe (especially Jean Piaget's genetic epistemology), the UK (e.g., Sir Frederic Bartlett's appeal to schemas to explain memory distortions and Donald Broadbent's analyses of memory and attention), Germany and Austria (Gestalt psychology), and the Soviet Union (Lev Vygotsky and Alexander Luria). Within the US, psychophysics (and to some extent developmental, social, and clinical psychology) functioned largely outside behaviorism's influence. Several psychologists who later pioneered a more cognitive approach, including Miller, Ulric Neisser, and Donald Norman, received their training in S. S. Stevens's Psychoacoustic Laboratory at Harvard. Miller earned his Ph.D. in 1946 for research on optimal signals for spot jamming of speech. Just 10 years later, he was talking about the structure of internal information processing systems, such as the 'seven plus or minus two' limitation in such domains as short-term memory. In 1960, Miller, Eugene Galanter, and Karl Pribram broke new ground in their *Plans and the Structure of Behavior*. In the same time frame, Miller's Harvard colleague Jerome Bruner was pioneering several strands of cognitive research: he showed that internal mental states influence perception and, arguing that categories are central to thought, Bruner, Goodnow, and Austin traced how people acquire them in their 1956 book, *A Study of Thinking*.

1.3 Neuroscience

Research into the brain was long thought to be relevant to understanding mental processes. One line of research focused on deficits stemming from brain lesions, such as Broca's classic nineteenth century work lining articulate speech to what is now called Broca's area. Although a holistic tradition in early twentieth century brain research temporarily turned investigators away from localization studies, Norman Geschwind and others gave new life to this approach in the 1950s. As well, improvements in electrophysiological techniques, including brain stimulation, single cell recording, and EEG recording, provided additional clues. As evidenced by a 1948 conference, 'Cerebral Mechanisms in Behavior,' there was eager engagement at the time between neurophysiologists, biologically oriented psychologists, and computer scientists.

One of the fruitful products of this engagement in the 1940s to 1960s was the development of neural networks, a kind of computational modeling pioneered by neurophysiologist Warren McCulloch and logician Walter Pitts. Donald Hebb proposed to build cell-assemblies by strengthening connections between neurons that fired simultaneously, a technique still in use. Oliver Selfridge had layers of units competing in parallel to recognize patterns in his *Pandemonium* simulation. Frank Rosenblatt built layered networks that learned through error correction (*Perceptrons*). Neural networks lost influence due to a devastating critique of Perceptrons by Minsky and Seymour Papert in 1969, but were revived when more effective techniques became available in the 'new connectionism' of the 1980s and beyond.

1.4 Linguistics

Linguistics began to move towards a central role in the emerging interdisciplinary discussion of mind and brain around the time of the 1956 MIT conference. In the early decades of the twentieth century, linguistics had changed its emphasis from reconstructing the history of languages to studying the structure of languages. Structuralist linguists such as Franz Boas, Edward Sapir, and the positivist Leonard Bloomfield focused on lower-level structural units (phonemes and morphemes). In the 1950s, post-Bloomfieldian Zellig Harris turned his attention to syntax and introduced the idea of transformations that normalized complex sentences by relating them to simpler kernel sentences. This idea launched a revolution in linguistics when it was further developed by Harris's student Noam Chomsky at the University of Pennsylvania and then MIT. In his 1957 *Syntactic Structures*, Chomsky proposed the idea of a grammar as a generative system—a set of rules that would generate all and only members of the infinite set of grammatically well-formed sentences of a human language—and argued that finite state and phrase structure grammars, though generative, were inadequate. A series of transformations was needed to obtain an appropriate surface structure from an initial deep structure created by means of phrase structure rules.

2. The Maturation of Cognitive Science

If the 1956 symposium represented the birth of cognitive science, it had a lot of maturing to do before it solidified into a major recognizable area of scientific inquiry. It did not even obtain its name and institutional identity until the mid- to late 1970s. But in the intervening two decades, interaction and collaboration between computer science, psychology, and linguistics developed and began to bear fruit.

2.1 Artificial Intelligence

Though based in computer science, much artificial intelligence (AI) research was directed towards accounting for the kinds of behavior studied by psychologists. Newell and Simon soon went beyond their initial Logic Theorist program to a General Problem Solver they used in less formal domains, such as solving Tower of Hanoi problems. They developed such concepts as subgoals, heuristics, and satisficing and introduced the production system framework, which employs rules that operate on the contents of working memory when their antecedent conditions are satisfied. Their collaborative work culminated in their 1972 book *Human Problem Solving*, but each went on to develop further systems, such as SOAR and extensions of EPAM. At MIT McCarthy developed a list processing language (LISP), which became a standard tool of AI. Students working with him and Minsky wrote LISP programs to perform such tasks as retrieving semantic information (Raphael's SIR) and solving algebra word problems (Bobrow's STUDENT) and geometric analogies (Evans's ANALOGY). A 1968 book reporting this work also included a seminal chapter by Ross Quillian introducing semantic networks. At Stanford, a team headed by Charles Rosen built a computer-controlled robot named Shakey that could reason backwards from goals and take appropriate actions with boxes that were found in its environment. Working with a simulated box world rather than a physical one, Terry Winograd's SHRDLU at MIT offered innovations in data structures and planning and had the most successful natural language interface of the early 1970s. Around the same time William Woods developed Augmented Transition Network (ATN) grammars at Harvard and BBN. As the 1970s progressed, AI researchers recognized the limitations of reasoning with only atomized information. Some proposed larger-scale knowledge structures, such as Roger Schank's scripts and MOPs and Minsky's frames. Also, considerable progress was made in such specialized areas as expert systems, speech understanding programs, and computational linguistics.

2.2 Psycholinguistics

One of the most fruitful collaborations was between psychology and linguistics. Modern psycholinguistics had already begun to emerge in the early 1950s, especially in the context of a summer seminar sponsored by the Social Science Research Council in 1953. One of the aims of this interaction between post-Hullians and post-Bloomfieldians was to investigate the psychological reality of linguistic constructs such as phoneme. Though many of their empirical strategies still thrive in some form, the field was impacted by the echos of Chomsky's revolution in linguistics. In his 1959 review of B. F. Skinner's *Verbal Behavior*,

Chomsky emphasized not only that linguistic behavior does not consist in reproduction of acquired responses but is creative in the sense that there is no bound to the novel but grammatically well-formed sentences one might produce or hear. Focusing on the poverty of the stimulus argument (that the input to children is inadequate to induce a language), Chomsky also later argued for an innate language capacity (Universal Grammar). A long-standing conflict developed between Chomskian developmental psycholinguists and those taking a cognitive interactionist perceptive (e.g., Elizabeth Bates). Meanwhile, Chomkian inspired psychologists showed that sentences with more transformations in their derivation were more difficult to process. Later, changes in linguistic theory led to a more nuanced psycholinguistics, including some Chomskian approaches.

2.3 Psychology

Information processing psychology drew explicitly or implicitly on computational ideas from information theory and AI. Some of the first glimmers of an information processing approach to psychology appeared in the work of Miller and Bruner, who established a Center for Cognitive Studies at Harvard in 1960. Research in the center focused on a host of topics including conceptual organization, language processing and development, visual imagery, memory, and attention. Eleanor Rosch, a Bruner student, began work that led in the 1970s to a view of categories that emphasized prototypes, fuzzy boundaries, and the primacy of basic-level categories. And in 1967 Ulric Neisser, one of the Center's many research fellows and visitors, published *Cognitive Psychology*. This book introduced and synthesized the newly burgeoning work on information processing, particularly emphasizing attention and pattern recognition, and it quickly became the bible for a new generation of students.

Although the Center closed in 1970, information-processing approaches to psychology had already begun to spread to other universities. Stanford University, for example, built from its existing strength in mathematical psychology (including the work of William K. Estes) quickly to emerge as a premier center for information processing. In 1968 Richard Atkinson and Richard Shiffrin developed a model that integrated previous work on control processes, sensory memory (Sperling), short-term memory (Peterson and Peterson), and the distinction between short-term and long-term memory (William James; Waugh and Norman). Roger Shepard did elegant work in mathematical psychology (e.g., he pioneered nonparametric multidimensional scaling), but is best known for his research on mental imagery and mental rotation with such students as Lynn Cooper and Jacqueline Metzler. For example, they demonstrated that when subjects had to decide whether a comparison stimulus was a rotation or a mirror image of a geometrical form, their reaction times increased linearly with the degree of rotation. This suggested that subjects mentally rotated the comparison stimulus—an attention-grabbing claim at a time when mentalism was still suspect in many quarters. A third researcher, Gordon Bower, moved from mathematical models of learning towards more cognitively oriented work on the nature of mental representations. One of his students, John Anderson, worked with Bower on a very influential semantic network model (HAM), that was described in their 1973 book, *Human Associative Memory*. Later Anderson combined it with a production system component in ACT* and its predecessors.

Another exemplar is University of California, San Diego, where the trio of Peter Lindsay, Donald Norman, and David Rumelhart created a collaborative research group (LNR) in a new department and institution. In 1975 they published *Explorations in Cognition*, which ended with what may have been the first published use of the term cognitive science: 'The concerted efforts of a number of people from ... linguistics, artificial intelligence, and psychology may be creating a new field: cognitive science' (Norman et al. 1975). (A second candidate for first use is a 1975 book by Bobrow and Collins, *Representation and Understanding: Studies in Cognitive Science*.) In addition to work on varied topics including memory, word recognition, problem solving, imagery, and analogy, the group implemented an ambitious memory model, MEMOD. It featured active structural networks, which used a common semantic network format to represent both data and process (e.g., declarative and procedural knowledge). A decade later yet another collaborative group coalesced at UCSD around Rumelhart and James McClelland; known as the PDP (parallel distributed processing) group, it helped bring neural networks (connectionist models) back to center stage.

Sensing the potential to catalyze cognitive science programs at these and other universities, the Alfred P. Sloan Foundation launched an initiative that eventually provided $17.4 million over 10 years to such institutions as MIT and the University of California, Berkeley. During 1982–84 another foundation, The System Development Foundation, contributed $26 million for computational linguistics and speech, with its largest support going to the Center for the Study of Language and Information at Stanford.

During the same period, linguist-turned-computer-scientist Roger Schank, psychologist Allan Collins, and computer scientist Eugene Charniak began a new journal called *Cognitive Science*. Describing a converging view of natural and artificial intelligence in his introduction to the first issue in 1977, Collins wrote: 'This view has recently begun to produce a spate of books and conferences, which are the first trappings of an emerging discipline. This discipline might have been called applied epistemology or intelligence theory, but someone on high declared it should be cognitive science and so it shall. In starting the journal we are just adding another trapping in the formation of a new discipline.' Drawing upon some of the early Sloan money, Donald Norman and his colleagues at UCSD organized the La Jolla Conference on Cognitive Science. But as planning proceeded the idea of a new society germinated, and the conference (held August 13–16, 1979) became the first annual meeting of the Cognitive Science Society.

3. Developing New Identities

By 1980 cognitive science had developed an institutional profile and was the focus of serious funding initiatives. It also had an identity, one that emphasized computational modeling of cognitive and linguistic processes, but also incorporated linguistics and psycholinguistics. The subsequent two decades have seen major efforts to revise this initial identity. Three contributing factors, each involving perspectives from disciplines not central to the cognitive science of the 1970s, deserve brief mention. First, the development of cognitive science gave philosophers, long interested in issues surrounding the mind, a chance to address such issues in the context of ongoing empirical research. Jerry Fodor argued that cognitive processes are autonomous from the neural substrate and capable of being realized in multiple ways; this view, congenial to the cognitive science of the 1970s and 1980s, was subsequently challenged by Patricia and Paul Churchland, who have emphasized the co-evolution of cognitive science and neuroscience.

Second, mavericks in a variety of disciplines found cognitive science's nearly exclusive focus on processes within the head a limitation. Philosopher Hubert Dreyfus challenged the attempt to analyze cognition as formal computational processes. Neisser integrated information processing with the ecological psychology of James J. and Eleanor J. Gibson. Edward Hutchens and many others began to focus on how embodiment and the situatedness of agents contribute to their cognitive performance.

Finally, although study of the brain largely disappeared from cognitive science in the 1960s and 1970s, partly because research on brain processes seemed too remote to contribute to understanding cognitive operations, the late 1980s and 1990s saw the emergence of cognitive neuroscience. Michael Posner, Marcus Raichle, and Steven Petersen collaborated at Washington University to show how images from PET could be used to link brain processes to cognitive processes. More recently greater spatial resolution has been gained using fMRI and greater temporal resolution using EEG-based methods such as ERP. Whether cognitive science can successfully incorporate these pilgrimages out into the world and down into the brain, or whether it will ultimately fractionate, is a question still unanswered.

See also: Artificial Intelligence in Cognitive Science; Behaviorism, History of; Cognitive Neuroscience; Cognitive Psychology: History; Cognitive Science: Overview; Cognitive Science: Philosophical Aspects; Psychology: Historical and Cultural Perspectives; Neuroscience, Philosophy of

Bibliography

Baars B J 1986 *The Cognitive Revolution in Psychology*. Guilford Press, New York
Bechtel W, Abrahamsen A, Graham G 1998 The life of cognitive science. In: Bechtel W, Graham G (eds.) *A Companion to Cognitive Science*. Blackwell, Malden, MA
Gardner H 1985 *The Mind's New Science*. Basic Books, New York
Hirst W (ed.) 1988 *The Making of Cognitive Science*. Cambridge University Press, Cambridge, UK
Miller G A 1979 A Very Personal History (Occasional paper no. 1). Center for Cognitive Science, Cambridge, MA
Norman D A, Rumelhart D E, and the LNR Research Group 1975 *Explorations in Cognition*. Freeman, San Francisco, CA

W. Bechtel, A. Abrahamsen, and G. Graham

Cognitive Science: Overview

Cognitive science (CS) is a young discipline that emerged from a research program started in 1975. It partially overlaps with its mother disciplines: psychology, artificial intelligence, linguistics, philosophy, anthropology, and the neurosciences. By no means the only discipline dedicated to the study of cognition, cognitive science is unique in its basic tenet that cognitive processes are computations, a perspective which allows for direct comparison of natural and artificial intelligence, and emphasizes a methodology that integrates formal and empirical analyses with computational synthesis. Computer simulations as generative theories of cognition (see *Cognitive Modeling: Research Logic in Cognitive Science*) have therefore become the hallmark of CS methodology.

Today, CS is an internationally established field. The dominant tradition of the early years, close to artificial intelligence and its symbol-processing architectures, has been enriched by alternative computational architectures (e.g.; artificial neural networks) and by the recognition that natural, especially human cognition, rests on biological as well as on social and cultural foundations. CS studies cognitive systems, which may be organisms, machines, or any combination of these acting in an environment that may be open and dynamically changing. Cognition in CS denotes a class of advanced control mechanisms that allow for sophisticated adaptation to changing needs (e.g., learning and planning) through computations operating on mental representations. Cognition typically coexists with simpler regulatory mechanisms, like reflexes. CS recognizes that cognition in biological systems is implemented in brain processes, but emphasizes the importance of analyses at the functional level, with cognitive neuroscience relating both domains. Applications of cognitive science may be found in human–computer interaction and in the design of software and information systems, as well as in human factors engineering, health care, and, most notably, in education.

1. Cognition and the Cognitive Science Approach

Although reflection on the mind dates back at least to Plato, the term 'cognition,' etymologically based on ancient Greek *gignoskein* and Latin *cognoscere*, is relatively recent. It surfaces in nineteenth-century psychology, which exclusively dealt with the phenomenology of consciousness, e.g., in Spencer's characterization of the interrelations of human feelings. At about the same time, the triad of thinking, feeling, and willing of eighteenth century *Vermögenspsychologie* became the well-known taxonomy of the mind, dividing it into cognition, emotion, and volition.

We all have an intuitive understanding of what 'cognition' refers to, and there is common agreement that thinking, memory, and language, and 'the use or handling of knowledge' (Gregory 1987, p. 149) are correctly subsumed under that term. On the other side, it is difficult to define the term strictly. Minimalist approaches (e.g., Searle 1990) would like to reserve its use for the contents of consciousness, whereas a maximum approach has been taken by Maturana and Varela (1980, p. 13), where they claim that 'living as a process is a process of cognition' (cf., Boden 2000, for a critique). The leading opinion, however, will consider unconscious processes as well as conscious ones (Neisser 1967, Norman 1981) without attributing cognitive abilities to every living organism (e.g., a tree) and, indeed, without confining the use of the term to biological systems. Still, 'cognition' continues to be a rather ill-defined term, which even as ambitious a project as *The MIT Encyclopedia of the Cognitive Sciences* (Wilson and Keil 1999) has not dared to treat in an article of its own.

The hallmark of the CS approach to cognition is to identify cognitive processes with computation: cognition is information processing. Not every computation is cognition, however, which means that these computational processes must be characterized (Newell and Simon 1976), and further restrictions must be named, such as referential content or 'intentionality' (Fodor 1975), or system complexity (Smolensky 1988). The rest of this section will sketch the way towards a computational theory of mind.

1.1 Formal Approaches in Philosophy, Computing, and Neuroscience

The philosophical tradition on which CS draws may be traced from the invention of number systems to medieval algebra (Raimundus Lullus) and on to Descartes and Leibniz, and from the Aristotelian syllogisms to Frege's seminal work on formal logic. Apart from being a history of the development of formal systems, this philosophical tradition can be seen as an analysis of thinking and reasoning aimed at separating content and form of argumentation. The syllogisms of Aristotle, which continued to constitute the core of logic, virtually unchanged, over more than 2,000 years, are the first milestone: In analyzing an argument such as 'All human beings will die. Socrates is a human being. Therefore, Socrates will die' as $p \rightarrow q$, $p \therefore q$ (*modus ponens*) in the Aristotelian tradition (combined with the formal advancements of Lullus and Descartes), the specific content of the argument is separated from the form of reasoning, and it becomes clear that the latter is sufficient for warranting a true conclusion, provided that the input to this logical vehicle consists of premises that are true. An important generalization about reasoning had been found. It was Leibniz in the late-seventeenth century who advocated the use of formal reasoning in the hope that all fruitless discussions might be ended just by formalizing the arguments and computing the conclusions—hopelessly optimistic from our view (there would be endless debate on how to formalize the premises), but instrumental for an account of thinking as symbol processing.

Frege's (1879/1967) reformulation of logic laid the foundations of modern logical semantics and marks the beginning of the modern tradition that led to CS. The theory of symbol processing is formalized as a general theory of computation in the works of Gödel, Turing, Church, and Post between 1931 and 1943, soon to become the foundation of computer science and, especially, artificial intelligence. Logical positivism (as epitomized in Wittgenstein's *Tractatus*, written during World War I) and logical semantics (foremost, Tarski's work in the 1920s) constitute the philosophical legacy on which CS could draw.

The invention of computing machinery in the 1940s (Zuse, with Babbage as an isolated forerunner in the nineteenth century) was instrumental in promoting a computational perspective to cognition. A major step was the founding of artificial intelligence (AI) in 1956. The work done in AI, notably on human problem solving by Newell and Simon, may well be regarded as CS at a time when the term was not around yet.

The symbol processing tradition was complemented in the neurosciences by the invention of the formal neuron (an abstraction from biological neurons; McCulloch and Pitts 1943), as well as by analog approaches to computing and self-regulation and general systems theory (cybernetics; Wiener 1948).

The detection of representational functions of single neurons in the visual system (receptive fields; Hubel and Wiesel 1962) paved the way for a new, scientific approach to the concept of mental representation, while the development of artificial neural networks, notably the perceptron (Rosenblatt 1958), showed a possible way to combine these new discoveries with the idea of computation.

1.2 Other Disciplines: Linguistics and Anthropology

Linguistics made a huge step forward when researchers such as Jakobson and Troubetzkoy succeeded in discovering the common abstract structure behind the phonemes utilized in different languages. Linguistic structuralism, later to be applied to syntax by Harris and Chomsky, became another driving force in the development of CS, as well as structuralism developed in ethnology by Levi-Strauss, and in cognitive anthropology. In addition, analysis of formal languages (Chomsky 1959a) provided the link to computer science.

1.3 The Rise of Cognitive Psychology

Nineteenth-century psychology has only recently been rediscovered, but failed to contribute to CS's early development because it had been all but extinguished by behaviorism from about 1915 to 1960. Only the later behaviorists considered internal variables (notably Hull), or even memory and mental representation (Tolman). It was information theory (developed by Shannon 1948), or rather its insufficiency to explain central psychological phenomena such as the memory span, which brought G. A. Miller in the mid-1950s to reconsider human information processing. His collaboration with Noam Chomsky, and especially the latter's poignant critique of behaviorist approaches to language (Chomsky 1959b), served to reorient psychological research towards issues of internal storage and processing, towards a psychology that no longer ignored mind and consciousness, yet was careful to stay within the limits of scientific rigor (Miller et al. 1960). Cognitive psychology underwent a rapid development and in 1967, Ulric Neisser wrote the first textbook of the new field, coining its name. Gardner (1985) names further influential researchers in psychology, among them Bruner (notably his work on strategies) and Jean Piaget. Although Piaget's numerous monographs on cognitive development did not become available in English before the 1960s, he is certainly a forerunner of CS who always insisted on the importance of formal principles for explaining cognitive development.

1.4 The Origin of Cognitive Science

A state-of-the-art report on CS by the Alfred P. Sloan Foundation concludes that 'What has brought the field into existence is a common research objective: to discover the representational and computational capacities of the mind and their structural and functional representation in the brain' (Sloan Foundation 1978, p. 6). But it would not be false to say that the Sloan Foundation acted as midwife at the birth of CS. Its committee diagnosed convergent approaches visible across disciplines and went one step beyond that diagnosis to unite what still were very different approaches. Institutionalization followed soon: a journal first (*Cognitive Science*, in 1977), then, two years later, a society and a yearly conference and, still later, doctoral programs and research projects, all evolving into a flourishing new field.

2. The Basic Tenet: Cognition as Computation

The modern idea of computation was formulated in the 1930s. It owes much to Hilbert's program for the complete axiomization of mathematics, limited by Gödel's (1931) proof that not all theorems about a formal system are provable with the means provided by that very same system. Some people have tried to use this result against the idea that cognition could be computation, but did not realize that there may well be truths about the human mind that it fails to arrive at, let alone prove them formally.

The best-known definitions of computation rely on recursive functions (Church 1941), logical productions (Post 1943), or the abstract machine designed by Turing (1936). All these approaches have been proved to be equivalent in scope, and especially the Turing machine may be considered the direct forerunner of today's computers. The common core is the idea of a formal system that uses symbols, i.e., variables and operators combined to form symbolic expressions that are manipulated according to fixed rules and to the internal state of the system.

2.1 Physical Symbol Systems

When they received the Turing Award for their ground-breaking work in AI, Newell and Simon expanded the theory of symbol processing and coined the Physical Symbol Systems Hypothesis (PSSH): 'A physical symbol system has the necessary and sufficient means for intelligent action' (Newell and Simon 1976, p. 117).

A physical symbol system is a formal system. Like all formal systems, it has an 'alphabet' of (at least two) arbitrarily defined symbols, as well as operators to create and transform symbol structures (symbolic expressions) of arbitrary complexity from the elementary symbols of the alphabet according to syntactic rules. This system is 'physical' in the sense that it has been implemented in a suitable way. One such way is the encoding of the symbols as levels of voltages in an array of transistors, and the operations by hard-wired connections between transistors; thus it is done in semiconductor chips. A different way would be to encode the symbols as 'spikes' (action potentials) of neurons. Other ways are possible, but those two already show how the theory can be applied to organisms as well as to technical systems. The point is that a system like that needs the physical implementation in order to function in the real world and become more than just an idea. The kind of implementation is arbitrary, however, because the system is functioning according to its symbolic expressions and syntactic rules, completely independent of its implementation.

Symbols are arbitrary signs, but they designate objects or processes, including processes in the system itself. Their semantics is defined either by reference to an object (in the sense that depending on the respective symbolic expression, the system exerts an influence on the object or is influenced by it), or by the symbolic expression being executable as a kind of program.

Physical symbol systems may have a lot of symbol structures, which means that they need to have a symbol store, or memory, which is unlimited according to Newell and Simon. In fact, physical symbol systems are Turing-equivalent computing devices and, therefore, the PSSH is equivalent to the notion of cognition being computation. The PSSH cannot be proven, nor can it be refuted formally. It gained plausibility, however, through empirical studies of human problem solving and its simulation (Newell and Simon 1972). The PSSH has integrated AI into computer science through the common reference to the theory of automata, a platform which gives a foundation to CS as well. The distinction between functional and implementation levels, elaborated by Newell (1982) and Marr (1982), enabled CS as a science of biological as well as technical cognitive systems.

2.2 Philosophical Foundations: Functionalism and the Computational Theory of Mind

Mental states have been analyzed as 'intentional attitudes' in the philosophy of mind, consisting of a propositional content (e.g., $P =$ *the sun is shining*) and an attitude that characterizes one's own relation to that proposition (e.g., *I wish that P would become true*). Fodor (1975) developed this approach further, arriving at a 'language of thought' that treats the propositional content as data and the intentional relation as an algorithmic one.

If we accept these as the elements of a 'language of thought,' then the question arises of how mental states relate to brain states: a well-known problem in philosophy. Following Putnam (1960), Fodor and others conceptualize the relation between brain and mental states as being parallel to the relation between a computer (i.e., the hardware) and a program running on that computer: the mind as the software of the brain. This approach is known as the computational theory of mind. It fits well with the PSSH, and it soon became the dominant framework in CS. However, it addresses (potentially) conscious thought only, ignoring lower cognitive processes.

2.3 Achievements and Drawbacks of the Classical Symbol-processing Approach

From the twenty-first-century perspective, the PSSH and the computational theory of mind together constitute the classical period of CS, spanning the decade from 1975 to 1985. Within that period, cognitive modeling (see *Cognitive Modeling: Research Logic in Cognitive Science*) emerges as CS's characteristic methodology. Its applications include the following fields.

2.3.1 Problem solving. The former general model of problem solving as heuristic search (Newell and Simon 1972) was enlarged by recognizing the importance of domain-specific knowledge, which became the foundation of an AI technology (knowledge-based systems or 'expert systems'; Hayes-Roth et al. 1983, Buchanan and Shortliffe 1984) and inspired much psychological research on expertise (e.g., Ericsson and Smith 1991).

2.3.2 Cognitive architectures. Rule-based architectures evolved into ambitious models of human cognition in general, comprising memory, problem solving, learning, and some natural language processing. The best-known of these systems are SOAR (Laird et al. 1987, Newell 1990) and the impressive series of ACT, ACT*, and ACT-R frameworks, all developed by John Anderson (Anderson 1976, 1983, Anderson and Lebière 1998).

2.3.3 Natural language processing. From the late 1950s on, theoretical linguistics has been dominated by Noam Chomsky. His theories (notably Chomsky 1981) are framed as theories of human linguistic competence and have inspired CS research on human parsing (Frazier 1987, Mitchell 1994) and on language acquisition (Pinker 1984).

2.3.4 Computers and education. Knowledge-based systems have been built for purposes of instruction, so-called 'intelligent tutorial systems' (Psotka et al.

1988). Although their cost-efficiency relation turned out to be not well suited for general education, they have been used with success for the training of specialists.

The main drawback of research during the classical period of CS was that it excluded many important issues that could well have been covered by assuming mental representation and cognitive algorithms. The original objective for AI, stated by Simon (1955)—to address problems whose solution by a human being would lead us to attribute intelligence to that person—led CS and AI largely to ignore problems that do not seem to require intelligence in people. However, these problems turned out to be the real 'tough nuts,' e.g., navigation and other skilled action.

The computer technology of that period was still mainframe oriented, and interactive and graphic technologies were scarcely developed. This state of the art did not encourage researchers to model real-time agent–environment interaction, although there were some exceptions, e.g., Winograd (1972).

The 'methodological solipsism,' as advocated by Fodor (1980) in connection with his theory of mental representation, and the dominance of logic-based approaches in AI (especially during the 1980s) made CS researchers believe that all interesting aspects of cognition happened within a single symbol system.

In Fodor's 'language of thought,' content is defined as a truthful representation of (a part of?) the world, as in Tarski semantics and similar approaches, which unduly constrains mental representation and ignores its constructive nature.

To summarize, CS research in fact fell short of the scope even its original symbol-processing framework provided.

3. Alternative Computational Frameworks

From a very abstract viewpoint, a Turing machine is all one ever needs to compute. However, different architectures or virtual machines may make some computations easy and others difficult. Classical CS had adopted symbol-processing frameworks. There is a large gap, however, between a functional specification and the way in which a brain is built. The new connectionist movement, which surfaced in the mid-1980s, attempted to bridge the gap with a framework that was all but forgotten at that time.

3.1 Artificial Neural Networks: Connectionism

McCulloch and Pitts (1943) presented the biological neuron as an abstract computing device. Hebb (1949) added a lot of hypotheses, most of which turned out to be correct in the meantime (e.g., that enduring changes in the transmission efficiency of certain synapses are the neurophysiological basis of memory). Rosenblatt (1958) built a simple artificial neural network (ANN)

that could be used for pattern recognition, the 'perceptron.' Soon, connectionism (the name adopted for this line of research) flourished. Its boom came to an end, however, when perceptrons ran into trouble with certain distinctions, and their limitations were mathematically proven (Minsky and Papert 1969). From then on, only a few researchers, mostly in biology and biophysics, continued the connectionist tradition.

The sudden rebirth of connectionism started with the discovery of an architectural change—introduction of 'hidden layers' in ANNs—that overcame the limitations of the perceptron (Rumelhart, McClelland and the PDP group 1986). After a period of heated dispute, connectionism has now been integrated into mainstream CS. Numerous ANN architectures have been developed, and hybrid connectionist–symbolic systems have also been constructed.

3.2 Distributed Representations as Subsymbols

At the heart of the dispute over connectionism was the issue of mental computation. Symbolic and 'localist' connectionist architectures (see Page 2000 for an overview) maintain that variables (or the nodes of an ANN) can be interpreted as being meaningful. In 'parallel distributed processing' (PDP), however, entities are represented by patterns, usually by a 'feature vector' containing the activation values of formal neurons. Smolensky (1988) claimed that only the subsymbolic approach (referring to the elements of a feature vector) grasps the essence of cognition, whereas symbol processing approaches were confined to a mere approximation. To the contrary, Fodor and Pylyshyn (1988) argued that connectionism either was just an implementation of symbol processing (hence banal), or inadequate for modeling productivity and systematicity in natural language. The debate was never resolved, but it is generally recognized that suitability for cognitive modeling is more important than an abstract decision about which framework is 'better,' and that, in fact, both frameworks share important characteristics, being computational as well as representational.

3.3 Beyond Connectionism: Nonlinear Dynamics

Since the early 1990s, another computational framework has been claimed to be useful for cognitive modeling: the theory of nonlinear dynamic systems, initially known as 'chaos theory' (Port and van Gelder 1995). Fine-grained analyses of movement (e.g., in phonetics) and of developmental changes are the intended area of application. Although this renders a more precise picture of how cognitive processes are implemented (like the neural models used in biology are more detailed than connectionist accounts), it could well be that these characteristics are less important on the functional level (Eliasmith 2000).

4. The 'New' Cognitive Science: Interacting Cognitive Systems

The technical cognitive systems of classical AI and CS were systems that were *only* cognitive at their functional level. This is never the case in biological systems: animals live, move and eat, and reproduce. All this basic behavior is made possible without cognition in the sense of thoughtful decision (in lower animals, at least). Built-in physiological regulations, reflexes, instincts and species-specific behaviors serve to achieve the necessary adaptation. Learning in its most primitive form (classical conditioning) has been demonstrated in some worms and, of course, higher species; categorization of stimuli (the forerunner of concepts) in birds and mammals; episodic memory at least in some mammals, especially in apes; full-fledged language in humans only.

Cognition has evolved because of the adaptive value of learning (and the cultural tradition that is based upon it) and thinking (in mental simulation of an act and its consequences). But cognition came late; it has to coexist with those basic regulatory mechanisms mentioned above. In the human species, most of an individual's knowledge, and even specialized cognitive processes, e.g., reading and writing, have to be learned and trained within the culture that provides it. Sensorimotor processes (e.g., driving in a city) rely heavily on a system's interaction with its environment and with special tools (like a car). Also, we are embedded in a social world: many cognitive processes, foremost language, are acquired through social interaction. All this cannot be modeled adequately by a single symbol-processing system that scarcely (if at all) interacts with its environment and with other cognitive systems. In CS, this paradigm shift occurred gradually, starting in the mid-1980s. Having extended its scope since its classical period, modern CS appears as the science of cognitive systems in a fuller sense, as described above.

4.1 Situated Cognition

Using the methodology of field studies, Suchman (1987), Hutchins (1995a, 1995b) and others could demonstrate how much people rely on cues and representations provided by the environment. While traditional accounts of planning rely on mental representations and processes exclusively, human planning can be shown to rely on maps, road signs, guidance by other people, and other external sources. The importance of external representations in problem solving has been repeatedly demonstrated (Zhang 1997).

As is so often the case, 'situated cognition' was introduced as an alternative to the 'old' paradigm of CS. Vera and Simon (1993), however, insisted that CS from its very start (e.g., Newell and Simon 1976) does not exclude situatedness, but rather emphasizes its necessity. Indeed, to realize that cognition is situated can also solve the problem of symbol grounding: mental representations arise and get their meaning in the context of acting in the world (a solution already envisioned by Newell 1980). Situated cognition, it seems, highlights a formerly neglected aspect of CS.

Situatedness also includes the body, not only in the basic sense that cognition coexists with other, more basic processes in organisms. Rather, mental representations are in many ways influenced by the cognitive representation of the body, as Lakoff and Johnson (1980) have shown for metaphors.

4.2 The Social Aspects of Cognition

Culture, and social action, shape a lot of our thoughts and cognitive skills: 'Sociality and culture are made possible by cognitive capacities, contribute to the ontogenetic and phylogenetic development of these capacities, and provide specific inputs to cognitive processes' (Sperber and Hirschfeld 1999, p. cxi). By focusing on a single individual concerned with a single task only, CS had followed the model provided by experimental psychology, its most prominent source of empirical data. The recent change of view in favor of social and cultural factors was mainly due to work in an applied CS area where social interaction is central: education. Lave (1988) gives numerous demonstrations of cultural influences on the solution of apparently context-free tasks in mathematics. More generally, culture-oriented theories of development and learning (beyond sociobiology as in Lumsden and Wilson 1981) have been advanced by Cole (1991) and Tomasello et al. (1993).

Because of the sheer amount of detail provided in cultures, especially in modern industrial ones with libraries and a high degree of specialization in work, it is very difficult to integrate cultural aspects in cognitive theories. The problem is eased when analyses focus on narrowly defined tasks.

A related field is research on groups (e.g., in computer-supported cooperative work (CSCW); Olson and Olson 1997) and on teams of experts (Hinsz et al. 1997). Here, as well as in knowledge engineering (Strube et al. 1996), the task itself comprises the exchange of knowledge and, at least to a certain degree, the development of 'shared knowledge' or 'shared mental models' (Lewis and Sycara 1993).

4.3 A New Paradigm: Autonomous Social Agents and Mixed Groups

According to the dominant paradigm in CS, cognitive systems are conceived as autonomous social agents, situated in a complex dynamic environment. This view bears no accidental resemblance to the shift in AI instigated by new architectures in robotics (Brooks 1991) and the development of intelligent agents (see Wooldrige and Jennings 1995 for an overview).

Agent approaches emphasize the complex action control needed for an agent (robot or organism) that pursues its own goals, which are always many, and potentially conflicting (Maes 1990). Because of restricted resources, agents in the real world cannot be fully rational; however, 'bounded rationality' (Simon 1955) has been claimed a universal principle of human thought (Gigerenzer et al. 1999).

Distributed AI (Bond and Gasser 1988) studies cooperation and competition among agents. The biennial RoboCup contest (Kitano et al. 1997) epitomizes this line of research, having robot or simulated agent teams playing soccer games against each other. The relevance for CS lies in the development of integrated architectures that comprise cognitive and more primitive (so-called 'reactive') regulation, as well as social interaction. This fits well with the current emphasis on situated cognition and with applied problems of CS, e.g., in the field of office automation and cooperation in mixed groups that comprise human workers as well as technical systems, as in the case of air traffic (Hutchins 1995b).

5. Achievements and Present State

CS in the twenty-first century has grown from an innovative interdisciplinary field to an academic discipline of its own, albeit in a still early stage of institutionalization. CS has been evolving differently, however, in different parts of the world. It has a solid infrastructure of departments, graduate programs, etc., in the UK and North America, in France, and in some other countries, but remains still an early stage of institutionalization in Germany, for instance, and still less in many other different countries. In the USA, cognitive neuroscience has split away from cognitive science, at least organizationally. In other countries like France, however, it would be impossible to imagine CS without brain research and neuroscience. The necessity and importance of real-world applications of CS in education, industry, and other fields is generally recognized, but CS still lacks a well-developed professional profile. On the other hand, CS has an impressive record of success in research, an infrastructure of international and national academic societies (foremost the Cognitive Science Society, founded in 1979), international and national conferences, and dedicated CS journals (*Cognitive Science*, founded in 1977, and *Cognitive Science Quarterly*, founded in 2000). An analysis of publications in *Cognitive Science* in 1977–95 found evidence not only for a dominance of psychologists and computer scientists among the CS community, but also for CS

'as a discipline of its own [...] becoming increasingly more common' (Schunn et al. 1998, p. 117). CS, as it seems, is still but steadily evolving.

See also: Cognitive Psychology: History; Cognitive Psychology: Overview; Cognitive Science: History; Cognitive Science: Philosophical Aspects

Bibliography

Anderson J R 1976 *Language, Memory, and Thought*. Erlbaum, Hillsdale, NJ

Anderson J R 1983 *The Architecture of Cognition*. Harvard University Press, Cambridge, MA

Anderson J R, Lebière C 1998 *Atomic Components of Thought*. Erlbaum, Hillsdale, NJ

Boden M A 2000 Autopoiesis and life. *Cognitive Science Quarterly* **1**: 135–46

Bond A H, Gasser L (eds.) 1988 *Readings in Distributed Artificial Intelligence*. Kaufmann, San Mateo, CA

Brooks R A 1991 Intelligence without representation. *Artificial Intelligence* **47**: 139–59

Buchanan B G, Shortliffe E H 1984 *Rule-based Expert Systems*. Addison-Wesley, Reading, MA

Chomsky N 1959a On certain formal properties of grammars. *Information and Control* **2**: 137–67

Chomsky N 1959b Verbal behavior—Skinner B F. *Language* **35**: 26–58

Chomsky, N 1981 *Lectures on Government and Binding*. Foris, Dordrecht, The Netherlands

Church A 1941 *The Calculi of Lambda-Conversion*. Princeton University Press, Princeton, NJ

Cole M 1991 A cultural theory of development: what does it imply about the application of scientific research? Special issue: culture and learning. *Learning and Instruction* **1**: 187–200

Eliasmith C 2000 Is the brain analog or digital? The solution and its consequences for cognitive science. *Cognitive Science Quarterly* **1**: pp. 147–70

Ericsson K A, Smith J (eds.) 1991 *Toward a General Theory of Expertise: Prospects and Limits*. Cambridge University Press, Cambridge, UK

Fodor J A 1975 *The Language of Thought*. Crowell, New York

Fodor J A 1980 Methodological solipsism considered as a research strategy in cognitive psychology. *Behavioral and Brain Sciences* **3**: 63–73

Fodor J A, Pylyshyn Z W 1988 Connectionism and cognitive architecture: a critical analysis. *Cognition* **28**: 3–71

Frazier L 1987 Sentence processing: a tutorial review. In: Coltheart M (ed.) *The Psychology of Reading. Attention and Performance*. Erlbaum, Hove, UK, Vol. 12, pp. 559–86

Frege G 1879/1967 Begriffsschrift: a formula language, modeled upon that of arithmetic, for pure thought. In: van Heijenoort J (ed.) *From Frege to Gödel: a Source Book on Mathematical Logic, 1879–1931*. Harvard University Press, Cambridge, MA pp. 5–82

Gardner H 1985 *The Mind's New Science: a History of the Cognitive Revolution*. Basic Books, New York

Gigerenzer G, Todd P M, ABC Research Group 1999 *Simple Heuristics That Make Us Smart*. Oxford University Press, New York

Gödel K 1931 Über formal unentscheidbare Sätze der Principia Mathematica und verwandter Systeme. *Monatshefte für Mathematik und Physik* **38**: 173 98

Gregory R L (ed.) 1987 *The Oxford Companion to the Mind*. Oxford University Press, Oxford, UK

Hayes-Roth F, Waterman D A, Lenat D B 1983 *Building Expert Systems*. Addison-Wesley, Reading, MA

Hebb D O 1949 *The Organization of Behavior*. Wiley, New York

Hinsz V B, Tindale R S, Vollrath D A 1997 The emerging conceptualization of groups as information processors. *Psychological Bulletin* **121**: 43 64

Hubel D H, Wiesel T N 1962 Receptive fields, binocular interaction and functional architecture in the cat's visual cortex. *Journal of Physiology* **160**: 106–54

Hutchins E 1995a *Cognition in the Wild*. MIT Press, Cambridge, MA

Hutchins E 1995b How a cockpit remembers its speeds. *Cognitive Science* **19**: 265–88

Kitano H, Asada M, Kuniyoshi Y, Noda I, Osawa E, Matsubara H 1997 RoboCup: a challenge problem for AI. *AI Magazine* **18**: 73–85

Laird J E, Newell A, Rosenbloom P S 1987 SOAR: an architecture for general intelligence. *Artificial Intelligence* **33**: 1–64

Lakoff G, Johnson M 1980 *Metaphors We Live By*. Chicago University Press, Chicago

Lave J 1988 *Cognition in Practice: Mind, Mathematics and Culture in Everyday Life*. Cambridge University Press, Cambridge, UK

Lewis C M, Sycara K P 1993 Reaching informed agreement in multispecialist cooperation. *Group Decision and Negotiation* **2**: 279–99

Lumsden C J, Wilson E O 1981 *Genes, Minds and Culture*. Harvard University Press, Cambridge, MA

Maes P (ed.) 1990 *Designing Autonomous Agents. Theory and Practice from Biology to Engineering and Back*. MIT Press, Cambridge, MA

Marr D 1982 *Vision. A Computational Investigation into the Human Representation and Processing of Visual Information*. Freeman, San Francisco

Maturana H R, Varela F J 1980 *Autopoiesis and Cognition: the Realisation of the Living*. Reidel, Dordrecht, The Netherlands

McCulloch W S, Pitts W 1943 A logical calculus of the ideas immanent in nervous activity. *Bulletin of Mathematical Biophysics* **5**: 115–33

Miller G A, Galanter E, Pribram K H 1960 *Plans and the Structure of Behavior*. Holt, New York

Minsky M, Papert S 1969 *Perceptrons*. MIT Press, Cambridge, MA

Mitchell D C 1994 Sentence parsing. In: Gernsbacher M A (ed.) *Handbook of Psycholinguistics*. Academic Press, San Diego, CA, pp. 375–409

Neisser U 1967 *Cognitive Psychology*. Prentice-Hall, Englewood Cliffs, NJ

Newell A 1980 Physical symbol systems. *Cognitive Science* **4**: 135–83

Newell A 1982 The knowledge level. *Artificial Intelligence* **18**: 87–127

Newell A 1990 *Unified Theories of Cognition*. Harvard University Press, Cambridge, MA

Newell A, Simon H A 1972 *Human Problem Solving*. Prentice-Hall, Englewood Cliffs, NJ

Newell A, Simon H A 1976 Computer science as empirical enquiry: symbols and search. *Communications of the ACM* **19**: 113–26

Norman D A 1981 Categorization of action slips. *Psychological Review* **88**: 1–15

Olson G M, Olson J S 1997 Research on computer supported cooperative work. In: Helander M, Landauer T K, Prabhu P V (eds.) *Handbook of Human–Computer Interaction*, 2nd rev. edn. Elsevier, Amsterdam, pp. 1433–56

Page M 2000 Connectionist modelling in psychology: a localist manifesto. *Behavioral and Brain Sciences* **23**

Pinker S 1984 *Language Learnability and Language Development*. Harvard University Press, Cambridge, MA

Port R, van Gelder T J 1995 *Mind as Motion: Explorations in the Dynamics of Cognition*. MIT Press, Cambridge, MA

Post E 1943 Formal reductions of the general combinatorial decision problem. *American Journal of Mathematics* **65**: 197–268

Psotka J, Massey D L, Mutter S A (eds.) 1988 *Intelligent Tutoring Systems: Lessons Learned*. Erlbaum, Hillsdale, NJ

Putnam H 1960 Minds and machines. In: Hook S (ed.) *Dimensions of Mind*. New York University Press, New York, pp. 138–64

Rosenblatt F 1958 The perceptron: a probabilistic model for information storage and organization in the brain. *Psychological Review* **65**: 386–408

Rumelhart D E, McClelland J L & the PDP Group 1986 *Parallel Distributed Processing: Explorations in the Microstructure of Cognition*. MIT Press, Cambridge, MA

Schunn C D, Crowley K, Okada T 1998 The growth of multidisciplinarity in the Cognitive Science Society. *Cognitive Science* **22**: 107–30

Searle J R 1990 Consciousness, explanatory inversion, and cognitive science. *Behavioral and Brain Sciences* **13**: 585–95

Shannon C 1948 A mathematical theory of communication. *Bell System Technical Journal* **27**: 379–423, 623–656

Simon H A 1955 A behavioral model of rational choice. *Quarterly Journal of Economics* **69**: 99–118

Sloan Foundation 1978 *Cognitive Science 1978. Report of the State of the Art Committee*. Alfred P. Sloan Foundation, New York

Smolensky P 1988 On the proper treatment of connectionism. *Behavioral and Brain Sciences* **11**: 1–23

Sperber D, Hirschfeld L 1999 Culture, cognition and evolution. In: Wilson R A, Keil F C (eds.) *The MIT Encyclopedia of the Cognitive Sciences*. MIT Press, Cambridge, MA, pp. cxi–cxxxii

Strube G, Janetzko D, Knauff M 1996 Cooperative construction of expert knowledge: the case of knowledge engineering. In: Baltes P B, Staudinger U M (eds.) *Interactive Minds*. Cambridge University Press, Cambridge, UK, pp. 366–93

Suchman L A 1987 *Plans and Situated Actions: the Problem of Human–Machine Communication*. Cambridge University Press, New York

Tomasello M, Kruger A C, Ratner H H 1993 Cultural learning. *Behavioral and Brain Sciences* **16**: 495–511

Turing A 1936 On computable numbers, with an application to the Entscheidungs problem. *Proceedings of the London Mathematical Society (Series 2)* **42**: 230–65; **43**: 544–546 (addendum)

Vera A H, Simon H A 1993 Situated action: a symbolic interpretation. *Cognitive Science* **17**: 7–48

Wiener N 1948 *Cybernetics*. Wiley, New York

Wilson R A, Keil F C (eds.) 1999 *The MIT Encyclopedia of the Cognitive Sciences*. MIT Press, Cambridge, MA

Winograd T 1972 Understanding natural language *Cognitive Psychology* **3**(1)

Wooldridge M, Jennings N R 1995 Intelligent agents: theory and practice. *Knowledge Engineering Review* **10**: 115–52

Zhang J J 1997 The nature of external representations in problem solving. *Cognitive Science* **21**: 179–217

G. Strube

Cognitive Science: Philosophical Aspects

Cognitive science emerged as a distinct field in the middle 1950s influenced by two important developments. First was the construction of digital computers and their capacity to perform operations that apparently require intelligent thinking. Second was Noam Chomsky's idea that linguistic capacities involve in some sense *knowledge* of and conforming to unconscious grammatical rules and that at least some of this knowledge is innate. The first suggested that the mind's operations could be understood on the model of a computer implementing an internally represented program (Turing 1950). The second that mental capacities are best describable in *intentional* terms like 'knowledge,' 'belief,' and 'following a rule.' Both of these developments rejected behaviorism (Skinner 1953). In its extreme forms behaviorism endorsed the view that human (and other animal) mental capacities are best understood in terms of causal connections between stimuli and responses and that learning is best understood as the change of such connections under reinforcement. Behaviorists tended to reject questions about the internal structures and processes that mediated stimulus and responses. They viewed intentional concepts as meaningless and/or unscientific.

Some mental states are attributed to a person, e.g. beliefs, memories, perceptions, desires, while others are properly attributed only to subpersonal parts or faculties, e.g. the language faculty and the visual system. Both kinds of mental states and processes involving them are *intentional*. 'Intentionality' refers to the fact that mental states *represent*. For example, the thought that New York is tropical represents New York as being tropical. It has long been observed that a thought can represent what doesn't exist (e.g., thoughts about Santa Claus) and misrepresent what does exist. Intentional mental states possess *semantic* properties. They refer and are evaluable as true or false. The thought that New York is tropical refers to New York and is false. Semantic features are shared with natural language expressions and by other kinds of representations (e.g., maps and pictures). For example, *the belief* that New York is tropical and 'New York is tropical' possess the same semantic content. It is widely held that the semantic features of nonmental items are ultimately derived from intentional mental states. Many theories in cognitive science assume that mental processes consist of mental states that are connected by virtue of their semantic contents. Such processes include ones that are 'rational' in that they tend to produce true beliefs or promote survival. Mental information processing consists of sequences of rationally related mental states.

Most cognitive scientists assume that psychological states are part of the natural physical order. However it is usually thought that cognitive science will, like other special sciences, employ its own taxonomy of states, and in particular one that differs from that of neurophysiology. The 'received' view is that psychological states are certain kinds of functional states. A functional state or property is one that is individuated in terms of a causal role. For example, what makes something a carburetor is its causal role in taking gas and air as inputs and producing a mixture of the two as output. In the case of psychological states the causal role involves causal connections to other psychological states, to stimuli, and to behavior. An important feature of functionalist accounts is that physically different kinds of structures can *realize* a given functional state by satisfying its functional specification. Thus carburetors can be made out of metal or plastic and minds out of brains or computers.

There are three big issues in the philosophy of mind. How is rational thinking possible? How can the mind represent the world? What is consciousness? Cognitive science has much to say about the first and has given new twists to the second and third. Below are discussions of these and related issues.

(a) *Is cognitive science possible?* There are philosophical traditions which claim that there can be no science of the mind. The main contemporary objection revolves around the idea that intentionality and rationality are *normative* categories and this disqualifies them from being the subject of scientific laws and causal explanations. Ruminations along these lines can be found in Wittgenstein (1953) and Ryle (1949) and later taken up by philosophers as diverse as Kripke (1982), Davidson (1980), McDowell (1994), and Quine (1960). Davidson's arguments have been especially influential among philosophers. He (1969) argues that in attributing beliefs, thoughts, desires, and other propositional attitudes to one another we are engaged in a project of *interpretation*. Further, he claims that interpretation is guided by a holistic 'principle of charity.' This principle dictates that when attributing mental states we *ought*, other things being equal, to maximize the subject's rationality. Attributions guided by charity are holistic since whether or not a belief or preference, etc. is rational depends on other beliefs, etc. The normativity of *rationality* makes intentional states normative as well. Davidson claims that *interpretation* is so different from the way physical properties are assigned as to make it impossible for there to be any *strict* laws connecting intentional psychological states with physical states or with each other. But while Davidson's (and other such) arguments have been influential it is far from clear that they are sound or even whether if sound they really would undermine the employment of intentional vocabulary in scientific laws and explanations. In any case, cognitive scientists persist in employing intentional concepts in formulating explanations and theories. For example, there is a lively area of cognitive science concerning how people engage in everyday logical and statistical inference that proposes hypotheses concerning causes of errors, selection of conclusions, and so forth (Johnson-Laird 1983). The mental states and processes studied are, of course, intentional ones. The issues of whether the mind and what aspects of mentality can be scientifically studied and whether there are laws involving intentional states are more likely to be resolved by the success (or lack thereof) of the theories produced in the cognitive sciences than by philosophical argument.

Most cognitive scientists think that a science of the mind like other sciences contains laws, which explain psychological capacities and processes. The question arises of how such laws are related to biological laws. According to Fodor (1975), psychological laws are neurophysiologically implemented. In this view psychology is autonomous in that its taxonomy and laws are specific to it but every instance of a psychological law is also an instance of a more basic law or causal mechanism. If this is right then various kinds of mechanisms can implement psychological laws so psychology is not restricted to humans but can apply to Martians and computers. Cognitive scientists disagree about exactly how much can be learned about psychology by studying neurophysiology. 'Top down' theorists (Fodor 1981) think that very little beyond crude neural geography of mental capacities can be learned from neural sciences. At the other extreme, 'bottom up' theorists think quite a lot can be learned about the mind and perhaps even that neurophysiology should replace cognitive psychology.

(b) What is the status of folk psychology? The mental states people attribute to one another (and sometimes animals) include belief, knowledge, memory, desire, perception, and emotions. Normal humans are capable of attributing mental states with reliability and employing them in explaining other mental states and behaviors. Such explanations seem to conform to general principles like 'if a person wants q and believes that doing A is the only way to get q then unless she has a reason not to do A she will intend to do A' and also to somewhat more specific principles like 'if a person sees a friend coming then unless she has some special reason not to she will greet him.' The collection of such principles has come to be known as 'folk psychology.' One issue concerning folk psychology is whether it is approximately true. Fodor (1981, 1987) argues that it is and provides the appropriate starting place of a deeper theory of the mind. In contrast Churchland (1995) argues that folk psychological explanations are often mistaken or vacuous and predicts that a developed science of the mind will abandon it in much the same way that physics abandons folk physics. At the current stage of development many cognitive theories do employ folk psychological concepts (or refinements of them) and produce theories that sometimes explain folk psychological regularities.

(c) Are there unconscious and subpersonal mental states? Folk psychology recognizes that there are unconscious mental states and processes. For example, most of a person's memories are not present to consciousness and the mental processes a person engages in when driving a car might well be unconscious. Psychoanalytic theory, which to some extent has been appropriated by folk psychology, recognizes unconscious thoughts and desires that are not normally accessible to consciousness, at least not without therapeutic assistance. Theories in cognitive science go quite a bit further, often positing intentional states that are in principle inaccessible to consciousness and are properly attributed only to parts of the mind. For example, some psycholinguistic theories posit a language module that *cognizes* grammatical rules formulated in terms of concepts that are unknown to the person but in some way guide comprehension and production of her speech.

Some functional structures engage in mental processes relatively independently of others. Such structures are said to be *cognitively encapsulated modules.* The mental processing engaged in by many modules is not accessible to consciousness although the end product of the processing may be. For example, there is evidence that the mind contains a 'face detecting' module that is able to determine whether or not a person has seen a particular face previously. The picture of the mind that emerges from this is in which it consists of many modules each dedicated to a particular task (e.g., face recognition, speech production, character trait attribution) and a general reasoner which receives information from the modules and whose operations are (partly) consciously accessible. There are disagreements concerning the extent to which cognitive capacities are modularized. Some (e.g., Pinker 1995) seem to think that the mind is massively modularized, while others (Fodor 1983) ascribe much more importance to general reasoning capacities.

(d) What are propositional attitudes? Belief, knowledge, desire, and other folk psychological mental states are said to be *propositional attitudes.* The reason is the widely held view that the 'that' clauses used for attributing such states refer to propositions. There are various views about the nature of propositions but they all have in common that propositions are the part of the meaning of a sentence that is or determines the conditions under which the sentence is true. The question arises of exactly what it is to have a propositional attitude; for example, the belief that

New York is tropical. This question is often seen (e.g., Fodor 1981) as having two parts: (i) what is it to have a belief? (ii) what is it to have a belief that expresses a particular proposition? The most widely accepted answer to the first question is that a belief is a functional state, i.e., it has a certain causal role. One approach to answering the second question is that a belief expresses the proposition that p in virtue of involving a *representation* whose content is that of the intentional state. So to believe that New York is tropical is to be in a functional state (believing) that involves a representation that has the intentional content *that New York is tropical*. This provides a nice explanation of why beliefs are truth evaluable, are about things, can be involved in inferences, etc. It is because these are features of the representations that they contain. The view that the mind contains representations is usually called 'the representational theory of mind' or RTM. It should be cautioned that RTM is restricted to *explicit* beliefs. Implicit beliefs (e.g., your belief you had prior to reading this sentence that no giraffe is bigger than the empire state building) are dispositions to form explicit beliefs under suitable circumstances. This account of propositional attitudes is the beginning of an account of how mental states can have intentional content. It has its dissenters. Some philosophers (Dennett 1981) suggest that there may be no internal representations with the same content as that clause we use in attributing a belief, but it is still appropriate to attribute the belief because of the person's behavioral (including linguistic behavior) dispositions that themselves may involve states that represent at the subpersonal level.

(e) What is the nature of mental representations? Cognitive science is up to its neck (and beyond) in representations. Some representations are involved in propositional attitudes, others in relatively high-level unconscious cognitive systems like the language faculty, and others lower level systems that may implement the higher level systems. There are various views about the nature of these representations. One widely held view (Fodor 1975) is that most mental representations, at least those involved in propositional attitudes, belong to an internal language of thought, 'mentalese.' Mentalese contains basic expressions—predicates, names, connectives, etc. and rules of combination. The rules allow for the construction of a potential infinity of complex expressions from a finite basic vocabulary. There are important differences between a natural language like English and mentalese. The most important difference (as will be further discussed in item (g)) is that mentalese syntax is logical form. Whereas English can be used for communication, mentalese is used for thinking. Understanding a natural language can be accounted for in terms of processes that 'translate' natural language into mentalese. But understanding mentalese cannot be understood in the same way on the pain of regress. Rather mentalese is not literally 'understood' but rather is the language in which thinking and other mental processes take place. Whereas natural languages must be learned, many proponents of mentalese think that in some sense it is innate.

(f) What is thinking? Perception and rational thinking involve mental states that are semantically related. For example, a person sees Macguire swing at a ball and the ball go over the centerfield fence. He thinks that it is a home run number 62 and then that Macguire has broken Maris' home run record. On the representational theory of mind the process running from the visual perception to the thought that the home run record has been broken consists of many representations, e.g., a visual representation of shapes and colors, a perception that the ball is going over the fence, etc. These are not arbitrarily related but are related to each other by virtue of their *semantic* features. These semantic features involve relations to things external to the mind, e.g., to Macguire, the property of being a home run, and so on. How does the mind 'know' to go from a representation, which refers one thing to a representation that refers to a related thing if it has access only to the representations and not to their references? A closely related question is how can the mind engage in reasoning, which leads it from some true representations (say about light striking the retinas) to other true representations (say about the scene in front of the eyes). The computational theory of mind suggests answers to this question. It says that mental processes like thinking and perceiving are *computations* on mental representations. A computer is a device which is able to follow a program for manipulating representations on the basis of their syntax. So any relation which can be reduced to or encoded in syntactical relations can, in principle, be computed. Logical relations, e.g. logical implication, can be reduced to syntactical relations of sentences whose syntactic forms are logical forms (as is the case for Mentalese) computation can then account for logical inference. By encoding semantic features in syntax the computer can manipulate representations in ways that respect their semantics. Researchers in computer science have shown how many tasks that apparently require intelligence can be educed to computations.

According to the computational theory of mind (CTM), the mind is a computer and mental processes consist of computations on Mentalese representations. In this way the mind is able to manipulate representations that are semantically related. Of course there is a big difference between a computer and a mind. The computer is programmed by a human programmer who supplies interpretations for the symbols it manipulates. If the CTM is correct the mind that programs what the mind implements is a product of the structure of the brain and that, presumably, is at least partly dependent on evolution. The interpretation of the symbols that the mind manipulates is not provided by a programmer. Exactly what determines the semantic features of mental representations is discussed in item (i).

Not every cognitive scientist is impressed by CTM as an account of mental processes. Some go along with the idea that mental processes involve a kind of computation but conceive of computation very differently from the TM account. They suggest that the mind has a connectionist *architecture*. I discuss this view in the next section. The most famous philosophical objection to CTM is due to John Searle (1980). Suppose that understanding a language, e.g. Chinese, involves following a program. Searle argues that this cannot be correct since it is possible for a person who knows no Chinese but is able to follow program instructions just like a computer implements the program. The program is written so that questions in Chinese are input and answers in Chinese are output. Searle observes that although the man implements the program he clearly has no clue as to the meanings of the Chinese symbols. There have been many replies to this objection. Perhaps the most convincing from proponents of CTM is that implementing a program is necessary but not sufficient for language understanding. The language must also be translated into the person's Mentalese. Of course this still leaves open the question of what it is for a symbol of Mentalese to represent, which will be discussed in item (i).

A different worry about CTM is whether it can account for certain kinds of reasoning, specifically inductive inference. Inductive reasoning involves considering various hypotheses and coming up with the one that is best supported by the evidence. We employ it in producing explanations, identifying causes, and so forth. For example, Sherlock Holmes solved a case when he realized that the fact that no dog barked was evidence that the murderer was known to the dogs. The worry, which is sometimes called 'the frame problem' (Pylyshyn 1987), is that no computational program can realistically perform this kind of task. In inductive reasoning almost any bit of information may be relevant. We seem to have the ability to survey a great deal of what we know and come up with what is evidentially relevant. But a program that operated by having to survey a vast number of representations evaluating them for relevance would seem to be completely impractical. There are too many computations to be performed. One response to this is to think that CTM may provide good accounts of the information processing that occurs in mental modules but that it is not very good at accounting for the mental capacities of a general reasoner. Thus those who like CTM are attracted to the view that the mind is massively modular.

(g) Classical or connectionist architecture? In the classical account of computation discussed in item (f), the architecture of the mind is that of a classical computer (or system of such computers) and mental processes are operations on linguistic-like representations by virtue of their syntactic forms. There is an alternative account of cognitive structure and computation that has been developed called 'connectionist architecture.' Roughly, a connectionist system consists of a network of *nodes* joined together in a pattern of connections. Each node can be activated (or activated to a certain degree) and can receive signals and send signals to certain connected nodes. Whether or not a signal travels via a connection from node A to node N depends on the weight of the connection. Some nodes are activated by external stimuli (input nodes) and others send signals outside the network. At any time the state of the network is determined by the weights of the connections and the activation of the nodes. Signals that activate the input nodes are propagated throughout the system to the output nodes. Thus connectionist systems can be thought of as computing certain outputs given certain inputs. Further, the connectionist network can be 'trained' by altering the connection weights depending on whether or not a given output is 'appropriate' for a given input. Connectionist networks have been constructed that do a number of tasks e.g. recognize letters of the alphabet, 'read' text, recognize faces, and so forth by such training.

Connectionist cognitive architecture is apparently quite different from a classical computer. There is no 'executive' that is following a program. Computations are not performed on sentences but on the totality of connections among nodes. Although the state of a connectionist system can be thought of as a representation—say as representing that the cat is on the mat—unlike sentences of mentalese it needn't contain any parts that correspond to 'the cat,' 'is on,' and 'the mat.' Proponents of connectionism think that it provides a model of mental states and processes that is more plausible than classical accounts. One reason is that some find it difficult to believe in mentalese. Another is that it seems natural for connectionist systems to implement vague concepts since a connectionist system can be trained to respond in a graded manner. The holism of connectionist representation is also appealing to some and there are suggestions that its holistic features may help with the frame problem mentioned in item (f). Finally, connectionist networks are reminiscent of assemblies of neurons and so strike some as biologically realistic. Proponents of classicism point out that connectionism is more than reminiscent of behaviorism. Like behaviorism it is an *associacionist* psychology that construes mental processes in terms of establishing and modifying associations. Although it is in a sense holistic it is far from clear how that will help accounting for inductive inference. In fact critics of connectionism set up a dilemma (Fodor and Pylyshyn 1988, Fodor and McLaughlin 1990): either the connectionist architecture implements a classical architecture, in which case it is not really an alternative to classicism, or it fails to account for essential features of thought. These features are *productivity* and *syst-*

ematicity. Productivity involves the fact that once a thinker has basic concepts she is able to produce a potential infinity of novel thoughts involving those concepts. Systematicity is the feature that any thinker who can think a thought can think related thoughts that apparently have the same components. For example, if one can think Jack loves Jill then one can also think Jill loves Jack. These features are easily accounted for by classicism since the thoughts correspond to syntactically structured representations. But a connectionist system can be capable of being in a state that represents that Jack loves Jill without being capable of being in a state that represent Jill loves Jack since it need not have parts that correspond to *Jack*, *loves*, *Jill*. If the connectionist system does have such parts then it is merely implementing a classical system.

(h) What are concepts? The *concept* plays an important role in the cognitive sciences. Thoughts (beliefs, memories, desires, etc.) are composed of concepts and so what mental processes a thinker can engage in depends on what concepts she possesses. Developmental psychology is interested in how people acquire concepts and whether some concepts are innate. There are various views about the nature of concepts. Advocates of RTM think of concept tokens as representations but there is a wide diversity of views on what makes a particular representation a particular concept, say the concept *horse*. One view is that a concept is something like a definition. For example, the concept *horse* may be the definition *is a large land mammal that has been domesticated for riding*. To possess the concept *horse* is to know the definition. This view has come under much deserved criticism. One problem is that not all concepts can have definitions without circularity. More serious even is that most words (and the concepts they are associated with) do not seem to have definitions at all. There are horses that are not large and large animals that have been domesticated for riding (e.g., elephants) that are not horses. Another view is that concepts are prototypes. A prototype consists of a core exemplar—a representation of something that is a paradigm example of the concept—and then a similarity metric that determines how close something is to the paradigm. For example, the concept *bird* consists of the representation *robin* and a metric that makes eagles pretty good birds and penguins pretty bad ones. But while there is evidence that thinkers do judge instances of a concept as better or worse examples, the account faces some of the same difficulties faced by the definition account. A somewhat more general approach considers the inferences that a thinker is disposed to make concerning thoughts containing a concept as individuating the concept. Such 'conceptual role' theories of concepts face a dilemma. Either all of the inferences involving the concept are individuative of it (holism) or only some are (molecularism). If the first then, as our beliefs change so do our concepts and it is unlikely that two people ever share the same concept. If the second then the question arises of what makes some inferences concept constituting. There are arguments in the philosophical literature (Quine 1960, Fodor and LePore 1992) that there is no principled distinction between the two but also some proposals (Peacocke 1992) for how to make the distinction. Finally, there is the view that concepts are expressions in mentalese that are individuated by their syntax and by their reference (Fodor 1998). This view allows for thinkers with very different beliefs to share the same concept. But it also allows for the bizarre possibility of someone possessing the concept horse while believing that horses are edible fruits.

Cognitive theories that posit innate knowledge are also committed to the innateness of the concepts that constitute the knowledge. Some cognitive scientists go much further and claim that many of our concepts are innate. One reason for this is the difficulty in accounting for how concepts can be learned. As Fodor (1980) observed, they cannot be learned by testing various hypotheses about them since the formulation of the hypotheses already requires possessing the concept. At one time Fodor thought that this line of argument showed that even the concept *carburetor* is innate. Fodor has since moderated his view but there is no consensus concerning how concepts are acquired.

(i) How does the mind represent the world? What makes a component of a mental state a representation is that it possesses semantic properties, e.g., it refers, has truth-value, and so on. But what exactly determines that a given representation possesses a certain semantic property. The Cartesian tradition generally thought that intentionality is a distinct and basic feature of mental substance. But most philosophers of cognitive science who think that there are mental representations think that whatever determines semantic features has to be within the realm of natural science. On the view that was once widely held in philosophy that concepts are images the answer to this question is that resemblance makes for representation. But even cognitive scientists who posit mental images do not think that these literally resemble their references. The two views that are currently most widely advocated are *informational semantics* and *teleological semantics* or some combination of the two Millikan 1984, Fodor 1987, 1990, Loewer 1998). Simplified informational semantics says that the fact that a certain state carries certain information under certain circumstances or is reliably caused by certain properties under certain circumstances determines its semantic properties. *Teleological semantics* says that semantic properties of a representation are determined by its biological function. A simplified combined view is that the function of carrying certain information under certain circumstances determines representations of semantic properties. For example, it is not implausible that there is a certain system of a frog's brain with the function of being in a particular state R if and only if a fly is nearby when the circumstances are normal (e.g., in a pond, good light, etc.). If the circumstances are normal then an occurrence of R in the frog's brain carries the information (to other parts of the frog's brain) that a fly is present. This kind of account fits very nicely with the view that the mind is a kind of information processor. But whether it can be developed so as to provide a plausible account of the semantics of the mental representations involved in human thought is a big and very open question.

See also: Cognitive Modeling: Research Logic in Cognitive Science; Cognitive Neuroscience; Cognitive Psychology: Overview; Cognitive Science: History; Cognitive Science: Overview; Consciousness and Sensation: Philosophical Aspects; Intentionality and Rationality: A Continental-European Perspective; Intentionality and Rationality: An Analytic Perspective; Knowledge (Explicit and Implicit): Philosophical Aspects; Marr, David (1945–80); Reference and Representation: Philosophical Aspects

Bibliography

Block N 1995 On a confusion about a function of consciousness. *Behavioral and Brain Sciences* **18**: 227–47
Chomsky N 1954 *Syntactic Structures*. Mouton, The Hague
Chomsky N 1959 A Review of Skinner's Verbal Behavior. *Language* **35**: 26–58
Churchland P M 1995 *The Engine of Reason, The Seat of the Soul*. MIT Press, Cambridge, MA
Davidson D 1980 *Essays on Actions and Events*. Oxford University Press, Oxford, UK
Dennett D 1981 *Brainstorms*. MIT Press, Cambridge, MA
Dennett D 1994 *Consciousness Explained*. Little Brown, New York
Descartes R 1641/1970 Meditations on first philosophy. In: ES Haldane, Ross GRT (trans.) *The Philosophical Works of Descartes*, Cambridge University Press, Cambridge, UK, Vol. 1, pp. 131–200
Fodor J A 1975 *The Language of Thought*. Crowell, New York
Fodor J A 1981 *RePresentations: Philosophical Essays on the Foundations of Cognitive Science*. MIT Press, Cambridge, MA
Fodor J A 1983 *The Modularity of Mind*. MIT Press, Cambridge, MA
Fodor J A 1987 *Psychosemantics*. MIT Press, Cambridge, MA
Fodor J A 1990 *A Theory of Content: And Other Essays*. MIT Press, Cambridge, MA
Fodor J A 1998 *Concepts: Where Cognitive Science Went Wrong*. University Press, Oxford, UK
Fodor J A, LePore E 1992 *Holism: a Shopper's Guide*. Blackwell, Oxford, UK
Fodor J A, McLaughlin B 1990 Connectionism and the problem of systematicity. *Cognition* **35**(2): 185–204
Fodor J A, Pylyshyn Z 1988 Connectionism and cognitive architecture: a critical analysis. In: Pinker S, Mehler J (eds.) *Connections and Symbols*. MIT Press, Cambridge, MA

Johnson-Laird P 1983 *Mental Models: Towards a Cognitive Science of language, Inference, and Consciousness*. Cambridge University Press, Cambridge, UK
Kossylyn S M 1980 *Image and Mind*. Harvard University Press, Cambridge, MA
Kripke S A 1982 *Wittgenstein on Rules and Private Language*. Harvard University Press, Cambridge, MA
Loewer B 1998 Guide to naturalizing semantics. In: Hale B, Wright C (eds.) *The Companion to the Philosophy of Language*. Blackwell, Oxford, UK
Loewer B, Georges, Rey 1991 *Meaning in Mind*. Blackwell, Oxford, UK
Marr D 1982 *Vision*. Freeman and Co.
Millikan R 1984 *Language, Thought, and Other Biological Categories*. MIT Press, Cambridge, MA
McDowell J 1994 *Mind and World*. Harvard University Press, Cambridge, MA
Nagel T 1979 *Mortal Questions*. Cambridge University Press, Cambridge, UK
Peacocke C 1992 *A Study of Concepts*. MIT Press, Cambridge, MA
Pinker S 1997 *How the Mind Works*. Norton, New York
Pylyshyn Z W 1984 *Computation and Cognition*. MIT Press, Cambridge, MA
Pylyshyn Z W 1987 *The Robot's Dilemma: The Frame Problem in Artificial Intelligence*. Ablex, Norwood, NJ
Rey G 1997 *Contemporary Philosophy of Mind*. Cambridge, MA
Ryle G 1949 *The Concept of Mind*. Hutchenson's University Library, London
Quine W 1960 *Word and Object*. Technology Press of MIT, Cambridge, MA
Searle J 1980 Minds, brains, and programs with commentaries. *The Behavioral and Brain Sciences* **3**: 417–57
Searle J R 1992 *Rediscovery of the Mind*. MIT Press, Cambridge, MA
Skinner B P 1953 *The Science of Human Behavior*. Macmillan, New York
Smolenski P 1988 On the proper treatment of connectionism. *Behavioral and Brain Sciences* **11**: 1–74
Turing A 1950 Computing machinery and intelligence. *Mind* **59**: 433–60
Wittgenstein L 1953 *Philosophical Investigations* [trans. Anscombe GEM]. Macmillan, New York

B. Loewer

Cognitive Styles and Learning Styles

1. Style Differences in Cognition and Learning

The chorus line of a popular song once claimed that ... *it's not what you do but the way that you do it*. This idea—making the *how* as important as the *what*—is intriguing. Furthermore, as the song insists, the character of an individual is invariably woven into how a task is completed. This can be seen in any number of human endeavors, for example, sport, art, handwriting, thinking, learning, even conversation.

In any performance then, a sense of person, as well as context, combines to produce a typical pattern, hallmark, leit-motif, signature, or style. The very same idea underlies the suggestion that individuals possess a personal way of thinking (cognitive style) or learning (learning style). The following discussion will introduce the construct of style differences in cognition and learning and consider its significance for lifelong learning in both the world of education and workplace.

2. The Style Construct in Psychology

The term *construct* refers to a psychological idea or notion. Examples of constructs are intelligence, personality, or self-concept. A *style construct* appears in a number of academic disciplines—in psychology it has been used in a number of different areas such as personality, cognition, communication, motivation, perception, learning, and behavior.

The theory of style, unfortunately, has been characterized by a tendency for researchers to (a) work in isolation; (b) develop their own instruments for the assessment of style; and (c) the creation of independent style labels with little reference to the field. A widespread use of the term 'style' has led to a number of different definitions and terminology. Consequently, those interested in validity or verifiability, and an accepted nomenclature for a theory of style, have faced considerable difficulty. The idea of style in educational psychology, nonetheless, is recognized as a key construct of individual differences in human performance.

3. Cognitive Styles

While Allport (1937), in work which developed the idea of 'lifestyles,' was probably the first researcher to deliberately use the 'style' construct in association with cognition, the following key areas of psychology contributed to an emerging field of cognitive style.

3.1 Perception

Experimental work—reflecting an emphasis on the 'regularities' of information-processing which were derived from the German gestalt school of perceptual psychology—led to an early development of the 'style construct' of field dependence–independence (Witkin et al. 1971).

Individuals were found to rely upon the surrounding 'field' or 'context' to a greater or lesser extent, when reorienting an object relative to the vertical. This was subsequently found to correlate with competence in disembedding shapes from a field and experimental participants were found to either rely heavily on the field for orientation or shape discrimination (field-dependent) or little or not at all (field-independent).

3.2 Cognitive Controls and Cognitive Processes

A second significant influence in the development of cognitive style was the study of cognitive processes related to individual adaptation to the environment, exemplified by the work of Gardner and co-workers at the Messinger Clinic in the USA. This work was shaped, originally, by psychoanalytic theories of ego psychology—which was typified by studies focusing upon variables in ego adaptation to the environment.

This led to the identification of several cognitive processes including perceptual attitudes, cognitive attitudes, and cognitive controls. Further work related to this area led to several stylistic labels and models, supporting the general notion of a cognitive style (see Messick 1976).

3.3 Mental Imagery

A third key influence in the development of cognitive style reflected work looking at mental representation. Early in the scientific study of psychology, attention was given to the notion that some people have a predominantly verbal way of representing information in thought, while others are more visual or imaginal. Paivio (1971) further developed this notion with a dual coding measurement of mental imagery. Riding and Taylor (1976) identified, as fundamental to the construct of cognitive style, the verbal-imagery dimension of cognitive style.

3.4 Personality Constructs

A fourth and separate influence on the field of cognitive style involved researchers utilizing personality-based constructs to develop a model of learning style (Myers 1978). The most influential model was the Myers–Briggs Type Indicator, developed from Jung's typology of personality constructs and 'psychoanalytic ego psychology' (Jung 1923). It offered an alternative model of cognitive style in contrast to those flowing from cognitive psychology.

4. The Further Development of Cognitive Styles

A contemporary resurgence of interest in style differences over the last three decades has resulted in three distinct developments, all involving the generation of new models of cognitive style or learning styles.

The first development involved researchers independently constructing new models of individual difference in various aspects of cognitive functioning. This approach tended to conceptualize styles as the discovery of new psychological phenomena, for example, styles of thinking, intuition, creativity, decision-making, and motivation.

Examples of some of this work generating additional labels of cognitive style include a model of perceptual style (Gregorc 1982); the Adaptor–Innovator cognitive style of decision-making (Kirton 1994); and the Assimilator–Explorer cognitive style of creativity (Kaufmann 1989). Another more elaborate model of mental self-government presented by Sternberg (1996, 1997) represented a theory of style derived from notions of government. According to this theory, people can be understood in terms of mental government, that is, processes of function, form, level, scope, and learning, which impact upon thinking and learning.

The second development reflected work aimed at a synthesis of theory and a consensus in the understanding of cognitive style. This approach was characterized by a focus upon the construct validity of cognitive style and its application. The work of Curry (1987) and Rayner and Riding (1997), for example, both attempted to synthesize or integrate existing theory of cognitive and learning styles.

The work of Riding over 20 years involved a reclassification of cognitive style models (see Riding and Rayner 1998). The structure of cognitive style was defined as two-dimensional, comprising the Wholist–Analytic style dimension, relating principally to cognitive organization and the Verbal–Imagery style dimension, relating principally to mental representation.

An individual's cognitive style was defined as a person's tendency to process information wholistically or analytically, that is, either as a whole piece or piecemeal, while at the same time mentally representing information using imagery or language. While each dimension was thought to be independent, they were conceptualized as continua and it was not suggested that an individual could only use one or the other way of thinking.

The further development of a computer-based assessment for cognitive style analysis (CSA) by Riding reflected a deliberate attempt to integrate both the Wholist–Analytic and Verbal–Imagery dimensions of cognitive style (see Riding 1991). An extensive number of empirical studies over a number of years were conducted using the CSA at the University of Birmingham and provided evidence to support this model of cognitive style (see Riding and Rayner 1998).

5. Learning Styles

A third more widespread development in contemporary work on style differences in cognition and learning led to the generation of yet more labels, which were described as models of learning styles. This learning-centered tradition of 'style' is arguably distinguished by four major features:

(a) the intention of developing new concepts of learning to reduce reliance upon tests of intelligence or ability;

(b) a focus on the learning process and achievement;

(c) a primary interest in the effect of individual differences upon pedagogy;

(d) a parallel construction of new assessment instruments and models of learning style.

The primary concern for educationists working within this learning-centered tradition lay with the process of learning and its context. It focused on individual differences in the process of learning rather than within the individual learner. Models of learning styles in this tradition included the following four groups.

5.1 Models Focusing on the Learning Process—Based on Experiential Learning

These derived from a theory of experiential learning, and the most influential example was the work of Kolb (1976), who described learning style as the individual's preferred method for assimilating information, in an active learning cycle. Kolb constructed a two-dimensional model comprising perception (concrete/abstract thinking) and processing (active/reflective information processing) as fundamental aspects of an experiential learning cycle.

5.2 Models Focusing on the Learning Process—Based on Orientation to Study

These derived from a theory of information processing and learning processes, and the most influential example was developed by Entwistle called the 'Approaches to Study Inventory.' Entwistle (1981) found that approaches to study often reflected either a surface or deep engagement with the study task. This was later extended to include four key orientations to study: meaning, reproducing, achieving, and holistic. The model was further refined as an integrated conception of the learning process, which described a series of actions linked to specific learning strategies identified in his original model.

5.3 Models Focusing on Instructional-preference

These set out to measure a range of environmental or instructional factors affecting an individual's learning behavior. A leading example of this type was the Learning Styles Inventory (LSI) developed by Dunn et al. (1989). The learning style elements identified in the LSI were: *environmental stimulus* (light, temperature); *emotional stimulus* (persistence, motivation); *sociological stimulus* (peers, adults); *physical stimulus* (perceptual strengths, time of day—morning vs. afternoon); and *psychological stimulus* (global/analytic, impulsive/reflective).

5.4 Models Focusing on Cognitive Skills, and Learning Strategy Development

The fourth group of learning style labels focused on an individual's developing cognitive ability and repertoire of cognitive skills or ability to learn, together with related behavioral characteristics, which were understood to comprise an individual's learning profile. Learning style was typically perceived as a multimodal construct and understood to describe a range of intellectual functioning relating to the learning activity.

An example of this type of model was the Learning Styles Profile developed by the North American Association of Secondary School Principals (Keefe 1988). This style construct described 24 key elements in learning style, grouped into three categories: cognitive skills—relating to aspects of information processing; perceptual responses—encompassing perceptual responses to data; study and instructional preference—referring to motivational and environmental elements affecting learning preferences.

6. Cognitive Style or Learning Styles

The models in the learning-centered tradition shared several limitations. First, they reflected a construct that by definition was not stable—it was grounded in process and therefore susceptible to rapid change. Second, they did not describe a developmental rationale for the concept of learning style nor easily correspond to other models of assessment, thereby suggesting a problem for conceptual validity. Third, they attracted peer criticism for lacking psychometric rigor and a systematically developed theory supported by empirical evidence (see Grigerenko and Sternberg 1995).

The learning-centered tradition, however, reflected a continuing need for a theory of individual differences which could be applied to the learning context. It also reinforced previous work in the area of cognitive style and pointed to the potential for profiling the personal learning style of an individual (see Rayner 2000).

7. Implications of Style for Lifelong Learning

At the 1997 Seventh International Conference on Thinking, Howard Gardner argued that in the not too distant future people will look back to the end of this millennium, and laugh at the 'uniform school.' They will be greatly amused, he suggested, by the idea that educationists actually believed they could teach the same things to all children at the same time and in the same way. To believe that the *uniform school* can provide efficient or effective education, he concluded, was to endorse educational failure!

The extent to which an awareness of learning style or the self as a learner is currently considered and managed within the educational context raises key questions for the design of instruction and pedagogy, including a consideration of:

(a) assessment-based learning;
(b) differentiation in the curriculum;
(c) learning method routines;
(d) professional development.

Each of these approaches, if adopted with an eye to considering the benefit of a pedagogy which is style-friendly, encourages interactive learning, builds upon the principles of individual difference, and adopts the idea of developing a learning expertise within the learner, will provide a foundation for lifelong learning (see Rayner 2000).

Implicit in all of this work, and equally relevant to the classroom as to the workplace, is the notion of the *matching hypothesis*. The full value and significance to the professional of cognitive and learning styles rest ultimately with the belief that if it is possible to make a better match between person and environment, then performance will improve and achievement will be enhanced. Moreover, formal education might be made more effective by matching style to materials, to presentation, mode and structure, through nurturing strategy development to maximize style effectiveness.

The delivery of a curriculum, albeit for schooling or workplace training, will improve with an increasing depth of differentiation and a match between individual differences with targeted learning or activity. Such an approach will build upon personal strengths, sow seeds of success, and reap the benefits of learning enhancement.

The final word in offering an overview of style differences in thinking, learning, and behavior is left to Sternberg (1996, p. 363). He succinctly stated that in the world of learning and education, '*styles matter*'! This view mirrors that of many workers in the field who remain interested in knowing more about those individual differences which affect human performance.

See also: Mental Imagery, Psychology of; Mental Representations, Psychology of; Metacognitive Development: Educational Implications; Self-regulated Learning

Bibliography

Allport G W 1937 *Personality: A Psychological Interpretation.* H. Holt and Co., New York

Curry L 1987 *Integrating Concepts of Cognitive or Learning Style: A Review with Attention to Psychometric Standards.* Canadian College of Health Service Executives, Ottawa, ON, Canada

Dunn R, Dunn K, Price G E 1989 *Learning Styles Inventory.* Price Systems, Lawrence, KS

Entwistle N J 1981 *Styles of Learning and Teaching: An Integrated Outline of Educational Psychology for Students, Teachers and Lecturers.* Wiley, Chichester, UK

Gregorc A R 1982 *Style Delineator*. Gabriel Systems, Maynard, MA

Grigerenko E L, Sternberg R J 1995 Thinking styles. In: Saklofske D H, Zeidner M (eds.) *International Handbook of Personality and Intelligence*. Plenum, New York

Jung C G 1923 *Psychological Types*. Harcourt Brace, New York

Keefe J W 1988 *Profiling and Utilising Learning Style*. National Association of Secondary School Principals, Reston, VA

Kaufmann G 1989 *The Assimilator-Explorer Inventory*. University of Bergen, Bergen, Norway

Kirton J W (ed.) 1994 *Adaptors and Innovators*, 2nd edn. Routledge, London

Kolb D A 1976 *Learning Style Inventory: Technical Manual*. Prentice-Hall, Englewood Cliffs, NJ

Messick S 1976 *Individuality in Learning*, 1st edn. Jossey-Bass, San Francisco

Myers I 1978 *Myers–Briggs Type Indicator*. Consulting Psychologists Press, Palo Alto, CA

Paivio A 1971 Styles and strategies of learning. *British Journal of Educational Psychology* **46**: 128–48

Rayner S 2000 Reconstructing style differences in thinking and learning: profiling learning performance. In: Riding R, Rayner S (eds.) *International Perspectives on Individual Differences*. Ablex, Stanford, CT, Vol. 1

Rayner S, Riding R 1997 Towards a categorisation of cognitive styles and learning styles. *Educational Psychology* **17**: 5–28

Riding R J 1991 *Cognitive Styles Analysis*. Learning and Training Technology, Birmingham, UK

Riding R J, Rayner S G 1998 *Cognitive Styles and Learning Strategies*. David Fulton Publishers, London

Riding R J, Taylor E M 1976 Imagery performance and prose comprehension in 7 year old children. *Educational Studies* **2**: 21–7

Sternberg R J 1996 Styles of Thinking. In: Baltes P B, Staudinger U M (eds.) *Interactive Minds*. Cambridge University Press, Cambridge, UK

Sternberg R J 1997 *Thinking Styles*. Cambridge University Press, Cambridge, UK

Witkin H A, Oltman P, Raskin E, Karp S 1971 *A Manual for Embedded Figures Test*. Consulting Psychologists Press, Palo Alto, CA

S. G. Rayner

Cognitive Theory: ACT

ACT is a theory of human cognition that posits particular ways of representing knowledge and the mechanisms by which such knowledge is acquired and used (Anderson 1983, 1993, Anderson and Lebiere 1998). The theory is implemented as a computer simulation system that generates the theory's predictions, thereby facilitating quantitative comparisons with experimental data.

1. What's in a Name?

The etymology of the acronym ACT is the subject of some debate. The original definition, Adaptive Con-trol of Thought, has not been consistently used, and several books written about the theory suggest alternative candidates, e.g., *The Adaptive Character of Thought* (Anderson 1990) and *The Atomic Components of Thought* (Anderson and Lebiere 1998). However, these publications postdate ACT's modest beginnings by more than a decade, making the simpler moniker A Cognitive Theory seem the most parsimonious answer.

2. Architectures and Models

Among computational systems designed to model cognition, there is a critical distinction between a cognitive *architecture* and a cognitive *model* built within an architecture. A cognitive architecture defines a specific way of representing knowledge and a fixed set of mechanisms for processing knowledge. A cognitive model, on the other hand, specifies the knowledge that is required to perform a particular task. Any one architecture supports a wide variety of models, all of which use the same mechanisms to capture behavior in different tasks, just as the brain presumably employs a common set of mechanisms across a variety of tasks.

The ACT theory is a cognitive architecture. It provides mechanisms for the retrieval and learning of facts (declarative knowledge) and the selection, application, and learning of skills (procedural knowledge). All cognitive models built within ACT share these mechanisms; what differs across ACT models is the task-specific knowledge (i.e., the facts and skills themselves) input to the system. ACT models have successfully fit behavioral data across a wide variety of tasks, including arithmetic, navigation, categorization, and game playing (see Table 1). The success of these ACT models across such varied domains provides support not only for the models themselves but for the explanatory power of the ACT architecture.

This article focuses on the current version of the ACT theory, called ACT-R (Anderson and Lebiere 1998). Nevertheless, a historical sketch of the theory's evolution and how it relates to contemporary research are presented as well as a brief discussion of future research issues.

3. Basic Features of the Theory

The four main tenets of the ACT theory are as follows:

(a) the ability to perform a complex task can be decomposed into separate pieces of knowledge;

(b) these pieces of knowledge are learned through experience, i.e., using a piece of knowledge is akin to practice;

(c) at any given time, the current focus of attention (also called the goal) influences what knowledge is used; and

(d) there are two types of knowledge, *declarative* (for facts) and *procedural* (for skills), that have distinct representations and learning mechanisms.

Table 1

A list of tasks and phenomena modeled with the ACT theory

1	Visual search including menu search
2	Subitizing
3	Dual tasking including Psychological Refractory Period (PRP)
4	Similarity judgments
5	Category learning
6	List learning experiments
7	Paired-associate learning
8	The fan effect
9	Individual differences in working memory
10	Cognitive arithmetic
11	Implicit learning (e.g., sequence learning)
12	Probability matching experiments
13	Hierarchical problem solving tasks
14	Strategy selection
15	Analogical problem solving
16	Dynamic problem solving tasks including military command and control
17	Learning of mathematical skills including interacting with Intelligent Tutoring Systems (ITSs)
18	Development of expertise
19	Scientific experimentation
20	Game playing
21	Metaphor comprehension
22	Learning of syntactic cues
23	Syntactic complexity effects and ambiguity effects
24	Dyad communication

Declarative knowledge is represented as nodes in an associative network. The more activated a given node, the more easily the corresponding fact can be accessed. Each node has an associated base-level activation B that increases each time the fact corresponding to that node is accessed (learning) and decays with time (forgetting) according to the equation

$$B = \ln\left(\sum_j (t - t_j)^{-d} \right) \qquad (1)$$

where t is the current time, t_j is the time of the jth use of the node, and d is a global decay rate. The quantity B offers a summary description of a node's past history of use and hence a reasonable estimate of its likelihood to be needed in the future.

Each link between two nodes in the network has a continuous-valued quantity S that measures the strength of association between those two nodes. The current focus of attention works by selecting a subset of nodes in the network to be attended. Each attended node gets a share of a limited amount of attentional activation W. (Because attentional activation is lim-

ited, the more nodes in the focus, the less attentional activation for each.) This activation then propagates from each attended node to related nodes in the network in proportion to the corresponding link strengths. This attentional activation produces context effects because only those nodes related to the current focus of attention receive extra activation.

The *total* activation at node i is the sum of its base-level activation B_i and the attentional activation it receives from nodes in the focus of attention:

$$A_i = B_i + \sum_j W_j S_{ji} \qquad (2)$$

where the sum is over attended nodes j. Retrieval of facts is determined by the total activation of the corresponding nodes. Specifically, the node that is retrieved is the one whose total activation plus some added noise is highest, given that this sum is above a global threshold. This added noise represents stochasticity in the system. The time it takes to recall this node decreases exponentially as a function of its (noisy) activation which, combined with Eqn. (1), produces a power-law speedup with practice (see *Learning Curve, The*).

Procedural knowledge is represented by a set of condition–action pairs called production rules (e.g., IF the goal is to add two numbers a and b, and the fact that c is the sum of a and b can be recalled, THEN say c is the answer). Each production has several associated quantities that reflect how useful it has been in past applications. These quantities are learned by experience and used to compute an estimate of the expected gain from applying each rule. For example, the cost associated with a particular production rule is the weighted average of the rule's past costs of application (measured in units of time) and a prior estimate of cost. When several rules are candidates at the same time, the one whose expected gain plus some added noise is highest gets selected. In this way, production rules that have been more useful (i.e., more successful and less costly) in the past are more likely to be selected. In addition, each piece of procedural knowledge is strengthened with each application, and that strength decays with time. A production rule's speed of application increases exponentially with strength.

The ACT theory also posits more complicated mechanisms by which production rules and declarative nodes are initially created. In both cases, the goal plays an important role in the form that new knowledge takes. These separate mechanisms highlight ACT's distinction between acquiring new pieces of knowledge and refining the continuous quantities associated with each piece of knowledge. Moreover, these two modes of knowledge representation—symbolic (nodes, production rules) and sub-symbolic (activations, costs, strengths)—make ACT a *hybrid* system. This distinguishes it from wholly symbolic (e.g., Soar) and wholly sub-symbolic (e.g., connectionist) systems.

4. Historical Development

ACT has been under development since the 1970s. It began as a theory of semantic memory and now encompasses learning, memory, problem solving, attention, perception, and action. The following provides a brief sketch of its development and places each version of the theory in its historical context. Until the 1970s, mathematical models were the typical formalism used to describe and predict cognitive psychological phenomena. A disadvantage of mathematical models, however, is that they are limited in the complexity of processes they can describe. Thus, to provide a mechanistic account of complex cognitive processes, computational models began to be developed. The first well-defined version of the ACT theory, called ACTE (Anderson 1976), was one such model. It introduced the distinction between declarative (i.e., factual) and procedural (i.e., skill-based) memory and the notion of declarative activation.

By the 1980s, however, some researchers were questioning whether the development of computational models (and the theories they implemented) was sufficiently constrained to produce reasonable models of the 'true' underlying representations and processes (e.g., Anderson 1978, Newell 1973). One approach that reduces this problem involves developing models within a cognitive architecture, where a fixed set of representations and mechansims are used to test a variety of models. That is, models are constrained to work within the strictures of the architecture. The next version of the ACT theory, ACT* (Anderson 1983) was a cognitive architecture, like others developed around this time (see also *Cognitive Theory: SOAR*; Newell 1990). ACT* extended its predecessor by specifying an activation calculus for declarative knowledge and a new mechanism for acquiring procedural knowledge.

Besides using ACT* to model a variety of task domains—from language processing to paired-associate learning—this version of the theory was applied to the practical problem of improving computer-aided instruction. So-called 'intelligent' tutoring systems were built based on ACT* cognitive models of algebra problem solving, geometry theorem proving, and computer programming (e.g., Anderson et al. 1989, 1990). Because these models could solve the required problems in each domain, they enabled the corresponding tutoring systems to follow students' problem-solving, give feedback when students made a mistake, and offer hints when students were confused. Moreover, because these systems tracked the steps students were taking and hence the knowledge they were using, specific predictions of the theory could be generated and tested in this scaled-up, real-world learning context.

The latest incarnation of the ACT theory, ACT-R (Anderson 1993, Anderson and Lebiere 1998), was developed in the 1990s, inspired by a rational analysis of cognition (Anderson 1990). Among other things, ACT-R includes a refined activation calculus and a more plausible mechanism for acquiring procedural knowledge. These changes were designed to reflect the way human cognition adapts to the structure of the environment. In addition, ACT-R has been put to the toughest challenges in testing its fidelity to empirical data: ACT-R models have been able to fit fine-grained, multivariate data simultaneously across several experiments (e.g., Anderson and Matessa 1997), and they have captured patterns of performance in individual subjects across tasks (e.g., Lovett et al. 2000).

In sum, the ACT theory has evolved into its current form by virtue of the guiding force of several kinds of constraints. Throughout ACT's development, experimental data have been used to test the veridicality of the theory. In some cases, this empirical constraint has invoked a reevaluation of some aspect of the theory (e.g., single-trial learning of production rules). More generally, even when the theory's predictions have been met, refinements were made so that more detailed, fine-grained datasets could be modeled. Besides these empirical constraints on the theory there are theoretical constraints imposed top-down from the architectural status of ACT's claims. That is, an ACT model may need to be designed in a certain way so that the knowledge it specifies is sufficient to perform the given task when ACT mechanisms are applied. Finally, based on the rational analysis of cognition (Anderson 1990), constraints have been imposed on the theory so that it includes the kind of processing that is necessary and sufficient to meet the demands of the environment.

5. Future Issues

The ACT theory is still under active development. An extension has been added (called ACT-R/PM, Byrne and Anderson 1998) that incorporates perception and motor modules (e.g., eyes, ears, and hands). This extension enables the system to model interaction with the environment. In addition, ACT models have been developed for a variety of new domains, including complex, dynamic tasks such as air-traffic control. In some cases, the data sets being modeled even include eye-movement protocols. Yet another area of development involves exploring the relationship between the algorithmic level of description of the ACT-R computer simulation system (cf. Marr 1982) and a corresponding neural level implementation.

See also: Cognitive Psychology: History; Cognitive Psychology: Overview; Cognitive Theory: SOAR; Knowledge Spaces; Knowledge Representation; Logics for Knowledge Representation; Mathematical

Psychology; Problem Solving and Reasoning, Psychology of;

Bibliography

Anderson J R 1976 *Language, Memory, and Thought*. Erlbaum, Hillsdale, NJ

Anderson J R 1978 Arguments concerning representations for mental imagery. *Psychological Review* **85**: 249–77

Anderson J R 1983 *The Architecture of Cognition*. Harvard University Press, Cambridge, MA

Anderson J R 1990 *The Adaptive Character of Thought*. Erlbaum, Hillsdale, NJ

Anderson J R 1993 *Rules of the Mind*. Erlbaum, Hillsdale, NJ

Anderson J R, Lebiere C 1998 *The Atomic Components of Thought*. Erlbaum, Mahwah, NJ

Anderson J R, Boyle C F, Corbett A T, Lewis M W 1990 Cognitive modeling and intelligent tutoring. *Artificial Intelligence* **42**: 7–49

Anderson J R, Conrad F G, Corbett A T 1989 Skill acquisition and the LISP tutor. *Cognitive Science* **13**: 467–505

Anderson J R, Matessa M 1997 A production system theory of serial memory. *Psychological Review* **104**: 728–48

Byrne M D, Anderson J R 1998 Perception and action. In: Anderson J R, Lebiere C (eds.) *The Atomic Components of Thought*. Erlbaum, Mahwah, NJ

Lovett M C, Daily L Z, Reder L M 2000 A source activation theory of working memory: Cross-task prediction of performance in ACT-R. *Cognitive Systems Research* **1**: 99–118

Marr D 1982 *Vision*. Freeman, San Francisco

Newell A 1973 You can't play 20 questions with nature and win: Projective comments on the papers of this symposium. In: Chase W C (ed.) *Visual Information Processing*. Academic Press, New York

Newell A 1990 *Unified Theories of Cognition*. Harvard University Press, Cambridge, MA

M. C. Lovett

Cognitive Theory: SOAR

SOAR is a computational theory of human cognition that takes the form of a general cognitive architecture (Laird et al. 1987, Newell 1990, Rosenbloom et al. 1992). SOAR (not an acronym) is a major exemplar of the architectural approach to cognition, which attempts the unification of a range of cognitive phenomena with a single set of mechanisms, and addresses a number of significant methodological and theoretical issues common to all computational cognitive theories (Anderson and Lebiere 1998, Newell 1990, Pylyshyn 1984). SOAR is also characterized by a set of specific theoretical commitments shaped primarily by attempting to satisfy the functional requirements for supporting human-level intelligence, manifest in soar's parallel existence as a state-of-the art artificial intelligence system (Laird et al. 1987). This focus on functionality, and its attendant theoretical commitments, is what makes soar both distinctive and controversial in cognitive psychology. SOAR represents the last major work of Allen Newell, one of the founders of modern cognitive science and artificial intelligence, and a pioneer in the development of architectures as a class of cognitive theory.

1. Multiple Constraints on Mind and Computational Theories of Cognition

Newell (1980a, 1990) described the human mind as a solution to a set of functional constraints (e.g., exhibit adaptive (goal-oriented) behavior, use language, operate with a body of many degrees of freedom) and a set of constraints on construction (a neural system, grown by embryological processes, arising through evolution). The structure of SOAR is shaped primarily by three of the functional constraints: (a) exhibiting flexible, goal-driven behavior, (b) learning continuously from experience, and (c) exhibiting real-time cognition (elementary cognitive behavior must be evident within about a second).

The emergence of computational models of cognition in information processing psychology (and artificial intelligence) represented a significant theoretical advance by providing the first proposals for physical systems that could, in principle, satisfy the functional constraints of exhibiting intelligence (Newell et al. 1958, Newell and Simon 1972). However, they raised a set of difficult methodological and theoretical issues that cognitive science still grapples with today. Among these issues are: (a) the problem of irrelevant specification (in a complex computer program, which of the myriad aspects of the program carry theoretical content, and which are irrelevant implementation details) (Reitman 1965); (b) the problem of too many degrees of freedom (an unconstrained computer program can be modified to fit any data pattern); and (c) the problem of identifiability (any sufficiently general proposal for processing schemes or representations can mimic the input/output characteristics of any other general processing or representation scheme (Anderson 1978, Pylyshyn 1973).

2. SOAR as a Confluence of Five Major Technical Ideas in Cognitive Science

SOAR can be seen as a confluence of five major technical ideas in cognitive science, which, taken together, are intended to address the three functional constraints summarized above, as well as the fundamental methodological issues concerning computational models.

2.1 Physical Symbol Systems

SOAR is a physical symbol system. The physical symbol system hypothesis asserts that physical symbol systems are the only class of systems that can in principle satisfy the constraint of supporting intelligent, flexible behavior. Physical symbol systems are a reformulation of Turing universal computation (Church 1936, Turing 1936) that identifies symbol processing as a key feature of intelligent computation. The requirement is that the system be capable of manipulating and composing symbols and symbol structures—physical patterns with associated processes that give the patterns the power to denote either external entities or other internal symbol structures (Newell 1980a, 1990, Simon 1996). The key to the universality of Turing machines and physical symbol systems is their programmability: content can be added to the systems (in the form of programs) to change their behavior, yielding indefinitely many response functions.

2.2 Cognitive Architectures

SOAR is a cognitive architecture. A cognitive architecture is a theory about the fixed computational structure of cognition (Anderson and Lebiere 1998, Newell 1990, Pylyshyn 1984). Computational systems that are programmable must have some kind of fixed structure that processes the variable content: a set of primitive processes, memories, and control structures. The theoretical status of this underlying structure has not always been clear in cognitive models. For example, when a cognitive model is programmed in Lisp, the theorist intends to make some theoretical claims about the program (e.g., that the steps of the program corresponds in some way to the cognitive steps of the human performing the task), but probably intends to make no theoretical claims about Lisp as the architecture that executes the program (e.g., the fact that unused memory structure are reclaimed via a garbage collection process is theoretically irrelevant).

A cognitive architecture explicitly specifies a fixed set of processes, memories, and control structures that are capable of encoding content and executing programs. Cognitive models for specific tasks can be developed in such architectures by programming them. The theoretical status of various parts of a programmed implementation is now considerably clarified: what counts is the structure of the architecture (not its particular implementation), and the cognitive model's program, which makes a set of specific commitments about the form and content of knowledge used in a specific task. Thus, implemented cognitive architectures go a long way toward solving the irrelevant specification problem.

Cognitive architectures, especially those with temporal mappings and integrated learning mechanisms, can also address the degrees of freedom problem and identifiability problem in four ways. First, to the extent that architectures have a constrained temporal mapping, the space of possible programs that yield both the required functionality and temporal profile is

considerably reduced. Second, to the extent that architectures have learning components that can acquire new knowledge (e.g., about a specific task), the form of that knowledge is no longer freely under control of the theorist. Third, to the extent that architectures are programmable (and are also constrained by a temporal mapping or learning mechanism), they permit a single set of processing assumptions to be applied to a diverse range of tasks, constraining that theory by a broader range of data. Fourth, to the extent that cognitive architectures are comprehensive and include some perceptual and motor components, they can be used to provide closed-loop models of complete tasks, so that no explanatory power need be ascribed to anything external to the model.

2.3 Production Systems

All long-term memory in SOAR is held in the form of productions (Anderson 1993, Newell 1973). Each production is a condition-action pair. The conditions form access paths and the actions form the memory contents. Productions continuously match against a declarative working memory that contains the momentary task context, and matching productions put their contents (actions) back into the working memory. Productions are the lowest level of elementary memory access available in SOAR, and Newell's (1990) temporal mapping onto human cognition places them approximately at the 10 ms level. This mapping provides strong constraints on the shape of cognitive models built in SOAR that must operate in real time.

SOAR's productions form a recognition memory. Such recognition memories have a number of features that make them attractive as models of human memory: they are associational in nature (access is via the contents of working memory); they are fine-grained and independent (which makes them a good match for continuous, incremental learning mechanisms); they are dynamic (a production system by itself defines a computationally complete system that can yield behavior; other processes are not needed to access or execute the memory structures); and they are cognitively impenetrable (their contents and structure may not be arbitrarily searched over, examined, or modified, but only accessed via automatic association). All of these properties place them in sharp contrast to memories in digital computers, which are static structures (not processes), freely addressable by location.

3. Search in Problem Spaces Supported by a Two-level Automatic/Deliberate Control Structure

SOAR achieves all cognition by search in problem spaces, and architecturally supports this by a flexible, two-level recognize–decide–act control structure. Problem spaces are based in part on the idea that search in combinatoric spaces is the fundamental process for attainment of difficult tasks. The nature of such search is seen most easily in tasks like chess that have a well-defined set of operators and states. A search space consists of a set of (generated) representational states and operators that transition between states.

Problem spaces as realized in SOAR extend the standard notion of search in an important direction: problems spaces are taken to be the fundamental way that humans accomplish all cognitive tasks, including routine (i.e., well-practiced) tasks. SOAR is, therefore, one realization of the problem-space hypothesis (Newell 1980b), which asserts that all deliberate cognitive activity occurs in problem spaces. The key to this move lies in the role of knowledge in problem spaces: problem spaces freely admit of any amount of knowledge for guiding search, executing operators, or formulating the space initially in response to a task. Because SOAR provides a set of mechanisms (described next) that support this kind of knowledge use, behavior in SOAR spans the well-known continuum between knowledge-intensive processing (little search) and knowledge-lean processing (much search) (Newell 1990).

Supporting knowledge-driven search places strong functional demands on the architecture's control structure: at any step in the problem-solving process—selecting the next operator, generating the next state, etc.—any relevant knowledge must be brought to bear. There are two parts to the solution to this problem: the mechanisms for appropriate indexing of the knowledge, and the mechanisms for retrieving and applying the relevant knowledge during search. The indexing concerns learning, discussed below.

For retrieving and applying the knowledge during search, SOAR relies on a two-level control structure that separates the automatic access of knowledge via the productions from the deliberate level of problem solving. Each cognitive step is accomplished by a recognize–decide–act cycle. In the recognize phase, all productions that match the current state fire, producing new content in the working memory. Part of this retrieved content is about what the system should do next—the possible operators to try in the current state, the relative desirability of these operators (e.g., operator A is better than operator B), and so on. Next, in the decide phase, a fixed (domain independent) decision procedure sorts out these preferences in working memory to determine if they converge on a consistent decision. In the event that this processing clearly determines the next step, the decision procedure places in working memory an assertion about what that step should be. In the act phase, that step is taken (by additional production rule firings): the move to the next state in internal problem space search, or the release of motor intentions in external interaction. If it

is not clear what to do next (e.g., several operators have been proposed, but no knowledge is evoked to prefer one option to another, or there are conflicts in the retrieved knowledge), an *impasse* has arisen, and the decision procedure records in working memory the type of the *impasse*, and sets a subgoal of resolving that *impasse*. In this way, SOAR's problem solving gives rise automatically to a cascade of subgoals whenever the knowledge delivered by the recognition memory is insufficient for the current task.

The critical feature of this control structure is its run-time, least-commitment nature: each local decision in the problem space is made at execution time by assembling whatever relevant bits of knowledge can be retrieved (by automatic match) at that moment. Decisions are not fixed in advance, and there are no architectural barriers to the kinds of knowledge that can be brought to bear on the decisions.

3.1 Continuous, Impasse-driven Learning

SOAR continuously acquires new knowledge in its long-term memory through an experience-based learning mechanism called chunking (Laird et al. 1987, Rosenbloom and Newell 1983). This mechanism generates new productions in the long-term memory by preserving the results of problem solving that occurred in response to impasses. The conditions of the new production consist of aspects of the working memory state just before the impasse, and the actions of the production consist of the new knowledge that resolved the *impasse* (e.g., an assertion that one of the proposed operators is to be preferred to the other in the current situation). Upon encountering a similar situation in the future, the production will automatically match and retrieve the knowledge that permits SOAR to avoid the *impasse*. Thus, chunking is a mechanism that converts problem solving into recognition memory, continuously moving SOAR from knowledge-lean to knowledge-rich processing.

Chunking in SOAR has two important functional properties. First, it begins to provide a solution to the knowledge-indexing problem raised earlier. The system assembles its own indices out of the contents of working memory in a way that is directly aimed at making the knowledge retrievable when it is relevant to the immediate demands of the task at hand. Second, learning permeates all aspects of cognition in SOAR. Chunking applies to all kinds of impasses, so any problem space function is open to learning improvements: problem-space formulation, operator generation, operator selection, and so on.

4. Major Architectural Implications and Specific Domains of Application

SOAR can be used as a theory in multiple ways (Newell 1990). Qualitative predictions can be drawn from SOAR as a verbal theory, without actually running detailed computer simulations. These qualitative predictions can be both domain-general (cutting across all varieties of cognitive behavior) and domain-specific. The theory can be also be applied to specific domains by developing detailed computational models of a task; this involves programming SOAR by adding domain-specific production rules to its long-term memory, and generating behavioral traces.

4.1 Domain-independent Predictions

A principal prediction of a theory of human cognition is that humans are intelligent; the only way to clearly make that prediction is to demonstrate it operationally. SOAR makes this prediction only to the extent that the system has been demonstrated to exhibit intelligent behavior. As a state of the art AI system that has been applied to difficult tasks (ranging from algorithm design to scheduling problems), SOAR makes the prediction to a greater degree than other psychological theories.

SOAR makes a number of general predictions related to long-term memory and skill (Newell 1990). These include the prediction that procedural skill transfer is essentially by identical elements, and will usually be highly specific (Singley and Anderson 1989, Thorndike 1903); the bias of *Einstellung* will occur—the preservation of learned skill when it is no longer useful (Luchins 1942); the encoding specificity principle (Tulving 1983) holds; and recall will generally take place by a generate-and-recognize process (Kintsch 1970). The best known of SOAR's general predictions is the power law of practice, which relates the time to do a task to the number of times the task has been performed (Newell and Rosenbloom 1981, Snoddy 1926).

4.2 Domain-specific Predictions

SOAR models have been constructed across a range of task domains, and the behavior of the models has been compared with human data on those tasks. One area that has received considerable attention is human-computer interaction (HCI). Some of the successes in this area, such as a detailed model of transcription typing (John 1988), are a result of SOAR inheriting the results of the GOMS theory (Goal, Operators, Methods, and Selection rules), a theory developed in HCI to predict the time it takes expert users to do routine tasks (Card et al. 1983). (GOMS can be seen at one level as a specialization of SOAR, missing features such as learning and impassing.) Other SOAR HCI models depend crucially on SOAR's real-time interruptability (a func-

tion of the two-level control structure) and SOAR's learning mechanism. SOAR models have been developed of real-time interaction and learning in video games (John et al. 1994), novice-to-expert transitions in computer menu navigation (Howes and Young 1997), and a programmer's interaction with a text editor (Altmann and John 1999), among others.

SOAR models have also been developed of problem solving (Newell 1990), sentence processing (Lewis 2000), concept acquisition (Miller and Laird 1996), and interaction with educational microworlds (Miller et al. 1999). In all SOAR models (as with any cognitive model), the explanatory power is shared to varying degrees by both the content posited by the theorist for the particular task and the architectural mechanisms. For example, in the sentence processing model, SOAR's control structure and learning mechanism, coupled with the real-time constraint, lead directly to a theory of ambiguity resolution that yields a novel explanation of apparent modularity effects and their malleability (Lewis 1996a, Newell 1990), but the architecture provides little apparent constraint on the choice of grammatical theory, which also plays a role in the empirical predictions (Lewis 1996b). Similarly, the general theory of episodic indexing of attention events embodied in the text editor model depends critically on SOAR's continuous chunking mechanism (Altmann and John 1999), while the specific behavioral traces are a function, in part, of task strategies that could be accommodated by alternative architectures.

5. Critiques of SOAR, and Future Directions

Critiques of SOAR fall into three major classes: critiques of specific models built within SOAR, critiques of the architecture itself, and critiques of the general methodological approach of building comprehensive architectural theories. For example, specific empirical critiques have been made of SOAR models of the Sternberg memory search task (Lewandowsky 1992) and immediate reaction tasks (Cooper and Shallice 1995). The theoretical challenge is understanding the extent to which the empirical problems can be resolved within the existing architecture, or whether they point back to problems in the architecture itself (Newell 1992b). (The fact that the latter is a real possibility demonstrates that the architectural approach has made some headway on the identifiability and degrees of freedom problems.)

At the architectural level, nearly every major assumption of SOAR has been challenged in the literature (see the multiple book review in BBS for a range of assessments; Newell 1992a). Many of these architectural-level criticisms have been aimed at the *uniformity* assumptions in SOAR (all tasks as problem spaces, all long-term memory as productions, all learning as chunking), which appear at first to run strikingly against the prevailing mode of theorizing in both cognitive psychology and cognitive neuroscience, which emphasizes functional specialization and distinctions over computational generality. The evaluation of SOAR in light of these concerns is not always transparent, however. For example, the analysis of SOAR's implications for modularity (particularly in language processing) revealed that SOAR is not only consonant with, but even predicts, many of Fodor's diagnostics of modular systems (Lewis 1996a, Newell 1990).

Finally, the general approach to cognitive theory that SOAR embraces has come under sharp criticism (most notably by Cooper and Shallice 1995) for not living up to the promise of addressing the methodological concerns identified above, and for not yielding theories with deep empirical coverage that clearly gain their explanatory power from general architectural mechanisms. To the extent that these critiques depend on practice with the SOAR theory specifically, their implications for the broader approach are insecure. Other architectural theories (e.g., ACT (Anderson and Lebiere 1998) and EPIC (Meyer et al. 1995)) exist in the field, and each has adopted somewhat different ways of dealing with these methodological issues that may or may not make them suspect to the same criticisms.

The evolution of SOAR as a theory, and its broader role in cognitive science, is likely to proceed along two fronts. First, SOAR will remain an important source of ideas for developing theories of complex cognition, even for those theorists who do not embrace the architecture whole cloth, or reject the architectural methodology. A harbinger of this can be seen in cognitive neuroscience: as researchers begin to tackle the problem of understanding the nature of 'executive' processes and their realization in the brain, models like SOAR can provide concrete proposals for a set of functionally sufficient mechanisms for the control of deliberate cognition; (see the recent volume on working memory and executive control for evidence of such interaction by Miyake and Shah 1999). Second, SOAR will continue to evolve as a unified set of mechanisms itself, informed in part by the continued application of SOAR to difficult AI problems, and in part by the continued construction and empirical evaluation of detailed models of cognitive tasks that focus on unique aspects of the architecture.

See also: Artificial Intelligence: Connectionist and Symbolic Approaches; Artificial Intelligence in Cognitive Science; Artificial Intelligence: Search; Cognitive Theory: ACT; Deductive Reasoning Systems; Expert Systems in Medicine; Intelligence: History of the Concept; Production Systems in Cognitive Psychology; Scientific Discovery, Computational Models of

Bibliography

Altmann E M, John B E 1999 Episodic indexing: A model of memory for attention events. *Cognitive Science* **23**(2): 117–56

Anderson J R 1978 Arguments concerning representations for mental imagery. *Psychological Review* **85**(4): 249–77

Anderson J R 1993 *Rules of the Mind*. Erlbaum, Hillsdale, NJ

Anderson J, Lebiere C 1998 *Atomic Components of Thought*. Erlbaum, Hillsdale, NJ

Card S K, Moran T P, Newell A 1983 *The Psychology of Human–Computer Interaction*. Erlbaum, Hillsdale, NJ

Church A 1936 An unsolvable problem of elementary number theory. *The American Journal of Mathematics* **58**: 345–63

Cooper R, Shallice T 1995 SOAR and the case for unified theories of cognition. *Cognition* **55**(2): 115–49

Howes A, Young R M 1997 The role of cognitive architecture in modelling the user: SOAR's learning mechanism. *Human–Computer Interaction* **12**: 311–43

John B E 1988 *Contributions To Engineering Models of Human–Computer Interaction*. Carnegie Mellon University, Pittsburgh, PA

John B E, Vera A H, Newell A 1994 Toward real-time GOMS: A model of expert behavior in a highly interactive task. *Behavior and Information Technology* **13**: 255–67

Kintsch W 1970 Models for free recall and recognition. In: Norman D A (ed.) *Models of Human Memory*. Academic Press, New York

Laird J E, Newell A, Rosenbloom P S 1987 SOAR: An architecture for general intelligence. *Artificial Intelligence* **33**: 1–64

Lewandowsky S 1992 Unified cognitive theory: Having one's apple pie and eating it. *Behavioral and Brain Sciences* **15**(3): 449–50

Lewis R L 1996a Architecture matters: What SOAR has to say about modularity. In: Steier D M, Mitchell T M (eds.) *Mind Matters: Contributions to Cognitive and Computer Science in Honor of Allen Newell*. Lawrence Erlbaum Associates, Mahwah, NJ

Lewis R L 1996b Interference in short-term memory: The magical number two (or three) in sentence processing. *Journal of Psycholinguistic Research* **25**(1): 93–115

Lewis R L 2000 Specifying architectures for language processing: Process, control, and memory in parsing and interpretation. In: Crocker M W, Pickering M, Clifton C Jr (eds.) *Architectures and Mechanisms for Language Processing*. Cambridge University Press, Cambridge, UK

Luchins A S 1942 Mechanization in problem solving. *Psychological Monographs* **54**(6): no. 28

Meyer D E, Kieras D E, Lauber E, Schumacher E H, Glass J, Zurbriggen E, Gmeindl L, Apfelblat D 1995 *Adaptive Executive Control: Flexible Human Multiple-task Performance Without Pervasive Immutable Response-selection Bottlenecks*. University of Michigan, Ann Arbor, MI

Miller C S, Laird J E 1996 Accounting for graded performance within a discrete search framework. *Cognitive Science* **20**: 499–537

Miller C S, Lehman J F, Koedinger K R 1999 Goals and learning in microworlds. *Cognitive Science* **23**(3): 305–36

Miyake A, Shah P (eds.) 1999 *Models of Working Memory: Mechanisms of Active Maintenance and Executive Control*. Cambridge University Press, Cambridge, UK

Newell A 1973 Production systems: Models of control structures. In: Chase W G (ed.) *Visual Information Processing*. Academic Press, New York

Newell A 1980a Physical symbol systems. *Cognitive Science* **4**: 135–83

Newell A 1980b Reasoning, problem solving and decision processes: The problem space as a fundamental category. In: Nickerson R (ed.) *Attention and Performance VIII*. Erlbaum, Hillsdale, NJ

Newell A 1990 *Unified Theories of Cognition*. Harvard University Press, Cambridge, MA

Newell A 1992a Precis of unified theories of cognition. *Behavioral and Brain Sciences* 15(3): 425–92

Newell A 1992b SOAR as a unified theory of cognition: Issues and explanations. *Behavioral and Brain Sciences* 15(3): 464–92

Newell A, Rosenbloom P 1981 Mechanisms of skill acquisition and the law of practice. In: Anderson J R (ed.) *Cognitive Skills and Their Acquisition*. Erlbaum, Hillsdale, NJ

Newell A, Shaw J C, Simon H A 1958 Elements of a theory of human problem solving. *Psychological Review* 65: 151–66

Newell A, Simon H A 1972 *Human Problem Solving*. Prentice-Hall, Englewood Cliffs, NJ

Pylyshyn Z W 1973 What the mind's eye tells the mind's brain: A critique of mental imagery. *Psychological Bulletin* 80(1): 1–24

Pylyshyn Z W 1984 *Computation and Cognition*. Bradford/MIT Press, Cambridge, MA

Reitman W 1965 *Cognition and Thought*. Wiley, New York

Rosenbloom P S, Laird J E, Newell A (eds.) 1992 *The SOAR Papers: Research on Integrated Intelligence*. MIT Press, Cambridge, MA

Rosenbloom P S, Newell A 1983 The chunking of goal hierarchies: A generalized model of practice. In: Michalski R S, Carbonell J, Mitchell T (eds.) *Machine Learning: An Artificial Intelligence Approach II*. Morgan Kaufman, Los Altos, CA

Simon H A 1996 The patterned matter that is mind. In: D a M Steier T (ed.) *Mind Matters: Contributions to Cognitive and Computer Science in Honor of Allen Newell*. Erlbaum, Hillsdale, NJ

Singley M K, Anderson J R 1989 *The Transfer of Cognitive Skill*. Harvard University Press, Cambridge, MA

Snoddy G S 1926 Learning and stability. *Journal of Applied Psychology* 20: 1–36

Thorndike E L 1903 *Educational Psychology*. Lemke and Buechner, New York

Tulving E 1983 *Elements of Episodic Memory*. Oxford University Press, New York

Turing A M 1936 On computable numbers, with an application to the Entscheidungsproblem. Paper presented at the Proceedings of the London Mathematics Society

R. L. Lewis

Cognitive Therapy

1. Definition

Cognitive therapy is one of a large number of psychotherapy approaches that was developed in the latter part of the twentieth century. It is associated principally with its originator, Dr. Aaron Beck. The treatment model falls within a broader class of treatments, which are referred to as the cognitive-behavioral therapies (Dobson, 2001). The cognitive-behavioral therapies share certain theoretical underpinnings, notably: (a) that cognitive events affect behavior (the mediational hypothesis); (b) that cognitive events can be assessed and systematically modified (the accessibility hypothesis); and (c) that cognitive change can be employed to cause therapeutic changes in behavior or adaptive functioning. In this regard, cognitive therapy is similar to other schools of cognitive-behavioral psychotherapy, such as rational-emotive psychotherapy.

Cognitive therapy distinguishes itself from other cognitive-behavioral therapies by the particular organization of its theoretical constructs. The model proposes that the manner in which an individual views, appraises, or perceives events around himself/herself is what dictates their subsequent emotional responses and behavioral choices. Although the content of situation-specific appraisals will vary as a function of the person's activities, the model also posits that these appraisals may be accurate or distorted, positive or negative. For example, an individual reacts to what another individual said in an interpersonal interaction, as well as to what he or she thinks about those statements.

The extent to which the individual sees situations accurately, or conversely may be distorting, is in part a function of the individual's core beliefs (also referred to as underlying assumptions, or schemas). These core beliefs are hypothesized to be intrapsychic phenomena that emerge over the person's lifetime, based on their experiences. Once established, these beliefs not only increase the likelihood of certain cognitive reactions to life events, but also then influence proactively the way in which an individual chooses to spend their time, career, partner choices, etc., which also tend to reinforce these beliefs. Thus, over time cognitive beliefs become the basic factor in what may become an increasingly negative and closed feedback loop (see Fig. 1).

Cognitive therapy is a systematic treatment, which is founded on the cognitive model of distress. The principal emphases in therapy are assisting the patient to identify, evaluate, and modify the potentially faulty information processing they engage in, as well as the underlying beliefs or schemas that drive that information processing. This process typically begins with an assessment of adaptive functioning and behavioral patterns that might either enhance or interfere with the process of treatment. In the case of depression, the patient may be encouraged to increase their activities to alleviate negative mood, and to ensure that the patient is at least engaged in their life sufficiently to generate negative information processing that can then be the focus of treatment. In the case of marital distress, negative interactional patterns (e.g., fighting, spousal abuse) will be assessed and modified before interventions aimed at relationship beliefs will be attempted.

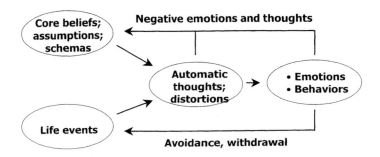

Figure 1
The cognitive therapy model of emotional distress

Once the patient is able to engage in a review of their negative thinking, a number of methods can be employed to assess this thinking. Strategies include counts of particular thoughts, questioning in the therapy session, thoughts about imagined situations, or the use of a written thought record (J. Beck 1995). Dependent on the pattern of dysfunctional thinking that is identified, various therapeutic techniques can be employed to change these patterns. For example, if a patient recurrently believes they 'cannot' be assertive with certain people, the therapist and patient can collaborate to set up circumstances in which they can test this idea empirically. In doing so, adaptive thinking and various behavioral competencies can be enhanced.

At a certain stage of treatment, it is typically the case that a patient's situation-specific automatic thoughts are accurate and adaptive, and that they are functioning more adaptively than when they first arrived for treatment. At this stage of treatment, the focus will move to the more general beliefs that prompted the patient's problems in the first instance. This work includes a search for the common themes underlying specific thoughts. These themes can take the form of beliefs about how 'the world' operates, or schemas that have developed about the self. Techniques that can be used include inductive questioning, a review of the negative thinking patterns seen by the therapist and patient, examination of historical patterns of thought and behavior, and a review of life events related to the problem. Once identified, dysfunctional beliefs can be challenged systematically through behavioral experiments, bibliotherapy, open discussion with key people in the patient's life, and other 'assumptive techniques' (J. Beck 1995).

In summary, cognitive therapy is a systematic and progressive form of treatment that typically includes assessment and modification of adaptive functioning, situation-specific automatic thinking, and more engrained, long-term beliefs and self-schemas. The cognitive content of various forms of disorders is increasingly understood, and it includes themes of danger in anxiety (Beck and Emery 1985), loss in

depression (Beck et al. 1979, Clark et al. 1999), and transgression in anger (Beck 1999). Further, the cognitive processes associated with various disorders (e.g., magnification of perceived danger in anxiety) are also increasingly understood.

2. Intellectual Context

Beck's original interest was in understanding and treating depression. He began his departure from his original psychoanalytic training through a series of studies of the dreams and daytime thoughts of depressed patients, in which he discovered that the content of these thoughts had stereotypical content. Further, he hypothesized that these depressed patients engaged in negative distortions of their world in order to obtain these thoughts. Based on these observations, he developed a treatment in which the negative cognitions were systematically tested, in order to undermine cognitive distortions and the negative thinking seen in depression (Beck et al. 1979).

The early formulation of cognitive therapy was put to its first empirical test in an outcome study in the late 1970s. Based on a developed treatment manual, cognitive therapy was contrasted with antidepressant medication. This study revealed that cognitive therapy had equal outcome to medication in the short term and superior outcome at follow-up. As a consequence of the original success of cognitive therapy, a number of outcome studies were conducted in the area of depression in subsequent years.

The first meta-analysis of these studies (Dobson 1989) used a standard outcome measure, the Beck Depression Inventory, and compared cognitive therapy to other forms of treatment. This analysis revealed that cognitive therapy patients ended treatment 0.5 standard deviations less depressed than patients receiving other treatments. Further, compared to wait list or placebo conditions, the effect size for cognitive therapy indicated that it was over 2 standard deviations superior to no treatment. Although the results of the above meta-analysis were criticized due to questions about the selection process for including studies, the conclusion that cognitive therapy is at least equal to pharmacotherapy has not been challenged seriously. Further, a more recent meta-analysis (Gloaguen et al. 1998) has confirmed the results found earlier by Dobson (1989).

More specifically, Gloaguen et al. (1998) found similar effect sizes to the earlier analysis, although the overall magnitude of these effects was somewhat attenuated. Notably, in an examination of long-term effects, it was also reported that relapse rates from cognitive therapy were approximately one-half of those observed for drug therapy for depression. Most recently, DeRubeis et al. (1999) conducted a 'mega-analysis' of treatment for depression, in which they collapsed the data from four outcome studies and analyzed the effects of cognitive therapy for depression, relative to drug therapy. They concluded that these two forms of therapy were equally effective, even for severely depressed patients. As such, it is an established fact that cognitive therapy is an effective treatment for clinical depression.

Notwithstanding the demonstrated efficacy of cognitive therapy for depression, a number of questions continue to require theoretical and empirical attention. The model underlying cognitive therapy states that cognitive distortions and situation-specific negative thoughts emerge from an interaction between core beliefs (also referred to as cognitive schemas, or underlying assumptions) and the life events that impinge on these beliefs. Once the core beliefs are activated and negative cognitions are produced, the emotional and behavioral consequences of these thoughts naturally flow (see Fig. 1). This mediational model, while intuitive and having lead to a successful treatment technology, has yet to be validated through research. In fact, based on a comprehensive examination of the research that has tested the various assumptions of cognitive therapy (Clark et al. 1999), the conclusion is that cognitive mediation remains to be proven.

Another challenge for the cognitive therapy of depression model comes from a component analysis of this treatment. Jacobson et al. (1996) conducted a randomized clinical trial in which depressed patients received either only the behavioral interventions associated with cognitive therapy, behavioral interventions and those aimed at situation-specific distortions, or the complete cognitive therapy program. Contrary to predictions, all three treatment conditions had equal outcomes, both in the short term and at up to two years follow-up. This study suggests that the cognitive interventions that are the hallmark features of the treatment may not, in fact, contribute to outcome more than the behavioral components of the treatment. If replicated, these results suggest that the active ingredients of cognitive therapy should be reconceptualized.

Further issues exist with regard to cognitive therapy of depression. These include the role of patient characteristics that potentially effect treatment outcome, the role of life stress in depression, the recent focus on schema-focused cognitive therapy (Clark et al. 1999), the risk of relapse relative to other treatments, and assessment issues relative to the adherence and competence of therapists in providing cognitive therapy.

3. Changes in Focus or Emphasis Over Time

Branching out from the early work on depression (Beck et al. 1979), Beck and his colleagues extended the cognitive model to other clinical conditions. Beck and Emery published a treatment manual for anxiety disorders in 1985, which was followed by works dedicated to marital disorder (Beck 1988), personality disorders (Beck et al. 1990), substance use and abuse (Beck et al. 1993), and—most recently—anger and aggression (Beck 1999). Other works on cognitive therapy have appeared for bipolar disorder, as well as numerous chapters in various sources (see J. Beck 1995 for a review).

Throughout the development of cognitive therapy, some features have remained constant. First, while the *content* of cognition related to various forms of disorders necessarily varies, there has been a consistent emphasis on the *process* of thinking in cognitive therapy that permits many of the treatment techniques to be applied across disorders. For example, a common intervention in cognitive therapy is assessing the reality basis, or veridicality, of certain perceptions. This intervention can be used successfully in many forms of anxiety disorders, depression, marital distress, and anger-related problems.

A second consistent emphasis in cognitive therapy has been a focus on treatment efficacy. From the outset of the development of cognitive therapy, Beck and colleagues have maintained that efficacy studies are required to establish the clinical utility of cognitive therapy. No doubt it is in part due to this emphasis that many of the psychological treatments now being recognized as empirically supported are variants of cognitive therapy.

4. Methodological Issues or Problems

Two primary sets of methodological issues have constrained the development of cognitive therapy. The first of these is related to the methodological issues inherent in clinical research. The randomized clinical trial methodology, which has become the standard in the development of psychotherapy, makes a number of requirements on investigators. These include the need for a well-defined independent variable, which in the context of psychotherapy means a treatment manual. Unfortunately, a consequence of this requirement is that fully developed treatment manuals are often developed before the research that is needed to substantiate them has been conducted. A second requirement of clinical trials is that the subject group be clearly specified. In psychotherapy research, this requirement has often been translated into using diagnostically related groups, ideally with few or no complicating co-morbid conditions. The relative homogeneity of research participants, while providing a good test of the intervention, unfortunately leads to what may be relatively poor generalizability of research findings. The requisite training for research trials has also been controversial. A fourth area of controversy surrounds the measurement and evaluation of outcome. Typically, the outcomes of a given treatment can be assessed in a number of ways (diagnostically, at the symptom level, or using specialized assessment tools), and the analysis of the outcomes can also be handled in several ways. As a consequence of these various strategies to conduct clinical trials, the scientific status of various treatments can be challenged. Given that most psychological treatments are developed in universities with publicly funded grants, and further given the necessarily limited set of questions that any one treatment study can address, it is not surprising that considerable efficacy and effectiveness research in the area of cognitive therapy is needed.

The second major methodological issue for cognitive therapy is the measurement of mechanisms of change. The cognitive model of distress makes a series of assumptions about the nature of cognitive processes involved in the development and treatment of various disorders (see Fig. 1). The measurement of cognition has been a difficult task, however—particularly as some of the constructs in the model are hypothetically latent until activated (Ingram et al. 1998). Even in the area of depression, where the greatest concentration of work has taken place to assess these constructs, some of the hypothesized mechanisms of change have yet to be established (Clark et al. 1999, Ingram et al. 1998). Research from the level of both theory and therapy are required to further evaluate the relationship between cognitive change and other parameters of clinical change in cognitive therapy.

5. Probable Future Directions of Theory And Research

Despite the success of cognitive therapy, and its phenomenal growth over the past two decades, there is no doubt that considerable development remains (Dobson and Khatri 2000). Some of the directions for this work that have been identified in the literature include:

(a) A need for continued emphasis on efficacy research, particularly as cognitive therapy is applied to new and innovative areas.

(b) A need for effectiveness research that assesses such issues as the utility of cognitive therapy relative to other treatments, the clinical acceptability of treatment to patients, and other issues that affect how practical the treatment is to apply in varied clinical contexts.

(c) Continued work on the measurement of cognition (Ingram et al. 1998) and the mechanisms of change in cognitive therapy is clearly warranted. Cognitive therapy is a complex, multi-component treatment, the mechanisms of which are only beginning to be studied. The results of this research will contribute both to the theory and application of the treatment.

(d) Theoretical therapy development and efficacy work are needed to address the issue of whether cognitive therapy is an exhaustive theory that can integrate other models (Dobson and Khatri, 2000), or whether it might be integrated optimally into other treatment models.

(e) There is a need for research that assesses the success and failure of cognitive therapy for patients of diverse backgrounds. This 'aptitude by treatment' research will help the theory of cognitive therapy to develop, as well as to ensure the most appropriate treatment is provided to different patient populations.

(f) Predicated on the assumption that cognitive therapy continues to enjoy strong clinical outcomes and popularity in the treatment community, further research is needed to understand the optimal method to disseminate this treatment approach. Tied to this development are issues related to how to best measure therapist adherence and competence in cognitive therapy.

See also: Behavior Psychotherapy: Rational and Emotive; Behavior Therapy: Psychiatric Aspects; Behavior Therapy: Psychological Perspectives; Cognitive and Interpersonal Therapy: Psychiatric Aspects; Depression, Clinical Psychology of

Bibliography

Beck A T 1988 *Love is Never Enough*. Harper and Row, New York
Beck A T 1999 *Prisoners of Hate: The Cognitive Bases of Anger, Hostility and Violence*. Harper Collins, New York
Beck A T, Emery G 1985 *Anxiety Disorders and Phobias: A Cognitive Perspective*. Basic Books, New York
Beck A T, Freeman A et al. 1990 *Cognitive Therapy of Personality Disorders*. Guilford Press, New York
Beck A T, Rush A J, Shaw B F, Emery G 1979 *Cognitive Therapy of Depression*. Guilford Press, New York
Beck A T, Wright F D, Newman C, Liese B S 1993 *Cognitive Therapy of Substance Abuse*. Guilford Press, New York

Beck J 1995 *Cognitive Therapy: Basics and Beyond*. Guilford Press, New York

Clark D A, Beck A, Alford B A 1999 *Cognitive Theory and Therapy of Depression*. Wiley, New York

DeRubeis R J, Gelfand L A, Tang T Z, Simons A D 1999 Medications vs. cognitive behavioral therapy for severely depressed outpatients: A mega-analysis of four randomized comparisons. *The American Journal of Psychiatry* **156**: 1007–13

Dobson K S 1989 A meta-analysis of the efficacy of cognitive therapy for depression. *Journal of Consulting and Clinical Psychology* **57**: 414–9

Dobson K S (ed.) 2001 *Handbook of Cognitive-behavioral Therapies*, 2nd edn. Guilford Press, New York

Dobson K S, Khatri N 2000 Cognitive therapy: Looking backward, looking forward. *Journal of Clinical Psychology* **56**: 907–23

Gloaguen V, Cottraux J, Cucherat M, Blackburn I 1998 A meta-analysis of the effects of cognitive therapy in depressed patients. *Journal of Affective Disorders* **49**: 59–72

Ingram R, Miranda J, Segal Z V 1998 *Cognitive Vulnerability to Depression*. Guilford Press, New York

Jacobson N S, Dobson K S, Truax P, Addis M, Koerner K, Gollan J, Gortner E, Prince S 1996 A component analysis of cognitive behavioral treatment for depression. *Journal of Consulting and Clinical Psychology* **64**: 295–304

K. S. Dobson